Hawaii

Jeff Campbell
Glenda Bendure, Sara Benson, Amanda C Gregg, Ned Friary,
Scott Kennedy, Ryan Ver Berkmoes, Luci Yamamoto

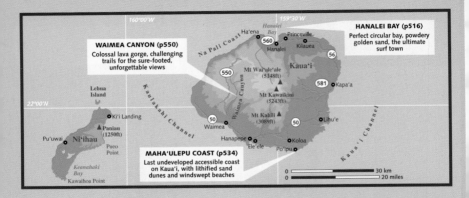

WAIMEA CANYON (p550)
Colossal lava gorge, challenging trails for the sure-footed, unforgettable views

HANALEI BAY (p516)
Perfect circular bay, powdery golden sand, the ultimate surf town

MAHA'ULEPU COAST (p534)
Last undeveloped accessible coast on Kaua'i, with lithified sand dunes and windswept beaches

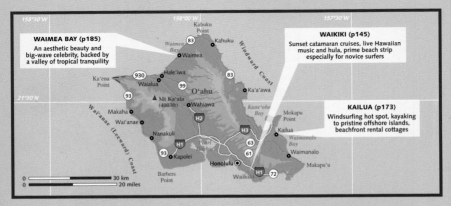

WAIMEA BAY (p185)
An aesthetic beauty and big-wave celebrity, backed by a valley of tropical tranquility

WAIKIKI (p145)
Sunset catamaran cruises, live Hawaiian music and hula, prime beach strip especially for novice surfers

KAILUA (p173)
Windsurfing hot spot, kayaking to pristine offshore islands, beachfront rental cottages

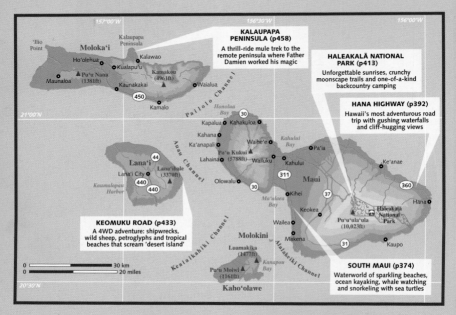

KALAUPAPA PENINSULA (p458)
A thrill-ride mule trek to the remote peninsula where Father Damien worked his magic

HALEAKALĀ NATIONAL PARK (p413)
Unforgettable sunrises, crunchy moonscape trails and one-of-a-kind backcountry camping

HANA HIGHWAY (p392)
Hawaii's most adventurous road trip with gushing waterfalls and cliff-hugging views

KEOMUKU ROAD (p433)
A 4WD adventure: shipwrecks, wild sheep, petroglyphs and tropical beaches that scream 'desert island'

SOUTH MAUI (p374)
Waterworld of sparkling beaches, ocean kayaking, whale watching and snorkeling with sea turtles

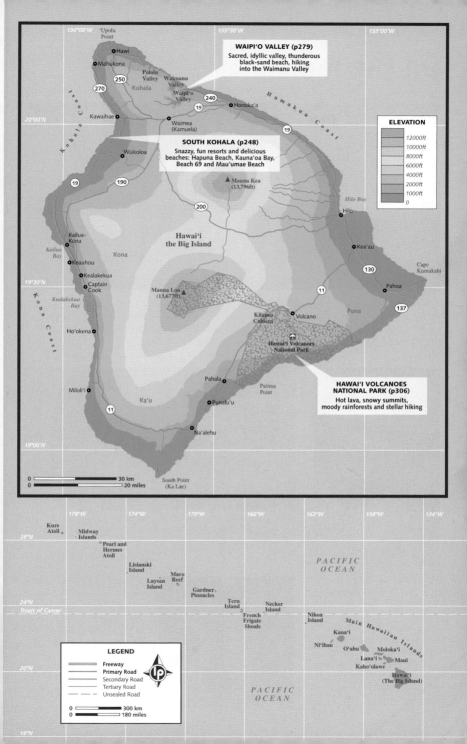

WAIPI'O VALLEY (p279)
Sacred, idyllic valley, thunderous
black-sand beach, hiking
into the Waimanu Valley

SOUTH KOHALA (p248)
Snazzy, fun resorts and delicious
beaches: Hapuna Beach, Kauna'oa Bay,
Beach 69 and Mau'umae Beach

**HAWAI'I VOLCANOES
NATIONAL PARK (p306)**
Hot lava, snowy summits,
moody rainforests and stellar hiking

Hawai'i
the Big Island

ELEVATION

12000ft
10000ft
8000ft
6000ft
4000ft
2000ft
1000ft
0

'Upolu
Point
Hawi
Mahukona
Pololu
Valley
Waimanu
Valley
250
Kohala
270
Waipi'o
Valley
240
Honoka'a
Kawaihae
19
19
Waimea
(Kamuela)
Kohala
Coast

Hamakua
Coast

Waikoloa
19
190
Mauna Kea
(13,796ft)
Hilo Bay
200
Hilo

Kailua-
Kona
Kailua
Bay
Kona
Kea'au
130
Keauhou
Cape
Kumukahi
Kealakekua
Captain
Cook
Mauna Loa
(13,677ft)
Pahoa
11
137
Kealakekua
Bay
Kilauea
Caldera
Volcano
Puna

Ho'okena
Hawai'i Volcanoes
National Park

Kona
Coast

Pahala
Palima
Point
Miloli'i
Ka'u
Punalu'u
11
Na'alehu

0 —— 30 km
0 —— 20 miles

South Point
(Ka Lae)

Kure
Atoll
Midway
Islands
Pearl and
Hermes
Atoll
Lisianski
Island
Maro
Reef
Laysan
Island
Gardner
Pinnacles
Tern
Island
Necker
Island
Nihoa
Island
Main
Hawaiian
Islands
Kaua'i
Ni'ihau
O'ahu
Moloka'i
Lana'i
Maui
Kaho'olawe
Hawai'i
(The Big Island)
French
Frigate
Shoals

*PACIFIC
OCEAN*

Tropic of Cancer

*PACIFIC
OCEAN*

LEGEND
Freeway
Primary Road
Secondary Road
Tertiary Road
Unsealed Road

0 —— 300 km
0 —— 180 miles

On the Road

JEFF CAMPBELL Coordinating Author
On top of Mauna Kea (p269) I took a ton of lousy pictures. The sunset and the mountains are just too big. I need a lens like the ones in the golf balls – the observatories. Later, I grew dizzy trying to take in the night sky, though I discovered that the moon really is made of cheese.

SCOTT KENNEDY A few days before the start of the Triple Crown of Surfing I found myself at Pipeline (p186). The beach was all but deserted, but just off shore, the best surfers in the world were catching waves and getting ready for the big comp. There I was front-row-center for a private session – classic!

NED FRIARY I've always been interested in herbal medicine. Strolling Maui Nui Botanical Gardens (p365), I'm thinking this place is ancient Hawaii's version of a pharmacy and the odiferous *noni* (Indian mulberry) tree was surely a big seller. One quick sniff of the pungent fruit and I get a jolt – wow, that's potent stuff.

SARA BENSON It's Sunday morning in Honolulu (p113), following a very late Saturday night spent researching Waikiki (p145). Here I am, sitting in an industrial-looking microbrewery out toward the airport. Although beer is not exactly my beverage of choice at the moment, I'll do anything for guidebook research – and for you, dear readers. Aloha!

GLENDA BENDURE I love the vibe at the aloha-filled Maui Swap Meet (p368). After chatting up island farmers – which papayas are ripe but not overripe? Which Kula strawberries the sweetest? – I come across drinking coconuts and can't resist. The woman who machetes it open tells me the coconuts come from her backyard.

LUCI YAMAMOTO Kaua'i's roads aren't exactly bike-friendly. But now there's a fantastic coastal path (p502) – no motorized vehicles allowed. When complete, it'll cover 16 miles. On a coaster bike, outside the confines of a car, the island comes alive – the breezes and heat and constant crashing surf.

AMANDA C GREGG Views of the Na Pali are that much sweeter when you've hiked to get there. After a short jaunt along the Pihea Trail (p556) in Koke'e State Park (p553), the clouds parted and the leg work paid off: views of the greenest of valleys, the bluest of oceans and the most breathtaking of sunsets capped off a perfect Westside day.

RYAN VER BERKMOES On my many visits to Moloka'i's isolated Halawa Beach (p453) I have always been a crowd of one (or if personally lucky, two). But the surf's roar doesn't drown out the voices of the generations of Hawaiians who grew taro in the tropical valley for centuries, and I can't escape feeling surrounded by ancient mysteries.

For full author biographies see p587.

LEI & ALOHA

Land in O'Hare, Houston, La Guardia, Sea-Tac and what do you find? Not a greeting of flowers, that's for sure – you won't see men and women waiting for their luggage with garlands of orchids draped around their necks.

No, lei signify Hawaii. They symbolize the spirit of aloha that animates the islands. Fragrant and ephemeral, lei embody the beauty of nature and the embrace of the community, freely given and freely shared. Placed on the traveler, they ask only that this embrace, this kindness, be returned – a small price to pay for a vacation in paradise.

O'ahu

If you want to take the measure of multi-ethnic, multiracial Hawaii, which has long chuckled over the neat categories of census takers, explore O'ahu. Three-quarters of state residents call the island home, and everyone rubs elbows – on the beach and the bus, on city sidewalks and country lanes. Here, East and West merge, and ancient Hawaii greets the 21st century.

1 Hanauma Bay

O'ahu's most famous fishbowl is Hanauma Bay (p166); its coral gardens and universities of fish amaze everyone from novice snorkelers to grizzled divers.

2 Waikiki

The cliché of 'Hawaii as paradise' was first concocted on the idyllic beaches of Waikiki (p149), where bartenders still serve up the stereotype with tacky tiki cocktails and fruity concoctions. But Waikiki is reinventing itself, and for a thrilling experience of hula and Hawaiian music (p160), it's still hard to beat.

3 Honolulu

This teeming metropolis is a cultural feast. Hawaii's complex history is on vivid display at 'Iolani Palace (p116), the Bishop Museum (p126), and more. Vibrant Chinatown (p120) is a gourmand's delight, while gourmets can catch a wave of local-grown Pacific fusion cuisine (p132).

4 North Shore

In winter, the North Shore (p184) becomes a thunderous place, a mecca of big-wave surfing, but the calm of summer shows its gentler side, allowing snorkelers, divers and swimmers to enjoy its gorgeous beaches and country life.

5 Kailua Bay

If the impersonal, high-rise Waikiki scene isn't for you, come to laid-back Kailua (p173) and its homey B&Bs. Kailua Bay has lovely swimming beaches, great coral reefs and wicked kitesurfing. There's also kayaking to uninhabited islands and fantastic bird-watching.

6 Pearl Harbor

Hawaii's many active US military bases, particularly on O'ahu, signal its continued strategic importance. For the most dramatic reminder of why, visit the USS Arizona Memorial (p142), a significant site commemorating WWII history.

Hawai'i the Big Island

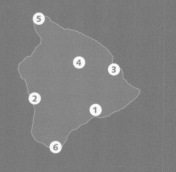

Among the Neighbor Islands (the five populated islands not named O'ahu) this is the only island still growing: Kilauea, the world's most active volcano, adds acreage daily. But that's not why it's called 'big.' Ancient temples, rugged adventure, beaches, museums, *paniolo* culture, artists villages, working-class towns: it's all here.

① Hawai'i Volcanoes National Park

No luau fire-twirler can match the show put on in this tremendous national park (p306). Even when you can't walk right up to hot lava (see p309), you can hike to smoking craters, lava deserts, dripping rainforests and heart-stopping coastal plains.

② South Kona Coast

The Big Island's famous coffee country (p230) offers much more than world-class java: enjoy Japanese home cooking, cozy B&Bs, snorkeling in Kealakekua Bay (the site of Captain Cook's demise, p236), and the ancient place of refuge, Pu'uhonua o Honaunau (p239).

③ Hilo

Next time they hand out nicknames, Hilo (p285) should pick something besides 'Rainiest City in the USA.' Perhaps, 'Hawaii's Most Charming Tsunami Survivor,' or 'Best Farmers Market, Museum and Gallery Scene on the Big Island.'

④ Mauna Kea

Standing on the sacred summit of Mauna Kea (p269) – the earth's largest volcanic mountain – is a preeminent collection of astronomical observatories (p272). Bring a jacket, and enjoy perhaps the clearest night sky on the planet.

⑤ North Kohala

Why isn't North Kohala (p257) better known? From moody Mo'okini Heiau (p259) to the misty, verdant Pololu Valley (p263), from the artists and writers who inhabit Kapa'au (p261) to the gourmet restaurants at Hawi (p259), it satisfies any number of traveler desires.

⑥ Ka'u

Rural Ka'u (p321) isn't for everyone, and locals like it that way. Come to feel the sweeping loneliness of South Point (p323), to seek out green-sand beaches and lava-tube caves, and to get far from the madding crowd.

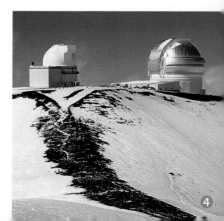

Maui

Sigh. It's a wonder this island isn't heart-shaped, it gets so much love. Even the humpbacked whales are frisky. First you get punch-drunk on the gorgeous beaches, then swept away by your encounters with sealife, and finally all snuggly-happy as you greet the new day in the 'house of the sun,' Haleakalā. Maui turns everyone into a romantic.

① Road to Hana
When they said it's not the destination but the journey, they could have been talking about the cliff-hugging Road to Hana (p392): 54 bridges, 600 curves, waterfalls galore and two sweaty palms gripping the wheel.

② Ka'anapali
We think the colors for tequila sunrise were inspired by the sunsets at Ka'anapali beaches (p351) – plush resorts, ocean sports and nearby Lahaina restaurants (p344) have inspired more romance than last dance at the prom.

③ Ho'okipa Beach
Combine the windsurfing theatrics of Ho'okipa Beach (p388) with the funky vibe and excellent eats of nearby Pa'ia (p388), and you've got a tough-to-beat combo.

④ Haleakalā National Park
Normally, we leave getting up before dawn to the sporty types, but for sunrise at Haleakalā Crater (p413), a jaw-dropping 7.5 miles wide, we make an exception. Still, we don't hit the trails until after breakfast.

⑤ Molokini Crater
A partially submerged volcanic crater (p379) halfway to Kaho'olawe, Molokini is an epic underwater experience, offering a chance to spot sea turtles, manta rays, sharks, black coral – and even unexploded bombs.

⑥ Makena
Makena (p385) is the destination for idyllic beaches free of condos and resorts. The area is crazy with snorkeling, and if you want to see whales, nearby Kihei (p375) is the whale sanctuary headquarters.

Kaua'i

Think old age isn't beautiful? Consider Kaua'i, the eldest island sibling, whose extinct volcanoes show the caresses of millenia. Here, nature's fingers have dug deep creases and fluted sharp edges, sculpting an intricate, emerald-bright jewel in the sea. Bring your boots, for this art gallery is all outdoors.

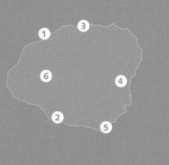

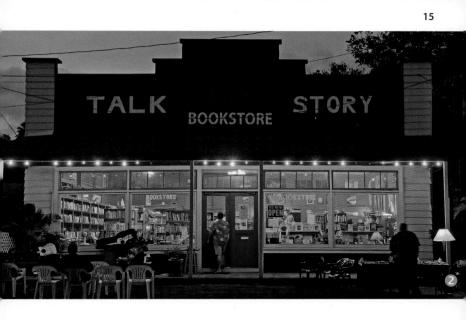

① Na Pali Coast

Kaua'i's most dramatic, wrinkled face is the daunting Na Pali Coast (p525). Hike the cliffs along the Kalalau Trail (p525) or admire them from a kayak (p519), but don't miss them.

② Hanapepe

Hawaii's plantations are mostly gone, but plantation towns remain. At their best, as in Hanapepe (p542), they've retained their rural character and local flavor while becoming thriving artists colonies.

③ Hanalei Bay

The North Shore's Hanalei Bay (p516) cradles the surf-bum town Hanalei (p516) and a cornucopia of adventures: surfing, kayaking, snorkeling and diving.

④ Wailua River

Age has endowed Kaua'i with a bounty of navigable rivers. The Wailua River (p492) is so popular with kayakers and tours it is now regulated; other waterways to traverse include the Hule'ia River (p482) and the Hanalei River (p518).

⑤ Maha'ulepu Coast

The undeveloped Maha'ulepu Coast (p534) is famous for its unique, lithified sand-dune cliffs and for the monk seals who rest in its secluded coves.

⑥ Waimea Canyon

Known as the 'Grand Canyon of the Pacific,' spectacular Waimea Canyon (p550) is not quite *that* big, but campers and hikers will still run out of days before they run out of trails.

Moloka'i & Lana'i

Hawaii's two smallest inhabited islands present a striking contrast: Moloka'i remains the most Hawaiian island and is only modestly developed for tourism. Lana'i, once awash in pineapple fields, has been reinvented as an upscale tourist retreat and now may be the least Hawaiian island. Yet both are off-the-beaten-path destinations offering seclusion to da max.

❶ Kalaupapa Peninsula
The mule ride down the steep cliffs to the Kalaupapa Peninsula (p458), a historic leprosy settlement and now national park, is Moloka'i's signature experience: moving, tragic, beautiful and adventurous.

❷ Eastside Beaches
For seclusion in a tropical paradise, head for Shipwreck Beach (p433) and Halepalaoa Beach (p434) on Lana'i's eastside.

❸ Lana'i City
Lana'i's only town, Lana'i City (p428) is one of Hawaii's most evocative historic plantation towns. It still feels like 50 years ago, with tin-roofed houses, simple wooden facades and no stoplights.

❹ Halawa Valley
To get to know Moloka'i, drive the eastern side of the island (p449), stopping for sacred heiau (ancient temples), historic fishponds, quiet beaches and local communities, on your way to the stunning Halawa Valley (p453).

Contents

Regional Map Contents

Papahanaumokuakea

Kaua'i
p469

Ni'ihau

O'ahu
pp102–3

Moloka'i
p440–41

Maui
p329

Lana'i
p426

Kaho'olawe

Hawai'i
the Big Island
pp206–7

Destination Hawaii

It is easy to see why Hawaii has long been synonymous with 'paradise.' Just look around – at the sugary beaches and rustling palms, at the sculpted emerald cliffs, at the coral reefs and smoking volcanoes. The natural beauty of these scattered islands in the cobalt blue Pacific Ocean is heavenly without the need for promotional embellishment.

Hawaii is that rare place where uniqueness abounds. It is certainly the USA's most unique state, but even within Polynesia it stands out. The islands' Native Hawaiian culture distinguishes it, of course, but nowhere else will you find its particular blend of ethnicities, its pidgin tongue, its amalgam of East and West. Almost halfway between continental Asia and North America, Hawaii lives at the edge of both, yet fashions its own fluid center in the middle of the sea.

What is unique, though – what is endemic to a particular ecosystem – can be easily knocked out of balance and lost. Hawaii has never been more aware of its own fragility. This applies to its environment, which modern industry and invasive species threaten daily; to its economy, which is not built for the long-term sustainability of either the land or its residents' quality of life; and to its multiethnic society and its 'aloha spirit' – that much-abused shorthand for the inherited ancient Hawaiian traditions of reciprocity, openness and mutual loving care.

These issues are not unique to Hawaii, but Hawaii's island ecology makes them unusually urgent. Like a canary in a coal mine, Hawaii is sounding a warning about the need to adopt a self-sustaining island mentality. For half a millennium Hawaii existed in complete isolation and its people flourished; today the state imports over 85% of its food and fuel, and residents like to ask, 'Could we survive if the boats stop coming?' The answer, right now, is 'no'. But Hawaii sees what it must do to change, and there has been no greater validation of its perspective than the 2008 election of Hawaii-born Barack Obama as the 44th US president.

Hawaii is naturally proud simply to have one of its own in the White House – someone who appreciates shave ice and can bodysurf like a local. Born and mostly raised on Oʻahu, the child of a white American mother and a black Kenyan father, Obama attended the exclusive Punahou School, where he graduated from high school in 1979 (for a tour of Obama's old neighborhood, see p126). After that, he left Hawaii, getting a law degree at Harvard and a political education in Chicago, but as First Lady Michelle Obama has said, 'You can't really understand Barack until you understand Hawaii.'

For Hawaii residents, a lot of what that means is understanding the dynamics of a multicultural household and a multiracial heritage. Hawaii was the last state to join the Union in 1959, largely because of US political reluctance to embrace its ethnically mixed population. Now, 50 years later, President Obama's calls for consensus-building and respect for diversity, his emphasis on renewable energy, his hopes to build a balanced economy that sustains all peoples and environments – these national aspirations also exemplify, and may in part arise from his upbringing in, Hawaii.

Sustainability is the mantra on every Hawaii politician's lips. Since 2005, the state has been developing a comprehensive sustainability plan – called Hawaiʻi 2050 – that, when passed, will be used to help guide the legislature in its decision making. As much as its specific proposals, the novel, statewide effort to define sustainability – agreeing to a vision of Hawaii's ideal self and

FAST FACTS

Population: 1,288,198

Gross state product: $63.4 billion

Median household income: $63,750 (5th in the US)

Miles of coastline: 750

Size: 6450 sq miles (the USA's fourth smallest state)

Percentage of marriages that are interethnic: about 50%

Percentage of residents who want mandatory recycling: over 80%

Energy produced from oil: 89%

Energy from alternative sources: 5%

Average number of tourists in Hawaii each day: 180,000

Cans of Spam consumed in Hawaii annually: 7 million

then establishing concrete ways of measuring it – is helping instill that ethic in every community.

Hawaii's economy is overdependent on tourism, construction and real estate – three entwined activities that take a heavy toll on the environment and are particularly sensitive to recession. When recession then swept the nation in 2008, Hawaii's tourism nose-dived and construction stalled, and by year's end state revenue shortfalls had soared to nearly $2 billion. Much like President Obama, Hawaii's governor Linda Lingle has proposed that Hawaii spend its way out of trouble, and she's offered a $1.8 billion stimulus plan to fund a host of public works. New highways and bridges are the main focus, but improving Hawaii's communication infrastructure, to attract high-tech industry and help diversify the economy, is another goal. Supporting small-farm agriculture, and emphasizing a 'buy local' mentality, will also hopefully increase economic stability by decreasing Hawaii's reliance on others.

Though the recession will clearly slow certain changes, one area where Hawaii is not waiting is energy. In 2008 Governor Lingle signed the Hawai'i Clean Energy Initiative (HCEI), which sets the goal of having a 70% clean energy economy by 2030. Hawaii is the USA's most oil-dependent state (spending $7 billion annually on foreign oil), and it has the high utility bills to prove it. With HCEI, it's now pursuing every renewable and clean energy option available – wind farms on Maui, geothermal and biomass on the Big Island, electric cars on O'ahu, in addition to remaking its electricity grid. If it succeeds, Hawaii would become the first economy based primarily on clean energy (see http://hawaii.gov/dbedt/info/energy/hcei).

This would be revolutionary. However, lower bills and less pollution won't solve Hawaii's dire fight against invasive species. In fact, recession-inspired budget cuts may gut eradication efforts, despite the fact that Hawaii's unique ecosystems – in which 90% of all species are endemic – cannot survive intact without human intervention.

Intertwined with these issues is the one of quality of life. Tourism brings in about 7 million visitors annually, five times the state population. This impacts on everyday life – crowding the roads, the beaches, the surfing spots and driving up the price of real estate. Among cities, Honolulu has the third-highest cost of living in the country. While residents accept with equanimity a certain 'paradise tax,' there's the uncomfortable sense that costs have become too high.

Maintaining Hawaii's cultural identity is intimately linked to the health of the Native Hawaiian community, whose income levels and educational achievements typically fall below state averages. Recent years have seen some improvements (like increased dispersal of Hawaiian Home Lands and the continued funding of Hawaiian Charter Schools), but state programs like these aimed solely at helping Native Hawaiians have given rise to controversies over race-based preferential treatment. Many feel the solution to this is for Native Hawaiians to be federal recognized as an indigenous people who could, similar to Native American tribes, maintain some form of sovereign self-government. Legislation asking for this, the Akaka Bill, has sat before the US Congress since 2000. Yet there is now excited hope that it might soon be passed because the nation's new president is someone who 'understands Hawaii' and has pledged to support it.

Ask locals about all this and they freely acknowledge the challenges facing their state. They are also quick to add that they wouldn't live anywhere else. Hawaii may be endangered, but it possesses a beauty and spirit that can be found nowhere else. Plus, if Hawaii can achieve a sustainable balance, it may do more than save itself. It may become a model for the nation.

Getting Started

As tropical getaways go, Hawaii couldn't be easier or more varied. It's not always cheap, and it's a long way from anywhere, but whether you want to trek an urban jungle or a cloud forest, a snowy mountain or a nude beach, it's here.

With so many possibilities, and so many ways to blow a budget, careful planning is essential. To make the best use of your time, a good rule of thumb is to allow at least four to seven days for each of the four main islands. It's much more satisfying to see one island well than to madly island hop to fit more in. In fact, on Oʻahu, Maui, Kauaʻi and the Big Island even a week can feel rushed; you won't be sorry to spend two weeks on any of these islands.

Visiting two islands, even in only a week, is easy to do. However, we don't recommend trying for three islands in less than two weeks, and going for four islands really increases logistics and costs. For instance, the islands are small, but unless you're sticking to a resort, you'll need a car to get around. How many cars do you want to rent? The only place where Hawaii's public bus system is good enough to dispense with renting a car is Honolulu. For itinerary suggestions, see p30.

Also, as you know, Hawaii is popular. Make reservations early for the things you don't want to miss, particularly in high season. That said, if you're flexible, it's also possible to wing it; there's usually a hotel room somewhere, and many outdoor activities need booking only a day or two in advance. If you have kids, no worries; it's easy for families to travel in Hawaii.

WHEN TO GO

There is no bad time to be in Hawaii. The busiest seasons are mid-December through March and June through August – but this has more to do with weather and vacation schedules *elsewhere*. The weather in Hawaii varies only a little year-round – a bit rainier in winter, a bit hotter in summer.

For certain activities, however, the seasons are a consideration: the biggest waves hit the islands in winter, which makes it prime time for surfers. Windsurfers will find optimal conditions in summer. Whale watching happens mainly from January to March. For more on activities, see p73.

See Climate Charts (p563) for more information.

Bargain hunters should target April to May and September to mid-November, when you have the best chance of netting off-season rates in lodgings, plus everything is a little more relaxed.

Prices spike around the big holidays – Thanksgiving, Christmas, New Year's and Easter – and during special events. Unless you specifically want to see the North Shore's Triple Crown of Surfing (p189) or Hilo's Merrie

---

DON'T LEAVE HOME WITHOUT...

- Beach clothes and sun protection: hat, sunglasses, sunscreen, UV shirts; and, you know, a swimsuit
- Light jacket, fleece layers and rain gear for evenings and inland adventures
- Binoculars for wildlife watching, snorkel gear, and flashlights for lava tubes and hiking
- Rubbah slippahs and hiking boots (for safe hiking gear, see p86), because beachwear and trail-wear don't mix
- A takeout meal kit: reusable utensils, paring knife and plastic bags for leftovers
- Canvas bag for farmers markets and groceries
- A spirit of aloha and a hang-loose attitude

Monarch Festival (p294), avoid these places at these times. For Hawaii's top festivals and events, see p27.

COSTS & MONEY

Hawaii, as a rule, is an expensive destination: most things come at a premium – flights, groceries, gas, hotel rooms – but budget travelers can still fashion an economical trip to paradise. It all depends on your needs and style of travel.

The cost of flights has varied wildly recently, due to oscillations in the US economy and fare wars. In general, flights from the mainland USA (p572) run from around $500 to $1000. Interisland flights (p573) run from $60 to $90, but advance-purchase discounts can make them cheaper. For more on airfares, see p571.

On average, Hawaii travelers spend $180 per day per person on everything else. For a couple, that means budgeting $360 a day, and this gets you an enjoyable midrange trip with a few splashy meals and/or guided trips. It's very easy to spend more (particularly in Honolulu and Waikiki, and at resorts), and it's also easy to spend half that – bring a tent and a camp stove. When comparing islands, O'ahu is more expensive than the Neighbor Islands, and the Big Island is the least expensive.

Rental cars cost from $160 to $240 per week (see also p576); the only place to even think of doing without one is Honolulu.

Each island has the full range of sleeping options (see p560). All have state and county campgrounds costing $10 a night or less; Maui and the Big Island have excellent national parks with free camping. Hostel dorm beds run to around $20. In hostels, rural B&Bs and spartan hotels, you can find private rooms for $60 to $80. For nice midrange hotels, expect to pay from $120 to $200-plus nightly. At deluxe beachfront hotels, rates start around $250 and go up. Celebrating that special romantic occasion? Hawaii has some of the world's finest hostelries, and they are yours for $250 to $1000 a night. Some places offer weekly discounts (always ask), and weekly or monthly condo rentals offer good value.

Where you eat has a big impact on your budget. Since Hawaii has the highest grocery prices in the US, cooking your own food (whether camping or in a condo) isn't always *that* much cheaper than a diet of plate lunches, saimin (local-style noodle soups) and local *grinds* (food). However, inexpensive farmers markets are common. Midrange dinners run from $20 to $30 per person, and gourmet cuisine comes with gourmet prices – but you know that. For more on food, see p61.

SUSTAINABLE TRAVEL

'Sustainability' is the buzzword in Hawaii today, particularly when it comes to tourism. Green travel and ecotourism is booming, and all travelers to Hawaii can do their part – by buying local, choosing less-polluting activities (like hiking over helicopters), and patronizing ecofriendly businesses.

For Hawaii's own definition of sustainability, see p97. For a general overview, pick up *50 Simple Things You Can Do to Save Hawai'i* by Gail Grabowsky.

The **Hawaii Ecotourism Association** (www.hawaiiecotourism.org) certifies and lists green businesses – particularly hotels and tour operators – and keeps a list of further resources. Local communities are also establishing their own certification programs, such as the Big Island's **Kuleana Green Business Program** (www.kona-kohala .com/kuleana-green-business-program.asp). In this book, check out the GreenDex (p614), which lists the ecofriendly businesses we recommend, and for a short list of ways to go green, see p26. For advice about low-impact activities see p94.

Agricultural tourism in Hawaii is growing along with the increasing number of organic small farms. The **Hawai'i Agritourism Association** (www.hiagtourism.org) facilitates farm visits and stays, and it maintains a list of farmers markets. When

HOW MUCH?

Aloha shirt $20-70

Mai tai $5-7

Hawaii Regional Cuisine dinner for two: $120-160

Shave ice $2.50-5

Half-day snorkel cruise $90-110

shopping in grocery stores, the 'Apple Mountain' brand designates local products, and check out the product directory of the **Hawaii Organic Farmers Association**
(www.hawaiiorganicfarmers.org). See also Hawaii's Locavore Movement, p63.

Takeout food containers seem like a little thing, but they are a nightmare
for Hawaii's limited landfills. Look for, and patronize, places that use bio-
degradable takeout-ware. Two companies that make it are **Sustainable Island
Products** (www.sustainableislandproducts.com) and **Styrophobia** (http://styrophobia.com); their
websites list participating restaurants. On Maui, the town of Pa'ia has gone
the whole hog and banned plastic bags (www.nomoplasticbag.com).

To play a more active role in sustaining Hawaii, there are a wealth of
volunteer opportunities that can fit inside a standard vacation. See p570 for
a list of recommendations and contacts.

TRAVEL LITERATURE

In 1866 Mark Twain traveled to the 'Sandwich Isles' and sent back rollicking
dispatches from paradise, now collected as *Letters from Hawaii*. Twain's wit
and wisdom remain as dry as ever – whether he's turning up his nose at raw
fish, visiting 'Pele's furnaces' or witnessing the 'lascivious hula-hula.' There's
even a primer on whaling slang.

In *Blue Latitudes* (2002), Tony Horwitz sails in Captain Cook's wake over
200 years later. As he hops around the Pacific Ocean, ending in Hawaii,
Horwitz evaluates Cook's impact and legacy while contrasting Cook's then
with his own jet-assisted travels through Polynesia's now.

David Gilmore did what most only fantasize about: moved to Puna on the
Big Island to build his dream home in Hawaii. However, too cynical for paradise, Gilmore's dream became a nightmare of contractors, coqui frogs and local
Punatics, a hilarious tale he relates with good gay humor in *HomoSteading at
the 19th Parallel* (2007); see also www.nineteenthparallel.com.

In the compelling, poetic memoir *West of Then* (2004), Tara Bray Smith
searches for her homeless, drug-addicted mother in the public parks of
Honolulu. To unravel and understand how mother and daughter came to this,
she carefully places her family's sugar-plantation heritage within 20th-century
island history. This is unlike any other depiction of Hawaii you'll read.

For a glimpse of Native Hawaiian culture today, pick up *Voices of Wisdom:
Hawaiian Elders Speak* by MJ Harden. In it 24 *kupuna* (elders – including
well-known folk like Herb Kawainui Kane) discuss nature, activism, hula,
spirituality, music and more.

Exploring Lost Hawaii (2008) by Ellie Crowe ties ancient Hawaiian history
to the preserved cultural sites you can visit today, mixing in interviews with
locals and modern travel tales. It's a nice, personable companion.

It sounds incongruous, but *Hawaii's Best Spooky Tales*, a long-running
series edited and collected by Rick Carroll, is ideal beach reading. These
goofy, short, modern-day 'chicken-skin' stories are told by locals, and every
one is real! Okay, well, maybe some are a *little* exaggerated.

INTERNET RESOURCES

Alternative Hawaii (www.alternative-hawaii.com) A one-stop site for ecotourism, with hotels,
restaurants, info and more.
Hawaii Ecotourism Association (www.hawaiiecotourism.org) This nonprofit organisation
certifies and lists outfitters, tours and hotels committed to ecotourism.
Hawaii Visitors & Convention Bureau (www.gohawaii.com) The state's official tourism site.
Honolulu Advertiser (www.honoluluadvertiser.com) The state's main daily newspaper.
Lonely Planet (www.lonelyplanet.com) Hawaii travel news and links to other useful web resources.
Resource 4 Hawaii (www.resource4hawaii.com) Check out the gorgeous 360-degree-view
photos of Hawaii beaches and sights.

TOP PICKS

HAWAII

BEACHES

Let's make this simple. Go here. These are the top beaches by island. Of course, many, many more beaches deserve your attention, but you can't miss at these sandy beauties.

- O'ahu, Kailua Bay (p174)
- O'ahu, Waimea Bay (p185)
- O'ahu, Makaha Beach (p198)
- The Big Island, Hapuna Beach (p254)
- The Big Island, Makalawena Beach (p245)
- The Big Island, Waipi'o Valley (p282)
- Maui, Big Beach (p386)

- Maui, Ho'okipa Beach (p388)
- Maui, Malu'aka Beach (p385)
- Kaua'i, Hanalei Bay (p516)
- Kaua'i, Po'ipu Beach (p530)
- Kaua'i, Ke'e Beach (p524)
- Moloka'i, Halawa Beach (p453)
- Lana'i, Hulopo'e Beach (p432)

WAYS TO GO GREEN

It's easy to go green in Hawaii – and getting easier all the time. Here are some specific suggestions that show just how simple it is. For more on sustainable travel, see p24.

- Sleep off the grid on the Big Island: go primitive at Lova Lava Land (p325) or plush at Waianuhea B&B (p278).
- Rent a biofuel car on Maui: drive an eco-friendly VW Beetle from Bio-Beetle (p368).
- Learn about Native Hawaiian culture in Honolulu: visit the Bishop Museum (p126), take a class at Native Books/Nã Mea Hawai'i (p131) and attend Waikiki's Kuhio Beach Torch Lighting & Hula Show (p160).

- Use foot, pedal and wind power on Kaua'i: walk the Na Pali Coast (p525), bike the paved Ke Ala Hele Makalae trail (p502) and sail in a Polynesian canoe (p518).
- Become a locavore: get yourself some lunch at a farmers market (for a multi-island list, see p68).
- Give back: count whales or weed invasive plants...lots of organizations could use volunteers (see p570).

WILDLIFE WATCHING

By wildlife we mean the big fellas – humpback whales, dolphins – and endangered native species like the nene (native goose), Hawaii's state bird.

- Whale watching: Maui's West Coast (p334), the Big Island's Kona Coast (p220), Kaua'i's West Side (p540).
- Bird watching: Maui's Kealia Pond National Wildlife Refuge (p372); O'ahu's James Campbell National Wildlife Refuge (p185) and Goat Island (p184); Kaua'i's Kilauea Point National Wildlife Refuge (p507) and Alaka'i Swamp (p556); the Big Island's Hawai'i Volcanoes National Park (p314) and Hakalua Forest National Wildlife Refuge (p270); Moloka'i's Kamakou Preserve (p455).
- Manta ray gawking: the Big Island's Kona Coast (p218), Maui's Molokini Crater (p379).

- Sea turtle spotting: Maui's Malu'aka Beach (p385), the Big Island's Punalu'u Beach (p322) and Hilo-area beaches (p292), Kaua'i's Po'ipu Beach (p530), Oahu's Hanauma Bay (p166), Lana'i's Polihua Beach (p435).
- Monk seal spying: Maui's Wai'anapanapa State Park (p396), Kaua'i's Kilauea Point National Wildlife Refuge (p507) and Po'ipu-area beaches (p530).
- Dolphin glimpsing: Maui's Makena Bay (p385) and Honolua-Mokule'ia Bay (p358), the Big Island's Kealakekua Bay (p234).

Events Calendar

Hawaii is an almost year-round festival, with far too many to list. Here are some of the state's major festivals and cultural highlights. For more, see the destination chapters. Also check out the events calendars maintained by the **Hawaii Visitors & Convention Bureau** (www.gohawaii .com) and **Hawaii Magazine** (www.hawaiimagazine .com/events). For holidays, see p566.

JANUARY–FEBRUARY

CHINESE NEW YEAR   mid-Jan–mid-Feb
In Hawaii, everyone is Chinese for the Chinese New Year! For a week or two expect parades, street fairs and firecrackers – and lots of cleaning house. Honolulu (p131) is the biggest, but Lahaina on Maui (p343) and Hilo on the Big Island are notable.

KA MOLOKA'I MAKAHIKI   late Jan
The ancient *makahiki* festival – a time for sporting competitions and harvest celebration – still lives on in Moloka'i (p446).

WAIMEA TOWN CELEBRATION   mid-Feb
For two days Waimea (p547) on Kaua'i hosts over 10,000 folks for the island's biggest festival – with canoe and foot races, a rodeo, lei and hula competitions, live music and much more.

GREAT MAUI WHALE FESTIVAL   Feb
Maui celebrates its famous humpback whales with a diverse slate of events throughout the month (www.mauiwhalefestival.org), including a fun run, parade, whale count and kids' activities.

MARCH–APRIL

CHERRY BLOSSOM FESTIVAL   Mar
Though there are cherry blossom celebrations island-wide, this Japanese-culture festival is biggest in Honolulu (for details, see http://cbf hawaii.com). Events begin in February, but the biggies – the Heritage Fair and Festival Ball – are in March.

HONOLULU FESTIVAL   mid-Mar
For three days, this festival (p131) in Honolulu and Waikiki promotes the harmony of Pacific Rim cultures; it's a uniquely Hawaiian blend of Japan, Tahiti, China, Korea, the Philippines, Australia, the US and more, culminating in a huge parade.

MERRIE MONARCH FESTIVAL   from Easter Sun
The Big Island's renowned Merrie Monarch Festival starts on Easter Sunday in Hilo (p294). This week-long celebration of Hawaiian culture culminates in the Olympics of hula competitions; hula doesn't get any better. Reserve your hotel room early!

EAST MAUI TARO FESTIVAL   weekend in Apr
On Maui, the Hawaiian town of Hana throws its biggest party (p398) for two days in April. It's a great introduction to Native Hawaiian culture, with outrigger canoe races, poi (fermented taro) making, hula dancing and lots of Hawaiian music.

WAIKIKI SPAM JAM   late Apr
How much does Hawaii love Spam? Apparently, residents consume seven million cans a year. This one-day festival (p153) probably accounts for 10,000 all by itself, prepared hundreds of ways. Thankfully, there's no Spam-eating contest!

MAY–JUNE

MAY DAY LEI DAY   May 1
Across Hawaii, the ancient, beautiful tradition of lei making gets its own day on May 1. On Kaua'i, Lihu'e holds a festival and competition (p484), and Hilo on the Big Island (p294) hosts lei demonstrations, hula and more.

MOLOKA'I KA HULA PIKO   mid-May
According to oral history, Moloka'i is the birthplace of hula, and this three-day hula festival (p446) is one of the best on the islands for its sacred, traditional hula performances and Native Hawaiian *ho'olaule'a* (celebration).

**INTERNATIONAL FESTIVAL
OF CANOES**   2 weeks in May
Lahaina hosts Maui's biggest cultural event (p344), which features master carvers from around the Pacific carving outrigger canoes, then launching them. There are lots of festivities, but don't miss the Parade of Canoes.

PAN-PACIFIC FESTIVAL   1st weekend in Jun

True to its name, this three-day festival in Honolulu and Waikiki (p131) combines celebrations of Japanese, Hawaiian and South Pacific cultures, with hula, *taiko* drumming, a craft fair and a block party.

KING KAMEHAMEHA HULA
COMPETITION   early Jun weekend

For traditional hula, this is one of Hawaii's biggest contests (p132), with hundreds of dancers.

JULY–AUGUST

INDEPENDENCE DAY   Jul 4

Across the islands, Fourth of July celebrations inspire fireworks and fairs, but the most fun is had at the July 4 rodeos held in the *paniolo* (Hawaiian cowboy)–friendly towns of Waimea on the Big Island (p266) and Makawao on Maui (p406).

PINEAPPLE FESTIVAL   Jul 4

This festival (p430), celebrating Lana'i's special relationship with the pineapple, is the island's main bash. But guess what? They now have to import their pineapples.

PRINCE LOT HULA FESTIVAL   late Jul

One of Hawaii's premier Hawaiian cultural festivals, Prince Lot (p132) is notable for its noncompetitive hula event, which gives it an even more graceful, traditional feeling.

KOLOA PLANTATION DAYS
CELEBRATION   late Jul

On Kauai's south shore, this nine-day festival (p528) is a huge celebration of sugar-plantation heritage and island life. It's like a state fair, Hawaii-style, with diverse events including a parade, rodeo, canoe race, *keiki* (children's) hula, music and much more.

HAWAIIAN INTERNATIONAL
BILLFISH TOURNAMENT   late Jul–Aug

Kailua-Kona, on the Big Island, is the epicenter of big-game fishing – particularly for Pacific blue marlin – and for 50 years this has been Hawaii's grand tournament (p221). It's accompanied by a week of festive entertainment.

MAUI ONION FESTIVAL   weekend in Aug

For a weekend in August, Maui's famously sweet onions inspire delicious events, appealing to gourmet and gourmand alike. It's held in Ka'anapali's Whalers Village (p353).

SEPTEMBER–OCTOBER

ALOHA FESTIVALS   Sep-Oct

Begun in 1946, Aloha Festivals is the state's premier Hawaiian cultural festival, an almost nonstop, two-month series of events across the islands. On each island, the signature event is a Native Hawaiian royal court procession; these occur at 'Iolani Palace (p116), Hawai'i Volcanoes National Park (p318) and Lihu'e (p484), among others. For a complete listing of events, see the website http://alohafestivals.com.

QUEEN LILI'UOKALANI
CANOE RACE   Labor Day weekend

Outrigger canoeing is alive and well, and fall is the season for long-distance events – beginning with the Queen Lili'uokalani (p208), two days of outrigger canoe races along the Big Island's Kona Coast.

KAUA'I MOKIHANA FESTIVAL   mid-late Sep

On Kaua'i, the week-long Mokihana Festival includes an exceptional three-day hula competition in Po'ipu (p534), and in Lihu'e, the Kaua'i Composers Contest & Concert (p484). Both are fantastic opportunities to experience contemporary Hawaiian artistry and culture. The festival culminates in a royal court procession.

NA WAHINE O KE KAI   late Sep

This is the all-women sister event (p446) of the all-male Moloka'i Hoe (opposite). Both are legendary long-distance outrigger canoe races that traverse the 41-mile Ka'iwi Channel between Moloka'i and O'ahu.

COCONUT FESTIVAL   early Oct

You can't call yourself a Coconut Festival (p502) and not get a little nutty. In fact, Kapa'a on Kaua'i gets downright silly, with two days of pie-eating contests, coconut crafts, a huge cook-off and entertainment.

EO E EMALANI I ALAKA'I   early Oct

On Kaua'i, Koke'e State Park (p557) reenacts Queen Emma's historic 1871 journey to Alaka'i Swamp, with a one-day festival full of hula and Hawaiian music and crafts.

IRONMAN WORLD CHAMPIONSHIP   early Oct

On the Big Island (p221), this legendary triathlon is the ultimate endurance contest, combining a 2.4-mile ocean swim, 112-mile bike race and 26.2-mile marathon. Watch 1700 athletes wear themselves to the nub. (For more triathlons, see p87.)

MOLOKA'I HOE
mid-Oct

Like Na Wahine O Ke Kai (opposite), this is the men's version of the grueling outrigger canoe race (p446) between Moloka'i and O'ahu.

HAWAII INTERNATIONAL FILM FESTIVAL
late Oct

This highly regarded celebration of Pacific Rim cinema screens some 150 films in a dozen venues statewide. The focus is on Asian-, Polynesian- and Hawaiian-focused and -made films, by emerging filmmakers. The main action is in Honolulu (p132); see www.hiff.org for more details.

HALLOWEEN
Oct 31

On Maui, Lahaina's Halloween celebration (p344) was once so huge it was dubbed 'the Mardi Gras of the Pacific.' It's been scaled back, but it still includes a great street festival. Other towns also celebrate All Hallow's Eve.

NOVEMBER–DECEMBER

MOKU O KEAWE
early Nov

This new, three-night international hula competition on Hawai'i the Big Island (p250) has a sister hula festival in Japan and it draws top Japanese hula troupes.

KONA COFFEE CULTURAL FESTIVAL
early Nov

For a fortnight during the harvest season, the Big Island celebrates its renowned Kona coffee with parades, concerts, a cupping competition, a coffee-picking race, block parties and lots more (p221). For complete details, see www.konacoffee fest.com.

'UKULELE & SLACK KEY GUITAR MASTERS CONCERT
early Nov

On the Big Island, Waimea hosts two nights of concerts with Hawaii's ukulele and slack key guitar legends, who also hold workshops and master classes (p266).

TRIPLE CROWN OF SURFING
Nov-Dec

The North Shore in O'ahu– specifically Hale'iwa, Sunset Beach and Pipeline – hosts three of surfing's ultimate contests from November through December, which are known as the Triple Crown of Surfing (p81); for complete details, see http://triplecrownofsurfing.com.

E HO'OULU ALOHA
late Nov

In Wailuku on Maui, this concert (p369) – its name means 'To Grow in Love' – features Hawaiian singers and ukulele masters, as well as hula, crafts, food and more.

HONOLULU MARATHON
2nd Sun in Dec

The Honolulu Marathon (www.honolulumarathon .org) is without a doubt Hawaii's biggest and most popular, attracting 23,000 to 25,000 runners every year, making it one of the top 10 marathons worldwide. Anyone can enter. (For more marathons, see p87.)

CHRISTMAS SEASON
Dec

Hawaii hosts a range of Christmas celebrations. Honolulu has Honolulu City Lights, starting in early December with a parade and concert and greeting New Year's with fireworks. Other towns, notably Holualoa on the Big Island and Lahaina on Maui (p344), have tree-lighting festivals.

Itineraries

On the four main islands, one to two weeks allows a full experience of each island. To create your own multi-island trips, combine the shorter itineraries suggested in each chapter.

CLASSIC ROUTES

O'AHU
One to Two Weeks

Immerse yourself in **Honolulu** (p113) and **Waikiki** (p145) for four days. Between sessions at Waikiki's beaches (p149), eat your heart out in the city, tour **Chinatown** (p130), visit the **Bishop Museum** (p126) and **'Iolani Palace** (p116), see **Pearl Harbor** (p141), enjoy some live **Hawaiian music and hula** (p160) and tour Doris Duke's incomparable **Shangri La** (p165). Now relax. Heading east: spend a day snorkeling at **Hanauma Bay** (p166). Then surf, kayak or windsurf at the beaches along **Kailua Bay** (p174). Wind your way along the rural **Windward Coast** (p169), saving a day or two to enjoy the **North Shore** (p184) and the famous beaches around **Waimea** (p185). In winter, watch big-wave surfers carve; in summer, snorkel with sea turtles. If the clock's run out, drive along the scenic Kamehameha Hwy through **central O'ahu** (p195) and hit the airport; otherwise, veer west on H1 and explore the **Wai'anae Coast** (p197). Hike to **Ka'ena Point** (p200), watch (or join) the surfers at **Makaha Beach** (p198) and give thanks to the gods at **Makaha Valley's** beautifully restored sacred site, **Kane'aki Heiau** (p199).

A week or two on O'ahu gives unrepentant urbanites a chance to combine big city and big waves – enjoying world-class snorkeling, windsurfing and, of course, surfing without sacrificing gourmet *grinds* (food), hula, ancient heiau or the concrete jungle. You'll drive 125 miles or so.

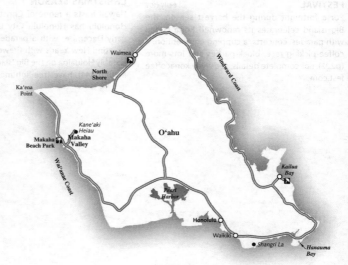

THE BIG ISLAND
One to Two Weeks

The Big Island can fill two weeks and then some. Base yourself in **Kailua-Kona** (p214) the first four days or so, combining trips to the beach – specifically, **Manini'owali Beach** (p246), **Kahalu'u Beach** (p226), **Hapuna Beach** (p254) and **Kauna'oa Bay** (p254) – with the art galleries and coffee farms in **Holualoa** (p228), the ancient mana (spiritual essence) of **Pu'uhonua o Honaunau National Historical Park** (p239), and a snorkel at **Kealakekua Bay** (p234). Then, spend two days in **North Kohala** (p257): hike into **Pololu Valley** (p263), visit **Mo'okini Heiau** (p259) and enjoy great eats in **Hawi** (p259). Or sightsee in North Kohala and save your appetite for **Waimea** (p263), which also has a nice selection of B&Bs. Is that a week already? Well, keep going. Take a leisurely drive along the **Hamakua Coast** (p277), making sure to at least peek into **Waipi'o Valley** (p279). Spend two days in **Hilo** (p285), exploring its downtown area, the farmers market and the excellent museums, particularly **'Imiloa** (p288). If you have extra time, detour either up to **Mauna Kea** (p269) for an evening of stargazing or venture into **Puna** (p300), lingering along **Red Road** (p304) and perhaps getting naked at **Kehena Beach** (p305). But leave at least two days for **Hawai'i Volcanoes National Park** (p306): hike the **Kilauea Iki Trail** (p315), drive along the **Chain of Craters Road** (p313), and hopefully trek to see some **hot lava** (p309). While adventuring, stay in one of the lovely **Volcano B&Bs** (p319). We understand that some have a plane to catch, but with another day or two for **Ka'u** (p321), you can admire sea turtles at black-sand **Punalu'u Beach** (p322), get in a last hike to **Green Sands Beach** (p324) and say good-bye from moody **Ka Lae** (p324).

The Big Island offers a continent's diversity within an island's circumference. In 320 miles, go from rain forests to snowy summits, from pastureland to dolphin-filled bays, from green-sand to black-sand to white-sand beaches, from artists villages to a working-class city, and from volcanic craters to hot lava.

MAUI

One to Two Weeks

You're on your honeymoon, right? Well, we're not waiting around for laggards. Just keep up. Start off in the old whaling town of **Lahaina** (p336) and explore its treasure trove of **historic sites** (p342), perhaps celebrating your special occasion with the superb **Old Lahaina Luau** (p347). Head north into **west Maui** (p348). In winter, spot whales breaching offshore, particularly at **Papawai Point** (p350) and take a **whale-watching tour** (p343). Naturally, at a time like this, money is no object, so indulge in a resort at **Ka'anapali** (p351) and enjoy its excellent beaches; spend two days (three if you're really in love), but then let's go! Drive around the peninsula, stopping at gorgeous **Kapalua Beach** (p358), and, OK, snorkel with spinner dolphins at **Slaughterhouse Beach** (p358), but eventually get on the scenic **Kahekili Highway** (p361). Stop to admire the legendary jade spire of **'Iao Valley State Park** (p371), then keep going to **south Maui** (p374): book a snorkel cruise to **Molokini Crater** (p379), check out more whales at **Kihei** (p375), and either snorkel around **Makena** (p385) or perhaps sunbathe au naturel at **Little Beach** (p386). Oh my, look at the time – only a day left!? Get thee to **Haleakalā National Park** (p413) before you go. Those staying longer should spend two days **hiking** (p417) this awesome crater and catching the **sunrise from the summit** (p419). Then drive the cliff-hugging **Road to Hana** (p392), stopping frequently to gape in wonder. Those smart enough to stay the full two weeks can lounge around at hip **Pa'ia** (p388), enjoying delicious eats and admiring the daredevil windsurfers at **Ho'okipa Beach Park** (p388); overnight in **Hana** (p396); and do some windsurfing yourself at **Kanaha Beach** (p365) before departure time. And by the way, congratulations!

For an adventure-packed holiday that doesn't skimp on the pampering, Maui combines comfy resorts with splendid beaches, whale watching, unbelievable snorkeling and windsurfing, the world's largest volcanic crater and the harrowing Hana Hwy. Activity hounds: 300-plus miles of driving.

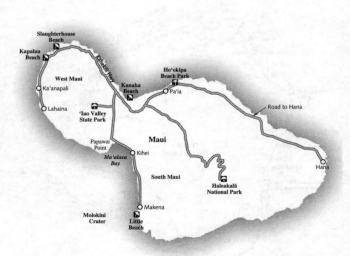

KAUA'I

One to Two Weeks

If you've chosen Kaua'i, you're looking for adventure, but let's start off nice and easy in **Po'ipu** (p530). Nap off your jet lag for a day or two on the sunny beaches here. For a taste of where we're headed, go to nearby Port Allen for a **Na Pali Coast snorkeling tour** (p540); scuba divers can take this chance to dive into the waters around **Ni'ihau** (p533). Now, lace up your hiking boots and spend the next two (or three) days in **Waimea Canyon State Park** (p550) and **Koke'e State Park** (p553): trek the bogs of the **Alaka'i Swamp** (p557), traverse knife-edge 2000ft cliffs on the **Awa'awapuhi Trail** (p556) and wear yourself out on the **Kukui Trail** (p551). If you aren't camping, then stay in **Waimea** (p545) and eat and shop in funky **Hanapepe** (p542); if it's Friday, chill out in **Hanapepe's art galleries** (p544). Well rested, head east: hit **Wailua** (p488) and kayak the **Wailua River** (p492) or the less crowded **Hule'ia River** (p482). If you have kids, don't miss **Lydgate Beach Park** (p489). If time is tight, skip Wailua and giddy-up to the **North Shore** (p507), which deserves three or four days. Get in some snorkeling and windsurfing at **'Anini Beach** (p511), and check out the surf-bum town of **Hanalei** (p516), while surfing and kayaking in **Hanalei Bay** (p516). Scenic drives hardly get more scenic than driving the 'End of the Road' to **Ha'ena State Park** (p524); mix in snorkeling at **Ke'e Beach** (p524) with a visit to beautiful **Limahuli Garden** (p524). OK, ready? **Na Pali Coast State Park** (p525) is all that's left: if it's May to September, **kayak** (p519) 17 miles along the coast; otherwise, hike the **Kalalau Trail** (p525). Either way, you've saved the best for last and have your story to dine out on.

Kaua'i is Hollywood's ready-made set whenever it needs a 'tropical paradise.' This faceted jewel of canyons, cliffs, waterfalls, rivers, bays and beaches is more than a backdrop for pretty actors, however. It's one of Hawaii's best, most soulful adventures. You'll drive 175 miles.

ISLAND HOPPING

You've got time, you've got money and you want culture, outdoor adventure and peaceful relaxation in equal measure. Combine O'ahu, Maui and Lana'i – half the time, you won't even need to drive. You get Hawaii's only metropolis, its fluffiest beaches and its quietest island. It's 300 miles, more or less.

O'AHU, MAUI & LANA'I   Two Weeks

This trip is for lovers, culture vultures and anyone happy to spend a little more for plush lodgings and gourmet eats. Start on O'ahu, basing yourself in **Waikiki** (p145) for a week. Among the major cultural sights in **Honolulu** (p113), don't miss the **Bishop Museum** (p126), **'Iolani Palace** (p116), the **Honolulu Academy of Arts** (p123) and **Pearl Harbor** (p141). Along with time spent on Waikiki's beaches, snorkel at **Hanauma Bay** (p166) and hike the **Mt Tantalus** (p129) and **Makiki Valley** (p128) trails, after visiting the **Lyon Arboretum** (p125). End each day exploring **Honolulu's dining scene** (p132) and enjoying lots of good **Hawaiian music and hula** (p160).

Now go to Maui for four or five days. Again, make it easy: get a nice room, for the duration of your visit, at **Lahaina** (p336) or **Ka'anapali** (p351). Immerse yourself in Lahaina's whaling history in town and at Ka'anapali's **Whalers Village Museum** (p352), enjoy some old-school aloha at the **Old Lahaina Luau** (p347), take a **whale-watching cruise** (p343), and for a thrill, try **ziplining** (p353). As for beach time, make do with **Kapalua Beach** (p358), **Ka'anapali Beach** (p351) and **Honolua Bay** (p358), and take one afternoon to visit **Haleakalā National Park** (p413).

Finally, stay in one of **Lana'i's world-class resorts** (in Lana'i City, p430; at Hulopo'e and Manele Bays, p433) for three or four nights. Things have been a little hectic so far, so play a round of **golf** (p430), snorkel at **Hulopo'e Beach** (p432) or take in the vistas from the **Munro Trail** (p436). To really get away, rent a 4WD and head for the **Garden of the Gods** (p435) and **Polihua Beach** (p435).

See the Transportation chapter for details on island hopping by air (p573) and/or boat (p575).

THE BIG ISLAND, MOLOKA'I & KAUA'I   Two to Three Weeks

This trip is for those who consider a six-hour hike a half-day's work and who prefer their 'view lanai' to be a patch of grass outside their tent flap. Don't camp the whole way; mix in enough hotels to keep this a vacation. Start on the Big Island and get a comfy B&B in **South Kona** (p230) for a few nights. For ocean adventures, hike to secluded, gorgeous **Makalawena Beach** (p245), kayak and snorkel at **Kealakekua Bay** (p232) and snorkel or dive at night with **manta rays** (p219) around Kailua-Kona. In **Ka'u** (p321), bunk in a **VW bus at Lova Lava Land** (p325), and go **caving at Kula Kai Caverns** (p325), hike to **Green Sands Beach** (p324), and take the **Road to the Sea** (p325). Then spend three nights camping and hiking in **Hawai'i Volcanoes National Park** (p306). Spend a night or two in **Hilo** (p285), and day-hike one of the big mountains, either **Mauna Kea** (p269) or **Mauna Loa** (p275). Next, camp at **Laupahoehoe Point** (p283) or **Kalopa State Park** (p283), and explore **Waipi'o Valley** (p279). If you've got the time, consider backpacking to **Waimanu Valley** (p282).

Next, spend three to four days on Moloka'i. Good camping is scarce, so stay in a condo or B&B in **Kaunakakai** (p446). Day one: explore **East Moloka'i** (p449), checking out **Halawa Valley** (p453) and perhaps **Moa'ula Falls** (p453). Day two: penetrate the raw forests of the **Kamakou Preserve** (p455). Day three: trek to the **Kalaupapa Peninsula** (p458).

With five or six days in Kaua'i, spend three camping and hiking at **Koke'e State Park** (p553) and **Waimea Canyon State Park** (p550), then boogie up to the **North Shore** (p507), mixing some camping at **'Anini Beach** (p511) or **Ha'ena Beach** (p524) with lodgings in **Hanalei** (p519). Swim, snorkel and surf, but don't leave without tackling the Na Pali Coast's *amazing* **Kalalau Trail** (p525). All in all, this trip is a hiker's dream.

If you want to live in the scenery (not just admire it), consider combining the Big Island, Moloka'i and Kaua'i, which offers the hiking and backcountry adventure of a lifetime plus lots of ancient and modern-day Hawaiian culture. It's 550 miles (that's driving, not hiking).

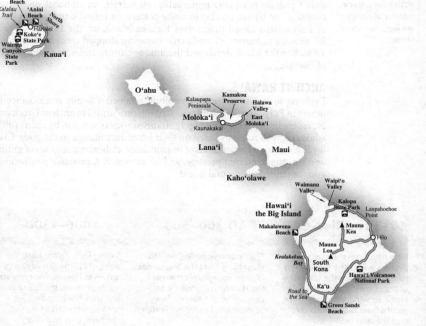

History

Want a history of Hawaii you can finish on the plane flight over? Grab A *Concise History of the Hawaiian Islands* (1999) by Phil Barnes, which captures a surprising amount of nuance in 90 crisp pages.

POLYNESIAN VOYAGERS

To ancient Polynesians, the Pacific Ocean was a passageway, not a barrier, and the islands it contained were connected, not isolated. Sailing double-hulled canoes fashioned without the benefit of metals, they settled an immense continent consisting largely of water. Sometime between AD 300 and 600, they made their longest journey yet and discovered the Hawaiian Islands. This would mark the northern reach of their migrations, which were so astounding that Captain Cook – the first Western explorer to take their full measure – could not conceive of how they did it, settling 'every quarter of the Pacific Ocean' and becoming 'by far the most extensive nation upon earth.'

Almost nothing is known about the first wave of Polynesians (likely from the Marquesas Islands) who settled Hawai'i except that the archaeological record shows that they were here. A second wave of Polynesians from the Tahitian Islands began arriving around AD 1000, and they conquered the first peoples and obliterated nearly all traces of their history and culture. Later Hawaiian legends of the *menehune* – an ancient race of little people who mysteriously built temples and great stoneworks overnight – may in fact refer to these original inhabitants.

For 300 years, regular voyaging occurred between Polynesia and Hawai'i, and Polynesians brought to the islands their religious beliefs, social structures and over two dozen food plants and domestic animals. But what they didn't possess is equally remarkable: no metals, no alphabet or written language, no wheel, no clay to make pottery. In Hawai'i, the second wave of Polynesians called themselves Kanaka Maoli, or 'the People.' When, for reasons unknown, cross-Pacific voyaging stopped completely around 1300, Kanaka Maoli developed the unique culture endemic to the islands of Hawaii.

Well designed, succinct and informative, Hawaii History.org (www.hawaiihistory.org) is an interactive timeline of Hawaii's history that makes it easy to browse quickly or delve deeply into events, with lots of links.

ANCIENT HAWAI'I

Evolving in isolation, Hawaiian culture retained a family resemblance to others in Polynesia, which all bear striking similarities to ancient Greek and Norse traditions: Hawai'i's highly stratified society was run by chiefs (*ali'i*) whose right to rule was based on their hereditary lineage to the gods. Clan loyalties trumped expressions of individuality, elaborate traditions of gifting and feasting conferred prestige, and an extremely humanlike pantheon of gods inhabited the natural world.

TIMELINE

40–30 million BC	AD 300–600	1000–1300
Kure rises from the sea, appearing where the Big Island is today, beginning the formation of the current island chain; borne by wind, wing and wave, plants, insects and birds colonize the new land.	The first wave of Polynesians, most likely from the Marquesas Islands, voyage by canoe to the Hawaiian Islands – a half-century before Vikings leave Scandinavia to plunder Europe.	Sailing from Tahiti, a second wave of Polynesian voyagers arrives in Hawaii. Their tools are made of stone, shells and bone, and they bring taro, sweet potato, sugarcane, coconut, chickens, pigs and dogs.

VOYAGING AMONG THE STARS

In 1976, the 62ft double-hulled canoe *Hokule'a*, a reproduction of an ancient Hawaiian long-distance sailing vessel, set off to do what no one had done in over 600 years: sail 2400 miles to Tahiti without benefit of radar or compass, satellites or sextant.

Hokule'a's Micronesian navigator, Mau Piailug, wasn't without tools. He knew how to use horizon or zenith stars – those that always rose over known islands – as a guide, then evaluate currents, winds, landmarks and time in a complex system of dead reckoning to stay on course. In the mind's eye, the trick is to hold the canoe still in relation to the stars while the island sails toward you. In ancient times, Hawai'i's horizon star was called Hokule'a, the Star of Gladness.

After 33 days at sea, *Hokule'a* reached its destination, where it was greeted by 20,000 Tahitians. This historic achievement swelled all Polynesians with pride and led to a new appreciation and interest in Polynesian and Hawaiian cultures.

Hokule'a and the Polynesian Voyaging Society (http://pvs.kcc.hawaii.edu) have been sailing by the stars ever since. They made a second Tahitian voyage in 1980 – with Hawaiian Nainoa Thompson, who apprenticed under Piailug, as *Hokule'a*'s master navigator – followed by six more throughout Polynesia and the Northwestern Hawaiian Islands. The most recent voyage was a five-month, 9500-mile trip to Micronesia and Japan in 2007.

Several layers of *ali'i* ruled each island, and life was marked by much warring as they jockeyed for power and status. The basic political subdivision was the *ahupua'a*, a wedge-shaped slice of land from the mountains to the sea that contained all the resources each chiefdom needed. Below the chiefs were the ka-huna (experts or masters), who included both the priests and the guildmasters – canoe makers, healers, navigators, and so on. *Maka'ainana* (commoners) did most of the physical labor, and below all was a small class of outcasts *(kaua)*.

A culture of mutuality and reciprocity infused what otherwise resembled a feudal agricultural society: chiefs were custodians of their people, and humans custodians of nature, all of which was sacred – the living expression (or mana, spiritual essence) of the universe's immortal soul. Everyone played their part, through work and ritual, to maintain the health of the community and its relationship to the gods; when needs and honor were satisfied, Hawaiians enjoyed themselves immensely, cultivating rich traditions in music, dance, sport and competition. Change was only marked by the seasons. If chiefs abused their power or failed their duties, commoners were free to move to other chiefdoms.

Nevertheless, in practice, a very strict code of ritualized behavior – the kapu system – governed every aspect of daily life; violating the kapu meant death. Further, in a society based on mutual respect, slights to honor – whether of one's chief or extended family – could not be abided. As a result, ancient Hawai'i was both a gracefully unselfish and fiercely uncompromising place.

Don't miss artist, historian and voyager Herb Kawainui Kane's beautiful history *Ancient Hawai'i* (1997). The 11 paintings that inspired this book are on display at the Four Seasons Resort Hualalai (p247).

1778–79	1810	1819
Captain Cook visits Hawaii twice, the first foreigner to reach the islands. After being warmly welcomed, Cook loses his temper over a stolen boat and is killed by Hawaiians.	Fourteen years after conquering the other islands, King Kamehameha the Great negotiates peacefully to take control of Kaua'i, uniting all the islands under one kingdom for the first time.	King Kamehameha dies 'in the faith of his fathers'; a few months later, his son, the new king Liholiho, breaks the kapu on eating with women, repudiating the Hawaiian religion, but with nothing to replace it.

CAPTAIN COOK & THE DISCOVERY OF THE WEST

Britain's greatest explorer, Captain James Cook, spent a decade traversing the Pacific Ocean over the course of three voyages. His ostensible goal was to locate a fabled 'northwest passage' between the Pacific and Atlantic Oceans. However, his were also self-conscious voyages of discovery, and he sailed with a full complement of scientists and artists to document the places, plants and peoples they found. In 1778, on the third trip, and quite by accident, Cook found the Hawaiian Islands.

In *Cook* (2003), Nicholas Thomas seeks the breathing present-tense man behind the controversial legend, retelling the story of Captain Cook's Pacific voyages with nuance and sensitivity to all perspectives.

Cook's arrival ended nearly 500 years of isolation, and it's impossible to overstate the impact of this, or even to appreciate now what his unexpected appearance meant to Hawaiians. Cook, of course, was well familiar with Polynesian peoples, but Hawaiians knew nothing of the metal, guns, gods, diseases and races his ships carried, not to mention the world view they represented: Hawaiians lived in an island world inseparable from the spiritual world, while Cook embodied a continental consciousness steeped in the individualism of Europe's Enlightenment, in which gods ruled only heaven and only men ruled earth.

In January 1778, Cook dropped anchor off O'ahu, and as he had elsewhere in the Pacific, he bartered with the indigenous peoples for badly needed food and fresh water. Then he left to hunt again for the northwest passage. He returned to the islands in November, this time sighting Maui. However, he didn't land, but kept moving, circling the Big Island – continuing to trade for fresh supplies as he went – until he stopped in Kealakekua Bay in January 1779.

For a fuller story of what happened next, see p236. Cook's ships were greeted by a thousand canoes, and Hawaiian chiefs and priests honored Cook with rituals and deference suggesting they perhaps considered him a god. The Hawaiians were so unrelentingly gracious, in fact – so fair in their dealings, so agreeable in every respect, including the eagerness of Hawaiian women to have sex – that Cook and his men felt safe to move about unarmed.

However, when Cook set sail some weeks later, he encountered storms that damaged his ships and forced him to return. Suddenly, the mood had changed: no canoes rowed out to meet them, and mistrust replaced welcome. A series of small conflicts escalated into an angry confrontation on the beach, and Cook, in an ill-advised fit of pique, shot and killed a Hawaiian while surrounded by thousands of natives. The Hawaiians immediately descended on Cook, killing him in return.

KAMEHAMEHA THE GREAT

In the years following Cook's death, a small, steady number of trading ships sought out Hawaii as a mid-Pacific supply point, and increasingly the main item Hawaiian chiefs traded for was firearms. Bolstered with muskets and

1820	1826	1828
The first Christian missionaries arrive in Hawaii; King Liho-liho eventually allows leader Hiram Bingham to establish his missionary headquarters in Honolulu.	Missionaries formulate a 12-letter alphabet (plus glottal stop) for the Hawaiian language and set up the first printing press. It's said that Queen Ka'ahumanu learns to read in five days.	Missionary Sam Ruggles introduces the first coffee tree as a garden ornamental; coffee doesn't become a commercial crop until the 1840s, when hundreds of acres are planted on the Big Island.

cannons, Kamehameha, one of the chiefs on the island of Hawai'i, began a tremendous military campaign in 1790 to conquer all the Hawaiian Islands. Other chiefs had tried this and failed, but Kamehameha not only had guns, he was prophesied to succeed and possessed an unyielding, charismatic determination. Within five bloody years he conquered all the main islands but Kaua'i (which eventually joined peacefully); for more, see p261.

Kamehameha was a singular figure whose reign established the most peaceful era in Hawaiian history. A shrewd politician, he configured multi-island governance to mute competition among the *ali'i*. A savvy businessman, he created a highly profitable monopoly on the sandalwood trade in 1810 while protecting trees from overharvest. He personally worked taro patches as an example to his people, and his most famous decree – Ka Mamalahoe Kanawi – established a kapu that protected innocent travelers from harm on the road.

Most of all, Kamehameha successfully absorbed growing foreign influences while fastidiously honoring ancient religious customs. He did this despite creeping doubts among his people about a divine social hierarchy and system of punishment that seemed oddly limited to Hawaiians. When Kamehameha died in 1819, he left the question of how to resolve this discrepancy in the hands of his son and heir, 22-year-old Liholiho.

Within the year, pressured by his stepmother Queen Ka'ahumanu and other powerful leaders, Liholiho deliberately broke the kapu and willingly abandoned Hawaii's gods in one sweeping, stunning act of repudiation (see the boxed text, p40). Suddenly and unexpectedly unmoored from its spiritual anchor, Hawaiian society immediately drifted into confusion.

> Of Hawaii's eight ruling monarchs, only King Kamehameha I begot children who inherited the throne.

MISSIONARIES & WHALERS

Into the midst of this upheaval, on April 19, 1820, the brig *Thaddeus* landed in Kailua on the Big Island, delivering a group of New England missionaries at a fateful moment. The missionaries' Christian zeal to save pagan souls was, however, matched by a deep disdain of Hawaiians themselves and of nearly every aspect of their traditional culture, which they soon worked tirelessly to stamp out.

The missionaries arrived expecting the worst, and that's what they found: public nakedness, 'lewd' hula dancing, polygamy, gambling, drunkenness, fornication with sailors. To them, all kahuna were witch doctors, and Hawaiians hopelessly lazy. Converts to Christianity came, since the missionaries' god was clearly powerful, but these conversions were not deeply felt; Hawaiians often abandoned the church's teachings to enjoy their typical lives. However, the missionaries found one thing that attracted avid, widespread interest: literacy.

The missionaries established an alphabet for the Hawaiian language, and with this tool, Hawaiians learned to read with astonishing speed. In their

> In 1839, New England missionaries needed five months to sail to Hawaii, and later steamships took five weeks. Today, airplanes can cross the continent and the ocean nonstop in half a day.

1830	1846	1848
To control dangerous herds of feral cattle (originally a gift from Vancouver to Kamehameha), Hawaii imports Spanish-Mexican cowboys, dubbed 'paniolo,' who introduce Hawaiians to the guitar.	At the height of the whaling era, a record 736 whaling ships stop at Hawaii ports. Ultimately, four of the Big Five sugar plantation companies get their start supplying whalers.	King Kamehameha III institutes the Great Mahele, which (along with the 1850 Kuleana Act) for the first time allows commoners and foreigners to own land in Hawaii.

DESTRUCTION OF THE TEMPLES

The purpose of the ancient Hawaiian kapu system was to preserve mana, or the manifest spirit of the gods animating the world. Mana could be strong or weak, won or lost; it expressed itself in one's talents and the success of a harvest or battle. Chiefs inherited mana through their lineage to the gods, and maintaining this was most important of all.

The kapu system kept ali'i from mingling with commoners and men from eating with women (to avoid dissipating mana). It kept women from eating pork and shark and from entering luakini heiau, or sacrificial temples. Chiefs could declare temporary kapus, and they punished with death even small infractions, say, a commoner stepping on an ali'i's shadow.

However, white foreigners, once they arrived in Hawaii, were clearly not governed by nor held accountable to the kapu system. Lesser ali'i saw you could possess power without following it, and women saw that breaking it – such as by secretly eating with sailors – didn't incur the gods' wrath. Kamehameha's unruly, powerful wife, Ka'ahumanu, particularly chafed under the kapu, as it kept her and all women from becoming leaders equal to men.

Eventually, even Hawaii's head priest, Hewahewa, couldn't justify the system. Upon Kamehameha's death in 1819, he and Ka'ahumanu convinced Liholiho, Kamehameha's heir, that the time had come. After observing the traditional mourning period, they arranged a huge feast where Liholiho was to sit and eat with women, thereby breaking and renouncing the kapu.

Such an act – effectively ending Hawaii's religion – was nearly beyond the young king. He dawdled for several months, and the day before, to bolster his courage, he drank himself into a royal stupor. But act he did. To the shock of the gathered ali'i, Liholiho helped himself to food at the women's table. Then Hewahewa, signaling his approval, noted that the gods could not survive without the kapu. 'Then let them perish with it!' Liholiho is said to have cried.

Immediately, and for months afterward, Ka'ahumanu and others set fire to the temples and pulled down and destroyed images of the gods. Most Hawaiians were happy to be released from the kapu, but many also continued to venerate the gods and secretly preserved religious idols.

Some, in fact, openly rebelled. Led by Hawaii's second-highest priest, Kekuaokalani, a small army gathered to defend the gods, but in battle, Liholiho's superior forces defeated them in fusillades of musket fire.

---

oral culture, Hawaiians were used to prodigous feats of memory, and ali'i understood that literacy was a key to accessing Western culture and power. Within a decade, two-fifths of the population was literate, and by the mid-1850s, Hawaii had a higher literacy rate than the United States and supported dozens of Hawaiian-language newspapers.

At the same time, Pacific whaling ships found Hawaii an ideal place to reprovision and transfer their catch to ships heading for America. By 1824, over 100 ships were arriving annually, and this number grew exponentially for the next three decades. Particularly once the sandalwood trade collapsed in 1830 (after profligate ali'i allowed the trees to be pillaged to pay off their debts), whaling became the economic backbone of the islands,

1852	1873	1879
The first sugar plantation contract laborers arrive from China; most Asian immigrants are single men who, upon completing their contract, often stay in Hawaii, starting families and small businesses.	A Belgian Catholic priest, Father Damien Joseph de Veuster, arrives at Moloka'i's leprosy colony to aid the sick. He stays for 16 years, dying of leprosy (now Hansen's disease) himself in 1889.	King Kalakaua lays the cornerstone for a new 'Iolani Palace, a lavish, four-story building with ornate throne room, running water and electric lights; it costs $350,00 and is completed in 1882.

especially in ports like Honolulu and Lahaina. Supplying the whalers also influenced island agriculture – since sailors didn't want poi (fermented taro) and breadfruit; they wanted beef, potatoes and green vegetables.

Additionally, sailors tended to conflict with the missionaries, since they enjoyed all the pleasures the missionaries censured. Amid these influences, it became clear to Hawaiian leaders that the only way to survive in a world of more-powerful nations was to adopt Western ways and styles of government.

MONARCHY & THE GREAT MAHELE

Born and raised in Hawaii after Western contact, King Kamehameha III (Kauikeaouli) struggled to retain traditional Hawaiian society while evolving the political system to better suit foreign, and frequently American, tastes. Hawaii's absolute monarchy denied citizens a voice in their government or the right to own land. Traditionally, no Hawaiian ever 'owned' land, but *ali'i* managed it in stewardship for all. However, none of this sat well with US patriots who, but a generation before, had fought a revolution to prove that representative government and private property were the *sine qua non* of civilization.

So, in 1840, Kauikeaouli promulgated Hawaii's first constitution, which established a constitutional monarchy with limited citizen representation. Given an inch, foreigners pressed for a mile, and in 1848, Kauikeaouli followed this with a revolutionary land reform act that was known as the Great Mahele (the great division).

This act took Hawaii and divided it three ways: into crown lands (owned by the kings and their heirs), chief lands (*ali'i* holdings within traditional *ahupua'a*), and government lands (to be held for the general public). This was followed in 1850 by the Kuleana Act, which awarded 30,000 acres of government lands to Hawaiian commoners, and it gave foreigners the right to purchase some lands.

The hope was that the Great Mahele would create a nation of small freeholder farmers, but instead it was an utter disaster – for Hawaiians, at least. Confusion reigned over boundaries and surveys. Unused to the concept of private land, and sometimes unable to pay the tax, many Hawaiians simply failed to follow through on the paperwork to claim their titles. Many of those who did – perhaps feeling that life as a taro farmer wasn't the attraction it once was – immediately cashed out, selling their land to eager and acquisitive foreigners.

Within 30 to 40 years, despite supposed limits, foreigners owned fully three-quarters of Hawaii, and Hawaiians, who had relinquished so much of their culture so quickly, had now lost their sacred connection to the land. As historian Gavan Daws wrote, 'The great division became the great dispossession.'

Born and raised on a Kona coffee farm, Gerald Kinro brings personal insight and scholarship to *A Cup of Aloha* (2003), a wonderful portrait of the Kona coffee industry and Hawaii's agricultural life.

For a century, the trip to Moloka'i's Kalaupapa Peninsula wasn't an adventure but a death sentence. In *The Colony* (2006), John Tayman tells this incredible story with dignity, compassion and unflinching honesty.

1893	1895	1898
On January 17, the Hawaiian monarchy is overthrown by a group of American businessmen, supported by US Marines. Queen Lili'uokalani acquiesces peacefully but under protest. Not a shot is fired.	Robert Wilcox leads a group of Hawaiian royalists in a failed counter-revolution to restore the monarchy. The deposed queen, charged with being a coconspirator, is placed under house arrest in 'Iolani Palace.	On July 7, President McKinley signs the resolution annexing Hawaii as a US territory; this is formalized by the 1900 Organic Act establishing the territorial government.

KING SUGAR & THE PLANTATION ERA

In another fateful moment of synchronicity, 1848 was the year gold was discovered in California – spurring the gold rush and Manifest Destiny, which swept west across North America and leapt from the coast to land on Hawaii's shores.

American entrepreneurs, increasingly landowners, discovered it was cheaper to supply California's gold miners from Hawaii than from the US East Coast. Foreign-controlled shipping, banking and agriculture grew, along with a struggling effort to make sugar commercially viable. All these shifts accelerated in the 1860s: the whaling industry collapsed (due to whale declines and the discovery of oil) at the same time that the American Civil War created a sharp demand for sugar in the north. In short order, sugar became Hawaii's staple export.

In 1860, 12 plantations exported under 1.5 million pounds of sugar; by 1866, 32 plantations were exporting nearly 18 million pounds. After the war, the demand for Hawaiian sugar dropped and the industry languished. When King Kalakaua was elected to the throne in 1874, he immediately lobbied the United States for a reciprocity treaty that would end foreign import taxes on sugar (thus ensuring profits). The United States agreed in 1876, and sugar production instantly skyrocketed, rising to 58 million pounds in 1878 and 114 million pounds in 1883.

Abundant supplies of low-cost labor were also necessary to make sugar plantations profitable. The first and natural choice was Hawaiians, but even when willing, they were not enough. Due primarily to introduced diseases – like typhoid, influenza, smallpox and syphilis – the Hawaiian population had steadily and precipitously declined. An estimated 800,000 people lived in the islands before Western contact, and in just two decades, by 1800, the Hawaiian population had dropped by two-thirds, to around 250,000. By 1860, Hawaiians numbered fewer than 70,000.

Beginning in the 1850s, plantation owners encouraged a flood of immigrants from China, Japan, Portugal and the Philipines to come to Hawaii to work the cane fields. These immigrants (see the boxed text, opposite), along with the culture of plantation life itself, transformed Hawaii into the multicultural, multiethnic society it's known as today.

Five sugar-related holding companies, known as the Big Five, quickly rose to dominate all aspects of the industry: Castle & Cooke, Alexander & Baldwin, C Brewer & Co, American Factors, and Theo H Davies & Co. All these companies were run by white businessmen, many the sons and grandsons of missionaries. While their focus shifted from religion to business, they reached the same conclusion as their forebears: Hawaiians could not be trusted to govern themselves. So, behind closed doors, the Big Five openly mused about whether Hawaiians should be relieved of that responsibility.

The plantations are gone, but Moloka'i and Lana'i both have big pineapple hangovers. *Hawai'i's Pineapple Century* (2004) by Jan Ten Bruggencate is a highly readable account of how the spiky fruit changed life across Hawaii.

1909	1912	1916
In Hawaii's first major labor strike, 5000 Japanese plantation workers go on strike, protesting their low pay and harsh treatment compared to Portuguese workers. The strike ultimately fails, winning no concessions.	Duke Kahanamoku wins gold and silver medals in freestyle swimming at the Stockholm Olympics; he goes on to become the ambassador of surfing around the world.	Hawai'i National Park, the nation's 12th national park, is established. It initially encompasses Haleakalā on Maui and Kilauea and Mauna Loa on the Big Island; these later become separate parks.

HAPA CHILDREN, PIDGIN TONGUES

Hawaii's unique multiethnic society was an unplanned accident of 19th-century sugar plantation economics. Needing cheap labor, plantations encouraged successive waves of immigrants who, stirred together for a century in the bubbling kettle of plantation life, emerged intermingled and increasingly intermarried, each generation inheriting a maligned mutt of a language, pidgin, that crossed cultural divides.

Typically, plantations offered laborers two- or three-year contracts, which included monthly wages, housing and medical expenses. When their contracts expired, some workers returned home, some moved to the US mainland, but the majority stayed in Hawaii.

In the 1850s, Chinese immigrants were the first to come in great numbers, eventually reaching about 45,000 before the USA's 1882 Chinese Exclusion Act dampened arrivals. All immigrant groups left their cultural stamp on the islands, and one change the Chinese spurred was replacing taro with rice.

Eventually totalling about 180,000 immigrants from the late 1860s to the 20th century, Japanese would become the largest ethnic group. 'Hawaii *netsu*,' or Hawaii fever, was encouraged by the Japanese government; most immigrants were single men, which led to the mail-order 'picture bride' phenomenon among those who stayed. Japanese also established themselves as independent coffee farmers on Hawai'i island.

The next major group (totalling about 20,000) was Portuguese, who were actively recruited beginning in 1878. In part because they were Europeans, Portuguese were treated better than Asians – they were paid more, and were often made supervisors over Asian field workers. Japanese complaints over these unfair discrepancies led to Hawaii's first organized labor strike in 1909.

After the turn of the century, Koreans and then a huge influx of Filipinos arrived. Totalling about 100,000, Filipinos found, as others had before them, that plantation life was much harsher than promised, and they were another prominent force in Hawaii's budding labor movement.

By the 1930s, immigration slowed to a trickle, though the sugar plantations would remain Hawaii's economic backbone and cultural melting pot for another 30 to 40 years.

OVERTHROW & ANNEXATION

As much as any other monarch, King Kalakaua fought to restore Hawaiian culture and native pride. With robust joy, he resurrected hula and its attendant arts from near extinction – earning himself the nickname 'the Merrie Monarch' – much to the dismay of white Christians. But he cared not a whit about placating the plantation oligarchy.

He spent money lavishly, piling up massive debts. Kalakaua wanted Hawaii's monarchy to be equal to any in the world, so he built a new 'Iolani Palace, beginning in 1879, and held an extravagant coronation in 1883. Foreign businessmen considered these to be egotistical follies, but worse, Kalakaua was a mercurial decision-maker given to summarily replacing his entire cabinet on a whim.

A secret, antimonarchy group called the Hawaiian League formed, and in 1887 they presented Kalakaua with a new constitution. This one stripped

1921	**1927**	**1941**
The Hawaiian Homes Commission Act is passed. This sets aside 200,000 acres for homesteading by Hawaiians with 50% or more native blood, granting 99-year leases costing $1 a year.	The $4-million, Moorish-style Royal Hawaiian Hotel, dubbed the 'Pink Palace' for obvious reasons, opens in Waikiki, inaugurating an era of steamship tourism to the islands.	On December 7, Pearl Harbor is attacked by Japanese forces, catapulting the US into WWII. The sinking of the battleship USS *Arizona* kills 1177 crew members.

the monarchy of most of its powers, making Kalakaua a figurehead, and it changed the voting laws to exclude Asians and include only those who met certain income and property requirements – effectively disenfranchising all but wealthy, mostly Caucasian business owners. Finally, since the Treaty of Reciprocity had run out, this renewed it by accepting US demands to give America permanent rights to Pearl Harbor. To ensure the profitability of its businesses, the Hawaiian League was ready to pay the price of Hawaiian sovereignty.

In *Legends and Myths of Hawaii*, King David Kalakaua captures the shimmering nature of ancient Hawaiian storytelling by seamlessly mixing history (of Kamehameha, Captain Cook, the burning of the temples) with living mythology.

Under threat of violence and against his wishes, Kalakaua signed, leading this to become known as the 'Bayonet Constitution.' When King Kalakaua died in 1891, his sister and heir, Princess Lili'uokalani, ascended the throne. The queen fought against foreign intervention and control, and she secretly drafted a new constitution to restore Hawaiian voting rights and the monarchy's powers. However, in 1893, before Lili'uokalani could present this, a hastily formed 'Committee of Safety' put in motion the Hawaiian League's long-brewed plans to overthrow the Hawaiian government.

First, the Committee requested support from US Minister John Stevens, who allowed 150 marines to come ashore in Honolulu Harbor 'only to protect American citizens in case of resistance.' The Committee's own 150-strong militia then surrounded the palace and ordered Queen Lili'uokalani to step down. With no standing army, and wanting to avoid bloodshed, Lili'uokalani acquiesced under protest.

After the coup, the Committee of Safety formed a provisional government and immediately requested annexation by the US. However, much to their surprise, new US President Grover Cleveland reviewed the situation and refused: he condemned the coup as illegal, conducted under false pretext and against the will of the Hawaiian people, and he requested Lili'uokalani be reinstated. Miffed but unbowed, the Committee instead established their own government, the Republic of Hawaii.

Shoal of Time by Gavan Daws (1968) remains perhaps the most well-written account of Hawaiian history from Captain Cook's arrival to statehood in 1959.

For the next five years, Queen Lili'uokalani pressed her case (for a time from prison) – even collecting an anti-annexation petition in 1897 signed by the vast majority of Native Hawaiians – to no avail. In 1898, spurred by new US President William McKinley, the US approved a resolution for annexing the Republic of Hawaii as a US territory. In part, the US justified this colonialism because the ongoing Spanish-American War had highlighted the strategic importance of the islands as a Pacific military base. Indeed, some feared that if America didn't take Hawaii, another Pacific Rim power (like Japan) just might.

PEARL HARBOR & THE JAPANESE PROBLEM

In the years leading up to WWII, the US government became obsessed with the Hawaiian territory's 'Japanese problem.' That is, they asked, what were the true loyalties of 40% of Hawaii's population, the first-generation

1946	1949	1959
On April 1, the most destructive tsunami in Hawaii history (generated by an earthquake in Alaska) kills 176 people across the islands, 96 in Hilo, and causes $10.5 million in property damage.	Dockworkers stage a 177-day strike that halts all shipping to and from the islands; this is accompanied by plantation worker strikes that win concessions from the Big Five companies.	Hawaii becomes the 50th state in the Union (a decision Hawaiians ratify by a margin of 17 to 1), and Hawaii's Daniel Inouye becomes the first Japanese American elected to the US Congress.

(issei) and second-generation (nisei) Japanese? During a war, would they sabotage Pearl Harbor for Japan or defend the US? Neither fully Japanese nor American, nisei also wondered about their identity.

Then, on December 7, 1941, a surprise Japanese invasion, consisting of 47 ships and submarines and 441 aircraft, bombed and attacked military installations across O'ahu. The main target was Pearl Harbor, the USA's most important Pacific naval base: among other damage, nine battleships and other ships were sunk; seven battleships, cruisers and destroyers were damaged; and over 3000 military and civilians were killed or injured. For more on the attack, see p142.

This devastating attack instantly propelled the USA into WWII. In Hawaii the army took control of the islands, martial law was declared, and civil rights were suspended. Immediately following the Pearl Harbor attack, around 1500 Japanese residents were rounded up, arrested and placed in internment camps.

However, a coalition of forces in Hawaii successfully resisted immense government pressure, including from President Roosevelt himself, to follow this with a mass internment of Japanese on the islands, to match what was being done on the US West Coast. Ultimately, around 110,000 Japanese were interned on the US mainland, but the majority of Hawaii's 160,000 Japanese citizens were allowed to live independently – though they suffered sometimes-intense racial discrimination and deep suspicions over their loyalties.

Further, in 1943, the government was persuaded to reverse itself and approve the formation of an all-Japanese combat unit, the 100th Infantry Battalion. Over 10,000 nisei volunteered for the 3000-soldier unit. This was sent, along with the all-Japanese 442nd Regimental Combat Team, to fight in Europe, where they became two of the most decorated units in US military history. By the war's end, Roosevelt proclaimed these soldiers were proof that 'Americanism is a matter of the mind and heart,' not 'race or ancestry.'

The 1950s would test this noble sentiment, but Hawaii's unique multiethnic society emerged from the war severely strained but not broken. Afterward, Japanese nisei and war veterans became some of Hawaii's most prominent politicians and businessmen.

THE 50TH STATE IS PARADISE

The Territory of Hawaii had lobbied for statehood ever since it was created, but statehood bills always failed mostly because of US political reluctance to accept its multiethnic, Asian-majority population on equal terms. After WWII and during the Cold War, Southern Democrats in particular raised the specter that Hawaiian statehood would leave the US open not just to the 'Yellow Peril' (embodied, as they saw it, by imperialist Japan) but to Chinese and Russian communist infiltration through Hawaii's labor unions. Further, they feared that Hawaii would elect Asian politicians who would seek to

Memoirs of a Buddhist Woman Missionary in Hawaii (1991) by Shigeo Kikuchi is a fascinating firsthand account of Japanese sugar plantation life and of the fears and prejudice suffered by Japanese in Hawaii during WWII.

The Island Edge of America (2003) by Tom Coffman tells the story of 20th-century Hawaii, emphasizing the impact of Japanese immigration and WWII on island politics.

1961	1962	1968
Elvis Presley stars in *Blue Hawaii*, the first of Elvis' three Hawaii movies. Along with *Girls! Girls! Girls!* and *Paradise, Hawaiian Style,* these set the mood for Hawaii's post-statehood tourism boom.	Democrat John Burns is elected as governor, and Democrats take control of all three branches of state government (including the House and Senate), a stranglehold on power they maintain until 2002.	*Hawaii Five-0* begins its 12-year run, becoming one of American TV's longest-running crime dramas. The iconic theme song soon epitomizes Hawaii, along with main character Steve McGarrett's unflappable hair and his tagline, 'Book 'em, Danno.'

end the USA's then-legal segregation. Conversely, proponents of statehood increasingly saw it as a necessary civil rights step to prove that the US actually practiced 'equality for all.'

In the late 1950s, both Hawaii and Alaska (which had suffered similar denials) were competing to be admitted as the 49th state. Alaska won, being approved in June 1958, but Hawaii was not disappointed long; eight months later, in March 1959, Congress voted again and finally admitted Hawaii. On August 21, President Eisenhower signed the bill that officially made Hawaii the 50th state of the USA.

A few years later, surveying Hawaii's relative ethnic harmony, President John Kennedy pronounced, 'Hawaii is what the United States is striving to be.' More than optimistic symbolism, Hawaii's two new senators (along with those from Alaska) helped secure the passage of America's landmark civil rights legislation in the 1960s.

As was the hope, statehood had an immediate economic impact, and once again, Hawaii's timing was remarkably fortuitous.

The decline of sugar (and pineapples) in the 1960s (due in part to the labor concessions won by Hawaii's unions) left the state scrambling economically – and just then the advent of the jet airplane (and of disposable incomes) meant tourists could become Hawaii's next staple crop. Tourism exploded, which naturally led to a building boom, in an ongoing cycle. In 1959, 175,000 visitors came, and by 1968, there were 1.2 million a year. By 1970, tourism was contributing $1 billion annually, four times what agriculture produced.

Ever since Mark Twain had visited in the 1860s, Hawaii had lived in the popular imagination as an earthly paradise, a lush, sensuous-yet-safe (and English-speaking) tropical idyll. Hawaii now gave rise to a full-blown tiki craze, in which the culture of Native Hawaiians was appropriated and commercialized to fulfill the romantically exotic, cross-cultural fantasies of vacationing Westerners.

In 1936, designer Ellery Chun updated the 'palaka,' a solid-colored plantation worker shirt, with a tropical print and a more casual style, which he dubbed the 'aloha shirt.' The rest is history.

HAWAIIAN RENAISSANCE

By the 1970s, Hawaii's rapid growth was making the state dizzy. New residents and visitors crowded the beaches and the roads, and rampant construction was transforming places like Waikiki so much they hardly resembled themselves. Ironically, the relentless peddling of 'aloha' got everyone wondering: did it actually exist, or was it just a marketing gimmick?

In fact, what did it mean to be Hawaiian? In the 1970s and 1980s, this question became a quest for Native Hawaiians, who turned to elders and the past to recover their essential selves, and by doing so became more politically assertive.

Up to now, no one had ever satisfactorily answered Cook's question: was it really possible that ancient Polynesians voyaged to Hawaii deliberately, or were they blown there by accident? In 1973, three men formed the Polynesian

Native Books Na Mea Hawai'i (www.native bookshawaii.com) is a fantastic resource for both well-known and hard-to-find books about Hawaii and Native Hawaiian culture.

1971	1976	1978
The Merrie Monarch hula festival, begun in 1964, holds its first competitive hula competition; the festival, part of a Hawaiian cultural resurgence, becomes Hawaii's proving ground for serious hula.	Activists illegally occupy Kaho'olawe, and *Holuke'a* – a reproduction of an ancient Polynesian voyaging canoe – sails to Tahiti. These events spur a Native Hawaiian cultural and political rennaissance.	The 1978 Constitutional Convention establishes the Office of Hawaiian Affairs (OHA), which holds the Hawaiian Home Lands in trust to ensure they are used for the benefit of Native Hawaiians.

HAWAIIAN SOVEREIGNTY & THE AKAKA BILL

In February 2009, Hawaii Senator Daniel Akaka reintroduced into the US Congress the Native Hawaiian Government Reorganization Act – aka the Akaka Bill. This seeks to establish the legal framework through which a Native Hawaiian government can be formed and thereby gain federal recognition of Native Hawaiians as the indigenous people of Hawaii. This would, in essence, finally put them on the same legal footing as the over 500 federally recognized Native American tribes.

Federal recognition of Native Hawaiians is widely supported in Hawaii (including by Governor Lingle), but there is lots of controversy and disagreement over what shape 'Hawaiian sovereignty' should ultimately take. As a result, the bill's sponsors emphasize what the legislation does *not* do: it doesn't establish a government (it provides the means for doing so); it doesn't settle any reparation claims; it doesn't take private land or create a 'reservation'; it doesn't authorize gambling; and it doesn't allow Hawaii to secede from the US.

Establishing a Native Hawaiian government, as Senator Akaka has said, 'is important for all people of Hawaii, so we can finally resolve the longstanding issues relating from the overthrow of the Kingdom of Hawai'i.'

The two main options are the semi-autonomous 'nation-within-a-nation' model, similar to Native Americans, and outright sovereignty, in which Native Hawaiians would have full autonomy over portions of land within the state of Hawaii.

Either option raises thorny, complex questions about who would be included and what land would be used. However, there are starting points for addressing both. First, the state of Hawaii holds in trust over a million acres of 'ceded lands,' which by law are to be used for the benefit of Native Hawaiians, in addition to the island of Kaho'olawe (p422). Second, extensive Native Hawaiian genealogical databases already exist, since the separate dispersal of Hawaiian Home Lands requires that applicants prove they are at least 50% Native Hawaiian.

Today, with Hawaii-born President Barack Obama indicating his support, hopes run high that the Akaka Bill might soon be passed. For legislation updates, see the Office of Hawaiian Affairs website www.nativehawaiians.com.

Voyaging Society, and they researched and built a replica of an ancient voyaging canoe, *Hokule'a* (see p37). In 1976, they sailed it to Tahiti using only the stars for a compass – and thus proved the Polynesians' feat and became Hawaiian cultural heroes.

That same year, an even more important spark was struck: a group of Moloka'i activists illegally occupied Kaho'olawe (p422), aka 'Target Island,' which the US government took during WWII and ever since had used for bombing practice. During a fourth landing/occupation in 1977, two Hawaiian activists disappeared at sea under mysterious circumstances, instantly becoming martyrs. After that, saving Kaho'olawe became a rallying cry, and it radicalized the nascent Native Hawaiian rights movement.

When the state held its landmark Constitutional Convention in 1978, it passed a number of important Native Hawaiian amendments, such as

1983	1992	1993
Kilauea Volcano begins its current eruption cycle, now the longest in recorded history. Eruptions destroy the village of Kalapana, various subdivisions, the coastal road to Puna, and other sites.	On September 11, Hurricane 'Iniki slams into Kaua'i, demolishing 1300 buildings and damaging 5000, causing a total of $1.6 billion in damage. Miraculously, only four people are killed.	On the 100-year anniversary of the overthrow of the Hawaiian monarchy, President Clinton signs the 'Apology Bill,' in which the US government acknowledges its role in the illegal takeover of the kingdom.

making Hawaiian the official state language (along with English) and mandating that Hawaiian culture be taught in public school. All these efforts led to a Native Hawaiian cultural revival, with a surge of residents, of all ethnicities, enrolling in hula schools, playing Hawaiian music, resurrecting the language, and rediscovering traditional crafts like lei-making and *lauhala* (leaf) weaving.

The Hawaiian Independence website (www .hawaii-nation.org) is an excellent source for current news and information on the Hawaiian Sovereignty movement, with clear descriptions of the issues and links to many perspectives and voices.

SEEKING A SUSTAINABLE BALANCE

By the 1990s, Hawaii was discovering the limits of its island resources. Its economy, now inextricably bound up with tourism, felt increasingly like a devil's bargain. By 1990, seven million tourists arrived annually, and tourism contributed $10 billion. The state population had doubled since 1959, to 1.3 million, but still, on any given day one out of nine people on O'ahu was a tourist; on Maui, one out of three.

Hawaii's unique environment and endemic species were being threatened by invasive species and loss of habitat, and off-island real-estate speculators and escalating housing prices were threatening to do the same to island residents, who couldn't afford to live in paradise anymore. Hawaii had sold itself too well. And for the first time, no ready economic savior presented itself.

The Office of Hawaiian Affairs (OHA; www.oha .org) posts up-to-date news and overviews of Native Hawaiian issues on its website, and publishes the monthly *Ka Wai Ola*.

Further, in 1993, President Bill Clinton signed Public Law 103-150, which was a formal apology from the US government to Native Hawaiians for the illegal overthrow of the Hawaiian monarchy 100 years prior. The apology gave new fuel to the Hawaiian sovereignty movement, a diverse collection of sometimes conflicting groups all agitating for Native Hawaiian self-government. The most high-profile effort that emerged was the Akaka Bill, which Senator Daniel Akaka first submitted to Congress in 2000 (see p47).

As Hawaii entered the 21st century, the state found itself seeking not yet another societal transformation, but a sustainable balance, one that preserved equally Hawaii's diverse culture, its unique environment and its residents' quality of life.

2000	2002	2008
Senator Daniel Akaka introduces the Native Hawaiian Government Reorganization Act (the 'Akaka Bill'), asking for federal recognition of Native Hawaiians as the islands' indigenous peoples.	In part as a response to Democratic corruption scandals, Republican Linda Lingle is elected governor, Hawaii's first Republican governor in 40 years. She is reelected in 2006.	Born and raised on O'ahu, Barack Obama is elected the first Hawaii-born president of the United States. In the election, Obama wins 72% of the vote in Hawaii, the most of any state.

The Culture

There's a great divide between the Hawaii of popular culture – that seductive vision of paradise – and the actual islands, a regular place where people live regular lives. Both exist, sometimes side by side; they may even share the same white-sand beach. But to grow up here, to be *kama'aina*, a 'child of the land,' is to see and experience Hawaii differently. This shared experience bonds locals despite their incredible diversity. Residents love Hawaii in all its imperfect, polyglot everydayness because they know – no matter how messy and mundane life is – it always beats the movie version.

REGIONAL IDENTITY

Plunk in the middle of the Pacific Ocean, Hawaii has its own fluid yet distinct sense of self. Poi (fermented taro), Spam, shave ice, volleyball, surfing, ukulele, hula, pidgin, broken-down sandals – these are the commonplace touchstones of everyday life. Island style is easygoing, low-key, casual; even guitar strings are more relaxed. Most distinctive of all – from a mainland US perspective – is that one's ethnicity – whatever it is – is usually unremarkable.

How different is Hawaii? During the 2008 US presidential election, island residents were thrilled that someone from Hawaii might be president, but much ink was spilled debating Barack Obama's 'localness.' As in: he has roots here, he is a *kama'aina* by birth, but leaving after high school, never coming back... that's often enough to lose your local cred. Still, he was and is embraced by locals because his unflappable cool and his respect for diversity resonate with Hawaii, he knows how to bodysurf, and he displayed true devotion to his grandmother, Toots (who lived in Honolulu and died days before the election).

In Hawaii, these are the things that count. That Obama is mixed race was an afterthought, almost unimportant. *Of course* he's mixed race – who isn't in Hawaii? One of the legacies of the plantation era is Hawaii's unselfconscious mixing of ethnicities; cultural differences are freely acknowledged, even carefully maintained, but they don't cleave society or the classroom. For residents, these two things – a relaxed lifestyle and inclusive cultural values – are probably the most defining, best-loved aspects of Hawaii.

As a state, Hawaii often feels overlooked by the nation, and yet it's protective of its separateness, its difference. Mainland transplants tend to stick out. For instance, as a rule (especially among seniors and Asians), loud assertiveness is looked down on. It is better to avoid embarrassing confrontations and 'save face' by keeping quiet. In a stereotype that's often true, the most vocal, liberal and passionate speakers – at a community meeting, a rally – are often pushy New Yorkers or California activists who just moved. No matter how long they live here, these folks will never be considered 'local.'

Of course, globalization and the internet age have meant a creeping sameness to culture everywhere. Locals love Costco and Wal-Mart; pop and Jawaiian (Hawaiian Island–style reggae) music can drown out traditional sounds. Some island stereotypes are fading. Then again, fast-food chains like McDonald's appeal to local tastes by adding rice, Spam and teriyaki burgers to their menus. The influence works both ways.

Within Hawaii, the biggest difference is between Honolulu and the Neighbor Islands. A huge metropolis, Honolulu is cosmopolitan, technologically savvy and fashion conscious. It has the major sports stadiums, the main university and an actual nightlife. Affluent city residents are more likely to share the upwardly mobile, professional aspirations of their mainland

What does it mean to be Hawaiian today? Read the wonderful, sharp-eyed journalist Sally-Jo Bowman's *The Heart of Being Hawaiian* (2008), a moving collection of articles and interviews that circle this question with unsentimental tenderness.

Tireless, much-loved cultural preservationist Mary Kawena Pukui's *Folktales of Hawai'i* (1995), illustrated by Sig Zane, is a delightful, bilingual collection of ancient teaching stories and amusing tall tales.

counterparts; they are more likely to wear business suits and travel. Though, travel often means Las Vegas (aka 'the ninth Hawaiian island'), for gambling and talking story with its large community of Hawaii expats.

Neighbor Islands are considered 'country' or even *da boonies* (the boondocks). In general, Neighbor Islanders tend to dress more casually, speak more pidgin, be more working-class and preserve plantation-era distinctions. Status isn't a Lexus but a monster truck. Family is important everywhere, but on Neighbor Islands it may be the center of one's life. When locals first meet, they don't ask 'What do you do?' but 'Where you wen' grad?'; like ancient Hawaiians comparing genealogies to find common bonds, locals identify themselves by listing the communities they're from – extended family, island, town, high school – not their accomplishments. Locals don't migrate restlessly; they find their place and stay, and they may be complete strangers to other parts of their island. Tourist hot spots create exceptions to these generalizations, but their influence is surprisingly limited.

In *Folks You Meet in Longs* (2005), *Honolulu Advertiser* columnist Lee Cataluna captures the flavor, and above all the voice, of working-class Hawaii in these painfully funny, exquisitely real first-person vignettes.

LIFESTYLE

Lifestyles differ between Honolulu and the Neighbor Islands just as city and rural lifestyles do anywhere. But even in Honolulu, people generally live more balanced and relaxed lives than in comparable US cities. In Hawaii, local life is relatively simple and often family-oriented. School sports events are packed with eager parents, plus the gamut of aunties and uncles (whether actual relatives or not). Working overtime is the exception, not the rule; weekends are for play and potlucks at the beach. Locals are of course not immune to natural beauty and balmy weather: life is lived outdoors, and golfing, fishing and surfing rule.

By most social indicators, life is good. Hawaii has been ranked the second-healthiest state in the nation, with a low uninsured population. Almost 90% of residents have a high-school degree, and almost 30% have a bachelor's degree (both above the national average). Rates of violent crime are nearly half what they are on the mainland. In 2007 Hawaii's median household income ($63,746) ranked fifth, and its poverty rate (8%) was third lowest, among US states.

Why is Hawaii the best? Hawaii residents have the longest life expectancy in the US: 81 years, compared with the US average of 78. Doctors credit a clean environment and healthy living.

However, incomes get spent quickly. Utility bills average three times higher than the mainland and grocery bills are exorbitant (since 85% of all food is imported). Honolulu has the third-highest cost of living among US cities (behind New York and San Francisco). Sky-high real-estate prices keep many locals from being able to buy their own home; though it's fallen recently, the median price of a home on Oʻahu was $625,000 in 2008. As one indication of the burden of housing costs, one study found that nearly 50% of renters and homeowners spent 30% or more of their income on housing. On Neighbor Islands, most affordable housing isn't near the majority of jobs (near resort areas), resulting in long commutes and increasing traffic jams.

Native Hawaiians also have some glaring disparities in their quality of life. They make up a disproportionate number of homeless and impoverished. Native Hawaiian schoolchildren, on average, lag behind state averages in reading and math, and they are much more likely to drop out of school. Hawaiian charter schools were created to address this problem, and they have demonstrated some remarkable success (using alternative, culturally focused methods). However, many Native Hawaiians feel that some form of sovereignty is necessary to give them control over their own circumstances (see p47).

These stresses – along with having to deal with a constant flow of travelers looking for paradise – can sap the aloha of residents. In recent years, there's a hard-to-quantify feeling that life isn't as good as it once was, which is partly why the state is so focused on developing a sustainability plan (see p97).

THE MOST AUTHENTIC LUAU IN HAWAII

Like getting sunburnt and wearing an aloha shirt, attending a commercial luau is something most visitors can't leave Hawaii without doing. Some are better than others, but none are truly 'authentic' – in the sense of representing the Hawaiian celebration they're named after. The modern resort-style luau is Hawaiian dinner theater – a huge buffet feast followed by a high-energy variety show featuring sexy performers and flashy dance numbers interspersed with vaudeville humor, cultural presentations, and the classic call-and-response: 'AloooooooooHA!'.

On the Big Island, the Kona Village Resort's luau (p247) is considered one of the best, and we spoke with the resort's longtime Hawaiian Cultural Historian and luau hostess Lani 'Opunui. Winner of a 2008 'Keep It Hawai'i – Lehua Maka Noe' award, Lani researches Hawaiian and Polynesian culture, and consults with other practitioners, to ensure she presents 'the dance and the culture from which it comes as accurately as possible.' The luau producers also try to match performers with dances appropriate to their heritage, but 'it's always a struggle. There's always a push to do the Waikiki-type show, the driving-it-home kind of show.' Kona Village's Wednesday-night luau 'has more meat to it,' she says. 'I go through the changes that affected Hawaiian hula, but the fire knife is the big show.'

And how authentic is that dramatic finish? Lani laughs: 'I used to explain this bit of history. It was developed by a Samoan in San Francisco. He combined fire twirling with juggling the ancient knife.' So, call it authentic Samoan entertainment.

Lani suggests that the best way to judge a good luau is by its food. When deciding where to go, compare luau menus, and choose the one with the greatest number of Hawaiian and local dishes – and skip any that don't cook a pig in an *imu* (underground earthen oven).

Even here, though, judging what's 'authentic' is tricky. At everyday luaus, Lani says, 'two of the most popular dishes besides *kalua* pig are chicken long rice and *lomilomi* salmon (minced, salted salmon, diced tomato and green onion). Except for chicken, neither have any Hawaiian ingredients. Even the word *kaukau* – as in, "We go *kaukau*" or "Let's go eat" – is not Hawaiian. It has a Chinese root. Also, I know it's sacrilegious, but sometimes I'll put sugar on my poi.'

Lani says, 'Hawaiians are not above adjusting. We're a very adaptive people. That's why we survived like we have.'

In regular life, luaus are thrown 'for graduation, major birthday, first birthday of a kid – or baby luau – weddings. They are not everyday and they're expensive.' Typically, it's a three-day event, with family and helpers cooking the day before and cleaning the day after, with an enormous party in the middle. While there's music and hula, it's casual and everyone joins in. The main focus is eating and celebrating. As one local told us, 'an "authentic" luau is when you and your friends make the food.'

And yet, no matter what difficulties arise, finding someone who'd actually prefer to live somewhere else is hardest of all.

ECONOMY

For decades the Hawaii economy has rested on four main pillars: tourism; construction and real estate; the military; and agriculture. Tourism is Hawaii's leading employer and accounts for 20% of all economic activity, and since 2002 it's enjoyed a spectacular boom – that is, until the 2008 recession brought it, and the state economy, to a screeching halt.

Perhaps 'halt' is overstating it, since in 2008, 6.8 million people visited the islands and spent $11.3 billion. But this was the first year since 2004 that visitation dropped below seven million, and visitor spending dropped $1.2 billion from 2007. Similarly, construction job growth galloped at 8% annually up until 2008, when it reported its first decline in six years. Home foreclosures also shot up: in 2007, the state ranked 43rd nationwide for fewest foreclosures; by fall 2008 it was ranked 20th.

Hawaii currently has no industry that can pick up the slack when tourism and real estate falter. The military (the state's second-largest employer) is subject to

Hawaii leads the nation in shared housing: 6.6% live with parents or relatives, compared with 2.6% nationally.

the budgetary whims of military agencies, and expansions (such as the training of Stryker brigades) create a host of environmental concerns (see p95).

Since the demise of the plantation era, Hawaii agriculture has been diversifying with macadamia nuts, coffee, floriculture, papayas and more. Sugarcane, once the king, is now commercially harvested on only one Maui plantation; likewise, only one pineapple plantation survives – and both are struggling financially. Agriculture accounts for less than 1% of Hawaii's gross domestic product, but reviving small farms is seen as an essential aspect of building a sustainable economy – one that could literally feed itself.

Hawaii is also looking to attract clean energy and high-tech industries as a way to diversify, since the state recognizes that continued growth in tourism (and more low-wage service sector jobs) no longer supports Hawaii's long-term health.

How did ancient Hawaii turn into mai tais, resort luau and tiki bars? Find out in *Tiki of Hawaii: A History of Gods and Dreams* (2005) by Sophia V Schweitzer, which succinctly captures the post-WWII tiki craze.

POPULATION

Over 70% of Hawaii's 1.3 million residents live on O'ahu, making Honolulu Hawaii's only real city. On O'ahu, population density is nearly 1500 people per sq mile, compared with 109 on Maui and 37 on the Big Island. Yet, in terms of its share of Hawaii's population, the Big Island has grown the fastest since 1990.

Ethnically, Hawaii is unique. First, it is among only four US states in which whites do not form a majority. Second, it has the largest percentage of Asian Americans (55%, predominantly Japanese and Filipino) among all states. Third, Hawaii has the highest mixed-race percentage (18.5%) among all states, and nearly half of all marriages are mixed race. Fourth, Hawaii was the first majority-minority state in the USA since the early 20th century – and its current minority (nonwhite) population constitutes a whopping 75%.

Today roughly 80,000 of Hawaii's people identify themselves solely as Native Hawaiian. However, about 250,000 identify themselves as all or part Hawaiian, while some estimate that the number of pure Native Hawaiians is actually less than 8000. Interestingly, Hawaii only contains an estimated 60% of Native Hawaiians worldwide, and the percentage off-island is growing as Native Hawaiians increasingly leave Hawaii (usually for economic reasons).

WHO'S WHO

- haole – white person (except local Portuguese); further defined as 'mainland' or 'local' haole.'

- *hapa* – person of mixed ancestry, commonly referring to *hapa haole* (part white and part Asian).

- Hawaiian – person of Native Hawaiian ancestry. It's a faux pas to call any Hawaii resident 'Hawaiian' (as you would a Californian or Texan), thus semantically ignoring indigenous people.

- *kama'aina* – person who is native to a particular place; literally, 'a child of the land.' A Hilo native is a *kama'aina* of Hilo and not of Kona. It assumes a deep knowledge of and connection to the place. In the retail context, '*kama'aina* discounts' apply to any resident of Hawaii (ie anyone with a Hawaii driver's license).

- local – person who grew up in Hawaii. Locals who move away retain their local 'cred,' at least in part. But longtime transplants (see below) never become local. To call a transplant 'almost local' is a welcome compliment, despite emphasizing the insider-outsider mentality.

- Neighbor Islander – person who lives on any Hawaiian Island other than O'ahu.

- transplant – person who moves to the islands as an adult.

Note: in this book, Hawai'i (with the *'okina* punctuation mark) refers to the island of Hawai'i (Big Island), while Hawaii (without the *'okina*) refers to the state. We use this distinction to avoid confusion between the island and the state, but the *'okina* spelling is officially used for both.

While Hawaii ranks last among states in its percentage of those who identify as all or part white (42%), whites (of one race) nevertheless comprise the largest single ethnic group, averaging 29% of the population in the islands, with higher numbers on Neighbor Islands. African Americans account for only 3%, and only 8% identify as Hispanic.

The median age in Hawaii is 38, with 22% under 18 years old and 14% over 65. However, Hawaii's population is definitely getting older. Since 2000, the senior population has grown at 1.9% annually – over twice the statewide growth rate of 0.8% – and estimates are that by 2030 over 25% of people in Hawaii may be 60 years and older.

MULTICULTURALISM

Hawaii's diversity is both eclectic and narrow at once. That's because Hawaii is uniquely positioned between and yet isolated from the Asian and North American continents. Depending on your perspective, Honolulu is either the USA's most Asian city, or it's Polynesia's most American city. When comparing US states, Hawaii is as ethnically diverse as – and more racially intermixed than – California, Texas and Florida, but it's nearly missing the African American and Mexican Hispanic populations that help define those states and most mainland multiculturalism.

Among older locals, plantation-era stereotypes still inform social hierarchies and interactions. During plantation days, whites were the wealthy plantation owners, and for years afterward, minorities would joke about their privileges as the white 'bosses.' As the Japanese rose to economic and political power after WWII, they tended to capitalize on their status as 'minorities' and former plantation laborers. But in a growing cultural divide, Hawaii's younger generation often dismisses these distinctions and alliances, even as they continue to speak pidgin, the plantation era's linguistic legacy.

Any tensions among ethnicities are quite benign compared with racial strife on the US mainland. Locals seem slightly perplexed at the emphasis on 'political correctness.' Among themselves, locals good-naturedly joke about island stereotypes, eg talkative Portuguese, stingy Chinese, goody-goody Japanese and know-it-all haole. Hawaii's much-loved comedians of the 1970s and 1980s – Andy Bumatai, Frank DeLima and Rap Reiplinger – used such stereotypes to hilarious comic effect.

Things shift when nonlocals enter the picture, since they don't share island history and don't always appreciate island ways. For instance, while the acceptability of pidgin as a language has many critics, the loudest complaints often arise from mainland haoles who don't speak it to begin with. In general, tourists and transplants are welcomed but have to earn trust and respect.

If you're called a haole, don't worry. It's rarely an insult (if it is, you'll know). Instead, like *pake* (Chinese), *Japanee* (Japanese), *hapa* (mixed race), *portagee* (Portuguese) and so on, haole is usually just a thick-skinned pidgin term that simply describes who you are.

RELIGION

Ancient Hawaiian religion fell to the wayside when the kapu system collapsed and Christian missionaries arrived (see the boxed text, p40). But it never died completely, and today Hawaiian traditions and ritual are increasingly incorporated into public life. Christian sermons often include both Hawaiian and English words, and civic ceremonies, such as ground breaking, feature a kahuna (priest) to bless the land.

Today, while most locals do not claim adherence to a particular faith, religion remains quite significant as a social force. Undoubtedly the largest group in Hawaii is Roman Catholic, with roughly 240,000 adherents, a large

In the tremendously moving *No Footprints in the Sand: A Memoir of Kalaupapa* (2006), Henry Nalaielua describes living with Hansen's disease in Moloka'i's famous leprosy colony, where he still lives today.

Following in Mary Kawena Pukui's footsteps, Davianna McGregor examines 'cultural *kipuka*' in *Na Kua'aina: Living Hawaiian Culture* (2007), which traces how cultural 'islands' of traditional rural Hawaiian life, like Waipi'o Valley, survive within modernity's incessant flow.

In *Change We Must* (1989), revered *kupuna* (elder) Nana Veary describes her spiritual journey, a path that embraces Pentecostal, metaphysical and Zen beliefs but never strays from Hawaiian spirituality and aloha.

SOUVENIRS & OFFERINGS: PROTOCOL FOR SACRED PLACES

Aloha 'aina and *malama 'aina,* or love and stewardship of the land, are two intertwined principles that permeate Native Hawaiian culture. When entering sacred places, starting new projects, or simply picking flowers for leis, Hawaiians often observe traditional protocols. These blessings or rituals are reminders that all nature is a living manifestation of the divine *(kino lau)* and commands respect.

Protocols don't have to be complicated. As the famed Hawaiian spiritual teacher Nana Veary said, 'Ask permission and give thanks – that was the Hawaiian protocol that extended to every aspect of life in nature.'

By following this protocol themselves, travelers to Hawaii can avoid inadvertently disturbing or desecrating sacred Hawaiian places. For instance, if you want to pick flowers, first ask permission of the flower or the forest; if you receive a sign or internal sense of welcome, give thanks. If, for some reason, you don't, then don't pick the flower.

Travelers often like to place 'rock *laulau*' (rocks wrapped in *ti* leaves) as offerings at heiau or altars. This can disturb places by both moving rocks you shouldn't and putting them where they shouldn't be. Instead, offer words, since the intention, not the object, is what's important.

Of course, the most famous legend is that if you take lava rocks, Pele will visit you with misfortune. Hawaiians themselves are baffled by this folktale and dismiss it. If you want a lava rock, they say, ask Tutu Pele's permission; if she says yes, then take it and don't worry.

The only caveat: don't do this in a national park. Pele may not get you, but – since it's illegal to disturb or remove anything on federal lands – park rangers might.

---

percentage of whom are Filipino immigrants. The next-largest group is the Church of Jesus Christ of Latter-Day Saints, with around 43,000 adherents, including many converts from the South Pacific.

As for Protestant Christianity, the mainstream, less conservative groups – including the United Church of Christ, which arrived with the early missionaries – are struggling with declining membership. Conversely, nondenominational and evangelical churches are burgeoning.

Buddhists number an estimated 100,000 in Hawaii, the highest statewide percentage of Buddhists in the USA, but they struggle to attract young adherents.

ARTS
Music

To learn more about slack key guitar, start at George Winston's Dancing Cat label, www .dancingcat.com. An online community for guitar and ukulele players is available at www .taropatch.net.

The most direct experience of the gentle, sweet soul of Hawaii is through her music, which resonates with the *oli* (chants) and *mele* (songs) of ancient Hawaii and hula and with the longing, troubles and rowdy humor of the rural countryside. The traditional Hawaiian sound incorporates falsetto singing and often features three instruments: steel guitar, slack key guitar and ukulele.

Mexican cowboys first introduced the guitar to Hawaiians in the 1830s. Fifty years later, young Joseph Kekuku (born 1874) began playing a guitar flat on his lap, sliding a knife or comb across the strings. At Kamehameha School for Boys, a shop teacher helped him create a steel bar and a converter nut to lift the strings off the fretboard. Thus, the Hawaiian steel guitar *(kika kila)* was born; among Hawaii's greatest musical contributions, it inspired the creation of resonator guitars such as the Dobro, now integral to bluegrass, blues and other genres, and country music's lap and pedal steel guitar.

Kekuku and other Hawaiians burst onto the international scene, introducing the steel guitar and *hapa haole* (Hawaiian music with predominantly English lyrics) sounds during the early 1900s. Today influential steel guitarists include Alan Akaka, Bobby Ingano and Gregory Sardinha.

Universally beloved is the ukulele, derived from the *braguinha*, a Portuguese stringed instrument introduced to Hawaii in the late 19th century. Ukulele means 'jumping flea' in Hawaiian, referring to the way players' deft fingers swiftly 'jump' around the strings. The ukulele is currently enjoying a revival as a young generation of ukulele virtuosos, such as Jake Shimabukuro and David Kamakahi, emerges.

Today the most famous and commercially successful Hawaiian genre is slack key guitar (*ki ho'alu*, which means 'loosen the key'), a fingerstyle method in which the strings are slacked from their standard tuning. Traditionally, slack key tunings were closely guarded family secrets.

Among the most influential steel and slack key guitarists was Gabby Pahinui (1921–80). When they emerged in the 1970s, Gabby and his legendary band the Sons of Hawai'i embraced the traditional Hawaiian sound, and they spurred a renaissance in Hawaiian music that continues to this day. The list of slack key masters is long and ever growing, including Dennis Kamakahi, Keola Beamer, Ledward Ka'apana, Ray Kane, Sonny Chillingsworth, Ozzie Kotani, Martin and Cyril Pahanui and more.

Today, Hawaiian singer-songwriters have also made a name for themselves – most famously Jack Johnson – and 'Jawaiian,' an infectious blend of Hawaiian and reggae, is all over the radio. For recommended albums and artists, see the boxed texts Modern Mele, p57, and Island Sounds, p161.

> An artful, beautiful blend of botany and culture, *Na Lei Makamae: The Treasured Lei* (2003) by Marie McDonald and Paul Weissich surveys Hawaiian flowers traditionally used in leis, their meaning and mythology.

Hawaiian Arts & Crafts

The 1970s Hawaiian renaissance sparked renewed interest in traditional Hawaiian arts and crafts. Today, these are wildly popular and inspire a flood of cheap imports (many from the Philippines), so shop carefully.

HAWAII'S FIERY GODDESS: PELE

In the pantheon of Polynesian gods, Pele was by all accounts a latecomer. Like her people, she voyaged from the South Pacific sometime in the 12th century and was, according to King Kalakaua, a real woman whose only supernatural attribute was her exceptional beauty. Eventually, Pele and her extended family (including three siblings) settled on the Big Island, near Kilauea.

Events took a fateful turn when Pele was romantically pursued by the brutish O'ahu chief Kamapua'a. Pele haughtily rebuffed him, and Kamapua'a threatened to kidnap her. So Pele and her family escaped and hid in a lava cave. But Kamapua'a found them and began digging his way in when a volcanic eruption forced them to flee – and buried everyone inside.

Afterward, it was said Pele herself commanded the lava flow to chase Kamapua'a away, and in death she and her family were reborn as gods, her life expanding into legend. As the ruler of volcanoes, Pele was given five brothers and eight sisters who, among other things, controlled all aspects of eruptions, such as creating steam, explosions and thunder, hurling lava and breaking canoes.

Hi'iaka, Pele's favorite sister, became a goddess and patroness of hula, along with Pele herself and another sister, Laka. Kamapua'a became a boarlike demigod associated with rain and forests, and their epic romance captured Hawaii's violent symbiosis of fire and fertility. Meanwhile, Pele's competitions with her greatest rival, the snow goddess Poliahu (who lives atop Mauna Kea), became a metaphorically accurate account of island geology.

In this way, Pele became a truly Hawaiian goddess, with the fulsome dualities of her myths embodying the complexities and soul-shaking experience of these volcanic islands. Peek into her house – Halema'uma'u Crater (p311) – and it's easy to understand why she has endured, why she seemingly *still* lives, and why she is so honored.

Sometimes, locals say, she still appears, often as an old woman dressed in white who warns of an impending disaster or asks for help. If you think you see her it's best to stop, because after all you never know, and Pele hates to be refused.

THE KUMULIPO: THE HAWAIIAN CREATION STORY

Born was the coral polyp, born was the coral, came forth
Born was the starfish, his child the small starfish, came forth
Born was the sea cucumber, his child the small sea cucumber, came forth
Born was the mother-of-pearl, his child the oyster, came forth

Born was the Ekaha moss living in the sea
Guarded by the Ekahakaha fern living on land
Darkness slips into light
Earth and water are food of the plant
The god enters, man cannot enter
Man for the narrow stream, woman for the broad stream
Born was the tough seagrass living in the sea
Guarded by the tough landgrass living on land

These lines from the opening of the *Kumulipo* give a sense of the most famous ancient Hawaiian genealogical chant to survive. In over 2000 lines, it traces the birth of the world, the gods, and humans, thus linking the chief's child who inspired the poem to the origins of the universe. While genealogies like this were used to bolster political claims to a chiefdom, they were also the natural expression of a culture in which religion was so enmeshed there was no separate word for it.

King David Kalakaua, claiming it represented his lineage, published the poem in Hawaiian in 1889, and in 1897, while imprisoned within 'Iolani Palace by US annexationists, his sister, Queen Lili'uokalani, translated it into English.

The chant's second half contains 1100 lines of pure genealogy that might tax the patience of a Mormon, but the poem's remarkable creation story tells of how Papa, the earth mother, was created in darkness, then Wakea – light or the sky father – was created, and 'from this union of opposites was created a universe of opposites,' as historian Herb Kane writes.

In form, the chant mirrors the stages of human growth, from single-cell polyp to fetus to child to adult, while pairing and relating sea and land creatures. Intriguingly, this unfolding process also resembles biological evolution. Long before Darwin, it seems, Hawaiians recognized that sacred life evolves.

Ancient Hawaiians were expert woodworkers, carving canoes out of logs and hand-turning lustrous bowls from a variety of hardwoods, such as koa, kou, milo and mango. *Ipu* (or gourds) were also dried and used as containers and as drums for hula. Contemporary woodworkers now take native woods and craft traditional bowls, exquisite furniture, jewelry and freeform artworks.

Worn daily, leis were integral to ancient society; they were also central to hula and made as special gifts for loved ones and the gods, practices that continue today. With their choice of materials, lei-makers tell a story – since flowers and plants embody place and myth – and express their feelings for the recipient. Lei materials can include feathers, *kukui* (candlenuts), shells, seeds, vines, *ipu*, leaves and fruit, in addition to flowers. In general, it's no longer common to make one's own lei, unless you're in a hula troupe; for ceremonial hula (as opposed to competitions or entertainment), performers are often required to make their own lei.

Tiny Ni'ihua developed its own tradition of intricate shell lei. Today, these are appraisable artworks protected by state law; leis must be made with at least 80% Ni'ihua shells, and prices range from $125 to $50,000.

The making of *kapa* (barkcloth) for clothing and artworks and *lauhala* weaving are two other ancient crafts. Weaving the *lau* (leaves) of the *hala* (pandanus) tree is the fun part, while preparing the leaves, which have razor-sharp spines, is messy work. Traditionally *lauhala* served as floor mats, canoe sails, protective capes and more. Today, the most common *lauhala* items are hats, placemats and baskets. Most are mass-produced; look for specialty shops like the Big Island's Kimura Lauhala (p230).

Missionaries introduced quilting to the islands in the 1800s. As Hawaiians adapted their *kapa*-cloth designs to appliqué quilts, they created a distinctive, beautiful quilting tradition. As with all traditional crafts, designs held symbolic meaning and quilts were imbued with the spirit of the crafter.

Hawaii has been home to a number of lauded painters, such as Herb Kane and Madge Tennent, among others. For a proper introduction to contemporary art, visit the Honolulu Academy of Arts (p123) and the Hawai'i State Art Museum (p116) in Honolulu, and the Isaacs Art Center (p265) on the Big Island.

Literature

Until the late 1970s, Hawaii literature was dominated by nonlocal Western writers observing Hawaii's exotic-seeming world from the outside; favorites are James Michener's well-researched saga *Hawaii* and Paul Theroux's caustically humorous *Hotel Honolulu*.

Since then, local-born writers have created a true Hawaii literature that evokes island life from the inside. Leading this has been Bamboo Ridge Press (www.bambooridge.com), which for over 30 years has published contemporary local fiction and poetry in a biannual journal, *Bamboo Ridge*, and launched the careers of many Hawaii writers.

In 1975, *All I Asking for Is My Body* by Milton Murayama vividly captured sugar plantation life for Japanese nisei (second-generation Japanese) around WWII. Murayama's use of pidgin opened the door to an explosion of vernacular literature, particularly since the 1990s. Lois-Ann Yamanaka has won widespread acclaim for her poetry (*Saturday Night at the Pahala Theatre*, 1993) and novels (*Wild Meat and the Bully Burgers*, 1996), in which pidgin embodies her characters like a second skin.

Indeed, redeeming pidgin – long dismissed by academics and disparaged by the upper class – has been a cultural and political cause for some.

One of the most highly regarded traditional Hawaiian quilters, Poakalani Serreo (www.nvo.com/poakalani) runs a website that has everything: classes, shops, patterns, history and more.

MODERN MELE

Ideally, this guidebook would come bundled with a CD and ukulele. Instead, here's a list of essential Hawaiian music, past and present:

- Genoa Keawe, *Party Hulas* – 'Aunty Genoa' and her signature falsetto epitomized old-school Hawaiian hula music, and this sets the standard.
- Raiatea Helm, *Hawaiian Blossom* – The *Village Voice* compared young Helm to Diana Krall with a ukulele, and her soaring falsetto is Aunty Genoa reborn.
- Gabby Pahinui, *Gabby* – No self-respecting slack key music collection is complete without this seminal album.
- Dennis and David Kamakahi, *'Ohana* – Father Dennis and son David are two of Hawaii's best musicians, here combining their talents on slack key guitar and ukulele, respectively.
- Israel Kamakawiwo'ole, *Facing Future* – 'Braddah Iz' touched Hawaii's soul with songs like 'Hawai'i '78,' and this has become Hawaii's all-time best-selling album.
- Jake Shimabukuro, *Walking Down Rainhill* – Check out Jake's ukulele cover of 'While My Guitar Gently Weeps' on YouTube, then buy this.
- Keali'i Reichel, *Kawaipunahele* – Charismatic vocalist and *kumu hula* (hula teacher), Reichel combines ancient chanting and soulful ballads.
- HAPA, *In the Name of Love* – Cross a New Jersey slack key guitarist and a Hawaiian vocalist, and you get HAPA's contemporary yet traditional, pop-flavored fusion.
- John Cruz, *One of these Days* – Cruz is a classic singer-songwriter crafting modern, blues-tinged Hawaiian-style songs.

The most notorious 'pidgin guerrilla' has been Lee Tonouchi. A prolific writer and playwright, his hilarious stories (*Da Word*, 2001) and essays (*Living Pidgin*, 2002) argue that pidgin is essential to understanding local culture and is a legitimate language. Other great introductions to pidgin are *Growing Up Local* (1998), an anthology published by Bamboo Ridge Press, and *Da Jesus Book*, a warm-hearted pidgin 'translation' of the New Testament.

Other important Hawaii writers include Nora Okja Keller, whose first novel, *Comfort Woman*, won the 1998 American Book Award, and Kiana Davenport, whose *Shark Dialogues* (1994) is a sweeping multigenerational family saga entwined with island history.

Meanwhile, new Hawaii writers abound: some, like Mia King (*Good Things*, 2007) and Joe Tsujimoto (*Morningside Heights*, 2008), eschew purely ethnic or Hawaii-centered narratives, while others – like Kaui Hart Hemmings (*House of Thieves*, 2005) and Mavis Hara (*An Offering of Rice*, 2007) – continue to explode the 'paradise myth' as they explore real Hawaii.

> More than a pidgin dictionary, *Pidgin to Da Max* by Douglas Simonson (aka Peppo) is a side-splitting primer on local life that's knocked around forever because it (and its sequels) are so damn funny.

Cinema & TV

Nothing cemented the fantasy of Edenic Hawaii in the popular imagination as firmly as Hollywood. Today, the 'dream factory' continues to peddle variations on a 'South Seas' genre that first swept theaters in the 1930s.

Whether the mood is silly or serious, whether Hawaii is used as a setting or a stand-in for someplace else, the story's familiar tropes hardly change: white men arrive in a languid tropical paradise to be tempted by,

---

HULA: LANGUAGE OF THE HEART

In ancient Hawaii, hula was as much a way of life as a performing art. Sometimes hula was solemn ritual, in which *mele* (songs or chants) had to be word-perfect as an honor to a chief or an offering to the gods. At other times hula was lighthearted entertainment, in which amateur and professional, chief and commoner, danced together. In many ways, hula embodied the community – telling stories of and celebrating itself.

Dancers trained rigorously in *halau* (schools) under *kumu hula* (hula teachers), so their hand gestures, expressions and rhythms were exact. Still, in a culture without written language, the chants were equally important, giving intention and meaning to the movements. Songs often contained *kanoa* – veiled or hidden meaning. This could be spiritual, but it could also be amorous or sexual. *Hula ma'i* was an entire tradition devoted to metaphorical praise of the chief's genitals.

One can only imagine how hard Christian missionaries blushed. Their efforts to suppress hula were aided by Christian convert Queen Ka'ahumanu, who banned hula in 1830. In the 1880s, King Kalakaua revived it, saying famously, 'Hula is the language of the heart and therefore the heartbeat of the Hawaiian people.' Then the monarchy was overthrown, and hula faded again, until a revival in the 1950s brought it back for good.

Today, *hula halau* run by revered *kumu hula* are thriving, as hula competitions blossom and people once again adopt hula as a life practice. In hula competitions, dancers vie in *kahiko* (ancient) and *'auana* (modern) categories. *Kahiko* performances are raw and primordial, accompanied only by chanting and thunderous gourd drums; costumes are traditional, with *ti*-leaf leis, primary colors and sometimes lots of skin.

'Auana can include all manner of Western, contemporary influences. English singing, stringed instruments, pants, pop culture jokes, sinuous arm movements and smiling faces – all may be included. Some troupes flirt with postmodern dance, creating what's been dubbed 'Cirque du Soleil hula.'

Among festivals, the Olympics of hula is the Merrie Monarch Festival (p294), but hula competitions and celebrations fill island calendars year-round. For a selection of the biggest, see the Events Calendar (p27).

and consequently to ravish, island women, updating the original Garden of Eden soap opera and providing a romantic gloss to the real history of colonizers and continents on the islands.

Hollywood first arrived in 1913, and Hawaii has been catnip ever since. By 1939, over 60 movies had been shot here, including classics like *Mutiny on the Bounty* (1935) and *Waikiki Wedding* (1937), in which Bing Crosby crooned the Oscar-winning song 'Sweet Leilani.' Later favorites include *From Here to Eternity* (1953), *South Pacific* (1958) and Elvis Presley's *Blue Hawaii* (1961).

Today, Hawaii actively encourages and supports the lucrative film industry by maintaining state-of-the-art production facilities and providing tax incentives. Hundreds of feature films have been shot in the state, including box-office hits like *Raiders of the Lost Ark, Godzilla, Pearl Harbor* and *Jurassic Park*. Kaua'i is the most prolific island 'set' and has appeared in over 70 films, including 2008's *Tropic Thunder* (p482); avid fans can tour Kaua'i movie sites (see p501).

Hawaii has hosted 23 major TV series since 1968. The most famous and perhaps least sentimental was *Hawaii Five-O*, an edgy cop drama featuring Honolulu's gritty side; in the 1980s, Tom Selleck's *Magnum PI* was almost campy by comparison. Currently O'ahu is being used as the location for – spoiler alert! – ABC's hit series *Lost*, which like *Gilligan's Island* (whose pilot was filmed on Kaua'i) is about a group of island castaways trying to get home. To find *Lost* locations, visit www.lostvirtualtour.com; and see the boxed text, p180.

For a Hawaii filmography, and more on the industry, visit the Hawaii Film Office (www.hawaiifilmoffice.com).

> Kaui Hart Hemmings' first novel, *The Descendants: A Novel* (2007), has a dissolute, sickly-sweet Southern Gothic air, as the children of haole plantation owners and a Hawaiian princess lose their inheritance and their way in a crumbling paradise.

SPORTS

The dearth of professional sports teams in Hawaii has everything to do with cost and logistics and absolutely zero to do with the local love of sports, which is intense and abiding. For 30 years, the National Football League's Pro Bowl played to sellout crowds at O'ahu's Aloha Stadium, but February 2009 was the last; the NFL decided to move the game to Miami to lower costs and increase exposure.

Similarly, Hawaii has an on-again, off-again relationship with Major League Baseball, which in 2008 ended its minor-league Winter Baseball league on O'ahu. Minor-league pro ball had prospered in the 1990s, too – drawing major-league talent from Japan and America – only to fall prey to Hawaii's inconvenient location.

So locals lose their voices rooting for University of Hawai'i sports (UH; http://hawaiiathletics.com). While women's and men's volleyball have long boasted powerhouse teams, and are closely followed, UH Warriors football is the only National Collegiate Athletic Association (NCAA) Division I program, and the Warriors regularly attract thousands of fans to Aloha Stadium.

The Warriors have recently enjoyed banner years. In 2006, the team had its best year to date and won the year-end Hawaii Bowl (www.sheraton hawaiibowl.com). Then in 2007, they went undefeated in the regular season and became only the second WAC (Western Athletic Conference) team invited to play in the Bowl Championship Series, where they suffered a crushing loss to Georgia in the Sugar Bowl.

The two hottest sports locals love to play (and watch) are surfing and golf. O'ahu's North Shore (p184) is legendary and hosts the Triple Crown of Surfing Championship and the Quiksilver In Memory of Eddie Aikau Invitational in November and December. For more on surfing, see the boxed text, p81.

> Too old to surf? In *Surfing for Life* (www.surfingfor life.com), documentary filmmaker David L Brown profiles 10 lifelong surfers, champions in their youth and still catching waves in their 70s, 80s and 90s.

ANCIENT EXTREME SPORTS

Never let it be said that ancient Hawaiians didn't know how to play. Every ruler had to prove his prowess in sports – to demonstrate his chiefly mana (spiritual essence) – and the greater the danger, the better. Wave sliding, or surfing, was integral to society; then as now, when surf was up, everyone left the taro fields to grab the biggest waves. In boxing matches, combatants didn't dodge the blows. Kamehameha once demonstrated his skill by having six spears thrown at him at once – he caught two and deflected the rest.

No chiefly contest topped the *holua* – an ancient sled that was 6in to 8in wide and 6ft to 12ft long. That's right, it was about as wide as this book's height and raced down a mountain at speeds of up to 50mph. The longest course, near Keauhou on the Big Island, descended a mile before plunging into the sea. Losing your balance could mean death – but greatness isn't proved without risk, right?

Not every sport was potentially deadly, though many involved gambling – like foot and canoe racing, wrestling, cockfighting and stone bowling. As for the gods, no athlete could top Lono, who could kill sharks with stones, and one legend tells of a young chief who casually dismissed a frail old woman's challenge to a *holua* race. She then transformed into a very angry Pele – who with thunder under her feet and lightning in her hair, surfed a crested wave of lava down the mountain, killing all who'd laughed at her.

Hawaii's latest sports star is Maui native and baseball player Shane Victorino, 'the flying Hawaiian,' who won a Gold Glove on his way to helping the Philadelphia Phillies win the 2008 World Series.

Golf is wildly popular among all ages, and fan favorites include Tiger Woods and Michelle Wie, a 2007 Punahou graduate who turned heads when she went pro at age 16. In January, two major PGA tournaments draw spectators: the Sony Open in Hawaii at Wai'alae Country Club on O'ahu and the Mercedes-Benz Championship at Kapalua Plantation Course (p360) on Maui.

Other major sporting events include the Ironman Triathlon World Championship (p221) and the EA Sports Maui Invitational (www.maui invitational.com), the nation's premier preseason college basketball tournament.

Food & Drink

'Dis is seriously *broke da mout!*' You're likely to hear this ultimate compliment if you hang around locals long enough. It means that something is so delicious, it breaks the mouth. And that's no exaggeration. Here, people go crazy over food.

Defining 'Hawaii food' requires a look at Hawaii's multicultural immigrants. Before human contact, the only indigenous edibles were ferns and *ohelo* berries. The Polynesians brought *kalo* (taro), *'ulu* (breadfruit), *'uala* (sweet potato), *mai'a* (banana), *ko* (sugarcane) and *niu* (coconut), plus chickens, pigs and dogs for meat – and they enjoyed an abundance of seafood.

The island diet expanded when Westerners brought cattle and horses, salted salmon and fruits such as pineapple and guava that now connote Hawaii. When the sugar industry rose to its peak in the late 1800s, bringing waves of immigrants from China, Japan, Portugal, Puerto Rico, Korea and the Philippines, Hawaii's cuisine developed an identity all its own. It took the plantation-era ethnic ingredients (including rice, soy sauce, ginger and chili pepper) but never abandoned Native Hawaiian *kalua* pork (rich and smoky, traditionally roasted underground) and *poke* (marinated chunks of raw fish).

Hawaii food is multiethnic, yet distinct from classic ethnic cooking. But rather than discounting the island dishes as inauthentic, recognize that they are meant as island renditions (which locals might call improvements!). Sample this unique, Asian-inspired mélange at celebrated restaurants featuring Hawaii Regional Cuisine (HRC, p62) and also in everyday *grinds* (food), such as *saimin* noodle soup and Spam *musubi* (rice ball).

This glorious mishmash of cuisines has turned locals into adventurous samplers and passionate eaters. Seek, as they do, that knockout mouthful. *Broke da mout!*

Among the dozens of Hawaii food blogs, two O'ahu-based notables are The Tasty Island at www .tastyisland.wordpress .com (by a *kama'aina*) and Ma'ona at www .maona.net (by a transplant), featuring compelling restaurant reviews and local commentary.

THE ISLAND DIET

Hawaii is a US state, so Americans will find the familiar: fast-food chains, supermarkets stocked with national brands, and conventional menus of pancakes and Caesar salads. But if you plunge in and go local, you'll find that the food gives real insight into the people, the history and the land. (What a fantastic excuse to eat up!)

Actually, you'll find many parallels between Hawaii favorites and Western classics. If you like hamburgers, try a juicy teriyaki burger in Hawaii. If you like beef-barley stew, try local-style beef stew with rice. If you like tuna sandwiches, try a seared-ahi wrap instead. You get the picture.

TOP PICKS – FOODIE TRENDS

- **gelato and sorbetto** made with local (often organic) fruits
- **evolved plate lunches** with two-scoop brown rice and steamed veggies or tossed greens instead of mayo-laden macaroni salad
- **izakaya (Japanese pubs serving tapas-style food)**, which are now ubiquitous across Honolulu and Waikiki
- **big-name chefs**, such as DK Kodama and Peter Merriman, expanding their empires to Neighbor Islands
- **locally grown, caught and raised** produce, fish and meats

Pick up a free copy of *Edible Hawaiian Islands* (www.ediblehawaiian islands.com), a colorful quarterly magazine focusing on Hawaii's locavore movement and other foodie trends.

Still, there are three notable characteristics of iconic local food. First, the primary starch is sticky, medium-grain, white rice. Jasmine rice is tolerated with Thai food, but flaky rice is considered *haole* (Caucasian) food (and instant rice is inedible).

Second, the top condiment is soy sauce (ubiquitously called by its Japanese name, *shōyu*), which combines well with sharp Asian flavors such as ginger, green onion and garlic.

Third, meat, chicken or fish is often integral to a dish. For quick, cheap eating, locals devour anything tasty, from Portuguese sausage to hamburger steak to corned beef. But the dinner-table highlight is always seafood, especially succulent, fresh-caught ahi.

Finally, don't bother with nonlocal classics (such as pizza and bagels), which are usually disappointing. Also bear in mind the idiosyncratic local definitions: In Hawaii, 'barbecue' typically means teriyaki-marinated.

Hawaii Regional Cuisine

Almost two decades old, Hawaii Regional Cuisine (HRC) is entering a new, 21st-century phase. The birth of Hawaii's now-iconic cuisine is well documented: in the late 1980s, a dozen or so of Hawaii's top chefs partnered with local farmers, ranchers and fishers to gather the freshest ingredients, which they fashioned into island- and Asian-influenced creations. Gone was the same-old continental cuisine of the past. Suddenly macadamia-crusted mahimahi, seared ahi, miso glaze and *liliko'i* (passion fruit) anything were all the rage.

Back then HRC was rather exclusive, found at destination restaurants and created by celebrity chefs. Its hallmark was elaborate fusion preparation. By the 2000s the focus began shifting toward the ingredients, which ideally are locally grown, organic, seasonal and handpicked. Today, individual farms are lauded like designer brands. (The single-estate trend in premium coffee has spread to the tomatoes and arugula in your locavore salad.)

The upshot? Hawaii Regional Cuisine is now more encompassing. The top restaurants are still its mainstay, but that little bistro or even plate-lunch stand might fall under the HRC umbrella if it satisfies locavore requirements.

When deciding on a main course, remember that almost all meats, poultry and shellfish are imported. If they're local, they'll probably be labeled as such. To experience the crux of Hawaii's finest cuisine, you should partake in ingredients that start and end here.

TOP PICKS – HAWAII REGIONAL CUISINE

Hawai'i
- **Merriman's** (p268)
- **Daniel Thiebaut** (p267)
- **Hilo Bay Café** (p297)

Maui
- **Mala Wailea** (p384)
- **Ka'uiki** (p399)
- **I'O** (p346)

Kaua'i
- **Bar Acuda Tapas & Wine** (p521)
- **Beach House Restaurant** (p537)
- **Hukilau Lanai** (p497)

O'ahu
- **Town** (p137)
- **Downtown** (p133)
- **Pineapple Room** (p135)

Roy's (p159, at Waikiki Beach and across the islands) remains a standout for impeccable preparations across the islands. But can a chain that overnight-delivers fresh Hawaii fish to worldwide outposts really fit the locavore model?

ISLAND BOUNTY

Locally grown basics such as cabbage, tomatoes, bell peppers, bananas and avocados are found across the islands. But each island has its star crops (and, often, brand names that you might notice on menus). There are too many notables to name, but here's a starting point:

- Hawai'i – mushrooms from Hamakua Mushrooms; tomatoes and salad greens from Hamakua Springs Country Farms; vanilla from Hawaiian Vanilla Company; Ka'u oranges; *kampachi* (yellowtail) from Kona Blue Water Farms; lobster from Kona Cold Lobster; abalone from Big Island Abalone; Kona or Ka'u coffee; yellow-flesh Solo papayas
- Kaua'i – goat cheese from Kaua'i Kunana Dairy; beef from Medeiros Farm; organic ginger from Kolo Kai Organic Farm; Kilauea honey; Hanalei-grown taro; red-flesh Sunrise papayas
- Maui – beef from Maui Cattle Co; lavender from Ali'i Kula Lavender; goat cheese from Surfing Goat Dairy; elk from 'Ulupalakua Ranch; strawberries from Kula Country Farms; sugar from Maui Brand Hawaiian Raw Sugar
- Moloka'i – coffee from Coffees of Hawai'i; sea salt from Pacifica Hawai'i; macadamia nuts from Purdy's; Moloka'i Purple–variety sweet potatoes from L&R Farms
- O'ahu – salad greens from Nalo Farms; beef from North Shore Cattle Co; tomatoes from North Shore Farms; Ewa-grown melons; North Shore–grown supersweet corn

---

HAWAII'S LOCAVORE MOVEMENT

A hot issue across the islands is food security. A whopping 80% to 90% of Hawaii's food is imported, despite its natural biodiversity. Now, a growing contingent of small-scale farmers is trying to shift the agriculture industry away from the model of corporate-scale, industrialized monocropping (eg sugar and pineapple) enabled by chemical fertilizers, pesticides and herbicides. Instead, family farms are growing diverse crops for the table or for sale locally.

This push for sustainable agriculture coincided with best-selling books like *The Omnivore's Dilemma* and *The 100-Mile Diet*, making it a fortuitous time for 'locally grown' to catch the public's fancy. On the Big Island, especially, diversified agriculture is booming, not just with its signature coffee and macadamia nuts, but a range of edibles from mushrooms to shellfish. With the only two cattle dairies left statewide, the Big Island produces 95% of its residents' milk consumption, while the other islands rely on 100% imported milk (which is always repasteurized, a process that adds eight days before the product reaches the consumer!).

Even with a local bounty, building a solid consumer market isn't easy. Safeway and island-based supermarket chains typically prefer the blemish-free consistency of Sunkist oranges and California grapes –an exception is the Big Island's KTA Super Stores (p297), which carries a commendable 90% locally grown produce. At the same time, locals tend to buy whatever's cheapest. Further, while tourists are eager to buy star fruit and avocados, locals often balk at paying for fruit they see falling off neighborhood trees.

As for imported staples such as wheat and other grains, some ask if we need them. Why not substitute native starches such as breadfruit, taro and sweet potato? Well, rice is king among local staples and can single-handedly keep Matson and Young Brothers (shipping barges) in business!

Bottom line: the only way that small-scale farmers can thrive is to sell their products. Buy local!

Learn more about local agriculture, farm tours and farmers markets at www.hiagtourism.org. It's not exhaustive but it's a good start.

Local Food

Cheap, filling and tasty, local food is the stuff of cravings and comfort. Such food might be dubbed 'street food' but street vendors are uncommon, except at farmers markets. No list is complete without that classic plate lunch, a fixed-plate meal containing 'two-scoop rice,' macaroni/potato salad and your choice of a hot protein dish, such as *tonkatsu* (breaded, fried pork cutlets), fried mahimahi or teriyaki chicken. Often eaten with disposable chopsticks on disposable plates, they pack a flavor (and caloric) punch, and are generally fried, salty, gravy-laden and meaty. Healthful plates are now available, too.

The local palate prefers hot rice or noodle mains to cold cuts and sliced bread. Thus another favorite is saimin, a soup of chewy Chinese egg noodles and Japanese broth, garnished with colorful toppings such as green onion, dried nori, *kamaboko* (steamed fish cake), egg roll and *char siu* (barbecued pork).

In a hurry, pick up a *bentō* (Japanese-style box lunch containing rice, meat or fish), and Japanese garnishes such as pickles, at deli counters and corner stores. And you can't go home without trying a Big Island invention called *loco moco*, a bowl of rice, two eggs (typically fried over easy) and hamburger patty, topped with brown gravy and a dash of *shōyu*.

Consider yourself lucky if you snag an invitation to a *pupu* (appetizer) party at a local home. Go casual and expect an endless spread of grazing foods (forget the cheese and crackers), such as fried shrimp, edamame (boiled soybeans in the pod) and *maki* (rolled) sushi. A must-try is *poke* (pronounced '*po-keh*'), Hawaii's soul food, a savory dish of bite-sized raw fish (typically ahi), seasoned with *shōyu*, sesame oil, green onion, sea salt, *ogo* (seaweed) and '*inamona,* a flavoring made of roasted and ground *kukui* (candlenut).

Nowadays kids veer toward mainstream candy and gum, but the traditional local treat is mouth-watering Chinese crack seed, preserved fruit (typically plum, cherry, mango or lemon) that, like Coca-Cola or curry, is impossible to describe. It can be sweet, sour, salty, or licorice-spicy. Sold prepackaged at grocers or by the pound at specialty shops, crack seed is mouthwatering and addictive.

On a hot day, nothing can beat shave ice, a mound of ice, shaved as fine as powdery snow, packed into a cup and drenched with sweet syrups in eye-popping hues. Purists stick with only ice but, for added decadence, try sweet azuki-bean paste or ice cream underneath.

Finally, no list of local *grinds* is complete without a mention of Spam *musubi*, a local 'delicacy' comprising a rice ball topped with sautéed Spam and wrapped with sushi nori (dried seaweed). Locals of all stripes savor this only-in-Hawaii creation, which is somewhat akin to an easy, satisfying PB&J sandwich. Spam has been Hawaii's comfort food since the plantation era, when canned meat was cheap and convenient for workers' lunchboxes.

Native Hawaiian Food

Utterly memorable in rich, earthy flavors and native ingredients, Hawaiian food is like no other. Today several dishes are staples in the local diet, but they're generally harder to find than other cuisines. The best venues for good, authentic Hawaiian food are plate-lunch shops, diners, fish markets and supermarket delis. Commercial luau buffets include all the notable dishes, but the quality can be mediocre or haole-fied (watered down for Caucasians).

Lighten up your cookbook library with *Hawai'i Cooks with SPAM: Local Recipes Featuring Our Favorite Canned Meat* (Muriel Miura), filled with trivia, history and remarkably flattering glossy photographs.

TOP PICKS – SHAVE ICE

- **Itsu's Fishing Supplies** (Hawai'i the Big Island; p299)
- **Jo-Jo's Anuenue Shave Ice & Treats** (Kaua'i; p549)
- **Tom's Mini-Mart** (Maui; p370)
- **Waiola Bakery & Shave Ice II** (O'ahu; p157)

IS CHOCOLATE THE NEW COFFEE?

The world's 'chocolate-growing belt' extends 20 degrees north and south of the equator. Today's key producers are West Africa, Brazil, Ecuador, Malaysia and Indonesia, but the Hawaiian Islands, which fall at the belt's northern edge, are inching their way into the industry. Cacao is among the specialty crops that sustainable-agriculture proponents are touting for Hawaii's next generation of farmers.

The forerunner is the Big Island's Original Hawaiian Chocolate Factory (p281), a mom-and-pop-run outfit that's been producing 100% Kona chocolate since 2000. Making chocolate is no cheap or overnight venture, and it's commendable that they do all of their own processing, packaging and marketing, while growing cacao on their six-acre farm and buying the rest from 60 farmers on the island.

Since 2005, a second company, O'ahu's Waialua Estate (on the Dole Plantation, p196), started growing cacao, which it now ships to San Francisco's Guittard Chocolate Company for roasting, grinding and final processing. Both companies sell their chocolate online.

On Kaua'i, cacao remains in the simmering stage (it takes thousands of mature plants to produce enough cacao for steady commercial production), but Steelgrass Farm (p490) already offers a fascinating farm tour that traces how cacao beans transform into chocolate bars.

Note: there are many fine chocolate makers (using imported chocolate) across the Islands. But if you're curious about *100% Hawaii-grown chocolate,* your choices dwindle to a handful.

Perhaps the most famous (or infamous) Hawaiian dish is poi, steamed and mashed wetland taro, which was sacred to Hawaiians. Locals savor the bland-to-mildly-tart flavor as a starchy palate cleanser, but its slightly sticky and pasty consistency can be off-putting to nonlocals. Taro is highly nutritious, low in calories, easily digestible and versatile to prepare. Also try taro chips (made with dryland/upland 'Chinese' taro) at local grocers.

Locals typically eat poi as a counterpoint to strongly flavored fish dishes such as *lomilomi* salmon (minced salted salmon tossed with diced tomato and green onion) and *poke* (see opposite). In case you're wondering, salmon is an import, first introduced to Hawaiians by whaling ships.

No Hawaiian feast is complete without *kalua* pig, which is traditionally roasted whole underground in an *imu,* a sealed pit of red-hot stones. Cooked this way, the pork is smoky, salty and succulent. Nowadays *kalua* pork is typically oven-roasted and seasoned with salt and liquid smoke. At commercial luau, a pig placed in an *imu* is only for show (and it couldn't feed 300-plus guests anyway).

A popular restaurant dish is *laulau,* a bundle of pork or chicken and salted butterfish, wrapped in taro leaves and steamed in *ti* leaves. When cooked, the melt-in-your-mouth taro leaves blend perfectly with the savory meats.

Another food hardly seen on menus is raw *'opihi,* which you might see locals picking off shoreline rocks.

DRINKS

Fruit trees thrive in Hawaii, so you'd expect to find fresh juices everywhere. Alas, most supermarket cartons contain imported purées or sugary 'juice drinks.' Avoid canned juices altogether. Find real, freshly squeezed or blended juices at fruit stands, health food stores, farmers markets and specialty bars. Don't assume that the fruit is local. Also, bear in mind that the ancients never tasted that succulent mango or tangy pineapple. One juice-bar standout is Lanikai Juice (O'ahu, p176).

Hawaii's original intoxicants were fruit juices, *'awa* (kava), a mild sedative, and *noni* (Indian mulberry), which some consider a cure-all. Both fruits are pungent, if not repulsive, in smell and taste, so they are typically mixed with other juices.

Coffee

World-renowned Kona coffee typically costs $20 to $40 per pound, depending on the grade. Aficionados rave about its mellow flavor that has no bitter after-taste. The upland slopes of Mauna Loa and Hualalai in the Big Island's Kona district offer the ideal climate (sunny mornings and rainy afternoons) for cof-fee cultivation. While Kona coffee has the most cachet, recent crops from Ka'u (the southernmost district on Hawai'i) have won accolades and Ka'anapali Estate's MauiGrown Coffee (p347) has impressed many aficionados.

Café culture has taken root, with baristas brewing espresso at deli counters, indie hangouts and, of course, Starbucks. Local old-timers balk at paying $3-plus for coffee, but today's youth are eager converts to cappuccinos and their ilk.

The Hawai'i Beer Book (Cheryl Chee Tsutsumi) is a nifty primer on the major eight microbrewer-ies across the islands. Aficionados won't need the 'Beer Appreciation 101' chapter but might appreciate the tasty *pupu* (appetizer) recipes.

Beer

In Hawaii, beer is the everyman, everyday drink. National brands such as Coors are popular but once-novel microbreweries are now firmly established across the islands. Brewmasters claim that the high mineral content and purity of Hawaii's water makes for excellent-tasting beer. Another hallmark of local microbeer is the addition of a tropical hint, such as Kona coffee, honey or *liliko'i*.

The biggest companies also run lively brewpubs, where you should try the following picks: Pipeline Porter by Kona Brewing Company (p223) on the Big Island, Coconut Porter by Maui Brewing Company (p357), Kaka'ako Cream Ale by Sam Choy's Big Aloha Brewery (p138) on O'ahu and Liliko'i Ale by Waimea Brewing Company (p548) on Kaua'i.

Wine

Did you know? Hawaii is the only US state com-mercially growing coffee and chocolate. Since the early 2000s, it's been one of only two states cultivating tea (the other is South Carolina).

Among mainland transplants and the upper-income, professional crowd, wine is growing in popularity. Wine-tasting parties and clubs are proliferating, wine sales have skyrocketed and wine bars have opened in Honolulu. As for locally made wine, head to Maui for pineapple wine at Tedeschi Vineyards (p412) and to the Big Island for the imaginative guava or macadamia-honey concoctions of Volcano Winery (p319).

CELEBRATIONS

To celebrate is to feast. Whether it's a 300-guest wedding or an intimate birthday party, a massive spread is mandatory. If not, why bother? Most gatherings are informal, held at parks, beaches or homes, featuring a potluck buffet of homemade dishes. On major American holidays, mainstream foods

---

TOP PICKS – PLATE LUNCH

- **Big Island Grill** (Hawai'i the Big Island; p223)
- **Ishihara Market** (Kaua'i; p548)
- **Pono Market** (Kaua'i; p503)
- **Aloha Mixed Plate** (Maui; p345)
- **Kualapu'u Cookhouse** (Moloka'i; p456)
- **Me BBQ** (O'ahu; p158)
- **Poke Stop** (O'ahu; p145)

TOP PICKS – POKE

- **Suisan Fish Market** (Hawai'i the Big Island; p297)
- **Koloa Fish Market** (Kaua'i; p529)
- **Eskimo Candy** (Maui; p380)
- **Ono Seafood** (O'ahu; p158)

---

appear (eg Easter eggs and Thanksgiving turkey) alongside local fare such as rice (instead of mashed potatoes), sweet-potato tempura (instead of yams) and hibachi-grilled teriyaki beef (instead of roast beef).

Luau

In ancient Hawaii, a luau commemorated auspicious occasions, such as births, war victories or successful harvests. In modern times, the 'commercial luau' arose in the 1970s and '80s on the four largest islands. Today, only such commercial shows (at $75 to $100 per person) offer the elaborate Hawaiian feast and Polynesian dancing that folks expect. Bear in mind, the all-you-can-eat buffet of luau standards is toned down for the Western palate, eg poi, *kalua* pig, steamed mahimahi, teriyaki chicken and *haupia* (coconut custard).

Alas, most commercial luau are overpriced and overly touristy, but two stand out: the Old Lahaina Luau (Maui, see p347) and the Kona Village luau (Hawai'i the Big Island, see p247). On Kaua'i, try Kilohana Plantation's theatrical Luau Kalamaku (p487), or for nostalgia's sake, the show at Smith's Tropical Paradise (p497).

Private luau celebrations, typically for weddings or first birthdays, are often large banquet-hall gatherings. The menu might be more daring (and include raw *'a'ama* (black crab) and *'opihi* (limpet) and the entertainment more low-key (no fire eaters).

Learn about the luau's cultural significance on p51.

Festivals & Events

Food festivals often showcase island crops, such as the Kona Coffee Cultural Festival (p221), East Maui Taro Festival (p398), Maui Onion Festival (p353), Wahiawa Pineapple Festival (www.hawaiipineapplefestival.com) and the biennial (even-numbered years) Hanalei Taro Festival (p519). Beer drinkers should mark their calendars for the Kona Brewers Festival (p221). Only in Hawaii will you find the Aloha Festivals Poke Contest (p255) and the Waikiki Spam Jam (p153).

Gourmet culinary events are all the rage across the islands; they vary in price and formality. On O'ahu, Restaurant Week Hawaii (p132) is a great chance to check out the gamut of venues offering special menus and deals. Maui boasts a spate of such events, including the Kapalua Wine & Food Festival (p360). Kaua'i's Spring Gourmet Gala (p484) and Taste of Hawaii (p495) bring top chefs to the island, while the Big Island's A Taste of the Hawaiian Range (p250) is an affordable treat for the carnivorous. Search for others at www.calendar.gohawaii.com.

WHERE TO EAT & DRINK

The dining scene is like night and day between Honolulu and the Neighbor Islands due to restaurant quantity and variety. On Kaua'i, we can count the number of established Japanese restaurants on one hand, while O'ahu's selection will number in the hundreds, from impeccable sushi bars to noodle shops to trendy *izakaya* (which by and large have not reached the

Hawaii's homegrown cornucopia comes to life in *The Hawai'i Farmers Market Cookbook* (Hawaii Farm Bureau), which features handy tips and recipes from top local farmers and chefs.

Neighbor Islands yet). That said, the Big Island and especially Maui are closer to O'ahu as trendsetters, whether they be boutique farms or four-star dining rooms.

Still across the islands you'll find similar types of restaurants. For sit-down meals, there is a big divide between highbrow restaurants that could rival mainland counterparts and lowbrow diner-type, family restaurants that serve classic, plantation-style cookery, loved for familiar flavors and generous portions. In either category, there are gems and duds. If you want to splurge on a meal, pick the foodie darlings rather than any oceanfront resort restaurant (for which you're paying mainly for the view).

Find fantastic prices on fresh fish at indie fish markets, which typically sell *poke,* seared ahi and fish plates. If calories are no concern, go for true local *grinds* at '70s-style drive-ins (for plate lunches and *loco moco*). Ideal for picnics are *okazu-ya* (Japanese takeout) lunch shops, mainly in Hilo and Honolulu.

While all-night eateries are readily found in Honolulu, Neighbor Island restaurants typically open and close (by 10pm) early. For late-night dining, you'll have to seek out bars or the rare 24-hour coffee shop. In general, locals tip slightly less than mainlanders do, but still up to 20% for good service and at least 15% for the basics.

Local produce is surprisingly pricey and hard to find except at farmers markets, fruit stands and some locally owned supermarkets (see the boxed text, below). Both residents and tourists cannot resist the deals at Costco (which actually has an impressive deli serving *poke* that garners raves from locals).

HABITS & CUSTOMS

In traditional households, home cooking is integral to daily life, perhaps owing to the slower pace, backyard gardens and obsession with food. Meals are early and on the dot: typically 6am breakfast, noon lunch and 6pm dinner.

At home, locals rarely serve formal sit-down meals with individual courses. Even when entertaining, meals are typically served potluck style with a spread of flavorful dishes that to the unfamiliar palate will seem ridiculously clashing. If you're invited to a local home, show up on time, bring dessert, and remove your shoes at the door. Locals are generous with leftovers and might insist that you take a plate (along with homegrown fruits) with you.

TOP PICKS – PRODUCE MARKETS

Here's a list of recommended farmers markets, produce stands and grocers that stock a lot of locally grown produce. Beware of markets selling imported produce, flowers and manmade junk. For a complete list of farmers markets, see www.ediblehawaiianislands.com.

Hawai'i the Big Island
- Hilo Farmers Market (p290)
- Waimea Farmers Market (p265)
- Keauhou Farmers Market (p227)

Kaua'i
- Kilauea Neighborhood Center Sunshine Market (Kilauea Neighborhood Center, Keneke St; Thursday, 4.30pm)
- Kapa'a New Park Sunshine Market (p504)
- Banana Joe's Fruitstand (p509)

Maui
- Maui Swap Meet (p368)
- Huelo Lookout (p392)
- Laulima Farms (p402)

Moloka'i
- Saturday morning market (p449)

O'ahu
- Saturday Farmers Market at KCC (p165)
- People's Open Market (p133 and p158)
- Kokua Market (p136)

MUST-TRY TASTES

- Leonard's *malasadas,* Portuguese fried dough, served warm and sugar-coated (O'ahu; p157)
- Two Ladies Kitchen *mochi,* Japanese sticky-rice cake (Hawai'i the Big Island; p299)
- Kumu Farms Macadamia Nut Pesto, sold at Friendly Market (Moloka'i; p448)
- frozen-fruit frosties at Banana Joe's (Kaua'i; p509)
- Sam Sato's *manju,* Japanese cake filled with sweet bean paste (Maui; p370)
- *manapua* (Hawaii version of Chinese-style steamed or baked buns) in local flavors (eg *kalua* pig, sweet potato, coconut) from Royal Kitchen (O'ahu; p133) or Chun Wah Kam Noodle Factory (O'ahu; p144)
- coconut macaroons from Icing on the Cake (Kaua'i; p496)
- Bubbies *mochi* ice cream (O'ahu; p136)
- Molokai Roadside Marinade, sold at Friendly Market (Moloka'i; p448)
- seared ahi wraps at Kilauea Fish Market (Kaua'i; p509)
- Surfing Goat Dairy chevre cheese (Maui; p408)
- *loco moco* at Café 100 (Hawai'i the Big Island; p296)

While standard cutlery (forks, spoons, knives) is the norm, you'll also see chopsticks widely used. Considering the number they go through, Hawaii must have a stake in disposable wooden chopsticks.

When dining out, you might find that even top-end restaurants are relatively casual (called 'island casual' here), with no jackets or ties required. Tourists can even get away with neat khaki shorts and an aloha shirt at resorts. In general, service at fancy restaurants might seem a tad unpolished (although polite) to those harking from big cities.

VEGETARIANS & VEGANS

While locals are diehard eaters of sashimi and Spam, vegetarians and vegans won't go hungry. Top-end restaurants almost always include meatless selections (such as grilled vegetable, garden pastas, creative uses of tofu). The multitude of Asian eateries ensures vegetable and tofu options, even in rural towns, while healthy versions of traditional local fare are now available, especially at establishments run by mainlanders influenced by 'California cuisine.' Popular offerings include tofu (or fresh ahi for fish-only eaters) wraps, meal-sized salads and grilled-vegetable sandwiches or plates (often with wholewheat bread or brown rice).

That said, finding an exclusively vegetarian restaurant isn't easy. Vegans, especially, must seek out the few eateries that use no animal products. When ordering at restaurants, be sure to ask whether a dish is indeed meatless; soups and sauces often contain meat, chicken or fish broth.

The most economical way to ensure no meat or animal ingredients: forage at farmers markets and health food stores.

EATING WITH KIDS

Hawaii is a family-oriented and unfussy place, so all restaurants welcome children. High chairs are usually available, but it pays to inquire ahead of time. Even the finest resort restaurants accommodate children (often with kid-specific menus). That said, consider your child's temperament: neighboring tables will not appreciate noisy interruptions during their four-star, wallet-draining meal.

GO FISH

Fresh sashimi-grade ahi for $10 per pound? You're not dreaming. Perhaps that's why locals eat twice as much seafood as the per-capita US national average. Ahi is the local favorite for eating raw, but mahimahi and *ono* are also popular for cooking.

The **Hawai'i Seafood Buyers' Guide** (www.hawaii-seafood.org) is a fascinating, one-stop resource (whether you're interested in the catching, the selecting or, of course, the eating of island fish).

The species most commonly eaten in Hawaii:

ahi – yellowfin or bigeye tuna, red flesh, excellent raw or rare

aku – skipjack tuna, red flesh, strong flavor; *katsuo* in Japanese

'ama'ama – mullet, delicate white flesh

awa – milkfish, tender white flesh

kajiki – Pacific blue marlin; *a'u* in Hawaiian

mahimahi – dolphin fish or dorado, firm pink flesh, popular cooked

moi – threadfish, flaky white flesh, rich flavor

monchong – pomfret, mild flavor, firm pinkish-white flesh

nairage – striped marlin; *a'u* in Hawaiian

'o'io – bonefish

onaga – red snapper, soft and moist; *'ula'ula* in Hawaiian

ono – wahoo, white-fleshed and flaky

opah – moonfish, firm and rich

'opakapaka – pink snapper, delicate flavor, premium quality

'opelu – mackerel scad, pan-sized, delicious fried

papio – jack fish; also called ulua

shutome – swordfish, succulent and meaty

tako – octopus, chewy texture; *he'e* in Hawaiian

tombo – albacore tuna, light flesh, mild flavor, silky texture

If restaurant dining is inconvenient, no problem: eating outdoors is among the simplest and best island pleasures. Pack finger foods for a picnic, stop for smoothies at roadside stands, and order plate lunches or fish wraps at patio counters. If you really want to act local, buy a *goza* (inexpensive roll-up straw mat sold at ABC Stores and Longs Drugs) and set up your cooler and fixings at the best nearby park. Accommodations with full kitchens are convenient for eat-in breakfasts, especially if you stock up on fruit at farmers markets.

The food itself should pose little trouble, as grocers stock mainstream national brands. A kid who eats nothing but Honey Nut Cheerios will not go hungry here. But the local diet, with its variety of cuisines and plethora of sweet treats, will probably tempt kids away from mainstream habits.

At hotel luau, kids receive a discount (and sometimes free admission when accompanied by a paying adult). Commercial luau might seem like cheesy Vegas shows to adults, but kids will probably enjoy the flashy dances and fire tricks.

EAT YOUR WORDS
Food Glossary

Hawaii cuisine is multiethnic and so is the lingo. In addition to this glossary, see the Language (p582) and Glossary (p584) chapters for pidgin and Hawaiian pronunciation tips.

adobo – Filipino chicken or pork cooked in vinegar, *shōyu*, garlic and spices

arare – *shōyu*-flavored rice crackers; also called *kaki mochi*

'awa – kava, a native plant used to make an intoxicating drink

bentō – Japanese-style box lunch
broke da mout – delicious; literally 'broke the mouth'
char siu – Chinese barbecued pork
crack seed – Chinese-style preserved fruit; a salty, sweet and/or sour snack

donburi – meal-sized bowl of rice and main dish

furikake – a catch-all Japanese seasoning or condiment, usually dry and sprinkled atop rice; in Hawaii, sometimes used for *poke*

grind – to eat
grinds – food; see *'ono kine grinds*
guava – fruit with green or yellow rind, moist pink flesh and lots of edible seeds

haupia – coconut-cream dessert
hulihuli chicken – rotisserie-cooked chicken

imu – underground earthen oven used to cook *kalua* pig and other luau food
inamona – roasted and ground *kukui* (candlenut), used to flavor *poke*
izakaya – a Japanese pub serving tapas-style dishes

kalo – Hawaiian word for taro
kalua – Hawaiian method of cooking pork and other luau food in an *imu*
kaukau – food
kamaboko – cake of puréed, steamed fish; used to garnish Japanese dishes
katsu – Japanese deep-fried cutlets, usually pork or chicken; see *tonkatsu*

laulau – bundle of pork or chicken and salted butterfish, wrapped in taro and *ti* leaves and steamed
li hing mui – sweet-salty preserved plum; type of crack seed; also refers to the flavor powder
liliko'i – passion fruit
loco moco – dish of rice, fried egg and hamburger patty topped with gravy or other condiments
lomilomi salmon – minced, salted salmon, diced tomato and green onion
luau – Hawaiian feast

mai tai – 'tiki bar' drink typically containing rum, grenadine, and lemon and pineapple juices
malasada – Portuguese fried doughnut, sugar-coated, no hole
manapua – Chinese steamed or baked bun filled with *char siu*
manju – Japanese steamed or baked cake, often filled with sweet bean paste
mochi – Japanese sticky-rice cake

nishime – Japanese stew of root vegetables and seaweed
noni – type of mulberry with smelly yellow fruit, used medicinally
nori – Japanese seaweed, usually dried

ogo – crunchy seaweed, often added to *poke; limu* in Hawaiian
ohelo – shrub with edible red berries similar in tartness and size to cranberries
'ono – delicious
'ono kine grinds – good food

pho – Vietnamese soup, typically beef broth, noodles and fresh herbs
poi – staple Hawaiian starch made of steamed, mashed taro
poke – cubed, marinated raw fish
pupu – snacks or appetizers

Did you know? *Manapua,* the local term for Chinese *bao* (steamed filled bun) derives from either of two Hawaiian phrases: *mea 'ono pua'a* ('good pork thing') or *mauna pua'a* ('mountain of pork').

saimin – local-style noodle soup

shave ice – cup of finely shaved ice sweetened with colorful syrups

shōyu – soy sauce

soba – thin Japanese buckwheat-flour noodles

star fruit – translucent green-yellow fruit with five ribs like the points of a star, and sweet, juicy pulp

taro – plant with edible corm used to make poi and with edible leaves eaten in *laulau; kalo* in Hawaiian

teishoku – Japanese set meal

teppanyaki – Japanese style of cooking with an iron grill

tonkatsu – Japanese breaded and fried pork cutlets, also prepared as chicken katsu

tsukemono – Japanese pickled vegetables

ume – Japanese pickled plum

unagi – freshwater eel, usually grilled and served with sweet sauce over sushi rice

Outdoor Activities & Adventures

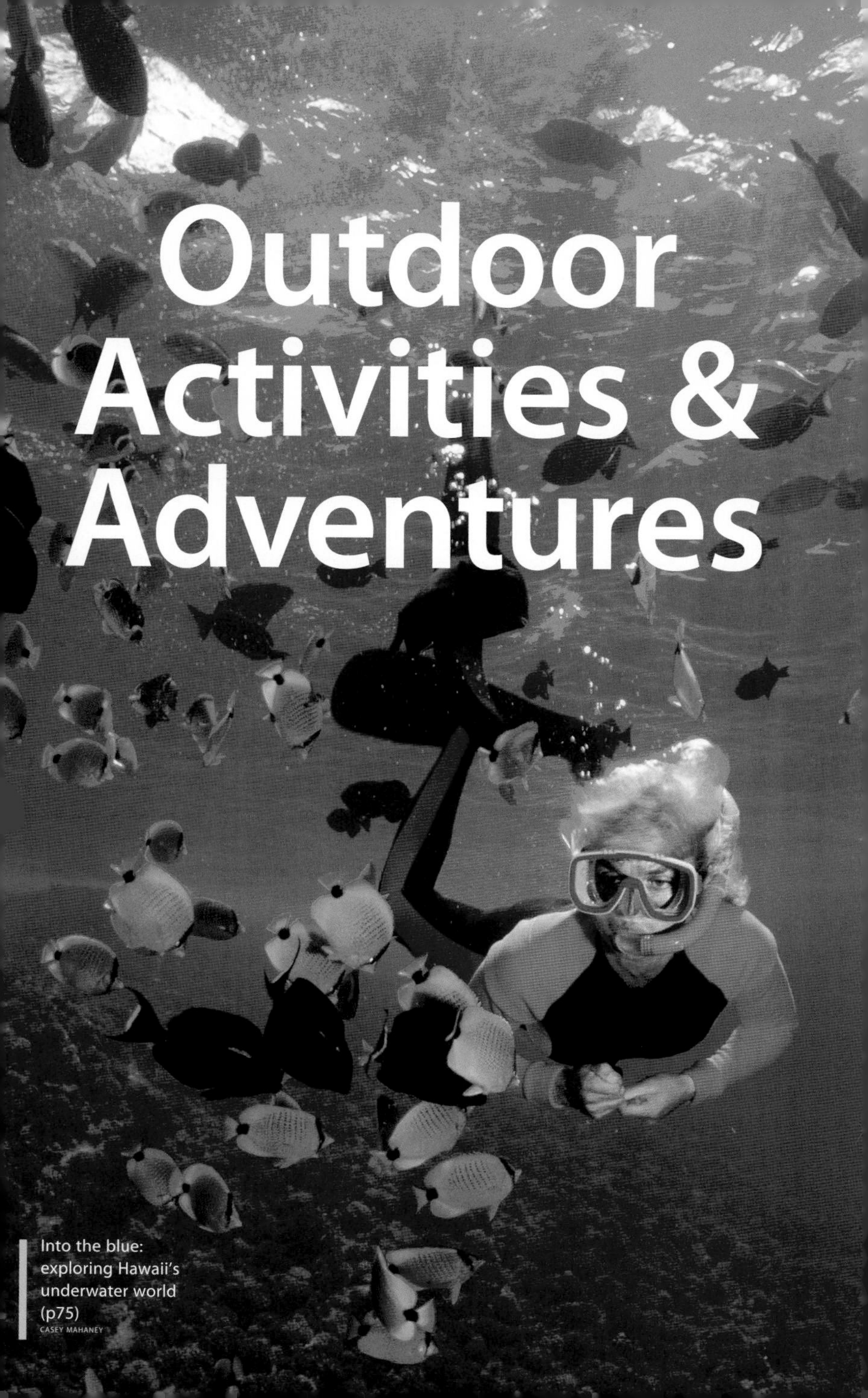

Into the blue:
exploring Hawaii's
underwater world
(p75)
CASEY MAHANEY

Are you coming to Hawaii to luxuriate in sensuous nature while having the outdoor adventures of a lifetime? Of course you are. The real question is – how much time have you got?

Mother Nature has bestowed these lonely Pacific isles with such divine scenery, with such a rare and delicate grace, you could do nothing but lie on your towel and still return home with stories to tell. But we feel certain you didn't come all this way merely to rest on your elbows.

In Hawaii, life is lived outdoors. And as in days of old, whether locals are surfing, swimming, fishing or picnicking with the entire 'ohana (family), every encounter with sacred nature is infused with the Hawaiian sensibilities of aloha 'aina and malama 'aina – love and care for the land. To appreciate the landscape is also to preserve it, and travelers should approach their Hawaii adventures in the same spirit.

Hopefully, this chapter will whet your appetite. Then turn to the island chapters, which open with an activities map and fuller details on the parks and unforgettable experiences that await.

TOP HAIR-RAISING ADVENTURES

- surf the waves of Jaws, off Maui (p410)
- night dive with manta rays on the Big Island (p219)
- ride a mule down the Kalapaupa Peninsula on Moloka'i (p461)
- count Laysan albatross on Midway Island (p559)
- kayak the Na Pali Coast on Kaua'i (p519)
- zipline the slopes of Haleakalā (p410)

Kayaking in Kailua (p174), O'ahu

ANN CECIL

At Sea

The Pacific Ocean. You probably noticed it on the flight over. Here are all the ways you can play in it.

BODYSURFING & BODYBOARDING

Sure, locals bodysurf like ballet dancers, but anybody can do it. Bodyboarding is even easier, giving you a slice of foam to hang on to. Best of all, except in the gnarliest or calmest surf, you can do both on almost any beach. If you're new, don't underestimate small-looking waves – they can roll you just like the five-footers.

Board rider, Makapu'u Beach (p168), O'ahu
ANN CECIL

Places known for bodysurfing include Brennecke's Beach (p530) and Kalapaki Beach (p479) on Kaua'i; White Sands Beach (p218) on Hawai'i the Big Island; Big Beach (p386) on Maui; and Sandy Beach Park (p168), Makaha Beach Park (p198) and Kapahulu Groin (p150) on O'ahu.

DIVING

Truly, the scenery under the water is every bit the equal of what's on land, and sometimes even more amazing. How do you beat diving shipwrecks and lava tubes, listening to whale-song and going nose to nose with sharks and manta rays?

If you don't already know how to dive, Hawaii is a great place to learn. Most dive companies offer both 'intro' dives for beginners and reasonably priced open-water certification courses. Experienced divers just need to bring their certification card; everything else is easily rented. Dive costs range widely depending on gear, dive length, location and so on, but in general, one-tank dives run from $90 to $130, two-tank dives $110 to $160, and PADI certification courses $450 to $650.

Every island has highly recommended dive spots for all abilities – how to choose? O'ahu's Hanauma Bay (p166) and the Big Island's Kona Coast (p207) are particularly good places for novice divers. The Big Island also offers nighttime sojourns with manta rays (p219), while in summer O'ahu's top spots include the caves and ledges of Three Tables and Shark's Cove in Waimea (p187).

Off Maui, the biggest fishbowl of all is crescent-shaped Molokini (see p379), and nearby Lana'i offers the grottoes, caves and arches of Cathedrals (p432) in Hulopo'e Bay. Kaua'i has excellent diving off the south coast near Po'ipu (p530) and fantastic trips to neighboring Ni'ihau (p528).

It takes planning, time and money, but recently reopened Midway Island (p559) in the Northwestern Hawaiian Islands is an epic experience.

OUTRIGGER CANOEING: THE ORIGINAL SUPERFERRY

Hawaii was settled by Polynesians paddling outrigger canoes across 2000 miles of open ocean, so you could say canoeing was Hawaii's original sport. Europeans, who marveled at so much when they first arrived, were awestruck at the skill Native Hawaiians displayed in their canoes near shore – timing launches and landings perfectly, and paddling for play among the waves like dolphins.

Today, over 40 canoe clubs keep outrigger canoeing alive and well, mainly through racing in single, double and six-person canoes. The main season is from January to May; many races are open to nonresidents. A great all-round resource, with links to canoe clubs and race schedules, is www.y2kanu.com. Major island-specific organizations include **Kanaka Ikaika** (www.kanakaikaika .com), **Hawaii Island Paddlesports Association** (www.kaikahoe.org) and **Maui Canoe & Kayak** (http://mauicanoeandkayak.org).

The most impressive long-distance events, though, happen in the fall. On the Big Island in early September, the **Queen Lili'uokalani** (www.kaiopua.org) races 18 miles from Kailua Bay to Honaunau Bay. Then, in late September and early October, men and women compete separately in a 41-mile race across the channel from Moloka'i to O'ahu (p446).

To dip a paddle yourself, outrigger canoe trips are offered at Waikiki's Kuhio Beach (p150), on Kaua'i's Wailua River (p492) and at Kihei on Maui (p377). Certainly, don't miss Maui's mid-May International Festival of Canoes (p344) in Lahaina, where master carvers create the boats, then launch them.

The **Professional Association of Diving Instructors** (PADI; ☎ 800-729-7234; www.padi.com) and the **National Association of Underwater Instructors** (NAUI; www.naui.org) certify scuba divers.

For more on Hawaii dive spots, pick up Lonely Planet's *Diving & Snorkeling Hawaii*.

FISHING

The sea has always been Hawaii's breadbasket. Today, approximately 30% of Hawaii households fish recreationally, and 10% still practice some subsistence fishing. You will see locals everywhere casting from shore (shorefishing), and no fishing license is required to join them (only freshwater fishing requires a license). However, regulation upon regulation governs what you can catch and when; see the website of the state **Division of Aquatic Resources** (http://hawaii. gov/dlnr/dar).

Most visiting anglers are more interested in deep-sea sportfishing charters for such legendary quarry as ahi (yellowfin tuna), swordfish, spearfish, mahimahi (dolphinfish) and, most famous of all, Pacific blue marlin, which can reach 1000lb ('granders'). Hawaii has some of the world's best sportfishing, chiefly off the Big Island's Kona Coast (p220), Moloka'i (p439) and Kaua'i (p483).

KAYAKING

Only Kaua'i offers river kayaking, but the entire wide blue ocean surrounding each sculpted emerald isle invites paddlers. Indeed, there are numerous beaches, bays and valleys that can be reached in no other way but from the sea.

Kayakers will find heavenly bits of coastline reserved for them on every island. Kaua'i is famous for its 17-mile, summer-only paddle along the beautiful Na Pali Coast (p519), while Kaua'i's famous Wailua River (p492) is so popular it is now almost entirely restricted to guided tours. Other riverine choices include the Hanalei River (p518) and the Hule'ia River (p482).

From O'ahu's Kailua Beach Park (p174), kayakers can reach three deserted islands that are now seabird sanctuaries. On the Big Island, kayaking is the best method to reach the snorkeling cove in Kealakekua Bay (p235).

On Maui, kayakers can sport with sea turtles, spinner dolphins and, in winter (see p80), with humpback whales at Makena (p385) and Honolua Bay (p358). On Moloka'i, experienced sea kayakers can launch from Halawa Beach (p453) and certainly shouldn't miss the dizzying sea cliffs at Kalaupapa (see the boxed text, p454).

For outrigger canoeing, see opposite.

KITESURFING

Kitesurfing, also called kiteboarding, is a little like strapping on a snowboard, grabbing a parachute and sailing over the water. It's a very impressive feat to watch, and if you already know how to windsurf, surf or wakeboard, there's a good chance you'll master it quickly.

Any place that's good for windsurfing is good for kitesurfing. This means that Maui should dominate the attention of kitesurfers, aspiring or otherwise. In fact, 'Kite Beach' is the nickname for the southwestern end of Kanaha Beach Park (p365), where you can find instruction and rentals. O'ahu's Kailua Beach Park (p174) is also a great place to learn. Windy Moloka'i calls to pros (p440); on Kaua'i, Kawailoa Bay (see the boxed text, p534) is popular; and kitesurfers can safely forget about the Big Island.

SAILING

The most common sailing excursion is a two-fer: a catamaran trip that doubles as a snorkel, dive or whale-watching cruise. Sometimes nonsnorkeling and nondiving passengers pay a reduced fare. But if your sole desire is to feel the sails luff with wind as you tack into the open ocean, then seek out each island's small boat harbor and start talking to captains. In this book, catamarans and sailboats may be listed under Activities or Tours.

On Maui, the Lahaina small-boat harbor (p343) is the prime destination, but nearby Ka'anapali also offers sailing trips (p353). Meanwhile, in Wailea, Hawaiian Sailing Canoe Adventures (p384) offers trips in a traditional Hawaiian outrigger sailing canoe.

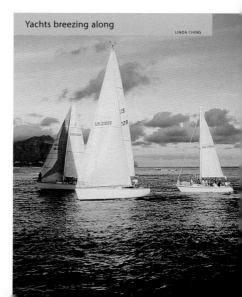

Yachts breezing along

LINDA CHING

On Kaua'i's Hanalei Bay, Island Sails (p518) also offers trips in a Hawaiian sailing canoe; for traditional sailboats, head for Po'ipu's Kukui'ula Harbor (p534).

On O'ahu, Waikiki is flush with 'booze cruise' catamarans (see the boxed text, p150), and sailing is big on the Big Island (p208); all kinds of boats can be chartered from Kailua-Kona's Honokohau Harbor (p241).

Finally, Lana'i's Manele Harbor (p432) has lots of sailboats.

SNORKELING

Coming to Hawaii and not snorkeling is like climbing the Eiffel Tower and closing your eyes – the most bright and beautiful city in the world lies at your feet, and all you need is some molded plastic and antifog gel to see it. If you can walk, you can climb the steps to admire Paris; if you can swim, Hawaii's magnificent coral reefs are yours.

In addition to over 500 species of sometimes neon-colored fish, sea turtles are increasingly common, and you may see manta rays, spinner dolphins, jacks, sharks and other predators. Even better, snorkeling is cheap. A weekly rental – including snorkel, mask, fins and usually a bag to carry them in – averages out at $2 to $4 a day, depending on the quality of the gear. But it's a worthwhile investment to buy your own high-quality mask.

Each island has fantastic shoreline snorkeling spots, in addition to snorkeling cruises that get you places you can't swim to. On O'ahu, Hanauma Bay (p166) is legendary, and in summer North Shore beaches (p186) are a snorkeler's delight. On Maui, don't miss Malu'aka Beach (p385), which is also known as 'Turtle Beach' for self-evident reasons. From Maui, cruises also get you to the partly submerged volcanic crater of Molokini (p330).

The Big Island has both coral reefs, as at Kealakekua Bay (p235), and lava-rock tide pools, as at Kapoho (p304). Top spots on Kaua'i include Ke'e Beach (p524) and Makua (Tunnels) Beach (p524). Lana'i and Moloka'i also have world-class snorkeling, at Hulopo'e Beach (p432) and Dixie Maru Beach (p465).

As a rule, snorkel early – morning conditions are often best, and if everyone else is sleeping, they won't be crowding the water. Also, review the advice in the boxed text, opposite; snorkelers are notorious for – whoops! – forgetting about the waves and the weather.

Eye to eye with a peacock flounder
CASEY MAHANEY

Tide pool, Puako (p253), Big Island
CASEY MAHANEY

There are like a million marine life and snorkel guides to Hawaii, but photographer John Hoover publishes some great ones: snorkelers and divers should pick up *Hawaii's Fishes*, tide-pool enthusiasts might grab *Hawaii's Sea Creatures*, and his new *Ultimate Guide* covers everything.

SURFING

Native Hawaiians invented surfing, and in Hawaii today, surfing is both its own intense subculture as well as a casual part of everyday life. Many island kids learn to surf the same way Canadians learn to ski – from the moment they can stand.

For an introduction to the sport and its place in Hawaiian history, see *Surfer* magazine editor Jake Howard's special section (p81). Each chapter also contains a boxed text by Jake describing that island's particular surf scene and its most notable surfing spots.

OCEAN SAFETY

Never turn your back on the ocean. You hear this a lot in Hawaii because locals know firsthand just how dangerous the ocean can be. Waves and water conditions can change abruptly, so always pay attention and never swim alone. Drowning is the leading cause of accidental death for visitors.

- **Rip currents** Rips, or rip currents, are fast-flowing ocean currents that can drag swimmers out into deeper water. Anyone caught in one should either go with the flow until it loses power or swim parallel to shore to slip out of it.
- **Rogue waves** All waves are not the same. They often come in sets, some bigger, some smaller, and sometimes, one really big 'rogue wave' sweeps in and literally catches sunbathers napping.
- **Shorebreaks** Waves breaking close to shore are called shorebreaks. Smaller ones are great for bodysurfing. Large shorebreaks, though, can slam down hard enough to knock you out.
- **Undertows** Particularly on sloped beaches, undertows occur when large waves wash back directly into incoming surf. If one pulls you under the water, don't panic. Go with the current until you get beyond the wave.
- For information about tsunamis, see p565.

With their attention focused under the waves, snorkelers need to be extra cautious. Meanwhile, scuba divers have an additional set of concerns; contact **Divers Alert Network** (DAN; ☎ 919-684-8111, 800-446-2671; www.diversalertnetwork.org) for advice on diving emergencies, insurance, decompression services and injuries. For coral-reef etiquette, see the boxed text, p94.

Hawaii's biggest waves roll into the north shores of the islands from November through February. Summer swells, which break along the south shores, aren't as frequent or as large as their winter counterparts.

When it comes to surfing, Oʻahu stands head and shoulders above the Neighbor Islands. With its excellent and wide variety of surf spots, Oʻahu is where all the major competitions happen; its epic North Shore (p184) is home to surfing's 'Triple Crown.' All the other islands have good, even great, surfing, but they tend to be more laid-back.

The latest fad is stand up paddle surfing – which, as the name implies, means standing on the surfboard and using a paddle to propel yourself into waves. It's great for less-limber folks, since you don't need to pop up into a stance; it takes coordination to learn, but isn't harder than regular surfing. Kauaʻi's Hanalei Bay (p518) and the Big Island's Kahuluʻu Bay (p220) are two places with stand up paddle lessons. Of course, regular surfing lessons and board rentals are available at just about every tourist locale with rideable waves.

The **Surf News Network** (www.surfnewsnetwork.com) provides a comprehensive weather-and-wave report. **Surfrider** (www.surfrider.org) is a nonprofit organization helping protect oceans and beaches. For a great guide to the best waves, pick up *Surfer's Guide to Hawaii* by Greg Ambrose.

SWIMMING

When it comes to swimming beaches in Hawaii, you're spoiled for choice. Coastal strands come in a rainbow of hues and an infinite variety of textures – with sand that's white, tan, black, charcoal, green, orange, sea-glass, pebbled, rocky and cratered with lava-rock tide pools. Water temperatures are idyllic, ranging from 72°F to 80°F year-round.

And yet, swimming is not ideal in the same place year-round. The islands have four distinct coastal areas – north shore, south shore, leeward (west) coast and windward (east) coast – and each has its own peculiar weather and water conditions. As a general rule, the best places

Diving humpback whale, West Maui (p348)
GREG ELMS

to swim in the winter are along the south shores, and in the summer, the north shores. When it's rough or rainy on one side, it's usually calm and clear on another, and so on.

The only island where swimming isn't great is Moloka'i, where incessant winds often make waters rough. Otherwise, no worries! Hawaii's most famous beach is Waikiki (p145) – and it's still a quintessential experience. Maui is often credited with having the 'best beaches,' and who are we to quibble with its succulent array? But don't dismiss the Big Island or Kaua'i, which both have their share of egregiously soft, silken strands kissed nightly by the same radiant sunset. For our humble list of the best beaches by island, see p26.

WHALE WATCHING

Each winter, mainly from January to March, about two-thirds of the entire North Pacific humpback whale population (roughly 10,000 whales) comes to the shallow coastal waters off the Hawaiian islands for breeding, calving and nursing. Five main areas are protected as the **Hawaiian Islands Humpback Whale National Marine Sanctuary** (http://hawaiihumpbackwhale.noaa .gov). Visiting the sanctuary waters at this time is a hot-ticket item. The western coastline of Maui (see p334) and the eastern shore of Lana'i are the chief birthing and nursing grounds, but the Big Island's west coast also sees lots of activity, including the acrobatic 'breaching' displays, for which humpbacks are famous. All islands offer whale-watching tours and have areas where you can spot whales from shore. Sanctuary headquarters are in Kihei (p375) on Maui; if you're really keen, volunteer for the annual Sanctuary Ocean Count (p570).

WINDSURFING

Hawaii ranks as one of the world's premier places for windsurfing. In general, the best winds blow from June through September, but tradewinds keep windsurfers happy all year. As O'ahu's North Shore is to surfing, so Maui's Ho'okipa Beach (p388) is to windsurfing: it is the sport's Everest, its Olympics – a dangerous, fast arena where the top international windsurfing competitions sort out who's best. Mere mortals might prefer windsurfing Maui's Kanaha Beach Park (p365) and Ma'alaea Bay (p372). The other islands have windsurfing, but they don't reach the pinnacle of Maui. Only Moloka'i, bracketed by wind-whipped ocean channels, provides an equivalent challenge for experts. If you're looking to learn, O'ahu's Kailua Beach Park (p174) is consistently good year-round and is home to top-notch schools. Other recommended spots include Diamond Head Beach Park (p165) and the North Shore's Sunset Beach Park (p186). Kaua'i has only one prime spot for windsurfers: 'Anini Beach (p511), which has lessons and rentals. On the Big Island, conditions are consistent at 'Anaeho'omalu Bay (p249), but currently the island has no rentals – so you must DIY or not do it at all.

WELCOME TO HAWAII, WHERE THE SURF'S ALWAYS UP
Jake Howard, Surfer magazine

Nowhere is there a better, more idyllic place to be a surfer than the islands of Hawaii. With a plethora of schools and rental outfitters, it's the perfect locale to get your feet – and your board – wet. Paddle out into that luxurious 75°F water once and you'll understand why it's impossible to conceive of a Hawaii without surfing, and surfing without Hawaii.

Island-specific surfing information can be found in each island's chapter.

Early Riders
The exact date of surfing's inception is unknown, but researchers have traced petroglyphs and oral chants to approximately AD 1500, which leads them to believe that surfing existed in Polynesian culture long before that. One thing they are sure of is that wave riding was an integral part of the old Hawaiian kapu (taboo) system of governing.

In ancient Hawaii, kings didn't have castles, they had surfboards. The *ali'i* (royalty) sought the finest craftsmen to transform just the right *wili wili* tree into a 14ft to 16ft *olo* (a primitive long-board that weighed in excess of 100lb). Once ground smooth by *pohaku puna* (granulated coral) and *oahi* (rough stone), the new boards were adorned with a dark stain derived from *ti* root and polished with *kukui* (candlenut) oil until gleaming with a glossy finish. This ceremonial process ended with the board being 'christened' before its first ride.

In 1778, when Captain Cook and his ships arrived in Hawaii (p38), Europeans beheld the wonder of surfing for the first time. Nothing much changed until New England missionaries arrived in 1820. The missionaries promptly started stamping out the 'hedonistic' act of surfing and, save a few holdouts, by 1890 surfing was all but extinct.

Then, in the early 1900s, modern surfing's first icon, Duke Kahanamoku, stepped off the beach into history. Kahanamoku grew up in Waikiki, where he swam, fished, dove and rode the reefs on traditional *olo*-style boards. In 1911 Duke and the Waikiki beachboys caught the attention of author Jack London, whose detailed accounts in *Cruise of the Snark* captured the imagination of the Western world. From then on, Kahanamoku spread the gospel of surfing, traveling the world demonstrating the Hawaiian 'Sport of Kings.'

Modern Masters
Understandably, Hawaii is home to some of the best surfers in the world, who remain at the forefront of their sport. In the 1960s, surfing became overwhelmingly popular, thanks largely to early surf films – particularly Bruce Brown's *The Endless Summer* (1964) – and the emergence of *Surfer* magazine. Hawaii quickly became the premier destination for traveling surfers, and the roots of professional surfing took hold on O'ahu. Local stars of the day, such as Gerry Lopez and Rory Russell, were the first to bring home legitimate paychecks for simply going surfing. Due to his casual grace and effortless style in the hollow waves of the Banzai Pipeline (p186), Lopez established himself as Mr Pipeline.

Pipeline remained the surf scene's focal point, led by local riders such as Dane Kealoha, Johnny Boy Gomes, and brothers Michael and Derek Ho. In 1993 Derek became Hawaii's first, but not last, world champion. Sunny Garcia, a strong-willed youngster from O'ahu's west side, ascended the world ranks until he claimed the title in 2000. Shortly thereafter, Kaua'i-born brothers Bruce and Andy Irons rose in prominence. Bruce quickly developed into one of the best free surfers in history, and Andy went on a competitive tear, winning three world titles in a row from 2002 through 2004.

To claim the **Triple Crown of Surfing** (www.triplecrownofsurfing.com) is one of surfing's most distinguished accomplishments. The three contests, which take place every winter on O'ahu's North Shore at Hale'iwa, Sunset Beach and Pipeline, showcase the world's top surfers on the world's top waves. Notable Triple Crown champions include nine-time world champion Kelly Slater, Andy Irons and Sunny Garcia.

Girls in Curls

Surfing has long been dominated by men. But in 2002, *Blue Crush,* a big-budget film about three surfer girls trying to make it on O'ahu's North Shore, led to a '*Blue Crush* boom,' as women around the country flocked to surfing.

Women in Hawaii, though, have always been riding waves. They rode with men in ancient times, and in the 1890s, Princess Ka'iulani, riding her *olo,* almost single-handedly saved the sport from extinction, influencing Duke and his contemporaries.

Seventy years later another woman emerged as a beacon of the aloha spirit. Makaha's Rell Sunn, or 'Auntie Rell,' started an unknowable number of young surfers on their paths. Sunn gave the gift of surfing to as many underprivileged island children as she could, most notably through her annual *menehune* contest (named after Hawaii's legendary 'little people'), which she ran from 1976 until she succumbed to cancer in 1998. Even today Sunn's surf contest remains a can't-miss event for the kids of O'ahu's Makaha.

Following in Sunn's footsteps, China Uemura's Wahine Classic runs in Waikiki every year, fostering youth and women's surfing. The torch has also been passed to teen talents such as Carissa Moore and Coco Ho (daughter of Pipe Master Michael Ho), two girls who are helping redefine women's pro surfing.

Nuts & Bolts

For a 'surfari' in paradise, few places are easier than Hawaii. You can forget everything from surf wax to your toothbrush, and you'll survive. Granted, it's one of the more expensive places to visit, but nearly every town can equip the traveling surfer with what they need.

It may be cheaper to bring your own boards, but before you fly, check airline baggage fees. (Check interisland carrier policies too; some have board restrictions.) Most airlines charge from $50 to $100 per board. Plus they're notoriously bad about handling board bags; damage is common.

If you don't want the hassle of flying with boards, some of the best surfboards in the world are hand-shaped in Hawaii. On O'ahu's North Shore, traveling professional surfers will often put their boards up for sale in local surf shops after their stay, and it's quite easy to find quality used boards. On average a brand-new surfboard runs at about $400, while used boards vary from $150 to $350 depending on condition.

Local board and surf shops are also great centers of information. Whether you're curious about conditions, looking for sunscreen or needing lessons, surf shops are the nerve centers for the wave-bound community.

To find out about surf and weather conditions, www.surfline.com offers top-of-the-line webcams and forecasts, but it is a for-fee service. For free but less in-depth reports and forecasts, try www .wavewatch.com. **North Shore lifeguards** (www.northshorelifeguards.com) are another great source of information. Also, the **Honolulu Advertiser** (www.honoluluadvertiser.com/section/surf) posts daily surf reports online.

It's All about Respect

As a tourist in Hawaii, there are some places you go, and some places you don't go. For many local families the beach parks are meeting places where generations gather to celebrate life under the sun. They're tied to these places by a sense of community and culture. Residents are usually welcoming and willing to share surf spots that, over time, have become popular tourist destinations, but they reserve the right to protect other 'secret' and sacred surf grounds. They don't want to feel pushed out by outsiders. As a conscious traveler it's important to understand this.

In the water, basic surf etiquette is vital. The person 'deepest,' or furthest outside, has the right of way. When somebody is already up and riding, don't take off on the wave in front of them. Also, as a visitor in the lineup, don't expect to get every wave that comes your way. There's a definite pecking order and, frankly, tourists are at the bottom. That being said, usually if you give a wave, you'll get a wave in return. In general, be generous in the water, understand your place and surf with a smile, and you should be fine.

On Land

As Hawaii's volcanic mountains rise above the waterline, they evolve into one of the planet's richest and most varied ecosystems – or what's also been called 'paradise.'

CAVING

Funny thing, lava. As the top of a flow cools and hardens, the molten rock beneath keeps moving. Then, when the eruption stops and the lava drains, what's left behind is an underground maze of tunnels like some colossal ant farm.

Being the youngest and still-active sibling, Hawai'i island is a caving mecca, containing six of the world's 10 longest lava tubes. Many of these are cultural as well as ecological wonders, since ancient Hawaiians used lava tubes as burial chambers, water caches, temporary housing and more. On the Big Island, check out the Kanohina cave system in Ka'u (p325), with 25 miles of complex tunnels; the Kazumura system in Puna (p300); and book a ranger-led tour in Hawai'i Volcanoes National Park (see the boxed text, p316). For more information, visit the **Cave Conservancy of Hawai'i** (www.hawaii caves.org).

Other islands have fewer opportunities, but along Maui's Road to Hana (p395) is a tube system once used as a slaughterhouse!

CYCLING & MOUNTAIN BIKING

Quality trumps quantity when it comes to cycling and mountain biking in Hawaii. Cyclists will find the friendliest roads and the most organizational support on O'ahu (p105) and the Big Island (p209), but all islands have rentals, trails and 4WD roads that double as two-wheel, pedal-powered adventures.

As the home of the Ironman Triathlon World Championships (p221), the Big Island is very welcoming to cyclists. Top cycling destinations include Hawai'i Volcanoes National

Light at the end of the tunnel, Kula Kai Caverns (p325), Ka'u, Big Island

GREG ELMS

Park (p306), the 45-mile Mana Rd (see the boxed text, p270) circling Mauna Kea and the 6.5-mile beach trail to Pine Trees (p244) on the Kona Coast.

On Oʻahu, popular coastal rides include Kaʻena Point (p200), while in the hills above Pearl Harbor, aim for the Waimano Trail (see the boxed text, p144).

Mountain bikers should also set their sights on Molokaʻi (p441), which has over 40 miles of trails, plus the dirt roads of the Molokaʻi Forest Reserve (p454).

On Maui, the legendary sunrise descent from the top of Haleakalā has been suspended indefinitely (see the boxed text, p415), but experienced riders can still get their adrenaline pumping on the national park's Skyline Trail (p419).

Kauaʻi roads have no bike lanes, but the island is paving a great new coastal trail, Ke Ala Hele Makalae (see the boxed text, p502), plus mountain bikers can pedal the Waimea Canyon Trail (p553) and the ridge-top Powerline Trail (p495).

A good mountain-bike trail guide covering all the islands is *Mountain Biking the Hawaiian Islands* by John Alford (www.bikehawaii.com). Also get advice from the **Hawaii Bicycling League** (www.hbl.org).

GOLF

Golfing is as popular with locals as with the PGA Tour, which always finds some excuse – any excuse – to visit Hawaii. Island resorts baby some of the world's most lauded, challenging and beautiful greens. While spoiling a good walk on one of these elite, professionally designed courses costs upwards of $150 to $200 a round, Hawaii is also silly with well-loved, affordable municipal courses ($35 to $50 a round) boasting scenery you probably can't get back home. Hey, Kauaʻi's **Kukuiolono Golf Course** (p539) costs only $8!

See the island chapter Activities sections for specific recommendations, and for a statewide overview, visit **Tee Times Hawaii** (www.teetimeshawaii.com). Playing in the afternoon is usually discounted.

Helicopter tours, Kauaʻi (p472)

HOLGER LEUE

HANG GLIDING & PARAGLIDING

Remove the engine, and flying becomes a wonderfully ecofriendly adrenaline rush. Oʻahu (p108) has ideal cliffs for hang gliding along the southwest coast, while glider rides (and skydiving) are offered at the North Shore's Dillingham Airfield (p194).

On Maui, tandem paraglide rides can be had near Polipoli Spring State Recreation Area (p411), and on Kauaʻi, you can book a ride in an ultralight – a powered hang glider – in Hanapepe (p543).

HELICOPTER & AIRPLANE TOURS

Far and away the most popular places to visit by air are Kauaʻi's almost inaccessible Na Pali Coast (p472) and the Big Island's

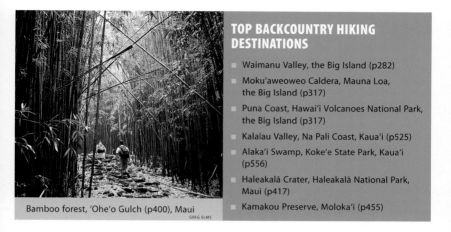

TOP BACKCOUNTRY HIKING DESTINATIONS

- Waimanu Valley, the Big Island (p282)
- Moku'aweoweo Caldera, Mauna Loa, the Big Island (p317)
- Puna Coast, Hawai'i Volcanoes National Park, the Big Island (p317)
- Kalalau Valley, Na Pali Coast, Kaua'i (p525)
- Alaka'i Swamp, Koke'e State Park, Kaua'i (p556)
- Haleakalā Crater, Haleakalā National Park, Maui (p417)
- Kamakou Preserve, Moloka'i (p455)

Bamboo forest, 'Ohe'o Gulch (p400), Maui

GREG ELMS

lava-spewing volcanoes (see the boxed text, p214). Visiting these areas by air provides unforgettable vantages and experiences you can't get any other way. Helicopter tours are also popular ways to see Maui (p366), and some Maui tours include a jaunt over to Moloka'i's towering Pali Coast. Then again, simply flying to visit Moloka'i constitutes an air tour (p442).

That said, helicopter tours – in fuel burned and noise generated – have a high impact on Hawaii's environment; for an overview, see the boxed text, p483.

HIKING & BACKPACKING

Hikers will find that, pound for pound, these tiny islands simply cannot be topped for heart-stopping vistas and soulful beauty. And being small, even the most rugged spots are usually accessible as day hikes. Backpacking is rarely necessary, though when it is, the rewards so outstrip the effort it's ludicrous.

Begin any exploration of Hawaii's trails by visiting **Na Ala Hele** (www.hawaiitrails.org), which maintains 97 public trails and 85 access roads (totaling 675 miles) statewide. For an overview of Hawaii's parks and land-management agencies, see p94.

For pure variety, Hawai'i the Big Island wins by a nose. Hawai'i Volcanoes National Park (p306) contains an erupting volcano, for goodness sake, plus steaming craters, lava deserts and native rainforests. Then, there are the two nearly 14,000ft mountains to scale – Mauna Loa (p275) and Mauna Kea (p269) – and, if that isn't enough, the haunting Waipi'o Valley (p279).

Kaua'i's legendary Kalalau Trail (p525) on the Na Pali Coast edges spectacularly fluted sea cliffs, while an abundance of trails crisscross Koke'e State Park (p553) and cavernous Waimea Canyon State Park (p550). The Maha'ulepu Coast (see the boxed text, p534) is also highly recommended.

Maui's volcano may be dormant, but Haleakalā National Park (p413) provides awe-inspiring descents across the caldera's enormous moonscape. The death-defying Hana Highway (p392) offers many short excursions; those looking for seclusion can visit gorgeous Polipoli Spring State Recreation Area (p411).

A spread of sea, sky and forest: view from the Kalalau Trail (p525), Na Pali Coast State Park, Kaua'i

On O'ahu, you can escape Honolulu in a hurry along the lush trails in the Manoa and Makiki Valleys around Mt Tantalus (p128). Other recommended destinations are the Kuli'ou'ou Ridge Trail (p166) and the Ka'ena Point Trail (p202).

Moloka'i's Kalaupapa Trail descends into historic Kalaupapa National Historical Park (p458), and Pepe'opae Trail in the Kamakou Preserve (p455) is 'verdant' defined.

What of Lana'i? It has only one first-rate hike, but take the Munro Trail (p436) on a clear day and you'll survey all the main islands but distant Kaua'i.

For more, check out Lonely Planet's *Hiking in Hawaii*.

Hiking Safety

Paved nature trails require no 'preparations' to speak of, but anyone looking to spend hours (or days) on dirt trails should bring sturdy hiking boots, rain gear and a fleece sweater – weather is changeable, and trails can be rocky, uneven and muddy. If you'll be tackling a mountain, bring a winter coat (even in summer). And always carry a flashlight: in the middle of the ocean, it gets dark fast once the sun sets. Of course, a hat, sunscreen and lots of water are mandatory; coastal trails can bake you to a crisp.

Specific safety advice varies with the hike (see details in the destination sections): potential hazards range from volcanic fumes, flash floods and crumbling cliffs to hypothermia and heatstroke. All freshwater – whether flowing or from a pond – must be treated before drinking. Keep in mind that true wilderness abuts civilization throughout Hawaii. Prepare for an hour-long hike outside Honolulu the same as you would for a backpack across a lava desert.

HORSEBACK RIDING

All the islands have ranch country and offer memorable horseback rides. But cattle, cowboys and rodeos have a long history – and still play large roles – on the Big Island (p211) and on Maui (p333), so they have more extensive riding opportunities and a richer *paniolo* (Hawaiian cowboy) culture. One memorable alternative is taking a mule ride to the Kalaupapa Peninsula (p461) on Moloka'i.

RUNNING & MARATHONS

Hawaii enhances any sport, and running is no exception. Marathons are quite popular, and each of the main islands has its signature race, plus a slew of smaller races year-round.

However, one of Hawaii's most famous series of races – the Kilauea Volcano Runs (www.volcanoartcenter.org) through Hawai'i Volcanoes National Park – was canceled in 2009, and if it returns, the races will be rerouted outside the park (to lessen environmental impacts). See the website for updates.

Here is a list of major marathons:

Big Island International Marathon (www.hilomarathon.org) March
Kaua'i Marathon (www.thekauaimarathon.com) September
Maui Marathon (www.mauimarathon.com) September
Honolulu Marathon (www.honolulumarathon.org) December

Of course, no discussion of races is complete without mentioning the **Ironman Triathlon World Championship** (http://ironman.com), held each October on the Big Island (p221). In addition to running 26.2 miles, contestants bike 112 miles and swim 2.4 miles in one of sport's ultimate endurance contests. If you think you're up for half an Ironman, enter May's **Ironman 70.3** (www.ironman703hawaii.com). Or, halve the 70.3 and you've got Honolulu's **Tinman Triathlon** (http://tinmanhawaii.com) in July and Maui's **Xterra World Championship** (p386) in October – which almost sound reasonable.

STARGAZING

Astronomers are drawn to Hawaii's night sky the way surfers are drawn to Hawaii's big waves. Mauna Kea (p269) on the Big Island is unmatched in clarity and has more astronomical observatories than any mountain on earth; the visitor center hosts excellent nightly stargazing programs (p274). Hilo also has a tremendous astronomy museum, 'Imiloa (p288).

Interestingly, astronomical observatories on Maui's Haleakalā Summit study the sun, but the park also hosts public stargazing nightly (p415).

Otherwise, across the state, though particularly on the Big Island and Maui, top-end resorts usually offer stargazing programs with high-quality telescopes.

TENNIS

If you bring your own racket and balls, free public tennis courts are available in just about every town of any size (usually bundled with the town pool and gym in community centers); these are noted throughout the island chapters.

Zipping above the treetops (p410), Haleakalā National Park, Maui

GREG E

However, as with golf courses, upscale resorts really pull out the stops, and at many of these you'll find immaculate tennis courts of professional-level quality, sometimes along with pro shops, round-robin tournaments and partner-matching. Resorts and hotels often reserve courts for guests only, but some allow visitors to rent court time.

YOGA, SPAS & RETREATS

Yoga studios thrive across the islands, allowing you to keep up with your practice while on holiday, and full-on retreats turn meditation into your vacation. Meanwhile, spas often highlight traditional Hawaiian healing arts, like *lomilomi* and hot-stone massage, and herbal treatments. Spas reach their pinnacle at luxury resorts.

On O'ahu, Waikiki resort hotels are famous for their spas (p151), while Kailua has an impressive selection of yoga studios (p174).

The Big Island has good yoga studios in Kailua-Kona (p221), Hilo (p294) and elsewhere, while Puna (p300) is the main destination for retreats. Kaua'i and Maui have fewer yoga studios, but still plenty to keep you limber. Even Moloka'i offers a recommended yoga retreat (p441).

ZIPLINING

Another fad that's growing in Hawaii is ziplining – a thrilling ride among the treetops that was first developed in the forests of Costa Rica and is infiltrating jungles everywhere. The only skill required is the ability to hang on (to your lunch). Currently, only Kaua'i (p473) and Maui (p334) offer ziplining, but they have multiple outfits to choose from. However, rumblings from the Big Island's North Kohala district indicate that ziplining may arrive there soon.

Environment

We tend to think of the Hawaiian Islands as tiny rafts of white sand and tiki bars sailing westward inch-by-inch to Japan. In fact, they are the palm-fringed tops of the earth's largest mountain range, something whales appreciate better than we do. For 70 million years, a 'hot spot' beneath the earth's mantle has operated like a volcanic conveyor belt, manufacturing a 3000-mile string of shield volcanoes that bubble out of the sea in the most geographically isolated spot on the planet – about 2400 miles from the closest continent. This profound isolation has created a living textbook of evolution. Over 90% of Hawaii's native species are endemic – occurring nowhere else in the world – yet endemics are easily threatened by changes to their environment. Consequently, Hawaii has become the 'endangered species capital of the world' (with 329) as well as the 'extinction capital of the US' (accounting for 75% of the nation's documented extinctions). Few places feel humanity's footprint as deeply as Hawaii.

A World Between Waves, edited by Frank Stewart, is a great essay collection covering everything from volcanoes to whales, including a fantastic account of Captain Cook's first voyage from the perspective of his naturalists.

THE LAND

The Hawaiian archipelago is made up of over 50 volcanoes (and 137 islands and atolls) that extend 1600 miles; it's part of the larger and mostly submerged Hawaiian-Emperor Seamount chain, which extends over 3000 miles. The volcanoes are created by a rising column of molten rock – a 'hot spot' – under the Pacific Plate; as the plate moves westward (at a rate of about 3.2in a year), the magma pierces through the crust like a sewing needle, creating volcanoes.

As each volcanic island moves off the hot spot, it stops erupting and starts eroding. At the far northwestern end of the chain, the islands have receded below the ocean surface to become seamounts. Moving eastward from Kure Atoll, the islands get progressively taller and younger until you reach Hawai'i the Big Island, the still-growing, million-year-old child of the group. Straddling the hot spot, Hawai'i's Kilauea is the world's most active volcano. All Hawaiian volcanoes are shield volcanoes that erupt with effusive lava (creating gentle dome-shaped mountains), though they have an explosive side, as Kilauea reminded everyone in 2008 (p306).

The ongoing Kilauea eruption, which began in 1983, is the most voluminous outpouring of lava on the east rift zone in 500 years; it's added well over 500 acres of new land to the Big Island.

Under the sea about 20 miles east of Hawai'i, however, a new volcano is erupting – Lo'ihi. In 30,000 years or so, it will emerge from the water to become the newest island in the Hawaiian chain.

Within the state of Hawaii, there are eight main islands, only seven of which are populated. West of Kaua'i, the minuscule islands and atolls of the Northwestern Hawaiian Islands (p558) stretch for a thousand miles. In all, Hawaii constitutes only 6423 sq miles. This accounts for about 1% of the total US landmass, an area slightly larger than the state of Connecticut. On the Big Island, Ka Lae is the southernmost point in the US, a latitude equivalent to Hong Kong, Bombay and Mexico City.

WILDLIFE

Born barren, the Hawaiian Islands were originally populated only by those plants and animals that could traverse the ocean – flying themselves, floating along the jet stream, or riding the waves. Seeds came in bird wings, insects on driftwood. Most species that landed didn't survive. Scientists estimate that successful species were established maybe once every 35,000 to 70,000 years – and they included no amphibians, no browsing animals, no pines, no mosquitoes and only two mammals: a bat and a seal.

SACRED HONU

Native Hawaiians revere the green sea turtle, which they call *honu*. Often considered a personal *'aumakua* (protective deity), *honu*'s image frequently appears in petroglyphs (and today in tattoos). For ancient Hawaiians, sea turtles were a delicious and prized source of food, but their capture and consumption were typically governed by strict religious and traditional codes.

As with all seven types of sea turtles (four of which can be found in Hawaii), the green sea turtle is now endangered and protected by federal law. Adults can grow over 3ft long and weigh more than 300lb. Young turtles are omnivorous, but adults (unique among sea turtles) become strict vegetarians. This turns their fat green – hence their name.

Green sea turtles can be found throughout the Hawaiian Islands; they are often seen feeding in shallow lagoons, bays and estuaries. However, their main nesting sight is the French Frigate Shoals in the Northwestern Hawaiian Islands (p558). Here, up to 700 females (90% of the population) come to lay their eggs every year.

However, the flora and fauna that made it occupied an unusually rich, diverse land, containing nearly every ecological or life zone. In a prime example of 'adaptive radiation,' the 250 flowering plants that arrived evolved into 1800 native species; 20 kinds of land snails became a thousand species. Lacking predators or much competition, new species dropped defensive protections: thorns, poisons and strong odors disappeared. This process accounts for why such high percentages of native Hawaiian species are endemic, or unique to the islands, and why they fare so poorly against modern invaders.

When Polynesians arrived, they brought new animals and plants (sometimes called 'canoe plants'). These 'Polynesian introductions' included pigs, chickens, rats, coconuts, bananas, taro and about two dozen other plants, not to mention people. Most of these species mixed comfortably with preexisting native species, though humans and their agriculture significantly altered low-elevation environments. This caused the first wave of species extinctions, including perhaps 40 birds that were extinct by the time of Captain Cook's arrival.

So-called alien or nonnative species refer to those introduced after late-18th-century Western contact. They include relatively benign crops and ornamental plants, as well as notoriously invasive and devastating pests – such as cattle, ants, fountaingrass and ivy gourd. Delicately balanced ecosystems have been decimated by even a single invader (for instance, rabbits on Laysan Island, see p559). Today, over two-thirds of known birds, over half of known snails and about 10% of endemic plant species are extinct.

Progress reports can make depressing reading, but success stories do occur, proving that with sufficient effort and the right conditions, nature can rehabilitate itself. In many ways, the Hawaiian Islands are a unique laboratory in the global effort to discover 'sustainable' methods of conservation – preserving diversity, and by extension our own skins.

Animals

Prior to the arrival of humans, the islands were home primarily to birds, snails, insects and spiders.

BIRDS

Many of Hawaii's birds are spectacular examples of adaptive radiation. For instance, all 57 species of endemic Hawaiian honeycreepers most likely evolved from a single finch ancestor. Today, over half of those bright-colored species – along with two-thirds of all native Hawaiian birds – are extinct, the victims of more aggressive, nonnative birds, predatory feral

Even visiting Midway might not provide as intimate a portrait of the Northwestern Hawaiian Islands as *Archipelago* by David Liittschwager and Susan Middleton. Island denizens pose for close-ups while the authors share tales of their adventures.

animals (like mongooses) and infectious avian diseases against which they have no immunity (see the boxed text, below). Over 30 bird species remain endangered.

The endangered nene, Hawaii's state bird, is a long-lost cousin of the Canada goose. Nene usually nest in sparse vegetation on rugged lava flows, to which their feet adapted by losing most of their webbing. While eight other species of Hawaiian geese (now extinct) became flightless, nene remain strong flyers. Nene once numbered as many as 25,000 on all the islands, but by the 1950s there were only 30 left. Intensive breeding programs have raised their numbers to around 2000 on Hawai'i, Maui, Kaua'i and Moloka'i.

The only hawk native to Hawaii, the 'io was a symbol of royalty and often an 'aumakua (protective deity). They breed only on the Big Island; their numbers have held steady at over 3000 for the last decade, and in 2008 the 'io was proposed for delisting from the endangered species list.

> The Hawaii Audubon Society (www.hawaii audubon.com) publishes the best bird guide and its website has bird-viewing suggestions for each island, and a good image gallery.

LAND MAMMALS

In modern times, nearly every animal introduction – whether rabbits, goats, sheep, pigs or horses – has led to devastating environmental damage. Some, like Maui axis deer and Big Island cattle, were sent as 'gifts' to Hawaiian kings that spun off out-of-control feral populations. The ubiquitous mongoose was originally introduced to control sugarcane rats, but have become a worse plague than the rats. Today, feral animals are the most destructive force in Hawaii, and getting rid of them is central to reestablishing native landscapes and saving certain endangered species.

The endangered 'ope'ape'a (Hawaiian hoary bat), one of Hawaii's two endemic mammals, has reddish-gray, white-tinged fur, making it appear 'hoary' (grayed by age). With a foot-wide wingspan, these tree-dwellers exist predominantly around forests on the leeward sides of the Big Island, Maui and Kaua'i.

OF PIGS, MOSQUITOES & HONEYCREEPERS

How delicately interdependent are Hawaiian ecosystems? Consider how pigs are driving Hawaiian birds to extinction. Not directly, of course, but the chain of cause and effect is undeniable.

Most likely the descendants of domestic pigs brought by early European explorers, feral pigs in fact cause such complete and widespread devastation to native wet forests that Mardy Lane, a ranger at Hawai'i Volcanoes National Park, says, 'Pigs are public enemy number one.' Despite the park's ongoing eradication and fencing program, thousands still live within its boundaries. Asked if feral pigs will ever be eliminated, Lane shrugs in frustration: 'I don't know.'

Outside of federal lands, eradication efforts are few, and one estimate is that there may be one feral pig for every 20 state residents.

Pigs trample and kill native fauna, destroy the forest understory and spread far and wide the seeds of invasive plants. They love native tree-fern stems, knocking them over and eating the plants' tender insides and the bowl-like cavities left behind catch rainwater and create ideal breeding pools for mosquitoes.

These common mosquitoes – presumed to have arrived in water casks in 1826 – pick up avian malaria and avian pox (also introduced from the European continent) and spread it to native birds, particularly honeycreepers, who lost their natural immunity to these diseases as they evolved.

Even in wet forests, water typically drains into the porous volcanic soil, and mosquitoes have trouble breeding. It's a simple equation: no feral pigs, far fewer mosquitoes, far less avian malaria and far more honeycreepers.

Lane is not alone in her feelings. As the eminent historian Gavan Daws wrote: 'To the Hawaiian forest, the pig is death.'

MARINE MAMMALS

No one knows why
spinner dolphins spin, but
one likely explanation
is that they are simply
having fun, and this
friendly play enhances
group cohesion.

Up to 10,000 migrating North Pacific humpback whales come to Hawaiian waters for calving each winter (January through March), and whale watching (p80) is a major highlight. The fifth largest of the great whales, the endangered humpback can reach lengths of 45ft and weigh up to 45 tons. Other whales (such as rarely seen blue and fin whales) migrate through, and Hawaii is home to a number of dolphins, the most notable of which is the intelligent spinner dolphin, so named for its acrobatic leaps from the water.

Hawaii's other endemic mammal, the Hawaiian monk seal, breeds primarily in the remote Northwestern Hawaiian Islands. Adults are 7ft and 600lb of tough, some with the scars to prove they can withstand tiger shark attacks. Once nearly driven to extinction, monk seals number around 1300, and they have recently been appearing more regularly on Waikiki and Big Island beaches.

FISH

Hawaiian monk seals
migrated to the Hawaiian
islands over 10 million
years ago, evolving into
a unique species that's
been called a 'living
fossil.'

Hawaii's coral reefs constitute 84% of all US reefs, and they are home to over 500 species, of which 30% are endemic. However, the contrast between the variety and numbers of fish in the main Hawaiian Islands and the protected Northwestern Hawaiian Islands (p558) is stunning. For instance, the weight of fish per acre in the Northwestern Hawaiian Islands is 2000lb, but it's 600lb in the main islands, and only 250lb on O'ahu; meanwhile, predators like sharks, jacks and parrotfish are 15 times as numerous in the Northwestern Hawaiian Islands' shallow reefs, where they dominate life.

That said, protected main-island coral reefs – such as at Hanauma Bay (p166) and Kealakekua Bay (p235) – teem with vast numbers of tropical fish: bright yellow tangs, striped butterflyfish and moorish idols, silver needlefish, and gape-mouthed moray eels. Neon-colored wrasse have more species (43) than any other Hawaiian reef fish. The saucy wrasse mate daily and change sex (and color) as they mature; most start female and become male.

Plants

Mile for mile, Hawaii has the highest concentration of climate or ecological zones on earth. And whether you're in tropical rain forests or dry forests, high-altitude alpine deserts or coastal dunes, marshes or grassy plains – extravagantly diverse flora occupies every niche.

Of course, what we see today is not what the first Polynesians saw. Most 'Hawaiian' agricultural products are imports – papayas, pineapples, mangoes, bananas, macadamia nuts, coffee. Also, over half of Hawaii's native forest is now gone – due to logging, conversion to agriculture, invasive species and so on – and only 10% of Hawaii's dry forest remains. As a rule, low-lying areas have been more heavily altered by human development and invasive species than higher-altitude terrains. Of Hawaii's 1300 endemic native plant species, over 100 are extinct and 273 are endangered.

FLOWERS

For a fun, gorgeous
'What's that?' guide to
native flora, Flowers and
Plants of Hawaii by Paul
Wood is a winner.

What's wrong with a place where it's common to wear flowers in your hair and around your neck? The classic hibiscus is native to Hawaii, but many varieties have also been introduced, so that now more than 5000 varieties grow on the islands. However, it's perhaps fitting that the state flower, the yellow *Hibiscus brackenridgei,* was added to the endangered species list in 1994. The *koki'o ke'oke'o,* a native white hibiscus tree that grows up to 40ft high, is the only Hawaiian hibiscus with a fragrance. Other common native plants include the yellow *'ilima,* popular for making leis, and the seed-filled *liliko'i* (passion fruit).

DARWIN'S DREAM: HAWAIIAN INSECTS

The Hawaiian islands are home to an estimated 10,000 native insects, 98% of which are endemic. These creepy-crawlies evolved from a mere 350 to 400 colonizing species; on average, every bug that was tossed into the jet stream and crash-landed successfully became two dozen new bugs uniquely adapted to various niches in Hawaii's diverse island ecosystems.

What puzzles scientists, though, is that there is no average rate. Some species hardly evolved at all, while others are off-the-charts: *Drosophila* flies evolved into over 600 species; *Hyposmocoma* moths evolved into over 350 species. Eight other insects account for over 100 species, some particular to only an acre or two.

One of the most common adaptations was losing wings, or flightlessness. Most of Hawaii's insects arrived by air – mainly beetles, small flies, wasps, moths, bugs and leafhoppers. Hawaii has no native ants, termites or cockroaches (or mayflies or bumble bees, or 85% of the world's insect families). In some places, like lava tubes, the evolutionary process is so accelerated that flighted, flightless and intermediary species exist in a single cave, the evolutionary puzzle pieces napping side by side.

Saltwater species adapted to freshwater, and vice versa, and the occasional shift from herbivore to carnivore was not unknown. In Hawaii, rather than eat the leaves they sit on, 18 moth caterpillar species learned to ambush and eat flies. Similarly, the wekiu – a quarter-inch-long bug endemic to high-altitude Mauna Kea – learned to catch and eat wind-blown insects swept up from the lowlands. The wekiu also developed 'antifreeze' blood to keep it from crystallizing in Mauna Kea's subfreezing climate.

Arctic winter is a rare problem in Hawaii, but if Hawaii's insects illustrate anything, it's that life changes as it must.

Strangely enough, while Hawaii's climate is ideal for growing orchids, there are only three native species – apparently orchids didn't travel well on their own. In the 1800s Chinese immigrants began bringing them, and today a thriving orchid industry helps define the 'orchid isles.' Hawaii is also abloom with scores of introduced ornamental and exotic tropical flowers, including blood red anthuriums with heart-shaped leaves, brilliant orange-and-blue bird-of-paradise and a myriad drooping heliconia.

TREES

The most bewitching of native Hawaiian trees is the koa, nowadays found only at higher elevations. Growing up to 100ft high, this rich hardwood is traditionally used to make canoes, surfboards and even ukuleles. The endemic *wili wili* is a lightweight wood that's also popular for surfboards and canoes.

Hawaii was once rich in fragrant *'iliahi* (sandalwood) forests, but these were sold off to foreign traders by the mid-19th century. Rare nowadays, these tall trees are found in Hawai'i Volcanoes National Park.

The widespread and versatile ohia is one of the first plants to colonize lava flows. Its distinctive tufted flowers *(lehua)* consist of petalless groups of red, orange, yellow and (rarely) white stamens; the flowers are considered sacred to Pele and are one of the most popular flowers in leis. Native forests of ohia and *hapu'u* (tree ferns) are vital, endangered habitats.

Brought by early Polynesian settlers, the *kukui* (candlenut tree) has light silver-tinged foliage that stands out brightly in the forest. The oily nuts from Hawaii's state tree are used for making leis and dyes and can be burned like candles.

Other notable trees include ironwood, a nonnative conifer with drooping needles, which acts as a natural windbreak and prevents erosion from beaches; majestic banyan trees, which have a canopy of hanging aerial roots with trunks large enough to swallow small children; and towering

Ancient Hawaiians didn't have metals and never developed pottery, so plants fulfilled most of their needs. Ethnobotanist Beatrice Krauss describes this fascinating history in *Plants in Hawaiian Culture*.

STEP LIGHTLY

So many travelers come to enjoy Hawaii's legendary scenery and wildlife that only strict protections keep certain extremely popular, beautiful places – like O'ahu's Hanauma Bay – from being loved to death. But many equally scenic and fragile areas have fewer regulations, or little oversight, and the question becomes: just because you can do something, should you? What are the impacts, and what are the best ways to experience nature without harming it in the process?

For many activities, there isn't a single definitive answer, but here we highlight a few universal guidelines and impacts to consider. Among other things, Hawaii is a high-profile test case in whether humans can maintain a truly sustainable relationship with nature.

■ **Coral-reef etiquette** When snorkeling or diving, never touch the coral reef. It's that simple. Coral polyps are living organisms, so oil from fingers and broken pieces create wounds and openings for infection and disease. Watch your fins; avoid stirring up clouds of sand, which can settle on and damage reef organisms. Don't feed fish.

■ **Dive etiquette** Practice proper buoyancy control to avoid hitting the reef. Don't use reef anchors or ground boats over coral. Limit time in caves, as air bubbles can collect on roofs and leave organisms high and dry.

■ **Encountering wild turtles, seals and dolphins** Federal and state laws protect all wild ocean mammals and turtles from 'harassment.' Legally, this means approaching them closer than 50yd or doing anything that disrupts their behavior. If these animals approach you, simply admire them. The most important actions to avoid are pursuing wild dolphins to get close to them, and disturbing seals or turtles resting on beaches.

■ **Captive dolphin swims** Boat tours promising swims with wild dolphins are notorious for ignoring both federal law and dolphin welfare. What about swims with captive dolphins? Some feel reputable companies are no different than zoos, and some feel that captivity itself is too harmful to justify. For more, see p171.

■ **Helicopter rides** Some places you can't reach except by air. However, as air tours increase (as on Kaua'i; see p483), aircraft noise disturbs visitors on the ground, and it may stress bird populations.

■ **ATVs and 4WDs** As a rule, nonmotorized travel has less impact than motorized; avoid driving if you can walk. However, when using 4WDs, always stay on the road; avoid creating or adding to braided trails. Off-roading with ATVs, even on private land, can cause scars that take decades to heal.

For more sustainable travel advice, see Getting Started, p24, and the boxed text, p54.

monkeypods, a common shade tree that has dark glossy green leaves, puffy pink flowers and longish seed pods.

NATIONAL, STATE & COUNTY PARKS

Hawaii has two national parks: Haleakalā National Park on Maui and Hawai'i Volcanoes National Park on the Big Island. Both have volcanoes as centerpieces, contain an astonishing range of environments and provide some of the best hiking in the islands. Hawai'i Volcanoes was named a Unesco World Heritage Site in 1987; it receives 1.6 million visitors a year and is Hawaii's most popular tourist sight.

In addition, the islands have five national historical parks, sites and memorials, all but one preserving ancient Hawaiian culture: three are on the Big Island, notably Pu'uhonua o Honaunau (Place of Refuge; p239); one is on Moloka'i, Kalaupapa Peninsula (p458); and in Honolulu is the famed USS *Arizona* Memorial (p142), dedicated to WWII's Pearl Harbor attack. For information on Hawaii's national parks, visit www.nps.go v/state/hi.

Hawaii has nine **national wildlife refuges** (NWR; www.fws.gov/pacific/refuges) on five of the main islands: O'ahu, Maui, Moloka'i, Kaua'i and Hawai'i. Most are open to the public; since their primary focus is preserving endangered plants and waterbirds, they are a delight for bird-watchers.

Hawaii has 55 state parks and recreational areas on five islands (excluding Lana'i). These diverse parks include some absolutely stunning places (like Waimea Canyon on Kaua'i; see p550); a few also have campsites and cabins. They are managed by the **Division of State Parks** (☎ 587-0300; www.hawaiistateparks .org), which has local offices on each island that issue camping permits. Finally, each island also has county beach-parks and other areas, many of which allow camping; see each island chapter for contact information. For general questions about state-managed areas, the website for the **Department of Land & Natural Resources** (DLNR; ☎ 587-0400; www.state.hi.us/dlnr; Kalanimoku Bldg, 1151 Punchbowl St, Honolulu) has an extensive FAQ that can answer most questions. DLNR's **Division of Forestry & Wildlife** (Map pp118-19; DOFAW; ☎ 587-0062; http://hawaii .gov/dlnr/dofaw; Suite 132, 567 S King St, Honolulu) manages Hawaii's 109,000-acre **Natural Area Reserves System** (http://hawaii.gov/dlnr/dofaw/nars); the system's 19 reserves are open to hiking, but other activities are restricted.

For a list of Hawaii's top 20 natural areas, see p96.

ENVIRONMENTAL ISSUES
Environmental concerns are entangled in just about every issue facing Hawaii. However, more people and organizations than ever before are raising environmental alarms, educating the public and working toward solutions.

There is widespread agreement that the two most dire problems facing native landscapes are feral animals (from goats to mongooses) and the introduction and uncontrolled proliferation of invasive, habitat-modifying plants; today, from 20 to 50 new species arrive in Hawaii every year. Even in Hawaii's most protected areas (national parks and state reserves) inadequate budgets hamper eradication and rehabilitation efforts, and the recession that began in 2008 will slash budgets even more. The **Nature Conservancy** (www .nature.org/hawaii), a nonprofit organization that purchases land to protect rare ecosystems, is very involved in Hawaii, and it has its own ecoregional plan (www.hawaiiecoregionplan.info).

In contrast to the land, Hawaii's coral reefs are comparatively healthy. Overfishing, though, is a major concern. Three-quarters of main island reef fish species are in critical or depleted conditions; not surprisingly, the most dire cases are those fish popular for aquariums or for eating (like moi, jacks and bonefish). **Fair Catch** (www.faircatchhawaii.org) is leading the effort to ban lay gill nets (indiscriminate mesh nets whose use was restricted in 2007) and restore reef fish.

In recent years, rising populations and real estate profits have spurred a building boom, some of it by off-island speculators with little concern for environmental impacts. New sprawling subdivisions and resorts have put even more pressure on a limited watershed and nearly full landfills. Plus, construction frequently uncovers and disturbs archaeological and ancient cultural sites like heiau, petroglyphs and burial mounds; protecting sites and repatriating remains can become a contentious issue that delays road building and construction for years.

The long-standing friction over Hawaii's military presence continues. The military is notoriously noncompliant with environmental regulations, and its training maneuvers frequently have a substantial impact on cultural sights and local communities. For instance, in 2005 it was discovered that the army dumped 8000 tons of chemical weapons off western O'ahu during WWII; the first deep-water surveys are now being conducted to assess what's

Hawaii: The Islands of Life has strikingly beautiful photos of the flora, fauna and landscapes being protected by the Nature Conservancy of Hawaii, with text by Gavan Daws.

The Native Hawaiian, grassroots activist organization Kahea (www .kahea.org) tackles a wide range of environment, development and cultural rights issues, such as those surrounding Mauna Kea and the Northwestern Hawaiian Islands.

HAWAII'S TOP 20 NATURAL AREAS

Natural area	Features	Activities	Best time to visit	Page
O'ahu				
Hanauma Bay Nature Preserve	enormous coral reef in volcanic ring	snorkeling, swimming	year-round	p166
Malaekahana State Recreation Area	sandy beach, Moku'auia bird sanctuary(Goat Island)	swimming, snorkeling, camping, bird-watching	May-Oct	p183
Big Island				
Hawai'i Volcanoes National Park	lava fields, milewide craters, fern forests	hiking, camping	year-round	p306
Kealakekua Bay	pristine waters, coral reefs, underwater caves	snorkeling, diving, kayaking	year-round	p234
Laupahoehoe Point	ragged coast, steep cliffs, restless sea	camping	year-round	p283
Mauna Kea	Hawaii's highest peak, ancient Hawaiian sites	hiking, stargazing	year-round	p269
Pololu Valley	scalloped seacliff views, remote valley, black-sand beach	hiking	year-round	p263
Waipi'o Valley	remote, historic valley, black-sand beach, waterfalls	hiking, backcountry camping	year-round	p279
Moloka'i				
Kalaupapa National Historic Park	historic & remote leprosy colony, mule riding	hiking, touring	year-round	p458
Kamakou Preserve	pristine rain forest, gorgeous valley vistas, waterfalls, montane bog	hiking, bird-watching	May-Oct	p455
Maui				
Haleakalā National Park (Kipahulu Section)	towering waterfalls, cascading pools, ancient sites	hiking, swimming	year-round	p400
Haleakalā National Park (Summit Section)	large dormant volcano	hiking, camping	year-round	p413
Makena State Park	glorious, unspoiled, expansive beaches (one is clothing-optional)	swimming, sunset watching	year-round	p386
Hana Hwy	38 miles of rugged steep cliffs, green valleys, waterfalls	hiking, camping	year-round	p392
Lana'i				
Hulopo'e Beach	dolphins frolicking in a pristine bay	swimming, snorkeling	year-round	p432
Kaua'i				
Koke'e State Park	waterfalls, trails for overnighters & day-trippers	hiking	year-round	p553
Na Pali Coast	beaches, waterfalls, classic 11-mile backpack trek	hiking, camping, swimming, snorkeling	May-Oct	p525
Hanalei Bay	gorgeous crescent-shaped bay, Hanalei River	surfing, bodyboarding, kayaking, summer swimming	year-round	p516
Waimea Canyon	unbeatable views of 'Grand Canyon of the Pacific'	hiking, mountain biking, camping	Apr-Nov	p550
Northwestern Hawaiian Islands				
Midway Island	Laysan albatross colony, epic coral reef, WWII history	bird-watching, snorkeling, hiking	Nov-Jul	p559

there, while underwater robots are being tested as a way to clean up Oʻahu's 'Ordnance Reef,' a shallow reef littered with conventional bombs.

In 2006 and 2007, after years of denial, the army admitted to using depleted uranium (banned under the Geneva Convention) at Oʻahu's Schofield Barracks and the Big Island's Pohakuloa Training Area. Conflicts also arose over the military's planned expansions to conduct maneuvers with 325 Stryker combat vehicles (for use in Iraq) on Oʻahu and the Big Island; in 2008 a lawsuit was settled allowing the military to move ahead when it agreed to let Native Hawaiians survey proposed training areas for cultural sites.

Future development of Mauna Kea's summit (p269) is another hot-button topic. Environmental groups and Hawaiians adamantly oppose any new astronomical observatories. In 2006, a proposal to build six new 'outrigger' telescopes around the Keck observatories was abandoned after a judge ruled that nothing new could be built without first developing a comprehensive summit management plan and environmental impact statement. In 2008, however, still lacking such a plan, scientists began considering whether to build a new Thirty Meter Telescope – the largest in the world – on the summit.

Hawaii's Superferry raised similar complaints that it was rushed into service in 2007 without properly studying its environmental and community impacts. Indeed, in 2009, the State Supreme Court ruled that Superferry had to

The Pacific Basin Information Node (http://pbin .nbii.gov/) sounds like a conspiracy, but it's a fantastic network of sources for information on all aspects of Hawaii's environment.

HAWAI'I 2050: CREATING A SUSTAINABLE FUTURE

How exactly do you tackle restoring the well-being of an entire society? First, you need a shared sense of purpose and a plan.

Hawaii has made great strides with both, with its Hawaiʻi 2050 Sustainability Plan (www .hawaii2050.org), which is the culmination of dozens and dozens of community meetings held over two years and involving over 10,000 Hawaii residents. Dubbed 'the people's plan,' Hawaiʻi 2050 is the first statewide planning effort since the 1978 Constitutional Convention. As the plan itself states: this 'is not an academic or political exercise; it is a matter of the survival of Hawaiʻi as we know it.'

The first task was defining 'sustainability' in Hawaii-specific terms. What came out of those 10,000 conversations was a 'triple bottom line' that recognized the interdependence of Hawaii's economic, cultural and environmental health. This is expressed in five goals. To quote from the plan:

1. Living sustainably is part of our daily practice in Hawaiʻi.
2. Our diversified and globally competitive economy enables us to meaningfully live, work and play in Hawaiʻi.
3. Our natural resources are responsibly and respectfully used, replenished and preserved for future generations.
4. Our community is strong, healthy, vibrant and nurturing, providing safety nets for those in need.
5. Our Kanaka Maoli [Native Hawaiian] and island cultures and values are thriving and perpetuated.

Since meaningful change requires specific, measurable action, the plan laid out nine urgent priorities for 2020 (covering affordable housing, education, energy, the environment), establishing benchmarks for progress and 55 indicators to measure Hawaii's health. The plan also recommended creating a Sustainability Council to promote and coordinate state efforts.

In 2008, the plan was presented for approval to the state legislature, which praised the effort but asked that it be made even more concrete. The revised Hawaiʻi 2050 plan is to be presented to the Hawaii legislature again in 2010. However, one of Hawaiʻi 2050's central goals – to plant a sustainability ethic within residents islandwide – is already bearing fruit.

halt service until the legally mandated studies were complete, and Superferry may very well never run again. For more see the boxed text, p474.

Hawaii's shorelines are in danger as well. The threat of rising seas due to global warming and persistent beach erosion (particular at Waikiki) are raising alarm bells. Recent studies have found that 25% of O'ahu and Maui beaches have been lost in the last 50 years; meanwhile, if tides rise a foot (as some predict they will), half of Waikiki hotels would be under water.

The **Sierra Club** (www.hi.sierraclub.org) is perhaps Hawaii's most active environmental organization, with groups on O'ahu, Maui, Kaua'i and Hawai'i. In addition to political lobbying and legal actions, it publishes an informative newsletter and sponsors activities and outings. The **Hawaii Audubon Society** (www.hawaiiaudubon.com) is also very active and provides good opportunities for visitors to get involved.

Two more good sources of information are **Environment Hawai'i** (www.environ ment-hawaii.org), a watchdog group that publishes a wide-ranging monthly newsletter, and **Hawaii Ecosystems at Risk** (www.hear.org), whose diverse website focuses on invasive species and eradication efforts.

Hawaiian Natural History, Ecology, and Evolution (2002) by Alan Ziegler is a great comprehensive study of the complex interaction of Hawaiian ecosystems, over time and with human society.

O'ahu

Nicknamed 'The Gathering Place,' O'ahu is home to nearly three out of every four Hawaii residents. In this jangling nerve center of the archipelago, you can come face-to-face with contemporary Hawaii as it really is, without pretense. O'ahu, especially in the capital city of Honolulu, has the most complex, multiethnic society in the islands, and through it all pulses the lifeblood of Hawaiian traditions, from ancient heiau (stone temples) to Ka'ena Point, which legends say was the jumping-off point for souls leaping into the afterlife.

For some, O'ahu is just a transit point en route to the Neighbor Islands. For others, it's the place for thrill-of-a-lifetime adventures. Here you can surf the giant waves of the North Shore, dive into the outdoor fishbowl of Hanauma Bay, go windsurfing or kayak to uninhabited islands off Kailua Beach, and still be back in Waikiki in time for sunset drinks, torchlit hula and live tunes by some of Hawaii's most iconic musicians. No worries, brah.

Landing at Honolulu's airport plunges you into the urban jungle, but relax, this is still Polynesia. Even among the high-rises of downtown Honolulu you'll find power brokers in breezy aloha shirts, and the pungent, chaotic markets of Chinatown taste more like Asia than the USA. Even in this modern 21st-century city, some places manage to feel timeless, like the harborfront and the hills, where hiking trails lead deep into the lush Ko'olau Range and its knife-edged *pali* (cliffs) that officially divide the 'city' from the 'country.'

Everything you've ever dreamed about Hawaii, you can find it here.

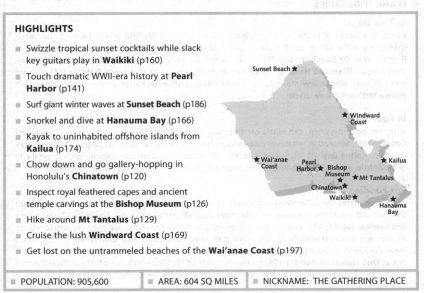

HIGHLIGHTS

- Swizzle tropical sunset cocktails while slack key guitars play in **Waikiki** (p160)
- Touch dramatic WWII-era history at **Pearl Harbor** (p141)
- Surf giant winter waves at **Sunset Beach** (p186)
- Snorkel and dive at **Hanauma Bay** (p166)
- Kayak to uninhabited offshore islands from **Kailua** (p174)
- Chow down and go gallery-hopping in Honolulu's **Chinatown** (p120)
- Inspect royal feathered capes and ancient temple carvings at the **Bishop Museum** (p126)
- Hike around **Mt Tantalus** (p129)
- Cruise the lush **Windward Coast** (p169)
- Get lost on the untrammeled beaches of the **Wai'anae Coast** (p197)

Sunset Beach ★

★ Windward Coast

★ Wai'anae Coast

Pearl Harbor ★

★ Kailua

Bishop Museum ★

★ Mt Tantalus

Chinatown ★

Waikiki ★

Hanauma Bay ★

■ POPULATION: 905,600 ■ AREA: 604 SQ MILES ■ NICKNAME: THE GATHERING PLACE

O'AHU

HISTORY

Around AD 1350, Ma'ilikukahi, the ancient *mo'i* (king) of O'ahu, moved his capital to Waikiki, a bounteous coastal wetland known for its fertile farmlands and abundant fishing, as well as for being a place of recreation and healing. O'ahu's fall to Kamehameha the Great in 1795 signaled the beginning of a united Hawaiian kingdom. In 1809 Kamehameha moved his royal court from Waikiki to Honolulu ('Sheltered Bay') to control the vigorous international trade taking place in the harbor.

First established in the 1830s, sugar plantations soon became O'ahu's major industry. Contract workers from Asia, North America and Europe were brought in to fill the island's labor shortage, as evidenced today by the island's ethnic diversity. The 19th century ended with the overthrow of the Hawaiian monarchy and the institution of a short-lived republic, until the USA annexed Hawaii in 1898.

Honolulu's electric streetcars reached Waikiki Beach in 1901, which was the same year that Waikiki's Moana Hotel opened, spurring a tourism boom interrupted only by the Great Depression and WWII. During the war, O'ahu was placed under martial law. As civil rights were suspended, a detention center for Japanese Americans and resident aliens was established on Honolulu's Sand Island, and later an internment camp was established in the Honouliuli area of Kunia Rd in central O'ahu. The US federal government did not apologize for WWII internment camps in Hawaii and on the mainland until 1988.

Modern jet-age travel and baby-boom prosperity after the war provided O'ahu with a thriving tourism industry that conveniently replaced its declining shipping industry. In the '60s and '70s, the Hawaiian renaissance flowered here, especially on the University of Hawai'i's Manoa campus and after the successful voyage of the *Hokule'a* (p37), first launched from Kualoa on the island's Windward Coast.

In 1971 the first Hawaiian Masters surfing competition was held on O'ahu's North Shore. By the 1980s, rampant tourist development had overbuilt Waikiki and turned some of O'ahu's agricultural land into water-thirsty golf courses and sprawling resorts. The island's last remaining sugar mills closed in the 1990s, leaving O'ahu more heavily dependent on tourism than ever. Debates about economic diversification, sustainable tourism and also the continuing US military presence continue today.

O'AHU ITINERARIES

In Two Days

Got only a weekend in the sun? Then it's all about you and **Waikiki** (p145). Laze on the beach (p149), enjoy the sunset torch lighting and hula show at **Kuhio Beach Park** (p160) and dine at **Roy's – Waikiki Beach** (p159). The next day get up early to snorkel at **Hanauma Bay** (p166), then hike up **Diamond Head** (p165) or out to the lighthouse at **Makapu'u Point** (p168). Reward yourself later with a few mai tais on a **catamaran cruise** (p150) or at the Halekulani's posh **House Without a Key** (p160).

In Four Days

With two extra days, you can rent a car and drive to the **North Shore** (p184) and the **Windward Coast** (p169). Stop off at whatever beaches catch your eye – especially, say, around **Waimea Bay** (p186) or **Kailua Bay** (p174). Spend at least a full morning or afternoon exploring the capital city of **Honolulu** (p113), with its impressive museums, historical sites and revitalized Chinatown.

For Foodies

O'ahu dominates the other Hawaiian Islands when it comes to food. Taste goodness straight from the land and sea at the Diamond Head **farmers market** (p165), Kaimuki's **Town** (p137) restaurant and **Lanikai Juice** (p176) over on the Windward Coast. *Izakaya* (Japanese pubs serving food) are all the rage across **Honolulu** (p132), while pan-Asian eateries inhabit **Chinatown** (p133). Don't leave the island without trying traditional Hawaiian cuisine, not at a touristy luau (Hawaiian feast) but at **Ono Hawaiian Food** (p158) on the outskirts of Waikiki, which has plenty of local flavor if you know where to look. When the bikini gets tight, you've conquered the island.

CLIMATE

O'ahu has two barely discernable seasons: summer (May to October), when higher humidity is likely, and winter (November to April), when it rains more frequently. Year-round, air temperatures vary between approximately 70°F and 80°F.

O'ahu has microclimates, governed by the weather patterns of the tradewinds and their interaction with the island's two mountain ranges. The prevailing tradewinds move across the island from the northeast, where most of the moisture is deposited, making the Windward Coast and eastern Ko'olau Range lush and relatively cooler.

The winds then move westward across the interior of the island, bumping against the Wai'anae Range, which exacts any remaining moisture, leaving the west side (also known as the Wai'anae or Leeward Coast) and coastal Honolulu and Waikiki dry and warm. During the winter months, Kona winds reverse all of these trends, bringing heavy rain to normally dry parts of the island. O'ahu's homes are traditionally built with louvered windows to catch the tradewinds, but air-con is a welcome modern convenience in hot-and-sweaty Honolulu and Waikiki.

The National Weather Service provides recorded **weather forecasts** (☎ 973-4381) and **marine conditions** (☎ 973-4382) for O'ahu. See p563 for more climate information.

NATIONAL, STATE & COUNTY PARKS

Even though O'ahu is Hawaii's most populous island, nature sits right outside of Honolulu's glass skyscrapers and Waikiki's high-rise hotels. About 25% of the island is protected natural areas. The entire coastline is dotted with beaches, while the lush mountainous interior is carved by hiking trails, including in forest reserves around Mt Tantalus (p129), where you'll find city skyline views and the jungly Lyon Arboretum (p124).

Most county beach parks are well maintained with free parking, rest room facilities, outdoor showers, lifeguards and picnic areas. These parks also function as communal backyards, where families celebrate birthdays with barbecues and go camping on weekends. Smack-dab in Honolulu is Ala Moana Beach Park (p123), one of the prettiest beaches this side of the equator. Waikiki's famous strand of white sand is also protected as public parks (p149).

On the Windward Coast, Waimanalo Beach Park (p171) and Kailua Beach Park (p174) are a paradise of gentle waves, while east of Hanauma Bay, Sandy Beach Park (p168) has beautifully violent waves beloved by bodysurfers. Some of the most famous North Shore surfing breaks occur just offshore from modest county beach parks, including 'Ehukai Beach Park (p186), home to Pipeline. Pupukea Beach Park (p187) is a conservation success story of protecting tide pools and sea turtles. The Wai'anae Coast doesn't register on many tourists' itineraries, but its beach parks are blessedly free of crowds, save for territorial locals.

State parks include iconic Diamond Head State Monument (p165), with hiking trails that summit the landmark volcanic tuff cone. Farther east is idyllic, crescent-shaped Hanauma Bay (p166), the island's premier snorkeling spot. On the Windward Coast there's the wild and rugged coastline of Malaekahana State Recreation Area (p183). Occupying the sacred northwestern tip of the island, Ka'ena Point State Park (p200) is a spectacular sight of lava cliffs and furious crashing waves. Political tensions exist between some state parks and some rural communities over land-use rights, especially in the Windward Coast's remote valleys.

Although O'ahu has no national parks, the federal government oversees the USS Arizona Memorial (p142) at Pearl Harbor, the Windward Coast's James Campbell National Wildlife Refuge (p185) and the Hawaiian Islands Humpback Whale National Marine Sanctuary (p80), which encompasses some of O'ahu's offshore waters.

Camping

For general information about camping in Hawaii, including safety tips and advice, see p561.

On O'ahu, you can pitch a tent at many county and some state parks that are fairly evenly spread around the island, but none are close to Waikiki. All county and state park campgrounds on O'ahu are closed on Wednesday and Thursday nights. Some are open only on weekends.

Ostensibly, this is for park maintenance, but also to prevent permanent encampments by homeless people, especially along the Wai'anae Coast, where camping by nonlocals

O'AHU

O'AHU

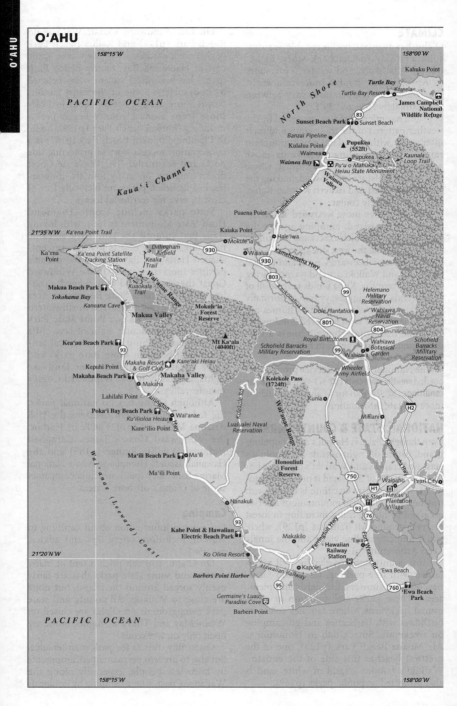

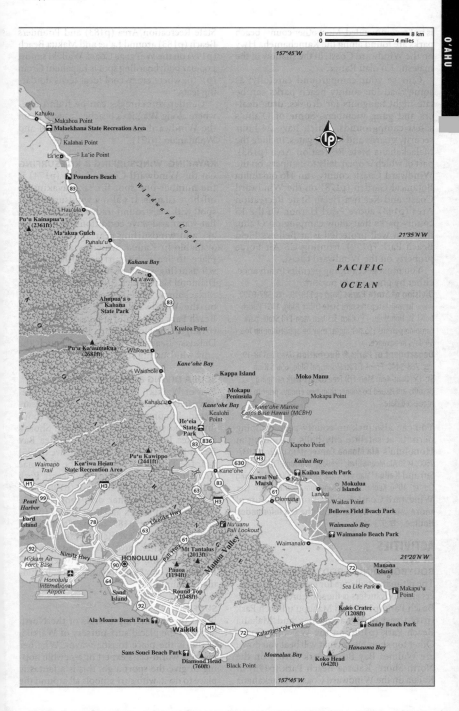

0 ____ 8 km
0 ____ 4 miles

157°45'W

Kahuku
Makahoa Point
Malaekahana State Recreation Area
Kalahai Point
La'ie — La'ie Point
Pounders Beach
83
Hau'ula
Pu'u Kainapua'a
(2361ft)
Ma'akua Gulch
Punalu'u
Kahana Bay
Ka'a'awa
83
Ahupua'a o
Kahana
State Park
Kualoa Point
Pu'u Ka'aumakua
(268ft)
Waikane
Kane'ohe Bay
Waiahole
Kappa Island
Moko Manu
Mokapu
Peninsula
Kahalu'u
Kane'ohe Bay Kane'ohe Marine
Kealohi Corps Base Hawaii (MCBH)
He'eia Point
State
Park
83 836
Kapoho Point
Pu'u Kawippo
(2441ft)
Waimano Kea'iwa Heiau 630
Trail State Recreation Area Kane'ohe Kawai Nui Kailua Beach Park
H1 Marsh Kailua
H3 63 83 Mokulua
99 H3 61 Islands
Pearl Olomana Lanikai
Harbor 78 Likelike Hwy Wailea Point
Ford 63 Bellows Field Beach Park
Island 61 Nu'uanu
92 Pali Lookout Waimanalo Bay
Nimitz Hwy Waimanalo Beach Park
Hickam Air 90 HONOLULU Mt Tantalus Waimanalo
Force Base (2013ft)
64 Pauoa Manana
Honolulu (1194ft) 72 Island
International Round Top
Airport Sea Life Park Makapu'u
92 (1048ft) Point
Sand
Island Koko Crater
Ala Moana Beach Park (1208ft)
Waikiki Sandy Beach Park
72 Kalaniana'ole Hwy
Sans Souci Beach Park H1 Hanauma Bay
Diamond Head Moanalua Bay Koko Head
(760ft) Black Point (642ft)

157°45'W

PACIFIC
OCEAN

Windward Coast

21°35'N'W

21°20'N'W

is not recommended. Most other county beach parks are found along the Kamehameha Hwy on the Windward Coast, in the shadow of the majestic Ko'olau Range.

Choose your campground carefully, as some roadside county beach parks can be late-night hangouts for drunks, drug dealers and gang members. Some of O'ahu's safest campgrounds, which have 24-hour security guards and locked gates, include the Malaekahana State Recreation Area (p183), part of which is open daily to campers, on the Windward Coast; county-run Ho'omaluhia Botanical Garden (p178) on the Windward Coast; and Kea'iwa Heiau State Recreation Area (p143) above Pearl Harbor. Of the 15 county parks that allow camping on O'ahu, the most well-protected is at Bellows Field Beach Park (p172), fronting US Air Force property on the Windward Coast.

You must get camping permits in advance, either by phone or in person:

Division of State Parks (Map pp118-19; ☎ 587-0300; www.hawaiistateparks.org; State Office Bldg, 1151 Punchbowl St, Honolulu; ☼ 8am-3:30pm Mon-Fri) State-park camping permits ($5 per night) may be applied for up to 30 days in advance.

Department of Parks & Recreation (Map pp118-19; ☎ 768-3440; Frank F Fasi Municipal Bldg, 650 S King St; ☼ 8am-4pm Mon-Fri) Free county-park camping permits are issued no sooner than two Fridays prior to the requested date.

You can also pick up county-park camping permits at satellite city halls, including at Honolulu's **Ala Moana Center** (Map p122; ☎ 937-2600; 1450 Ala Moana Blvd; ☼ 9am-5pm Mon-Fri, 8am-4pm Sat) and **Kailua** (Map p170; ☎ 261-8575; Keolu Shopping Center, 1090 Keolu Dr; ☼ 8am-4pm Mon-Fri) on the Windward Coast. For locations and hours of more satellite city halls, call the **City Information Hotline** (☎ 973-2600).

ACTIVITIES
At Sea
BODYBOARDING & BODYSURFING
The ultimate challenge for expert bodyboarders and bodysurfers is the shorebreaks at Sandy Beach Park (p168) and Makapu'u Beach Park (p168) east of Hanauma Bay and Makaha Beach Park (p198) on the Wai'anae Coast. Other top shorebreaks that will beat you down are Waimea Bay Beach Park (p187) on the North Shore; Kalama Beach Park (p175) in Kailua on the Windward Coast; Malaekahana

State Recreation Area (p183) and Pounders Beach (p183) around La'ie; and Makua Beach (p199) on the Wai'anae Coast. Waikiki's most popular bodyboarding spot is Kapahulu Groin (p150), where crazy-cool local teens do daring feats.

Gentler shorebreaks can be found elsewhere along Waikiki's beaches, as well as on the Windward Coast at Kailua (p174) and Waimanalo (p171).

KAYAKING, WINDSURFING & KITESURFING
On the Windward Coast, Kailua (p174) is the number-one spot for sea kayaking to offshore islands. It's also a windsurfing hot spot, with year-round tradewinds and good flat-water and wave conditions. Rental kayaks and windsurfing gear and lessons are available in Kailua, which is also a great place to learn kitesurfing. Other prime windsurfing spots around O'ahu include Diamond Head Beach (p165) east of Waikiki; Malaekahana State Recreation Area (p183) on the Windward Coast; and Mokule'ia Beach Park (p194) and at Sunset Beach Park (p186) on the North Shore. In Waikiki, Fort DeRussy Beach (p149) is pretty much the only windsurfing spot.

SCUBA DIVING & SNORKELING
East of Waikiki, Hanauma Bay Nature Preserve (p166) offers excellent snorkeling year-round. In summer, follow the locals (both divers and snorkelers) to the North Shore's Pupukea Beach Park (p187), Waimea Bay Beach Park (p187) and Kuilima Cove (p185) near the Turtle Bay Resort. On the Wai'anae Coast, try Hawaiian Electric Beach Park (p198) and Makaha Beach Park (p198).

O'ahu's top summer dive spots include the caves and ledges at Three Tables (p187) and Shark's Cove (p187) on the North Shore, and the Makaha Caverns off Makaha Beach (p198). In winter, most divers head to wrecks off Waikiki and farther east between Black Point and Koko Head Regional Park, including Hanauma Bay.

SURFING
From the thundering barrels of the North Shore to the placid surf-nursery of Waikiki, O'ahu is the place to ride waves. Whether you're a world-class expert or a newbie hoping to give the sport a go, this is a fantastic place to do it, with surf schools all around the

island. On the international surfing circuit, itinerant wave riders show up for the North Shore's massive winter breaks and high-profile competitions. Other breaks around O'ahu have their own personalities and status in the surfing hierarchy; see the boxed text, p108, for a rundown.

SWIMMING
O'ahu is ringed by more than 50 gorgeous white-sand beaches, most with rest rooms, showers and sometimes lifeguards. Different coastal areas together provide year-round swimming; when it's rough or rainy on one side of the island, it's generally calm and sunny on another.

As a general rule, the best places to swim in winter are along the south shore. After Waikiki (p149), Honolulu's top swimming spot is Ala Moana Beach Park (p123). On the Windward Coast, Waimanalo Beach Park (p171), Kailua Beach Park (p174), Kualoa Regional Park (p180) and Malaekahana State Recreation Area (p183) are favorites.

North Shore beaches, while too rough for swimming much of the winter, can be calm during summer. The Wai'anae Coast extends from Ka'ena Point to Barbers Point, with the best year-round swimming at Poka'i Bay Beach Park (p198), and at the artificial Ko Olina Lagoons (p197).

WHALE WATCHING
Between late December and mid-April, humpback whales and their newly birthed offspring visit the harbors of northern and western O'ahu. Hawaiian spinner dolphins are year-round residents of the Wai'anae Coast. Well regarded for its environmental stewardship, the North Shore's Deep Ecology

(p192) offers whale- and dolphin-watching boat tours. For more about wild-dolphin swims and captive-dolphin 'encounters', see p171.

On Land
BIRD-WATCHING
Most islets off O'ahu's Windward Coast are sanctuaries for seabirds including terns, noddies, shearwaters, Laysan albatrosses, boobies and 'iwa (great frigate birds). Moku Manu (Bird Island) off the Mokapu Peninsula near Kane'ohe has the greatest variety of species, including a colony of 'ewa'ewa (sooty terns) that lay their eggs in ground scrapes. Although visitors are not allowed on Moku Manu, birders can visit Moku'auia (Goat Island) offshore from Malaekahana State Recreation Area (p183), north of La'ie.

Farther north along the Windward Coast, the James Campbell National Wildlife Refuge (p185) encompasses a native wetland habitat protecting some rare and endangered waterbird species. In Kailua, just over the *pali* (mountains) from Honolulu, the Hamakua Marsh Wildlife Sanctuary (p175) is another place to see Hawaiian waterbirds in their natural habitat.

Hikers who tackle O'ahu's many forest-reserve trails, especially around Mt Tantalus (p128), can expect to see 'elepaio (Hawaiian monarch flycatcher), a brownish bird with a white rump, and 'amakihi, a yellow-green honeycreeper, the most common endemic forest birds on O'ahu. The 'apapane, a bright red honeycreeper, and the 'i'iwi, the scarlet Hawaiian honeycreeper, are more rare.

For birding checklists and group field trips, contact the **Hawaii Audubon Society** (Map pp118-19; ☎ 528-1432; www.hawaiiaudubon.com; 850 Richards St, Honolulu).

CYCLING & MOUNTAIN BIKING
For cycling as a means of transportation around O'ahu, see p111. The **Hawaii Bicycling League** (Map p114; ☎ 735-5756; www.hbl.org; 3442 Wai'alae Ave, Honolulu) organizes rides around O'ahu on most weekends and some weekdays, ranging from 10-mile jaunts to triathlon trainers. Honolulu's **Bike Shop** (Map p122; ☎ 596-0588; 1149 S King St, Honolulu; ⏰ 9am-7pm Mon-Fri, to 5pm Sat, 10am-5pm Sun) also organizes weekend group rides. **Bike Hawaii** (☎ 734-4214, 877-682-7433; www.bikehawaii.com) offers mountain-biking and multisport tours of the island; the company

O'AHU ACTIVITIES

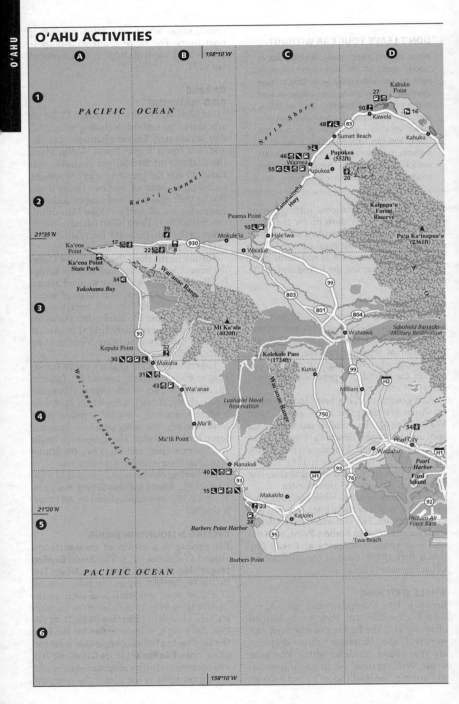

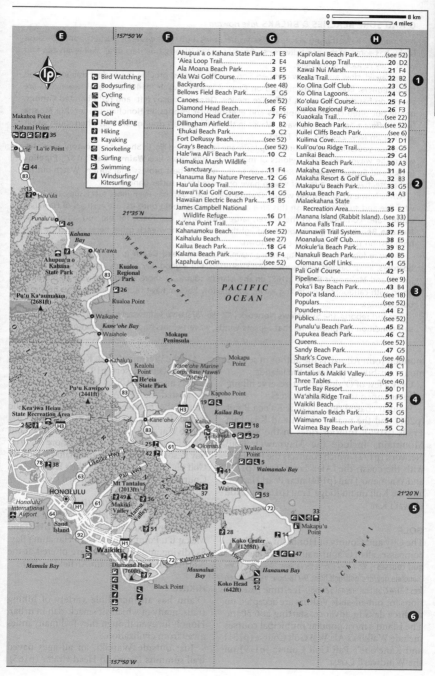

0 — 8 km
0 — 4 miles

Legend:
- Bird Watching
- Bodysurfing
- Cycling
- Diving
- Golf
- Hang gliding
- Hiking
- Kayaking
- Snorkeling
- Surfing
- Swimming
- Windsurfing/Kitesurfing

Ahupua'a o Kahana State Park....1 E3
'Aiea Loop Trail....................2 E4
Ala Moana Beach Park............3 E5
Ala Wai Golf Course..............4 F5
Backyards.........................(see 48)
Bellows Field Beach Park.........5 G5
Canoes............................(see 52)
Diamond Head Beach..............6 F6
Diamond Head Crater.............7 F6
Dillingham Airfield...............8 B2
'Ehukai Beach Park...............9 C2
Fort DeRussy Beach.............(see 52)
Gray's Beach.....................(see 52)
Hale'iwa Ali'i Beach Park........10 C2
Hamakua Marsh Wildlife
    Sanctuary.....................11 F4
Hanauma Bay Nature Preserve...12 G6
Hau'ula Loop Trail................13 E2
Hawai'i Kai Golf Course..........14 G5
Hawaiian Electric Beach Park....15 B5
James Campbell National
    Wildlife Refuge...............16 D1
Ka'ena Point Trail................17 A2
Kahanamoku Beach...............(see 52)
Kaihalulu Beach..................(see 27)
Kailua Beach Park................18 G4
Kalama Beach Park...............19 F4
Kapahulu Groin..................(see 52)

Kapi'olani Beach Park............(see 52)
Kaunala Loop Trail...............20 D2
Kawai Nui Marsh.................21 F4
Kealia Trail......................22 B2
Ko Olina Golf Club...............23 C5
Ko Olina Lagoons................24 C5
Ko'olau Golf Course..............25 F4
Kualoa Regional Park............26 F3
Kuaokala Trail...................(see 22)
Kuhio Beach Park................(see 52)
Kuilei Cliffs Beach Park..........(see 6)
Kuilima Cove.....................27 D1
Kuli'ou'ou Ridge Trail............28 G5
Lanikai Beach....................29 G4
Makaha Beach Park..............30 A3
Makaha Caverns.................31 B4
Makaha Resort & Golf Club......32 B3
Makapu'u Beach Park............33 G5
Makua Beach Park...............34 A3
Malaekahana State
    Recreation Area..............35 E2
Manana Island (Rabbit Island)..(see 33)
Manoa Falls Trail.................36 F5
Maunawili Trail System..........37 F5
Moanalua Golf Club..............38 E5
Mokule'ia Beach Park............39 B2
Nanakuli Beach Park.............40 B5
Olomana Golf Links..............41 G5
Pali Golf Course..................42 F5
Pipeline..........................(see 9)
Poka'i Bay Beach Park...........43 B4
Popoi'a Island....................(see 18)
Populars.........................(see 52)
Pounders........................44 E2
Publics...........................(see 52)
Punalu'u Beach Park.............45 E2
Pupukea Beach Park.............46 C2
Queens..........................(see 52)
Sandy Beach Park................47 G5
Shark's Cove.....................(see 46)
Sunset Beach Park...............48 C1
Tantalus & Makiki Valley.........49 F5
Three Tables.....................(see 46)
Turtle Bay Resort................50 D1
Wa'ahila Ridge Trail..............51 F5
Waikiki Beach....................52 F6
Waimanalo Beach Park..........53 G5
Waimano Trail...................54 D4
Waimea Bay Beach Park.........55 C2

O'AHU SURF BEACHES & BREAKS *Jake Howard*

Nicknamed 'The Gathering Place,' O'ahu has become a hub for the islands' surf economy. Because O'ahu has some of the most diverse surf breaks in the islands, boarders of all skill levels can find what they're looking for here.

In Waikiki, slow and mellow combers (long curling waves) provide the perfect training ground for beginners. Board rentals abound on Central Waikiki Beach (p149) and local beachboys are always on hand for lessons at spots like mellow **Queens**, mushy left- and right-handed **Canoes**, gentle but often crowded **Populars** and ever-popular **Publics**. In Honolulu proper, **Ala Moana** (p123) offers a heavy tubing wave. Waves in this area are best during summer, when south swells arrive from New Zealand and Tahiti.

Reckon yourself a serious surfer? A pilgrimage to the famed North Shore is mandatory. In winter, when the waves can reach heights of more than 30ft, spots like **Waimea Bay** (p187), **Pipeline** (p186) and **Sunset Beach** (p186) beckon to the planet's best professional surfers. Watch out for turf-protective locals, a few of whom have organized into surfer gangs.

While home to some great waves, O'ahu's Wai'anae Coast has even more turf issues; the locals who live and surf here cherish this area and are trying to hold onto its last vestiges of Hawaiian culture and community. In the winter, large west swells can make for big surf at places like **Makaha Beach Park** (p198), but tread lightly: the locals know each other here, so there will be no question that you're from out of town.

If you're looking for a multipurpose wave, **Diamond Head Beach** (p165) is friendly to short-boarders, longboarders, windsurfers and kitesurfers. For a good day of bodysurfing, **Sandy Beach** (p168) and **Makapu'u Beach** (p168) on the island's southeast shore are ideal. If you go out here, do so with caution: the pounding waves and shallow bottom have caused some serious neck and back injuries.

For surf reports, the **Surf News Network** (☎ 596-7873; www.surfnewsnetwork.com) runs a recorded surf-condition telephone line that reports winds, wave heights and tide information.

founder, John Alford, is the author of several mountain-biking guides to the islands.

Only a few of O'ahu's forest-reserve hiking trails are open to mountain bikers.

Popular coastal rides include Ka'ena Point (p201) and the nearby Kealia and Kuaokala Trails (p195). Interior rides in the Ko'olau Mountains include the Maunawili Trail Network (p172), which connects the Pali Hwy with the coast; the 'Aiea Loop Trail (p143) and Waimano Trail (p144) near Pearl Harbor; and the Kuli'ou'ou Ridge Trail (p166) outside Hawai'i Kai.

GOLF

The City and County of Honolulu, which en-compasses all of O'ahu, maintains six **municipal golf courses** (☎ 733-7386, reservations 296-2000; www .honolulu.gov/des/golf/golf.htm; 9-/18-hole visitor green fees $21/42, incl cart rental $29/58). Tee-time reservations for out-of-state visitors are accepted up to three days in advance, starting at 6:30am. The island's most popular municipal courses include Waikiki's Ala Wai Golf Course (p151) and Kane'ohe's Pali Golf Course (p179) on the Windward Coast.

On the Wai'anae Coast, Ko Olina Golf Club at the Ko Olina Resort (p197) was *Golf Digest*'s pick as one of the USA's top 75 resort courses; it's hosted the LPGA Tour and senior PGA Tour. Other notable courses open to the public include the Makaha Resort & Golf Club (p199) on the Wai'anae Coast; the Arnold Palmer and Greg Fazio Courses at North Shore's Turtle Bay Resort (p185); and Waimanalo's Olomana Golf Links (p172) and Kane'ohe's Ko'olau Golf Course (p179) on the Windward Coast.

HANG GLIDING & SKYDIVING

For experts, O'ahu's top hang gliding is from the cliffs opposite Sandy Beach Park (p168) and Makapu'u Point (p168) east of Hanauma Bay. Skydiving and glider rides are offered at the North Shore's Dillingham Airfield (p194).

HIKING

O'ahu has an incredible variety of hiking trails, many of which sit smack-dab in urban Honolulu, even though they feel many miles away from civilization.

Just outside Waikiki, an all-ages paved trail summits Diamond Head Crater (p165), making a touristy version of a pilgrimage that ends with sweeping ocean views. The lush forest-reserve trails in the upper Manoa and Makiki Valleys around Mt Tantalus (p128) are pleasantly devoid of crowds –waterfalls, native flora and fauna (especially myriad birdlife) and head-spinning lookouts are among the rewards of this extensive trail network.

The Kuli'ou'ou Ridge Trail (p166) outside Hawai'i Kai and Kea'iwa Heiau State Recreation Area (p143) near Pearl Harbor offer more opportunities to climb into the windswept Ko'olau Range, while a paved trail leads out to the lighthouse at Makapu'u Point (p168). The winding Maunawili Trail System (p172) connects the Pali Hwy with coastal Waimanalo, passing near a small pooling waterfall. Farther north, a wet, verdant scramble leads through Ahupua'a o Kahana State Park (p181), while the thickly forested Hau'ula Loop (p182) peeps into the untrammeled Kaipapa'u Valley.

A wild and ocean-whipped landscape unfolds along the Ka'ena Point Trail (p202) on the remote Wai'anae Coast. On the opposite side of the point, the Kealia and Kuaokala Trails (p195) climb above Dillingham Airfield to gorgeous views of the ocean and mountains. Elsewhere on the North Shore, the Kaunala Loop Trail (p189) overlooks Waimea Bay and the entire Wai'anae Range.

This book sketches O'ahu's most popular and accessible hikes. For more trails, check out *O'ahu Trailblazer* by Jerry and Janine Sprout, *O'ahu Trails* by Kathy Morey or *The Hikers Guide to O'ahu* by Stuart Ball. **Na Ala Hele** (www.hawaiitrails.org) offers free online trail maps, information and tips. For group hikes and guided tours, check the calendar in the free *Honolulu Weekly*, distributed around the island.

The following organizations also organize group hikes (reservations usually required), as well as educational and 'voluntourism' opportunities:

Hawai'i Nature Center (Map p125; ☎ 955-0100, 888-955-0104; www.hawaiinaturecenter.org; 2131 Makiki Heights Dr) Low-cost family-oriented hikes and environmental programs.

Hawaiian Trail & Mountain Club (http://htmclub.org) Volunteer-run community organization offers guided hikes and extensive online resources.

Sierra Club (Map pp118-19; ☎ 538-6616; www.hi .sierraclub.org/oahu; 1040 Richards St, Honolulu) Leads weekend hikes and other outings around O'ahu.

For bird-watching walks, see p105. For commercial guided hikes around O'ahu, see p112.

HORSEBACK RIDING

O'ahu's ranch country spreads along the Windward Coast and North Shore. Easy trail rides geared mostly for tourists, not *paniolo* (Hawaiian cowboys), are given at Turtle Bay Resort (p185) and Kualoa Ranch (p180).

RUNNING

In the Waikiki area, Ala Moana Beach Park (p123), Kapi'olani Park (p151) and the Ala Wai Canal are favorite jogging spots, as is the 4.6-mile run around Diamond Head crater. O'ahu has over 50 foot races each year, culminating in mid-December's **Honolulu Marathon** (www.honolulu marathon.org); for a complete list of events, contact Waikiki's **Running Room** (☎ 737-2422; www .runningroomhawaii.com; 819 Kapahulu Ave; ✆ 10am-7pm Mon-Fri, to 5pm Sat & Sun), a retail shop.

TENNIS

O'ahu has almost 200 public tennis courts. In Waikiki, the most convenient public courts are across the canal at Ala Moana Beach Park (p123) and at Kapi'olani Park (p151) toward

---

O'AHU FOR CHILDREN

- Outrigger canoe rides, pools and a sunset torch lighting and hula show at Waikiki's **Kuhio Beach Park** (p150)
- Touch tanks at the **Waikiki Aquarium** (p151)
- Planetarium shows, exploding faux volcanoes and more at Honolulu's **Bishop Museum** (p126)
- Petting critters at Waikiki's **Honolulu Zoo** (p152)
- Hiking up **Diamond Head** (p165)
- Snorkeling at **Hanauma Bay** (p166)
- Calm, shallow swimming at **Ko Olina Lagoons** (p197)
- Train rides and a giant maze at the **Dole Plantation** (p196)
- Movie and TV filming tours at **Kualoa Ranch** (p180)
- Rainy-day indoor fun at the **Hawaii Children's Discovery Center** (p131)

Diamond Head. Many resort hotels also have private courts for guests.

YOGA & SPAS
Many of O'ahu's most famous spas are found inside Waikiki resort hotels; see p151. On the Windward Coast, Kailua has the most yoga studios on O'ahu, along with sunrise and sunset sessions right on the beach (p174).

GETTING THERE & AWAY
Air
The vast majority of flights into Hawaii (see p571) land at **Honolulu International Airport** (Map p114; HNL; www.honoluluairport.com; ☎ 836-6413; 300 Rodgers Blvd, Honolulu), 6 miles west of downtown Honolulu and 9 miles west of Waikiki. O'ahu's only commercial airport, it's also a hub for interisland flights (see p573), offering frequent services to all of the Neighbor Islands. Free **Wiki-Wiki shuttle buses** (🕑 6am-10pm) around the airport stop curbside at ground level outside the terminals.

Foreign-currency exchange counters are located in strategic sections of the airport; in the international arrivals hall, most operate 6am to midnight. ATMs are scattered throughout the airport. You'll find visitor information booths near baggage claim, the international-arrivals area, the interisland terminal, and at both ends of the main lobby. Counters for car-rental agencies and courtesy phones are located near baggage claim. A **business center** (☎ 831-3600; 🕑 8am-5pm) in the main lobby offers telephone and postal services, as well as computer workstation rentals.

GETTING AROUND
O'ahu is an easy island to get around, whether by public bus or rental car.

To/From the Airport
From Honolulu International Airport, you can reach Honolulu or Waikiki by airport shuttle or public bus. Cab fares from the airport will cost about $30 to $35. For other points around O'ahu, it's usually more convenient to rent a car. You can travel to downtown Honolulu, the Ala Moana Center and Waikiki via TheBus 19 or 20 from the airport. Buses often fill up, so catch them at the first stop at the airport in front of Lobby 4. Buses run every 20 minutes from 5am to 11:30pm daily; the regular fare is $2. Luggage is restricted to what you can hold on your lap or stow under the seat. In Waikiki, buses stop every couple of blocks along Kuhio Ave.

There are several door-to-door airport shuttles. **Roberts Hawaii** (☎ 954-8652, 866-898-2519; www.robertshawaii.com) operates 24-hour shuttles between the airport and Waikiki hotels. For airport arrivals, proceed to the ground-transportation median outside baggage claim. Shuttles pick up passengers every 20 minutes; the fare is $9/15 one-way/round-trip, not including surcharges for bicycles, surfboards, baby gear or extra baggage. The ride from the airport to Waikiki averages 20 and 45 minutes, depending on your destination and

---

BE YOUR OWN TOUR GUIDE

Unlike on many of the other Hawaiian Islands, you won't need to rent a car or take a boring ol' bus tour around O'ahu. You can travel at your own pace and save not only money, but also the environment by circling the island on O'ahu's public transit system, TheBus.

Starting from the Ala Moana Center just outside Waikiki, the No 52 Wahiawa Circle Isle bus goes clockwise up Hwy 99 to Hale'iwa and along the North Shore. At the Turtle Bay Resort, on the island's northern tip, it switches signs to No 55 and comes down the Windward Coast to Kane'ohe and back over the Pali Hwy to Ala Moana. The No 55 Kane'ohe Circle Isle bus does the same route in reverse. These buses operate every 30 minutes from 6:30am to around 10pm daily. If you take the circle-island route nonstop (though why would you, since the point is to get off and look around along the way?), it takes about four hours.

For a shorter excursion from Waikiki, you can make a stunning loop around southeast O'ahu by taking 'The Beach Bus' No 22 (no service on Tuesday) or No 23 to Sea Life Park, then transfer to No 57 bound for Kailua and back over the Pali Hwy to the Ala Moana Center. Because you'll need to change buses, ask the driver for a free transfer when you first board. With fast connections, this loop takes about 2½ hours, but allow extra time at the end to catch one of the many frequent buses from the Ala Moana Center back to Waikiki.

USEFUL BUS ROUTES

Route No	Destination
A City Express!	University of Hawai'i, Ala Moana Center, Downtown Honolulu, Chinatown, Aloha Stadium
B Country Express!	Waikiki, Honolulu Academy of Arts, Downtown Honolulu, Chinatown, Bishop Museum
E Country Express!	Waikiki, Ala Moana Center, Aloha Tower, Downtown Honolulu
2 & 13	Waikiki, Honolulu Convention Center, Honolulu Academy of Arts, Downtown Honolulu, Chinatown; also Waikiki Aquarium and Bishop Museum (No 2) and Kapahulu Ave (No 13)
4	Waikiki, University of Hawai'i Queen Emma Summer Palace, Downtown Honolulu, Foster Botanical Garden
6	University of Hawai'i, Ala Moana Center, Downtown Honolulu
8	Waikiki, Ala Moana Center, Ward Centers, Downtown Honolulu, Chinatown
19 & 20	Waikiki, Ala Moana Center, Ward Centers, Restaurant Row, Aloha Tower, Downtown Honolulu, Chinatown, Honolulu International Airport
22	Waikiki, Diamond Head, Koko Marina, Hanauma Bay (no service Tue)
23	Ala Moana, Waikiki, Diamond Head, Hawai'i Kai, Sea Life Park
42	Waikiki, Ala Moana, Downtown Honolulu, Chinatown, USS Arizona Memorial (limited hours)
52 & 55	Circle Isle buses: Ala Moana Center, North Shore, Windward Coast
57	Ala Moana, Kailua, Waimanalo, Sea Life Park

traffic. For return trips to the airport, make reservations at least 48 hours in advance.

If you're driving yourself, the easiest way to Waikiki is via the Nimitz Hwy (92), which turns into Ala Moana Blvd. Although this route hits more local traffic, it's hard to get lost on it. For the fast lane, take the H-1 Fwy eastbound, then just follow the signs 'To Waikiki.' On the return trip to the airport, beware of the poorly marked interchange where H-1 and Hwy 78 split; if you're not in the right-hand lane at that point, you could easily end up on Hwy 78. It takes about 25 minutes to get from Waikiki to the airport via H-1 *if* you don't hit traffic; allow extra time during morning and afternoon rush hours.

Bicycle

It's possible to cycle around O'ahu, but consider taking TheBus to get beyond Honolulu metro-area traffic. Most buses have bicycle racks, which can carry two bicycles at no extra charge. The state's **Department of Transportation** (www.state.hi.us/dot/highways/bike/oahu) publishes a free *Bike O'ahu* map with recommended routes, including road-safety tips. You can pick up a printed copy at Honolulu's **Bike Shop** (Map p122; ☎ 596-0588; 1149 S King St, Honolulu; 9am-7pm Mon-Fri, to 5pm Sat, 10am-5pm Sun), which provides top-quality rentals and sales.

Bus

O'ahu's extensive public bus system, **TheBus** (www.thebus.org), is easy to use. Routes link Honolulu with Waikiki, beach parks in Kailua, the surf scene on the North Shore and the snorkeling spot of Hanauma Bay, just to name a few. Most hiking trails and some of the island's best viewpoints are beyond reach of TheBus, however.

The Ala Moana Center (Map p122) is Honolulu's central transfer point. Each bus route can have a few different destinations, and buses generally keep the same number whether inbound or outbound. If you're in doubt, ask the bus driver. They're used to disoriented and jet-lagged visitors. All buses are wheelchair-accessible and have front-loading racks that can accommodate two bicycles at no extra charge (let the driver know first). Be prepared for frigid air-conditioning; a public bus in Honolulu is probably the coldest place on O'ahu, regardless of the season.

See above for useful routes covering the Honolulu metro area, including Waikiki.

FARES & PASSES

The one-way fare for all rides is $2 for adults, $1 for children aged six to 17 (children under six ride free). You can use either coins or $1 bills, but bus drivers don't give change. One free transfer (with a two-hour time limit) per paid fare is available.

For short-term visitors, the O'ahu Discovery Passport ($20) is valid for unlimited rides over four consecutive days and can be purchased at any of Waikiki's ubiquitous ABC Stores or at **TheBus Pass Office** (Map p114; ☎ 848-4444;

811 Middle St; 7:30am-4pm Mon-Fri). A monthly bus pass ($40), which is valid for unlimited rides during a calendar month (not just any 30-day period), can be purchased at TheBus Pass Office, 7-Eleven convenience stores and Foodland or Star supermarkets.

Seniors (65 years and older) and anyone with a physical disability can buy a $10 discount card at TheBus Pass Office, which entitles them to pay $1 per one-way fare or $5/30 for a pass valid for unlimited rides during one calendar month/year.

SCHEDULES & INFORMATION

Schedules vary depending on the route. Many routes operate from about 5am to 9pm daily, though some main routes, such as Waikiki, continue until around 11pm. Buses run reasonably close to scheduled times, although if you set your watch by TheBus, you'll end up with Hawaii Time. Waiting for the bus that isn't full, especially along Waikiki's Kuhio Ave, can be frustrating.

TheBus has a great **route information service** (☎ 848-5555; 5:30am-10pm). As long as you know where you are and where you want to go, the staff will tell you which bus to catch and when the next one will arrive. This same service also has a TDD service for hearing-impaired travelers.

Routes and timetables are available on TheBus website or you can pick up free timetables for individual routes from public libraries, any satellite city hall (including at the Ala Moana Center) and at **McDonald's** (Map pp146-7; 2136 Kalakaua Ave) in Waikiki.

Car, Motorcycle & Moped

For general information about rental cars, including toll-free reservations numbers and websites for agencies, see p576.

Avis, Budget, Dollar, Enterprise, National and Hertz have rental cars available at Honolulu International Airport. Alamo and Thrifty have operations about a mile outside the airport, off Nimitz Hwy. All things being equal, try to rent from a company with its lot inside the airport – it's more convenient, because on the way back to the airport, all highway signs lead to in-airport car returns. Driving around looking for a lot outside the airport when you're trying to catch a flight can be stressful.

Most major car-rental agencies have multiple branch locations in Waikiki, usually in the lobbies of larger hotels. The best rental rates

DRIVING DISTANCES & TIMES

Although actual times vary depending upon traffic conditions, here are some average driving times and distances from Waikiki to points of interest around O'ahu:

Destination	Miles	Time
Diamond Head	2	10min
Hale'iwa	33	50min
Hanauma Bay	11	25min
Honolulu International Airport	9	20min
Ka'ena Point State Park	43	70min
Kailua	15	30min
Kapolei	26	40min
La'ie	34	65min
Makaha Beach	38	1hr
Makapu'u Point	14	25min
Nu'uanu Pali Lookout	8	20min
Sunset Beach	39	1hr
USS Arizona Memorial	12	25min
Waipahu	17	30min

are usually offered at the airport, however. Independent car-rental agencies in Waikiki may offer even lower rates, though, especially for one-day rentals and 4WD vehicles like Jeeps. They are also more likely to rent to drivers under 25. Many independent agencies also rent mopeds and motorcycles, but these two-wheeled rides can be more expensive than renting a car.

Taxi

Taxis are readily available at the airport and at larger hotels and shopping centers, but otherwise you'll probably have to call for one. Taxis have meters and charge a flag-down fee of $3, plus another $3 per mile and 50¢ for each suitcase or backpack. Because island taxis are often station wagons or minivans, they're good for groups.

Tours

For do-it-yourself circle-island tours by public bus, see p110.

Mauka Makai Excursions (Map p122; ☎ 734-8414, 866-896-0596; www.hawaiianecotours.net; Suite 106, 350 Ward Ave, Honolulu; adult/child from $52/42) Hawaiian-owned and operated cultural ecotour company offers a few bus and hiking trips around the island; rates include Waikiki hotel pick-ups.

Polynesian Adventure Tours (☎ 833-3000, 800-622-3011; www.polyad.com) Conventional bus and van sightseeing tours of O'ahu, including exhausting full-day

'Circle Island' trips (adult/child from $71/42) and eclectic options like a half-day 'President Obama' tour (adult/child $39/22) or evening 'Ali'i Ghost' tour (adult/child $49/39).

HONOLULU

pop 375,570

Three out of every four O'ahuans lives in Honolulu, so you can't claim to have really gotten to know the island if you never even leave Waikiki. Ever since Kamehameha the Great conquered O'ahu and the first foreign trading ships arrived, Honolulu has been the nerve center of the island and in truth, the entire archipelago. It's a laid-back Polynesian island capital, where Victorian-era buildings stand in the shadow of sleek modern high-rises.

Venture downtown not just for its unmatched collection of historic sites, museums and gardens, but also to eat your way through O'ahu's intoxicating blend of ethnic cultures, from the pan-Asian alleyways of Chinatown where 19th-century whalers once brawled, to hole-in-the-wall diners where local kids slurp saimin (local-style noodle soup), to haute cafés dishing up the freshest bounty from land and sea.

Then escape the concrete jungle for a hike up into the lush valleys nestled beneath the jagged Ko'olau Mountains, especially in the forest preserves encircling Mt Tantalus, traditionally known as Pu'u 'Ohi'a. Around sunset, cool off with a breezy walk along Honolulu's historic harborfront or splash into the Pacific at Ala Moana Beach Park, a rare beauty. After dark, hit Chinatown's edgy nightlife scene. You won't even miss Waikiki, we promise.

HISTORY

In 1793 the English frigate *Butterworth* became the first foreign ship to sail into what is now Honolulu Harbor. In the 1820s, Honolulu's first bars and brothels opened to international whaling crews. Protestant missionaries began arriving around the same time. Today, Hawaii's first church is just a stone's throw from 'Iolani Palace.

In 1843, ancient Hawai'i's only formal military 'invasion' by a foreign power occurred when George Paulet, an upstart British commander upset about a petty land deal involving a British national, sailed into Honolulu and seized O'ahu for six months. He proceeded to anglicize street names, seize property and collect taxes. Upon hearing

of his actions, Queen Victoria quickly dispatched Admiral Richard Thomas to restore the kingdom's independence.

Honolulu replaced Lahaina as the capital of the kingdom in 1845. Increasingly, Western expatriates came to dominate local affairs. It's no coincidence that the names of some of Honolulu's richest and most powerful families – Alexander, Baldwin, Cooke and Dole – read like rosters from the first mission ships. In 1893 a small group of new citizens overthrew Queen Lili'uokalani and declared their own 'republic' on the steps of Ali'iolani Hale in Honolulu. The queen was tried and placed under house arrest at 'Iolani Palace.

In December 1899 bubonic plague broke out in Chinatown. As the plague spread, the all-powerful Board of Health ordered the Honolulu Fire Department to burn the wooden buildings on the *mauka* (inland) side of Beretania St between Nu'uanu Ave and Smith St. But the wind suddenly picked up and the fire spread out of control, racing toward the waterfront on January 20, 1900. Nearly 40 acres of Chinatown burned to the ground, leaving 4000 residents temporarily homeless.

In the early 1900s, Honolulu continued to grow as a commercial center. The next decades saw a revival of Hawaiian culture, as the sounds of falsetto voices and steel guitars filled the airwaves of territorial radio. Following the Japanese attack on Pearl Harbor on December 7, 1941, Honolulu experienced a cultural, political and economic clampdown on Japanese American residents by military leaders.

Today this modern metropolis dominates the government and cultural life of the state. Environmental issues are often at the forefront of the agenda, including questions about where to build new landfills without polluting groundwater, whether garbage should just be shipped to the US mainland, and how the environmental impacts of cruise ships docked at Honolulu Harbor can be mitigated. In 2008 voters approved a controversial new commuter-rail system that has yet to be built.

ORIENTATION

The City & County of Honolulu sprawls along the south shore of O'ahu. The city proper is generally considered to extend west to the airport and east to Kaimuki.

Two major thoroughfares run the length of the city: Ala Moana Blvd (Hwy 92) skirts the coast from the airport to Waikiki, and the

O'AHU

GREATER HONOLULU & PEARL HARBOR

INFORMATION		
Hyperbaric Treatment Center	1	B2
Japan Consulate	2	C2
Korea Consulate	3	C2
Main Post Office	(see 15)	

SIGHTS & ACTIVITIES		
Bishop Museum	4	C2
Diamond Head State Monument	5	D3
Hawaii Bicycling League	(see 25)	
Hawaii Children's Discovery Center	6	C3
Moanalua Golf Club	7	B1
National Memorial Cemetery of the Pacific	8	C2
Pacific Aviation Museum	9	A1
USS Arizona Memorial	10	A1
USS Arizona Memorial Visitor Center	11	A1
USS Bowfin Submarine Museum & Park	12	A1
USS Missouri Memorial	13	A1

SLEEPING		
Best Western Plaza Hotel	14	B2
Ohana Honolulu Airport Hotel	15	B2

EATING		
Helena's Hawaiian Food	16	C2
Liliha Bakery	17	C2
Nico's at Pier 38	18	C2
Town	19	D3
Whole Foods	20	D3

DRINKING		
La Mariana Sailing Club	21	B2
Sam Choy's Big Aloha Brewery	22	B2

ENTERTAINMENT		
Movie Museum	23	D3
Pipeline Cafe	24	C3

SHOPPING		
Montsuki	25	D3

TRANSPORT		
AAA	(see 18)	
The Bus Pass Office	26	B2

H-1 Fwy runs east–west between the beach and the mountains. In between are several grids bisected by one-way streets overlapping at irregular angles, making navigation within central Honolulu difficult.

Heading into downtown Honolulu, King St (one-way heading southeast) and Beretania St (one-way heading northwest) are primary conduits. Downtown houses O'ahu's government buildings, including the state capitol, and 'Iolani Palace.

Chinatown is immediately north of downtown Honolulu, roughly bounded by the harbor, Bethel St, Vineyard Blvd and River St. The landmark Aloha Tower and cruise-ship terminals sit *makai* (oceanside, or seaward) of Chinatown.

Kapi'olani Blvd and University Ave are the main thoroughfares connecting the Ala Moana area and University of Hawai'i campus, situated in the Manoa Valley underneath the Ko'olau Mountains.

Southeast of downtown Honolulu, Waikiki is the tourist epicenter, and just beyond it is Diamond Head, a striking geological landmark. Waikiki is contained within the boundaries of Honolulu, but is covered later in this chapter (see p145).

INFORMATION
Bookstores

Bestsellers (Map pp118-19; ☎ 528-2378; 1001 Bishop St; ⏰ 7:30am-5:30pm Mon-Fri, 9am-3pm Sat) Good selection of travel guides, novels and maps.

Borders (Map p122; ☎ 591-8995; Victoria Ward Centre, 1200 Ala Moana Blvd; ☒ 10am-11pm Mon-Thu, 10am-midnight Fri, 9am-midnight Sat, 9am-10pm Sun; ☎) Extensive newspaper, magazine and travel sections.

Native Books/Nā Mea Hawaii (Map p122; ☎ 597-8967; www.nativebookshawaii.com; Ward Warehouse, 1050 Ala Moana Blvd; ☒ 10am-9pm Mon-Sat, to 6pm Sun) Specializes in Hawaiiana books, CDs/DVDs and gifts; also holds cultural performances, author readings and classes (see p131).

Rainbow Books & Records (Map p122; ☎ 955-7994; www.rainbowbookshawaii.com; 1010 University Ave; ☒ 10am-10pm Sun-Thu, to 11pm Fri & Sat) New and used books, CDs and records near the University of Hawaiʻi.

Emergency

Police (☎ 529-3111) For nonemergencies.
Police, Fire & Ambulance (☎ 911) For emergencies.

Internet Access

FedEx Office (www.fedex.com; per hr $6-12) Ala Moana (Map p122; ☎ 944-8500; 1500 Kapiʻolani Blvd; ☒ 7am-11pm Mon-Thu, 7am-9pm Fri, 9am-9pm Sat & Sun); Downtown (Map pp118-19; ☎ 528-7171; 590 Queen St; ☒ 7am-11pm Mon-Fri, 8am-7pm Sat, 7am-7pm Sun); University Area (Map p122; ☎ 943-0005; 2575 S King St; ☒ 24hr) Self-serve, pay-as-you-go computer terminals and wi-fi, plus digital-photo printing and CD-burning stations.

Netstop Coffee (Map p122; ☎ 955-1020; 2615 S King St; per hr $6; ☒ 7:30am-midnight) Casual cybercafé with internet terminals and wi-fi near the University of Hawaiʻi.

Hawaii State Library (Map pp118-19; ☎ 586-3500; www.librarieshawaii.org; 478 S King St; ☒ 10am-5pm Mon & Wed, 9am-5pm Tue, Fri & Sat, 9am-8pm Thu) The main branch of the state system; there are also 23 neighborhood library branches around Oʻahu. All provide free reservable internet terminals (see p568); some offer free wi-fi.

Media

NEWSPAPERS & MAGAZINES

There are several free glossy tourist magazines like *This Week Oʻahu* and *101 Things to Do* listing events, visitor information and coupons, all available at the airport.

Honolulu Advertiser (www.honoluluadvertiser.com) Honolulu's morning newspaper; the TGIF events-and-entertainment section is published every Friday.

Honolulu Magazine (www.honolulumagazine.com) Monthly magazine covers arts, culture, fashion and cuisine.

Honolulu Star-Bulletin (www.starbulletin.com) Honolulu's afternoon newspaper.

Honolulu Weekly (www.honoluluweekly.com) Free weekly tabloid covering progressive politics and entertainment.

RADIO & TV

The following radio and TV stations broadcast local news, music and programs.

KHPR (88.1FM) Hawaii Public Radio.
KHET (cable channel 10) Hawaii public TV (PBS).
KIKU (cable channel 9) Multicultural TV programming.
KINE (105.1FM) Classic and contemporary Hawaiian music.
KIPO (89.3FM) Hawaii Public Radio.
KTUH (90.3FM) University of Hawaiʻi student-run radio station.

Medical Services

Hyperbaric Treatment Center (Map p114; ☎ 851-7030, 851-7032; www.hyperbaricmedicinecenter.com; 275 Puʻuhale Rd) For divers with the bends.

Longs Drugs (Map p122; ☎ 947-2651; 2220 S King St; ☒ 24hr) Convenient pharmacy near the University of Hawaiʻi.

Queen's Medical Center (Map pp118-19; ☎ 538-9011; 1301 Punchbowl St) Oʻahu's biggest, best-equipped hospital has a 24-hour emergency room.

Straub Clinic & Hospital (Map p122; ☎ 522-4000; 888 S King St) Operates a 24-hour emergency room and neighborhood clinics around the island.

Money

Banks with convenient branches and ATMs around the island:

Bank of Hawaii (☎ 888-643-3888; https://www.boh.com)
First Hawaiian Bank (☎ 844-4040; www.fhb.com)

Post

For post office locations and hours, call ☎ 800-275-8777 or visit www.us ps.com.

Ala Moana post office (Map p122; ground fl, Ala Moana Center, 1450 Ala Moana Blvd; ☒ 8:30am-5pm Mon-Fri, to 4:15pm Sat)

Chinatown post office (Map pp118-19; 100 N Beretania St; ☒ 9am-4pm Mon-Fri)

Downtown post office (Map pp118-19; ground fl, 335 Merchant St; ☒ 8am-4:30pm Mon-Fri) In the Old Federal Building.

Main post office (Map p114; Honolulu International Airport, 3600 Aolele St, Honolulu, HI 96820; ☒ 7:30am-3pm Mon-Fri) General-delivery (poste-restante) mail is only accepted at this location; it's normally held for 10 days (up to 30 days for international mail).

Moʻiliʻili post office (Map p122; 2700 S King St ☒ 9:30am-4:15pm Mon-Fri) Near the University of Hawaiʻi.

Tourist Information

Oʻahu Visitors Bureau (Map pp118-19; ☎ 524-0722, 877-525-6248; www.visit-oahu.com; Suite 1520, 733 Bishop St, Honolulu; ☒ 8am-4pm) Excellent online information, but no walk-in visitor center.

DANGERS & ANNOYANCES

Drug dealing and gang activity are prevalent on the north side of Chinatown, particularly along Nu'uanu Stream and the River St pedestrian mall, which should be avoided after dark. Chinatown's skid rows include blocks of Hotel St.

SIGHTS

Honolulu's compact downtown area was the stage for the rise and fall of the 19th-century Hawaiian monarchy, all just a lei's throw from the harborfront. Nearby, the buzzing streets of Chinatown are packed with noodle shops, dim-sum palaces, antiques shops and art galleries. East of downtown, the University of Hawai'i area is a gateway to the Mt Tantalus green belt, not far north of Waikiki. A few outlying sights, including the Bishop Museum, are worth a detour.

Downtown
'IOLANI PALACE

Perhaps no other place evokes a more poignant sense of Hawaii's history than this **royal palace** (Map pp118-19; info ☎ 538-1471, tickets ☎ 522-0832/0823; admission to grounds free, basement galleries adult/child 5-12 $6/3, tours adult/child 5-12 self-guided audio $12/5, guided $20/5; ☽ grounds sunrise-sunset, basement galleries 9am-5pm Tue-Sat, tours guided every 15min 9am-11:15am Tue-Sat, self-guided every 10min 11:45am-3:30pm Tue-Sat,), where plots and counterplots simmered.

The regal palace was built by King David Kalakaua in 1882. At that time, the Hawaiian monarchy observed many of the diplomatic protocols of the Victorian world. The king traveled abroad meeting with leaders around the globe and received foreign emissaries at 'Iolani Palace. Although the palace was modern and opulent for its time, it did little to assert Hawaii's sovereignty over powerful US-influenced business interests, who overthrew the Kingdom of Hawai'i in 1893.

Two years after the coup, the former queen, Lili'uokalani, who had succeeded her brother David to the throne, was convicted of treason and spent nine months as a prisoner in her former home. The palace later served as the capitol of the republic, then the territory and later the state of Hawaii. In 1969 the government finally moved into the current state capitol, leaving 'Iolani Palace a shambles. It has since been painstakingly restored to its former glory, although many of the original royal artifacts were lost or stolen over the years.

The only way to see the palace's handsome interior is to join a tour (children under five are not allowed). Sometimes you can join a tour on the spot, but it's advisable to call ahead for reservations and to double-check tour schedules, especially during peak periods. If you're short on time, just browse the historical exhibits in the basement, including royal regalia and reconstructions of the kitchen and chamberlain's office.

Outside on the palace grounds, the former Royal Household Guards **barracks** is now the ticket booth. The domed **pavilion** was originally built for the coronation of King Kalakaua. Underneath a huge **banyan tree** thought to have been planted by his wife Queen Kapi'olani, the Royal Hawaiian Band usually gives free concerts from noon to 1pm every Friday.

HAWAI'I STATE ART MUSEUM

With its vibrant, thought-provoking collections, this eclectic **art museum** (Map pp118-19; ☎ 586-0900; www.hawaii.gov/sfca; 2nd fl, No 1 Capitol District Bldg, 250 S Hotel St; admission free; ☽ 10am-4pm Tue-Sat, 5-9pm 1st Fri of each month) showcases traditional and contemporary art from Hawaii's diverse multiethnic communities. It inhabits a 1928 Spanish Mission–style building, formerly a YMCA. Revolving exhibits of paintings, sculptures, fiber art, photography and mixed media reveal how a blending of Western, Asian and Polynesian art forms and traditions have shaped a unique island aesthetic that really captures the soul of the islands and the hearts of the people. Drop by at noon on the last Tuesday of the month for free 'Art Lunch' lectures.

MISSION HOUSES MUSEUM

Occupying the original headquarters of the Sandwich Islands Mission that forever changed the course of Hawaiian history, this modest **museum** (Map pp118-19; ☎ 447-3910; 553 S King St; grounds admission free, temporary-exhibit galleries $6, 1hr guided tour adult/student & child 6-18 $10/6; ☽ 10am-4pm Tue-Sat, tours usually 11am, 1pm & 2:45pm Tue-Sat) is authentically furnished with handmade quilts on the beds and iron cooking pots in the stone fireplaces. The **Printing Office** houses a lead-type press first used to print the Bible in Hawaiian.

The first missionaries packed more than their bags when they left Boston; they actually brought a prefabricated wooden house, now called the **Frame House**, with them around the Horn. Designed to withstand cold New England winter winds, the small windows instead block out Honolulu's cooling tradewinds, keeping the two-story house hot and stuffy. Erected in 1821, it's the oldest wooden structure in Hawaii.

The coral-block **Chamberlain House** was the early mission's storeroom, a necessity as Honolulu had few shops in those days. Upstairs are hoop barrels, wooden crates packed with dishes, and the desk and quill pen of Levi Chamberlain. He was appointed by the mission to buy, store and dole out supplies to missionary families, who survived on a meager allowance – as the account books on his desk testify.

KAWAIAHA'O CHURCH

O'ahu's oldest Christian **church** (Map pp118-19; ☎ 522-1333; 957 Punchbowl St; admission free; ☺ 8am-4pm Mon-Fri, worship service 9am Sun) stands on the site where the first Protestant missionaries built a grass-thatch church shortly after their arrival in 1820. The original structure seated 300 Hawaiians on *lauhala* mats, woven from *hala* (screwpine) leaves.

This 1842 New England Gothic–style church is made of 14,000 coral slabs, which divers chiseled out of O'ahu's underwater reefs – a task that took four years. The clock tower was donated by Kamehameha III, and the old clock, installed in 1850, still keeps accurate time. The rear seats of the church, marked by *kahili* (feather staffs) and velvet padding were for royalty and are still reserved for their descendants today.

The **tomb of King Lunalilo**, the short-lived successor to Kamehameha V, stands near the main entrance to the church grounds. The **cemetery** at the rear of the church is almost like a who's who of colonial history. Early missionaries are buried alongside other important figures of the day, including infamous Sanford Dole, who became the first Hawai'i's first territorial governor after Queen Lili'uokalani was overthrown.

ALOHA TOWER

Built in 1926 at the edge of downtown Honolulu, this 10-story **landmark** (Map pp118-19; ☎ 537-9260; Pier 9; admission free; ☺ 9am-5pm; P) was once the city's tallest building. In the golden days when all tourists to Hawaii arrived by ship, this pre-WWII waterfront icon greeted every visitor. Today cruise ships still

disembark at the terminal beneath the tower. Take the elevator to the top-floor tower observation deck for sweeping 360-degree views, then peek through the cruise-ship terminal windows back below and outside on ground level to see colorful murals depicting bygone Honolulu. There's pay parking at the Aloha Tower Marketplace next door.

HAWAI'I MARITIME CENTER

A great place to get a sense of Hawaii's history, this educational **museum** (Map pp118-19; ☎ 523-6151; www.bishopmuseum.org; Pier 7; adult/child 6-17/senior $8.50/5.50/7; ☺ 9am-5pm; P) covers everything from the arrival of Captain Cook and 19th-century whaling ships to modern-day windsurfing. Displays on early tourism include a reproduction of a Matson liner stateroom and historical photos of Waikiki from the early 20th century, when only the Matson-built Moana and Royal Hawaiian hotels shared the horizon views with Diamond Head.

The museum's centerpiece is *Hokule'a*, a traditional double-hulled sailing canoe that has repeatedly sailed from Hawaii to the South Pacific and back, retracing the routes of the islands' original Polynesian settlers using only ancient methods of wayfaring (navigation that relies on the sun, stars and wind and wave patterns; see p37).

Outside, climb aboard the *Falls of Clyde*, the world's last four-masted, four-rigged ship. Built in 1878 in Glasgow, the ship once carried sugar and passengers between Hilo on the Big Island of Hawai'i and San Francisco, then oil, before finally being stripped down to a barge. Today you can stroll the deck and explore the cargo holds of this restored, floating National Historic Landmark. Three-hour validated parking ($5) is available nearby.

The museum announced a temporary closure just as this book went to press, so call ahead before you visit.

CONTEMPORARY MUSEUM AT FIRST HAWAIIAN CENTER

Inside the headquarters of the First Hawaiian Bank, this downtown **art gallery** (Map pp118-19; ☎ 526-1322; www.tcmhi.org; 999 Bishop St; admission free; ☺ 8:30am-4pm Mon-Thu, to 6pm Fri) fills the briefcase district with modern and contemporary art. Changing exhibits feature renowned international and local artists. The building itself boasts a four-story-high art-glass wall

O'AHU

DOWNTOWN HONOLULU & CHINATOWN

INFORMATION
Australia Consulate...........................1 D3
Bestsellers...................................(see 57)
Canada Consulate.......................(see 1)
Chinatown Post Office...................2 D2
Department of Parks & Recreation.3 F5
Division of Forestry & Wildlife....(see 4)
Division of State Parks....................4 F5
Downtown Post Office...................5 D4
FedEx Office..................................6 E6
France Consulate............................7 D4
Hawaii State Library.......................8 E5
Italy Consulate...............................9 C4
Netherlands Consulate..................10 C4
O'ahu Visitors Bureau..................(see 9)
Queen's Medical Center...............11 F4

SIGHTS & ACTIVITIES
Ali'iolani Hale...............................12 D5
Aloha Tower...................................13 B4
Anna Li Clinic of Chinese
  Medicine....................................14 D3
Atlantis Adventures.......................15 C5
Chinatown Cultural Plaza.............16 D2
Contemporary Museum at First
  Hawaiian Center.........................17 D4
Dr Sun Yat-sen Statue...................18 D2
Father Damien Statue....................19 E4
Foster Botanical Garden................20 E1
Hawaii Audubon Society...............21 D4
Hawai'i Heritage Center................22 C2
Hawai'i Maritime Center...............23 C5
Hawai'i State Art Museum.............24 E3
Honolulu Hale (City Hall)..............25 E5
'Iolani Palace................................26 E4
Izumo Taisha.................................27 D1
Kamehameha the Great Statue.....28 D5
Kawaiaha'o Church........................29 E5
Kekaulike Market...........................30 C2
King Lunalilo Tomb........................31 E5
Kuan Yin Temple............................32 E1
Leanne Chee Chinese Herbs &
  Acupuncture...............................33 D2
Maunakea Marketplace.................34 C2
Mission Houses Museum................35 E5
O'ahu Market.................................36 C2
Queen Lili'uokalani Statue............37 E4
St Andrew's Cathedral...................38 E3
Sierra Club..................................(see 44)
State Capitol.................................39 E4
Taoist Temple................................40 D1
Washington Place..........................41 E4
Yat Tung Chow Noodle Factory..42 C2

EATING
Ba Le...43 C2
Cafe Laniakea...............................44 D4
Downtown...................................(see 24)
Duc's Bistro...................................45 D2
Hiroshi Eurasian Tapas.................46 D6
Honolulu Café...............................47 C4
Indigo...48 D3
Legend Seafood Restaurant..........49 D2
Legend Vegetarian Restaurant.....50 D2
Little Village Noodle House..........51 D2
Maunakea
  Marketplace.............................(see 34)
Mei Sum Dim Sum.........................52 D2
Royal Kitchen................................53 D1
Soul de Cuba.................................54 D3
Sun Chong Co...............................55 C2
To Chau...56 C2
'Umeke Market & Deli...................57 D3
Vino..(see 46)
Vita Juice......................................58 D3

DRINKING
Bar 35..(see 63)
Gordon Biersch Brewery
  Restaurant..................................59 B4
Green Room Lounge &
  Opium Den...............................(see 48)
Hank's Cafe Honolulu...................60 C3
Honolulu Coffee Company.........(see 57)
Smith's Union Bar..........................61 C2
The Loft...62 C2
thirtyninehotel..............................63 C3

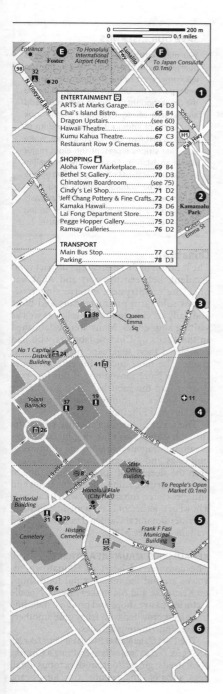

incorporating 185 prisms, designed by NYC architect James Carpenter.

STATE CAPITOL
Built in the architecturally interesting 1960s, Hawaii's **state capitol** (Map pp118-19; ☎ 586-0178; 415 S Beretania St; admission free; ☯ 8am-5pm Mon-Fri, tours usually 1:30pm Mon, Wed & Fri) is not your standard gold dome. It's a poster-child of conceptual postmodernism: the two cone-shaped legislative chambers represent volcanoes; the supporting columns symbolize palm trees; and a large pool encircling the rotunda represents the Pacific Ocean surrounding the Hawaiian Islands.

In front of the capitol stands a **statue of Father Damien**, the Belgian priest who lived and worked among patients with Hansen's Disease (formerly called leprosy) who were forcibly exiled to the island of Moloka'i beginning in 1866 (see p459). The highly stylized sculpture was created by Paris-born Venezuelan artist Marisol Escobar.

Symbolically positioned between the palace and the state capitol is a bronze **statue of Queen Lili'uokalani**, Hawaii's last reigning monarch. Lili'uokalani holds the constitution that she wrote in 1893, in a failed attempt to strengthen Native Hawaiian rule; 'Aloha 'Oe,' a popular song she composed; and *Kumulipo* the traditional Hawaiian chant of creation.

ALI'IOLANI HALE
The first major government **building** (Map pp118-19; ☎ 539-4994; 417 S King St; admission free; ☯ 8am-4pm Mon-Fri) constructed by the Hawaiian monarchy in 1874, the 'House of Heavenly Kings' was designed by Australian architect Thomas Rowe to be a royal palace, although it was never used as such. It was on these steps in January 1893 that Sanford Dole proclaimed the end of the Hawaiian monarchy. Today, this dignified Italianate structure houses the Hawaii Supreme Court. Step inside for historical displays about Hawaii's judicial history.

Outside, a **statue of Kamehameha the Great** faces 'Iolani Palace. Every year on June 11, a state holiday honoring the king, the statue is ceremoniously draped with layers of colorful leis.

WASHINGTON PLACE
Formerly the governor's official residence, this historic **home** (Map pp118-19; ☎ 586-0248; admission by donation; ☯ by appt Mon-Fri) is now a museum.

Surrounded by stately trees, this large colonial-style mansion was erected in 1846 by US sea captain John Dominis. The captain's son, also named John, became the governor of O'ahu and married the Hawaiian princess who later became Queen Lili'uokalani. After the queen was released from house arrest, she lived at Washington Place until her death in 1917. A plaque near the sidewalk is inscribed with the words to 'Aloha 'Oe,' the farewell song Liliu'okalani composed. For tour reservations, call at least 48 hours in advance.

ST ANDREW'S CATHEDRAL
This French Gothic **cathedral** (Map pp118-19; ☎ 524-2822; 229 Queen Emma Sq; 🕙 9am-5pm, tours usually 11am Sun; (P)) was King Kamehameha IV's personal homage to the architecture and faith of the Church of England. The king and his consort, Queen Emma, founded the Anglican Church in Hawaii in 1861. The cornerstone was laid four years after the death of Kamehameha IV on St Andrew's Day – hence the church's name. Historical tours usually meet by the pulpit after the 10am Sunday worship service, but call ahead to confirm schedules. For a free concert, the largest pipe organ in the Pacific is sonorously played every Wednesday starting at 12:15pm. Limited free parking.

HONOLULU HALE
Designed and built in 1927 by CW Dickey, Honolulu's then-famous architect, **City Hall** (Map pp118-19; ☎ 523-2489; 530 S King St) is now on the National Register of Historic Places. Its Spanish Mission Revival–style architecture features a tiled roof, decorative balconies, arches and pillars, some ornate frescoes, and an open-air courtyard occasionally used for concerts and art exhibits. On the front lawn, an eternal-flame memorial honors the victims of the September 11 terrorist attacks on the US mainland.

TOP PICKS – FREE STUFF IN HONOLULU

- ■ **Ala Moana Beach Park** (p123)
- ■ **Hawai'i State Art Museum** (p116)
- ■ **First Friday Gallery Walk** in Chinatown (p124)
- ■ **Aloha Tower** (p117)
- ■ **Nu'uanu Valley Lookout** (p128)

SAVE OUR...ISLANDS

You may notice that Hawaii's state flag is quartered with the Union Jack in the top left corner next to the flagpole. Hawaii was never part of the UK, although Kamehameha the Great thought the Union Jack would add an element of regal splendor, so he took the liberty of adding it to the Kingdom of Hawai'i's first flag. The horizontal red, white and blue stripes represent the eight major Hawaiian Islands. Today Native Hawaiian sovereignty activists often fly the flag upside down, a time-honored symbol of distress, as happened when small groups of activists occupied the palace grounds twice during 2008, bringing attention to their cause.

Chinatown
The location of this mercantile district is no accident. Between the port and what was once the countryside, enterprising businesses sold farm products, nuts and bolts and daily services to the city folks, as well as visiting ship crews. Many were established in the 1860s by Chinese laborers who had completed their sugarcane plantation contracts. The most successful entrepreneurs have long since moved out of this low-rent district into the suburbs, making room for newer waves of immigrants: Vietnamese, Laotians and Filipinos.

The scent of burning incense still wafts through Chinatown's buzzing markets, fire-breathing dragons spiral up the columns of buildings and steaming dim sum awakens even the sleepiest of appetites. Take time to explore: peruse cutting-edge art galleries and antiques stores, rub shoulders with locals over a bowl of noodles and take a meditative stroll in Foster Botanical Garden. For a self-guided walking tour, see p130.

KEKAULIKE & MAUNAKEA STREETS
The commercial heart of Chinatown revolves around the markets and food shops on Kekaulike and Maunakea Streets. Noodle factories, pastry shops and produce stalls line the streets crowded with feisty grandmothers and errand-running families.

The 1904 **O'ahu Market** (Map pp118-19; cnr Kekaulike & N King Sts; 🕙 7am-5pm) sells everything a Chinese cook needs: ginger root, fresh octopus, quail eggs, slabs of tuna, jasmine rice, long beans and salted jellyfish. You owe yourself a bubble tea if you spot a pig's head among the stalls.

A block away is **Yat Tung Chow Noodle Factory** (Map pp118-19; ☎ 531-7982; 150 N King St; ⏰ 6am-3pm Mon-Sat, to 1pm Sun), one of the neighborhood's half-a-dozen family-run noodle factories. Stop by in the early morning when a cloud of flour covers every surface.

The pedestrian lane of Maunakea St is bookended by the vibrant **Kekaulike Market** (Kekaulike St, btwn King & Hotel Sts; ⏰ 7am-5pm) and **Maunakea Marketplace** (Map pp118-19; 1120 Maunakea St; ⏰ 7am-5pm), with its bustling food court (p133).

FOSTER BOTANICAL GARDEN

Tropical plants you've only ever read about can be spotted in all their lush glory at this **botanical garden** (Map pp118-19; ☎ 522-7066; www.co.honolulu .hi.us/parks/hbg/fbg.htm; 180 N Vineyard Blvd; adult/child 6-12 $5/1; ⏰ 9am-4pm, guided tour usually 1pm Mon-Sat; P), which took root here in 1850. Among its rarest specimens are the Hawaiian *loulu* palm and the East African *Gigasiphon macrosiphon*, both thought to be extinct in the wild. Several of the garden's towering trees are the largest of their kind in the USA. Oddities include the cannonball tree, the sausage tree and the double coconut palm capable of producing a 50lb nut – watch your head! Follow your nose past fragrant vanilla vines and cinnamon trees in the spice and herb gardens, then pick your way among the poisonous and dye plants. Don't miss the blooming orchid gardens. All of the species are labeled, and a free self-guided tour booklet is available at the garden entrance.

CHINATOWN CULTURAL PLAZA

Covering the better part of a city block, this open-air mall (Map pp118–19) doesn't have the character of nearby antiques shops, but it's still quintessentially Chinatown, with tailors, acupuncturists and calligraphers working alongside travel agencies and dim-sum restaurants. In the small courtyard, elderly Chinese come daily to light incense at a statue of Kuan Yin. Outside, a **bronze statue of Dr Sun Yat-sen** stands watch near the start of the River St pedestrian mall, where senior citizens play checkers and mah-jongg on shady benches alongside Nu'uanu Stream. Parking available.

HAWAI'I HERITAGE CENTER

Local volunteers with family ties to the community run this friendly **gallery** (Map pp118-19;

FLOWER POWER

Chinatown herbalists are both physicians and pharmacists, with walls full of small wooden drawers, each filled with a different herb. They'll size you up, feel your pulse and listen to you describe your ailments before deciding which drawers to open, mixing herbs and flowers and wrapping them for you to take home and boil together. Find traditional herbalists at the Chinatown Cultural Plaza, **Leanne Chee Chinese Herbs & Acupuncture** (Map pp118-19; ☎ 533-2498; 1159 Maunakea St) or **Anna Li Clinic of Chinese Medicine** (Map pp118-19; ☎ 537-1133; 1121 Nu'uanu Ave).

☎ 521-2749; 1040 Smith St; ⏰ 9am-2pm Mon-Sat) that offers changing exhibitions on O'ahu's Chinese and other ethnic communities. The center also organizes historical walking tours (see p131).

KUAN YIN TEMPLE

With its green ceramic-tile roof and bright red columns, this ornate Chinese **Buddhist temple** (Map pp118-19; ☎ 533-6361; 170 N Vineyard Blvd; admission free; ⏰ sunrise-sunset) is Honolulu's oldest. The richly carved interior is filled with the sweet, pervasive smell of burning incense. The temple is dedicated to Kuan Yin, goddess of mercy, whose statue is the largest in the interior prayer hall. Devotees burn paper 'money' for prosperity and good luck, while offerings of fresh flowers and fruit are placed at the altar. The large citrus fruit stacked pyramid-style is pomelo, a symbol of fertility because of its many seeds. Respectful visitors are welcome.

IZUMO TAISHA

Across the river, this **shintō shrine** (Map pp118-19; ☎ 538-7778; 215 N Kukui St; admission free; ⏰ 9am-4pm) was built by Japanese immigrants in 1906. During WWII the property was confiscated by the city; it wasn't returned to the community until 1962. The 100lb sacks of rice near the altar symbolize good health. Ringing the bell at the shrine entrance is considered an act of purification for those who come to pray and seek blessings, especially on January 1, when the temple heaves with celebrants from all around O'ahu.

TAOIST TEMPLE

Founded in 1889, the Lum Sai Ho Tong Society was one of more than 100 societies

O'AHU

ALA MOANA & UNIVERSITY AREA

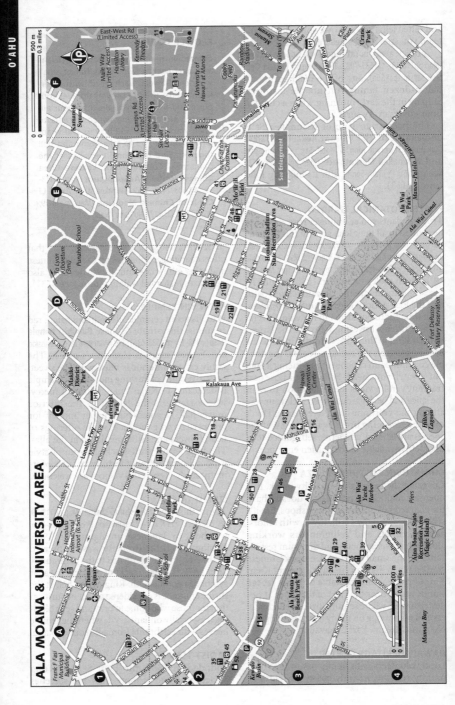

started by Chinese immigrants in Hawaii to help preserve their cultural identity. This one was for the Lum clan, hailing from west of the Yellow River. At one time the society had more than 4000 members, and even now there are nearly a thousand Lums in the Honolulu phone book.

The society's Taoist **temple** (Map pp118-19; 1315 River St) honors the goddess Tin Hau, a Lum child who rescued her father from drowning and was later deified. Some believers still claim to see her apparition when traveling by boat. The temple is not usually open to the public, but you can admire the colorful exterior while walking by.

Ala Moana & University Area

Meaning 'Path to the Sea,' Ala Moana is the nickname of the area west of Waikiki, which includes Honolulu's largest beach park and Hawaii's largest shopping center.

ALA MOANA BEACH PARK

Opposite Ala Moana Center mall, this **park** (Map p122; 1201 Ala Moana Blvd; admission free; **P**) claims a nearly mile-long golden beach buffered from passing traffic by shade trees. Honolulu residents go jogging, play volleyball and enjoy weekend picnics here, yet it never feels too crowded. The beach is safe for swimming and a good spot for distance laps. However, at low tide the deep channel running the length of the beach can be a hazard if you don't realize it's there – it drops off suddenly to overhead depths. The park has full beach facilities, 10 **tennis courts** lighted for night play and free parking.

The peninsula jutting from the east side of the park is 'Aina Moana State Recreation Area, aka **Magic Island**. High-school outrigger-canoe teams often practice here in the late afternoon during the school year. In summer it's a hot surfing spot. There's an idyllic walk around the perimeter of the peninsula. It's especially picturesque at sunset, with sailboats pulling in and out of Ala Wai Yacht Harbor.

HONOLULU ACADEMY OF ARTS

This exceptional **museum** (Map p122; ☎ 532-8700; www.honoluluacademy.org; 900 S Beretania St; adult/senior & student $10/5, child under 13 free, all free 1st Wed & 3rd Sun of each month; ☼ 10am-4:30pm Tue-Sat, 1-5pm Sun; **P**) may be the biggest surprise of your trip to O'ahu. It covers the artistic traditions of almost every continent, playing a leading role in the area of Asian art. Here you can see masterpieces by Monet, Matisse and Gauguin; galleries of Greek and Roman antiquities and

CRUISING FOR ART

Smart urban professionals now flock to once-seedy Nu'uanu Ave in Chinatown for a dose of art and culture, socializing, live music and bar-hopping. The city's **First Friday Gallery Walk** (🕙 5–9pm 1st Fri of each month) is prime time for Chinatown's art galleries, which set out free *pupu* (appetizers) and host entertainment to lure browsers. Pick up a walking map from any of two dozen art galleries; most are in a two-block radius of the landmark Hawaii Theatre (p139).

A good place to start is at **Pegge Hopper Gallery** (Map pp118-19; ☎ 524-1160; 1164 Nu'uanu Ave), which represents the namesake artist's distinctive prints and paintings depicting voluptuous island women. **Bethel St Gallery** (Map pp118-19; ☎ 524-3552; 1140 Bethel St) is an artist-owned cooperative displaying a mixed plate, from blown-glass sculptures to abstract painting. **Ramsay Galleries** (Map pp118-19; ☎ 537-2787; 1128 Smith St) specializes in detailed pen-and-ink drawings and works by well-known Hawaii artists. For übercool 'lowbrow' art and one-of-a-kind customized surfboards, drop by the **Chinatown Boardroom** (Map pp118-19; ☎ 585-7200; 1160 Nu'uanu Ave).

Escape the culture vultures at Hank's Cafe Honolulu (p137), which serves thirsty locals shots of art, spirits and live jazz at the Dragon Upstairs (p138), or grab dinner at a neighborhood restaurant (p133) before hitting the nightclub and lounge scene (p137) that cranks up later in the evening.

Italian Renaissance paintings; major works of American modern art; ancient Japanese woodblock prints by Hiroshige and Hokusai; Ming dynasty–era Chinese calligraphy and painted scrolls; Indian temple carvings; war clubs and masks from Papua New Guinea – and so much more.

As explained by museum director Stephen Little, 'The museum was founded in 1927 by Anna Rice Cooke to create an art collection that would reflect the diversity of the local population. She wanted this to be a place where children who are born here could come and examine their own cultural roots through the window of works of art and just as importantly discover something about their neighbors.'

Plan on spending a couple of hours here, maybe stopping for lunch at the Pavilion Café (p135) and joining a tour out to Shangri La (p165), Doris Duke's enchanting estate near Diamond Head. Four-hour validated parking at the nearby Art Center lot costs $3.

UNIVERSITY OF HAWAI'I AT MANOA

Born too late for the tweedy academic architecture of the mainland, **University of Hawai'i at Manoa** (UH; Map p122; ☎ 956-8111; www.uhm.hawaii.edu; cnr University Ave & Dole St; 🅿), the central campus of the statewide university system, is filled with shade trees and well-bronzed students, including from around Polynesia. UH Manoa has strong academic programs in astronomy, geophysics, marine sciences, and Hawaiian and Pacific studies.

Staff members at the **UH Information & Visitor Center** (Map p122; ☎ 956-7236; Room 212, Campus Center; 🕙 8:30am-4:30pm Mon-Fri) offer campus maps and free one-hour **walking tours** of the campus, emphasizing history and architecture. Tours leave from Campus Center at 2pm on Monday, Wednesday and Friday; to join a tour, show up 10 minutes beforehand. A *Campus Art* brochure, also available at the information center, outlines a self-guided walking tour of outdoor sculptures and other works by distinguished Hawaii artists.

A short walk downhill, the **John Young Museum of Art** (Map p122; ☎ 956-8866; Krauss Hall, 2500 Dole St; admission free; 🕙 11am-2pm Mon-Fri, 1-4pm Sun) houses a 20th-century Hawaii painter's eclectic collection of artifacts from Pacific islands, Africa and Asia, including impressive ceramics, pottery and sculpture. Although it fills only two rooms, it's worth a quick look.

On the east side of campus, the **East-West Center** (Map p122; ☎ 944-7111; www.eastwestcenter.org; 1601 East-West Rd) aims to promote mutual understanding among the peoples of Asia, the Pacific and the USA. Changing exhibitions of art and culture are displayed in the center's **gallery** (Map p122; ☎ 944-7177; Burns Hall; admission free; 🕙 8am-5pm Mon-Fri, noon-4pm Sun). The center also hosts multicultural programs, including lectures, films, concerts and dance performances.

On-campus parking costs $3 before 4pm on weekdays; otherwise it's free.

Upper Manoa Valley, Tantalus & Makiki Heights

Welcome to Honolulu's green belt. The verdant Upper Manoa Valley climbs beyond the UH Manoa campus through exclusive residential neighborhoods into forest reserve land high in the Ko'olau Range above Honolulu. For popular hiking trails, including to Manoa Falls and the Nu'uanu Valley Lookout, turn to p128.

LYON ARBORETUM

Beautifully unkempt walking trails wind through this highly regarded 200-acre **arboretum** (Map p125; ☎ 988-0456; wwwdev.hawaii.edu/lyonarboretum; 3860 Manoa Rd; admission by donation; ☽ 9am-4pm Mon-Fri; ℗), founded in 1918 and managed by the University of Hawai'i. This is not your typically precious landscaped island tropical flower garden, but a mature and largely wooded arboretum, where related species are clustered in a seminatural state.

Among the plants in the Hawaiian ethnobotanical garden are *'ulu* (breadfruit), *kalo* (taro) and *ko* (sugarcane) brought by early Polynesian settlers; *kukui*, once harvested to produce lantern oil; and *ti*, which was used for medicinal purposes during ancient times and for making moonshine after Westerners arrived. If you walk uphill for about a mile along a dirt jeep road, a narrow, tree root–entangled footpath leads to seasonal 'Aihualama Falls, a lacy cliffside cascade (no swimming).

From the Ala Moana Center, catch TheBus No 5 to Manoa Valley and get off at the last stop, then walk 0.5 miles uphill to the end of Manoa Rd. There is limited free parking available.

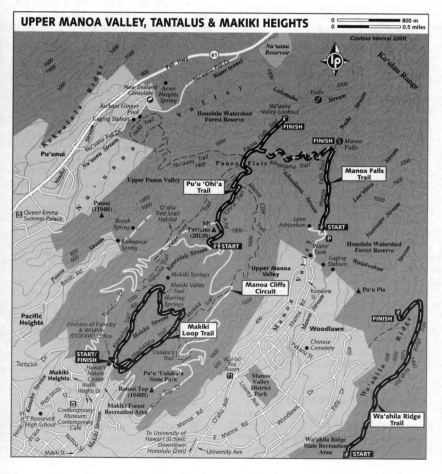

UPPER MANOA VALLEY, TANTALUS & MAKIKI HEIGHTS

MR OBAMA'S NEIGHBORHOOD

If you want to follow in the footsteps of US President Barack Obama, who grew up in Honolulu's Makiki Heights neighborhood, here are a few of his favorite places on O'ahu:

- **Manoa Falls** (p128)
- **Rainbow Drive-In** (p157)
- **Kapi'olani Beach Park** (p150)
- **Hanauma Bay** (p166)
- **Sandy Beach** (p168)
- **Olomana Golf Links** (p172)

To learn more about the 44th US President's childhood in Hawaii, read *The Dream Begins: How Hawaii Shaped Barack Obama* by Stu Glauberman and Jerry Burris.

CONTEMPORARY MUSEUM

Inside an estate house with meditative sculpture and flowering gardens, this engaging **art museum** (Map p125; TCM; ☎ 526-1322; www.tcmhi.org; 2411 Makiki Heights Dr; adult/senior & student/child under 13 $5/3/free, all free 3rd Thu of each month; ☾ 10am-4pm Tue-Sat, noon-4pm Sun, tours usually 1:30pm Tue-Sun; ℗) features changing exhibits of paintings, sculpture and other artwork dating from the 1940s onward by Hawaii-born, mainland and international artists.

A newer building on the lawn holds the museum's most prized piece, an environmental installation by David Hockney based on sets for *L'Enfant et les Sortilèges*, Ravel's 1925 opera. The refreshing Contemporary Café (p136) prepares lunch and packs romantic picnic baskets that you can enjoy alfresco.

From Waikiki, take either TheBus 2 or B Country Express! toward downtown Honolulu and get off at Beretania and Alapa'i Sts; walk one block toward the ocean along Alapa'i St and transfer to TheBus 15, which stops at the museum. If you're driving, follow Makiki St north of S Beretania St (see Map p122), then turn left onto Makiki Heights Dr. There's free parking.

PU'U 'UALAKA'A STATE PARK

For a remarkable panoramic view across Honolulu, detour to this tiny **park** (Map p125; admission free; ☾ 7am-7:45pm Apr-Aug, to 6:45pm Sep-Mar; ℗). The entrance is 2.5 miles up Round Top

Dr from Makiki St. It's half a mile in to the lookout; bear to the left when the road forks. The sweeping views extend from Diamond Head on the far left, across Waikiki and downtown Honolulu, to the Wai'anae Range on the right. To the southeast is the University of Hawai'i at Manoa, easily recognized by its sports stadium. To the southwest you can see clearly into the green mound of Punchbowl crater. The airport is visible on the coast, with Pearl Harbor beyond that.

Greater Honolulu

BISHOP MUSEUM

Like Hawaii's version of the Smithsonian Institute in Washington, DC, this **museum** (Map p114; ☎ 847-3511; www.bishopmuseum.org; 1525 Bernice St; adult/senior & child 4-12 $16/13; ☾ 9am-5pm; ℗) showcases a remarkable array of cultural and natural history and science exhibits. It is often ranked as the finest Polynesian anthropological museum in the world. Founded in 1889 in honor of Princess Bernice Pauahi Bishop, a descendant of the Kamehameha dynasty, it originally housed only Hawaiian and royal artifacts.

The recently renovated main gallery, the **Hawaiian Hall**, resides inside a dignified three-story Victorian building. Displays covering the cultural history of Hawaii include a *pili*-grass thatched house, carved *ki'i akua* (temple images), *kahili* (feathered staffs used at royal funerals and coronations), shark-toothed war clubs and traditional *tapa* cloth made by pounding the bark of the paper mulberry tree. Don't miss the feathered cloak once worn by

---

DETOUR: TANTALUS–ROUND TOP SCENIC DRIVE

Two miles above downtown Honolulu, a narrow switchback road cuts its way up into the forest-reserve land of the Makiki Valley (Map p125). Rewarding drivers with skyline views, it climbs almost to the top of Mt Tantalus (2013ft), aka Pu'u 'Ohi'a. Bamboo, ginger, elephant-eared taro and eucalyptus trees are among the profusion of tropical plants along the way. Vines climb to the tops of telephone poles and twist their way across the wires. This 8.5-mile circuit is a two-way loop that's called Tantalus Dr on the western side and Round Top Dr on the east.

Kamehameha the Great, created entirely of the yellow feathers of the now-extinct *mamo* – some 80,000 birds were caught and plucked to create this single adornment. Upper-floor exhibits delve into the relationships between Native Hawaiians and the land, as well as the diversity of contemporary society in Hawaii.

The two-story exhibits inside the adjacent **Polynesian Hall** cover the myriad cultures of Polynesia, Micronesia and Melanesia. You could spend hours gazing at astounding and rare ritual artifacts, from elaborate dance masks and ceremonial costumes to carved canoes and tools of warfare. The museum's more modern wing, the **Castle Memorial Building**, has changing traveling exhibitions next door.

Across the Great Lawn, the state-of-the-art, family-oriented **Science Adventure Center** uses interactive multimedia exhibits and demonstrations to explain Hawaii's natural environment, letting kids walk through an erupting volcano or take a minisub dive. The museum is also home to O'ahu's only **planetarium** (☎ 848-4136), which highlights traditional Polynesian methods of wayfaring (navigation), along with astronomy and the telescope observatories atop Mauna Kea. Shows are usually held at 11:30am, 1:30pm and 3:30pm, and are included in the museum admission price. A **gift shop** off the lobby sells books on the Pacific not easily found elsewhere, as well as some high-quality Hawaiian crafts and souvenirs.

On-site parking is free. From Waikiki or downtown Honolulu, take TheBus 2 School St-Middle St or B City Express! to Kapalama St, then walk one block *makai* and turn right on Bernice St. By car, take the eastbound H-1 Fwy exit 20, go *mauka* on Houghtailing St and turn left on Bernice St.

NATIONAL MEMORIAL CEMETERY OF THE PACIFIC
A mile north of downtown Honolulu surrounded by freeways and residential neighborhoods is a bowl-shaped crater poetically named Punchbowl, formed by a long-extinct volcano. Sitting at an elevation of 500ft, this geologic souvenir offers impressive views of the city, out to Diamond Head and the Pacific beyond. The early Hawaiians called the crater Puowaina, the 'hill of human sacrifices.' It's believed there was once an ancient heiau here and that the slain bodies of *kapu* (taboo) breakers were ceremonially cremated upon an altar.

TOP PICKS – PLACES TO LEARN ABOUT HAWAIIAN CULTURE

- **Bishop Museum** (opposite)
- **Native Books/Nā Mea Hawai'i** (p115)
- **Kumu Kahua Theatre** (p139)
- **Kuhio Beach Torch Lighting & Hula Show** (p160)
- **Na Lima Mili Hulu No'eau** (p162)
- **Ono Hawaiian Food** (p158)
- **Kea'iwa Heiau** (p143)
- **Kane'aki Heiau** (p199)

Today at this **cemetery** (Map p114; ☎ 532-3720; 2177 Puowaina Dr; admission free; 🕙 8am-5:30pm Oct-Feb, to 6:30pm Mar-Sep; 🅿), ancient Hawaiians sacrificed to appease the gods share the crater floor with almost 50,000 US soldiers, many of whom were killed in the Pacific during WWII. The remains of Ernie Pyle, the distinguished war correspondent who covered both world wars and was hit by machine-gun fire on Ie-shima during the final days of WWII, lie in section D, grave 109. Five stones to the left, at grave D-1, is the marker for Ellison Onizuka, the Big Island astronaut who perished in the 1986 *Challenger* space-shuttle disaster. For plum views of the city and Diamond Head, head up to the **lookout** by bearing left after passing through the main cemetery gates.

If you're driving to Punchbowl, there's a marked exit as you start up the Pali Hwy – watch closely, because it comes up quickly! Then just follow the signs through a series of narrow residential streets. Parking is free. From Waikiki, take TheBus 2 toward downtown Honolulu and get off at Beretania and Alapa'i Sts, walk one block *makai* along Alapa'i St and transfer to TheBus 15, then the bus driver where to get off. From the bus stop, it's about a 15-minute uphill walk to the cemetery entrance.

QUEEN EMMA SUMMER PALACE
In the heat and humidity of summer, Queen Emma, the royal consort of Kamehameha IV, used to slip away to this genteel hillside retreat, now a **historical museum** (Map p125; ☎ 595-6291; www.daughtersofhawaii.org; 2931 Pali Hwy; adult/child $6/1; 🕙 9am-4pm; 🅿). The exterior somewhat resembles an old Southern plantation house,

O'AHU

with its columned porch, high ceilings and louvered windows catching the breezes.

Forgotten after Queen Emma's death in 1885, this stately home was slated to be razed and the estate turned into a public park. The Daughters of Hawai'i, whose members are all descendants of early missionary families, rescued it. The interior now looks much as it did in Queen Emma's day, decorated with period furniture, including a koa-wood cabinet displaying a set of china from England's Queen Victoria and feather cloaks and capes once worn by Hawaiian royalty.

To get here, take TheBus 4 from Waikiki, or bus 56 or 57A from the Ala Moana Center. Be sure to let the bus driver know where you're going, so you don't miss the stop. If you're driving, look for the entrance near the 2-mile marker on the Pali Hwy (Hwy 61); free parking is limited.

ACTIVITIES

UH's Campus Center Leisure Programs (p131) runs a variety of public classes and trips, from snorkeling excursions ($25) and half-day introductory bodyboarding classes ($20) to intensive one-week PADI certification courses ($210).

Swimming & Surfing

Hands down, Honolulu's best ocean swimming is at Ala Moana Beach Park (p123). There are intermediate-level surf breaks just off Ala Moana Beach Park, while those off **Kaka'ako Waterfront Park** (Map p114) are for advanced surfers only. Rent surfboards near UH Manoa from **Aloha Board Shop** (Map p122; ☎ 955-6030; www.alohaboardshop.com; 2600 S King St; 3-day/weekly rental $60/100; ☺ 10am-7pm Mon-Sat, 11am-5pm Sun).

Hiking

You could spend days enjoying the solitude of the hills surrounding the city. Inside the Makiki Forest Recreation Area, Hawaii's **Division of Forestry & Wildlife** (Map p125; DOFAW; ☎ 973-9778; www.hawaiitrails.org; 2135 Makiki Heights Dr; ☺ 7:45am-4:30pm Mon-Fri) distributes free trail maps. Outside the office, next to a soda-vending machine, there's a drinking fountain good for filling water bottles. For directions to this office, see the Makiki Valley Loop trail section, right. For island hiking clubs, see p108. For guided hiking tours, see p112.

MANOA FALLS & NU'UANU VALLEY LOOKOUT

Maybe Honolulu's most rewarding short hike, the 1.5-mile round-trip **Manoa Falls Trail** (Map p125) runs above a rocky streambed through lush vegetation. Tall tree trunks line the path, including *Eucalyptus robusta*, with soft, spongy, reddish bark; flowering orange African tulip trees; and other lofty varieties that creak like wooden doors in old houses. Wild orchids and red ginger grow near the falls, which drop 100ft into a small, shallow pool. Falling rocks and the risk of leptospirosis (see p579) make swimming inadvisable. Beware that the trail is often a bit muddy and slippery.

Just before reaching Manoa Falls, the inconspicuous **'Aihualama Trail** branches off west of a chain-link fence, offering broad views of Manoa Valley starting just a short way up the path. After a five-minute walk, you'll enter a bamboo forest with some massive old banyan trees, that contours around the ridge, then switchbacks up. You can hike the trail as a side spur from the Manoa Falls trail or orchestrate a 5.5-mile round-trip hike by connecting with the **Pauoa Flats Trail**, which leads up to the **Nu'uanu Valley Lookout**, from where it's possible to peer through a gap in the steep *pali* (cliffs) over to the Windward Coast.

By car from Waikiki, take McCully St heading into Honolulu and turn left onto Wilder Ave, then right onto Punahou St. Take the left fork when the road splits in two, following Manoa Rd up to the trailhead parking lot ($5). From the Ala Moana Center, take TheBus 5 Manoa Valley bus to the end of the line, from where it's a 10-minute uphill walk.

MAKIKI VALLEY LOOP & MANOA CLIFFS CIRCUIT

A favorite workout for city dwellers, the 2.5-mile **Makiki Loop Trail** (Map p125) links three Tantalus area trails. The loop cuts through a lush and varied tropical forest, mainly composed of nonnative species introduced to reforest an area denuded by the *'iliahi* (sandalwood) trade in the 19th century. Keep an eye out for the archaeological remains of ancient Hawaiian stone walls and a 19th-century coffee plantation. These trails are usually muddy, so wear shoes with traction and pick up a walking stick.

Starting past the Hawaii Nature Center, the **Maunalaha Trail** crosses a small stream, passes

O'AHU

JEWELS OF THE FOREST

O'ahu has an endemic genus of tree snail, the *Achatinella*. Island forests were once loaded with these colorful snails, which clung like gems to the leaves of trees. They were too attractive for their own good, however, and hikers collected them by the handfuls around the turn of the 20th century. Even more devastating has been the deforestation of habitat and the introduction of a cannibal snail and predatory rodents like mongoose. Of O'ahu's 41 *Achatinella* species, only 19 remain today – and all are endangered.

taro patches and climbs up the eastern ridge of Makiki Valley, passing Norfolk pine, banyans and bamboo, with some clear views along the way. After 0.7 miles, you'll come to a four-way junction. Continue uphill on the 1.1-mile **Makiki Valley Trail**, which traverses small gulches and across gentle streams bordered by patches of ginger. Edible yellow guava and strawberry guava also grow along the trail, which offers glimpses of the city below. The **Kanealole Trail** begins as you cross Kanealole Stream, then follows the stream back to the baseyard, 0.7 miles away. This trail leads down through a field of Job's tears; the beadlike bracts of the female flowers of this tall grass are often used for leis.

From the same trailhead, a more strenuous 6.2-mile hike leads to sweeping views of the valley and the ocean beyond. This **Manoa Cliffs Circuit**, aka the Big Loop, starts on the same Maunalaha Trail, then takes the Moleka Trail to the Manoa Cliff, Kalawahine and Nahuina Trails. At the Kalawahine Trail intersection, detour to the right along the Pauoa Flats Trail up to Nu'uanu Valley Lookout (see opposite). From the lookout, backtrack to the Kalawahine Trail, which connects with the Kanealole Trail back down to the forest baseyard.

The starting point for both hikes is the Makiki Forest Recreation Area baseyard, about 0.5 miles up Makiki Heights Dr, if you're approaching from Makiki St. The forest baseyard turnoff is a little lane at a sharp bend in the main road. Park along the shoulder before reaching the Hawaii Nature Center and a branch office of Hawaii's Division of Forestry & Wildlife (see p109). From downtown Honolulu, take TheBus

15, which runs into Pacific Heights. Get off near the intersection of Mott-Smith and Makiki Heights Drs and walk about a mile further along Makiki Heights Dr to the baseyard. From Waikiki, take TheBus 4 Nu'uanu-Dowsett/Pauoa to the corner of Wilder Ave and Makiki St, then walk a mile up Makiki St.

PU'U 'OHI'A (MT TANTALUS) TRAIL

Along the Tantalus–Round Top loop drive (see p126), a network of hiking trails littered with fragrant *liliko'i* (passion fruit) encircles Mt Tantalus, offering contemplative forest hikes with city views. The hardy **Pu'u 'Ohi'a Trail** (Map p125), in conjunction with the Pauoa Flats Trail, leads up to the Nu'uanu Valley Lookout (see opposite), traveling nearly 2 miles each way. You'll find this trailhead at the very top of Tantalus Dr, 3.6 miles up from Makiki Heights Dr; there's a large turnoff for parking opposite the trailhead.

The trail begins with reinforced log steps, leading past fragrant ginger, musical bamboo groves and lots of eucalyptus, a fast-growing tree planted to protect the watershed. After 0.5 miles, the trail summits **Mt Tantalus** (2013ft), also called Pu'u 'Ohia. From below Mt Tantalus, the trail leads back onto a service road that ends at a telephone relay station. Behind the building, the trail continues until it reaches the **Manoa Cliff Trail**, where you'll go left. At the next intersection, turn right onto the Pauoa Flats Trail, which leads to the Nu'uanu Valley Lookout high in the Ko'olau Range. The flats area can be muddy; be careful not to trip on exposed tree roots.

You'll pass two trailheads before reaching the lookout. The first is Nu'uanu Trail, on the left, which runs 0.75 miles along the western side of the upper Pauoa Valley, offering broad views of Honolulu and the Wai'anae Range. The second is the 'Aihualama Trail, a bit further along on the right, which takes you 1.3 miles through tranquil bamboo groves and past huge old banyan trees to Manoa Falls (see opposite).

WA'AHILA RIDGE TRAIL

Popular with families, the boulder-strewn **Wa'ahila Ridge Trail** (Map p125) offers a cool retreat amid Norfolk pines and endemic plants, with ridgetop views of Honolulu and Waikiki. The 4.8-mile trail covers a variety of terrain in a short time, making an enjoyable afternoon's walk for novice hikers. Look for the Na Ala Hele trailhead sign just past the picnic tables deep inside Wa'ahila Ridge State Recreation Area, at the back of the St Louis Heights subdivision, east of Manoa Valley.

By car, follow Wai'alae Ave east of Waikiki into the Kaimuki neighborhood (see off-map arrow, Map p122), then turn left onto St Louis Dr. Turn right near the top of Peter St, then left onto Ruth Pl, which runs west into the park. From Waikiki, TheBus 14 St Louis Heights stops at the intersection of Peter and Ruth Sts, about a 15-minute walk from the trailhead.

Whale Watching

From late December through mid-April, **Atlantis Adventures** (Map pp118-19; ☎ 973-1311, 800-548-6262; www.atlantisadventures.com; Pier 6, Aloha Tower Dr) offers naturalist-led whale-watching cruises aboard the *Navatek I*, a sleek, high-tech catamaran designed to minimize rolling. Tours (2½-hour tour including buffet lunch adult/child $65/33) usually depart at noon daily. Reservations are recommended.

Cycling

The **Bike Shop** (Map p122; ☎ 596-0588; 1149 S King St; rentals per day $20-40; ☺ 9am-7pm Mon-Fri, 9am-5pm Sat, 10am-5pm Sun) rents top-quality road bikes and can provide maps of suggested cycling routes to match your interest. Cyclists often head up to the scenic Tantalus–Round Top loop road (p126) for an athletic workout.

Golf

Hawaii's oldest golf course is the nine-hole/par 36 **Moanalua Golf Club** (Map p114; ☎ 839-2411; http://moanaluagolfclubhawaii.com; 1250 Ala Aolani St; green fees $25-40; ☺ by appt Mon-Fri). Built in 1898 by a missionary family, it's a fairly quick course with an elevated green, straight fairways and nine holes that can be played twice around.

WALKING TOUR

Honolulu's most foot-trafficked neighborhood is Chinatown (p120), filled with bustling markets and eateries, nostalgic antiques shops and nouveau art galleries.

Start at **Chinatown Gateway Plaza** (1), where stone lions mark the neighborhood's official entrance. Walk northeast along Bethel St to the neoclassical 1922 **Hawaii Theatre** (2; p139). Nicknamed the 'Pride of the Pacific,' it showed movies until Waikiki's more modern cinemas

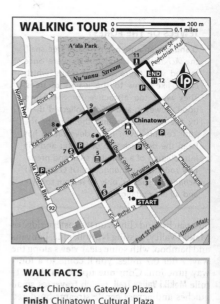

WALK FACTS
Start Chinatown Gateway Plaza
Finish Chinatown Cultural Plaza
Distance 1 mile
Duration one or two hours

brought down the curtain in the 1970s. Now gloriously restored, the performing-arts theater sometimes offers one-hour guided tours ($5) at 11am on Tuesday mornings; call ahead to confirm schedules.

Proceed up Pauahi St and turn left on Nu'uanu Ave, where you'll see the now-abandoned **Pantheon Bar** (3), Honolulu's oldest watering hole and a favorite of sailors in days past. The granite-block sidewalks of Nu'uanu Ave are also relics, built with the discarded ballasts of 19th-century trading ships that brought tea from China in exchange for 'iliahi (sandalwood). At the corner of King St, peek into the **First Hawaiian Bank** (4), with its antique wooden teller cages. Incidentally, Kate's bank robbery scene in the TV show *Lost* was shot here.

Turn right onto King St, then right on Smith St. Poke your head into the **Hawai'i Heritage Center** (5; p121). Soon you'll intersect seedy N Hotel St, undergoing a transformation from a red-light district into a row of nightclubs and lounges. Turn left onto N Hotel St and walk to the corner of Maunakea St, where the ornate facade of the **Wo Fat Building** (6) resembles a Chinese temple. Turn left and walk down Maunakea St, then right onto N King St.

Walk past the red pillars coiled with dragons outside the **Bank of Hawaii (7)** and keep going to the corner of Kekaulike St and the bustling **O'ahu Market (8**; p120), where boxes of iced fish and fresh produce await eager morning shoppers. Walk north up the Kekaulike St pedestrian mall to **Maunakea Marketplace (9**; p133). Stroll past its dozen pan-Asian lunch counters, turning right as you emerge onto Pauahi St.

At the corner of Pauahi and Maunakea Sts, O'ahu's thriving lei industry is in full bloom. You'll pass clusters of tiny **lei shops (10)** where skilled artisans, some with glasses studiously tilted down, string and braid blossom after blossom, filling the air with the scents of pikake and ginger. Turn left onto Maunakea St, then left again onto N Beretania St.

Down by the riverside, the **Dr Sun Yat-sen statue (11)** honors the Chinese revolutionary. The utilitarian modern building next door is **Chinatown Cultural Plaza (12**; p121), where you can feast at dim-sum palaces and bite into Buddhist vegetarian fake meats or *manapua* (island-style steamed or baked buns with various fillings).

COURSES

Native Books/Nā Mea Hawaii (Map p122; ☎ 596-8885; www.nativebookshawaii.com; Ward Warehouse, 1050 Ala Moana Blvd) This bookstore hosts free classes, workshops and demonstrations in hula dancing, Hawaiian language, traditional feather lei–making and ukulele playing.

our pick **Campus Center Leisure Programs** (Map p122; ☎ 956-6468; www.hawaii.edu/cclp; Room 101, Hemenway Hall, 2445 Campus Center Rd; classes from $20) UH Manoa offers a variety of short-term courses open to the public. Some courses, including hula, yoga and slack key guitar, meet a couple of times a week during a month-long session.

HONOLULU FOR CHILDREN

For endless sand and calm waters, take your *keiki* to **Ala Moana Beach Park** (p123), where local families hang out. The **Bishop Museum** (p126) is entertaining for kids of all ages. There's an interactive family art center in the basement of the **Honolulu Academy of Arts** (p123).

For more of O'ahu's great outdoors, head up into the Upper Manoa Valley to the **Lyon Arboretum** (p124), then hike to pretty **Manoa Falls** (p128).

For the best islandwide activities for kids, see p109.

Hawaii Children's Discovery Center

On a rainy day when you can't go to the beach, take your tots to this hands-on, family-oriented **museum** (Map p114; ☎ 524-5437; www .discoverycenterhawaii.org; 111 'Ohe St; adult/senior/child 1-17 $8/6/8; ♥ 9am-1pm Tue-Fri, 10am-3pm Sat & Sun; **ⓟ**). Occupying a 38,000-sq-ft waterfront site, this was once the city's garbage incinerator, as evidenced by the surviving smokestack reaching skyward.

Interactive exhibits are geared toward elementary school–aged children and preschoolers. **Fantastic You!** explores the human body, allowing kids to walk through a mock human stomach. More traditional displays are found in the **Your Town** section, where kids can drive an interactive fire engine or conduct TV interviews. Two other sections, **Hawaiian Rainbows** and **Your Rainbow World**, touch on Hawaii's multicultural heritage.

From Waikiki, take TheBus 19 or 20; it's a five-minute walk from the nearest bus stop on Ala Moana Blvd. If you're driving, there's limited free parking.

TOURS

For a self-guided walking tour of Chinatown, see opposite. For more conventional bus tours, see p112.

Hawaii Food Tours (☎ 926-3663, 800-715-2468; www .hawaiifoodtours.com; tours incl transportation $99-$149) Former chef and restaurant critic for the *Honolulu Advertiser* runs a four-hour lunchtime tour sampling Chinatown's ethnic hole-in-the-walls; a three-hour evening tour delves into traditional Hawaiian and contemporary island cuisine.

Hawai'i Heritage Center (Map pp118-19; ☎ 521-2749; 1117 Smith St; ♥ 9:30-11:30am Wed & Fri; tours $10) Insightful walking tours of Chinatown depart from the storefront gallery.

FESTIVALS & EVENTS

Year-round, festivals and events take place at various venues all over the city, including in Waikiki (p153).

Chinese New Year (☎ 533-3181; www.chinatownhi .com) Between late January and mid-February, Chinatown festivities include a parade, lion dances and firecrackers.

Honolulu Festival (☎ 926-2424; www.honolulufestival .com) Two days of Asian-Pacific cultural exchange with music, dance and drama performances in mid-March.

Pan-Pacific Festival (☎ 926-8177; www.pan-pacific -festival.com) Three days of Japanese, Hawaiian and South

O'AHU

Pacific entertainment in early June, with music, dancing and *taiko* drumming at the Ala Moana Center.

King Kamehameha Hula Competition (☎ 586-0333; http://hawaii.gov) One of Hawaii's biggest hula contests, with hundreds of dancers competing at the Neal S Blaisdell Center (Map p122) in early June.

Prince Lot Hula Festival (☎ 839-5334; www.mgf-hawaii.org) The state's oldest and largest noncompetitive hula event at the Moanalua Gardens (Map p114) in late July.

Hawaii Dragon Boat Festival Colorful dragon boats race to the beat of island drummers at Ala Moana Beach Park (Map p122) in late August.

Talk Story Festival (☎ 768-3003; www.co.honolulu.hi.us/parks/programs) Storytellers gather at Ala Moana Beach Park (Map p122) in mid-October; Friday is usually spooky stories.

Hawaii International Film Festival (www.hiff.org) This celebration of celluloid screens Pacific Rim and homegrown films in late October.

King Kalakaua's Birthday Victorian-era decorations and a concert of traditional monarchy-era music by the Royal Hawaiian Band at 'Iolani Palace (p116) on November 16.

SLEEPING

Downtown Honolulu doesn't have much in the way of accommodations. That's because Waikiki functions as the nearest bedroom community for tourists. The Ala Moana Center has a few options right outside Waikiki by the island's central bus terminal. Otherwise, unless you have business downtown or are visiting relatives, you're probably better off in Waikiki.

Hostelling International–Honolulu (Map p122; ☎ 946-0591; www.hostelsaloha.com; 2323-A Seaview Ave; dm $20-23, r $46-52; ◷ reception 8am-noon & 4pm-midnight; P ☜ ▣) This small, tidy house is hidden in a residential neighborhood near UH Manoa, just a short bus ride from Waikiki. Sex-segregated dorms are sunny and breezy. Some students use this as a landing pad before finding an apartment, so it's often full. There's a kitchen, laundry room, lockers and limited free parking.

Central Branch YMCA (Map p122; ☎ 941-3344; www.ymcahonolulu.org; 401 Atkinson Dr; s with/without bathroom $45/37; ▣ ☜ ▣) Walking distance to Waikiki, the good ol' Y is a reliable deal, as long as you're not fussy. Basic rooms with shared bathrooms are for men only, while infinitesimally larger rooms which come with bathrooms are available to women too. Bonus perks include the use of an Olympic-sized swimming pool and the modern, fully-equipped gym.

Pagoda Hotel (Map p122; ☎ 923-4511, 800-472-4632; www.pagodahotel.com; 1525 Rycroft St; r $95-169, 1br $105-185; P ▨ ▣ ☜ ▣) This mid-20th-century survivor has terribly outdated decor but a kitschy sense of place. The no-frills Pagoda is divided into a 12-story hotel tower and a nearby apartment complex with kitchenettes. It's mostly popular with Neighbor Islands visitors, mainly as an alternative to the hectic Waikiki scene. Surcharge applies for in-room wired high-speed internet access, and lobby and poolside wi-fi.

Ala Moana Hotel (Map p122; ☎ 955-4811, from Neighbor Islands 800-446-8990, from US mainland & Canada 800-367-6025; www.alamoanahotel.com; 410 Atkinson Dr; r $149-330, ste from $300; P ▨ ▣ ☜ ▣) Looming above the Ala Moana Center, this multistory condotel near the convention center has executive-strength rooms with bland trimmings. Prices rise as you climb higher up in the tower to gain a city or ocean view. You'll share the check-in line with airline crews and conventioneers. Free in-room wired internet; lobby wi-fi costs extra.

For overnight layovers near the airport, these places offer complimentary 24-hour airport shuttles:

Best Western Plaza Hotel (Map p114; ☎ 836-3636, 800-800-4683; www.bestwesternhawaii.com; 3253 N Nimitz Hwy; r $129-159; P ▨ ▣ ☜ ▣) Top pick among airport-area hotels, though noisy rooms front the highway; parking $5.

Ohana Honolulu Airport Hotel (Map p114; ☎ 836-0661, 866-968-8744; www.ohanahotels.com; 3401 N Nimitz Hwy; r $139-209; ▨ ▣ ☜ ▣) Also near the airport, with free lobby wi-fi and wired in-room high-speed internet; parking $15.

EATING

You might sleep and play in Waikiki, but you should definitely eat in Honolulu, where a bounty of restaurants reflect the city's multi-ethnic population. We'd like to think that if Hawaii wasn't so far away from the US mainland, you'd hear a lot more buzz about this chowhound capital. During **Restaurant Week Hawaii** (www.restaurantweekhawaii.com), usually held in mid-November, some local restaurants offer a plethora of dining-out discounts, including prix-fixe dinners.

Downtown

Many restaurants are only open on weekdays for the lunchtime office crowd. After dark, Restaurant Row has new hot spots worth trying, despite its checkered history. The harborfront Aloha Tower Marketplace is great for sunset drinks and *pupu* (appetizers), but not so much for full meals.

Honolulu Café (Map pp118-19; ☎ 533-1555; ground fl, Pacific Guardian Center, 741 Bishop St; mains $4-10; ⏰ 7:45am-4pm Mon-Fri) In a breezy walkway through the Dillingham Building, formerly a hub for US 'robber barons' who once ruled Hawaii's economy, this chef-owned café is an easy walk from the Aloha Tower. Daily specials are adventurous; creative grilled panini and entrée salads are almost always delish.

Downtown (Map pp118-19; ☎ 536-5900; 1040 Richards St; mains $6-15; ⏰ lunch Mon-Fri) Inside the Hawai'i State Art Museum, this arty café is an outpost of Kaimuki's ultratrendy Town restaurant (p137). Market-fresh salads, soups, sandwiches and creative plate lunches break through barriers – just consider the cantaloupe sorbet, lotus-root chips and 'ahi club sandwiches.

Cafe Laniakea (Map pp118-19; ☎ 538-7061; 1040 Richards St; mains $8-12; ⏰ 11am-2pm Mon-Fri) Unpretentious and health-conscious, this café runs with an entirely different crowd than your average 'Y' mess hall. Set in the courtyard of the historic Julia Morgan–designed YWCA, it has a changing menu committed to locally grown, often organic ingredients such as 'Nalo greens and North Shore free-range, grass-fed beef.

Hiroshi Eurasian Tapas (Map pp118-19; ☎ 533-4476; Restaurant Row, 500 Ala Moana Blvd; mains $22-37; ⏰ 5:30-9:30pm) A legend on the Honolulu foodie scene, Hiroshi Fukui (former chef of L'Uraku) puts a Japanese twist on Pacific Rim fusion styles, from crab cannelloni swirled with miso sauce to smoked *hamachi* (yellowtail) spiced with habanero peppers and a garlic kicker. You can order tropically flavored martinis and house-made fruit-purée sodas at the bar, or duck next door to vivacious Vino, a wine bar and Italian tapas restaurant.

Also recommended:

People's Open Market (off Map pp118-19; ☎ 522-7088; City Hall parking lot deck, cnr Alapa'i & Beretania Sts; ⏰ 10-11am Wed) Farmers market sells fresh bounty from the land and sea.

'Umeke Market & Deli (Map pp118-19; ☎ 522-7377; 1001 Bishop St; ⏰ 7am-4pm Mon-Fri) Organic island-grown produce, natural-foods groceries and a vegan-friendly takeout deli.

Vita Juice (Map pp118-19; ☎ 526-1396; 1111-C Fort St Mall; items $4-6; ⏰ 7am-5pm Mon-Fri, 9am-3pm Sat) Exotic smoothie bar mixes up 'brain food' and sells home-made cookies.

Chinatown

This historic downtown neighborhood is packed with markets, hole-in-the-wall eateries, noodle factories, dim-sum palaces, pan-Asian kitchens and trendy upscale fusion restaurants.

BUDGET

Royal Kitchen (Map pp118-19; ☎ 524-4461; Chinatown Cultural Plaza, 100 N Beretania St; items from $1; ⏰ 5:30am-4pm Mon-Fri, 6:30am-4:30pm Sat, 6:30am-2pm Sun) This humble takeout shop is worth fighting Chinatown's snarled traffic just to try its famous *manapua* with an inventive variety of fillings such as *char siu* (Chinese barbecue pork), chicken curry, sweet potato, *kalua* pig or black sugar.

Ba Le (Map pp118-19; ☎ 521-3973; 150 N King St; mains $3-9; ⏰ 6am-5pm Mon-Sat, to 3pm Sat) Its name a corruption of the word 'Paris,' this fluorescent-lit bakery-café is an island-born chain, best known for its chewy baguette sandwiches. For a caffeine jolt, there's an equally chewy cup of coffee served either hot or iced, with loads of sugar and milk. Yeehaw!

To Chau (Map pp118-19; ☎ 533-4549; 1007 River St; mains $5-8; ⏰ 8am-2:30pm) Always packed, this Vietnamese restaurant holds fast to its reputation for serving Honolulu's best *pho* (Vietnamese noodle soup). Beef, broth and vegetables – the dish is a complete meal in itself, but the menu includes other Vietnamese standards too. Just 16 tables means long lines.

Mei Sum Dim Sum (Map pp118-19; ☎ 531-3268; 65 N Pauahi St; dim-sum dishes $2-4, mains $6-12; ⏰ 7am-8:45pm) Where else are you gonna go to satisfy that crazy craving for dim sum after noon? This no-nonsense corner shop cranks out cheap, delectable little plates. It has also got a full spread of Chinese mains; order the secret garlic eggplant that's not on the menu.

Maunakea Marketplace (Map pp118-19; 1120 Maunakea St; meals from $6; ⏰ 7am-3:30pm) At this back-alley food court, mom-and-pop vendors dish out home-style Chinese, Filipino, Thai, Vietnamese, Korean and Japanese fare. You can chow down at tiny wooden tables crowded into the central walkway.

Legend Vegetarian Restaurant (Map pp118-19; ☎ 532-8218; Chinatown Cultural Plaza, 100 N Beretania St; dim-sum dishes from $2.50, mains $8-13; ⏰ 10:30am-2pm Thu-Tue) This 100% Buddhist Chinese vegetarian, lunch-only spot is known for its extensive menu of fake seafood and meat dishes using tofu and wheat gluten to mimic island classics like sweet-and-sour pork or butterfish.

ourpick Little Village Noodle House (Map pp118-19; ☎ 545-3008; 1113 Smith St; mains $8-15; ☻ 10:30am-10:30pm Sun-Thu, to midnight Fri & Sat) Forget about chop suey: any fish in black-bean sauce here is Honolulu's gold standard. On the eclectic pan-Chinese menu, dishes are served garlicky, fiery or with just the right dose of saltiness. It's full of more surprises, including air-con and free parking out back behind the restaurant. Make reservations.

Also recommended:

Sun Chong Co (Map pp118-19; ☎ 537-3525; 127 N Hotel St; ☻ 7am-5pm) Come early for almond cookies, moon cakes and candied ginger and tropical fruits.

Legend Seafood Restaurant (Map pp118-19; ☎ 532-1868; Chinatown Cultural Plaza, 100 N Beretania St; dim-sum dishes $2.50-4, mains $8-20; ☻ 10:30am-2pm Mon-Fri, 8am-2pm Sat & Sun, 5:30-9:30pm daily) Impersonal banquet hall wheels heavily laden dim-sum carts for connoisseurs.

MIDRANGE & TOP END

Soul de Cuba (Map pp118-19; ☎ 545-2822; 1121 Bethel St; mains $7-22; ☻ 11:30am-10pm Mon-Thu, to 11pm Fri & Sat) Sate your craving for Afro-Cuban food and out-of-this-world *mojitos* inside this restauro-lounge near Chinatown's art galleries, often with live music. Stick with family-recipe classics like *ropa vieja* (shredded beef in tomato sauce) and black-bean soup.

Duc's Bistro (Map pp118-19; ☎ 531-6325; 1188 Maunakea St; mains lunch $12-19, dinner $16-32; ☻ 11am-2pm Mon-Fri, 5-10pm Mon-Sat) Honolulu's power brokers hang out at this swank French-Vietnamese bistro, an escape from the seediness just outside. Flat-iron steaks, buttery escargots, fire-roasted eggplant with lime dressing, and pan-fried fish with mango relish round out a haute fusion menu. A small jazz combo serenades most evenings. Reservations recommended.

Indigo (Map pp118-19; ☎ 521-2900; 1121 Nu'uanu Ave; mains $18-30; ☻ 11:30am-2pm Tue-Fri, 6-9:30pm Tue-Sat) Once a standard-bearer for a revitalized Chinatown, this still-busy eatery has let its lunch slide to a buffet level. Creative dim-sum appetizers still include 'ahi tempura rolls and goat-cheese wontons. Dinner features Pacific Rim and Asian fusion fare such as cocoa-bean seafood curry and little-known classics like Malaysian beef *rendang*.

Ala Moana

The bulk of local restaurants are found on side streets around the Ala Moana Center.

BUDGET

Makai Market (Map p122; 1st fl, Ala Moana Center; mains $6-12; ☻ 9am-9pm Mon-Sat, to 7pm Sun) Would you rather die than be caught eating at a shopping-mall food court? Let your preconceptions fly out the window at this Asian-spiced marketplace with air-con comfort. Fave spots include Yummy Korean BBQ, Japanese-style CoCo Curry House and Donburi Don-Don, and Hawaii-flavored Lahaina Chicken and the Poi Bowl.

Da Spot (Map p122; ☎ 941-1313; 908 Pumehana St; smoothies $5, plate lunches $7-10; ☻ 10am-9:30pm Mon-Wed, Fri & Sat, to 4pm Thu) This neighborhood storefront is home base for an enterprising chef duo, crafting smoothies and plate lunches that feature island tastes and around-the-world flavors like Egyptian chicken, Southeast Asian curries and Turkish baklava.

Also recommended:

Foodland (Map p122; ☎ 949-5044; Ala Moana Center, 1450 Ala Moana Blvd; ☻ 6am-10pm Mon-Fri, 7am-10pm Sat, 7am-8pm Sun) Full-service supermarket at Hawaii's biggest mall; free parking.

Ward Farmers Market & Marukai Market Place (Map p122; ☎ 593-9888; Ward Gateway, 1020 Auahi St; ☻ 7am-8pm Mon-Sat, to 6pm Sun) Local-style and Asian fresh produce and prepared meals.

Kua 'Aina (Map p122; ☎ 591-9133; Victoria Ward Centre, 1200 Ala Moana Blvd; mains $5-9; ☻ 10:30am-9pm Mon-Sat, to 8pm Sun) Branch of Hale'iwa's gourmet burger joint, serving crispy matchstick fries.

MIDRANGE

Gyu-Kaku (Map p122; ☎ 589-2989; 1221 Kapi'olani Blvd, enter off Hopaka St; shared dishes $4-21; ☻ 5-11pm Sun-Thu, to midnight Fri & Sat) Who doesn't love a good grill-it-yourself Asian barbecue place? Settle in with your entourage for Kobe rib-eye steak, *kalbi* short ribs, garlic shrimp and enoki mushrooms, all served with plentiful sweet and spicy marinades and dips.

Shokudo Japanese (Map p122; ☎ 941-3701; Ala Moana Pacific Center, 1585 Kapi'olani Blvd; shared dishes $7-17; ☻ 11:30am-1am Sun-Thu, to 2am Fri & Sat) Knock back sake-tinis at this sleek Japanese-esque restaurant always filled to the rafters with island families, urbane couples and late-night clubbers. A mixed menu of island-style and traditional Japanese dishes is the main event, with silky homemade tofu the show stealer.

Side Street Inn (Map p122; ☎ 591-0253; 1225 Hopaka St; plate lunches $6-8, shared dishes $8-18; ☻ 10am-1:30pm Mon-Fri, 4pm-midnight daily) The outside looks like hell, and the sports-bar atmosphere wouldn't rate on a Zagat's survey, but this late-night mecca is where you'll find some of Honolulu's top chefs hanging out in the Naugahyde booths up front after work. Divinely tender *kalbi* short ribs and pork chops are the most famous dishes. Look for a new branch opening on Waikiki's Kapahulu Ave soon.

Sushi Izakaya Gaku (Map p122; ☎ 589-1329; 1329 S King St; shared dishes $8-25; ⏱ 5-11pm Mon-Sat) Popularized by word-of-mouth, this *izakaya* (Japanese pub serving food) beats the competition with adherence to tradition and supremely fresh sushi and sashimi. A spread of savory and sweet hot and cold dishes includes hard-to-find specialties like *chazuke* (tea-soaked rice porridge) and *natto* (fermented soybeans). Reservations are recommended.

Jimbo Restaurant (Map p122; ☎ 947-2211; 1936 S King St; mains $9-15; ⏱ 11am-3pm daily, 5-10pm Sun-Thu, 5-10:30pm Fri & Sat) Folks from around O'ahu drop by for handmade soba and thick *udon* noodles, all made fresh daily, and always fresh and flavorful. Order them cooked in hot broth on rainy days or chilled on a summer's afternoon, then slurp your way to happiness.

Pavilion Café (Map p122; ☎ 532-8734; Honolulu Academy of Arts, 900 S Beretania St; mains $9-15; ⏱ 11:30am-1:30pm Tue-Sat) Looking out onto courtyard fountains, this lovely museum café offers a tantalizing light variety of market-fresh salads and sandwiches, decadent desserts and a refreshing wine list. It's an indulgent way to support the arts. Reservations are recommended, particularly during special events and exhibitions.

our pick Pineapple Room (Map p122; ☎ 945-6573; 3rd fl, Macy's, Ala Moana Center, 1450 Ala Moana Blvd; prix-fixe lunch $22, dinner mains $19-35; ⏱ 11am-8:30pm Mon-Fri, 8am-8:30pm Sat, 9am-3pm Sun) Although Honolulu foodies may howl in disagreement, we prefer Alan Wong's dressed-down café to his

eponymous King St restaurant. Besides, you'll pay less here. All of Chef Wong's classics are made in the exhibition kitchen, along with island-style comfort food like the *kalua* pig BLT sandwich. Desserts are killer, especially the five-sorbet sampler with knock-out pairings of fresh fruit, nuts and candy. Reservations recommended.

TOP END

Alan Wong's (☎ 949-2526; www.alanwongs.com; 1857 S King St; mains $27-52; ⏱ 5-10pm) One of O'ahu's most celebrated chefs, Alan Wong offers his creative, occasionally whimsical interpretations of Hawaii Regional cuisine with extra emphasis on fresh seafood and local produce, especially at bimonthly 'farmers series' dinners. Skip the daily tasting menus, however. Instead rely on signature dishes like ginger-crusted *onaga* (red snapper) and twice-cooked *kalbi* short ribs. Reservations are essential; request a windowside table.

Chef Mavro (Map p122; ☎ 944-4714; 1969 S King St; 4-course dinner without/with wine pairings $69/108; ⏱ 6:30-9:30pm) At Honolulu's most avant-garde restaurant, maverick chef George Mavrothalassitis creates conceptual dishes like abalone ceviche with red *chimichurri* (Argentine herb sauce) paired with Old and New World wines. Textures and fragrances are as important as flavor, which unfortunately means that the cuisine, like the half-empty atmosphere, may fall flat.

University Area

Near the University of Hawai'i's Manoa campus is a cluster of ethnic restaurants that'll go easy on your wallet. It's just a short bus ride from Waikiki.

Well Bento (Map p122; ☎ 941-5261; 2nd fl, 2570 S Beretania St; meals $7-13; ⏱ 10:30am-9pm) This inconspicuous hole-in-the-wall takeout kitchen is the Zen macrobiotic alternative to the plate

---

LATE-NIGHT BITES

An easy walk from the Ala Moana Center, Shokudo Japanese (opposite) and the Side Street Inn (opposite) both keep their kitchens open later than the sleepy-headed island norm, and so do these places:

Liliha Bakery (Map p114; ☎ 531-1651; 515 N Kuakini, cnr Liliha St; mains $6-10; ⏱ nonstop 6am Tue-8pm Sun) All-night diner and bakery causes traffic jams for its coco puff pastries.

Sorabol (Map p122; ☎ 947-3113; 805 Ke'eaumoku St; mains $10-37; ⏱ 24hr) Feeds lunching ladies by day and bleary-headed clubbers before dawn.

Yanagi Sushi (Map p122; ☎ 597-1525; 762 Kapi'olani Blvd; dinner mains $15-31; ⏱ 11am-2pm daily, 5:30pm-2am Mon-Sat, 5:30pm-10pm Sun) 'Late bird' specials available after 10:30pm daily, except Sunday.

TOP PICKS – LOCALS' HANGOUTS IN HONOLULU

- **Ala Moana Beach Park** (p123)
- **Chinatown Cultural Plaza** (p121)
- **Makiki Valley Loop** (p128)
- **Side Street Inn** (p134)
- **Movie Museum** (p139)
- **Town** (opposite)
- **thirtyninehotel** (opposite)
- **La Mariana Sailing Club** (p138)
- **Jazz Minds Art & Cafe** (p138)
- **Aku Bone Lounge** (p138)

lunch, serving veggies and grilled tofu, as well as seared chicken or fish, all free of refined sugar or dairy products. Cash only.

Shōchan Hiroshima-Yaki (Map p122; ☎ 947-8785; 1035 University Ave; mains $8-12; 11:30am-10pm Wed-Mon) Talk about a niche market: this sunny café grills up Hiroshima-style *okonomiyaki* (savory Japanese pancakes) layered with cabbage and barbecue-sauced yakisoba or *udon* noodles topped off by a crepe-thin fried egg. Kids love the *mochi* (Japanese pounded-rice cake) and cheese version. Last order 9pm.

Kiawe Grill BBQ & Burgers (Map p122; ☎ 955-5500; 2334 S King St; mains $8-12; 10am-9pm Mon-Sat, to 8pm Sun) Step into a 1950s time warp. Here green Formica tables heave with plastic plates of exotic venison, ostrich, buffalo and Kobe beef burgers piled high with steak fries or spicy Korean vegetables. Warning: you'll smell like BBQ smoke for the rest of the day.

Spices (Map p122; ☎ 949-2679; 2671-D S King St; mains $11-14; 11:30am-2pm Tue-Fri, 5:30-9:30pm Tue-Sat, 5-9pm Sun) Setting a neighborhood-friendly table free of suffocating ethnic kitsch, this modern Southeast Asian kitchen charges more than the competition, but the variety of Thai curries, Lao soups and Burmese noodles is worth it.

Tsukuneya Robata Grill (Map p122; ☎ 949-0390; 1442 University Ave; shared dishes $4-38; 5pm-midnight Wed-Mon, to 1am Fri & Sat) Imported from Nagoya, this Japanese skewers, grills and deep-fries carnivorous delights. The tender *tsukune* (meatballs) are cooked in a dozen different styles. Kahuku shrimp from the Windward Coast and spicy Hawaiian *'ahi* served on hot lava-rock platters are also specialties of this samurai-worthy house.

our pick **Imanas Tei** (Map p122; ☎ 941-2626; 2626 S King St; shared plates $5-30; 5-11:30pm Mon-Sat) It is no longer Honolulu's top izakaya, but this long-standing spot tucked behind Puck's Alley still draws a crowd. Staff members will shout a raucous chorus of '*Irrashaimase!*' as you walk in the door, then make your way over to tatami-mat tables and booths. Sushi and sake fans can booze it up while they graze their way through an endless menu of epicurean Japanese pub grub, including crowd-pleasing *nabemono* (clay-pot meat and vegetable soups).

Also recommended:

Down to Earth Natural Foods (Map p122; ☎ 947-7678; 2525 S King St; 7:30am-10pm) This natural-foods supermarket also has a vegetarian-friendly salad bar and deli.

Kokua Market (Map p122; ☎ 941-1922; 2643 S King St; 8:30am-8:30pm) Hawaii's only natural-foods co-op offers an organic salad bar and vegan-friendly deli.

Bubbies (Map p122; ☎ 949-8984; Varsity Center, 1010 University Ave; dishes $3-6; noon-midnight Mon-Thu, to 1am Fri & Sat, to 11:30pm Sun) Homemade ice cream in luscious tropical flavors, including made with *mochi*.

Upper Manoa Valley, Tantalus & Makiki Heights

Although hiking boots may look out of place at these genteel cafés, they're convenient places for refueling either before or after hiking around Mt Tantalus.

Waioli Tea Room (Map p125; ☎ 988-5800; 2950 Manoa Rd; mains $6-13; 10:30am-3:30pm Mon-Fri, 8am-3:30pm Sat & Sun) If 19th-century author Robert Louis Stevenson were still hanging around Honolulu today, this is where you'd find him. Set in the verdant Manoa Valley, this restaurant exudes period charm and its open-air dining room overlooks gardens. Light eats like cinnamon-apple waffles and chicken curry sandwiches are served, but the real event is afternoon high tea (reservations required).

Contemporary Café (Map p125; ☎ 523-3362; Contemporary Museum, 2411 Makiki Heights Dr; mains $8-10; 11am-2:30pm Tue-Sat, noon-2:30pm Sun) In the exclusive Makiki Heights neighborhood, this breezy museum café is open to the public – no need to pay the admission fee. Country-club fare like focaccia sandwiches and chocolate gâteau taste even more delectable when packed into romantic picnic baskets for two to enjoy on the garden lawns. Reservations recommended.

Greater Honolulu

In low-key Kaimuki east of Waikiki, Wai'alae Ave is Honolulu's homegrown 'restaurant row,' full of cozy bistros, cafés and old-school bakeries.

Whole Foods (off Map p114; ☎ 738-0820; 4211 Wai'alae Ave; ⊙ 7am-10pm) Near Kaimuki is this organic grocery store with a takeout deli. More off-the-beaten path eateries are scattered around the city, from *mauka* to *makai*.

Helena's Hawaiian Food (Map p114; ☎ 845-8044; 1240 N School St; dishes $2-10; ⊙ 10:30am-7:30pm Tue-Fri) This humble Honolulu institution dates back to 1946. The menu is mostly à la carte dishes, some smoky and salty, others sweet or spicy. Start with *poi* (fermented taro), then add some *pipi kaula* (beef jerky), *kalua* pig, fried butterfish or squid cooked in coconut milk, and you've got a mini-luau for about $12. It's east of Houghtailing St.

Nico's at Pier 38 (Map p114; ☎ 540-1377; 1133 N Nimitz Hwy; mains $4-10; ⊙ 6:30am-5pm Mon-Fri, to 2:30pm Sat) French chef Nico marries classical French cooking with Hawaii culinary traditions and fresh seafood from Honolulu's nearby fish auction. Look for steak frites, tropical fish sandwiches, chicken katsu and hoisin BBQ chicken. Casual outdoor tables are within view of the Pacific. West of Alakawa St.

our pick Town (Map p114; ☎ 735-5900; 3435 cnr Wai'alae Ave & 9th Ave; mains lunch $6-15, dinner $15-22; ⊙ 6:30-9:30pm Mon-Thu, to 10pm Fri & Sat) The motto at this buzzing Kaimuki bistro is 'local first, organic whenever possible, with aloha always.' On the daily-changing menu of boldly flavored cooking are burgers and steaks made from North Shore free-range cattle and salads that taste as if the ingredients were just plucked from a backyard garden. The urban coffee shop decor – stainless steel tables, dark wood tables and original artwork – attracts surfers, yoga teachers and sometimes *Lost* cast members.

DRINKING & ENTERTAINMENT

For up-to-date listings of live-music gigs, DJ clubs, movies, theater and cultural events, check the free tabloid newspaper *Honolulu Weekly,* published every Wednesday, and *Honolulu Advertiser's* TGIF section, which comes out on Friday.

Cafés

Glazer's Artisan Coffee (Map p122; ☎ 391-6548; 2700 S King St; ⊙ 6:30am-11pm Mon-Thu, 6:30am-9pm Fri, 9am-11pm Sat & Sun; 📶) Nobody in Honolulu seems to be more serious about brewing the perfect line-up of espresso drinks than this university-student hangout, with comfy sofas and jazzy artwork on the walls. Free wi-fi.

Honolulu Coffee Company (Map pp118-19; ☎ 521-4400; 1001 Bishop St; ⊙ 6am-5:30pm Mon-Fri, 7am-noon Sat; 📶) Overlooking Bishop Sq with city skyline views, take a break for a java jolt brewed from handpicked, hand-roasted 100% Kona estate–grown beans. Free wi-fi. Also at the Ala Moana Center (Map p122).

Bars, Lounges & Clubs

The hippest nightlife scene revolves around revitalized N Hotel St and Nu'uanu Ave in Chinatown, once the city's notorious red-light district. Wherever you go in Honolulu, any self-respecting bar or lounge has a *pupu* menu to complement the liquid sustenance, and some bars are as famous for their appetizers as their good-times atmosphere. A key term to know is *pau hana* (literally 'stop work'), which is Hawaiian pidgin for happy hour.

Green Room Lounge & Opium Den (Map pp118-19; ☎ 521-2900; Indigo, 1121 Nu'uanu Ave; ⊙ 4-11:30pm Tue-Wed, to 2am Thu-Sat) Divided into different theme lounges, Indigo restaurant mixes martinis in the Opium Den and spins tunes in the Green Room. Jazz and live music are featured during the week, with electronica DJs slotted in for the weekend.

The Loft (Map pp118-19; ☎ 688-8813; 115 N Hotel St; ⊙ 9pm-2am Wed-Sun) Situated on a seedy stretch of Hotel St, where dive bars are the order of the day, this ultra lounge set above a bakery is a svelte retreat, with glowing paper lanterns. DJs spin mostly downtempo house and techno.

thirtyninehotel (Map pp118-19; ☎ 599-2552; 39 N Hotel St; ⊙ 4pm-2am Tue-Sat) More arty than clubby, this multimedia space is a gallery by day and low-key dance space at night. Guest DJs don their aloha wear for special weekend appearances, while rock bands test the acoustics on some weeknights. Next-door Bar 35 stocks over 100 bottled beers to choose from, along with chef-made gourmet pizzas.

Hank's Cafe Honolulu (Map pp118-19; ☎ 526-1410; 1038 Nu'uanu Ave; ⊙ 3pm-1am) You can't get more low-key than this neighborhood bar on the edge of Chinatown. Owner Hank Taufaasau is a jack-of-all-trades when it comes to the barfly business: the walls are decorated with Polynesian-themed art, live music rolls in nightly and regulars call it home.

ONLY-IN-HAWAII BREWS

Truth be told, O'ahu's microbrew scene is still a work in progress. If you can't make it out to the Big Island's Kona Brewing Company (p166) outpost in Hawai'i Kai, sample Hawaii-brewed beers here:

Varsity (Map p122; ☎ 447-9244; 1015 University Ave; ☼ 10am-2am) Formerly Magoo's, this UH student-friendly bar has open-air sidewalk tables and plenty of microbrews from Hawaii and the US mainland on tap.

Sam Choy's Big Aloha Brewery (Map p114; ☎ 545-7979; 580 N Nimitz Hwy; ☼ 10:30am-9:30pm Sun-Thu, to 10pm Fri & Sat) At the back of Sam Choy's Breakfast, Lunch & Crab restaurant, sip Kaka'ako Cream Ale and Kiawe Honey Porter next to the shiny vats they were brewed in.

Gordon Biersch Brewery Restaurant (Map pp118-19; ☎ 599-4877; 1st fl, Aloha Tower Marketplace, 1 Aloha Tower Dr; ☼ 10am-11pm Sun-Thu, to midnight Fri & Sat) Fresh lagers made according to Germany's centuries-old purity laws, with harborfront tables and live music on weekends.

On Waikiki Beach Walk, check out the Yard House (p161), a mainland chain that stocks microbrews from the US and around the world.

---

ourpick La Mariana Sailing Club (Map p114; ☎ 848-2800; 50 Sand Island Access Rd; ☼ 11am-9pm Sun-Thu, to midnight Fri & Sat) Who says all the great tiki bars have gone to the dogs? Irreverent and kitschy, this 1950s joint by the lagoon is filled with yachties and long-suffering locals. Classic mai tais are as good as the other signature tropical potions, complete with tiki-head swizzle sticks. Grab a waterfront table and dream of sailing to Tahiti.

Mai Tai Bar (Map p122; ☎ 947-2900; Ho'okipa Terrace, 3rd fl, Ala Moana Center; ☼ 4pm-midnight) A happening bar in the middle of a shopping center? We don't make the trends, we just report 'em. During Friday happy hours, this suburban-style bar is packed with a see-and-flirt crowd. There's live island-style music nightly.

Aku Bone Lounge (Map p122; ☎ 589-2020; 1201 Kona St; ☼ 5pm-2am) This down-home dive bar with a tasty *pupu* menu and a rubbah-slippah (rubber flip-flops) crowd believes in 'keeping Old Hawaii alive, one beer at a time.' Weekends are for karaoke, sung by patrons from the comfort of their own tables. Live Hawaiian music takes over on weeknights.

Smith's Union Bar (Map pp118-19; ☎ 538-9145; 19 N Hotel St; ☼ 6pm-midnight) You have to be a dive-bar aficionado to appreciate Smith's Union, which first opened in 1935 when this section of Chinatown was a red-light district and playground for merchant seamen. For wage-slave hipsters, it's a cheap front-loading hangout before hitting the clubs.

Live Music

If it is traditional and contemporary Hawaiian music you want, look no further than Waikiki (p160). But if it's jazz, alt-rock and punk sounds you're after, then venture outside the tourist zone in Honolulu's other neighborhoods.

ourpick Chai's Island Bistro (Map pp118-19; ☎ 585-0011; Aloha Tower Marketplace, 1 Aloha Tower Dr; ☼ 11am-10pm Tue-Fri, 4-10pm Sat-Mon) When the sun sets over Honolulu Harbor, you'll find some of Hawaii's top contemporary musicians performing here, including the Brothers Cazimero and Jerry Santos. Come for the drinks and the music, not the food.

Jazz Minds Art & Café (Map p122; ☎ 945-0800; 1661 Kapi'olani Blvd; ☼ 9pm-2am Mon-Sat) Don't let the nearby strip clubs turn you off. Intimate and subdued, this speakeasy lounge pulls in Honolulu's top jazz talent – big band, bebop, salsa and minimalist sounds are all heard here.

Dragon Upstairs (Map pp118-19; ☎ 526-1411; http://the dragonupstairs.com; 2nd fl, 1038 Nu'uanu Ave; ☼ usually Wed-Sat) This hideaway above Hank's Cafe Honolulu has a sedate vibe, plus funky artwork and lots of mirrors. An intimate space, it hosts a rotating line-up of local jazz cats, from experimental bands to bop trios to piano and vocal soloists.

Anna Bannanas (Map p122; ☎ 946-5190; 2440 S Beretania St; ☼ 9pm-2am Thu-Sat) A reliable college bar, part roadhouse and part arthouse, Anna Bananas goes beyond its retro-1960s 'Summer of Love' atmosphere to put island reggae, alt-rock, punk and metal bands on stage. Too bad they haven't brought back those hookah pipes yet.

Pipeline Cafe (Map p114; ☎ 589-1999; http://pipeline cafehawaii.com; 805 Pohukaina St; ☼ varies) A gargantuan warehouse on an industrial side street, this place has a punk-rock heart but also opens for hip-hop and heavy metal bands. You don't need multiple face piercings to blend in, but it doesn't hurt. There's often a cover charge, depending on the band.

Wards Rafters (☎ 735-8012; 3810 Mauna Loa Ave; ☯ 3-6pm Sun) Make your way to a family affair in Kaimuki, where Jackie Ward opens up her converted attic to O'ahu's tight-knit jazz community. It's a word-of-mouth place that informs regulars of gigs via an email list. You can call with questions and please be generous with your cash donations to the musicians. We've left this place unmapped to better protect its invite-only status. BYOB.

Performing Arts

Hawaii's capital city is home to a symphony orchestra, an opera company, ballet troupes, chamber orchestras and over a dozen diverse community theater groups.

ourpick Hawaii Theatre (Map pp118-19; ☎ 528-0506; www.hawaiitheatre.com; 1130 Bethel St) In a beautifully restored historic building in Chinatown, this is a major venue for dance, music and theater. Performances range from local live music and international touring acts, to modern dance, contemporary plays and film festivals. The theater also hosts the Ka Himeni 'Ana competition in which famous musicians play in traditional Hawaiian styles.

Neal S Blaisdell Center (Map p122; ☎ 591-2211; www.blaisdellcenter.com; 777 Ward Ave) A cultural liynchpin for the city, this performing-arts center stages symphonic and chamber-music concerts; opera performances and ballet recitals; prestigious hula competitions; Broadway shows; family-friendly events; and arts-and-crafts fairs. Occasionally big-name rock musicians such as Sting play here instead of at Aloha Stadium (Map p114).

ARTS at Marks Garage (Map pp118-19; ☎ 521-2903; www.artsatmarks.com; 1159 Nu'uanu Ave) On the cutting edge of Chinatown's arts scene, this community gallery and performance space puts on a cornucopia of live shows, from poetry slams and conversations with island-born artists to live jazz and Hawaiian music.

Kumu Kahua Theatre (Map pp118-19; ☎ 536-4441; www.kumukahua.org; 46 Merchant St) In the Kamehameha V Post Office building, this little 100-seat treasure is dedicated to pre-

miering works by Hawaii's playwrights, often focusing on the multicultural complexities of contemporary island life and peppered richly with Hawaiian pidgin.

HawaiiSlam (Map p122; ☎ 387-9664; www.hawaii slam.com; 2nd fl, Honolulu Design Center, 1250 Kapi'olani Blvd; admission $3-5; ☯ 8:30pm 1st Thu of month) One of the biggest poetry slams in the USA, here international wordsmiths, artists, musicians, MCs and DJs share the stage inside the Cupola Theatre. Sign-up for aspiring poetry-slam stars starts at 7:45pm.

For more multicultural theater productions and musical concerts:

Doris Duke Theatre (Map p122; ☎ 532-8768; www .honoluluacademy.org; Honolulu Academy of Arts, 900 S Beretania St)

East-West Center (Map p122; ☎ 944-7111; www.east westcenter.org; 1601 East-West Rd)

Cinemas

Doris Duke Theatre (Map p122; ☎ 532-8768; www.hono luluacademy.org; Honolulu Academy of Arts, 900 S Beretania St) Inside an art museum, this intimate movie house showcases homegrown and imported independent cinema, foreign films and avant-garde and experimental shorts. Look for screenings of ground-breaking Hawaii and Pacific Rim documentaries here.

Movie Museum (Map p114; ☎ 735-8771; www .kaimukihawaii.com; 3566 Harding Ave; ☯ noon-8pm Thu-Mon) This Kaimuki neighborhood spot is a very social place to watch classic oldies, foreign flicks and indie films (including Hawaii premieres) in a theater equipped with just 20 comfy Barcalounger chairs. Reservations strongly recommended.

Megaplexes showing first-run Hollywood movies:

Restaurant Row 9 Cinemas (Map pp118-19; ☎ 526-4171; Restaurant Row, 500 Ala Moana Blvd)

Ward Stadium 16 (Map p122; ☎ 593-3000; 1044 Auahi St)

SHOPPING

Although not the shopping powerhouse that Waikiki is, Honolulu has more than a few unique shops offering plenty of local flavor, from traditional flower lei and ukulele makers to antiques stores and island-style clothing boutiques.

Shopping Malls

Ala Moana Center (Map p122; ☎ 955-9517; 1450 Ala Moana Blvd; ☯ 9am-9pm Mon-Sat, to 6pm Sun) Holy

TOP PICKS – HONOLULU & WAIKIKI HAWAIIANA SHOPS

- Bishop Museum (p126)
- Native Books/Nā Mea Hawai'i (p115)
- Cindy's Lei Shop (below)
- Na Lima Mili Hulu No'eau (p162)
- Bailey's Antiques & Aloha Shirts (p162)
- Kamaka Hawaii (right)
- Manuheali'i (right)
- Antique Alley (opposite)
- Hula Supply Center (right)
- Hawai'i State Art Museum (p116)

fashion! This open-air shopping mall and its department stores could compete on an international runway with some of Asia's most famous malls. A favorite stop for local color is the Crack Seed Center, where you can scoop from jars full of pickled mangoes, dried plums, candied ginger and dozens more exotic tropical flavors.

our pick **Ward Warehouse** (Map p122; ☎ 591-8411; cnr Ward Ave & Kamake'e St; ☺ 10am-9pm Mon-Sat, to 6pm Sun) Just across the street from Ala Moana Beach Park, this minimall is home to more one-of-a-kind island-born shops, including Native Books/Nā Mea Hawaii (see p115), which sells gourmet foodstuffs, wooden koa bowls, hand-carved fishhook jewelry, authentic Hawaiian quilts and oodles of books, CDs and DVDs.

Aloha Tower Marketplace (Map pp118-19; ☎ 528-5700; 1 Aloha Tower Dr; ☺ 9am-9pm Mon-Sat, to 6pm Sun) Beside the landmark Aloha Tower (p117), this harborfront shopping center has 50 shops varying in quality from kitschy to high-end, with barely an off-island chain among them. Hula dancers welcome arriving cruise ships on the pier, usually from 4:30 to 5:30pm almost daily.

Art & Hawaiian Crafts

For Chinatown's art galleries, see the boxed text on p124.

Cindy's Lei Shop (Map pp118-19; ☎ 536-6538; 1034 Maunakea St; ☺ 6am-8pm Mon-Sat, 6:30am-6pm Sun) This friendly, inviting little place sells leis made of maile (a native twining plant), lantern ilima (a native ground cover) and Micronesian

ginger, as well as more common orchids and plumeria.

Kamaka Hawaii (Map pp118-19; ☎ 531-3165; 550 South St; ☺ 8am-4pm Mon-Fri) Skip right by those shops selling cheap plastic and wooden ukuleles. Kamaka specializes in handcrafted ukuleles made on O'ahu since 1916, with prices starting at around $500. Their signature is an oval-shaped 'pineapple' ukulele that has a more mellow sound.

Hula Supply Center (Map p122; ☎ 941-5379; 2338 & 2346 S King St; ☺ 9am-5:30pm Mon-Fri, to 5pm Sat) For over 60 years, Hawaiian musicians and dancers have come here to get their kukui (candlenut) leis, calabash drum gourds, Tahitian grass skirts, nose flutes and the like. If you're not a dancer, they've also got aloha shirts, Hawaiiana books, CDs and DVDs.

Jeff Chang Pottery & Fine Crafts (Map pp118-19; ☎ 599-2502; 808 Fort St Mall; ☺ 10am-5pm Mon-Fri) Not everything at this downtown gallery is island-made, but it's all handcrafted. Striking raku pottery molded by Chang himself sits beside hand-turned bowls of tropical hardwoods, art jewelry and blown glass by some of Hawaii's finest artisans. Also at Ward Warehouse (left).

Clothing & Shoes

Island Slipper (Map p122; ☎ 593-8229; Ward Warehouse, 1050 Ala Moana Blvd; ☺ 10am-9pm Mon-Sat, to 6pm Sun) There are scores of stores selling flip-flops (aka 'rubbah slippah') across Honolulu, but nobody carries such ultracomfy suede and leather styles, some made right here in the islands, let alone such giant sizes.

Locals Only (Map p122; ☎ 942-1555; Ala Moana Center, 1450 Ala Moana Blvd; ☺ 9:30am-9pm Mon-Sat, 10am-7pm Sun) Around since 1981, this homegrown brand's name says it all. Rayon reproductions of vintage aloha shirts and casual T-shirts speak to island lifestyles – our fave is a Rastafarian-colored shaka sign with the logo 'Keep Hawaii Green.'

Manuheali'i (Map p122; ☎ 942-9868; 930 Punahou St; ☺ 9:30am-6pm Mon-Fri, 9am-4pm Sat, 10am-3pm Sun) Look to this island-born shop for original and modern designs. Hawaiian musicians often sport Manuheali'i's bold-print silk aloha shirts. Flowing rayon dresses take inspiration from the traditional muumuu, but are transformed into spritely contemporary looks.

Cinnamon Girl (Map p122; ☎ 947-4332; Ala Moana Center, 1450 Ala Moana Blvd; ☺ 9:30am-9pm Mon-Sat, 10am-7pm Sun) From the whimsical genius of O'ahu fashionista Jonelle Fujita, flirty rayon dresses that are cool, contemporary and island-made hang on the racks here, while feminine sandals, bejeweled necklaces and sweet floppy sun hats line the shelves.

T&L Muumuu Factory (Map p122; ☎ 941-4183; 1423 Kapi'olani Blvd; ☽ 9am-6pm Mon-Sat, 10am-4pm Sun) So much flammable aloha wear in one space! This is a shop for *tutu* (grandmothers), to whom polyester represents progress. Bold-print muumuus run in sizes from supermodel skinny to queen, and *pu'u* skirts are just funky enough to wedge into an urban outfit.

Montsuki (Map p114; ☎ 734-3457; 1148 Koko Head Ave; ☽ 10pm-5pm) In the low-key Kaimuki neighborhood east of Waikiki, the mother-daughter design team of Janet and Patty Yamasaki refashions classic kimono and *obi* designs into modern attire. East-West wedding dresses, formal wear or sleek day fashions can all be custom-crafted.

Antiques

Antique Alley (Map p122; ☎ 941-8551; 1347 Kapi'olani Blvd; ☽ 11am-5pm) Delightfully crammed full of rare collectibles and other cast-off memorabilia from Hawaii through the decades, its co-op vendors sell everything from poi pounders to vintage hula dolls and Matson cruise liner artifacts.

Lai Fong Department Store (Map pp118-19; ☎ 781-8140; 1118 Nu'uanu Ave; ☽ 9am-7:30pm Mon-Sat) This family-owned Chinatown shop sells a hodge-podge of antiques and knickknacks in all price ranges, from Chinese silk and brocade clothing to vintage postcards of Hawaii from the early 20th century. Tailor-made apparel can be custom ordered.

GETTING THERE & AROUND
To/From the Airport

For transportation options and driving directions to and from Honolulu International Airport, see p110.

Bus

The Ala Moana Center, just northwest of Waikiki, is the central transfer point for TheBus, O'ahu's public transportation network. From Ala Moana, you can connect to dozens of routes across the Honolulu metro area, and other parts of the island. For general information about TheBus, including useful routes, schedules, fares and passes, see p111.

Private trolleys also trundle between Honolulu and Waikiki (see p163).

Car

Directions in Honolulu are often given using landmarks. If someone tells you to 'go 'Ewa' (west of Honolulu) or 'go Diamond Head' (east of Waikiki), it just means to head in that general direction.

Honolulu traffic jams up during rush hours, from 7am to 9am and 3pm to 6pm on weekdays. Expect heavy traffic in both directions on the H-1 Fwy during this time, as well as on the Pali and Likelike Hwys headed into Honolulu in the morning and away from the city in the late afternoon.

Downtown Honolulu and Chinatown are full of one-way streets, traffic is thick and parking can be tight, so consider taking the bus. N Hotel St is open to bus traffic only. Expensive hourly parking is available at several municipal parking lots and garages, including at Chinatown Gateway Plaza and ARTS at Mark Garage. On-street metered parking is hard to find on weekdays, easier on weekends; bring lotsa quarters.

On the outskirts of downtown, the Neal S Blaisdell Center offers all-day parking for $6. Major shopping centers offer free parking for customers, including at Ala Moana Center and the Ward Centers. The Aloha Tower Marketplace has validated paid parking – just make sure to have your parking ticket stamped after making a purchase. On weekdays after 3pm and all day on weekends and holidays, a flat rate of $2 applies; before 3pm on weekdays, it costs $2 for the first three hours, then $3 for each additional 30-minute period.

Taxi

Phone **City Taxi** (☎ 524-2121), **TheCab** (☎ 422-2222) or **Charley's** (☎ 531-1333, from payphones ☎ 877-531-1333). For metered rates, see p112.

PEARL HARBOR AREA

The WWII-era rallying cry 'Remember Pearl Harbor!' that once mobilized an entire nation dramatically resonates on O'ahu. It was here that the surprise Japanese attack on December 7, 1941 hurtled the USA into war in the Pacific. Every year 1.5 million tourists visit Pearl Harbor's unique collection of war memorials and museums, all clustered around a quiet bay where oysters were once farmed, just west of Honolulu.

O'AHU

A DAY OF INFAMY

December 7, 1941 – 'a date which will live in infamy,' President Franklin D Roosevelt later said – began at 7:55am with a wave of over 350 Japanese planes swooping over the Ko'olau Range headed toward the unsuspecting US Pacific Fleet in Pearl Harbor.

The battleship USS *Arizona* took a direct hit and sank in less than nine minutes, trapping its crew beneath the surface. The average age of the 1177 enlisted men who died on the ship was just 19 years. It wasn't until 15 minutes after the bombing started that American anti-aircraft guns began to shoot back at the Japanese warplanes. Twenty other US military ships were sunk or seriously damaged and 347 airplanes were destroyed during the two-hour attack.

In hindsight, there were two significant warnings prior to the attack that were disastrously dismissed or misinterpreted. Over an hour before Japanese planes arrived, USS *Ward* spotted a submarine conning tower approaching the entrance of Pearl Harbor. The *Ward* immediately attacked with depth charges and sank what turned out to be one of five midget Japanese submarines launched to penetrate the harbor. At 7:02am a radar station on the north shore of O'ahu reported planes approaching. Even though they were coming from the west rather than the east, it was assumed that the planes were from the US mainland.

For more on Hawaii's WWII-era history, see p44.

Today Pearl Harbor (Map p114) is still home to an active and mind-bogglingly enormous US naval base. Anyone looking for a little soul-soothing peace and quiet, especially after a solemn visit to the USS Arizona Memorial, can head up into the misty Ko'olau Mountains above the harbor, where an ancient Hawaiian medicinal temple and forested hiking trails await.

INFORMATION

Strict security measures are in place at all of Pearl Harbor's memorials, museums and visitor centers. You are not allowed to bring in any items that allow concealment, including purses, camera bags, fanny packs, backpacks and diaper bags. Personal-sized cameras and camcorders are allowed. Do not lock any valuables in your car. Instead use the **baggage-storage facility** (per item $3; ☼ 6:30am-5:30pm) at the entrance to Bowfin Park, near the Ford Island shuttle bus stop and visitor parking lot.

SIGHTS & ACTIVITIES

The offshore shrine at the sunken USS *Arizona* is Hawaii's most-visited tourist attraction. Nearby are two other military historic sites: the USS *Bowfin* submarine, aka the 'Pearl Harbor Avenger,' and the battleship USS *Missouri*, where General Douglas MacArthur accepted the Japanese surrender at the end of WWII. Together, for the US, these historical sites represent the beginning, middle and end of the war. To visit all three, as well as the Pacific Aviation Museum,

dedicate at least a half-day, preferably in the morning when it's less crowded. All Pearl Harbor attractions are wheelchair-accessible and closed on Thanksgiving, Christmas and New Year's Day.

USS Arizona Memorial

One of the USA's most significant WWII sites, this somber **memorial** (☎ 422-0561; www.nps.gov /usar; 1 Arizona Memorial Dr, 'Aiea; admission free; ☼ visitor center & museum 7:30am-5pm, last boat tour 3pm) narrates the history of the Pearl Harbor attack and commemorates its fallen service members. Run by the National Park Service (NPS), the memorial comprises a **visitor center** and offshore shrine. On land inside the visitor center, a **museum** presents rare WWII memorabilia and a model of the battleship and shrine, as well as historical photos.

The offshore **shrine** was built over the midsection of the sunken USS *Arizona*, with deliberate geometry to represent initial defeat, ultimate victory and eternal serenity. In the farthest of three chambers inside the shrine, the names of crewmen killed in the attack are engraved onto a marble wall. In the central room are cutaway well sections that allow visitors to see the skeletal remains of the ship, which even now oozes about a quart of oil each day into the ocean. In its rush to recover from the attack and prepare for war, the US Navy exercised its option to leave the servicemen inside the sunken ship. They remain entombed in its hull, buried at sea. Visitors are asked to maintain respectful silence at all times, although some tour groups and their guides don't always comply.

Boat trips to the shrine depart from the visitor center every 15 minutes from 7:45am until 3pm on a first-come, first-served basis (weather permitting). At the visitor center, you'll be given a ticket stating exactly when your 75-minute tour program, which includes a documentary film on the attack, will begin. In the afternoon, waits of a couple hours are not uncommon. In peak summer months, 4500 people take the tour daily, and the day's allotment of tickets is often gone by noon.

USS Bowfin Submarine Museum & Park
If you have to wait an hour or two for your USS Arizona Memorial tour to begin, the adjacent **USS Bowfin Submarine Museum & Park** (☎ 423-1341; www.bowfin.org; 11 Arizona Memorial Dr, 'Aiea; park admission free; museum & self-guided submarine audio tour adult/child 4-12/senior $10/3/7; ☺ 8am-5pm) contains the moored WWII-era submarine USS Bowfin and a niche **museum** that traces the development of submarines from their origins to the nuclear age, including footage from real-life wartime submarine patrols. Last entry 4:30pm.

The highlight of the park is clambering aboard the historic **submarine**. Lunched on December 7, 1942, one year after the Pearl Harbor attack, the USS Bowfin completed nine war patrols and sank 44 enemy ships in the Pacific by the end of WWII. A self-guided audio tour explores the life of the crew – remember to watch your head below deck! Children under the age of four are not allowed on the submarine.

As you stroll around the surrounding waterfront **park**, you can peer through periscopes and inspect a Japanese kaiten (suicide torpedo), the marine equivalent of a kamikaze pilot and his plane, developed as a last-ditch effort by the Japanese military near the end of WWII.

If you plan on visiting the Battleship Missouri Memorial and/or Pacific Aviation Museum, purchase tickets here first at Bowfin Park; discount combos are available.

Battleship Missouri Memorial
The last battleship built at the end of WWII, the **USS Missouri** (☎ 455-1600, 877-644-4896; www .ussmissouri.com; 63 Cowpens St, Ford Island; adult/child 4-12 $16/8, with guided tour from $23/15; ☺ 9am-5pm, last entry 4pm) provides a unique historical 'bookend'

to the US campaign in the Pacific during WWII. Nicknamed the 'Mighty Mo,' this decommissioned battleship (incidentally, it's bigger than the RMS Titanic) saw action during the decisive WWII battles of Iwo Jima and Okinawa.

The USS Missouri is now docked on Ford Island, just a few hundred yards from the sunken remains of the USS Arizona. You can poke about the officers' quarters, browse exhibits on the ship's history and walk the deck where General Douglas MacArthur accepted the Japanese surrender on September 2, 1945. Worthwhile guided tours are led by friendly and knowledgeable docents, often military veterans themselves.

To visit the memorial, you must first buy tickets at Bowfin Park, then board the mandatory shuttle bus to Ford Island.

Pacific Aviation Museum
Still a work-in-progress, this military aircraft **museum** (☎ 441-1000; www.pacificaviationmuseum.org; 319 Lexington Blvd, Ford Island; adult/child 4-12 $14/7, with guided tour $21/14; ☺ 9am-5pm) covers the period from WWII through the US conflicts in Korea and Vietnam. Already the first aircraft hangar has been outfitted with exhibits on the Pearl Harbor attack, the Doolittle Raid on mainland Japan in 1942 and the pivotal Battle of Midway, when the tides of WWII in the Pacific turned in favor of the Allies. Authentically restored planes on display here include a Japanese Zero and a Dauntless navy dive bomber. Last entry 4pm.

To visit the museum, you must first buy tickets at Bowfin Park, then board the mandatory shuttle bus to Ford Island.

Kea'iwa Heiau State Recreation Area
In the hills above Pearl Harbor, this **park** (Map pp102-3; ☎ 587-0300; off 'Aiea Heights Dr, 'Aiea; admission free; ☺ 7am-7:45pm April-early Sep, 7am-6:45pm early Sep-Mar) protects **Kea'iwa Heiau**, an ancient Hawaiian stone temple used by kahuna lapa'au (herbalist healers). The kahuna used hundreds of medicinal plants and grew many on the grounds surrounding the heiau. Among those still found here are noni (Indian mulberry), whose pungent yellow fruits were used to treat heart disease; kukui (candlenuts), a laxative; and ti leaves, which were wrapped around a sick person to break a fever. Not only did these herbs have medicinal value, but the heiau itself was believed

O'AHU

DETOUR: WAIMANO TRAIL

Starting above 'Aiea, the challenging 14.5-mile round-trip **Waimano Trail** (Map pp102–3) is a boulder-hopping, bush-whacking, stream-crossing and rope-assisted climbing adventure that scales knife-edged ridges prone to mudslides, all in pursuit of a spectacular lookout atop the Ko'olau Range.

It's a stretch to do the entire trail in one day. Think about camping overnight in the backcountry with a free advance permit from the **Division of Forestry & Wildlife** (DOFAW; Map pp118–19; ☎ 587-0166; Kalaniomoku Bldg, Room 325, 1151 Punchbowl St, Honolulu; ◷ 7:45am-4:30pm), then hike to the *pali* lookout the next morning and back to the trailhead in the afternoon.

For a shorter day hike, it's 3 miles round-trip from the trailhead to Waimano Pool, reached via steep 'Cardiac Hill,' where local kids go for waterfall swimming. To reach the trailhead, take the H-1 Fwy west from Honolulu to Moanalua Rd (exit 10); at the first stoplight, turn right onto Waimano Home Rd. Park at the end of the road in a dirt pull-out before reaching a security guardhouse.

---

to possess life-giving energy that could be channeled by the kahuna.

For hikers and mountain bikers, the park's scenic 4.5-mile **'Aiea Loop Trail** starts from the top of the paved loop road and ends at the campground, about 0.3 miles below the trailhead. Along the way you'll get sweeping vistas of Pearl Harbor, Diamond Head and the Ko'olau Range. About two-thirds of the way along, the wreckage of a C-47 cargo plane that crashed in 1943 can be spotted through the foliage on the east ridge.

The park's few **campsites** are maintained well, but there's not a lot of privacy. In winter bring waterproof gear, as it rains frequently at this elevation. The park has picnic tables, BBQ grills, rest rooms, showers, drinking water and a payphone. There's a resident caretaker by the front gate, which is locked at night for security. Camping is not permitted on Wednesday and Thursday nights, and advance permits are required (see p101).

From Honolulu or Waikiki, drive west on the H-1 Fwy, then merge onto Hwy 78 and take the exit 13A 'Aiea turnoff onto Moanalua Rd. Turn right onto 'Aiea Heights Dr at the second traffic light. The road winds up through a residential area for about 2.5 miles to the park.

From downtown Honolulu, TheBus 11 'Aiea Heights ($2, 35 minutes, hourly) stops about 1.3 miles downhill from the park entrance.

TOURS

Pearl Harbor tours that are widely advertised in Waikiki range from shuttle buses to excursions in WWII-era amphibious armored vehicles (aka 'ducks'). These tours don't add much, if anything to the experience of visiting the memorials and museums, however. Pearl Harbor boat cruises do not allow disembarking at the USS Arizona Memorial.

EATING

Bowfin Park has concession stands. The Battleship Missouri Memorial and Pacific Aviation Museum have fast-food cafés. Downhome local eateries are flung farther east along the Kamehameha Hwy (Hwy 99) near the Pearlridge Center mall.

Chun Wah Kam Noodle Factory (☎ 485-1107; Waimalu Shopping Center, 98-040 Kamehameha Hwy, 'Aiea; items from $1, meals $5-12; ◷ 7:30am-6:30pm Mon-Sat, 8:30am-4pm Sun) In a minimall chockablock with Asian takeout joints, fanatics will line up for these *manapua* stuffed with anything from *char siu* pork or *kalua* pig to black sugar or taro. Generous mix-and-match plate lunches could easily feed two people.

Kuru Kuru Sushi (☎ 484-4596; Pearl Kai Shopping Center, 98-199 Kamehameha Hwy; items $2-8; ◷ 11am-9pm Sun-Thu, to 10pm Fri & Sat) This island chain of sushi bar runs its classic Japanese *nigiri* sushi, *kalbi* short-rib rolls, vegetable croquettes and fruit-jelly desserts around a conveyor belt. Plates are color-coded by price, so staff can quickly total up your bill after you're stuffed to the gills.

Forty Niner Restaurant (☎ 484-1940; 98-110 Honomanu St, 'Aiea; mains $3-10; ◷ 7am-2pm daily, 5-8pm Mon-Thu & 5-9pm Fri & Sat) This little 1940s noodle shop may look abandoned, but it's a jewel-in-the-rough for anyone craving old-fashioned saimin (local-style noodle soup), made here with a secret-recipe broth. The garlic chicken and hamburger steaks aren't half bad. No air-con, though.

our pick **Poke Stop** (Map pp102-3; ☎ 676-8100; Waipahu Town Center, 94-050 Farrington Hwy, Waipahu; dishes $4-10, meals $9-14; ⏰ 8am-7pm Mon-Sat) It's a longer detour west of Pearl Harbor, but we'd drive all the way across the island just to bite into these spicy eggplant fries, deconstructed sushi bowls, gourmet plate lunches and over 20 kinds of *poke* – the *furikake* salmon and 'Da Works' *'o'io* (bonefish) will leave you salivating for more.

GETTING THERE & AWAY

The USS Arizona Memorial visitor center and Bowfin Park are off the Kamehameha Hwy (Hwy 99) southwest of Aloha Stadium. Coming from Honolulu or Waikiki, take the H-1 Fwy west to exit 15A (Arizona Memorial/Stadium), then follow the signs for the USS Arizona Memorial, not Pearl Harbor; the latter lead onto the military base. There's ample free parking outside the visitor center and Bowfin Park.

From Waikiki, TheBus 42 'Ewa Beach is the most direct route, making stops outside the USS Arizona Memorial visitor center between 7:15am and 3pm, taking about an hour each way. TheBus 20 Airport-Pearlridge detours to the airport, taking about 15 minutes longer. Both routes run at least twice hourly. Slightly quicker **VIP Trans** (☎ 836-1037, 866-836-0317) shuttle vans depart from Waikiki area hotels every 30 minutes starting around 7am, costing $6/11 one-way/round-trip.

Civilians are not allowed to drive onto Ford Island, an active military base. Instead, a frequent free shuttle bus picks up ticketholders outside Bowfin Park, stopping at the Battleship Missouri Memorial, then the Pacific Aviation Museum.

WAIKIKI

pop 27,500

Waikiki – just the name alone will have you thinking of boundless horizons, Pacific sunsets and hula dancers gently swaying to the beat of island rhythms. Once the playground of Hawaiian royalty, this remains O'ahu's quintessential beach.

After emerging from the long shadow of WWII, Waikiki recaptured the popular imagination as an idyllic tropical island vacation complete with flower leis, aloha shirts and romance. Celebrities like Elvis sang about it and strummed ukuleles, while bronzed beachboys walked on water thanks to their long wooden surfboards.

Today Waikiki is experiencing a renaissance. Although tacky tiki drinks and luau buffets featuring Samoan fire-dancing are still a fixture on the scene, this enclave is moving beyond plasticky mass tourism, with boutique hotels, sophisticated restaurants and stylish lounges. Like Palm Springs, Waikiki has reinvented itself.

A lazy day of lying on the beach here is really just the beginning of all the fun. When the sun sinks below the horizon, Waikiki becomes even more of a playground by night than it is by day. Let yourself be mesmerized by hula troupes performing on the beach or contemporary Hawaiian musical icons playing at oceanfront hotel bars. No matter where you go, Waikiki will put a spell on you.

HISTORY

Fed by mountain streams from Manoa Valley, Waikiki ('Spouting Water') was once a fertile wetland of *kalo lo'i* (taro fields) and fishponds. In 1795 when Kamehameha the Great conquered O'ahu, he built his royal court here. For almost the next century, Waikiki was a privileged royal retreat. But by the 1880s, Honolulu's wealthier citizens started building gingerbread-trimmed cottages along the narrow beachfront.

Tourism started booming in 1901, when the Moana opened its doors as Waikiki's first luxury hotel, built on a former royal compound. A tram line was built to connect Waikiki with downtown Honolulu, and city folk crowded aboard for weekend beach outings. Tiring quickly of the pesky mosquitoes that thrived in Waikiki's wetlands, early beachgoers petitioned to have the 'swamps' brought under control. In 1922 the Ala Wai Canal was dug to divert streams and dry out the wetlands.

Old Hawaii lost out: local farmers had the water drained out from under them and water buffaloes were quickly replaced by tourists. In 1927 the Royal Hawaiian Hotel opened to serve passengers arriving on luxury ocean liners from San Francisco. During WWII, this 'Pink Palace' was turned into an R&R playground for US sailors on shore leave. As late as 1950, surfers could still drive their cars right up onto Waikiki Beach and park on the sand.

O'AHU

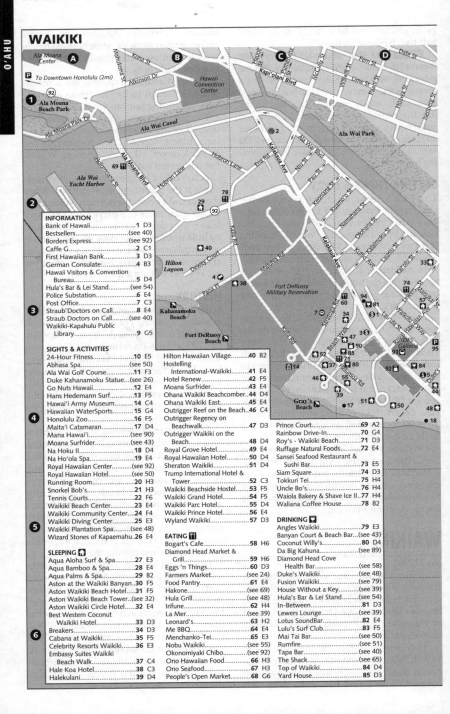

WAIKIKI

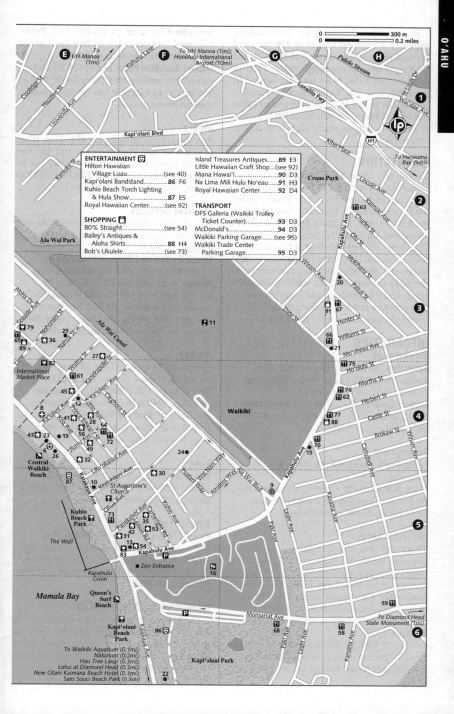

ENTERTAINMENT
Hilton Hawaiian
  Village Luau....................(see 40)
Kapi'olani Bandstand.............86 F6
Kuhio Beach Torch Lighting
  & Hula Show.....................87 E5
Royal Hawaiian Center........(see 92)

SHOPPING
80% Straight......................(see 54)
Bailey's Antiques &
  Aloha Shirts.....................88 H4
Bob's Ukulele...................(see 73)

Island Treasures Antiques......89 E3
Little Hawaiian Craft Shop....(see 92)
Mana Hawai'i.......................90 D3
Na Lima Mili Hulu No'eau.....91 H3
Royal Hawaiian Center..........92 D4

TRANSPORT
DFS Galleria (Waikiki Trolley
  Ticket Counter)...............93 D3
McDonald's.........................94 D3
Waikiki Parking Garage.......(see 95)
Waikiki Trade Center
  Parking Garage.................95 D3

O'AHU

By that time, passenger jets were making regularly scheduled flights to Hawaii, and tourism once again boomed along with the USA's postwar prosperity, especially after statehood in 1959. Mass tourism landed in the 1960s and '70s. Only a lack of available land finally halted Waikiki's expansion at the end of the 1980s – the only place left to go was up, which is why so many high-rises cluster here today.

ORIENTATION

Technically Waikiki is only a district of Honolulu. It's bounded by the Ala Wai Canal, the ocean and Kapi'olani Park. Three parallel roads cross Waikiki: Kalakaua Ave, the beach road; Kuhio Ave, the main drag for Waikiki's buses; and Ala Wai Blvd, bordering the canal. This forms the tight nucleus of tourist hotels, restaurants and bars. Inland Kapahulu Ave and Monsarrat Ave have more local eateries and shops. In central Waikiki, walking along the beach and its paved seaside footpaths sometimes may be faster than navigating the overcrowded sidewalks of busy Kalakaua Ave.

INFORMATION
Bookstores
Bestsellers (☎ 953-2378; Rainbow Bazaar, Hilton Hawaiian Village, 2005 Kalia Rd; ☼ 8am-10pm) Vends Hawaiiana books, travel guides and maps.
Borders Express (☎ 922-4154; Royal Hawaiian Center, 2201 Kalakaua Ave; ☼ 9:30am-9:30pm) A smaller but well-stocked version of Borders.

Emergency
Police, Fire & Ambulance (☎ 911) For all emergencies.
Police Substation (☎ 529-3801; 2405 Kalakaua Ave; ☼ 24hr) If you need help, or just friendly directions, there's a small police station at Kuhio Beach.

Internet Access
There are lots of cybercafés along Kuhio Ave and inside the Lemon Rd backpacker hostels, but few offer wi-fi; surfing costs an average of $6 to $12 per hour. Many hotels have wired high-speed connections in guest rooms, but limited wi-fi only in the lobby or poolside areas; daily surcharges of around $10 may apply.
Caffe G (☎ 979-2299; 1888 Kalakaua Ave; per hr $6; ☼ 8am-10pm Mon-Fri, 10am-10pm Sat, 8:30am-10pm Sun) High-speed internet terminals with ethernet cables for laptops.

Hula's Bar & Lei Stand (☎ 923-0669; 2nd fl, Waikiki Grand Hotel, 134 Kapahulu Ave; ☼ 10am-2am) Free wi-fi and internet terminals inside the bar (p154).
Waikiki-Kapahulu Public Library (☎ 733-8488; www.librarieshawaii.org; 400 Kapahulu Ave; ☼ 10am-5pm Tue, Wed, Fri & Sat, noon-7pm Thu) Free wi-fi and reservable internet terminals.

Media
Freebie tourist magazines like *This Week O'ahu* and *101 Things to Do* and the free tabloid newspaper *Honolulu Weekly* can be found on street corners and in hotel lobbies throughout Waikiki. See also p115.

Medical Services
For all-night pharmacies and hospitals with 24-hour emergency rooms elsewhere in Honolulu, see p115.
Straub Doctors on Call (www.straubhealth.org) North Waikiki (☎ 973-5250; 2nd fl, Rainbow Bazaar, Hilton Hawaiian Village, 2005 Kalia Rd; ☼ 8:30am-4:30pm Mon-Fri); South Waikiki (☎ 971-6000; Sheraton Princess Kaiulani, 120 Ka'iulani Ave; ☼ 24hr) These walk-in non-emergency clinics currently accept Blue Cross/Blue Shield, Medicare and some travel health insurance policies.

Money
There are 24-hour ATMs all over Waikiki, including at these full-service banks:
Bank of Hawaii (☎ 543-6900; 2228 Kalakaua Ave; ☼ 8:30am-4pm Mon-Thu, 8:30am-6pm Fri, 9am-1pm Sat)
First Hawaiian Bank (☎ 943-4670; 2181 Kalakaua Ave; ☼ 8:30am-4pm Mon-Thu, 8:30am-6pm Fri) Lobby displays Hawaii history murals by French artist Jean Charlot.

Post
Post office (☎ 800-275-8777; 330 Saratoga Rd; ☼ 8am-4:30pm Mon-Fri, 9am-1pm Sat) In the center of Waikiki, with free parking for customers.

Tourist Information
Hawaii Visitors & Convention Bureau (HVCB; ☎ 923-1811, 800-464-2924; www.gohawaii.com; Suite 801, Waikiki Business Plaza, 2270 Kalakaua Ave, Waikiki; ☼ 8am-4:30pm Mon-Fri) Visitor information office offers brochures and free maps.

DANGERS & ANNOYANCES
It can be risky to walk along the beach or the Ala Wai Canal after dark, whether alone or in groups. Day or night, you can't walk down Kalakaua Ave without encountering timeshare salespeople, often sitting behind the desk of an 'activity center' advertising free luau, sunset

cruises or $5-per-day car rentals. At night, especially along Kuhio Ave, prostitutes cruise for well-dressed tourists.

SIGHTS & ACTIVITIES

Let's be honest: you're just here for the beach. But Waikiki's other diversions include historical hotels, resort spas, a popular golf course and an ecofriendly aquarium.

Beaches

The 2-mile stretch of white sand commonly referred to as Waikiki Beach runs from Hilton Hawaiian Village in the west to Kapi'olani Park in the east. Along the way, the beach changes names and personalities. In the early morning, the quiet seaside path belongs to walkers and joggers. By midmorning it looks like a normal resort beach – surfboard concessionaires, bronzed beachboys and lots of tourist bodies. By noon it's challenging to walk along the packed beach without stepping on anyone.

Offshore Waikiki is good for swimming, bodyboarding, surfing, sailing and other water sports most of the year, and there are lifeguards and showers scattered along the shore. Between May and September, summer swells make the water rougher for swimming, but great for surfing (for surfing lessons and board rentals, see p151). For snorkeling, head to Sans Souci Beach or Queen's Surf Beach. For windsurfing, go to Fort DeRussy Beach.

The following beaches run from northwest to southeast.

KAHANAMOKU BEACH

Fronting Hilton Hawaiian Village, Kahanamoku Beach is protected by a breakwater at one end and a pier at the other, with a coral reef running between the two. It's a calm swimming area with a gently sloping sandy bottom. The beach is named for Duke Kahanamoku (1890–1968), the legendary Waikiki beachboy, champion surfer and Olympic gold medal–winning swimmer whose family once owned this land.

FORT DERUSSY BEACH

An overlooked beauty, this seldom-crowded beach borders a US military reservation. The only area off-limits to civvies is Hale Koa Hotel backing onto the beach. The water is usually calm and good for swimming, but shallow at low tide. When conditions are right, windsurfers, bodyboarders and board surfers play here. There are two beach huts, both open daily, which rent windsurfing equipment, bodyboards, kayaks and snorkel sets. In addition to lifeguards and showers, you'll find an inviting grassy lawn with palm trees offering some sparse shade, an alternative to frying on the sand. Public fee parking is available in front of the Hawai'i Army Museum (p152).

GRAY'S BEACH

Near the Halekulani Hotel, Gray's Beach has suffered some of the Waikiki strip's worst erosion. Because the seawall in front of the Halekulani was built so close to the waterline, the part of the beach facing the hotel is often totally submerged, though the waters off the beach are shallow and calm. What little remains preserves the memory of a boarding house called Gray's-by-the-Sea established here during the 1920s.

CENTRAL WAIKIKI BEACH

Between the Royal Hawaiian Hotel and the Moana Surfrider, Waikiki's busiest section of sand and surf is great for sunbathing, swimming and people watching.

Most of the beach has a shallow bottom with a gradual slope. The only drawback for swimmers is the beach's popularity with beginner surfers and the occasional catamaran landing. **Queens** and **Canoes**, Waikiki's best-known surf breaks, are just offshore, and sometimes there are scores of surfers lined up on the horizon waiting to catch a wave. A longer paddle offshore is **Populars** (aka 'Pops'), favored by longboarders.

There are rest rooms, showers, a snack bar, surfboard lockers and rental stands at **Waikiki**

GROANING ABOUT WAIKIKI'S GROINS

After Waikiki tourism took off in the 1950s, the beachfront inevitably became more developed. Private landowners haphazardly constructed seawalls and offshore barriers (called groins) to protect their properties, thus blocking the natural forces of sand accretion, making erosion a serious problem. Today, some of Waikiki's legendary white sands have actually been barged in from Papohaku Beach on the island of Moloka'i.

Beach Center. On the Diamond Head side of the police station, you'll see four boulders, known as the **Wizard Stones of Kapaemahu**, said to contain the secrets and healing powers of four sorcerers who visited from Tahiti in the 16th century.

Just east of the stones is a bronze **statue of Duke Kahanamoku** standing with one of his longboards. Considered the father of modern surfing, Duke made his home in Waikiki and gave surfing demonstrations around the world, from Sydney, Australia, to Rockaway Beach, New York. Many local surfers have taken issue with the placement of the statue; Duke is standing with his back to the sea, a position they say he never would have assumed in real life.

KUHIO BEACH PARK

For everything from protected swimming to outrigger canoe rides, this beach is marked on its eastern end by **Kapahulu Groin**, a walled storm drain with a walkway on top that juts out into the ocean. A low stone breakwater, called **the Wall**, runs out from Kapahulu Groin, parallel to the beach. It was built to control sand erosion and, in the process, two nearly enclosed swimming pools were formed.

Local kids walk out on the Wall, but it can be dangerous, due to a slippery surface and breaking surf. The pool closest to Kapahulu Groin is best for swimming, with the water near the breakwater reaching overhead depths. However, because circulation is limited, the water gets murky, with a noticeable film of suntan oil. The 'Watch Out Deep Holes' sign refers to holes in the pool's sandy bottom created by swirling currents, so waders should be cautious in the deeper part of the pool.

Kapahulu Groin is one of Waikiki's hottest bodyboarding spots. If the surf's right, you can find a few dozen bodyboarders, mostly teenagers, riding the waves. These experienced local kids ride straight for the groin's cement wall and then veer away at the last moment, thrilling tourists watching them from the little pier above.

KAPI'OLANI BEACH PARK

Starting at Kapahulu Groin and extending down to the Natatorium, this stretch of beach is backed by banyan trees and grassy lawns. It's a relaxed place with far less of the hubbub by Waikiki's beachfront hotels. It's a popular weekend picnicking spot for families, who unload the kids to splash in the water while they fire up the barbecue grills.

Queen's Surf Beach is the common name given to the widest section of Kapi'olani Beach. There are rest rooms and showers at the Queen's Surf pavilion. The stretch in front of the pavilion is popular with the gay community, and its sandy bottom offers decent swimming. The beach between Queen's Surf and the Wall is shallow and has broken coral. The surfing area offshore is called **Publics** and sees some good waves in winter.

SANS SOUCI BEACH PARK

Also called **Kaimana Beach** because of its proximity to the New Otani Kaimana Beach Hotel, Sans Souci attracts sunbathers and swimmers who want to escape Waikiki's frenzied scene. Facilities include a lifeguard station and outdoor showers. Locals come here for their daily swims. A shallow coral reef close to shore makes for calm, protected waters and provides reasonably good snorkeling. More coral can be found by following the Kapua Channel as it cuts through the reef, although if you swim out, beware of strong currents that can pick up. Check conditions with the lifeguard before venturing out.

CRUISING WAIKIKI

Several catamaran cruises leave right from Waikiki Beach – just walk down onto the sand, step into the surf and hop aboard. A 90-minute, all-you-can-drink 'booze cruise' costs around $25 to $30 per person.

Maita'i Catamaran (☎ 922-5665, 800-462-7975; www.leahi.com) Look for the white catamaran with green sails pulling up on the beach between the Halekulani and Sheraton Waikiki hotels. This company offers the biggest variety of trips, including reef snorkeling, moonlight sails and a sunset 'booze cruise'; call ahead for schedules and reservations.

Na Hoku II (www.nahokuii.com) With its yellow-and-red–striped sails, this frat boy–friendly, hard-drinkin' catamaran departs five times daily between 9:30am and 5:30pm, shoving off in front of Duke's Waikiki (p160).

Other Activities
In the mornings, runners pound the pavement next to Ala Wai Canal, while in the late afternoon outrigger canoe teams ply the canal's waters en route to Ala Wai Yacht Harbor. **Kapi'olani Park** (right) has sports fields for soccer and softball, even cricket. For an indoor workout, **24-Hour Fitness** (☎ 923-9090; 2490 Kalakaua Ave; daily/weekly pass $25/69; ☽ 24hr) has a small, fully-equipped gym and group classes.

SURFING
For a complete rundown on Waikiki's surfing hot spots, see the Beaches section (p149). For surfing lessons (two-hour group classes from $80) and board rentals (from $20 per day), try the following:
Go Nuts Hawaii (☎ 926-3367; www.gonuts-hawaii.com; 159 Ka'iulani Ave; ☽ 8am-9pm)
Hans Hedemann Surf (☎ 924-7778; www.hhsurf.com; 2586 Kapahulu Ave; ☽ 9am-5pm)
Hawaiian WaterSports (☎ 739-5483; www.hawaiianwatersports.com; 415 Kapahulu Ave; ☽ 9am-5pm)

For lessons taught by real-life firefighters, **Hawaiian Fire Surf School** (☎ 737-3743, 888-955-7873; www.hawaiianfire.com; 2hr lessons group/private $99/179) offers free pick-ups from Waikiki and transportation to/from a quiet beach near Barbers Point on the Wai'anae Coast.

SCUBA DIVING & SNORKELING
The best snorkeling is toward Diamond Head at Sans Souci Beach (opposite) and Queen's Surf Beach (opposite), but to really see the gorgeous stuff – coral gardens, manta rays and exotic tropical fish – you should go on a boat dive. For equipment rentals and/or boat trips:
Snorkel Bob's (☎ 735-7944; www.snorkelbob.com; 702 Kapahulu Ave; snorkel-set rental per day $2-11, per week $9-44; ☽ 8am-5pm) Rates vary depending on the quality of the gear and accessories packages.
our pick Waikiki Diving Center (☎ 922-2121; www.waikikidiving.com; 424 Nahua St; snorkel trip $35, 2-tank/wreck dive $115/125; ☽ 7am-5pm) Reliable full-service dive shop offers small-group boat dives and open-water PADI certification courses ($350).

GOLF
With views of Diamond Head, the 18-hole/par 70 **Ala Wai Golf Course** (☎ 733-7387; 404 Kapahulu Ave) scores a Guinness World Record for being the world's busiest golf course. For tee-time reservations, green fees and general information, see p108. If you get there early in the day and get on the waiting list, you'll probably get playing time later in the day, as long as your entire party waits at the course.

SPAS
What's a beach vacation without a little pampering? Especially with Hawaii's traditions of *lomilomi* ('loving touch') and *pohaku* (hot-stone) massage, coupled with gentle aloha spirit. Call ahead for appointments, including at these places:
Abhasa Spa (☎ 922-8200; www.abhasa.com; Royal Hawaiian Hotel; 2259 Kalakaua Ave) Hawaiian massage in cabanas amidst tropical gardens.
AquaSPA (☎ 924-2782; www.aquaresorts.com; various locations) Intimate boutique-hotel cabana massages, often at discounted rates.
Na Ho'ola Spa (☎ 923-1234; http://waikiki.hyatt.com; Hyatt Regency Waikiki Beach Resort & Spa, 2424 Kalakaua Ave) Seaweed, mud and *ti*-leaf wraps, plus mac-nut exfoliation and coconut moisturizers.
Waikiki Plantation Spa (☎ 926-2880, 866-926-2880; www.waikikiplantationspa.com; Outrigger Waikiki on the Beach, 2335 Kalakaua Ave) Holistic Hawaiian spa therapies with penthouse views.

Kapi'olani Park
At the Diamond Head end of Waikiki, opposite Kapi'olani Beach Park (opposite), Hawaii's first public park is the city's communal backyard, hosting outdoor concerts, festivals, farmers markets, arts-and-crafts fairs and family picnics under shady banyan trees. Opposite Waikiki Aquarium there are four **tennis courts** lighted for night play; they're free and first-come, first-served, but you'll need your own equipment.

WAIKIKI AQUARIUM
Next to a living reef on Waikiki's shoreline, this modern university-managed, kid-friendly **aquarium** (☎ 923-9741; www.waquarium.org; 2777 Kalakaua Ave; adult/child 4-13/child over 13 $9/2/4; ☽ 9am-5pm) features a jaw-dropping shark gallery and dozens of tanks that re-create different Pacific Ocean reef habitats. It's a great place to identify colorful coral and fish you've seen while snorkeling. Check the website for special family-friendly events and programs such as 'Aquarium After Dark.'

There are rare Hawaiian fish species such as the bearded armorhead, as well as hypnotic moon jellies and flashlight fish that host bioluminescent bacteria. Especially noteworthy

O'AHU

are the Paluan chambered nautiluses with their unique spiral shells; this eco-conscious aquarium was the world's first to breed these endangered creatures in captivity. An outdoor tank out back is home to a pair of rare and endangered Hawaiian monk seals, which typically breed on the remote Northwestern Hawaiian Islands, but have recently hauled out on some of O'ahu's beaches.

HONOLULU ZOO
This fairly respectable **zoo** (☎ 971-7171; www .honoluluzoo.org; adult/child 6-12 $6/1; 🕙 9am-4:30pm), on the north side of Kapi'olani Park, features some 300 species spread across over 40 acres of tropical greenery. Although small, a highlight is the African Savanna section, next to a small petting zoo. In the aviary near the entrance you'll spot native birds, including the *ae'o* (Hawaiian black-necked stilt), *nene* (Hawaiian goose) and *'apapane,* a bright red Hawaiian honeycreeper. Check the website for schedules of family-friendly twilight tours, overnight campouts and 'breakfast with a keeper' events (reservations recommended). The zoo is wheelchair-accessible.

Historical Sites
The Royal Hawaiian and Moana Surfrider hotels, both on the National Register of Historic Places, are within walking distance of each other on Kalakaua Ave.

MOANA SURFRIDER
Christened the Moana Hotel when it opened in 1901, this **hotel** (☎ 922-3111; www.moana-surf rider.com; 2365 Kalakaua Ave; free tours usually 11am & 5pm Mon, Wed & Fri) is built in the civilized style of an old plantation inn. The Moana joined what was then an exclusive neighborhood for Hawaiian royalty and business tycoons. Early guests included aristocrats, princes and Hollywood movie stars. If you don't join a tour, visit the mezzanine **museum**, which displays period photographs and hotel memorabilia, including scripts from the *Hawaii Calls* radio show, broadcast from here between 1935 and 1975.

ROYAL HAWAIIAN HOTEL
With its Moorish-style turrets and archways, this 1927 art deco **hotel** (☎ 923-7311; www.royal-hawaiian.com; 2259 Kalakaua Ave; free tours usually 2pm Mon, Wed & Fri) is a landmark. During the days of luxury ocean liners, the hotel became

an extension of the cruise ships run by the Matson Navigation Company. Dubbed the 'Pink Palace,' its guest list once read like a who's-who of A-list celebrities, from royalty to Rockefellers, plus pop-culture stars like Charlie Chaplin and Babe Ruth. Today, historic tours explore the architecture and lore of this grand dame. Ask the concierge for a self-guided walking tour brochure before visiting the hotel's flowering gardens.

HAWAI'I ARMY MUSEUM
Of interest mainly to specialists, this **museum** (☎ 955-9552; www.hiarmymuseumsoc.org; Kalia Rd; admission by donation; 🕙 10am-4:15pm Tue-Sun; P) traces the military history of consolidation of power under King Kamehameha in the late 18th century through life under martial law during WWII and the US army's ongoing role on O'ahu. Located at Fort DeRussy Military Reservation, the museum occupies Battery Randolph, erected in 1911. The battery once held two formidable guns with an impressive 14-mile range, designed to recoil into the concrete walls for reloading after firing, which shook the whole neighborhood. A Cobra helicopter and various military tanks and machinery are also on display. There's free parking with validation.

NATATORIUM
At the Diamond Head end of Kapi'olani Beach Park (p150), this broken-down, padlocked **building** (http://natorium.org) houses a 100m-long saltwater swimming pool constructed as a memorial for WWI veterans. Two Olympic gold medalists – Johnny Weissmuller and Duke Kahanamoku – trained in the tide-fed pool. There were once hopes of hosting the Olympics on O'ahu, with this pool as the focal point. Although the Natatorium is now on the National Register of Historic Places, restoration projects have been repeatedly stalled by political bureaucracy.

COURSES
Mana Hawai'i (☎ 923-2220; www.waikikibeachwalk .com; 226 Lewers St) Hawaiiana shop (p162) offers free weekly classes in Hawaiian language, hula dancing, ukulele playing and *lauhala* leaf weaving and occasional workshops in traditional Hawaiian spiritual practices.
Royal Hawaiian Center (☎ 922-2299; www.royal hawaiiancenter.com; 2201 Kalakaua Ave) Shopping mall offers free Hawaiian cultural classes and demonstrations in arts and crafts, including quilts, leis, *kapa* (pounded-bark

cloth), hula, ukulele and *lomilomi* massage; check the website or call for schedules.

Waikiki Community Center (☎ 923-1802; www .waikikicommunitycenter.org; 310 Pa'oakalani Ave; lesson $3-15) Try your hand at mah-jongg, the ukulele, hula or other island arts and crafts. Instructors at this homespun community center are brimming with aloha. Most classes are held on weekdays; call or go online for schedules.

FESTIVALS & EVENTS

Waikiki loves to party. Every Friday night at 7:30pm from October to March (from 8pm April to September), the Hilton Hawaiian Village shoots off a big ol' fireworks display, visible from the beach. For festivals and events elsewhere around Honolulu, see p131.

Ala Wai Challenge (☎ 923-1802; www.waikikicom munitycenter.org) Outrigger canoe races, local food, games and live entertainment in January.

Honolulu Festival (☎ 926-2424; www.honolulufest ival.com) Cultural performances at Waikiki Beach Walk and a festive parade along Kalakaua Ave in mid-March.

Waikiki Spam Jam (www.spamjamhawaii.com) Late April sees a street festival devoted to Hawaii's favorite tinned meat product: Spam.

Pan-Pacific Festival (☎ 926-8177; www.pan-pacific -festival.com) Hula dancing, *taiko* drumming, an arts-and-crafts fair and a huge *ho'olaule'a* (block party) in early June.

Hawaiian Slack Key Guitar Festival (☎ 226-2697; www.slackkeyfestival.com) Traditional Hawaiian guitar and ukulele music at Kapi'olani Park in mid-August.

Aloha Festivals (http://alohafestivals.com) During a statewide cultural festival, Waikiki is famous for its *ho'olaule'a* in mid-September.

SLEEPING

Waikiki's main beachfront strip, Kalakaua Ave, is lined with high-rise resort hotels. Be aware that 'ocean view' and its cousins 'ocean front' and 'partial ocean view' are all liberally used and often require a periscope to spot the waves. 'City', 'garden' or 'mountain' views may be euphemisms for overlooking a parking lot. When making reservations, check hotel room maps online or call a hotel reservation agent to ask.

If you don't mind walking a few minutes to the beach, there are some inviting small hotels on Waikiki's backstreets. Some near Kuhio Ave and up by the Ala Wai Canal have rooms as lovely as the beachfront properties, but for half the price. Others are just grotty renovated apartment buildings or aging 1960s and '70s high-rises. Waves of chic boutique-styled hotels are just starting to come ashore in Waikiki.

For a modicum of style on a budget, look into **Aqua Hotels & Resorts** (www.aquaresorts.com), the best of which offer free high-speed internet, complimentary continental breakfast, tiny pools and small workout rooms; they're also gay-friendly and designed for both business and leisure travelers. A more massive local chain is **Outrigger Hotels & Resorts** (www.outrigger .com), which also owns Waikiki's **Ohana Hotels & Resorts** (www.ohanahotels.com). Outrigger gives back to the local community through volunteer work and charity donations.

Wherever you stay in Waikiki, make reservations in advance. Overnight parking costs $5 to $25, whether for valet or self-parking. Increasingly, many hotels are also charging for mandatory 'resort fees,' which tack another $5 to $25 per day onto your final bill. Resort fees may cover internet connections, local and toll-free phone calls and fitness room access, or no extra perks at all, but regardless, you'll have to pay.

Waikiki has far more hotel rooms than condos. For condo rentals, which are not as easy to come by on O'ahu as on some Neighbor Islands, contact the following:

Pacific Islands Reservations (☎ 808-262-8133; www.waikiki-condo-rentals.com)

Aloha Waikiki Vacation Condos (☎ 924-0433, 800-655-6055; www.waikiki-condos.com)

Hawaiian Beach Rentals (☎ 800-853-0787; www .hawaiianbeachrentals.com)

For more short-term vacation rentals and sublets, browse listings online at **Vacation Rentals By Owner** (www.vrbo.com) or **Craigslist** (http://honolulu .craigslist.org).

Budget

Lemon Rd, an alley set back from the Diamond Head end of the beach, is filled with backpacker hostels catering to global nomads and a twenty-something party crowd.

Hostelling International-Waikiki (☎ 926-8313; www.hostelsaloha.com; 2417 Prince Edward St; dm $25-28, d $58-64; ✿ reception 1pm-3am; ℗ ▣) Occupying a converted low-rise apartment building, this tidy hostel has single-sex dormitories, a common kitchen and bodyboards to borrow. The accommodations are adequate but won't have you jumping for joy. Unlike most mainland HI hostels, there's no dormitory lockout or curfew. No alcohol allowed.

Waikiki Beachside Hostel (☎ 923-9566, 866-478-3888; www.waikikibeachsidehostel.com; 2556 Lemon Rd; dm $26-35, semiprivate r $67-76; P 🖳 ☎) Travelers report that security and cleanliness can be lax, but discounts on surfboards, bodyboards, snorkel sets and moped rentals are perks. Rooms are more expensive than at neighboring hostels because each dorm (co-ed or female-only) comes equipped with a full kitchen and phone. Free wi-fi in common areas.

Royal Grove Hotel (☎ 923-7691; www.royalgrovehotel.com; 151 Uluniu Ave; r with kitchenette $55-100; ☒ 🖳 ☒) No frills but plenty of aloha characterize this fabulously pink low-rise motel, a favorite of 'snowbird' retirees who return each winter to this home-away-from-home complete with a pet bird and a piano in the lobby. Economy rooms in the older Mauka Wing have no air-con and suffer heavy traffic noise. Weekly off-season discounts available.

Waikiki Prince Hotel (☎ 922-1544; 2431 Prince Edward St; r $65-100; P ☒ ☎) What ocean views? Never mind the cramped check-in office either. This 1970s apartment complex on an anonymous side street is a standout budget option, as some of the two dozen compact, cheerful rooms have kitchenettes. Free lobby wi-fi.

Midrange

Waikiki sits firmly in the lap of middle-class standards. Thankfully, a few boutique properties rise above the generic hotel herd.

Celebrity Resorts Waikiki (☎ 923-7336, 866-507-1428; www.celebrityresorts.com; 431 Nohonani St; r $85-130,
1br $105-140; P ☒ 🖳 ☎ ☒) With an easy-to-miss sign under a green awning, this low-key, three-story hotel merits a second look. With impromptu pizza nights and sing-alongs by the tropical garden-shaded pool, guests act just like neighbors and old friends. Motel-style rooms deliver rattan furnishings, kitchenettes and noisy air-con.

Aqua Aloha Surf & Spa (☎ 923-0222, 866-406-2782; www.aquaresorts.com; 444 Kanekapolei St; r incl breakfast $85-175; P ☒ 🖳 ☒) If you don't mind being beside Ala Wai Canal, this lively, surf-themed hotel can be a bargain. Although kinda bland, shoebox-sized contemporary rooms each have a microwave, minifridge and coffeemaker, plus free wired internet. Offsite parking lot.

Ohana Waikiki East (☎ 922-5353, 866-968-8744; www.ohanahotels.com; 150 Ka'iulani Ave; r $99-329, 1br & 2br available by request; P ☒ 🖳 ☎ ☒) Centrally located, this entirely nonsmoking hotel lacks the historical charm and oceanfront setting of nearby hotels, but actual room quality is just as good – and for much less money. Some rooms have kitchenettes. A downstairs coffee shop sells Hawaii-grown brews and snacks. Free in-room wired internet, and lobby and poolside wi-fi.

Aqua Palms & Spa (☎ 406-2782, 866-406-2782; www.aquaresorts.com; 1850 Ala Moana Blvd; r incl breakfast $115-175; P ☒ ☒ ☒) A short walk from the Ala Moana Center mall, this boutique hotel feels more functional than fun, but still delivers bang for your buck. Smallish rooms lack tropical panache but you can't fault those plush beds, sofas or fluffy robes for comfort. There's a postage stamp–sized swimming pool and workout room. Free in-room wired internet.

our pick Best Western Coconut Waikiki Hotel
(☎ 923-8828, 866-406-2782; www.aquaresorts.com; 450 Lewers St; r incl breakfast $115-195; P ⊠ ☐ ⧈ ⊠) Don't let the chain-gang name fool you: this Aqua-managed property has hip, edgy decor: atomic starburst mirrors in the hallways, and cool mint green rooms, each with private lanai. Designed with business travelers in mind, rooms have ergonomic work desks, microwaves and minifridges. The exercise room is small, but well equipped.

✗**Ohana Waikiki Beachcomber** (☎ 922-4646, 866-968-8744; www.ohanahotels.com; 2300 Kalakaua Ave; r $119-229; P ⊠ ☐ ⧈ ⊠) On Waikiki's main strip, this modern nonsmoking hotel is remarkable for its prime location and subprime rates. This-could-be-anywhere-in-the-world rooms have been renovated with flat-screen TVs and alarm clocks with MP3 player plug-ins. Free in-room wired internet and lobby wi-fi.

Breakers (☎ 923-3181, 800-426-0494; www.breakers-hawaii.com; 250 Beach Walk; r $120-150; P ⊠ ⊠) You'll either love it or hate it: this older, Polynesian-style hotel is a throwback to earlier times, with a petite garden and floor-to-ceiling louvered windows. Very old, creaky rooms all have kitchenettes; those on the second-floor also have Japanese-style *shōji* (translucent paper-covered wooden sliding doors).

✗**Aqua Bamboo & Spa** (☎ 922-7777, 866-406-2782; www.aquabamboo.com; 2425 Kuhio Ave; r $120-160, 1br $215-285, all incl breakfast; P ⊠ ☐ ⧈ ⊠) Looking for a meditative retreat from Waikiki's urban jungle? An intimate boutique hotel, the Bamboo has stylishly minimalist rooms and a small saltwater pool, should you tire of the ocean. Free in-room wired internet and wi-fi in lobby and poolside.

✗**Wyland Waikiki** (☎ 954-4000, 877-995-2638; www.outrigger.com; 400 Royal Hawaiian Ave; r $129-355; P ⊠ ☐ ⧈ ⊠) Named after the cheesy muralist; the ocean theme is pervasive here, starting from the lobby aquarium. Fresh, contemporary rooms may be smallish, but have flat-screen TVs and some kitchenettes; they're only good value at under $200 per night. Free in-room wired internet and lobby and poolside wi-fi.

our pick Hotel Renew (☎ 687-7700, 888-485-7639; www.hotelrenew.com; 129 Pa'oakalani Ave; r incl breakfast $149-209; P ⊠ ☐ ⧈) Just a half-block from the beach, this eco-conscious boutique hotel has attentive concierge staff who can be

counted on to provide all of the little niceties, from chilled drinks upon arrival to beach mats and bodyboards to borrow. Design-savvy accommodations come with platform beds, projection-screen TVs, spa robes, earth-toned furnishings and *shōji* sliding screens. It's romantic enough for honeymooners, and also gay-friendly.

✗**Aston Waikiki Circle Hotel** (☎ 923-1571, 877-997-6667; www.astonhotels.com; 2464 Kalakaua Ave; r $150-220; P ⊠) Tired of square boxes? This circular building must have been *très chic* back in the playful era of postmodernism, but today this survivor is all about value not fashion. About half of the rooms, complete with lanai, get a full ocean view. The drawback is that they aren't big enough to practice your hula dancing in. In-room wired internet costs extra.

Cabana at Waikiki (☎ 926-5555, 877-902-2121; www.cabana-waikiki.com; 2551 Cartwright Rd; 1br incl breakfast $159-255; P ⊠ ☐ ⧈ ⊠) Waikiki's only exclusively gay-owned and -operated hotel is only minutes from Hula's bar, Queen's Surf Beach and a 24-hour gym. Each of the 15 comfy units has a king-size bed, full-size sofa bed and either a kitchenette or full kitchen. An eight-man hot tub awaits in the tropical garden.

Waikiki Grand Hotel (☎ 923-1814, 888-336-4368; www.waikikigrand.com; 134 Kapahulu Ave; r $139-199, ste $159-350; P ⊠ ⊠) Best known for Hula's, a popular gay bar, this condotel is just a minute's walk from Queen's Surf Beach. Individually owned units (some kitchenettes) vary from horrifying to heavenly, so view the online photo with some skepticism. Weekly discounts available.

Aston at the Waikiki Banyan (☎ 922-0555, 877-977-6667; www.astonhotels.com; 201 Ohua Ave; 1br $190-295; P ⊠ ☐ ⧈ ⊠) This all-suite, high-rise hotel is a short walk from the aquarium, the zoo and of course, the beach. Roomy suites have a handy sofabed in the living room. Kids get a free souvenir sand pail full of cool, fun stuff at check-in, and the pool deck has a playground, tennis and basketball courts, and a putting green. In-room wired internet and common-area wi-fi cost extra.

✗**New Otani Kaimana Beach Hotel** (☎ 923-1555, 800-356-8264; www.kaimana.com; 2863 Kalakaua Ave; r $190-440; P ⊠ ☐ ⧈) Just half a mile from the throbbing hub of Waikiki, this low-key hotel sits oceanside in front of Sans Souci Beach Park. Book early, because repeat guests also crave the seclusion and idyllic

O'AHU

TOP PICKS – WAIKIKI'S FAMILY-FRIENDLY HOTELS

■ **Hilton Hawaiian Village** (below)

■ **Sheraton Waikiki** (right)

■ **Royal Hawaiian Hotel** (p152)

■ **Aston Waikiki Beach Hotel** (right)

■ **Aston at the Waikiki Banyan** (p155)

■ **Outrigger Reef on the Beach** (below)

■ **Embassy Suites Waikiki Beach Walk** (below)

■ **Ohana Waikiki East** (p154)

---

beach access. The rooms are small, but the view is big, and all rooms have private lanai. Japanese is spoken here.

Embassy Suites Waikiki Beach Walk (☎ 921-2345, 800-362-2779; www.embassysuiteswaikiki.com; 201 Beach Walk; 1br incl breakfast $209-329; P ✕ ▯ ⬚ ⬚) Enviably near the beach, restaurants and nightlife, this brand-new chain property has no-nonsense, tropically inspired suites big enough for families. All come with microwaves, minifridges, coffeemakers, flat-screen TVs and radio/alarm clocks with MP3 input jacks. There's also a professionally equipped fitness room. Free in-room wired internet and common-area wi-fi.

Outrigger Reef on the Beach (☎ 923-3111, 866-956-4262; www.outriggerreef.com; 2169 Kalia Rd; r $209-465; P ✕ ▯ ⬚ ⬚) Forget the hoity-toity attitudes of the Outrigger's higher-priced beachfront neighbors. Here the Hawaiiana flows from the handmade outrigger canoe in the Polynesian-style lobby through free hula, ukulele and lei-making classes. Rooms are modern and functional enough for a mostly suburban crowd. Free in-room wired internet and lobby and poolside wi-fi.

Waikiki Parc Hotel (☎ 921-7272, 800-422-0450; www.waikikiparc.com; 2233 Helumoa Rd; r $215-415; P ✕ ▯ ⬚) Near its more upmarket sister resort, the Halekulani, the Parc is an affordably hip hangout that oddly mixes nostalgic touches like plantation-shuttered windows with minimalist contemporary furnishings. Although the staff pamperings, guest rooms are not as chic as the common areas or Nobu Waikiki (p159) sushi bar and lounge.

Hilton Hawaiian Village (☎ 949-4321, 800-445-8667; www.hawaiianvillage.hilton.com; 2005 Kalia Rd; r $219-850; P ✕ ▯ ⬚ ⬚) On the Fort DeRussy side of

Waikiki, the Hilton is Waikiki's largest hotel – practically a self-sufficient tourist fortress of towers, restaurants, bars and shops. It's geared almost entirely for families and package tourists. Expect check-in lines to move as slowly as TSA airport-security checkpoints.

Aston Waikiki Beach Hotel (☎ 922-2511, 800-877-7666; www.astonhotels.com; 2570 Kalakaua Ave; r incl breakfast $225-425; P ✕ ▯ ⬚ ⬚) With cheery surf-themed decor and a rooftop bar lit by tiki torches, this contemporary number opposite the beach is frequently sold out, especially on internet-booking sites. If you get a discount, you too will be a devotee. Free souvenir soft-sided cooler bags can be filled with breakfast goodies to take to the beach. In-room wired internet and lobby and poolside wi-fi costs extra.

Also recommended:

Hale Koa Hotel (☎ 955-0555, 800-367-6027; www.halekoa.com; 2055 Kalia Rd; r $87-277; P ✕ ▯ ⬚) Reserved for active and retired US military personnel; ask for renovated Ilima Tower rooms.

Lotus at Diamond Head (☎ 922-1700, 800-367-5004; www.castleresorts.com; 2885 Kalakaua Ave; r $189-850; P ✕) Well-worn boutique hotel is still a mod sanctuary by Sans Souci Beach.

Top End

Waikiki's most historic hotels and top-tier resorts all cluster by the beach.

Outrigger Regency on Beachwalk (☎ 922-3871, 866-956-4262; www.outrigger.com; 255 Beach Walk; 1br $245-399, 2br $379-499; P ✕ ▯) This sleek modern high-rise is designed with earth- and jewel-toned furnishings, marble baths and bold artwork. Spacious condo-style suites all have full kitchens; some also have private lanai with partial ocean views. Step outside the downstairs lobby, and you're right on buzzing Waikiki Beach Walk. Free in-room wired internet.

Moana Surfrider (☎ 922-3111, 866-716-8109; www.moana-surfrider.com; 2365 Kalakaua Ave; r $265-510; P ✕ ▯ ⬚ ⬚) Waikiki's most historic hotel retains most of its colonial character in the common areas, with high plantation-style ceilings, Hawaiian artwork on the walls and koa-wood rocking chairs beckoning on the front veranda. Compact rooms have been recently upgraded with 21st-century amenities. In-room wired internet and lobby and poolside wi-fi cost extra. Self-parking is offsite.

Sheraton Waikiki (☎ 922-4422, 866-716-8109; www.sheraton-waikiki.com; 2255 Kalakaua Ave; r $380-735; P ✕ ▯ ⬚) This chain megahotel looms over the historic Royal Hawaiian Hotel with modern utilities and is ginormous enough to accommodate package-tour groups and conferences. Facing the beach, a 'superpool' amphibious playground will keep the kiddos entertained. Online booking discounts of 50% are commonly available; otherwise, don't bother.

Royal Hawaiian Hotel (☎ 923-7311, 866-716-8110; www.royal-hawaiian.com; 2259 Kalakaua Ave; r $380-855; P ✂ 🖥 🛜 🍴) The aristocratic Royal Hawaiian was Waikiki's first true luxury hotel and now it looks better than ever, thanks to multimillion-dollar renovations. The pink Moorish-style building is all ambience, with airy walkways and soaring ceilings. Rooms in the historic section maintain classic appeal, though many prefer ocean-view rooms in the modern high-rise tower. In-room wired internet and limited common-area wi-fi cost extra.

our pick **Halekulani** (☎ 923-2311, 800-367-2343; www.halekulani.com; 2199 Kalia Rd; r $425-750; P ✂ 🖥 🍴 🛜) With modern sophistication, this resort hotel lives up to its name, which means 'House Befitting Heaven.' It's an experience of gracious living, not merely a place to crash. Peaceful rooms are equipped with modern gadgets, such as high-tech entertainment centers, deep soaking tubs and expansive lanai. Eclectic luxury suites include one personally designed by Vera Wang. Warning: this is one of O'ahu's few resorts where evening dress codes are in effect.

Also recommended:

Aston Waikiki Beach Tower (☎ 926-6400, 877-997-6667; www.astonhotels.com; 2470 Kalakaua Ave; 1br & 2br $495-815; P ✂ 🍴) Full-service apartment-style hotel in the heart of Waikiki, perfect for family reunions.

Trump International Hotel & Tower (☎ 212-299-1062; www.trumpwaikikihotel.com; 223 Saratoga Rd; P ✂ 🖥 🍴) Luxury high-rise boasts an infinity pool and apartment-style suites with panoramic windows, full kitchens and marble baths. Call for room rates.

EATING

Early-bird specials and mediocre buffets are still the standard in Waikiki. Along Kalakaua Ave, suburban chains like the Cheesecake Factory overflow with hungry tourists, although a few beachfront hotel restaurants are run by star chefs. A block farther inland, Kuhio Ave is filled with cheap grazing choices, especially ethnic takeout joints to fuel an afternoon of surfing. On the outskirts of

Waikiki, you can dig up delicious neighborhood eateries, drive-ins and bakeries along Kapahulu Ave heading toward the university. Otherwise, you're better off getting out of Waikiki and eating in other neighborhoods of Honolulu (see p132).

Budget

Yes, you can eat cheaply in Waikiki, if you know where to look.

Leonard's (☎ 737-5591; 933 Kapahulu Ave; pastries 75¢-$2; 🕑 6am-9pm Mon-Thu, to 10pm Fri & Sat) This Portuguese bakery with a vintage 1950s neon sign is known throughout O'ahu for its *malasadas*, a type of sweet, fried dough rolled in sugar. Try the *haupia malasada*, with coconut-cream filling, and you'll be hooked.

Waiola Bakery & Shave Ice II (☎ 949-2269; 525 Kapahulu Ave; items $2-4; 🕑 7:30am-6pm) Developing a shave-ice palate is a point of pride for the locals. This modest storefront delivers superfine shave ice and a large assortment of add-ons including azuki beans, condensed milk, *mochi* (sticky-sweet Japanese pounded-rice cakes) and island-style *li hing mui* crack seed.

Tokkuri Tei (☎ 739-2800; 611 Kapahulu Ave; shared dishes $3-15; 🕑 11am-2pm Mon-Fri, 5:30pm-midnight Mon-Sat, 5-10pm Sun) Under-the-radar neighborhood *izakaya* offers upbeat contemporary versions of Japanese standards. Paper lanterns hang overhead and bookcases store customers' private bottles of sake and *shōchū* (potato liquor). Try the house spider *poke* with fish roe, grilled *kushiyaki* skewers or soft-shell crab drizzled with sweet-chili vinaigrette.

Rainbow Drive-In (☎ 737-0177; 3308 Kanaina Ave; meals $4-7; 🕑 7:30am-9pm) Started by an island-born US Army cook after WWII, this classic Hawaii drive-in wrapped in rainbow-colored neon is a throwback to another era. From the takeout counter, construction workers and gangly surfers order all the local favorites: *loco moco*, teriyaki burgers and mixed-plate lunches.

Ruffage Natural Foods (☎ 922-2042; 2443 Kuhio Ave; items $4-8; 🕑 9am-6pm) This pint-sized health-food store whips up taro burgers, veggie burritos, vegan chili and real-fruit smoothies that will revitalize your whole bod. At night, the shop shares space with a tiny, backpacker-friendly sushi bar run by a Japanese chef.

Eggs 'n Things (☎ 949-0820; 343 Saratoga Rd; mains $4-10; 🕑 6am-10pm) Never empty, this diner dishes up reliable banana macnut pancakes topped

O'AHU

with your choice of honey, guava or coconut syrup and fluffy omelets with Portuguese sausage for jet-lagged tourists, graveyard shift workers and postclubbers.

Me BBQ (☎ 926-9717; 151 Uluniu Ave; plate meals $4-12; ☽ 7am-9pm Mon-Sat) This streetside takeout counter has zero atmosphere, but service is lightning-fast and there are plastic picnic tables where you can chow down. Succulent *kalbi* short ribs and spicy kim chi are house specialties, but the wall-sized picture menu also includes island plate-lunch combos with chicken katsu, shrimp tempura and more.

Diamond Head Market & Grill (☎ 732-0077; 3158 Monsarrat Ave; meals $4-15; ☽ 6:30am-9pm) This takeout counter and market with a bakery and gourmet deli inside feeds neighborhood hipsters and families who don't want to heat up the kitchen. Try the *char siu* pork plate lunches, portabello-mushroom burgers and tropical pancakes. There are picnic tables beside the parking lot for immediate consumption.

Bogart's Cafe (☎ 739-0999; 3045 Monsarrat Ave; mains $5-10; ☽ 6am-6:30pm Mon-Fri, to 6pm Sat & Sun) Where surfers, artists and dot-com millionaires all get their caffeinated jolts, this neighborhood espresso bar in a minimall is a popular breakfast spot, especially for fruit-topped Belgian waffles and crab-and-avocado omelets. At lunch, there's veggie wraps and salads. If you're not local, service can take forever.

Waliana Coffee House (☎ 955-1764; 1860 Ala Moana Blvd; mains $5-15; ☽ 24hr) Opposite the Hilton Hawaiian Village, this all-night coffee shop is stuck in the 1970s with its Naugahyde booths and counter stools and serves heaping portions of greasy-spoon fare and tropical fruity drinks. Waitstaff all know the regulars by name. Go sing karaoke with the locals in the cocktail lounge.

Menchanko-Tei (☎ 924-8366; Waikiki Trade Center, 2255 Kuhio Ave; mains $8-12; ☽ 11am-11pm) Japanese

expats head to this unassuming kitchen for their fix of Hakata-style ramen soup with freshly made noodles, citrus pepper and a creamy broth. This place also makes a mean *tonkatsu* (deep-fried pork cutlet), *gyōza* and Nagasaki-style *sara-udon* (fried noodles with stir-fried veggies).

Also recommended:

Farmers Market (☎ 923-1802; Waikiki Community Center, 310 Pa'oakalani Ave; ☽ 7am-1pm Tue & Fri) Fresh produce stands set up in the parking lot.

Food Pantry (☎ 923-9831; 2370 Kuhio Ave; ☽ 6am-1am) More expensive than chain supermarkets, which are all outside Waikiki, but cheaper than convenience stores.

Ono Seafood (☎ 732-4806; 747 Kapahulu Ave; items $2-12; ☽ varies) An addictive, made-to-order *poke* shop – get there early before the fresh fish runs out.

People's Open Market (☎ 522-7088; cnr Monsarrat & Paki Aves, Kapi'olani Park; ☽ 10-11am Wed) Farmers market for fresh bounty from land and sea.

Midrange

Many of Waikiki's middle-of-the-road restaurants are overpriced and not worth it, no matter how enticing the ocean views. But we've listed a few standout exceptions here.

Siam Square (☎ 923-5320; 2nd fl, 408 Lewers St; mains $11-16; ☽ 11am-11pm Mon-Sat, to 10pm Sun) This is Waikiki's most authentic Thai restaurant. You want it spicy? Good, because that's the only way you're going to get your larb pork salad or fried fish with chili sauce here. Service is smiley, but standoffish.

Uncle Bo's (☎ 735-8311; 559 Kapahulu Ave; shared dishes $6-14, mains $11-26; ☽ 5pm-2am) Inside a divey-looking storefront, boisterous groups of friends devour an endless list of *pupu* crafted here with island flair, like baby-back ribs with Maui onions or *kalua* pig nachos with won-ton chips. For dinner, pastas and steaks take a backseat to market-fresh seafood like Chinese-style steamed *opakapaka* (pink snapper).

Ono Hawaiian Food (☎ 737-2275; 726 Kapahulu Ave; combination plates $12-16; ☽ 11am-8pm Mon-Sat) This little diner concentrates on homegrown Hawaiian fare. In between crowded, aging tables and sports paraphernalia, locals and tourists shoehorn themselves in for *kalua* pig, *lomilomi* salmon, or *laulau* (meat wrapped in *ti* leaves and steamed) served with poi or rice. Arrive early to avoid a long wait. Cash only.

Irifune (☎ 737-1141; 563 Kapahulu Ave; mains $12-18; ☽ 11:30am-1:30pm & 5:30-9:30pm Tue-Sat) Follow local families to this cramped eatery, decorated with Japanese country kitsch and serving up creative appetizers like *gyōza* (fried dumplings) stuffed with tofu and cream cheese. Top dinner choices are garlic *'ahi*, seared ever so gingerly, and a variety of combination plates. BYOB (beer only).

Sansei Seafood Restaurant & Sushi Bar (☎ 931-6286; 3rd fl, Waikiki Beach Marriott Resort, 2552 Kalakaua Ave; mains $16-35; ⊙ 5:30-10pm Sun-Thu, to 1am Fri & Sat) From the mind of one of Hawaii's hottest chefs, DK Kodama, this Pacific Rim fusion menu rolls out everything from traditional sashimi to Dungeness crab ramen with black-truffle butter sauce. Tables on the torchlit veranda enjoy prime sunset views. Queue for early-bird specials, available from 5pm to 6pm on Sunday and Monday, or enjoy 50% off all food after 10pm on Friday and Saturday nights.

Hula Grill (☎ 923-4852; 2nd fl, Outrigger Waikiki on the Beach, 2335 Kalakaua Ave; breakfast à la carte items $2-7, dinner mains $17-34; ⊙ breakfast & dinner) Come early to score a table on a wraparound lanai and watch the sun set over the beach. Reward yourself with 'wrong island' ice teas and island-style *pupu* such as mango-barbecued ribs. Breakfast offers some refreshingly healthy, if pricey options.

Okonomiyaki Chibo (☎ 922-9722; 3rd fl, Royal Hawaiian Center, 2201 Kalakaua Ave; lunch $10-20, dinner mains $18-38; ⊙ lunch Mon-Sat, dinner daily) With a sleek dark-wood interior, this high-end Japanese *teppanyaki* grill is a standout for its customized chef-made *okonomiyaki* (savory cabbage pancakes). Go traditional and order one made with *buta* (pork) or *ika* (squid), or splurge on steak, scallops and prawns. Lunch is a fair deal, but dinner is overpriced.

Top End

Reservations are recommended for all of these restaurants, except the buffets.

Nobu Waikiki (☎ 237-6999; Waikiki Parc Hotel; 2233 Helumoa Rd; shared dishes $2-48, mains $32-40; ⊙ 5:30-10pm Sun-Wed, to 11pm Thu-Sat, lounge till midnight) Iron Chef Matsuhisa's Japanese fusion restaurant has made a big splash in Waikiki, where his hybrid dishes taste right at home. Broiled black cod with miso sauce, Japanese-Peruvian *tiradito* (ceviche) and seafood tartar are among Nobu's signature tastes. The chic attached lounge serves appetizers and 'sake-tinis.'

our pick **Roy's – Waikiki Beach** (☎ 923-7697; 226 Lewers St; mains $28-40; ⊙ dinner) This latest incarnation of Roy Yamaguchi's island-born chain is perfect for a flirty date or just celebrat-

TOP PICKS – HONOLULU & WAIKIKI FOODIE FAVES

- **Roy's – Waikiki Beach** (left)
- **Alan Wong's** (p135)
- **Town** (p137)
- **Hiroshi Eurasian Tapas** (p133)
- **Sansei Seafood Restaurant & Sushi Bar** (left)
- **Duc's Bistro** (p134)
- **Chef Mavro** (p135)

ing the good life with friends. The groundbreaking chef doesn't actually cook in the kitchens here, but his signature *misoyaki* butterfish, blackened *'ahi*, macnut-encrusted mahimahi and deconstructed sushi rolls are always on the menu. Molten-chocolate soufflé for dessert is a must.

Hau Tree Lanai (☎ 921-7066; New Otani Kaimana Beach Hotel, 2863 Kalakaua Ave; dinner mains $30-44; ⊙ breakfast 7-10:45am daily, lunch 11:45am-2pm Mon-Sat & noon-2pm Sun, dinner 5:30-9pm daily) A seductive setting under an arbor of hau trees is the draw at this delightful breakfast spot on Sans Souci Beach. The menu abounds in local flavor, everything from poi pancakes to seafood omelets. More mediocre, but globally spiced surf-and-turf dinners are serenaded by the sounds of the surf and Hawaiian music nightly except Sunday.

Prince Court (☎ 944-4494; Hawaii Prince Hotel Waikiki, 100 Holomoana St; buffet breakfast/brunch/dinner $21/35/44; ⊙ breakfast 6-10:30am Mon-Sat & 6-8:30am Sun, brunch 10am-1pm Sun, dinner 5:30-9:30pm Fri-Sun) The posh Prince Court restaurant offers serene yacht-harbor views and fully loaded buffets of Asian and American cuisine. Weekend seafood dinner buffets bring out a Vietnamese *pho* station and tropical desserts. Inside the more generic hotel, Hakone restaurant puts on an authentic Japanese buffet nightly, including *shabushabu* (hot-pot dishes).

La Mer (☎ 923-2311; Halekulani, 2199 Kalia Rd; 2-/3-/4-course dinner $90/120/135, 9-course tasting menu $150; ⊙ 6-10pm) La Mer boasts a spectacular view of Diamond Head through swaying palms. A neoclassical French menu puts the emphasis on Provençal cuisine and adds fresh Hawaii-grown ingredients. Wines are perfectly paired. Formal is the byword: either a jacket or collared long-sleeved shirt is required for men.

DRINKING & ENTERTAINMENT

There's no denying it: Waikiki is tourist central with all the telltale signs: weak alcoholic fruity umbrella drinks and a unique culture sometimes reduced to a coconut bra. But underneath all of the commoditized cheesiness, you'll find both traditional and contemporary Hawaiian music and hula dancing making a real comeback. Most of these live performances are free too. For LGBT nightlife, see p154.

Hawaiian Music & Hula

Performances are free, unless otherwise noted. All schedules are subject to change.

ourpick Kuhio Beach Torch Lighting & Hula Show (☎ 843-8002; www.honolulu.gov/moca; Kuhio Beach Park; ☽ 1hr show usually starts btwn 6pm & 7pm) Some of O'ahu's top hula troupes perform at the hula mound near the Duke Kahanamoku Statue on the Waikiki strip. It all starts off with a traditional torch lighting and conch shell ceremony and is accompanied by Hawaiian music.

House Without a Key (☎ 923-2311; Halekulani Hotel, 2199 Kalia Rd; ☽ 7am-9pm, live music 5:30-8:30pm) Named after a 1925 Charlie Chan novel set in Honolulu, this classy open-air oceanfront bar sprawled beneath a century-old kiawe tree simply has no doors to lock. Come for sunset cocktails, live music and solo hula dancing by two former Miss Hawaii pageant winners.

Banyan Court & Beach Bar (☎ 922-3111; Moana Surfrider, 2365 Kalakaua Ave; ☽ 10:30am-midnight, live music 6-10pm) Soak up the sounds of contemporary Hawaiian music beneath the same old banyan tree where *Hawaii Calls* broadcast its nationwide radio show for four decades beginning in 1935. Friday is usually hula dancing, while famous island musicians take over on Saturday and Sunday nights.

Duke's Waikiki (☎ 922-2268; Outrigger Waikiki, 2335 Kalakaua Ave; ☽ 4pm-midnight) It's a raucous, surf-themed party scene mostly for baby boomers, with lots of drunken souvenir photo-taking and vacationland camaraderie. Weekend afternoon concerts featuring big names like Henry Kapono can't help but spill onto the beach.

Mai Tai Bar (☎ 923-7311; Royal Hawaiian Hotel, 2259 Kalakaua Ave; ☽ 10:30am-12:30am, live music 6-10pm) At the Royal Hawaiian's low-key bar (no preppy resort wear required), catch some great island musical groups and a view of the breaking surf down to Diamond Head. The signature Royal mai tai packs a punch.

Tapa Bar (☎ 949-4321; Tapa Tower, Hilton Hawaiian Village, 2005 Kalia Rd; ☽ 3-11pm, live music 8-11pm) On Friday nights, head to the gargantuan Hilton Hawaiian Village complex, not just for the free beachfront fireworks show, but also to see Jerry Santos and Olomana usually play a few sets.

Rumfire (☎ 922-4422; Sheraton Waikiki, 2255 Kalakaua Ave; ☽ 4pm-midnight Sun-Thu, to 2am Fri & Sat, live music 5pm-7pm daily) If cabinets full of vintage rum aren't tempting enough, there are also flirty beachfront fire pits with ocean views. The cabanalike Sand Bar out back also has live Hawaiian music nightly, usually from 6pm to 8:30pm.

Royal Hawaiian Center (☎ 922-2299; 2201 Kalakaua Ave; ☽ schedule varies) This shopping mall may not have oceanfront panache, but you can still find Hawaiian music and hula performances by top island talent here, including by performers from the Polynesian Cultural Center (p183) in La'ie.

Royal Hawaiian Band (☎ 922-5331; www.co.honolulu.hi.us/rhb; Kapi'olani Park; ☽ 2-3pm Sun) Performing classical music from the monarchy era, Hawaii's 'official' band takes over the Kapi'olani Bandstand on Sunday afternoons. It's a quintessential island scene that caps off with the audience joining hands and singing Queen Lili'uokalani's 'Aloha 'Oe.' Other concerts around O'ahu include at 'Iolani Palace (p116).

Bars & Lounges

For more spring-break party spots and dive bars, hit Kuhio Ave after dark.

ourpick Diamond Head Cove Health Bar (☎ 732-8744; 3045 Monsarrat Ave; ☽ 10am-8pm Mon, Fri & Sat, to midnight Tue-Thu & Sun) Why rot your guts with the devil's brew when you can chill-out with a coconut-husk bowl of 'awa (kava), Polynesia's spicy, mildly intoxicating elixir made from the *Piper methysticum* plant? Local musicians jam here some nights.

Lewers Lounge (☎ 923-2311; Halekulani, 2199 Kalia Rd; ☽ 7:30pm-midnight) Waikiki as an aristocratic playground is kept alive at this sophisticated lounge. Cocktails are made from scratch using fresh (not canned) juices, including tropical lychee and ginger. Smooth-jazz combos serenade most nights.

The Shack (☎ 921-2255; Waikiki Trade Center, 2255 Kuhio Ave; cover free-$10; ☽ 11am-4am) If you're wondering where Waikiki's hotel bartenders go after their shifts, check out this tiki-esque

ISLAND SOUNDS

You might be surprised to learn that some of Hawaii's leading local musicians play regular gigs at Waikiki's resort hotels and bars. Here are some stars to watch out for.

- Jake Shimabukuro – The 'Jimi Hendrix of the uke' has been lured away from the islands by record companies, but sometimes plays live shows in his hometown, Honolulu.
- Henry Kapono – This Kapahulu-born singer-songwriter is O'ahu's renaissance man, putting out innovative Hawaiian rock albums since the 1970s.
- Brothers Cazimero – The O'ahu-born, Hawaiian heritage–conscious duo (12-string guitar and bass) played in Peter Moon's legendary Sunday Manoa band in the early '70s.
- Kapena – The group Kapena may not have won O'ahu's high-school battle of the bands back in the day, but founding member Kelly Boy De Lima is a ukulele star.
- Jerry Santos and Olomana – Traditional and contemporary ukulele and falsetto performers from Windward O'ahu have been performing for decades.
- Martin Pahinui – The son of late slack key master Gabby Pahinui is a gifted vocalist and often performs with guitarist George Kuo and former Royal Hawaiian Band leader Aaron Mahi.
- Keawe 'Ohana – Some say the granddaughter of the late great *ha'i* (high falsetto) singer Genoa Keawe sounds just like Genoa in her younger days.
- Sam Kapu III – Part of a musical dynasty, Sam Kapu performs traditional ukulele music and contemporary three-part harmonies with his trio.
- Po'okela – A contemporary trio fronted by Honolulu-born slack-key artist Greg Sardinha, who studied with the late great steel-guitar player Jerry Byrd.
- Makana – An O'ahu-born singer-songwriter who studied guitar with Sonny Chillingworth and is a leading proponent of slack key fusion rock.
- Ka'ala Boys – At the moment, they're Honolulu's fave 'Jawaiian' island reggae group.

sports bar with huge TVs, a waterfall and live music most Wednesday to Saturday nights, often 'Jawaiian' island reggae groups.

Yard House (☎ 923-9273; 226 Lewers St; ☑ 11am-1am) The busiest bar on Waikiki Beach Walk, this raucous mainland chain with big-screen sports TVs pours gigantic glasses of microbrewed draft beer made in North America, Europe and around the Hawaiian Islands – Big Swell IPA or Mehana Volcano Red, anyone? The classic-rock soundtrack never dies.

Da Big Kahuna (☎ 923-0333; 2299 Kuhio Ave; ☑ 7am-4am) For frat boys, this tiki bar serves fruity, Kool-Aid–colored drinks with names like 'Da Fish Bowl' in ceramic mugs carved with the faces of Polynesian gods, plus there are pool tables and a full menu of food served till 3am.

Top of Waikiki (☎ 923-3877; 18th fl, Waikiki Business Plaza, 2270 Kalakaua Ave; ☑ 5-9:30pm) Spinning at just one revolution per hour, this tower cocktail lounge and restaurant absorbs a 360-degree view from *mauka* to *makai* and back again. There's so-so food involved, but the novelty is the slow-motion sit-and-spin.

Nightclubs

The nightclub scene has migrated elsewhere in Honolulu (p137), but if you don't feel like making the trek, there are still a few dance floors here for getting your ya-yas out. For weekly and monthly DJ party-circuit events, check **Metromix Honolulu** (http://honolulu.metromix.com).

ourpick **Lotus SoundBar** (☎ 924-1688; Waikiki Town Center, 2301 Kuhio Ave; cover $10-20; ☑ 9pm-2am Sun-Wed, to 4am Thu-Sat) Cutting-edge DJs spin at this tri-level club with plush, dark decor. Get down to soulful hip-hop, chill-out grooves, drum 'n' bass and pure house sounds, all courtesy of a killer sound system.

Restaurants by day, dance clubs by night: **Coconut Willy's** (☎ 921-9000; 227 Lewers St; ☑ 11am-4am) Live bands, dancing and drinkin' on Waikiki Beach Walk.

Lulu's Surf Club (☎ 926-5222; 2586 Kalakaua Ave; ⊗ 24hr) DJs usually spin after 10pm on weekends for a beach-party crowd.

Luau

If your Hawaii vacation just won't be complete without taking in a luau, you can choose from a Waikiki resort-hotel production right on the beach or a big bash outside town, for which tourists are picked up at central Waikiki hotels and shuttled to Kapolei, taking about an hour each way. Alternatively, visit La'ie's **Polynesian Cultural Center** (p183) on the Windward Coast.

Hilton Hawaiian Village Luau (☎ 949-4321, 800-862-5335; 2005 Kalia Rd; adult/child 4-11 $95/45; ⊗ 5:30-8:30pm Wed & Sun) Waikiki's only beachside luau at press time features a buffet-style dinner of Hawaiian food and just one complimentary mai tai. The enthusiastic, if not very authentic Polynesian show, with Samoan fire dancing and mid-20th-century *hapa haole* hula, is a crowd-pleaser, especially for kids.

Commercial luau outside Waikiki:

Germaine's Luau (Map pp102-3; ☎ 949-6626, 800-367-5655; www.germainesluau.com; 91-119 Olai St, Kapolei; adult/youth 14-20/child 6-13 $75/65/55; ⊗ 5:15-9pm) Nightly dinner buffet and Polynesian-style show on the beach.

Paradise Cove (Map pp102-3; 842-5911, 800-775-2683; www.paradisecove.com; 92-1089 Ali'inui Dr, Kapolei; adult/youth 13-18/child 3-12 $80/70/60; ⊗ 5-9pm) Like Germaine's, but also includes demonstrations of Hawaiian games and crafts.

SHOPPING

Catwalk designer boutiques are found inside the DFS Galleria at the north end of Kalakaua Ave, while some only-in-Hawaii stores lining Waikiki Beach Walk. Not feeling flush? Waikiki's ubiquitous ABC Stores are the handiest place to pick up beach mats, sunblock, snacks and sundries, 'I got lei'd in Hawaii' T-shirts and motorized grass-skirted hula girls for the dashboard of your car back home.

our pick **Bailey's Antiques & Aloha Shirts** (☎ 734-7628; 517 Kapahulu Ave; ⊗ 10am-6pm) There's no place like Bailey's, which has without a doubt the finest aloha shirt collection on O'ahu. Racks are crammed with thousands of collector-worthy vintage aloha shirts in every conceivable color and style, from 1920s kimono-silk classics to 1970s polyester specials. Of the new generation of shirts, Bailey's only carries Hawaii-made labels, including Kona Bay and RJC. Prices

vary from five bucks up to several hundred or thousand dollars.

our pick **Na Lima Mili Hulu No'eau** (☎ 732-0865; 762 Kapahulu Ave; ⊗ 9am-5pm Mon-Sat) Aunty Mary Louise Kaleonahenahe Kekuewa and her daughter Paulette keep alive the ancient craft of feather lei-making at this humble storefront, the name of which means 'the skilled hands that touch the feathers.' Their previously self-published book *Feather Lei as an Art* has revived this exquisite Hawaiian art.

Mana Hawai'i (☎ 923-2220; 2nd fl, Waikiki Beach Walk; ⊗ 9am-10pm) Unlike many other shops on Waikiki Beach Walk, this airy space displays authentic Hawaii-made products such as island woodcarvings, fine-art photography and Hawaiiana books and CDs. It also hosts free Hawaiian cultural classes (see p152).

Royal Hawaiian Center (☎ 922-2299; 2201 Kalakaua Ave; ⊗ 10am-10pm) Waikiki's biggest shopping center has mostly name-brand international chains, but also some Hawaii-born labels like Crazy Shirts and Honolua Surf Co. The Little Hawaiian Craft Shop displays cheap Hawaiiana trinkets next to high-quality koa bowls, Ni'ihau shell-lei necklaces and other pan-Polynesian artisan crafts.

Island Treasures Antiques (☎ 922-8223; 2nd fl, Waikiki Town Center, 2301 Kuhio Ave; ⊗ 2-8pm Tue-Sat, to 6pm Sun) Ride the wave of Waikiki's retro vibe at this mid-20th-century antiques mall, stocking everything from old Hawaii license plates to nostalgic memorabilia from vintage resort hotels and hip-shaking hula dolls.

Bob's Ukulele (☎ 372-9623; Waikiki Beach Marriott Resort, 2552 Kalakaua Ave; ⊗ 9am-noon & 5-9pm) Avoid those cheap, flimsy imported ukuleles sold at so many Waikiki shopping malls. Instead let the knowledgeable staff here show you island-made ukes handcrafted from native woods, including by Kamaka Hawaii (p140).

GETTING THERE & AROUND

Taxis are available at larger resort hotels and shopping malls; otherwise, you'll probably need to call for one (see p112).

To/From the Airport

See p110 for transportation options and driving directions to/from Honolulu International Airport.

Bicycle

You can easily rent beach cruisers or commuter bikes from several places, costing around $20 per day, with discounts for multi-day and weekly rentals. For top-quality rentals and sales of road and mountain bikes, head to Honolulu's **Bike Shop** (Map p122; ☎ 596-0588; 1149 S King St, Honolulu; ✆ 9am-7pm Mon-Fri, 9am-5pm Sat, 10am-5pm Sun).

Bus

O'ahu's public bus system, TheBus, runs frequent routes through Waikiki, with the most bus stops along Kuhio Ave. Just outside Waikiki, the Ala Moana Center is O'ahu's central bus terminal and transfer point to other lines across Honolulu and around the island. For general information about TheBus, including useful routes, schedules, fares and passes, see p111.

Car, Motorcycle & Moped

Most hotels charge $15 to $25 per night for valet or self-parking. At the east end of Waikiki, there's a free parking lot along Monsarrat Ave beside Kapi'olani Park with no time limit. Waikiki's cheapest metered lot (25¢ per hour) is along Kapahulu Ave next to the zoo. More centrally located, the **Waikiki Trade Center Parking Garage** (2255 Kuhio Ave, enter off Seaside Ave) and next-door **Waikiki Parking Garage** (333 Seaside Ave) usually offer Waikiki's cheapest flat-rate day, evening and overnight rates.

Several Waikiki-based car-rental offices are affiliated with international agencies, but lines tend to be long on weekends and rates are usually higher than at the airport (see p112). For general rental-car information and toll-free reservations numbers, see p576.

Mopeds may seem like a great way of getting around Waikiki, but they're really best suited to those who already have experience riding in city traffic. Motorcycles rent for about $65 per four hours, and mopeds for $35 to $50 per day, the latter of which may be as much or more than a rental car.

Trolley

Trolley-style buses shuttle between Waikiki, Honolulu and outlying tourist sights, mostly running only during the daytime. These services don't offer much in the way of value compared to TheBus, but they are tailored to tourists and thus may seem more convenient.

Waikiki Trolley (☎ 593-2822; www.waikikitrolley .com; adult/child 4-11/senior 1-day pass $27/13/20, 4-day pass $48/20/28) runs four color-coded lines that connect Waikiki with downtown Honolulu, the Ala Moana Center and O'ahu's Southeast Coast. Single-ride tickets ($2) are available only on the Pink and Yellow Lines. Purchase passes online or at the **DFS Galleria Waikiki** (330 Royal Hawaiian Ave), Hilton Hawaiian Village or Ala Moana Center.

Red Line (Honolulu City Line) Starts at the Hilton Hawaiian Village, runs along Kalakaua Ave, loops around Kuhio Ave into Honolulu via S Beretania St stopping at the Honolulu Academy of Arts, 'Iolani Palace, Foster Botanical Garden, Bishop Museum, Aloha Tower, Chinatown, Ward Centers and Ala Moana Center. Trolleys run every 40 minutes from 9:10am to 5:30pm; the entire route takes two hours.

Blue Line (Ocean Coast Line) Starts at DFS Galleria Waikiki, runs along Kalakaua Ave to the Honolulu Zoo, Waikiki Aquarium, Diamond Head, Kahala Mall, Koko Marina Center, Hanauma Bay (photo-stop only – no disembarking), Halona and Makapu'u Lookouts and Sea Life Park. Trolleys run hourly from 8:30am to 6:15pm; the entire route takes three hours. An express service to Diamond Head runs four times daily.

Pink Line (Ala Moana Shopping Shuttle) Starts at DFS Galleria Waikiki, runs along Kalakaua Ave, loops around Kuhio Ave to Ala Moana Blvd past the Hilton Hawaiian Village to the Ala Moana Center. Trolleys run every 10 minutes from 9:30am to 9:45pm (to 7:45pm Sunday); the entire route takes one hour.

Yellow Line (Local Shopping and Dining Line) Loops between Ala Moana Center and Ward Centers every 45 minutes from 12:30pm to 7:45pm (to 7pm Sunday); the entire route takes 45 minutes.

SOUTHEAST COAST

You can pretend to be the star of your own movie on O'ahu's most glamorous stretch of coastline, starting just outside Waikiki. Cruise past the mansion-filled suburbs of Kahala and Hawai'i Kai along the Kalaniana'ole Hwy (Hwy 72), a serpentine coastal drive that swells and dips like the sea itself as it rounds Koko Head, formed by volcanic activity about 10,000 years ago.

The snorkeling hot spot of Hanauma Bay, hiking trails to the top of Diamond Head and the windy lighthouse at Makapu'u Point, and O'ahu's most famous bodysurfing beaches are just a short bus ride or drive from Waikiki. Save time for the coast's more hidden delights such as billionaire Doris Duke's former mansion – a world-class trove of Islamic art – and a fragrant botanical garden hidden inside a volcanic crater.

O'AHU

SOUTHEAST COAST

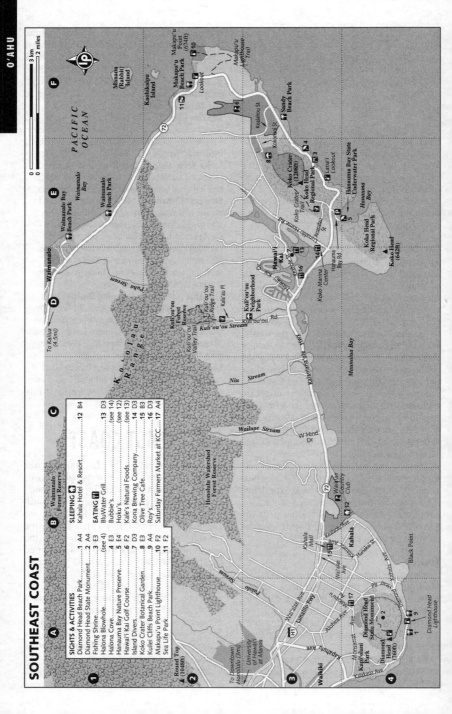

DIAMOND HEAD & KAHALA

A massive backdrop to Waikiki and the wealthy Kahala neighborhood, Diamond Head is O'ahu's best-known landmark. It's a tuff cone and crater formed by a violent steam explosion long after most of the island's other volcanic activity had stopped. Ancient Hawaiians called it Le'ahi and at its summit they built a *luakini* heiau, a temple dedicated to the war god Ku and used for human sacrifices.

Ever since 1825, when British sailors found calcite crystals sparkling in the sun and mistakenly thought they'd struck it rich, it's been called Diamond Head. In the early 1900s the US Army began building Fort Ruger at the edge of the crater. They constructed a network of tunnels and topped the rim with cannon emplacements, bunkers and observation posts. Reinforced during WWII, the fort is a silent sentinel whose guns have never been fired.

Sights & Activities
DIAMOND HEAD STATE MONUMENT
This **state monument** (☎ 587-0300; pedestrian/vehicle $1/5; ☯ hiking 6am-6pm, last trail entry 4:30pm) is popular mostly for its hiking trail. The trail to the summit was built in 1910 to service the military observation stations along the crater rim. Although it's a fairly steep 0.8-mile hike to the top, the trail is fully paved and plenty of people of all ages make it. The return trip takes about an hour; definitely bring water. The trail, which passes through several tunnels and up dizzying staircases, is mostly open and hot, so wear plenty of sunscreen too. The windy summit affords fantastic 360-degree views of the southeast coast to Koko Head and west to the Wai'anae Range. A lighthouse, coral reefs and surfers waiting to catch a wave are visible below.

From Waikiki, take TheBus No 22 or 23, which run twice hourly; from the bus stop, it's a 20-minute walk to the trailhead. By car, take Monsarrat Ave to Diamond Head Rd, then turn right after Kapi'olani Community College into the parking lot.

SHANGRI LA
Once called 'the richest little girl in the world,' heiress Doris Duke (1912–93) had a lifelong passion for Islamic art and architecture that was first inspired by a visit to the Taj Mahal during her honeymoon voyage to India in 1935. During her honeymoon, she also stopped on O'ahu, fell in love with the island and decided to build Shangri La, a private seasonal residence on Black Point. Over the next 60 years, she traveled the globe from Indonesia to Istanbul, collecting priceless art en route.

Doris made Shangri La into an intimate sanctuary rather than an ostentatious mansion. One of the true beauties of the place is the way it harmonizes with the natural environment. Finely crafted interiors open to embrace gardens and fountain courtyards. Collections blend with the architecture to represent a theme or region, for instance in the Damascus Room, the restored interior of a 19th-century Syrian merchant's house. Duke's extensive collections included gemstone-studded enamels, glazed ceramic paintings and silk *suzanis* (intricate needlework tapestries).

You can visit Shangri La only on a guided **tour** (☎ 866-385-3849; www.shangrilahawaii.org; 2½hr tour $25; ☯ usually 8:30am, 11am & 1:30pm Wed-Sat late Sep–late Aug), departing from the Honolulu Academy of Arts (p123) in central Honolulu. Tours aren't recommended for children under 12; reservations are essential. Although Shangri La is not air-conditioned, fetching souvenir paper fans are provided.

BEACHES
Southwest of the lighthouse, **Diamond Head Beach Park** draws surfers, snorkelers and tidepoolers, plus a few picnickers. The narrow strand is popular with gay men, who pull off Diamond Head Rd onto short, dead-end Beach Rd, then walk north along the shore to find a little seclusion and (illegally) sunbathe au naturel.

Nearby **Kuilei Cliffs Beach Park** draws experienced windsurfers when the tradewinds are blowing. When the swells are up, surfers take over the waves. This little beach has showers, but no other facilities. Park off Diamond Head Rd just beyond the lighthouse, then walk east past the end of the lot to the paved trail down to the beach.

From Waikiki, TheBus No 14 runs by both beaches once or twice hourly.

Sleeping & Eating
There's a luxury hotel by the beach, and more restaurants around the Kahala Mall.

Saturday Farmers Market at KCC (☎ 848-2074; Parking Lot C, Kapi'olani Community College, 4303 Diamond

Head Rd; ⏰ 7:30am-11:30am Sat) At O'ahu's premier gathering of farmers and their fans, everything sold is local and has a loyal following, including 'Nalo greens and North Shore avocados. Different restaurants each week are invited to sell tasty takeout meals.

Olive Tree Cafe (☎ 737-0303; 4614 Kilauea Ave, cnr Pahoa Ave; mains $5-12; ⏰ 5-10pm) Hidden on the east side of Kahala Mall, this always-packed Mediterranean restaurant swears by the motto 'Mostly Greek, not so fast food.' Try the succulent chicken souvlaki and *dolmadakia* (stuffed grape leaves). The next-door Greek deli has a cache of imported wines for BYOB.

Kahala Hotel & Resort (☎ 739-8888, 800-367-2525; www.kahalaresort.com; 5000 Kahala Ave; r $380-845; Ⓟ 🍴 💻 📶 🐬) Nestled on a private beach, about a 15-minute drive from Waikiki, this swank resort is an intimate haven for rich-and-famous folks who crave seclusion above all. The price tag is high for such small standard rooms, especially those without views. Open for dinner Tuesday through Saturday, Hoku's restaurant is revered for its East-West fusion; make reservations and inquire about the dress code.

HAWAI'I KAI
pop 29,000

With its marina and picturesque canals surrounded by mountains, bays and beach parks, this meticulously planned suburb designed by steel tycoon Henry J Kaiser (he's the Kai in Hawai'i Kai) is a nouveau-riche scene. Everything revolves around megashopping centers off the Kalaniana'ole Hwy (Hwy 72). If you're driving around Southeast O'ahu, this is convenient stop for either a bite to eat or sunset drinks, or both.

Activities

An established five-star PADI operation, **Island Divers** (☎ 423-8222, 888-844-3483; www.oahuscubadiving .com; Hawai'i Kai Shopping Center, 377 Keahole St; 2-tank boat dive $125-160, ride-along per snorkeler $50) offers boat dives for all levels, including expert-level wreck dives. If you're a novice, staff can introduce you to calm, relatively shallow waters.

Often-overlooked hiking trails climb dramatically into the Ko'olau Range. West of Hawai'i Kai, the 5-mile round-trip **Kuli'ou'ou Ridge Trail** is open to hikers and mountain bikers. It travels up forested switchbacks, then makes a stiff, but satisfying ascent along a ridgeline to a windy summit for 360-degree views of Koko Head, Makapu'u

Point, the Windward Coast, Diamond Head and Honolulu. The trail, which may be partly overgrown with vegetation, starts from the **Na Ala Hele** (www.hawaiitrails.org) trailhead sign at the end of Kala'au Pl, which branches right off Kuli'ou'ou Rd, just over a mile north of the Kalaniana'ole Hwy (Hwy 72). From Waikiki, take TheBus No 22 or 23 to Kuli'ou'ou Rd; from the bus stop, it's a 1-mile walk inland to Kala'au Pl.

About 4 miles east of town, **Hawai'i Kai Golf Course** (☎ 395-2358; www.hawaiikaigolf.com; 8902 Kalaniana'ole Hwy; green fees incl cart $70-110) features a challenging par-72 championship course with Koko Head views, and a smaller par-54 course designed by Robert Trent Jones Sr back in the 1960s. Call ahead for tee-time reservations; club rentals available.

Eating & Drinking

The original Roy's restaurant (see p159) still stands at Hawai'i Kai Towne Center.

Kona Brewing Company (☎ 394-5662; Koko Marina Center, 7192 Kalaniana'ole Hwy; mains $11-25; ⏰ 11am-9pm Sun-Thu, to 10pm Fri & Sat) This Big Island import is known for its microbrews, like Longboard Lager and Castaway IPA, and live Hawaiian music on weekends, including by big-name musicians like slack key guitar and ukulele master Led Ka'apana. Island-style *pupu*, wood-fired pizzas, burgers and salads are so-so.

BluWater Grill (☎ 395-6224; Hawai'i Kai Shopping Center, 377 Keahole St; mains lunch $10-18, dinner $20-32; ⏰ 11am-11pm Mon-Thu, 11am-midnight Fri & Sat, 10am-11pm Sun) Perfect for chilling out with a cocktail, this breezy open-air restaurant overlooks the waterfront and dishes up kiawe-grilled fare such as seafood kebabs and chicken with papaya-ginger glaze. Sunday brunch features spicy 'ahi eggs Benedict, haute *loco moco* and a pancake bar with tropical toppings.

Also recommended:

Bubbie's (☎ 396-8722; Koko Marina Center, 7192 Kalaniana'ole Hwy; items $2-6; 10am-11pm Sun-Thu, to midnight Fri & Sat) Tropically flavored and *mochi*-mixed ice cream, with a Foodland supermarket nearby.

Kale's Natural Foods (☎ 396-6993; Hawai' Kai Shopping Center, 377 Keahole St; ⏰ 9am-8pm Mon-Fri, to 5pm Sat & Sun) Near both a Safeway supermarket and The Shack sports bar for burgers and beer.

HANAUMA BAY NATURE PRESERVE

A stunning ensemble of sapphire and turquoise hues all mix together in modern-art abstractions in this bowl-shaped bay, ringed by the remnants of an eroded volcano. Just below the sparkling surface are coral reefs, some of which are 7000 years old. These craggy and ancient underwater formations are a city for fish, providing food, shelter and an interspecies 'pick-up' scene. You'll see schools of glittering silver fish, bright blue flashes of parrotfish and perhaps sea turtles so used to snorkelers that they'll go eyeball to face mask with you. Despite its protected status as a marine-life conservation district since 1967, this beloved bay is still a threatened ecosystem, constantly in danger of being loved to death by the huge number of annual visitors – an average of 3000 people hit the beach each day to snorkel and dive here.

Information

Hanauma Bay is both a county beach park and a state underwater **park** (☎ 396-4229; www .honolulu.gov/parks/facility/hanaumabay, www.soest .hawaii.edu/seagrant/education/Hanauma; adult/child under 13 $5/free; ☑ 6am-6pm Wed-Mon Nov-Mar, to 7pm Wed-Mon Apr-Oct, also to 10pm on 2nd & 4th Sat of each month). To beat the crowds, especially during peak summer season, arrive early (around 6am) when all the locals show up, and avoid Mondays and Wednesdays.

Sights & Activities

Past the ticket booth at the entrance is an award-winning **educational center** run by the University of Hawai'i. It features modern interactive, family-friendly displays that teach about the geology and ecology of the bay. All visitors are expected to watch a video, intended to stagger the crowds and inform you about environmental precautions. Down below at beach level are snorkel-gear rental concessions, lockers, lifeguards and bathrooms.

The bay is well protected from the vast ocean by various reefs and the inlet's natural curve, making conditions favorable for snorkeling year-round. The fringing reef closest to shore has a large, sandy opening known as the **Keyhole Lagoon**, which is the best place for novice snorkelers. The deepest water is 10ft, though it's very shallow over the coral. The Keyhole is well protected and usually very calm. Because most visitors are beginners, this is also the most crowded part of the bay later in the day and visibility can be poor from swimming. Be careful not to step on the coral or to accidentally

knock it with your fins. Feeding the fish is strictly prohibited.

For confident snorkelers and strong swimmers, it's better on the outside of the reef, where there are large coral heads, bigger fish and fewer people; to get there follow the directions on the signboard or ask the lifeguard at the southern end of the beach. There are two channels on either side of the bay that experience very strong currents. Don't attempt to swim outside the reef when the water is rough or choppy.

If you're scuba diving, you have the whole bay to play in, with crystal-clear water, coral gardens and sea turtles. Beware of currents when the surf is up, especially surges near the shark-infested Witches Brew, on the right-hand side of the bay, and the Moloka'i Express, a treacherous current on the left-hand side of the bay's mouth.

Getting There & Away

Hanauma Bay is about 10 miles east of Waikiki along the Kalaniana'ole Hwy (Hwy 72). The parking lot sometimes fills by mid-morning, after which drivers will be turned away, so the earlier you get there the better. From Waikiki, TheBus No 22 (nicknamed the 'Beach Bus') runs hourly to Hanauma Bay, except on Tuesday when the park is closed; the one-way trip takes about an hour. Buses leave Waikiki between 8am and 4pm (till 4:45pm on Saturday and Sunday); the corner of Kuhio Ave and Namahana St is the first stop, and buses often fill up shortly thereafter. Buses back to Waikiki leave Hanauma Bay between 10:45am and 5:25pm (to 6pm on weekends).

KOKO HEAD REGIONAL PARK

With mountains on one side and a sea full of bays and beaches on the other, the drive along this coast rates among O'ahu's best. The highway rises and falls as it winds its way around the tip of the Ko'olau Range, looking down on stratified rocks, lava sea cliffs and other fascinating geological formations. At last, you'll truly feel like you've left the city behind.

Less than a mile east of Hanauma Bay, the roadside **Lana'i Lookout** offers a panorama on clear days of several Hawaiian islands: Lana'i to the right, Maui in the middle and Moloka'i to the left. About 0.5 miles further east, at the highest point on a sea cliff known locally as Bamboo Ridge, look for a temple-like mound of rocks surrounding a statue of

O'AHU

Jizō, a Japanese Buddhist deity and guardian of fishers. This **fishing shrine** is often decked in colorful leis and surrounded by saké cups.

Halona Blowhole & Cove

Follow all of the tour buses to find the **Halona Blowhole**. Here the water surges through a submerged tunnel in the rock and spouts up through a hole in the ledge. It's preceded by a gushing sound, created by the air that's being forced out by the rushing water. The action depends on water conditions – sometimes it's barely discernible, while at other times it's a showstopper. Ignore the temptation to ignore the warning signs and walk down toward the blowhole, as several people have been fatally swept off the ledge by rogue waves.

Down to the right of the lookout parking lot is **Halona Cove**, the gem-like beach where the steamy love scene with Burt Lancaster and Deborah Kerr in *From Here to Eternity* (1953) was filmed. There's no lifeguard on duty, and when the surf's up, this beach really earns its nickname 'Pounders,' so never turn your back on the sea.

Sandy Beach Park

Here the ocean heaves and thrashes like a furious beast. This is one of O'ahu's most dangerous beaches, with a punishing shore-break, powerful backwash and strong rip currents. Expert bodysurfers spend hours trying to mount the skull-crushing waves, as crowds gather to watch the daredevils being tossed around. When the swells are big, bodyboarders hit the left side of the beach.

Sandy Beach is wide, very long and, yes, sandy, but this is no place to frolic. Dozens of people are injured at Sandy Beach each year, some with just broken arms and dislocated shoulders, but others with serious spinal injuries. Red flags flown on the beach indicate hazardous water conditions. Even if you don't see flags, always check with the lifeguards before entering the water.

Not all the action is in the water. The grassy strip on the inland side of the parking lot is used by people looking skyward for their thrills – it's both a hang-glider landing site and a popular place for flying kites. On weekends, you can usually find a food wagon selling plate lunches in the beach parking lot. The park has rest rooms and showers.

From Waikiki, TheBus No 22 stops here approximately hourly.

Koko Crater

According to Hawaiian legend, Koko Crater is the imprint left by the magical flying vagina of Kapo sent from the Big Island to lure the pig-god Kamapua'a away from her sister Pele, goddess of fire and volcanoes.

One of O'ahu's tallest and best-preserved tuff cones, Koko Crater now embraces a small county-run **botanical garden** (☎ 522-7063; end of Kokonani St; admission free; ☺ sunrise-sunset), planted with plumeria, oleander and cacti and other native and exotic dryland species. You'll probably have the garden's interconnecting loop trails to yourself.

To get here, turn inland off the Kalaniana'ole Hwy (Hwy 72) onto Kealahou St, opposite the north end of Sandy Beach. After 0.5 miles, turn left onto Kokonani St. From Waikiki, TheBus No 23 stops at the corner of Kealahou St and Kokonani St, about 0.3 miles from the garden entrance, but service is infrequent; the trip takes about an hour each way.

MAKAPU'U POINT

The coastal **lighthouse** at the tip of Makapu'u Point marks O'ahu's easternmost point. The gate to the mile-long service road is locked to keep out private vehicles, but hikers can park off the highway just beyond and walk in. Although not a difficult hike, it's a steady uphill walk and conditions can be hot and windy. The path and the lighthouse lookout provide spectacular coastal views of Hanauma Bay and Koko Head, and, during winter, you may spot migratory whales offshore.

A little further along the highway, a scenic **roadside lookout** gazes down at aqua-blue waters outlined by white sand and black lava beds – an even more spectacular sight when hang-gliders take off from the cliffs. Offshore is **Manana Island (Rabbit Island)**. This aging volcanic crater is populated by feral rabbits and wedge-tailed shearwaters The island looks vaguely like the head of a rabbit, ears folded back. In front of it is the smaller, flat **Kaohikaipu Island**.

Opposite Sea Life Park and just within view of the lighthouse is **Makapu'u Beach Park**, one of the island's top winter bodysurfing spots, with waves reaching 12ft and higher. It also has the island's best shorebreak. As with Sandy Beach, Makapu'u is strictly the domain of experienced bodysurfers, who can handle rough water and dangerous currents. Board surfing is prohibited. In summer, when the wave action disappears, calmer waters may afford good swimming. Two native Hawaiian plants are plentiful here – yellow-orange *'ilima*, O'ahu's official flower, by the parking lot and *naupaka*, a native shrub with a five-petaled white flower that looks as if it has been torn in half, by the beach.

SEA LIFE PARK

More like a circus than an aquarium, Hawaii's only **marine park** (☎ 259-2500, 866-393-5158; www.sealifeparkhawaii.com; 41-202 Kalaniana'ole Hwy; adult/child 3-11 $29/19; ◷ 10:30am-5pm) offers a mixed bag of attractions that, frankly, aren't worth your time. The theme-park entertainment includes choreographed shows and pool encounters with imported Atlantic bottlenose dolphins, a controversial activity (see the boxed text, p171).

The park's 300,000-gallon aquarium is filled mostly with marine animals not found in Hawaiian waters, including rays and sharks. There's also a penguin habitat, a turtle lagoon and a seabird 'sanctuary' with native *'iwa*. The park does maintain a breeding colony of green sea turtles, releasing young hatchlings back into their natural habitat each year. But if you really want to learn about Hawaii's marine life, visit the Waikiki Aquarium (p151).

Although parking in the main lot costs $3, if you continue past the ticket booth to an area marked 'additional parking,' there's typically no fee. TheBus No 22 (Beach Bus), 23 (Hawai'i Kai–Sea Life Park) and 57 (Kailua–Sea Life Park) all stop here.

GETTING AWAY FROM IT ALL

WINDWARD COAST

More than anything, this lush coast is defined by the dramatic Ko'olau Range, where the *pali* (cliffs) are shrouded in mist as often as they are bathed in glorious sunshine. Tropical rain showers guarantee that everything shares a hundred different shades of green, even more dazzling when set against turquoise bays and white-sand beaches. Repeat visitors to O'ahu often make this side of the island their adventure base camp, whether they've come to kayak, windsurf, snorkel, dive or just laze on the sand.

Although some enticing beaches are here, especially around Waimanalo and Kailua Bays, keep in mind that many spots farther north along the coast are too silted to be much more than a snapshot. Swimmers should keep a careful eye out for the stinging Portuguese man-of-wars that are sometimes washed in during storms.

Once you've left behind the affluent suburbs of Kailua and Kane'ohe, which are less than 10 miles over the *pali* from metro Honolulu, the rest of the coast is surprisingly rural, with humble roadside shops, small farms and taro patches. The Kamehameha Hwy becomes a modest two-lane road that runs the length of the entire coast, doubling as Main St for each of the small towns along the way.

Three highways cut through the Ko'olau Range from central Honolulu to the Windward Coast. The Pali Hwy (Hwy 61) goes straight into Kailua center. The Likelike Hwy (Hwy 63) runs directly into Kane'ohe, although it doesn't have the scenic lookouts that the Pali Hwy has. The H-3 Fwy begins near Pearl Harbor and cuts through the mountains directly to Kane'ohe.

THE PALI HIGHWAY

This scenic highway is the perfect vantage point for marvelling at the emerald Ko'olau Range, which it slices right through. If it has been raining heavily every fold and crevice of each hoary *pali* will have a lacy waterfall streaming down its face.

The highway's official purpose is to link Honolulu with Kailua on the Windward Coast. An ancient footpath once wound its way perilously over these cliffs. In 1845 the path was widened into a horse trail and, later again, into a cobblestone road that would

O'AHU

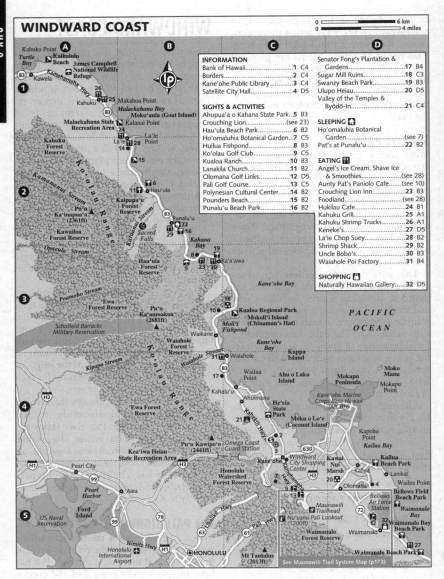

WINDWARD COAST

0   6 km
0   4 miles

INFORMATION
Bank of Hawaii....................................1 C4
Borders...2 C4
Kane'ohe Public Library....................3 C4
Satellite City Hall.............................4 D5

SIGHTS & ACTIVITIES
Ahupua'a o Kahana State Park......5 B3
Crouching Lion.............................(see 23)
Hau'ula Beach Park..........................6 B2
Ho'omaluhia Botanical Garden.....7 C5
Huilua Fishpond................................8 B3
Ko'olau Golf Club.............................9 C5
Kualoa Ranch...................................10 B3
Lanakila Church...............................11 B2
Olomana Golf Links.........................12 D5
Pali Golf Course...............................13 C5
Polynesian Cultural Center............14 B2
Pounders Beach...............................15 B2
Punalu'u Beach Park........................16 B2

Senator Fong's Plantation &
  Gardens..17 B4
Sugar Mill Ruins...............................18 C3
Swanzy Beach Park..........................19 B3
Ulupo Heiau.....................................20 D5
Valley of the Temples &
  Byōdō-In...21 C4

SLEEPING
Ho'omaluhia Botanical
  Garden...(see 7)
Pat's at Punalu'u.............................22 B2

EATING
Angel's Ice Cream, Shave Ice
  & Smoothies..............................(see 28)
Aunty Pat's Paniolo Cafe.........(see 10)
Crouching Lion Inn.........................23 B3
Foodland......................................(see 28)
Hukilau Cafe....................................24 B1
Kahuku Grill....................................25 A1
Kahuku Shrimp Trucks....................26 A1
Keneke's...27 D5
La'ie Chop Suey...............................28 B2
Shrimp Shack...................................29 B2
Uncle Bobo's....................................30 B3
Waiahole Poi Factory......................31 B4

SHOPPING
Naturally Hawaiian Gallery............32 D5

PACIFIC

OCEAN

See Maunawili Trail System Map (p173)

allow carriage traffic to pass. The **Old Pali Highway** was built along the same route in 1898. It was abandoned in the 1950s after tunnels were blasted through the Ko'olau Range for the present multilane highway.

You can still drive a scenic stretch of the Old Pali Hwy now called **Nu'uanu Pali Dr** (Map p125) by turning east off the Pali Hwy (Hwy 61) half a mile north of the Queen Emma Summer Palace (p127). The drive takes you through a cathedral of trees draped with hanging vines and philodendrons. The lush vegetation includes banyans with hanging aerial roots, bamboo groves and Cup of Gold, a tall climbing vine with large golden flowers.

This short detour returns you to the Pali Hwy just in time to exit at the **Nu'uanu Pali Lookout** (Map p114) for its sweeping view of the Windward Coast from a height of 1200ft. From this popular lookout, you can see Kane'ohe straight ahead, Kailua to the right, and Mokoli'i Island and the coastal fishpond at Kualoa Regional Park to the far left. The winds that funnel through the *pali* here are so strong that you can sometimes lean against them; it's usually cool enough that you'll want a jacket.

A pedestrian-only section of the Old Pali Hwy winds down from the right of the lookout, ending abruptly at a barrier near the current highway about a mile away. Few people realize the road is here, let alone venture down it – and thus miss out on the magnificent views looking back up at the snaggle-toothed Ko'olau Range and out across the broad valley. It's worth walking just five minutes down the paved path for a photo-op.

As you get back on the highway, it's easy to miss the sign leading you out of the parking lot, and instinct could send you in the wrong direction. As you drive out of the parking lot, go left if you're heading toward Kailua and right toward Honolulu. Several TheBus routes travel the Pali Hwy, but none stop at the lookout.

WAIMANALO
pop 3600

A breadbasket of small family farms, this proud Hawaiian community sprawls alongside O'ahu's longest beach, with white sands stretching 5.5 miles all the way to Makapu'u Point (p168). What could be just the usual palm-fringed beach and sparkling sea is prettily punctuated by offshore islands and a coral reef a mile offshore that keeps the breaks at a reasonable distance. As elsewhere, don't leave valuables in your car, as break-ins and theft are common.

Sights & Activities
WAIMANALO BEACH PARK
By the side of the highway, this strip of soft white sand has little puppy waves that are excellent for swimming. The park has a shady patch of ironwood trees and views of Manana Island and Makapu'u Point to the south. This is an in-town roadside county

---

CLOSE ENCOUNTERS: DOLPHIN SWIMS

You might want to think twice before signing up for a dolphin swim in the Hawaiian Islands, especially on O'ahu. Although many of these 'dolphin encounter' programs claim to be ecofriendly and educational, the realities of this for-profit business are more complex.

In the wild, acrobatic spinner dolphins are nocturnal feeders that come into sheltered bays during the day to rest. Although it may look tempting to swim out and join them, these intelligent animals are very sensitive to human disturbance. That's why it's illegal to approach them too closely. Some tour boats allow swimmers to approach the dolphins much closer than the federal guideline of 50yd. Even when wild dolphins appear frolicsome and 'happy' to see you, as swimmers commonly report, encountering humans tires them out, according to many marine biologists, so that the dolphins may not have enough energy later to feed or defend themselves. Repeated encounters with humans have driven some dolphins out of their natural habitats to seek less-safe resting places.

In captivity, dolphins are trained to perform for humans using a variety of techniques, ranging from positive behavioral training to food deprivation. Instead of encouraging natural behaviors, captive dolphins are sometimes subjected to artificial routines that can be painful and cause the animals to exhibit signs of stress. Programs that let children or even adults 'ride' the dolphins by hanging onto the animals' dorsal fins are the most questionable, as some captive dolphins have had to undergo surgery to repair damaged fins. On average, captive dolphins die faster than their wild cousins, mostly due to exposure to human-borne illnesses and bacteria. Before signing up for an expensive 'dolphin encounter,' you may want to visit the facility first and ask questions about the animals' care and training.

The success of dolphin swim programs in Hawaii and elsewhere in the USA has led to copycat programs worldwide, in which wild dolphins are sometimes 'harvested' and forced into captivity. The 2008 documentary *The Cove*, directed by a former dolphin trainer, takes a hard-hitting look at the 'dolphinarium' biz and the global industry invested in keeping dolphins in captivity.

park with a grassy picnic area, playground, lifeguards, rest rooms and showers. Camping is allowed in an open area near the road, but it's pretty uninviting.

WAIMANALO BAY BEACH PARK
A mile north of Waimanalo Beach Park, Waimanalo Bay's biggest waves break on-shore here, drawing dedicated board surfers and bodysurfers. Through a wide forest of ironwoods, you'll find a thick mane of blond sand for long walks and ocean ogling. There are lifeguards, a picnic area with barbecue grills, rest rooms, showers and fewer than a dozen just-OK campsites.

BELLOWS FIELD BEACH PARK
Fronting Bellows Air Force Station, this is a long beach with fine sand and a natural setting backed by ironwood trees. The small shorebreak waves are good for beginner bodysurfers and board surfers. The beach is open to civilians only on national holidays and weekends, usually from noon Friday until 8am Monday. There are lifeguards, showers, rest rooms, drinking water and 60 attractive campsites nestled among trees and by the beach. Buses stop in front of the park entrance road, just north of Waimanalo Bay Beach Park; from the bus stop, it's a 1.5 mile walk to the beach.

HIKING
To reach a small pooling waterfall alongside a muddy, mosquito-infested stream, the 2.5-mile round-trip **Maunawili Falls Trail** is a family-friendly trail. It's also the most popular segment of the panoramic 10-mile hiking and mountain-biking **Maunawili Trail System** (Map p173), which gently contours around a series of *pali* lookouts through the Ko'olau Range from the west off the Pali Hwy to the east near Waimanalo town. To reach the main falls trailhead, drive the Pali Hwy from Honolulu toward the coast, then take the second right-hand exit onto A'uloa Rd. At the first fork veer left onto Maunawili Rd, which ends in a residential subdivision; look for a gated trailhead access road on your left.

GOLF
With the dramatic backdrop of the Ko'olau Range, 18-hole/par-72 **Olomana Golf Links** (☎ 259-7926; 41-1801 Kalaniana'ole Hwy; green fees incl cart rental from $80, club rental $35) is where LPGA star Michelle Wie got her start. The two challenging nine-hole courses are played together as a regulation 18-hole course. Facilities include a driving range and Sakura restaurant serving beer and local grinds.

Sleeping & Eating
All three of Waimanalo's beach parks allow camping; for information on obtaining advance permits, see p101. Just north of Waimanalo Beach Park, **Keneke's** (☎ 259-9811; 41-857 Kalaniana'ole Hwy; mains $4-8; ☷ 9:30am-5:30pm) drive-in cooks up island-style barbecue, plate lunches (try the *mochiko* chicken), pineapple smoothies and rainbow-colored shave ice.

Shopping
Set inside a converted gas station, **Naturally Hawaiian Gallery** (☎ 259-5354; www.naturally hawaiian.com; 41-1025 Kalaniana'ole Hwy; ☷ usually 10am-6pm) sells handmade works by O'ahu artists, including wooden koa bowls,

---

THE BATTLE OF NU'UANU
O'ahu was the final island conquered by Kamehameha the Great in his campaign to unite all of the Hawaiian Islands under his rule. On the pastoral beaches of Waikiki, Kamehameha landed his fleet of canoes to battle Kalanikupule, the *mo'i* (king) of O'ahu.

Heavy fighting started around Puowaina (Punchbowl), and continued up Nu'uanu Valley. But O'ahu's spear-and-stone warriors were no match for Kamehameha's troops, which included a handful of Western sharpshooters. The defenders made their last stand at the narrow ledge along the current-day Nu'uanu Pali Lookout. Hundreds were driven over the top to their deaths. A century later, during the construction of the Old Pali Hwy, more than 500 skulls were found at the base of the cliffs.

Some O'ahu warriors, including their king, escaped into upland forests. But when Kalanikupule surfaced a few months later, he was sacrificed by Kamehameha to the war god, Ku. Kamehameha's taking of O'ahu marked the last battle ever fought between Hawaiian forces.

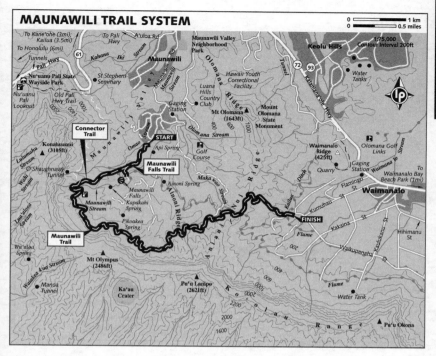

MAUNAWILI TRAIL SYSTEM

carved bone fishhook pendants and other jewelry. Owner Patrick Ching, a former park ranger and cowboy, also sells his own naturalist paintings, prints and illustrated books here.

Getting There & Away

TheBus No 57, which runs between Waimanalo and Honolulu's Ala Moana Center (one hour) and Sea Life Park via Kailua (25 minutes), makes stops along the Kalania'ole Hwy (Hwy 72) through town, running once or twice hourly.

KAILUA
pop 49,250

Kailua is windward O'ahu's largest town, which is a fairly easy title to win. A long graceful bay protected by a coral reef is Kailua's claim to fame, and many repeat visitors to O'ahu leapfrog over touristy Waikiki to hang out in laid-back surf style here instead.

That's because the weather and wave conditions are ideal for swimming, kayaking, windsurfing and kitesurfing. Along the shore,

mid-20th-century cottages, most cooled by tradewinds and not air-conditioning, crowd into little neighborly lanes. The exclusive enclave of Lanikai is where you'll find million-dollar views – and homes that easily cost at least that much.

In ancient times Kailua (meaning 'two seas') was a place of legends and home to several Hawaiian chiefs, serving as a political and economic center for the region. Rich in stream-fed agricultural land, fertile fishing grounds and protected canoe landings, it supported at least three temples, one of which you can still visit today.

Information

Bank of Hawaii (☎ 266-4600; 636 Kailua Rd; ☺ 8:30am-4pm Mon-Thu, to 6pm Fri)
Bookends (☎ 261-1996; Kailua Shopping Center, 600 Kailua Rd; ☺ 9am-8pm Mon-Sat, to 5pm Sun) Next to Times Supermarket, this indie bookstore sells new and used titles, plus newspapers and maps.
Kailua Information Center & Chamber of Commerce (☎ 261-2727; www.kailuachamber.com; Kailua Shopping Center, 600 Kailua Rd; ☺ 10am-4pm Mon-Fri, to 2pm Sat) Hands out free maps and local information.

O'AHU

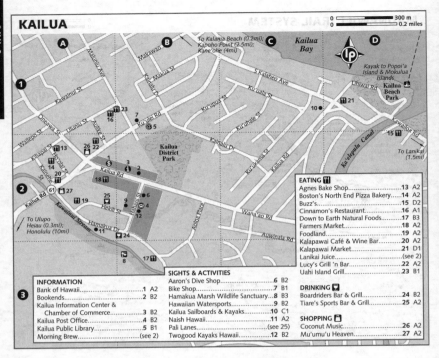

KAILUA

INFORMATION
Bank of Hawaii...........................1 A2
Bookends...................................2 B2
Kailua Information Center &
   Chamber of Commerce............3 B2
Kailua Post Office......................4 B2
Kailua Public Library.................5 B1
Morning Brew........................(see 2)

SIGHTS & ACTIVITIES
Aaron's Dive Shop.....................6 B2
Bike Shop.................................7 B1
Hamakua Marsh Wildlife Sanctuary..8 B3
Hawaiian Watersports................9 B2
Kailua Sailboards & Kayaks.........10 C1
Naish Hawaii...........................11 A2
Pali Lanes..........................(see 25)
Twogood Kayaks Hawaii.............12 B2

EATING
Agnes Bake Shop......................13 A2
Boston's North End Pizza Bakery......14 A2
Buzz's....................................15 D2
Cinnamon's Restaurant..............16 A1
Down to Earth Natural Foods........17 B3
Farmers Market.......................18 A2
Foodland...............................19 A2
Kalapawai Café & Wine Bar........20 A2
Kalapawai Market....................21 D1
Lanikai Juice.......................(see 2)
Lucy's Grill 'n Bar...................22 A2
Uahi Island Grill.....................23 B1

DRINKING
Boardriders Bar & Grill..............24 B2
Tiare's Sports Bar & Grill...........25 A2

SHOPPING
Coconut Music........................26 A2
Mu'umu'u Heaven.....................27 A2

Kailua Post Office (☎ 800-275-8777; 335 Hahani St;
☺ 8:30am-5pm Mon-Fri, 9am-4pm Sat)
Kailua Public Library (☎ 266-9911; 239 Ku'ulei Rd;
☺ 10am-5pm Mon, Wed, Fri & Sat, 1-8pm Tue & Thu)
Free reservable internet terminals (see p568).
Morning Brew (☎ 262-7770; Kailua Shopping Center,
600 Kailua Rd; per hr $6; ☺ 6am-9pm Sun-Thu, to 10pm
Fri & Sat) Fee-based internet terminals or free wi-fi with
purchase.

Sights & Activities

A wide arc of white sand drapes around the
jewel-colored waters of Kailua Bay with formidable volcanic headlands pinning either side.
Sea turtles poke their heads above the gentle
waves, while residents swap gossip during
early morning dog walks along the beach. The
beaches have gently sloping sandy bottoms
with usually calm waters, good for swimming year-round. In the afternoons, winds
transform the bay into a windsurfing and
kitesurfing rink. For sunrise or starlight yoga
on the beach, check out the rotating schedule
of classes, styles and teachers with **Kailua Beach
Yoga** (☎ 722-8923; www.kailuabeachyoga.com); beginners are welcome – just bring your own mat.

KAILUA BEACH PARK

This is the primary access point for visitors
and has the usual public facilities. Three of the
pretty little offshore islands are seabird sanctuaries and only accessible by kayak. Landings
are allowed on **Popoi'a Island** (Flat Island), directly off the south end of Kailua Beach Park.
Twin **Mokulua Islands**, Moku Nui and Moku
Iki, sit directly off Lanikai. It's possible to
kayak from Kailua Beach Park to Moku Nui,
but landings are prohibited on **Moku Iki**, the
smaller of the two islands. Landings are allowed on **Moku Nui**, which has a beautiful beach
for sunbathing and snorkeling.

A few kayaking, windsurfing and kitesurfing outfitters have rental-gear concession
stands by the beach and in-town shops where
you can arrange for group or private lessons
and guided tours:

our pick **Hawaiian Watersports** (☎ 262-5483; www
.hawaiianwatersports.com; 354 Hahani St; kayak rentals
$50-65; ☺ 9am-5pm) Gives discounts for online bookings.
Kailua Sailboards & Kayaks (☎ 262-2555, 888-457-
5737; www.kailuasailboards.com; Kailua Beach Center, 130
Kailua Rd; kayak rentals $40-60; ☺ 9am-5pm) A short
walk from the beach.

Naish Hawaii (☎ 262-6068; www.naish.com; 155 Hamakua Dr; windsurfing rig rentals $45-55; ☺ 9am-5:30pm) Owned by windsurfing champion Robbie Naish.
Twogood Kayaks Hawaii (☎ 262-5656; www.two goodkayaks.com; 345 Hahani St; kayak rentals $40-60; ☺ 9am-6pm Mon-Fri, 8am-6pm Sat & Sun) Free delivery next to Kailua Beach Park.

LANIKAI BEACH
By following the coastal road southeast of Kailua Beach Park, you'll soon enter Lanikai, fronted by what was once one of Hawaii's prettiest stretches of powdery white sand. Today the beach is shrinking, as nearly half of the sand has washed away as a result of retaining walls built to protect the neighborhood's multimillion-dollar mansions. Still, it's a rare beauty, and at its best during full-moon phases. Beyond Kailua Beach Park, the coastal road turns into one-way A'alapapa Dr, which loops back around as Mokulua Dr, passing 11 narrow public-access walkways to the beach. The most luxurious stretches of sand are the farthest southeast toward Wailea Point.

KALAMA BEACH PARK
On the northern side of the bay, this beach has the roughest shorebreak and is popular with experienced bodyboarders. Surfers usually head for the northernmost tip of Kailua Bay at Kapoho Point or further still to Zombies Break.

SCUBA DIVING
Sea caves, lava tubes, coral gardens and WWII-era shipwrecks can all be explored courtesy of **Aaron's Dive Shop** (☎ 262-2333, 888-847-2822; www.hawaii-scuba.com; 307 Hahani St; 2-tank boat dive $115-125; ☺ 7am-7pm Mon-Fri, to 6pm Sat, to 5pm Sun), a five-star PADI operation. Discounts may be available for booking online; inquire about free Waikiki hotel pick-ups.

BIRD WATCHING
Kawai Nui Marsh is one of Hawaii's largest freshwater marshes and provides flood protection for the town of Kailua.

The inland water catchment is also one of the largest remaining fishponds used by ancient Hawaiians. Legend says the edible mud of the ancient fishpond was once home to a *mo'o* (lizard spirit).

Downstream is the smaller **Hamakua Marsh Wildlife Sanctuary** (http://hamakuamarsh.com; admission free; ☺ sunrise-sunset), which provides habitat for some rare waterbirds, including the *koloa maoli* (Hawaiian duck), *ae'o* (Hawaiian black-necked stilt), *'alae kea* (Hawaiian coot) and *kolea* (Pacific golden plover). Birders flock to the sanctuary after rainstorms. You can park for free behind the Down to Earth Natural Foods store off Hamakua Dr.

Sleeping
Kailua has no hotels, but what it does have in abundance is suburban home-style B&Bs and vacation rentals either on the beach or within walking distance. Most are nonsmoking, don't accept credit cards, require an advance deposit and multiple-night stays, add a cleaning fee surcharge and are legally prohibited from displaying signs or offering a hot breakfast. Call ahead (not just from the airport or the road!) a few days, weeks or months in advance for reservations and directions. For camping, head west to Kane'ohe (p179) or south to Waimanalo (p172).

Manu Mele Bed & Breakfast (☎ 262-0016; www.pixi.com/~manumele; 153 Kailuana Pl; d $100-120; ⊠ ⊠) A little out of the way but still just steps from the beach, these simply decorated guest rooms in the contemporary home of English-born host Carol Isaacs appeal. Each has a private entrance, refrigerator, microwave, coffeemaker and cable TV. Smoking allowed only in the garden.

DETOUR: ULUPO HEIAU

The building of this imposing platform **temple** (☎ 587-0300; admission free; ☺ sunrise-sunset) was traditionally attributed to *menehune*, the 'little people' who legends say created much of Hawaii's stonework, finishing each project in one night. Fittingly, Ulopo means 'night inspiration.' In front of the temple, thought to have been a *luakini* (place used for human sacrifice), is an artist's rendition of the site as it probably looked in the 18th century. This heiau is a mile west of Kailua, behind the YMCA at 1200 Kailua Rd. Coming down the Pali Hwy from Honolulu, take Uluoa St, the first left after passing the Hwy 72 junction, then turn right on Manu Aloha St and right again on Manu O'o St.

TOP PICKS – O'AHU B&B AND VACATION-RENTAL AGENCIES

- **Affordable Paradise** (☎ 261-1693; www.affordable-paradise.com) Books Kailua's widest range of B&B rooms, apartments, bungalows and rental houses.
- **Pat's Kailua Beach Properties** (☎ 261-1653; www.patskailua.com) Over 30 options on or near Kailua Beach, from studios to large houses.
- **Lanikai Beach Rentals** (☎ 261-7895; www.lanikaibeachrentals.com) Beautiful, contemporary island-style studio and multibedroom apartments.
- **Hawaii's Best Bed & Breakfast** (☎ 263-3100, 800-262-9912; www.bestbnb.com) Handpicked, high-quality B&Bs, condos and vacation-rentals on the Windward Coast and North Shore.
- **Bed & Breakfast Hawaii** (☎ 822-7771, 800-733-1632; www.bandb-hawaii.com) Books B&B rooms, suites and cottages in Kailua and around Hawai'i Kai.
- **Vacation Rentals by Owner** (www.vrbo.com) For finding scores of vacation-rental houses, condos and cottages all around O'ahu.

Sheffield House (☎ 262-0721; www.hawaiisheffield house.com; 131 Ku'ulei Rd; d $105-125; 🛜) Around the corner from Kailua Beach, this kid-friendly place has tasteful kitchenette units. The smaller guest room is a studio with a wheelchair-accessible bathroom and built-in bookshelves full of beach reading. The one-bedroom suite has a foldout futon and a peaceful garden lanai with a barbecue grill.

Beach Lane B&B (☎ 262-8286; www.beachlane.com; d incl breakfast $105-145; 🖳) Just a short walk from the beach, this sweet little cottage B&B has breezy rooms on the upper floor of a contemporary home, which are best suited for couples. Out back a pair of airy studios each has a kitchenette. Bodyboards and beach chairs can be freely borrowed. Danish, German, Norwegian and Swedish spoken.

Paradise Palms Bed & Breakfast (☎ 254-4234; www.paradisepalmshawaii.com; 804 Mokapu Rd; d $110-120; 🎮) You'll feel like you're visiting newfound relatives at this tidy suburban home. The beds claim most of the floor space, although the efficiency studios with private entrances also have kitchenettes.

Papaya Paradise Bed & Breakfast (☎ 261-0316; www.kailuaoahuhawaii.com; 395 Auwinala Rd; d incl breakfast from $125; 🏊) A half-mile from the beach, this suburban home run by a retired couple has a big outdoor sitting area, a shared fridge and microwave, and quiet lodgings best suited to more mature audiences. The backyard has a handsome view of Mt Olomana.

ourpick Kailua Guesthouse (☎ 261-2637, 888-249-5848; www.kailuaguesthouse.com; d $129-159; 🛜) Not far from downtown, this contemporary home rents out two blissfully quiet apart-

ment-style suites with handmade Hawaiian quilts and lanai overhung with plumeria blossoms. Modern amenities include flat-screen TVs with DVD players, digital in-room safes and shared washer-dryer access. Japanese spoken.

Tee's at Kailua (☎ 261-0771; www.teesinn.com; 771 Wana'ao Rd; d incl breakfast $215; 🎮 🖳) This pampering suburban home rents out just one deluxe guest room, decorated with tropical hardwood furnishings, a king-size sleigh bed and Aveda products in the bathroom. Breakfast includes homegrown organic teas. Japanese spoken.

Eating

Kailua has dozens of places to eat, from fast-food joints to upscale restaurants, but most are mediocre. We've reviewed some standout exceptions here.

Agnes Bake Shop (☎ 262-5367; 46 Ho'olai St; items from 75¢; ⏰ 6am-6pm Tue-Sat, to 2pm Sun) This bakery makes Portuguese sweetbread, chocolate–macnut log pastries and tempting Portuguese *malasadas* (allow 10 minutes, or call ahead to pre-order).

Kalapawai Market (☎ 262-4359; 306 S Kalaheo Ave; items $1-8; ⏰ 6am-9pm, deli 7am-6pm) En route to the beach, everyone stops at this 1930s landmark to stock their picnic basket with made-to-order sandwiches and market-fresh salads. Early-morning regulars often toast their own bagels while helping themselves to fresh coffee. The market's in-town cafe and wine bar serves haute bistro dinners.

ourpick Lanikai Juice (☎ 262-2383; Kailua Shopping Center, 600 Kailua Rd; items $3-8; ⏰ 6am-8pm Mon-Fri, 7am-7pm Sat & Sun) With fresh fruit grown by local farmers and biodegradable cups, this addictive juice bar blends yogi-worthy smoothies with names like Ginger 'Ono and Kailua Monkey. In the morning, join all the locals at sunny sidewalk tables while devouring overflowing bowls of granola topped with *açai* berries, apple bananas and grated coconut.

Boston's North End Pizza Bakery (☎ 263-8005; 31 Ho'olai St; slices $4-6; ❧ 11am-8pm Sun-Thu, to 9pm Fri & Sat) Along with enormous handmade pies, this authentic place dishes up supersized slices with thick, chewy crusts that are equal in size to a quarter of a pizza – surely enough to fuel an afternoon of windsurfing.

Cinnamon's Restaurant (☎ 261-8724; 315 Uluniu St; mains $5-12; ❧ 7am-2pm) Locals pack this humble family-friendly café for standouts like guava chiffon pancakes, Portuguese sweet-bread French toast, eggs Benedict ma-himahi, curried chicken-and-papaya salad, and frittatas with sun-dried-tomato pesto and artichoke hearts.

Uahi Island Grill (☎ 266-4646; 307 Uluniu St; meals $6-11; ❧ 10:30am-8pm Mon & Wed-Sat, to 2:30pm Tue) Get your fresh, flavorful and healthy plate-lunch fix at this corner spot. *Furikake* tofu *poke*, red seafood curry, garlicky chicken, brown rice and vegan desserts all come packaged in biodegradable containers.

Buzz's (☎ 261-4661; 413 Kawailoa Rd; mains lunch $9-15, dinner $15-36; ❧ 11am-3pm & 4:30-9:30pm) By the canal across the road from the beach, this locals' hangout has a tiki-lit lanai and a straightforward menu of charbroiled fish and burgers at lunch and kiawe-grilled surf-and-turf at dinner. Waits are usually long; service can be lousy. Cash only.

Lucy's Grill 'n Bar (☎ 230-8188; 33 Aulike St; mains $16-32; ❧ 5-10pm) A dressed-down contemporary bistro, Lucy's mingles tastes from the Pacific Rim, Southeast Asia and the Americas, like 'ahi-crab cakes with chipotle aioli or grilled fish with lemongrass-curry glaze and Moloka'i sweet-potato mash on the side. If you like exotic bar drinks, check out the pineapple martini and *li hing mui* margarita.

Also recommended:

Down to Earth Natural Foods (☎ 262-3838; 201 Hamakua Dr; ❧ 8am-10pm) Natural-foods grocery store with a takeout deli and hot-and-cold salad bar.

Farmers Market (☎ 848-2074; parking garage behind Longs, 591 Kailua Rd; ❧ 5-7:30pm Thu) Artisan breads, organic fruit and veggies and island-style plate meals.

Foodland (☎ 261-3211; 108 Hekili St; ❧ 24hr) Look for a gourmet wine-and-food specialty shop inside this supermarket.

Drinking & Entertainment

Though it's not a huge party spot like Waikiki, Kailua has the Windward Coast's most happening bars.

Boardriders Bar & Grill (☎ 261-4600; 201 Hamakua Dr; ❧ noon-2am) Has live bands and dancing most weekends.

Tiare's Sports Bar & Grill (☎ 230-8911; 120 Hekili St; ❧ 2pm-4am) Next to Pali Lanes bowling alley, this has live bands, along with karaoke, pool tables and sports TV.

Shopping

Downtown has plenty of thrift shops, antique stores and island-art galleries.

Mu'umu'u Heaven (☎ 263-3366; Davis Bldg, 767 Kailua Rd; ❧ 10am-6pm Mon-Sat, 11am-4pm Sun) Hidden behind the fine-arts Nohea Gallery, this chic contemporary boutique vends flowing tropical-print dresses, skirts and feminine tops all handmade from vintage muumuus, as glimpsed in fashion and style mags like *Lucky*.

Coconut Music (☎ 262-9977; 418 Ku'ulei Rd; ❧ 10am-6pm Mon-Sat) This island-born guitar shop carries name-brand ukuleles – including Kamaka, handmade in Honolulu (p140) – and vintage ukes from the early 20th century. Next-door Hungry Ear Records stocks new, used and collectible Hawaiian music CDs and vinyl records.

Getting There & Away

From Honolulu's Ala Moana Center, TheBus routes No 56 and 57 run to downtown Kailua every 15 minutes, taking about 45 minutes (longer during rush hours). To get to Kailua Beach Park or Lanikai, get off in downtown Kailua at the corner of Kailua Rd and Oneawa St and transfer to TheBus No 70, which runs every 60 to 90 minutes.

You can avoid parking headaches and traffic jams by cycling around town:

Bike Shop (☎ 261-1553; 270 Ku'ulei Rd; per day/week from $20/100; ❧ 10am-7pm Mon-Fri, 9am-5pm Sat, 10am-5pm Sun) Top-quality rentals, repairs and cycling gear.

Kailua Sailboards & Kayaks (☎ 262-2555, 888-457-5737; Kailua Beach Center, 130 Kailua Rd; per half-day/full day/week $15/25/85; ❧ 8:30am-5pm) Rents single-speed beach cruisers.

O'AHU

KANE'OHE
pop 37,070
Although Kane'ohe is blessed with Hawaii's biggest reef-sheltered bay, its largely silty waters are not good for swimming. Outside the military base, this workaday town doesn't receive nearly as many tourists as the surf-and-sun village of Kailua, but it does have a few attractions worth stopping briefly for on a round-the-island tour.

Orientation & Information
Two highways run north–south through Kane'ohe. The coastal Kamehameha Hwy (Hwy 836) is slower, but more scenic. The inland Kahekili Hwy (Hwy 83) intersects the Likelike Hwy (Hwy 63) and continues north past Valley of the Temples. Both highways merge into a single route, the Kamehameha Hwy (Hwy 83), a few miles north of Kane'ohe. Kane'ohe Marine Corps Base Hawaii (MCBH) occupies the entire Mokapu Peninsula; the H-3 Fwy terminates at its gate.

Bank of Hawaii (☎ 233-4670; 45-1001 Kamehameha Hwy; ☼ 8:30am-4pm Mon-Thu, 8:30am-6pm Fri, 9am-1pm Sat) Has a 24-hour ATM.

Borders (☎ 235-8803; Windward Mall, 46-056 Kamehameha Hwy; ☼ 9am-10pm Sun-Thu, to 11pm Fri & Sat) Stocks Hawaii-related books and maps and some mainland and international newspapers.

Kane'ohe Public Library (☎ 233-5676; 45-829 Kamehameha Hwy; ☼ 10am-8pm Mon & Wed, 10am-5pm Tue, Thu & Sun, 1-5pm Fri;) Free wi-fi and reservable internet terminals (see p568).

Sights & Activities
VALLEY OF THE TEMPLES & BYŌDŌ-IN
The Valley of the Temples is an interdenominational cemetery that is famously home to the **Byōdō-In** (☎ 239-8811; 47-200 Kahekili Hwy; adult/senior & child under 13 $3/2; ☼ 9am-5pm), a replica of a 900-year-old temple in Uji, Japan. The temple's symmetry is a classic example of Japanese Heian architecture, with its rich vermilion walls set against the verdant fluted cliffs of the Ko'olau Range. In the main hall, a 9ft-tall Lotus Buddha, covered in gold leaf, is positioned so as to catch the first rays of morning sunlight. Outside, wild peacocks roam beside a carp pond and a garden designed to symbolize the Pure Land of Mahayana Buddhism. The three-ton brass bell is said to bring peace and good fortune to anyone who rings it – and so, of course, everyone does.

From Honolulu's Ala Moana Center, TheBus No 65 stops near the cemetery entrance on Kahekili Hwy, from where it's a 0.7-mile walk winding uphill to the temple.

HO'OMALUHIA BOTANICAL GARDEN
Set against a dramatic backdrop of *pali* at the foot of the Ko'olau Range, O'ahu's biggest **botanical garden** (☎ 233-7323; www.co.honolulu.hi.us /parks/hbg; 45-680 Luluku Rd; admission free; ☼ 9am-4pm) is planted with over 400 acres of trees and shrubs from the world's tropical regions and was originally designed by the US Army Corps of Engineers as flood protection for the valley.

This peaceful nature preserve is networked by sporadically marked, delightfully grassy and often muddy trails winding around an artificial reservoir (no swimming). A small **visitor center** features displays on the park's history, flora and fauna, and Hawaiian ethnobotany. Call ahead to register for two-hour guided nature hikes, usually offered at 10am Saturday and 1pm Sunday. The park allows camping (see opposite).

The park is at the end of Luluku Rd, over a mile *mauka* from the Kamehameha Hwy. TheBus No 55 stops at the Windward City Shopping Center, opposite the start of Luluku Rd, from where the visitor center is a 2-mile uphill walk.

SENATOR FONG'S PLANTATION & GARDENS
A labor of love by Hiram Fong (1907–2004), the first Asian American elected to the US Senate, these flowering **gardens** (☎ 239-6775; www.fonggarden.net; 47-285 Pulama Rd; adult/child 5-12/ senior $14.50/9/13; ☼ 10am-2pm, tours usually 10:30am & 1pm) aims to preserve Hawaii's plant life for future generations. The Fong family offers informal lei-making classes ($6.50) and 90-minute, 1-mile guided tours that wind past tropical flowers, sandalwood and palm trees, and other endemic plants. The gardens are 0.8 miles *mauka* of the Kamehameha Hwy – watch for the signed turnoff around a half-mile north of Sunshine Arts Gallery, which is painted with eye-catching colorful murals.

HE'EIA STATE PARK
Despite looking abandoned, this park offers picturesque views of **He'eia Fishpond**, an impressive survivor from the days when stone-walled ponds used for raising fish for royalty were common on Hawaiian

TOP PICKS – O'AHU'S GARDENS & GREEN SPACES

- Lyon Arboretum (p125)
- Foster Botanical Garden (p121)
- Ho'omaluhia Botanical Garden (p178)
- Koko Crater Botanical Garden (p168)
- James Campbell National Wildlife Refuge (p185)
- Waimea Valley (p187)
- Waihaiwa Botanical Garden (p196)
- Honouliuli Forest Reserve (p196)

hores. It remains largely intact despite invasive mangrove.

Just offshore to the southeast, **Moku o Lo'e** was a royal playground. Its nickname 'Coconut Island' comes from the trees planted there by Princess Bernice Pauahi Bishop in the mid-1800s. During WWII, the US military used it for R&R. Today the Hawai'i Institute of Marine Biology occupies much of the island, which you might recognize from the opening scenes of the *Gilligan's Island* TV series.

Near the park entrance, there's a traditional Hawaiian canoe shed and workshop.

GOLF
It's no contest: 18-hole/par-73 **Ko'olau Golf Club** (☎ 247-7088; www.koolaugolfclub.com; 45-550 Kionaole Rd; green fees $59-145) is O'ahu's toughest course, scenically nestled beneath the Ko'olau Range. Nearby, the municipal 18-hole/par-72 hillside **Pali Golf Course** (☎ 266-7612; www.co.honolulu.hi.us/des /golf; 45-050 Kamehameha Hwy; green fees $21-42) also has stunning views, stretching from the mountains across to Kane'ohe Bay. For tee-time reservations, green fees and general information, see p108. Club and handcart rentals are available at both of these courses.

Sleeping & Eating
Before your circle-island tour, you're better off eating in nearby Kailua (p176).

County-run **Ho'omaluhia Botanical Garden** (☎ 233-7323; www.co.honolulu.hi.us/parks/hbg; 45-680 Luluku Rd; campsites free) allows camping from 9am Friday until 4pm Monday. With an overnight guard and gates that open after-hours only for pre-registered campers, it's among O'ahu's safest places to camp. You can get a permit in advance at any satellite city hall (see p101), or

simply go to the park's visitor center between 9am and 4pm, but call first to confirm that space is available. No alcohol allowed.

Getting There & Away
TheBus No 55 and 65 leave from Honolulu's Ala Moana Center every 20 minutes, taking just under an hour to reach Kane'ohe. From Kailua, TheBus No 56 runs once or twice hourly to Kane'ohe. TheBus No 55 trundles north from Kane'ohe along the Kamehameha Hwy to Turtle Bay (p185), taking about an hour to reach La'ie; this route usually operates every 30 minutes or so until after 6pm, then approximately hourly until 10:45pm.

WAIAHOLE & WAIKANE
Traveling north along the Kamehameha Hwy across the bridge beside Kahulu'u's Hygienic Store is a physical and cultural departure from the gravitational pull of Honolulu. Now you've officially crossed into 'the country,' where the highway becomes a two-laner and the ocean shares the shoulder. You'll cruise through sun-dappled valleys inhabited by small towns and farms. A roadside landmark, the **Waiahole Poi Factory** (48-140 Kamehameha Hwy) opens a couple of days each week to sell bags of poi and Hawaiian plate lunches.

Not everything in these parts is as peaceful as the *lo'i kalo* (taro fields) however. Large tracts of the Waikane Valley were taken over by the US military during WWII for training and target practice, which continued into the 1960s. The government claims the land has so much live ordnance that it can't be returned to the families it was leased from, a source of ongoing contention with locals, who resent that much of the valley remains off-limits. Not surprisingly, you will encounter quite a few Hawaiian sovereignty activists here. Anti-development signs and bumper stickers with slogans like 'Keep the Country Country' are everywhere you look.

KUALOA
Although there's not a lot to see nowadays, in ancient times Kualoa was one of the most sacred places on O'ahu. When a chief stood on Kualoa Point, passing canoes lowered their sails in respect. The children of royalty were brought here to be raised, and it may have been a place of refuge where *kapu* (taboo) breakers and fallen warriors could seek reprieve from traditional Hawaiian law.

Kualoa Regional Park

Offering an expansive vista of offshore islands, this **park** (☎ 237-8525; 49-479 Kamehameha Hwy; admission free; ☿ sunrise-sunset) is backed by magnificent mountain scenery. Palm trees shade a narrow white-sand beach that offers safe swimming, but watch out for jellyfish in summer. There are picnic areas, barbecue grills, rest rooms, showers and sometimes a lifeguard.

Birders will want to stroll south along the beach to **'Apua Pond**, a 3-acre brackish salt marsh on Kualoa Point, and a nesting area for the endangered *ae'o* (Hawaiian black-necked stilt). Further down the beach, you can spot **Moli'i Fishpond**, its rock walls covered with mangrove.

That eye-catching peaked islet you see off-shore is **Mokoli'i** ('little lizard'). According to legend, it's the tail of a *mo'o* (lizard spirit) slain by the goddess Hi'iaka and thrown into the ocean. Following the immigration of Chinese laborers to Hawaii, this cone-shaped island also came to be called 'Chinaman's Hat,' a nickname that persists today, regardless of political correctness.

Roadside camping is allowed, but beware that this county park is often a hangout for drinking and carousing at night. For camping permits, see p101.

Kualoa Ranch

A wholeheartedly touristy attraction, to be sure, but with an almost irresistibly scenic location, as you may recognize from movies and TV shows. Tour groups, especially Japanese, make up the bulk of visitors at this island-style dude **ranch** (☎ 237-7321, 800-231-7321; www.kualoa.com; 49-560 Kamehameha Hwy; tours $21-145; ☿ 9am-3pm). If you want to see where Hurley built his *Lost* golf course, Godzilla left his footprints or the *Jurassic Park* kids hid from dinosaurs, take a jeep or ATV tour of the movie-set sites. Forget the ranch's horseback trail rides, which lack much giddy-up. Inside the visitor center, cafeteria-style **Aunty Pat's Paniolo Café** lays out a supersized barbecue lunch buffet ($16) between 10:30am and 1:30pm daily.

Back in 1850 Kamehameha III leased over 600 acres of this land to Dr Judd, a missionary doctor who became one of the king's advisers. Judd planted the land with sugarcane, built flumes to transport it and imported Chinese laborers to work the fields. Drought spelled the end of O'ahu's first sugar plantation in 1870. Today you can still see the **ruins** of the mill's stone stack, and a bit of the crumbling walls, about a half-mile north of the beach park and the main ranch entrance.

KA'A'AWA

Here the road really hugs the coast and the *pali* move right on in, with barely enough space to squeeze a few houses between the base of the cliffs and the road. **Swanzy Beach Park**, a narrow neighborhood beach used mainly by fisher-folk, is fronted by a shore wall. Across the road from the park is a convenience store, a gas station and a hole-in-the-wall post office – pretty much the center of town, such as it is. **Uncle Bobo's** (☎ 237-1000; 51-480 Kamehameha Hwy; mains $7-12; ☿ 10:30am-7pm Tue-Sun) drive-in fills beachgoers up with barbecue, burgers, hot dogs and shave ice.

A DO-IT-YOURSELF 'LOST' TOUR

Figuring out exactly where on O'ahu scenes from TV's smash-hit series *Lost* are filmed is almost as much of a local pastime as reading about the exploits of the cast, four of whom have been arrested for DUI (and perhaps not coincidentally, as local media has speculated, three of those arrested soon saw their characters killed off on the show).

Some of the most easily recognized *Lost* filming locations are at **Kualoa Ranch** (above), which offers guided tours. You can roam the beach where the main *Lost* survivors set up camp for free – it's **Mokule'ia Beach** (p194), on the North Shore, out toward Ka'ena Point. On the Windward Coast, **Byōdō-In** (p178) represented Korea during some scenes with Jin and Sun.

On the other side of the island east of Hanauma Bay, the sculpted rocks of the **Lana'i Lookout** (p167) are unmistakable during some of the backstory scenes about 'The Others,' while aerial cliffside views from the lighthouse at **Makapu'u Point** (p168) were shared by Hurley, Locke and Sawyer. Many jungle scenes were shot along hiking trails around Honolulu's **Mt Tantalus** (p128). Finally, just outside Waikiki, the **Hawaii Convention Center** (Map pp146–7) has stood in for Sydney's airport, where the *Lost* survivors boarded doomed Oceanic Airlines Flight 815.

The **Crouching Lion** is a rock formation just north of the 27-mile marker. The Hawaiian version of the legend goes like so: a demigod from Tahiti was cemented to the mountain during a jealous struggle between the volcano goddess Pele and her sister Hi'iaka. When he tried to free himself by crouching, he was turned to stone. To find him, stand at the restaurant sign with your back to the ocean and look straight up to the left of the coconut tree at the cliff above.

Sharing real estate with the famous landmark, the recently renovated **Crouching Lion Inn** (☎ 237-8511; 51-666 Kamehameha Hwy; mains $11-24; ☻ 11am-10pm) has country roosters parading around the parking lot. During the day, busloads of day-trippers stop in for a light lunch of predictable salads and sandwiches. In the evening, tiki torches are lit for surf-and-turf dinners on a sunset-view lanai.

KAHANA VALLEY

In ancient Hawaii, all of the islands were divided into *ahupua'a* – pie-shaped land divisions that ran from the mountains to the sea – providing everything Hawaiians needed for subsistence. Modern subdivisions and town boundaries have erased this traditional organization everywhere except here, O'ahu's last publicly owned *ahupua'a*.

Before Westerners arrived, the Kahana Valley was planted with wetland taro, which thrived in the rainy valley. Archaeologists have identified the remnants of more than 130 agricultural terraces and irrigation canals, as well as the remains of a heiau, fishing shrines and numerous *hale* (house) sites.

In the early 20th century the lower valley was planted with sugarcane, which was hauled north to Kahuku via a small railroad. During WWII the upper valley was taken over by the US military and used to train soldiers in jungle warfare. It remains undeveloped today, used mostly by locals who come to hunt feral pigs on weekends.

Kahana Bay Beach Park

While many archaeological sites are hidden inaccessibly deep in the valley, Kahana's most impressive site, **Huilua Fishpond**, is readily visible from the main road and can be visited simply by walking down to the beach. This county park is a locals' hangout that offers mostly safe swimming with a gently sloping sandy bottom. Watch out for the riptide near the reef

WHOSE VALLEY IS IT ANYWAY?

When the state bought the Kahana Valley in 1969 in order to preserve it from development, it also acquired tenants, many of whom had lived in the valley for a long time. Rather than evict a struggling rural population, the state agreed to let some of the residents stay on the land, hoping to eventually incorporate the families into a 'living park,' with residents acting as interpretive guides. According to local opinion and an official 2001 governmental report, that long-term plan has failed. At press time, Hawaii's legislature was preparing to vote on whether or not the last remaining families, some of whom had been living here illegally without leases, should be evicted.

break at the south end of the beach. The park has rest rooms, showers, drinking water and picnic tables. Roadside campsites don't offer much privacy, and are mostly used by island families; for camping permits, see p101.

Ahupua'a o Kahana State Park

In spite of political controversy, this **park** (☎ 237-7766; www.hawaiistateparks.org; Kamehameha Hwy; admission free; ☻ sunrise-sunset) is currently open to visitors, although wandering around may feel like intruding on someone's private home. Look for the signposted entrance about a mile north of Crouching Lion Inn.

Starting from the orientation center, the gentle, 1.2-mile **Kapa'ele'ele Trail** runs along a former railbed and visits both a fishing shrine and the bay-view **Keaniani Kilo** lookout, then follows the highway back to the park entrance. Starting 1.3 miles farther up the rough, unpaved valley road, the **Nakoa Trail** is a 2.5-mile rain forest loop that crisscrosses Kahana Stream, passing by a swimming hole next to an artificial dam. Both trails can be very slippery and muddy when wet.

PUNALU'U
pop 895

This inconspicuous seaside community is just another string of houses along the highway that most visitors drive by en route to the North Shore. But it's close enough to the surf scene, and offers more affordable accommodations. **Punalu'u Beach Park** has a long, narrow swimming beach with an offshore reef that

O'AHU

protects the shallow waters in all but stormy weather. Be cautious of strong currents near the mouth of the stream and in the channel leading out from it, especially during high surf.

Sleeping & Eating

Punalu'u Guesthouse (☎ 946-0591; 53-504 Kamehameha Hwy; dm $20-23) Cheap without being a flophouse, this three-bedroom house has been converted into an informal hostel. Because it's a cozy situation, the hostel prescreens potential guests, so most folks come here after a stay at HI–Honolulu (p132), and walk-ins are not accepted. There's a communal kitchen, an on-site house 'parent' and guests often get together at dinnertime.

Pat's at Punalu'u (Map p170; ☎ 255-9840; http://pats atpunaluu.org; 53-567 Kamehameha Hwy; 🍴) Largely residential and looking a bit neglected on the outside, this oceanfront condominium houses privately owned units that are spacious, if well worn. There's no front desk; instead, rental arrangements are handled either by realty agents or private owners, including through Vacation Rentals by Owner (www.vrbo.com).

Shrimp Shack (☎ 256-5589; 53-352 Kamehameha Hwy; mains $8-16; ⏱ 11am-5pm) Next door to Ching's general store, you'll find this sunny yellow truck which sells *mochi* (sticky-sweet Japanese pounded-rice cakes) for dessert. Order some deep-fried coconut shrimp imported from Kaua'i or more seafood plate lunches, from snow-crab legs to mussels, all made to order and served piping hot.

For condo rentals at Pat's:

Paul Comeau Condo Rentals (☎ 293-2624, 800-467-6215; www.patsinpunaluu.com; studio/1br/2br $100/150/250, plus cleaning fee $50-150; 🍴) Three-day minimum stay; weekly and monthly discounts available.

Papaya Paradise (☎ 261-0316, 262-1008; http://kai luaoahuhawaii.com; studio d $125, plus cleaning fee $75; 🍴) Kailua B&B owners (p176) rent two studio condos at Pat's.

HAU'ULA
pop 3690

Aside from a couple of gas pumps, a general store and a 7-Eleven store, the only point of interest in this small coastal town is the stone ruins of **Lanakila Church** (c 1853), perched on a hill next to newer Hau'ula Congregational Church. Across the road is shallow-rocky-bottomed **Hau'ula Beach Park**. Roadside camping is allowed, though it's mostly the domain of folks living out of their cars; for county permits, see p101.

Behind Hau'ula's soggy commercial strip is a scenic backdrop of hills and majestic Norfolk pines. The **Kaipapa'u Forest Reserve** offers two secluded hiking trails with ocean vistas that head deeper into the Ko'olau Range. The signposted trailhead is at a bend in Hau'ula Homestead Rd, just 0.25 miles above the Kamehameha Hwy, starting north of Hau'ula Beach Park. Follow the paved access road inland, past the hunter-hiker check-in station that marks the start of the reserve.

Both trails share the same access point and head into the lush foothills of the Ko'olau Range. The tranquil **Hau'ula Loop**, which clambers through Waipilopilo Gulch and onto a ridge over Kaipapa'u Valley, is better maintained and more rewarding, both for its views and the native flora along the way, including sweet-smelling guava, ohia trees with feathery red blossoms and thick groves of shaggy ironwood trees. This moderate 2.5-mile lollipop loop hike takes about 1½ hours.

LA'IE
pop 4640

Feeling almost like a big city compared to its rural neighbors, life here in La'ie revolves around Brigham Young University (BYU)–Hawaii, where scholarship programs recruit students from islands throughout the Pacific. Many students help pay for their expenses by working as guides at the Polynesian Cultural Center, a tourist mega complex that draws nearly a million visitors each year.

The first Mormon missionaries to Hawaii arrived in 1850. After an attempt to establish a 'City of Joseph' on the island of Lana'i failed amid a land scandal, the missionaries moved to La'ie. In 1919 they constructed a smaller, but still showy version of their Salt Lake City, Utah temple here at the foot of the Ko'olau Range. This dazzlingly white temple at the end of a wide boulevard may be the Windward Coast's oddest sight. There's a temple visitor center where volunteers will tell you about their faith, but nonbelievers are not allowed inside the temple itself.

Information

Restaurants, shops and services cluster in the Lai'e Shopping Center, a half-mile north of the Polynesian Cultural Center.

O'AHU

Bank of Hawaii (☎ 293-9238; 55-510 Kamehameha Hwy; ☽ 8:30am-4pm Mon-Thu, to 6pm Fri) Has a 24-hour ATM.

La'ie Post Office (☎ 800-275-8777; 55-510 Kamehameha Hwy; ☽ 9am-3:30pm Mon-Fri, 9:30-11:30am Sat)

Sights & Activities
POLYNESIAN CULTURAL CENTER

A nonprofit theme park showcasing the cultures of Polynesia, this **center** (PCC; ☎ 293-3333, 800-367-7060; www.polynesia.com; 55-370 Kamehameha Hwy; park admission & evening show adult/child 3-11 $60/45; ☽ 11am-9pm Mon-Sat, villages noon-6pm only) is owned by the Mormon Church and is one of O'ahu's biggest attractions, second only to the USS Arizona Memorial at Pearl Harbor.

Continually overrun by tour-bus crowds, the park revolves around seven theme 'villages' representing Samoa, Aotearoa (New Zealand), Fiji, Tahiti, Tonga, the Marquesas and Hawaii. The villages contain authentic-looking huts and ceremonial houses, many elaborately built with twisted ropes and hand-carved posts. BYU–Hawaii students dressed in native garb gamely demonstrate poi pounding, coconut-frond weaving, handicrafts and games. There's also a replica of a 19th-century mission house and chapel.

Although steep, the basic admission price also includes a winding boat ride through the park, ocean-themed movies at the IMAX theater and in the evening, a Polynesian song-and-dance revue that's partly authentic, partly Bollywood-style with creative sets and costumes, and BYU college students animatedly performing on stage.

BEACHES

La'ie's beaches are more attractive than those to the immediate south, but they're not as amazing as Malaekahana State Recreation Area (right), just north of town.

A half-mile south of the PCC's main entrance, **Pounders Beach** is an excellent bodysurfing beach, but the shorebreak, as the name of the beach implies, can be brutal. Summer swimming is generally good, but watch out for strong winter currents. The area around the old landing is usually the calmest.

Crashing surf, a lava arch and a slice of Hawaiian folk history await at **La'ie Point**. The tiny offshore islands are said to be the surviving pieces of a *mo'o* (lizard spirit) slain by a legendary warrior. The islet to the left with the hole in it is **Kukuiho'olua** (Puka

Rock). To get here from the Kamehameha Hwy, head seaward on Anemoku St, opposite La'ie Shopping Center, then turn right on Naupaka St.

Sleeping & Eating

Laie Inn (☎ 293-9282, 800-526-4562; www.laieinnhawaii .com; 55-109 Laniloa St; d incl breakfast $75-85; ☒ ☒ ☒) Next to the Polynesian Cultural Center, this bedraggled two-story motel surrounding a courtyard swimming pool is slated to be demolished and replaced with a new Courtyard by Marriott hotel in 2010. Expect standards – and room rates – to rise significantly.

La'ie Chop Suey (☎ 293-8022; La'ie Shopping Center, 55-510 Kamehameha Hwy; mains $7-10; ☽ 10am-8:45pm Mon-Sat) No place in town gets more packed than this family-owned Chinese kitchen, with its long menu of Americanized and island-flavored dishes, ranging from lemon chicken to pot-roast pork.

Hukilau Cafe (☎ 293-8616; 55-662 Wahinepe'e St; mains $4-8; ☽ 7am-2pm Tue-Fri, to 11:30am Sat) Just north of town, this hole-in-the-wall is the kind of place locals like to keep to themselves. (And no, it's not the same place depicted in the movie *50 First Dates*.) Island-sized breakfasts and lunches, including sweet-bread French toast, *loco moco* and teriyaki burgers, are mostly right on.

Also recommended:

Angel's Ice Cream, Shave Ice & Smoothies (☎ 293-8260; La'ie Shopping Center, 55-510 Kamehameha Hwy; items $3-6; ☽ 10am-10pm Mon-Thu, to 11pm Fri & Sat) Cool off with an 'Angel's Halo' shave ice or real-fruit smoothie.

Foodland (☎ 293-4443; La'ie Shopping Center, 55-510 Kamehameha Hwy; ☽ 6am-11pm) Supermarket has a bakery and deli, but no alcohol (this is Mormon country).

MALAEKAHANA STATE RECREATION AREA

You'll feel all sorts of intrepid pride when you discover this wild and rugged beach, just north of town. A long, narrow strip of sand stretches between Makahoa Point to the north and Kalanai Point to the south with a thick inland barrier of ironwoods.

Swimming is generally good year-round, although there are occasionally strong currents in winter. This popular family beach is also good for many other water activities, including bodysurfing, board surfing and windsurfing. Kalanai Point, the main section of the park, is less than a mile north of La'ie and has picnic tables, BBQ grills, camping, rest rooms and showers.

Moku'auia (Goat Island), a state bird sanctuary just offshore, has a small sandy cove with good swimming and snorkeling. It's possible to wade over to the island when the tide is low and the water's calm. Be careful of the shallow coral (sharp) and sea urchins (sharper). When the water is deeper, you can swim across, but beware of a rip current sometimes present off the island's windward side. Before going out, ask the lifeguard about water conditions and the advisability of crossing.

Sleeping

Malaekahana has the best public campgrounds on the northern Windward Coast. Camping at **Kalanai Point** is free with an advance state-park permit (see p101). As with all public campgrounds on O'ahu, camping is not permitted on Wednesday and Thursday nights.

You can also let the surf be your lullaby at Makahoa Point, about 0.7 miles north of the park's main entrance. **Friends of Malaekahana** (☎ 293-1736; 56-335 Kamehameha Hwy; tent site per person $8.50, cabins $50-150; ☽ office 10am-4pm Mon-Fri) maintains this end of the park, offering tent sites, very rustic 'little grass shacks' and eco-cabins, plus 24-hour security and hot showers. Reservations are strongly recommended; there's a two-night minimum stay. Gates are locked after 7pm.

KAHUKU

pop 1780

Kahuku is a former sugar-plantation town, its roads lined with wooden cane houses. Most of the old sugar mill that operated here until 1996 has been knocked down, but the remnants of the smokestack and the old iron gears can be seen behind the post office. The rest of the former mill grounds have been transformed into a small shopping center containing the town's bank, gas station and grocery store.

Today locals are once again looking to the land for their livelihoods. Roadside stands sell Kahuku corn on the cob, a famously sweet variety of corn that gets name-brand billing on Honolulu menus. Shrimp ponds at the north side of town also supply O'ahu's top restaurants, while colorful lunch trucks that cook up the crustaceans – in sweet-and-spicy sauce, for example, or fried with butter and garlic – are thick along the highway. But be forewarned that not all of these trucks serve shrimp and prawns that were actually raised here. Some import the crustaceans from around the islands, or even from overseas.

You'll probably be in for a long wait at Kahuku's most famous shrimp trucks, including **Romy's** (☎ 232-2202; 56-781 Kamehameha Hwy), just north of town, and **Giovanni's** (☎ 293-1839), near the old sugar mill. Next to Giovanni's, **Famous Kahuku Shrimp** (☎ 389-1173; 56-580 Kamehameha Hwy) offers a few more menu choices like hot-'n'-spicy squid. All of these shrimp trucks are usually open 10am to 6pm daily, depending upon supply and demand. Expect to pay at least $12 per dozen shrimp or prawns with two-scoop rice.

Back in the middle of town, at the back of the shopping center, **Kahuku Grill** (☎ 293-2110; 55-565 Kamehameha Hwy; mains $5-12; ☽ 8am-7pm) looks like a tidy farmhouse kitchen and has true aloha spirit. The pancakes are fluffy, the handmade beef burgers juicy and the coconut-encrusted shrimp delicately fried – yum, yum.

NORTH SHORE

pop 18,380

You don't have to know much about the world of surfing to know a few things about the North Shore. Iconic breaks such as Pipeline, Sunset and Waimea are known all over the globe as must-surf locations. In winter the big swells come in and the wave heights reach truly gigantic proportions. The ocean rears its head in either profound beauty or utter terror – depending on your point of view.

To say that the North Shore is just about big waves is misleading – the beaches are stunning by anyone's standards and the sleepy rural lifestyle sits in harmony with its bohemian underpinnings. In summer the waves peter out and the surf tribe migrates to the next big break – in their wake all that is left is calm water, perfect for snorkeling, and those same stunning beaches.

Before the surfing revolution of the 1950s the North Shore was little more then a collection of fishing villages, sugarcane plantations and dilapidated houses. The rebirth of board riding saw the arrival of surfers, surf competitions and eventually those eager to cash in on the trend.

DETOUR: JAMES CAMPBELL NATIONAL WILDLIFE REFUGE

Signposted 2 miles north of Kahuku, this wildlife refuge (☎ 637-6330; www.fws.gov /jamescampbell; admission free; ☒ varies) encompasses freshwater wetland habitat for four of Hawaii's six species of endangered waterbirds: the *'alae kea* (Hawaiian coot), *ae'o* (Hawaiian blacknecked stilt), *koloa maoli* (Hawaiian duck) and *'alae 'ula* (Hawaiian moorhen). During stilt nesting season, normally from mid-February to mid-October, the refuge is off-limits to visitors. The rest of the year, free guided tours are given (reservations required).

The North Shore is far from a sellout though – there is a strong current within the local community to keep 'The North Shore Country'. Development is frowned upon and conservation is the coolest concept in town.

TURTLE BAY

Sitting upon the crown of northeastern O'ahu, the coves and lava beds that define the area in and around Turtle Bay (Kawela Bay) is a stunning marker between the Windward Coast and the North Shore. The Turtle Bay Resort claims a portion of this landscape with a view-perfect hotel, golf course, condo village and public access to the nearby beaches. There are rumors of expansion afoot – while the resort is dead keen, the locals are almost unanimously opposed. Time will tell if the development goes through and if tough economic times are enough to sway the locals.

Beaches

Kuilima Cove, with a beautiful little beach known as **Bay View Beach**, is a stunner. Like a good beach should, it has something for everyone, and there is plenty of sand to stretch out on, which should keep the placid placated. An outer reef that not only knocks down the waves but facilitates some great snorkeling – and, in winter some nice moderate surf – can be found on the right-hand side of the bay.

Just a mile east of Kuilima Cove is **Kaihalulu Beach**, a beautiful, curved, white-sand beach backed by ironwoods. The rocky bottom makes for poor swimming, but the

shoreline attracts morning beachcombers. Go another mile east to reach scenic **Kahuku Point**, where local fishers cast throw-nets and pole fish from the rocks.

Turtle Bay Resort

Out-of-sync with the North Shore's beatnik reputation, the **Turtle Bay Resort** (Map p170; ☎ 293-6000; www.turtlebayresort.com; 57-091 Kamehameha Hwy, Kahuku) has brought all the modern conveniences of resort life to an unlikely corner of the island. The resort has two top-rated 18-hole courses (one designed by George Fazio and the other by Arnold Palmer); 10 tennis courts (highly rated by *Tennis* magazine) and horseback riding on slow-paced trails and sunset rides.

SLEEPING & EATING

The sleeping options at the resort include the multistory **hotel** (☎ 293-6000; r from $460; ☒ ☒ ☒) and the adjacent **condominiums** (studios from $110; 1br from $135; 2br from $190). Each of the hotel rooms has a lanai with a breathtaking ocean view. Booking arrangements for the condos are handled by **Turtle Bay Condos** (☎ 293-2800, 888-266-3690; www.turtlebaycondos.com) or **Estates at Turtle Bay** (☎ 293-0600, 888-200-4202; www.turtlebay-rentals.com). Team Real Estate at Hale'iwa (p192) also deals with Turtle Bay condo bookings.

21 Degrees North (☎ 293-8811; Turtle Bay Resort, 57-091 Kamehameha Hwy; mains $28-40; ☒ 6-10pm Tue-Sat) has big windows filled with views of the ocean – the hallmark of this fine-dining establishment. Well-prepared seafood with a local flavor makes for a memorable dining experience.

WAIMEA
pop 2450

The tiny community of Waimea is little more then a collection of a few houses and shops, across the road from one of the best surf breaks in the world.

Revered the world over for its monster winter waves, it's a sort of loose gathering point for the world's best surfers, ardent fans and enthusiastic wannabes. Beyond the beach, which shouldn't be ignored, lies a pocket of lush green beauty. Even if you don't surf, there's enough here worth spending some time in the area – the surrounding hills are home to lush rainforest, archeological treasures and a charming little town.

NORTH SHORE

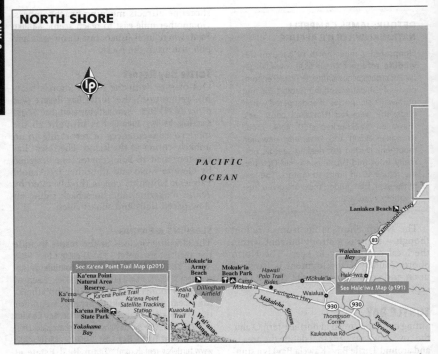

Two hundred years ago the Waimea Valley was heavily settled, the lowlands terraced in taro, the valley walls dotted with houses and the ridges topped with heiau sites. Waimea River, now blocked at the beach, originally opened into the bay and was a passage for canoes traveling to villages upstream. Surfing has been associated with Waimea since the 15th century, when Hawaiians took to *he'e nalu* (traditional Hawaiian term for board surfing).

Sights & Activities
SUNSET BEACH PARK
Like many beaches on the North Shore, Sunset Beach has a split personality depending on the time of year. In the winter the big swells come in and the sand is pounded into submission by spectacularly large waves. It's a hot spot for the top wave riders and the posse of followers that these rockstars of the sea attract.

In the summer the waves calm down and the beach increases in size, thanks to the lack of pounding. Though the water is more inviting, be aware that there are still some nasty currents about.

The beach has rest rooms, showers and a lifeguard tower. If the beachside parking is full, you can find parking in the lot across the street.

BACKYARDS
A smokin' surf break off Sunset Point at the northern end of the beach, Backyards draws top windsurfers. There's a shallow reef and strong currents to contend with, but also the island's biggest waves for sailing.

'EHUKAI BEACH PARK
'Ehukai Beach, aka Banzai Pipeline, aka Pipeline, aka Pipe – call it what you want, but if it's big surf you seek, this is *the* place. Pipeline is known the world over as one of the biggest, heaviest and closest-to-perfect barrels in all of wave riding. When the strong westerly swells kick up in winter the waves jack up to monster size, often reaching over 15ft before breaking on the ultrashallow reef below. For those who know what they're doing (and no, a day at Waikiki beach doesn't count) this could very well be the holy grail of surfing.

their loyalty, Pele gave her followers immortality by turning them to stone.

There are showers and rest rooms in front of Old Quarry; TheBus 52 stops out front.

Shark's Cove

Shark's Cove is beautiful both above and below the water's surface. The naming of the cove was done in jest – sharks aren't a problem. In summer, when the seas are calm, Shark's Cove has super snorkeling conditions, as well as O'ahu's most popular cavern dive. A fair number of beginner divers take lessons here, while the underwater caves will thrill advanced divers.

To get to the caves, swim out of the cove and around to the right. Some of the caves are very deep and labyrinthine, and there have been a number of drownings, so divers should only venture into them with a local expert.

Three Tables

Three Tables gets its name from the flat ledges rising above the water. In summer when the waters are calm, Three Tables is good for snorkeling and diving. It is possible to see some action by snorkeling around the tables, but the best coral and fish, as well as some small caves, lava tubes and arches, are in deeper water further out. This is a summer-only spot. In winter dangerous rip currents flow between the beach and the tables. Watch for sharp rocks and coral – and, as always, don't touch the reef.

WAIMEA VALLEY

The perfect antithesis to the beach, this complex and endearing **park** (☎ 638-9199; 59-864 Kamehameha Hwy; adult/child 4-12 $8/3; ☯ 9:30am-5:30pm) across from Waimea Bay Beach Park is a sanctuary of tropical tranquility. You have the option to wander among the gardens or even take a dip at the base of the 60ft waterfall. Amongst the foliage you'll find up to 6000 plant species and replicas of the buildings the early Hawaiians dwelled in.

WAIMEA BAY BEACH PARK

It may be a beauty but it's certainly a moody one. Waimea Bay changes dramatically with the seasons: it can be tranquil and flat as a lake in summer, then savage in winter, with incredible surf and the island's meanest rip currents.

Winter is prime time for surfers. On the calmer days bodyboarders are out in force, but

For the non-world-class surfer this is a great venue to watch the best do their thing – the waves break only a few yards off shore, so you really are front-row and center. In the summer months everything is calm and there is even some decent snorkeling to be done off this beach – oh how the seasons change!

The entrance to 'Ehukai Beach Park is opposite Sunset Beach Elementary School. At the beach, there's a lifeguard, rest rooms and showers.

PUPUKEA BEACH PARK

Pupukea Beach Park is a long beach further south along the highway that includes Three Tables to the south, Shark's Cove to the north and Old Quarry in between. Pupukea, meaning 'white shell,' is a very scenic beach, with deep blue waters, a varied coastline and a mix of lava and white sand. The waters off Pupukea Beach are protected as a marine-life conservation district.

The large boulders on the end of Kulalua Point, which marks the northernmost end of the beach, are said to be followers of Pele, the Hawaiian volcano goddess. To acknowledge

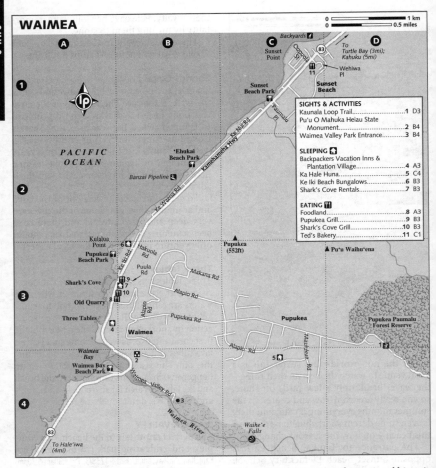

WAIMEA

SIGHTS & ACTIVITIES
Kaunala Loop Trail.........................1 D3
Pu'u O Mahuka Heiau State
  Monument................................2 B4
Waimea Valley Park Entrance...........3 B4

SLEEPING
Backpackers Vacation Inns &
  Plantation Village.....................4 A3
Ka Hale Huna..............................5 C4
Ke Iki Beach Bungalows.................6 B3
Shark's Cove Rentals.....................7 B3

EATING
Foodland..................................8 A3
Pupukea Grill.............................9 B3
Shark's Cove Grill.......................10 B3
Ted's Bakery.............................11 C1

even then sets come in hard and people get pounded. Winter water activities at this beach are *not* for novices. Usually the only time it's calm enough for swimming and snorkeling is from June to September.

Given Waimea Bay's position as the most popular North Shore beach, parking is often tight. Don't park along the highway, even if you see others doing so; police are notorious for towing away dozens of cars at once, particularly when surf competitions are taking place. Facilities here include showers, rest rooms and picnic tables, and a lifeguard is on duty daily.

PU'U O MAHUKA HEIAU STATE MONUMENT
A stellar view of the coast and a stroll around the grounds of O'ahu's largest temple reward

those who venture up to this national historic landmark, perched on a bluff above Waimea. The temple's stacked stone construction is attributed to the legendary *menehune* (the 'little people' who, according to legend, built many of Hawaii's fishponds, heiaus and other stonework), who are said to have completed their work in just one night. Pu'u O Mahuka means 'hill of escape,' and it was a *luakini* heiau, where human sacrifices took place.

The terraced stone walls are a couple of feet high of rough dilapidated stone. Collectively, the three adjoining enclosures that form the main body of the heiau are more than 550ft in length. This was a dramatic site for a temple, and it's well worth the drive for the commanding view, especially at sunset.

To get there, turn up Pupukea Rd at the Foodland supermarket. The heiau turnoff is half a mile up, and from there it's 0.7 mile to the site.

KAUNALA LOOP TRAIL

Little-known Kaunala Loop Trail sits quietly above Waimea Valley, a good place to mix an easy valley walk with a moderate ridge climb for sweeping views of Waimea Bay. After seeing the beauty of the bay from viewpoints high atop this trail, it's easy to see why Hawaiian royalty considered it sacred.

To get to the trailhead, turn up Pupukea Rd at the Foodland supermarket and continue for 2.5 miles, where the road ends at a Boy Scout camp. Park in the camp parking lot and follow the Na Ala Hele signs to the trailhead. This 4.5-mile hike averages about two hours. This trail is officially open to the public only on weekends and state holidays. Hunting is also allowed in this area, so hikers should wear bright colors and avoid wandering off the trail.

Festivals & Events

The kickoff leg of the world's premier surfing event, the **Triple Crown of Surfing**, is the Reef Hawaiian Pro held at Hale'iwa Ali'i Beach Park in mid-November. The O'Neill World Cup of Surfing (late November to early December) is the second leg of the competition and takes place at Sunset Beach. Then the final leg, the Billabong Pipeline Masters, is in early to mid-December at Banzai Pipeline, with the world's top pros vying for a $275,000 purse.

Sleeping

The bulletin board at Pupukea's Foodland supermarket has notices of roommates wanted and the occasional vacation rental listing, so check it out if you're thinking of staying a while. There are also a number of private home owners who rely on word-of-mouth advertising, as well as vacation-rental agencies (see p192).

Backpackers Vacation Inns & Plantation Village (☎ 638-7838; http://backpackers-hawaii.com; 59-788 Kamehameha Hwy; dm/d/studio $30/72/120; 🖥) Travelers looking for a good budget choice on the North Shore are in luck. This friendly backpacker-style place is your one and only option and thankfully it's also a groovy place to stay. In keeping with the local vibe, the digs are modest to the point of ramshackle, but if you don't mind the odd bit of peeling paint and an eclectic decor you'll feel right at home. The location is superb and there is a variety of rooming options, from bunk rooms through to private cabins on the beach.

Shark's Cove Rentals (☎ 638-7980, 888-883-0001; www.sharkscoverentals.com; 59-672 Kamehameha Hwy; r $75-185; 🖥) This well-managed property consists of four adjacent houses that are directly across from Pupukea Beach Park. The houses are divided into apartment-style dorms: each of the self-contained apartments has three private bedrooms with bunk beds, shared bathroom and shared kitchen. In the main house, overlooking the water, the units have a private bathroom but shared kitchen and common space. The owners are enthusiastic about their guests and their enjoyment of the North Shore.

THE EDDIE

Every winter a very special surf contest takes place. Named in honor of the late Eddie Aikau, this big-wave surfing event is perhaps the most prestigious and spiritual surf contest anywhere.

Eddie Aikau was a legendary waterman and Waimea lifeguard. You only have to see Waimea on a big day to know the courage it takes to wade into the water to save a swimmer in trouble.

In 1978 Eddie joined an expedition to re-create the Polynesian journey to Hawaii – by sailing a replica double-hulled canoe from O'ahu to Tahiti and back. Soon after the craft left the shore it was in trouble and capsized in rough water. Eddie decided to go for help – he grabbed his surfboard and set off to paddle the 12 miles to shore to raise the alarm. Eddie was never seen again. His companions survived, but the legendary waterman was gone.

As a tribute the supposedly annual Eddie Aikau surf contest at Waimea Bay is an invitation-only event that only runs when the waves are big enough (ie 30ft minimum), meaning the Bay picks the day. It doesn't happen every year and you can't predict the waves – but that's somehow fitting. People like Eddie are one in a million, and the waves that befit his legend are worth the wait.

Ka Hale Huna (☎ 638-7924; www.vrbo.com/59784; off Pupukea Rd; studios $125) Perched on the mountain that overlooks the sea, this private home rents out a very private studio with a lanai facing a wooded canyon filled with bird activity. The unit has a kitchenette, a sun-filled room, outdoor BBQ grill and access to the shade and fruit trees of the garden. The beach is a five-minute drive away and it's a great place to spend the winter. There is a 30-day minimum stay.

Ke Iki Beach Bungalows (☎ 638-8229; www.keiki beach.com; 59-579 Ke Iki Rd; 1br $145-215, 2br $165-230; ⌘) This hideaway retreat fronts a beautiful white-sand beach just north of Pupukea Beach Park. The 11 units are comfortably furnished with a tropical decor of floral prints and rattan chairs that fits the setting like a glove. Each unit has a full kitchen, TV and phone, and guests have access to a barbecue, picnic tables and hammocks strung between coconut trees. The location is an absolute gem – the beachside units are right on the sand, the others just a minute's walk from the water.

Eating

Foodland (☎ 638-8081; 59-720 Kamehameha Hwy; ◷ 6am-11pm) This modern supermarket opposite Pupukea Beach Park has everything you need for a beachside picnic, a quick snack or more elaborate DIY meals.

Ted's Bakery (☎ 638-8207; 59-024 Kamehameha Hwy; items $1-7; ◷ 7am-4pm) World famous in Hawaii, Ted's is the place to go on the North Shore for a quick bite. The chocolate-coconut pie is legendary and there is a decent selection of savories and deli choices to satisfy every taste.

our pick **Shark's Cove Grill** (☎ 638-8300; Kamehameha Hwy; dishes $5-8; ◷ 8:30am-7pm) You can't get more North Shore than this quintessential joint. The little blue shack on the roadside cranks out great breakfasts, sandwiches, mixed plates and smoothies. Pull up a seat of ramshackle patio furniture, watch the waves and dig in.

Pupukea Grill (Kamehameha Hwy; mains from $8; ◷ 11am-9:30pm) This place is not much more then a collection of picnic tables in front of a permanently parked truck on the side of the highway. Shave ice, panini, wraps, mixed plates and nachos are all served with a great outlook onto Shark's Cove.

HALE'IWA
pop 2500

The best way to know if the surf's up is by how busy Hale'iwa is. If the town is alive with ac-

tivity, hustle and bustle, then chances are the surf is flat. Arrive into town and find it eerily quiet – then check the beach, as odds are the waves are pumping. It's that sort of town: it's all about the surf and everyone knows it.

There is a laid-back ambience to the place that sits in perfect concert with the rest of the North Shore. As the biggest center on the coast, this is where to come to find a decent meal, get a new T-shirt or rent out a longboard for the day.

Orientation

Most of Hale'iwa's shops are situated along Kamehameha Hwy, the main street. Hale'iwa has a picturesque boat harbor bounded on both sides by beach parks, including Hale'iwa Ali'i Beach Park, known for the North Shore's safest year-round swimming conditions.

The Anahulu River, flowing out along the boat harbor, is spanned by the Rainbow Bridge. In 1832 John and Ursula Emerson, the first missionaries to come to the North Shore, built Hale'iwa, meaning house (hale) of the great frigate bird ('iwa), a grass house and missionary school on the riverbank, which gave its name to the village.

Information

Coffee Gallery (☎ 637-5355; North Shore Marketplace, 66-250 Kamehameha Hwy; per 10min $1; ◷ 7am-8pm) Internet access and free wi-fi is available at this café.

First Hawaiian Bank (☎ 637-5034; 66-135 Kamehameha Hwy; ◷ 8:30am-4pm Mon-Thu, to 6pm Fri) Just north of the Hale'iwa Shopping Plaza.

Post office (☎ 637-1711; 66-437 Kamehameha Hwy; ◷ 8am-4pm Mon-Fri, 9am-noon Sat) At the south side of town.

Hale'iwa Pharmacy (☎ 637-9393; 66-149 Kamehameha Hwy) In Hale'iwa Shopping Plaza.

Dangers & Annoyances

Because there is a transient population on the North Shore, car and vacation rental break-ins are common. Don't leave any valuables in your car when parked at beach parks and follow all the safety regulations required by the rental agencies.

Sights
BEACHES

The in-town beach parks provide a nice patch of green to host family luau and community

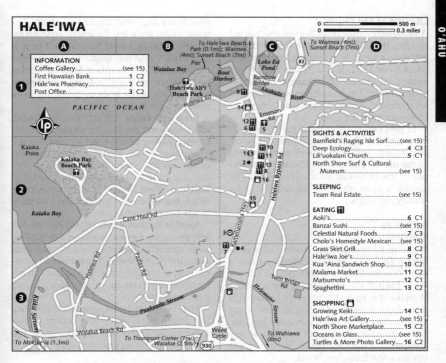

soccer scrimmages. Although these beach parks are close to the harbor, the wave action does attract annual surf competitions and lots of local attention.

On the northern side of Waialua Bay, the **Hale'iwa Beach Park** is protected by a shallow shoal and breakwater so the water is usually calm, and a good choice for swimming. There's little wave action, except for the occasional north swells that ripple into the bay.

Although the beach isn't as pretty as Hale'iwa's other strands, this 13-acre park has a broad range of facilities, as well as basketball and volleyball courts, an exercise area and a softball field. It also offers a good view of Ka'ena Point.

Hale'iwa Ali'i Beach Park is home to some of the best surf on the North Shore and as a result is a popular spot for surf contests. In late November the Triple Crown of Surfing gets underway on this break – bringing in the best surfers in the world. The waves here can be huge, with double or triple overhead tubes not uncommon.

When it's flat, the local kids rip it up with their bodyboards and mere mortals test their skills on the waves. The 20-acre beach park has rest rooms, showers, picnic tables and lifeguards. The shallow areas on the southern side of the beach are generally the calmest places to swim.

Those wanting to get away from Hale'iwa can head a mile or so west of town to the **Kaiaka Bay Beach Park**. There are a few more trees here, so it's a good option when the mercury climbs and shade is necessary. The swimming is better at the other local beaches, so look elsewhere if you're looking to get wet. Kaiaka has rest rooms, picnic tables, showers, drinking water and campsites.

NORTH SHORE SURF & CULTURAL MUSEUM
It's impossible to separate surfing from the culture of the North Shore – the best place to see how deep that connection runs is this **museum** (☎ 637-8888; 66-250 Kamehameha Hwy; admission by donation; ☼ 11am-5:30pm Wed-Mon) in the North Shore Marketplace. The little museum is packed with vintage boards, fading photographs and some great stories. They have some cool vintage bits of memorabilia for too. Definitely worth a wander.

LILI'UOKALANI CHURCH

Although the current building was constructed in 1961, the **Lili'uokalani Church** (☎ 637-9364; 66-090 Kamehameha Hwy; ☺ most mornings) congregation dates from 1832. It is a Protestant church named for Queen Lili'uokalani, who spent summers on Anahulu River and attended services here. Services were held entirely in Hawaiian until the 1940s.

In 1892 Queen Lili'uokalani gave the church its seven-dial clock, which shows the hour, day, month and year, as well as the phases of the moon. The queen's 12-letter name replaces the numerals on the clock face. The church is open whenever the minister is in, usually mornings.

Activities
SURFING

If you're a beginner, the North Shore does have a few tame breaks, including Chun's Reef, Pu'uena Point and Hale'iwa Ali'i Beach Park. Even if you've ridden a few waves in Waikiki, it is advisable to take a lesson with one of the many freelancing surfers to get an introduction to the underwater hazards. Everyone offers lessons on the side, so ask around for recommendations or keep an eye out for homemade brochures.

SNORKELLING

During the winter, North Shore dive operators take trips to Shark's Cove (p187) in the summer months and to South Shore wrecks in the winter. Between Christmas and April, humpback whales visit the harbors of northern and western O'ahu.

Deep Ecology (☎ 637-7946, 800-578-3992; www.deepecologyhawaii.com; 66-456 Kamehameha Hwy; 2-tank dive $139; ☺ 9am-5pm Mon-Sat, to 4pm Sun) If you'd rather get under the waves as opposed to on top of them, the folks at Deep Ecology can sort you out. With a strong ecological bent, these divers are concerned about the ocean and lead dive trips with that in mind.

CYCLING & MOUNTAIN BIKING

Bike riding on the North Shore ranges from paved bike paths next to the Kamehameha Hwy to challenging tracks above Waimea Bay and wider trails around Ka'ena Point (p200).

Sleeping

Except for Turtle Bay Resort, there are no official hotels on the North Shore. Vacation rentals are the most common lodging options. There are a few European-style B&Bs, as well as budget-style hostels, and people occasionally rent out rooms in their homes; check the bulletin boards at Malama Market in Hale'iwa or Foodland supermarket in Pupukea. See under Waimea (p189) for more sleeping options.

Team Real Estate (☎ 637-3507, 800-982-8602; www.teamrealestate.com; North Shore Marketplace; 66-250 Kamehameha Hwy; vacation homes per night from $65) This place handles a couple dozen vacation rentals on the North Shore, including several one- and two-bedroom apartments in Hale'iwa. Most budgets can be accommodated, but it's best to get in early, especially in the busy winter season.

SandSea Vacation Homes (☎ 637-2568, 800-442-6901; www.sandsea.com; beachfront houses $175-750) This outfit specializes in renting beachfront homes along the North Shore. It has about 20 properties in all, ranging from places that can accommodate just two people to those that can sleep up to 20.

Hale'iwa's only camping option is at Kaiaka Bay Beach Park, where the county allows camping on Friday to Tuesday nights. For details on obtaining a permit, see p101.

Eating
BUDGET

Celestial Natural Foods (☎ 637-6729; 66-443 Kamehameha Hwy; ☺ 9am-6pm Mon-Sat, to 5pm Sun) For those in search of karmicly cool organic produce and health foods this is the place. There is a tiny veggie-friendly deli out back for a quick meal.

Malama Market (☎ 637-4520; 66-190 Kamehameha Hwy; ☺ 7am-9pm) If you're looking to self-cater, get the picnic gear in order or grab a quick bite from the deli. You'll find all the right ingredients at this modern supermarket.

Spaghettini (☎ 637-0104, 66-200 Kamehameha Hwy; pizza slices $2.50-3, pizza $10-$16; ☺ 11am-8pm) Don't be fooled by its unassuming looks – this place serves up the best pizza in all O'ahu. For a quick, delicious lunch try a veggie slice loaded with spinach, olives and garlic. Forget the pasta – pizza is the real prize.

Kua 'Aina Sandwich Shop (☎ 637-6067; 66-160 Kamehameha Hwy; sandwiches $4-8; ☺ 11am-8pm) Want the best burgers in all of O'ahu? Look no further then this North Shore überclassic burger joint. Kua 'Aina has a list of burgers and sandwiches a mile long, so there is bound

---

SWEET TREAT

The circle-island drive isn't complete without stopping for shave ice at **Matsumoto's** (☎ 637-4827; 66-087 Kamehameha Hwy; snacks $2-5) tin-roofed general store. Often Honolulu families drive to the North Shore with one goal only in mind: to stand in line here and walk out with a dripping, delicious shave ice cone, drenched with island flavors, such as *liliko'i* (passion fruit), banana, mango and pineapple.

Hawaii's shave ice is drenched with industrial-strength sweet syrup, like the snow cones found on the US mainland, but it's much better because the ice is more finely shaved. A medium-sized cone with a combination of flavors usually costs about $2 – a bit more if you add a local favorite, red azuki bean. The entire concoction begins dripping into a sticky mess the second you get it, so don't dawdle.

Most tourists flock to Matsumoto's, but many North Shore locals prefer **Aoki's** (66-117 Kamehameha Hwy; snacks $1.50-3).

---

to be at least a few things to tickle your fancy. We find the mahimahi sandwich particularly scrumptious.

Grass Skirt Grill (☎ 637-hula; 66-214 Kamehameha Hwy; lunch/dinner from $10) It's the micro-tiki room, with retro surf decor on the walls, which fits right in with the traditional fare of mixed plates and seafood specialities. Popular with locals and great for a takeout meal bound for the beach.

MIDRANGE & TOP END

Hale'iwa Joe's (☎ 637-8005; 66-001 Kamehameha Hwy; appetizers $5-12, lunch mains $7-16, dinner mains $14-28; ☺ 11:30am-9:30pm Sun-Thu, to 10:30pm Fri & Sat) With a superb location overlooking the marina and some of the best food on the North Shore, Hale'iwa Joe's shouldn't be missed. While much of the dining in town reflects the laid-back feel of the area, the food here takes it up a notch. Brilliantly prepared seafood and hearty steaks pepper the menu. Freshness is key, with much of the fish coming from the boats you can see out the windows.

Cholo's Homestyle Mexican (☎ 637-3059; North Shore Marketplace; 66-250 Kamehameha Hwy; combination plates $8-17; ☺ 10am-9pm) Solid home-style Mexican food is what attracts such a big crowd of locals and tourists alike. If you've never tried a fresh *'ahi* taco or a grilled *'ahi* burrito, here's your chance to get one done to perfection. It serves good fajitas and chimichangas as well.

Banzai Sushi (☎ 637-4404; 66-246 Kamehameha Hwy; mains from $10; ☺ lunch & dinner) Hidden at the back of the shopping plaza, this sushi place does it right. It has a big menu filled with the classic rolls you'll be looking for, but try the signature dish, the Banzai sushi and sashimi set – it's the perfect postsurf scarf.

Shopping

Hale'iwa shopping ranges from the trendy to the quirky, and most of the shops and galleries are either in or nearby the **North Shore Marketplace** (66-250 Kamehameha Hwy).

Oceans in Glass (637-3366; North Shore Marketplace, 66-250 Kamehameha Hwy) Who says glass figurines are just for Nana? These handmade fish, turtles and dolphins are made before you eyes and, even better, are replaced for free if you break 'em on the way home.

Hale'iwa Art Gallery (☎ 353-5763, North Shore Marketplace, 66-252 Kamehameha Hwy) At this gallery featuring the works of 20-plus local and regional artists, you're sure to find something you like. There are a variety of styles on offer – everything from dreadful through to dramatic.

Turtles & More Photo Gallery (☎ 741-3510; 66-218 Kamehameha Hwy) If your holiday snaps don't measure up, the photos in here will surely impress the gang back home, with stunning underwater images of sea life and some killer surfing shots thrown in. There are various sizes up for sale to suit most budgets.

Growing Keiki (☎ 637-4544; 66-051 Kamehameha Hwy) This kids' shop has gear for junior surf grommets and budding beach bunnies, including mini aloha shirts, trunks and toys.

Barnfield's Raging Isle Surf (☎ 637-7797; www .ragingisle.com; North Shore Marketplace, 66-250 Kamehameha Hwy; ☺ 10am-6:30pm) Packed full of beachwear, surfboards, skateboards and anything else you might need for life on the North Shore.

WAIALUA
pop 3761

For travelers that are seeking to really get a~ from it all or for those that find the re'

O'AHU

slow pace of life on the North Shore just too hectic – head to Waialua. This sugar-mill town ground to a halt in 1996, when the mill shut for good. Since then, precious little has happened here and the cracks in the pavement are starting to sprout weeds.

The **Waialua Sugar Mill** (www.sugarmillhawaii.com) has been redeveloped into a model center for locally owned shops and businesses. While much of the North Shore has a distinctly rustic flavor, take one step into **Hawaiian Bath & Body** (☎ 637-8400; Old Sugar Mill, 67-106 Kealohanui St; ⏰ 9am-5pm) and you are transported into a bubble of aromatic opulence. Peek through the glass and watch the soapmakers craft their bars, all made with local ingredients such as *kukui* (candlenut tree) nuts.

The rambling warehouse known as **Island X Hawaii** (☎ 637-2624; Old Sugar Mill, 67-106 Kealohanui St; ⏰ 9am-3:30pm Mon-Fri, 8:30am-noon Sat) has everything from reasonably priced aloha shirts to wooden handicrafts and pieces of original and vintage art. Tucked in the corner is a little coffee shop that has Waialua coffee on the boil – this local brew is grown in the hills above town.

On Saturdays from 8:45am to noon the **Waialua Farmers Market** sets up in the parking lot of the sugar mill to show off the wares of local farmers. Many of the former plantation workers now farm small plots of land leased from the Dole pineapple corporation, an agreement that was reached to help workers retrenched as a result of the sugar mill's closure. There are also small-scale surfboard makers and other light-industry operations keeping the old mill decidedly brawny.

If you miss the farmers market, stop in at **Brown Bottle** (☎ 637-6728; 67-292 Goodale Ave; ⏰ 7am-10:30pm), a liquor store that sells fresh produce grown by a local farmer.

The Waialua area remains economically depressed, with many of the surrounding fields overgrown with feral sugarcane. Other sections are newly planted with coffee trees – a labor-intensive crop that holds promise for job creation. You can see the coffee trees, planted in neat rows, as you come down the slopes into Waialua.

Sleeping

Camp Mokule'ia (Map pp186-7; ☎ 637-6241; www .campmokuleia.com; 68-729 Farrington Hwy; campsites per person $10, r from $65, cottages from $85; 🏊) Those wanting to really escape from the tourist scene can find solace here. This church-run camp is open to travelers as long as there isn't a prebooked group on the site. The amenities are basic, with BBQ facilities, a pool, tent sites, a few rooms and couple of cottages. It's easy to find, sitting right across the road from Dillingham Airfield.

MOKULE'IA TO KA'ENA POINT

Here's to the end of the road! This section describes the last few stretches of human habitation before the island terminates in the deep and fearsome ocean. The Farrington Hwy (930) is your honorable guide; it runs west from Thompson Corner to Dillingham Airfield and Mokule'ia Beach. Both this road and the road along the Wai'anae (Leeward) Coast are called Farrington Hwy, but they don't connect, as each side reaches a dead end about 2½ miles short of Ka'ena Point.

Mokule'ia Beach Park

Keen windsurfers often congregate on this stretch of shore, taking advantage of the consistent winds. The beach park sports a large grassy area with picnic tables, rest rooms and showers. The beach itself is a nice sandy stretch but the rocky seabed makes for poor swimming conditions. Come wintertime the currents pick up and entering the water isn't advisable.

Dillingham Airfield

The trade winds that visit O'ahu create perfect conditions for sailplanes to glide over the scenic North Shore. All sailplane operations on the island are headquartered at Dillingham Airfield, at the west end of the Farrington Hwy, just past Mokule'ia Beach Park.

Original Glider Rides (☎ 637-0207) offers scenic glider rides that last anywhere from 10 minutes to an hour. The silent flight is a peaceful and scenic way to see the island. On the other hand, if that all sounds too placid, things can be spiced up with some aerobatics. Prices start at $60 for 10 minutes and go to $250 for an aerobatic hour of flight. Be sure to call ahead, as flights are weather-dependant.

Skydive Hawaii (☎ 637-9700; www.hawaiiskydiving .com; jumps 150; ⏰ 8am-3pm) will toss you out of a perfectly good airplane, preferably with a parachute attached. It offers tandem jumps, where you're attached to an instructor who does all the mental heavy lifting, then you jump from a stomach-turning 13,000ft, free-fall for a minute and pull the chute and glide down for 15 minutes. You have to be 18 or over, and under 200lb. If you know what you're doing they can also sort out a lift for experienced jumpers so that they can take the leap on their own.

Mokule'ia Army Beach to Ka'ena Point

Mokule'ia Army Beach, opposite the western end of Dillingham Airfield, has the widest stretch of sand on the Mokule'ia shore. Once reserved exclusively for military personnel, the beach is now open to the public, although it is no longer maintained and there are no facilities. The beach is unprotected and has very strong rip currents, especially during high surf in winter.

From Army Beach you can proceed another 1.5 miles down the road, passing still more white-sand beaches with aqua blue waters. You'll usually find someone shore-casting and a few folks living out of their cars. The terrain is scrubland reaching up to the base of the Wai'anae Range, while the shoreline is wild and windswept. The area is not only desolate, but can also be a bit trashed.

The Farrington Hwy ends at the beginning of the dirt path leading to rocky Ka'ena Point (p201), which connects to the Wai'anae (Leeward) Coast. You can hike or mountain bike around the point but you can't drive. To get to the other side by car, you'll have to backtrack to the highways that buzz through Central O'ahu.

Hiking

The 5-mile **Kealia Trail** (Map pp102–3) ascends from Dillingham Airfield up a cliff-face and through a forest of ironwoods and *kukui* trees. The snaking trail switchbacks its way up the cliff, offering ocean views along the way, but the real prize is its connection to the **Kuaokala Trail** (Map pp102–3), which brings hikers to a justly celebrated viewpoint over Makua Valley and the Wai'anae Range. The Kealia Trail is best for those wishing to avoid the hassle of securing a permit and driving up the Wai'anae (Leeward) Coast just to hike the Kuaokala Trail, a 5.5-mile loop trail accessible from the Ka'ena Point Satellite Tracking Station. The trailhead to Kealia Trail begins in the back of the airfield; head west 2 miles past the main airfield entrance and just before the airfield ends, take the road marked Gate D and follow it inland 0.4 miles. Just before the air control tower parking lot, there's an access road on the right. Walk around the old storage hangar to begin the trail. Give yourself about three hours to walk the Kealia Trail and back, and another three hours if you add on the Kuaokala loop.

If all that walking sounds like too much work, all of the trails are also open to mountain bikes.

CENTRAL O'AHU

Always the bridesmaid, never the bride – Central O'ahu is the forgotten region of the island. Squashed between the buzzing south and the hip north it's more of a thoroughfare then a destination unto itself. Take heed – for those with the time and the inclination there are some worthy stops along the way.

Three routes lead north from Honolulu to Wahiawa, the region's central town. The freeway, H2, is the fastest route, whereas Kunia Rd (750), the furthest west, is the most scenic. The least interesting of the options, Farrington Hwy (93), catches local traffic. From Wahiawa two routes, Kaukonahua Rd (803) and Kamehameha Hwy (99), lead through scenic pineapple country to the North Shore.

HAWAII'S PLANTATION VILLAGE

The lives of the people who came to Hawaii to work on the sugarcane plantations are showcased at **Hawaii's Plantation Village** (Map pp102–3; ☎ 677-0110; www.hawaiiplantationvillage.org; 94-695 Waipahu St, Waipahu; adult/child 4-11 $13/5; ☼ tours on the hr 10am-2pm Mon-Sat). The setting is particularly evocative, as Waipahu was one of O'ahu's last plantation towns, and its rusty sugar mill, which operated until 1995, still looms on a knoll directly above this site.

The place encompasses 30 buildings typical of a plantation village of the early 20th century, including a Chinese cookhouse, a Japanese shrine and authentically replicated homes of the ethnic groups – Hawaiian, Japanese, Chinese, Korean, Portuguese, Puerto Rican and Filipino – that lived on the plantations.

To get there by car from Honolulu, take the H1 to exit 7, turn left onto Paiwa St, then right onto Waipahu St, continue past the sugar mill and turn left into the complex. Otherwise, take TheBus No 42 from various Waikiki locations to get there.

O'AHU

HONOULIULI FOREST RESERVE

Honouliuli Forest Reserve is home to nearly 70 rare and endangered plant and animal species. The land once belonged to Hawaiian royalty and was named Honouliuli – meaning dark harbor – for the dark, fertile lands that stretch from the waters of Pearl Harbor to the summit of the Wai'anae Range.

The **Nature Conservancy** (☎ 587-6220; www.nature .org\hawaii) leads monthly hikes on trails in the Honouliuli Forest Reserve on the slopes of the Wai'anae Range north of Kapolei. Check out the website for upcoming hikes and general information about joining.

KUNIA ROAD (HIGHWAY 750)

If you're not in a hurry (and why would you be?) this slightly longer route through the center of the island is a scenic alternative. It may add a few minutes to your drive from Hololulu, but the scenery along the way is far more interesting compared to the H2 speedway. Follow H1 from Honolulu to the Kunia/Hwy 750 exit, 3 miles west of where H1 and H2 divide.

The drive starts in sprawling suburbia but soon breaks free into an expansive landscape with 360-degree views. As you gain altitude, views of Honolulu and Diamond Head emerge below; be sure to stop off somewhere and look back at the landscape. Cornfields give way to enormous pineapple plantations, all hemmed in by the mountains to the west.

The rural landscape continues until you pass by Schofield Barracks Military Reservation. This massive army base is the largest on the island and is a hive of activity – it's not uncommon to be passed on the highway by camo-painted Humvees while a Black Hawk chopper hovers overhead.

At 1724ft, **Kolekole Pass** occupies the gap in the Wai'anae Range that Japanese fighter planes flew through on their way to bomb Pearl Harbor. Film buffs may recognize the landscape, as the historic flight was re-created here 30 years later for the classic war film *Tora! Tora! Tora!*

Kolekole Pass, on military property above Schofield Barracks, can be visited as long as the base isn't on military alert. Access is through Lyman Gate on Hwy 750, 0.7 miles south of Hwy 750's intersection with Hwy 99. Follow Lyman Rd for 5.25 miles, passing a military golf course and bayonet assault course, to reach the pass.

In Hawaiian mythology, the large, ribbed stone that sits atop the ridge here is the embodiment of a woman named Kolekole, who took the form of this stone in order to become the perpetual guardian of the pass.

WAHIAWA
pop 16,151

Wahiawa isn't the sort of destination that most travelers seek out. That is, of course, unless you are looking for a new tattoo, some used stereo equipment or a meal from a chain fast-food establishment. There is one notable exception – the serene Botanical Garden, which shines all the more for its contrasting surrounds.

Sights & Activities
WAHIAWA BOTANICAL GARDEN

While much of Wahiawa is drab, grey and bordering on ugly, this **botanical garden** (☎ 621-7321; 1396 California Ave; admission free; ☼ 9am-4pm) a mile east of Kamehameha Hwy (Hwy 83) is a slice of arboreal heaven. Nature lovers and gardeners will delight in the rollicking grounds that stretch for at least 27 acres. There is a mix of the manicured, with beautiful lawns and pruned ornamental plants, and the wild, with a gully of towering hardwoods, tropical ferns and forests of bamboo.

The garden has a long and interesting history – started 80 years ago as an experiment by the local sugarcane farmers, it has evolved into a striking oasis of horticultural perfection. There are several paths that weave their way through the garden, about half of which are wheelchair-friendly. An enthusiastic volunteer staff is on hand to answer questions and point you in the right direction.

DOLE PLANTATION

This busy **complex** (☎ 621-8408; 64-1550 Kamehameha Hwy 'Hwy 99'; admission free; ☼ 9am-5:30pm) has a split personality – outside the maze and train are great fun for the kids and the young at heart. Meanwhile inside the gift shop is overflowing with pineapple-flavored tacky tourist items. It's a sickly sweet overdose of everything pineapple – the final touch being the pineapples for sale for 20% more than the grocery store in town!

The pineapple industry in O'ahu was established in 1901 by James D Dole, a cousin of Sanford B Dole, then president of the Republic of Hawaii after the overthrow of the queen. Not only was Dole successful at growing pineapples in the temperamental soil but he introduced industrialization into the time-consuming process of canning the fruit, so that it could reach the mainland market faster and cheaper.

Getting hopelessly lost has never been more fun then here in the 'world's largest' **maze** (adult/child $6/4). This claim to fame has been verified by the good folks at Guinness World Records. It truly is a gigantic undertaking, with over a mile and a half of pathways to lose your way in. The goal is to find six different stations before making your way out. You better be quick if you want to beat the current record of six minutes – most people take 30 minutes and the geographically challenged can take *hours*.

Thomas fans unite! A vintage **steam train** (adult/child $7.75/5.75) grinds a groove around the plantation, taking budding engineers and conductors for a 20-minute ride. The kids will love it and parents will have a place to sit for 20 minutes.

WAI'ANAE (LEEWARD) COAST

The Wai'anae (or Leeward) Coast is a one of contrasts. On one side of the Farrington Hwy (Hwy 93) are some of the nicest beaches on the island, yet on the other side, dilapidated houses and scruffy businesses dominate the region. There is a collective feeling of the forgotten over here – with the wealthy of Honolulu sweeping what they don't want in their backyard under the Wai'anae rug. You'll find the garbage dump, the power plant and the economically depressed all living here.

While one might assume that this makes for a depressing experience, it's quite the contrary. The Wai'anae (Leeward) Coast is in many ways the heart and soul of the island. You'll find more Native Hawaiians here then anyplace else and with that, a cultural pride permeates the area.

The land is dry and the mountains seem to push you into the sea – but the beaches are wide, untouched by tourism and the communities are nothing if not authentic.

Farrington Hwy runs the length of the coast, scooting past squatty towns and liquor stores on one side and white-sand beaches

on the other. Further up the coast habitation yields to the velvet-tufted mountains and rocky coastal ledges leading all the way to the sacred tip of the island at Ka'ena Point.

KO OLINA RESORT

No beach? No problem. All it takes is a little bit of lateral thinking and a couple of thousand tons of imported sand. When this resort was still on the drawing board it lacked the signature feature that is key for all Hawaiian resorts – a beach. A deal was struck and in exchange for public access, investors were allowed to carve out four kidney-shaped lagoons and line them with soft white sand. These four man-made beaches are well worth a visit – the calm waters are perfect for kids. Even if you're not keen to get wet the ample recreation opportunities make this resort a worthy stop. There's a great golf course for the energetic and a decadent spa for those in need of pampering.

The key feature to the resort is the **Ko Olina Lagoons** – four purpose-built beaches that are an indulgent treat. The largest of the bunch is the lagoon that sits in front of the JW Marriott Ihilani Resort & Spa. At nearly 200yd across – it's a nice little fake beach. The islands that block the open sea from the lagoons help with water circulation and are also great places for spotting fish. Keep an eye on the kiddies though – the current picks up near the opening to the open sea.

There is a wide and comfortable path that connects the lagoons, which is a great venue for a lazy stroll. Limited free parking can be found at each of the lagoons.

Sleeping

JW Marriott Ihilani Resort & Spa (☎ 679-0079, 800-626-4446; www.marriotthotels.com; Ko Olina Resort, 92-1001 Olani St; r from $295, with ocean view from $340; 🐕 🖥 🔊) Seated right on the beach, this attractive property is palatial, expansive and architecturally pleasing to the eye. It's popular with families and those wanting to avoid the Waikiki scene and still have all the trappings of mainstream luxury. Hollywood has checked in here, hence it's somewhat familar appearance – it was the workplace of the surfer girls in the hit movie *Blue Crush*.

KAHE POINT

A hulking power plant complete with towering smokestacks isn't the best neighbor t~

beach, but as they say, you can't pick your neighbors. Called the **Kahe Point Beach Park**, there isn't actually a beach here, just a rocky point that's popular with fishermen. However, there are great views to the north, as well as running water, picnic tables and rest rooms.

Hawaiian Electric Beach Park is the name on the map, but all the locals refer to this stretch of sand as Tracks. This colloquial name stems from the train that transported beachgoers here prior to WWII. The sandy shores are good for swimming in the summer and great for surfing in the winter.

NANAKULI

Nanakuli, the biggest town on the Wai'anae (Leeward) Coast, is the site of a Hawaiian Homesteads settlement, having one of the largest Native Hawaiian populations on O'ahu. It also has supermarkets, a courthouse, a bank and fast-food joints.

Nanakuli Beach Park is a broad, sandy beach park that lines the town, offering swimming, snorkeling and diving during the calmer summer season. In winter high surf can create rip currents and dangerous shorebreaks. As an in-town community park, it has a playground, sports fields and beach facilities. To get to the beach park, turn *makai* at the traffic lights on Nanakuli Ave.

MA'ILI BEACH PARK

Ma'ili has a long, grassy roadside park with a seemingly endless stretch of white beach. Like other places on this coast, the water conditions are often treacherous in winter (which pleases the local surfers), but calm enough for swimming in summer. There's a lifeguard station and run-down facilities; coconut palms provide shade.

WAI'ANAE

pop 10,814

Wai'anae is the second-largest town on the coast and has the greatest concentration of everyday services: from grocery stores to the commercial boat harbor and a well-used beach park.

Protected by Kane'ilio Point and a long breakwater, **Poka'i Bay Beach Park** features the calmest year-round swimming on the Wai'anae Coast. Waves seldom break inside the bay, and the sandy sea floor slopes gently, making the beach a popular spot for families. Snorkeling is fair near the breakwater, where

fish gather around the rocks. You can watch local canoe clubs rowing in the late afternoon and lots of family luau on weekends. There are showers, rest rooms and picnic tables, and a lifeguard on duty daily.

Kane'ilio Point, along the south side of the bay, is the site of **Ku'ilioloa Heiau**. Partly destroyed by the army during WWII, this stone temple has been reconstructed by local conservationists. To get there, turn onto Lualualei Homestead Rd from Farrington Hwy and head toward the sea.

Eating

Barbeque Kai (☎ 696-7122; 85-973 Farrington Hwy; mains $3-7; ☼ 8am-8pm) On a nice day the tables in front of this grungy little lunch bar are overflowing with the local crew. Don't come here expecting fine china or reusable silverware – but if you want a good feed for a couple of bucks, this is the place – cheap-as-chips mixed plates, burgers and other local favorites populate the menu.

Surfah Smoodeez (☎ 478-9088; 85-979 Farrington Hwy; smoothies $5; ☼ 10:30am-7pm Mon-Fri, to 5:30pm Sat) This nondescript, low-key little shop is a hidden gem and just what the doctor ordered on a hot day, with its fresh-fruit smoothies a refreshing treat. It's just south of the highway's intersection with Wai'anae Valley Rd.

Tacos & More (☎ 697-8800; 85-993 Farrington Hwy; mains $5-10; ☼ 10am-8pm Mon-Fri, 2-8pm Sat) A great Mex place with plenty of aloha – owned by a family who started out in Mexico City – this ever-expanding eatery with vegetarian options has retained its delicious reputation and continues to be a local favorite.

MAKAHA

pop 7753

Makaha means 'ferocious,' and in days past the valley was notorious for the bandits who waited along the cliffs to ambush passing travelers. Today Makaha is best known for its world-class surfing, fine beach and O'ahu's best-restored heiau. If you're looking for accommodation, this area offers the coast's best options.

Sights & Activities
MAKAHA BEACH PARK

Makaha Beach has a history of big-wave surfing that ranks amongst the richest on the island. It's a beautiful arcing beach with a stunning stretch of sand that entices you to spread out your towel and spend the day.

Makaha leapt to fame in the 1950s when it hosted Hawaii's first international surfing competition. The long point break here produced the waves that inspired the first generation of big-wave surfers. It's still possible to rekindle that pioneering feeling as (except on the biggest days) you're likely to have the place virtually to yourself. Winter months bring big swells and preclude swimming much of the time – the golden sand however, is a permanent feature. The beach has showers and rest rooms, and lifeguards are on duty daily.

KANE'AKI HEIAU

Set within the Makaha Valley the **Kane'aki Heiau** (☎ 695-8174; admission free; ☷ 10am-2pm Tue-Sun) is one of the best restored sacred sites on the island. According to legend the rain goddess was impressed with the fishing prowess of a local chief. His generous offering of fish was reciprocated with generous rainfall to the parched valley and in turn a heiau was built in her honor. The site was later used as a *luakini*, a type of temple dedicated to the war god Ku and a place for human sacrifices. Kamehameha worshipped here and it remained in use until the time of his death in 1819.

Restoration, undertaken by the Bishop Museum and completed in 1970, added two prayer towers, a taboo house, drum house, altar and god images. The heiau was reconstructed using traditional ohia tree logs and *pili* (a type of Hawaiian grass used for thatching buildings) from the Big Island. The immediate setting surrounding the heiau remains undisturbed, though it's in the midst of a residential estate.

To get there, take Kili Dr to the Makaha Valley Towers condominiums, and turn right onto Huipu Dr. Half a mile down on the left is Mauna Olu St, leading into Mauna Olu Estates. The guard at the Mauna Olu Estates gatehouse grants entry to nonresidents who are visiting the heiau, a short drive past the gatehouse. Following rain, access is difficult, so call in advance.

Sleeping

Makaha accommodations options include several beachside condos that are rented out by realty agents, as well as an inland resort hotel. While most condo rates are quoted for monthly stays, you may be able to negotiate shorter periods.

Hawaii Hatfield Realty (☎ 696-7121, 696-4499; www.hawaiiwest.com; Suite 201, 85-833 Farrington Hwy, Wai'anae; units from $500 per week) Hawaii Hatfield arranges long-term rentals for Makaha Shores, a condo complex at the northern end of Makaha Beach.

Makaha Resort & Golf Club (☎ 695-9544; www.makaharesort.net; 84-626 Makaha Valley Rd; r from $130; ✖ ✖ ☷) Straight from the 1970s, this decidedly retro establishment is the place to be for the sporting set. With a golf course right out the door plus a batting cage, tennis court, basketball court and pool at your disposal you might actually forget to relax. There are great panoramic views of the valley and the ocean far below. The rooms themselves are spacious and tidy. Rates can really vary here – it's best to hunt for specials.

MAKUA VALLEY

Scenic Makua Valley opens up wide and grassy, backed by a fan of sharply fluted mountains. It serves as the ammunition field of the Makua Military Reservation. The seaside road opposite the southern end of the reservation leads to a little graveyard that's shaded by yellow-flowered trees. This site is all that remains of the Makua Valley community, which was forced to evacuate during WWII when the US military took over the entire valley for bombing practice. War games still take place in the valley, which is fenced off with barbed wire and signs that warn of stray explosives.

Kea'au Beach Park

This beach park is a long, open, grassy strip that borders a rocky shore. It has rest rooms, showers, drinking water and picnic tables, making it a good place to unpack that picnic lunch. A sandy beach begins at the very northern end of the park, although a rough reef, sharp drop and high seasonal surf make swimming uninviting.

North along the coast you'll see lava cliffs, white-sand beaches and patches of kiawe, while on the inland side you'll glimpse a run of little valleys.

Makua Beach

This beach has an interesting history – way back in the day it was a canoe landing site for interisland travelers. In the late '60s it wa?

HOMELESS IN PARADISE

Every big city in the USA has a homeless population, due in part to an inadequate mental health-care system, drug and alcohol abuse and a certain cultural legacy of wanderers and drifters. But in O'ahu, where many of the city-managed beach parks have become permanent homeless encampments, the profile of the average homeless person is quite different from that of the mainland. Many in this group are low-income families who have been pushed out by the island's housing boom.

The state doesn't have an accurate figure of how many people are living at the parks, but 2006 estimates put the number at about 1000 people living on the beach of the Wai'anae (Leeward) Coast. Other sources quote between 12,000 to 15,000 islandwide and include extended families living together in cramped quarters.

With the state's strong economy and increasing national housing prices, many rental properties, especially in the now-gentrifying Wai'anae (Leeward) Coast, have been sold to owner-occupiers, thus diminishing the available rental accommodations and driving up rents. A studio apartment that cost $400 per month in Makaha a few years ago now costs about $800.

Many low-income families – some with service-industry or construction jobs, others receiving some form of government assistance – can't afford the increase and can't find alternatives within the state's public-housing system or the federally funded housing-assistance program. Another aggravating factor is the state's diminishing stock of public housing, with no new construction in the past decade.

With the economic downturn affecting O'ahu both directly and indirectly due to a reduction in tourist numbers, the number of homeless people living on the Wai'anae (Leeward) Coast is bound to increase.

used as the backdrop for the movie *Hawaii*, starring Julie Andrews. These days there is little here beyond a nice stretch of sand opposite the Makua Military Reservation.

Locals crawl out from their nine-to-five lives on holiday weekends to absorb the sun and spirit of the beach. The powerful shore-breaks are popular with bodyboarders and high surf waves appear in winter and spring. Spinner dolphins are frequent visitors and snorkeling is good at the northern end.

There are two parking lots on either side of the beach, but no facilities.

Kaneana Cave

Two miles north of Kea'au Beach Park sits this giant stone amphitheater. Carved out by the incessant waves through centuries of pounding, this enormous cave sits dry by the roadside. The waves that created the cave have receded and now the highway sits between it and the seashore.

Kahuna once performed rituals inside the cave's inner chamber. Older Hawaiians consider it a sacred place and won't enter the cave for fear that it's haunted by the spirits of deceased chiefs. Judging by the collection of broken beer bottles and graffiti inside, it's obvious not everyone shares their sentiments.

Ka'ena Point Satellite Tracking Station

The US Air Force operates a satellite tracking station high on the ridge of O'ahu's north-westernmost tip. It was originally built for use in the country's first reconnaissance satellite program (known as Corona), but now supports weather, early warning and communications systems. The station is not open to the public but the surrounding acreage is managed by the **Division of Forestry & Wildlife** (☎ 587-0166), which can issue hiking permits to the trail system that connects the Wai'anae (Leeward) Coast to the North Shore. Part of the land is also open to hunting and is popularly used by locals.

The dusty 2.5-mile **Kuaokala Trail** (Map pp102–3) follows a high ridge to Mokule'ia Forest Reserve. At the trail's highest point (1960ft) is an overlook with great views. On a clear day hikers can see Mt Ka'ala (4040ft), the highest peak on O'ahu, and part of the Wai'anae Range. The trail connects to the Kealia Trail (p195), whose trailhead starts near the Dillingham Airfield in the North Shore.

KA'ENA POINT STATE PARK

Running along both sides of the westernmost point of O'ahu, Ka'ena Point State Park is an undeveloped 853-acre coastal strip.

Until the mid-1940s the O'ahu Railway ran up here from Honolulu and continued around the point, carrying passengers on to Hale'iwa on the North Shore. The gorgeous, mile-long sandy beach on the southern side of the point is Yokohama Bay, named for the large numbers of Japanese fishers who came here during the railroad days.

Rest rooms, showers and a lifeguard station are at the southern end of the park. It's best to bring food and drinks with you, though occasionally a lunch wagon parks here selling beef stew and smoothies.

Incidentally, those domes sitting above the park that resemble giant white golf balls belong to the Air Force's Ka'ena Point Satellite Tracking Station.

Sights & Activities
YOKOHAMA BAY

Locals say this is the best sunset spot on the island. It certainly has the right orientation and an attractive mile-long sandy beach, and its status as the last sandy beach on the Wai'anae (Leeward) Coast adds to the symbolic appreciation of the setting sun.

Winter brings huge pounding waves, making Yokohama a popular seasonal surfing and bodysurfing spot best left to the experts because of the submerged rocks, strong rips and the dangerous shorebreak.

Swimming is limited to the summer and then only when calm. When the water's flat, it's possible to snorkel. The best spot with the easiest access is at the south side of the park. Rest rooms, showers and a lifeguard station are at the south end of the park.

KA'ENA POINT

You don't have to be well versed in Hawaiian legends to know that something mystical occurs at this dramatic convergence of land and sea at the far northwestern tip of the island. Powerful ocean currents altered by the O'ahu landmass have been battling against each other for millennia. The watery blows crash onto the long lava bed fingers, sending frothy explosions skyward. All along this untamed coastal section, nature is at its most furious and beautiful – an incongruous harmony.

Early Hawaiians believed that when people went into a deep sleep or lost consciousness,

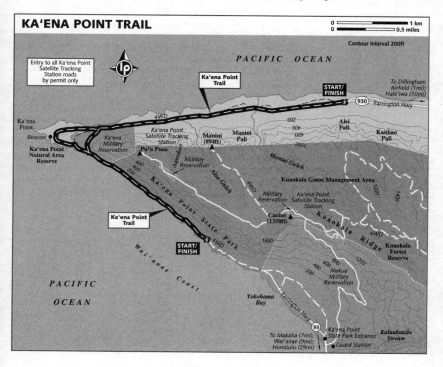

their souls would wander. Souls that wandered too far were drawn west to Ka'ena Point. If they were lucky, they were met here by their *'aumakua* (guardian spirit), who led their souls back to their bodies. If unattended, their souls would be forced to leap from Ka'ena Point into the endless night, never to return.

The 2.5-mile (one-way) coastal **Ka'ena Point Trail** runs from Yokohama Bay to Ka'ena Point, and around the point to the North Shore, utilizing the old railroad bed. Most hikers take the trail, which begins from the end of the paved road at Yokohama Bay, as far as the point and then come back the same way; it takes about three to four hours round-trip. This easy-to-follow hike offers fine views the entire way, with the ocean on one side and the

lofty cliffs of the Wai'anae Range on the other. Along the trail there are tide pools, sea arches and a couple of lazy blowholes that occasionally come to life on high-surf days.

The trail is exposed and lacks shade (Ka'ena means 'the heat'), so take sunscreen and plenty of water. Be cautious near the shoreline, as there are strong currents, and the waves can reach extreme heights. In fact, winter waves at Ka'ena Point are the highest in Hawaii, sometimes towering in excess of 50ft.

Don't leave anything valuable in your car. Telltale mounds of shattered windshield glass litter the road's-end parking area used by most hikers. Parking closer to the rest rooms or leaving your doors unlocked can decrease the odds of having your car windows smashed.

Hawai'i the Big Island

Kamehameha the Great named the Kingdom of Hawaii after his home island, a synecdoche that still rings true today. While Moloka'i is often called 'the most Hawaiian island,' the rich diversity of Hawai'i island's landscapes and people make it feel convincingly emblematic of the entire state.

First, there's so much space. Hawai'i is twice as big as the other islands combined. It's the only island where you feel you're on a road trip. Hawaii's peoples have room to be themselves, and they ring the Big Island with personality: from multiethnic, working-class Hilo to Waimea's *paniolo* (cowboy) country, from funkadelic Puna to rural, off-the-grid Ka'u, from South Kona's Japanese coffee farmers to North Kohala's writers and artists. Hawai'i is steeped in ancient history. The first Polynesians landed here, and Kamehameha was born here. So many ancient sites are preserved, and so well, that it takes little imagination to conjure helmeted warriors and Captain Cook, bays full of outrigger canoes and the terror of the gods. Without question, Pele still lives here. Her home is Kilauea, and try as one might, it is impossible not to personify the fiery volcanoes and their creative-destructive power, which is everywhere evident – in burnt, blackened landscapes and in the ongoing eruption giving birth to the islands.

Hawai'i is a place you can return to again and again, always finding something new, and always deepening and broadening your understanding of what 'Hawaii' means.

HIGHLIGHTS

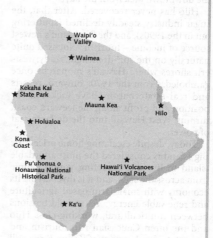

- Hike the smoking craters and lava terrain of **Hawai'i Volcanoes National Park** (p306)
- Brush bellies, almost, with **Pacific manta rays** (p219) while snorkeling
- Soak up the sun and swim at the idyllic white-sand beaches of **Kekaha Kai State Park** (p245)
- Get a shot of both art and caffeine at the galleries and coffee farms of **Holualoa** (p228)
- Commune with the ancients at **Pu'uhonua o Honaunau National Historical Park** (p239)
- Watch the sun set and the stars blaze from **Mauna Kea** (p269)
- Discover historic downtown **Hilo** (p285) – its museums, historic buildings and ice shave
- Indulge your inner gourmet, *paniolo*-style, in **Waimea** (p263)
- Lounge with wild horses on the black-sand beach in **Waipi'o Valley** (p282)
- Explore the underground realm of **lava tubes** (p325) in Ka'u

Map labels:
★ Waipi'o Valley
★ Waimea
Kekaha Kai ★ State Park
★ Mauna Kea
★ Hilo
★ Holualoa
Kona Coast
Pu'uhonua o Honaunau National Historical Park
Hawai'i Volcanoes National Park
★ Ka'u

| POPULATION 173,000 | AREA: 4028 SQ MILES | NICKNAME: ORCHID ISLE |

HISTORY

The modern history of the Big Island is a tale of two cities – Kailua-Kona and Hilo – which represent the island's split personality: West Hawai'i and East Hawai'i. Kamehameha the Great, born in West Hawai'i, lived out the end of his life in Kailua, and throughout the 19th-century, Hawaiian royalty enjoyed the town as a leisure retreat, using Hulihe'e Palace as a crash pad.

Yet, during the same period, Hilo emerged as the more important commercial harbor. The Hamakua Coast railroad connected Hilo to the island's sugar plantations, and its thriving wharves became a hub for agricultural goods and immigrant workers. By the 20th century the city was the Big Island's economic and political center of power, and Hilo remains the official seat of island government.

Then, on April 1, 1946, the Hamakua Coast was hit by an enormous tsunami that crumpled the railroad and devastated coastal communities (such as Laupahoehoe; see p285). Hilo got the worst: its waterfront was completely destroyed, killing 96 people. The city rebuilt, but 14 years later, in 1960, it happened again: a deadly tsunami splintered the waterfront. This time, Hilo did not rebuild, but left a quiet expanse of parks separating the downtown area from the bay.

Hilo has never recovered. After that, the sugar industry steadily declined (sputtering out in the 1990s), and the Big Island's newest source of income – tourism – focused quite naturally on the sun-drenched, sandy western shores where Hawaii's monarchs once gamboled. From the 1970s onward, resorts and real-estate barons have jockeyed for position and profit along the leeward coast, turning West Hawai'i into the de facto seat of power.

Today, despite escalating home prices, the Big Island is considered the most affordable island to live on, attracting young people from across the state, and it is diversifying its economy with small farm-based agriculture and renewable energy. Yet the old tensions between multicultural, working-class Hilo and the often Caucasian-run tourism and real-estate development of Kailua-Kona still define much of present-day Big Island politics. Indeed, the current effort to fix Saddle Rd (p276) is an explicit attempt to literally and metaphorically reconnect the island's long-divided east and west.

CLIMATE

The Big Island climate is fairly stable year round. As a rule, it's cooler as you move inland and up, and it's wetter on the windward north and east coasts. The Kona Coast is perennially sunny and hot, though things cool off quickly just a few miles upland in coffee country. However, air quality in South Kona and Ka'u has been increasingly troubled by persistent 'vog' (volcanic smog; see p217).

On the eastern coast, Hilo is notoriously rainy, with an annual rainfall of over 100in. But temperatures remain balmy and, except for rainstorms, the typical drizzle is innocuous and short-lived. Few risk predicting Windward Coast weather; newspapers simply print endless variations on 'sunny, with a chance of rain.'

At 4000ft, Hawai'i Volcanoes National Park has similar weather to Hilo, but is noticeably cooler. Yet the island's coolest town is Waimea, where many an afternoon receives a blanket of chilly fog.

On the windward side of Mauna Kea, along the northeastern Hamakua Coast, around 300in of rain falls annually – but this water usually gets squeezed out on the mountain's flanks, at around 2500ft, and both the coast and the summit remain clear. In fact, only about 15in of precipitation falls on the summits of Mauna Kea and Mauna Loa, mostly as winter snow capping the peaks with white.

In January the average daily high temperature is 65°F at Hawai'i Volcanoes National Park, 79°F in Hilo and a toasty 81°F in Kailua-Kona. August temperatures rise only 5°F or so. Nighttime lows are about 15°F less. For more on climate, see p23.

The National Weather Service Hilo provides recorded forecasts for the Big Island (☎ 961-5582) and for island water conditions (☎ 935-9883). **Hawai'i Volcanoes National Park** (☎ 985-6000) has recorded information on eruption activity and viewing points.

NATIONAL, STATE & COUNTY PARKS

Hawai'i Volcanoes National Park (p306) is one of the Big Island's main attractions and one of the USA's most interesting and varied national parks. Over a million visitors come annually to (hopefully) witness flowing lava and to drive and hike this lava and rain-forest wonderland.

The Big Island is notable for its wealth of ancient Hawaiian sights, which are preserved in several national and state historical parks. The most famous is Pu'uhonua o Honaunau (p239), an ancient place of refuge in South Kona. But Native Hawaiian history and moody landscapes can be found at remote Mo'okini Heiau (p259) in North Kohala; kayak-friendly Kealakekua Bay (p234), where Captain Cook met his demise; the restored fishponds of Kaloko-Honokohau (p243) near Kailua-Kona; and the imposingly majestic Pu'ukohola Heiau (p256).

Many of the island's finest beaches lie within parkland, such as the world-renowned Hapuna Beach (p254). The beaches within Kekaha Kai State Park (p245) are also idyllic, though only Manini'owali is accessible by paved road.

Other parks worth seeking out on the Windward Coast are Kalopa (p283), preserving a native forest; Laupahoehoe (p283), site of a tsunami disaster; and Akaka Falls (p284), the prettiest 'drive-up' waterfalls in Hawai'i. Though not a designated park, Waipi'o Valley (p279) shouldn't be missed.

Camping

Hawai'i has enough good campgrounds that you can enjoyably circumnavigate the island in a tent, plus several highly memorable backcountry camping opportunities. Some parks also offer simple cabins.

NATIONAL PARKS

Hawai'i Volcanoes National Park has two good, free, drive-up campgrounds, some A-frame cabins for rent and great backcountry camping. See p318 for details.

STATE PARKS

Three state parks allow camping: highly recommended Kalopa State Park (p283), which has well-kept facilities, and both MacKenzie State Recreation Area (p305) and Manuka State Wayside Park (p326), neither of which is well cared for, nor recommended. Permits are required; the fee is $5 per family campsite.

There are recommended cabins in three state parks. Hapuna Beach State Recreation Area (p254) has six A-frame cabins sleeping up to four people ($20 per night). Kalopa State Park (p283) has two group cabins sleeping up to eight people ($55 per night). Mauna Kea State Recreation Area (p275) maintains five cabins sleeping up to six people ($35 per night, Friday to Sunday only).

To make a reservation and obtain a permit, contact the **Division of State Parks** (Map p287; ☎ 974-6200; www.hawaiistateparks.org/parks/hawaii; Suite 204, 75 Aupuni St, PO Box 936, Hilo, HI 96721; 🕑 8am-3:30pm Mon-Fri), which accepts reservations in order of priority: first walk-ins, then mail requests, then phone requests – though the phone is rarely answered and long-distance calls aren't returned. The website has an application form you can print and mail in, and the office has a binder with photos of campsites and cabins. The maximum length of stay per permit is five consecutive nights. You can obtain another permit for the same park only after 30 days have passed.

Cabins are popular with locals and require booking well in advance (up to one year ahead). Cancellations do occur; if you're flexible, you might get one without advance reservations.

COUNTY PARKS

The county allows camping at 10 of its beach parks. Proceeding clockwise around the island, these are: Spencer (p255) in South Kohala; Mahukona (p258) and Kapa'a (p258) in North Kohala; Laupahoehoe (p283) and Kolekole (p284) on the Hamakua Coast; Isaac Hale (p305) in Puna; Punalu'u (p322) and Whittington (p322) in Ka'u; and Miloli'i (p241) and Ho'okena (p240) in South Kona.

County parks can be noisy places, particularly on weekends when they're popular with late-night revelers. Only three parks have security guards (Spencer, Isaac Hale, and Ho'okena) who help keep a lid on things. For detailed recommendations, see specific parks. Facilities and upkeep range from good to minimal, with the exception of newly renovated Isaac Hale, which is sparkling. Some parks are isolated, raising concerns about personal safety. If you can, see the park before committing. The only park to expressly avoid is Miloli'i.

Camping permits are required, and can be obtained (up to a year in advance) by mail, online or in person from the **Department of Parks & Recreation** (Map p287; ☎ 961-8311; www.hawaii-county.com/parks/parks.htm; Suite 6, 101 Pauahi St, Hilo, HI 96720; 🕑 7:45am-4:30pm Mon-Fri). The website lists facilities and availability at each county park. You can make reservations through the Hilo office and pick up the permit at the department's branch offices around the island. The Hilo office has binders with photos of each campsite; staff offer helpful advice about noise and safety issues.

HAWAI'I THE BIG ISLAND

HAWAI'I THE BIG ISLAND

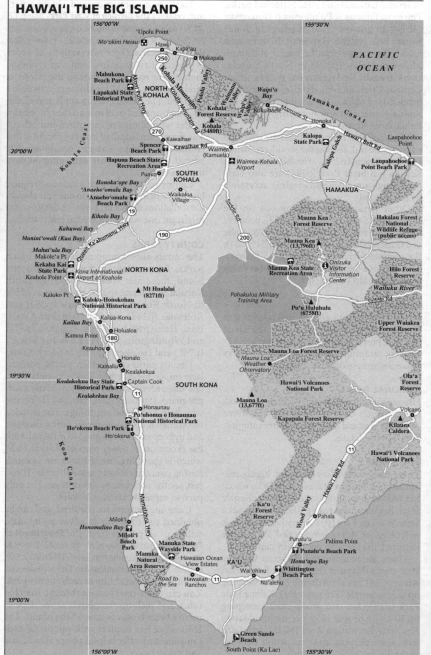

156°00'W

'Upolu Point
Mo'okini Heiau
Hawi   Kapa'au
250   Makapala

Mahukona
Beach Park
Lapakahi State
Historical Park

NORTH
KOHALA

Kohala Mountains

Pololu Valley
Waipi'o
Valley
Waimanu Valley
Kohala
Forest Reserve
Kohala
(5480ft)

Waipi'o
Bay

Kukuihaele

Hamakua Coast

Honoka'a

PACIFIC
OCEAN

155°30'N

Laupahoehoe
Point

270   Kawaihae
Spencer   Kawaihae Rd
Beach Park
Hapuna Beach State
Recreation Area
Puako

Waimea
(Kamuela)

Waimea-Kohala
Airport

Kalopa
State Park

Kalopa Gulch   Hawai'i Belt Rd

Laupahoehoe
Point Beach Park

20°00'N

SOUTH
KOHALA

HAMAKUA

Honoka'ope Bay
'Anaeho'omalu Bay
'Anaeho'omalu
Beach Park

Waikoloa
Village

Kiholo Bay

Kahuwai Bay

Manini'owali (Kua Bay)
Mahai'ula Bay
Makole'a Pt
Kekaha Kai
State Park
Keahole Point

Kaloko Pt

19   Saddle Rd

190   200

NORTH KONA

Kona International
Airport at Keahole

Mt Hualalai
(8271ft)

Mauna Kea
Forest Reserve

Mauna Kea
(13,796ft)

Mauna Kea State
Recreation Area

Onizuka
Visitor
Information
Center

Hakalau Forest
National
Wildlife Refuge
(public access)

Hilo Forest
Reserve

Wailuku River

Kaloko-Honokohau
National Historical Park

Kailua Bay   Kailua-Kona
Holualoa
Kamoa Point
180   Keauhou
Honalo
Kainaliu
Kealakekua
Kealakekua Bay State   Captain Cook
Historical Park
Kealakekua Bay   11
Honaunau
Pu'uhonua o Honaunau
National Historical Park
Ho'okena Beach Park
Ho'okena

Pohakuloa Military
Training Area

Pu'u Huluhulu
(6785ft)

Mauna Loa Forest Reserve

Mauna Loa
Weather
Observatory

Mauna Loa
(13,677ft)

Hawai'i Volcanoes
National Park

Kapapala Forest Reserve

Upper Waiakea
Forest Reserve

Ola'a
Forest
Reserve

Volcano

Kilauea
Caldera

SOUTH KONA

11

Hawai'i Volcanoes
National Park

19°30'N

Miloli'i
Honomalino Bay
Miloli'i
Beach
Park
Manuka
Natural
Area Reserve

Manuka State
Wayside Park

Hawaiian Ocean
View Estates

Road to
the Sea

Hawaiian
Ranchos

11

Ka'u
Forest
Reserve

Wai'ohinu

KA'U

Na'alehu

Wood Valley

Pahala

Punalu'u   Palima Point
Punalu'u Beach Park
Honu'apo Bay
Whittington
Beach Park

19°00'N

Green Sands
Beach
South Point (Ka Lae)

156°00'W   155°30'W

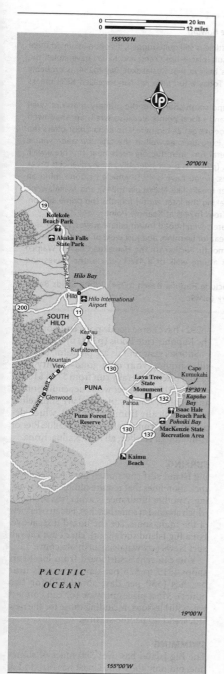

Daily camping fees are $5 for adults, $2 for teens and $1 for children 12 and under; internet bookings cost $1 more. Camping per site is allowed for up to two weeks, except between June and August, when the limit is one week.

ACTIVITIES

The Big Island is heaven for activity hounds. When it comes to the water, Hawai'i's western shore has top-quality choices, and when it comes to hiking, the Big Island suffers no comparison: where else can you walk from the snowcapped summits of the world's largest volcanoes to live lava at the coast?

At Sea
DIVING

Along the Kona Coast diving conditions are first class, with warm, calm waters and, frequently, 100ft visibility. One of the best spots is Ka'awaloa Cove (p235) in the Kealakekua Bay; most snorkel spots also provide good dives. In Kailua-Kona you can arrange a thrilling night dive to see manta rays (p219). The best conditions are in spring and summer, but diving is decent year round. On the Hilo side, the diving conditions tend to be mediocre, but good dives are possible (p293). Most dive outfits are located in Kailua-Kona (see p220) and charge from $110 to $160 for a two-tank dive; Hilo has two dive shops (p293).

FISHING

Deep-sea fishing is an obsession on the Kona Coast, which is the world's number-one spot for catching Pacific blue marlin. The waters are also rich with ahi (yellowfin tuna) and *aku* (bonito or skipjack tuna), swordfish, spearfish and mahimahi (white-fleshed fish also called 'dolphin'). June to August typically sees the biggest hauls of blue marlin, while January to June is the best time for striped marlin. Most of the world records for catches of such fish belong to Kona fishers. For charter tours, see p220. You can also try your hand at spearfishing (p293).

For Kona fishing reports, the ubiquitous **Jim Rizzutto** (www.fishinghawaiioffshore.com) lets you know who's catching what. For tournament schedules, check the **Hawaii Big Game Fishing Club** (www.hbgfc.org).

KAYAKING

Kayaking in lovely Kealakekua Bay (p235) is a must. The most popular launching spot is Napo'opo'o Beach, where you paddle across

BIG ISLAND SURF BEACHES & BREAKS *Jake Howard*

Because Hawai'i is the youngest island and its coastline is still quite rugged, it's often assumed there isn't much in the way of surfable waves. As a result, places like O'ahu and Kaua'i have stolen the surf spotlight, but archaeologists and researchers believe that Kealakekua Bay (p234) is probably where ancient Polynesians started riding waves. Today a fun little left-hander called Ke'ei breaks near the bay.

Unlike its neighboring islands, whose north and south shores are the primary center of swell activity, the east and west shores are the Big Island's focal points. Because swells are shadowed by the other islands, as a general rule the surf doesn't get as big here. The Kona Coast offers the best opportunities, with north and south swell exposures, as well as the offshore trade winds. Kawaihae Harbor (p256) is surrounded by several fun, introductory reefs near the breakwall, while further south, near Kekaha Kai State Park (p245), is a considerably more advanced break that challenges even the most seasoned surfers. If you have a 4WD vehicle or don't mind an hour-long hike, be sure to check out heavy reef breaks like Mahai'ula (p245) and Makalawena (p245). They break best on northwest swells, making the later winter months the prime season. A hike or 4WD is also necessary to reach Pine Trees (p244) at Keahole Point.

On East Hawai'i, just outside of Hilo (p292), are several good intermediate waves. Richardson Ocean Park is a slow-moving reef break that's great for learning, and just west of town is Honoli'i, a fast left and right peak breaking into a river mouth. Further up the Hamakua Coast is Waipi'o Bay (p279); while access to the beach requires a long walk or a 4WD vehicle, the waves and scenery are worth the effort.

Top bodyboarding and bodysurfing spots include Hapuna Beach (p254), White Sands Beach (p218) and the beaches at Kekaha Kai State Park (p245).

the bay toward the Captain Cook Monument for snorkeling and explorations.

To watch or join outrigger canoe racing, contact the **Hawai'i Island Paddlesports Association** (www.kaikahoe.org) for its January to May race schedule. And don't miss the **Queen Lili'uokalani outrigger race** (www.kaiopua.org) on Labor Day weekend.

SAILING
Most catamaran trips focus on fishing, snorkeling, or whale watching, with sailing itself a pleasant add-on. If sailing is your *main* pleasure, try Kamanu Charters (p219), and ask around at Kailua-Kona's Honokohau Harbor (p241). Another company to consider is **Maile Charters** (800-726-7245; www.adventuresailing.com; 3½hr cruises from $1300), which sails out of Kawaihae.

SNORKELING
The best snorkeling is south of Kailua-Kona: head straight for Kahalu'u Beach Park (p226) in Keauhou; Two-Step (p240), north of Pu'uhonua o Honaunau; and Kealakekua Bay (p235).

That said, there are wonderful places elsewhere: north of Kailua, check out the Kekaha Kai beaches (p245), the tide pools of Puako (p253), and Mahukona (p258). Hilo's beaches

(p292) have some good spots, and don't miss the Kapoho Tide Pools (p304) in Puna.

Snorkel gear rentals are plentiful, but consider buying your own good-quality gear. Rental prices generally run from $7 to $10 per day and $15 to $45 per week, depending on kit and quality. Equally plentiful are snorkeling tours (typically from $80 to $90), which depart mainly from Keauhou Bay, Kailua Pier or Honokohau Harbor, all near Kailua-Kona.

SURFING
Big Island surf spots often have rugged lava-rock shorelines that require nimble maneuvering. Another hindrance is *wana* (sea urchins), which abound at some beaches. For an overview of the main spots, see the boxed text, above. For a Big Island surf report, check out Hawaii Surf News (www.hawaiisurfnews.com).

You can rent a surfboard from local surf shops ($15 to $25 per day) or stands near beaches ($30 per day; about $20 for two hours). Most places provide (or can connect you with) lessons, including those for the new fad, stand up paddle surfing.

SWIMMING
The Big Island has over 300 miles of shoreline, but only the Kona Coast has the kind of

dreamy white-sand beaches that grace tourist brochures. The best swimming spots are in South Kohala and North Kona: top picks are Hapuna Beach (p254), Manini'owali (p246) and Kauna'oa Bay (p254).

Elsewhere, the coast can be rocky and the seas rough, but protected coves can be found. Time it right, and Hilo's beaches (p292) can be great; nearby Puna has a hot pond (p304) and lava tide pools (p304).

There are recommended public swimming pools in Hilo (p293), Kailua-Kona at the Kailua Park Complex (p218), Kapa'au (p261), and Pahoa (p302). For directions and open-swim schedules, call the county **Aquatics Division** (☎ 961-8694).

On Land
CAVING
The Big Island has six of the 10 longest lava tubes in the world, as well as a growing number of guided tours. At Kaumana Cave near Hilo (p293), you just drive up and walk in (with a flashlight, of course). Others include the culturally rich thousand-year-old Kanohina cave system in Ka'u (p325); the Kazumura cave system in Puna (p301); and the lava tubes in Hawai'i Volcanoes National Park – Thurston Lava Tube (p311) and Pua Po'o (p316).

CYCLING & MOUNTAIN BIKING
With wide-open spaces, the Big Island is ideal for both road and mountain biking. Outside Kailua-Kona, Hwy 19 has bicycle lanes, and cyclists can enjoy Crater Rim Drive in Hawai'i Volcanoes National Park (p310). Avid mountain bikers can tackle the 45-mile Mana Rd loop (p270) circling Mauna Kea and the 6.5-mile beach trail to Pine Trees (p244) on the Kona Coast, plus plenty more miles of 4WD roads and rocky trails. To find out more about Big Island cycling, contact **People's Advocacy for Trails Hawaii** (☎ 936-4653; www.pathhawaii.org) or the **Hawaii Cycling Club** (www.hawaiicyclingclub.com), based in Kona, which hosts fun rides, organizes races and offers advice for nonmembers. The island's biggest event, of course, is the Ironman Triathlon (p221).

For Big Island cycling tours, contact **Orchid Isle Bicycling** (☎ 327-0087, 800-219-2324; www.cyclekona .com; day tour $125-145), which offers set and custom-designed trips. **Volcano Bike Tours** (☎ 934-9199; www.bikevolcano.com; day tour $130) seeks out hot lava. For week-long tours, try **Woman Tours**

(☎ 800-247-1444; www.womantours.com; tours $2700), for women only, and **Common Circle Expeditions** (www.commoncircle.com; tours $1000), which focuses on sustainability and green living.

For bicycle rentals, head to the main towns, Hilo (p300) and Kailua-Kona (p225).

GOLF
The Big Island boasts more than 20 golf courses, including the world-class courses at the South Kohala resorts. The five that get the most press are the Mauna Kea & Hapuna Golf Courses (p255), the Mauna Lani golf course (p252) and Waikoloa Beach & Kings' Courses (p250). The Four Seasons Hualalai Course (p247), designed by Jack Nicklaus, is also highly regarded but open only to club members and hotel guests.

You'll find the best prices at the Hilo Municipal Golf Course (p293) and the scenic Volcano Golf & Country Club (p319), near the national park; both courses are dear to the hearts of locals.

HIKING
Hikers will find the widest variety of trails and terrain at Hawai'i Volcanoes National Park (p314): hot lava, rain forests, lava deserts, steaming craters, mountain summits, grassy plains and more.

Hawai'i has not one but two nearly 14,000ft summits that can be day hiked: Mauna Loa (p275) and Mauna Kea (p272). Want verdant valleys? Try the relatively short hike to Pololu Valley (p263) in North Kohala, or, from the Hamakua Coast, drop into wondrous Waipi'o Valley (p279), which can be extended into a two-night backpack to Waimanu Valley (p282). More good trails await at Kalopa State Recreation Area (p283).

The website for **Na Ala Hele** (www.hawaiitrails.org) lists more trails. It is also working to restore the 175-mile **Ala Kahakai National Trail** (www.nps .gov/alka), which, when finished, will edge the island from Hawai'i Volcanoes National Park, around South Point and up the Kona Coast to 'Upolu Point; for now, only a couple of dozen miles are accessible along the Kona Coast.

For hiking tours (including hikes to hot lava), **Hawaiian Walkways** (☎ 775-0372, 800-457-7759; www.hawaiianwalkways.com) and **Hawaii Forest & Trail** (☎ 331-8505, 800-464-1993; www.hawaii-forest.com) are the Big Island's best outfits; both are winners of Hawaii Ecotourism Board awards, and offer guided hikes to places you wouldn't see

THE BIG ISLAND ACTIVITIES

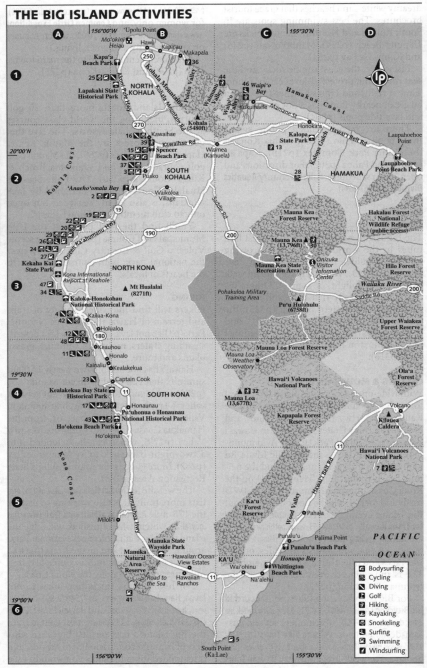

Legend:

- Bodysurfing
- Cycling
- Diving
- Golf
- Hiking
- Kayaking
- Snorkeling
- Surfing
- Swimming
- Windsurfing

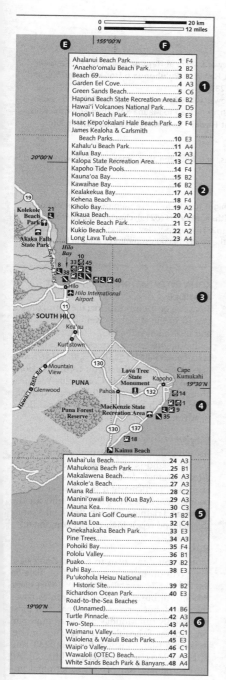

Ahalanui Beach Park	1	F4
'Anaeho'omalu Beach Park	2	B2
Beach 69	3	B2
Garden Eel Cove	4	A3
Green Sands Beach	5	C6
Hapuna Beach State Recreation Area	6	B2
Hawai'i Volcanoes National Park	7	D5
Honoli'i Beach Park	8	E3
Isaac Kepo'okalani Hale Beach Park	9	F4
James Kealoha & Carlsmith Beach Parks	10	E3
Kahalu'u Beach Park	11	A4
Kailua Bay	12	A3
Kalopa State Recreation Area	13	C2
Kapoho Tide Pools	14	F4
Kauna'oa Bay	15	B2
Kawaihae Bay	16	B2
Kealakekua Bay	17	A4
Kehena Beach	18	F4
Kiholo Bay	19	A2
Kikaua Beach	20	A2
Kolekole Beach Park	21	E2
Kukio Beach	22	A2
Long Lava Tube	23	A4

Mahai'ula Beach	24	A3
Mahukona Beach Park	25	B1
Makalawena Beach	26	A3
Makole'a Beach	27	A3
Mana Rd	28	C2
Manini'owali Beach (Kua Bay)	29	A3
Mauna Kea	30	C3
Mauna Lani Golf Course	31	B2
Mauna Loa	32	C4
Onekahakaha Beach Park	33	E3
Pine Trees	34	A3
Pohoiki Bay	35	F4
Pololu Valley	36	B1
Puako	37	B2
Puhi Bay	38	E3
Pu'ukohola Heiau National Historic Site	39	B2
Richardson Ocean Park	40	E3
Road-to-the-Sea Beaches (Unnamed)	41	B6
Turtle Pinnacle	42	A3
Two-Step	43	A4
Waimanu Valley	44	C1
Waiolena & Waiuli Beach Parks	45	E3
Waipi'o Valley	46	C1
Wawaloli (OTEC) Beach	47	A3
White Sands Beach Park & Banyans	48	A4

otherwise. The Sierra Club's **Big Island Moku Loa Group** (☎ 965-5460; www.hi.sierraclub.org/Hawaii/outings.html; suggested nonmember donation $3) offers a range of hiking tours. For all, reserve in advance.

HORSEBACK RIDING
The Big Island is *paniolo* country, and the pastureland of Waimea (p266) and North Kohala (p265) are perfect for horseback riding. Horseback trips in Waipi'o Valley are also fun (p282).

STARGAZING
Few places on earth get closer to the stars than Mauna Kea's summit (p274). However, night skies are clear all over the Big Island, and most of the South Kohala resorts have public stargazing programs.

TENNIS
Many county parks have well-maintained public tennis courts. Call the **Department of Parks & Recreation** (☎ 961-8311) in Hilo for a list. Large hotels and resorts sometimes allow non-guests to rent court time.

GETTING THERE & AWAY
Air
An increasing number of flights go directly to Kona and Hilo airports, though many flights also route through Honolulu first. Kona is the busier airport, with the bulk of mainland and international flights.

Hilo International Airport (ITO; ☎ 934-5840; http://hawaii.gov/dot/airports/ito) Off Hwy 11, just under a mile south of the intersection of Hwys 11 and 19.

Kona International Airport at Keahole (KOA; ☎ 329-3423; http://hawaii.gov/dot/airports/koa) On Hwy 19, 7 miles north of Kailua-Kona. For directions to/from the airport, see p212.

See p571 for airline contact details, and more information on flights to the Big Island.

With the demise of Aloha Airlines in 2008, only two major interisland carriers remain: **Hawaiian Airlines** (☎ 800-367-5320; www.hawaiianair.com) and **Go!** (☎ 888-435-9462; www.iflygo.com). Both have multiple interisland flights daily, though Go! has more direct flights, while many of Hawaiian's require a stopover in Honolulu. Current fares range from $60 to $90 one way, though advance-purchase fare wars can bring prices down to $40 one way.

Another option is **Island Air** (☎ 800-652-6541; www.islandair.com), which offers a few direct

---

BIG ISLAND ITINERARIES

In Two Days

If you arrive in **Kona** (p214), spend your days leeward: swim at **Hapuna Beach** (p254), kayak and snorkel at **Kealakekua Bay** (p234), visit ancient Hawaii at **Pu'uhonua o Honaunau** (p239), and tour coffee farms and galleries in **Holualoa** (p228).

If you arrive in **Hilo** (p285), stay windward. Browse Hilo's **farmers market** (p290); while exploring Hilo's historic downtown, visit **'Imiloa** (p288), dedicated to Mauna Kea. Then enter the wilds of **Puna** (p300) and pay your respects to Pele at **Hawai'i Volcanoes National Park** (p306).

In Four Days

Combine the leeward and windward itineraries, and between them make sure to visit either **Mauna Kea** (p269) or **Waipi'o Valley** (p279).

For Nonstop Adventure

Did you come to play hard? In a week, you might just fit in these unforgettable adventures: **kayaking** (p235) Kealakekua Bay, **snorkeling with manta rays** (p219), **charter fishing for marlin** (p220), **riding horses** (p265) in Kohala, **hiking** (p281) Waipi'o Valley, seeing hot lava at **Hawai'i Volcanoes National Park** (p309), and reaching the nearly 14,000ft summits of **Mauna Kea** (p272) or **Mauna Loa** (p275).

---

flights daily from Hilo to Honolulu, Maui and Moloka'i, and one from Kona to Kaua'i. Fares are typically $70 to $90 one way.

See p573 for more on interisland flights.

GETTING AROUND

The Big Island is divided into six districts: Kona, Kohala, Waimea, Hilo, Puna and Ka'u. The Hawai'i Belt Rd circles the island, connecting the main towns and sights. It's possible but neither efficient nor convenient to get around by bus. If you want to explore, you really need a car.

The best foldout map is the Hawaii Street Guide *Big Island Manini Map*. This is a slimmer version of the *Ready Mapbook* series' encyclopedic books covering east and west Hawai'i (bulky for short visits, but very useful for longer stays). Another good foldout map is Nelles' *Hawai'i: The Big Island*. The colorful Franko's map of *Hawai'i, the Big Island* features watersports and is sold at dive shops.

To/From the Airports

Most Big Island visitors rent cars, and car-hire booths for the major agencies (see opposite) line the road outside the arrivals area at both airports.

HILO INTERNATIONAL AIRPORT

Taxis can be found curbside; the approximate fare from Hilo airport to downtown Hilo is between $18 and $20.

KONA INTERNATIONAL AIRPORT AT KEAHOLE

Taxis can be found curbside; the approximate fare from the airport to Kailua-Kona is $30, and to Waikoloa it's $55.

Shuttle-bus services typically cost as much as taxis. **Speedi Shuttle** (☎ 329-5433, 877-242-5777; www.speedishuttle.com) will get you to destinations up and down the Kona Coast, plus Waimea, Honoka'a and Hawai'i Volcanoes National Park (though that'll cost $165-plus). Book in advance.

Bicycle

As your primary transportation, cycling around the Big Island is easiest with the support of a tour. Though do-able on one's own, it's a challenge, particularly if the weather doesn't cooperate. However, Kona, the hub for the Ironman Triathlon, has top-notch bike shops that sell and repair high-caliber equipment.

Bus

Unless you don't plan to go far, don't base your trip on using the county-run **Hele-On Bus** (☎ 961-8744; www.heleonbus.org; ⏰ 7:45am-4:30pm Mon-Fri). All buses are free, and routes cover the island, but service is minimal, and most routes only run Monday to Friday; none run on Sunday. Schedules are available online, at the Big Island Visitors Bureau (p288) and at Hilo's Mo'oheau bus terminal (p300). All buses originate from Mo'oheau terminal, unless otherwise noted. You need permission from the driver to board with a surfboard or bodyboard; these items, as well as luggage, backpacks and bicycles, are charged at $1 per item.

Car & Motorcycle

From Kona to Hilo, the northern half of the belt road is 92 miles, and the nonstop journey takes over two hours. The southern Kona-Hilo route is 125 miles and takes approximately three hours nonstop.

Before renting a car, consider whether you want to drive Saddle Rd, the only route to Mauna Kea and Mauna Loa. Though the condition and reputation of this road is improving (see p276), some rental companies still prohibit driving on it. Currently, Harper, National, Dollar and Alamo allow driving on Saddle Rd; Avis allows driving to the Mauna Kea visitor center, but only from the Hilo side; and only Harper rents 4WDs that can be driven past Mauna Kea's visitor center to the summit.

There are car-hire booths at Kona and Hilo airports for the following companies:

Alamo (☎ in Hilo 961-3343, in Kona 329-8896)
Avis (☎ in Hilo 935-1290, in Kona 327-3000)
Budget (☎ in Hilo 935-6878, in Kona 329-8511)

Dollar (☎ Hawaii reservations 800-367-7006)
Enterprise (☎ in Hilo 934-0359, in Kona 331-2509) Both are located off-airport.
Hertz (☎ in Hilo 933-2566, in Kona 329-3567)
National (☎ in Hilo 935-0891, in Kona 329-1674)
Thrifty (☎ in Hilo 877-283-0898)

For more on the national chains, including toll-free numbers and websites, see p576. **Harper Car & Truck Rentals** (Map p287; ☎ 969-1478, 800-852-9993; www.harpershawaii.com; 456 Kalaniana'ole Ave, Hilo) is the local car-hire agency. It's the only company renting 4WDs that can be driven to Mauna Kea's summit, but they are expensive and the insurance coverage (which is supplemental, not primary) has a high deductible. Rates fluctuate greatly by season and demand, but for a 4WD anticipate spending at least $130 per day, and always ask for rate quotes that include taxes.

Taxi

In Hawai'i, cabbies are typically locals who often act as island tour guides. It's easy to find a cab at either airport, but most companies are small, with no advertisements or *Yellow Pages* listings. Cabs don't run all night or cruise for passengers, so in town call ahead. The standard flag-down fee is $2, plus $2 per mile thereafter.

DRIVING DISTANCES & TIMES

From Hilo

Destination	Miles	Time
Hawi	86	2¼hr
Honoka'a	40	1hr
Kailua-Kona	92	2½
Na'alehu	64	1¾hr
Pahoa	16	½hr
Hawai'i Volcanoes National Park	28	½hr
Waikoloa	80	2¼hr
Waimea	54	1½hr
Waipi'o Lookout	50	1¼hr

From Kailua-Kona

Destination	Miles	Time
Hawi	51	1¼hr
Hilo	92	2½hr
Honoka'a	61	1½hr
Na'alehu	60	1½hr
Pahoa	108	3hr
Hawai'i Volcanoes National Park	98	2½hr
Waikoloa	18	¾hr
Waimea	43	1hr
Waipi'o Lookout	70	1¾hr

FLY LIKE AN 'IO

For a thrilling bird's-eye view of the island and its red-hot volcanoes, try a helicopter tour. Lava tours leave from Hilo – most fly over Kilauea Caldera, the active Pu'u 'O'o vent and then hover over live lava flows. Before booking, confirm what you'll see, and make sure all seats are window seats; some also offer 'doors off' tours, and noise-canceling headsets are nice. Other helicopter tours (some leaving from Kona) take in the valleys along the Kohala and Hamakua Coasts. Helicopter tours will fly if it's cloudy (but not if it's raining); wait for a sparkling clear day if you can.

Without discounts, expect to pay $165 to $210 for a 45- to 55-minute lava tour, while two-hour valley trips run between $400 and $450. Most companies offer advance-purchase internet deals, and free tourist magazines have discount coupons. (For an overview of the environmental impacts of helicopter tours, see the boxed text, p483.)

Blue Hawaiian Helicopters (☎ 961-5600, 800-745-2583; www.bluehawaiian.com) Reliable, dependable and high volume.

Iolani Air Tour Company (☎ 329-0018, 800-538-7590; www.iolaniair.com) Has cheaper 50-minute 'flight-seeing tours' by small prop plane.

Paradise Helicopters (☎ 969-7392, 866-876-7422; http://paradisecopters.com) A good reputation for more personal tours.

Safari Helicopters (☎ 969-1259, 800-326-3356; www.safarihelicopters.com)

Sunshine Helicopters (☎ 270-3999, 866-501-7738; www.sunshinehelicopters.com) Also has snorkel combo tours.

Tropical Helicopters (☎ 866-961-6810; www.tropicalhelicopters.com) Also does custom charters.

Tours

Several long-time tour operators offer around-the-island tours, which are essentially a mad dash through Kailua-Kona, Hawai'i Volcanoes National Park, Punalu'u black-sand beach, Hilo's Rainbow Falls, the Hamakua Coast and Waimea. They provide a quick glimpse of the island's buffet.

Roberts Hawaii (☎ 954-8652, 866-898-2519; www.robertshawaii.com), **Jack's Tours** (☎ 969-9507, 800-442-5557; www.jackshawaii.com) and **Polynesian Adventure Tours** (☎ 833-3000, 800-622-3011; www.polyad.com) offer day-long circle-island bus tours (with variations) that cost from $70 to $85. All three companies pick up passengers at hotels in Waikoloa, Kailua-Kona and Keauhou; the exact time varies, but expect to leave around sunrise and get back around sunset.

Other region- and activity-specific tours are mentioned throughout the chapter. For helicopter tours, see above; and for agricultural tours, see p281.

KAILUA-KONA

pop 10,000

In 1866, Mark Twain described Kailua-Kona as 'a little collection of native grass houses reposing under tall coconut trees – the sleepiest, quietest, Sundayest looking place you can imagine.' My, how things have changed.

Kailua (or Kona) now has the worst traffic, the most hotels and condos, the most tourists, the most souvenirs per square foot, and is in fact the most likely place on the entire island to find businesses open on a Sunday. Along the waterfront's meandering Ali'i Drive, Kailua works hard to evoke the nonchalance of a sun-drenched tropical getaway, but in an injection-molded, bargain-priced way. It's the inevitable result of having to efficiently absorb and satisfy cruise-ship arrivals carrying fantasy expectations borne from the seed of Twain's wry amusement.

Which isn't to say Kailua isn't fun. Most Big Island visitors pass through at some point, if only to finish their gift shopping, and Kailua can make an affordable, pleasant base from which to enjoy the Kona Coast's nearby beaches, its fantastic snorkeling and watersports, and its preeminent ancient Hawaiian sites. Amid the town's forgettable dross, there are some delicious restaurants and cool shops and, of course, plenty of chances to share your adventures with fellow travelers over a coconut full of kava or an umbrella-shaded, sunset-colored cocktail.

ORIENTATION

The highways and major roads in the Kona district parallel the coastline, making navigation easy. Kailua-Kona is south of the airport on Hwy 19 (Queen Ka'ahumanu Hwy), which becomes Hwy 11 (Mamalahoa Hwy) at Palani Rd; expansion of the highway near town has been ongoing, and road construction will likely continue to snarl commuter traffic for the forseeable future.

From the highway, Kaiwi St, Palani Rd and Henry St are the primary routes into town. Ali'i Dr is Kailua's main street; the first mile, from Palani Rd to Kahakai Rd, is a pedestrian-friendly ramble lined with shops, restaurants and hotels. Ali'i Dr then continues another 4 miles along the coast to Keauhou, and is shoulder-to-shoulder with condo complexes, vacation rentals, B&Bs, hotels and private homes. A sometimes quicker route through town is Kuakini Hwy, which parallels Ali'i Dr and eventually flows into Hwy 11 to the south.

INFORMATION

Bookstores

Borders Books Music & Café (☎ 331-1668; cnr Henry St & Hwy 11; 🕑 9am-9pm) Kailua-Kona's largest bookseller, with 'plenny' magazines and coffee.

Kona Bay Books (☎ 326-7790; www.konabaybooks.com; 74-5487 Kaiwi St; 🕑 10am-6pm) The island's best used-book store, with a nice selection of Hawaiian titles, plus used CDs.

Emergency

Police (☎ 935-3311) For nonemergencies.

Sexual Assault Hotline (☎ 935-0677)

Internet Access

Island Lava Java (☎ 327-2161; Ali'i Sunset Plaza, 75-5799 Ali'i Dr; per 20min $4; 🕑 6am-10pm) Wireless, plus three computer terminals.

Kona Business Center (☎ 329-0006; www.konacopy.com; Suite B-1A, Kona International Market, 74-5533 Luhia St; per 30min $5.25, per hr $10; 🕑 8:30am-5:30pm Mon-Fri) Complete business services; internet and wi-fi.

Scandinavian Shaved Ice Internet Café (☎ 331-1626; 75-5699 Ali'i Dr; per hr $8; 🕑 10am-9:30pm Mon-Sat, noon-9:30pm Sun) Terminals in the café and in a separate computer room.

Internet Resources

Big Island Visitors Bureau (www.bigisland.org)

Kona Web (www.konaweb.com).

Media

NEWSPAPERS

Hawaii Tribune-Herald (www.hawaiitribune-herald.com) The Big Island's main daily newspaper.

West Hawaii Today (www.westhawaiitoday.com) Kona Coast's daily newspaper.

RADIO

A station guide is available at http://diallists.hawaiirad iotv.com/BigIsleRadio.html.

KAGB 99.1 FM (www.kaparadio.com) The Kona-side home of effervescent KAPA – Hawaii and island music.

KKUA 90.7 FM (www.hawaiipublicradio.org) Hawaii Public Radio; classical music, talk and news.

KLUA 93.9 FM Native FM (previously 'Da Beat') plays island and reggae tunes.

Medical Services

Kona Community Hospital (☎ 322-9311; www.kch.hhsc.org; 79-1019 Haukapila St, Kealakekua) Located about 10 miles south of Kailua-Kona.

West Hawaii Medical Group (☎ 329-6355; 77-6447 Kuakini Hwy; 🕑 8am-5pm Mon-Fri, 9am-5pm Sat) For nonemergency medical care. Appointments recommended.

Longs Drugs (☎ 329-1380; Lanihau Center, 75-5595 Palani Rd; 🕑 8am-9pm Mon-Sat, to 6pm Sun) Centrally located drugstore and pharmacy.

Money

Bank of Hawaii (☎ 854-2150; Lanihau Center, 75-5595 Palani Rd) Has a 24-hour ATM.

First Hawaiian Bank (☎ 329-2461; 74-5593 Palani Rd) Has a 24-hour ATM.

Post

Post office (☎ 331-8307; 74-5577 Palani Rd; 🕑 8:30am-4:30pm Mon-Fri, 9:30am-1:30pm Sat) Access is via the Lanihau Center.

Tourist Information

Oddly, Kona has no official tourist office. Flyer racks are ubiquitous along Ali'i Dr, and the tour booth at the Kailua Pier is usually staffed.

DANGERS & ANNOYANCES

'Tourist information' or 'discount activities' storefronts along Ali'i Dr are most often fronts for aggressive salespeople looking to push condominium time-shares. Caveat emptor.

SIGHTS

Kailua is a breezy waterfront tourist town. Its main attractions are the sparkling Pacific Ocean and tourism itself. Kailua holds a few historic buildings well worth seeing, but it's only crowded because of its proximity to sunny beaches and watersports north and south.

Hulihe'e Palace

Hawai'i's second governor, 'John Adams' Kuakini, built this simple two-story, lava-rock

HAWAI'I THE BIG ISLAND

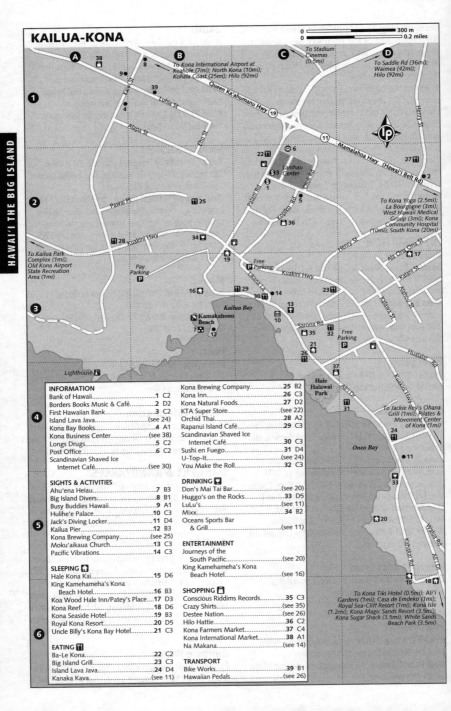

KAILUA-KONA

Lighthouse

Hale Halawai Park

Kailua Bay

Kamakahonu Beach

Oneo Bay

To Kona International Airport at
Keahole (7mi); North Kona (10mi);
Kohala Coast (25mi); Hilo (92mi)

To Stadium
Cinemas
(0.5mi)

To Saddle Rd (36mi);
Waimea (42mi);
Hilo (92mi)

To Kona Yoga (2.5mi);
La Bourgogne (3mi);
West Hawaii Medical
Group (3mi); Kona
Community Hospital
(10mi); South Kona (20mi)

To Kailua Park
Complex (1mi);
Old Kona Airport
State Recreation
Area (1mi)

To Jackie Rey's Ohana
Grill (1mi); Pilates &
Movement Center
of Kona (1mi)

To Kona Tiki Hotel (0.5mi); Ali'i
Gardens (1mi); Casa de Emdeko (1mi);
Royal Sea-Cliff Resort (1mi); Kona Isle
(1.2mi); Kona Magic Sands Resort (3.5mi);
Kona Sugar Shack (3.5mi); White Sands
Beach Park (3.5mi)

A VOGGY DAY IN KONA TOWN

Living with an active volcano means a lifetime of secondhand smoke. The Big Island has always had to deal with vog (short for volcanic smog). However, since early 2008, when Kilauea changed its eruption pattern (p306), vog has affected the island much more seriously. For some, living downwind has become unbearable, forcing them to leave the island. For farmers in affected areas it's a bona fide disaster, with sometimes 90% of their crops wilting as if doused by gasoline.

Steady southwest trade winds typically blow vog away from Hilo and south around Mauna Loa. The mountain then becomes a windbreak allowing vog to gather thickly over Ka'u and South Kona, though Kailua-Kona also gets plenty. Rarer Kona winds blow vog the other way, and local winds around Hawai'i Volcanoes National Park can send blinding clouds over roadways, like you're driving through a forest fire.

According to park rangers, Kilauea's vog output has more than doubled, and air monitoring in Captain Cook and Pahala show double to quadruple the usual amounts of sulfur dioxide. South Kohala and the Hamakua Coast are rarely affected, and North Kohala never gets any. For daily monitoring and health advice, see http://hawaii.gov/gov/vog.

No one knows how long this will continue; it could easily be years. For visitors, short-term exposure is more a nuisance – perhaps, spoiling a sunny day – than a health concern, though if you have respiratory issues, stick to clearer parts of the island.

Then again, as Mark Twain once quipped upon visiting Kilauea, 'The smell of sulphur is strong, but not unpleasant to a sinner.'

---

house as his private residence in 1838. After Kuakini's death in 1844, it became the favorite vacation getaway for Hawaiian monarchs. In the mid-1880s, Hulihe'e Palace was thoroughly renovated by the well-traveled King David Kalakaua, who felt it needed more polish. He stuccoed the lava rock outside, plastered it inside, and added decorative ceilings, gold-leaf picture moldings and crystal chandeliers.

Hard times befell the monarchy in the early 20th century, and the house was sold and the furnishings and artifacts were auctioned off by Prince Kuhio in 1914. Luckily, his wife and other royalty meticulously numbered each piece and recorded the names of bidders. In 1925, the Territory of Hawaii purchased the house to be a museum run by the Daughters of Hawai'i, a women's group dedicated to the preservation of Hawaiian culture and language. This group tracked down the furnishings and royal memorabilia and persuaded many to donate pieces, such as a table inlaid with 25 kinds of native woods and several of Kamehameha the Great's war spears.

Unfortunately, the building suffered major structural damage during an earthquake in 2006, and the **museum** (☎ 329-1877; www.daughtersofhawaii.org; 75-5718 Ali'i Dr) has since been closed for repairs and reconstruction. Check with the Daughters of Hawai'i for updates on its reopening.

Ahu'ena Heiau

After uniting the Hawaiian islands, Kamehameha the Great established his kingdom's royal court in Lahaina on Maui, but he continued to use Ahu'ena Heiau as his personal retreat and temple. This is where he died in May 1819, and where his body was prepared for burial, though in keeping with tradition, his bones were secreted elsewhere, hidden so securely no one has ever found them.

Reconstructed with palm-leaf shacks and carved wooden *ki'i* (statues), the small, dramatically positioned heiau (ancient stone temple; closed to the public) sits next to Kailua Pier, and the adjacent King Kamehameha Beach Hotel uses it as a backdrop for its luau. The heiau's tiny cove doubles as a placid saltwater pool where locals fish, children swim and seniors lounge on its comma of sand, **Kamakahonu Beach**.

Moku'aikaua Church

On April 4, 1820, the first Christian missionaries to the Hawaiian Islands sailed into Kailua Bay. When they landed, they were unaware that Hawai'i's old religion had been abolished on that very spot just a few months before. King Liholiho gave them this site, just a few minutes' walk from Kamehameha's Ahu'ena Heiau, to establish Hawai'i's first Christian church.

Completed in 1836, the **church** (☎ 329-1589; www.mokuaikaua.org; 75-5713 Ali'i Dr) is a handsome building with walls of lava rock held together by sand and coral-lime mortar. The posts and beams, hewn with stone adzes, and smoothed with chunks of coral, are made from ohia, and the pews and pulpit are made of koa, the most prized native hardwood. The steeple tops out at 112ft, making the church the tallest structure in Kailua. The church is popular for weddings, and inside is a dusty model of the missionaries' ship, *Thaddeus*, and a history of their arrival.

Kailua Pier

The town's pier, built in 1915, was once a major cattle-shipping area. Cattle driven down from hillside ranches were stampeded into the water and forced to swim out to waiting steamers, where they were hoisted aboard by sling and shipped to Honolulu slaughterhouses.

As sportfishing charters now use Honokohau Harbor north of town, Kailua Pier is mainly used by dive boats and cruise ships, though its hoist and scales are still used for weigh-ins during billfish tournaments. A staffed information booth helps orient newly landed cruise-ship arrivals.

Beaches

WHITE SANDS BEACH PARK

This small but gorgeous beach (also called La'aloa Beach) has crystal-clear turquoise waters and tall palms (but little shade). During high winter surf the beach can lose its sand literally overnight, earning it nicknames like Magic Sands and Disappearing Sands. When its rocks and coral are exposed, the beach becomes too treacherous for most swimmers. Gradually the sand returns, transforming the shore back into its former beachy self. White Sands is always packed and is an extremely popular bodyboarding and bodysurfing spot. Facilities include rest rooms, showers, picnic tables and a volleyball court; a lifeguard is on duty. The park is about 4 miles south of the center.

OLD KONA AIRPORT STATE RECREATION AREA

Maybe it's the name, but visitors often overlook this quiet, 217-acre park (Map p242) a mile from downtown. The old airport runway skirts a long, sandy beach laced with thick strips of black lava rock. Granted, this doesn't make for good swimming, but low tide reveals countless aquariumlike **tide pools**. Bring a picnic, meander through the pools and enjoy a little solitude. Just inside the

southern entrance gate, one pool is large and sandy enough to be the perfect *keiki* (child) pool. The waters offshore are a marine-life conservation district.

A few breaks in the lava allow entry into the water, but fishing is the main activity. Scuba divers and confident snorkelers can make for **Garden Eel Cove**, a short walk from the north end of the beach. The reef fish are large and plentiful, and a steep coral wall in deeper waters harbors moray eels and small caves. When the surf's up, local surfers flock to an offshore break here.

Facilities include rest rooms, showers and covered picnic tables on a lawn dotted with beach heliotrope and short coconut palms. The former runway disposes of parking worries, and locals enjoy a mile-long jogging track here.

Adjacent to the recreation area is the county's **Kailua Park Complex** (☎ 327-3500; ◐ 6:30am-7:30pm Mon-Fri, 8:30am-5:30pm Sat & Sun). The extensive facilities include a toddler playground, an attractive Olympic-size lap pool and kids' pool (get your swim in here), soccer and softball fields, four night-lit tennis courts and a gym. To get here, follow Kuakini Hwy to its end.

ACTIVITIES

Most of Kailua's activities focus on the sea. Coconut Grove on Ali'i Dr has a sandy volleyball court (BYO volleyball or join a pickup game). Hikers can aim for the parks in North Kona. To rent a bicycle, see p225.

The area's snorkeling and diving tours are gathered here, so you can see the range of options on offer. Descriptions note whether tours leave from Kailua Pier, Honokohau Harbor (p241) to the north or Keauhou Harbor (p227) to the south. For kayaking, see the listings in Kealakekua Bay (p235).

Snorkeling

Some of the island's best, most accessible snorkeling is an easy drive from Kona: to the south, check out Kahalu'u (p226), Two-Step (p240) and Kealakekua Bay (p235), and to the north try Mahukona (p258).

If you prefer a snorkeling boat cruise (aka 'dolphin cruise'), these are plentiful around Kailua, with good reason. A half-day (four-hour) cruise offers snorkeling in otherwise inaccessible places, the chance to spot whales and dolphins, and knowledgeable guides.

THE BIG ISLAND FOR CHILDREN

For babysitting services in Kona, **Busy Buddies Hawaii** (☎ 334-1800; Kaiwi Sq, 74-5565 Luhia St; per hr $5-7.50; ⏰ 7am-6pm Mon-Fri, 8am-5pm Sat) is a clean, reliable day-care center that welcomes drop-ins.

- Get underwater with **Atlantis Submarines** (p221).
- Say 'hi' to Max at **Pana'ewa Rainforest Zoo** (p291).
- Bodyboard at **White Sands Beach** (opposite).
- Go tide-pooling at **Kapoho Tide Pools** (p304) and **Puako** (p253).
- Snorkel and swim with the sea turtles at **Hilo's beaches** (p292), **Kahalu'u Beach Park** (p226) or the **'Ai'opio Fishtrap** (p243).
- Picnic and swim at **Lili'uokalani Park** (p290).
- Catch a $1 movie at Hilo's **Kress Cinema** (p298).
- Enjoy the warm waters of Puna's **'hot pond'** (p304).

When choosing, always opt for morning departures, when water conditions are best.

Ultimately, the captain decides the best destination for the day's conditions, but by far the most common (and crowded) snorkeling spot is Kealakekua Bay. However, the coast south of Kailua has beautiful lava cliffs and caves, while the northern coast is a flat lava shelf with great snorkeling aplenty.

For a truly amazing experience, do a **night snorkel or dive with Pacific manta rays**. The ocean at night is spooky enough, but to see a handful of these graceful, gentle creatures (with 8ft to 14ft wing spans) glide out of the darkness and spin cartwheels as they feed is unforgettable. The main manta ray location is in front of the Sheraton Keauhou Bay Resort (p227). For more information on manta rays, see www.mantapacific.org.

Other details aside, cruises come in two main types: small Zodiac rafts, which can zip into sea caves but lack shade or toilets; and large catamarans, which have a smoother, comfier ride but aren't as nimble around small coves. Cruise prices usually include snorkeling gear, beverages and snacks. Most offer internet discounts.

Recommended Zodiac operators include the following:

Captain Zodiac (☎ 329-3199; www.captainzodiac.com; half-day cruise adult/child 4-12 $93/78) In business since 1974, Captain Zodiac makes daily trips to Kealakekua Bay in 24ft rigid-hull inflatable Zodiacs with up to 16 passengers and a jaunty pirate theme. Departs from Honokohau Harbor.

Sea Hawaii Rafting (☎ 325-7444; www.seahawaii rafting.com; half-day $95, charters per hr $400) With over 15 years of experience in Kona's waters, excellent guide Kris Henry can tailor trips to your preferences. His rigid-hull, inflatable Zodiac can accommodate up to 20 passengers, with a trip minimum of four. Knowledgeable, friendly owner. Departs from Kailua Pier, with other departure points possible.

Sea Quest (☎ 329-7238, 888-732-2283; www .seaquesthawaii.com; morning cruise adult/child $92-109/75-89, afternoon cruise $72/62) Sea Quest has four rigid-hull inflatable rafts that take up to six or 14 passengers. All half-day cruises visit Kealakekua Bay, while two morning cruises add more sites and stops, like Honaunau Bay. Departs from Keauhou Bay.

For catamarans, try the following:

Fair Wind (☎ 345-0268, 800-677-9461; www.fair-wind .com) The *Fair Wind II*, a scrappy 100-passenger catamaran with two kickin' 15ft slides and a BBQ, sails daily to Kealakekua Bay (adult/child $75/45, including meal adult $109 to $119, child four to 12 years $69 to $75). Cruises on the luxury Hydrofoil catamaran *Hula Kai* (per person including meal $125 to $155) are longer and look for the day's best, most crowd-free spots. The *Hula Kai* also does a night manta trip (snorkel $89, dive $120 to $135). Divers are accommodated. Book in advance, as Fair Wind does the area's highest volume. Departs from Keauhou Bay.

Kamanu Charters (☎ 329-2021, 800-348-3091; www .kamanu.com; adult/child $80/50) Snorkel without crowds at Pawai Bay, just north of the protected waters of the Old Kona Airport State Park. The 36ft catamaran, which motors down and sails back, takes a maximum of 24 people. Has a night manta snorkel ($80), and boat can be privately chartered. Departs from Honokohau Harbor.

our pick **Sea Paradise** (☎ 322-2500, 800-322-5662; www.seaparadise.com; adult/child snorkel cruise incl 2 meals $99/59, manta snorkel $89/59, 2-tank dive $145, manta dive $110) Highly recommended Sea Paradise offers morning snorkel cruises to Kealakekua Bay, dive trips and a sunset dinner sail on a classy 46ft catamaran with a fun and professional crew. The manta night cruises include James Wing, a manta ray expert and professional videographer, and are the area's best. Departs from Keauhou Bay.

Diving

Near the shore, divers can see steep drop-offs with lava tubes, caves and diverse marine life. In deeper waters there are 40 popular boat-dive areas, including an airplane wreck off Keahole Point.

One well-known dive spot is **Red Hill**, an underwater cinder cone about 10 miles south of Kona. It has beautiful lava formations (including ledges and lots of honeycombed lava tubes) as well as coral pinnacles and brightly colored nudibranchs (mollusks).

Two-tank dives range from $110 to $160. One-tank night dives and manta ray dives cost between $100 and $130. The larger five-star PADI operations offer certification courses for $500 to $650.

See the list of snorkel outfits, p218, as some accommodate divers; conversely, some dive companies accommodate snorkelers. Kailua-Kona's dive operations are numerous, and largely have great reputations:

Aloha Dive Company (☎ 325-5560, 800-708-5662; www.alohadive.com) A personable small company run by local Native Hawaiian Mike Nakachi and Earl and Chris Kam. Groups are limited to six on the 28ft boat.

Big Island Divers (☎ 329-6068; www.bigislanddivers .com; 74-5467 Kaiwi St) Personable staff with expansive shop; all boat dives are open to snorkelers. Specializes in night and manta dives, including black night dives.

Dive Makai (☎ 329-2025; www.divemakai.com) A small, friendly operation run by a husband-and-wife team with a 31ft boat. In business for nearly three decades, they provide thorough predive briefings, have a diver-to-guide maximum ratio of 6:1 and keep dives unstructured. Offers night and manta ray dives.

our pick **Jack's Diving Locker** (☎ 329-7585, 800-345-4807; www.jacksdivinglocker.com; Coconut Grove Marketplace, 75-5813 Ali'i Dr) One of the best outfits for introductory dives and courses, with extensive programs for kids. Housed at a 5000ft-deep facility, with a store, classrooms, a tank room and a 12ft-deep dive pool. Offers boat and shore dives, as well as night manta-ray dives; snorkelers welcome on many trips. Its five boats (from 23ft to 46ft) handle groups of six to 18 divers. Jack's has a reputation for preservation and setting up moorings.

Whale Watching

The season for humpback whales usually starts around January and runs to March or April. While many snorkeling, diving or fishing operations add whale-watching trips in season, we recommend marine mammal biologist Dan McSweeney's **Whale Watch** (☎ 322-0028, 888-942-5376; www.ilovewhales.com; 3hr cruise adult/child $80/70; ☺ Jul, Aug & Nov-Apr). An active researcher, he leads educational excursions where observing whales is always the main focus. Several other types of whales, and five species of dolphin, can also be seen in Kona waters year round. Hydrophones allow passengers to hear whale songs.

Fishing

Kona has hundreds of charter fishing boats; many are listed in the *Fishing* freebie available around town. The standard cost to join an existing party starts at $100 per person for a four-hour (half-day) trip. Otherwise, a charter for up to six people runs between $450 and $600 for a half-day, and $700 and $3000 for a full day, depending on the boat. Prices include equipment.

Next to the weigh station at Honokohau Marina, the **Charter Desk** (☎ 329-5735, 888-566-2487; www.charterdesk.com) is the main booking service; it can match you with 50 or more boats. Another matching service is **Charter Services Hawaii** (☎ 800-567-2650; www.konazone.com), with about a dozen boats in its 'fleet.'

Surfing

What little surf there is on the Leeward Coast is not in Kailua-Kona. **Banyans**, near the banyan tree north of White Sands Beach (p218), has some waves. The best wave for beginners, and those who want to try stand up paddle surfing, is at Kahalu'u Beach (p226), while getting to Pine Trees (p244) requires a hike or 4WD. Right in Kailua, friendly and family-run **Pacific Vibrations** (☎ 329-4140; pacvibe@hawaii.rr.com; 75-5702 Likana Lane; board per day $15-20; ☺ 10am-5:30pm Mon-Fri, to 3:30pm Sat) has board rentals, clothes, and tips.

Across the road from Kahalu'u Bay, **Kona Surf School** (Map p231; ☎ 217-5329; www.konasurfschool.com; 78-6685 Ali'i Dr; board rental $25/day, surf lessons $100-130; ☺ 8:30am-5pm) offers board rentals and regular lessons daily (reservations required), including stand up paddle surfing ($75). Another outfit for lessons is **Ocean Eco Tours** (☎ 324-7873; www.oceanecotours.com; Honokohau Harbor; surf lessons $95), the only operator permitted to surf within the boundaries of Kaloko-Honokohau National Historical Park.

Yoga

In a private home, **Yoga Hale** (☎ 938-9980; www
.yogahale.com; 77-6530 Naniloa Dr; drop-in class $15) offers
a variety of yoga classes and styles, such as
Vinyasa, Ashtanga and hot yoga. **Kona Yoga**
(☎ 331-1310; www.konayoga.com; Sunset Shopping Plaza,
77-6425 Hwy 11, D202; drop-in class $15) is a no-frills
studio with a limited schedule, but owner
Barbara Uechi teaches Iyengar-inspired
classes with lots of care and humor.

For more of a workout, stop by **Pilates &
Movement Center of Kona** (☎ 329-3211; www.konapi
lates.com; 75-5995 Kuakini Hwy; drop-in class $20), which
offers 'yoga in motion' (or Gyrokinesis) and
Pilates classes in an attractive studio.

TOURS

Atlantis Submarines (☎ 329-6626, 800-548-6262;
www.atlantisadventures.com; adult/child $89/45; ⏱ sub-
marine rides 10am, 11:30am & 1pm) Rides last 35 minutes
and descend 100ft into a coral crevice in front of the Royal
Kona Resort. The sub has 26 portholes and carries 48
passengers.

Kailua Bay Charter Company (☎ 324-1749; www
.konaglassbottomboat.com; 50min tour adult/child $30/15;
⏱ tours hourly from 10:30am) See Kailua's coastline, and
its underwater reef and sea life, from a 36ft glass-bottom
boat with a pleasant crew and onboard naturalist. Easy
boarding for elderly or mobility-impaired passengers.

Kona Brewing Company (☎ 334-2739; North Kona
Shopping Center, 75-5629 Kuakini Hwy; www.konabrew
ingco.com; admission free; ⏱ tours 10:30am & 3pm Mon-
Fri) Founded in 1995, the Big Island's first microbrewery
now ships its handcrafted brews throughout the islands
and beyond. Tours of this family-run Kona icon are free,
and include sampling.

Kona Historical Society (☎ 323-3222, 938-8825;
www.konahistorical.org; 75min tour $15) This worthwhile
and informational walking tour covers historical sites
in downtown Kailua-Kona, and includes a book. Four-
person minimum and a cruise-ship maximum. Tours by
apppointment.

FESTIVALS & EVENTS

Hawaiian International Billfish Tournament

(☎ 836-3422; www.hibtfishing.com) Late July to August.
'The grandfather of all big game fishing tournaments' is
also Kona's most prestigious. It's accompanied by a week of
festive entertainment; 2009 marked its 50th anniversary.

Ironman Triathlon World Championship (http://
ironman.com) Early October. This legendary event combines a 2.4-mile ocean swim, 112-mile bike race and
26.2-mile marathon – the ultimate race. About 1700 men
and women from around the world qualify to compete
each year, finishing with times from eight to 17 hours.

Kona Brewers Festival (☎ 331-3033, 334-1884;
www.konabrewersfestival.com; admission $40) Mid-
March. This 'just folks' festival features samples from over
30 craft breweries and gourmet eats from scores of local
restaurants. Proceeds benefit local environmental and cultural organizations. Get your tickets early or you'll miss out.

Kona Coffee Cultural Festival (☎ 326-7820; www
.konacoffeefest.com) For 10 days during harvest season in
November the community celebrates Kona coffee pioneers
and their gourmet brew. Events include a cupping competition (like a wine tasting), art exhibits, farm tours, parades,
concerts and a coffee-picking race.

SLEEPING

The quality of hotels and condos along Ali'i
Dr in the walkable center of Kailua-Kona is
only fair to middling. More attractive offerings are just outside town (in all directions).
Since convenience is a siren song, reservations
for all Kailua properties are recommended in
high season.

Condos tend to be cheaper than hotels for
longer stays, and they offer more amenities.
Condo vacation rentals are handled directly
by owners or by property management agencies. In addition to the agencies listed here,
also check the listings on **Alternative Hawaii**
(www.alternative-hawaii.com).

ATR Properties (☎ 329-6020, 888-311-6020; www
.konacondo.com)

Kona Hawaii Vacation Rentals (☎ 329-3333, 800-
244-4752; www.konahawaii.com)

Knutson & Associates (☎ 329-1010, 800-800-6202;
www.konahawaiirentals.com)

**SunQuest Vacations & Property Management
Hawaii** (☎ 329-6438, from US 800-367-5168; www
.sunquest-hawaii.com)

Budget

Koa Wood Hale Inn/Patey's Place (☎ 329-9663; www
.alternative-hawaii.com/affordable/kona.htm; 75-184 Ala Ona
Ona St; dm/s/d from $25/55/65; 🖳) This well-managed
hostel is Kona's best budget deal, offering
basic, quiet and clean dorms and private
rooms (all with shared baths, kitchens and
living rooms) on a residential street that's
walking distance to Ali'i Dr. Hostel travelers
young and old create a friendly, low-key vibe.
No drugs, alcohol or shoes indoors.

our pick **Kona Tiki Hotel** (☎ 329-1425; www.konatiki
.com; 75-5968 Ali'i Dr; r incl breakfast $72-86, with kitchenette
$96; 🅿 🆂) The nothing-special rooms (with
refrigerator, but no TV or phone) in this older
three-story building would be forgettable if the
intimate hush of crashing waves didn't tuck

you in every night. Snug on a restless cove, the Kona Tiki is acceptably well-kept and friendly; that it is also surprisingly romantic is all about the setting. No credit cards.

CONDOMINIUMS

Kona Isle (☎ 329-6311; 75-6100 Ali'i Dr; 1br $90-135; P 🞨 🞨) That Kona Isle feels like a residential apartment complex is either its draw or its drawback; it makes an inoffensively plain but clean home base for exploring. Saltwater pool.

Midrange & Top End

King Kamehameha's Kona Beach Hotel (☎ 329-2911, reservations 800-367-2111; www.konabeachhotel.com; 75-5660 Palani Rd; r $120-180; P 🞨 🞨 🞨) Thankfully, new owners are in the midst of overhauling Kailua's signature hotel, which anchors the top of Ali'i Dr. However, until renovations on the first tower are complete (call to check), it makes for a dreary stay that even steep online discounts don't fix. Rooms have been tired for years, but now the abandoned 1st-floor shops and dusty displays give the King Kam a forlorn air.

Kona Sugar Shack (☎ 895-2203, 877-324-6444; www.konasugarshack.com; 77-6483 Ali'i Dr; r $150-400; P 🞨 🞨 🞨) Your friendly, artistic hosts have created an attractively funky yet homey three-room 'shack' (really a B&B without breakfast), mostly solar powered, with shared outdoor kitchen, a miniscule pool, eclectic furnishings and lots of amenities. Also, they love kids. What will you say when you see the location (and views) almost directly across from White Sands Beach? Sweet.

Royal Kona Resort (☎ 329-3111, reservations 800-222-5642; www.royalkona.com; 75-5852 Ali'i Dr; r $185-285, ste $300-430; P 🞨 🞨 🞨) You can't miss the Royal Kona, thrusting like a ship's prow, and whose '70s Polynesian kitsch is so over-the-top you half expect the Brady Bunch to come tumbling out of the elevator – making this Kailua's most enjoyable big hotel. The good-sized rooms are attractive and more neutrally decorated, with nice touches like wood-shutter closet doors; corner room lanais have tremendous views. Ask for the more recently renovated Lagoon and Alii Towers; the Bay Tower is older (and $30 to $60 cheaper).

If you're desperate to stay downtown, you might consider these two functional standbys. Both offer 15% to 30% discounts online:
Kona Seaside Hotel (☎ 329-2455, 800-560-5558;

http://seasidehotelshawaii.com; 75-5646 Palani Rd; r $120-150; P 🞨 🞨) The Garden Wing is quietest; rooms with a view aren't worth the extra cash.
Uncle Billy's Kona Bay Hotel (☎ 329-1393, 800-367-5102; www.unclebilly.com; 75-5744 Ali'i Dr; r $95-120; P 🞨 🞨 🞨 🞨) Looks retro-cool outside, but badly designed inside; too much street noise.

CONDOMINIUMS

Casa de Emdeko (☎ 329-6311, 329-6020; www.casademdeko.org; 75-6082 Ali'i Dr, 1br & 2br from $95-150; 🞨 🞨) With Spanish-tile roofs, white stucco, immaculate gardens and two pools, this vacation rental complex is stylish and restful. Units are overall up-to-date, well cared for, and nicely priced. The off-highway location means no noise except wind, surf, and tinkling chimes.

Kona Magic Sands Resort (☎ 329-6311, office 326-5622; www.konahawaii.com/ms.htm; 77-6452 Ali'i Dr; studio units $110-150; P 🞨 🞨) This three-story building is an ugly cinderblock shoebox, but the compact studios are surprisingly cool and quiet. Each has a full kitchen and an oceanfront lanai. White Sands Beach next door is an important plus.

Hale Kona Kai (☎ 329-2155, 800-421-3696; www.halekonakai-hkk.com; 75-5870 Kahakai Rd; 1br $160-185; P 🞨) Quietly positioned on a hidden lane just walkable to downtown, this three-story block of frequently upgraded units is a satsifying choice. All face the ocean and have lanais.

Kona Reef (☎ 329-2959, 800-367-5004; www.kona-reef.com; 75-5888 Ali'i Dr; 1br $250-305, 2br $410-510; P 🞨 🞨 🞨) The condos here are spacious and well-kept, but the complex itself is boring – dated, nondescript, lacking greenery and in need of a makeover. While you won't be unhappy with the room itself, it's a better deal with an extended-stay or internet discount.

Royal Sea-Cliff Resort (☎ 329-8021, 800-688-7444; www.outrigger.com; 75-6040 Ali'i Dr; studios $225, 1br $265-365, 2br $305-399; P 🞨 🞨 🞨 🞨) Outrigger runs the condo side of this seven-floor time-share complex like an upscale hotel, giving you the best of both worlds. Immaculate units are generous-sized and uniformly appointed with pretty furniture and lots of amenities – well-stocked kitchens, washers and dryers, sauna and two oceanfront pools. You can't go wrong.

EATING

Kailua-Kona's eateries show a curiously inverse relationship between quality and price:

with a few exceptions, it seems the more you spend, the less satisfying your meal. So while in Kona, save your money and frequent those unassuming local joints hiding in plain sight in malls and former fast-food franchises.

Budget

Scandinavian Shaved Ice Internet Café (☎ 331-1626; 75-5699 Ali'i Dr; shave ice $2.50-6; 10am-9:30pm Mon-Sat, noon-9:30pm Sun) Shave ice is served in huge, psychedelic-colored mounds that are as big as your head. There is an orgy of syrup choices. At night, folks sometimes break out board games.

You Make the Roll (☎ 326-1322; Kona Marketplace, 75-5725 Ali'i Dr; sushi rolls $5-6.50; 11am-7pm Mon-Fri, to 4pm Sat) This high-concept hole-in-the-wall presents 20 sushi ingredients you can combine however you like. Fat loose rolls, low prices, lots of fun and a hidden location: it's a budgeteer's dream.

U-Top-It (☎ 329-0092; Ali'i Sunset Plaza; meals $5-10; 7:30am-2:30pm, 5-9pm Tue-Sat, 7:30am-2:30pm Sun) For hearty breakfasts with a local twist, order up taro pancakes, crepes, eggs and *loco moco* (rice topped with hamburger, fried egg and brown gravy) at this unpretentious restaurant. The diverse menu pleases a range of palates. It's behind Island Lava Java.

Island Lava Java (☎ 327-2161; Ali'i Sunset Plaza, 75-5799 Ali'i Dr; meals $8-20; 6am-10pm;) This café is a favorite gathering spot for sunny breakfasts with a killer bay view. The food aims for upscale diner; if it sometimes hits closer to greasy spoon, no one minds. Use the internet, linger over a copy of *West Hawaii Today* and enjoy waking up to another day in paradise.

Ba-Le Kona (☎ 327-1212; Kona Coast Shopping Center, 74-5588 Palani Rd; sandwiches $5-7.50; soups & plates $9-13; 10am-9pm Mon-Sat, 11am-7pm Sun) Don't let the fluorescent-lit, cafeterialike dining room and polystyrene plates fool you: Ba-Le serves up rave-worthy Vietnamese fare. Flavors are simple, refreshing and bright, from the green-papaya salad to traditional *pho* (Vietnamese noodle soup) and saimin (local-style noodle soup), and rice plates of spicy lemongrass chicken, tofu, beef or roast pork. Nestle those same proteins in freshly baked French bread or croissants, and *that's* a sandwich to take to the beach.

Orchid Thai (☎ 327-9437; Kuakini Center, 74-5555 Kaiwi St; lunch specials $10, dinner $10-16; 11am-3pm, 5-9pm Mon-Sat) Orchid Thai is the neighborhood

stalwart locals seek when they need a curry fix. The classic preparations are handled well and without fuss. Strip mall location, but fake brick and eggplant-colored curtains warm up the interior. Bring your own alcohol.

Big Island Grill (☎ 326-1153; 75-5702 Kuakini Hwy; plate lunches $10, mains $10-19; 6am-9pm Mon-Sat) Everyone loves this spot, which serves Hawaii's comfort foods – aka, plate lunches and *loco moco* – as fresh and flavorful as home cooking. *Whaaa?* What's a plate lunch? Choose from fried chicken katsu (deep-fried fillets), fried mahimahi, shrimp tempura, beef teriyaki, *kalua* (traditional method of cooking) pork, and more; all come with two scoops of rice, potato-mac salad, and rich gravy. It's always packed, but swift service is warm with aloha.

our pick Kanaka Kava (☎ 327-1660; www.kanakakava.com; Coconut Grove Marketplace, 75-5803 Ali'i Dr; à la carte $4-5, mains $13-16; 10am-10pm, to 11pm Thu-Sat) Follow the strains of Jawaiian music to this tiny counter serving kava (the mashed root of the 'awa plant and water) in coconut cups. Granted, kava tastes like dirt, but give it a chance and its legendary relaxing qualities become evident. Hang out, talk story, and sample the top-notch Hawaiian food: the Waipi'o Valley poi (fermented taro) is delightful, as is the homemade *poke* (cubed raw fish mixed with shōyu and other ingredients), taro, 'opihi (edible limpet) and more. Cash only.

Midrange & Top End

Rapanui Island Café (☎ 329-0511; Banyan Court mall, 75-5695 Ali'i Dr; lunch $6-8, dinner mains $12-16; 11am-2pm, 5-9pm Mon-Fri, 5-9pm Sat) The New Zealand owners know curry, which they prepare with a delicious tongue-tingly warmth. Choose from various satays, spiced pork, chicken, and seafood. Order the house coconut rice; and wash it down with lemongrass ginger tea or a New Zealand wine.

Sushi en Fuego (☎ 331-2200; www.sushienfuegokona.com; 75-5770 Ali'i Dr, Waterfront Row; sushi & tapas $6-16; 11:30am-9pm) 'Sushi on fire' is a newfangled Spanish/sushi fusion restaurant where nearly every dish has a kick. Creative, delicious rolls and tapas have amusing names like Squid Vicious and Hot Piece of Bass. Plus, for romantic sunsets, the 2nd-floor tiki-torch deck overhangs the ocean. Lengthy happy hour (11:30am to 6pm daily, till 9pm Monday) with watery $2 mai tais.

Kona Brewing Company (☎ 334-2739; www.konabrewingco.com; 75-5629 Kuakini Hwy; sandwiches & salads

$11-16, pizzas $15-26; ⊙ 11am-9pm Sun-Thu, to 10pm Fri & Sat) The Big Island's first microbrewery pleases everyone, making for one of Kona's liveliest scenes. Award-winning specialty ales include Pipeline Porter (made with Kona coffee) and Longboard Lager. Either at the bright bar or on the torch-lit patio, diners enjoy meal-sized salads, juicy burgers and thin-crust pizzas from a stone oven. Make reservations.

Jackie Rey's Ohana Grill (☎ 327-0209; Sunset Shopping Plaza, 75-5995 Kuakini Hwy; mains lunch $11-15, dinner $15-28; ⊙ lunch 11am-5pm Mon-Fri, dinner 5-9pm daily) Jackie Rey's is a casual surf-and-turf with Polynesian flair and a fun retro Hawaii vibe. Christmas lights, butcher-paper tablecloths, and aloha shirts set the mood for glazed short ribs, wasabi-seared ahi, tempura vegetables, chops and steaks. Kids get their own menu, and adults get a decent wine list and microbrews on tap.

Kona Inn (☎ 329-4455; Kona Inn Shopping Village, 75-5744 Ali'i Dr; mains lunch $10-16, dinner $20-35; ⊙ 11:30am-9pm) For a more conventional surf-and-turf (as in, pick your fish, choose your preparation) the Kona Inn is a reliable favorite with a pretty dining room and nice views. No surprises, but few disappointments.

La Bourgogne (☎ 329-6711; Kuakini Plaza, 77-6400 Nalani St, at Hwy 11; mains $28-36; ⊙ 6-10pm Tue-Sat) Kona's best choice for special occasion fine dining is this classic French restaurant, where the cuisine and the presentation exude skill and refinement. Expect baked brie in puff pastry, roast duck, rabbit in white wine, foie gras and Kona's best wine list. The dining room is Parisian-intimate, and the service is good, if not always up to the food. Reservations are a must.

Groceries

For groceries, **KTA Super Store** (☎ 329-1677; Kona Coast Shopping Center, 74-5594 Palani Rd; ⊙ 5am-midnight) and **Kona Natural Foods** (☎ 329-2296; Crossroads Shopping Center, 75-1027 Henry St; ⊙ 8:30am-9pm Mon-Sat, to 7pm Sun, deli to 4pm daily) should have everything you need. Each has a deli, and at KTA you'll find sushi, *poke*, kimchi (seasoned vegetable pickle) and other local specialties.

DRINKING

The Big Island has no nightlife scene comparable to Waikiki or Maui. For sheer number of bars, Kailua-Kona is as good as it gets, but most are fairly touristy sports bars. Don't forget the Kona Brewing Company (p223).

LuLu's (☎ 331-2633; Coconut Grove Marketplace, 75-5819 Ali'i Dr; ⊙ 11am-10pm) Second-floor, open-air LuLu's is guarded by an Elviki head, and walls are crowded with dollar bills, signed celebrity photos and dozens of sports TVs. You get the picture. You can tell if LuLu's dance floor is happening from down the street.

Oceans Sports Bar & Grill (☎ 327-9494; Coconut Grove Marketplace, Ali'i Dr; ⊙ 11am-2am) Locals seem to favor Oceans, keeping it hopping even when other places are dead. It's got two pool tables, sports TVs (typically with surfing), good food and a friendly vibe.

Mixx (☎ 329-7334; www.konawinemarket.com; King Kamehameha Mall, 75-5626 Kuakini Hwy; pupu $6-15; ⊙ noon-late Mon-Sat) Mixx is a small spot that's tucked in a shopping mall and attracts a local crowd; often it's a quiet place for wine and *pupu* (snacks), but if there's a DJ or salsa, it gets lively.

Huggo's on the Rocks (☎ 329-1493; 75-5828 Kahakai Rd; ⊙ 11:30am-11pm Sun-Thu, to midnight Fri & Sat) Right on the water, with a thatched-roof bar and live music nightly, Huggo's is an ideal sunset spot. Whether it's worth staying longer depends on who's playing and who shows up.

Don's Mai Tai Bar (☎ 329-3111; www.royalkona.com; 75-5852 Ali'i Dr; ⊙ 10am-10pm) For pure kitsch, nothing beats the shameless lounge-lizard fantasy of Don's in the Royal Kona (p222). Isn't Hawaii all about grimacing tiki, an umbrella-shaded mai tai and the great wide ocean?

ENTERTAINMENT

Luau

Kailua-Kona's two hokey, cruise-ship friendly luau include a ceremony, a buffet dinner with Hawaiian specialties, an open bar and a Polynesian dinner show featuring a cast of flamboyant dancers and fire twirlers. Instead, consider the Kona Village luau (p247).

Journeys of the South Pacific (☎ 329-3111; www.konaluau.com; Royal Kona Resort; adult/child 6-11 $63/24; ⊙ 6pm Mon, Wed & Fri)

King Kamehameha's Kona Beach Hotel (☎ 329-4969; www.islandbreezeluau.com; adult/child 5-12 $69/35; ⊙ 5pm Tue-Fri & Sun)

Cinemas

First-run Hollywood films dominate the 10 screens at **Stadium Cinemas** (☎ 327-0444; Makalapua Shopping Center; 74-5469 Kamaka'eha Ave).

SHOPPING

Kailua-Kona is swamped with run-of-the-mill, dubious-quality Hawaiiana, but there's good stuff, too. You never know when you'll find that perfectly sublime kitschy-tacky something.

Kona farmers market (Ali'i Dr; ⏰ 7am-5pm Wed-Sun) First, wander through this market where craft stalls outnumber produce stands two to one. Get your coconut purses, cheap kids wear, and koa wood Harleys here.

Kona International Market (☎ 329-6262; 74-5533 Luhia St; ⏰ 9am-5pm Tue-Sun) Five large warehouse buildings make up this expansive, attractive complex, where individual stalls sell everything imaginable: beach gear, fresh fish, boutique clothing, and music, gifts and crafts galore. Has a food court and ample parking.

Ali'i Gardens (☎ 334-1381; 75-6129 Ali'i Dr; ⏰ 9am-5pm) This pretty outdoor market gathers two dozen vendors selling mostly clothing and an interesting mix of moderately priced imported and local crafts.

Na Makana (☎ 326-9552; 75-5722 Likana Lane; ⏰ 9am-5pm) This odds-and-ends shop is a rarity in Kailua – offering authentic Hawaii-made gifts, books and collectibles, with unusual finds like Japanese glass fishing floats. Opening hours vary according to owner's schedule.

Hilo Hattie (☎ 329-7200; www.hilohattie.com; Kopiko Plaza; 75-5597 Palani Rd; ⏰ 9am-6:30pm) This Kona outlet of the famous Hilo store sells decent quality Hawaiian clothes for the whole family.

Crazy Shirts (☎ 329-2176; www.crazyshirts.com; Kona Marketplace, 75-5719 Ali'i Dr; ⏰ 9am-9pm) The iconic T-shirt company, founded in 1964, offers unique island designs on heavyweight cotton. The quality shows, and just for fun, shirts are dyed in coffee, beer, tea, volcanic ash and more!

Destee Nation (☎ 327-4478; www.desteenation.com; 75-5744 Ali'i Dr; ⏰ 9am-9pm) Using the logos of longtime Big Island companies, Destee Nation makes classy, retro-cool T-shirts you won't see anywhere else.

Conscious Riddims Records (☎ 326-7685; Kona Marketplace, Ali'i Dr; ⏰ 10am-6pm Sun-Fri) A wide selection of reggae and Jawaiian music, plus clothing and *pakalolo* (marijuana) activism.

GETTING THERE & AWAY
Air
The island's primary airport is **Kona International Airport at Keahole** (KOA; ☎ 329-3423; www.hawaii.gov /dot/airports/hawaii/koa; Hwy 19), located 7 miles north of Kailua-Kona. When booking flights keep

in mind that late afternoon weekday traffic is brutal on southbound Hwy 19.

Bus
The free Hele-On Bus (see p212) runs from Kailua-Kona to Captain Cook several times daily on weekdays, and once on Saturday (1½ hours). Twice daily, it runs to Pahala (two hours, Monday to Saturday) and South Kohala (1½ hours, Monday to Saturday). Once daily, it runs to Hilo (3½ hours, Monday to Saturday) and Waimea (1½ hours, Monday to Friday).

Another option between Kailua-Kona and Keauhou is the Honu Express (p228), a free shuttle that runs daily between Kailua Pier and Keauhou Shopping Center.

Car
The trip from Hilo to Kailua-Kona is 92 miles and takes 2½ hours; for other driving times and distances, see p213.

GETTING AROUND
To/From the Airport
If you're not picking up a rental car, taxis can be found curbside; the fare averages $25 to Kailua-Kona and $45 to Waikoloa. **Speedi Shuttle** (☎ 329-5433, 877-242-5777; www.speedishuttle .com) charges about the same, and only charges a couple of dollars for each additional person. Book in advance.

Bicycle
Bicycle is an ideal way to get around Kailua. **Hawaiian Pedals** (☎ 329-2294; www.hawaiianpedals .com; Kona Inn Shopping Village, 75-5744 Ali'i Dr; per day $20; ⏰ 9am-9pm) rents well-used hybrid bikes for cruising. Affiliated **Bike Works** (☎ 326-2453; www.bikeworkskona.com; 74-5583 Luhia St; per day $40-60; ⏰ 9am-6pm Mon-Sat) rents high-quality mountain and touring bikes for the serious cyclist; offers multiday discounts. Rentals include helmet, lock, pump and patch kit.

Car
Ali'i Dr, in downtown Kailua-Kona, gets very congested in the late afternoon and evening. Free public parking is available in a lot between Likana Lane and Kuakini Hwy. Shopping centers along Ali'i Dr usually provide free parking for patrons behind their center.

The highways running past Kailua experience horrific commuter gridlock. Avoid southbound Hwy 19 and Hwy 190 between 4pm and

6pm, and northbound Hwy 11 between 6am and 8am. Radar speed traps are common on Hwy 19 between Kailua and the airport.

Bus
The free Hele-On Bus (see p225) and the Honu Express (see p228) both make stops within Kailua-Kona.

Taxi
Call ahead for pickups from the following companies:
Aloha Taxi (329-7779; 5am-10pm)
D&E Taxi (329-4279; 6am-9pm)

AROUND KAILUA-KONA
South of Kailua-Kona is the upscale Keauhou resort area, while in the mountains to the southeast is the dropped-in-amber town of Holualoa, now an intriguing artists community.

KEAUHOU RESORT AREA
Keauhou has no town center, unless you count the shopping mall. Rather, it is a collection of destinations: Keauhou Harbor for boat tours, Kahalu'u Beach for snorkeling and surfing, two resorts and condos for sleeping, a farmers market and good restaurants, and a significant ancient Hawaiian settlement.

Information
The following are in the **Keauhou Shopping Center** (Map p231; 322-3000; www.keauhoushopping center.com; cnr Ali'i Dr & Kamehameha III Rd):
Bank of Hawaii (322-3380; 9am-6pm Mon-Fri, 9am-2pm Sat & Sun) Has a 24-hour ATM.
Longs Drugs (322-5122; 8am-9pm Mon-Sat, to 6pm Sun) A drugstore with a pharmacy.
Post office (800-275-8777; 9am-4pm Mon-Fri, 10am-3pm Sat)

Sights & Activities
ST PETER'S CHURCH
The 'Little Blue Church' is one of Hawai'i's most photographed, and a favorite for weddings. The striking sea-green and white building sits almost in Kahalu'u Bay.

Built in the 1880s, St Peter's was moved from White Sands Beach to this site in 1912. It now sits on an ancient Hawaiian religious site, Ku'emanu Heiau. Hawaiian royalty, who surfed Kahalu'u Bay, prayed for good surf at this temple before hitting the waves.

KAHALU'U BEACH PARK
One of the island's most thrilling and easy-access snorkeling spots, **Kahalu'u Bay** (p231) is a giant natural aquarium loaded with colorful marine life. It's the classic medley of rainbow parrotfish, silver needlefish, brilliant yellow tangs, and Moorish idols, plus green sea turtles often swim in to feed and rest on the beach. An ancient breakwater, which according to legend was built by the *menehune* (Hawaii's mythical race of little people), is on the reef and protects the bay.

This is a favorite **surf spot** that, when conditions are mellow, is ideal for beginners and for learning to stand up paddle; when surf is high, strong rip currents make it challenging. Talk to a lifeguard if you're unsure.

One thing not to come for is peace and quiet. The tiny salt-and-pepper beach is hemmed in on all sides: by the busy highway, by the adjacent resort, by the covered pavilion with picnicking families, and by the throngs of snorkelers constantly paddling in and out of the water. Come early; the parking lot can fill up by 10am. Facilities include showers, rest rooms, picnic tables, grills and snorkel and locker rentals. A lifeguard is on duty.

ANCIENT HEIAUS & HISTORICAL SITES
Kahalu'u Bay is adjacent to the Outrigger Keauhou Beach Resort (opposite), which sits where a major ancient Hawaiian settlement once existed. An easy path leads from the beach into and around the protected sites – the front desk has displays and a map brochure.

At the north end are the ruins of **Kapuanoni**, a fishing heiau, and a replica of the **summer beach house of King Kalakaua** next to a spring-fed pond, once either a fishpond or a royal bath. To the south are two major heiaus. The first, **Hapaiali'i Heiau**, was built 600 years ago and in 2007 was completely restored by dry-stack masonry experts into a 15,000-sq-ft platform; speculation is that the heiau was used as a calendar to mark the solstice and equinox. Next to Hapaiali'i is the even larger **Ke'eku Heiau**, which is in the middle of restoration. Legends say that Ke'eku was a *luakini* (temple of human sacrifice); most famously, a Maui chief who tried to invade the Big Island was sacrificed here, and his grieving dogs guard the site still. Nearby petroglyphs, visible only at low tide, tell this story.

To learn more about the restoration of Keauhou's heiaus, visit the **Keauhou Kahalu'u**

Heritage Center (10am-5pm), unstaffed and with no phone, in the Keauhou Shopping Center; it's near KTA Super Store. Displays and videos also describe *holua*, the ancient Hawaiian sport of sledding.

KEAUHOU BAY
This bay, with a small boat harbor and launch ramp, is one of the most protected on the west coast. There's no real reason to come unless you've booked, or want to book, a tour. However, there's a small grassy area with picnic tables, showers and rest rooms, a sand volleyball court, and the headquarters of the local outrigger canoe club. To get to the bay, turn *makai* (seaward) off Ali'i Dr onto Kamehameha III Rd. See p218 for information about excursions out of this harbor.

HAWAIIAN CLASSES, CRAFTS & TOURS
On Monday from 4:30pm to 8pm on the grounds of the Outrigger Keauhou Beach Resort, Keala Ching, a wonderful Native Hawaiian *kumu* (teacher), holds a series of Hawaiian language, hula and chanting classes. Visitors are allowed to watch respectfully or, with the permission of the *kumu*, to join in.

At 8am every Tuesday and Thursday, Outrigger conducts a free one-hour cultural tour of its grounds, including the restored heiaus.

On Friday the Keauhou Shopping Center offers ukulele lessons, a lei-making class, and other craft classes, from 10am to around noon. At 6pm, it hosts a Polynesian dance show. All are free; BYO ukulele.

FARMERS MARKET
One of the Big Island's best farmers markets is held at the Keauhou Shopping Center every Saturday morning (8am to noon). Though not large, it focuses almost solely on high-quality organic produce and products from local small farms. The warm community feeling is enhanced by live Hawaiian music and presentations by local chefs. Grab a coffee and come early!

Festivals & Events
The **Kona Chocolate Festival** (987-8722; www.kona chocolatefestival.com; Outrigger Keauhou Beach Resort; gala $50; late Mar/early Apr) is a weekend-long event that's only getting bigger. It includes a three-day 'chocolate symposium' of workshops and culminates in a gala evening celebration, with

live music and a chocolate cook-off among island chefs.

Sleeping
Outrigger Keauhou Beach Resort (Map p231; 322-3441, reservations 800-688-7444; www.outrigger.com; 78-6740 Ali'i Dr; r $190-270; P   ) Not a true 'resort,' this attractive, full-amenity oceanfront hotel has a great (if small) pool, tennis courts and a tremendous coastal vantage point, experienced to full effect in the breezy, wall-less 1st-floor public areas. While room decor is hotel standard (and bathrooms a bit small), it is nevertheless neat and fresh, with soothing sea-green tones. Most rooms have great views, and some take in the restored heiaus, adding gravitas to your horizon. The manicured grounds include tide pools.

Sheraton Keauhou Bay Resort (Map p231; 930-4900, 866-716-8109; www.sheratonkeauhou.com; 78-128 'Ehukai St; r $350-460;   ) The only bona fide resort in the Kailua-Kona area, the Sheraton boasts a sleekly modern (if starchily corporate) design, over 500 rooms, upscale spa, fine dining, and massive riverine pool (with spiral slide) threading through the canyonlike atrium, but no beach. The grand, theatrical atmosphere is topped off by the manta rays, which gather offshore nightly. Internet rates are surprisingly affordable.

CONDOMINIUMS
For a list of property management agencies, see p221.

Outrigger Kanaloa at Kona (Map p231; 322-9625, reservations 800-688-7444; www.outrigger.com; 78-261 Manukai St; 1br $295-365, 2br $325-499;   ) These tropical townhouse-style condominiums are simply splendid. Large, immaculate and fully stocked, units are gathered in small, well-designed clusters that afford privacy. One-bedroom units can easily fit a family of four, and you'll want to rip the kitchen out to take home. A daily maid service is included.

Eating
Habaneros (324-4688; Keauhou Shopping Center; à la carte $3-7, plates $7.50-9; 9am-9pm Mon-Sat) Add Habaneros to the list of decent taquerias that bless the Big Island. Its fresh, flavorful burritos, tacos and fajitas have a loyal following. Cash only.

Peaberry & Galette (322-6020; Keauhou Shopping Center; crepes $8-14; 9:30am-8pm Mon-Thu, to 10pm Fri

& Sat, to 6pm Sun) For a dose of European hipness, order a sweet or savory crepe here. The quality of the salads and quiches is above average and the espresso machine hisses constantly, of course.

Kama'aina Terrace (☎ 322-3441; Outrigger Keauhou Beach Resort; Friday buffet adult/child 6-12 $35/17.50; ⏰ 6:30-10:30am & 5:30-9pm) The Outrigger's oceanfront dining room offers an uncompelling surf-and-turf, except on Friday nights, when it hosts a lavish seafood and prime-rib buffet that includes traditional Hawaiian dishes and sushi. It is like a luau spread, sans fire-twirlers.

our pick **Kenichi Pacific** (☎ 322-6400; Keauhou Shopping Center; sushi $7-15, mains $26-43; ⏰ 4-9:30pm, dinner from 5pm) Kenichi prepares well-executed and beautifully presented Pacific fusion cuisine. Highlights include scallops in red curry over soba noodles, grilled ono with a ponzu glaze and sweet potatoes, and sauteed shiitake mushrooms over spaghettini. It also prepares extremely fresh sushi and sashimi. While the mall setting doesn't affect the sleek, stylish dining room, it kills the outdoor terrace. Don't miss happy hour (4pm to 6pm), with half-price sushi rolls and drink specials.

For groceries and deli takeout, head for **KTA Super Store** (☎ 322-2311; Keauhou Shopping Center; ⏰ 7am-10pm) or **Kona Natural Foods** (☎ 322-1800; Keauhou Shopping Center; ⏰ 10am-7pm Mon-Sat, to 5pm Sun).

Drinking & Entertainment

Verandah Lounge (☎ 322-3441; Outrigger Keauhou Beach Resort; ⏰ 4-10pm Tue-Sat) Waves crashing just below greatly enhances the atmosphere of this wraparound bar. Live Hawaiian music sets the tone from 7pm to 10pm Friday and Saturday.

Firenesia (☎ 326-4969; www.firenesia.com; adult/child 5-12 $80/50; ⏰ 4:30pm Mon) The Sheraton replaced its old luau with this Polynesian-focused show (another Island Breeze production).

Keauhou Cinema (☎ 324-0172; Keauhou Shopping Center) Hollywood flicks fill seven screens.

Shopping

Kailua Village Artists Gallery (☎ 324-7060; Outrigger Keauhou Beach Resort; ⏰ 9:30am-5:30pm Sat-Thu, till 7pm Fri) In the Outrigger hotel, this co-op gallery represents a wide range of professional local artists and photographers. It's fun browsing even if you're not buying.

Getting Around

A free shuttle (called the Honu Express) runs between Keauhou Shopping Center and Kailua Pier in Kailua-Kona, stopping at the Keauhou resorts and White Sand Beach, among other stops, between 7:30am and 8:30pm daily. It makes 10 trips into downtown Kailua-Kona. Anyone can ride; to pick up a schedule, visit the **shopping center** (www.keauhoushoppingcenter.com) or any Keauhou hotel.

HOLUALOA
pop 6100

Holualoa, at 1400ft on the lush slopes of Mt Hualalai above Kailua-Kona, appears almost unchanged from its days as a tiny, one-donkey coffee village. Appearances can be deceiving, however. The Holualoa area is now one of West Hawaii's prime addresses, and the town's ramshackle buildings hold a stunning collection of sophisticated artistowned galleries. Preserving the village's historic atmosphere and community spirit while building one of the Big Island's most vibrant art colonies (at the same time keeping tour buses at bay) has been a tightrope walk since the 1980s. Today, the Old Mamalahoa Hwy's designation as the Kona Heritage Corridor (see opposite) should help this quirky town retain its unique flavor.

For more information, see www.holualoa hawaii.com. Most businesses close on Sunday and Monday. During November's Kona Coffee Cultural Festival (p221), Holualoa hosts a day-long block party called the **Coffee & Art Stroll**; the **Music & Light Festival** is a wonderful Christmas celebration.

Sights & Activities
DONKEY MILL ART CENTER

Today, the only donkey you're likely to see is on the roof of this fantastic **art center** (☎ 322-3362; www.donkeymillartcenter.org; 78-6670 Hwy 180; admission free; ⏰ 10am-4pm Tue-Sat), which is 3 miles south of the village and run by the Holualoa Foundation for Arts & Culture. The unpretentious center is a working studio that hums with activity and offers a diverse slate of recommended classes; many are taught by the same artists (like Hiroki Morinoue, Sam Rosen and Michael Harburg), whose works fill the town's galleries. A small permanent gallery, gift shop and revolving art shows mean there's always something to see.

KONA HERITAGE CORRIDOR & COFFEE FARM TOUR

The Kona Heritage Corridor was created to help preserve and promote the historic village of Holualoa and its surrounding coffee farms. It encompasses the 10-mile section of the Old Mamalahoa Hwy (Hwy 180) between Hwys 190 and 11, but efforts are underway to have a 60-mile portion of the Mamalahoa Hwy designated a national scenic byway. Incredibly, it would be Hawaii's first.

Brochures (in town and at visitors centers) describe the route and the region's history. For more on Holualoa, see opposite. The following are a few of the several coffee farms where you can learn firsthand about the meticulous handpicking, sun-drying and roasting of the renowned Kona coffee. All give free tours and tastings without reservations. Begin this tour in the north, at the junction of Hwys 190 and 180.

Hula Daddy Kona Coffee (☎ 327-9744, www.huladaddy.com; 74-4944 Hwy 180; ⏲ 10am-2pm Tue-Sat) The attractive tasting room is the place for cupping seminars.

Kona Blue Sky Coffee (☎ 877-322-1700; www.konablueskycoffee.com; 76-973A Hualalai Rd; ⏲ 9am-3:30pm Mon-Sat) In Holualoa village, this estate's tour includes the traditional open-air drying racks and a video; it has a nice gift shop.

Holualoa Kona Coffee Company (☎ 322-9937, 800-334-0348; www.konalea.com; 77-6261 Hwy 180; ⏲ 8am-4pm Mon-Fri) The Kona Le'a Plantation does not use pesticides or herbicides on its beautiful organic farm; the tours are excellent.

Sugai Coffee Farm (Map p231; ☎ 322-7717, 800-566-2463; www.sugaikonacoffee.com; Hwy 180; ⏲ 8am-2pm Mon-Fri) Just north of Hwy 11 junction, this third-generation, family-owned Japanese coffee farm has been here for a century. The tour is a basic presentation; roastings are from Monday to Wednesday mornings.

For a comprehensive description of Kona coffee country, see www.konacoffeefest.com/driving tour.

MALAMA I'KA OLA HOLISTIC HEALTH CENTER

This **health center** (☎ 324-6644; 76-5914 Hwy 180) offers yoga classes and massage, in addition to alternative skin and healthcare treatments.

Sleeping & Eating

Kona Hotel (☎ 324-1155; Hwy 180; s/d with shared bathroom $30/35-40) This shockingly pink historic boarding house (c 1926) is not for everyone. The amazing views might distract you from the barely adequate rooms, but it's hard to look past the dirty communal bathrooms. Rooms cannot be locked (they latch from inside), and the Inaba family usually insists on seeing you before saying whether you can stay, so don't bother calling ahead.

our pick **Holualoa Inn** (☎ 324-1121, 800-392-1812; www.holualoainn.com; 76-5932 Hwy 180; r $270-310, ste $295-345, both incl breakfast; 🏊) At the other extreme, the Holualoa Inn is one of the island's classiest, most romantic properties. From the gleaming eucalyptus floors to the unwoven *lauhala* (hala leaf) walls to the river-rock showers, serene beauty and comfort shines in every detail; several gorgeous public rooms graced with tasteful Asian art and exquisite carved furniture segue seamlessly into the outdoor gardens and pool, while the rooftop gazebo surveys the world. The six rooms don't disappoint, making this peaceful, intimate retreat one you'll long remember. No TVs, phones, or children under 13.

Holuakoa Gardens & Café (☎ 322-2233; Hwy 180; brunch $11-15, dinner $22-32; ⏲ cafe 6:30am-3pm Mon-Fri, 8am-3pm Sat & Sun, restaurant brunch 10am-2:30pm Tue-Sat, 9am-2pm Sun, dinner 5:30-8:30pm Wed-Sat) The coffee-shop in front serves espressos and sandwiches, while the organic, slow-food restaurant in the garden dishes up French-influenced cuisine that, like the town itself, is far more sophisticated than first glance would suggest. The menu is constantly changing, but homemade gnocchi with morels, leeks and edamame (boiled soybeans) – or grilled ahi with roasted fig and ginger fried-rice – indicate the creative approach. Book ahead for dinner.

Shopping

Ipu Hale Gallery (☎ 322-9069; Hwy 180; ⏲ 10am-4pm Tue-Sat) This gallery sells *ipu* (gourds) decoratively carved with Hawaiian imagery using an ancient method unique to the Hawaiian island of Ni'ihau. Lost after the introduction of Western crockery, the art form was revived by a Big Island scholar just 15 years ago, and is now practiced by Michael Harburg, artist and co-owner of the gallery.

Holualoa Ukulele Gallery (☎ 324-4100; Hwy 180; 🕙 10:30am-4:30pm Tue-Sat) In the historic Holualoa post office building, Sam Rosen sells his hand-crafted ukuleles, and those of other artists, for the serious musician. Sam himself is rarely serious; he's happy to talk story all day and show you his workshop. Drop by Wednesday nights (6pm to 8:30pm) for a ukelele jam, or if you have two weeks, take a class and build your own.

Studio 7 Gallery (☎ 324-1335; 🕙 11am-5pm Tue-Sat) Holualoa would not be what it is without Hiroki Morinoue, who led the town's artistic renaissance in the 1980s. Morinoue became world-renowned for Japanese wood-blocks, and his serene gallery showcases his modern, sophisticated works in all media, along with the accomplished pottery of his wife, Setsuko.

Kimura Lauhala Shop (☎ 324-0053; cnr Hualalai Rd & Hwy 180; 🕙 9am-5pm Mon-Fri, to 4pm Sat) Three generations of Kimuras weave *lauhala* products here, as they have since the 1930s. Originally, they purchased *lauhala* products from Hawaiian weavers to sell. When demand increased they took on the production themselves, assisted by local farming wives, who do piecework at home outside of coffee season. Don't fall prey to cheap imports – the *lauhala* hats, placemats, baskets and floor mats sold here are the real deal.

Also recommended:

Dovetail (☎ 322-4046; www.dovetailgallery.net) Funky and cool Asian and Hawaiian-style art.

Holualoa Gallery (☎ 322-8484; www.lovein.com) Matt and Mary Lovein specialize in whimsical, oversized paintings and raku pottery.

Shelly Maudsley White Gallery (☎ 322-5220; www .shellymaudsleywhite.com) White paints bright, bold island images in hyper-real colors.

Getting There & Away

From Kailua-Kona, turn *mauka* (inland) on Hualalai Rd off Hwy 11, and wind 3 miles (including hairpin turns) up to Hwy 180; turn left for most sights. If coming from North Kona, Hina Lani St and Palani St are straighter shots to Hwy 180 than Hualalai Rd, though they are a little indirect. From South Kona, head up Hwy 180 immediately north of Honalo.

SOUTH KONA COAST

After leaving Kailua-Kona, Hwy 11 climbs steadily, slipping back in time as you gain elevation. In South Kona it's as if old Hawaii is rooted too deeply to be overrun by modern life. Past and present coexist dreamily on the steep mountainsides, where ominous gray clouds daily threaten the impossibly verdant slopes, while nary a drop of rain falls on the blazing coast.

This is the acclaimed Kona Coffee Belt, consisting of 22 miles patchworked with hundreds of small coffee farms. That there is no cost-efficient way to industrialize the hand-picking and processing of the beans contributes to the time-warp quality of local life. But the reasons are also cultural. At the turn of the 20th century, thousands of Japanese immigrants arrived to labor as independent coffee farmers, and their influence – along with that of Chinese, Filipino and Portuguese workers – remains richly felt in Buddhist temples, fabric stores and restaurant menus.

Meanwhile, traditional Hawaiian lifestyles are jealously guarded in coastal villages like Miloli'i, and ancient Hawaiian sites resonate with peculiar force – such as when snorkeling in the shadow of Pu'uhonua o Honaunau, and kayaking in the bay where Captain Cook met his grisly demise.

So if you occasionally have to shake your head to clear the ghosts at the edges of your vision, it's just old Hawaii going about its eternal business.

HONALO
pop 2000

At a bend in the road past the intersection of Hwys 11 and 180, little Honalo is your first sign that more than miles separate you from touristy Kailua. The first building you see is the **Daifukuji Soto Mission** (322-3524; www.daifukuji .org; 79-7241 Hwy 11; 🕙 8am-4pm Mon-Sat), a humble-looking Buddhist temple. Slip off your shoes and admire the two ornate, lovingly tended altars. Everyone is welcome to join the twice weekly **Zen meditation** (🕙 6am Wed, 7pm Thu) session, and *taiko* (Japanese drum) groups practice in the early evenings. If you have young kids, return north a mile or so and enjoy shady **Higashihara Park** (🕙 7am-8pm). Its unique Hawaii-themed wooden play structure is

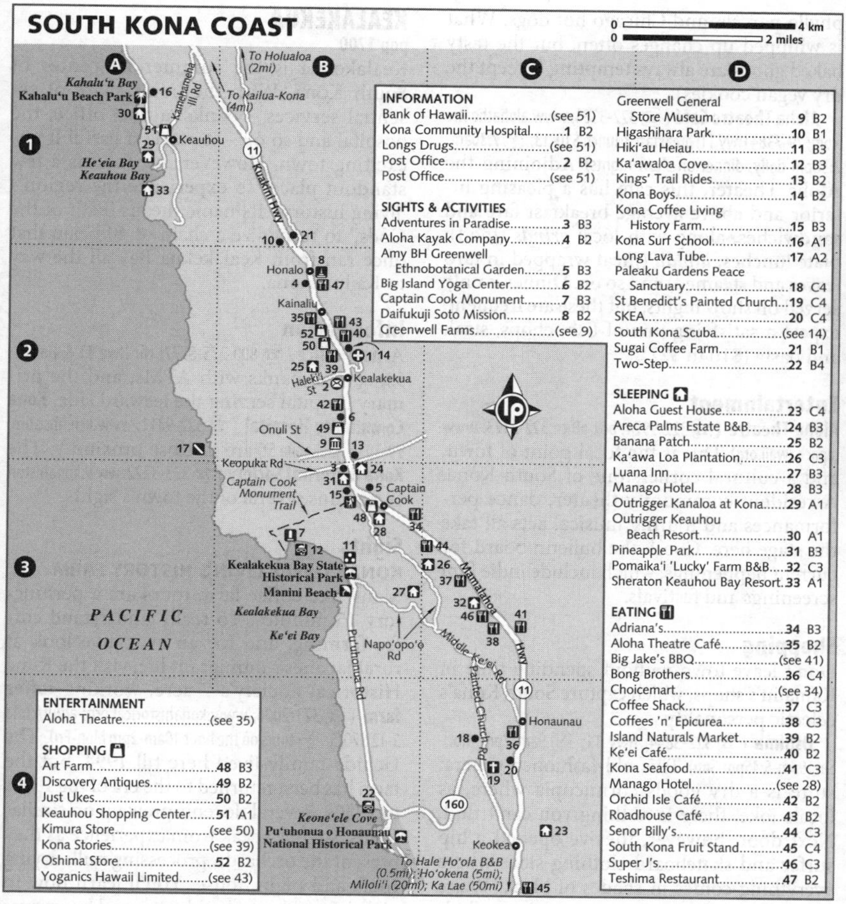
SOUTH KONA COAST
0 4 km
0 2 miles
A
B
C
D
1
2
3
4
To Holualoa (2mi)
To Kailua-Kona (4mi)
Kahalu'u Bay
Kahalu'u Beach Park
Kamehameha III Rd
Keauhou
He'eia Bay
Keauhou Bay
Kuakini Hwy
Honalo
Kainaliu
Haleki'i St
Kealakekua
Onuli St
Keopuka Rd
Captain Cook Monument Trail
Captain Cook
Kealakekua Bay State Historical Park
Manini Beach
Kealakekua Bay
Ke'ei Bay
PACIFIC OCEAN
Mamalahoa Hwy
Pu'uhonua Rd
Napo'opo'o Rd
Middle Ke'ei Rd
Painted Church Rd
Honaunau
Keone'ele Cove
Pu'uhonua o Honaunau National Historical Park
Keokea
To Hale Ho'ola B&B (0.5mi); Ho'okena (5mi); Miloli'i (20mi); Ka Lae (50mi)
INFORMATION
Bank of Hawaii (see 51)
Kona Community Hospital 1 B2
Longs Drugs (see 51)
Post Office 2 B2
Post Office (see 51)
SIGHTS & ACTIVITIES
Adventures in Paradise 3 B3
Aloha Kayak Company 4 B2
Amy BH Greenwell Ethnobotanical Garden 5 B3
Big Island Yoga Center 6 B2
Captain Cook Monument 7 B3
Daifukuji Soto Mission 8 B2
Greenwell Farms (see 9)
Greenwell General Store Museum 9 B2
Higashihara Park 10 B1
Hiki'au Heiau 11 B3
Ka'awaloa Cove 12 B3
Kings' Trail Rides 13 B2
Kona Boys 14 B2
Kona Coffee Living History Farm 15 B3
Kona Surf School 16 A1
Long Lava Tube 17 A2
Paleaku Gardens Peace Sanctuary 18 C4
St Benedict's Painted Church 19 C4
SKEA 20 C4
South Kona Scuba (see 14)
Sugai Coffee Farm 21 B1
Two-Step 22 B4
SLEEPING
Aloha Guest House 23 C4
Areca Palms Estate B&B 24 B3
Banana Patch 25 B2
Ka'awa Loa Plantation 26 C3
Luana Inn 27 B3
Manago Hotel 28 B3
Outrigger Kanaloa at Kona 29 A1
Outrigger Keauhou Beach Resort 30 A1
Pineapple Park 31 B3
Pomaika'i 'Lucky' Farm B&B 32 C3
Sheraton Keauhou Bay Resort 33 A1
EATING
Adriana's 34 B3
Aloha Theatre Café 35 B2
Big Jake's BBQ (see 41)
Bong Brothers 36 C4
Choicemart (see 34)
Coffee Shack 37 C3
Coffees 'n' Epicurea 38 C3
Island Naturals Market 39 B2
Ke'ei Café 40 B2
Kona Seafood 41 C3
Manago Hotel (see 28)
Orchid Isle Café 42 B2
Roadhouse Café 43 B2
Senor Billy's 44 C3
South Kona Fruit Stand 45 C4
Super J's 46 C3
Teshima Restaurant 47 B2
ENTERTAINMENT
Aloha Theatre (see 35)
SHOPPING
Art Farm 48 B3
Discovery Antiques 49 B2
Just Ukes 50 B2
Keauhou Shopping Center 51 A1
Kimura Store (see 50)
Kona Stories (see 39)
Oshima Store 52 B2
Yoganics Hawaii Limited (see 43)

both attractive and endlessly climbable. It is on the *makai* side, between mile marker 114 and 115.

For a real window into local life, reserve a table at **Teshima Restaurant** (☎ 322-9140; Hwy 11; mains $13-23; 🕒 6:30am-1:45pm & 5-9pm), which has served up delicious Japanese comfort food since the 1940s. Local families crowd in for the unpretentious country cooking, which isn't done better – order *donburi* (bowl of rice and main dish), sashimi, fried fish and teriyaki, or better yet, sample a bit of everything with a *teishoku* (set meal). However, it's the patina of many hands that makes this low-key place special. Four generations of Teshimas keep guests happy, but the star is Grandma Teshima, the delightful centenarian owner who still clears tables when regulars aren't insisting she sit and talk story. Cash only.

KAINALIU

Hwy 11 is a beautiful, relaxing drive, but you know you've reached Kainaliu when you get caught in traffic. New road construction may one day solve the town's strangely persistent congestion. Best advice: park as soon as possible and walk. Kainaliu's main street is a tightly packed retail corridor.

Eating

Roadhouse Café (Hwy 11; sandwiches $5.25; 🕒 11am-4pm Mon-Fri) Cheeky signs keep customers amused as they order bargain-priced gourmet sandwiches (such as Thai sweet chili chicken), phyllo parcels, and Chicago hot dogs. What is whipped up changes often, but the tasty baked goods are always tempting (except the dry vegan cookies).

Aloha Theatre Café (☎ 322-3383; www.alohatheatre .com; 79-7384 Hwy 11; breakfast & lunch $10-13; ☼ 7:30am-2:30pm daily, dinner on show nights) Adjoining the Aloha Theater, this café has a pleasing interior and above average breakfast fare and sandwiches, along with local *grinds* (food): plate lunches, *laulau* (meat wrapped in taro leaves and steamed) and so on. Dinner is only served on show nights, but these are frequent; expect a satisfying mix of fish, chops, steak and pasta ($16 to $22).

Entertainment

Aloha Theatre (☎ 322-9924, box office 322-2323; www .apachawaii.org) This is the focal point of town, and a cultural cornerstone of South Kona. A resident community theater, dance performances and touring musical acts all take the stage here. Check the bulletin board for current happenings, which include indie film screenings and festivals.

Shopping

Don't leave town without spending time in Kainaliu's shops, which capture South Kona's eclectic personality.

Oshima (☎ 322-3844; Hwy 11; ☼ 9am-7pm Mon-Sat, 9am-5:45pm Sun) This old-fashioned general store is a dry goods cornucopia where, as locals joke, there is nothing you can't find. Next door, however, they've opened a hip surfer and skateboard clothing store where everything comes in shades of black. We're guessing grandparents go one way, grandkids the other.

Kimura Store (☎ 322-3771; Hwy 11; ☼ 9am-5:30pm Mon-Sat, noon-3:30pm Sun) This fabric store is stuffed with bolts of Hawaiian and island-style prints to make your own aloha wear.

Just Ukes (☎ 322-0808; Hwy 11; ☼ noon-5pm Mon & Wed-Fri, 1-6:30pm Tue, noon-4pm Sat) Pick up a good quality but affordable ukelele ($100 and up), along with sheet music and Hawaiian CDs. It's also a gallery for photographer Kim Taylor Reece, whose sexy hula portraits are everywhere.

Yoganics Hawaii Limited (☎ 322-0714; Hwy 11; ☼ 10am-5pm Mon-Fri) This eco-boutique carries bamboo T-shirts and Organiks brand clothing; an attached studio has yoga and Pilates classes (drop-in $15).

KEALAKEKUA
pop 1700

Kealakekua is the commercial center of South Kona. With the lion's share of essential services – banks, a post office, the hospital and so on – it makes a useful if unexciting town. However, it contains a few standout places to experience the region's 'living history.' Its name means 'Path of the Gods,' to recognize a chain of 40 heiau that once ran from Kealakekua Bay all the way to Kailua-Kona.

Information

A **post office** (☎ 800-275-8777; cnr Hwy 11 & Haleki'i St), several banks with ATMs, and the primary hospital serving the leeward side, **Kona Community Hospital** (☎ 322-9311; www.kch.hhsc.org; 79-1019 Haukapila St) are in close proximity. The **Kona Historical Society** (☎ 323-3222; www.konahistori cal.org) runs several of the town's sights.

Sights

KONA COFFEE LIVING HISTORY FARM
Many free coffee farm tours are a perfunctory 15 minutes. To really understand coffee farming, and for an evocative look at rural Japanese-immigrant life, visit the Kona Historical Society's 7-acre, working **coffee farm** (☎ 323-2006; www.konahistorical.org; adult/child 5-12 $20/5; ☼ tours on the hour 10am-2pm Mon-Fri). The Uchida family lived here till 1994, but the farm has been returned to the era of the 1920s to 1940s. Several docents grew up on similar farms, so they speak from experience as they present the orchards, processing mill, drying roofs and main house. You'll learn how to pick, how to heat a bathhouse, and how wives prepared *bentō* (Japanese-style box lunch) for the field. It's worth the high ticket price. Call ahead, as time slots can fill up.

GREENWELL GENERAL STORE MUSEUM
Next door to Greenwell Farms (right), the Kona Historical Society has turned the 1890 stone-and-mortar Greenwell General Store into a very clever **museum** (adult/child $7/3; ☼ 10am-2pm Mon-Fri). Shelves and walls are meticulously stocked with brand new or re-created dry goods and farm equipment authentic to the period. Inside, docents hand you a shopping list and a 'character' (based on actual customers from Henry Greenwell's journals). Then, you shop, learning as you do. On Thursday afternoon, the Portuguese oven turns out fresh-baked bread.

It's between the 110- and 111-mile markers; the society's headquarters are behind it.

GREENWELL FARMS

This is one of Kona's oldest coffee farms, and it's still run by the Greenwells. Established in 1850, their beautiful 35-acre farm (☎ 888-592-5662; www.greenwellfarms.com; Hwy 11; ☼ 8:30am-4pm Mon-Fri, 8:30am-3pm Sat) became known worldwide as a large-scale producer of quality Kona coffee. Henry Greenwell achieved this fame by trading dry goods from his general store for other farmers' coffee cherry, which he blended with his own. As the line of farm trucks during harvest season indicates, that practice continues today; if it smells like burnt sugar on a stove, they're roasting. The free tour includes the wet mill (which other coffee-farm tours skip) and information on family history.

AMY BH GREENWELL ETHNOBOTANICAL GARDEN

Without pottery or metals, ancient Hawaiians fashioned most of what they needed from plants. This ethnobotanical garden (☎ 323-3318; www.bishopmuseum.org/greenwell; suggested donation $4; ☼ 8:30am-5pm Mon-Fri, free guided tours 1pm Wed & Fri, 10am 2nd Sat of month) preserves Hawaii's original native and Polynesian-introduced plants in a typical ahupua'a, the ancient land division system that ensured all Hawaiians had access to everything they needed. Plaques are informative, but guided tours are helpful to appreciate the humble grounds. Bring insect repellant. The garden is just south of the 110-mile marker.

Activities

MAMALAHOA HOT TUBS & MASSAGE

Soak away your worries in one of two jarrah wood tubs at Mamalahoa Hot Tubs & Massage (☎ 323-2288; www.mamalahoa-hottubs.com; hot tub per hr $30; ☼ by appointment noon-8pm Wed-Sat), set in a lush garden. The tubs, sheltered by thatched roofs that allow for stargazing, are open yet private. Hawaiian hot stone and lomilomi (traditional Hawaiian massage) are offered. A half-hour tub and one-hour massage package costs $95.

BIG ISLAND YOGA CENTER

For Iyengar yoga, Big Island Yoga Center (☎ 329-9642; www.bigislandyoga.com; 81-6623 Hwy 11; drop-in class adult $14) is the place. The studio occupies the 2nd floor of a beautiful old house, and is bright and stocked with mats and props.

TOP PICKS – ROMANTIC B&BS

- Holualoa Inn (p229)
- Ka'awa Loa Plantation (p237)
- Aloha Guest House (p239)
- Kalaekilohana B&B (p325)
- Shipman House (p295)
- Hilo Honu Inn (p295)
- Art & Orchids B&B (p301)
- Waianuhea B&B (p278)
- Aaah, the Views B&B (p267)

Sleeping

While Kailua-Kona has hotels and condos, South Kona is stocked with B&Bs.

Pineapple Park (☎ 323-2224, 877-800-3800; www.pineapple-park.com; 81-6363 Hwy 11; dm $25, r with/without bathroom $85/55; ☼ office 7am-8pm; 💻 📶) South Kona's only hostel is nothing special but cozy enough. Dorms are the essence of basic; eight private rooms are comfortable (if slightly overpriced), and the shared baths and showers are not for the shy. The best things: the nice porch area and roomy kitchens. It's between the 110- and 111-mile markers; look for the kayaks (singles/doubles $30/55).

Banana Patch (☎ 322-8888, 800-988-2246; www.bananabanana.com; studio $100, 1br/2br cottage $125/150; ♿) A clothing-optional jungle retreat in the midst of a staid suburban neighborhood? Indeed, tropical foliage surrounds these three attractive, individual units so thickly you can, if you wish, prance nude worry-free. Each has lovely furnishings and funky charm, with flagstone decks, full kitchens, plush carpets, stained-glass lamps and, naturally, private hot tubs. The two-bedroom Bungalow Hideaway is the star, with a luscious outdoor shower and sleeping porch. Nightly rates are based on a one-week stay.

Areca Palms Estate B&B (☎ 800-545-4390, 323-2276; www.konabedandbreakfast.com; Hwy 11; r incl breakfast $110-145; 💻) A wide, neatly trimmed lawn surrounds this B&B shaded by giant areca palms. The owners, from Oregon, prove you need not be local-born to epitomize the aloha spirit. Their immaculate house resembles an airy cedar lodge, with loads of natural wood and country-style furnishings. A large common living room, an outdoor Jacuzzi and thick robes add comfort; breakfast is a highlight.

Eating

Orchid Isle Café (☎ 323-2700; 81-6637 Hwy 11; snacks $5-8; ☼ 6am-4pm Mon-Fri, 7am-2pm Sat & Sun; ▣) Hang out, surf the internet (per hour $10), enjoy the views and refuel with coffee and an inexpensive sandwich at this relaxed coffeehouse.

Ke'ei Café (☎ 322-9992; 79-7511 Hwy 11; mains $15-23; ☼ 11am-2pm & 5-9pm Tue-Fri, 5-9pm Sat) The menu is all over the map – Greek salad, Brazilian seafood chowder, red Thai curry, pasta primavera, fajitas, pork chops – but the kitchen is largely up to the challenge; dishes can be uneven but are largely successful. A local favorite for a nice meal, Ke'ei Café has a warm dining room, with wood floors and colorful artwork. Reservations are recommended for dinner. It's just south of the 113-mile marker.

Island Naturals Market (☎ 930-7550, Mango Court shopping center, Hwy 11; ☼ 7:30am-7:30pm Mon-Sat, 8am-7pm Sun) For groceries, this is a nice organic market with bulk grains and locally grown produce on offer.

Shopping

Kona Stories (☎ 324-0350; www.konastories.com; 79-7460 Mango Court shopping centre, Hwy 11; ☼ 9:30am-6pm Mon-Fri, 9:30am-4pm Sat) This independent bookstore carries a great selection of Hawaii titles and kids books, and it hosts author readings.

Discovery Antiques (☎ 323-2239; Hwy 11; ☼ 11am-5pm Mon-Sat, 11:30am-4pm Sun) Tin toys and aloha shirts, bric-a-brac and boxing gloves – who knows what you'll find at this secondhand antiques and curiosities shop.

CAPTAIN COOK
pop 3200

As Hwy 11 winds southward, as the greenery gets thicker and the ocean views more compelling, as businesses ebb and flow, it can be hard to tell where towns start and stop. Captain Cook is signaled by the historic Manago Hotel, which began in 1917 as a restaurant catering to salesmen on the then-lengthy journey between Hilo and Kona. The stout building remains a regional touchstone for travelers and residents alike. Captain Cook is also where you access Kealakekua Bay, and the area offers a great selection of B&Bs and down-home cooking.

Sights
KEALAKEKUA BAY STATE HISTORICAL PARK

Kealakekua Bay is a wide, calm bay shouldered by a low lava point to the north, tall reddish *pali* (cliffs) in the center and miles of green mountain slopes to the south. The bay is both a state park and a marine-life conservation district, and it is famous for its rich variety of sea life, including spinner dolphins.

Napo'opo'o Rd, off Hwy 11, winds 4.5 miles down to the bay, leaving behind the lush foliage of the rainier uplands for the perpetually sunny coast; never assume that rain on the highway means rain on the bay. The road ends at the parking lot for Napo'opo'o Beach and Wharf, the kayak launch (opposite). Veer right at the base of Napo'opo'o Rd to reach public rest rooms and **Hiki'au Heiau**, a large platform temple. In front of the heiau, a stone beach makes a moody perch from which to observe the stunning scenery, but the surf is too rough to swim. Veer left at the parking lot for Manini Beach and Ke'ei Bay.

At the bay's north end is the protected Ka'awaloa Cove (opposite), a good diving and legendary snorkeling spot; most access this by sea, but you can also hike. The fish and coral are absolutely wonderful, and those with iron stomachs can swim out 100ft to hang over the blue abyss. The cove is easily identified by the **Captain Cook Monument**, a 27ft white obelisk marking the spot where Captain Cook was killed in 1779 (see p236). In 1877, as an act of diplomacy, the Kingdom of Hawai'i gifted the 16 sq ft of land the monument stands on to Britain; as the grafitti scars make clear, not everyone has been pleased with this. Behind the monument are the ruins of the ancient village of Ka'awaloa; avoid climbing on this sacred site.

Pali Kapu o Keoua, or the 'sacred cliffs of Keoua,' were named for a chief and rival of Kamehameha I. Numerous caves in the cliffs were the burial places of Hawaiian royalty, and it's speculated that some of Captain Cook's bones were placed here as well. High, inaccessible caves probably still contain bones.

On its southern shoreline, Kealakekua Bay is rocky and exposed to regular northwest swells, making for poor swimming and snorkeling conditions. However, **Manini Beach** makes a highly scenic, shady picnic spot, and confident swimmers use a small break in the lava (to the right) to access the water. Surfers head to the point just south of Manini Beach. The park has portable toilets and picnic tables. From Napo'opo'o Rd, turn left on Pu'uhonua Rd, then right on Kahauloa Rd; after a quarter-mile, turn right on Manini Beach Rd and park at the blue house.

Further south on Pu'uhonua Rd is attractive **Ke'ei Bay**, which, while popular with surfers and kayakers, is rough for swimming. To get there, take the very ragged dirt road past the turnoff for Manini Beach (if you reach Ke'ei Transfer Station, you've gone too far). If you don't have high-clearance, park along the dirt road and walk. At the bay, there's a beach, a small canoe launch and a few shacks, but no facilities – be respectful of residents.

Pu'uhonua Rd continues for several miles south through scrub brush to Pu'uhonua o Honaunau National Historical Park (p239).

Activities

SNORKELING

Ka'awaloa Cove, in Kealakekua Bay, is among the island's (and Hawaii's) premier snorkeling spots. The water is protected from ocean swells and is exceptionally clear. Snorkeling is limited to a narrow section along the shore, where sea stars and eels weave through coral gardens, and schools of colorful fish sweep by. Confident swimmers can seek out an underwater lava arch toward the point. If you're lucky, sea turtles and spinner dolphins might join you – but remember to keep your distance from these mammals (see p94), and avoid stepping on coral.

There are three ways to get to Ka'awaloa Cove: rent a kayak (below), take a snorkeling cruise (p218), or hike the Captain Cook Monument Trail (p236). Morning is best, when the winds are calm and sunny skies the most reliable.

KAYAKING

The calm waters of Kealakekua Bay make for a great paddle, even for novices. Outfitters along Hwy 11 rent kayaks and snorkeling kits, as do a few free agents around the parking lot. All outfitters should include paddles, life jackets, backrests, and scratch-free pads for strapping the kayak to your car; make sure to get a dry bag (unless you want mongoose to steal your lunch). It's forbidden to launch kayaks around Hiki'au Heiau – the **Napo'opo'o Wharf** provides a launching point for independent kayakers. Locals may offer to help lift your kayak in and out of the water (a boon for solo kayakers); if you accept, it's the expected courtesy to tip a buck or two.

The paddle to the cove, typically into the wind, takes about half an hour, less returning. Arrive before 9:30am to beat the snorkel cruises, when the cove can become a zoo of bobbing bright-colored noodle-assisted swimmers. Pull your kayak up on the lava rocks to the left of the monument (and tie it to a tree limb). Note that it is illegal for guided kayak tours (but not individuals) to launch from Napo'opo'o Wharf. Kayak tours must launch from private land or through other waters.

The following outfitters all have good reputations:

Adventures in Paradise (☎ 323-3005, 866-824-2337; www.bigislandkayak.com; 81-6367 Hwy 11, Kealakekua; single/double/triple kayak rental $37/64/90, tours $80-110; ☒ 8am-4pm) Friendly and professional, this outfitter makes sure beginners know what they're doing. It runs both kayak snorkel and boat snorkel tours to Kealakekua Bay. At the intersection of Hwy 11 and Keopuka Rd.

Aloha Kayak Company (☎ 322-2868, 877-322-1444; www.alohakayak.com; Hwy 11, Honalo; single/double kayak rental full day $35/60, half-day $25/45, tours $65-160; ☒ 8am-5pm) This popular, Hawaiian-owned outfit knows local waters, has half-day rentals (from noon) and rents glass-bottomed kayaks. Kayak tours to Kealakekua Bay, Keauhou Bay and other destinations, seeking out sea caves and cliff jumping.

Kona Boys (☎ 328-1234; www.konaboys.com; 79-7539 Hwy 11, Kealakekua; single/double kayak rental $47/67, tours $125-350; ☒ 7:30am-5pm) This laid-back yet professional outfit is the area's largest. Its kayak tours include private and group paddles to Kealakekua Bay, sunset paddles and overnight camping.

DIVING

Between the Napo'opo'o landing and the southern tip of Manini Beach, marine life abounds amid coral, caves, crevices and ledges in waters up to 30ft deep. But the bay's best diving spot is Ka'awaloa Cove, where depths range from about 5ft to 120ft – the diversity of coral and fish is exceptional.

The aptly named **Long Lava Tube**, just north of Kealakekua Bay, is an intermediate dive site. Lava 'skylights' allow light to penetrate through the ceiling, yet nocturnal species are often active during the day, and you may see crustaceans, morays and even Spanish dancers. Outside are countless lava formations sheltering critters such as conger eels, triton's trumpet shells and schooling squirrelfish.

For dive shops, see p220. Also check out **South Kona Scuba** (☎ 322-5012; www.southkonascuba.net; 79-7539 Hwy 11, Kealakekua; 2-tank dive $100, intro dive $125), where dive master Tim Folden does only individual (never group) dives.

OF LONO, NAILS & CAPTAIN COOK'S BONES

On January 17, 1779, Captain Cook sailed into Kealakekua Bay, on his second visit to Hawaii in a year (see p38), touching off one of the strangest and most controversial months in Hawaii's incredible history.

Both of Cook's visits coincided with the annual *makahiki*, a four-month period when all warfare and heavy work was suspended to pay homage to Lono – the god of agriculture and peace – so Lono could fertilize the land. *Makahiki* was marked by an islandwide procession to collect the chief's annual tribute, which set off celebrations, sexual freedom and games.

Cook's welcome in Kealakekua Bay was spectacular: over 1000 canoes surrounded his ships, with 9000 more people on shore. Cook wrote in his journal, 'I had nowhere in the course of my voyages seen so numerous a body of people assembled in one place.'

Once landed, Cook was treated with supreme deference and led by a wizened kahuna (priest) through clearly religious ceremonies. The supposition has long been that Hawaiians regarded Cook as Lono incarnate, fulfilling prophecies Lono would one day return. This view is now vigorously disputed – on the grounds that Hawaiians could distinguish between gods and men. Instead, Cook was being feted as any ruling chief would be.

Either way, the Hawaiians threw huge celebrations and gave Cook and his men overwhelming offerings of food. The Hawaiians also bartered for goods – particularly for metals, which they'd never seen before. Though Cook tried to keep his sailors from having sex with Hawaiian women – from past experience he knew it spread deadly venereal disease – he failed utterly and gave up: Hawaiian women flocked to the boats, having sex freely and frequently in exchange for nails. Officers wrote that sailors would have pulled the ships apart if not stopped.

On February 4, restocked and ready to go, Cook departed Kealakekua Bay. But only a short way north, he encountered a huge storm, and the *Resolution* broke a foremast. Unable to continue, Cook returned to the safety of Kealakekua Bay on February 11.

HIKING

To snorkel Kealakekua Bay's Ka'awaloa Cove without renting a kayak or taking a boat tour, hike the **Captain Cook Monument Trail.** The trail itself is not especially interesting – and can be hot and buggy – but it leads right to the snorkeling cove. The way down is an easy hour, but after a morning of snorkeling, the uphill return seems twice as steep; allow two hours to return.

To get to the trailhead, turn *makai* off Hwy 11 onto Napo'opo'o Rd; within the first tenth of a mile, park along the road wherever it is safe. To find the trail entrance, count four telephone poles from the start of the road, and it's *makai* across from three tall palm trees. The trail is clear and easy to follow going down; when in doubt at a confusing spur, stay to the left. The trail ends at the place where kayaks pull up on the rocks. There are no facilities at the bottom; bring lots of water.

Returning uphill, stay right at the fork (back onto the lava ledge); left is a 4WD road that continues north along the coast for miles.

HORSEBACK RIDING

Kings' Trail Rides (☎ 323-2388, 345-0661; www.kona cowboy.com; 81-6420 Mamalahoa Hwy; rides Mon-Fri $135, Sat & Sun $150; ✆ 9am-4pm Mon-Fri) Kings' leads horseback trips to the coastline just north of Kealakekua Bay. Trips include lunch and possibly snorkeling if waters are calm. It's at the 111-mile marker.

Sleeping

Manago Hotel (☎ 323-2642; www.managohotel.com; Hwy 11; s/d $56-61/59-64, with shared bathroom $33/36, Japanese-style $75/78) The Manago is an absolutely classic Hawai'i experience. The shared-bath boarding-house rooms are the same today as they were over 80 years ago (but with more highway noise). A more modern block of motel-style rooms sits behind the historic building; the 2nd and 3rd floors are the hotel's quietest and enjoy ocean views. All are plain, no-frills, but well-kept rooms, with nothing to disturb your sleep – except for South Kona's roosters, which don't seem to understand the concept of crowing only at dawn. It's between the 109- and 110-mile markers.

Pomaika'i 'Lucky' Farm B&B (☎ 328-2112, 800-325-6427; www.luckyfarm.com; 83-5465 Mamalahoa Hwy; d incl breakfast $80-105) New owners, a genial father-daughter team from Virginia, have resuscitated this quirky property. One room shares

This time, no canoes rowed out in greeting. Chief Kalaniopu'u, nonplussed by Cook's return, seemed to indicate he'd worn out his welcome. For one, supplying Cook had already depleted the Hawaiians supplies of food, and they had little left to give. But also, the *makahiki* season had now ended; the party was over.

As Hawaiian generosity decreased, petty thefts increased; insults and suspicion replaced politeness on both sides. After a cutter (rowboat) was stolen, an agitated Cook ordered a blockade of Kealakekua Bay and decided to take chief Kalaniopu'u hostage until the boat was returned, a tactic that had worked well for him on other islands.

At dawn, Cook woke up Kalaniopu'u and, as a ruse, convinced him to come to the *Resolution* to resolve their disputes. But as they walked to shore, Kalaniopu'u received word that sailors had shot and killed a lower chief attempting to exit the bay in his canoe. At this, Kalaniopu'u apparently sat and refused to continue, as a large angry crowd gathered.

Thinking to frighten the Hawaiians, Cook fired his pistol, killing one of the chief's bodyguards. Incensed, the Hawaiians attacked. In the deadly melee, Captain Cook was stabbed with a dagger (made from metal from his own ship) and clubbed to death.

Cook's death stunned both sides and ended the battle. In the days afterward, the Hawaiians took Cook's body and dismembered it in the custom reserved for high chiefs. The Englishmen demanded Cook's body back, and in a spasm of gruesome violence torched homes and slaughtered anyone – women and children included. Eventually, the Hawaiians returned some bits and pieces – a partial skull, hands and feet – which the Englishmen buried at sea, as per naval tradition. However, the Hawaiians kept the bones – like femurs – that held the most mana (spiritual essence).

According to legend, for years afterward Cook remained part of the annual temple-to-temple *makahiki* procession, with priests carrying his dried bones in a red feather–covered wicker basket.

the main house, while attached are two pleasant 'Greenhouse' rooms with queen beds and screened windows. Separate and hidden by banana plants, the 'Barn' is a charmingly unadorned shack with screened, half-open walls and an outdoor shower; when you're snuggled under comforters, this is a budget traveler's jungle fantasy. Families are particularly welcome, and breakfast is a social occasion.

Luana Inn (☎ 328-2612; www.luanainn.com; 82-5856 Napo'opo'o Rd; r incl breakfast $180-200; 🅿 💻 🛜 🐾) Everything about this B&B is spacious, uncluttered and tastefully understated. Furnishings are modern, with muted colors and accent pieces, and all guest rooms have private entrances and stocked kitchenettes. Your hosts are a gracious, attentive young couple who are quite knowledgeable about the island and pride themselves on their gourmet-style breakfast. Best of all, the grassy grounds and sunny circular pool have an unforgettable sweeping view of Kealakekua Bay.

our pick Ka'awa Loa Plantation (☎ 323-2686; www.kaawaloaplantation.com; 82-5990 Napo'opo'o Rd; r incl breakfast $125-145, cottage $150, ste $195; 💻 🛜) This rambling plantation home, set in lush jungle gardens with towering mango trees, is one of South Kona's most romantic stays. Perhaps it's the dramatic four-poster beds, or the living room fireplace, or the tasteful art and fine linens, or the divine outdoor shower, or the hot tub and Hawaiian steam box. It certainly has to do with the aloha and attention to detail of the hosts. Or maybe it's just watching the sunset from the wraparound lanai, with seemingly the entire coast below. The suite has the only full bath (it's a doozy), and a separate cottage has a kitchenette but no views.

Eating

South Kona Green Market (🕙 9am-1pm Sun) Across from the Manago Hotel, this is a new farmers market – an interesting mix of organic produce, local specialties and funky crafts, plus pony rides for the kids.

Coffees 'n' Epicurea (☎ 328-0322; 83-5315 Hwy 11; 🕙 6:30am-6pm) A coffee-tasting room is an unlikely place for this sublime patisserie with flaky pastries, delicate éclairs and gorgeous pies. (The baker defected from the Kohala Coast resorts.) There's also a gift shop. It's on the *makai* side at the 106-mile marker.

Adriana's (☎ 217-7405; 936-8553; Kealakekua Ranch Center, Hwy 11; meals $3-6; 🕙 10am-5pm Mon-Fri,

10am-2pm Sat) These days, coffee pickers tend to hail from Mexico and Central America, which explains South Kona's several good taquerias. Adriana's mom, Juanita, rules the kitchen, serving delicious enchiladas, tacos and tamales from a takeout window. Cash only.

Super J's (☎ 328-9566; 83-5409 Hwy 11; plate lunches $3.50-9; ☷ 10am-6pm Mon-Sat) Stop in for takeout plate lunches of *laulau*, poi and *kalua* pig at this simple but friendly Hawaiian food stand. It's south of the 107-mile marker; cash only.

Kona Seafood (☎ 328-9777; 83-5308 Hwy 11; ☷ 10am-6pm Mon-Fri, 10am-5pm Sat & Sun) This tiny storefront is a must for fresh *poke* and other local specialties, plus fish and seafood to cook yourself. It's at the 106-mile marker.

Big Jake's BBQ (☎ 328-1227; Hwy 11; meals $6.50-16; ☷ 11am-6pm) Next to Kona Seafood, Big Jake's serves a flavorful pulled pork sandwich, along with other deliciously greasy delicacies cooked in the fat black barrel smoker out front.

ourpick Manago Hotel (☎ 323-2642; Hwy 11; breakfast $4-6, dinner mains $8-14; ☷ 7-9am, 11am-2pm & 5-7:30pm Tue-Sun) Like Teshima's, Manago's dining room is a quintessential South Kona experience. Part of its scuffed charm is that it still feels like a roadhouse, with a menu board and food rolling out on metal carts. Large Hawaiian and Japanese families know the dishes by heart, and the swift efficient service is based on a simple premise: order a main dish (fish, steak, teriyaki, burgers or the famous pork chops), which comes with several sides of the kitchen's choosing. Typically, it's some combination of pickled *ogo* (seaweed), potato-mac salad, baked beans, sweet black-eyed peas, a vegetable and white rice. The fish is excellent, but the lightly breaded and fried pork chops are Manago's signature; the owner says the secret is the pans, which were purchased in the 1920s from the Hilo Iron Works and are never used for anything else.

Coffee Shack (☎ 328-9555; 83-5799 Hwy 11; meals $9-14; ☷ 7:30am-3pm) Perched precariously next to the highway, the Shack is famous for the insane views of Kealakekua Bay from its open-air deck; you may never have a cup of coffee with a view to rival this one. However, the service and the food (omelettes, pizza and salads) can be inconsistent, and the prices high. It is definitely worth stopping, but save your real appetite. It's between the 108- and 109-mile markers.

Senor Billy's (☎ 323-2012; Hwy 11; mains $9-14; ☷ 11am-9pm) Turning this former fast-food joint inside out, Senor Billy's is an upscale taqueria with a groovy beach-shack vibe and a menu featuring a dozen tasty specialty burritos. No place in South Kona stays open as late, it mixes margaritas and other cocktails, and the black beans are flavored with whole garlic cloves – what's not to like?

South Kona's largest grocery store is **Choicemart** (☎ 323-3994; Kealakekua Ranch Center, Hwy 11; ☷ 6am-9pm Mon-Sat, to 8:30pm Sun).

Shopping

Art Farm (☎ 323-3495; Hwy 11; ☷ 10am-5pm Mon & Wed-Fri, 9am-4pm Sun) If this feels like a San Francisco art gallery, that's because the owner – who creates weird sheet metal paintings – hails from the 'City by the Bay.' The unique works by local artists will have you scratching your head, reaching for your wallet, or both.

HONAUNAU

pop 2450

Tiny Honaunau has no true village center; for travelers, it's more a loose collection of businesses along the highway, and is indistinguishable from Captain Cook.

Sights

ST BENEDICT'S PAINTED CHURCH

John Berchmans Velghe was a Catholic priest who came to Hawai'i from Belgium in 1899. Upon taking responsibility for St Benedict's **church** (☎ 328-2227; 84-5140 Painted Church Rd; admission free), he moved it 2 miles up from its original location on the coast near the *pu'uhonua* (place of refuge). It's not clear whether he did this as protection from tsunami or as an attempt to rise above – both literally and symbolically – what Christians considered pagan native culture.

Father John then painted the walls with a series of biblical scenes (now deteriorated) to aid in teaching the Bible. On columns topped with palm fronds are sayings in Hawaiian (with the admonishment 'Begone Satan!' among others).

PALEAKU GARDENS PEACE SANCTUARY

Near the church on Painted Church Rd, these tranquil seven-acre **gardens** (☎ 328-8084; www.paleaku.com; 83-5401 Painted Church Rd; admission $5; ☷ 9am-4pm Tue-Thu) contain shrines to the world's religions and an intriguing 'Galaxy Garden,' in which famous space painter Jon Lomberg has created a scale model of the

Milky Way – in plants. It's indeed a meditative, peaceful sanctuary.

Courses

SKEA (Society for Kona's Education & Art; ☎ 328-9392; www.skea.org; 84-5191 Mamalahoa Hwy) is a hotbed of activity, with Pilates, Polynesian dance and Japanese ink-painting classes, plus pidgin poetry readings and concerts on the lawn. Check the calendar, and look for it between the 105- and 106-mile markers.

Sleeping

Hale Ho'ola B&B (☎ 328-9117, 877-628-9117; www .hale-hoola.com; 85-4577 Mamalahoa Hwy; r incl breakfast $110-150; 💻 🛜) This friendly B&B makes for a homey, relaxed stay, with three small but comfortable rooms downstairs from the main house. Rooms have nice beds and lanais, but are positioned close together – though this makes for a more social atmosphere, particularly when everyone gathers for the generous breakfast.

our pick **Aloha Guest House** (☎ 328-8955, 800-897-3188; www.alohaguesthouse.com; 84-4780 Mamalahoa Hwy; r incl breakfast $140-280; 💻 🛜) Lose yourself, quite literally, in South Kona's lush upper slopes at this egregiously stylish five-room B&B. The commanding coastal views are unforgettable, whether from the cozy upstairs lanai or, in the upstairs rooms, while snuggled beneath your bed's gorgeous quilts. A relaxed elegance graces everything, from the open glass-block showers to the sage-and-copper hues to the gourmet breakfasts. Downstairs rooms (no view) are a bargain. Plus, there's an outdoor Jacuzzi, and your sophisticated, eco-conscious hosts know the Big Island intimately. Ask for directions; it's *mauka* 1 mile along local roads from Hwy 11.

Eating

South Kona Fruit Stand (☎ 328-8547; 84-4770 Hwy 11; smoothies $5.25-6.25, sandwiches $7-8.50 🕙 9am-6pm Mon-Sat, café 10am-4pm) This chichi organic fruit-and-vegetable stand sells only the cream of the crop. The café whips up heavenly fruit smoothies and good sandwiches; there are nice views from the outdoor patio. The stand is between the 103- and 104-mile markers.

Bong Brothers (☎ 328-9289; www.bongbrothers .com; Hwy 11; deli items $3-5; 🕙 9am-6pm Mon-Fri, 10am-5:30pm Sun) Food is politics at Bong Brothers, a small organic health food store and vegetarian takeout deli in an historic 1929 building.

The fresh-made curries, soups and salads are mouthwateringly delicious, even when served with ornery aloha by unrepentant agricultural activists. Bong Brothers has cool gift items, too.

PU'UHONUA O HONAUNAU NATIONAL HISTORICAL PARK

This impressive **national park** (☎ 328-2288, 328-2326; www.nps.gov/puho; 1-week pass adult/car $3/5; 🕙 7am-8pm, visitor center 8am-5:30pm) fronting Honaunau Bay provides one of the state's most evocative experiences of ancient Hawaii. The park's tongue-twister name simply means 'place of refuge at Honaunau.' In 2008, the park acquired 238 more acres, doubling its size; expect changes and new trails in the near future.

History

In ancient Hawai'i, the kapu system (strict ancient Hawaiian social and religious system) regulated daily life. A common person could not look at the *ali'i* (chief) or walk in his footsteps. Women could not prepare food for men or eat with them. One could not fish, hunt or gather timber except during certain seasons.

If one broke the kapu, the penalty was death, and kapu violators were hunted down and killed. This was done to appease the gods, who otherwise would become angry and possibly visit destruction upon the entire community – with famine, tidal waves or volcanic eruptions.

However there was one escape. Commoners who broke a kapu could get a second chance if they reached the sacred ground of a *pu'uhonua*. A pu'uhonua also gave sanctuary to defeated warriors, deserters and other men unable to fight (being, perhaps, too old or too young) during times of war.

To reach the *pu'uhonua* was a challenge. Since the grounds immediately surrounding the refuge were royal and therefore couldn't be crossed, kapu breakers had to swim through open ocean, braving sharks and currents, to reach safety. Once inside the sanctuary, priests performed ceremonies of absolution to placate the gods. Kapu breakers could then return home for a fresh start. The *pu'uhonua* at Honaunau was used for several centuries before being abandoned around 1819.

Sights

A half-mile **walking tour** encompasses the park's major sites – the visitor center hands

HAWAI'I THE BIG ISLAND

out a brochure map with cultural information. Avoid midday, as the park gets hot and is only partially shaded. While most of the sandy trail is accessible by wheelchair, sites near the water require traversing rough lava rock.

You enter the national park in the village-like royal grounds, where Kona ali'i (chiefs) and their warriors lived; this area's quiet spiritual atmosphere is greatly enhanced by the gently breaking waves and wind-rustled palms. **Hale o Keawe Heiau**, the temple on the point of the cove, was built around 1650 and contains the bones of 23 chiefs. It was believed that the mana (spiritual essence) of the chiefs remained in their bones and bestowed sanctity on those who entered the grounds. A fishpond, lava tree molds, a hand-carved koa canoe, and a few thatched huts and shelters are scattered through here. The royal canoe landing, a tongue of sand called **Keone'ele Cove**, is a favorite resting spot for sea turtles.

Carved wooden ki'i (deity images) standing up to 15ft high front an authentic-looking heiau reconstruction. Leading up to the heiau is the **Great Wall** separating the royal grounds from the pu'uhonua. Built around 1550, this stone wall is more than 1000ft long and 10ft high. Inside the wall are two older heiau platforms and legendary standing stones.

Just south of the park's central village area, an oceanfront palm tree grove holds one of South Kona's choicest **picnic areas**. Parking, picnic tables and BBQs face a wide slab of pa-hoehoe (smooth-flowing) lava, which is pock-marked with busy **tide pools** and littered with wave-tumbled lava rock boulders. Swimming is possible but can be dicey; judge the surf and entry for yourself.

Activities

Beyond the main village site, the park has one hiking trail and one of the island's best snorkeling spots. The park also holds traditional **hula and chanting classes** on Friday, usually between 4pm and 8pm; these are taught by the highly respected hula kumu Keala Ching, who is very welcoming of beginners. Respectful observers are also permitted.

SWIMMING & SNORKELING
Immediately north of the park is **Two-Step**, a stellar snorkeling spot that is also popular with divers and kayakers. Leave your car in the park's lot, and hang a left outside the entrance.

There's no beach – snorkelers step off a lava ledge beside the boat ramp into about 10ft of water, which quickly drops to about 25ft. Some naturally formed steps (hence the spot's name) make it fairly easy to get in and out of the water.

Visibility is usually excellent, especially with the noon sun overhead; good-sized reef fish and a fine variety of corals are close to shore. When the tide is rising, the water is deeper and it brings in more fish. The predatory 'crown of thorns' starfish can be seen here feasting on live coral polyps. Cool, freshwater springs seep out of the ground, creating blurry patches in the water. Divers can investigate a ledge a little way out that drops off about 100ft.

HIKING
The **1871 Trail** is a pretty hike (2-miles return) that leads to the abandoned village of Ki'ilae. The visitor center lends a trail guide describing the marked archaeological sites along the way; in all, it takes about an hour. However, the park's recent expansion was largely aimed at protecting more of this village site, and plans are underway to extend this trail.

Among other things, you pass a collapsed lava tube and a tremendous, if overgrown, holua (sled course) that ali'i raced sleds down. The steep **Alahaka Ramp** once allowed riders on horseback to travel between villages, and halfway up the ramp, the **Waiu o Hina lava tube** opens to the sea. Once an unofficial cliff-jumping site, it's now permanently closed (with bars).

From the top of the ramp, the incredible vista of ocean coves and ragged cliffs is a trail highlight; for confident snorkelers, some of these coves can provide water access in calm seas. Continuing on, you reach a gate that once marked the park's boundary; this is the current Ki'ilae Village site, where the ruins are pretty ruined, with almost nothing to see.

Festivals & Events
On the weekend closest to July 1, the park puts on a **cultural festival** with traditional displays and food, hukilau (net fishing) and a 'royal court.'

HO'OKENA
Ho'okena is a tiny, impoverished fishing village with no businesses to speak of, but it fronts a beautiful bay with a popular charcoal-sand **beach park**. This is primarily a locals'

spot, where large families picnic and teens hang out, blaring music from car speakers. Unlike Miloli'i, the vibe is mellow and open to outsiders and, particularly during the day, travelers should have no qualms about hanging out.

Ho'okena was once a bustling village. King Kalakaua dispatched his friend Robert Louis Stevenson here in 1889 to show him a typical Hawaiian village; Stevenson then wrote about Ho'okena in *Travels in Hawaii*. In the 1890s, Chinese immigrants moved into Ho'okena, a tavern and a hotel opened, and the town got rougher and rowdier. In those days, Big Island cattle were shipped from the Ho'okena landing, but when the circle-island road was built, the steamers stopped coming and people moved away. By the 1920s, the town was all but deserted.

Ho'okena's modest-sized beach is backed by a steep green hillside. The bay's waters are often calm and great for swimming and kayaking. The snorkeling is decent, though it drops off pretty quickly. There are strong currents further out. When the winter surf is up, local kids hit the waves with bodyboards.

The beach park has a picnic pavilion, bathrooms, showers and a concession stand, but no drinking water. Camping is right on the sand, at the base of the cliffs. Sites are awesome, but be warned that the beach is very isolated at night, and it's a favorite late-night drinking spot. Campers have occasionally been hassled. While there's now a security guard patrolling the park, survey the scene before committing yourself. A county permit (p561) is required.

The signed turnoff is between the 101- and 102-mile markers. A narrow road winds 2 miles down to the beach. Veer left at the bottom.

MILOLI'I

Miloli'i residents highly prize the traditional lifestyle of their modest fishing village, and they are very protective of it. Compared to Ho'okena, Miloli'i feels quite prosperous, with new homes dotting the hillsides (and a 1926 lava flow), well-kept churches, and fishermen zipping around in motorized boats – along with makeshift shacks and older fishermen patiently fixing their nets by the water. Miloli'i means 'fine twist,' and historically the village was known for its skilled sennit twisters, who used bark from the *olona* (a native shrub) to make fine cord and highly valued fishnets.

But Miloli'i is also known for its resistance to, and lack of, tourism. Villagers prefer their isolation and are not enthusiastic about visitors strolling through town. At the end of the steep, winding 5-mile road to the village is a small county **beach park** with bathrooms, a covered pavilion and camping (with a county permit; see p561). It's a beautiful spot with lots of tide pools, but it's also tiny and intimate, and you feel a bit like a stranger crashing a family reunion. In a way you are, and it may be most respectful to honor residents' desire for solitude.

The turnoff is just south of the 89-mile marker.

NORTH KONA COAST

As your plane lands on a cleared patch of runway in a barren landscape scoured by tongues of black lava, it's clear that Mt Hualalai rules the North Kona Coast. This arid, gently sloping terrain is so forbidding that modernity has made little headway domesticating it. A few resorts have bulldozed their way to the water's edge – where the sharp contrast of turquoise water, white sand, swaying palms and black rock make a paradisical scene. The only other thing catching your eye along the highway is the endless coral rock graffiti, shouted messages edging an existential landscape.

Were it not for those gorgeous beaches and those upscale resorts, North Kona would be a place to drive through without pausing, except for snapshots. For the best photo-ops take the upland Mamalaho Hwy (Hwy 190).

Also, according to scientists, the still-active Mt Hualalai isn't finished. On average the volcano erupts every 200 years, and the last eruption was in 1801 – the same flow, in fact, where the Kona airport now sits.

HONOKOHAU HARBOR

This small-boat harbor, Kona's largest, was built in 1970 to alleviate traffic off Kailua Pier. It is the main launching point for fishing charters, but other tours leave from here as well. To reach the harbor, from Hwy 19, turn *makai* on Kealakehe Parkway just north of the 98-mile marker.

Sights & Activities

To witness the sometimes dramatic weigh-ins from charter fishing boats, head to the

HAWAI'I THE BIG ISLAND

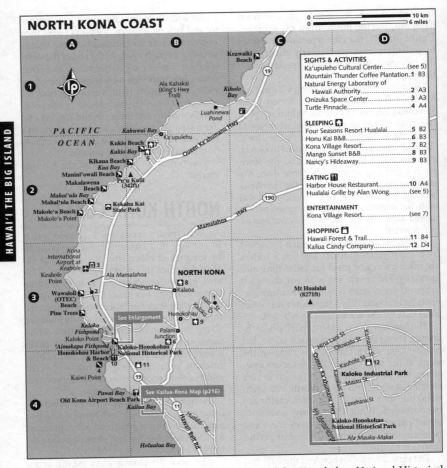

NORTH KONA COAST

SIGHTS & ACTIVITIES
Ka'upuleho Cultural Center..............(see 5)
Mountain Thunder Coffee Plantation.**1** B3
Natural Energy Laboratory of
   Hawaii Authority.........................**2** A3
Onizuka Space Center.......................**3** A3
Turtle Pinnacle..................................**4** A4

SLEEPING
Four Seasons Resort Hualalai.............**5** B2
Honu Kai B&B...................................**6** B3
Kona Village Resort...........................**7** B2
Mango Sunset B&B............................**8** B3
Nancy's Hideaway..............................**9** B3

EATING
Harbor House Restaurant..................**10** A4
Hualalai Grille by Alan Wong.........(see 5)

ENTERTAINMENT
Kona Village Resort.......................(see 7)

SHOPPING
Hawaii Forest & Trail.......................**11** B4
Kailua Candy Company.....................**12** D4

far side of the harbor, near the gas station; the weigh-in station is behind the deli. Charters typically arrive around 3:30pm, sometimes at 11am too, but call the Charter Desk first (☎ 329-5735); they'll know if any boats will be coming in. Boats fly flags to signal their catch: blue is marlin, white is ahi, and red is shark.

For information about snorkeling and diving tours and fishing charters departing from this harbor, see p218.

SNORKELING & DIVING
The area south of Honokohau Harbor all the way to Kailua Bay is a marine-life conservation district (accessible by boat); diving here is better than snorkeling, though also see the Kaloko-Honokohau National Historical Park (opposite).

Straight out from Honokohau Harbor, **Turtle Pinnacle** is a premier dive site for spotting turtles, which congregate here to let small fish feed off the algae and parasites on their shells.

Off **Kaiwi Pt**, south of Honokohau Harbor, sea turtles, large fish and huge eagle rays swim around some respectable drop-offs. Nearby is **Suck 'Em Up**, a couple of lava tubes. The swell pulls divers through like an amusement-park ride.

Eating
Harbor House Restaurant (☎ 326-4166; harbor complex; mains $7-18; 🕙 11am-7pm Mon-Sat, to 6pm Sun)

TOP PICKS – BEST BEACHES

- **Hapuna Beach** (p254)
- **Kauna'oa Bay** (p254)
- **Beach 69** (p254)
- **Waipi'o Valley** (p279)
- **Manini'owali Beach** (p246)
- **Makalawena Beach** (p245)
- **Green Sands Beach** (p324)
- **Kukio Bay Beaches** (p246)

After fishing, the place to spin your tale is at a wharfside table here. Order a happy hour schooner (18oz beer for $2.50; 4pm to 6pm Monday to Saturday, to 5:15pm Sunday), a burger or the excellent fish and chips, and start exaggerating. Service is good.

Shopping

Kailua Candy Company (☎ 329-2522, 800-622-2462; www.kailua-candy.com; cnr Kamanu & Kauhola Sts, Kaloko Industrial Park; ⏲ 8am-6pm Mon-Sat, noon-4pm Sun) Detour to this chocolate shop before boarding your flight home. Its celebrated chocolate-covered macadamia-nut *honu* ('turtles') are seriously yum, as are the Kona coffee swirls and truffles. They give good samples. Turn *mauka* on Hina Lani St off Hwy 19 and right on Kamanu St.

Hawaii Forest & Trail (☎ 331-8505, 800-464-1993; www.hawaii-forest.com; 74-5035B Hwy 19; ⏲ 7am-6pm Mon-Fri, 7am-5pm Sat & Sun) This tour company's headquarters is also a retail store selling high-quality outdoor gear and clothing, plus topo maps and a full range of outdoor guides. It has gas canisters, stoves, binoculars, packs and more. It's in a shopping center on Hwy 19 just south of Honokohau Harbor.

KALOKO-HONOKOHAU NATIONAL HISTORICAL PARK

Just north of Honokohau Harbor, this 1160-acre **national park** (☎ 329-6881; www.nps.gov/kaho; ⏲ visitor center 8:30am-4pm, park 24hr) is probably the island's most under-appreciated ancient Hawaiian site. The main draws are two ancient fishponds and a *honu*- (green sea turtle) friendly beach, but it also preserves ancient heiau and house sites, burial caves, petroglyphs, *holua,* and a restored 1-mile segment of the ancient King's Trail footpath. It's speculated that the bones of Kamehameha the Great were secretly buried near Kaloko.

The park takes its name from the two *ahupua'a* (ancient land divisions) it occupies. These comprise a seemingly desolate expanse of black lava, perhaps explaining the lack of visitation. But no worries. If the relatively short, hot trails through this otherworldly wasteland don't appeal (we actually like them), you can drive and see the highlights with hardly any hiking at all.

At the park's northern end is **Kaloko Fishpond**; it's the most interesting because its massive rock retaining wall is being completely rebuilt, so that the fishpond can once again be worked in the traditional way. It's wide enough to walk on, and provides gorgeous views. From the park's visitor center, drive north on Hwy 19 till you reach a separate gated entrance.

At the southern end is **'Aimakapa Fishpond**, the largest on the Kona Coast. Separated from the ocean by a high berm, it resembles a rectangular lake and is home to *ae'o* (Hawaiian black-neck stilt) and *'alae kea* (Hawaiian coot), which are both endangered native waterbirds. Adjacent to the fishpond is the salt-and-pepper **Honokohau Beach**, which is ideal for sunning, strolling and even swimming when waters are calm.

At the southern end of the beach is a heiau and the partially submerged **'Ai'opio Fishtrap**. In ancient times, fish swam into an opening in the rock wall at high tide and were trapped inside when the tide fell. Now it's a favorite spot for green sea turtles, who feed and rest by the handful. Humans are also allowed to swim (and snorkel) within the fishtrap's protected waters. It makes an ideal shallow *keiki* pool; just don't climb on the rocks or disturb the turtles. The south side has the sandiest entrances. There are pit toilets, but the only drinking water is at the visitors center. To drive to Honokohau Beach, enter Honokohau Harbor on Kealakehe Parkway, take the first right and follow signs to the entrance.

The main entrance to the park's visitor center is off Hwy 19 between the 96- and 97-mile markers.

KEAHOLE POINT

At Keahole Point the seafloor drops steeply just offshore, providing a continuous supply of both cold water from 2000ft depths and warm surface water. These are ideal conditions for –

you'll never guess – ocean thermal-energy conversion (OTEC).

Sights & Activities
NATURAL ENERGY LABORATORY OF HAWAII AUTHORITY
The **Natural Energy Laboratory of Hawaii Authority** (Nelha; www.nelha.org) was created by the state in 1974 to research OTEC and related technologies. Nelha has successfully generated electricity and continues to research methods to transform OTEC into an economically viable energy resource. **Public lectures** (☎ 329-8073; www .keaholepoint.org; per person $8; ☑ 10-11:30am Tue-Thu) are held (reservations required).

Today Nelha also sponsors a variety of commercial ventures, including aquaculture production of *ogo*, algae, abalone, lobster and black pearls. One of Nelha's tenants is a Japanese company that desalinates pristine Hawaiian seawater and sells it as a tonic in Japan. Their huge ponds are hard to miss.

The signed turnoff to Nelha is between the 94- and 95-mile markers.

WAWALOLI (OTEC) BEACH
The Nelha access road leads to Wawaloli Beach, perfectly positioned for sunset and containing oodles of tide pools along its rocky lava coastline. Swimming conditions are poor, but the quiet beach has bathrooms and outdoor showers. Enjoy a late-afternoon picnic as waves crash, the sun falls and the kids play in a protected *keiki* pool (best at high tide). Never mind the airplanes.

PINE TREES
Pine Trees, one of west Hawai'i's best **surfing breaks**, is just south of Nelha. Why Pine Trees? Early surfers spied mangrove trees near the break, which they thought were pines. No mangroves (or pines) are visible today, but the name stuck.

The break stretches along a pretty beach that is rocky enough to make swimming difficult. There is surf at a number of points depending on the tide and swell. The final bay gets the most consistent yet more forgiving waves. An incoming midtide is favorable, but as the swell picks up in winter these breaks often close out. This place attracts a crowd, so if you plan to paddle out, respect the priority of locals.

When the access road to Nelha veers to the right, look left for an extremely rutted dirt road leading about 2 miles further south to Pine Trees. You need a high-clearance 4WD to make it, or you can walk, but it's hot. Gates close between 8pm and 6am.

ONIZUKA SPACE CENTER
Astronaut Ellison S Onizuka Space Center (☎ 329-3441; Kona Airport; adult/child under 12 $3/1; ☑ 8:30am-4:30pm) pays tribute to the Big Island native who perished in the 1986 *Challenger* space shuttle disaster. The little museum has interesting astronaut and space exhibits and sits between the airport's departure and arrival buildings. Don't make a special trip, but it's worth finding if you're waiting for a flight.

MT HUALALAI SLOPES
To trek around Mount Hualalai, which is largely private land, you need to join a tour; contact either **Hawaii Forest & Trail** (☎ 331-8505, 800-464-1993; www.hawaii-forest.com) or **Hawaiian Walkways** ☎ 800-457-7759; www.hawaiianwalkways.com); see p209 for details.

Sights & Activities
MOUNTAIN THUNDER COFFEE PLANTATION
At an elevation of 3200ft, this organic **coffee farm** (☎ 325-2136; 888-414-5662; www.mountainthunder .com; 73-1944 Hao St; ☑ 9am-4pm, last tour 4pm) grows and roasts some of Kona's best coffee (with the awards to prove it). The key is the elevation, which allows the beans to ripen more slowly, and a commitment to quality, since each acre yields less. Mountain Thunder also offers the most-involved tours. The free 20-minute tour (every hour) is good (and wheelchair accessible), but the recommended two-hour VIP Tour (per person $30, reserve ahead, lunch extra) takes in the whole operation. Become Roast Master for a Day (call for rates), and you roast 5lb of your own beans. Call for directions.

KONA CLOUD FOREST SANCTUARY
Above 3000ft on the slopes of Mt Hualalai, the Kaloko Mauka subdivision contains this spectacular 70-acre **forest sanctuary** (www.kona cloudlforest.com) protecting an unusual 'cloud forest' ecosystem, where plants absorb moisture from clouds rather than from rain (hence the name), creating a lush haven for native plants and birds. The sanctuary also contains demonstration gardens of non-native species, such as over 100 varieties of bamboo, which horticulture expert Norm Bezona is studying for their viability and use on the Big Island. To

visit, contact **Hawaiian Walkways** (☎ 800-457-7759; www.hawaiianwalkways.com; tour adult/child $120/100), which has a daily morning tour, including a stop at Mountain Thunder Coffee.

Sleeping

Mango Sunset B&B (☎ 325-0909; www.mangosunset .com; 73-4261 Mamalahoa Hwy; r $95-110; 🖳 🛜) The organic Lyman Kona Coffee Farm also runs this three-room B&B. The gregarious owner reserves coffee tours for guests only; the estate does everything from seed to cup. The small, plain rooms are tightly bunched, but they are nicely cared for and share a lanai with sweeping coastal views. Two rooms share a bath, and all share a partial kitchen and grill. Breakfasts are a gourmet feast.

Nancy's Hideaway (☎ 325-3132, 866-325-3132; www.nancyshideaway.com; 73-1530 Uanani Pl; studio/cottage incl breakfast $130/150) If you're looking for peace and quiet, the two unfussy, unpretentious rooms in this pretty residential neighborhood are for you. Both the one-bedroom cottage and the studio have kitchenettes and plenty of room to get comfortable; furnishings are nice but plain. Since there are no lanais or shared spaces, you enjoy full privacy; a continental breakfast is left in the room. Call for directions.

Honu Kai B&B (☎ 329-8676; www.honukaibnb.com; 74-1529 Hao Kuni St; d incl breakfast $140-175; 🖳 🛜) Another get-away-from-it-all choice is this attractive four-room B&B. New owners have renovated rooms so they're plush and upscale, with rich fabrics, carved bed frames and Asian and Hawaiian decor; only the bathrooms remind you this is a suburban home. A separate cottage has full kitchen, and the well-tended gardens afford privacy and seclusion, whether lounging on the huge porch or in the Jacuzzi. Your hostess, to her chagrin, is a former Dallas Cowboys cheerleader.

KEKAHA KAI STATE PARK

The gorgeous beaches of **Kekaha Kai** (🕙 9am-7pm Thu-Tue) are all the more memorable for being tucked on the far side of a vast desert of unforgiving black lava. This nearly undeveloped 1600-acre park has four beaches, only one of which has paved access. The others are best approached with a 4WD or on foot, but if you hike, be prepared with good shoes, food and lots of water. It can be brutally hot, and once you reach the sand, you'll want to stay till the last drop of sunlight.

Sights & Activities
MAHAI'ULA BEACH

The park's largest, this rough, salt and pepper–sand **beach** is not the best for swimming. Kayakers put in here; during winter swells, surfing is popular on the bay's north side. The beach has shaded picnic tables and pit toilets. However, walk a few minutes north along the coast and you reach a second, less rocky, curved tan beach with soft sand (called Magoon's) that is perfect for sunning and swimming.

Mahai'ula Beach is at the end of the park's main entrance – a ragged 1.5-mile dirt road between the 90- and 91-mile markers. A 4WD is recommended; attempting it in a 2WD is just asking for a punctured oil pan (trust us, we know). The end of this road is the junction for Makalawena and Makole'a Beaches.

MAKALAWENA BEACH

Just before the parking lot for Mahai'ula, the road junction offers two choices: go south for Makole'a Beach, or go north for Makalawena Beach. If what you're after is an almost deserted, postcard-perfect strand of pristine white-sand beach, edged by ivy-covered dunes and cupping brilliant blue-green water, head north.

The service road to Makalawena Beach is cabled off, so you have to park and walk. Either follow the service road or follow the coastline from Mahai'ula Beach (a much nicer route), and aim for the abandoned red houses; north of these, a mile-long trail continues through nasty 'a'a (rough, jagged type of lava) to Makalawena.

After the broiling hike, it's shocking to emerge at this series of idyllic, scalloped bays with almost-glowing velvety white sand. If it's midweek, you might be the only one here. Swimming is splendid, though the surf can get rough, and bodyboarding and snorkeling are also attractive; sea turtles seem to prefer the furthest cove. Some like to rinse off in a brackish pond behind the southernmost cove. There is no official camping, though locals sometimes do, and they don't always appreciate fellow tenters.

MAKOLE'A BEACH

At the road junction, you can drive south to Makole'a Beach, but this section of road is definitely 4WD only; in fact, it's wise to park the 4WD after 1000yd, where coral marks the path

HAWAI'I THE BIG ISLAND

KONA COFFEE

From Puna to Ka'u, award-winning coffee is grown all over the Big Island, but it's unlikely that any region will ever dethrone Kona as the producer of Hawaii's most-famous cup of joe. Kona has been commercially producing coffee for over 160 years, and it's more successful today than ever.

Kona coffee accounts for less than 1% of coffee produced worldwide, and all of it comes from a strip of land just 2 miles wide and 22 miles long on the slopes of Hualalai and Mauna Loa – what's known as the Kona Coffee Belt. This region is patchworked with over 700 independent coffee farms, most covering only 3 to 10 acres. Because of the steep terrain, it's still necessary to hand-pick the beans, which are often dried the old-fashioned way: in the sun.

Coffee was introduced to the Big Island in 1828 by missionary Samuel Ruggles, who thought it made a pretty garden ornamental. By the 1840s coffee was being grown on plantations as a commercial crop and soon became a vital agricultural industry. In the 19th century, coffee was so important that cash-poor farmers used it as currency for buying groceries, and until 1969 public school 'vacations' were timed so that kids could help with the fall coffee harvest.

However the instability of world coffee prices eventually drove all the large plantations out of business, and the industry periodically struggled. Only the extraordinary high quality of Kona coffee allowed increasing numbers of independent, often immigrant farmers to survive, as some have for five generations and counting.

Why is Kona coffee so special? First and foremost, the climate. Sunny mornings usually give way to cloudy or rainy afternoons, while temperatures remain mild and frost-free. _Coffea arabica_ flourishes in these conditions, which occur in Kona at elevations between 800ft and 2800ft. Plus, there's the rich volcanic soil and a commitment to excellence: only superior beans (called 'Kona Typica') are grown, and cultivation and roasting remains a meticulous, handcrafted process.

In recent decades, there's been a surge in certified coffee estates – which do everything from seed to cup – and increased efforts to preserve Kona's reputation by protecting its label against deceptive 'Kona blends,' which by law need only contain 10% Kona beans. When shopping, look for the **Kona Coffee Council** (www.kona-coffee-council.com) seal of approval, and for more information, visit www.konacoffeefarmers.org. For a Hualalai coffee tour, see p229.

to the ocean. You won't get lost walking: either follow the road or follow the coastline from Mahai'ula Beach and make for the lone tree.

Lacking shade and too rocky for good swimming, this black-sand beach is most popular with local fisherman, but its beauty rewards those who make the effort.

MANINI'OWALI BEACH (KUA BAY)

Manini'owali Beach, also called Kua Bay, is another vision of paradise: a crescent-shaped white sand beach with sparkling turquoise waters that makes for first-rate swimming and bodyboarding, and even decent snorkeling when waters are calm. But unlike Makalawena, a paved road (built by the Kukio Bay resorts as a 'give back' to the community) leads right to it; the parking area has bathrooms and showers. Thus, Manini'owali draws major crowds, especially on weekends; arrive late, and cars will be parked a half mile or more up the road – meaning you have to hike here, too, but for the wrong reason.

To get here, take the paved access road between the 88- and 89-mile markers (north of the main Kekaha Kai entrance).

KA'UPULEHU

Once one of a string of fishing villages, Ka'upulehu was destroyed by the 1946 tsunami and abandoned until the Kona Village Resort opened here in 1965. It was joined by the Four Seasons Hualalai in 1996, and these resorts are the poshest on the island. By law the resorts must provide public access to the coast, meaning that anyone can enjoy the beautiful beaches on Kukio Bay for the cost of asking.

Sights & Activities
BEACHES

On the south end of Kukio Bay, **Kikaua Beach** is accessed through a private country club. Come early, as beach parking is limited to 28 stalls and can fill up. This lovely, quiet, tree-shaded beach contains a protected cove where kids can swim and snorkel in bathtub-calm water; around the kiawe-covered point, sea turtles line up to nap. Both this and Kukio Beach have bathrooms, showers and drinking water. Access is via Kuki'o Nui Rd near the 87-mile marker; request a pass at the gate.

From Kikaua Beach, you can see (and walk to) the bay's northern **Kukio Beach**, which is within the grounds of the Four Seasons. This brochure-worthy crescent of sand is great for swimming or lounging away a perfectly good afternoon. You can follow a paved footpath north past some intriguing lava rock coastline to another beach. To drive here, turn onto the (unsigned) Ka'upulehu Rd between the 87- and 86-mile markers; go to the Four Seasons gate and request a beach pass. Public parking accommodates 50 cars and almost never fills up.

KA'UPULEHO CULTURAL CENTER
Don't miss this often-overlooked Native Hawaiian **cultural center** (☎ 325-8520; Four Seasons Resort; admission free; ✆ 8:30am-4pm Mon-Fri) on the grounds of the Four Seasons. Excellent displays are organized around the center's incredible collection of 11 original paintings by Herb Kawainui Kane (which the Four Seasons commissioned in 1995). Each work portrays an ancient craftsman or elder, and is accompanied by a hands-on exhibit: shake an *'uli'uli* (feathered hula rattle), test the heft of a *kapa* (mulberry tree bark) beater or war club, examine adze heads and pandanus paint brushes. It's run by Hawaiian cultural practitioners who actively link the present with the past. The center holds classes (usually open to resort guests only), but they'll happily refer you to *kumu* directly. At the Four Seasons gate, tell them you're visiting the center.

Sleeping
Four Seasons Resort Hualalai (☎ 325-8000; 888-340-5662; www.fourseasons.com/hualalai; 72-100 Ka'upulehu Dr; r $775-1155, ste from $1525; ✆ 🖥 📶 📺) The only five-diamond resort on the Big Island, the Four Seasons exudes taste, luxury and class. Service is impeccable, accommodations are without flaw, and the tone – from the PGA-tour golf course to the luxurious spa to the world-class restaurant to the last detail of the sumptuous furnishings – is one of understated elegance. The resort aims to please those who don't need to be impressed, but simply want everything perfect. It is only overpriced if you have to worry about price.

Kona Village Resort (☎ 325-5555, 800-367-5290; www.konavillage.com; 1 Kahuwai Bay Dr; 1-room hale $660-$1200, 2-room hale $975-1475; 📶 📺) When this 82-acre hideaway resort opened in 1965 it was so isolated guests had to fly in. That 'lost' feeling is cultivated today. Kona Village is a truly unplugged resort: accommodations are individual thatch-roof *hale* (houses) lacking TVs, phones, radios and wi-fi (cell phones are forbidden from being used outside them). The sprawling layout ensures a maximum of privacy, and service is genuinely friendly and professional without the stuffy corporate deference of other resorts. Plus, rates include three meals a day and special events like the luau and BBQ night; kids programs are free. Guests are encouraged, in other words, to relax, whether they're rock stars, senators, or average joes. And don't worry: *hale* interiors are stylishly luxurious; some have the ocean practically lapping at their lanai. Kona Village is an oasis from modern life, and when you do the math, a surprisingly affordable one at that.

Eating
Hualalai Grille by Alan Wong (☎ 325-8525; Golf Clubhouse, Four Seasons Resort Hualalai; mains $30-56; ✆ 5:30-9pm) Nicknamed the '19th Hole,' the Hualalai Grille was under the direction of celebrity chef Alan Wong till 2008, when he passed the ladle to *chef du cuisine* James Ebreo. Ebreo promises to continue emphasizing 'farm-to-table island cuisine' – which Wong elevated to the best fine dining on the island – while using locally grown produce as much as possible. Expect to see Kona *kampachi* (yellowtail) and ahi and Keahole lobster as the menu evolves. The bar opens at 2pm with a limited menu of Kobe beef sliders and lobster wontons. Reservations are highly recommended.

Drinking & Entertainment
Kona Village Resort (☎ 325-5555, 800-367-5290; 1 Kahuwai Bay Dr; adult/child 3-5/child 6-12 $97/40/67; ✆ from 6pm Wed & Fri) What really sets this commercial luau apart is the food, which offers a wide selection of better-prepared Hawaiian specialties. The shows are also excellent: the Wednesday show focuses on the history of Hawaiian hula, and the Friday show is the more typical Polynesian buffet of sexy dancing and fire twirlers. Only one (one!?) cocktail is included. Reserve ahead.

KIHOLO BAY

With its pristine turquoise waters and shoreline fringed with coconut trees, dramatic **Kiholo Bay** (☉ 7am-7pm) is yet another oasis. Indeed, Kiholo Bay makes a good alternative to Kekaha Kai beaches, since the graded access road is kind to 2WD and the black-sand beach is remarkably uncrowded.

The 2 mile–wide bay rewards explorers. The main beach (near the parking lot) is pebbly, and swimming is fine when seas are calm. Follow a trail south over the lava to find secluded pockets of fine black sand, and further south, a coconut grove surrounding **Luahinewai**, a lovely spring-fed pool. Walking north, low tide reveals tide pools that are popular feeding and napping grounds for sea turtles and offer plenty of snorkeling possibilities. Inland near the end of the gravel path is a lava tube filled with clear freshwater; adventurous swimmers can check it out. You'll pass a gargantuan private estate with a yellow mansion and tennis courts, and at the northern end, you can walk across a shallow channel to a small island with white sand.

To get here, turn *makai* on the graded gravel road between the 82- and 83-mile markers. Follow the road for a mile, taking the left-hand fork and parking at the abandoned roundhouse.

For a little more adventure and even more solitude, check out **Keawaiki Beach** just north of Kiholo Bay. This secluded black-sand strand fronts the former estate of Francis I'i Brown, an influential 20th-century Hawaiian businessman. It's fine for swimming when calm, but wear reef shoes, as sea urchins like the rocks. To get here, park between the 78- and 79-mile markers on Hwy 11; there's a small lot in front of a boulder-blocked gravel road. Walk the road to the estate's fence, then follow the trail to the right around the fence to the beach.

SOUTH KOHALA

What began in North Kona continues in South Kohala: the sometimes plumb-straight highway cuts through sweeping coastal plains. Stark lava fields alternate with barren pastures, all baking under a relentless sun. Punctuating the drive, a series of sumptuous resorts have carved green oases at the water's edge on some of the island's best beaches – making their own beaches, if necessary. This region is known as the Gold

TOP PICKS – SCENIC DRIVES

- **Chain of Craters Road** (p313)
- **Kohala Mountain Road** (p259)
- **Highway 270 from Hawi to Pololu Valley** (p263)
- **Saddle Road** (p276)
- **South Point Road** (p323)
- **Highway 19 along the Hamakua Coast** (p277)
- **Old Mamalahoa Highway from Waimea to Holualoa** (p269)
- **Red Road in Puna** (p304)

Coast, but whether that's for the sun, the prevalence of yellow tang in the waters or the wealth generated by tourism, it's hard to say.

In contrast to the very modern world of the resorts, South Kohala also contains numerous ancient Hawaiian sights. Apparently, the Kohala Coast (including North Kohala) was more populated then than now, and the region is packed with village sites, heiau, fishponds, petroglyphs and historic trails.

WAIKOLOA RESORT AREA
pop 4800

The celebrated Waikoloa Resort area has a lot to offer and makes a compelling destination: in addition to two huge first-rate resorts – along with their golf courses, spas and gourmet restaurants – there are two wide-ranging and attractive outdoor shopping malls, regular cultural events and entertainment, a good beach and a huge petroglyph field.

Inland from the resort area is Waikoloa Village; this 'town' of condo complexes was originally meant to be affordable housing for resort workers, but it's now become more an upscale haven for retirees. The village contains a range of shops and services, but nothing you can't get in the resort area.

Sights & Activities
WAIKOLOA PETROGLYPH PRESERVE

A lava field etched with impressive petroglyphs, many dating back to the 16th century, is located beside the Kings' Shops. Some are graphic (humans, birds, canoes) and others cryptic (dots, lines); some from the 19th century are the English-lettered names of the men who made the King's Road along here. From

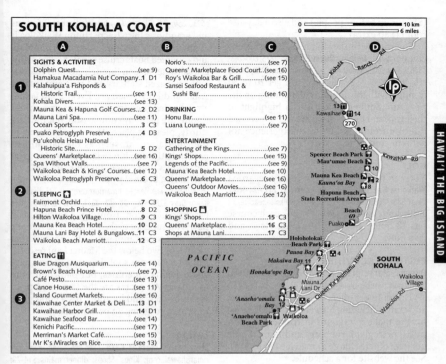

HAWAI'I THE BIG ISLAND

the Kings' Shops outdoor malls, a five-minute walk along a signposted path leads to the first of the etchings. Stay on the path to avoid damaging the petroglyphs, and bring water and a hat, as it's hot and exposed.

The Kings' Shops offers a free, one-hour **petroglyph tour** (☺ tours 10:30am Thu-Sun).

'ANAEHO'OMALU BEACH PARK

Dubbed 'A Bay' by the linguistically challenged, this artificial **beach** (☺ 6am-8pm) feels like the thin drawn line of a draftsman's pencil – one that in winter must be protected by a three-foot berm of sand to keep from being washed away. Nevertheless, it's a perfectly lovely narrow strip with shady palms separating an extremely calm bay from two ancient fishponds. It's popular with families, swimmers and picnickers; snorkeling is decent at the north end, in front of the sluice gate. You can also follow the coast south and discover more sandy patches, while a short footpath with interpretive plaques passes ancient Hawaiian fishponds, caves, ancient house platforms and a shrine. Drinking water, showers and bathrooms are available.

At the northern end, next to a fitness area and volleyball net, is **Ocean Sports** (☎ 886-6666, ext 2; www.hawaiioceansports.com; ☺ 8:30am-5pm), which rents kayaks (single/double per hour $18/$22), hydro-bikes and snorkel gear at scandalous prices. It also offers scuba-diving and surfing lessons, as well as a variety of activity and sunset cruises.

To get here, turn left off Waikoloa Beach Dr opposite the Kings' Shops.

HILTON POOLS & DOLPHIN SWIM

The grounds of the Hilton Waikoloa Village (p250) both feel and operate like a theme park. There's a man-made beach on a protected lagoon (frequented by sea turtles and tropical fish), two ridiculously enormous serpentine pools (with multiple waterslides, waterfalls, hot tubs, and sandy toddler areas), and a minigolf course. The centerpiece, though, is the large enclosed pond holding a handful of playful bottlenose dolphins. Nonguests are welcome to stroll the grounds and watch the dolphin shows for free. To swim in the pools and lagoon (catnip to kids), you can buy a nonguest pool pass

($80 for up to four people) and also a day-use room ($80 extra).

To swim with the dolphins, book an encounter with **Dolphin Quest** (☎ 886-2875, 800-248-3316; www.dolphinquest.org; per person from $200, family of up to 6 $1300; ☯ 8:30am-5pm). You get 20 to 30 minutes with the dolphins, depending on the program. Some consider this a highlight of their trip, and the dolphins are well supervised during encounters, but it's an experience not without controversy (see p171).

GOLF
You can't go wrong at the highly regarded **Waikoloa Beach & Kings' Courses** (☎ 877-924-5656, Kings' 886-7888, beach 886-6060; www.waikoloabeachresort .com/golf.php; guests/nonguests $130/195); each course has 18 holes' worth of stunning views and lava flows.

CULTURAL ACTIVITIES
Queens' Marketplace (☎ 886-8822; www.waikoloa beachresort.com/big-island-shopping; 201 Waikoloa Beach Dr; ☯ 11:30am-1:30pm) offers daily cultural activities and crafts, including hula and ukulele lessons, how to make *ipu* (gourd instrument used in hula), petroglyph rubbings and more. Some are free; others charge a small fee ($5 to $15). See the website for a schedule.

Festivals & Events
Great Waikoloa Food, Wine & Music Festival
(☎ 886-1234, www.dolphindays.com; Hilton Waikoloa Village; admission $120) On the third Saturday in June, this festival is the culmination of the Hilton's four-day Dolphin Days event. It combines two dozen of the state's prominent chefs with an array of fine wines and boutique brews, plus jazz music.

A Taste of the Hawaiian Range (☎ 322-4892; www .ctahr.hawaii.edu/taste/; Hilton Waikoloa Village; admission $35) Held in early October. Celebrated Big Island chefs work magic with local range-fed meats and local produce at this food event. Portions are generous and the price is right.

Moku O Keawe (☎ 886-8822; www.mokif.com; Waikoloa Resort Area; hula competition admission per night $15) Held in early November. Established in 2006, this three-night international hula competition includes *kahiko* (ancient), *'auana* (modern) and *kapuna* (elder) categories; gets top Japanese hula troupes and includes wonderful hula arts workshops. A great, less-crowded alternative to the iconic Merrie Monarch Festival (p294).

Sleeping
Hilton Waikoloa Village (☎ 886-1234, 800-445-8667; www.hiltonwaikoloavillage.com; 69-425 Waikoloa Beach Dr;

r $230-650; ⊠ ▢ 🛜 ⌨) Gleefully ostentatious and grandiose, the 62-acre Hilton Waikoloa is as much event as accommodation. A monorail and canopied boats cruise canals past an artificial saltwater lagoon through grounds studded with oversized statuary and museum-quality Asian and Polynesian art. Every bend is theatrically designed to elicit ooohs and ahhhs. Rooms are plain by comparison, but they are sturdy, pleasing places to rest in between all the entertainment, such as the gargantuan pools and the dolphin swims (p249). It's great for families, but watch out for extra fees.

Waikoloa Beach Marriott (☎ 886-6789, 877-924-5656; www.waikoloabeachmarriott.com; 69-275 Waikoloa Beach Dr; r $284-550; ⊠ ▢ ⌨) The Marriott's beachside location, fronting 'Anaeho'omalu Bay, is far superior to the Hilton's, and recently renovated rooms are a notch above as well (but a notch or two below the Mauna Lani resorts). Muted colors are soothing, and rooms have good-quality amenities, but bathrooms are mundane. All rooms are the same size; price varies by view and location. It's a good place to save by forgoing an ocean vista.

Eating
Merriman's Market Café (☎ 886-1700; www.mer rimanshawaii.com; Kings' Shops; dinner mains $14-28; ☯ 11:30am-9:30pm) This Kings' Shops location of the famous Merriman's in Waimea (p268) is more low-key and casual, but it serves similar Mediterranean-influenced dishes featuring organic island-grown produce, locally caught fish and artisanal breads, cheeses and wines. The dinner menu includes a range of delicious midpriced tapas and salads to tide you over while shopping, but the mall setting undercuts its ambience.

our pick Sansei Seafood Restaurant & Sushi Bar (☎ 886-6286; www.sanseihawaii.com; Queens' MarketPlace; sushi $4-22, mains $20-40; ☯ 5:30-10pm, till 1am Fri & Sat) Celebrity chef DK Kodama opened this Big Island outlet of his lauded Maui restaurant to great acclaim. Promising 'new wave sushi,' Sansei delivers fun, innovative, fusion Japanese cuisine. Signature dishes – like the panko-crusted ahi roll with spinach – have visual panache and vibrant flavors. Even seaweed salad comes in a martini glass. The dining room is bright, loud and upbeat, encouraging a good time rather than intimate conversation.

Roy's Waikoloa Bar & Grill (☎ 886-4321; Kings' Shops; mains $26-35; ☯ 5-9:30pm) The renowned Roy Yamaguchi opened his first restaurant over

20 years ago, leading a wave of Hawaiian fusion cuisine. Today, Hawaiian fusion is everywhere (and his restaurant is an international chain), but Roy's still sets the standard. You will appreciate delicate blackened ahi all over again, and dishes like rack of lamb in a *liliko'i* (passion fruit) cabernet sauce will knock your socks off.

Queens' Marketplace (☎ 886-8822; www.waikoloa beachresort.com/big-island-shopping; 201 Waikoloa Beach Dr; ⏰ food court 7:30am-9:30pm) has a budget-friendly fast-food court (Subway, Dairy Queen etc) and **Island Gourmet Markets** (☎ 886-3577; ⏰ 7am-10pm), an enormous upscale grocery store with fresh produce and tons of picnic-ready takeout: sushi, poke, *bentō*, Spam *musubi* (fried Spam and rice sushi), and more.

Entertainment

The Waikoloa luaus are crowd-pleasers, but neither serves food as good as that at the Kona Village luau (p247).

Legends of the Pacific (☎ 886-1234, ext 54; Hilton Waikoloa Village; adult/child 5-12 $99/59; ⏰ shows 6pm Tue & Fri) The Hilton's luau includes a colorful show, one cocktail and a dinner buffet with a lavish dessert selection.

Waikoloa Beach Marriott (☎ 886-6789, 888-924-5656; adult/child 6-12 $88/40; ⏰ shows 5pm Sun & Wed) The open bar at this luau makes the Hawaiian-style dinner buffet seem even tastier and the show even more vibrant.

Queens' Marketplace (☎ 886-8822; www.waikolo abeachresort.com/big-island-shopping) A hub of entertainment. In the mall's central pavilion, hula and Hawaiian music performances occur daily (shows from 5pm Monday to Friday, 2pm to 4pm Saturday and Sunday), while Queens' Outdoor Movies (Friday at dusk) shows free family-friendly, second-run Hollywood flicks on an outdoor screen; chairs provided. The marketplace also has a new outdoor stage, Queens' Gardens, that books rock concerts and cultural events; for a schedule, check Waikoloa Nights (www.waikoloanights.com).

Kings' Shops (☎ 886-8811; www.kingsshops.com; ⏰ shows 6pm Mon-Fri, 4pm Sat & Sun) Has free performances of Hawaiian music and dance daily; try to catch excellent local slack key guitarist John Keawe, who's a regular.

Shopping

Kings' Shops (☎ 886-8811; www.kingsshops.com; 250 Waikoloa Beach Dr; ⏰ 9:30am-9:30pm) Satisfy your inner clothes horse at the designer boutiques and cute shops – like Louis Vuitton, L'Occitane, Cinnamon Girl, Crazy Shirts – at this outdoor shopping mall.

Queens' Marketplace (☎ 886-8822; www.waikoloa beachresort.com/big-island-shopping; 201 Waikoloa Beach Dr; ⏰ 9:30am-9:30pm) This newer shopping complex offers more affordable island fashion and gifts, at stores like like Giggles and Reyn's.

MAUNA LANI RESORT AREA

The Mauna Lani resort area is home to two large hotels, 36 holes of golf, condo complexes, a shopping mall and nice beaches. But it deserves special attention for the significance of its historical sites, as well as for the Mauna Lani Bay Hotel's refreshingly open attitude toward nonguests who wish to explore its beach, trails, ancient sites and petroglyph preserve.

Sights

BEACHES

The long and lovely beach fronting the Mauna Lani Bay Hotel is protected, but the gentle water is rather shallow; snorkelers might prefer exploring a coral reef beyond the inlet. Also, a 10-minute walk south of the hotel (take the trail past the fishponds), **Makaiwa Bay** protects a small placid cove in front of the Mauna Lani Beach Club condos.

If you keep walking south along the old coastal trail, after about a mile you reach **Honoka'ope Bay**. This salt-and-pepper beach has nice swimming and snorkeling when seas are calm. If you want to drive, take the road to the golf courses and turn left at Honoka'ope Rd.

At the Fairmont Orchid, the public access beach on **Pauoa Bay** is shunted to the side of the lovely, protected cove with the best snorkeling; nonguests can snorkel too, but have to pay.

Holoholokai Beach Park

North of the Fairmont Orchid, this beach is a rocky stretch of coral chunks and lava. It makes for great picnicking but lousy swimming, though snorkeling is fine during calm surf. Facilities include showers, drinking water, rest rooms, and picnic tables.

To get there, take Mauna Lani Dr and turn right at the rotary, then right again on the beach road immediately before the Fairmont Orchid. The park leads to the Puako petroglyphs.

HAWAI'I THE BIG ISLAND

TOP PICKS – SUSHI FEASTS

- **Sushi Rock** (p260)
- **Sansei Seafood Restaurant & Sushi Bar** (p250)
- **Norio's** (opposite)
- **Sushi en Fuego** (p223)
- **Kenichi Pacific** (p228)
- **Sushi Bar Hime** (p296)

KALAHUIPUA'A FISHPONDS

These ancient **fishponds** lie along the beach just south of the Mauna Lani Bay Hotel, partly shaded by a grove of coconut palms and *milo* (native hardwood) trees. They are among the few still-working fishponds in Hawai'i, and are stocked, as in ancient times, with *awa* (Hawaiian milk fish). Water circulates from the ocean through traditional *makaha* (sluice gates), which allow small fish to enter but keep mature, fattened catch from leaving. The rock walls of the sluice gates hide moray eels; drop in some *poke* and watch a dozen gape-jawed heads emerge.

KALAHUIPUA'A HISTORIC TRAIL

This easy **trail** begins on the inland side of the Mauna Lani Bay Hotel, at a marked parking lot opposite the resort's little grocery store. Pick up a free, self-guided trail map from the concierge desk.

The first part of the trail meanders through a former Hawaiian settlement dating from the 16th century, passing lava tubes once used as cave shelters and a few other archaeological sites marked by interpretive plaques.

The trail then skirts fishponds lined with coconut palms and continues out to the beach, where there's a thatched shelter with an out-rigger canoe and a historic cottage with a few Hawaiian artifacts. Continue southwest past the cottage to loop around the fishpond and back to your starting point – a round-trip of about 1.5 miles.

PUAKO PETROGLYPH PRESERVE

With more than 3000 **petroglyphs**, this preserve is one of the largest collections of ancient lava carvings in Hawai'i, and it makes for a thought-provoking experience. The simple, linear human figures are among the oldest examples of such drawings in Hawai'i; some date

to 1000 AD. The symbols are tantalizingly evocative, but like all ancient petroglyphs, their meaning remains enigmatic.

The trail begins at the *mauka* end of the Holoholokai Beach parking lot. The initial section is paved and wheelchair accessible, and it leads to a collection of stunning petroglyphs arranged in a circle. The well-marked, extremely dusty trail then leads another 1300yd through a moody kiawe forest to the main site. Here, a basketball court–size field is crammed with etchings and figures like some crazy ancient census. Wear shoes (not rubbah slippahs) and avoid midday, as it gets dry and hot.

Activities

GOLF

Golfers can certainly spoil a good walk on the challenging **Francis I'i Brown North & South Courses** (☎ 885-6655; www.maunalani.com; green fee guest/non-guest $145/210). The South Course has a signature 15th-hole featuring a tee shot over crashing surf. The North Course has a par-three 17th hole within an amphitheater of black lava rock. Some golfers dream their whole lives of playing on carpetlike greens like these.

SPAS

While the husband's away...the **Mauna Lani Spa** (☎ 881-7922; Mauna Lani Bay Hotel & Bungalows; massages from $145, facials from $155; ⏰ treatments 9am-5:30pm) awaits. It's a visual delight, with extravagant tropical landscaping, a lava-rock sauna and calm pools for water therapy. Treatments are equally elaborate.

The Fairmont Orchid's **Spa Without Walls** (☎ 887-7540; www.fairmont.com/orchid; Fairmont Orchid; indoor/outdoor massages from $159/169, facials from $145; ⏰ treatments 8am-7pm) conducts business in alfresco *hale* hidden amid orchids, coconut palms, waterfalls and lily ponds.

Sleeping

our pick **Mauna Lani Bay Hotel & Bungalows** (☎ 885-6622, 800-367-2323; www.maunalani.com; 68-1400 Mauna Lani Dr; r $445-935, ste from $985; 🅿 🖳 🛜 🆒) The vaulted interior lobby sets the tone, creating an airy, serene space to relax while *honu* nibble lettuce in lazy pools nearby. The architecture feels a bit retro, but rooms are nicely appointed and positioned (most have ocean views; mountainside rooms are slightly bigger), with first-rate amenities and decor. Attractive baths have sliding wood–shutter doors, and his- and her- vanities. The feeling of aloha is enhanced by the considerate staff, the commitment to Hawaiian culture and the resort's eco-conscious approach: it makes significant use of solar power, plants drought-resistant grass, uses recycled water for irrigation and participates in a reforestation program. Most basic services (parking, phone, wi-fi etc) are included.

Fairmont Orchid (☎ 885-2000, 800-845-9905; www .fairmont.com/orchid; 1 N Kaniku Dr; r $500-900, ste from $1100; 🅿 🖵 🛜 🐾) Rooms at the Orchid are equivalent to the Mauna Lani in terms of amenities, but decor is just that little bit nicer: a medley of warm browns and oranges, classy furnishings, and egregiously nice marble baths with separate tub, shower and toilet. There is a corporate edge to the pampering, but it is an indulgent embrace nonetheless; the resort offers every sort of activity, an all-day kids program, and can no doubt satisfy any whim you dream up. As at the Mauna Lani, the grounds are luscious and idyllic.

Eating

Kenichi Pacific (☎ 881-1515; Shops at Mauna Lani; sushi $7-16, mains $28-44; 🕑 5-9:30pm Tue-Sat) The Mauna Lani branch of this Keauhou favorite (see p228) offers an almost identical menu and the same excellent happy hour (4pm to 6pm Tuesday to Friday). The mall setting isn't swoon-worthy, but your palate will still get the flutters: order favorites like *ono tataki* (seared wahoo), diver scallop curry, and spicy tuna tempura rolls.

Norio's (☎ 887-7320; Fairmont Orchid; sushi rolls $11-22, mains $29-46; 🕑 6-9pm Thu-Mon) Chef Norio Yamamoto specializes in classic Japanese cuisine, especially sushi and sashimi featuring fresh locally caught seafood. Don't expect wild invention, just perfectly done preparations and rich entrées like grilled Kobe-style beef and seared foie gras sushi.

Canoe House (☎ 885-6622; Mauna Lani Bay Hotel & Bungalows; mains $29-49; 🕑 6-9pm) The outdoor oceanfront patio of the Mauna Lani's signature restaurant almost catches the mist from breaking waves (lit at night). This tranquil romantic mood is only enhanced by the food, which doesn't turn cartwheels to get your attention. Instead, expect classic entrées like rib-eye steak, blackened ahi and scallops, and BBQ rack of lamb with local-grown and island touches – adding Hamakua mushrooms here and Waipi'o Valley fern shoots there.

Brown's Beach House (☎ 887-7368; Fairmont Orchid; mains $32-68; 🕑 5:30-9pm) At the Orchid, Brown's enjoys an envy-inducing seaside position, while its imposing menu is designed to impress gourmets and high rollers. The chef turns out high-end cuisine highlighting Big Island produce and the freshest local seafood. Keahole lobster is prepared several ways, and the crab-encrusted fresh catch with mango beurre blanc is widely acclaimed.

Foodland Farms (☎ 887-6101; 🕑 5am-11pm) For groceries or a takeout lunch, head to this full-service gourmet supermarket at the Mauna Lani shopping mall.

Drinking & Entertainment

Gathering of the Kings (☎ 326-4969; http://island breezeluau.com/gotk; Fairmont Orchid; adult/child 6-12 $99/65; 🕑 Tue & Sat) This luau spins a thread of storytelling to highlight slightly modernized versions of Polynesian and Hawaiian dance and music; it's notable for its above average Polynesian dinner buffet and an open bar.

Honu Bar (☎ 885-6622; Mauna Lani Bay Hotel; 🕑 5:30-11pm) Fans spin over wooden floors and comfy chairs at this bar with a garden view. The hotel atrium has live Hawaiian music and hula dancing nightly from 6pm to 9pm.

Luana Lounge (☎ 885-2000; Fairmont Orchid; 🕑 4-11pm) This casual indoor-outdoor patio is a cozy spot to enjoy sunset with a drink and appetizers.

SHOPPING

Shops at Mauna Lani (☎ 885-9501; 68-1330 Mauna Lani Dr) This upscale mall is similar to Kings' Shops in Waikoloa. A small stage has a free hula show, Ho'oilina (at 7pm Monday, Wednesday and Friday), a fun if silly concoction of sexy hula set against film clips of exploding lava and movies from Hollywood's golden age.

PUAKO
pop 430

Puako is a tiny beach town that's lucky to remain off the beaten track. The main road is two miles of modest homes interspersed with signed 'shoreline access' points. A small general store is open daily.

Sights & Activities

The main attraction at Puako is giant **tide pools**, set in the swirls and dips of *pahoehoe* (smooth-flowing type of lava) coastline. Some pools are deep enough to shelter live coral. There's no sandy beach; instead a narrow strip of pulverized coral and lava lines much of the shore. Snorkeling can be excellent off Puako, but the surf is usually too rough in winter.

There are numerous access points. At road's end, near the 'Road Closed 500 Feet' sign, is a small cove with the most parking and easy water access. This spot is popular with both snorkelers and shore divers; be careful of the undertow. Walk a couple of minutes north to see a few petroglyphs and tide pools deep enough to cool off in.

Nearby, beautiful white-sand **Beach 69** (gate 7am-8pm) is on a calm bay ideal for swimming and snorkeling. The beach is shaded by low, thick kiawe trees, some bleached like beseeching arms and one with a rope-swing over the surf; the trees create private pockets. Low rock ledges provide kids with modest 'cliff jumping,' and all in all, this strand pleases just about everyone and can get insanely crowded. In case you're wondering, telephone pole 69 was once the marker for the beach, hence the name. Facilities include bathrooms, showers and drinking water.

To get to Puako and the tide pools, turn *makai* down Puako Beach Rd between the 70- and 71-mile markers and keep going straight. For Beach 69, take the first right turn onto Old Puako Rd. An access road from Hapuna Beach State Recreation Area leads to both Puako and Beach 69.

HAPUNA BEACH STATE RECREATION AREA

It's one thing to be popular, but when *Condé Nast Traveller* names you one of the world's best beaches, it can be the kiss of death. Thankfully, **Hapuna Beach** (gate 7am-8pm) has shoulders broad enough to handle it. A long, wide swath of fluffy golden sand caressed by clear waters and fringed by palms, Hapuna is the movie brought to life – the one popular culture placed in your head, entitled 'Hawaiian paradise.'

Hapuna's surf changes dramatically with the seasons. In calm summer, swimming, snorkeling and diving are excellent (though fish populations have declined). When the surf's up in winter, bodysurfers and bodyboarders get their turn. High winter surf can produce strong currents close to shore and a pounding shorebreak; numerous tourists

unfamiliar with the water conditions have drowned here. Lifeguards are on duty.

With drive-up access and a legendary reputation, Hapuna is extremely popular; arrive early to score parking and stake out your spot. However, with so many people (and perpetually strained state budgets), park facilities are run-down. Up from the beach is a shaded, scrabbly hillside picnic area with covered tables, two pavilions, showers, drinking water and grungy rest rooms. A concession stand sells snacks and rents boogie boards, snorkels and umbrellas. Don't leave valuables in your car.

Equally famous among campers are the park's six A-frame cabins ($20), up the hill from the park, with fabulous views. The cabins are little more than dilapidated wooden teepees with screened half-walls that let in the breeze (and highway noise); they have electricity, drinking water, a picnic bench and two sleeping ledges. There are shared bathrooms with showers and a cooking pavilion with a stove and fridge (but no pots, pans, plates or utensils). Yet, for self-sufficient folks with their own bedding, this is heaven. An advanced permit is required (see p205) but the camp host (on duty 8am to 4pm) will issue a same-day, one-night permit after 2pm if space is available. Tent camping is not permitted, but you can always beg.

MAUNA KEA RESORT AREA

The granddaddy of the Kohala Coast resorts, the Mauna Kea Beach Hotel was built in 1965 by the late Laurance Rockefeller and was the first luxury hotel on the Neighbor Islands. Naturally, other resorts followed, and they eventually surpassed Mauna Kea in size and luxury. But no money in the world could buy or build its beach, which is just as Hollywood gorgeous as neighboring Hapuna. Now, in 2009, after closing due to earthquake damage in 2006, the Mauna Kea has been renovated and reopened, ready to restake its claim. The turnoff is just north of the 68-mile marker.

Sights & Activities

Take Hapuna Beach and ever-so-gently bend it like an archer's bow and you have **Kauna'oa Bay** (aka Mauna Kea Beach), a stunning crescent-shaped cove with silky sand and gradual slope that fosters excellent swimming conditions most of the year. On the north end, snorkeling conditions are good during calm waters.

Just north of Mauna Kea Beach is delightful **Mau'umae Beach**, with soft white sand, shady trees and protected blue waters with good snorkeling. Locals are proprietary about this beach, so be respectful when visiting. To visit either beach, you must get a parking pass at the Mauna Kea Beach Hotel gate; specify Mau'umae Beach if that's what you want, since otherwise your pass will only be for Mauna Kea Beach. To get to Mau'umae, drive toward the hotel, turn right on Kamahoi and cross two wooden bridges. Look for telephone pole 22 on the left and park. Walk down the trail to the Ala Kahakai sign and turn left toward the beach.

Golfers will be itching to play the combined 36 holes of the **Mauna Kea & Hapuna Golf Courses** (☎ 882-5400; Hapuna course guest/nonguest $125/165). The Hapuna course was designed by Arnold Palmer and Ed Seay, and Mauna Kea is a 72-par championship course that is currently being redesigned by Rees Jones (call for fees and opening); it consistently ranks among the top 10 courses in the world.

All the resorts offer excellent tennis courts with pro shops, but the **Seaside Tennis Club** (☎ 882-5420; per person per day $20; ☷ 7am-6pm) offers 13 Plexipave oceanside tennis courts, holds round-robin tournaments and arranges partners.

Festivals & Events
In September locals flock to the annual **Poke Contest** (☎ 880-3424; www.pokecontest.com; admission $5), which is the 'signature event' of the Hapuna Beach Prince Hotel's Aloha Festival. Several dozen professional and amateur chefs compete and sample out their concoctions after the judging concludes.

Sleeping & Eating
Hapuna Beach Prince Hotel (☎ 880-1111, 866-774-6236; www.princeresortshawaii.com; r $415-725, ste $1350; ☐☲) With the reopening of the Mauna Kea, Hapuna Beach seems more than ever in need of a makeover. This 'sister' hotel opened in 1995 and immediately impresses with its grand architecture and enviable position on Hapuna Beach. But the seams are showing (sometimes literally) in the rooms; while they are good-sized with great bathroom layouts, the decor feels washed-out and the furniture tired – particularly for the rate. Score an internet deal. Hapuna Beach offers several restaurants and bars, a beautiful pool and various entertainment, such as traditional Hawaiian music and hula.

Mauna Kea Beach Hotel (☎ 882-7222, 866-977-4589; www.maunakeabeachhotel.com; 62-100 Mauna Kea Beach Dr; r $450-850, ste from $800; ☐☲☲) The Mauna Kea had its grand reopening in March 2009 (after this book was researched), and initial reviews have been mixed. For some, the renovations haven't quite met the high expectations of a flagship resort (nor matched the high-end competition), while other long-time guests have been enchanted and grateful to have the old lady back in action. Rooms have been enlarged, and the decor and amenity upgrades aim for a more contemporary feel, while maintaining the 'understated elegence' the hotel is known for. Certainly, book an ocean-view deluxe, and the lanai baths with their 'wall-less showers' will leave a stunning impression. Of course, the beach hasn't changed.

Entertainment
Mauna Kea Beach Hotel (☎ 882-5810; 62-100 Mauna Kea Beach Dr; adult/child luau 5-12 $86/43; ☷ 5:30pm Tue) The Mauna Kea luau, which resumed shortly after this book went to press, was always one of the island's best.

SPENCER BEACH PARK
Kids and families love to swim in the gentle waters at Spencer Beach, and its campground is the best place along this stretch of coast to sleep under the stars. That said, the waters are silty (Kawaihae Harbor blocks the clearing currents) and, though pretty, the beach seems dowdy compared to its fashion-plate siblings just south.

The park infrastructure is great, and better kept than most; there's a lifeguard station, picnic tables and a pavilion, BBQ grills, rest rooms, showers, drinking water, basketball and volleyball courts, and an on-site camp host. Plus, a short hike south, along the shady coastal Ala Kahakai Trail, leads to Mau'umae Beach (left); look for the 'Na Ala Hele' sign near the pavilion.

Two areas allow camping: one is within low trees by the water, and the other is an exposed, dirt picnic area. Regular winds kick up the dust here, the only real downfall. A county permit is required (see p205), but the camp host sells one-night permits.

The turnoff to Spencer Beach Park (and Pu'ukohola Heiau National Historic Site) is off Hwy 270, between Kawaihae and the intersection with Hwy 19.

PU'UKOHOLA HEIAU NATIONAL HISTORIC SITE

By 1790 Kamehameha the Great had conquered Maui, Lana'i and Moloka'i. However, power over his home island of Hawai'i proved to be a challenge. When a prophet said that if he built a heiau dedicated to his war god Kuka'ilimoku, he'd rule all the islands, Kamehameha immediately went to work building **Pu'ukohola Heiau** (☎ 882-7218; www.nps.gov/puhe; admission free; ☽ 7:45am-4:55pm).

According to legend, Kamehameha labored alongside his men in a human chain 20 miles long, transporting rocks hand to hand from Pololu Valley in North Kohala. After finishing the heiau by the summer of 1791, Kamehameha held a dedication ceremony and invited his rival and cousin, Keoua, the chief of Ka'u. Keoua accepted, understanding his fate: when Keoua's patroness, Pele, destroyed a portion of his army in an eruption earlier that same year, he knew it was a sign that Kamehameha was destined to win; see p261). When Keoua arrived at Pu'ukohola, he was killed and taken to the *luakini* as the first offering to the gods. Kamehameha, now sole ruler of the Big Island, eventually united all the islands by 1810.

With a prime coastal vantage, Pu'ukohola Heiau is perhaps the most physically majestic heiau on the Big Island, standing 224ft by 100ft, with 16ft-to-20ft walls. Though unadorned today, it once held wooden *ki'i* and thatched structures, including an oracle tower, an altar, a drum house and a shelter for the high priest. Original paintings by Herb Kane, the highlight of the revamped visitors center, bring this to life.

In addition to excellent exhibits, the visitors center has a variety of videos on Hawaiian history and culture. Short, easy, sun-baked trails lead to the heiau and past the ruins of **Mailekini Heiau**, which predates Pu'ukohola. A third temple, **Hale o Kapuni Heiau**, dedicated to shark gods, lies submerged offshore.

Unfortunately, the 2006 earthquake damaged both Pu'ukohola and Mailekini Heiau, and they are in the middle of a multiyear repair project using *olokea*, or traditional ladders, to put the stones back in place. Even when repairs are finished, it's doubtful the public will be allowed to walk on the heiau again.

In August, the park has a free **cultural festival**, with double-hull canoe rides, craft demonstrations, Hawaiian food and entertainment.

Traditionally, a Hawaiian group also re-enacts a royal court procession and battles; for now they're using the festival as an opportunity to rebuild the heiau.

KAWAIHAE

Kawaihae is the Big Island's second-largest deepwater commercial harbor, and at first glance it's just an unsightly industrial dock. What an unexpected surprise, then, to discover this sun-bleached hamlet contains destination-worthy eats and the island's best (make that only) live jazz supper club.

Sights & Activities

Outside the harbor, North Kohala has healthy reef ecosystems – with numerous lava tubes, arches and pinnacles – that make for great, uncrowded diving and snorkeling. To explore this part of the coast, visit **Kohala Divers** (☎ 882-7774; www.kohaladivers.com; Kawaihae Center, Hwy 270; snorkeling $75, dives $100-140), which offers dive, snorkeling and seasonal whale-watching tours (plus gear rental). Dive groups are kept small (with a six-to-one diver-to-guide ratio).

South of Kawaihae, stop by the locally owned **Hamakua Macadamia Nut Company** (☎ 882-1690, 888-643-6680; www.hawnnut.com; Maluokalani St; admission free; ☽ 8am-5:30pm) for a quick, personal tour, generous samples and tasty gifts. The eco-conscious company halves its fuel use by burning ground mac-nut shells. To get here, turn *mauka* just north of the 4-mile marker.

Eating & Drinking

Mr K's Miracles on Rice (☎ 882-1511; Kawaihae Center; donburi & plate lunches $6.50-10; ☽ 8am-4pm Mon-Fri) Friendly, fresh, and quick, this hole-in-the-wall takeout window serves delicious *donburi*, sushi, Spam *musubi* and fruit smoothies. For on-the-go lunches, it's hard to find better.

Café Pesto (☎ 882-1071; www.cafepesto.com; Kawaihae Center, Hwy 270; lunch $11-14, pizza $9-20, dinner mains $17-33; ☽ 11am-9pm Sun-Thu, to 10pm Fri & Sat) This fun, stylish restaurant is a well-loved favorite, serving eclectic, innovative cuisine you might call Mediterranean with an Asian twang, or Italian with an island twist. Choose from curries and Greek salads, seafood risotto and smoked salmon alfredo, piping hot calzones and thin-crust gourmet pizza. Walls are crowded with lively art, and the comfy lounge is a perfect cocktail-hour destination.

Kawaihae Seafood Bar (☎ 880-9393; Hwy 270; pupu $9-16, mains $15-27; ☺ 11am-11:30pm) Upstairs from the Kawaihae Harbor Grill, this spot draws a rowdier crowd for drinks, and upscale bar food like *poke* burger and ginger steamed clams.

Kawaihae Harbor Grill (☎ 882-1368; Hwy 270; breakfast $9-16, dinner $27-33; ☺ 7am-9:30pm) The Grill has developed a loyal following for its reliably prepared fresh seafood, pastas and steaks, and for its family-friendly atmosphere. It also serves a full diner-style breakfast.

Kawaihae Center (Hwy 270) For simple groceries and sandwiches, this place has a small market and deli.

ourpick Blue Dragon Musiquarium (☎ 882-7771; www.bluedragonhawaii.com; 61-3616 Kawaihae Rd; mains $15-36; ☺ 5-10pm, bar till 11pm Wed-Sun) Glowing blue, this roofless restaurant under towering palms books live jazz music almost nightly – as well as local slack key favorites like John Keawe – creating a mood so upbeat and friendly that (aided by potent specialty cocktails) even the shyest couples can't resist the scallop of a dance floor. Food is sourced locally and well-prepared into an eclectic mix of stir-fries and curries, rib-eye steaks and teriyaki. Service is casual (and a bit distracted). Music ends at 10pm, but the bar goes as long as you do.

NORTH KOHALA

Slow-paced, attractive North Kohala has a distinct flavor all its own – a charming, successful mix of rural farmers and local artists, of Native Hawaiians and haole transplants, of tidy suburban homes, plantation-era storefronts, green valleys and ancient temples.

Few visitors, and indeed few Big Island residents, make the detour off the Hawai'i Belt Rd to experience it, which irks locals, who feel North Kohala is unfairly overlooked.

Geologically the oldest part of the Big Island, the North Kohala Coast is rich in ancient history, including the birthplace of King Kamehameha I. In modern times, North Kohala was sugar country until the Kohala Sugar Company closed in 1975. Today, the small historic towns of Hawi and Kapa'au contain smart galleries and boutiques, creative eateries and enough eccentrics to keep things interesting.

Rounding the peninsula's thumb on Hwy 270, you leave the Kohala Mountain's rain shadow, and the land shifts steadily from bone dry to lushly tropical. By the time you reach road's end, the wet landscape has been carved into ever more dramatic contours, culminating in the Pololu Valley, the jewel of North Kohala.

AKONI PULE HIGHWAY

The land along the Akoni Pule Hwy (Hwy 270) remains largely undeveloped, affording spectacular coastal views that make Maui seem but a short swim away.

Pua Mau Place

Who takes 15 acres of the driest land on the island to prove it can support a flowering, eco-friendly **botanic garden** (☎ 882-0888; www.puamau .org; Ala Kahua Dr; admission adult/child 6-16 $15/5; ☺ 9am-4pm)? Virgil Place, that's who, and his vision has largely been realized in this blooming, heartfelt oasis. Live peacocks and oversized animal and insect sculptures add fun, and the visitor center affords tremendous coastal views. Bring a picnic! Ala Kahua Dr intersects the highway just north of the 6-mile marker.

Lapakahi State Historical Park

This 262-acre **park** (☎ 882-6207; admission free; ☺ 8am-4pm, gate closes 3:30pm, closed holidays) was a remote, successful fishing village 600 years ago. Eventually, as some villagers moved to the wetter uplands to farm, they began trading their crops for fish with those on the coast, thereby creating an *ahupua'a*, a wedge-shaped land division radiating from sea to mountain. When the freshwater table dropped in the 19th century, the village was abandoned.

From the abundant, unrestored foundations of the ancient village, it is easy to

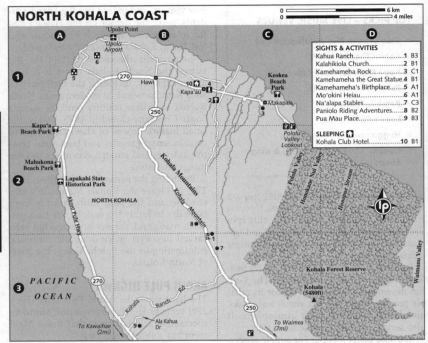

NORTH KOHALA COAST

0 — 6 km
0 — 4 miles

SIGHTS & ACTIVITIES	
Kahua Ranch	1 B3
Kalahikiola Church	2 B1
Kamehameha Rock	3 C1
Kamehameha the Great Statue	4 B1
Kamehameha's Birthplace	5 A1
Mo'okini Heiau	6 A1
Na'alapa Stables	7 C3
Paniolo Riding Adventures	8 B2
Pua Mau Place	9 B3

SLEEPING	
Kohala Club Hotel	10 B1

conjure traditional life on the beautiful cove. The unshaded, 1-mile **loop trail** meanders past low stone walls, house sites, canoe sheds and fishing shrines. Displays show how fishers used lift nets to catch 'opelu (pan-sized mackerel scad), a technique still practised today, and how the salt used to preserve the fish was dried in stone salt pans. You even stumble across ancient Hawaiian games, like konane (Hawaiian checkers) and 'ulu maika (stone bowling).

Lapakahi's clear waters are loaded with tropical fish and are part of a marine-life conservation district. Swimming and snorkeling are theoretically possible, but it's a sensitive issue, since areas of the park are considered sacred, and are still used, by Native Hawaiians. Ask first, if you want to enter the water; park staff request that you not use sunscreen or towels, as these affect the fish. (Better yet, snorkel at Mahukona, below.)

The park is located just south of the 14-mile marker.

Mahukona Beach Park

This **park** has no beach, and its campground is unappealing, but it contains an old boat landing (which was once used by the Kohala Sugar Company) that provides easy-access snorkeling, spearfishing, diving and swimming. A metal ladder makes water entry simple (and ideal for kids), and the rocky sea bottom attracts colorful fish and provides hidey-holes for eels. Near the landing, you can follow an anchor chain out to a submerged boiler and the remains of a ship in about 25ft of water. You can rinse off at a shower near the ladder. Winter seas can sometimes be too rough for swimming.

Separate from the landing is a dusty oceanfront picnic area with a ratty wooden pavilion, picnic tables and unkempt bathrooms (no drinking water). Camping is allowed with a county permit (see p205), but it's not recommended because of the run-down facilities, the park's isolation, and, in late summer, the biting flies.

Kapa'a Beach Park

This relatively unused park has a rock-lined shore (no sandy beach) that fronts clear waters with great snorkeling. Water access over the rocks is tricky, however, and virtually impossible when the surf picks up. If that's the case, try Mahukona (opposite).

Otherwise, there's just a parking lot, a falling down wooden picnic pavilion (with lovely views) and portable toilets. Camping with a county permit (see p205) is allowed, but this park is even more isolated than Mahukona.

The signed entrance is almost exactly at the 16-mile marker.

Mo'okini Heiau

Near 'Upolu Point at the northern tip of the Big Island, this **heiau** (☎ 373-8000; admission free; ☽ dawn-dusk) is one of the oldest and most historically significant temples in the Hawaiian islands. Measuring about 250ft by 125ft, with walls 6ft high, the massive structure sits solitary and brooding on a wind-rustled grassy plain, contemplating distant Maui and, in winter, humpback whales. There are no facilities.

A 'closed' temple reserved for *ali'i nui* (high chiefs), the heiau was dedicated to the god Ku, and built from 'sunrise to first light' by up to 18,000 'little people' passing water-worn basalt stones in complete silence from Pololu Valley – a distance of 14 miles – under the supervision of Kuamo'o Mo'okini. According to Mo'okini genealogical charts, the heiau was built around AD 480.

Five hundred years later Pa'ao, a priest from Samoa, raised the walls to 30ft and changed the altar to a scalloped shape as his *ho'okupu* (offering) to the gods. He was the first to introduce human sacrifices in an effort to stem dilution of the royal bloodlines and to enforce stricter moral codes of conduct (making this the first *'luakini'* heiau)

In 1963 the National Park Service designated Mo'okini Heiau as Hawaii's first registered National Historic Landmark. Fifteen years later, it was deeded to the state.

About 1000yd down a dirt road below the heiau are stone-walled foundations that are believed to be the **site of Kamehameha's birth** (see p261). As the legend goes, when Kamehameha was born on a stormy winter night in 1758, his mother was told by a kahuna that her son would be a powerful ruler and conquer all the islands. Upon hearing this, the ruling high chief of Hawai'i ordered all male newborns killed. Thus, after Kamehameha was taken to the Mo'okini Heiau for his birth rituals, he was spirited away into hiding.

The current *kahuna nui* (high priestess), Leimomi Mo'okini Lum, is the seventh high

priestess of the Mo'okini bloodline serving the temple. In 1978 she lifted the kapu that restricted access to the temple, thereby opening it to visitors. In 1994, she rededicated the heiau to 'the children of the world,' and she requests that visitors bring a flower lei or blossom (symbolizing a child of the land) and leave it as a gift to the heiau. You are allowed to enter the stone fence surrounding the heiau, but *do not climb* on the heiau.

The heiau suffered minor damage during the 2006 earthquake, but Lum doesn't want it repaired, and the state will honor her request. At the time she said: 'It has been here 1500 years. I'm not going to change it. I'm 80. I don't look that good, but I looked good when I was 20.'

Getting There & Away

There are two routes to the heiau. The first and most convenient is to turn *makai* off the highway onto Old Coast Guard Station Rd, between the 18- and 19-mile markers. Follow the one-lane paved, potholed road for just over a mile. Turn right onto a red-cinder road, which is blocked by a locked cattle gate. If you call ahead, the gate will be left open and you can drive in, but you are also welcome to park here (without blocking the gate) and walk the rest of the way to the heiau (about 15 minutes). The alternative route is to drive toward 'Upolu Airport, then turn south on the coastal dirt road. This rough 4WD road is impassable after rain.

HAWI
pop 940

Little Hawi (hah-*vee*), which is a former sugar-company town, has been remade into a rustic, picturesque two blocks of artful, upscale fun exuding a certain northern California vibe. Even a rainy day doesn't spoil the pleasure of walking among the attractive shops (browsing for cigars, fudge, Japanese tea and hand-carved koa bowls) and getting a gourmet bite. Stay for a day or two and you'll soon feel like a regular.

South of Hawi, Hwy 250 (Kohala Mountain Rd) to Waimea is one of the most scenic drives on the island: with Mt Hualalai, Mauna Kea and Mauna Loa posing in a CinemaScope panorama.

Hawi has a post office, grocery store and gas station to round out town services. A cool and shady **park** with giant banyan trees is on

Hwy 250. Behind it is the old sugar-mill tower, a remnant of the town's former mainstay. The Kohala Town Theater, behind the Kohala Village Inn, shows second-run Hollywood **movies** (tickets $3; ☺ 7:30pm) on Friday night.

Sleeping

Kohala Village Inn (☎ 889-0404; www.kohalavillageinn .com; 55-514 Hawi Rd; s $65, d $75-85, ste $110; ☐ ☎) The inn's 19 cozy rooms are much nicer than the plantation-era, motel-style building suggests. Inside each are attractive plank floors, tile baths, warm furniture, soft towels and cable TV. The hotel is a short walk from the main strip.

Plantation House (☎ 889-0404; www.hawiplantation house.com; house $800, with cottage $900, cottage alone $150; ☐ ☎ ☒) The Kohala Village Inn also rents this enormous six-bedroom, six-bathroom plantation home (sleeping 14) that would make a memorable group retreat. Rented separately, the detached cottage becomes a secluded romantic hideaway.

Eating & Drinking

For its size, Hawi serves a ridiculous amount of good food.

Kava Kafé (☎ 889-0505; Kohala Trade Center, Hwy 270; kava $5-10; ☺ 4:21-8:59pm Mon-Fri) Try kava at this local hole-in-the-wall. Don't like the taste? Try its dolled-up Maya Chocolate – kava with coconut milk, ginger, chocolate, cayenne and cinnamon.

Kohala Coffee Mill (☎ 889-5577; Akoni Pule Hwy; snacks $3-8; ☺ 6:30am-6pm Mon-Fri, 7am-5:30pm Sat & Sun) This comfy little espresso shop has smoothies and muffins, burgers and bagels, plus heavenly Tropical Dreams ice-cream.

Upstairs at the Mill (☎ 889-5015; Kohala Coffee Mill; ☐ ☎) Enjoy fudge, shave ice and internet access (per 30 minutes $5) at this spot.

Short 'n' Sweet (☎ 889-1444; www.shortnsweet.biz; Kohala Trade Center, Hwy 270; salads & panini $7-9; ☺ 9am-3pm-ish) Everything is delectable and homemade at this tiny two-table bakery. Ease into the day with a breakfast panini or delicate, French-style croissant and pastries, and at midday nosh on house-made focaccia-bread sandwiches and organic salads. On Friday evening (4:30pm to 7:30pm) locals pack in for pizza made from scratch. Or skip all that and go straight for the rich, decadent sweets.

Luke's Place (☎ 889-1155; 55-514 Hawi Rd; mains $7-19; ☺ 11:30am-'till pau,' or 10pm-ish) This new restaurant is still looking for its groove, with a menu of predictable standards. No such problem troubles the attached, thatch-roof Tiki Bar, which books a wide range of live music most nights and makes a convivial local watering hole.

Bamboo (☎ 889-5555; www.bamboorestaurant .info/restaurant.htm; Hwy 270; lunch $9-14, dinner $14-35; ☺ 11:30am-2:30pm & 6-8pm Tue-Sat, 11:30am-2:30pm Sun) Bamboo enjoys abiding affection as a highly regarded local institution, one that promises East-meets-West fusion cuisine delivered with 'fresh island style.' It's a winning combination, and done well. Still, it's less innovative than it once was, and not every dish or side arrives equally refined. However, the relaxed, friendly setting – a cheery mix of suspended Balinese umbrellas, twinkling Christmas lights, and the warm wood interior of the historic building – is pure Hawi, particularly on weekends when live music sweeps everyone up in a tide of aloha.

our pick Sushi Rock (☎ 889-5900; Hwy 270; sushi $7-17, mains $22-26; ☺ noon-3pm, 5:30-8pm Thu-Tue) In this tiny shack of a restaurant, evenings dissolve into cross-table chattering; no one stays a stranger long. After all, youthful owner-chef Rio Miceli, a Hawi native, has created a sushi maven's dream: Miceli's traditional and new-wave sushi has real personality and a playful creativity, with local ingredients, nuanced flavors and a casual artistry. Generous rolls don't toss in every fish and slap on a goofy name. Seared beef melts like butter, and you can order pure wasabi – the ground root, not the paste. Plus, there's a full bar, cooked entrées and occasional live music. Arrive early.

Takata Store (☎ 889-5413; Akoni Pule Hwy; ☺ 8am-7pm Mon-Sat, to 1pm Sun) Between Kapa'au and Hawi, this is a decent, family-run market for groceries.

Shopping

L Zeidman Gallery (☎ 889-1400; www.lzeidman.com; Hwy 270; ☺ 10am-6pm Tue-Sat, 10am-5pm Sun-Mon) Most people can only afford to browse the exquisitely crafted wood bowls and sculpture at this gallery, which sells museum-quality pieces by island artists.

As Hawi Turns (☎ 889-5023; Hwy 270; ☺ 10am-6pm Mon-Sat, 11am-5pm Sun) Come here for stylish women's wear and eclectic fun stuff.

Gallery at Bamboo (☎ 889-1441; www.bamboo restaurant.info/gallery.htm; Hwy 270; ☺ 11:30-8pm Tue-Sat, 11:30am-2:30pm Sun) The Old General Store

THE LONELY ONE: KAMEHAMEHA THE GREAT

When Kamehameha was born in 1758 near Mo'okini Heiau (p259), a kahuna prophesied he would one day rule all of Hawaii, and he was taken away before jealous island chiefs could kill him. Kamehameha was then raised in secret in North Kohala's valleys, including Waipi'o Valley (p279), where years later the high chief Kalaniopu'u appointed him the guardian of the war god, Kuka'ilimoku, the 'snatcher of land.'

Kamehameha emerged as Kalaniopu'u's fiercest, most ambitious general. As King David Kalakaua later described him (in *Legends and Myths of Hawaii*), 'his features were rugged and irregular, and he held in contempt the courtly graces.' After Kalaniopu'u's death in 1782, Kamehameha led his warriors against Kalaniopu'u's son, Kiwalao, who had taken the throne. Kiwalao was killed, and Kamehameha emerged as ruler of the Kohala region and one of the ruling chiefs of the Big Island.

In 1784 the prophet Keaulumoku predicted that Kamehameha, whom he dubbed 'the lonely one,' would conquer Hawaii. Keaulumoku also prophesied Hawaii's eventual domination by the white race, the destruction of the temples, and the decline of the Hawaiian people.

Emboldened by his apparent destiny, Kamehameha continued to wage war. In 1790, with the aid of a captured foreign schooner and two shipwrecked sailors, Isaac Davis and John Young, whom he used as gunners, Kamehameha attacked and conquered the island of Maui.

Kamehameha was on Moloka'i preparing for an invasion of O'ahu when he learned that Keoua Kuahu'ula, his cousin and chief of the Ka'u region, was attacking the Hamakua Coast. An angry Kamehameha set sail for home, and Keoua's soldiers beat a quick retreat back to Ka'u. But when the withdrawing troops passed beneath the slopes of Kilauea, the volcano suddenly erupted, engulfing and killing many of the warriors with toxic fumes and ash. Still, Keoua remained undefeated, and Kamehameha sought advice from the prophet Kapoukahi, who told him he would finally prevail if he built a heiau (stone temple) to honor his war god, Kuka'ilimoku.

Kamehameha immediately began constructing Pu'ukohola Heiau (p256) in Kawaihae. When it was finished in 1791, Kamehameha sent word to Keoua, asking him to meet at the heiau for reconciliation. It's believed that Keoua understood and accepted his fate, for he prepared for death and willingly sailed to Kawaihae. Upon landing with his party, Keoua was killed, becoming the *luakini* heiau's first sacrifice. With this, Kamehameha became sole ruler of the Big Island.

By 1795, Kamehameha conquered all the islands except Kaua'i, which peacefully joined the others in 1810. Kamehameha named the entire kingdom after his home island, Hawai'i.

contains Bamboo (opposite) and this gallery, chock-full of paintings, photos, funky art and high-end gifts. Don't miss upstairs.

KAPA'AU
pop 1160

Kapa'au is another former sugar town refashioned into an attractive tourist destination, though it's not as adorably quaint as Hawi. Kapa'au is North Kohala's civic center, with a courthouse, police station, library and bank (with ATM). North Kohala was Kamehameha's childhood home, so the June **King Kamehameha Day** festivities have extra significance here.

Sights & Activities

Kamehameha Park is an ideal place to let the kids run loose: there are large fields, tennis courts, a play structure and a small, but nice, swimming pool.

KAMEHAMEHA THE GREAT STATUE

This **statue** on the front lawn of the North Kohala Civic Center may look familiar. Its lei-draped and much-photographed twin stands opposite Honolulu's 'Iolani Palace (p116).

The statue was made in 1880 in Florence by American sculptor Thomas Gould. When the ship delivering it sank off the Falkland Islands, a second statue was then cast from the original mold. The duplicate statue arrived at the islands in 1883 and took its place in downtown Honolulu. Later the sunken statue was recovered from the ocean floor and completed its trip to Hawaii. It was then sent here, to Kamehameha's childhood home. A notice board tells the full story.

KENJI'S HOUSE

Not famous, Kapa'au native Kenji Yokoyama (1931–2004) was an avid free diver and obsessive collector of rocks, driftwood and shells, which he fashioned into little sculptures and naive artworks. Set in Kenji's home, this very personal, intimate exhibit honors this humble, thoughtful man, who made art out of his North Kohala life. Upstairs is the equally interesting **North Kohala Artists Cooperative Gallery** (☎ 884-5556; www.kohalaartists.com; Akoni Pule Hwy; admission free; 11am-5pm Wed-Mon), which displays the high-quality works (at affordable prices) of North Kohala artists. The site also includes a restaurant, Pico's Bistro (right).

KALAHIKIOLA CHURCH
Protestant missionaries Elias and Ellen Bond built this church in 1855. Unfortunately, large portions of three of the church's walls crumbled in the 2006 earthquake, and they still await repair. Towering banyan trees and peaceful macadamia-nut orchards surround the church, making this a worthwhile detour.

The church is 900yd up 'Iole Rd, which is on the *mauka* side of the highway between the 23- and 24-mile markers.

KOHALA YOGA COMMUNITY CENTER
This **center** (☎ 889-0583; Sakamoto Bldg, 55-3877 Hwy 270; drop-in class $15) offers classes in yoga and dance.

KAMEHAMEHA ROCK
Sure, it is just a rock by the side of the road. But if legends are to be believed, Kamehameha carried this rock from the beach below to demonstrate his great strength. Much later, a road crew attempted to move the rock, and it stubbornly fell off the wagon – a sign that it wanted to stay put. Not wanting to upset Kamehameha's mana, the workers left it in place. The rock is on the *mauka* side of Hwy 270, on a curve that is just past a small bridge, about 2 miles east of Kapa'au. Just past this, on the cliff above, is the striking green-and-red **Tong Building**, an old Chinese hall.

Sleeping & Eating
Kohala Club Hotel (889-6793; www.kohalaclubhotel.com; 54-3793 Hwy 270; d $56) These aging plantation-worker cottages hold basic, perfunctory shared-bath accommodations, the equivalent of private rooms at a hostel. They are clean, affordable beds for budget travelers. Look for the sign suspended over a driveway on the *makai* side, south of mile-marker 23.

Kohala Country Adventures Guest House (☎ 889-5663, 866-892-2484; www.kcadventures.com; d $85-135, ste $175;) This guesthouse surrounded by fruit-filled tropical gardens offers three pleasing rooms with private entrances and homey decor. The smallest has no view, but from the other two you can see Maui on a clear day. The suite is the nicest, with a huge private deck and mini-kitchen. Families could bunk here very comfortably.

Sammy D'S (☎ 889-5288; 54-3854 Akoni Pule Hwy; meals $7-9; 11am-8pm Tue-Sat, 11am-4pm Sun) This clean, friendly café dishes up no-muss, no-fuss local *grinds*, plate lunches and sandwiches.

Pico's Bistro (☎ 884-5555; Kenji's House, Akoni Pule Hwy; mains $9-12; 11:30am-8pm) With a roof-shaded open patio and a teeny kitchen, Pico's resembles a beachside food stand. But the menu is a gourmet Greek feast – try lamb kebabs, falafel, spanakopita, Greek salad and quiche. Everything is fresh, organic and homemade. Uses biodegradable cutlery and containers.

Shopping
Kohala Book Shop (☎ 889-6400; www.kohalabooks .com; Hwy 270; 11am-5pm Mon-Sat) One of the Big Island's best bookstores (with new, used and rare books), this has a fantastic Hawaiiana collection. Kohala is home to several well-known novelists – like Kiana Davenport and Mia King – and this is their literary gathering place.

Ackerman Galleries (☎ 889-5137; www.ackerman galleries.com; Akoni Pule Hwy; 9:30am-6pm) This large upscale gallery has a wide range of authentic crafts, carvings, jewelry and quilts.

Elements (☎ 889-0760; www.kahiko; 54-3885 Akoni Pule Hwy; 10am-6pm Mon-Sat) Specializing in locally handcrafted jewelry, Elements is stocked with lots of attractive finery.

MAKAPALA
After Kapa'au, the highway narrows, sloping and winding deeper into the jungle. A few single-lane bridges add to the sensation that the end of the road is near. The village of Makapala has only a few hundred residents and no town center.

Take in the awesome mana of the North Kohala Coast at **Keokea Beach Park** (gate 7am-11pm), where reddish-orange cliffs enclose a rock-lined bay. The surf really surges with a west swell, attracting experienced local surfers. Swimming is sketchy due to dangerous shore breaks and strong currents, but a protected boat launch with an envelope of sand provides entry. Run-down facilities include grills, showers and portable toilets. A pavilion with two tables on a small rise is a prime picnic spot. The park is signed from the highway down a 1-mile road.

Bright as a tropical bird, the tiny yellow-and-green **Makapala Store** (☎ 884-5686; Hwy 270; snacks $4-6; ☺ 9am-3pm-ish Mon-Sat) is your last chance to get shave ice, smoothies or a tuna sandwich before reaching Pololu Valley. It plans to offer horseback rides and ziplines.

POLOLU VALLEY

Hwy 270 becomes increasingly evocative until it reaches its dramatic climax at secluded Pololu Valley, where a cliff-top viewpoint overlooks the steeply scalloped coastal cliffs, which recede in the mist to the east. Smaller and more intimate, Pololu Valley makes a scenic bookend with the more famous and historic Waipi'o Valley.

Pololu was once thickly planted with wetland taro. The Pololu Stream fed the valley, carrying water from the remote, rainy interior to the valley floor. When the Kohala Ditch was built, it siphoned off much of the water for sugarcane and put an end to taro production. The last islanders left the valley in the 1940s, and the valley slopes are now forest-reserve land. The ditch continued to be a water source for Kohala ranches and farms until it was busted by the 2006 earthquake. Multimillion-dollar repairs are ongoing.

Sights & Activities

From the lookout, **Pololu Valley Trail** switchbacks steeply down to the valley floor. It's short enough not to be truly daunting – about 15 minutes going down and perhaps twice as long coming back up. It's rocky in spots, and after rain it gets very muddy; let it dry for an afternoon before attempting it. There are no facilities.

At the mouth of the valley lies a gorgeous black-sand **beach.** The surf can get rough, particularly in winter, with rip currents year round, so be cautious and swim with care. Behind the beach, a hillocky ironwood forest vibrates like some Tolkien-inspired shire wood. Deeper valley explorations are blocked by a pond, beyond which cattle roam freely (an indication you shouldn't drink the water).

Normally, intrepid hikers can continue to the next valley, **Honokane Nui**. The trailhead is up from the beach, within the forest. The steep, frequently slippery trail ascends 600ft over the ridge (traversing private property) and eventually drops into Honokane Nui Valley; allow two to three hours for the roundtrip. However, the 2006 earthquake caused landslides that damaged the trail, which is currently closed for repairs. For updates call **Surety Kohala** (☎ 889-6257), which helps manage the property.

Tours

Hawaii Forest & Trail (☎ 331-8505, 800-464-1993; www.hawaii-forest.com; waterfall tour adult/child under 13 $135/99, 4WD tour adult/child 6-12 $115/89) offers two tours in the Kohala area. One is a hike along the Kohala Ditch Trail to waterfalls, and includes transportation from the Waikoloa Resort Area. The other is through the Pololu Valley in a six-wheel off-road vehicle and on foot.

WAIMEA (KAMUELA)

pop 7030

The cool, green rolling pastureland surrounding Waimea is perhaps Hawai'i's most unexpected face. This is cattle and cowboy country, and nearly all of it, including Waimea itself, is owned, run or leased by Parker Ranch, one of the largest ranches in the USA. Covering about 175,000 acres, Parker Ranch land constitutes about 10% of the Big Island and is about twice the size of Lanai.

In a familiar Hawaii story, it all began because an introduced species – seven longhorn cattle given as a gift to King Kamehameha in 1793 – reproduced to become a pest. In 1809 the king commissioned 19-year-old John Palmer Parker to thin and control the wild herd. The skillful Parker did so, and he further secured his future by marrying one of Kamehameha's granddaughters. As Parker's holdings grew, he brought three Mexican-Spanish cowboys over to better train his Hawaiian ranch hands. The *paniolos*, as the newcomers were called, also brought their guitars – and Hawaiians quickly adapted the instrument into their own distinctive and now famous 'slack key' style.

Beyond this interesting slice of island history, Waimea offers travelers great lodgings, first-rate art galleries and gourmet eats. So long as you don't mind the fog and brisk afternoon winds, Waimea makes an appealing base for exploring the nearby Kohala and Hamakua Coasts.

ORIENTATION

Waimea is also referred to as Kamuela, which is the Hawaiian spelling of Samuel; most claim it's for Samuel Parker of Parker Ranch fame. Maps usually list both names, the phone book and post office only use Kamuela, and, yes, it gets confusing.

The junction of Hwys 19 and 190 is the center of town; most businesses and sights are near it. From Hilo, Hwy 19 is commonly called the Mamalahoa Hwy, though west of Hwy 190, Hwy 19 becomes Kawaihae Rd, while Hwy 190 continues as the Mamalahoa Hwy. If you've followed this, remember that, further east, a section of the 'Old Mamalahoa Hwy' intersects and parallels Hwy 19.

INFORMATION

Big Island Visitors Bureau (☎ 885-1655; www.big island.org; Suite 27B, Waimea Center, 65-1158 Mamalahoa Hwy; ☼ 8am-4:30pm Mon-Fri) Though a sales office, it welcomes walk-in visitors; in the mall, around the corner from KTA.

Emma's Waimea Washerette (☎ 345-8213; Kawaihae Rd; ☼ 6am-9pm, till 11pm Fri & Sat) Across from Tako Taco.

KTA Super Store (☎ 885-8866; Waimea Center, 65-1158 Mamalahoa Hwy; ☼ 6am-11pm) Has a pharmacy.

North Hawaii Community Hospital (☎ 885-4444; 67-1125 Mamalahoa Hwy) Emergency services available 24 hours.

Post office (☎ 800-275-8777; 67-1197 Mamalahoa Hwy; ☼ 8am-4:30pm Mon-Fri, 9am-noon Sat) Address all Waimea mail to Kamuela.

www.ahualoa.net Visit this website for a more personal window into local (particularly agricultural) life.

www.kamuela.com The town's official website is a good source of information.

SIGHTS
Parker Ranch Historic Homes

Immerse yourself in the Parker family's epic saga by visiting the Parker Ranch's two 19th-century **homes** (☎ 885-5433; www.parkerranch.com; 67-1435 Mamalahoa Hwy; adult/child 4-12 $9/5, family $23; ☼ 10am-5pm, last entry 4pm), less than a mile south of the intersection of Hwys 190 and 19. In 2008, the Parker Ranch Museum closed, and all the family's heirlooms and memorabilia were moved here. Visits begin with a 20- to 30-minute docent presentation, after which visitors explore on their own.

Built in 1962, **Pu'uopelu** is the estate's sprawling 8000-sq-ft grand manor. It's packed with amazing historical artifacts, ornate furnishings and some show-stopping art. The ranch owns one of the largest French, postimpressionist and Oriental collections in Hawaii – courtesy of Parker Ranch's last owner, Richard Smart. Another room celebrates Smart's theatrical career on Broadway and in Europe. Adjacent to the main house is **Mana Hale**, the koa wood, saltbox-style home John Parker built in the

WAIMEA (KAMUELA)

Merriman's..................................	12 A1
Pau..	(see 12)
Waimea Coffee Company...........	(see 15)
Waimea Ranch House................	(see 16)
Yong's Kal-Bi..............................	(see 16)

ENTERTAINMENT
Kahilu Theatre...........................	13 B1

SHOPPING
Crackseed, Etc............................	(see 11)
Gallery of Great Things..............	(see 15)
Giggles.......................................	(see 14)
Parker Ranch Center...................	14 B1
Parker Square.............................	15 B1
Reyn's..	(see 14)
Waimea Center..........................	16 B1

Parker Ranch Historic Homes.....	5 A1
Ulu La'au Waimea Nature Park....	6 B1
WM Keck Observatory Office......	7 C1

SLEEPING
Kamuela Inn...............................	8 A1
Waimea Country Lodge...............	9 B1

EATING
Daniel Thiebaut.........................	10 B1
Hawaiian Style Cafe....................	11 B1
KTA Super Store.........................	(see 16)
Lilikoi Café.................................	(see 14)

INFORMATION
Big Island Visitors Bureau.........(see 16)
KTA Super Store.......................(see 16)
North Hawaii Community Hospital...1 C1
Post Office...............................2 B1

SIGHTS & ACTIVITIES
Imiola Congregational Church....3 C1
Isaacs Art Center......................4 B1

--

NORTH KOHALA UPCOUNTRY RIDES

Get a feel for Hawaii's *paniolo* culture through a horseback ride or visit to one of North Kohala's upcountry ranches. The riding is open range, not nose-to-tail, and there are trotting and cantering opportunities on all rides. Riders must be at least eight years old and 4ft tall.

Paniolo Riding Adventures (☎ 889-5354; www.panioloadventures.com; Hwy 250; rides $69-159) Offers short, long, picnic and sunset rides over 11,000-acre Ponoholo Ranch, a working cattle ranch. Horses are all riding horses, and they're selected for the rider's experience, from 'city slicker' to 'wrangler.'

Na'alapa Stables (☎ 889-0022; www.naalapastables.com; Hwy 250; rides $68-89, wagon tour adult/child $37/18) Na'alapa Stables organizes rides across the pastures of the 8500-acre Kahua Ranch, affording fine views of the coast from its 3200ft elevation. Also offered is a narrated historical tour of the ranch aboard an 1860s-style farm wagon.

Evening at the Ranch (☎ 987-2108; www.evening-at-kahua.com; Kohala Ranch Rd; adult/child under 12 $104/55) This is essentially a cowboy luau at Kahua Ranch, with a Western-style BBQ dinner and an open beer and wine bar. A guitar-playing *paniolo* provides entertainment, while activities include roping, branding a souvenir shingle, playing horseshoes, line dancing and stargazing. Naturally, the evening ends with marshmallows around a campfire. It's great fun, if a decidedly family affair.

1840s. The gleaming interior is original – it was dismantled board by board and rebuilt here. Period furnishings, photos of the hardy Parker clan and exhibits on ranch life fill the handful of rooms.

In addition, the estate maintains beautiful gardens, and visitors to the homes are welcome to picnic on the grounds.

Isaacs Art Center

With a stunning collection of significant and historic Hawaiian paintings and artifacts, this art center (☎ 885-5884; www.isaacsartcenter.org; 65-1268 Kawaihae Rd; admission free; ☼ 10am-5pm Tue-Sat) more resembles a museum than a traditional gallery, and is perhaps the best outside of the Honolulu Academy of Arts. It's housed in a 1915 plantation schoolhouse (now on the historic register), whose single row of six classrooms makes an ideal exhibition space. The center owns the entire collection of Madge Tennent, and highlights include Tennent's *Lei Queen Fantasia*, Jules Tavernier's *Kilauea by Moonlight*, and especially Herb Kawainui Kane's *The Arrival of Captain Cook at Kealakekua Bay in January 1779*. Many other important artists (not all Hawaiian) are represented. Sales benefit the attached Hawai'i Preparatory Academy, which runs the center and uses it to teach art to its students. Don't miss it.

Waimea Farmers Market

Waimea's farmers market (☼ 7am-noon Sat) is an island highlight and certainly the town's most vibrant and fun community event. Locals turn out in droves to stock up on fresh produce and recent gossip. A wide selection of food stalls emphasize organic produce and specialty items: fresh eggs, herbs and plants, local meat and honey, beautiful flowers and plenty of cooked food. There's a smaller selection of high-quality craft stalls. The market is in front of the Hawaiian Home Lands office, near the 55-mile marker on Hwy 19.

WM Keck Observatory Office

The lobby of this working office (☎ 885-7887; www.keckobservatory.org; 65-1120 Mamalahoa Hwy; ☼ 8:30am-4:30pm Mon-Fri) is open to the public. It's worth visiting if you won't be going to Mauna Kea's Onizuka Center (p271). A computer station and video nicely overview the twin Kecks and their astronomical work, plus there are pretty photos, scale models and a telescope trained on Mauna Kea.

Church Row

Conveniently enough, the historic churches of Waimea are gathered along the same street just off Mamalahoa Hwy. In the park that fronts the 'row,' a display describes all five, which include Baptist, Buddhist, Mormon and Hawaiian Christian places of worship. All hold services.

The Imiola Congregational Church (☼ services 9:30am) was constructed in 1857 and restored in 1976. The beautiful interior was built mainly of koa, which glows unadorned by stained glass or painted scenes. In the churchyard is the grave of missionary Lorenzo Lyons, who arrived in 1832 and spent 54 years in Waimea. Lyons wrote many of the hymns that are still sung in Hawaiian here each Sunday. Also in the garden is the church bell, which is too heavy for the church roof to support.

Anna Ranch Heritage Center

The life and times of Hawaii's 'first lady of ranching,' Anna Leialoha Lindsey Perry-Fiske, are celebrated at this 14-room **historic ranch house** (☎ 885-4426; www.annaranch.org; 65-1480 Kawaihae Rd; tours $7; ⏰ by appointment Wed, Fri & Sat), which is stuffed with memorabilia. It makes an interesting alternative to Parker Ranch. Tours must be booked in advance.

ACTIVITIES

Ulu La'au Waimea Nature Park (☎ 885-5210; www .waimeaoutdoorcircle.org; ⏰ 7am-5:30pm), which is off Hwy 190, is a 10-acre, lovingly tended community garden (featuring native plants) that's perfect for a picnic. If you have young kids, head for the excellent playground in **Waimea Park** on Kawaihae Rd.

Of course, horseback riding is quite popular in Waimea, and a great outfit is near town. our pick **Dahana Ranch Roughriders** (☎ 885-0057, 888-399-0057; www.dahanaranch.com; rides per 1½hr $70, 2hr $100; ⏰ tours 9am, 11am, 1pm & 3pm), owned by a Native Hawaiian family, is both a working ranch and the most established horseback tour company on the Big Island. It breeds, raises, trains and uses only its own American quarter horses for its tours; reservations required. Horses cross the open range of a working cattle ranch rather than follow trails, and you can trot, canter and gallop. For a special 'city slicker' adventure (four-person minimum), you can help drive a 100-head herd of cattle ($130). Dahana is also the only outfit that lets very young children (aged three and up) join in. It's located 7.5 miles east of Waimea, off Old Mamalahoa Hwy.

To book **Parker Ranch horseback rides** (☎ 885-7655, 877-855-7999; www.parkerranch.com; horseback rides $79; ⏰ 8:15am & 12:15pm), contact the 'Gear Up and Go' desk in the Parker Ranch store in Parker Ranch Shopping Center. The two-hour rides (age seven and up) focus on ranch history and include visits to the stone corrals and the arena. Parker Ranch also offers, by reservation only, a variety of hunting trips For Parker Ranch tours, see below.

TOURS

Parker Ranch tours (☎ 885-7655, 877-855-7999; www .parkerranch.com) come in two sizes. First, there's

the 1½-hour Mana Rd Tour (per person $75; Monday to Saturday), which includes a snack and visits ranch operations not open to the public, like the working corrals and the *paniolo* workstation. Then there's the four-hour Cattle Country Tour (per person $140; Tuesday to Saturday), which includes a light lunch, a personalized tour of the main estate, and a more customized and involved tour of the private ranch. On both there's the chance, but not the promise, that you'll meet a working *paniolo*. Both tours have a minimum of two people and a maximum of six.

A number of small farms in the region welcome visitors; see p281.

FESTIVALS & EVENTS

Small rodeo events occur year round.
Fourth of July Parker Ranch Rodeo (☎ 885-2303) A uniquely Waimea event, with cattle roping, bull riding, horse races and other hoopla at the Rodeo Arena.
Aloha Festivals Ho'olaule'a (http://alohafestivals .com) Held during the statewide Aloha Festivals in August and September, with food, games, art and crafts, and entertainment, plus the Aloha Festival Paniolo Parade, which has marching bands, floats, *taiko* drumming and equestrian units.
Round-Up Rodeo (☎ 885-5669) Held on Labor Day weekend (first Monday in September). Another whip-cracking Parker Ranch rodeo, this one lasting two days.
'Ukulele & Slack Key Guitar Masters Concert (☎ 885-6017; www.kahilutheatre.org) Early November. Two nights of concerts gather uke and slack key guitar legends, like Cyril Pahinui, Ozzie Kotani and HAPA, and include a *kanikapila* (open-mike jam). Fantastic workshops range from beginner to master classes.

SLEEPING

Kamuela Inn (☎ 885-4243, 800-555-8968; www.hawaii -bnb.com/kamuela.html; 1600 Kawaihae Rd; r $60-85, ste $90-185) This motel is definitely the best deal in town. The 31 rooms aren't fancy and walls are thin, but they are clean and modestly attractive, and all have TV and private bath. Within the complex, room sizes and situations vary; spending a little more can significantly improve your experience.

Waimea Country Lodge (☎ 885-4100, 800-367-5004; www.castleresorts.com; 65-1210 Lindsey Rd; r $120-140) This 21-room motel makes an acceptable, if overpriced, backup if other lodging is booked: rooms are scuffed, tired and suffer from street noise, but they are clean enough and don't lack for space.

Waimea Gardens Cottages (☎ 885-8550; www .waimeagardens.com; cottage d incl breakfast $150-180; 🖳 🛜) For a private romantic getaway, book one of the three rooms here. Two are detached cottages, all have private entrances, and each is attractively decorated and stocked with amenities. Two (Kohala and Garden) have fun outdoor showers; Kohala cottage adds a full kitchen and whirlpool bath. Breakfast is left in your room's refrigerator, encouraging late mornings. It's 2 miles west of downtown (near the intersection of Kawaihae Rd and Hwy 250).

Jacaranda Inn (☎ 885-8813; www.jacarandainn.com; 65-1444 Kawaihae Rd; r $160, ste $180-200) The eight romantic rooms here are indulgent, antique-filled visions, a mix of four-poster beds, opulent tiled baths, carved furniture, Jacuzzi tubs and oriental rugs over hardwood floors. No two are alike. Call ahead; the property is for sale, but promises to continue as an inn.

our pick Aaah, the Views B&B (☎ 885-3455; www .aaahtheviews.com; 66-1773 Alaneo St; d incl breakfast $150-195; 🛜) This funky, supremely cozy B&B certainly earns its name – it's a memorable combination of aaah-some mountain views, romantic indulgence and a relaxed, friendly atmosphere. Of the two view rooms, the Dream Room is a favorite, adding a tasty outdoor shower and luscious bath, while Treetop has two sleeping lofts (great for families) and a private deck. The equally nice Garden Room lacks a view, but it *does* have an in-room sauna. The affable, eco-conscious owners make sure everyone is ready for their day with large breakfasts and banter on the view-licious common porch.

EATING

Waimea restaurants serve some of the Big Island's best eats.

Waimea Coffee Company (☎ 885-8915; www.waimea coffeecompany.com; Parker Sq, Kawaihe Rd; sandwiches $7-8.50; 🕙 7am-5:30pm Mon-Fri, 8am-4pm Sat, 10am-3pm Sun; 🛜) This upscale coffee shop has a devoted following for its espresso drinks and panini.

Tako Taco (☎ 887-1717; 64-1066 Mamalahoa Hwy; dishes $3-11; 🕙 11am-8:30pm Mon-Sat, noon-8pm Sun) Good taquerias are a salve to the soul, and this brightly decorated choice serves burritos, quesadillas and fish tacos that put you right. For that warm yet eye-watering kick, request the habanero salsa. A full selection of beers and occasional live music.

Lilikoi Cafe (☎ 887-1400; Parker Ranch Center, 67-1185 Mamalahoa Hwy; mains $5-11.50; 🕙 7:30am-4pm Mon-Sat) For healthy and delicious fresh juices, tons of creative salads and an eclectic range of hot food (lasagna, meatloaf, crepes) seek out this hidden café. It's great for takeout (it uses compostable tableware).

Hawaiian Style Cafe (☎ 885-4295; Hayashi Bldg, 64-1290 Kawaihae Rd; dishes $6-9; 🕙 7am-1:30pm Mon-Sat, to noon Sun) The screen door, its springs shot, slams constantly as locals gather around the horseshoe-shaped counter. This favorite island-style greasy spoon plates generous portions of *loco moco*, pancakes, *laulau*, poi, fried rice, burgers and much more. Heed the sign: 'Come early. When food is *pau*…there is no more!'

Yong's Kal-Bi (☎ 885-8440; Waimea Center, Mamalahoa Hwy; mains $9-12; 🕙 10am-9pm Mon-Sat) This busy Korean cafeteria whips up delicious tender BBQ and rich soups. Yong's is appetizing, efficient and well-priced – a great combo.

Pau (☎ 885-6325; http://paupizza.com; Opelo Plaza, 65-1227 Opelo Rd; sandwiches & pizza $9-24; 🕙 11am-8pm Mon-Sat) 'Casual gourmet' sums up the almost off-hand deliciousness of this stylish, low-key newcomer. Fresh soups, grilled fish sandwiches, perfect thin-crust pizza – nothing disappoints, and local ingredients grace everything. Even the side salads are crisp and well made.

Huli Sue's (☎ 885-6268; www.hulisues.com; 64-957 Mamalahoa Hwy; mains $12-24, BBQ $15-19; 🕙 11:30am-8:30pm Mon-Sat, noon-8pm Sun) Huli Sue's kiawe-smoked BBQ is sweet (not hot) and can be greasy. However, the sides – like corn pudding, onion rings and garlic mashed potatoes – are rave-worthy and the salad bar is awesome. Weekly specials can see curry and other Indian food added to the menu.

Waimea Ranch House (☎ 885-2088; Waimea Center, 65-1144 Mamalahoa Hwy; mains $15-33; 🕙 11am-1:30pm & 5-8:30pm Wed-Mon) When you need a flawlessly grilled rib-eye steak, come here. All the locals do. There's a down-home bar and a more formal dining room, but steak prepared without fuss and as rare as you dare is the only meal to order. Yes, it does other things, and quite well, we're told; but maybe next time.

Daniel Thiebaut (☎ 887-2200; www.danielthiebaut .com; 65-1259 Kawaihae Rd; mains lunch $11-14, dinner $21-45; 🕙 11am-1:30pm Mon-Fri, 10am-1:30pm Sun, 3:30-9pm daily) Chef/owner Daniel Thiebaut seems to remake the menu at his namesake restaurant every other year. But whatever he serves in the rambling, attractively restored historic building is sure to be good. Happy

HAWAI'I THE BIG ISLAND

hour (3:30pm to 5:30pm) is a great start, with tasty *pupu* and creative cocktails. Lunch is relaxed and informal, while dinner creates a more romantic, special-occasion mood. Thiebaut has a way with seafood, which is always excellent, and the current menu adds curries, steaks, pad thai (Thai noodle stir-fry) and creative pastas.

our pick **Merriman's** (☎ 885-6822; www.merriman shawaii.com; Opelo Plaza, 65-1227 Opelo Rd; mains lunch $12-18, dinner $30-45; ☺ 11:30am-1:30pm Mon-Fri, 5:30-9pm daily) An innovator of Hawaii Regional Cuisine, chef-owner Peter Merriman created the Big Island's first gourmet restaurant devoted to organic, island-grown produce and meats. Romance infuses the dining room, and the service is perfect, but the proof is on the plate: Hawaiian- and Asian-influenced dishes like ponzu-marinated mahimahi, wok-charred ahi and Big Island filet steak with Hamakau mushrooms are gems. Merriman's signature coconut crème brûlée still only wants for two spoons.

The **KTA Super Store** (☎ 885-8866; Waimea Center, 65-1158 Mamalahoa Hwy; ☺ 6am-11pm) has 'plenny' *poke* (and a pharmacy).

ENTERTAINMENT

Kahilu Theatre (☎ 885-6017, box office 885-6868; www .kahilutheatre.org; Parker Ranch Center, 67-1186 Lindsey Rd; admission $35-45; ☺ showtimes vary) Waimea may not be hopping with nightlife, but it enjoys a first-class year-round slate of dance, music and theater. Past performers at Kahilu have included Chick Corea, Paul Taylor Dance Company, Laurie Anderson, Chanticleer and the Harlem Gospel Choir. A big draw is the annual 'Ukulele & Slack Key Guitar Masters Concert (p266).

SHOPPING

Three shopping malls line Hwy 19 through town: **Parker Ranch Center** (67-1185 Mamalahoa Hwy), where the stop signs say 'Whoa,' **Waimea Center** (65-1158 Mamalahoa Hwy) and **Parker Square** (65-1279 Kawaihae Rd). The first two have groceries and basics, in addition to gift shops; Parker Square aims for the more discriminating, upscale gift buyer.

Gallery of Great Things (☎ 885-7706; www.gal leryofgreatthings.com; Parker Sq; ☺ 9am-5:30pm Mon-Sat, 10am-4pm Sun) This standout gallery carries over 200 artists and is crammed with antiques, high-quality art and collectibles from Hawaii, Polynesia and Asia.

TOP PICKS – GOURMET CUISINE

- **Hualalai Grille by Alan Wong** (p247)
- **Merriman's** (left)
- **Daniel Thiebaut** (p267)
- **Hilo Bay Cafe** (p297)
- **Brown's Beach House** (p253)
- **Roy's Waikoloa Bar & Grill** (p250)

Reyn's (☎ 885-4493; www.reyns.com; Parker Ranch Center; ☺ 9:30am-5:30pm Mon-Sat, to 4pm Sun) If you want to dress like a local, shop at Reyn's. Its classic, understated aloha shirts (which use Hawaiian fabrics in reverse) never go out of style.

Giggles (☎ 885-2151; Parker Ranch Center; ☺ 9am-5:30pm Mon-Sat, to 5pm Sun) A must for affordable, baby- and kid-size aloha shirts and dresses, plus cool toys and Hawaiian Hello Kitty items.

Crackseed, Etc (☎ 885-6966; Hayashi Bldg, Kawaihae Rd; ☺ 9:30am-4:30pm Mon-Fri, 10am-4pm Sat) Need bulk quanitites of that addictive Chinese dried fruit called 'crack seed' (see p64)? Get them here. Crackseed also carries a nice selection of gift items, like authentic fishhook carvings and stylish clothes.

Dan DeLuz's Woods (☎ 885-5856; 64-1013 Mamalahoa Hwy; ☺ 9am-5pm) The Waimea shop of this famous local woodworker (see p301) contains one-of-a-kind handcarved bowls and sculptures of the highest quality.

GETTING THERE & AROUND

Waimea-Kohala Airport is south of town, but you aren't likely to fly there. From Monday to Saturday the free Hele-On bus (p212) goes from Waimea to Kailua-Kona on its 16 Kailua-Kona route (65 minutes), and to Hilo on its 7 Downtown Hilo route (one hour 20 minutes). The bus stops at Parker Ranch Center.

The drive from Kailua-Kona is 37 very scenic miles along Hwy 190; you ascend into grassy rangeland studded with prickly-pear cacti and enjoy great coastal views. From Hilo, the drive is 51 miles along Hwy 19 around the Hamakua Coast.

Though Waimea isn't large, you need a car to get around. There's ample parking, but peak commuter times create terrible traffic jams.

AROUND WAIMEA

KOHALA FOREST RESERVE

One of the Big Island's best short hikes is the **Kohala Forest Reserve Trail**, leading several miles through an ohia forest to stunning views of the back of Waipi'o Valley. However, the trail was closed due to damage from the 2006 earthquake and has not reopened. Apparently, property owners (tired of careless hikers leaving trash and cattle gates open) want access through their land closed indefinitely. Call the **Department of Land & Natural Resorces** (DLNR; ☎ 794-4221) for updates.

Should it reopen: to get there, from Waimea head east on Hwy 19 for about 3 miles (past mile marker 54), then turn left (or north) on White Rd. Drive about a mile to the end of the road, park at the gate, and enter on foot (closing the gate behind you). Walk past Waimea Reservoir; in about 1.5 miles a sign lets you know you've entered the Kohala Forest Reserve (Map p277).

OLD MAMALAHOA HIGHWAY

If you're driving between Waimea and Honoka'a, consider taking this portion of the Old Mamalahoa Hwy (Map p277), a 10-mile detour off Hwy 19 (from Waimea, enter at the 52-mile marker; from Honoka'a, enter at the 43-mile marker across from Tex Drive-In). This winding, unhurried road provides a soothing glimpse of surrounding ranchland, horses, and herds of cattle; to deepen the experience, consider taking an agricultural tour at one of the small farms in this area (see p281).

MAUNA KEA

At 13,796ft, Mauna Kea is Hawai'i's highest peak, but measured from its beginnings on the ocean floor, it adds another 15,000ft, becoming the world's tallest mountain (just edging out Mauna Loa). Size, however, is just one measure of Mauna Kea's stature. Here, nature, spirituality and science converge and sometimes conflict in vivid ways. This dormant volcano's harsh environment once sported a glacier and is home to numerous endangered endemic species. Mauna Kea is also one of the holiest places in traditional Hawaiian spirituality, and on its most sacred spot – the summit – has gathered the greatest collection of major astronomical telescopes in the world.

The Hilo museum 'Imiloa (p288) provides a wonderful introduction to the mountain and its history, but a visit to Mauna Kea itself, particularly the summit, is an unforgettable experience. All of Hawaii lies below (not to mention 40% of earth's atmosphere) as the sun sinks into an ocean of clouds – while the telescopes silently unshutter and turn their unblinking eyes to the heavens. Even though it means long pants, a winter coat, some careful arrangements and a little luck, you won't be sorry you left the beach to make the pilgrimage.

HISTORY

Mauna Kea rose to become the tallest peak in Polynesia. Between 40,000 and 13,000 years ago, ice-age glaciers covered the summit, beneath which lava continued to erupt. Mauna Kea's last eruption was around 4500 years ago; it has since slid off the hot spot and is considered 'dormant.'

Certain plants and animals adapted to this unique environment. Ascending the mountain, biological zones shift from rain forest to koa-and-ohia forest to open woodland to shrubs and finally (above 11,500ft) to alpine desert. Every elevation has numerous species endemic to Hawai'i, and some found only on Mauna Kea. Plants endemic to the summit include the dramatic Mauna Kea silversword, which takes 50 years to flower, and does so only once (see p418).

Summit creatures are restricted mostly to insects. Strangest by far is the endemic *wekiu*, a bug that adapted by changing from a herbivore to a bug-eating carnivore, and by developing 'antifreeze' blood to survive the subfreezing temperatures. Further down the mountain, several of Hawai'i's endemic birds call Mauna Kea home, such as the nene, the *palia* (honeycreeper) and the endangered Hawaiian bat, the *'ope'ape'a*.

When Polynesians arrived on Hawai'i, Mauna Kea came to play a central role in Hawaiian cosmology. Mauna Kea is believed to be the firstborn child of the gods Wakea and Papa, who also gave birth to taro and the first human (from whom Hawaiians and all people descend). The mountain is also considered a sacred realm of the gods (where people are not meant to live), and the summit is the place were sky and earth separated to create heaven.

DETOUR: HAKALAU FOREST NATIONAL WILDLIFE REFUGE

The Hakalau Forest National Wildlife Refuge (Map p277) is a place few people, even locals, ever venture. This extremely remote refuge protects a portion of the state's largest koa-ohia forest, which provides a habitat for endangered bird species. About 7000 acres are open to public access, but only on weekends and state holidays.

Adventurous souls with a 4WD (or a mountain bike) can visit on their own. From Waimea, a rough dirt road runs 44 miles around Mauna Kea; from Hwy 19 at the 55-mile marker near Waimea, turn south onto Mana Rd. However, if it's rained, don't attempt this – the mud bogs are said to be bottomless. The refuge has no facilities, signage or trails. To get a permit, call or write to the **refuge manager** (☎ 933-6915; www.fws.gov/pacificislands/wnwr/bhakalaunwr.html; 32 Kino'ole St, Hilo, HI 96720; ☑ 8am-4pm Mon-Fri).

A much easier way to experience this pristine wilderness is to take a tour with **Hawaii Forest & Trail** (☎ 331-8505, 800-464-1993; www.hawaii-forest.com; tours $160).

Three sister goddesses call the summit home; the most famous is the snow goddess Poliahu, who lives in Pu'u Poliahu. In legends, Poliahu often competes with Pele, and their snow-and-lava tussles are a metaphorically correct depiction of Mauna Kea's geology. For Hawaiians, Mauna Kea was (and remains) a temple, a place of worship and a sacred burial site.

The arrival of Westerners in the late 1700s also meant the introduction of feral cattle, goats and sheep on Mauna Kea. By the early 20th century these animals had decimated the mountain's natural environment; animal eradication efforts, begun in the 1920s and continuing today, have helped nature to partly restore itself.

In 1960 astronomer Gerard Kuiper placed a telescope on Pu'u Poliahu and announced that 'the mountaintop is probably the best site in the world from which to study the moon, the planets and stars.' Kuiper turned out to be right.

In 1968, the same year the first Mauna Kea observatory was built, the University of Hawai'i (UH) was granted a 65-year lease to the summit area, now called the 'Mauna Kea Science Reserve.' The university leases property to others, and 13 telescopes are currently in operation, which is more than on any other single mountain. They include three of the world's largest, and their combined light-gathering power is 60 times greater than the Hubble Space Telescope.

All this building and development on such an environmentally fragile and culturally sacred place has led to heated conflicts (see opposite). Today, concerted efforts are being made to balance the needs of all stakeholders on Mauna Kea, so that the environment is protected, Hawaiian culture is respected and cutting-edge astronomy continues. It's a three-sided conflict that often defines modern-day Hawaii.

ORIENTATION & INFORMATION

The Mauna Kea Summit Rd is near mile marker 28 on Saddle Rd (for more on driving this road with a rental car, see p276). From the Saddle Rd junction, it's paved for 6 miles to the Onizuka Visitor Information Station (see opposite).

Any standard car can drive this far; it takes about 50 minutes from Hilo or Waimea and 1½ hours from Kailua-Kona. Past the visitor center, it's another 8 miles (half unpaved) and nearly 5000ft to the summit; only 4WD vehicles should be used from this point on. To visit the summit without a 4WD, you will need to join a Mauna Kea tour (for more information see p274), hike, or beg a lift at the visitor center from someone with a 4WD (you sometimes get lucky).

Note that the Mauna Kea summit is not a national, state or county park. There are no restaurants, gas stations or emergency services. Weather conditions can change rapidly, and daytime temperatures range from 50°F to below freezing. The summit can be windy, and observatory viewing rooms are just as cold as outside. Bring warm clothing, a heavy jacket, sunglasses and sunscreen. Call the **recorded hotline** (☎ 935-6268) for info on weather and road conditions.

DANGERS & ANNOYANCES

The Onizuka Visitor Information Station is at 9200 ft, and even here some visitors might experience shortness of breath and mild altitude sickness. At the 13,796ft summit, atmospheric pressure is 60% what it is at sea level, and altitude sickness is common. Symptoms include nausea, headaches, drowsiness, impaired reason, loss of balance, shortness of breath and dehydration. The only way to recover is to descend. Kids under 16, pregnant women, and those with high blood pressure or circulatory conditions should not go to the summit. Nor should you scuba dive within 24 hours of visiting Mauna Kea.

The best way to avoid altitude sickness is to ascend slowly. All hikers and travelers to the summit should stop first at the visitor center for at least 30 minutes to acclimatize before continuing.

SIGHTS
Onizuka Visitor Information Station

Officially the Onizuka Center for International Astronomy, the **center** (☎ 961-2180; www.ifa .hawaii.edu/info/vis; ☽ 9am-10pm) was named for Ellison Onizuka, a Big Island native, and one of the astronauts who perished in the 1986 *Challenger* space shuttle disaster.

In itself, the Onizuka Visitor Information Station is rather modest, but its one room is packed with information: videos on astronomy, computer feeds and virtual tours of several observatories, and exhibits on the mountain's history, ecology and geology. The rangers, interpretive guides and volunteers are extremely knowledgeable about astronomy and Mauna Kea's cultural significance,

---

THE PLACE BETWEEN HEAVEN & EARTH

On Mauna Kea's summit, the first snow of winter is falling.

Near the visitor center, Ranger James Keali'i Pihana – known affectionately as 'Kimo' – is blocking the frozen road in his pickup and trying to explain to a haole (Caucasian) writer what Mauna Kea means to Hawaiians.

'To us, Mauna Kea is not "White Mountain," it is "the heavens." It is the "Mount of Waikea," the place between heaven and earth. The *Kumulipo* tells the creation story of these islands, the first creation of man, and Mauna Kea is the center of our "Bible story."'

Beneath his stiff ranger cap, long gray hair curls over Kimo's collar. His dark eyes are intense as his thick laborer's hands gently conjure visions in the air.

'Mauna Kea is the home of the snow goddess, Poliahu, Pele's sister. Ceremonies are still conducted: equinox, solstices, first light, pray to the sun. In the old days, common people could only go up as far as the visitor center today. Lake Waiau is sacred water. Umbilical cords were put in the lake for the protection of children. My son's umbilical cord is in the lake right now.'

Officially, Kimo is Mauna Kea's resident 'Hawaiian cultural practitioner,' but he doesn't need the title. 'My authority comes from the ruling chiefs of Hawaii. I'm the conscience of the Hawaiian people up here.'

An elder and priest – kahuna – Kimo and others walked up the mountain in 1998 to voice their deep concern over the 'golf balls' – the observatories. Sacred places and burial sites had been built on and disturbed, and new observatories were going up without communicating with or consulting Native Hawaiians.

'We found astronomers were not having respect for the mountain.' A rally was held, and Kimo says, 'I scolded all of them, from the governor on down. Our people were ready to shut the road down.'

It was a pivotal moment, and the politicians and astronomers responded. A Native Hawaiian advisory council was created, Kimo conducted 'cleansing rituals to forgive and repent,' and then he applied for a job. He now spends his days like any other ranger, but his more important duty is communicating with Hawaiian leaders about what's happening on their sacred mountain.

He says, 'There is much more cooperation today. The directors acknowledge they need to respect Hawaiian protocol. Locals are accepting of astronomy. The mountain is calm.'

As he talks, two Japanese men approach the truck; despite the weather, they still want to drive to the top. One pleads, 'We've traveled very far.'

Kimo shakes his head. 'The mountain rules' is all he says.

On this night, Poliahu is spreading her white robe over the summit, and Kimo doesn't seem at all sad to be the one making sure no one disturbs her homecoming.

and they are eager to help with hiking and driving advice.

Also, you can purchase (and heat in a microwave) coffee, hot chocolate and instant noodles, or munch on freeze-dried astronaut food, and there are books and gifts for sale. Several hikes are possible from the visitor center (see right), and at night the free stargazing program (see p274) is held here.

Summit Observatories

If you have a 4WD, you may drive to the summit in the daytime, and you are allowed to stay until a half-hour after sunset. Since vehicle headlights interfere with astronomical observation, all cars are asked to leave before nightfall. It takes about half an hour to drive the 8-mile summit road; the first 4.5 miles are gravel.

Just before the pavement begins, the area on the east side of the road is dubbed 'moon valley,' because it's where the Apollo astronauts rehearsed with their lunar rover before their journey to the real moonscape.

Just past the 6-mile marker is a parking area; below this is the trailhead to Lake Waiau and to the ancient adze quarry Keanakako'i. Getting to both takes about an hour, depending on your rate of acclimatization. During Mauna Kea's ice age, when molten lava erupted under the glaciers, it created an extremely hard basalt, which ancient Hawaiians chipped into sharp adzes at **Keanakako'i**. These tools were fashioned on the mountain and traded throughout the islands. Entering the fragile quarry is highly discouraged.

Nearby, sitting in Pu'u Waiau at 13,020ft, is **Lake Waiau**. This unique alpine lake is the third-highest in the USA. Thought by ancient Hawaiians to be bottomless, it is actually only 10ft deep and, despite desert conditions, never dry. Clay formed from ash holds the water, which less fed by melted snow, permafrost and less than 15in of rainfall annually. To Hawaiians, these sacred waters are considered the 'umbilical cord' (*piko*) connecting heaven and earth, and a traditional practice is to place a baby's umbilical cord in the water to assure good health.

On the summit are the massive dome-shaped observatories, which rise up from the stark terrain like some futuristic human colony on another planet. Unfortunately, you can't see much inside the observatories. Currently only two have visitor galleries, and they're minimal: the **WM Keck Observatory visitor gallery** (www.keckobservatory.org; admission free; 10am-4pm Mon-Fri) includes a display, a 15-minute video, public bathrooms and a plexiglass-enclosed viewing area inside the Keck I dome; and the **University of Hawai'i 2.2m Telescope** (admission free; 9:30am-3:30pm Mon-Thu), which has displays and a view of the telescope room.

The short 200yd trail to Mauna Kea's true summit begins opposite the University of Hawai'i telescope; it's harder than it looks, and it's not necessary to go to see the sunset. The summit is marked by a US Geological Survey (USGS) summit benchmark and a Native Hawaiian altar. Given the biting winds, high altitude and extreme cold, most people don't linger.

From the summit, the breathtaking sunsets leave everyone speechless; look east to see 'the shadow,' or the gigantic silhouette of Mauna Kea looming over Hilo. Moonrises can be equally as impressive: the high altitude can make the moon appear squashed and misshapen, or sometimes resemble a brushfire.

ACTIVITIES
Hiking

Several short walks begin at the Onizuka Visitor Information Station. Off the parking lot is an area protecting the endemic, dramatic silversword, while across from the visitor center, a 10-minute uphill hike on a well-trodden trail crests **Pu'ukalepeamoa**, a cinder cone that offers the best sunset views near the center. Several moderate hikes also begin from the summit road (see left).

Then there is the 6-mile **Humu'ula-Mauna Kea Summit Trail**, which climbs nonstop about 4600ft to the top of Mauna Kea. This is a very strenuous, all-day, high-altitude hike up such steep, barren slopes you sometimes feel you might step off the mountain into the sky. Utterly exposed to winds and the changeable weather, it makes for an eerie, primordial experience.

To do this trail, start early – by 6am if possible. It typically takes five hours to reach the summit, and half as long coming down, and you want time to explore in between. Consult with rangers for advice, and before hiking, get a map and register at the center's outdoor trail kiosk.

Park at the Onizuka Center and walk 1000ft up the road; where the pavement ends, go left

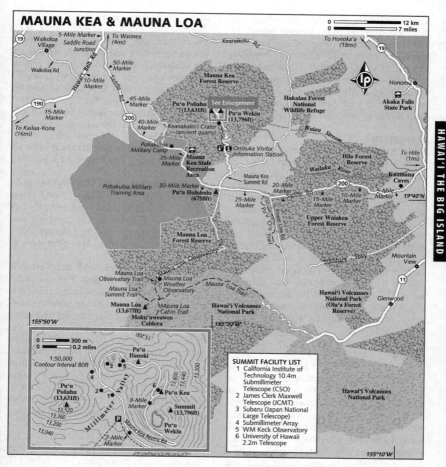

MAUNA KEA & MAUNA LOA

SUMMIT FACILITY LIST
1 California Institute of Technology 10.4m Submillimeter Telescope (CSO)
2 James Clerk Maxwell Telescope (JCMT)
3 Subaru (Japan National Large Telescope)
4 Submillimeter Array
5 WM Keck Observatory
6 University of Hawaii 2.2m Telescope

on the dirt road, following several **Humu'ula Trail** signs to the trail proper. Reflective T-posts and cairns mark the route; after about an hour the summit road comes back into view on your right, and the vegetation starts to disappear. As you weave around cinder cones and traipse over crumbled 'a'a and slippery scree, you pass various spur trails; all lead back to the access road.

Most of the way you will be passing through the **Mauna Kea Ice Age Natural Area Reserve**. After about three hours, a sharp, short ascent leads to Keanakako'i (see opposite), the adze quarry, which is off to the right; look for large piles of bluish-black chips. Do not enter, or remove anything from, this protected area.

The hardest, steepest part of the trail is now behind you. After another mile you reach a four-way junction, where a 10-minute detour to the left brings you to Lake Waiau (see opposite). Return to the four-way junction and head north (uphill) for the final push to meet the Mauna Kea Access Rd at a parking area. Suddenly the observatories are visible on the summit, and straight ahead is Millimeter Valley, nicknamed for its three submillimeter observatories (among them the James Clerk Maxwell Telescope). The trail officially ends at the access road's 7-mile marker, but the top of the mountain still snickers at you another 1.5 miles away.

You didn't come this far not to reach the true summit, so soldier on till you reach the

University of Hawai'i 2.2m Telescope, where the short spur trail to the summit begins.

When descending, return along the shoulder of the access road rather than retracing the trail. Though the road is 2 miles longer, it's easier on the knees and easier to follow as sunlight fades. Also, it's common for hikers to get offered a lift downhill; sticking to the road increases your chances.

Stargazing

The Onizuka Visitor Information Station offers a free stargazing program from 6pm to 10pm, weather permitting (bad weather prevents stargazing only two to three nights per month). There are no reservations, but you could call the visitor center to confirm that the program is on that evening. At 9200ft the skies are among the clearest, driest and darkest on the planet. In fact, at the station you're above the elevation of most major telescopes worldwide. This is the *only* place you can use telescopes on Mauna Kea; there are no public telescopes on the summit. How much you'll see depends on cloud cover and moon phase. The busiest nights are Friday and Saturday.

Skiing

You brought your skis to Hawai'i, right? For a month or two (beginning in January or February), enough snow usually falls on Mauna Kea's heights to allow for winter sports. Snowboards are preferred over skis, but on a nice day the 'slopes' can get crowded with locals using surfboards, bodyboards, inner tubes – whatever! One popular tradition is to fill a truck bed with snow, drive to the beach and build a snowman.

Skiing Mauna Kea is a novelty experience and entirely DIY. There are no groomed trails, no lifts, no patrols; exposed rocks and ice sheets are constant dangers. The snow isn't exactly Utah powder, either – more like milky granola. Note that commercial ski tours on Mauna Kea are prohibited.

TOURS

The Onizuka Visitor Information Station offers **free summit tours** (admission free; ⏱ 1pm Sat & Sun), but you must provide your own 4WD transportation. No reservations are needed; simply arrive at the visitor center by 1pm to join the tour. (You might hitch a ride with a friendly person with a 4WD, but don't count

on it.) The first hour is spent watching videos about Mauna Kea as you acclimatize, then you caravan to the summit, where you hear a talk on the history and workings of the summit telescopes. The tours then visit one or two telescopes: the University of Hawai'i's 2.2m telescope and/or WM Keck's 10m telescope. Tours depart from the summit at about 4:30pm, but most people stay for sunset and come down on their own. Pregnant women, children under 16, and those with circulatory and respiratory conditions are not allowed, and tours don't go in bad weather, so call ahead.

Subaru Telescope (☎ 934-5056; www.naoj.org/Information/Tour/Summit; ⏱ tours 10:30am, 11:30am & 1:30pm) offers 30-minute summit tours up to 15 days per month, in English and in Japanese. You must make reservations (by internet only), and you need your own transportation to the summit.

A highly recommended alternative is taking a **sunset summit tour.** The two most recommended companies, Hawaii Forest & Trail and Mauna Kea Summit Adventures (see below), have excellent guides who know their history and astronomy; aided by 11-inch, satellite-guided telescopes, their stargazing sessions make the sky come alive. They also have comfortable vans, and provide gloves and parkas, a tasty hot dinner and snacks. Their tours typically start in early afternoon, include a meal stop, arrive at the summit just before sunset (staying about 40 minutes, which doesn't allow for hiking), return to the Onizuka Center for private stargazing, and get you home after 9pm. All require participants to be at least 16 years old, and all but Arnott's pick up from the Kona, Waikoloa and Waimea areas.

Arnott's Lodge (☎ 969-7097; www.arnottslodge.com; 98 Apapane Rd, Hilo; guests/nonguests $70/100) Arnott's tour is more for budget hikers than stargazers. It's cheaper, leaves from Hilo and encourages hiking to the true summit; astronomy is bare bones, with guides relying mostly on laser pointers. BYO food and warm clothes.

our pick **Hawaii Forest & Trail** (☎ 331-8505, 800-464-1993; www.hawaii-forest.com; tours $170) This excellent tour company has the nicest meal stop (at a private ranch outpost); its guides and equipment are both top-notch.

Mauna Kea Summit Adventures (☎ 322-2366, 888-322-2366; www.maunakea.com; tours $178) Mauna Kea was the first company to do summit tours, starting over 20 year ago. It remains a high-quality outfit; meals are outside at the Onizuka Center. Book online two weeks in advance for a 15% discount.

FESTIVALS & EVENTS

Every Saturday night at 6pm the Onizuka center hosts a rotating series of lectures and events:

'The Universe Tonight' First Saturday of the month. Astronomy lecture.

University of Hawai'i Hilo Astrophysics Club Second Saturday of the month. Students assist with stargazing.

Malalo I Ka Lani Po Third Saturday of the month. Culture lecture.

University of Hawai'i Hilo music program Fourth Saturday of the month. All genres.

During big meteor showers, the center staffs its telescopes for all-night star parties; call for details.

SLEEPING

At the 35-mile marker, Mauna Kea State Recreation Area maintains five simple cabins ($35 per night, Friday to Sunday only), which have three twin beds and a bunk bed, flush toilets, a kitchen, lights, electricity and a space heater. However, they have no drinkable water (or showers), kitchens come unequipped, and nearby military maneuvers and seasonal hunting could intrude on your solitude. For reservations, contact the **Division of State Parks** (Map p287; ☎ 974-6200; www.hawaii.gov/dlnr/dsp; PO Box 936, Hilo, HI 96721; ✹ 8am-3:30pm Mon-Fri).

GETTING THERE & AROUND

From Kona, Saddle Rd (Hwy 200) starts just south of the 6-mile marker on Hwy 190. From Hilo, drive *mauka* on Kaumana Dr, which becomes Saddle Rd (Hwy 200). All drivers should start with a full tank of gas, as there are no gas stations on Saddle Rd (see p276).

As described in the Orientation section (see p270), past the visitor center the road is suitable only for 4WD vehicles. Over half the road is gravel, sometimes at a 15% grade, and the upper road can be covered with ice. When descending, drive in low gear (or you can ruin your brakes), and pay attention for any signs of altitude sickness. Driving when the sun is low – in the hour after sunrise or before sunset – can create hazardous blinding conditions.

AROUND MAUNA KEA

MAUNA LOA'S NORTHERN FLANK

Several exceptional hikes are possible from Saddle Rd. The most legendary and rewarding is the route to Mauna Loa's summit, which is the only way to get to the top in a single day.

Hiking
PU'U HULUHULU TRAIL

Just off Saddle Rd and directly across from the Mauna Kea Access Rd, **Pu'u Huluhulu** (meaning 'shaggy hill') is a bushy, foliage-covered cinder cone that stands out on the saddle's flat plain. An easy short hike surmounts and circles it, providing splendid mountain views in all directions. If you're heading for the Mauna Loa summit, this makes a reflective way to spend 30 minutes acclimatizing to the high altitude first. There's a parking lot and pit toilet at the trailhead.

PU'U 'O'O TRAIL

For a more substantial but equally peaceful ramble, try the Pu'u 'O'o Trail (also called the Power Line Rd Trail), a 7-mile loop traversing meadows, old lava flows and a pretty koa-and-ohia *kipuka* forest (an 'island' of older vegetation surrounded by newer lava) filled with the birdsong of Hawaiian honeycreepers. This is a different trail from Hawai'i Volcanoes National Park's Pu'u 'O'o Trail.

The signed trailhead (with a small parking area) is almost exactly halfway between the 22- and 23-mile markers on Saddle Rd. The trail is marked by *ahu* (stone cairns) and white-painted trail tags on lava rocks; it's initially easy to follow, but can get confusing around the *kipuka*. If in doubt, simply retrace your steps the way you came. Eventually, the trail connects with Power Line Rd (marked with a PLR sign), a 4WD road that can be used as the return route. Note, though, that the road returns you about half a mile away from the trailhead parking area.

MAUNA LOA OBSERVATORY TRAIL

This trail is the most recommended way to summit Mauna Loa; those who prefer a challenge above all else might consider taking the daunting, multiday Mauna Loa Trail (see p317). However, make no mistake: the Observatory Trail is a difficult, all-day adventure, but few 13,000ft mountains exist that are

HAWAI'I THE BIG ISLAND

RIDIN' THE SADDLE

True to its name, Saddle Rd (Hwy 200) runs along a saddle-shaped valley between the island's two highest points, Mauna Kea and Mauna Loa. It's an extremely scenic drive: sunrise and sunset bathe these majestic, cinder cone–studded mountains in a gentle glow, and on clear days the vistas extend forever (at least to Maui).

But this 53-mile, mostly two-lane paved road was until recently an accident-prone nightmare: frequently narrowing to one lane, winding and hilly, with blind turns, no lights, sometimes thick fog, and with potholed, deteriorated pavement so bad locals dangerously hugged the center line – leading to its nickname 'Straddle Road.' At one time, all national car-rental companies forbade driving it.

However, its condition and reputation have changed dramatically. The county is spending hundreds of millions to repave and widen the road, so that it might finally function as a practical, safe connector between the island's east and west sides. Today, only the first 10 miles or so from the Kona side recall the good-old bad days. From Hilo, clean smooth pavement gets you over the top, past the Mauna Kea summit turnoff, and down to the Pohakuloa Military Training Area. Work is ongoing (including a realignment around the military base), but the finish date isn't known, since funding is ongoing, too.

Slowly, some national car-rental companies are relaxing their restrictions, so you don't have to feel the outlaw to drive it, but always ask local offices about current policies (see p213 for specifics).

Finally, Saddle Rd contains no services or gas, so fill up, check your spare tire, pack a lunch and don't forget your camera.

---

so accessible to the average hiker. This is a rare and unforgettable experience.

Day hikers do not need a permit, but if you would like to overnight at Mauna Loa Cabin (p317), register the day before at the Kilauea Visitor Center in Hawai'i Volcanoes National Park (see p308).

To reach the trailhead, take the unsigned Mauna Loa Observatory Rd near the 28-mile marker on Saddle Rd; it's nearly opposite the Mauna Kea Access Rd and adjacent to Pu'u Huluhulu. The single-lane, 17.5-mile asphalt road is passable in a standard car but, except for the first 4 miles, it's in terrible condition and full of blind curves. Allow an hour; the squiggled white line is to aid drivers in the fog. The road ends at a parking area just below the weather observatory at 11,150ft. There are no visitor facilities or bathrooms. From the observatory, the Mauna Loa Observatory Trail climbs up to the mountaintop.

Begin hiking early, preferably by 8am; you want to be off the mountain or descending if afternoon clouds roll in. The trail is marked by cairns, which disappear in the fog. If this happens, stop hiking; find shelter in one of several small tubes and hollows along the route until you can see again, even if this means waiting till morning.

It is nearly 4 miles to the trail junction with the **Mauna Loa Trail**. Allow three hours for this gradual ascent of nearly 2000ft. If it weren't for the altitude, this would be a breeze. Instead, proceed slowly but steadily, keeping breaks short. If you feel the onset of altitude sickness (p270), descend. About two hours along, you re-enter the national park, and the lava erupts in a rainbow of colors: sapphire, turquoise, silver, ochre, orange, gold, magenta.

Once at the trail junction, the majesty of the summit's **Moku'aweoweo Caldera** overwhelms the imagination. Day hikers have two choices: proceed another 2.6 miles and three hours along the **Summit Trail** to the tippy-top at 13,677ft (visible in the distance), or explore the caldera itself by following the 2.1-mile **Mauna Loa Cabin Trail**. If you can stand not summiting, the second option is extremely interesting, leading to even grander caldera views and a vertiginous peek into the awesome depths of **Lua Poholo**.

Descending takes half as long as ascending: depending on how far you go, prepare for a seven- to 10-hour round-trip hike. Bring copious amounts of water, food, a flashlight and rain gear, and wear boots, a winter coat and a cap – it's cold and windy year round.

HAMAKUA COAST

On the Big Island, where do you find that lush tropical paradise pictured on magazine covers, the one untouched by the ironic ringtones of the 21st century? Come to the Hamakua Coast. From Waipi'o Valley to Hilo, the Big Island's windward face tells a tale of rain. Innumerable streams gush down the flanks of Mauna Kea, carving deep ravines and tumbling over thousand-foot cliffs. Farmers still work ancient taro patches, and well-preserved sugar plantation towns recall the region's economic heyday, when steam trains rumbled across the sweeping cantilevered bridges. These and other ghosts – from Kukuihaele's legendary night marchers to Laupahoehoe schoolchildren – haunt this fertile region, where along overgrown, forgotten roads it seems as if only a gauzy veil separates then from now.

HONOKA'A

pop 2240

Tiny Honoka'a has done a good job picking itself up from the collapse of the local sugar industry in the 1990s. Gleaming with fresh paint, its false-front, Western-style plantation architecture, a legacy of the sugar boom in the 1920s and 1930s, is Hawai'i's best surviving example of a rural plantation town. Having remade itself into a low-key tourist destination, Honoka'a's raised sidewalks now hold a browser's delight of funky shops run by friendly locals who hardly need an excuse to drop everything and talk story.

Meanwhile, in the fertile countryside that's around town, small-farm agriculture is surging; organic Hamakua produce is often the star of farmer's markets and gourmet menus island-wide. Visiting these farms is another interesting window on local life (see p281).

While here, make sure to visit the small **Katsu Goto Memorial**, on Mamane St next to the library, which honors one of Hawaii's first union activists. A Japanese cane-field worker, Goto was hanged by Honoka'a sugar bosses in 1889 for his attempts to improve labor conditions on Hamakua plantations.

Information

Honoka'a has all the basics: banks with ATMs, a grocery store, a coin laundry and a **post office**

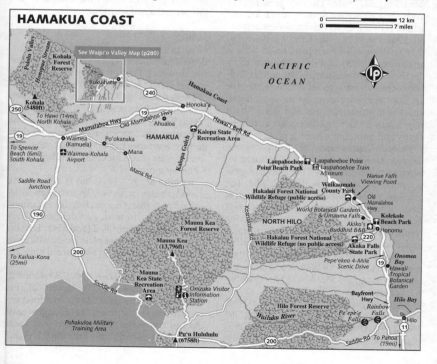

HAWAI'I THE BIG ISLAND

(☎ 800-275-8777; cnr Lehua & Mamane Sts; ☼ 9am-4pm Mon-Fri, 8:15-9:45am Sat). The town's website (www.honokaahawaii.com) is packed with wonderful photos.

Festivals & Events

Hamakua Music Festival (☎ 775-3378; http://ha makuamusicfestival.com; Honoka'a People's Theater, Mamane St; admission $30-40) Late November to early December. A premier music event combining Hawaiian, jazz and classical music and gathering such world-class talents as Cedar Walton and James Moody. The festival also awards scholarships to music students and funds music teachers in public schools.

Honoka'a Western Week (☎ 933-9772; Mamane St; admission free) Late May. An annual event that awakens the usually sleepy Mamane St with a BBQ, a parade, a country dance, a rodeo and entertainers such as local icon Melveen Leed.

Sleeping

The Honoka'a area has some great sleeps and makes a good base for Waipi'o Valley adventures.

Hotel Honoka'a Club (☎ 775-0678, 800-808-0678; www.hotelhonokaa.com; Mamane St; dm & r with shared bathroom $15-35, r $50-70, ste $85) The only game right in town, these plantation workers' rooms are old-school Hawai'i. Expect clean, decent accommodations with lived-in charm – plain decor, thin walls, scuffed furniture, so-so beds – and an atmosphere of warm aloha created by the friendly owner, Annelle. The quieter 2nd-floor ocean-view rooms are definitely the best; 1st-floor no-view rooms get the most noise; and the downstairs dorm and shared-bath rooms can be skipped. Breakfast is simple, chatty and homespun, like the place.

Mountain Meadow Ranch (☎ 775-9376; www.moun tainmeadowranch.com; 46-3895 Kapuna Rd, Ahualoa; ste incl breakfast $115, cottages $150; ☞) For a private getaway, this 7-acre ranch is almost idyllic. The gracious owners, who train quarter horses, have turned the lower level of their redwood home into a spacious B&B suite, with living room, dry-heat sauna, skylights, refrigerator and microwave. The freestanding, family-friendly two-bedroom cottage (three-night minimum) has full kitchen, wood stove and laundry. Mountain Meadow is 3 miles southwest of Honoka'a.

Waipi'o Wayside B&B (☎ 775-0275, 800-833-8849; www.waipiowayside.com; Hwy 240; r incl breakfast $100-170; ☐ ☞) This attractively furnished 1932 plantation house is a cozy B&B that works equally well for couples and families. The five rooms differ markedly, but each enjoys intriguing touches, like iron bed frames, a wooden Chinese barber chair, shower skylight and hardwood floors. The relaxed common room has a library and large-screen TV (with DVDs), and there's a lounge-worthy, secluded lanai. The delicious highlight, though, is the full, homemade organic breakfast. It's between the 3- and 4-mile markers on Hwy 240.

our pick Waianuhea B&B (☎ 775-1118, 888-775-2577; www.waianuhea.com; 45-3503 Kahana Dr; r $195-400; ☐ ☞) Solar-powered, off-the-grid living doesn't get more artfully luxurious than this. Enjoy magazine-quality interior design in each of the five rooms, with color schemes playing off dramatic art pieces. Amenities include flat-screen TVs, cell phones, robes and yoga mats; several have wood stoves, one a view from its soaking tub. The gracious, relaxing public areas and expansive, hidden grounds include a tremendous common room with marble fireplace, outdoor hot tub, lily pond, spacious lanai, downstairs room with carved Balinese bed and more. Toss in a three-course gourmet breakfast (from the restaurant-certified kitchen) and afternoon wine and *pupu*, and this place is a real knockout.

Eating

Honoka'a has a natural foods grocery, an independent butcher and a supermarket; near the Honokaa Trading Company, a farmers market is held on Saturday from 7:30am.

Simply Natural (☎ 775-0119; www.hawaiisimplynatu ral.com; Mamane St; dishes $4-10; ☼ 8am-3pm Mon-Sat, 9-11:30am Sun; ☞) Order up organic, wholesome taro pancakes, tempeh eggs, fruit smoothies and fresh sandwiches at this good-vibe café; free internet access for customers. Live music Saturday mornings.

Tex Drive-In (☎ 775-0598; Hwy 19, mile marker 43; sandwiches & plate lunches $4-9; ☼ 6:30am-8pm-ish) A *malasada* is just a donut, but Tex is famous for making them fresh and delicious. They come plain (96¢) or filled (add 35¢). Tex also serves an above average plate lunch, with crisp green salads; burgers on sweetbread buns are good, too.

Café il Mondo (☎ 775-7711; 45-3626A Mamane St; sandwiches $7, pizza $12-15; ☼ 11am-8pm Mon-Sat) This casual Italian restaurant takes a slow-food approach to its classic renditions of lasagna, roast chicken and pastas. The excellent pizzas and calzones are flavorful (if a little oily); BYOB.

Entertainment

Honoka'a People's Theater (☎ 775-0000; Mamane St; adult/child $6/3) Catch a first-run movie in this atmospheric 1930s theater. It also hosts occasional events, including the not-to-be-missed Hamakua Music Festival (opposite).

Shopping

Honokaa Trading Company (☎ 775-0808; Mamane St; ⏱ 10:30am-4:30pm, hours vary) Whole afternoons can be lost rummaging through the dusty treasures, used books and aloha shirts in this secondhand store. It's worth stopping just for the vintage signs.

Kama'aina Woods (☎ 775-7722; www.hulihands.com; Lehua St; ⏱ 9am-5pm Mon-Fri) This workshop creates some of the finest koa woodwork you'll find. The store also sells smaller items to go with its gems, like a koa concert ukulele.

Honokaa Marketplace (☎ 775-8255; 45-3586 Mamane St; ⏱ 9am-5:30pm) Amazing handmade Hawaiian quilts, bright painted bedspreads and sheets.

LalaSun Designs (☎ 775-1818; www.lalasun.com; 45-3577 Mamane St; ⏱ 11am-5pm Mon & Wed-Fri, 10am-2pm Sat) Gorgeous and unique handmade batik clothes for men and women.

Taro Patch (☎ 775-7228; Mamane St; ⏱ 10am-5pm) This upscale gift store has a little of everything, so you're sure to find something.

Hamakua Fudge Shop (☎ 775-1430; 45-3611 Mamane St; ⏱ 10:30am-4:30pm Mon-Sat, noon-3pm Sun) Creamy fudge ($14 per pound), all made here, with unusual island variations. There's no finer use of the mac nut.

Getting There & Away

From Monday to Saturday the free Hele-On Bus (p212) arrives from Kona on the 7 Downtown Hilo route, then continues on to Hilo. From Hilo, take either the 31 Honoka'a route or the 16 Kailua–Kona route (which continues to Kona). It takes an hour or so from either direction.

KUKUIHAELE

pop 320

This tiny village, about 7 miles from Honoka'a on a loop road off Hwy 240, consists of two shops, a post office mail drop, and a few places to stay – if you dare. Kukuihaele means 'traveling light' and refers to the 'night marchers': the ghosts of Hawaiian warriors carrying torches on their way to Waipi'o Valley, which contains a hidden entrance to the netherworld.

According to legend, if you look directly at them or get in their way, you'll die. It's possible to survive if your ancestor is a marcher, or if you lie face down on the ground.

Sleeping

Hale Kukui Orchard Retreat (☎ 775-7130, 800-444-7130; www.halekukui.com; 48-5460 Kukuihaele Rd; studio $160, 2-room ste $180, 1-room cottages $195) These three secluded, comfortable rooms have amazing views, but the perspective of Waipi'o from the detached cottage is unforgettable. All are nicely, but not plushly, decorated and have TV, phone, kitchen, private bath and private jet tubs on the decks.

Oceanview House (☎ 775-9098, 866-492-4746; www.hawaiioceanviewhouse.com; Hwy 240; house $165) For a house to call your own, this is a stellar choice. It has attractive furnishings and decor, a fully equipped kitchen, two bedrooms, a living room, a laundry, a TV, a phone and geckos aplenty – plus a gorgeous view of the endless Pacific with a peek of Waipi'o Valley. There's nothing not to like. If the Cliff House is booked, you won't regret this choice.

Cliff House Hawaii (☎ 775-0005, 800-492-4746; www.cliffhousehawaii.com; Hwy 240; house $199) You want views? While the layout and level of decor are identical to the Oceanview House, *your* sweeping view is like a private perch over Waipi'o. Book *way* in advance.

Shopping

Neptune's Garden Gallery at Last Chance Store (Map p280; ☎ 775-1343; www.neptunesgarden.net; ⏱ 9am-2:30pm Mon-Sat) The Last Chance Store is a gallery for the owner's stained-glass artworks. If only to continue tradition, the store also still sells bottled water, soda, snacks and ice-cream.

Waipio Valley Artworks (Map p280; ☎ 775-0958, 800-492-4746; www.waipiovalleyartworks.com; ⏱ 8am-5pm) This is a great gift shop and gallery, with lots of koa and ceramic art, plus an excellent selection of books and prints. The shop has a slightly larger selection of sandwiches, muffins, coffee, and ice-cream. It allows Waimanu campers to park here overnight for $15 per night.

WAIPI'O VALLEY

Hawaii contains many beautiful places, but a select few pulsate with a special aura, like dreams sprung to life. The largest of seven spectacular amphitheater valleys on the windward side of the Kohala Mountains, Waipi'o

HAWAI'I THE BIG ISLAND

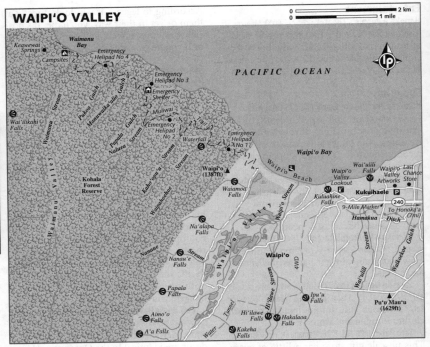

WAIPIʻO VALLEY

embodies the Hawaii of fantasy: white waterfalls trickle down near-vertical emerald cliffs (some 2000ft high), while on the valley floor a tangle of jungle, flowering plants and ancient taro patches is edged with a black-sand beach pounded by frothy waves. Ever since Hawaiians first encountered it, Waipiʻo has been considered a sacred place, and was long a seat of power, but you don't need to know any of that to understand what's meant by mana.

That feeling is, of course, enhanced by descending into the valley, which requires work and planning. The valley is the abrupt end to Hwy 240, and to continue down the precipitous winding road to the bottom requires a 4WD or two sturdy knees. The valley itself contains no lodging or services. Most people content themselves with the views from the lookout, which has a parking lot, phone, bathroom, and trail board. A ranger (8am to 4pm) is also on hand to answer questions and give advice.

History

In ancient times Waipiʻo Valley was the political and religious center of Hawaiʻi; it was nicknamed the 'Valley of Kings' because so many chiefs and aliʻi ruled from here. Kamehameha the Great was raised in secret in the valley, which is where he received the statue of his fearsome war god, Kukaʻilimoku.

Waipiʻo ('curving water') is ideal for growing taro, from which poi is made, and the valley supplied the islands with this important Hawaiian staple crop. According to oral histories, over 4000 people lived in this fertile valley before the arrival of Westerners. Waipiʻo's sacred status is evidenced by a number of important heiau. The most sacred, Pakaʻalana, was also the site of one of the island's two major puʻuhonua (the other is now the Puʻuhonua National Historical Park, p239), but today its location has been lost.

In the 19th century Waipiʻo Valley's population dropped, despite an influx of Chinese immigrants. Nevertheless, the valley still supported schools, restaurants and churches, as well as a hotel, post office and jail.

In 1946 Hawaiʻi's most devastating tsunami slammed great waves far back into the valley (see p285). Coincidentally or not, no one in this sacred place perished. But businesses and farms were ruined, and Waipi'o has been sparsely populated ever since.

Today, about 50 people live in the valley, most of them working some 150 acres of taro patches (many laid out in the 16th century). Other Waipi'o crops include lotus root, avocados, breadfruit, oranges, limes and *pakalolo*.

Dangers & Annoyances

Waipi'o Stream divides the beach in half; take care crossing it, as it is full of ankle-twisting, slippery rocks. It's usually better to cross in deeper, slower-moving water away from the surf. In the winter rainy season the stream can swell till it's impassable, with occasional flash floods. In fact, all valley streams along the Windward Coast are susceptible to flash floods; be watchful for rising waters, and wait to cross. Floods usually subside in a few hours.

As for the surf, it is extremely rough year round, with a tremendous undertow, hidden rocks and rogue waves.

Finally, don't drink from *any* creeks or streams without first boiling or treating the water. Feral animals roam the area, making leptospirosis a real threat (see p579).

Activities

Locals enjoy **surfing** at Waipi'o, but it's not for novices or newcomers; watch the waves for an afternoon and talk to locals before putting your board in the water.

Time the waves and you can certainly take a dip, but rough surf discourages real swimming; use extreme caution in or near the water.

Besides hanging out, most people **hike**. In addition to walking into and out of the valley, the beach area has enjoyable explorations. If you want more, consider tackling the Muliwai Trail (p282). This challenging two- or three-day trip starts from the far end of Waipi'o Valley and leads to the adjacent Waimanu Valley.

WAIPI'O VALLEY HIKE

Spending a day in Waipi'o Valley is reason enough to come to the Big Island. From the lookout a very steep, 1-mile paved road de-

---

SMALL FARMS, BIG ISLAND

With its sugar plantations long gone, Hawai'i is experiencing a surge in small-farm agriculture. Many farms focus on high-end, specialized products using organic, sustainable methods. Many also welcome visitors and are eager to join the growing wave of agricultural tourism.

One company specializing in these tours is **Hawaii AgVentures** (☎ 885-5580, 800-660-6011; www.hawaiiagventures.com), which can tailor specific trips. Another excellent resource is **Hawai'i's Slow Food Convivium** (www.slowfoodhawaii.org). It has regular food events and can connect you to local producers. To ensure you're buying local, look for the words 'Island Fresh' and the 'Hawaii Seal of Quality.'

Three farms have teamed up along the Old Mamalahoa Hwy outside Honoka'a: in one morning, you can visit **Long Ears Hawaiian Coffee** (☎ 775-0385; www.longearscoffee.com), **Volcano Island Honey** (☎ 775-1000, www.volcanoislandhoney.com), which makes highly regarded white honey, and **Mauna Kea Tea** (☎ 775-1171, www.maunakeatea.com). The three-farm tour ($75) starts at 8:45am and lasts till 12:30pm; to book, visit www.visitahualoa.com, or contact the farms directly.

In fact, on the Big Island, tea may soon be the new coffee: a dozen small tea farms, most in East Hawai'i, now focus on growing the highest quality *Camellia sinensis* possible. One is **Tea Hawaii** (☎ 967-7637; www.teahawaii.com) in Volcano village, which does a joint tour with **Volcano Winery** (p319). Another is **Onomea Tea** (www.onomeatea.com) near Onomea Bay on the Hamakua Coast. For coffee farm tours, see p229.

Also on the Hamakua Coast is the **Hawaiian Vanilla Company** (☎ 776-1771; www.hawaiianvanilla .com; ⏰ 10am-5pm Mon-Fri), which was the first commercial vanilla farm in the US. It has regular tastings and culinary events at the mill, and it conducts a Hamakua mushroom tour, with a gourmet dinner.

Finally, chocolate lovers shouldn't miss the **Original Hawaiian Chocolate Factory** (☎ 322-2626, 888-447-2626; www.originalhawaiianchocolatefactory.com), on the slopes of Mt Hualalai. It grows, harvests, processes and packages only Big Island cocoa, and if you're nice, you might even be given a taste.

scends to the valley floor. You can jiggle-jog down the 25% grade in about 20 minutes, but it's a 40-minute thigh-burn return uphill; if you're lucky, someone will offer you a lift.

At the bottom, turn *mauka;* in five minutes you reach perfect views of ribbony **Hi'ilawe Falls**, which at over 1200ft is Hawai'i's highest free-fall waterfall. There's no trail or public access to the falls themselves. You're free to follow the road up-valley; you pass private homes and taro fields. However, you soon reach a deep stream crossing, and past that, a growing sense of privacy. Respect all 'Kapu – No Trespassing' signs.

Back at the main junction, turn *makai* along a muddy dirt road to reach sublime **Waipi'o Beach** in about 10 minutes. The sparkling black-sand beach is lined with graceful ironwood trees, and free-roaming horses often walk the roads and rest on the sand beside you. Bucolic **Waipi'o Stream** enters the ocean (see p281), splitting the rockier eastern strand from the sandy western end.

At the far east end, it's possible to boulder for 20 minutes around the coast to **Kaluahine Falls** (it's sometimes dry) with views of distant **Wai'ulili Falls** cascading into the sea. However, you'll need luck, agility and good timing; the large rocks are unsteady and huge waves can crash up to the cliff face. Be extremely cautious, and never take your eyes off the sea.

MULIWAI TRAIL TO WAIMANU VALLEY

For some, the Zorro-like scratch of the Z trail on the far cliff will beckon, and, by all means, strap on your boots and day-hike a portion of the Muliwai Trail. Just 15 steep minutes yields unparalleled valley views, and more gorgeous sights await once you've crested the cliff. However, getting all the way to Waimanu Valley and back in a day is unrealistic. Depending on pace and fitness, the total 9.5-mile hike from the Waipi'o Lookout takes six to eight hours one way. Backpackers should really consider this a two-night trip, so you can enjoy a full day in timeless Waimanu Valley, which is like a mini Waipi'o. Before starting, spend time reviewing the lookout trailboard; the ranger can also give advice.

At the far west end of the beach, just inland, the trail begins to the right of a locked gate; in a few feet, you come to a Na Ala Hele and state forestry sign. Proceed uphill. In 30 minutes or so, an ironwood grove provides delicious shade, and the first break in the grove signals

your last and best view of Waipi'o – rest here and take it in.

After another 15 minutes in the ironwoods, the trail heads inland, into pine forest, and levels out; you've climbed over 1200ft in about a mile! You quickly reach Helipad 1, and from here the trail dips in and out of stream gulches for about 5 miles. Hugged by cliffs, surrounded by forest, periodically swarmed by mosquitoes, you get only peekaboo views of the ocean until the end.

Compensating for this, in the shadiest heart of each gulch are some of the prettiest cascading rivulets imaginable; some become waterfalls, some burble in quiet pools. If treated, the water is drinkable. At Helipad 2, you are about halfway there; at Helipad 3 is a trail shelter (where you can camp if you have a Waimanu permit); and soon after Helipad 4 the difficult descent into Waimanu Valley begins.

The final mile of the trail can be badly maintained and entails a steep, slippery and exposed descent of 1200ft. Fatigue (and recent rainy weather) can make this particularly treacherous, so go slow. If it's too sketchy, stay overnight at the Helipad 3 trail shelter.

On weekends and holidays you may be shocked to arrive and find the camping area is crowded; local kayakers sometimes come with tons of gear. Arrive midweek and you might have the black-sand beach and waterfalls to yourself.

Tours

Taking a guided tour is another popular option for experiencing the valley; reserve all in advance.

Hawaiian Walkways (☎ 775-0372, 800-457-7759; www.hawaiianwalkways.com; guided hikes $120) Takes you on a hike through private land along the valley rim to waterfalls and pools, where you can swim.

Na'alapa Stables (☎ 775-0419; www.naalapastables .com; rides $89; ✆ departures 9:30am & 1pm Mon-Sat) This outfit also offers a 2½-hour horseback ride; children must be at least eight years old.

Waipi'o on Horseback (☎ 775-7291, 877-775-7291; www.waipioonhorseback.com; Hwy 240, past mile marker 7; rides $85; ✆ rides 9:30am & 1:30pm) The WOH Ranch runs 2½-hour horseback rides on the valley floor. It also offers ATV rides of its ranch ($100), and runs combo tours with Hawaiian Walkways and Paradise Helicopters.

Waipio Ridge Stables (☎ 775-1007, 877-757-1414; www.waipioridgestables.com; rides $85-165; ✆ departures 8:45am) Horseback-riding tours follow a 2½-hour valley-rim route, or go on a five-hour trot deeper into the rain forest and end with a picnic and a swim at a hidden waterfall.

Waipio Valley Shuttle (☎ 775-7121; adult/child 3-11 $50/25; ⏰ departures 9am, 11am, 1pm & 3pm Mon-Sat) Runs 90-minute 4WD taxi tours; allows drop-offs/pickups (each way $30).

Waipi'o Valley Wagon Tours (☎ 775-9518; www .waipiovalleywagontours.com; adult/child 4-12 $55/25; ⏰ departures 10:30am, 12:30am & 2:30pm Mon-Sat) For a quaint experience, this 1½-hour jaunt in an open mule-drawn wagon carts visitors over rutted roads and rocky streams.

Sleeping

No camping is allowed in Waipi'o Valley; the beach area has portable toilets, but no water or other facilities. Backcountry camping is allowed in Waimanu Valley with a free state permit (six-night maximum). Facilities include nine campsites, two composting outhouses, and fire pits, but no drinking water. Reservations are taken no more than 30 days in advance by the **Division of Forestry & Wildlife** (☎ 974-4221; www.dofaw.net; 19 E Kawaili St, Hilo, HI 96720; ⏰ 7:45am-4:30pm Mon-Fri). With two weeks' notice, the permit can be mailed to you.

KALOPA STATE RECREATION AREA

This 100-acre state park preserves a beautiful, rare example of a native forest *almost* as it was before Polynesians arrived. Few people venture up here, and the quiet enhances the moody sensation of stepping back in time. To get here, turn *mauka* off Hwy 19 at the Kalopa Dr sign and drive 3 miles.

Near the cabins, a three-quarter-mile loop **nature trail** guides you through an old, scruffy ohia forest thick with *hapu'u* (tree ferns). Don't miss the dramatic strangler fig, a sci-fi-scary specimen emblematic of Hawaii's invasive flora; you may also hear the occasional, heart-stopping grunt of a wild boar. Two native birds call the forest home, the *'io* (Hawaiian hawk), and the small *'elepaio* (Hawaiian monarch flycatcher).

For a longer hike, take the pretty **Kalopa Gulch Trail**, which enters the adjoining forest reserve and edges Kalopa Gulch for about a mile. The trail begins next to the campground entrance (a trailboard and maps are near the cabins). While the main trail is recommended and clearly marked, side trails (such as Silk Oak and Blue Gum Lanes) are badly maintained and hard to follow. Plan for a 3-mile hike.

Kalopa has three great tent sites; each is a covered concrete patio in a pretty grassy area with well-kept facilities. Rest rooms have indoor showers, and covered picnic pavilions have running water and BBQ grills. In a separate area, simple but nice cabins have bunk beds, linens and blankets, hot showers, and access to a fully equipped kitchen. For permits, see p205.

LAUPAHOEHOE

pop 470

Laupahoehoe means 'leaf of pahoehoe lava,' an apt name for the evocative **Laupahoehoe Point**, a flat peninsula that's tucked beneath cliffs and battered relentlessly by the sea. Legend has it that Poliahu, the snow goddess, was sledding down Mauna Kea one day when her ever-jealous sister, Pele, decided to compete with her. One thing led to another, as it often does, and the goddesses were soon fighting, lava melting snow and snow freezing lava, until finally Poliahu forced Pele all the way down Mauna Kea and into the sea, leaving behind this spit of land, which, in fact, is the result of a late-stage Mauna Kea eruption.

Until 1946 the point contained a small but thriving plantation town, however, that year a tsunami struck and destroyed most of it (see p285); afterward the town moved 'topside.' Today a monument commemorates the event, and the point is a county beach park with some of the island's prettiest camping (for information on permits, see p205).

The park has rest rooms, outdoor showers, water, covered pavilions and electricity. Weekends can be busy with locals and families; midweek is quieter. There's no swimming.

Up by the highway the **Laupahoehoe Train Museum** (☎ 962-6300; www.thetrainmuseum.com; adult/ child 4-18 $4/2; ⏰ 9am-4:30pm Mon-Fri, 10am-2pm Sat & Sun) lovingly preserves Hawai'i's long-gone railroad and sugar plantation era – it's chock-full of photos and ephemera, including 'Rusty' the switch engine and a model railroad. The porch has model trains for kids to play with. Continue past the museum into town, and you'll find a '50s-style diner.

Laupahoehoe is on Hwy 19, midway between Honoka'a and Hilo. Near the 27-mile marker a 'Laupahoehoe Point' sign leads you down the steep winding road to the coast, while the museum is visible from the highway between the 25- and 26-mile markers.

KOLEKOLE BEACH PARK

This grassy park set dramatically beneath a highway bridge is great for an afternoon picnic. Facilities are run down (there's no drinking water), but there's nothing wrong with the trim wide lawn, Kolekole Stream or the rocky beach. Locals love to bodyboard and surf here, but it's not good for ocean swimming.

You can tent camp with a county permit (see p205), but weekends sees this spot get crowded with picnicking families. There are better choices.

To get here, turn inland off Hwy 19 at the southern end of the Kolekole Bridge, south of the 15-mile marker.

HONOMU
pop 540

Like Honoka'a, Honomu is an old sugar town whose neat, false-fronted buildings could pass for an old Western movie set. It's a pleasurable stop on your way to or from Akaka Falls; the single main street holds a bakery, pizza parlor, Buddhist temple and several gift shops. The town, falls and Hwy 220 (which leads to both) are clearly signed from Hwy 19 between the 13- and 14-mile markers.

Woodshop Gallery & Cafe (☎ 963-6363; www.wood shopgallery.com; lunch dishes $6-9; ☺ 11am-5:30pm) is the largest gallery, with an excellent selection of prints, crafts and wood carvings. The small café isn't bad, serving an above average ahi sandwich, plate lunches and burgers.

You needn't be a Buddhist to stay at **Akiko's Buddhist B&B** (963-6422; www.alternative-hawaii .com/akiko; s/d $65/75, cottages $65-85), but it helps to want a humble meditative retreat. Accommodations are clean-swept but bare bones. Monastery rooms lack doors and have futons on the floor; the adjacent house provides twin beds and all share baths. Two solar-powered cottages are simplicity itself. Truly, the draw is the atmosphere. The monastery, a former gas station, is now, Akiko says, a 'human service station' for those needing a 'tune up.' Akiko's is in Wailea, 2 miles north of Honomu; call for directions.

AKAKA FALLS STATE PARK

The only way these impressive falls could be easier to reach would be to put them in the parking lot – but then you'd miss the enchanting half-mile loop **trail** through the rain forest, whose dense foliage includes banyan and monkeypod trees, massive philodendrons, fragrant ginger, dangling heliconia, orchids and gigantic bamboo groves.

Follow the park's advice and start by heading to the right: you come first to 100ft **Kahuna Falls**, which strikes you as the perfect Hawaiian cascade, for about as long as it takes to reach its neighbor. Then, when you see 420ft **Akaka Falls**, you can swoon properly: the water tumbles majestically down a moss and fern-draped cliff, its spray sometimes painting a rainbow.

From Hwy 19 the falls are about 4 miles inland on Hwy 220.

PEPE'EKEO 4-MILE SCENIC DRIVE

Between Honomu and Hilo, a 4-mile scenic loop off Hwy 19 is a majestic tropical drive; from the north, between the 10- and 11-mile markers, look for the scenic drive and Onomea Bay signs.

Stop at **What's Shakin'** (☎ 964-3080; snacks $6.50-10; ☺ 10am-5pm) for all-fruit smoothies almost too thick for the straw. Eat lunch on the covered porch while perusing the venue's hula kitsch.

Like the Old Mamalahoa Highway (see p286), the road crosses a string of one-lane bridges over little streams through humid jungle, while African tulip trees drop their orange flowers onto the road.

An overabundant nature preserve with 2500 species of tropical plants from around the world, **Hawaii Tropical Botanical Garden** (☎ 964-5233; www.hawaiigarden.com; adult/child 6-16 $15/5; ☺ 9am-4pm) is an entertaining spectacle that epitomizes 'tropical jungle': a mile-long paved path winds amid streams, pretty waterfalls, ocean view points, dangling heliconia, dazzling blossoms, towering palms – all of it a quivering, crowded mass of photosynthesis and Kodachrome moments.

On either side of the gardens are **Na Ala Hele trailheads** leading to rugged Onomea Bay. The southern trailhead has easier parking and access, and the trails themselves connect, leading quickly to rocky coves, a stream, waterfalls and a dramatic finger of land jutting into the turtle- and shark-filled bay. Divers like this spot, but rough surf and the 'tax collectors' (sharks) tend to discourage swimming and snorkeling.

On Hwy 19 between the 6- and 7-mile marker, near the drive's southern entrance, **Baker Tom's** (☎ 964-8444, 27-2111 Mamalahoa Hwy; malasada $1.35-3; ☺ 6am-6pm Mon-Fri, 7am-5pm Sat & Sun) is a fantastic roadside *malasada* stand. Get these fresh-from-the-oven puff pastries fruit-filled or savory, but get them.

HILO

pop 41,000

Hilo and Kona are like mismatched cops in a Hollywood buddy movie: Kona is the sunny optimist, the blonde-haired, good-looking goof-off always flirting with the doe-eyed suspects. Hilo is the cranky realist in the ill-fitting gray suit suspiciously poking holes in everyone's alibi, the one who cracks the case and, as credits roll, gets stuck with the paperwork.

Yet Hilo is comfortable being the unglamorous one. Perhaps that's because it knows life is tough: it's been knocked down twice by tsunamis (in 1946 and 1960), threatened by Mauna Loa lava flows (most recently in 1984), and it gets rained on two out of three days a year (statistically speaking). Its population – a polyglot mix of Japanese, Chinese, Korean, Filipino, Portuguese, Puerto Rican and Caucasian immigrants, in addition to Native Hawaiians – is largely working or mid-dle class. Many families came originally to work the sugar plantations, and they stayed because the community became their life.

So if tourists prefer Kona two to one, Hilo residents just shrug. Who can blame them? Sure, Hilo's walkable downtown has an unpolished weathered charm, full of historic buildings, interesting museums, art galleries and great local food. Yes, it's perched on a crescent-shaped bay cradled by lush rain forests, and is close to Hawai'i Volcanoes National Park, Mauna Kea, the offbeat wilds of Puna and the Hamakua Coast. And certainly, Hilo wouldn't mind more tourists, but not if it means changing (or more traffic, or higher real estate prices). Residents would rather live in 'scruffy old Hilo' – a real place with real people – than remake their home into a fantasy to satisfy visitors and mainland transplants.

In fact, 'the rainiest city in the USA' has a lot to offer: sandy coves flecked with sea turtles, a wealth of friendly B&Bs, the island's best farmers

APRIL FOOL'S DAY, 1946

On the morning of April 1, 1946, Hawaii's worst tsunami struck without warning. Along the Big Island's Windward Coast it destroyed railroad bridges and Hilo's bay front, and 159 people died. In Waipi'o, the water filled the valley like it was a bowl, but no one perished. At the plantation town of Laupahoehoe many homes and the schoolhouse were swept away, and 35 people were killed. Most of these were children who, on their way to school, had detoured to wonder at something strange – the sea was disappearing. Survivor Bunji Fujimoto remembers: 'Somebody started yelling, "Oh, there's no water in the ocean." Being that it was April Fool's Day, half of us didn't believe what they were saying. Then, we saw the water receding out. We went down towards the park, where the monument is now, to see what's it all about.'

A crowd gathered at the shore: for 300yd or more there was only ocean bottom, with bright red moss and stranded flapping fish. The water then filled in and receded several times.

Says survivor Joseph Ah Choy: 'We was just running back and forth when the wave come up. We go run to the grandstand. When the wave go back, we follow. When the water come up again, we run again. We had about seven or eight small kine waves coming in and out. I don't know what made me run straight from the last one.'

This time, says Fujimoto, 'the wave was like filling a cup with water, but when it reaches the brim, it doesn't stop.' As the children raced away like mad, some fell and others hid again in the grandstand. Running without stopping, Fujimoto says, 'I saw the bleachers collapse like a house of matchsticks, making terrifying cracking sounds. The other thing I remember was one of the teachers' cottages sailing through the coconut trees.'

In eerie silence, successive waves picked up people and buildings, leaving some stranded uphill while dragging everything else out to sea. Over 20 people were never found. One woman and two boys floated for nearly three days before being rescued.

Afterward, the town relocated topside. The Hamakua Coast railroad never ran again, and two years later an official tsunami-warning system was created. A memorial was erected on Laupahoehoe Point to honor the town's victims, and since then the community gathers there every April Fool's Day to eat, play music and listen to survivors 'talk story.'

The quotes above are taken from the book *April Fool's*, an award-winning oral history compiled by Laupahoehoe school students in 1996. Copies are available at the train museum (p283).

HAWAI'I THE BIG ISLAND

DETOUR: OLD MAMALAHOA HIGHWAY

The Hamakua Coast is perfect for those who like exploring neglected old roads just to see what you can find. This 4-mile portion of the bypassed Old Mamalahoa Hwy (near Honomo) satisfies that itch. However, don't miss the bridge over **Nanue Falls** on Hwy 19 between the 18- and 19-mile markers; park south of the bridge and walk back for vertiginous views of the steep gulch.

Coming from the north, turn off Hwy 19 at the 19-mile marker, following the sign for **Waikaumalo County Park**. Here, a grassy slope (with picnic area) leads to a pretty stream, which, if you're so inclined, is tailor-made for muddy jaunts upstream.

Driving on, Old Mam Hwy becomes a one-lane road, which dips into a series of stream gulches overhung with thick foliage; it's sometimes possible to pull over next to the bridges and explore. Out of the gulches, you pass small bucolic farms and ocean views. A little less than halfway along, keep an eye out for **Honohina Cemetery**, a historic Japanese graveyard full of crumbling, kanji-covered headstones.

The south end of the road is anchored by the **World Botanical Gardens** (☎ 963-5427; www .wbgi.com; adult/child 6-12/child 13-17 $13/3/6; ☒ 9am-5:30pm), which is signed on Hwy 19 at the 16-mile marker. The fee is a bit steep for the modest gardens, even including access to the beautiful, three-tiered **Umauma Falls**, but if you're jonesing for a walk, you'll get your money's worth.

---

market, and much more. What about the rain? Hilo's secret is that most showers pass quickly, leaving balmy, sunny afternoons in their wake. When they don't? Open your umbrella.

For an overview of Hilo's history, see p204.

ORIENTATION

Hilo's compact downtown is about six square blocks on the southwest side of the bay. Called the 'bayfront,' it lies between Kamehameha Ave and Kino'ole St (both parallel to the bay) and between Waianuenue Ave and Mamo St. On the bay's southeast side, small Waiakea Peninsula is rimmed by Banyan Dr, which contains Hilo's modest hotel row. Most B&Bs are in residential neighborhoods closer to downtown.

From the Hamakua Coast, Hwy 19 enters Hilo from the north, passes downtown, then meets Hwy 11 at the intersection with Banyan Dr. Hwy 11 goes south and is called Kanoelehua Ave in town; further south, it becomes the Hawai'i Belt Rd and leads to the Puna district, Hawai'i Volcanoes National Park and Ka'u. South of the airport, Kanoelehua Ave is lined with shopping malls; this is Hilo's main retail district, complete with a Wal-Mart, a multiplex cinema and all the other big-box stores.

INFORMATION
Bookstores

Basically Books (Map p289; ☎ 961-0144, 800-903-6277; 160 Kamehameha Ave; ☒ 9am-5pm Mon-Sat, 11am-3:30pm Sun) One of the island's best bookstores; carries the full range of Hawaiian titles, plus kids' books, music, travel guides and topo maps.

Book Gallery (Map p289; ☎ 935-4943; 259 Keawe St; ☒ 9:30am-5pm Mon-Fri, 9:30am-3pm Sat) Also excellent; specializes in local press and Hawaiian titles and kids' books.

Borders Books Music & Café (Map p287; ☎ 933-1410; Waiakea Center, 301 Maka'ala St; ☒ 9am-9pm) Full-service chain selling books, CDs, periodicals and Starbucks coffee.

Emergency

Police (Map p287; ☎ 935-3311; 349 Kapi'olani St) For nonemergencies.
Sexual Assault Hotline (☎ 935-0677)
Suicide Prevention Hotline (☎ 800-753-6879)

Internet Access

The public library is a great option if you need internet access.

Bytes & Bites (Map p289; ☎ 935-3520; www.bytesand bites.net; 179 Kilauea Ave; per 15min $2.50, per hr $8; ☒ 9:30am-9:30pm Mon-Fri, 10:30am-3:30pm Sat & Sun) Small downtown business center with terminals and wi-fi.

Library

Hilo Public library (Map p289; ☎ 933-8888; www .librarieshawaii.org; 300 Waianuenue Ave; ☒ 11am-7pm Tue & Wed, 9am-5pm Thu & Sat, 10am-5pm Fri) To use the free internet terminals or borrow books, purchase a three-month nonresident library card ($10). The pretty interior courtyard is a pleasant place to write and read.

Media
NEWSPAPERS

The *Hawaii Tribune-Herald* (www.hawaiitrib une-herald.com) is the Big Island's main daily newspaper.

HILO

HAWAI'I THE BIG ISLAND

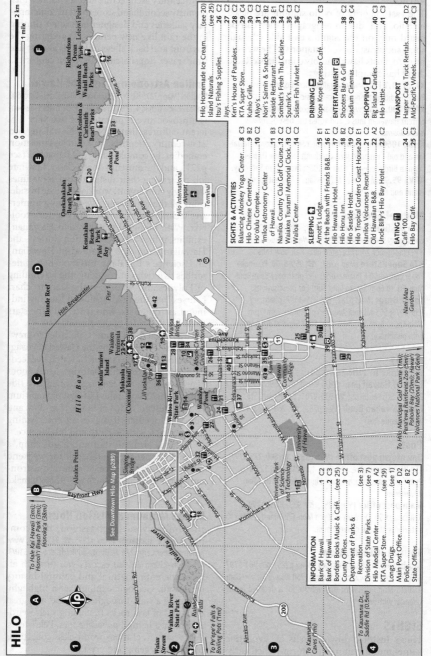

INFORMATION
Bank of Hawaii	1 C2
Bank of Hawaii	2 C3
Borders Books Music & Café	(see 25)
County Offices	3 C2
Department of Parks & Recreation	(see 3)
Division of State Parks	(see 7)
Hilo Medical Center	4 A2
KTA Super Store	(see 29)
Longs Drugs	5 D2
Main Post Office	6 B2
Police	7 C2
State Offices	

SIGHTS & ACTIVITIES
Balancing Monkey Yoga Center	8 C3
Hilo Chinese Cemetery	9 B2
Ho'olulu Complex	10 C2
'Imiloa Astronomy Center of Hawaii	11 B3
Naniloa Country Club Golf Course	12 C2
Waiakea Tsunami Memorial Clock	13 C2
Wailoa Center	14 C2

SLEEPING
Arnott's Lodge	15 E1
At the Beach with Friends B&B	16 F1
Hilo Hawaiian Hotel	17 C2
Hilo Honu Inn	18 B2
Hilo Seaside Hotel	19 C2
Hilo Tropical Gardens Guest House	20 E1
Naniloa Volcanoes Resort	21 C2
Old Hawaiian B&B	22 A2
Uncle Billy's Hilo Bay Hotel	23 C2

EATING
Café 100	24 C2
Hilo Bay Café	25 C2
Hilo Homemade Ice Cream	(see 20)
Island Naturals	(see 25)
Itsu's Fishing Supplies	26 C2
Jays	27 C2
Ken's House of Pancakes	28 C3
KTA Super Store	29 C4
Kuhio Grille	30 C2
Miyo's	31 C2
Nori's Saimin & Snacks	32 B2
Seaside Restaurant	33 E1
Sombat's Fresh Thai Cuisine	34 C2
Sputnik's	35 C3
Suisan Fish Market	36 C2

DRINKING
Kope Kope Espresso Café	37 C3

ENTERTAINMENT
Shooters Bar & Grill	38 C2
Stadium Cinemas	39 C4

SHOPPING
Big Island Candies	40 C3
Hilo Hattie	41 C3

TRANSPORT
Harper Car & Truck Rentals	42 D2
Mid-Pacific Wheels	43 C3

To Hale Kai Hawaii (3mi); Honoli'i Beach Park (3mi); Honoka'a (38mi)

To Pe'epe'e Falls & Boiling Pots (1mi)

To Kaumana Dr, Saddle Rd (0.5mi)

To Kaumana Caves (7mi)

To Hilo Municipal Golf Course (1mi); Panaewa Rainforest Zoo (5mi); Pahoehoe Bay (20mi); Hawai'i Volcanoes National Park (26mi)

See Downtown Hilo Map (p289)

RADIO

The vast majority of radio stations are based in Hilo, and, due to geography, they can be heard only on the island's east side (though some simulcast on Kona stations). The website http://diallists.hawaiiradiotv.com/BigIsleRadio .html has complete listings.

KANO 91.1 FM (www.hawaiipublicradio.org) Hawai'i Public Radio featuring classical music and news.

KAPA 100.3 FM (www.kaparadio.com) The best for current Hawaiian music, and voted the best by *Hawaii Island Journal*.

KHBC 1060AM (www.khbcradio.com) Traditional Hawaiian and old-fashioned jazz; check out longtime DJ Mel 'Mynah Bird Medeiros' 6am to 10am Monday to Saturday.

KPVS 95.9 FM Native FM (previously Da Beat) plays island and reggae tunes.

Medical Services

Hilo Medical Center (Map p287; ☎ 974-4700, emergency room 974-6800; 1190 Waianuenue Ave; ☺ emergency 24hr) Located near Rainbow Falls.

KTA Super Store (Map p287; ☎ 959-8700; Puainako Town Center, 50 E Puainako St; ☺ pharmacy 8am-8pm Mon-Fri, to 6pm Sat, to 5pm Sun) For prescriptions.

Longs Drugs (Map p287; ☎ 935-3357, pharmacy 935-9075; 555 Kilauea Ave; ☺ pharmacy 7am-7pm Mon-Fri, to 6pm Sat, 8am-5pm Sun) General drugstore with pharmacy.

Money

All banks in Hilo have 24-hour ATMs.

Bank of Hawaii (Map p287) Kawili St (☎ 961-0681; 417 E Kawili St); Pauahi St (☎ 935-9701; 120 Pauahi St)

First Hawaiian Bank (Map p289; ☎ 969-2222; 120 Waianuenue Ave)

Post

Downtown post office (Map p289; ☎ 800-275-8777; 154 Waianuenue Ave; ☺ 9am-4pm Mon-Fri, 12:30-2pm Sat) Conveniently located in the Federal Building downtown.

Main post office (Map p287; ☎ 933-3019; 1299 Kekuanaoa St; ☺ 8am-4:30pm Mon-Fri, 9am-12:30pm Sat) Holds general delivery mail.

Tourist Information

Big Island Visitors Bureau (Map p289; ☎ 961-5797, 800-648-2441; www.bigisland.org; 250 Keawe St; ☺ 8am-4:30pm Mon-Fri) Check the website for a detailed events calendar with links.

SIGHTS

Hilo's historic downtown is an evocative, sometimes urban mix of storm-lashed early-20th-century architecture and abandoned lots, of musty secondhand stores next to contemporary galleries and designer boutiques shining in the rain like new pennies. Wandering the bayfront and back alleys of Hilo is almost like time travel, hopscotching between centuries.

'Imiloa Astronomy Center of Hawaii

'Imiloa (Map p287; ☎ 969-9700; www.imiloahawaii.org; 600 'Imiloa Pl; adult/child 4-12 $17.50/9.50; ☺ 9am-4pm Tue-Sun) is a provocative exploration of two very different cultures: that of Native Hawaiians and 21st-century scientists. This odd juxtaposition embodies the complex story of Mauna Kea (see p271), and the museum does a classy, first-rate job presenting their distinct (and sometimes strikingly convergent) world views side by side, using all the whiz-bang, eye-popping immersive technology in the modern curator's toolbox. With bilingual (English and Hawaiian) exhibits, it first tells two creation stories – the Hawaiian *Kumulipo* (chanted in Hawaiian) and science's Big Bang theory. Then it describes two types of voyaging: the wayfinding of Polynesians, who used the stars to chart courses into the unknown, and the wayfinding of astronomers, who reach into the stars to divine the order of the cosmos.

Grab a seat in a 'Cosmic Cab,' listen to crewmembers describe sailing the Hawaiian voyaging canoe *Hokule'a* (see p37), watch live feeds from Mauna Kea observatories, learn about Hawaiian music and language, and hitch a ride into the night sky in the 120-seat planetarium (which presents shows at 11am, 1pm, 2pm and 3pm). Altogether, it makes an entertaining journey, rich with warmth and intelligence.

There is also a restaurant, a gift shop, a Hawaiian language center (call for weekend class schedules) and once-a-month astronomy presentations (call ☎ 969-9711 to make reservations).

Lyman Museum & Mission House

In admirably succinct fashion, this comprehensive **museum** (Map p289; ☎ 935-5021; www .lymanmuseum.org; 276 Haili St; adult/child 6-17 $10/3; ☺ 10am-4:30pm Mon-Sat) escorts you through almost the entire natural and cultural history of Hawaii. Geologic exhibits are a highlight, including a walk-through 'lava tube' and great examples of lava rocks (including such weirdness as lava bombs, *pahoehoe* toes, Pele's tears, Pele's hair). It also has world-class collections of seashells, gems and crystals.

Exhibits on ancient Hawaiian life are well done, describing everything from simple daily tasks – such as how adzes, feather lei, *kapa* (cloth made by pounding the bark of paper mulberry), and thatched homes were made – to ancient sports, religious worship and the mysteries of the kapu system. Exhibits also look at the immigrants who created Hawaii's

multiethnic society. If the old-fashioned cultural displays now feel like museum pieces themselves, don't worry – mysterious but exciting plans are underway to completely redesign them to, as one curator told us, 'tell the history in a whole new way.'

Adjacent to the museum (and included in the admission) is the **Mission House**, which was

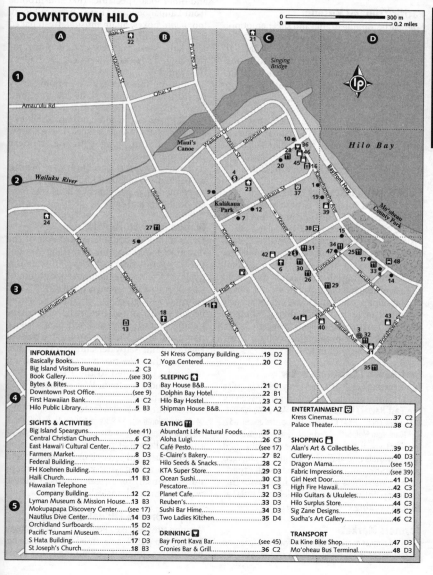

DOWNTOWN HILO

INFORMATION
Basically Books..................................1 C2
Big Island Visitors Bureau..................2 C3
Book Gallery................................(see 30)
Bytes & Bites...................................3 D3
Downtown Post Office..................(see 9)
First Hawaiian Bank..........................4 C2
Hilo Public Library.............................5 B3

SIGHTS & ACTIVITIES
Big Island Spearguns....................(see 41)
Central Christian Church....................6 C3
East Hawai'i Cultural Center..............7 C2
Farmers Market...............................8 D3
Federal Building...............................9 B2
FH Koehnen Building.......................10 C2
Haili Church....................................11 B3
Hawaiian Telephone
  Company Building........................12 B3
Lyman Museum & Mission House....13 B3
Mokupapapa Discovery Center......(see 17)
Nautilus Dive Center........................14 D3
Orchidland Surfboards.....................15 D2
Pacific Tsunami Museum..................16 C2
S Hata Building...............................17 D3
St Joseph's Church..........................18 B3

SH Kress Company Building............19 D2
Yoga Centered................................20 C2

SLEEPING
Bay House B&B...............................21 C1
Dolphin Bay Hotel...........................22 B1
Hilo Bay Hostel...............................23 C2
Shipman House B&B........................24 A2

EATING
Abundant Life Natural Foods..........25 D3
Aloha Luigi.....................................26 C3
Café Pesto...................................(see 17)
E-Claire's Bakery.............................27 B2
Hilo Seeds & Snacks........................28 C2
KTA Super Store..............................29 D3
Ocean Sushi...................................30 C3
Pescatore.......................................31 C3
Planet Cafe....................................32 D3
Reuben's...33 D3
Sushi Bar Hime...............................34 D3
Two Ladies Kitchen.........................35 D4

DRINKING
Bay Front Kava Bar......................(see 45)
Cronies Bar & Grill..........................36 C2

ENTERTAINMENT
Kress Cinemas.................................37 C2
Palace Theater................................38 C2

SHOPPING
Alan's Art & Collectibles..................39 D2
Cutlery...40 D3
Dragon Mama.............................(see 15)
Fabric Impressions.......................(see 39)
Girl Next Door.................................41 D4
High Fire Hawaii..............................42 C3
Hilo Guitars & Ukuleles....................43 D3
Hilo Surplus Store...........................44 C3
Sig Zane Designs.............................45 C2
Sudha's Art Gallery.........................46 C2

TRANSPORT
Da Kine Bike Shop...........................47 D3
Mo'oheau Bus Terminal...................48 D3

built by the Reverend David Lyman and his wife, Sarah, in 1839. The modest house reflects the missionaries themselves; it contains many original furnishings, including Sarah Lyman's melodeon, rocking chair, china and quilts. Docents do a good job of evoking missionary life and the role the Lymans played on the Big Island; there are free tours several times daily.

Pacific Tsunami Museum

For heart-stopping drama and sheer emotion, it's hard to top this tidy **museum** (Map p289; ☎ 935-0926; www.tsunami.org; 130 Kamehameha Ave; adult/child 6-17 $7/2; ☒ 9am-4pm Mon-Sat), which brings to life the destructive horror of a Pacific Ocean tsunami. Multimedia exhibits are excellent (including chilling computer simulations, videos, documentaries, dioramas and more), but it's the first-person accounts by survivors that grab you. Some docents are Hilo tsunami survivors. Though focused on the tsunami, displays amount to a de facto history of Hilo; ask for the free tsunami sites walking-tour brochure.

Mokupapapa Discovery Center

The best, and surely the easiest, way to visit the long string of islands and atolls that make up the Northwestern Hawaiian Islands is to visit this **museum** (Map p289; ☎ 933-8190; www .hawaiireefnoaa.gov; 308 Kamehameha Ave; admission free; ☒ 9am-4pm Tue-Sat). It packs a lot in a small space, describing all the islands and their abundant marine life through videos, films, displays, maps and interactive exhibits, such as a mock-up of the *Pisces V* diving submersible, with workable robotic arms. It hosts evening scientific presentations on the third Thursday of every month.

East Hawai'i Cultural Center

In its own quiet, 'who-me?' way, Hilo is quite the art town, and the scene is largely driven by the **East Hawai'i Cultural Center** (Map p289; ☎ 961-5711; www.ehcc.org; 141 Kalakaua St; suggested donation $2; ☒ 10am-4pm Mon-Sat). Dedicated to promoting local artists, it presents a range of established professionals and skilled amateurs, all engaged in celebrating and digesting the Hawaii experience. It also offers workshops and classes (including painting, drawing, ukulele and hula) as well as evening events and live music.

Farmers Market

Hilo's **farmers market** (Map p289; www.hilofarmersmar ket.com; cnr Mamo St & Kamehameha Ave; ☒ 6am-3pm

Wed & Sat) is over 20 years old and an island-wide event – drawing folks from as far away as Kona. It's also Hilo's liveliest scene, with everyone and their auntie mingling, tasting, buying and gossiping. Covered stalls sell the gamut of fresh produce: pick up papayas, *liliko'i*, breadfruit, apple bananas, mangoes, Asian greens, organic vegetables and other local specialties (like mushrooms from Laupahoehoe). There's prepared food, too: *bentō* boxes, Spam *musubi*, fresh baked breads, kimchi, sweet desserts, fresh juices and jams, and machete-cut coconuts for drinking. Tropical flowers can be had by the armful.

Opposite this scene, an enormous array of craft and clothing stalls lay out their wares: browse for sarongs and T-shirts, rubbah slippahs and wood carvings, shell jewelry and coconut-leaf baskets. There's some wonderful stuff along with the standard cheap souvenirs.

It may not happen soon, but long-term plans are to build a $5 million, LEED-certified, three-story building to permanently house the market on the current site.

Wailoa River State Park

Drive along Kamehameha Ave east of the downtown area, and the first thing you notice about this **state park** (Map p287) is its imposing 14ft, Italian-made bronze statue of Kamehameha the Great; erected in 1997, and restored with gold leaf in 2004, the statue beckons with an outstretched arm, perhaps inviting you to enjoy the lovely park's lawns, ponds and arched bridges. Spring-fed **Waiakea Pond** contains saltwater and brackish-water fish, and there are two **memorials**: a tsunami memorial dedicated to the 1946 and 1960 victims, and a Vietnam War memorial with an eternal flame.

Adjacent, the **Wailoa Center** (Map p287; ☎ 933-0416; admission free; ☒ 8:30am-4:30pm Mon, Tue, Thu & Fri, noon-4:30pm Wed) is an eclectic, small state-run art gallery that provides fun local color. Multicultural exhibits change monthly and there's no telling what you'll find: perhaps quilts, bonsai, historical photos, Chinese watercolors or whimsical mixed media.

Banyan Drive & Lili'uokalani Park

Around tiny Waiakea Peninsula curves **Banyan Drive** (Map p287), so-named for the massive banyan trees lining it, containing Hilo's short 'hotel row.' Royalty and celebrities planted the trees in the 1930s, and plaques identify the honorees: Babe Ruth, Amelia Earhart, King George and Mrs Cecil B DeMille, among a number of others.

Banyan Dr also skirts around the nine-hole Naniloa Golf Course (p293) and the 30-acre, Japanese-style **Lili'uokalani Park** (Map p287). This lovely green oasis is named for Hawai'i's last queen. It contains manicured lawns, saltwater ponds, patches of bamboo, quaint arched bridges, stone lanterns, pagodas and a teahouse. With 2 miles of paths and idyllic views of Hilo and (on a clear day) Mauna Kea across the bay, it's perfect for a sunset stroll or an early morning jog.

If you have kids, don't miss the tiny island of **Mokuola** (Map p287), aka 'Coconut Island,' a separate county park connected to the gardens by a footbridge. Sandy pockets provide access to calm, protected waters for swimming, and trim grass calls out for blankets and games of chase. Facilities include covered pavilions, bathrooms and outdoor showers. Local anglers love this spot too.

Not really on the peninsula, but fronting Kamehameha Ave on the park side, close to Manono St, is the **Waiakea Tsunami Memorial Clock** (Map p287). The clock is stuck at 1:05, the exact moment, in the predawn hours of May 23, 1960, when Hilo's last major tsunami swept ashore.

Pana'ewa Rainforest Zoo

Upon entering this modest 12-acre **zoo** (Map p294; ☎ 959-9233; www.hilozoo.com; admission free; ⏲ 9am-4pm, petting zoo 1:30-2:30pm Sat), visitors receive a cheerful 'Hi! How are you?' from Max, the zoo's talking parrot and official goodwill ambassador. The zoo's real pride, however, is a white Bengal tiger, in a large grassy enclosure. You need only an hour or two to tour the landscaped tropical grounds, which feature several endangered Hawaiian birds, monkeys, reptiles, a pygmy hippo, a Monarch butterfly house and gaggles of free-roaming peacocks and chickens. To get here, turn off Hwy 11 at W Mamaki St, just past the 4-mile marker; the zoo is another mile west.

Historic Buildings

Compact downtown Hilo, with its historic buildings and panoramic bay, rewards wanderers; pick up a free historic sites legend at the visitor center.

Sitting on the corner of Kamehameha and Waianuenue Aves, the **FH Koehnen Building** (Map p289) is a stylish 1910 building with interior koa walls and ohia floors (housing an interior-design store). East on Kamehameha Ave at the corner of Kalakaua St, the **Pacific Tsunami Museum** (opposite) occupies the 1930 First Hawaiian Bank Building, which was built by renowned Honolulu architect CW Dickey. Another block east on Kamehameha Ave is the art deco **SH Kress Company Building** (Map p289). Built in 1932, it fell into disrepair in the 1980s but was restored in 1990. Along with a movie theater and shops, it now houses a 245-student public-charter school. Further east on Kamehameha Ave (near Mamo St), the 1912 **S Hata Building** (Map p289) is a fine example of renaissance-revival architecture. The US government seized the building from the original Japanese owner during WWII; after the war, the owner's daughter bought it back and restored it.

From Kamehameha Ave, Haili St is interesting. The first notable building is Hilo's 1925 **Palace Theater** (p298); renovated in the late 1990s, it evokes the faded elegance of a bygone era, when it was the Big Island's first deluxe theater showing silent movies with live organ music. Over the next two blocks you pass the simple, Victorian-style **Central Christian Church** (Map p289), built by Portuguese immigrants in the early 1900s; 1859 **Haili Church** (Map p289), which wouldn't look out of place in the New England countryside; and Catholic **St Joseph's Church** (Map p289), a 1919, pink paean of Spanish-mission design. Just past St Joseph's is the 1839 **Lyman Mission House**, which is now part of the Lyman Museum (p288).

Side by side on Kalakaua St, south of Keawe St, are two striking structures. First is the **East Hawai'i Cultural Center** (opposite), which served as the Hilo police station until 1975; its hipped roof and covered lanai were common features in 19th-century island homes. Next door, the handsome 1920s **Hawaiian Telephone Company Building** (Map p289) is another CW Dickey creation that displays Spanish, Italian and Californian mission influences.

Outside of downtown, on Ululani St near Ponahawai St, the **Hilo Chinese Cemetery** (Map p287) is announced by a gorgeous, green-and-red temple building. The board out front lists the names, dates and villages of the Chinese immigrants buried here.

HAWAI'I THE BIG ISLAND

Beaches

Hilo is no beach town. But when the sun shines, grab your suit, make haste for 4-mile Kalaniana'ole Ave (Hwy 19; east of Banyan Dr), and you won't be disappointed. Here, a string of intriguing pockets provide sand enough for sunning, swimming, snorkeling, surfing and diving. Rough surf can stir up these spots, making swimming dangerous, so assess conditions carefully.

About 1.5 miles east of Banyan Dr along Kalaniana'ole Ave, across from Baker Ave, **Keaukaha Beach Park** (Map p287) on Puhi Bay is the smallest spot. A semiprotected cove is often filled with kids, and on the east side is a good beginner dive site, 'Tetsu's Ledge,' at 30ft.

Further east, **Onekahakaha Beach Park** (Map p287) should be the destination for families with small children, who can splash safely in a broad, shallow, sandy-bottomed pool (with steps) that is well protected by a rock wall. On calm days, an unprotected cove on the Hilo side is good for snorkeling. The park has life-guards on weekends and holidays, rest rooms, showers, grassy lawns, covered pavilions and the Hilo Horseshoe Club.

Older kids and snorkelers should aim for the adjacent **James Kealoha and Carlsmith Beach Parks** (Map p287). On the east side, Carlsmith contains a shallow, protected tub of aquama-rine water, white sand and sea turtles. Tropical fish are sparse, and cold currents can obscure visibility, but snorkeling with the ancient *honu* is dreamy. James Kealoha, on the western side, is rocky and faces the open ocean; winter waves are popular with surfers, and locals net fish. There are rest rooms, covered pavilions, a coconut grove and weekend lifeguards.

Another mile eastward are the adjacent **Waiolena and Waiuli Beach Parks** (formerly Leleiwi Beach; Map p287). This pretty stretch of ragged coastline gets waves big enough to attract surfers, and it's known as the best place to shore-dive in Hilo. The entrance is a bit tricky; ask for advice at Nautilus Dive Center (opposite).

Just beyond these, near the end of the road, **Richardson Ocean Park** (Map p287) has just enough black-sand beach to inspire sun-bathing. So long as it's calm, swimming is fine and snorkeling is super at the warmer, eastern end among the lava rocks; in late af-ternoon sea turtles often nestle here. When surf is rough, bodyboarders take to the waves (called a 'junk wave' by local surfers). There are rest rooms, showers, picnic tables and a daily lifeguard.

North of downtown Hilo, the protected cove at **Honoli'i Beach Park** (Map p294) has Hilo's best bodyboarding and surfing, and it has the crowded lineups to prove it. A lovely grassy picnic area fronts the beach, with fantastic views of Hilo, plus there are rest rooms, out-door showers and a lifeguard. Honoli'i isn't the best for swimming, as the adjacent river often muddies the waters. From Hilo, take Hwy 19 north; after the 4-mile marker, turn right onto Nahala St, then left onto Kahoa St. People park on the roadside and walk down to the park.

Waterfalls

These three waterfalls are a few minutes from downtown along Waianuenue Ave.

RAINBOW FALLS

Providing the sort of instant gratification that's a godsend to parents and tour-bus op-erators, this delightful cascade (Map p287), adjacent to the parking lot, winks a rainbow in the morning when the sun is right. The cave beneath the falls is said to have been the home of Hina, mother of Maui. You can't get to the cave, but a short, unpaved path leads from the parking lot to the top of the falls, where there are some inviting pools with a rope swing. The trail passes a tremendous banyan tree, whose thick canopy blocks the sun and whose roots could swallow children. It's great to play on, but be prepared for mosquitoes.

PE'EPE'E FALLS & BOILING POTS

Along Waianuenue Ave, 2 miles past Rainbow Falls, this waterfall (Map p294) is prettier still, a series of dramatic falls that create swirling, bubbling pools (or 'boiling pots'). A grassy lawn and bathrooms make a good picnic spot, but a better one is down the slippery, rocky trail by the water's edge. However, don't dis-miss the 'No Swimming' sign. Drownings do occur, and stagnant water can carry a risk of leptospirosis.

WAI'ALE FALLS

Less than a mile further you'll cross a bridge in front of Wai'ale Falls, which are not on any tour bus itinerary. A 'Dangerous Swimming' sign marks the uneven, buggy, 15-minute trail through the forest to the top of the falls, where lava-encased swimming holes and a view to the ocean make a wonderful retreat. Locals think so too; come midweek for the quietest experience.

Kaumana Caves

These caves (Map p294) are actually a large lava tube formed by an 1881 Mauna Loa eruption. The tube is extensive (enter the left or right opening), but it narrows periodically and lengthy explorations require some crawling; it's a much more evocative experience than Thurston Lava Tube in Hawai'i Volcanoes National Park. Bring two flashlights (in case one goes out). The caves are signposted about 4 miles along Kaumana Dr (Hwy 200).

Mauna Loa Macadamia-Nut Visitor Center

Hershey-owned **Mauna Loa** (Map p294; ☎ 966-8618, 888-628-6256; www.maunaloa.com; Macadamia Rd; ⏰ 8:30am-5:30pm) provides huge windows on its working factory, where you can watch the humble mac nut as it moves along the assembly line from cracking to roasting to chocolate dipping and packaging. The gift shop, of course, has every variation ready for purchase, with tasters. The factory is well signed about 5 miles south of Hilo; the 3-mile access road dips through acres of macadamia trees.

HILO FOR CHILDREN

If it's sunny (or at least not raining), Hilo has a great selection of parks and outdoor amusements. Topping the list is Hilo's **Pana'ewa Rainforest Zoo** (p291), just south of town; time your visit for Saturday's petting zoo. As for parks, **Lili'uokalani Park** (p290) is the prettiest and offers the most, but **Wailoa River State Park** (p290) has plenty of space to run, and **Kalakaua Park** (Map p289) has a majestic, shady banyan tree perfect for a picnic, plus a time capsule and carp pool. Don't forget Hilo's **beaches** (opposite) or its **farmers market** (p290), which provides the memorable opportunity to drink from a fresh-cut coconut. If you visit in September, the annual **Hawai'i County Fair** (p294) is a great old-fashioned event with carnival rides.

Of course, if it *is* raining, well, it only costs a buck to take in a movie at downtown's **Kress Cinemas** (p298). If you don't like what's playing there, check out **Stadium Cinemas** (p298) in Prince Kuhio Plaza, which also has a video arcade.

ACTIVITIES

Swimming

For lap swimming, the **Ho'olulu Complex** (Map p287; ☎ 961-8698; Kalanikoa St) has an impressive, Olympic-sized, open-air pool (with high dive but no kiddie pool). Open swim times vary; call for hours.

For information about beach swimming around Hilo, see opposite.

Diving

The best spot near Hilo is at Waiolena and Waiuli Beach Parks (Map p287), with depths of 10ft to 70ft, while **Pohoiki Bay** (Map pp206-7), in the nearby Puna district, is the best dive site in East Hawai'i, with depths of between 20ft and 100ft. Both have an impressive variety of marine life.

Long the only dive shop in Hilo, the good folks at **Nautilus Dive Center** (Map p289; ☎ 935-6939; www.nautilusdivehilo.com; 382 Kamehameha Ave; scuba package from $35, dives $85-105; ⏰ 9am-4pm Mon-Sat) are reliable, friendly and generous with advice. It runs a variety of dives (including a beginner's intro dive) and has PADI certification courses.

Big Island Spearguns (Map p289; ☎ 961-9061; www.bigislandspearguns.com; 207 Kilauea Ave; trips from $150; ⏰ 10am-4pm Mon-Fri, 9am-3pm Sat) is a gay-friendly shop specializing in spearfishing trips, but it offers scuba dive trips as well. Three-hour spearfishing tours are one-on-one, and scuba dive trips are also personalized. It hires out snorkel gear.

Surfing

The best surfing spot near Hilo is Honoli'i Cove at Honoli'i Beach Park (Map p294), but see opposite for other spots.

Stop by **Orchidland Surfboards** (Map p289; ☎ 935-1533; www.orchidlandsurf.com; 262 Kamehameha Ave; ⏰ 9am-5pm Mon-Sat, 10am-3pm Sun) for surfboard (per day $20) and bodyboard (per day $12) rentals and to buy surf gear and clothes. Owner Stan Lawrence is an expert surfer, and he opened the Big Island's first surf shop in 1972. Check his website for surf reports and cool videos.

Golf

Golf is cheap – at least in Hilo. Local duffers adore their 18-hole **Hilo Municipal Golf Course** (Map p294; ☎ 959-7711; 340 Haihai St; $29 Mon-Fri, $34 Sat & Sun), but another option is the nine-hole **Naniloa Country Club Golf Course** (Map p287; ☎ 935-3000; 9-/18-hole green fees $25/45).

HAWAI'I THE BIG ISLAND

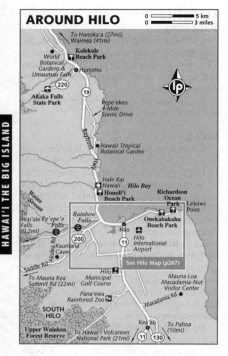

AROUND HILO

0 — 5 km
0 — 3 miles

To Honoka'a (27mi);
Waimea (41mi)

Kolekole
Beach Park

World
Botanical
Gardens &
Umauma Falls

Honomu

Akaka Falls
State Park

19

Pepe'ekeo
4-Mile
Scenic Drive

Hawaii Tropical
Botanical Garden

Hale Kai
Hawaii   Hilo Bay
Honoli'i
Beach Park

Richardson
Ocean
Park   Leleiwi
Point

Wailuku
Stream

To
Wai'ale Pe'epe'e
Falls
(0.2mi)

Pe'epe'e
Falls

Rainbow
Falls

Kaumana
Caves

200

Onekahakaha
Beach Park

Hilo

Hilo
International
Airport

11

See Hilo Map (p287)

Saddle Rd

To Mauna Kea
Summit Rd (22mi)

Hilo
Municipal
Golf Course

Pana'ewa
Rainforest Zoo

Mauna Loa
Macadamia-Nut
Visitor Center

Macadamia Rd

SOUTH
HILO

Upper Waiakea
Forest Reserve

To Hawai'i Volcanoes
National Park (21mi)

Kea'au

11   130

To Pahoa
(10mi)

Yoga
The attractive **Yoga Centered** (Map p289; ☎ 934-7233; www.yogacentered.com; 37 Waianuenue Ave; drop-in class $14) studio emphasizes Vinyasa (flowing sequences of poses) classes, plus it sells high-quality yoga gear.

Run out of the owner's home, **Balancing Monkey Yoga Center** (Map p287; ☎ 936-9590; www.balancingmonkey.com; 65 Mohouli St; drop-in class $14) offers more casual, 90-minute classes in the Ashtanga, Vinyasa and Iyengar methods.

FESTIVALS & EVENTS
For a complete listing of Big Island events, visit www.gohawaii.com.

Merrie Monarch Festival (☎ 935-9168; www.merriemonarchfestival.org; 2-night admission general/reserved $10/15) Starts Easter Sunday. Hilo's biggest event is a week-long cultural festival that culminates with a spirited hula competition. The islands' best hula troupes vie in *kahiko* and *'auana* (modern) categories, with a skill and seriousness that puts hotel hula shows to shame. Other events include a *ho'olaule'a* (celebration), a Miss Aloha Hula contest and a parade. Tickets go on sale at the end of December and sell out within a month.

May Day Lei Day Festival (☎ 934-7010; www.hilopalace.com; admission free) On the first Sunday in May, the art of lei making is celebrated with incredible displays, demonstrations, live music, hula and more at the Palace Theater.

Big Island Hawaiian Music Festival (☎ 961-5711; www.ehcc.org) Mid-July. A two-day concert featuring accomplished ukulele, steel guitar and slack key guitar players from across the islands.

Aloha Festival (http://alohafestivals.com) During the August/September statewide Aloha Festival, Hilo jumps in with an outdoor concert and a festival honoring Queen Lili'uokalani.

Hawai'i County Fair September. The fair comes to town on the grounds of the Afook-Chinen Civic Auditorium (Map p287). It's pure rural nostalgia, with carnival rides, cotton candy, orchid shows and agricultural exhibits.

SLEEPING
The resorts and 'vacation rental' condos of the Kona Coast are nonexistent in Hilo. Instead, you'll find more affordable standard hotels and a wonderful selection of homey B&Bs.

Budget
Hilo Bay Hostel (Map p289; ☎ 933-2771; www.hawaiihostel.net; 101 Waianuenue Ave; dm $20, r with/without bathroom $60/50; ☐) Put simply, this hostel is great. Perfectly situated downtown, it occupies an airy historic building with hardwood floors, well-maintained rooms and real character. A diverse crowd of older, international travelers and a welcoming staff keep the mood low-key, relaxed and friendly. The attractive common room has TV and internet computers (per hour $5). Private rooms are a great deal (room 9 holds a surprise in the exterior mural), though street noise can intrude at night.

Hilo Tropical Gardens Guest House (Map p287; ☎ 217-9650; www.hilogardens.com; 1477 Kalaniana'ole Ave; camping $15, dm $25, r with shared bathroom $65, huts $100; ☐ ☎) Near Onekahakaha Beach and tucked within an atmospheric jungly garden, this small well-managed hostel offers dorms, private rooms, two free-standing huts and campsites. The common kitchen is limited, but the on-site ice-cream shop compensates, making this a lovely budget hideaway.

Arnott's Lodge (Map p287; ☎ 969-7097; www.arnottslodge.com; 98 Apapane Rd; tent sites $10, dm/r with shared bathroom $25/60, r/ste $70/130; ☐ ☎) Known as Hilo's 'party hostel,' Arnott's is fine if you just want a bed and the conviviality of young fellow travelers. The separate 'deluxe' rooms are most comfortable; others occupy a worn-out, cement-block motel. Tents crowd an open lawn, with access to outdoor showers. Staff can be grumpily rule-oriented. There's a movie room, coin laundry, and shuttles to downtown (round-trip $3); ask about free airport pickups (until 7:30pm).

Old Hawaiian B&B (Map p287; ☎ 961-2816, 877-961-2816; www.thebigislandvacation.com; 1492 Wailuku Dr; r incl breakfast $80-110; 🛜) In a private home in a neighborhood above downtown, these three cozy rooms are great value, offering pretty furnishings, a sense of seclusion, and a sociable morning over a generous breakfast on the backyard lanai. Room sizes vary.

Midrange & Top End

Dolphin Bay Hotel (Map p289; ☎ 935-1466; www.dolphinbayhotel.com; 333 Iliahi St; studios $100-110, 1br/2br $140/160) The glowing 'lava-fall' framing the office is your first clue that the owner loves volcanoes and has fashioned the Dolphin Bay into an ideal base for East Hawai'i adventures. In a residential neighborhood walkable to downtown, the 18 unfussy, functional rooms with full kitchens make comfortable crash pads after a day spent exploring. In the morning, fresh fruit and coffee are available, along with slightly charred walking sticks.

Hale Kai Hawaii (☎ 935-6330; www.halekaihawaii.com; 111 Honoli'i Place; r $145-165; 🛜 🐬) For memorable views of Hilo across the bay, book one of the four rooms here, which your talented, well-traveled hosts have decorated with their own art. Smallish rooms have character, with pretty quilts and bright color schemes; all open onto a shared lanai. A hot tub and tiny pool look out onto sweeping views, and they provide a convivial gourmet breakfast. Hale Kai overlooks Honoli'i Beach Park, north of downtown Hilo.

Bay House B&B (Map p289; ☎ 961-6311, 888-235-8195; www.bayhousehawaii.com; 42 Pukihae St; r incl breakfast $150; 🖥) Across the Singing Bridge, these three attractive tropical-themed rooms offer generous lanai with bay views, the serenade of restless waves and luscious privacy. Indeed, the gracious owner, making sure nothing disrupts your quiet escape, leaves a breakfast basket in your room.

our pick Hilo Honu Inn (Map p287; ☎ 935-4325; www.hilohonu.com; 465 Haili St; r incl breakfast $140-250; 🐬 🖥 🛜) On the hill above downtown, this remodeled 1933 home has three custom-designed guest rooms. All are wonderful, with mosaic-tile baths and memorable furnishings.

However, the top-floor Samurai Suite is a memorable standout. The house's original Japanese tea room, it boasts authentic Japanese furnishings, including tatami mat floor, sliding paper-screen doors, awesome sled bed, *furo* (soaking tub), and sweeping, 180-degree views of Hilo Bay. The engaging hosts make you feel at home, and they serve one mean breakfast.

Hilo Hawaiian Hotel (Map p287; ☎ 935-9361, 800-367-5004; www.castleresorts.com; 71 Banyan Dr; r $155-205; 🐬 🖥 🛜) The Hilo Hawaiian is Banyan Dr's best big hotel. Rooms are pleasing, if standard – neat and clean, with a tropical floral decor. Ocean-view rooms really deliver and are the real draw. The expected comforts and amenities – a freshwater pool, decent restaurant etc – seem better with an internet discount.

At the Beach with Friends B&B (Map p287; ☎ 934-8040; www.hiloinn.com; 369 Nene St; r incl breakfast $170-190; 🖥 🛜) Across from the beaches on Kalaniana'ole Ave, with jungly grounds that include an anchialine (a mixture of seawater and freshwater) pond swimming with fat koi, this three-room B&B feels a world away from Hilo. Carved Bali doors, bamboo bed frames and mosaic-tile baths set the tone for rooms packed with Hawaiiana. Breakfast is a buffet, and it's fully wired for business travelers.

Shipman House B&B (Map p289; ☎ 934-8002, 800-627-8447; www.hilo-hawaii.com; 131 Ka'iulani St; r incl breakfast $210-250; 🖥 🛜) This gracious, stately Victorian mansion, still run by Shipman heirs, is Hilo's most historic property. Play the grand piano Queen Lili'uokalani entertained on, and sleep where Jack London once lay his head; the family's museum-quality collection of antiques and artifacts fills every nook. The three main-house rooms are the most memorable, but two rooms in the nearby 1910 guest cottage are no slouch either: all rooms have nice baths, high ceilings, vintage furnishings, hardwood floors covered with *lauhala* mats, and refrigerators. A delicious breakfast is served on a spacious patio with thrilling views, and the owner hosts a hula class Wednesday night.

Several more Banyan Dr hotels can be OK, but only with an internet deal:

Hilo Seaside Hotel (Map p287; ☎ 935-0821, 800-560-5557; www.hiloseasidehotel.com; 126 Banyan Dr; r $85-120; 🐬 🐬) Bland, boring but adequate; view rooms are disappointing, so save your money.

Uncle Billy's Hilo Bay Hotel (Map p287; ☎ 935-0861, 800-442-5841; www.unclebilly.com; 87 Banyan Dr; r $90-130; 🐬 🖥 🐬) Uncle Billy's kitschy Polynesian decor doesn't extend to the tired, plain rooms. Spring for a room with a view.

Naniloa Volcanoes Resort (Map p287; ☎ 969-3333; www.hottours.us; 93 Banyan Dr; r $110-150) Newly renovated rooms are sleekly contemporary but feel done on the cheap; great views are worth the extra cost. Ongoing construction could be disruptive.

EATING

Hilo restaurants aim to satisfy local palates, not visitor desires, so it has a surfeit of wonderful neighborhood eats and a dearth of upscale cuisine. Many restaurants are closed Sunday.

Budget

Café 100 (Map p287; ☎ 935-8683; 969 Kilauea Ave; loco moco $2-5.25, plate lunches $6-7; ☽ 6:45am-8:30pm Mon-Sat) This legendary drive-in popularized the *loco moco* – rice topped with hamburger, fried egg and brown gravy. It's fast food Hawaiian-style, with dozens of varieties: Spam, mahimahi, teriyaki beef, a hot dog, even a garden burger. Portions aren't big; go crazy, order two!

Planet Cafe (Map p289; ☎ 640-1777; 187 Kilauea Ave; mains $6-9; ☽ 7am-8pm Mon-Fri, 9am-3pm Sat) This gay-friendly vegetarian café is a gathering spot for Hilo's hip, alternative-lifestyle contingent. Dishes have culinary flair, like banana pancakes, bagels with mac-nut pesto spread, homemade soups and veggie quesadilla with brie and roasted garlic. Cash only.

Nori's Saimin & Snacks (Map p287; ☎ 935-9133; Suite 124, Kukuau Plaza, 688 Kino'ole St; noodle soups $5.50-9; ☽ 10:30am-11pm Tue-Sat, 10:30am-10pm Sun) A Hilo institution run by a local celebrity chef, Nori's is all about saimin, that Japanese soup for the soul. Look past the strip-mall setting, perfunctory dining room and spotty service; steaming bowls are packed with goodies (get the wontons with sinus-clearing mustard). The saimin is irresistibly chewy and satisfying.

Aloha Luigi (Map p289; ☎ 934-9112; 264 Keawe St; mains $7.50-12; ☽ 9am-3pm Mon & Tue, 9am-7pm Wed-Sat) Sometimes enthusiasm and cheerful decor beat finesse and refinement, and so it is at this bus-your-own-tray place: order either Mexican or Italian, and you won't want for flavor. The garlicky Caesar salad is a highlight, but there's nothing wrong with the parmigiana sub or mahimahi burrito. Hit the outdoor patio when the sun shines.

Ken's House of Pancakes (Map p287; ☎ 935-8711; 1730 Kamehameha Ave; meals $7-13; ☽ 24hr) Strand a New Jersey diner in the tropics and you get a mile-long menu filled with mac-nut pancakes, fat crab omelettes, sweetbread French toast, oxtail stew and *kalua* pig dinners. In other words, it's 'ono, brah! Local families keep it packed night and day, and it's the perfect place to bring yours (particularly pint-sized fussy eaters).

Miyo's (Map p287; ☎ 935-2273; Waiakea Villa, 400 Hualani St; mains $8-13; ☽ 11am-2pm & 5:30-8:30pm Mon-Sat) Overlooking Waiakea Pond, Miyo's resembles a rustic Japanese teahouse and evokes a warm, even romantic, atmosphere. It dishes up tasty renditions of Japanese country cooking – tempura, sesame chicken, beef teriyaki, *donburi*, sashimi and more. Call ahead to reserve a coveted window table. It's in the first complex of buildings adjacent to the pond as you enter Waiakea Villa.

Kuhio Grille (Map p287; ☎ 959-2336; Suite A106, Prince Kuhio Plaza; mains $8-18; ☽ 6am-10pm Sun-Thu, to midnight Fri) Locals needing a fix of traditional Hawaiian comfort food gather at the family-run Kuhio Grille. Its specialty is the filling 1lb *laulau* (various meats wrapped in taro leaves and steamed). However, all the favorites are here, such as poi, *lomilomi* (minced, salted salmon), *kalua* pig, saimin and *loco moco*. Behind Prince Kuhio Plaza.

Midrange & Top End

Reuben's (Map p289; ☎ 961-2552; 336 Kamehameha Ave; meals $11-17; ☽ 11am-9pm Mon-Sat, till 10pm Fri & Sat) With plates as cheesy as its velvet paintings of Zapata, Reuben's dishes up satisfyingly greasy renditions of *chillies rellenos*, fish tacos and enchiladas. Service may be slow, but that's why Mexico invented the margarita ($5).

Ocean Sushi (Map p289; ☎ 961-6625; 250 Keawe St; rolls $4-7, bentō $12-14; ☽ 10am-2pm & 5-9pm Mon-Sat) Zip atmosphere, rushed service, linoleum floors – but this sushi joint is always packed. Rolls ($4 to $7) show an island influence – with mac nuts, tropical fruit, and *poke* – but mainly they're priced so you can order a bunch.

Sushi Bar Hime (Map p289; ☎ 961-6356; 14 Furneaux Lane; sushi & sashimi $3-9; ☽ 11:30am-1:30pm & 5:30-8pm Tue-Sat, noon-3pm Sun) This hole-in-the-wall with three tiny tables and four stools is an outstanding classic sushi bar. With consummate skill, the understated preparations allow the fresh, high-quality fish to shine. Go figure: the sweetheart owners cashed out of the Maui rat-race to live the simple life in Hilo.

Sombat's Fresh Thai Cuisine (Map p287; ☎ 936-9336; www.sombats.com; 88 Kanoelehua Ave; dishes $12-18; ⏱ 10:30am-2pm Mon-Fri, 5-8:30pm Mon-Sat) Sombats serves above average Thai classics made with local produce and fresh herbs (grown by the chef). Soups are aromatic, curries piquant and as hot as you like. The lunch buffet ($7 to $9) is a great deal. The only drawback is the fluorescent-lit, bare dining room in a deserted commercial building.

Pescatore (Map p289; ☎ 969-9090; 235 Keawe St; pizzas $9-13, mains $16-28; ⏱ 11am-9pm Mon-Fri, 7:30am-9pm Sat & Sun) The ideal neighborhood restaurant, with attentive service and quality ingredients prepared simply, Pescatore satisfies any Italian cravings. The ahi carpaccio is a star, the sausage is homemade, and the authentic fare includes cioppino, *fra diavolo* and eggplant parmesan. The lounge and bar make waiting a pleasure.

Café Pesto (Map p289; ☎ 969-6640; 308 Kamehameha Ave; pizzas $12-19, dinner mains $17-30; ⏱ 11am-9pm Sun-Thu, to 10pm Fri & Sat) Housed in a beautifully renovated historical building, Café Pesto has a varied but accomplished menu. It started as a pizza place – and the crisp gourmet-style pies remain noteworthy – but there are delectable risottos, fresh stir-fries, interesting pastas and more, many featuring seafood. With weekend guitarists and a lively mix of locals, a friendlier scene can't be found downtown.

Jays (Map p287; ☎ 955-8880; 782 Kilauea Ave at Aupuni; tapas $6-12, mains $19-27; ⏱ 11am-2pm & 5:30-9pm Mon-Sat) This newcomer has made a splash on the dining scene with a robust menu of hearty entrées and oversized tapas. Dishes aim for satisfying, big flavors: crab cakes, 1lb of steamed clams, steak and onions on a sizzling platter, and Hamakua mushroom lobster ravioli. The attractive dining room sports white tablecloths, lazy ceiling fans, colorful art and a dark wood bar.

our pick **Hilo Bay Café** (Map p287; ☎ 935-4939; Waiakea Center, 315 Maka'ala St; mains $16-30; ⏱ 11am-9pm Mon-Sat, 5-9pm Sun) Hilo's only true gourmet destination, Hilo Bay Café serves inventive Hawaiian-infused cuisine that holds its own. Dishes are complex but always perfectly balanced. The crab cakes and the seared macadamia nut–crusted scallops alone are worth the trip. The changing menu includes BBQ ribs, Hamakua mushroom risotto, pork chops with red curry and *poke*. Service is excellent and friendly, and the short wine list makes choosing easy: all vintages are priced the same.

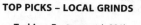

TOP PICKS – LOCAL GRINDS

- **Teshima Restaurant** (p231)
- **Manago Hotel** (p238)
- **Hawaiian Style Cafe** (p267)
- **Big Island Grill** (p223)
- **Kanaka Kava** (p223)
- **Café 100** (opposite)
- **Kuhio Grille** (opposite)

The only knock is the mall setting; despite the restaurant's stylish modern interior, it isn't as warmly romantic as the food deserves.

Seaside Restaurant (Map p287; ☎ 935-8825; 1790 Kalaniana'ole Ave; mains $21-35; ⏱ 5-8:30pm Tue-Sun, to 9pm Fri & Sat) This old favorite is as comfortable as a rubbah slippah. Its calling card is that its mullet and *aholehole* (flagtail) are raised in its own fishponds. The traditional preparation (steamed in *ti* leaves) is good, but 'Chinese-style' is a flavorful variation. If *moi* is on the menu, order it; this delectable reef fish was once reserved for Hawaiian royalty. It also has the full range of seafood, great *poke* appetizers and a full bar, but service can be uneven.

Groceries

Picnics that are the stuff of legend can be assembled in Hilo. First stop is always the extensive farmers market (p290).

Suisan Fish Market (Map p287; ☎ 935-9349; 93 Lihiwai St; ⏱ 8am-5pm Mon-Fri, to 4pm Sat) For just-caught seafood, go here. It has an attention-grabbing variety of *poke* and will fry whole fish on-the-spot next door.

KTA Super Store Downtown (Map p289; ☎ 935-3751; 321 Keawe St; ⏱ 7am-9pm Mon-Sat, to 7pm Sun); Puainako Town Center (Map p287; ☎ 959-9111; 50 E Puainako St; ⏱ 5:30am-midnight) For regular groceries, Hilo shoppers prefer KTA. The downtown store is as cramped as the Puainako location is enormous; downtown sells out of the good stuff early, but Puainako has such an extensive selection of *poke*, *bentō* and other local treats that you needn't worry.

For organic foods, bulk grains, fruit smoothies and travel-ready salads, head for **Abundant Life Natural Foods** (Map p289; ☎ 935-7411; 292 Kamehameha Ave; ⏱ 8:30am-7pm Mon, Tue, Thu & Fri, 7am-7pm Wed & Sat, 10am-5pm Sun) in downtown Hilo; it also has a simple café. **Island Naturals** (Map p287; ☎ 935-5533; Waiakea Center, 303 Maka'ala St; ⏱ 7:30am-8pm Mon-Sat, 9am-

7pm Sun), near the Hwy 11 malls, has a nice salad bar and good to-go and bakery items.

DRINKING & ENTERTAINMENT

The words 'Hilo' and 'nightclubbing' never rub together. There are a few bars downtown and at the Banyan Dr hotels, and some live music – but even then, when it's slow, places shut early. Often, the only ones making noise after 10pm are the coqui frogs.

Bars & Nightclubs

Shooters Bar & Grill (Map p287; ☎ 969-7069; 121 Banyan Dr; admission $5; ⏱ 9pm-2am Wed, 10pm-3am Thu-Sat) This is the most reliable spot for local 20-somethings who want to drink, flirt and dance to DJ-spun tunes.

Cronies Bar & Grill (Map p289; ☎ 935-5158; 11 Waianuenue Ave; ⏱ 11am-10pm Mon-Sat) With big windows looking out on the bayfront, Cronies is a bright, TV-festooned sports bar with occasional live music and a full menu (meals $9 to $18). It's the biggest, most welcoming spot downtown.

Coffeehouses

Kope Kope Espresso Café (Map p287; ☎ 933-1221; www.kopekopeespresso.com; Hilo Shopping Center, 1261 Kilauea Ave; ⏱ 6:30am-7pm Mon-Wed, 6:30am-9pm Thu-Sat, 7:30am-6pm Sun; 🖥 🛜) This hip Seattle-ish coffeehouse with couches, simple eats and internet access hosts a daily lunchtime music series, and live entertainment on weekend evenings. It could be jazz, slack key guitar, ukelele or swing dancing.

Bayfront Kava Bar (Map p289; ☎ 935-1155; 155 Kamehameha St; snacks $4-8; ⏱ 10am-9pm Mon-Sat) It looks like an upscale coffeeshop, but that's kava in those coconut cups. Order your mashed 'awa straight up or with coconut milk (for a slightly sweeter dirt taste). Relax, that's what kava's for, and enjoy live music most nights. This place also serves espresso, tea and a few munchables.

Theaters & Cinemas

our pick **Palace Theater** (Map p289; ☎ 934-7010; box office 934-7777; www.hilopalace.com; 38 Haili St; tickets $7) The resurrected, historic Palace Theater is Hilo's cultural crown jewel. Its eclectic programming includes arthouse and silent films (accompanied by the house organ), music and dance concerts, Broadway musicals, and various cultural festivals. Every Wednesday morning it hosts the highly recommended 'Hawai'iana Live' ($5), a sweetly intimate, personal, 45-minute sampling of Hawaiian culture.

Kress Cinemas (Map p289; ☎ 935-6777; 174 Kamehameha Ave; tickets $1) Second-run films are only one buck (!) during the week at Kress Cinemas, and a whole $1.50 on evening weekends (blame inflation).

Stadium Cinemas (Map p287; ☎ 961-3456; Prince Kuhio Plaza, 111 E Puainako St; adult/child 3-11/matinee $9.25/5.75/6.75) New Hollywood releases are shown at this plush, up-to-date multiplex cinema.

SHOPPING

Downtown Hilo has some of the coolest gift stores and boutiques on the island. It's got a great gallery scene if you're hunting for local and/or fine art; cruise the corner of Mamo St and Kilauea Ave, in addition to bayfront's Kamehameha Ave.

Sudha's Art Gallery (Map p289; ☎ 934-0009; www.sudhaachar.com; 100 Kamehameha Ave; ⏱ 11am-4pm Tue-Sat) Run by the former chairman of the East Hawai'i Cultural Center, this fine art gallery sells contemporary paintings, sculpture and woodworking. Upstairs, you'll find secondhand books.

High Fire Hawaii (Map p289; ☎ 935-8380; www.highfirehawaii.com; 114 Haili St; ⏱ 11am-6pm Mon-Sat) This tiny shop represents only local ceramicists, painters, and jewelry-makers. Quality is high, and prices are reasonable; it also holds ceramics classes.

Sig Zane Designs (Map p289; ☎ 935-7077; www.sigzane.com; 122 Kamehameha Ave; ⏱ 9:30am-5pm Mon-Fri, 9am-4pm Sat) Famous statewide, Sig Zane custom designs his own fabrics and styles, lifting the humble aloha shirt and tropical-flower dress into the realm of fashion.

Cutlery (Map p289; ☎ 934-7500; www.upinthecutlery.com; 141 Mamo St; ⏱ 11am-6pm Mon-Fri) Urban, hip male clothes by local indie designers fill this ultra-cool shop owned by Kuhau Zane (son of Sig Zane). These are Hawaiian T-shirts even Manhattanites would wear.

Girl Next Door (Map p289; ☎ 933-1460; 223-B Kilauea Ave; ⏱ 10am-6pm Mon-Fri) This amusingly naughty, gay-friendly shop (advertising 'objects of virtue') sells sex toys, steamy videos and saucy souvenirs – along with legitimate kids toys. Only in Hilo. It's a good place to connect with the local gay scene and grab a copy of *Da Kine*.

Hilo Hattie (Map p287; ☎ 961-3077; www.hilohattie.com; Prince Kuhio Plaza; ⏱ 8:30am-6pm) Good-quality

SWEETS & SNACKS

No question, Hilo has a sweet tooth, and many ways to satisfy it.

our pick **Two Ladies Kitchen** (Map p289; ☎ 961-4766; 274 Kilauea Ave; 8-piece boxes $7; ⏲ 10am-5pm Wed-Sat) is leading a 'confection revolution' with its Japanese *mochi* (sweet rice dessert) and *manju* (baked adzuki bean-filled cake). These pillowy confections come in a happy pastel rainbow of traditional and creative flavors – some filled with red bean paste, others with tropical fruits, brownie, and marshmallow. *Mochi* has a short shelf life, so buy a beautifully packaged mixed box for yourself. At the very least order a single strawberry *mochi*. This handmade delight is a prize possession.

At the closet-sized **Hilo Seeds & Snacks** (Map p289; ☎ 935-7355; 15 Waianuenue Ave; snacks under $5; ⏲ 9:30am-5pm Mon-Fri) you can try 'crack seed,' a bizarre Chinese dried-plum snack that some find addictive and others find…well, try it yourself. The friendly owner will explain the overwhelming variety of types: salty, sour, sweet, some medicinal and others mild. Mango with *li hing* (preserved plum flavor powder) is a tasty choice.

When O'Keefe's bakery closed, the 'cake lady' opened her own tiny, takeout shop, **E-Claire's Bakery** (Map p289; ☎ 961-3848; 268 Waianuenue Ave; items $1-5, cakes $15-25; ⏲ 7am-5pm Mon-Fri, 7am-3pm Sat). Grateful locals now come here for her delectable flaky pastries, tarts, eclairs and one-serving pies – in addition to her cakes and cheesecakes. Cash only.

What E-Claire's doesn't do are buttermilk doughnuts. For these, head to **Sputnik's** (Map p287; ☎ 961-2066; 811 Laukapu St; doughnuts 95¢; ⏲ 6:30am-1:30pm Mon-Fri), a third-generation family business that makes a limited supply of these moist, hearty fried beauties every weekday morning. Come early, they sell out.

The best ice-cream and sorbet on the island comes from a Kawaihae creamery that produces two equally yummy premium lines: Hilo Homemade (classic flavors) and Tropical Dreams (fusion flavors). Many places in town sell them, but if it's a hot day at the beach (it happens!), head for **Hilo Homemade Ice Cream** (Map p287; ☎ 217-9650; 1477 Kalaniana'ole Ave; scoops from $3; ⏲ 11am-6pm).

Finally, no visit to Hilo is complete without a stop at **Itsu's Fishing Supplies** (Map p287; ☎ 935-8082; 810 Pi'ilani St; ice shave $1.50-3.25; ⏲ 8am-5pm Mon-Fri) – yes, a fishing-supply store! – which sells Hilo's best ice shave (note: Hilo folks call it 'ice shave,' not 'shave ice'). The ice shave is hand-cranked off an ice block, scooped into a cone and topped with your choice of sweet syrups – double your pleasure and get ice-cream inside.

Hawaiian wear for the whole family. Styles range from tacky to retro kitschy to almost understated old-school aloha.

Dragon Mama (Map p289; ☎ 934-9081; www.dragonmama.com; 266 Kamehameha Ave; ⏲ 9am-5pm Mon-Fri, to 4pm Sat) Luscious kimonos, unique shirts and custom-made pillows from imported Japanese fabrics; also check out the gorgeous tea sets.

Fabric Impressions (Map p289; ☎ 961-4468; 206 Kamehameha Ave; ⏲ 9:30am-5pm Mon-Fri, 9am-4:30pm Sat) It has everything for the DIY quilter (attractive fabrics, tropical squares and patterns), plus finished quilts and adorable handmade gifts: pot holders, luggage tags, tea cozies, *bentō* carriers and more.

Hilo Guitars & Ukuleles (Map p289; ☎ 935-4282; www.hiloguitars.com; 56 Ponahawai St; ⏲ 10am-5pm Mon-Fri, 10am-4pm Sat, noon-4pm Sun) All musicians, budding and otherwise, should come here for top-quality ukes (from $90), steel guitars and Hawaiian sheet music. Knowledgeable staff will steer you to the right instrument.

Big Island Candies (Map p287; ☎ 935-8890, 800-935-5510; www.bigislandcandies.com; 585 Hinano St; ⏲ 8:30am-5pm) This candy factory makes stylishly packaged confections and shortbread – watch them hand-dip chocolate from behind picture windows. One visit makes short work of your gift list.

Hilo Surplus Store (Map p289; ☎ 935-6398; 148 Mamo St; ⏲ 8am-5pm Mon-Sat) This vintage army surplus store is *the* place for jungle-grade machetes or a bolt of camouflage Gore-Tex. Campers will find a good selection of gear, in addition to authentic mess kits.

Alan's Art & Collectibles (Map p289; ☎ 969-1554; 202 Kamehameha Ave; ⏲ 10am-4:30pm Mon & Wed-Fri, 1-4:30pm Tue, 10am-3pm Sat) Time travel through Hawai'i's past in this secondhand shop full of coconut ashtrays, bowling trophies, Elvis posters and kitschy treasures.

HAWAI'I THE BIG ISLAND

GETTING THERE & AWAY
Air
Although most Big Island visitors fly into Kona airport, Hilo airport (Map p287) is also busy. See p211 for more information.

Bus
The main Hilo station for the **Hele-On Bus** (☎ 961-8744; www.heleonbus.org; ☺ 7:45am-4:30pm Mon-Fri) is at **Mo'oheau terminal** (Map p289; 329 Kamehameha Ave). All intra-island buses originate here. Routes connect to Kona and most towns in between, and they connect to Pahoa and Hawai'i Volcanoes National Park. See individual destinations for details on specific routes to/from Hilo.

GETTING AROUND
For directions to/from the airport, see p212.

Bicycle
Biking around Hilo is fun – when it isn't raining.
Da Kine Bike Shop (Map p289; ☎ 934-9861; 18 Furneaux Lane; ☺ noon-6pm Tue-Fri, 9am-3pm Sat) Offers sales, advice, personal tours and, sometimes, rentals (per day from $15 to $30).
Mid-Pacific Wheels (Map p287; ☎ 935-6211; www .midpacificwheels.com; 1133-C Manono St; ☺ 9am-6pm Mon-Sat, 11am-5pm Sun) Hilo's most comprehensive bike shop rents wheels (per day from $25 to $35).

Car
Hilo is car-oriented. Shopping malls and businesses usually have ample lots, while most streets downtown allow free two-hour parking. On most days it's easy to find a space, but the bayfront area gets jammed during the Saturday and Wednesday farmers market (see p290).

Public Transport
The Hele-On Bus (above) has a few intracity routes, all free, operating Monday to Friday:
No 4 Kaumana Goes five times a day (from 7:35am to 2:20pm) to Hilo Public Library and Hilo Medical Center (near Rainbow Falls).
No 6 Waiakea-Uka Goes five times a day (from 7:05am to 3:05pm) to the University of Hawai'i at Hilo and Prince Kuhio Plaza.
No 7 Downtown Hilo Goes a dozen times a day (from 7am to 9pm) to Aupuni Center and Prince Kuhio Plaza.

Taxi
In Hilo, call **Marshall's Taxi** (☎ 936-2654) or **Percy's Taxi** (☎ 969-7060).

PUNA

Puna lives on Pele's skirt, and residing that close to such a volatile goddess must affect you. Puna is laid-back and cool, a live-and-let-live sort of place, but it's also intense. The land vibrates with energy; emotions and creativity run high. One settles here only by accepting wildness and impermanence as the price. Puna retains dense, unspoiled portions of sometimes hallucinatory jungle as well as neighborhoods now nothing more than imaginary property lines running beneath a thick mass of black lava.

Outlaws like it here, and nonconformists, and anyone looking to escape: Puna is home to mainland hippies, funky artists, alternative healers, Hawaiian sovereignty activists, *pakalolo* growers, organic farmers and off-the-grid survivalists. Sultry and hang-loose, Puna encourages travelers to ditch the guidebook and go with the flow.

Considering this, it is somewhat surprising that Puna is the fastest-growing district in the state. It has some of the state's most affordable land, in subdivisions that were marked out over 50 years ago and sparsely settled – until now. The northern half of Puna is becoming one unending subdivision, with home prices doubling and tripling, and the population poised to almost double within a decade. Most agree Puna faces an infrastructure crisis, not to mention an identity crisis.

That Puna will be different a decade from now goes without question, but whether by human design or Pele's whim, who knows?

KEA'AU
pop 2010
Just off Hwy 11, Kea'au is Puna's largest town, and it serves the major shopping and business needs of the district's burgeoning subdivisions – Hawaiian Paradise Park, Hawaiian Beaches, Hawaiian Acres and Orchidland Estates. For travelers, it's mainly useful for fresh provisions, particularly if you're headed to Volcano village, which lacks a decent grocery store.

Everything is near the main crossroads. The Kea'au Shopping Center has a laundry, an ATM, a large grocery store, a natural food store and a Longs drugstore (all open daily except Longs, which is closed Sun). Across the road, small **Kea'au Village Market** (☎ 966-4853; ☺ 7am-5pm) has outdoor stalls with fresh local produce, gift shops and a couple of lunch counters serving local *grinds*.

If you're looking for adventure, detour for some spelunking in the 500-year-old **Kazumura Cave**, which at 41 surveyed miles is the world's longest lava tube. **Kilauea Caverns of Fire** (☎ 217-2363; www.kilaueacavernsoffire.com; 1/3hr tours $29/79; ☺ by appointment) conducts two tours – an easy one-hour walk or a three-hour scramble. Call for reservations and directions; the entrance is on private land in Orchidland Estates.

Sleeping

ourpick **Art & Orchids B&B** (☎ 982-8197, 877-393-1894; www.artandorchids.com; 16-1504 39th Ave; r incl breakfast $90-115; ☺ ☒) The artistic, eco-conscious owners have created a dreamy, relaxed haven in an ohia forest. Three airy, tastefully decorated rooms include funky mosaic-tile baths and tons of amenities. The spacious common room has a full kitchen and cozy couches for reading and games. An unforgettable lava-rock-and-mosaic-tile swimming pool has a waterfall and hot tub. Papermaking and mosaic classes are given on request, and they'll happily babysit your kids and do art projects with them (per hour $20). The generous homemade breakfast includes fresh farm eggs. This is Puna at its best.

MOUNTAIN VIEW & AROUND

Along Hwy 11, west of Kea'au, are several notable stops along the northern edge of Puna. Just past Kurtistown is the **Fuku-Bansai Cultural Center** (☎ 982-9880; www.fukubonsai.com; 17-856 Ola'a Rd; admission free; ☺ 8am-4pm Mon-Sat). This working nursery cultivates the art of Japanese bonsai; tour impressive outdoor displays of these miniature trees. The specialty, dwarf schefflera, have aerial roots like handheld banyan trees; it's a kooky shift in perspective.

Just before Mountain View, after the 12-mile marker, visit **Dan DeLuz's Woods** (☎ 968-6607; Hwy 11; ☺ 9am-5pm). Dan is a master woodworker who takes native hardwoods such as koa, sandalwood, mango and banyan and crafts gorgeous bowls, platters and furniture. His store is an education in the art, and his workshop is next door. Adjacent **Koa Shop Kaffee** (☎ 968-1129; Hwy 11; mains $5-9; ☺ 7am-8pm, till 9pm Sat & Sun) is a home-style diner with average plate lunches and sandwiches.

A half-mile further, coffee addicts (or lovers, if you will) should put on the brakes for the **Hilo Coffee Mill** (☎ 968-1333; www.hilocoffeemill .com; 17-995 Hwy 11; ☺ 7am-4pm Mon-Fri, 8am-4pm Sat).

HAWAI'I THE BIG ISLAND

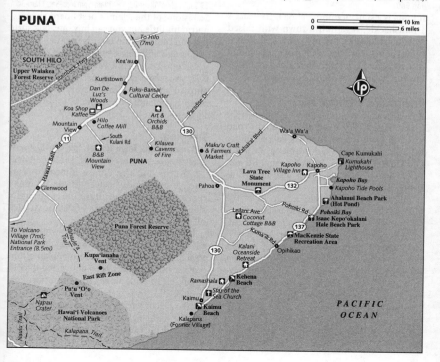

It's dedicated to promoting East Hawai'i coffee, which has begun rivaling Kona coffee for excellence. Free coffee tastings treat roasts like fine wine, and free tours include the roaster next door. The Mill sells a full range of beverages and whole beans.

Within the village of Mountain View (at the 14-mile marker), **Mountain View Bakery** (☎ 968-6353; Old Volcano Rd; items $4-6 ⏰ 7:30am-1pm Mon-Fri, 7:30am-1:30pm Sat) bakes its own pies, breads and its iconic 'stone cookies,' a crack-your-tooth biscotti-like confection. Try original, raisin, chocolate chip (our favorite) or, if you must, soft.

A peaceful retreat, **Bed & Breakfast Mountain View** (☎ 968-6868, 888-698-9896; www.bbmtview.com; r incl breakfast $90-110) offers four comfortable rooms in the warm home of famous Big Island artists Jane and Linus Chao. Hidden on a quiet road a mile from Hwy 11, surrounded by pretty landscaping, the Chaos' large house (built for grown kids who never stayed) is graced with their splendid art and genuine aloha.

PAHOA
pop 960

If Puna is a state of mind, Pahoa is its heart – a ramshackle, ragamuffin town with raised wooden sidewalks, peeling paint and an unkempt bohemian edge. It's full of oddballs and eccentrics and gentle, genuine aloha. No one's in a hurry, and you needn't be either.

Orientation & Information

Roads in and around Pahoa are known by many names. For example, the main road through town is signposted as Pahoa Village Rd but is also called Government Main Rd, Old Government Rd, Main St, Puna Rd and Pahoa Rd – but Hwy 130 is also known as Pahoa Rd!

Just off the main highway, north of the historic downtown, is Pahoa Marketplace – a shopping mall with a huge grocery store, hardware store and fresh-fish monger. Also here is **Aloha Outpost Internet Café** (Pahoa Marketplace; mains $5-8; internet per hr $7, wi-fi per day $10; ⏰ 6am-9pm; 💻 📶), with plenty of computers, inexpensive eats, an attached used bookstore and regular events. You could hang out all day.

Along the main street in town is a convenience store, banks, gas stations and a **post office** (☎ 965-1158; 15-2859 Pahoa Village Rd; ⏰ 8:30am-4pm Mon-Fri, 11am-2pm Sat), as well as **Sirius Coffee**

(☎ 965-8555; Pahoa Village Rd; ⏰ 7am-6pm Mon-Fri, 7am-4pm Sat, 7am-3pm Sun; 💻 📶) with internet access (per 30 minutes $2), espresso coffee and baked goods ($2 to $5).

Sights & Activities

Join the entire Puna 'ohana (family) at the **Maku'u Craft & Farmers Market** (☎ 896-5537; www.makuufarmersassociation.org; ⏰ 5:30am-2pm Sun) on Hwy 130 between the 7-mile and 8-mile markers. It's more like a massive village party than a market, and you'll find psychic channeling, wood carvings, massage, old junk, surfboard repair, orchids, organic honey, sarongs and jewelry, photos of the Kalapana eruption and even fruits and vegetables. Hot food includes Hawaiian, Samoan, Mexican and Thai cuisine, and more. Morning cultural workshops (9am) give way to live music through the afternoon. Don't miss it.

For swimming, head for the gorgeous outdoor, heated Olympic-size pool at **Pahoa Community Aquatic Center** (Kauhale St; ⏰ 9am-4:40pm), behind the Pahoa Neighborhood Facility; it has nice showers and a separate kids' pool.

Jeff Hunt of **Jeff Hunt Surfboards** (☎ 965-2322; 15-2883 Pahoa Village Rd; ⏰ 10am-5pm Mon-Sat, 11am-3pm Sun) is one of the island's best board shapers, and at his little hut you can buy one, talk surfing and rent soft-top boards (per day $20).

Though still being built at press time, the grassroots, nonprofit **Pahoa Museum** (☎ 965-0072; www.pahoamuseum.org; 15-2931 Pahoa Village Rd) aims to showcase Puna history and culture in all its splendid diversity, as told by local Punatics. It's due to open in 2009.

Sleeping

JoMamas Pahoa Town Hostel (☎ 430-1573; www.jomamahawaii.com; Pahoa Village Rd; dm $30, s/d $45/60; 📶) At the north end of downtown, this attractive, brand-new hostel is filled with funky carvings, imported furniture and community aloha. It's a welcoming, drug-free place to kick off your slippahs.

Island Paradise Inn (☎ 990-0234; www.islandparadiseinn.com; Pahoa Village Rd; d $40-60) Smack downtown, this inn is actually a row of former plantation-worker houses that's been converted into 12 small, clean and, above all, very affordable rooms, all with private bathroom and kitchenette. Decor varies; pleasing touches (fluffy towels, stained glass) are combined with secondhand bureaus and furniture displaying various nicks and scratches.

TOP PICKS – MEDITATIVE RETREATS

- **Wood Valley Temple** (p324)
- **Akiko's Buddhist B&B** (p284)
- **Kalani Oceanside Retreat** (p305)
- **Ramashala** (p305)
- **Volcano Rainforest Retreat** (p320)

Coconut Cottage B&B (☎ 965-0973, 866-204-7444; www.coconutcottagehawaii.com; 13-1139 Leilani Ave; r incl breakfast $110-140; ☐) South of Pahoa in a trim residential neighborhood, this four-room B&B is packed with sweet Balinese accents and little luxuries that set a romantic mood. The garden hot tub in a tiki hut and the breezy porch are attractive places to relax, a sensation that's cultivated by the warm, gracious hosts. Rooms are comfortably cozy; the largest is the detached bungalow with kitchenette. Breakfast is a feast.

Eating

Island Naturals (☎ 965-8322; 15-1403 Pahoa Village Rd; ⏲ 7:30am-7:30pm Mon-Sat, 8am-7pm Sun) For organic produce and picnic lunches; this place has a fresh, interesting range of sandwiches, packaged salads, baked goods and hot food.

Pahoa's Village Café (☎ 965-1133; 15-2471 Pahoa Village Rd; mains $7-13; ⏲ 8am-midnight Wed-Sat, 8am-9pm Sun) Recently renovated, this attractive café serves good-quality burgers, plate lunches, *loco moco*, salads and various specials. It also hosts evening entertainment – a mix of music, dancing and karaoke.

Luquin's Mexican Restaurant (☎ 965-9990; 15-2942 Pahoa Village Rd; mains $8-17; ⏲ 7am-9pm) Luquin's is the favorite local watering hole, serving a tasty variety of potent margaritas in pint glasses (from $5.50), along with premium tequilas. It serves decent versions of the standard Mexican combo plates – which is really all you need to soak up maybe just one more margarita.

Paolo's Bistro (☎ 965-7033; Pahoa Village Rd; mains $11-20; ⏲ 5:30-8:30pm Tue-Sun) Check tablecloths, an intimate dining room, and a well-executed short menu of authentic northern Italian cooking make for a satisfying Pahoa evening.

Kaleo's Bar & Grill (☎ 965-5600; 15-2969 Pahoa Village Rd; mains $9-25; ⏲ 11am-2pm Tue-Fri, 5-8:30pm daily) The menu tries to do too much; Kaleo falls short of its gourmet aims, but it gets points for creativity and for the romantic atmosphere. Stick to simpler preparations – ribs and steaks, penne vodka pesto, burgers – and you won't be disappointed. Live music most nights.

Getting There & Away

The free Hele-On Bus (p300) goes from Hilo to Kea'au and Pahoa six times a day Monday to Friday; take the 9 Pahoa.

LAVA TREE STATE MONUMENT

Entering this **park** beneath a tight-knit canopy of monkeypod trees is an otherworldly experience. A short, easy loop trail passes through a tropical vision of Middle Earth, full of ferns, orchids and bamboo, and takes you past unusual 'lava trees,' which were created in 1790 when a rain forest was engulfed in *pahoehoe* from Kilauea's East Rift Zone. The lava enveloped the moisture-laden ohia trees and then receded, leaving lava molds of the destroyed trees. These mossy shells now lie scattered like dinosaur bones, adding to the park's ghostly aura. In the late afternoon, the love songs of coqui (see p304) reverberate among the trees. To get here, follow Hwy 132 about 2.5 miles east of Hwy 130.

Lava Tree Tropic Inn (☎ 965-7441; www.lavatree tropicinn.com; 14-3555 Puna Rd, Pahoa; d $90-130, cottage $200; ☐ ☎) Next to the state monument, this B&B exudes a quirky European feel because of its gregarious Hungarian owner, who has converted the upstairs into five comfortable, homey rooms, adding funky touches like paintings and table lamps from Budapest. The suite has a fun powder room, a Jacuzzi tub and a bidet, while a detached, fully equipped cottage makes a perfect home base. Breakfast comes with Hungarian treats, while Tuesday is music night; bring your ukelele!

KAPOHO

Hwy 132 heads east until it meets Hwy 137 at what is called 'Four Corners' near Kapoho. This spot contained a farming town until Pele paid a visit in January 1960. A fissure opened up in the midst of a nearby sugarcane field; while the main flow of *pahoehoe* lava ran toward the ocean, a slower-moving offshoot of 'a'a lava crept toward the town, burying orchid farms in its path. Two weeks later the lava entered Kapoho and buried the town. A hot-springs resort and nearly 100 homes and businesses disappeared beneath the flow. Amazingly, when the lava approached the sea at Cape Kumukahi, it parted into two flows around the lighthouse, which alone survived. Old-timers say it's because, on the eve of the disaster, the lighthouse keeper offered a meal to Pele, who had appeared in the form of an old woman, and she spared the structure.

Most visitors turn right here and continue along Hwy 137, but this area has some interesting detours (see opposite).

On Hwy 132, **Kapoho Village Inn** (☎ 937-0588; www.kapohovillageinn.com; 14-4587 Kapoho-Pahoa Rd; r $89, ste $139) is an old Kapoho boardinghouse – which was spared in 1960 – that's been converted by an enthusiastic young couple into five attractive, breezy rooms with shared bathrooms and a common kitchen. All have fresh, simple decor, with bent-cane furniture, nice spreads, flat-screen TVs and screened windows. Tiled showers are sparkling clean, and there's a washer-dryer for guest use.

RED ROAD (HIGHWAY 137)

Scenic, winding Hwy 137 is nicknamed Red Road because its northern portion is paved with red cinder. It's a swooping, atmospheric drive that periodically dips beneath tunnel-like canopies of milo and *hala* (pandanus) trees.

Two side roads also make intriguing detours or shortcuts back to Pahoa: **Pohoiki Road** connects Hwy 137 with Hwy 132, and it is another of Puna's shaded, mystical roads, winding through thick forest dotted with papaya orchards and wild *noni* (Indian mulberry). Further south, Kama'ili Rd connects with Hwy 130, and though less moody, it's a pleasant country ramble.

Kapoho Tide Pools

The best snorkeling on the Big Island's windward side is this sprawling network of **tide pools**, which are officially named the Wai Opae Tide Pools Marine Life Conservation District. Here, Kapoho's lava-rock coast is a mosaic of protected, shallow, interconnected pools containing a rich variety of sea life. It's easy to pool-hop for hours, tracking saddle wrasses, Moorish idols, butterfly fish, sea cucumbers and much more.

From Hwy 137, a mile south of the lighthouse, turn onto Kapoho Kai Dr, which winds a little and dead-ends at Wai Opae; turn left and park in the lot (7am to 7pm). There are no facilities.

Ahalanui Beach Park

It's called 'the hot pond' because of its main attraction – a large, spring-fed **thermal pool** that's set in lava rock and deep enough for swimming. It's a pretty sweet bathtub: water temperatures average 90°F, cement borders make for easy access, tropical fish abound, and, though the ocean pounds the adjacent seawall, the pool is always calm. However, despite being regularly flushed by the sea, the pond contains a risk of bacterial infection. Don't enter if you have any cuts or a cold, and the prudent avoid low tide.

The park is officially open from 7am to 7pm, but the gates are never locked and nighttime soaks are possible. The park has picnic tables, portable toilets and a lifeguard daily. Don't leave valuables in your car.

NOISY LITTLE FROGS

Tourists love them because their bright chirping is like a tropical jungle soundtrack, but Hawai'i's cutest invasive species – the coqui – is a real pest. These tiny Puerto Rican frogs, most no bigger than a quarter, arrived on the island in 1990 and, finding no natural predators, proliferated wildly, mostly around Hilo and Puna. At Lava Tree State Monument densities are the highest in the state (up to 20,000 an acre) and twice that of Puerto Rico.

Within 2ft the coqui's sweet call can register between 90 and 100 decibels, and at a distance a chorus maintains 70 decibels – equivalent to a vacuum cleaner. To hear what you're in for, visit www.hear.org/AlienSpeciesInHawaii/species/frogs.

Locals tune them out like so much white noise. But they can't be ignored. With voracious appetites, they are eating all the bugs, endangering unique insect species and competing with birds for food. They're also getting bigger, and have started eating honey bees and geckos. They have affected the price of real estate, and they've hopped as far as O'ahu and Maui as well.

Eradication efforts are expensive, and so far incomplete and temporary. Places sprayed with citric acid solution have found the coquis returning in a few days. Currently, the federal EPA is considering whether to allow the Big Island to haul out the big gun: a 6% hydrated lime solution that is, apparently, 100% effective.

DETOUR: PUNA BACKROADS

The old lighthouse that Pele spared isn't much – just a tall piece of white-painted metal scaffolding. But it's still rewarding to head straight across 'Four Corners' from Hwy 132 and brave the rutted, 1.5-mile dirt road to the end of **Cape Kumukahi**. This is the easternmost point in the state, and the air that blows across it is the freshest in the world (so scientists say). Even better, the lava-covered cliffs make a gorgeous perch to contemplate this meeting of sky, sea and lava. From the parking area, walk the 4WD roads that crisscross the point.

Turn left, or north, at 'Four Corners,' and time will seem to slow to a stop as you enter a teeming, ancient, vine-draped forest pulsing with mana. The dirt road leads to **Wa'a Wa'a** and is passable for standard cars, but it's cratered, narrow and twisted. Mind the numerous 'Kapu' signs and go slow. After about 5 miles you reach a boulder **beach** shaded by ironwood trees; park here and scramble along the shore to find a spot for a quiet picnic lunch. Just past this, the paved road begins and you enter the Hawaiian Shores development (but you didn't want the easy way, right?).

Isaac Kepo'okalani Hale Beach Park

Renovations in 2008 have completely changed **Isaac Hale** (pronounced *ha*-lay). The rocky beach along Pohoiki Bay is of course the same, with waves usually too rough for swimming but great for bodyboarding and surfing. The boat ramp area is still a popular fishing spot, and beyond that, a well-worn path still leads (past a private house) to a small natural hot pond. And kids and families still create a frenzy of activity on weekends. But almost everything else is new: the parking lots, the walkways, the picnic tables, the outdoor showers and – most of all – the park across the road from the beach.

Here, the camping area is now a pristine lawn, trim as a putting green, with 22 sites, picnic tables, BBQs, and new bathrooms with flush toilets and drinking water. A security guard checks permits and ensures that the park's once semipermanent squatters do not return. What used to be a sketchy place campers had to avoid is now one of Puna's best camping spots (for permit information, see p205).

MacKenzie State Recreation Area

Puna does not lack for moody, mana-imbued settings, and yet another is this grove of ironwood trees edging sheer, 40ft cliffs above a restless ocean. During the day, this quiet, secluded park makes an unforgettable picnic spot. However, while camping is allowed (for permits, see p205), staying overnight is not recommended. Facilities are derelict (the pit toilets disgusting), and rare but serious crimes here underscore the unsettling isolation.

Kehena Beach & Around

If any place captures the friendly uninhibited intensity of Puna, it's this beautiful **black-sand beach** at the base of rocky cliffs and shaded by coconut and ironwood trees. All types and persuasions mix easily – hippies, Hawaiians, gays, families, teens, seniors, tourists. Many come to doff their clothes, but truly, no one cares if you don't. As the drum circle plays, old guys dance with their eyes closed while parents chase their kids in the surf – every generation nude – while others meditate, drink, swim, hang out. For a quieter experience, come early to greet the rising sun.

The surf is powerful, even when 'calm,' so swim with caution. Deaths occur here every year, and you shouldn't venture beyond the rocky point at the southern end. Kehena is immediately south of the 19-mile marker. From the small parking lot, a short, steep path leads down to the beach. Don't leave any valuables in your car.

Almost directly across from Kehena Beach is the laid-back retreat **Ramashala** (☎ 965-0068; www.ramashala.com; 12-7208 Hwy 137; r $65-225; ⊛). Among the red-shingled Balinese buildings, the seven rooms vary wildly: from a teeny-tiny hut in the middle of the lawn to spacious roosts with full kitchens. A couple of rooms share baths. Hardwood floors, furnishings and gorgeous grounds exude a spare, meditative elegence. There's a communal hot tub, and two studio spaces host weekly yoga classes and other events 'in a healing capacity.'

For the full-on retreat experience, head north up Hwy 137 (between the 17- and 18-mile markers) to **Kalani Oceanside Retreat** (☎ 965-7828, 800-800-6886; www.kalani.com; tents s/d $40/55, r &

cottage d $115-175, treehouse d $265; 🖳). Kalani occupies a sprawling compound that hums with activity and energy. It's a fun, communal place to stay even if you don't participate in the daily programs, which include yoga, meditation, dance, alternative healing and much more. Alternately, nonguests are free to use the facilities and enjoy the grounds (8am to 8pm). Kalani bills itself as a gay-friendly retreat, and the vibe is open and welcoming to all; the pool and sauna are clothing-optional after 3pm. An outdoor dining room (also open to nonguests) serves healthy buffet-style meals, while the rooms are all simple and breezy, with bright tropical spreads and plywood floors covered in *lauhala* mats. The camping area is a great place to park your tent. Ask about packages.

Kalapana (Former Village)

As with Kapoho in 1960, so it was for Kalapana 30 years later: in 1990 a redirection of the current ongoing eruption buried most of this village, destroying 100 homes and obliterating what was once Hawai'i's most famous black-sand beach, **Kaimu Beach**.

Today Hwy 137 ends abruptly at the eastern edge of what used to be Kalapana. A few houses here were spared and sit surrounded by devastation. The dead-end now contains two things: a modest complex catering to tourists and an outpost of the Hawaiian sovereignty movement. You can buy current lava photos and gifts, an ice shave or smoothie, and get a quite good burger or plate lunch at **Kalapana Village Cafe** (☎ 965-0121; mains $7.50-13; ☼ 8am-9pm). In the afternoon, sidle up to the outdoor **kava bar** (☼ 3-10pm), where you can try this ancient concoction and rub elbows with locals. One conversation starter is the adjacent billboard display promoting the establishment of the 'lawful Hawaiian government.' The display provides a full account of Hawaiian history, past and present, from a native perspective.

Finally, a short walk across the lava leads to a new **black-sand beach**, where hundreds of baby coconut palms surround a comma of sand. The water is too rough to swim, but it's a reflective spot, particular with the fat steam plume of a new Kalapana lava flow rising skyward a mile or so away (see the boxed text Hot Lava, p309).

HIGHWAY 130

Red Rd intersects Hwy 130 (Old Kalapana Rd), which leads north to Pahoa. At the 20-mile marker the 1929 **Star of the Sea Church** (☼ 9am-4pm) is noted for the naive-style paintings that cover the walls and the trompe l'oeil mural behind the altar, whose illusion of depth is remarkably effective. Inside, displays recount the history of the church and of the area's missionaries.

Sadly, bulldozers have recently leveled a steaming spatter cone that provided Puna with a locally famous natural (and au naturel) steam bath along Hwy 130. It was at the 15-mile marker, and marked by a blue 'Scenic Point' highway sign, but development has ended its days.

Hwy 130 ends at a gate protecting the destroyed Kalapana village, which is still private property off-limits to visitors. However, at the time of research, fresh lava was again flowing through the devastated Royal Gardens subdivision and entering the sea. The county had set up a public **lava viewing site** (☎ county updates 961-8093; www.lavainfo.us), which will remain as long as the flow does. Currently, the gate is open from 2pm to 10pm (the last car is allowed in at 8pm), and the large, staffed parking lot has portable toilets and vendors. The hike to the viewing area is less than a mile over *pahoehoe* lava. For more on lava viewing, see p309.

HAWAI'I VOLCANOES NATIONAL PARK

Of all of Hawaii's marvels, none equals the elemental grandeur and raw power of the two active volcanoes contained within Hawai'i Volcanoes National Park (HAVO). The entire island chain is the result of the volcanic processes on display here, which is nothing less than the ongoing birth of Hawaii.

The elder sibling is Mauna Loa, whose recumbent bulk slopes as gently as Buddha's belly, as if the earth's largest volcano (which constitutes over half of the Big Island's land mass) were nothing more than an overgrown hill. But, at 13,677ft, its navel is a frigid alpine desert that's snow-covered in winter.

The younger sibling is Kilauea – the earth's youngest and most active volcano. Within Kilauea Caldera, Halema'uma'u Crater is considered Pele's home, and in 2008, a new Halema'uma'u eruption signaled her return after 26 years away – though she wasn't very

HAWAI'I VOLCANOES NATIONAL PARK

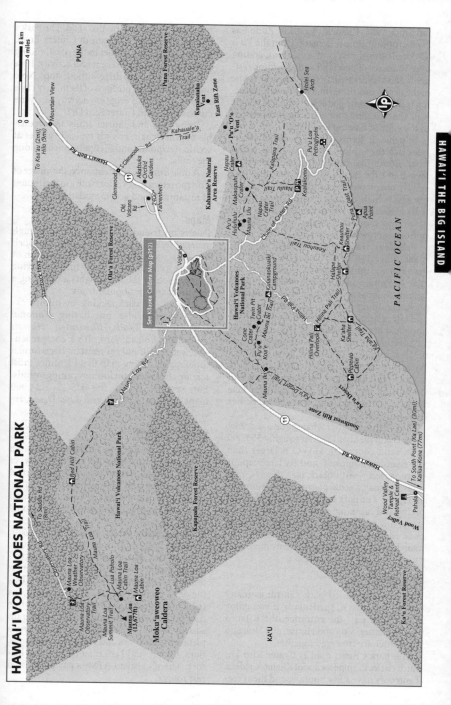

far. Since 1983, Kilauea's East Rift Zone has been erupting almost nonstop from the Pu'u 'O'o vent (northeast of the caldera), adding over 500 acres of new land and providing residents and visitors with a front-row seat at one of the best shows on earth. How accommodating is this fearsome goddess – who lets people walk the steaming roof of her house and even to the edge of flowing lava itself?

In geologic terms, Hawai'i's shield volcanoes lack the explosive gases of other volcanoes. Bomb-like explosions and geysers of lava aren't the norm. Most of the time lava simply oozes and creeps along till it reaches the sea, which creates arcs of steamy fireworks. Naturally, whenever Pele does send up dramatic curtains of fire, people stream in from everywhere to watch.

Pele does exact a price for this entertainment. Since 1983, this side of the island has been remade. In 1988 lava blocked the coastal road to Puna, and in 1990 it covered the village of Kalapana. Flows then crept further west, engulfing Kamoamoa Beach in 1994, and later claiming an additional mile of road and most of sacred Wahaula Heiau. In 2008, in addition to the Halema'uma'u eruption, a 'Thanksgiving Breakout' vent sent lava back through Kalapana (p306), and there is truly no telling how (or even if) lava will be flowing by the time you read this. Pele may be accommodating, but she keeps her own counsel.

However, no matter what the lava is doing, there is still plenty to see. At roughly 333,000 acres (and counting), HAVO is larger than the island of Moloka'i, and its landscape is more varied – with black-lava deserts, rain forests, grassy coastal plains, snowy summits and more. The park is Hawai'i's best place for hiking and camping, with about 140 miles of trails, but you don't *have* to break a sweat: good roads circle the caldera and take in the main highlights of what is certainly the USA's most dynamic national park.

ORIENTATION

This vast and varied park can fill as many days as you give it, particularly if you enjoy hiking. Just past the entrance, the Kilauea Visitor Center, Volcano House, and Volcano Art Center are clustered together.

The park's main road is Crater Rim Dr, which circles the moonscape of Kilauea Caldera. If you only have a few hours, spend them seeing the drive-up sites on this road. The park's other scenic drive is Chain of Craters Road, which leads south 20 miles to the coast, ending at the site of the most recent lava activity. It's a two-hour round-trip drive without stops. Note that these roads, or portions of them, may close at any time due to eruption activity (as is the current case with Crater Rim Dr).

Some sites and shorter trails are accessible by wheelchair; crowds typically gather at scenic viewpoints and dissipate quickly along the trails.

A mile from the park entrance, the village of Volcano serves park visitors with a nice selection of restaurants and accommodations.

Maps

Pele is no friend to cartographers; though generally reliable, park maps have a short shelf life. That said, the free color map given at the park's entrance is usually fine for driving around, seeing the main sights and hiking a few short and/or popular trails.

If you'll be backpacking or hiking extensively, consider purchasing *National Geographic's Trails Illustrated Hawaii Volcanoes National Park*. It's a comprehensive, waterproof and rip-resistant large-format topographic hiking map that identifies most terrain features, including campgrounds. For specific hikes, the USGS 1:24,000 maps *Kilauea*, *Volcano* and *Ka'u Desert* are also helpful.

INFORMATION

The **park** (☎ 985-6000; www.nps.gov/havo; 7-day pass per car $10, per person on foot, bicycle or motorcycle $5) never closes. The toll station also sells two annual passes: a three-park Hawaii pass ($25, including HAVO, Pu'uhonua o Honaunau, and Haleakalā on Maui) and one for all national parks ($80).

Kilauea Visitor Center (Map p312; ☎ 985-6017; ⌚ 7:45am-5pm) should be your first stop. Rangers can advise you on volcanic activity, air quality, trail conditions and the best things to see based on your time. A board lists the day's guided hikes and ranger programs (which are posted by 8:45am). Pick up free trail pamphlets and junior-ranger program activity sheets. The excellent bookstore has a plethora of volumes and videos on volcanoes, flora, hiking, and Hawaiian culture and history. There's also an ATM, a pay phone and rest rooms.

The park's **hotline** (☎ 985-6000; ☽ 24hr) provides daily recorded updates on park weather, road closures and lava-viewing conditions. The USGS also has eruption updates on its website (http://hvo.wr.usgs.gov). Note that the nearest gas station is in Volcano village.

At 4000ft above sea level, the Kilauea Caldera area is generally 10°F to 15°F cooler than Hilo or Kona, but weather is unpredictable and microclimates can vary dramatically within the park. Plan and prepare for hot sun, dry wind, fog, chilly rain and soaking downpours, all in a day. At a minimum, bring long pants, a jacket or sweater and a rain slicker.

The free Hele-On bus (p300) leaves once a day from Hilo (at 2:40pm) and arrives at the park visitor center an hour later; take the 23 Ka'u.

DANGERS & ANNOYANCES

Active volcanoes create a few unusual hazards. Though extremely rare and highly unlikely,

deaths have occurred on park visits (see boxed text, below). Statistics are of course in your favor (fatalities are *rare*), but it keeps you on your toes. Interestingly, molten lava is itself not the most threatening personal danger. Instead, deaths and injuries tend to occur when people venture too close to the active flow – and wind up on unstable 'benches' of new land that collapse, or get caught in steam explosions when lava enters the ocean.

As for less mortal dangers, remember that hardened lava is uneven and brittle; rocks can be glass-sharp. Thin crusts can give way over unseen hollows and lava tubes; the edges of craters and rifts crumble easily. Deep earth cracks may be hidden by plants. When hiking, abrasions, deep cuts and broken limbs are all possible. So, even more than most places, stay on marked trails and take park warning signs seriously. Blazing paths into unknown terrain can damage fragile areas, lead to injuries, and leave tracks that encourage others to follow.

HAWAI'I THE BIG ISLAND

HOT LAVA

If you're lucky, you'll get to see some good ol' red-hot molten lava while you're here. Even for island residents, it never gets old, and it changes all the time. Some tell of reading at home by the light of Kilauea's lava fountains in 1959, or of seeing homes burn, or of roasting chicken in a molten lava 'oven' (outside park boundaries, of course). Even at a distance, witnessing such an elemental act of creation inspires profound awe – seeing Pele's livid face in the roiling plume as lava greets the sea in violent sputtering showers. Watchers sometimes stand in silent reverence for hours, unable to tear themselves away from this once-in-a-lifetime experience.

Where the lava will be and the effort required to reach it are impossible to predict. When lava flows within national park boundaries, as it has almost continuously since 1983, the National Park Service facilitates **lava viewing** (☎ flow updates 967-8862; http://hvo.wr.usgs.gov). As of early 2009, it was possible to view the Halema'uma'u Crater eruption from the Jagger Museum, though no molten lava had yet emerged on the crater floor. Often it's possible to hike to flowing lava from the end of Chain of Craters Road (for facilities here, see p314). Occasionally, lava flows right at road's end, but more often reaching it involves a hike of one to several miles over a wracked lava landscape.

When lava flows outside park boundaries, viewing sites are managed by the county; as of early 2009, the county was maintaining a viewing area at Kalapana (see p306).

Whatever the hike, the best strategy is to come during daylight and stay through sunset, when the surreal orange glow illuminates the night. Trails are marked with temporary reflectors, and safe viewing areas are roped off. It is paramount that you respect these boundaries. Like moths to a flame, people want to get as close to the flow as possible, but when molten 2100°F rock meets the ocean, the explosions send showers of scalding water and lava chunks raining down. In 2000, two people were found scalded to death. New ledges or benches of lava can collapse without warning. In 1993 a bench collapse killed one person and seriously injured a dozen others; a 2007 bench collapse sent 58 acres into the sea (luckily injuring no one). In the excitement of the moment, don't forget to respect Pele's power.

Finally, come prepared. It may rain, so bring rain gear. Wear sturdy shoes, pants, and a hat, and bring water and one flashlight per person. You might also want a walking stick, gloves, first aid kit, and some food. Oh, and your camera (fully loaded).

HAWAI'I THE BIG ISLAND

Another major, constant concern is air quality. Halema'uma'u Crater and Pu'u 'O'o vent belch thousands of tons of sulfur dioxide daily. Where lava meets the sea, it also creates a 'steam plume,' which is a toxic cocktail of sulfuric and hydrochloric acid mixed with airborne silica (or glass particles). All this combines to create 'vog' (for more on vog, see p217), which depending on the winds can settle over the park. Before hiking, check the visitor center's air-quality monitor. In addition, steam vents throughout the park spew high concentrations of sulfuric fumes (which smell like rotten egg); Halema'uma'u Overlook (Map p312) and Sulphur Banks (Map p312) are prime spots. Given all this, people with respiratory and heart conditions, pregnant women, infants and young children should take special care when visiting.

Finally, vast areas of the park qualify as desert. Dehydration is common. Carrying two quarts of water per person is the standard advice, but bring more and keep a gallon in the trunk: you'll drink it.

If you plan to get out of your car, come prepared: bring hiking shoes or sneakers, long pants, a hat, sunscreen, water (and snacks), a flashlight with extra batteries and a first aid kit.

SIGHTS
Crater Rim Drive

This incredible 11-mile loop road skirts the rim of Kilauea Caldera. It passes the visitor center, a museum, a lava tube, steam vents, rifts, hiking trails and views of the smoking crater that'll knock your socks off. Don't miss it. Also, since it's relatively level, it's the park's best road for cyclists. This description starts at the visitor center and goes counterclockwise.

Note that as of early 2009, the portion of the road closest to Halema'uma'u Crater, including the Halema'uma'u Overlook, was closed due to eruption activity.

KILAUEA VISITOR CENTER

The tidy visitors center (Map p312) is an excellent place to start. A small **theater** shows free short films on Kilauea and the current eruption, with spectacular footage, on continuous rotation. Attractive, refurbished exhibits, listening stations and life-size dioramas introduce the area's geology, flora, fauna and conservation issues. Out front,

rangers give regular talks around the scale model of Hawaii.

VOLCANO ART CENTER

Next door to the visitors center, inside the 1877 Volcano House lodge, this **gallery shop** (Map p312; ☎ 967-7565, 866-967-7565; www.volcanoart center.org; ⏰ 9am-5pm) sells high-quality island pottery, paintings, woodwork, sculpture, jewelry, Hawaiian quilts and more. Browsing the stunning collection – which ranges from $8000 koa rocking chairs to $20 prints – is almost as satisfying as buying. The resident nonprofit arts organization hosts craft and cultural workshops, music concerts, plays and dance recitals, all listed in its free bimonthly *Volcano Gazette*.

SULPHUR BANKS

Nearby, wooden boardwalks weave through steaming Sulphur Banks, where numerous **holes and rocky vents** (Map p312) have been stained yellow, orange and neon green by the hundreds of tons of sulfuric gases released here daily. The smoldering, foul-smelling area looks like the aftermath of a forest fire. It's possible to walk here from the art center, cross the road, visit Steaming Bluff (below) and loop back on a portion of Crater Rim Trail.

STEAM VENTS & STEAMING BLUFF

At the next pull-off, these nonsulfurous steam vents (Map p312) make a good drive-up photo op; they are the result of rainwater that percolates down and is heated into steam by hot rocks underground. Much more evocative is the short walk to the crater rim at Steaming Bluff (Map p312), where the magnificent crater view feels infernolike as steam from the cliffs below pours over you. Cool early mornings or cloudy afternoons showcase the steam best.

JAGGAR MUSEUM

The exhibits at this small **museum** (Map p312; ☎ 985-6049; ⏰ 8:30am-8pm) are a nice complement to the visitor center: they introduce the museum's founder, the famous volcanologist Dr Thomas A Jaggar; overview the Hawaiian pantheon; and provide a deeper understanding of volcanic geology. Tracking Pele's heartbeat, a bank of real-time seismographs monitor the park's daily quota of earthquakes, which number from the tens to the hundreds.

When the Halema'uma'u Crater began erupting in 2008, the real show moved outside to the viewpoint. Museum hours were extended, and ranger talks expanded. It's a thrilling vantage that also constitutes – until the eruption stops – the end of the road from this direction.

Just before you reach the museum, the **Kilauea Overlook** (Map p312) provides another pause-worthy panorama, and a few miles south is the **Southwest Rift** (Map p312). This rocky fissure is more massive and long than it looks; it slices from the caldera summit all the way to the coast.

HALEMA'UMA'U OVERLOOK

On March 18, 2008, Halema'uma'u Crater shattered a quarter-century of silence with a huge steam-driven explosion that scattered rocks and Pele's hair (strands of volcanic glass) over 75 acres. A series of explosions followed, widening a 300ft vent in the crater floor, which as of early 2009 continued to spew a muscular column of smoke but no molten lava.

By November 2008, this officially became the longest continuous eruption since 1924. That's the year when Halema'uma'u ended over a century as a fiery lake of lava that alternately overflowed its rim and receded. No one knows if Pele is on the verge of filling her cup once more.

In 1823, missionary William Ellis first described the boiling goblet of Halema'uma'u, and this prodigious sight attracted travelers from all over the world. Looking in, some saw the fires of hell, others primeval creation, but none left unmoved. Mark Twain wrote that he witnessed:

Circles and serpents and streaks of lightning all twined and wreathed and tied together…I have seen Vesuvius since, but it was a mere toy, a child's volcano, a soup kettle, compared to this.

Then, in 1924, the crater floor subsided rapidly, touching off a series of explosive eruptions. Boulders and mud rained down for days. When it was over, the crater had doubled in size – to about 300ft deep and 3000ft wide. Lava activity ceased and the crust cooled.

Since then, Halema'uma'u has erupted 18 times; it's the most active area on the volcano's summit. During the last eruption, on April 30, 1982, geologists only realized something was brewing that morning as their seismographs went haywire. The park service quickly cleared hikers from the crater floor, and before noon a half-mile fissure broke open and spewed 1.3 million cubic yards of lava.

All of the Big Island is Pele's territory, but Halema'uma'u is her home. Ceremonial hula is performed in her honor on the crater rim, and throughout the year people leave offerings of flowers, leaf-wrapped rocks and gin to appease the goddess. However, as long as Pele's in the house, the overlook will remain closed. When it's open, this is one end of the Halema'uma'u Trail (Map p312).

DEVASTATION TRAIL

As of early 2009, this trail was open and accessible by driving driving south from the visitors center; the road west of the intersection with Chain of Craters Road was closed. At this intersection is one end of the half-mile Devastation Trail (Map p312); parking is also available at the trail's other end, the Pu'u Pua'i Overlook further east.

The wheelchair-accessible Devastation Trail is paved and passes through the fallout area of the 1959 eruption of Kilauea Iki Crater, which decimated this portion of the rain forest. This is a great trail to do on a guided ranger walk, since at first glance it's not half as dramatic as its name. The overlook provides a fantastic vantage into the crater, and it's a quick walk to see **Pu'u Pua'i**, which formed during the eruption.

THURSTON LAVA TUBE

East of the intersection with Chain of Craters Road you enter the rain forest of native tree ferns and ohia that covers Kilauea's windward slope.

Often crowded to the extreme, this lava tube (Map p312) is the end point of an enjoyable short walk through lovely, bird-filled ohia forest (it's a good place to spot the red-bodied 'apapane, a native honeycreeper). The lava tube itself is enormous – practically big enough for your car, much less yourself – and a short initial section is lighted.

Lava tubes are formed when the outer crust of a river of lava starts to harden but the liquid lava beneath the surface continues to flow through. After the flow has drained out, the hard shell remains. Eastern Hawai'i is riddled with lava tubes, and this is a grand example.

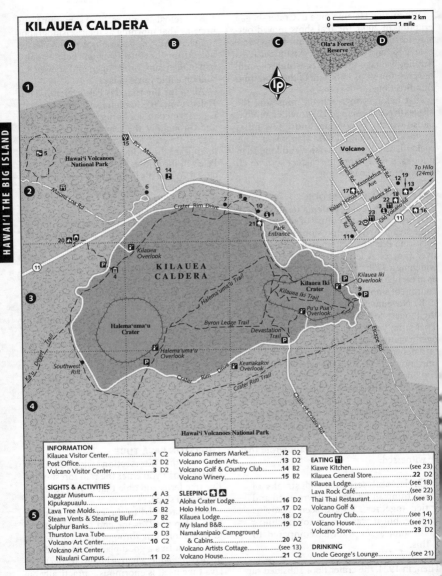

KILAUEA CALDERA

The tube extends for quite a way beyond the lighted area; with a flashlight it's easy to keep going – and highly recommended.

KILAUEA IKI CRATER

When Kilauea Iki (Little Kilauea) burst open in a fiery inferno in November 1959, the whole crater floor turned into a bubbling lake of molten lava. Its fountains reached record heights of 1900ft, lighting the evening sky with a bright orange glow for miles around. At its peak, it gushed out 2 million tons of lava an hour.

The overlook provides an awesome view of the mile-wide crater (Map p312), and the hike (p315) across its hardened surface i the park's most popular. One good strategy for visiting this often crowded, but scenic, portion of Crater Rim Drive is to park at the Kilauea Iki Overlook and walk the Crater Rim Trail to Thurston Lava Tube and back; it's about a mile all told and easy as pie.

Chain of Craters Road

This road (Map p307) gets shorter all the time (most recently in 2003). It currently winds about 19 miles down the southern slopes of Kilauea Volcano, ending abruptly at the latest East Rift Zone lava flow on the Puna Coast. It's paved but curvaceous; allow 45 minutes one way without stops.

For visual drama, the road is every bit the equal of Crater Rim Dr. As you descend toward the sea, panoramic coastal vistas open before you, revealing slopes covered in frozen fingers of blackened lava. Then, at the coast, you get to stare at those same flows from below, looking up to where they crested the cliffs and plunged across the land to meet the sea. Early morning and late afternoon are the best times to photograph this unique landscape, when sunlight slants off the lava.

The road takes its name from a series of small, drive-up craters that lie along the first few miles. In addition, the road provides access to several trails, a campground, petroglyphs and often to the active flow itself.

At one time, Chain of Craters Road connected to Hwys 130 and 137 in Puna. Lava flows closed the road in 1969, but, slightly rerouted, it reopened in 1979. Then Kilauea cut the link again in 1988, burying a 10-mile stretch of the road.

HILINA PALI ROAD

The first major intersection is this 9-mile, one-lane road (see Map p307). Four miles along this road is the small Kulanaokuaiki Campground (p318). The road itself is not very scenic, and it is so winding that the drive can take over 40 minutes one way. However, it ends at the **Hilina Pali Overlook**, a lookout of exceptional beauty. The grassy coastal plain below will beckon hikers to descend the steep Hilina Pali Trail here, but don't – unless you're prepared for a grueling all-day adventure or an overnight backpack. If not, be content to follow the trail for 100yd and sigh rapturously.

MAUNA ULU

In 1969, eruptions from Kilauea's east rift began building a new **lava shield** (Map p307), which eventually rose 400ft above its surroundings. It was named Mauna Ulu (Growing Mountain). By the time the flow stopped in 1974, it had covered 10,000 acres of parkland and added 200 acres of new land to the coast.

It also buried a 12-mile section of Chain of Craters Road in lava up to 300ft deep. A half-mile portion of the old road survives, and you can follow it to the lava flow by taking the turnoff on the left, 3.5 miles down Chain of Craters Road. Just beyond this is Mauna Ulu itself.

The easy **Pu'u Huluhulu Overlook Trail**, a 2.5-mile round-trip hike, begins at the parking area (which is also the trailhead for Napau Crater Trail, p316). The overlook trail ends at the top of a 150ft cinder cone, **Pu'u Huluhulu**, which is like a crow's nest on a clear day: the vista nets Mauna Loa, Mauna Kea, Pu'u 'O'o vent, Kilauea, the East Rift Zone and the ocean beyond. Just before you is the steamy teacup of Mauna Ulu crater. Nothing stops hikers from checking this out, but the park rangers would prefer if you didn't. The rim is fragile, for one, but also, those who watched it being born feel almost parentally protective.

KEALAKOMO

About halfway along the road is this coastal lookout (Map p307) – once nicknamed 'pizza hut' for its roof, now gone – with picnic tables and commanding views. The trailhead for the Naulu Trail is across the road. After Kealakomo, the road descends long, sweeping switchbacks, some deeply cut through lava flows.

PU'U LOA PETROGLYPHS

The gentle Pu'u Loa Trail leads less than a mile to the largest concentration of ancient petroglyphs in the state. At Pu'u Loa (Map p307), early Hawaiians chiseled more than 23,000 drawings into *pahoehoe* lava. Look around and it's easy to see why this spot might have been considered sacred. There are abstract designs, animal and human figures, as well as thousands of dimpled depressions (or cupules) that were receptacles for umbilical cords. Placing a baby's umbilical stump inside a cupule and covering it with stones was meant to bestow health and longevity on the child.

The parking area and trailhead are signed between the 16- and 17-mile markers. At the site, stay on the boardwalk at all times – not all the petroglyphs are obvious, and you are likely to trample (and damage) some if you walk over the rocks.

HOLEI SEA ARCH

Near the end of the road, across from the ranger station, is this sea arch (Map p307). This rugged section of the coast has sharply eroded lava cliffs, called Holei Pali, which are constantly being pounded by the crashing surf. The high rock arch, carved out of one of the cliffs, is impressive, although the wave action of Namakaokahai, goddess of the sea and sister to Pele, has numbered its days.

THE END OF THE ROAD

Chain of Craters Road ends abruptly wherever hardened lava covers the road. This is often the starting point for hikes to see the active flow (see p309). At road's end you'll find a ranger station (till 9pm daily), an information board with a four-minute safety video, portable toilets and a **snack shack** (☺ in theory noon-6pm) selling bottled water, candy and batteries. But if there's no active flow, there are no rangers or staff.

However, when there's no molten lava, this becomes one of the quietest, most dramatic day hikes in the park. There's no trail per se, but wander into the Mordor-like terrain until the surging, frozen, oily veins surround you, looking as if they cooled only yesterday.

Mauna Loa Road

If you really want to escape the crowds, explore the 11.5-mile Mauna Loa Rd, which begins off Hwy 11 outside the park entrance. The first turnoff leads to some neglected **lava tree molds** (Map p312), deep tubelike apertures formed when a lava flow engulfed the rain forest. Then, after a mile, there is a picnic area (with toilets) and just beyond this is **Kipukapuaulu** (Map p312), informally known as 'Bird Park.' This unique 100-acre sanctuary protects an island of ancient forest containing rare endemic plants, insects and birds. About 400 years ago a major Mauna Loa lava flow buried the land here, but Pele split the flow and saved this small island of vegetation; in Hawaiian these are known as a *kipuka*.

An easy 1-mile loop trail through the forest makes a very meditative walk, particularly in the morning surrounded by birdsong. You'll see lots of koa trees and pass a lava tube where a unique species of big-eyed spider was discovered in 1973.

About 1.5 miles past Bird Park, Mauna Loa Rd passes another *kipuka* (Kipuka Ki), and 2 miles later the road narrows to one lane. Go slow; it's winding, with potholes and lots of blind curves. Along the way are several places to pull over to admire the views and trails to explore – it's a wonderful diversion. By the end of the road, you've ascended to 6662ft; this is the start of the extremely difficult Mauna Loa Trail (p317) to the summit. Wander down the trail a few dozen yards for expansive southern vistas that include the smoking Kilauea Caldera far below.

ACTIVITIES

Hiking is the park's main activity, and there are trails to suit all abilities. Ranger-led walks occur daily and typically don't last longer than an hour; the visitor center (p308) posts a list (the Pua Po'o lava tube is highly recommended, p316). Or join a guided hike with outdoor-adventure companies **Hawaii Forest & Trail** (☎ 331-8505, 800-464-1993; www.hawaii-forest.com) or **Hawaiian Walkways** (☎ 775-0372, 800-457-7759; www.hawaiianwalkways.com); see p209. Note that trails may be closed due to ongoing eruptions, as were several, as noted, at the time of research.

Cyclists can enjoy circumnavigating Kilauea Caldera along Crater Rim Dr, and mountain bikes are allowed on a few firebreak roads, such as Escape Rd past Thurston Lava Tube. For guided cycles in the park and to the lava, contact **Volcano Bike Tours** (☎ 934-9199, 888-934-9199; www.bikevolcano.com; per person $130). Helicopter tours are also popular (see p214).

Hiking

If variety is the spice of life, park trails are a feast. You can hike to secluded beaches or the snowcapped 13,677ft summit of Mauna Loa; through lush native rain forests or barren lava wastelands; across the hardened top of the world's most active volcano; or sometimes, to the glowing flow itself.

There are excellent trails of every length and level of difficulty. Plus, many trails intersect, allowing the flexibility to design your own routes. Most of the park is accessible to day hikers, while most backcountry destinations require only a single overnight. However, if you wish, you can wander backcountry trails for days.

If you're interested in overnight backpacking, note that backcountry camping is limited and entirely first come, first served; backcountry trails contain hiking shelters, simple cabins or primitive campgrounds. All have pit toilets. Bring a stove, as open fires are prohibited. Almost no freshwater is available anywhere; some campgrounds have catchment water (always treat before drinking), and the visitor center posts a daily log of water levels. Overnight hikers must get a free permit (and register) at the visitor center no sooner than the day before their hike; each site has a three-day limit.

Following are some of the most popular and/or recommended day hikes, along with a few backcountry possibilities and variations. Some of the park's shortest hikes are mentioned in the descriptions of the park's main roads (see p310).

KILAUEA IKI TRAIL

If you have time for only one hike, choose this one. It's the park's most popular trail (Map p312) for good reason – it captures all the summit's drama and beauty in one manageable, moderate, 4-mile, two-hour package. The trail's glossy brochure ($2) is a good investment.

The loop trail has multiple start points and trail junctions (making the hike easy to expand). Park at Kilauea Iki Overlook (avoiding the Thurston Lava Tube madness) and proceed counterclockwise along the crater rim. Passing through an ohia forest, you can admire the mile-long lava bathtub below before descending into it.

After almost a mile you descend onto Waldron Ledge; multiple trail junctions allow for quick explorations of the main caldera rim (highly recommended), or extend your loop by connecting with the Halema'uma'u and Byron Ledge Trails for an all-day adventure. Either way, once you reach the west end of the crater, descend 400ft to the crater floor.

Across the *pahoehoe* crust the trail is easy to follow, and *ahu* aid navigation. It's possible to enter the vent beneath the Pu'u Pua'i cinder cone, where ohia trees now bloom. As you continue over the surface, consider that molten magma is a mere 230ft below (less than a football field). Once you reach the crater's east end, ascend 400ft up switchbacks to the

rim, and explore Thurston Lava Tube on your return to the Kilauea Iki Overlook.

HALEMA'UMA'U TRAIL

Halema'uma'u Crater was closed to hikers at the time of research, though portions of this trail along the rim were open. When open, this trail is an extremely rewarding 7-mile loop (Map p312) that starts near Volcano House (p318). It quickly passes through ohia forest, and spends the bulk of its time traversing the ragged blankets of lava that cover Kilauea Caldera. The trail is completely exposed; depending on the weather, it'll be hot and dry or chillingly damp. Bring lots of water.

If you think lava is simply lava, this hike will change your mind. You pass numerous flows on the trail – some old (1885) and some new (1982) – and the diversity is astonishing, as is the overall effect of the otherworldly landscape. Nearly 3 miles from the start, the trail ends at the steaming (currently closed) Halema'uma'u Overlook (see p311). You return on the Byron Ledge Trail, which allows for easy peeks of, or a side trip into, Kilauea Iki Crater.

CRATER RIM TRAIL

This 11.5-mile trek (Map p312) circles the summit, running roughly parallel to Crater Rim Drive (p310), and, as with the road, large portions of this trail were closed at the time of research. If you do the whole thing, plan for five or six hours, but many people hike only portions. Overall, the trail is mostly level. On the north side, the trail is busiest as it skirts the view-licious crater rim, while on the south side, it runs outside the paved road (and away from caldera views) and you will likely see no one. Lots of side trips are possible, and you pass through a wide variety of terrains; one of the most beautiful sections is the forested southeast portion. Note that it's acceptable – for hikers doing one-way hikes, either here or elsewhere – to hitch a ride to/from a trailhead, but it's best to park at the end and hitch to the start, so you hike *to* your car.

MAUNA IKI TRAIL

For solitude in a mesmerizing lava landscape, take this trail (Map p307) into the Ka'u Desert, but start from the north, along what is sometimes labeled the Footprints Trail. From this approach, the trailhead access is easier, your initial commitment is low and variations allow

---

LIFE UNDERGROUND

Lava tubes riddle the Big Island like holes in Swiss cheese, and these remarkable caves are high-powered incubaters of new species – blind spiders, wingless crickets, possibly cancer-curing bacteria, and more we don't even know about. In 1992, a pristine 500-year-old lava tube, **Pua Po'o**, was discovered in the national park, and it is the destination of a fascinating ranger-led **lava tube hike** (admission free; ☽ 12:30pm Wed).

The easy, 4-mile round-trip passes through ohia forest and involves about an hour underground exploring the cave's bizarre ecosystem. Though you learn about how Native Hawaiians used lava tubes to collect water and bury royalty, this cave holds no cultural significance. There's some stooping involved, but no serious crawling, and of course, everyone douses their headlamps once to experience a darkness deeper than night.

To protect the tube, only 12 people are allowed once a week, and participants are asked to keep the location secret. To sign up, call the **Kilauea Visitor Center** (☎ 985-6017) the week before, on Wednesday, at exactly 7:45am; slots fill up in about 15 minutes. Children must be at least 10 years old.

---

great extensions of your route. This hike can be an easy 3.5-mile sampling, a moderate 7- to 8-mile afternoon or an 18-mile overnight backpack. However, due to Halema'uma'u's current eruption, only the initial portion of this trail was open at the time of research.

On Hwy 11 between the 37- and 38-mile markers, look for the 'Ka'u Desert Trailhead' parking area. Start early, as midday can be brutally hot and dry. Initially, the trail is very clear, level and partly paved, threading through sand-covered *pahoehoe* flows. In 20 minutes you reach a structure protecting ancient footprints preserved in hardened ash; more footprints exist in the surrounding rock. Apparently, in 1790 the army of Hawaiian chief Keoua was marching to battle Kamehameha when a rare explosive eruption buried his soldiers, killing many of them and changing the course of island history (p261).

Past the hut, the trail is marked by easy-to-follow cairns. As you gradually ascend, views expand, with gentle giant Mauna Loa behind and the immense Ka'u Desert in front. After 1.8 miles you crest the rise at **Mauna Iki** (and the trail junction) and stand likely alone in the middle of a vast lava field.

From here, backpackers will turn right, following the Ka'u Desert Trail over 7 miles to Pepeiao Cabin. Day hikers can turn left, following the Ka'u Desert Trail for 1232yd to the junction with the official Mauna Iki Trail, which runs another 6.3 miles to Hilina Pali Rd (the other starting point). Hiking about halfway along the Mauna Iki Trail, to Pu'u Koa'e, makes a good end point.

The lava terrain is noticeably more intense and wild as you continue, with vivid colorful rents, collapsed tubes and splatter cones; in cracks you can find piles of golden Pele's hair. The discoveries are almost endless.

NAPAU CRATER TRAIL
The Napau Crater Trail (Map p307) is perhaps the most varied and satisfying all-day hike in the park. It passes lava fields, immense craters and thick forest, and it currently ends with distant views of Pu'u 'O'o, the source of Kilauea's ongoing 1983 eruption. Backcountry camping is available if you want to do this overnight; the distance to the campground (the current end of the trail) is 7 miles (or 5 miles from the Kealakoma starting point), making it a 10- to 14-mile adventure (about six to eight hours round-trip). Note that this is the only day hike that requires a permit; all hikers should register at the visitor center before heading out.

Rather than taking the Napau Crater Trail from its trailhead (the same one as for Pu'u Huluhulu Overlook Trail, p313), you'll save about 4 miles and several hours round-trip (and lose nothing in scenery) if you begin on the Naulu Trail, which leaves from Kealakomo (p313) on Chain of Craters Road. This route is described here.

For the first hour, you hike mostly sinuous, leathery *pahoehoe* lava, following sometimes difficult-to-see cairns. Then you enter some trees and (surprise!) stumble across paved portions of the old Chain of Craters Road, which was buried in a 1972 eruption. Follow the pavement (complete with dashed white line) past the junction with the unmaintained **Kalapana Trail**.

After a quick sprint across some 'a'a (which is exactly what you'll say if you trip), you enter moody fern-and-ohia forest; in less than a mile is the Napau Crater Trail junction – turn right.

Keep an eye on your left for openings to view the mile-wide Makaopuhi Crater. About 30 minutes later, low lava rock walls indicate the site of an old 'pulu factory.' Pulu is the golden, silky 'hair' found at the base of hapu'u (tree fern) fiddlehead stems. Ancient Hawaiians used pulu to embalm their dead, and in the late 1800s pulu was exported as mattress and pillow stuffing, until it was discovered that it eventually turned to dust.

You may think you're near the airport – considering the helicopter traffic – but in fact you're 10 minutes from the primitive **campground** (with pit toilet). Definitely take the spur to the Napau Crater **overlook** (to see steaming Pu'u 'O'o). At the time of research, the rest of this trail was closed due to a Pu'u 'O'o vent collapse and shifts in the eruption.

When open, the trail continues through a surreal, wondrous terrain of hummocks, vents and tree molds to and through **Napau Crater** itself. On the other side, the trail continues another few miles across the shattered landscape to gaping **Pu'u 'O'o**. As the recent vent collapse makes clear, this is a dangerous and volatile area; respect all park signs and use common sense.

KAHAUALE'A TRAIL

This troubled 4-mile trail (Map p307), the shortest route to the Pu'u 'O'o vent, has been closed indefinitely by the county. Partly this is due to the vent collapse. However, it was also because the county wasn't maintaining the trail and several hikers got lost and injured. If the county reopens the trail, it's worth remembering that the reassuring trailhead sign doesn't reflect the true condition of this often muddy pig-hunter's trail riddled with confusing spurs. Further, the trailhead is notorious for car break-ins. From Hwy 11, turn south on S Glenwood Rd and drive 3 miles till it dead ends.

MAUNA LOA TRAIL

Reaching the summit of 13,677ft Mauna Loa is a sublime experience, one that most everyday hikers would rank as one of the best treks of their lives. However, if you're an everyday hiker, you don't want to get there by way of the 19-mile Mauna Loa Trail (Map p307) that leaves from the end of the park's Mauna Loa Rd. Everyday hikers should instead tackle the 6.5-mile Observatory Trail (p275), which is accessed from Saddle Rd and leaves from the Mauna Loa Weather Observatory.

If you fall within that smaller class of extremely fit, elite hikers – for whom the easy way is no way at all – this is your trail. It ascends about 7000ft and, while it is not technically challenging, due to the high elevation and frequent subarctic conditions it takes at least three and usually four days. Two simple cabins with foam pad-covered bunks, new water-free toilets and catchment water (which must be treated) are located on the route; the first cabin sleeps eight, the second 12, and they are available on a first-come, first-served basis. Get a free backcountry permit, advice and water-level updates at the Kilauea Visitor Center (p308) the day before your hike.

Typically, the first day is spent hiking 7.5 miles to Pu'u 'Ula'ula at 10,035ft, where **Red Hill Cabin** is located. The next day is spent hiking 9.5 miles to Moku'aweoweo Caldera, and another 2 miles to **Mauna Loa Cabin** at 13,250ft; from here you can admire the summit directly across the caldera. On the third day, you hike nearly 5 miles around the caldera to reach the summit and return for a second night at Mauna Loa Cabin. On the fourth day, you descend.

Now, the fun part: altitude sickness is common, even expected; going slowly aids acclimatization. Nighttime temperatures are below freezing. Storms may bring snow, blizzards, whiteouts, rain and fog, all of which can obscure the ahu that mark the trail, making it impossible to follow. And don't forget that Mauna Loa is still active and, according to its 20-year cycle of eruptions, it's overdue.

PUNA COAST TRAILS

Three main trails (Map p307) take hikers down to the Puna Coast: the **Hilina Pali**, **Keauhou** and **Puna Coast Trails**. These trails start from vastly different places, but they each eventually intersect (with each other and even more trails), and they lead to four separate backcountry campgrounds or shelters. Because of steep elevation changes and distance, these trails are most commonly done as overnight backpacks.

This is also because, once you see the grassy, wind-swept coast, you won't want to leave. Talk to rangers about routes and water-catchment levels at the shelters. With lovely swimming and snorkeling, the Halape shelter is the most popular (and books up), with Keauhou a great second choice.

For day hikers, the Hilina Pali Trail looks easiest on the map (it's only 3.5 miles to snorkeling at Ka'aha), but it's actually the hardest, with a brutal initial cliff descent; the trailhead is at the end of Hilina Pali Rd (p313). Far gentler on the knees is the 6.8-mile Keauhou Trail, which takes about four hours to the stunning coast; the trailhead is past 6-mile marker on Chain of Craters Road.

FESTIVALS & EVENTS

Regular park programs include **After Dark in the Park** (Kilauea Visitor Center Auditorium; admission free; ☾ 7pm Tue), a series of free talks by experts on cultural, historic and geological matters, held two or three times monthly.

The **Volcano Art Center** (☎ 967-8222; www.volcanoartcenter.org) hosts a full slate of events year round. The following annual events are free with park admission.

Na Mea Hawaii Hula Kahiko Series Four times throughout the year, free hula *kahiko* performances are held outdoors overlooking Kilauea Caldera.

Annual Spring Dance Concert Last weekend in March. An event hosted by the Volcano Art Center, presenting works by Big Island choreographers and dancers.

Kilauea Volcano Wilderness Runs Late July. This popular marathon ran its last race in the national park in 2008, and is looking for a new route; call the art center for updates.

Aloha Festivals Ka Ho'ola'a o Na Ali'i (http://alohafestivals.com) Don't miss this brilliant Native Hawaiian royal court procession on the Halema'uma'u Crater rim, with ceremonial chanting and hula, during the August/September Aloha Festival.

SLEEPING

Accommodation options within the national park are limited; nearby Volcano village (opposite) has more choices.

Camping

The park has two free, first-come, first-served drive-up campgrounds. Facilities are well kept; expect nights to be crisp and cool. The only time the sites get full are busy holiday weekends. The campgrounds are only rarely closed due to volcanic activity.

Kulanaokuaiki Campground (Map p307; Hilina Pali Rd) About 4 miles along Hilina Pali Rd, this secluded, quiet, eight-site campground has pit toilets and picnic tables, but no water.

Namakanipaio Campground & Cabins (Map p312; ☎ cabin bookings 967-7321; cabins d $55, extra person $10) Between the 32- and 33-mile markers off Hwy 11, 3 miles west of the visitor center, this campground's two pleasant grassy meadows fill with as many tents as it will hold. It lacks privacy, but nice facilities include rest rooms, water, fireplaces, picnic tables and a covered pavilion. Adjacent to the campground, but with access to a separate bathroom (with showers), are 10 windowless, plywood A-frame cabins with a double bed, two single bunk beds, grills, picnic tables and electric lights, but no power outlets or heating. Volcano House takes bookings and provides linens, but bring a sleeping bag – it gets cold! Campers can access the cabin showers for $3 per person per day.

Top End

Volcano House (Map p312; ☎ 967-7321; www.volcanohousehotel.com; 1 Crater Rim Dr; r $100-230) Perched on the rim of Kilauea Caldera, Volcano House has a venerable history, but its accommodations are so bland and boring it's almost a crime. True, it's clean and certainly convenient, but the only thing to recommend it is the view – which the deluxe rooms deliver with a bang from huge picture windows. Then again, after dark, you're left with faded furniture and naked walls. Avoid the cheapest Ohia Wing rooms; they're below ground and poorly ventilated.

EATING & DRINKING

As with the rooms, so with the food. The restaurant at **Volcano House** (Map p312; ☎ 967-7321; www.volcanohousehotel.com; 1 Crater Rim Dr; buffet breakfast & lunch $13-17, dinner mains $17-30; ☾ 7-10:30am, 11am-2pm, 5:30-9pm) serves a cafeteria-quality buffet for breakfast and lunch, and dinner plates match what you'd expect at your uncle's second wedding – but the dining-room view is a knockout. There's a snack bar during the day, and at night **Uncle George's Lounge** (☾ 4:30-9pm) has a full bar. The high point of Volcano House is the lobby with its famous fireplace. At the end of the day, grab some firewater at Uncle George's Lounge, come sit in a leather couch under a Tavernier painting, and warm yourself in front of 'Pele's fireplace,' which according to legend is never allowed to go out.

HAWAI'I THE BIG ISLAND

GETTING THERE & AROUND
The national park is 29 miles (about 40 minutes) from Hilo and 97 miles (2½ hours) from Kailua-Kona. From either direction, you'll drive on Hwy 11. Volcano village is a mile east of the park entrance.

AROUND HAWAI'I VOLCANOES NATIONAL PARK

VOLCANO
pop 2230
The village of Volcano is a mystical place of giant ferns, giant *sugi* (Japanese evergreen) and ohia trees full of puffy red blossoms. Many artists and park employees enjoy the seclusion here.

Information
The visitor center and a laundromat (open daily) are located next to Thai Thai Restaurant (p320).
Post office (Map p312; ☎ 967-7611; 19-4030 Old Volcano Rd; ☯ 7:30am-3:30pm Mon-Fri, 11am-noon Sat) Down the street from the post office
Volcano Visitor Center (Map p312; ☎ 985-7422; Old Volcano Rd; ☯ 7am-7pm) This teensy unstaffed hut has brochures aplenty and an ATM; call for help booking a room.

Sights & Activities
One of the warmest community events on the island is the **Volcano Farmers Market** (Map p312; Cooper Community Center, Wright Rd; ☯ 5:30-9am Sun). If you've been in Volcano more than a day, you won't feel like a stranger here. Everyone comes (and comes early) to socialize and buy local organic produce, hot food, and local crafts you won't see everywhere. A bright play structure teems with children (as does the awesome skate park, outside market hours). There's even a used bookstore.

The very attractive **Volcano Winery** (Map p312; ☎ 967-7772; www.volcanowinery.com; 35 Pi'i Mauna Dr; ☯ 10am-5:30pm) grows only one variety of grape – symphony – and only one of its six vintages uses it exclusively. Others mix in jaboticaba berries and guava for sweet, unusual wine variations, and a rich honey wine is almost like mead. Free tastings let you try them all.

Artist Ira Ono and his voluptuous masks seem to be everywhere, and his gallery, **Volcano Garden Arts** (Map p312; ☎ 967-7261; www.volcanogardenarts.com; 19-3834 Old Volcano Rd; ☯ 10am-4pm Tue-Sun), is central to Volcano's burgeoning art scene. A cute café serves vegetarian gourmet lunches (and soon dinners as well), and it hosts poetry readings and arts events. A pottery studio is in the works.

At the glass-blowing studio **2400° Fahrenheit** (Map p307; ☎ 985-8667; www.2400F.com; Old Volcano Rd; ☯ 10am-4pm Thu-Mon), you can watch artists Michael and Misato Mortara create their mind-boggling glass bowls and vases (Thursday to Sunday). A tiny gallery displays finished pieces. It's outside of Volcano on Hwy 11, near the 24-mile marker.

Near 2400° Fahrenheit on Hwy 11, **Akatsuka Orchid Gardens** (Map p307; ☎ 967-8234, 888-967-6669; www.akatsukaorchid.com; Hwy 11; admission free; ☯ 8:30am-5pm) is famous for its unique hybrid orchids and its warehouse stuffed with 100,000 perennially blooming plants. It also carries seeds and starters for Kona coffee plants, hibiscus, plumeria and bamboo orchids, all ready for shipping.

Free half-mile nature walks are offered every Monday at 9:30am by the **Volcano Art Center's Niaulani Campus** (Map p312; ☎ 967-8222; www.volcanoartcenter.org; 19-4074 Old Volcano Rd), which also hosts a range of evening poetry readings, music, artist lectures and other events.

After a hard day's hiking, relax with a traditional Hawaiian massage or steam bath at **Hale Ho'ola Hawaiian Healing Arts Center & Spa** (☎ 756-2421; www.halehoola.net; 11-3913 7th St; 30-90min treatments from $45-110). The extensive menu has much more; appointments required.

A local favorite, the 18-hole **Volcano Golf & Country Club** (Map p312; ☎ 967-7331; www.volcanogolfshop.com; Pi'i Mauna Dr; green fees before/after noon $73/59) has majestic links, with views of Mauna Kea and Mauna Loa.

Sleeping
Volcano has a preponderance of nice B&Bs and vacation homes. **Volcano Gallery** (☎ 800-967-8617; www.volcanogallery.com) is a locally managed rental agency listing over two dozen good properties, many in the $145 to $165 range.

BUDGET
Holo Holo In (Map p312; ☎ 967-7950; www.enable.org/holoholo; 19-4036 Kalani Honua Rd; dm $19, r $50-65; ☐) Don't be put off by this small hostel's exterior. Inside, the two six-bed dorms and four private

rooms are meticulously cared for, sizable and pleasant. The kitchen is nicely equipped, and there's a laundry. It's a quiet, homey place tended by a gracious host.

MIDRANGE & TOP END

My Island B&B (Map p312; ☎ 967-7216; www.myislandinnhawaii.com; 19-3896 Old Volcano Rd; s $65-95, d $80-120, house d $150; ☎) In a historic 1886 house, this comfortable European-style B&B is run by a friendly family who know the volcano as intimately as any ranger. Gordon, the father, is a colorful raconteur who keeps things lively around the breakfast table. The three main-house rooms have character but are small (two share a tiny bathroom with a redwood-and-copper tub); two studio rooms in a separate building have TV and kitchenette. It also rents out a fully equipped three-bedroom house nearby.

Volcano Artists Cottage (☎ 967-7261; www.volcanoartistscottage.com; 19-3436 Old Volcano Rd; cottage incl breakfast $130; ☎) On the grounds of Volcano Garden Arts (p319), the caretaker's cottage of this former estate has been reimagined as a tiny retreat to restore your creative muse. Somehow it holds a fully functioning kitchen, dining table, comfy chair and queen bed (with delicious spreads), as well as an inspirational step-down, sea-green tile bathroom as big as the living area. Best for singles and intimate couples.

Aloha Crater Lodge (Map p312; ☎ 345-4449; www.alohacraterlodge.com; 11-3966 Lanihuli Rd; r $100-150; ☎) Families wanting a well-kept place to relax will find common cause with the enthusiastic young innkeepers. The new-built house has four well-insulated rooms with mini-kitchens and attractive, unpretentious decor. Ohia-trunk posts add character, as does the outdoor Jacuzzi. The forested property has an entrance to Kazumura Cave (p301).

Bamboo Orchid Cottage (☎ 985-9592, 877-208-2199; www.bambooorchidcottage.com; 11-3903 Tenth St; r incl breakfast $100-130, ste $180; ☎) Built to be a B&B, this house holds five well-designed rooms and a vaulted common area with wood fireplace. All rooms have lush bedspreads and attractive furnishings; three have propane fireplaces with mosaic-tile mantels. Add a shared BBQ and hot tub, and it's easy to bunk here.

Volcano Tree House (www.volcanotreehouse.com; 11-3860 Eleventh St; r $175-250; ☎) For a more private retreat, consider Bamboo Orchid's sister property. Set in a fern forest with raised cat-

walks among the trees, all three large rooms have a kitchen and TV.

Volcano Rainforest Retreat (☎ 985-8696, 800-550-8696; www.volcanoretreat.com; 11-3832 12th St at Ruby St; cottage d incl breakfast $140-260; ☎ ☎) For all the jungle with none of the sacrifice, book one of the four luxurious, individually designed cedar cottages at this meditation-minded B&B. Artfully positioned among giant *hapu'u*, cottages have huge windows and either outdoor hot tubs or Japanese-style soaking tubs to maximize your experience of nature. Some have kitchens. To complete the northern California vibe, it offers meditation retreats and on-call massage therapists.

our pick Kilauea Lodge (Map p312; ☎ 967-7366; www.kilauealodge.com; Old Volcano Rd; incl breakfast r $175-225, cottage d $185-300; ☎) Volcano's most attractive property is an old renovated YMCA camp that sleeps like a B&B with hotel services. The 12 rooms vary their offerings, but all embody upscale country romance with gas fireplaces, Hawaiian quilts, artistic stained glass, tall ceilings and bathroom skylights. A relaxing common room has a wood fireplace, and the manicured jungle gardens hold a gorgeous hot tub. It also rents three detached, fully equipped cottages.

Eating

Lava Rock Café (Map p312; ☎ 967-8526; Old Volcano Rd; mains $8-10; ☺ 7:30am-5pm Mon, to 9pm Tue-Sat, to 4pm Sun; ☎ ☎) Behind Kilauea General Store, this basic diner is nothing special, but it's the favored spot for breakfast or a burger. It has internet terminals (per hour $10) and wi-fi (per day $10).

Volcano Golf & Country Club (Map p312; ☎ 967-7331; Pi'i Mauna Dr; meals $6-10.50; ☺ restaurant 8am-3pm) Locals come here for affordable lunch specials and fresh mahimahi burgers while chatting around the attractive fireplace.

our pick Thai Thai Restaurant (Map p312; ☎ 967-7969; 19-4084 Old Volcano Rd; mains $15-23; ☺ 4-9pm) The owners get their spices directly from Thailand and craft destination-worthy Thai cuisine. Here, satay doesn't come on a stick, and the generous-portioned, attractively presented curries and soups arrive vibrantly flavored with a rich tingly warmth – we're guessing they could even impress Pele if she ordered 'Thai hot.'

Kiawe Kitchen (Map p312; ☎ 967-7711; cnr Old Volcano & Haunani Rds; pizzas $15-20, mains $24-32; ☺ 11am-2:30pm & 5:30-8:30pm) Locals call this pleasant café with big art and a nice patio 'the pizza place.' The thin-crust, gourmet-style pizza pies are good, but it also serves Italian-influenced, dependable entrées, like *fra diavolo*, shrimp scampi and rib-eye steak. A full bar completes the friendly atmosphere.

Kilauea Lodge (Map p312; ☎ 967-7366; www.kilauealodge.com; Old Volcano Rd; breakfast $8-10, dinner mains $25-30; ⏱ 7:30-10am & 5-9pm) The vaulted beamed ceiling, historic stone fireplace and eye-catching paintings create an upscale rustic atmosphere. The kitchen prepares gourmet versions of mostly German comfort food: *hasenpfeffer* (braised rabbit), venison, sausage and sauerkraut, and Parker Ranch steaks. Dinners come with fresh mini-loaves of bread, the wine list is extensive and service is attentive. In fact, for a romantic evening, you won't find better in East Hawai'i. Reservations advised. The restaurant is also open for breakfast.

For groceries, pickings are slim at both **Volcano Store** (Map p312; ☎ 967-7210; cnr Old Volcano & Haunani Rds; ⏱ 5am-7pm) and **Kilauea General Store** (Map p312; ☎ 967-7555; Old Volcano Rd; ⏱ 7am-7:30pm Mon-Sat, to 7pm Sun). The best trail lunch will be leftovers from the night before (hint: think Thai).

KA'U

Ancient Hawaiians considered the people who lived in Ka'u to be independent, even prickly folk who did things their way. It's no different today. At times, Ka'u (kah-*oo*) feels almost like the frontier, with off-the-grid living that's both practical necessity and political statement. Residents often say they feel called to live here, and they develop an abiding loyalty; they love and protect Ka'u fiercely, fending off developers and all other carpetbaggers.

Traveling east to west, Ka'u's landscape changes dramatically – fertile foothills become bucolic pasturelands around South Point, then everything swiftly dries out, turning into a parched lava rock desert. Upland are protected native forests.

Many travelers come to Ka'u to notch a travel milestone and set foot on the southernmost point in the USA – which is also considered the landing point of the first Polynesians to Hawaii. But Ka'u rewards those who linger. There is seclusion and enough quiet to think your own thoughts,

HAWAI'I THE BIG ISLAND

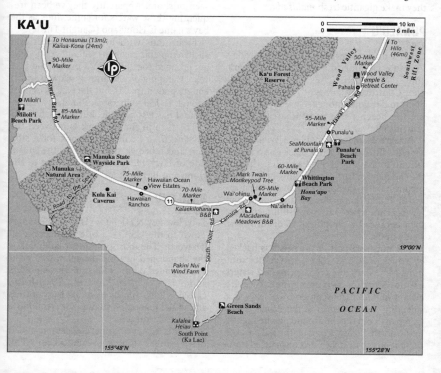

KA'U

HAWAI'I THE BIG ISLAND

and a close-knit community that understands that desire.

PAHALA
pop 1400

A former sugar town that's struggled through hard times, Pahala is making a comeback with small-farm agriculture, particularly macadamia nuts and coffee. This quiet town's main streets are lined with charming early-20th-century plantation homes, but it doesn't offer much for travelers beyond a peek at country life.

From Hwy 11, take the signed turnoff (between the 51- and 52-mile markers) on Kamani St, and take this to Pikake St, where you'll find Pahala's only shopping center, with a market, post office and bank. Nearby are a gas station and the **Ka'u Hospital** (☎ 928-2050; www.kau.hhsc .org; Kamani St).

Also in the shopping center is **Pahala Town Cafe** (☎ 928-8200; Pikake St; meals $5-10; ☻ 7am-7pm Sat-Thu, 7am-4pm Fri), the town's only eatery. Bright and clean, it serves decent food to a purely local crowd. The extensive menu has something for everyone. Friday to Monday they make gigantic fresh *malasada*.

PUNALU'U
pop 880

Once a major Hawaiian settlement, today Punalu'u is home to a popular beach park and SeaMountain, Ka'u's only condo complex. Controversy surrounds SeaMountain's plans to develop untouched areas surrounding the beach park, and the area's future remains unclear.

Punalu'u Beach Park provides easy access to a pretty little bay with a black-sand beach famous for basking green sea turtles. Though the endangered turtles seem unconcerned by picture-taking gawking humans, don't harass or touch them. Punalu'u is one of the few beaches where rare hawksbill turtles lay their eggs, so be careful not to disturb their sandy nests.

The northern part of the beach is backed by a duck pond and is the best place for sunning. Most days, the cold, spring-fed waters are not ideal for swimming, but there are always *malihini* (newcomers) who give it a shivering try. The ruins of the Pahala Sugar Company's old warehouse and pier lie slightly to the north. Follow a trail up the hill past the cement pier to find the unreconstructed ruins

of Kane'ele'ele Heiau in a vast 'a'a field; the trail continues to some secluded coves.

The park has several picnic pavilions, rest rooms, showers and drinking water. A concession stand is run by local aunties who happily talk story, and camping is allowed (with a county permit, see p205) throughout a grassy picnic area above the crashing waves. Camping is only so-so, with zero privacy: the exposed area gets some heavy winds, and the parking lot can attract carousing locals at night. Come morning, the park quickly fills with picnickers and tour buses.

SeaMountain's **golf course** (☎ 928-6222; green fees $47-50; ☻ 7am-6pm) has ocean views from each of its 18 holes.

There are two signed turnoffs for Punalu'u between the 56- and 57-mile markers.

WHITTINGTON BEACH PARK

This small beach park has tide pools to explore, and the cement pilings of an old pier that was used for shipping sugar and hemp until the 1930s. The ocean is usually too rough for swimming and, despite the name, there is no beach. Green sea turtles can sometimes be seen offshore. Apparently they've been frequenting these waters for some time, as the bay's name is Honu'apo (Caught Turtle).

Bathrooms with no potable water and sheltered picnic pavilions without good views are grouped together near a pretty, pondlike inlet. Camping on the grass is allowed with a county permit (p205), but the park is isolated enough to feel vulnerable; Punalu'u's campground has less solitude, but feels safer.

The turnoff for the park is between the 60- and 61-mile markers. Look for a stop sign and a brown park sign on the *makai* side of Hwy 11, just below the rise to the Honu'apo Bay lookout.

NA'ALEHU
pop 920

Tiny, low-key Na'alehu is 'The Southernmost Town in the USA' – a title it milks for all it's worth. The most prominent landmark is the abandoned historic theater with a giant *honu* painted on the roof, and movie posters announcing *Citizen Kane* and *The African Queen*. Along with its towering banyan trees and pastel plantation homes, Na'alehu has a lost-in-time rural feel.

This is Ka'u's commercial center, and it has a grocery store, a gas station, an ATM, a post office, a police station and a half-dozen churches.

Eating

Punalu'u Bakeshop (☎ 929-7343; www.bakeshophawaii.com; cnr Hwy 11 & Ka'alaiki Rd; sandwiches $4-6, plate lunches $8; 9am-5pm) Na'alehu's one bona fide tourist attraction and tour-bus stop is this sweetbread bakery, which supplies the island. The sweetbread comes plain or in brightly colored flavors like guava, *liliko'i* and taro. Snack on a pastry or *malasada*, or grab a salad or sandwich to go from the deli (steer clear of the mediocre plate lunches). A small garden area out back allows for picnicking.

Hana Hou (☎ 929-9717; Spur Rd; mains $10-16; 8am-3pm Mon-Thu, to 8pm Fri & Sat, to 5pm Sun) A community fixture, this friendly, homespun diner offers 'the best of everything…and plenty of it.' Indeed, portions are generous and dishes, though not fancy, rarely disappoint. The wide-ranging menu has the usual local *grinds* and fish plates plus stir-fries, chicken parmesan and other Asian-inspired specials.

Shaka Restaurant (☎ 929-7404; www.shakarestaurant.com; lunch $8-13, dinner $11-20; 10am-8:30pm) Na'ahlehu's other eatery serves mainly fryer and grill fare and has a hardworking bar.

A small but recommended **farmers market** (Hwy 11; 8am-noon Wed & Sat) is held across from the theater.

WAI'OHINU

Wai'ohinu has no commercial center. One sign you've reached it is when you pass the landmark **Mark Twain monkeypod tree**, which was planted by the author in 1866 and fell over in a 1957 hurricane. Hardy new trunks have sprung up and replaced it, and behind the tree is a macadamia-nut orchard. It's along Hwy 11, but there's no place to park.

Sleeping

Macadamia Meadows B&B (☎ 929-8097, 888-929-8118; www.macadamiameadows.com; d incl breakfast $89-129, ste $139;) Just half a mile south of town, a family of friendly macadamia-nut farmers rents rooms on the ground floor of their contemporary home. Room decor is country cozy – eclectic and relaxed, if not especially memorable. They are spacious and clean, with private entrances, lanai, cable TV, and other amenities. Guests receive a free tour of the surrounding organic orchard, and there's a pool and tennis court.

Margo's Corner (☎ 929-9614; www.margoscorner.com; Wakea St; cottages incl breakfast $90-130;) This gay-friendly guesthouse offers two bright, pleasing cottages, plus it accommodates tent campers. The Adobe Suite has a wall of windows, double beds in Star Trek–like berths and a private sauna. The lavendar Rainbow Cottage is smaller, and the garden setting is peaceful. Call for directions.

South Point Banyan Tree House (☎ 715-302-8180; www.southpointbth.com; cnr Pinao St & Hwy 11; house $185) Nestled high in the limbs of a huge banyan tree, this fun octagonal vacation rental offers the visually arresting illusion of a jungle escape. Fully equipped and flooded with light, it has a great kitchen, relaxed living room (with TV) and a hot tub on a hidden deck. Honeymoon, anyone?

SOUTH POINT

South Point is the southernmost point in the USA and a national historic landmark. In Hawaiian, it's known as Ka Lae, which means simply 'The Point'. In lava-covered rural Ka'u, only South Point looks like 'the country' – with sweeping grassy ranchlands dotted with grazing cattle and horses. It could be mistaken for the Midwest (even down to the shot-up road signs), except that the rolling hills slope toward rugged lava cliffs and a turbulent turquoise ocean. This is apparently where the first Polynesians landed.

To get here, take **South Point Rd** between the 69- and 70-mile markers. The 10-mile road is mostly one lane, so be polite, edge over to let folks pass and give a *shaka* (Hawaiian hand greeting sign).

Sights

PAKINI NUI WIND FARM

The winds are bracing here, as evidenced by tree trunks bent almost horizontal. After a few miles of scattered houses, macadamia-nut farms and grassy pastureland, you'll see the rows of high-tech windmills of this wind farm. Many are defunct leftovers from an older wind farm (Kama'oa), which was replaced in 2007 with 14 new turbines.

About 4 miles south of the wind farm are the abandoned buildings that once made up the Pacific Missile Range Station. Up until 1965, missiles shot from California to the Marshall Islands in Micronesia were tracked here.

DETOUR: WOOD VALLEY

Near Pahala, the Tibetan Buddhist **Wood Valley Temple & Retreat Center** (Nechung Dorje Drayang Ling; Map p321; ☎ 928-8539; www.nechung.org; requested donation $5; ⏰ 10am-5pm) makes a lovely escape from the modern world, whether for an hour or several days. The century-old, colorful temple contains a wonderfully ornate altar, which is all the more striking and exotic set against the backdrop of the center's lush 25-acre property. The temple's name, Nechung Dorje Drayang Ling, translates as 'Immutable Island of Melodious Sound,' and that perfectly captures the valley's meditative thrum of forest, wind and birdsong.

The temple was built around 1902 by Japanese sugarcane laborers. Later abandoned, it was rediscovered in the early 1970s and reestablished in the Tibetan Buddhist tradition by Tibetan lama Nechung Rinpoche. His Holiness the Dalai Lama has visited twice: in 1980 to dedicate the temple and again in 1994. Many well-respected Tibetan lamas conduct programs here.

Visitors are welcome to attend daily chanting and meditation sittings at 8am and 6pm (it might be just you and the Rinpoche!) or visit the temple and gift shop. In addition to a regular schedule of Buddhist teachings, Wood Valley also hosts nondenominational retreats.

For a personal retreat or meditative getaway, stay in the center's cheerfully painted **guesthouse** (dm/s/d with shared bathroom $65/75/85; ☎). Guests have the run of the huge building, which has a full kitchen and a screened-in dining hall and lanai with lush views, as well as several reading nooks. Rooms aren't spacious, but they are clean, simple and nicely furnished, with colorful details and new bamboo floors. Some rooms have only curtains, not doors. Though rains can create dampness, there is no musty air here. There's a three-night minimum; two nights are possible for an extra $25.

To get here, from Pahala's shopping center (see p322), follow Pikake St about 4.5 miles inland.

When the road forks, veer right for Ka Lae and left for Green Sands Beach.

KA LAE

The elemental simplicity of the incessant winds, steep cliffs and endless ocean make Ka Lae feel like the edge of the earth. Even with the rushing wind filling your ears, an odd stillness and silence steals over you. From the parking area, a short walk leads down to the southernmost tip itself, where there are no markers, no souvenirs, just wave after wave rushing across the ragged lava.

Not that you will be alone, necessarily. The confluence of ocean currents here makes this one of Hawai'i's most bountiful fishing grounds, and locals fish off the craggy cliff, some bracing themselves on tiny ledges partway down. The wooden platforms built on the cliff have hoists and ladders for small boats anchored below. Local kids like to **cliff jump** here, though you may want to poke your nose over the surging water and just imagine that heart-thumping trick. Behind the platforms, inside a large *puka* (hole), you can watch water rage up and recede with incoming waves. The only facilities are two portable toilets.

Near the parking area is **Kalalea Heiau**, classified as a *ko'a*, or a small stone pen designed to encourage fish and birds to multiply. Inside is a fishing shrine where ancient Hawaiians left offerings to Ku'ula, the god of fishermen. A standing rock below the heiau has several **canoe mooring holes.** Ancient Hawaiians would tether their canoes with ropes to these handles, then let the strong currents pull their canoes into the deep waters to fish.

GREEN SANDS BEACH

This legendary green sand **beach** on Mahana Bay is made of semiprecious olivine (a type of volcanic basalt), which erodes from the ancient littoral cone towering over it. The olivine sand mixes with black sand to create an unusual olive green that brightly sparkles in the sun, making this a fun, unique destination. However, the tiny strand is pounded by strong waves even on calm days, making swimming dubious, and high surf can flood it completely. Plus, its popularity guarantees other visitors. In fact, if the one-hour, 2.5-mile hike to reach it weren't so darn lovely, it wouldn't be half as satisfying.

The road to the beach ends at a turnaround with a grassy parking area; don't leave valuables in your car. Though a 4WD road continues to the beach (and locals with 4WDs sometimes wait here to sell rides), don't drive there. Braided tracks are tearing up the land, and you'll miss one of the best parts, the hike.

From here, walk toward the water, past the Kaulana boat ramp, and follow the rutted dirt road left through the metal gate. Then just keep going, enjoying the gorgeous undulating coastline and aiming for the uplifted, striated cliff-face in the distance. Once there, a slight scramble down the cliff is required to reach the beach.

Sleeping

our pick **Kalaekilohana B&B** (☎ 939-8052, 888-584-7071; www.kau-hawaii.com; 94-2152 South Point Rd; r incl breakfast $219; 🖥 🛜) It's a rare place that's so welcoming you feel at once like a special guest and a member of the family. But the *ho'okipa* (hospitality) extended by hosts Kilohana Domingo and Kenny Joyce does just that. Upstairs, four airy rooms feature gleaming hardwood floors, carved bed frames, open 'rainfall' shower and French doors opening onto large lanai. Amenities include guest laundry and locally made bath products. Downstairs, the gracious library/music room and the wide porch invite lingering long after the breakfast plates have been swept away. They are also the setting for occasional musical *kanikapila* (jam) nights, hula lessons and master lei-maker Domingo's workshops. Ask about multinight deals and packages.

OCEAN VIEW
pop 2180

Ocean View is largely comprised of two huge subdivisions that were bulldozed into the desolate black lava in the 1950s: Hawaiian Ocean View Estates (HOVE) and Hawaiian Ranchos. The lots were never fully settled, and they remain undersettled today, mainly because there's no water. Though the area is economically depressed and has suffered from drug problems in the past, residents are tight-knit and proud – far preferring the rough simplicity of their independent life to the 'rat race' in Kona and Hilo, where many work.

Across the highway from each other, two shopping centers – Pohue Plaza and Ocean View Town Center – make up the commercial center of Ocean View. They contain gas stations, grocery stores, simple restaurants, ATMs and a laundromat.

Activities

Explore a portion of the world's second-longest lava tube (with over 25 mapped miles) at **Kula Kai Caverns** (☎ 929-7539, 929-9725; www.kulakaicaverns.com; adult/child 6-12 tours from $15/10). Evidence of ancient Hawaiians extends throughout the thousand-year-old **Kanohina cave system**, and tours emphasize respectful stewardship of these 'living museums.' On the 40-minute tour, you enter a short, lighted section of the cave, as expert guides present both cultural and ecological history. There's also a longer 'crawling' tour (per person $30) and a two-hour extended tour (adult/child $95/65). Group sizes are quite small (with two- or four-person minimums); reservations required.

Sleeping & Eating

our pick **Lova Lava Land** (☎ 352-9097; www.lovalavaland.com; Hawaiian Ranchos; yurt $55, VW buses $35; 🛜) This off-the-grid 'eco-resort' (solar power, catchment water, composting toilet) is a hippie's dream: sleep in tricked-out VW buses in the middle of a lava flow and share a central compound with fully equipped kitchen, wi-fi and a (sometimes hot) lava rock shower. A single yurt is a cozy love nest, with a double bed, hardwood floors and moon roof. It's fun, well-planned DIY living.

Bougainvillea Bed & Breakfast (☎ 929-7089, 800-688-1763; www.bougainvilleabedandbreakfast.com; Hawaiian Ranchos; s/d incl breakfast $80/90; 🐾) The four rooms in this family home are comfortably furnished, with floral spreads, good mattresses and private entrances. It's an unpretentious place, with a small pool and Jacuzzi and a home-cooked breakfast.

Desert Rose Cafe (☎ 939-7673; Pohue Plaza; mains $9-21; ⏱ 7am-8pm) Ocean View doesn't have many dining options, but that's no knock on this local hangout, which serves a full range of good, fresh food: thick sweetbread French toast, tasty egg scrambles, fried chicken, fish specials, burgers and steaks. Order a beer and meet the locals.

Ocean View Pizzaria (☎ 929-9677; Ocean View Town Center; pizza $13-15, sandwiches $7-12; ⏱ 11am-7pm, till 8pm Fri & Sat) The submarine sandwiches are great, the pizza good, and the milkshakes fine indeed. But it's a place to eat, not linger.

ROAD TO THE SEA

The Road to the Sea has a name that calls adventurers, but it's not the human-free destination it once was, despite being an extremely rugged 4WD-only road. Brave the journey and you may have the beaches to yourself. Or you may find, after all that trouble, that you're alone because the sea is too rough to swim and the beach too windy to stay. Not that that should stop you; just be warned.

To get here, turn *makai* at the row of mailboxes (near the 'Ka Ulu Malu Shady Grove Farm') between the 79- and 80-mile markers and set your odometer. From here you cross 6 miles over a rudimentary, seemingly never-ending lava road. The first and smaller of the two beaches is at the end of this road; it takes 45 minutes or so, depending on your comfort level driving on rough terrain.

To reach the second beach, drive a half mile back inland. Skip the first left fork that appears (it's a dead end) and take the second left fork. Look for arrows that are painted on the lava rock. The road heads inland before heading toward the shore again, and the course isn't always apparent. There are many places where you can lose traction or get lost. Almost

a mile from the fork you'll reach a red *pu'u* (hill). Park here and walk down to the ocean. If you decide to walk the whole distance, it's about 1.5 miles. Bring as much water as you can carry; it's hot and shadeless.

Neither beach is named, but both have exquisite black-and-green sand, similar to Green Sands Beach, backed by looming cliffs. Low tide presents intriguing beach-trekking possibilities.

MANUKA STATE WAYSIDE PARK

The facilities at this 13.5-acre state park are forlorn and neglected. You can camp with a permit (see p205), but it's isolated and there's no drinking water (only pit toilets). However, it's worth coming for the easy 2-mile **nature walk**, which provides a rare (for Ka'u) hike in the woods. A handy trail guide identifies the many native Hawaiian and introduced species you encounter, and the trail passes several ancient Hawaiian sites and ruins. The entrance is off Hwy 11, just north of the 81-mile marker.

Maui

You'll notice it proudly displayed – from rusty bumpers of pickup trucks to glossy brochures: *Maui no ka 'oi*, meaning 'Maui is the best.' That's a big claim for an island with such pretty siblings. And yet, Maui's magnificent beaches could well make you giddy. The entire west coast is lined with golden sands, some backed by fancy resorts, some full of beach towels and boogie boards, some as naked as the day they were born. In midwinter, all you have to do is stare out to sea to spot humpback whales cavorting offshore. You can ride monster waves if you're a pro, learn to surf if you're not. Snorkel each day at a different site. Kayak with dolphins and sea turtles. Pin a sail to your board and fly with the wind.

A plethora of adventures await on land. Strap on a pair of boots and hike the crunchy lunarlike surface of the world's largest dormant volcano. Twist your way along the jungly cliff-hugging Hana Hwy, soaking up waterfalls and swimming holes. Explore the salt-sprayed whaling town of Lahaina. Foodies, take note. You could come to Maui to do nothing but eat, and not be disappointed. It doesn't hurt that the rich and famous favor Maui, which helps top-chef restaurants to thrive. But you don't need a fat wallet to treat your palate – just step into the tasty café-laden streets of Pa'ia, where everything's green, local and hip.

Add it all up and it's little wonder Maui draws more visitors than any other Neighbor Island.

MAUI

HIGHLIGHTS

- Catch a soulful crater-rim sunrise at **Haleakalā National Park** (p413)
- Dive the crystal-clear waters of **Molokini Crater** (p379)
- Wind across 54 one-lane bridges on the **Hana Highway** (p392)
- Slurp mango shave ice at **Tom's Mini-Mart** (p370)
- Snorkel the turtle town waters of **Malu'aka Beach** (p385)
- Ogle Maui's favorite green landmark at **'Iao Valley State Park** (p371)
- Bask in the aloha at the **Old Lahaina Luau** (p347)
- Swim in the cascading pools at **'Ohe'o Gulch** (p400)
- Pedal-power your own smoothie at off-the-grid **Laulima Farms** (p402)
- Watch the sunset from glorious **Big Beach** (p386)

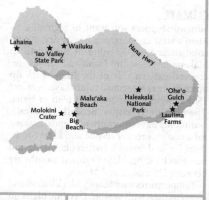

- POPULATION: 120,000
- AREA: 728 SQ MILES
- NICKNAME: VALLEY ISLE

HISTORY

Maui's early history mirrors the rest of Hawaii's, with warring chiefs, periods of peace, missionaries, whalers and sugarcane. At the time of statehood in 1959, Maui's population was a mere 35,000. In 1961 Maui retained such a backwater appearance that director Mervyn LeRoy filmed his classic *The Devil at 4 O'Clock* in Lahaina, where the dirt roads and untouristed waterfront offered a perfect setting for the sleepy South Pacific isle depicted in his adventure movie. Spencer Tracy and Frank Sinatra not only shot many of their scenes at Lahaina's Pioneer Inn, but slept there too, since the inn's two dozen rickety rooms represented the bulk of Maui's hotel options.

Enter sugar giant Amfac in 1962, which sweetened its pot by transforming 600 acres of canefields in Ka'anapali into Hawaii's first resort destination outside Waikiki. Things really took off in 1974 with the first non-stop flight between the mainland USA and Kahului. Maui soon blossomed into the darling of Hawaii's tourism industry.

Its growth spurt hasn't always been pretty. In the mid-1970s the beachside village of Kihei was pounced on by developers with such intensity it became a rallying call for antidevelopment forces throughout Hawaii. Much of the last decade has been spent catching up with Kihei's rampant growth, mitigating traffic and creating plans intent on sparing the rest of Maui from willy-nilly building sprees. More recent development has taken a decidedly upscale approach, leaving Maui with some fancy resorts and the highest room rates in Hawaii.

CLIMATE

Sun-worshippers will want to hightail it to Maui's west coast, which boasts dry, sunny conditions from Kapalua in the north to Makena in the south. Hana and the jungle-covered eastern side of the island pick up much more rain. Annual rainfall averages just 15in along the west coast but 69in in Hana. The Upcountry slopes, beneath Haleakalā, commonly have intermittent clouds, making for a cooler, greener respite and ideal conditions for land-based activities like hiking and horseback riding. Maui's rainiest months are between December and March.

Temperatures vary more with elevation and location than with season. Daytime highs on Maui vary only about 7°F between summer and winter, and coastal waters are always warm. Average daily temperatures in August hover around 80°F in Lahaina, Kihei or Hana, but only 50°F at Haleakalā summit. The lowest temperature ever recorded on Maui was 14°F at the summit of Haleakalā, where overnight lows dip below freezing and the volcano even gets an occasional winter snowcap.

See p563 for more climate information and climate charts. For an islandwide recorded weather forecast, call ☎ 866-944-5025.

NATIONAL, STATE & COUNTY PARKS

The crowning glory of Maui's parks, Haleakalā National Park embraces the lofty volcanic peaks that gave rise to east Maui. The park has two distinct faces. The main section (p413) encompasses Haleakalā's volcanic summit with its breathtaking crater-rim lookouts and lunar-like hiking trails. In the park's rainforested Kipahulu section (p400), you're in the midst of towering waterfalls, cascading pools and ancient Hawaiian archaeological sites.

A must-see among the Maui's state parks is 'Iao Valley State Park (p371), whose towering emerald pinnacle rises picture-perfect from the valley floor. For the ultimate stretch of unspoiled beach, head to Makena State Park (p386), the northern portion of which is a haunt for nude sunbathers. On the east side of the island, Wai'anapanapa State Park (p396) sits on a gem of a black-sand beach. To explore a dreamy cloud forest, head to Upcountry to Polipoli Spring State Recreation Area (p411), where a lightly trodden network of trails winds beneath lofty trees.

Maui's county parks center on beaches and include some hot places, like Kanaha Beach Park (p365) and Ho'okipa Beach Park (p388) for windsurfing and kitesurfing.

Camping

NATIONAL PARKS

For the best camping on Maui, head to Haleakalā National Park. Drive-up camping is available in both the summit (p420) and Kipahulu (p401) sections of the park, and no fees, reservations or permits are required. Haleakalā also offers free backcountry camping on the crater floor (with a permit), as well as high-demand $75 cabin rentals (p421).

STATE PARKS

Maui has two state parks with both campsites and cabins: Polipoli Spring State Recreation

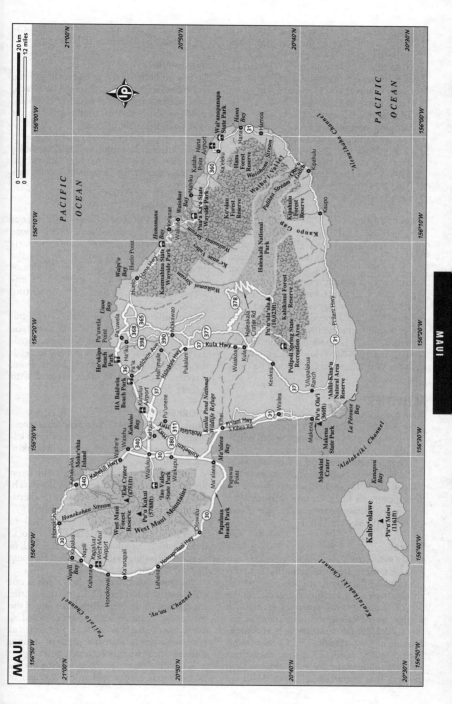

MAUI

Area (p412) and Wai'anapanapa State Park (p396). Polipoli, deep in the rain forest, has one primitive cabin at the end of a rough access road that usually requires a 4WD vehicle. If you're not a pig hunter, you'll find the dozen beachside cabins at Wai'anapanapa, just north of Hana, more to your taste. Book well in advance to avoid disappointment.

Camping permits are required for state parks. Tent camping costs $5 per day per site and cabins cost $45. For permits and cabin reservations, contact the **Division of State Parks** (☎ 984-8109; www.hawaiistateparks.org/camping; Room 101, State Office Bldg, 54 S High St, Wailuku, HI 96793; ☽ 8am-3:30pm Mon-Fri).

COUNTY PARKS
Kanaha Beach Park (p365) is just north of Kahului Airport and allows camping Wednesday through to Sunday; Papalaua Beach Park (p350) is on Hwy 30 south of Lahaina and allows camping Friday through Wednesday. Camping is limited to three consecutive nights. Permits cost $5 to $8 per adult per day ($2 to $3 for children under 18) and are available from the **Department of Parks & Recreation** (☎ 270-7232; www.co.maui.hi.us; 700 Hali'a Nakoa St, Wailuku, HI 96793; ☽ 8am-1pm & 2:30-4pm Mon-Fri) at the War Memorial Complex at Baldwin High School.

ACTIVITIES
Maui has primo conditions for virtually anything you can do in the water, from snorkeling to kiteboarding – and the surfing and windsurfing here is the stuff of legends.

The adventures on land are equally awesome. Haleakalā National Park boasts crater trails so unearthly that astronauts trained for their moonwalk there. Or take it airborne on a zipline rip above the treetops at eagle speed. On Maui, the sky's the limit.

At Sea
KAYAKING
Kayakers, there are some great places to dip your paddle. The top spot is Makena (p385), an area rich with marine life including sea turtles, dolphins and wintering humpback whales. In the calmer summer months, another exceptional destination is Honolua-Mokule'ia Bay Marine Life Conservation District (p358), north of Kapalua, where there are turtles aplenty and dolphin sightings. Keep in mind that water conditions on Maui are

usually clearest and calmest early in the morning, so that's an ideal time to head out.

KITESURFING
There's no better place to learn kitesurfing, also called kiteboarding, than at Kite Beach, at the southwestern end of Kanaha Beach Park (p365) in Kahului. Vans and instructors set right up in the parking lot.

You can get the lowdown on everything to do with kiteboarding from the **Maui Kiteboarding Association** (www.mauikiteboardingassociation.com) and **Maui Kitesurfing Community** (www.mauikitesurfing.org).

SCUBA DIVING
The granddaddy of Maui dives is the islet of Molokini (see the boxed text, p379), whose steep crater walls nurture an amazing variety of sea life. Another prime dive is at the untouched Cathedrals, on the south side of Lana'i, which takes its name from its underwater caverns, arches and connecting passageways.

Most dive operators on Maui offer a full range of dives as well as certification courses. And if you've never tried it before, introductory dives for beginners get you beneath the surface in just a couple of hours. Book directly, and don't monkey around with activity desks.

SNORKELING
Don a mask and fins and a whole other world opens up. The waters around Maui are a kaleidoscope of colorful fish, coral and honkin' big sea turtles.

For phenomenal snorkeling right from the beach, top spots include Malu'aka Beach, dubbed 'Turtle Beach' (p385), in Makena; 'Ahihi-Kina'u Natural Area Reserve (p387), south of Makena; Ulua Beach (p382) in Wailea; Pu'u Keka'a (p351), aka Black Rock, in Ka'anapali; Kapalua Beach (p358); and, in summer, Slaughterhouse Beach and Honolua Bay (p358), north of Kapalua.

Snorkelers should get an early start, as not only does the first half of the morning offer the calmest water conditions but some of the more popular places begin to get crowded by 10am. Snorkeling gear can readily be rented at reasonable prices from dive shops or at more inflated prices from hotel beach huts.

A terrific destination for snorkeling cruises is the largely submerged volcanic crater of

MAUI ACTIVITIES

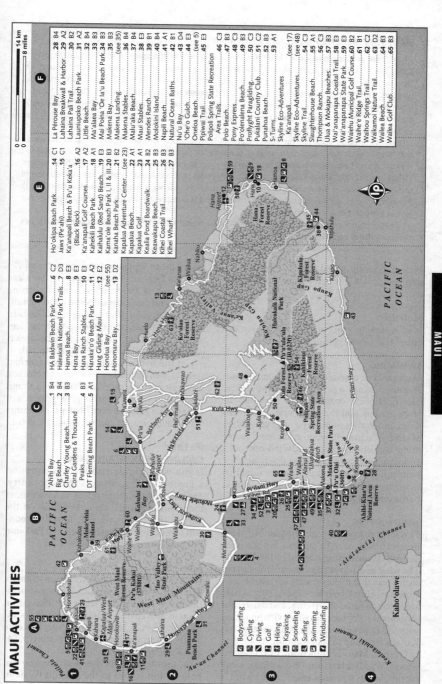

Bodysurfing
Cycling
Diving
Golf
Hiking
Kayaking
Snorkeling
Surfing
Swimming
Windsurfing

MAUI

MAUI

MAUI SURF BEACHES & BREAKS *Jake Howard*

While there are hippie holdouts from the 1960s who believe the spirit of Jimi Hendrix roams the Valley Isle's mountains, today Maui's beaches are where most of the island's action is found. On the north shore, near the town of Ha'iku (p408), is the infamous big-wave spot known as **Pe'ahi**, or **Jaws**. Determined pro surfers, such as Laird Hamilton, Dave Kalama and Derrick Doerner, have helped put the planet's largest, most perfect wave on the international map, appearing in everything from American Express commercials to mutual fund ads. Jaws' waves are so high that surfers must be towed into them by WaveRunners.

Not into risking your life on your vacation? No worries, there are plenty of other waves to ride. Maui's west side, especially around **Lahaina** (p336), offers a wider variety of surf. The fun reef breaks at **Lahaina Breakwall and Harbor** cater to both beginner and intermediate surfers. To the south is **Ma'alaea Pipeline**, a fickle right-hand reef break that is often considered one of the fastest waves in the world. On the island's northwest corner is majestic **Honolua Bay** (p358). Its right point break works best on winter swells and is considered one of the premier points not just in Hawaii, but around the world.

Gentler shorebreaks good for bodysurfing can be found around **Pa'ia**, **Kapalua** and the beaches between **Kihei** and **Makena**.

Molokini (see the boxed text, p379), off Maui's southwest coast. The best place to join a cruise is at Ma'alaea (p373).

SURFING
Maui's surfing spots are legendary. See the boxed text (above) for details.

SWIMMING
Maui makes a credible claim to being the top Hawaiian island when it comes to beaches. The northwest coast from Ka'anapali to Honolua Bay and the southwest coast from Kihei and Wailea to Makena offer you scores of sandy beaches with good year-round swimming conditions. The windward northern and eastern coasts are generally rough for swimming in winter but quieten down in summer, when they can become as calm as a swimming pool.

WINDSURFING
This sport reaches its peak on Maui. Ho'okipa Beach (p388), near Pa'ia, is so hot it's been dubbed 'Windsurfing Capital of the World.' The wind and waves combine at Ho'okipa in such a way that makes gravity seem arbitrary. However, Ho'okipa is for experts only as hazards include razor-sharp coral and dangerous shorebreaks. For kick-ass wind without taking your life in your hands, the place to launch is Kanaha Beach (p365) in Kahului.

Overall, Maui is known for its consistent winds. Windsurfers can find action in any month, but as a general rule the best wind is from June to September and the flattest spells are from December to February. At Ma'alaea (p372), where the winds are usually strong and blow offshore toward Kaho'olawe, conditions are ripe for advanced speed sailing. In winter, on those occasions when *kona* (leeward) winds blow, the Ma'alaea-Kihei area is often the only place windy enough to sail.

Get the inside scoop on the windsurfing scene at **Maui Windsurfing** (www.mauiwindsurfing.net). Most windsurfing shops are based in Kahului (p365) and handle rentals, give lessons, sell windsurfing gear and even book package tours that include gear, accommodations and car.

On Land
CYCLING & MOUNTAIN BIKING
If you want to ride into the wilderness on a mountain bike, head to the Upcountry. Experienced downhill riders will encounter the ultimate adrenaline-stoked thrill on the Skyline Trail (p419), which follows the mountain's spine from Haleakalā National Park into Polipoli Spring State Recreation Area.

GOLF
Golfers will find lots of pretty places to knock that little white ball around. The most prestigious of Maui's courses is the Plantation Course at Kapalua (p360), which kicks off the annual PGA tour. Only slightly less elite are the championship greens at Wailea (p384) and Ka'anapali (p353).

At the other end of the spectrum, you can enjoy a fun round at the friendly Waiehu

Municipal Golf Course (p361) and at lesser-known country clubs elsewhere around the island. Pick up the free tourist magazine *Maui Golf Review* for in-depth course profiles and tips on playing specific holes. Another good resource is **Golf Maui** (www.golf-maui.com).

HIKING

Hikers on Maui get to pick from an amazing diversity of trails that traverse coastal deserts, bamboo forests and lush green jungles. Hands down the most extraordinary trails are in Haleakalā National Park (p413) where hikes ranging from half-day walks to quad-busting multiday treks meander across the moonscape of Haleakalā Crater. In the Kipahulu section (p400) of the national park, a trail leads you beside terraced pools ideal for a dip and on to the towering waterfalls that feed them.

In Maui's Upcountry, Polipoli Spring State Recreation Area (p411) has an extensive trail system in a nice quiet cloud forest. North of Wailuku is the lofty Waiheʻe Ridge Trail (p361), which penetrates deep into the misty West Maui Mountains. Near Maʻalaea Bay, the challenging Lahaina Pali Trail (p373) follows an old footpath on the drier western slope of the same mountain mass.

Several pull-offs along the Hana Hwy offer short nature walks that lead to hidden waterfalls and unspoiled coastal views, including the Waikamoi Nature Trail (p393). A longer coastal trail between Waiʻanapanapa State Park (p396) and Hana Bay follows an ancient Hawaiian footpath past historic sights, as does the Hoapili (King's Hwy) Trail (p387) from La Pérouse Bay on the other side of the island.

Share the trails with other eco-minded hikers by joining one of the **Sierra Club's** (☎ 573-4147; www.hi.sierraclub.org/maui) guided hikes. These hikes are held mostly on weekends, and sometimes go into fascinating places that are otherwise closed to the public. Nonmembers are asked to pay $5 each; carpooling to trailheads may be available.

HORSEBACK RIDING

With its abundant ranches and a living cowboy culture, Maui's the perfect place to saddle up. Choose a ride based on the landscape you most want to explore, since all are good, reputable outfitters. The most unusual ride, offered by Pony Express (p410), meanders down into the belly of Haleakalā Crater. Maui Stables (p402), near Kipahulu, offers rides through rain forests to waterfalls. Makena Stables (p387) takes riders up the sunny volcanic slopes near La Pérouse Bay, while Mendes Ranch (p362) rides high atop the cliffs of the Kahekili Hwy. Families will like the gentle rides at Thompson Ranch (p412) in Keokea.

TENNIS

The county maintains tennis courts in several towns, free to the public on a first-come, first-served basis. Numerous hotels and condos have tennis courts for their guests. If you're looking to hone your game, you'll find world-class tennis clubs in Wailea (p384) and Kapalua (p360).

BEACH BEAUTIES

- **Ulua Beach** (p382), a favorite for morning snorkeling and diving
- **Hoʻokipa Beach** (p388), where the pros go for surfing and windsurfing
- **Kite Beach** (p365) for kickin' kitesurfing
- **Honolua Bay** (p358) offers top surfing in winter, snorkeling in summer
- **Kaʻanapali Beach** (p351), a happening resort beach with all the amenities
- **Kapalua Beach** (p358) for calm-as-a-lake swimming and snorkeling
- **Keawakapu Beach** (p375), the perfect place for a sunset swim
- **Charley Young Beach** (p375), a hidden gem in the heart of bustling Kihei
- **Big Beach** (p386) for long beach strolls and bodysurfing
- **Maluʻaka Beach** (p385), the best place to snorkel with turtles
- **Little Beach** (p386), a hang-out of the clothing-optional crowd
- **Paʻiloa Beach** (p396), Maui's most stunning black-sand beach

MAUI

A WHALE OF A TIME

It's not just honeymooners that flock here – turns out humpback whales prefer Maui too. In winter they can be spotted throughout Hawaii but the waters off western Maui are the favored haunt for mating and birthing.

Fortunately, humpbacks are coast-huggers, preferring shallow waters to protect their new-born calves. This makes for terrific whale watching opportunities whether you're on land or on water.

Whale-watching cruises are the easiest way to get close to the action, as the boats know all the best spots and offer a close-up view of humpbacks demonstrating their hulking presence in leaps and bounds. You can readily join a cruise from a green operator like Pacific Whale Foundation from either Lahaina or Ma'alaea harbor.

Not that you have to join a whale-watching cruise to see these 40-ton leviathans. If you're taking the Lana'i ferry in winter, a glimpse of breaching whales is a common bonus; snorkeling tours to Molokini sometimes have sightings en route; and ocean kayaking in south Maui packs good odds of seeing these colossals as close as you'd ever want.

From the shore, whale spotting abounds – cliff-side lookouts, west-facing beaches, the lanai of your oceanfront condo, most anywhere from Kapalua in the north to Makena in the south. Two particularly rewarding lookouts are Papawai Point (p350) north of Ma'alaea and the Wailea Beach Walk (p383) in Wailea.

Of course, binoculars will bring the action closer. If you're not carting along a pair, stop by the Hawaiian Islands Humpback Whale National Marine Sanctuary headquarters (p375) in Kihei where there's a seaside scope. While you're at it, check out the whale displays and scoop up the handy humpback brochure to discover the difference between a full breach, a spy hop and a peduncle slap.

Then there's the music. The Whalesong Project maintains an underwater hydrophone off Kihei – just log on at www.whalesong.net and listen to whales singing in real time. Lucky snorkelers and divers who happen to be in the water at the right time can hear them singing as well – Ulua Beach (p382) is a top spot for eavesdropping on their haunting music. Love songs, we presume.

ZIPLINING

Maui's ziplines let you soar freestyle over gulches, woods and waterfalls while strapped into a harness. The hardest part is stepping off the platform for the first zip – the rest is pure exhilaration!

The favorite is Skyline Eco-Adventures' Haleakalā Skyline Tour, but it often books out far in advance. The same company has zipped up to Ka'anapali (p353) and opened a second zipline in the hills above the resort, this one pricier but easier to book. Kapalua Adventure Center (p360), up the slopes from Kapalua, differs from the others by having a dual track allowing riders to zip side by side with a friend.

GETTING THERE & AWAY
Air

Most travelers to Maui land in Kahului, which has the busiest airport in Hawaii outside Honolulu. North of Lahaina in west Maui, the Kapalua/West Maui Airport is Maui's second largest airport but it's strictly for inter-island flights. Tiny Hana Airport sees only a few flights a day, all by prop plane.

Hana Airport (HNM; ☎ 248-8208) A single terminal off the Hana Hwy, about 3 miles north of Hana in east Maui.

Kahului International Airport (OGG; ☎ 872-3830) There's a small visitor information desk (☎ 872-3893; open 7:45am to 9:45pm) in the baggage-claim area. Nearby are courtesy phones for contacting accommodations and ground transportation, plus racks upon racks of free tourist magazines and brochures. In the departure area are gift shops, ATMs and eateries and a lounge. For information on getting to and from Kahului's airport, see opposite.

Kapalua/West Maui Airport (JHM; ☎ 669-0623) The terminal is off Hwy 30, about midway between Kapalua and Ka'anapali, within easy reach of Lahaina.

Several airlines provide direct flights from the US mainland to Maui, including **Hawaiian Airlines** (☎ 800-367-5320; www.hawaiianair.com), which also offers a full schedule of daily flights between Maui and the other Hawaiian islands. See p571 for airline contact details and more information on flights to Maui from the mainland and abroad. See p573 for more on interisland flights.

Sea

Interisland ferries to Moloka'i and Lana'i depart from Lahaina Harbor. For information on ferry schedules and ticket prices, see p442 for sailings of the *Moloka'i Princess* to Moloka'i and p427 for Expeditions' Maui–Lana'i ferry.

The Hawaii Superferry, which once connected Kahului and Honolulu, has ceased operations; for details, see the boxed text, p474.

GETTING AROUND

If you really want to explore Maui thoroughly, and reach off-the-beaten-path sights, you'll need to have your own wheels. Public transportation, while improving, is still limited to the main towns and tourist resorts.

Be aware that most main roads on Maui are called highways whether they're busy four-lane thoroughfares or just quiet country roads. What's more, islanders refer to highways by name, rarely by number. If you ask someone how to find Hwy 36, chances are they're going to stare at you blankly – ask for the Hana Hwy instead.

The most comprehensive road atlas available is *Ready Mapbook of Maui County,* which shows every road on the island and is sold in bookstores.

To/From the Airports

With either of the following Kahului Airport transfer services you can make advance reservations for your arrival to speed things along. Both have courtesy phones in the baggage-claim area.

Speedi Shuttle (☎ 871-7474, 877-242-5777; www .speedishuttle.com) is the largest airport-transfer

---

service on Maui. One advantage to Speedi is that they've converted to biodiesel using recycled vegetable oil to fuel their vehicles, so you'll be traveling green-friendly. Fares for one person from Kahului Airport cost $50 to Lahaina, $54 to Ka'anapali, $74 to Kapalua, $35 to Kihei and $40 to Wailea. Add $7 to $10 more per additional person.

Executive Shuttle (☎ 669-2300, 800-833-2303) is cheaper and sometimes less backlogged. Like Speedi, its price depends on the destination and the size of the group. For example, the cost for one person from Kahului Airport to Lahaina is $43, for two people $49.

Kahului Airport's taxi dispatchers are near the exit of the baggage-claim area. Approximate fares are: to Wailuku $20; to Pa'ia $25; to Kihei $40; and to Lahaina $75.

Taxi fares from the Kapalua/West Maui Airport average $18 to Ka'anapali and $25 to $35 for most other places along the west Maui coast. But check with your hotel first, as many resorts on the Ka'anapali coast offer free shuttles to/from the Kapalua/West Maui Airport.

Bicycle

Cyclists on Maui will face some challenges: narrow roads, an abundance of hills and mountains, and the same persistent winds that so delight windsurfers. Maui's stunning scenery will rev up hard-core cyclists, but casual riders hoping to use a bike as a primary source of transportation around the island may well find the conditions daunting.

However, getting around by bicycle within a small area can be a good option for the average rider. For example, the tourist enclave of Kihei is largely level and has cycle lanes on two main drags, S Kihei Rd and the Pi'ilani Hwy.

The full-color *Maui County Bicycle Map* ($6), available from bicycle shops, shows all the roads on Maui that have cycle lanes and gives other nitty-gritty details. Consider it essential if you intend to do your exploring by pedal power. For information on bicycle rentals, see specific destinations around the island.

Bus

With the exception of O'ahu, Maui has Hawaii's most extensive public bus system. But don't get too excited – the buses can take you between the main towns, but they're not going to get you to many of the prime out-of-the-way places, such as Haleakalā National

---

MAUI

Park, Hana or Makena's Big Beach. And some of the buses, like the one between Ma'alaea and Lahaina, make a direct beeline, passing trailheads and beaches without stopping.

Maui Bus (☎ 871-4838; www.mauicounty.gov/bus), the island's public bus system, operates a dozen routes, each of them daily. The main routes run once hourly throughout the day and several have schedules that dovetail with one another for convenient connections. The handiest buses for visitors are the routes Kahului–Lahaina, Kahului–Wailea, Kahului–Wailuku, Kahului–Pa'ia, Ma'alaea–Kihei, Lahaina–Ka'anapali and Ka'anapali–Napili. Fares are just $1 per ride. There are no transfers, however, so if your journey requires two separate buses, you'll have to buy a new ticket when you board the second bus. Monthly passes ($45) are also available.

Maui Bus also operates city loop routes in the towns of Lahaina, Wailuku and Kahului. These buses are mainly geared for local shoppers, but are free to everyone – just hop on.

All buses allow you to carry on only what fits under your seat or on your lap, so forget the surfboard.

In addition to the public buses, free resort shuttles take guests between hotels and restaurants in the Ka'anapali and Wailea areas.

Car & Motorcycle

See p576 for more information on the national car-rental chains, including their toll-free numbers and websites. **Alamo** (☎ 871-6235), **Avis** (☎ 871-7575), **Budget** (☎ 871-8811), **Dollar** (☎ 877-7227), **Hertz** (☎ 877-5167) and **National** (☎ 871-8851) all have booths at Kahului Airport. Alamo, Avis, Budget, Dollar and National also have offices on Hwy 30 in Ka'anapali and will pick you up at Kapalua/West Maui Airport. Dollar is the only rental agency serving Hana Airport.

In addition to the national chains, there are local car-rental agencies on the island. See p382 for rentals in Kihei and p368 in Kahului. For information on renting motorcycles, see p382 for Kihei and p355 for Ka'anapali.

Taxi

Companies with service throughout the island include **Royal Sedan & Taxi Service** (☎ 874-6900) and **Sunshine Cabs of Maui** (☎ 879-2220).

Tours

A handful of tour bus companies operate half-day and full-day sightseeing tours on Maui.

DRIVING DISTANCES & TIMES

Average driving times and distances from Kahului are as follows. Allow more time in the morning and late afternoon rush hours.

Destination	Miles	Time
Haleakalā Summit	36	1½hr
Hana	51	2hr
Ka'anapali	26	50min
Kapalua	32	1hr
Kihei	12	25min
Lahaina	23	45min
Makawao	14	30min
Makena	19	40min
'Ohe'o Gulch	61	2¾hr
Pa'ia	7	15min
Wailuku	3	15min

Roberts Hawaii (☎ 866-898-2591; www.roberts-hawaii.com; tours from $60-100), a giant among Hawaiian tour companies, typically offers the best prices and most variety. The most popular routes include day-long jaunts to Hana and a Haleakalā sunrise trip that takes in many of the Upcountry's sights. **Polynesian Adventure Tours** (☎ 877-4242, 800-622-3011; www.polyad.com; tours from $70-100) is the other big player and offers similar tours.

You'll pay a bit more but family-run **Ekahi Tours** (☎ 877-9775, 888-292-2422; www.ekahi.com; tours $95-135) offers similar runs with more local flavor and less canned commentary. Best of all it takes a deeper cultural slant on places visited, so you end up with more than just snapshots.

LAHAINA

pop 18,000

When you're ready for action, spring over to Lahaina. Wander its bustling streets awash with whaling-era sights, art galleries and trendy shops. Saunter down to the insanely picturesque harbor and hop on a catamaran for a whale watching cruise. Getting hungry? Some of Maui's top chef-driven restaurants line the shoreline vying for your attention. And the nightlife, while not exactly ripping, is nonetheless the island's hottest. Lahaina is a lot of things: touristy, yes; overly commercial, perhaps; busy, always. But you will never be bored.

HISTORY

In ancient times Lahaina housed a royal court for high chiefs and it was the breadbasket – or,

MAUI ITINERARIES

In Two Days
Start day one strolling the old whaling town of **Lahaina** (opposite), follow it with an afternoon whale watching cruise, then cap it off with a sunset dinner at one of Lahaina's fine waterfront restaurants. Still got jet lag? Good. On day two set the alarm early for the drive to **Haleakalā National Park** (p413) to catch a breathtaking sunrise and hike into the crater. On the way back, stop in **Pa'ia** (p388) for Maui's hippest café and shopping scene and to check on the surf action at **Ho'okipa Beach** (p388).

In Four Days
Plan your first two days as above. Day three winds past waterfalls galore on the most legendary drive in all Hawaii, the wildly beautiful **Road to Hana** (p392). It's going to be a big day – start early, bring a bathing suit and a sense of adventure. Day four is all about those gorgeous beaches. Begin by snorkeling with turtles at **Malu'aka Beach** (p385), followed by a picnic at magnificent **Big Beach** (p386). In the afternoon pop by **'Iao Valley State Park** (p371) to ogle central Maui's emerald gem, and then head over to **Kanaha Beach** (p365) for the sailboarding scene.

For Waterbabies
If you like your adventures wet, Maui dishes up the ultimate. Start with a plunge at **Molokini Crater** (p379) for dazzling snorkeling and diving. When you're ready to dip a paddle, launch your kayak at dolphin-rich **Makena Landing** (p385). For a taste of extreme sports, island style, try your hand kitesurfing at **Kite Beach** (p365) and windsurfing at nearby **Kanaha Beach** (p365). The adventure continues for bodysurfers in the smashing breaks of **DT Fleming Beach** (p358) and **Big Beach** (p386). What about surfing, you say. It takes newbies just two hours to be up and riding with lessons in **Lahaina** (p341). Surf pros head north to **Honolua Bay** (p358) for monster waves.

more accurately, the breadfruit basket – of west Maui. After Kamehameha the Great unified the islands he chose Lahaina as his base, and the capital remained there until 1845. The first Christian missionaries arrived in the 1820s and within a decade Hawaii's first stone church, first missionary school and first printing press were all in place in Lahaina.

Lahaina became the dominant port for whalers, not only in Hawaii but for the entire Pacific. The whaling years reached a peak in Lahaina in the 1840s, with hundreds of ships pulling into port each year. The town took on the whalers' boisterous nature, opening dance halls, bars and brothels. When the whaling industry fizzled in the 1860s, Lahaina all but became a ghost town. In the 1870s sugarcane came to Lahaina and it remained the backbone of the economy until tourism took over in the 1960s.

ORIENTATION
The focal point of Lahaina is its harbor and the adjacent Banyan Tree Sq. The main drag and tourist strip is Front St, which runs along the shoreline. Most of Lahaina's top sights, restaurants and entertainment venues are either on Front St or within a couple of blocks of it.

INFORMATION
Bookstores
Barnes & Noble (☎ 662-1300; Lahaina Gateway, cnr Keawe St & Honoapi'ilani Hwy) The island's largest bookstore has a first-rate Hawaii section.
Old Lahaina Book Emporium (☎ 661-1399; 834 Front St; ☒ 10am-7pm) Bookworms, you're in for a feast at Maui's finest independent bookstore: new and used volumes plus vintage Hawaiiana.

Emergency
Police (☎ 244-6400) For nonemergencies.
Police, Fire & Ambulance (☎ 911)

Internet Access
Buns of Maui (☎ 661-5407; Old Lahaina Center, 880 Front St; per min 8c; ☒ 7:30am-6pm) You'll find Maui's cheapest internet at this little café named for its delish cinnamon rolls.
Livewire Café (☎ 661-4213; 612 Front St; per 20min $3; ☒ 6am-9pm Mon-Sat, 7am-9pm Sun) Convenient location, good karma and coffee.

Laundry
Coin laundry (Limahana Pl; ☒ 24hr) Opposite the bakery.

LAHAINA

0 ——————— 500 m
0 ——————— 0.3 miles

INFORMATION
American Savings Bank............1 B4
Barnes & Noble.......................2 B2
Buns of Maui.......................(see 55)
Coin Laundry..........................3 B3
Downtown Post Office Station.4 B4
First Hawaiian Bank.................5 B3
Lahaina Public Library.............6 B5
Lahaina Visitor Center.............7 B5
Livewire Café..........................8 C5
Longs Drugs.......................(see 59)
Maui Medical Group................9 C5
Old Lahaina Book Emporium..10 B4

SIGHTS & ACTIVITIES
Atlantis Submarine...............(see 62)
Baldwin House.......................11 B5
Banyan Tree Gallery..............(see 7)
Banyan Tree Square...............12 B5
Bikram Yoga Lahaina............(see 52)
Brick Palace.........................(see 6)
Fort.......................................13 B5
Goofy Foot Surf School.........(see 57)

Hale Kahiko..........................14 B3
Hale Pa'ahao........................15 C5
Hale Piula............................16 C5
Hauola Stone........................17 B5
Holy Innocents' Episcopal
  Church...............................18 C5
Lahaina Breakwall.................19 B5
Lahaina Divers......................20 B4
Lahaina Heritage Museum.....(see 7)
Lahaina Jodo Mission............21 A3
Lahaina Lighthouse...............22 B5
Lahaina Public Library.........(see 6)
Maria Lanakila Church...........23 C4
Masters' Reading Room..........24 B4
Maui Dive Shop....................(see 2)
Moku'ula.............................25 C5
Old Lahaina Courthouse........(see 7)
Pacific Dive...........................26 C4
Pacific Whale Foundation......27 C5
Reefdancer..........................(see 62)
Royal Hawaiian Surf
  Academy............................28 C5
Seamen's Cemetery...............29 C4
Trilogy Excursions.................30 B4
Waine'e Church & Cemetery..31 C5
Wo Hing Museum..................32 B4

SLEEPING
Lahaina Inn...........................33 B4
Lahaina Shores......................34 C6
Makai Inn.............................35 A1
Pioneer Inn...........................36 B5
Plantation Inn.......................37 B4

EATING
Aloha Mixed Plate.................38 A2
Bakery..................................39 B3
Foodland............................(see 55)
Gerard's..............................(see 37)
I'O......................................(see 57)
Kahuna Kabobs.....................40 B4
Kimo's.................................41 B4
Lahaina Fish Co....................42 B4
Lahaina Grill.......................(see 33)
Mala Ocean Tavern...............43 A2
Maui Tacos...........................44 B4
Pacific'O.............................(see 57)
Penne Pasta Café...................45 C4
Safeway..............................(see 59)
Smokehouse BBQ Grill...........46 B3
Sunrise Café.........................47 B5
Thai Chef............................(see 55)
Ululani's Hawaiian Shave Ice.48 B4

DRINKING
Aloha Mixed Plate...............(see 38)
Bamboo Sports Bar...............(see 57)
Cool Cat Café.......................(see 61)
Front Street Grill...................49 C5
Lahaina Coolers....................50 C4
Pioneer Inn.........................(see 36)

ENTERTAINMENT
BJ's......................................51 B4
Feast at Lele.........................(see 57)
Hale Kahiko.........................(see 14)
Hard Rock Cafe.....................52 B4
Lahaina Cannery Mall...........(see 59)
Lahaina Store Grille & Oyster
  Bar.....................................53 B4
Moose McGillicuddy's............54 B4
Mulligans at the Wharf ....(see 61)
Old Lahaina Center...............55 B4
Old Lahaina Luau..................56 A2
'Ulalena.............................(see 55)

SHOPPING
505 Front Street....................57 C6
Aloha Shirt Museum.............(see 53)
Crazy Shirts..........................58 B4
Lahaina Arts Society.............(see 7)
Lahaina Cannery Mall............59 A2
Lahaina Printsellers..............(see 57)
MauiGrown Coffee.................60 C4
Needlework Shop.................(see 57)
Village Gifts & Fine Arts.......(see 24)
Wharf Cinema Center............61 C5

TRANSPORT
Lahaina Harbor.....................62 B5
West Maui Cycles..................63 B3

MAUI

To Lahaina Post Office
(0.8mi); Ka'anapali
(1.5mi); Kapalua/West
Maui Airport (3.5mi)

Fleming Rd

Honoapi'ilani Hwy

Ainakea St

Kapunakea St

Mala
Wharf

Front St

Keawe St

Ala Moana St

Puunoa Pl

Kenui St

Hinau St

Baker St

Sugar Cane Train

Limahana Pl

Lahaina
Station

Lahainaluna Rd

To Hale
Pa'i (1.2mi)

PACIFIC
OCEAN

Lahaina
Center

Papalaua St

Waine'e St

Lahainaluna Rd

Honoapi'ilani Hwy

Ferry to Moloka'i

Ferry to Lana'i

Dickenson St

Luakini St

Prison St

Wharf St

Malu'uluolele
Park

Kamehameha
Iki Park

Shaw St

Front St

'Au'au Channel

To Launiupoko
Beach Park (1mi);
Olowalu (5mi);
Ma'alaea (14mi);
Maui Memorial
Medical Center (26mi)

RIGHTEOUS & ROWDY

Lahaina owes much of its period appearance to two diametrically opposed groups of New Englanders who landed in the 1820s. In 1823 William Richards, Lahaina's first missionary, converted Maui's native governor, Hoapili, to Christianity and persuaded him to pass laws against 'drunkenness and debauchery.' After months at sea, however, sailors weren't looking for a prayer service when they pulled into port – to them there was 'no God west of the Horn.' Missionaries and whalers almost came to battle in 1827 when Governor Hoapili arrested a whaler captain for allowing women to board his ship. The crew retaliated by shooting cannonballs at Richards' house. The captain was released, but laws forbidding liaisons between seamen and Hawaiian women remained in force.

It wasn't until Governor Hoapili's death in 1840 that laws prohibiting liquor and prostitution were no longer enforced and whalers began to flock to Lahaina. Among the sailors who roamed Lahaina's streets was Herman Melville, who later penned *Moby Dick*.

Libraries

Lahaina Public Library (☎ 662-3950; 680 Wharf St; ⏲ noon-8pm Tue, 9am-5pm Wed & Thu, 12:30-4:30pm Fri & Sat)

Media

Lahaina News (☎ 667-7866; www.lahainanews.com) This free weekly, easily found around town, has the scoop on Lahaina's entertainment scene & local issues.

Medical Services

The Maui Memorial Medical Center in Wailuku (p368) is the nearest hospital in case of emergencies.

Longs Drugs (☎ 667-4384; Lahaina Cannery Mall, 1221 Honoapi'ilani Hwy; ⏲ 7am-midnight) Lahaina's largest pharmacy.

Maui Medical Group (☎ 249-8080; 130 Prison St; ⏲ 8am-9pm Mon-Fri, 8am-noon Sat & Sun) This clinic handles nonemergencies.

Money

Both banks have 24-hour ATMs.

American Savings Bank (☎ 667-9561; 154 Papalaua St)

First Hawaiian Bank (☎ 661-3655; 215 Papalaua St)

Post

Downtown post office station (Old Lahaina Center, 32 Papalaua St; ⏲ 8:15am-4:15pm Mon-Fri) Central if you're in town, but longer lines and fewer parking spaces than Lahaina Post Office.

Lahaina Post Office (☎ 661-0904; 1760 Honoapi'ilani Hwy, Lahaina, HI 96761; ⏲ 8:30am-5pm Mon-Fri, 9am-1pm Sat) You'll have to go to this post office north of town near the Lahaina Civic Center to pick up general-delivery mail (held 30 days) sent to Lahaina.

Tourist Information

Lahaina Visitor Center (☎ 667-9193; www.visitlahaina.com; 648 Wharf St; ⏲ 9am-5pm) The gift shop in the Old Lahaina Courthouse doubles as the visitor information center and distributes a free Lahaina pocket guide.

SIGHTS

Many of Lahaina's sightseeing attractions date to the whaling era and include the homes of missionaries, prisons for sailors and graveyards of both. See p342 for a recommended walking tour that takes them all in.

Banyan Tree Square

Forget water fountains and war memorials – the centerpiece of Lahaina's town square is the USA's largest banyan tree. And what a sight it is! Planted as a sapling on April 24, 1873, the tree now sprawls across the entire square, a virtual forest unto itself with 16 major trunks and scores of horizontal branches reaching across nearly an acre. This magnificent tree is so revered that throngs of townsfolk gather each year just to celebrate its birthday. When it's not hosting a party it makes a shady respite from the crowds on Front St. Grab a bench and enjoy the scene.

Old Lahaina Courthouse

Lahaina's **old courthouse** (648 Wharf St; ⏲ 9am-5pm), built in 1859, packs a wealth of history. It's no coincidence that it overlooks Lahaina's bustling harbor. Smuggling was so rampant during the whaling era that officials decided this was the perfect spot to house the customs operations, the courthouse and the jail – all neatly wrapped into a single building. It also held the governor's office and in 1898 the US annexation of Hawaii was formally concluded here.

The old jail in the basement has been turned into a gallery for the **Lahaina Arts Society** (p347) and the cells that once held drunken sailors now display fine artwork, making for fun browsing.

Lahaina Heritage Museum (☎ 667-1959; admission free; ☺ 9am-5pm) celebrates Lahaina's culture and history through changing exhibits. The focus could be on anything from ancient Hawaiians to 19th-century whaling, but whatever it is it's well worth hopping the stairs to the 2nd floor to check it out. And don't overlook the fascinating period photos of Lahaina in the 2nd floor hallway.

Wo Hing Museum

The most colorful building in town, this **museum** (☎ 661-5553; 858 Front St; admission $1; ☺ 10am-4pm) was originally a meeting hall and temple for the Chinese benevolent society Chee Kung Tong, providing Chinese immigrants with a place to preserve their cultural identity. After WWII Lahaina's Chinese population spread far and wide and the temple fell into decline. Now restored and turned into a cultural museum, it houses period displays and a Taoist shrine.

Whatever you do, don't miss the tin-roof cookhouse out the back, which holds a little theater showing fascinating films of Hawaii shot by Thomas Edison in 1898, soon after he invented the motion-picture camera. These grainy B&W shots capture poignant images of old Hawaii, with *paniolo* (Hawaiian cowhands) herding cattle, cane workers in the fields and everyday street scenes. Take a look at the wall behind the screen to find a collection of opium bottles unearthed during an excavation of the grounds.

Hale Pa'ahao

A curious remnant of the whaling days, this old **prison** (☎ 667-1985; cnr Prison & Waine'e Sts; admission free; ☺ 10am-4pm Mon-Sat) was built in 1852 by convicts who dismantled a harborside fort and carted the stones here to construct the 8ft-high prison walls. Hale Pa'ahao means 'Stuck-in-Irons House.'

Inside one of the whitewashed cells you'll find an 'old seadog' mannequin spouting a recorded description of 'life in this here calaboose.' Another cell displays a list of arrests for the year 1855. Top offenses were drunkenness (330 arrests), adultery and fornication (111) and 'furious riding' (89). Other wayward transgressions included profanity, aiding deserting sailors and drinking *'awa* (kava moonshine).

Baldwin House

The oldest Western-style building in Lahaina is the **Baldwin House** (☎ 661-3262; 696 Front St; adult/family $3/5; ☺ 10am-4pm). It was erected in 1834 by Reverend Dwight Baldwin, a missionary doctor. It served as both his home and Lahaina's first medical clinic. The coral and rock walls are a hefty 24in thick, which keeps the house cool year-round. The exterior walls are now plastered over, but you can get a sense of how they originally appeared by looking at the Masters' Reading Room next door.

Think your flight to Hawaii was long? It took the Baldwins 161 days to get here from their native Connecticut. These early missionaries traveled neither fast nor light, and the house still holds the collection of china and furniture they brought with them around the Horn.

Waine'e (Waiola) Church

Dating to 1832, Hawaii's first stone church, **Waine'e Church** (535 Waine'e St), was cursed with bad luck. The steeple collapsed in 1858. In 1894 royalists, enraged that the minister supported Hawaii's annexation, torched it to the ground. A second church, built to replace the original, burned in 1947, and the third was blown away in a storm a few years later. One might get the impression that the ancient Hawaiian gods didn't take kindly to the house of this foreign deity! The fourth version, now renamed Waiola Church, has been standing since 1953 and still holds Sunday services.

The adjacent **cemetery** holds as much intrigue as the church. Here lie several notables: Reverend William Richards, Lahaina's first missionary; Governor Hoapili, who ordered the original church built; and Queen Ke'opuolani, wife of Kamehameha the Great and the mother of kings Kamehameha II and III.

Library Grounds

History doesn't exist just in books at the **Lahaina Public Library** (p339). Although they don't reveal themselves at first glance, the grounds here hold a cluster of historic sites. The library yard was once a royal taro field, where Kamehameha III toiled in the mud to instill in his subjects the dignity of labor.

On the ocean side of the library sat the first Western-style building in Hawaii, the **Brick Palace**, erected by Kamehameha the Great around 1800 so he could keep watch on arriving ships. Despite the name, this 'palace' was a simple two-story structure built by a pair of ex-convicts from Botany Bay. All that remains today is the excavated foundation.

Walk to the nearby shoreline to see the **Hauola Stone**, a flat seat-shaped rock that early Hawaiians believed emitted healing powers to those who sat upon it. To spot this water-worn stone, look to the right as you face the ocean – it's just above the water's surface, the middle of three lava stones. In the 14th and 15th centuries royal women sat on the stone while giving birth to the next generation of chiefs and royalty.

About 100ft to the south stands the **Lahaina Lighthouse**, the site of the first lighthouse in the Pacific. Commissioned in 1840 to aid whaling ships pulling into Lahaina, it shone with a beam fueled by sperm-whale oil. The current structure dates from 1916.

Hale Kahiko

The three thatched houses at **Hale Kahiko** (Lahaina Center, 900 Front St; admission free; 9am-6pm) replicate a slice of an ancient Hawaiian village. The location at the back of a shopping center is not without its irony, but the site nonetheless offers an insightful glimpse of Hawaiian life before Western development swept through the landscape.

The *hale* (houses) were hand-constructed true to the period using ohia-wood posts, native pili grass thatch and coconut-fiber lashings. The grounds are planted in the types of native flora that Hawaiians relied upon for food and medicinal purposes. Each *hale* had a different function; one was used as the family sleeping quarters, one as a men's eating house, and the third as a workshop where women made tapa. Inside you'll find gourd containers, poi pounders and other essentials of Hawaiian life.

Hale Pa'i

Hawaii's first printing press was at **Hale Pa'i** (667-7040; 980 Lahainaluna Rd; admission by donation; 10am-4pm Mon-Fri), a cottage adjacent to Lahainaluna High School. Although its primary mission was making the Bible available to Hawaiians, the press produced many other works, including the first Hawaiian botany book and, in 1834, Hawaii's first newspaper.

So heavily used was the original Ramage press that it wore out in the 1850s, but several of the items printed from it are still on display.

Should you want to try your hand as a 19th-century pressman, a replica of the original equipment can be used to hand-press your own copy of a page from the first Hawaiian primer. Reprints of amusing 'Temperance Maps' ($5) drawn by an early missionary to illustrate the perils of drunkenness make unusual souvenirs.

Lahaina Jodo Mission

Enjoy a meditative moment at this **Buddhist mission** (12 Ala Moana St; admission free) where a 12ft-high bronze Buddha sits serenely in the courtyard looking out across the Pacific toward its Japanese homeland. Cast in Kyoto, the Buddha is the largest of its kind outside Japan and was installed here in 1968 to celebrate the centennial of Japanese immigration to Hawaii. The grounds contain a lofty pagoda and a 3-ton temple bell, which is rung 11 times every evening at 8pm.

ACTIVITIES

Lahaina is not known for its beaches, which are generally shallow and rocky. For swimming and snorkeling, head up the coast to neighboring Ka'anapali (p351). For whale watching and other boat tours, see p343.

Diving

Dive boats leave from Lahaina Harbor, with programs suited for all levels.

Lahaina Divers (667-7496, 800-998-3483; www.lahainadivers.com; 143 Dickenson St; 2-tank dives from $129; 8am-8pm), Maui's first PADI five-star center, offers a full menu of dives, from advanced night dives to 'discover scuba' dives for newbies. The latter goes out to a reef thick with green turtles and makes a great intro to the sport.

Maui Dive Shop (661-5388, 800-542-3483; www.mauidiveshop.com; Lahaina Gateway, cnr Keawe St & Honoapi'ilani Hwy; 2-tank boat dives from $140; 7am-9pm) is another reliable full-service operation with a dive geared for everyone.

Contact **Pacific Dive** (667-5331; www.pacificdive.com; 150 Dickenson St; shore dives from $59; 8am-6pm) if you just want an inexpensive dive from the beach.

Surfing

If you've never surfed before, Lahaina's the perfect place to learn, with skilled instructors, gentle waves and ideal conditions for beginners. The section of shoreline known as **Lahaina Breakwall**, north of Kamehameha Iki Park, is a favorite for novices. Surfers also take to the waters at Launiupoko Beach Park (p348).

Several places in Lahaina offer surfing lessons. Most guarantee you'll be able to ride a wave after a two-hour lesson, or there's no charge. Rates vary depending upon the number of people and the length of the class, but for a two-hour lesson expect to pay about $65 in a small group, $150 for a private lesson.

Goofy Foot Surf School (☎ 244-9283; www.goofyfootsurfschool.com; 505 Front St; ☟ 7:30am-9pm Mon-Sat) does a fine job of combining fundamentals with fun. In addition to lessons, it runs daylong surf camps and rents boards to experienced surfers.

Besides honing a solid reputation for its instruction, **Royal Hawaiian Surf Academy** (☎ 276-7873; 117 Prison St; ☟ 8am-5pm) has the coolest T-shirts. Look familiar? MTV focused its lens on Royal Hawaiian's surf instructors for its *Living Lahaina* reality series.

Yoga

If it's time to stretch, bring your mat and pop in to **Bikram Yoga Lahaina** (☎ 661-6828; www.bikramyoga.com; Lahaina Center, 900 Front St; class $16; ☟ schedule varies). Classes include a daily morning session at 8am (9am Sunday).

WALKING TOUR

Chockablock with historic sites, Lahaina just begs you to stroll around it.

Begin at **Banyan Tree Sq** (1; p339), taking in the Old Lahaina Courthouse (p339) and eclectic harbor sights. Quirkiest are the four waterfront cannons raised from an 1816 shipwreck that in a comical twist now point at Lahaina's small-boat harbor, which is jam-packed with sunset sailboats and windjammers.

At the corner of Wharf and Canal Sts stands a partial coral-block wall from an 1832 **fort** (2) built to keep rowdy whalers in line. Each day at dusk a Hawaiian sentinel beat a drum to alert sailors to return to their ships. Those who didn't make it back in time ended up imprisoned in the fort.

Continue up Canal St, which takes its name from the canal system that once ran through Lahaina. An enterprising US consul officer built the canal in the 1840s to allow whalers easier access to freshwater supplies – for a fee, of course. The canal turned into a breeding ground for mosquitoes, so it was eventually

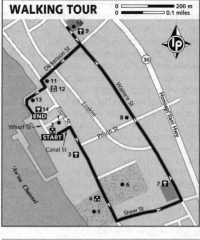

WALKING TOUR

0 ————— 200 m
0 ————— 0.1 miles

WALK FACTS

Start Banyan Tree Sq
Finish Pioneer Inn
Distance 1.5 miles
Duration 2-3 hours

filled in. The mosquito, incidentally, was introduced to Hawaii via the water barrels the whalers brought from North America.

Turn right on Front St to reach **Holy Innocents' Episcopal Church** (3; 561 Front St), which has a colorful interior depicting a Hawaiian Madonna, an outrigger canoe and Hawaiian farmers harvesting taro. The site was once a summer home of Hawaii's last monarch, Queen Lili'uokalani. South of the church you'll find a foundation, all that remains of **Hale Piula** (4), Lahaina's halfhearted attempt at a royal palace. It was abandoned in mid-construction because Kamehameha III preferred sleeping in a Hawaiian-style thatched house. The site, fronted by **Kamehameha Iki Park** (5), is now used by local woodcarvers to build traditional outrigger canoes.

Across the street is **Malu'uluolele Park** (6), which once held a pond-encircled island, Moku'ula, that was home to ancient kings and the site of an ornate burial chamber. In 1918 it was landfilled to make a county park containing ball fields, tennis courts and barely a hint of its fascinating past.

Turn left on Shaw St, then left on Waine'e St to reach **Waine'e Church** (7; p340). Stroll through the church's old cemetery, where several of the most pivotal figures in 19th-century Maui are buried. Evocative inscriptions and photo cameos adorn many of the old tombstones.

You'll find one of Lahaina's more notorious sights, **Hale Pa'ahao (8**; p340), on the corner of – guess where – Prison St. Take a peek into the old prison cells where drunken whalers once served time for debauchery.

Continue north along Waine'e St to reach the c 1846 **Maria Lanakila Church (9)**, Maui's first Catholic church. The adjacent **Seamen's Cemetery (10)**, despite its name, has only one seaman's tombstone identified. However, ship logs indicate that many whaling-era sailors were buried here, including a shipmate of Herman Melville's from the *Acushnet*.

Heading back toward the waterfront, on the corner of Front and Dickenson Sts, you'll reach the **Masters' Reading Room (11)**. This was an officers club during the whaling heyday, where captains could watch out for potential rabble-rousing in the nearby harbor. This coral block building and the adjacent **Baldwin House (12**; p340) museum now belong to the Lahaina Restoration Foundation, which oversees Lahaina's historical sites.

Return to the harbor, stopping to view the **Brick Palace (13**; p340) and the Hauola Stone at the rear of the library.

Cap off your tour with a cold brew at the atmospheric **Pioneer Inn (14**; p346), the most prominent landmark on the harborfront. For half a century this veranda-wrapped building was Lahaina's only hotel; Jack London slept here. Despite its whaling-era atmosphere, with swinging doors and ship figureheads, it was actually built in 1901, after the whaling days had passed, but nobody seems to notice or care.

LAHAINA FOR CHILDREN

Kids love that awesome banyan tree (p339), whose dangling aerial roots invite at least one Tarzan-style swing. Little tots will want to ride the Sugar Cane Train (below). The rest of the clan can take the plunge with a surfing lesson from kid-friendly Goofy Foot Surf School (p341). Prefer to go deeper? Atlantis Submarines (below) turns the ocean into a dazzling aquarium.

TOURS

Lahaina Harbor abounds with catamarans and other vessels catering to the tourist trade.

You'll find scores of day cruises, from whale-watchers and glass-bottomed boats to daylong sails to Lana'i.

Atlantis Submarines (☎ 667-2224, 800-548-6262; www.atlantisadventures.com; adult/child under 12 $90/45) See the world from a porthole aboard this 65ft sub that dives to a depth of 130ft to see coral, tropical fish and the sunken *Carthaginian*, the sailing brig that played a role in the 1965 movie *Hawaii*. Tours depart from 9am to 2pm from Lahaina Harbor.

Pacific Whale Foundation (☎ 879-8811, 800-942-5311; www.pacificwhale.org; 612 Front St; adult/child 7-12 from $32/16; ☼ 7am-6pm) The well-versed naturalists on this nonprofit foundation's cruises are Maui's best. Immensely popular are the whale watching cruises that sail out of Lahaina Harbor several times daily in winter. In the unlikely event you don't spot whales, your next trip is free. It also offers wild dolphin ecoadventures and snorkel tours year-round.

Reefdancer (☎ 667-2133; Lahaina Harbor; adult/child 6-12 per 1hr $33/20, 1½hr $45/25; ☼ departures 10am-2:15pm) This glass-bottomed boat has a submerged lower deck lined with windows. The views aren't as varied as on a submarine but the underwater scenes are still eye candy and you won't feel claustrophobic.

Sugar Cane Train (☎ 667-6851; www.mauisteamtrain.com; 975 Limahana Pl; adult/child 3-12 $22/15; ☼ 8am-5pm) The restored, century-old steam train that once carried cane from the fields to Lahaina's sugar mill now carries tourists on an hour-long trip between Lahaina and Ka'anapali. The ride's a bit poky and there's not really much to see, but kids will love it and steam-train buffs will no doubt want to hop aboard.

our pick **Trilogy Excursions** (☎ 661-4743, 888-225-6284; www.sailtrilogy.com; 180 Lahainaluna Rd; adult/child 3-15 $190/95) This first-rate operation specializes in eco-friendly catamaran tours to Lana'i that let you get your feet wet. The 6am trip from Lahaina to Lana'i's Hulopo'e Beach includes a BBQ lunch, beach volleyball and snorkel time; the 10am boat adds on dinner and sails back to Lahaina at sunset. In winter there's whale watching along the way.

FESTIVALS & EVENTS

Mauians love a party and Lahaina is party central. The top festivals draw huge crowds, with Front St closed to traffic during the events. For updated details on festivities, contact the **LahainaTown Action Committee** (☎ 667-9194, 888-310-1117; www.visitlahaina.com).

Chinese New Year On a weekend between mid-January and mid-February, Lahaina welcomes the lunar new year with a street festival on Front St, complete with colorful lion dances, martial-arts demos and an explosion of firecrackers.

Ocean Arts Festival The humpback whale migration is the theme of these festivities celebrated on a weekend in mid-March at Banyan Tree Sq with Hawaiian music, hula and games.

Banyan Tree Birthday Party Lahaina's favorite tree gets a two-day birthday party on the weekend closest to April 24, complete with a frosted cake and a serenade by island musicians. Kids will love the piñata smash.

International Festival of Canoes (www.mauica noefest.com) Maui's signature cultural event draws master carvers from around the Pacific to carve outrigger canoes. The whole log-to-launch process takes place right in the town center over two weeks in May, culminating with the Parade of Canoes down Front St and ceremonial launchings from Kamehameha Iki Park. Festivities include Hawaiian music and island grinds. Don't miss it.

Na Kamehameha Pa'u Parade & Ho'olaule'a Traditionally dressed Hawaiians on horseback, marching bands and floral floats take to Front St to honor Kamehameha the Great on this public holiday in mid-June. Festivities follow at Banyan Tree Sq.

Fourth of July Bands perform on the lawn of the public library from 5pm and fireworks light up the sky over the harbor at 8pm.

Halloween in Lahaina Once a huge bash dubbed 'Mardi Gras of the Pacific,' this street festival along Front St has been scaled back, but it's still *the* place to revel on October 31.

Holiday Lighting of the Banyan Tree Lahaina lights Hawaii's biggest tree on the first weekend in December with thousands of colorful lights, accompanied by musicians, carolers and a craft show. And, of course, Santa shows up for the *keiki* (children).

SLEEPING

Despite the flood of tourists filling Lahaina's streets, the town offers surprisingly few places to stay. All of west Maui's resort hotels are to the north, where the beaches are better. On the plus side, Lahaina's accommodations tend to be cozy and in tune with the town's historic character. The nearest campground (p350) is in Olowalu, 5 miles south of town. See p351 for midrange B&Bs between Lahaina and Ka'anapali.

Makai Inn (☎ 662-3200; www.makaiinn.net; 1415 Front St; r $105-180; P 💻) This family-run place is a gem, albeit not a highly polished one. It's an older condo and some of the furnishings could use a bit more luster, but it's got a pretty tropical garden and the oceanfront setting sparkles. All units have full kitchens. Price differences reflect the distance from the ocean, but even the cheapest rooms are a mere stone's throw from the water.

our pick Lahaina Inn (☎ 661-0577, 800-669-3444; www.lahainainn.com; 127 Lahainaluna Rd; r $150-170, ste $205; P 🔲 🛜) Forget cookie-cutter resorts – if you want an authentic taste of Lahaina book a room at this boutique hotel. Lahaina Inn was a labor of love by Crazy Shirts founder Rick Ralston, who spent millions painstakingly restoring this century-old place to its original character. The charm of an earlier era shines through in the hardwood floors, hand-stitched Hawaiian quilts and antique furnishings. No TV but you can sit in a rocking chair on the lanai and watch Lahaina unfold in the streets below.

Pioneer Inn (☎ 661-3636, 800-457-5457; www.pioneer innmaui.com; 658 Wharf St; r $160-215; 🔲 🛏) This historic harborfront hotel packs so much whaling-era personality you almost expect Herman Melville to mosey in. While the common space abounds in character, the rooms are disappointingly bland and lacking water views. But heck, you're in the hub of Lahaina, so who's hanging out in a room?

Plantation Inn (☎ 667-9225, 800-433-6815; www .theplantationinn.com; 174 Lahainaluna Rd; r incl breakfast $179-250, ste $275-300; P 🔲 🛜 🛏) Quiet yet central, this plantation-style inn fuses period elegance with modern amenities. The guest rooms are decked out in frilly Victorian decor with four-poster beds and matching upholstery and wallpaper. French doors open to balustered verandas and in the courtyard Lahaina's deepest swimming pool invites a dive.

Lahaina Shores (☎ 661-3339, 800-642-6284; www .lahainashores.com; 475 Front St; studios/1br from $189/290; P 🔲 🛏) The only oceanfront condo complex in Lahaina that's run hotel-style with a front desk and full services. Guests are next door to some of Lahaina's top restaurants, and the beach out the back offers night entertainment and good conditions for beginner surfers. The units are roomy, and even the studios have full kitchen and lanai.

EATING

Whether you're looking for tasty local grinds or five-toque nouvelle cuisine, it's all here. Just be aware that so many folks staying in Ka'anapali pour into Lahaina at dinnertime that the traffic jams up, so give yourself extra time and call ahead for reservations.

Budget

The Bakery (☎ 667-9062; 991 Limahana Pl; snacks $1.50-6, 🕐 5:30am-12:30pm Mon-Fri, to noon Sat) Lahaina's finest bakery is in a nondescript industrial park, but don't let that deter you. On the other side of the rickety screen door you'll find sinfully sweet pastries, crispy croissants and generously heaped sandwiches made to order.

Ululani's Hawaiian Shave Ice (819 Front St; shave ice $3.50-4.50; 11am-9:30pm) Cool off your afternoon with a heaping of fluffy shave ice dripping in a rainbow of tropical flavors.

Maui Tacos (661-8883; Lahaina Sq, 840 Waine'e St; mains $4-9; 9am-9pm) Here's proof that Mexican fare can be island-style healthy. The salsas and beans are prepared fresh daily, transfat-free oil replaces lard, and fresh veggies and local fish highlight the menu. Order the Ho'okipa surf burrito to see just how good it gets.

Sunrise Café (661-8558; 693-A Front St; mains $6-11; 6am-4:30pm) The dawn patrol loves this cozy mom-and-pop place near the harbor. Breakfasts (served till closing) have pizzazz: try the smoked salmon with eggs, Maui onions and lemon-caper hollandaise, or indulge in the decadent chocolate pancakes. The lunch menu covers the gamut from gourmet sandwiches to roast beef plates.

our pick Aloha Mixed Plate (661-3322; 1285 Front St; plates $6-14; 10:30am-10pm) Simply put, the best place on Maui to enjoy a Hawaiian-style meal in a beachside setting. Go local with the Ali'i Plate brimming with all manner of tasty traditional fare. Then there's the fab coconut prawns with pineapple chutney – order them as a *pupu* (snack) or as part of a mixed plate, but don't go away without trying them.

Smokehouse BBQ Grill (667-7005; 930 Waine'e St; mains $7-20; 11:30am-9pm Mon-Fri, 3-9pm Sat & Sun) Kiawe-smoked meats slow-cooked to perfection are the specialty at this family-run joint. Everybody orders the tender, meaty baby-back ribs, but the *kalua* (cooked in an underground pit) pork sandwiches are also excellent and the cornbread served warm with mac-nut honey is not to be missed.

Kahuna Kabobs (661-9999; 884 Front St; mains $8-15; 9am-9:30pm) Tucked into a courtyard off Front St, this hole-in-the-wall eatery rakes in the surfers with its killer blackened-ahi kebabs. There's lots of other options for both carnivores and vegetarians ranging from *kalua* pork to 'veggie hipster' falafel wraps.

Penne Pasta Café (661-6633; 180 Dickenson St; mains $8-17; 11am-9:30pm Mon-Fri, 5-9pm Sat & Sun) There's no view, and that's the key. To keep it affordable, chef Mark Ellman of Mala fame chose a side street location for this one and streamlined the menu. That said, the food's

anything but boring: garlic ahi atop pesto linguine, roasted beets with sesame butter and, of course, creamy tiramisu for dessert.

Thai Chef (667-2814; Old Lahaina Center, 880 Front St; mains $10-16; 11am-2pm Mon-Fri & 5-9pm daily) It may look like a dive from the outside, but this little place at the back of a shopping center has incredible food. Start with the crispy spring rolls served with pineapple dipping sauce and then move on to savory curries that explode with flavor. No alcohol on the menu but you can BYOB – pick up a bottle from the nearby Foodland.

Foodland (661-0975; Old Lahaina Center, 880 Front St; 6am-midnight) and **Safeway** (667-4392; Lahaina Cannery Mall, 1221 Honoapi'ilani Hwy; 24hr) supermarkets both have delis stocking all you need for a picnic lunch.

Midrange

Mala Ocean Tavern (667-9394; 1307 Front St; mains $15-30; 11am-10pm Mon-Fri, 9am-10pm Sat, 9am-9pm Sun) Pacific and Mediterranean influences fuse lusciously at this seaside bistro. Tapas like spiced lamb tzatziki and the crispy calamari steal the stage. Anything with fish is a sure pleaser, and the decadent 'caramel miranda' makes a sweet finale fit for two. Best time to come is at sunset, when you can watch turtles feeding and tiki torches light the lanai.

Lahaina Fish Co (661-3472; 831 Front St; lunch $9-15, dinner $16-30; 11am-10pm) Perched on a balcony above the surf you could practically drop a line and catch your own fish. But why wait for a bite? Just sit back and order. The seafood is fresh, the servings generous, so it's little wonder this place packs a crowd. Come early for a good table at sunset.

Kimo's (661-4811; 845 Front St; lunch $10-13, dinner $20-30; 11am-10:30pm) At this Hawaiian-style standby, you'll find reliable food, a superb water view and a family-friendly setting. Dishes include fresh fish, oversized prime ribs and good ol' teriyaki chicken. And you get your money's worth: all dinners come with Caesar salad and warm carrot muffins. Lunch ranges far and wide, from salads and sandwiches to seafood specials.

Top End

Pacific'O (667-4341; 505 Front St; lunch $13-16, dinner $26-38; 11:30am-4pm & 5:30-10pm) Contemporary regional cuisine with added bling jumps off the menu at this chic seaside restaurant. The dishes are bold and innovative – where else

MAUI

can you try a crispy coconut roll with seared scallops and arugula-lime pesto? Lunch is a tamer affair, with salads and sandwiches, but the same in-your-face ocean view. Live dinnertime jazz on the weekends cranks the hip atmosphere up a notch.

our pick I'O (☎ 661-8422; 505 Front St; mains $28-38; ☻ 5:30-10pm) If you're looking for Lahaina's best waterfront fine dining, stop the search here. The handiwork of chef James McDonald features Hawaii Regional Cuisine with scrumptious creations like seared fresh catch in mango cream, island-raised filet mignon with tempura Maui onions and guava-glazed coconut cheesecake. McDonald is so obsessed with freshness that he started an organic farm in Kula to grow his own veggies.

Lahaina Grill (☎ 667-5117; 127 Lahainaluna Rd; mains $28-45; ☻ 6-9:30pm) Beautiful people, beautiful food – this dinner restaurant at the historic Lahaina Inn offers the town's most sophisticated dining scene. The menu gives fresh local ingredients an innovative twist with dishes like Kona coffee–roasted rack of lamb. Although the food gets rave reviews, seating is limited and service can be rushed, so be prepared to hold on to your plates.

Gerard's (☎ 661-8939; 174 Lahainaluna Rd; mains $35-45; ☻ 6-9pm) Chef Gerard Reversade takes fresh Lahaina-caught seafood and infuses it with flavors from the French countryside in savory dishes such as Pacific bouillabaisse. Both the island-style French cuisine and the extensive wine lists have earned Gerard's top-of-the-line accolades. Add a quiet candlelit setting and it all makes for one romantic night out.

DRINKING

our pick Pioneer Inn (☎ 661-3636; 658 Wharf St; ☻ 11am-10pm) You couldn't be more in the middle of the action than at this century-old landmark overlooking the bustling harbor. It's all open air, making for great people watching, and the afternoon happy hour (3pm to 6pm) keeps it light on the wallet.

Aloha Mixed Plate (☎ 661-3322; 1285 Front St; ☻ 10:30am-10pm) This peppy beachside shack is the real deal. Let the sea breeze whip through your hair while lingering over a rainbow-hued tropical drink – come between 2pm and 6pm and they're half price. It really gets atmospheric after sunset, when you can listen to Old Lahaina Luau's music beating next door.

Cool Cat Café (☎ 667-0908; Wharf Cinema Center, 658 Front St; ☻ 11am-10pm) The cool '50s decor would make Elvis feel right at home. Whether you're looking for fountain drinks or hard-hitting cocktails, this breezy open-air spot is an ideal place to whet your whistle as the sun sets over the harbor. Live music nightly.

Lahaina Coolers (☎ 661-7082; 180 Dickenson St; ☻ 8am-2am) An eclectic open-air café, Lahaina Coolers attracts the 30-something crowd who come to mingle, munch *pupu* and sip wine coolers. As the town's late-night bar, it's the place to head after the dance floor has emptied.

Bamboo Sports Bar (☎ 667-0361; 505 Front St; ☻ 11am-2am) True to its motto 'where locals hang loose,' this is Lahaina's version of a *Cheers* bar. Tourists and locals alike come to watch sports on a big-screen TV, shoot a game of pool and have a few cold ones.

Front Street Grill (☎ 662-3003; 672 Front St; ☻ 10:30am-9:30pm) This balcony bar near the harbor is a hit with the college-age crowd, who beat a path here to listen to live music in the afternoon and down some brews.

ENTERTAINMENT

Front St is where the night scene's centered. Check the entertainment listings in the free *Lahaina News* or just stroll the main drag. Nightspots in Lahaina typically don't charge a cover unless there's a big-name performer.

Live Music

Lahaina Store Grille & Oyster Bar (☎ 661-9090; 744 Front St) A hot place to go after dark, this multistory restaurant and nightclub has live music and DJs nightly, with anything from top 40 to underground.

Moose McGillicuddy's (☎ 667-7758; 844 Front St) A hopping bar-cum-restaurant, Moose attracts a party crowd, out to drink and dance till they drop. With two dance floors, it jams with DJs nightly and live music on weekends.

BJ's (☎ 661-0700; 730 Front St) This place boasts an ocean view and live music from 7:30pm to 10pm nightly. Incidentally, back in the 1970s this was the legendary Blue Max, where Elton John and Stevie Nicks partied.

Hard Rock Cafe (☎ 667-7400; Lahaina Center, 900 Front St) There's not much that's Hawaiian about this rock-themed chain restaurant, but it does get jiggy with Marty Dread, the island's best reggae, on Monday from 10pm.

Mulligans at the Wharf (☎ 661-8881; Wharf Cinema Center, 658 Front St; ☛ 11am-midnight) Lahaina's friendly Irish pub has live music, typically Irish folk or Hawaiian, every night. Want to take the stage yourself? Swing by at 10pm Wednesday when it's open-mic night.

Luau, Hula & Theater

our pick Old Lahaina Luau (☎ 667-1998; www.old lahainaluau.com; 1251 Front St; adult/child under 12 $92/62; ☛ 5:15-8:15pm Oct-Mar, 5:45-8:45pm Apr-Sep) If you're ready to experience an authentic luau, this is as good as it gets. The food is terrific, the hula troupe and music are first rate and the beachside location fits the scene perfectly. No resort hotel luau even comes close. Get there early, before the seating takes place, to stroll the grounds and get a lesson in traditional poi pounding and hula dancing. One caveat: this luau often sells out weeks in advance, so book ahead.

Feast at Lele (☎ 667-5353; www.feastatlele.com; 505 Front St; adult/child under 12 $110/80; ☛ 5:30-9pm) This multicourse beachside dinner show takes your tastebuds on a sensual voyage. Hawaiian, Maori, Tahitian and Samoan dance performances are each paired to a food course. With the Hawaiian music, you're served *kalua* pork and taro; with the Maori, duck salad with poha berry dressing; and so on. Put on by the chefs at the celebrated I'O restaurant, it's a gourmet feast.

'Ulalena (☎ 661-9913; www.ulalena.com; Maui Theatre, Old Lahaina Center, 880 Front St; adult/child under 12 from $60/40; ☛ 6:30-8pm Tue-Sat) A high-energy performance, this Cirque du Soleil–style extravaganza pairs themes of Hawaiian history and storytelling with brilliant stage sets, acrobatics and elaborate costumes.

Free hula shows performed by children's troupes are held at **Lahaina Cannery Mall** (1221 Honoapi'ilani Hwy) at 1pm Saturday and Sunday and 7pm Tuesday and Thursday, and at **Hale Kahiko** (p341) at 2:30pm on Wednesday and 3:30pm Friday.

SHOPPING

Art galleries, souvenir shops and boutiques run thick along Front St, and you'll find lots of shops under one roof at the **Wharf Cinema Center** (☎ 661-8748; 658 Front St) and **Lahaina Cannery Mall** (☎ 661-5304; 1221 Honoapi'ilani Hwy).

Lahaina Arts Society (☎ 661-0111; 648 Wharf St) The perfect place to start any art browsing, this artists cooperative spreads its galleries across two

ARTY WEEKENDS

Every Friday night is 'Art Night' in Lahaina. Scores of galleries have openings, some with entertainment, wine and hors d'oeuvres. It's an ideal time to mingle with the Front St art scene, meet artists and nibble a little cheese. The action's from 7pm to 10pm and it's all free – that is, unless you see a treasure that catches your fancy.

On Saturday and Sunday the scene swings to Banyan Tree Sq, where from 9am to 5pm local artists and craftspeople set up stalls shaded by the sprawling tree, while Hawaiian musicians entertain.

floors of the Old Lahaina Courthouse. Works cover the gamut from avant-garde paintings to traditional weavings. Many of Maui's best-known artists got their start here, and there are some gems among the collection.

MauiGrown Coffee (☎ 661-2728; 277 Lahainaluna Rd; ☛ 6:30am-5pm Mon-Sat) On the mountain side of the highway, shaded by the old sugar mill's smokestack, this shop sells west Maui's newest homegrown crop, Ka'anapali Estate coffee. Buy it by the pound, or test it by the cup. Curious to see what a coffee tree looks like? Just wander out to the north side of the shop.

Lahaina Printsellers (☎ 667-5815; 505 Front St) Hawaii's largest purveyor of antique maps showcases fascinating originals dating back to the voyages of Captain Cook. The shop also sells affordable reproductions if you don't have a fat wad of cash on you.

Crazy Shirts (☎ 661-4775; 865 Front St) Not only will you find some really cool Hawaiian-designed T-shirts here, but the store itself is worth a look for its display of whaling-era artifacts. Step out to the back porch where there's a trypot once used for boiling down whale blubber.

Needlework Shop (☎ 662-8554; 505 Front St) Hawaiian quilting is a unique craft and this place is dedicated to spreading the art. Not only do they sell quilt kits but they'll also get you started with free quilting lessons. Gorgeous tropical print fabrics here too.

Aloha Shirt Museum (☎ 661-7172; 780 Front St) OK, despite the name it's really a shop, but the vintage shirts are indeed museum quality with prices running into the thousands. They also sell classy new aloha shirts from around $30.

MAUI

Village Gifts & Fine Arts (☎ 661-5199; cnr Front & Dickenson Sts) This one-room shop in the Masters' Reading Room sells prints, wooden bowls and glasswork, with a portion of the proceeds supporting the Lahaina Restoration Foundation.

GETTING THERE & AWAY
The Honoapi'ilani Hwy (Hwy 30) connects Lahaina with Ka'anapali to the north and with Ma'alaea to the south. Ferries to Lana'i (p427) and Moloka'i (p442) dock at Lahaina Harbor.

GETTING AROUND
To/From the Airport
To get to Lahaina from the Kapalua/West Maui Airport (p334) in Kahului, take Hwy 380 south to Hwy 30; by car or taxi, the drive takes about 45 minutes. For information on taxi services from the airport, see p335.

Bicycle
For bike rentals visit **West Maui Cycles** (☎ 661-9005; 1087 Limahana Pl; per day $20-50; ☼ 9am-5pm Mon-Sat, 10am-4pm Sun), which has quality mountain bikes, as well as cheaper cruisers that are fine for just kicking around town.

Bus
Maui Bus (☎ 871-4838) connects Kahului and Lahaina ($1, one hour) with a stop at Ma'alaea, where connections can be made to Kihei and Wailea. Another route connects Lahaina and Ka'anapali ($1, 30 minutes). Both routes depart from the Wharf Cinema Center hourly from 6:30am to 8:30pm. In addition, there's a free loop route that runs on the hour from 8am to 10pm from the Wharf Cinema Center to Lahaina Civic Center, making a half-dozen stops en route.

Car & Motorcycle
Most visitors rent cars upon arrival at Kahului Airport; see p336.

PARKING
Front St has free on-street parking, but there's always a line of cruising cars competing for spots. Your best bet is the large parking lot at the corner of Front and Prison Sts, where there's free public parking with a three-hour limit. There are also several private parking lots, averaging $8 per day, with the biggest one being Republic Parking on Dickenson

St. Otherwise, park at one of the shopping centers for free if you get your parking ticket validated by making a purchase.

Taxi
For a taxi, call **A Taxi Service** (☎ 661-1122) or **Ali'i Cab** (☎ 661-3688), which both operate out of Lahaina.

WEST MAUI

Sheltered by the West Maui Mountains, Maui's sunny northwestern side has been drawing visitors for a very long time. This is where the whalers pulled into port, where Hawaiian kings set up shop, and where Maui's first resort developments blossomed. For visitors today, it's jam-packed with things to see and do. Start with those gorgeous beaches, each with its own personality: quiet bays, bustling resort strands and scurry-down-the-cliff surfer haunts. The mountains looming inward hold adventures of their own, from quiet hiking trails to heart-pounding ziplines. Or just mellow out on a lounge chair, drink in hand, sailboats glistening past Lana'i, whales frolicking just offshore – no place stacks sunsets like west Maui. Lahaina is part of west Maui, too, but so much of a destination that it's got its own section (p336).

LAHAINA TO MA'ALAEA
The road between Lahaina and Ma'alaea offers fine mountain scenery, but during winter everyone is craning their necks toward the ocean to spot the humpback whales cruising just offshore.

Puamana & Launiupoko Beach Parks
Puamana Beach Park, 1.5 miles south of Lahaina, is rocky but sometimes has good conditions for beginner surfers – otherwise it's mostly a quick stop for an ocean view, especially at sunset.

A better bet is **Launiupoko Beach Park**, where even the rest rooms glow with murals of young surfers hitting the waves. The south side of the beach has small waves ideal for beginning surfers, while the north side ratchets it up for those who have honed their skills. Not that surfing is the only scene here – keiki have a blast wading in the large rock-enclosed shoreline pool, and good picnic facilities make it an ideal spot for families. Launiupoko is at the traffic lights at the 18-mile marker.

WEST MAUI

0 ————— 5 km
0 ————— 3 miles

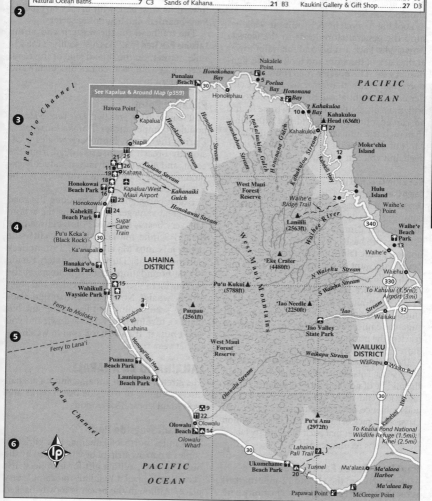

Olowalu

The West Maui Mountains form a scenic backdrop, giving Olowalu its very name, which means 'many hills.' The tiny village is marked by the Olowalu General Store and a fine chef-driven French restaurant, both at the 15-mile marker.

SIGHTS & ACTIVITIES

You'll notice snorkelers taking to the water near the 14-mile marker. Don't waste your time. The coral reef is shallow and silty and the 'Sharks May Be Present' signs lining the beach are the real thing – people have been chomped on here.

Looking to stretch? A 15-minute walk behind the general store leads to the **Olowalu Petroglyphs**. Park just beyond the water tower at the back of the store and look for the sign-posted gate. The quarter-mile route along an open road is easy to follow; just keep the cinder cone straight ahead of you as you go. As with most of Maui's petroglyphs, these figures are carved into the vertical sides of cliffs rather than on horizontal lava like on the Big Island. Most of the Olowalu figures have been damaged, but you can still make some out.

SLEEPING & EATING

Camp Olowalu (☎ 661-4303; www.campolowalu.com; 800 Olowalu Village Rd; campsite per person $10) Oceanfront camping and a friendly caretaker make this the best camping option in west Maui. Facilities are basic: cold-water showers, outhouses, picnic tables and drinking water. But hey, if you want to splurge, Chez Paul is just a half-mile walk away.

Olowalu Juice Stand (Olowalu Village Rd; smoothies $5; ☺ 9am-5:30pm) Refreshing tropical fruit smoothies made with squeezed-on-the-spot sugarcane juice are whipped up at this food truck at the north side of the Olowalu General Store. Fresh fruit is for sale, too.

Chez Paul (☎ 661-3843; 820 Olowalu Village Rd; mains $30-44; ☺ 5-9pm) This French provincial restaurant in the middle of nowhere attracts diners from far and wide. Old-world artwork and white linen add ambience, but it's the masterfully prepared classics like rack of lamb or caramelized salmon in Grand Marnier that pack those pretty tables. Reservations recommended.

Papalaua Beach Park & Around

Midway between the 11- and 12-mile markers is **Papalaua Beach Park**, a lackluster county park squeezed between the road and the ocean, though it does have firepits, toilets and tent camping (for permit information, see p330) under thorny kiawe trees. Campers take note: this place buzzes all night with traffic noise – better to skip it and head to Camp Olowalu (left).

Further north at the 12-mile marker is **Ukumehame Beach Park**. Shaded by ironwood trees, this sandy beach is OK for a quick dip, but because of the rocky conditions most locals stick with picnicking and fishing. Dive and snorkel boats anchor offshore at **Coral Gardens**. This reef also creates **Thousand Peaks** toward its west end, with breaks favored by long-boarders and beginning surfers.

The trailhead for the western end of the **Lahaina Pali Trail** (p373) is just south of the 11-mile marker, on the inland side of the road. Keep an eye out, as it comes up quickly and can be hard to spot.

Papawai Point

You're now in the area that gave rise to Maui's popular bumper sticker 'I brake for whales.' During the winter, humpback whales occasionally breach as close as 100yd from the coast, and 40 tons of leviathan suddenly exploding straight up through the water can be a real showstopper!

Beach parks and pull-offs along the road offer great vantages for watching the action. The very best is Papawai Point, between the 8- and 9-mile markers, where a cliff-side perch juts into Ma'alaea Bay, a humpback nursing ground. During the winter, Pacific Whale Foundation posts volunteers at the parking lot to share their binoculars and point out the whales. Note that the road sign reads simply 'scenic point,' not Papawai Point, but there's a turning lane, so slow down and you won't miss it. It's also a top spot to watch the sunset year-round.

LAHAINA TO KA'ANAPALI

The stretch between Lahaina and Ka'anapali offers a couple of roadside beach parks and west Maui's best B&B options.

Wahikuli Wayside Park

Two miles north of Lahaina, this park occupies a narrow strip of beach flanked by the busy highway. With a gift for prophecy, the Hawaiians named it Wahikuli, meaning 'noisy place.' Although the beach is mostly backed by a black-rock retaining wall, there's a small sandy area. Swimming conditions are usually fine, and when the water's calm, you can snorkel near the lava outcrops at the park's south end. The park has showers and rest rooms.

SLEEPING

These B&Bs are near each other in a residential neighborhood inland of Hwy 30, about 0.25 miles east of Wahikuli Wayside Park.

House of Fountains (☎ 667-2121, 800-789-6865; www.alohahouse.com; 1579 Lokia St; r incl breakfast $150-170; ❷ ❷) A Hawaiian theme resonates throughout, with hula rattles and warrior masks brimming from every corner, and even a hand-carved outrigger canoe hanging from the living room ceiling. The six guest rooms are nicely fitted with queen beds, refrigerators and DVD players. It's a kid-friendly place – the owners have kids of their own. German is spoken.

Guest House (☎ 661-8085, 800-621-8942; www.mauiguesthouse.com; 1620 'Ainakea Rd; r incl breakfast $169; ❷ ❷ ❷ ❷) The amenities here put the nearby resorts to shame. Each room has a 42in plasma TV, a hot tub and private lanai. Stained-glass windows and rattan furnishings reflect a tropical motif. The long list of free perks runs from wi-fi and beach gear to a guest shower you can use before your midnight flight home. And with access to a fully equipped kitchen you won't need to eat all your meals out.

Hanaka'o'o Beach Park

This long, sandy beach extending south from Ka'anapali Beach Resort has a sandy bottom and water conditions that are usually safe for swimming. However, southerly swells, which sometimes develop in summer, can create powerful waves and shorebreaks, while the occasional *kona* (leeward) storm can kick up rough water conditions in winter. Snorkelers head to the second clump of rocks on the south side of the park, but it really doesn't compare with sites further north. The park has full facilities and is one of only two beaches on the entire west Maui coast that has a lifeguard. Hanaka'o'o Beach is also called 'Canoe Beach,' as west Maui outrigger canoe clubs practice here in the late afternoons.

KA'ANAPALI

pop 1375

Ka'anapali, west Maui's first and foremost resort, spreads along three sparkling miles of sandy beach. With a dozen oceanfront hotels

and condos, two 18-hole golf courses and an oceanful of water activities, Ka'anapali is tricked out with everything you'd expect of a resort vacation. After you're done splashing around, kick back with a frosty drink topped by a little paper umbrella and enjoy the pretty views across the 'Au'au Channel to Lana'i and Moloka'i.

Sights
KA'ANAPALI BEACH

The long golden-sand strand fronting the Ka'anapali resort hotels is the liveliest stretch of beach on the west Maui coast. Dubbed 'Dig Me Beach' for all the well-waxed strutting that takes place, it's a happening scene with surfers, bodyboarders and parasailers ripping across the water, and sailboats pulling up on shore. However, swimmers should check with the hotel beach huts before jumping in, as water conditions vary and currents are sometimes strong.

The best underwater sights are at **Pu'u Keka'a**, also known as Black Rock, the lava promontory that protects the beach in front of the Sheraton. Novices snorkel along the sheltered southern side of Pu'u Keka'a, but the shallow coral in these waters has been stomped to death. If you're a confident swimmer, the less frequented horseshoe cove cut into the tip of the rock is the real prize, teeming with tropical fish, colorful coral and sea turtles. There's often a current to contend with off the point, which can make getting to the horseshoe a bit tricky, but when it's calm you can swim right in. Pu'u Keka'a is also a popular shore-dive spot; any of the beach huts can set you up.

KAHEKILI BEACH PARK

To leave the see-me crowd behind, head to this idyllic golden-sand beach at Ka'anapali's less-frequented north end. The swimming's better, the snorkeling's good and you'll find plenty of room to stretch without bumping into anyone else's beach towel. The park has showers, rest rooms, a sheltered pavilion and BBQ grills, making it perfect for a beachside picnic.

Snorkelers will find colorful coral and fish right in front of the beach and sea turtle sightings are common too. If you want to go a bit farther afield, you can swim north to Honokowai Point and then ride the current, which runs north to south, all the way back.

MAUI

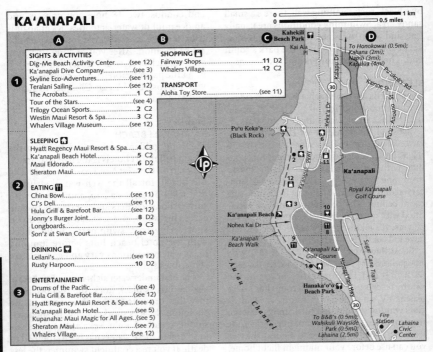

KA'ANAPALI

0 ____ 1 km
0 ____ 0.5 miles

SIGHTS & ACTIVITIES
Dig-Me Beach Activity Center........(see 12)
Ka'anapali Dive Company................(see 3)
Skyline Eco-Adventures..................(see 11)
Teralani Sailing..............................(see 12)
The Acrobats.....................................1 C3
Tour of the Stars............................(see 4)
Trilogy Ocean Sports.........................2 C2
Westin Maui Resort & Spa..................3 C2
Whalers Village Museum.................(see 12)

SLEEPING
Hyatt Regency Maui Resort & Spa.....4 C3
Ka'anapali Beach Hotel......................5 C2
Maui Eldorado...................................6 D2
Sheraton Maui...................................7 C2

EATING
China Bowl....................................(see 11)
CJ's Deli.......................................(see 11)
Hula Grill & Barefoot Bar...............(see 12)
Jonny's Burger Joint..........................8 D2
Longboards.......................................9 C3
Son'z at Swan Court.......................(see 4)

DRINKING
Leilani's..(see 12)
Rusty Harpoon................................10 D2

ENTERTAINMENT
Drums of the Pacific......................(see 4)
Hula Grill & Barefoot Bar...............(see 12)
Hyatt Regency Maui Resort & Spa..(see 4)
Ka'anapali Beach Hotel...................(see 5)
Kupanaha: Maui Magic for All Ages..(see 5)
Sheraton Maui................................(see 7)
Whalers Village..............................(see 12)

SHOPPING
Fairway Shops.................................11 D2
Whalers Village................................12 C2

TRANSPORT
Aloha Toy Store.............................(see 11)

Kahekili Beach Park
Kai Ala Pl
To Honokowai (0.5mi);
Kahana (2mi);
Napili (3mi);
Kapalua (4mi)
Pu'u Keka'a (Black Rock)
Ka'anapali
Royal Ka'anapali Golf Course
Ka'anapali Beach
Nohea Kai Dr
Ka'anapali Beach Walk
Ka'anapali Kai Golf Course
'Au'au Channel
Hanaka'o'o Beach Park
To B&B's (0.5mi);
Wahikuli Wayside Park (0.5mi);
Lahaina (2.5mi)
Fire Station
Lahaina Civic Center
Sugar Cane Train
Honoapi'ilani Hwy
Ka'anapali Pkwy
Keka'a Dr
Kapalua Rd

The wide beach, backed by swaying palms and flowering morning glory, is also ideal for strolling. It is about a 15-minute walk south to Pu'u Keka'a or a 20-minute walk north to Honokowai Point.

To get to the beach from the Honoapi'ilani Hwy, turn seaward about 0.2 miles north of the 25-mile marker onto Kai Ala Dr, then bear right.

WHALERS VILLAGE MUSEUM
Don't let the shopping center location fool you. This whaling **museum** (☎ 661-5992; Level 3, Whalers Village, 2345 Ka'anapali Pkwy; admission free; ☑ 10am-6pm) is one of the finest anywhere. Authentic period photographs, whaling ship logs and detailed interpretive boards sound the depths of whaling history. It's all rounded out with exhibits of harpoons, whale jawbones and a wild array of scrimshaw.

The character of the 19th-century whalers comes through, giving you a feel for how rough and dirty the work really was. Wages were so low that sailors sometimes owed the ship money by the time they got home and had to sign up for another four-year stint

just to pay off the debt. No wonder so many jumped ship when they reached Maui!

When you're done, walk out to the front entrance of the shopping center to find a full-size **sperm whale skeleton** on display.

KA'ANAPALI BEACH WALK
Bask in the sunny beach scene on this mile-long walk that runs between the Hyatt Regency Maui Resort & Spa and the Sheraton Maui, the lavish hotels that anchor the ends of Ka'anapali Beach. In addition to all the action on the beach, both the Hyatt and the Westin Maui Resort & Spa are worth a detour for their dazzling garden statuary and landscaping replete with free-form pools, rushing waterfalls and swan ponds. A walk through the Hyatt's rambling lobbies is a bit like museum browsing – the walls hang with everything from heirloom Hawaiian quilts to meditative Buddhas and Papua New Guinea war shields.

At the southern end of the walk the graceful 17ft-high bronze sculpture *The Acrobats*, by Australian John Robinson, makes a dramatic silhouette against the sunset. If you walk along the beach in the early evening, you'll often be treated to entertainment, most notably from the beachside restaurants at Whalers Village and from the Hyatt, which holds its luau on the oceanfront.

Activities

AT SEA

Dig-Me Beach Activity Center (☎ 661-5552; Whalers Village, 2345 Ka'anapali Pkwy; snorkel sets & boogie boards per hr/day $5/12; ☉ 8am-5pm), on the beach fronting the shopping center, has the best prices on beach gear rentals and arranges all manner of water activities.

Teralani Sailing (☎ 661-1230; www.teralani.net; Whalers Village, 2345 Ka'anapali Pkwy; outings $59-99; ☉ vary) offers a variety of catamaran sails from Ka'anapali Beach, including morning snorkel sails, sunset sails and whale watch outings. No matter what sail you take you can expect a helpful crew, free drinks and tasty munchies.

The pros at **Trilogy Ocean Sports** (☎ 661-7789; Ka'anapali Beach Walk; ☉ 8am-5pm), in a beach hut in front of the Ka'anapali Beach Hotel, can get you riding a board with a two-hour surfing lesson ($70) and rent snorkel sets and bodyboards for $15 a day.

If you've never been diving before, **Ka'anapali Dive Company** (☎ 661-4622; www.kaanapalidiveco.com; Westin Maui Resort & Spa; introductory dive $89; ☉ 9am-5pm) are the people you want to see. Their introductory dive begins with instruction in a pool and ends with a guided dive from the beach.

SPIRITS LEAP

In Hawaiian lore, Pu'u Keka'a (Black Rock), the westernmost point of Maui, is thought to be a place where the spirits of the dead leap into the unknown to be carried back to their ancestral homeland.

The rock is said to have been created during a scuffle between the demigod Maui and a commoner who questioned Maui's superiority. Maui chased the man to this point, then froze his body into stone and cast his soul out to sea.

A different kind of soul jumps into the water today. You'll often find a line of daring teens waiting for their turn to leap off the rock for a resounding splash into the cool cove below.

ON LAND

Skyline Eco-Adventures (☎ 662-1500; www.skyline hawaii.com; Fairway Shops; 4hr outing $140; ☉ departs 7am, 8am, 9am, 11am, noon & 1pm), Ka'anapali's new zipline, takes you on a free-glide above waterfalls, stream beds and green valleys in the hills above the resort. The scenery's not as wild as Skyline's wildly popular Haleakalā zipline (p410), but if this is the only one you can book, you won't be disappointed.

Ka'anapali Golf Courses (☎ 661-3691; www.kaa napali-golf.com; 2290 Ka'anapali Pkwy; green fees $195-235, after 1pm $95-125; ☉ first tee time 6:30am) consists of two courses. The more demanding Royal Ka'anapali Golf Course, designed by Robert Trent Jones, is tournament grade with greens that emphasize putting skills. The Ka'anapali Kai Golf Course is a bit shorter and more of a resort course.

Take it skyward at the Hyatt resort's rooftop **Tour of the Stars** (☎ 667-4727; 200 Nohea Kai Dr; admission $30-35). These astronomy programs, using a 16in-diameter telescope, are limited to 14 people and held at 8pm, 9pm and 10pm on clear nights. Romantic types should opt for the couples-only viewing at 11pm Friday and Saturday, which rolls out champagne and chocolate-covered strawberries.

Courses

Whalers Village (☎ 661-4567; www.whalersvillage.com; 2435 Ka'anapali Pkwy) offers free lei-making classes and hula lessons. Look for the schedule, which changes throughout the year, in the shopping center's magazine.

Festivals & Events

Maui Onion Festival (www.whalersvillage.com) Maui's famous pungent bulb takes center stage in cooking demonstrations and (gasp) raw-onion-eating contests at Whalers Village on a weekend in August.

Hula O Na Keiki (www.kbhmaui.com) Children perform at this hula dance competition in early November at Ka'anapali Beach Hotel, which features some of the best *keiki* dancers in Hawaii.

Na Mele O Maui (www.kaanapaliresort.com) This event, which translates as 'Song of Maui,' features children's choral groups singing traditional songs in Hawaiian. Lots and lots of aloha at this event held in mid-November at the Hyatt Regency Maui Resort & Spa.

Sleeping

In addition to the following resorts, there are recommendable B&Bs (p351) nearby between Ka'anapali and Lahaina.

MAUI

our pick **Ka'anapali Beach Hotel** (☎ 661-0011, 800-262-8450; www.kbhmaui.com; 2525 Ka'anapali Pkwy; r incl breakfast from $225; P ⊠ 🕾 🛜 🖭) If you're looking for aloha over ritz, this is the place. The rooms at this older hotel may not pack the same punch as the fancier neighbors but nightly hula shows and welcoming Hawaiian staff remind guests why they came to Maui in the first place. Heaps of family-oriented activities from lei-making to ukulele singalongs assure that the *keiki* will never be bored. And it borders one of the best sections of the beach for swimming and snorkeling.

Maui Eldorado (☎ 661-0021, 800-688-7444; www.outrigger.com; 2661 Keka'a Dr; studios/1br from $325/379; P ⊠ 🖭) Don't bother paying extra for the ocean view – this one's all about the greens. You can literally step off your lanai and onto the fairways at this quiet condo complex bordering the Royal Ka'anapali Golf Course. Best deal are the studios, which are very large and have kitchens set apart from the bedroom area. Online discounts typically knock about a third off the standard rates.

Hyatt Regency Maui Resort & Spa (☎ 661-1234, 800-233-1234; www.maui.hyatt.com; 200 Nohea Kai Dr; r from $450; P ⊠ 🖭) The most extravagant of the resorts, the Hyatt's lobby atrium overflows with orchids and artwork while the grounds are given over to lush gardens and swan ponds. Kids will thrill in the water world of meandering pools, swim-through grottos and towering water slides. For grown-ups, there's a swim-up bar and a pampering full-service spa.

Sheraton Maui (☎ 661-0031, 866-716-8109; www.sheraton-maui.com; 2605 Ka'anapali Pkwy; r from $500; P ⊠ 🖭) This smart resort enjoys a prime beach location, smack in front of Pu'u Keka'a (Black Rock). The rooms have rich wood tones and Hawaiian prints, and the grounds have night-lit tennis courts, a fitness center and a cool lava-rock swimming pool. Online deals can ease the price bite.

Eating

CJ's Deli (☎ 667-0968; Fairway Shops, 2580 Keka'a Dr; mains $6-12; 🕙 7am-8pm; 🛜) CJ's is the handiwork of Christian Jorgensen, a top chef who abandoned the snazzy resort scene to open his own homestyle eatery. Naturally the menu includes deli classics like hot pastrami on rye but it's the fully loaded omelettes in the morning and heaping servings of pot roast and other comfort food at dinner that draw the largest crowds.

Jonny's Burger Joint (☎ 661-4500; 2291 Ka'anapali Pkwy; burgers $7-10; 🕙 11:30am-2am) Shoot a game of pool while your burger is flipped at this combo eatery-bar at the entrance to Ka'anapali. These generous hand-patted burgers, served with caramelized Kula onions, are some of the best you'll find on Maui. Forget the fried dishes – Jonny's is all about the burgers.

China Bowl (☎ 661-0660; Fairway Shops, 2580 Keka'a Dr; mains $9-15; 🕙 10:30am-9:30pm) This simple family-friendly place wok-fries authentic Szechuan dishes with fiery peppers as well as Mandarin fare for tamer palates. The health-conscious will be happy to know MSG is banned from the kitchen. Parents will also like the kids' menu, which features a meal with a drink for just $6.

Longboards (☎ 667-8220; Marriott's Maui Ocean Club, 100 Nohea Kai Dr; light eats $8-14, dinner mains $18-30; 🕙 5-10pm) A fun surf motif, fab water view and 'hang loose' menu of beach fare like coconut shrimp, fish tacos and beer-battered onion rings make this Ka'anapali's hippest spot to kick back over a beer and light eats. If you want to get serious, a full menu of steaks, ribs and seafood is paddled out for dinner.

Hula Grill & Barefoot Bar (☎ 667-6636; Whalers Village, 2345 Ka'anapali Pkwy; grill menu $9-18, dinner mains $19-34; 🕙 11am-10pm) Sure, it's a bit contrived, but heck this is Ka'anapali and who doesn't want to dine on the beach? So grab a seat under one of the coconut-frond umbrellas and watch the swimsuit parade pass by as you dine on fun *pupu* like ahi *poke* (cubed raw fish) or *imu*-style BBQ ribs. Dinner kicks it up a notch with kiawe-grilled fresh catch and steaks.

Son'z at Swan Court (☎ 667-4506; Hyatt Regency Maui Resort & Spa, 200 Nohea Kai Dr; mains $30-48; 🕙 5:30-10:30pm) Between the waterfalls, the swan pond and tiki torches, this is Ka'anapali's most romantic dinner choice. The award-winning cuisine goes beyond the expected fine-dining steak and lobster offerings to include island touches like Maui goat cheese ravioli. It also boasts the largest wine cellar on Maui.

Drinking

Leilani's (☎ 661-4495; Whalers Village, 2345 Ka'anapali Pkwy) This open-air bar and restaurant right on the beach is the place to linger over a cool drink while catching a few rays.

Rusty Harpoon (☎ 661-3123; 2290 Ka'anapali Pkwy) If you don't want to get caught up in the beach scene, this open-air bar overlooking golf greens is the best place for a sunset drink.

Entertainment

There's always something happening at the hotels, ranging from music in the lounges and restaurants to luau and hula shows.

HULA & LIVE MUSIC

Ka'anapali Beach Hotel (☎ 661-0011; 2525 Ka'anapali Pkwy) 'Maui's most Hawaiian hotel' cheerfully entertains anyone who chances by between 6:30pm and 7:30pm with a free hula show. There's also music and dancing nightly in the hotel's Tiki Courtyard.

Sheraton Maui (☎ 661-0031; 2605 Ka'anapali Pkwy) Everybody swings by at sunset to watch the torch-lighting and cliff-diving ceremony from Pu'u Keka'a. It's followed by live music from 6:30pm to 9pm at the hotel's Lagoon Bar.

Hyatt Regency Maui Resort & Spa (☎ 661-1234; 200 Nohea Kai Dr) A free torch-lighting ceremony at 6:15pm is followed nightly by live Hawaiian music until 9:30pm.

Whalers Village (☎ 661-4567; 2435 Ka'anapali Pkwy) Ka'anapali's shopping center hosts Polynesian hula and Tahitian dance performances from 7pm to 8pm on Monday, Wednesday and Saturday (free).

Some of the beachside restaurants also have entertainment, including **Hula Grill & Barefoot Bar** (☎ 667-6636; Whalers Village, 2345 Ka'anapali Pkwy), which has a guitarist or ukulele player daily after 3pm.

LUAU & DINNER SHOWS

Drums of the Pacific (☎ 667-4727; Hyatt Regency Maui Resort & Spa, 200 Nohea Kai Dr; adult/child 6-12 $86/49; ☒ 5-8pm) Ka'anapali's best luau includes an *imu* ceremony (the unearthing of a roasted pig from an underground oven), an open bar, a Hawaiian-style buffet dinner, and a flashy South Pacific dance and music show.

Kupanaha: Maui Magic for All Ages (☎ 661-0011; Ka'anapali Beach Hotel, 2525 Ka'anapali Pkwy; adult/child 6-12 $79/29; ☒ Tue-Sat) Illusionists take a Hawaiian slant adding legends through hula and chants to the usual magic at this dinner show.

Shopping

You will find more than 50 shops at **Whalers Village** (☎ 661-4567; 2435 Ka'anapali Pkwy; ☒ 9:30am-10pm) shopping center, selling all sorts of goodies ranging from beach mats to designer clothing:

Blue Ginger (☎ 661-1666) For light and breezy women's wear, check out the cheery Hawaiian-designed blouses and dresses here.

Gecko Store (☎ 661-1114) Everything from T-shirts to toys crawls with pictures of friendly Hawaiian geckos. You'll be amazed at what geckos can do.

Honolua Surf (☎ 661-5455) This is the place to pick up Maui-style board shorts and other casual beachwear for both men and women.

Totally Hawaiian Gift Gallery (☒ 667-4070) If it's made in Hawaii, you'll find it at this shop, which sells everything from tropical decor to koa bowls.

Getting There & Around

Aloha Toy Store (☎ 662-0888; Fairway Shops, 2580 Keka'a Dr; ☒ 8am-5pm) rents Kawasaki motorcycles ($129) and Harleys ($169).

Maui Bus (☎ 871-4838; ride $1) connects the Whalers Village shopping center in Ka'anapali with the Wharf Cinema Center in Lahaina hourly from 6:30am to 8:30pm, and runs north up the coast to Kahana and Napili hourly from 6am to 8pm.

The free **Ka'anapali Trolley** (☎ 667-0648) runs between the Ka'anapali hotels, Whalers Village and the golf course about every 20 minutes between 10am and 10pm.

The resort hotels offer free beach parking, but the spaces allotted are so limited they commonly fill by mid-morning. Your best bet for beach parking is at the south end of the Hyatt, which has more slots than other hotels. Another option is the pay parking at Whalers Village – get your ticket validated by making a $10 purchase at any shop or restaurant and the first three hours are free. Parking is free at Kahekili Beach Park.

HONOKOWAI

pop 3000

Squeezed between its trendier neighbors Ka'anapali and Kahana, Honokowai is all but bypassed by most visitors. Granted it's condoville – a mile-long stretch of condos form the village center. But don't write it off as a place to stay – it's convenient, affordable and low-rise, and the ocean views are every bit as fine as in the upscale resorts to the south. Another perk: this is one of the best places on Maui to spot passing humpback whales right from your lanai.

Orientation

North of Ka'anapali, the road forks. If you want to zip up to the northern beaches, by-passing the condos and resorts, the main road is Honoapi'ilani Hwy (Hwy 30), which has a bicycle lane. The parallel shoreline

356 WEST MAUI •• Kahana

Book your stay at lonelyplanet.com/hotels
356 WEST MAUI •• Kahana

Book your stay at lonelyplanet.com/hotels

road is Lower Honoapi'ilani Rd, which leads into Honokowai.

Sights & Activities

In the center of town, **Honokowai Beach Park** has a fun playground for kids and makes a nice spot for picnics. Forget swimming, though. The water is shallow and the beach is lined with a submerged rock shelf. Water conditions improve at the south side of town, and you can walk along the shore down to lovely Kahekili Beach Park (p351) at the northern end of Ka'anapali. Rent a snorkel from **Boss Frog** (☎ 665-1200; 3636 Lower Honoapi'ilani Rd; per day from $3; ☺ 8am-5pm) before you set off.

Sleeping

Kuleana Maui (☎ 669-8080, 800-367-5633; www.kuleana resorts.com; 3959 Lower Honoapi'ilani Rd; 1br from $145; ☒) The most value for the buck in Honokowai. The rooms are a bit small but not claustrophobic and the amenities are generous, with full kitchens and entertainment centers. You'll find plenty of space to stretch out on the extensive palm-shaded grounds. Request an upper floor unit, which has the best views.

Noelani (☎ 669-8374, 800-367-6030; www.noelani -condo-resort.com; 4095 Lower Honoapi'ilani Rd; studios $157, 1br/2br/3br from $197/290/357; ☜ ☒) This ocean-kissing condo is so close to the water you can sit on your lanai and watch turtles swimming in the surf. There's no air-con but ceiling fans, sea breezes and surf lullabies should rock you to a cool night's sleep. The well-maintained units cover a wide gamut, ranging from cozy studios to three-bedroom suites that can handle an entire family.

Hale Kai (☎ 669-6333, 800-446-7307; www.halekai .com; 3691 Lower Honoapi'ilani Rd; 1br/2br/3br $160/210/310; ☜ ☒) Perched on the water's edge, you can step right off your lanai and onto the sand at this old-fashioned condo. Even the pool is shoreline here, with a splash of saltwater breaking over the edge. Best of all, the place abounds in Hawaiian accents, from the room decor to the lava-rock exterior. If you need extra space, go for the three-bedroom corner unit, which has a cool loft, wraparound ocean-view windows and all the character of a Hawaiian beach house.

Eating

Farmers Market Deli (☎ 669-7004; 3636 Lower Honoapi'ilani Rd; takeout items $5-8; ☺ 7am-7pm) Swing by this health food store to stock up on take-out fare for your beach outing. The salad bar includes organic goodies and hot veggie dishes, the smoothies are first-rate and Maui-made ice cream is sold by the scoop. It's even greener on Monday, Wednesday and Friday mornings, when vendors set up stalls to sell local produce in the parking lot.

Honokowai Okazuya (☎ 665-0512; 3600 Lower Honoapi'ilani Rd; mains $9-14; ☺ 10am-9pm Mon-Sat) The counter service is abrupt and the prices are high for a plate lunch, so why the crowds? It's all about the cooking. Plate lunch goes gourmet here, with heavenly sauces. The mahimahi lemon caper sauté is not to be missed. A strip of stools lines the wall if you want to feast on the spot, but most folks treat it as takeout.

Java Jazz & Soup Nutz (☎ 667-0787; Honokowai Marketplace, 3350 Lower Honoapi'ilani Rd; breakfast & lunch $6-12, dinner $12-30; ☺ 6am-9pm Mon-Sat, to 5pm Sun) As Bohemian as you'll find this side of Greenwich Village, this arty café has a menu as eclectic as its decor. Breakfast packs 'em in with everything from bagels to hearty omelettes; lunch revolves around specialty salads and innovative sandwiches. Dinner gets downright meaty with what may well be the finest flame-grilled filet mignon on Maui.

KAHANA

pop 2200

Kahana, the village north of Honokowai, boasts million-dollar homes, upscale beachfront condominium complexes and Maui's only microbrewery.

Information

The **Kahana Gateway** (4405 Honoapi'ilani Hwy) shopping center has a gas station, **Bank of Hawaii** (☎ 669-3922), **Kahana Koin-op Laundromat** (☎ 669-1587; ☺ last wash 8pm) and **Whalers General Store** (☎ 669-3700; ☺ 6:30am-11pm) for basic groceries and sundries. The center's **Hawaiian Village Coffee** (☎ 665-1114; per min 20¢; ☺ 6am-9pm) has online computers.

Sights & Activities

The sandy **beach** fronting the village offers reasonable swimming. Park at the seaside **Pohaku Park** and walk north a couple of minutes to access the beach. Pohaku Park itself has a gnarly offshore break called S-Turns that attracts lots of surfers. **Maui Dive Shop** (☎ 669-3800; Kahana Gateway shopping center, 4405 Honoapi'ilani Hwy; dives from $90; snorkel rentals per day $8; ☺ 8am-9pm) provides a full range of dives and rental gear.

Sleeping

Sands of Kahana (☎ 669-0423, 800-580-1006; www
.sands-of-kahana.com; 4299 Lower Honoapi'ilani Rd;
1br/2br/3br from $150/265/375; ❄ ➳) Among the
beachside condos in Kahana, this is easily the
best value. The huge one-bedroom units have
more space than the average two-bedroom
elsewhere – four people could happily coexist, as the living room sofabed is a long 25ft
from the bedroom. Room amenities include
a washer/dryer and ocean-view lanai; the
grounds have tennis courts, a fitness center
and a seaside restaurant.

Eating & Drinking

Hawaiian Village Coffee (☎ 665-1114; Kahana Gateway,
4405 Honoapi'ilani Hwy; snacks $2-6; ❄ 6am-9pm; ❄)
This little shop's all about local flavor with
Maui-grown coffee, Maui-made Roselani ice
cream – try the yummy *haupia* (coconut pudding) and homemade baked goods.

Maui Brewing Company (☎ 669-3474; Kahana
Gateway, 4405 Honoapi'ilani Hwy; mains $8-25; ❄ 11am-
1am) The food would be reason enough to
come to this microbrewery: whole-grain pizzas, Maui Cattle burgers, Thai egg rolls. But
it's the heady brews that really steal the show.
For something light, try the Bikini Blonde; for
more of a wallop, order the Coconut Porter.
Then set your drinks down on the frost rail –
a strip of white snow that lines the bar – and
meditate on why it's better to be in Maui
than Manitoba.

Roy's Kahana Bar & Grill (☎ 669-6999; Kahana
Gateway, 4405 Honoapi'ilani Hwy; mains $30-40; ❄ 5:30-
10pm) You'll find outstanding Hawaii Regional
Cuisine at this outpost of famed Honolulu-
chef-guru Roy Yamaguchi. His Maui flagship
woos diners with savory dishes like blackened ahi with Chinese mustard and the co-
riander pork chops in plum wine sauce. A
sweet deal is the prix-fixe three-course dinner
($40) available to those seated before 6:30pm.
Reservations advised.

NAPILI
pop 1600

Napili's lovely bay makes you want to stop and
stay awhile. Somewhat ironically, this little
seaside village owes its low-key appeal to its
early history of resort development. Its largest
hotel, Napili Kai Beach Resort, was built in
1962 as Maui's first hotel north of Ka'anapali.
To protect the bay, and its investment, Napili
Kai organized its neighbors and persuaded

the county to pass a zoning bylaw restricting
all Napili buildings to the height of a coconut
tree. The law passed in 1964, long before the
condo explosion took over the rest of west
Maui, and as a result Napili has preserved an
intimate scale that's been lost elsewhere.

Sights & Activities

The deep golden sands and gentle curves of
Napili Beach offer good beachcombing anytime and excellent swimming and snorkeling
when it's calm. Big waves occasionally make
it into the bay in winter, and when they do
it's time to break out the skimboards – the
steep drop at the beach provides a perfect
run into the surf.

Sleeping

Hale Napili (☎ 669-6184, 800-245-2266; www.halenapili
.com; 65 Hui Dr; studios/1br from $160/260) The aloha of
the Hawaiian manager ensures lots of repeat
guests at this well-maintained condo right on
the beach. The place is a welcome throwback
to an earlier era, when everything in Maui
was small and personable. The 18 units, each
roomy and neat as a pin, have tropical decor,
fully equipped kitchens and oceanfront lanai
with unbeatable sunset views.

Outrigger Napili Shores (☎ 669-8061, 800-688-
7444; www.outrigger.com; 5315 Lower Honoapi'ilani Rd;
studios from $219, 1br $299; ❄ ❄ ➳) This friendly
place packs a lot for a small resort. The palm-
filled grounds hold two solar-heated pools,
a hot tub and the area's coolest beachfront
eatery. The units are fresh off a renovation
that added top-of-the-line features including
granite countertops, flat-screen TVs and new
kitchens. Plantation-style shutters look out
upon waterview patios. Amenities include
free internet and voice mail.

Napili Kai Beach Resort (☎ 669-6271, 800-367-
5030; www.napilikai.com; 5900 Lower Honoapi'ilani Rd;
r/studios/1br from $235/335/475; ❄ ❄ ❄ ➳) Spread
across several waterfront acres, this pampering resort perched above the northern end of
Napili Bay has classic appeal. The units, which
tastefully blend Polynesian decor with Asian
touches, have ocean-view lanai and, in most
cases, kitchenettes.

Eating

our pick Gazebo (☎ 669-5621; Outrigger Napili Shores,
5315 Lower Honoapi'ilani Rd; meals $7-11; ❄ 7:30am-
2pm) There's no better place to start your
day than at this open-air place – literally a

gazebo, smack on the beach. Sweet tooths love the white chocolate mac-nut pancakes, while serious appetites dig into the mammoth omelettes. Arrive early, though, to beat the breakfast queue. Meal-size salads, hearty sandwiches and the *kalua* pig plate are the menu stars at lunch.

Mama's Ribs 'N Rotisserie (☎ 665-6262; Napili Plaza, cnr Napilihau St & Hwy 30; meals $7-12; ☼ 11am-8pm) This unpretentious mom-and-pop operation dishes up heaping portions of tasty BBQ ribs and rotisserie chicken. It's all home-style using heirloom family recipes for everything from the BBQ sauce to the flavorsome Portuguese bean soup.

Sea House Restaurant (☎ 669-1500; Napili Kai Beach Resort, 5900 Lower Honoapi'ilani Rd; dinner mains $25-35; ☼ 7am-9pm) The breezy seaside dining and flaming tiki torches add up to one romantic setting. If you're in a seafood mood, start with the *poke* nachos made from sashimi-grade ahi and move on to the taro-crusted sea bass topped with green papaya salad. The Sea House is open for breakfast and lunch too, but really, this place is all about dinner.

Entertainment

Masters of Hawaiian Slack Key Guitar Concert Series (☎ 669-3858; www.slackkey.com; Napili Kai Beach Resort, 5900 Lower Honoapi'ilani Rd; admission $45; ☼ 7:30pm Wed) Forget whatever else you had planned for the night – this cultural gem is worth going out of your way to experience. Top slack key guitarists such as Ledward Ka'apana and Dennis Kamakahi are monthly guests, and the Grammy award–winning George Kahumoku Jr is the weekly host. The intimate setting makes it feel like a family jam session. Seating is limited and sell-outs are the norm, so be sure to call ahead for reservations.

KAPALUA & AROUND

pop 600

Nestled in pineapple fields and overlooking beautiful beaches, Kapalua reigns as Maui's most exclusive destination. Its very name is synonymous with golf – Kapalua hosts the PGA Tour's opening tournament every January – but there's much more than just greens here. An awesome zipline is taking people skyward for new thrills and trails in a once-restricted forest that's been opened to hikers. Water-lovers will find ideal conditions for an array of splashy activities and the dining scene alone is worth a visit.

Sights
KAPALUA BEACH

This crescent-shaped beach, with its clear view of Moloka'i across the channel, is the perfect place to while away a sunny day. Long rocky outcrops at both ends protect the bay, making Kapalua Beach the safest year-round swimming spot on this coast. You'll find good snorkeling on the right side of the beach, where there's abundant tropical fish and orange slate-pencil sea urchins.

Take the drive immediately north of Napili Kai Beach Resort to get to the beach parking area, where there are rest rooms and showers. Look for the tunnel that leads from the parking lot north to the beach.

DT FLEMING BEACH PARK

No matter what you might think of Dr Beach, when he declares a place 'America's Best Beach' you're not going to just drive by, are you? Surrounded by ironwood trees and adjacent to an old one-room schoolhouse, this long, sandy beach feels like an outpost from another era. In keeping with its Hawaiian nature, the beach is the domain of wave riders.

Experienced surfers and bodysurfers find impressive wave action in winter. The shorebreaks can be brutal, however, and this beach is second only to Ho'okipa for injuries. It also has powerful currents, so check with the lifeguard before jumping in. The reef on the right is good for snorkeling when it's very calm.

The park has rest rooms, picnic facilities and showers. The access road is off Honoapi'ilani Hwy (Hwy 30), immediately north of the 31-mile marker.

SLAUGHTERHOUSE BEACH & HONOLUA BAY

Talk about split personalities. This double-bay conservation district can be tranquil and

---

TOP PICKS – FESTIVALS & EVENTS

- ▪ **International Festival of Canoes** (p343) in Lahaina
- ▪ **Makawao Rodeo** (p406) in Makawao
- ▪ **East Maui Taro Festival** (p398) in Hana
- ▪ **E Ho'oulu Aloha** (p369) in Wailuku
- ▪ **Ki Ho'alu Slack Key Guitar Festival** (p366) in Kahului
- ▪ **Art Night** (p347) in Lahaina

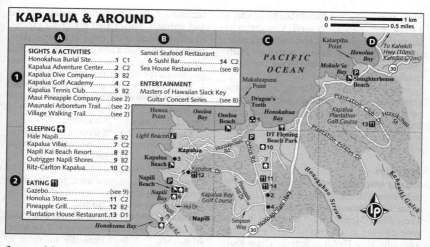

KAPALUA & AROUND

SIGHTS & ACTIVITIES
Honokahua Burial Site..........**1** C1
Kapalua Adventure Center.....**2** C2
Kapalua Dive Company.........**3** B2
Kapalua Golf Academy..........**4** C2
Kapalua Tennis Club.............**5** B2
Maui Pineapple Company......(see 2)
Maunalei Arboretum Trail.....(see 2)
Village Walking Trail............(see 2)

SLEEPING
Hale Napili.........................**6** B2
Kapalua Villas.....................**7** C2
Napili Kai Beach Resort.........**8** B2
Outrigger Napili Shores.........**9** B2
Ritz-Carlton Kapalua............**10** C2

EATING
Gazebo...............................(see 9)
Honolua Store......................**11** B2
Pineapple Grill......................**12** B2
Plantation House Restaurant..**13** D1

Sansei Seafood Restaurant
& Sushi Bar....................**14** C2
Sea House Restaurant..........(see 8)

ENTERTAINMENT
Masters of Hawaiian Slack Key
Guitar Concert Series.......(see 8)

MAUI

flat as a lake or savage with incredible surf, depending on the season. But no matter what the mood, you'll always find conditions ideal for some sort of activity.

Slaughterhouse Beach (Mokule'ia Bay) and Honolua Bay are separated by the narrow Kalaepiha Point and together form the Honolua-Mokule'ia Bay Marine Life Conservation District.

Honolua Bay is a surfer's dream. Like O'ahu's famed North Shore, it faces northwest and when it catches the winter swells it has some of the most gnarly surfing anywhere in the world. Honolua Bay is so hot it's been cover material for surfing magazines.

Slaughterhouse Beach is a first-rate body-surfing spot during the summer. Its attractive white-sand crescent invites sunbathing and exploring – look for glittering green olivine crystals in the rocks at the south end of the beach.

In summer snorkeling is excellent in both bays, thanks in part to prohibitions on fishing in the preserve. Honolua Bay is the favorite, with thriving reefs and abundant coral along its rocky edges. As an added treat, spinner dolphins sometimes hang out near the mouth of the bays, swimming just beyond snorkelers. When it's calm, you can snorkel around Kalaepiha Point from one bay to the other. The bays also offer excellent kayaking opportunities.

Just north of the 32-mile marker, there's public parking and a concrete stairway leading down the cliffs to Slaughterhouse Beach.

A half-mile past the 32-mile marker there's room for about half a dozen cars to park adjacent to the path down to Honolua Bay.

ONELOA BEACH

True to its name, Oneloa ('Long Sand') fringes a half-mile of Kapalua shoreline. Yet few tourists trip upon this beauty, backed as it is by gated resort condos and restricted golf greens.

Still, this white-sand jewel is too pretty to leave to the jet set. Cradled by sand dunes and beach morning glory, it's a superb place to soak up a few rays. On calm days swimming is good close to shore, as is snorkeling in the protected area along the rocky point at the north side of the beach. When there's any sizable surf, strong rip currents can be present.

The beach access requires a sharp eye; turn onto Ironwood Lane and immediately turn left into the parking lot opposite the Ironwoods gate. A footpath across the street leads down to the beach.

DRAGON'S TEETH

If you're ready for a Harry Potter moment, the Dragon's Teeth makes a fun diversion. Razor-sharp spikes crown rocky Makaluapuna Point, looking uncannily like the mouth of an imaginary dragon. What's the magic behind the run of 3ft-high teeth? It's the work of pounding winter waves that have ripped into the lava rock point, leaving only pointy spikes behind.

The walk out to this curious formation and back takes only 15 minutes return. En route you'll pass the **Honokahua burial site**, a 13-acre native burial ground. You can skirt along the outside of this area but don't enter sites marked 'Please Kokua,' which are easily visible islets of stones bordering the Ritz's manicured golf greens.

Start your detour by driving north to the very end of Lower Honoapi'ilani Rd, where you'll find parking and a plaque detailing the burial site. The path to the Dragon's Teeth leads down from the plaque along the north edge of the golf course.

Activities

Kapalua Adventure Center (☎ 665-4386; Office Rd; zipline outings $130-299; ☻ 7am-7pm) is the jumpoff point for zipline tours that soar across the West Maui Mountains. The thrills include nine ziplines in all, two of them extending a breathtaking 2000ft in length. These tours differ from other Maui ziplines in that there's a dual track allowing you to zip side by side with a friend.

The recently opened **Maunalei Arboretum Trail** (☎ 665-9110 for shuttle; Kapalua Adventure Center, Office Rd; admission free; ☻ 8am-3:30pm) cuts through an exotic arboretum planted a century ago by DT Fleming, the Scotsman who developed Maui's pineapple industry. This previously inaccessible forest sits above an exclusive gated development and access is strictly via a free shuttle that departs from the Kapalua Adventure Center at 8am and then every 90 minutes until 3:30pm. The hikes include a 2.5-mile ridge trail offering spectacular views and a pair of leisurely loop trails (1 mile and half a mile) that meander through the arboretum.

For an easy stroll, take the **Village Walking Trail** (☎ 665-4386; Kapalua Adventure Center, Office Rd; admission free; ☻ 7am-7pm Tue-Sun), a former golf course now quaintly overgrown and reincarnated as a hiking trail. It offers stunning scenery as it rises up the mountain slopes. For the best views, follow it all the way to the end, where there's a lake loop; it takes about two hours and covers 3.5 miles. Just check in at the Kapalua Adventure Center where the trail starts, sign their liability waiver and pick up a map.

Kapalua Golf (☎ 669-8044, 877-527-2582; www .kapaluamaui.com; Bay/Plantation course green fees before 2pm $215/295, after 2pm $130/150; ☻ 1st tee 6:45am) boasts two of the island's top championship golf courses, both certified by Audubon

International as sanctuaries for native plants and animals. How's that for green greens? The Bay course is the tropical ocean course, meandering across a lava peninsula. The challenging Plantation course sweeps over a rugged landscape of hills and deep gorges.

Want to hone your golf skills? **Kapalua Golf Academy** (☎ 669-6500; 1000 Office Rd; 1hr clinics from $35, lessons per hr $110; ☻ 7am-6pm), staffed by PGA pros, is Hawaii's top golf school.

Kapalua Tennis Club (☎ 669-5677; 100 Kapalua Dr; per day $16, racquet rental $6; ☻ 8am-6pm Mon-Fri, 8am-4pm Sat & Sun) is Maui's largest full-service tennis club, with 20 Plexipave courts and an array of clinics. If you're on your own, give the club a ring and they'll match you with other players for singles or doubles games.

Kapalua Dive Company (☎ 669-3448; www.kapalua dive.com; Kapalua Beach; snorkel rental per hr $8; kayak/snorkel tours $70; ☻ 7:30am-4:30pm) offers a range of water activities, including kayak tours that take you snorkeling, and a full menu of dive outings from beach dives ($75) to kayak dives ($99) and scooter dives ($110).

Tours

Maui Pineapple Company (☎ 669-5491; Office Rd; 2½hr tours $40; ☻ tours 9am & 11:45am Mon-Fri) opens its dusty red fields for pineapple-plantation tours led by seasoned workers who give you the lowdown on the pineapple biz and let you harvest one of those juicy delights to take home. Reservations are required, as are covered shoes…those spines are sharp!

Festivals & Events

Mercedes-Benz Championship (www.pgatour.com) Tiger and friends tee off at the PGA Tour's season opener in early January at the Plantation course, vying for a multi-million-dollar purse.

Celebration of the Arts (www.celebrationofthearts .org) This festival in April at the Ritz-Carlton celebrates traditional Hawaiian culture with workshops, hula demonstrations, chants and storytelling.

Kapalua Wine & Food Festival (www.kapaluamaui .com) A culinary extravaganza held over four days in late June at the Ritz-Carlton, it features renowned winemakers and Hawaii's hottest chefs in cooking demonstrations and wine tastings.

Billabong Pro Maui (www.billabongpro.com/maui) This annual women's title race, held at Honolua Bay when the surf's up in mid-December, showcases the world's top *wahine* (female) surfers. And as the final event of the World Championship Tour, it often determines the world's champion.

Sleeping

Kapalua Villas (☎ 669-8088, 800-545-0018; www.kapalu avillas.com; 500 Office Rd; 1br/2br from $319/419; ▣ ▣) OK, budget really isn't part of the vernacular in Kapalua, but if you have a small group, this is the most affordable way to go. Three luxury condominium complexes comprise Kapalua Villas, with some units on the golf course and others overlooking the beach. One-bedroom units sleep up to four; two-bedroom units sleep six. Amenities include free tennis and discounted golf.

Ritz-Carlton Kapalua (☎ 669-6200, 800-262-8440; www.ritzcarlton.com; 1 Ritz-Carlton Dr; r incl breakfast from $450; ▣ 🛜 ▣) This luxe hotel's low-keyed elegance attracts the exclusive golf crowd. On a hillside fronting the greens and the sea, the hotel has a heated multilevel swimming pool shaded by palm trees, a spa and a fitness club. Rooms have oversized marble bathrooms, goose-down pillows…you get the picture.

Eating

Honolua Store (☎ 669-6128; 502 Office Rd; lunches $5-7; 🕑 6am-8:30pm) A nod to normalcy in the midst of lavish exclusiveness, this general store's deli serves sandwiches and plate lunches. It's all takeout but there are picnic tables on the porch where you can chow down alongside the brawny construction workers who flock here at lunchtime.

our pick Sansei Seafood Restaurant & Sushi Bar (☎ 669-6286; 600 Office Rd; sushi $4-15, mains $17-32; 🕑 5-10pm Sun & Mon, 5:30-10pm Tue-Sat) The imaginative menu takes sushi to a whole different level. Feast on luscious creations like the ahi sashimi wrapped in a panko-crusted roll, or the island-style mango and crab sushi. Be sure to sample some of the non-sushi house specials too. A standout is the tempura rock shrimp in garlic aioli, which flawlessly blends Japanese and French flavors. Order before 6pm and all food is discounted 25%.

Pineapple Grill (☎ 669-9600; Kapalua Bay Golf Course clubhouse, 300 Kapalua Dr; lunch $10-16, dinner mains $28-40; 🕑 11am-2pm & 5-10pm) Pineapple Grill has it all, from a sweeping hilltop view to a sleek exhibition kitchen that whips up innovative fusion fare. Island flavor abounds from the Maui coffee–roasted duck breast to the fresh pineapple cake topped with macadamia nut ice cream. Come before 6pm to take advantage of the three-course ($32) sunset dinner specials.

Plantation House Restaurant (☎ 669-6299; 2000 Plantation Club Dr; breakfast & lunch $8-18, dinner mains $30-40; 🕑 8am-3pm & 5:30-9pm) This open-air restaurant above the golf course pairs reliably good food with a grand view clear out to the ocean. The breakfast and lunch menu highlights Hawaiian accents with dishes like seared ahi Benedict, while dinner takes a Mediterranean slant. Think fresh Hawaiian fish, pinot noir glaze and caramelized Maui onions.

KAHEKILI HIGHWAY

If you're hungry for an adventure, this razor-thin road traversing the rugged northern tip of the island will sate any appetite. Cliff-side views, hidden pools and ridgeline trails – the terrain's so ravishingly rural that it's hard to imagine trendy west Maui could hold such untouched country. The key to its preservation is the Kahekili Hwy (highway – ha!), which narrows to the width of a driveway, keeping construction trucks and tourist buses at bay.

Not for the faint of heart, sections slow to just 5mph as the road wraps around hairpin curves. Indeed, a two-mile stretch around the village of Kahakuloa is a mere one lane with cliffs on one side and a sheer drop on the other – if you hit oncoming traffic here you may be doing much of your traveling in reverse! But heck, if you can handle that, this largely overlooked route offers all sorts of thrills, from horseback riding to mighty blowholes.

Don't be fooled by car rental maps that show the road as a dotted line – it's paved and open to the public the entire way. There are no services, so gas up before heading off, and give yourself at least two hours' driving time, not counting stops.

Waiehu & Waihe'e

Navigating from the eastern end of the highway, you start just north of Wailuku where Waiehu Beach Rd turns into Kahekili Hwy. From here, it runs through the sleepy towns of Waiehu and Waihe'e where the county-run **Waiehu Municipal Golf Course** (☎ 243-7400; 200 Halewaiu Rd; green fees $50, optional cart $19), near the shore, is an affordable and easily walkable course.

WAIHE'E RIDGE TRAIL

Further west, this lightly trodden trail slices along a ridge top deep into the West Maui Mountains, rewarding hikers with breathtaking views along the way. The well-defined trail is a five-mile roundtrip and takes about three hours. It crosses forest reserve land, and though it's a bit steep, it's a fairly steady climb and not overly strenuous. Pack a lunch, as there's a primo picnic spot waiting at the end.

Starting at an elevation of 1000ft, the trail climbs a ridge, passing from pasture to cool forest. Guava trees and groves of rainbow eucalyptus are prominent along the way, and if you look closely you can usually find thimbleberries. From the 0.75-mile post, panoramic views open up with a scene that sweeps clear down to the ocean along the Waihe'e Gorge and deep into pleated valleys. As you continue, you'll enter ohia forest with native birds and get distant views of waterfalls cascading down the mountains. The ridge-top views are similar to those you'd see from a helicopter, though the stillness along this route can be appreciated only by those on foot. The trail ends at the 2563ft peak of Lanilili, where you'll enjoy awesome views in all directions.

To get to the trailhead, take the one-lane paved road just south of the 7-mile marker that leads up to the Boy Scouts' Camp Mahulia. The trailhead, marked with a 'Na Ala Hele' sign, is a mile up on the left just before the camp.

Waihe'e to Kahakuloa

For a real *paniolo* experience, saddle up at **Mendes Ranch** (☎ 871-5222; www.mendesranch.com; 3530 Kahekili Hwy; 2hr ride $110; ⊗ rides 8:15am & 12:15pm), a working cattle ranch near the 7-mile marker. The scenery on these rides includes everything from jungle valleys to lofty seacliffs and waterfalls.

For an Eden-like scene, stop at the pull-off 0.1 miles north of the 8-mile marker and look down into the ravine below to see a cascading **waterfall** framed by double pools.

Continuing around beep-as-you-go hairpin turns, the highway gradually levels out atop sea cliffs. Before the 10-mile marker is **Turnbull Studios & Sculpture Garden** (☎ 244-9838; ⊗ 10am-5pm Tue-Fri) where you can view Bruce Turnbull's ambitious bronze and wood creations, as well as the works of other area artists. Very cool stuff.

Just before the 14-mile marker, the hilltop **Kaukini Gallery & Gift Shop** (☎ 244-3371; ⊗ 10am-5pm) has works by island artists, with watercolors, native-fiber baskets and pottery. Also eye-catching is the view of Kahakuloa village from the shop grounds.

Kahakuloa Village

Cradled in a tidy valley and embraced by towering sea cliffs, remote Kahakuloa retains a solidly Hawaiian character. Farmers tend taro patches, poi dogs wander across the road, and a missionary-era church marks the village center.

You won't find any stores here, but villagers set up roadside stands selling snacks to day-trippers. For shave ice, hit Ululani's hot-pink stand. For delicious banana bread stop at Julia's lime-green sugar shack. In this one-road town, you can't miss 'em.

Heading up out of the valley a pull-off above the northern edge of town provides a bird's-eye view of the village and the surrounding coast. The rise at the backdrop of Kahakuloa Bay is **Kahakuloa Head** (636ft), once a favorite cliff-diving spot of Hawaiian chiefs. As you climb out of the valley, the terrain is hilly, with rocky cattle pastures punctuated by tall sisal plants. At a number of pull-offs, you can stop and explore. Lush pastures invite you to traipse down the cliffs and out along the rugged coastline.

Ocean Baths & Bellstone

One-tenth of a mile beyond the 16-mile marker, look to the right for a large dirt pull-off and a well-beaten path that leads 15 minutes down lava cliffs to **natural ocean baths** on the ocean's edge. Cut out of slippery lava rock and encrusted with olivine minerals, these incredibly clear pools sit in the midst of roaring surf. Some have natural steps, but if you're tempted to go in, size it up carefully – people unfamiliar with the water conditions here have been swept into the sea and drowned. If the rocks are covered in silt from recent storm runoffs, or the waves look high, forget about it – it's dangerous.

That huge boulder with concave marks on the inland side of the road just beyond the pull-off is **Pohaku Kani**, a bellstone. If you hit it with a rock on the Kahakuloa side, where the deepest indentations are, you might be able to get a hollow sound. It's a bit resonant if you hit it just right, though it certainly takes some imagination to hear it ring like a bell.

Nakalele Point

After the bellstone the mile markers change; the marker beyond 16 becomes 42 and the numbers go down from here. Just 0.2 miles after the 41-mile marker look for the **Ohai**

Viewpoint, on the *makai* (seaward) side of the road. The viewpoint won't be marked but there's a sign announcing the start of the Ohai Trail. Don't bother with the trail – it's not particularly interesting. Instead, bear to the left and walk out to the tip of the point just two minutes away for a jaw-dropping coastal view that includes a glimpse of the Nakalele Blowhole. If you have kids, be careful – the crumbly cliff has a sudden drop of nearly 800ft!

The **Nakalele Blowhole** roars when the surf is up but it's a sleeper when the seas are calm. To check on its mood park at the boulder-lined pull-off 0.4 miles beyond the 39-mile marker. It's a 15-minute walk down to the blowhole. You can get a glimpse of the action, if there is any, just a few hundred yards beyond the parking lot.

At the 38-mile marker, a mile-long trail leads out to a **light station** at the end of wind-swept Nakalele Point, where you'll find a coastline of arches and other interesting formations worn out of the rocks by the pounding surf. During winter you can sometimes spot humpbacks breaching offshore.

Punalau Beach

Back on the highway, Moloka'i comes into view as you make your way along Maui's northernmost point en route to Kapalua (p358). Ironwood-lined Punalau Beach, 0.3 miles after the 35-mile marker, makes a worthy stop if you're up for a solitary stroll. Swimming is a no-go though, as a rocky shelf creates unfavorable conditions for water activities.

CENTRAL MAUI

Your first look at Maui will likely be here, on the windswept flatlands that separate Maui's two mountain masses. Paradoxically, central Maui lays claim to both the island's largest urban sprawl and its greenest agricultural land. Fields of waving sugarcane stretch clear across the central plains from Kahului to Ma'alaea. But central Maui's claim to fame for travelers is found in the water. Anything with a sail rips in this wind-whipped region. Kanaha Beach has morphed into one of the hottest windsurfing and kiteboarding destinations on the planet, bursting each day into a colorful mile-long sea of sails. Central Maui

also holds other watery wonders: a dazzling tropical aquarium, two waterbird sanctuaries and rainforested 'Iao Valley.

KAHULUI

pop 20,150

All roads lead to Kahului. It's home to the island's gateway airport and cruise-ship ports. Just about everything that enters Maui comes through this workaday town thick with warehouses, big-box stores and shopping centers. Hardly a vacation scene, you say. True, but if you dig a little deeper you'll find more to your liking. You have to go island-style to have fun here: talk story with the locals at the Saturday swap meet, take in a concert on the lawn of the cultural center or join the wave-riding action at Kanaha Beach. There's a lot more to Kahului than first meets the eye.

History

Fronted by the island's deepwater harbor, Kahului has long been the commercial heart of Maui. In the 1880s it became headquarters to Hawaii's first railroad, built to haul sugar from the refineries to the port. In 1900 an outbreak of bubonic plague hit Kahului and the settlement that had grown up around the harbor was purposely burned to the ground.

Present-day Kahului is a planned community developed in the early 1950s by the Alexander & Baldwin sugar company. It was called 'Dream City' by cane workers, who had long dreamed of moving away from dusty mill camps in places like Pa'ia and Pu'unene into a home of their own.

Orientation

The airport is on the east side of town, connected to central Kahului by Keolani Pl, which leads to both the Haleakala Hwy (Hwy 37) and the Hana Hwy (Hwy 36). Ka'ahumanu Ave (Hwy 32) is Kahului's main artery, connecting Kahului to neighboring Wailuku. Dairy Rd, to the south, links to both Lahaina (take Hwy 380) and Kihei (take Hwy 311).

Information

Bank of Hawaii (☎ 871-8250; 27 S Pu'unene Ave)
Borders Books & Music Café (☎ 877-6160; Maui Marketplace, 270 Dairy Rd; ☷ 9am-10pm Sun-Thu, 9am-11pm Fri & Sat) Good selection of maps, Hawaiiana books and international newspapers.
Kahului Public Library (☎ 873-3097; 90 School St; ☷ noon-8pm Tue, 9am-5pm Wed-Sat)

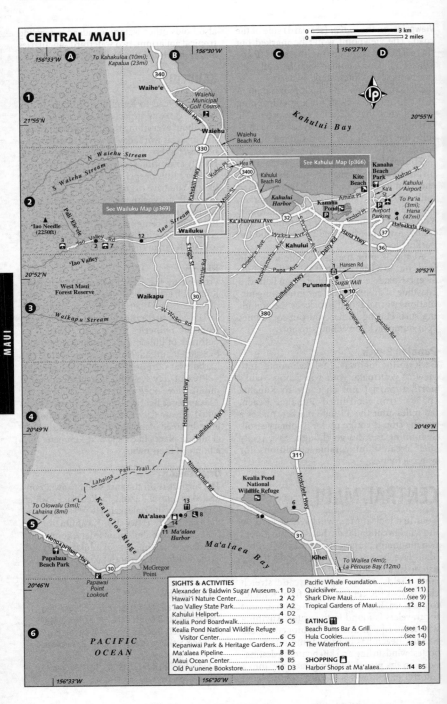

CENTRAL MAUI

| 0 | 3 km |
| 0 | 2 miles |

SIGHTS & ACTIVITIES	
Alexander & Baldwin Sugar Museum..	1 D3
Hawai'i Nature Center	2 A2
'Iao Valley State Park	3 A2
Kahului Heliport	4 D2
Kealia Pond Boardwalk	5 C5
Kealia Pond National Wildlife Refuge Visitor Center	6 C5
Kepaniwai Park & Heritage Gardens	7 A2
Ma'alaea Pipeline	8 B5
Maui Ocean Center	9 B5
Old Pu'unene Bookstore	10 D3
Pacific Whale Foundation	11 B5
Quicksilver	(see 11)
Shark Dive Maui	(see 9)
Tropical Gardens of Maui	12 B2

EATING	
Beach Bums Bar & Grill	(see 14)
Hula Cookies	(see 14)
The Waterfront	13 B5

SHOPPING	
Harbor Shops at Ma'alaea	14 B5

FedEx Kinko's (☎ 871-2000; Dairy Center, 395 Dairy Rd; per min 20¢; ☷ 7am-10pm Mon-Fri, 9am-9pm Sat, 9am-6pm Sun) Internet with no minimums.

Longs Drugs (☎ 877-0041; Maui Mall, 70 E Ka'ahumanu Ave; ☷ 7am-midnight) The town's largest pharmacy.

Maui Visitors Bureau (☎ 872-3893; www.visitmaui .com; Kahului Airport; ☷ 7:45am-9:45pm) This booth in the airport's arrivals area has tons of free tourist brochures.

Post office (☎ 871-2487; 138 S Pu'unene Ave, Kahului, HI 96732)

Sights

KANAHA BEACH PARK

On a windy day this place is a kaleidoscope of swirling sails. Both windsurfing and kite-surfing are so hot here that the beach has been divvied up, with kitesurfers converging at the southwest end, known as **Kite Beach**, and windsurfers hitting the water at the northeast end. Kanaha Beach is the best place in Maui for beginners to learn both sports, and most windsurfing and kitesurfing shops (right) give their lessons here.

A section in the middle of the beach is roped off for swimmers, but this place is really all about using wind power. The local facilities include rest rooms, showers and shaded picnic tables.

To get there, look for the shoreline access sign down by the car-rental lots at the airport, or if you're coming from downtown Kahului take Amala Pl.

KANAHA POND BIRD SANCTUARY

The first stop Audubon tours make when they arrive on Maui is at this **sanctuary** (Hwy 37; admission free; ☷ 6am-6pm), a haven for rare Hawaiian birds. Most notable is the *ae'o* (black-necked stilt), a wading bird with long orange legs that feeds along the pond's marshy edges. Even though this graceful bird has a population of just 1500 in the entire state, you can count on spotting it here.

An **observation deck** just beyond the parking lot offers the ideal lookout for spotting the *ae'o*, native coots and black-crowned night herons. Close the gate and walk into the preserve quietly; you should be able to make several sightings right along the shoreline.

Hiking is allowed on the sanctuary's service roads from September to March – when the birds aren't nesting – by obtaining a free permit from the **Department of Land & Natural Resources** (Map p369; ☎ 984-8100; Room 101, State Office Bldg, 54 S High St, Wailuku; ☷ 8am-4:30pm Mon-Fri).

MAUI NUI BOTANICAL GARDENS

If you're interested in the subtle beauty of native Hawaiian plants, this **garden** (☎ 249-2798; 150 Kanaloa Ave; admission free; ☷ 8am-4pm Mon-Sat) is a gem. Come here to view rare species and to identify plants you've heard about but haven't yet seen, such as *wauke* (paper mulberry, used to make tapa) and *'iliahi* (sandalwood). Don't expect it to be overly flowery, however. What you won't see here are the riotous colors of exotic tropicals that now dominate most Hawaiian gardens.

MAUI ARTS & CULTURAL CENTER

Maui's pride and joy, the state-of-the-art **Maui Arts & Cultural Center** (MACC; ☎ 242-2787; www .mauiarts.org; 1 Cameron Way; admission free; ☷ tour 11am Wed) is the island's premier concert venue. There are free tours (reservations are required) that include both the concert halls and the grounds, which have the remains of a heiau. The center's **Schaefer International Gallery** (☷ 11am-5pm Tue-Sat) features changing exhibits of works by both island and international artists.

Activities

WINDSURFING

Windswept Kahului is the base for Maui's main windsurfing operations. Board-and-rig rentals start around $50/300 per day/week. The business is competitive, so ask about discounts. If you're new to the sport, introductory classes are readily available, last a couple of hours and cost $80.

Reliable shops that sell and rent gear and arrange lessons:

Hawaiian Island Surf & Sport (☎ 871-4981, 800-231-6958; www.hawaiianisland.com; 415 Dairy Rd; ☷ 8:30am-6pm)

Hi-Tech Surf Sports (☎ 877-2111; www.htmaui.com; 425 Koloa St; ☷ 9am-6pm)

Second Wind (☎ 877-7467, 800-936-7787; www .secondwindmaui.com; 111 Hana Hwy; ☷ 9am-6pm)

KITESURFING

Kitesurfing has taken off big-time in Kahului. The action centers on Kite Beach, the southwest end of Kanaha Beach Park. If you've never tried it before, you can learn the ropes from some of the very pros who've made kite-surfing such a hot wave ride. Vans set up right at Kite Beach to offer lessons. Expect to pay about $275 for a half-day intro course. Check out the scene live at kitebeachcam.com.

MAUI

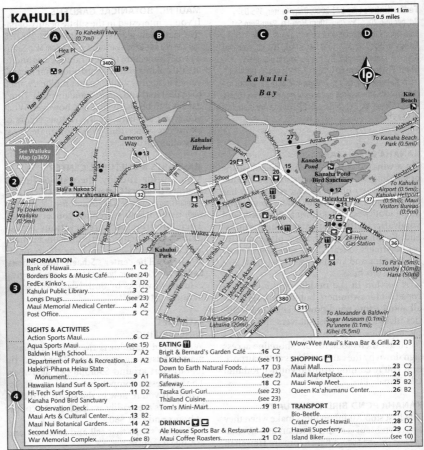

KAHULUI

Recommended:

Kiteboarding School Maui (☎ 873-0015; www
.ksmaui.com; Kite Beach)

Aqua Sports Maui (☎ 242-8015; www.mauikiteboard
inglessons.com; 111 Hana Hwy)

Action Sports Maui (☎ 871-5857; www.actionsports
maui.com; 96 Amala Pl)

HELICOPTER RIDES

Several companies, including **AlexAir** (☎ 871-
0792), **Blue Hawaiian** (☎ 871-8844), **Mauiscape**
(☎ 877-7272) and **Sunshine** (☎ 871-5600), offer
helicopter tours of Maui. All operate out of
the **Kahului Heliport** (1 Kahului Airport Rd), at the
southeast side of Kahului Airport. Typical
30-minute tours of the jungly West Maui
Mountains cost around $125 and one-hour

circle-island tours about $275. Discounts
abound. Companies advertise in the free tourist magazines, with all sorts of deals.

Festivals & Events

Ki Ho'alu Slack Key Guitar Festival (www.mauiarts
.org) At this event held on the lawn of the Maui Arts &
Cultural Center in late June, top slack key guitarists from
throughout Hawaii take the stage.

Maui Marathon (www.mauimarathon.com) Held
in mid-September, this road race begins at the Queen
Ka'ahumanu Center in Kahului and ends 26.2 miles later at
Whalers Village in Ka'anapali.

Sleeping

Kanaha Beach Park allows camping (see p330
for information about permits and fees) but

it's not recommended. The campsites are right beneath the airport's flight path with planes rumbling overhead from dawn to midnight. More importantly, folks down on their luck hang out here and personal safety is a real issue after dark.

The best place to stay in the area is in the nearby surfing haunt of Pa'ia (p388), just a 10-minute drive from Kanaha Beach.

Eating

Tasaka Guri-Guri (☎ 871-4513; Maui Mall, 70 E Ka'ahumanu Ave; scoop/quart 50¢/$5; ⏰ 10am-6pm Mon-Thu & Sat, to 8pm Fri, to 4pm Sun) For the coolest treat in town search out this hole-in-the-wall shop dishing up tangy homemade pineapple sherbet. The *guri-guri*, as it's called, is so wildly popular that locals pick up quarts on the way to the airport to take to friends on the Neighbor Islands.

Down to Earth Natural Foods (☎ 877-2661; 305 Dairy Rd; salad bar per lb $9; ⏰ 7am-9pm Mon-Sat, 8am-8pm Sun) Everything you'd expect from a good health food store including an excellent deli and robust salad bar. Take your goodies to the upstairs dining room or pack 'em for the beach.

Piñatas (☎ 877-8707; 395 Dairy Rd; mains $5-10; ⏰ 10:30am-8pm Mon-Sat, from 11am Sun) Join the surfers at this unpretentious cantina serving good Mexican food at honest prices. You'll find all the usual taco and enchilada combination plates, as well as its famed 'kitchen sink burrito,' a monstrous wrap stuffed with just about everything but the sink.

Da Kitchen (☎ 871-7782; 425 Koloa St; plate lunches $9-12; ⏰ 9am-9pm) Hawaiian decor and unbeatable local grinds make this a favorite meal stop. Da Lau Lau Plate, featuring steamed pork wrapped in taro leaves, is a top choice if you don't count calories. If you prefer it leaner, go for the teriyaki chicken. Expect a crowd at lunch but don't be deterred, as service is quick.

Thailand Cuisine (☎ 873-0225; Maui Mall, 70 E Ka'ahumanu Ave; mains $10-15; ⏰ 10:30am-3pm & 5-9:30pm) The readers of Maui's daily newspaper voted this family-run eatery the island's best ethnic restaurant. And yes, it lives up to the reputation. Start with the shrimp summer rolls, and then move on to the aromatic green curries and the tangy lemongrass chicken. Dozens of tasty vegetarian options feature on the menu too.

Brigit & Bernard's Garden Café (☎ 877-6000; 335 Ho'ohana St; mains $10-20; ⏰ 11am-2:30pm Mon-Fri & 5-9pm Wed-Sat) The 'garden' is laughable – this café overlooks a busy road in an industrial center. But the food is damn good and if you swing by at lunchtime you'll need to hustle just to find an empty table. The extensive menu runs from fresh salads and grilled local fish to authentic German dishes like Wiener schnitzel.

If you need to stock up the condo on the way in from the airport, the **Safeway** (☎ 877-3377; 170 E Kamehameha Ave; ⏰ 24hr) is in the town center and it never closes.

Drinking

Wow-Wee Maui's Kava Bar & Grill (☎ 871-1414; 333 Dairy Rd; ⏰ 11am-9pm Sun-Thu, to 11pm Fri & Sat; 🖳) This hip café serves up an intoxicating combination of kava and gourmet chocolate. A ceremonial drink in old Hawaii, the kava is an elixir made from the roots of the *Piper methysticum* plant. It gives a mild buzz – and yes, it's legal. Wow-Wee Maui's chocolate bars, some flavors spiked with kava, will also make you swoon.

Maui Coffee Roasters (☎ 877-2877; 444 Hana Hwy; ⏰ 7am-6pm Mon-Fri, 8am-5pm Sat, 8am-2:30pm Sun; 🖳 🛜) Good vibes and good java at this coffee shop where surfers linger over lattes while surfing on free wi-fi. Need to jumpstart your day? Step up to the bar and order a Sledge Hammer – a quadruple espresso with steamed half and half.

Ale House Sports Bar & Restaurant (☎ 877-9001; 355 E Kamehameha Ave) Wash-ashores from the mainland and locals alike gather here to watch sports on big-screen TVs. And to make sure everyone shows up, it offers $2.50 draft beers whenever a big game is on.

Entertainment

Maui Arts & Cultural Center (MACC; ☎ box office 242-7469; www.mauiarts.org; 1 Cameron Way) There's always something happening at this entertainment complex, which boasts two indoor theaters and an outdoor amphitheater, all with excellent acoustics. As Maui's main venue for music, theater and dance, it hosts everything from ukulele jams to touring rock bands. Check the schedule online for the latest lineup.

Shopping

Kahului has all of Maui's big-box discount chains and the island's two largest malls, **Queen Ka'ahumanu Center** (☎ 877-4325; 275 Ka'ahumanu Ave;

MAUI

9:30am-9pm Mon-Fri, to 7pm Sat, 9:30am-5pm Sun) and **Maui Marketplace** (☎ 873-0400; 270 Dairy Rd; ⏰ 10am-9pm Mon-Sat, to 7pm Sun).

Maui Swap Meet (☎ 877-3100; Maui Community College, 310 Ka'ahumanu Ave; admission 50¢; ⏰ 7am-1pm Sat) For a scene that glows with aloha, spend a Saturday morning chatting with local farmers and craftspeople at Maui's largest outdoor market. You'll not only find fresh organic Hana fruits, Kula veggies and homemade banana bread, but it's a fun place to souvenir shop for everything from Hawaiian tapa to Maui-designed T-shirts. Don't be mislead by the term 'swap meet' – most stands are selling quality local goods and every dollar you spend here stays in the community.

Getting There & Around
For information about travel through Kahului Airport see p335.

CAR
Instead of the usual car rental agencies at the airport, consider going green with **Bio-Beetle** (☎ 873-6121, 877-873-6121; www.bio-beetle.com; 55 Amala Pl; per day/week from $50/250), which rents Volkswagen Jettas and Beetles that run on recycled vegetable oil.

BICYCLE
Island Biker (☎ 877-7744; 415 Dairy Rd; per day/week $40/140; ⏰ 9am-5pm Mon-Fri, to 3pm Sat) rents quality mountain bikes and road-racing bikes.

Crater Cycles Hawaii (☎ 893-2020; 358 Papa Pl; per day downhill/electric bikes $75/20; ⏰ 10am-5pm Mon-Thu & Sat, 9am-noon Fri) are the people to go to for serious off-road bikes with full suspension and all the accoutrements. Non-diehards will like the electric bikes, which run 20 miles on a charge before pedal-power kicks in.

BUS
The **Maui Bus** (☎ 871-4838) connects Kahului with Ma'alaea, Kihei, Wailea, Makawao and Lahaina; each route costs $1 and runs hourly, except for Makawao, which runs every 90 minutes. There are also free buses that operate hourly between Kahului and Wailuku.

HALEKI'I-PIHANA HEIAU STATE MONUMENT
Overgrown and nearly forgotten, **Haleki'i-Pihana Heiau** (Map p366; Hea Pl; admission free; ⏰ sunrise-sunset) holds the hilltop ruins of two of Maui's most important temples.

The site was the royal court of Kahekili, Maui's last ruling chief, and the birthplace of Keopuolani, wife of Kamehameha the Great. After his victory at the battle of 'Iao in 1790, Kamehameha came to this site to worship his war god Ku, offering the last human sacrifice on Maui.

Haleki'i, the first heiau, has stepped stone walls that tower above 'Iao Stream, the source for the stone used in construction. The pyramidlike mound of **Pihana Heiau** is a five-minute walk beyond, but a thick overgrowth of kiawe makes it harder to discern.

Although it's all but abandoned, a certain mana (spiritual essence) still emanates from the site. To imagine it all through the eyes of the ancient Hawaiians, ignore the creeping suburbia and concentrate instead on the wild ocean and mountain vistas.

The site is about 2 miles northeast of central Wailuku. From Waiehu Beach Rd (Hwy 340), turn inland onto Kuhio Pl, then take the first left onto Hea Pl and drive up through the gates.

WAILUKU
pop 12,300
Unabashedly local, Wailuku is an enigma. As an ancient religious and political center, it boasts more sights on the National Register of Historic Places than any other town on Maui but sees the fewest tourists. As the county capital, its central area wears a modern facade of midrise office buildings, while its age-old backstreets hold an earthy mishmash of curio shops, galleries and mom-and-pop stores that just beg for browsing. If you are here at lunchtime you're in luck. Thanks to a combination of low rent and hungry government employees, Wailuku dishes up tasty eats at prices that shame Maui's more touristed towns.

Information
The county and state office buildings are adjacent on S High St, near its intersection with Main St.
First Hawaiian Bank (☎ 877-2377; 27 N Market St)
Maui Memorial Medical Center (Map p366; ☎ 244-9056; 221 Mahalani St; ⏰ 24hr) The island's main hospital is in the eastern suburbs of Wailuku.
Maui Visitors Bureau (MVB; ☎ 244-3530, 800-525-6284; www.visitmaui.com; 1727 Wili Pa Loop; ⏰ 8am-4:30pm Mon-Fri) Essentially an administrative office – you'll find better information at the airport booth (p363).
Post office (☎ 244-1653; 250 Imi Kala St)

Dangers & Annoyances

One caution: the town can get rough at night. The public parking lot on W Main St is an after-dark hangout that's rife with drug dealing and fights and gets more police calls than any other spot on Maui.

Sights

BAILEY HOUSE MUSEUM

This evocative **museum** (☎ 244-3326; 2375 W Main St; adult/child 7-12 $5/1; ⏰ 10am-4pm Mon-Sat) occupies the 1833 home of Wailuku's first Christian missionary, Edward Bailey. The second story, decorated with Bailey's sparse furnishings, reflects his era.

But it's the Hawaiian section on the ground floor that holds the real intrigue. Check out the display of spears and shark-tooth daggers (ouch!) used in the bloody battles at nearby 'Iao Valley. There's also a notable collection of native wood bowls, stone adzes, feather lei and tapa cloth.

Don't miss the 10ft redwood surfboard that surfing legend Duke Kahanamoku rode and the koa fishing canoe (c 1900), both in an outdoor exhibit near the parking lot.

KA'AHUMANU CHURCH

This handsome 19th-century **church** (cnr Main & High Sts) is named for Queen Ka'ahumanu, who cast aside the old gods and allowed Christianity to flourish. The clock in the steeple, brought around the Horn by early missionaries, still keeps accurate time. Hymns ring out in Hawaiian at Sunday morning services, but other times it's a look-from-outside sight, as the church is usually locked.

Festivals & Events

Maui County Fair (www.mauicountyfair.com) Get a feel for Maui's agricultural roots at this venerable fair held in late September at the War Memorial Complex (Map p366), with farm exhibits, tasty island grinds and a dazzling orchid display.

E Ho'oulu Aloha (www.mauimuseum.org) Translated as 'To Grow in Love,' this family-friendly festival held in November at the Bailey House Museum features hula, ukulele masters, crafts, food and more. You won't find a friendlier community scene.

Sleeping

Wailuku's two hostels are in older, termite-gnawed buildings that occasionally get a fresh coat of paint but are otherwise spartan. Because of frequent staffing changes it's hard to predict what your experience will be like. Best advice: size up the places when you arrive and don't dish out money for a lengthy stay in advance.

Northshore Hostel (☎ 986-8095, 866-946-7835; www.northshorehostel.com; 2080 E Vineyard St; dm $25, s/d with shared bathroom $50/65; 🖳 🛜) The smaller of the two hostels, it's a bit spiffier but leaner on the perks. Two considerations – the security is better and overseas travelers will like the free international calls.

Banana Bungalow (☎ 244-5090, 800-846-7835; www.mauihostel.com; 310 N Market St; dm $25, s/d with shared bathroom $60/71; 🖳 🛜) The dorms are cramped, but on the plus side amenities include a

MAUI

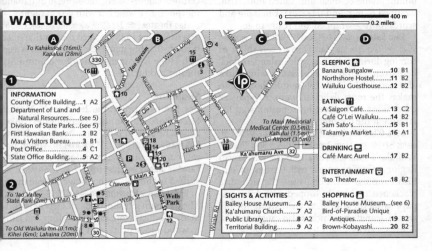

WAILUKU

0 ——— 400 m
0 ——— 0.2 miles

To Kahakuloa (16mi);
Kapalua (28mi)

To Maui Memorial
Medical Center (0.5mi);
Kahului Airport (3.5mi)

To 'Iao Valley
State Park (2mi)

To Old Wailuku Inn (0.1mi);
Kihei (6mi); Lahaina (20mi)

Chevron

Wells
Park

Ka'ahumanu Ave (32)

INFORMATION
County Office Building....1 A2
Department of Land and
Natural Resources......(see 5)
Division of State Parks...(see 5)
First Hawaiian Bank........2 B2
Maui Visitors Bureau......3 B1
Post Office....................4 C1
State Office Building........5 A2

SIGHTS & ACTIVITIES
Bailey House Museum....6 A2
Ka'ahumanu Church.......7 A2
Public Library................8 A2
Territorial Building..........9 A2

SLEEPING 🛏
Banana Bungalow..........10 B1
Northshore Hostel.........11 B2
Wailuku Guesthouse......12 B2

EATING 🍴
A Saigon Café...............13 C2
Café O'Lei Wailuku.......14 B2
Sam Sato's....................15 B1
Takamiya Market...........16 A1

DRINKING 🍷
Café Marc Aurel...........17 B2

ENTERTAINMENT 🎭
'Iao Theater.................18 B2

SHOPPING 🛍
Bailey House Museum...(see 6)
Bird-of-Paradise Unique
Antiques....................19 B2
Brown-Kobayashi..........20 B2

backyard hot tub, BBQ facilities, a shed for storing windsurfing gear and, best of all, free island tours.

Wailuku Guesthouse (☎ 877-986-8270; www.wailuku house.com; 210 S Market St; r $79-99; 🛜 📺) If you're on a budget and thinking of a private room, you'll get more bang for your buck at this family-run guesthouse than at the hostels. The simple, clean rooms have a bathroom, private entrance, refrigerator and coffeemaker. Guests have access to a BBQ and pool.

our pick **Old Wailuku Inn** (☎ 244-5897, 800-305-4899; www.mauiinn.com; 2199 Kaho'okele St; r incl breakfast $165-195; 📺) The finest period B&B in Maui, this elegant 1920s home retains the antique furniture and native hardwood floors of earlier times, while discreetly adding modern amenities. Each room is unique, but all are large and comfy with Hawaiian quilts warming the beds. Honeymooners love the 'Ilima Room, with its whirlpool tub right in the bedroom. A very classy place.

Eating

Tom's Mini-Mart (Map p366; ☎ 244-2323; 372 Waiehu Beach Rd; shave ice $2.50; 🕑 7am-6pm Mon-Sat) Search out this friendly neighborhood shop in the middle of nowhere for Maui's finest shave ice, soft and fluffy. They even make their own fruit syrups, which burst with tropical flavor. You gotta try the mango.

Takamiya Market (☎ 244-3404; 359 N Market St; takeout meals $4-8; 🕑 5:30am-6:30pm Mon-Sat) This old-time grocer specializes in all things Hawaiian. Lunchtime features ahi *poke*, *laulau* (steamed bundle made of meat and salted butterfish, wrapped in taro and *ti* leaves), *kalua* pig and scores more – wrapped and ready to go.

Sam Sato's (☎ 244-7124; 1750 Wili Pa Loop; mains $5-8; 🕑 7am-2pm Mon-Sat) Don't even think of coming during the noon rush – islanders flock here from far and wide for Sam's saimin-like 'dry noodles.' Maui's top noodle house also makes the most delicious *manju* (Japanese cakes filled with sweet bean paste), sold for takeout at the counter until 4pm.

Café O'Lei Wailuku (☎ 986-0044; 62 Market St; mains $7-14; 🕑 11am-3pm Mon-Fri & 5-8pm Thu-Sat) Wailuku's smartest restaurant serves Hawaii Regional Cuisine on par with the best of 'em. Fish connoisseurs, don't miss the signature blackened mahimahi topped with fresh papaya salsa; on your next visit, swing for the wasabi-seared ahi, which is also caught locally. Great specialty salads too.

> **BEAT YOUR OWN PATH**
>
> Ready to get down to some nitty-gritty exploring? Dusty Wailuku offers a bevy of historic treasures. Hawaii's best-known architect, Maui-born CW Dickey, left his mark in this town before moving on to fame in Honolulu. The c 1928 **public library** (cnr High & Aupuni Sts) is a classic example of Dickey's distinctive Hawaii regional design. Another Dickey creation, the **Territorial Building**, lies right across the street. Within a short walk are four more buildings on the National Register of Historic Places. To discover all the gems in town, pick up a copy of the free Wailuku Historic District walking map at the library or the Bailey House museum.

A Saigon Café (☎ 248-9560; cnr Main & Kaniela Sts; mains $7-20; 🕑 10am-9:30pm Mon-Sat, to 8:30pm Sun) The oldest and best Vietnamese restaurant on Maui has such a faithful local following that it's never even bothered to put up a sign, but it's well worth the effort to find. You'll love the food. Start with the green papaya salad, move on to the spicy *pho* (Vietnamese noodle soup) or perhaps the aromatic lemongrass chicken curry. To get there, take Central Ave to Nani St and turn south on Kaniela St.

Drinking & Entertainment

Café Marc Aurel (☎ 244-0852; 28 N Market St; 🕑 7am-at least 9pm Mon-Sat; 🛜) Proof positive that downhome Wailuku has its hip corners, this 'green certified' café brews organic espresso by day and morphs into a wine bar with jazz at night.

'Iao Theater (☎ 242-6969; www.mauionstage.com; 68 N Market St) This 1928 art-deco theater that once hosted such big names as Frank Sinatra and Bob Hope is now the venue for community theater productions.

Shopping

For the best browsing, head to N Market Street, lined with antique, clothing and trinket shops. Be sure to poke your head into **Brown-Kobayashi** (☎ 242-0804; 38 N Market St), which has museum-quality Asian antiques and **Bird-of-Paradise Unique Antiques** (☎ 242-7699; 56 N Market St), stuffed to the gills with vintage Hawaiiana.

Bailey House Museum (☎ 244-3326; 2375 W Main St) The museum gift shop sells all sorts of island-made products from salad dressings and jams to wood-block prints and koa bowls.

Getting There & Around

Maui Bus (☎ 871-4838) runs free buses between Wailuku and Kahului hourly from 8am to 9pm. Wailuku stops include the state office building and the post office.

'IAO VALLEY ROAD

'Iao Valley is such a sumptuous sight that in ancient times it was reserved for royalty. Today much of the upper valley's natural beauty is preserved as parkland, all reached via 'Iao Valley Rd, which ends at misty 'Iao Valley State Park.

Tropical Gardens of Maui

These fragrant **gardens** (☎ 244-3085; 200 'Iao Valley Rd; adult/child under 8 $5/free; ☯ 9am-4:30pm Mon-Sat), which straddle both sides of 'Iao Stream, showcase a superb orchid collection, endemic Hawaiian plants, brilliant bromeliads and a meditative bamboo grove with a trickling waterfall. See if you can find the world's largest orchid!

Kepaniwai Park & Heritage Gardens

This streamside county **park** (875 'Iao Valley Rd; ☯ 7am-7pm), 2 miles west of Wailuku, pays tribute to Hawaii's ethnic heritages. Sharing the grounds are a traditional Hawaiian *hale* (house), a New England–style missionary home, a Filipino farmer's hut, Japanese gardens and a Chinese pavilion with a statue of revolutionary hero Sun Yat-sen. 'Iao Stream runs through the park, bordered by well-used picnic shelters.

At the west end of the park is the **Hawai'i Nature Center** (☎ 244-6500; 875 'Iao Valley Rd; adult/child 5-12 $6/4; ☯ 10am-4pm), a nonprofit educational facility with interactive exhibits for young kids. For those over 10, more interesting are the center's two-hour **rain-forest walks** (adult/child $30/20) that climb into an otherwise inaccessible wilderness.

At a bend in the road about half a mile after Kepaniwai park, you'll likely see a few cars pulled over and their occupants staring off into Pali 'Ele'ele, a gorge on the right where a **rock formation** has eroded into the shape of a profile. Some legends associate it with a powerful kahuna (priest) who lived here during the 1500s, but today it bears an uncanny resemblance to former President John F Kennedy. If parking is difficult, continue on to 'Iao Valley State Park, as it's only a couple of minutes' walk back to the viewing site.

'Iao Valley State Park

Nowhere is Maui's verdant beauty better captured than at **'Iao Valley State Park** (admission free; ☯ 7am-7pm), where an emerald-green pinnacle shoots straight up from the valley floor. Nestled in the mountains, 3 miles west of Wailuku, the park extends clear up to Pu'u Kukui (5788ft), Maui's highest and wettest point.

'IAO NEEDLE

This rock pinnacle snuggled sensuously in the deep folds of velvety mountains takes its name from 'Iao, the beautiful daughter of Maui. The 2250ft 'Iao Needle is said to be 'Iao's clandestine lover, captured by an angry Maui and turned to stone. A monument to love, this is the big kahuna, the ultimate phallic symbol.

Whether you believe in legends or not, this place looks like something torn from the pages of a fairy tale. Clouds rising up the valley form an ethereal shroud around the top of 'Iao Needle. With a stream meandering beneath and the steep cliffs of the West Maui Mountains in the backdrop, it's easy to see why this is the most photographed scene on Maui. Just a few minutes' walk from the parking lot, you'll reach the bridge where most people snap their photos of the needle. A better idea is to take the walkway just before the bridge that loops downhill by the stream; this leads to the nicest photo angle, one that captures the stream, bridge and 'Iao Needle together.

If the water is high you'll see local kids taking bravado jumps from the bridge to the rocky stream below. You might be tempted to join them, but expect to get the stink eye – not to mention that the rocks below are potentially spine-crushing for unfamiliar divers. Better to take your dip in the swimming holes along the streamside path instead.

TRAILS

After you cross the bridge you'll come to two short trails that start opposite each other. Both take just 10 minutes to walk and shouldn't be missed. The upper path leads skyward up a series of steps, ending at a sheltered lookout with a closeup view of 'Iao Needle.

The lower path leads down along 'Iao Stream, skirting the rock-strewn streambed past native hau trees with hibiscus-like flowers. The path returns to the bridge via a garden of taro and a variety of other native Hawaiian plants.

MAUI

BLOODY WATERS

Filled now as it is with happy tourists and picnickers, it's hard to imagine 'Iao Valley was once the site of Maui's bloodiest battle. In 1790 Kamehameha the Great invaded Kahului by sea and routed the defending Maui warriors up into precipitous 'Iao Valley. Those unable to escape over the mountains were slaughtered along the stream. The waters of 'Iao Stream were so choked with bodies that the area was called Kepaniwai, meaning 'Dammed Waters'.

'Iao Valley Rd follows that same stream-side route, but today it's a delightful drive up to 'Iao Valley State Park and Maui's most famous landmark, 'Iao Needle.

PU'UNENE

Sugar's the lifeblood of Pu'unene. Endless fields of sugarcane expand out from the Hawaiian Commercial & Sugar (C&S) Company's mill that sits smack in the center of the village. If you happen to swing by when the mill is boiling down the sugarcane, the air hangs heavy with the sweet smell of molasses.

Pu'unene's main attraction is the **Alexander & Baldwin Sugar Museum** (☎ 871-8058; cnr Pu'unene Ave & Hansen Rd; adult/child 6-12 $7/2; ⏰ 9:30am-4:30pm Mon-Sat), an evocative collection in the former home of the mill's superintendent. Exhibits, including a working scale model of a cane-crushing plant, give the skinny on the sugarcane biz. But most interesting are the images of people. The museum traces how the privileged sons of missionaries wrested control over Maui's fertile valleys and dug the amazing irrigation system that made large-scale plantations viable. Representing the other end of the scale is an early-20th-century labor contract from the Japanese Emigration Company committing laborers to work the canefields 10 hours a day, 26 days a month for a mere $15.

KEALIA POND NATIONAL WILDLIFE REFUGE

A magnet for both birds and bird-watchers, this **national wildlife refuge** (☎ 875-1582; Mokulele Hwy; ⏰ 7:30am-4pm Mon-Fri) harbors native waterbirds year-round and migratory birds from October to April. In the rainy winter months Kealia Pond swells to 400 acres, making it one of the largest natural ponds in Hawaii. In summer it shrinks to half that size, creating the skirt of crystalline salt that gives Kealia (meaning 'salt-encrusted place') its name.

Birding is excellent from the boardwalk (see boxed text, opposite) on N Kihei Rd, as well as from the refuge's visitor center off Mokulele Hwy (Hwy 311) at the 6-mile marker. In both places, you're almost certain to spot wading Hawaiian black-necked stilts and Hawaiian coots, two endangered species that thrive in this sanctuary.

MA'ALAEA
pop 460

Ma'alaea literally means 'beginning of red dirt,' but once you're there you'll swear it means 'windy.' Prevailing trade winds funneling between Maui's two great rises, Haleakalā and the West Maui Mountains, whip down upon Ma'alaea. By midday you'll need to hold on to your hat. It's no coincidence that Maui's first windmill farm marches up the slopes above Ma'alaea.

Sights

Come eye to eye with all sorts of cool creatures at **Maui Ocean Center** (☎ 270-7000; www.maui oceancenter.com; 192 Ma'alaea Rd; adult/child 3-12 $24/17; ⏰ 9am-6pm Jul & Aug, to 5pm Sep-Jun). The largest tropical aquarium in the USA showcases Hawaii's dazzling marine life with award-winning style. The exhibits are laid out to take you on an ocean journey, beginning with nearshore reefs teeming with colorful tropical fish and ending with deep-ocean sealife.

For the spectacular grand finale, you walk along a 54ft glass tunnel right through the center of a massive tank as gliding stingrays and menacing sharks encircle you. It's as close as you'll ever get to being underwater without donning dive gear. And if you are a diver or snorkeler, the aquarium is an unbeatable place to identify the fish you've already seen.

Kid-friendly features abound, including interactive displays on whales, a touch pool and, best of all, *keiki*-level viewing ports that allow the wee ones to peer into everything on their own.

Activities
WINDSURFING & SURFING

Wicked winds from the north shoot straight out toward Kaho'olawe, creating some of the best **windsurfing** conditions on Maui. In winter, when the wind dies down elsewhere, windsurfers still fly along Ma'alaea Bay.

WALK ON WATER

You can tread gently into a fragile wildlife habitat thanks to an elevated boardwalk that's turned previously inaccessible marshland into a one-of-a-kind nature walk. The coastal marsh and dunes nestling Kealia Pond not only provide feeding grounds for native waterbirds but are also a nesting site for the endangered hawksbill sea turtle. The 2200ft boardwalk begins on N Kihei Rd just north of the 2-mile marker. Interpretive plaques and benches along the way offer opportunities to stop and enjoy the splendor, and in winter you might be able to spot passing humpback whales. You'll even find a turtle laying eggs at the end of the boardwalk. Say what? Go take a look…

The bay has a couple of hot surfing spots. The **Ma'alaea Pipeline**, south of the harbor, freight-trains right and is the fastest surf break in all Hawaii. Summer's southerly swells produce huge tubes. Ma'alaea Bay is fronted by a 3-mile stretch of sandy **beach**, running from Ma'alaea Harbor south to Kihei, which can be accessed at several places along N Kihei Rd.

SNORKEL & WHALE WATCHING CRUISES

Many of the boats going out to Molokini (see the boxed text, p379) leave from Ma'alaea. Afternoon trips are typically cheaper, but because that's when the wind picks up, it's rougher and murkier.

our pick **Pacific Whale Foundation** (☎ 249-8811, 800-942-5311; www.pacificwhale.org; Harbor Shops at Ma'alaea; adult/child 7-12 from $55/35; ⏱ 7am-6pm) has Naturalist-led tours, beginning with snorkeling classes on the boat. Snacks are provided and kids under 6 are free. Also done with style are the whale-watching cruises (adult/child $32/16) that sail from several times daily in the winter season.

If you want more of a party scene, hop aboard **Quicksilver** (☎ 662-0075, 888-700-3764; Slip 103 Ma'alaea Harbor; cruise $99), a sleek double-decker catamaran. Once you're done in the water your crew cranks up Jimmy Buffett and breaks out a BBQ lunch.

HIKING

Fine hilltop views of Kaho'olawe and Lana'i reward hikers along the **Lahaina Pali Trail**, which

follows an ancient footpath as it zigzags steeply up through native dryland. After the first mile it passes into open, sun-baked scrub, from where you can see Haleakalā and the fertile central plains. Ironwood trees precede the crossing of Kealaloloa Ridge (1600ft), after which you descend through Ukumehame Gulch. Look for stray petroglyphs and *paniolo* graffiti. Stay on the footpath all the way down to Papalaua Beach and don't detour onto 4WD roads. The 5.5-mile trail takes about 2½ hours each way.

You can hike in either direction, but starting off early from the east side of the mountains keeps you ahead of the blistering sun. The trailhead access road, marked by a 'Na Ala Hele' sign, is on Hwy 30, about 100yd south of its intersection with Hwy 380. If you prefer to start at the west end, the trailhead is 200yd south of the 11-mile marker on Hwy 30.

Eating

Hula Cookies (☎ 243-2271; Harbor Shops at Ma'alaea; snacks $2-5; ⏱ 10am-6pm Mon-Sat, to 5pm Sun) The perfect place to take the kids for a snack after the aquarium. The fresh-baked cookies and Maui-made ice cream are chockful of macadamia nuts, pineapple and mango.

Beach Bums Bar & Grill (☎ 243-2286; Harbor Shops at Ma'alaea; mains $10-20; ⏱ 11:30am-10pm) If BBQ is your thing, you'll love this harborfront eatery, which uses a wood-burning rotisserie smoker to grill up everything from burgers and ribs to turkey and Spam. Come between 3pm and 6pm for $2 drafts of Kona-brewed Longboard Lager.

GREEN POWER

Windy central Maui is a major league player in the field of alternative energy, producing some 20% of Maui's electricity needs from the windmills above Ma'alaea and a bagasse plant at Pu'unene's sugar mill. The mill's power plant is a thorough recycler, burning residue sugarcane fibers, called bagasse, to run the mill and pump excess juice into the island's electrical grid. But it's the windmills that hold the greenest future and a planned expansion of the wind farm could soon double the number of turbines at Ma'alaea. Meanwhile, a second commercial wind farm is in the planning stages for development on 'Ulupalakua Ranch property in the Upcountry

MAUI

MAUI

DETOUR: OLD PU'UNENE

You could drive through Pu'unene every day without realizing a slice of a bygone plantation village lies hidden behind the sugar mill. There, a long-forgotten church sits abandoned in a field of waving cane, across from the village's old schoolhouse. Still, the place isn't a ghost town. Out the back, just beyond the school, you'll find an old shack that has served as a used bookstore since 1913. It's a bit musty and dusty, but still sells books for a mere dime. To get there turn off Mokulele Hwy (Hwy 311) onto Hansen Rd and take the first right onto Old Pu'unene Ave, continuing past the old Pu'unene Meat Market building (c 1926) and the mill. Turn left after half a mile, just past a little bridge. Just before the pavement ends, turn right and drive behind the old school to reach the bookstore, which is open from 9am to 4pm Tuesday to Saturday.

The Waterfront (☎ 244-9028; Milowai Condominium, 50 Hauoli St; mains $26-35; ☷ 5-10pm) Central Maui's best seafood restaurant pairs fresh-off-the-boat fish with a breezy harbor view. The variety depends on what's reeled in each day, but the preparation choice – nine options in all – is yours. Maybe you're in a blackened Cajun mood. Perhaps island-style with gingered coconut jus. The wine selection is topnotch too.

Getting There & Away

Located at a crossroads, Ma'alaea has good connections to the rest of Maui's public bus system. **Maui Bus** (☎ 871-4838) connects the Harbor Shops at Ma'alaea with Lahaina, Kahului, Kihei and Wailea. Service depends on the route, but buses ($1) operate hourly from around 6am to 8pm.

SOUTH MAUI

If beaches are your thing, south Maui is your place. Whether you're into lazing on a glistening resort beach or kayaking into untouched bays, sunny south Maui offers up an amazing variety of aquatic adventures. 'Turtle town' snorkeling, coastline whale watching and coral garden dives are just a few of the attractions that have made this region such a hit with visitors. South Maui starts off with the 6 mile–long stretch of Kihei – often maligned as being congested and overbuilt, but oh-so family friendly and convenient. The honeymoon and celeb crowd favor Wailea's tony resort scene, while back-to-nature folks keep going straight to Makena with its untamed scenery.

KIHEI
pop 19,900

Graced with a string of golden-sand beaches and basking in near constant sunshine, it's easy to see why Kihei has boomed into Maui's largest tourist destination. Granted, its strip mall development is not Maui's finest look, but the town boasts everything needed for a seaside vacation. Good restaurant and accommodation options abound and just about everything is a mere sandal shuffle from the beach. And the views from the shoreline, looking across to Kaho'olawe and Lana'i, are as picturesque as they come.

Orientation

The Pi'ilani Hwy (Hwy 31) runs parallel to and bypasses the start-and-stop traffic of S Kihei Rd. Half-a-dozen crossroads connect the two, making it easy to zip in and out of Kihei efficiently.

Information

Bank of Hawaii (Map p376; ☎ 879-5844; Azeka Mauka, 1279 S Kihei Rd)

Coffee Store (Map p376; ☎ 875-4244; Azeka Mauka, 1279 S Kihei Rd; per min 20¢; ☷ 6am-6pm Mon-Sat, to 5pm Sun)

Hale Imua Internet Stop (Map p378; ☎ 891-9219; Kama'ole Shopping Center, 2463 S Kihei Rd; per 15min $3,

---

SWIM WITH THE FISHES

The sharks are circling. Some 20 of them, to be exact. Blacktip reef sharks, hammerheads and, gasp, a tiger shark. And you can jump in and join them. **Shark Dive Maui** (☎ 270-7000; 2hr dive $199; ☷ 8:15am Mon, Wed & Fri) takes intrepid divers on a daredevil's plunge into Maui Ocean Center's 750,000-gallon deep-ocean tank to swim with the toothy beasts as aquarium visitors gaze on in disbelief. You do need to be a certified diver and because it's limited to four divers per outing, advance reservations are essential.

then per min 15¢; ☺ 8am-9pm Mon-Fri, 10am-5pm Sat, 10am-9pm Sun)

Kihei Police District Station (Map p378; ☎ 244-6400; Kihei Town Center, 1881 S Kihei Rd; ☺ 7:45am-4:30pm Mon-Fri)

Lipoa Laundry Center (Map p378; Lipoa Center, 40 E Lipoa St; ☺ 8am-9pm Mon-Sat, to 5pm Sun)

Longs Drugs (Map p376; ☎ 879-2033; 1215 S Kihei Rd; ☺ 7am-midnight) Kihei's largest pharmacy.

Post office (Map p376; ☎ 879-1987; 1254 S Kihei Rd)

Urgent Care Maui Physicians (Map p378; ☎ 879-7781; 1325 S Kihei Rd; ☺ 7am-10pm) This clinic accepts walk-in patients.

Sights

KEAWAKAPU BEACH

The queen of Kihei's many attractive beaches, this sparkling stretch of sand extends south from the southernmost part of Kihei to Wailea's Mokapu Beach. Less visible than the main roadside beaches, Keawakapu Beach (Map p378) is also less crowded.

With its silky soft sand, it's a favorite place for people doing sunrise yoga and wake-up strolls and it's also an excellent spot for a sunset swim. Mornings are the best time for snorkeling; head to the rocky outcrops that form the northern and southern ends of the beach. If it's winter, keep an eye out for humpback whales that come amazingly close to shore here.

There are three beach access points, all with outdoor showers. To get to the south end, go south on S Kihei Rd until it dead-ends at a beach parking lot. Near the middle of the beach, there's a parking lot at the corner of Kilohana and S Kihei Rd; look for a blue shoreline access sign on the *makai* side of the street. At the northern end, beach parking can be found at the side of Mana Kai Maui.

KAMA'OLE BEACH PARKS

Kama'ole is one long beach divided into three sections (Kam I, II and III; Map p378) by rocky points. All three are lovely golden-sand beaches with full facilities, including lifeguards.

Water conditions vary with the weather, but swimming is usually good. For the most part, these beaches have sandy bottoms with a fairly steep drop, which tends to create good conditions for bodysurfing, especially in winter.

For snorkeling, the south end of Kama'ole Beach Park III has some nearshore rocks harboring a bit of coral and a few colorful fish,

though it pales in comparison to the snorkeling at beaches farther south.

KIHEI COASTAL TRAIL

Want to leave the crowds behind? Take this lightly trodden footpath (Map p378) that runs south from Kama'ole Beach Park III and winds a half-mile along coastal bluffs to Kihei Boat Ramp. At the start of the trail look for the burrows of 'ua'u kani (wedge-tailed shearwaters), ground-nesting seabirds that return to the same sites each spring and remain until November when the fledglings are large enough to head out to sea. Benches set in pretty places and interpretive plaques identifying native plants enhance the walk.

CHARLEY YOUNG BEACH

Hidden off a side street, this neighborhood beach is Kihei's least touristed strand. It's a real jewel in the rough, broad, sandy, and backed by swaying coconut palms. You're apt to find fishers casting their lines, families playing volleyball and someone strumming a guitar. It also has some of the better bodysurfing waves in Kihei. Beach parking is on the corner of S Kihei Rd and Kaia'u Pl. To get to the beach, simply walk to the end of Kaia'u Pl and follow the steps down the cliff.

HAWAIIAN ISLANDS HUMPBACK WHALE NATIONAL MARINE SANCTUARY

The **marine sanctuary headquarters** (Map p376; ☎ 879-2818; www.hawaiihumpbackwhale.noaa.gov; 726 S Kihei Rd; admission free; ☺ 10am-3pm Mon-Fri) is a great place to get acquainted with Hawaii's spectacular marine life. The center overlooks an ancient fishpond and its oceanfront lookout is ideal for sighting the humpback whales that frequent the bay during winter. There's even a free telescope set up for viewing. Displays on whales and sea turtles offer interesting

---

PLUGGING IN

- To local issues: **Maui News** (www.mauinews.com)
- To the environmental scene: **Sierra Club** (www.hi.sierraclub.org/maui)
- To the art scene: **Art Guide Maui** (www.artguidemaui.com)
- To the gay community: **Maui Pride** (www.pridemaui.com)

MAUI

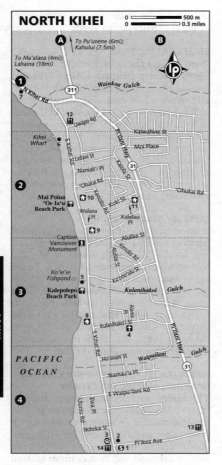

Places. Signboards at the park delve into its fascinating history.

MAI POINA 'OE IA'U BEACH PARK

This long sandy beach (Map p376) at the northern end of Kihei is a popular morning launch for outrigger canoes and kayaks. After the wind picks up in the afternoon it's Kihei's top windsurfing venue.

KALAMA PARK

A retaining wall runs along most of the shoreline, so the action here is best suited for land-lubbers. This expansive park (Map p378) has softball fields, tennis, basketball and volleyball courts, a skateboard park and a playground. There is a small beach behind the whale statue but a ditch carries runoff here after heavy rains, so best take your swim elsewhere.

DAVID MALO'S CHURCH

Philosopher David Malo built this church in 1853 and he wore many collars. He was the first Hawaiian ordained to the Christian ministry, coauthor of Hawaii's first constitution and an early spokesperson for Hawaiian rights. While most of Malo's original church has been dismantled, a 3ft-high section of the walls still stands beside a palm grove. Pews are lined up inside the stone walls, where open-air services are held at 9am Sunday by **Trinity Episcopal Church-by-the-Sea** (Map p376; 100 Kulanihako'i St).

background on the creatures you might spot here. And there's always a whale poster or other free handout available for the kids. Want to take it deeper? Swing by at 11am on Tuesday and Thursday for the center's '45-Ton Talks' on whales.

KALEPOLEPO BEACH PARK

Keiki, this one's for you. The calm, shallow waters at this beach park (Map p376) are perfect for children. The swimming area is essentially a big pool, because the waters are encircled by the stone walls of **Ko'ie'ie Fishpond**. The most intact fishpond remaining on Maui, Ko'ie'ie was built in the 16th century to raise mullet for the *ali'i* (royalty). The 3-acre fishpond is on the National Register of Historic

Activities

DIVING & SNORKELING

`our pick` **Maui Dreams Dive Company** (Map p378; ☎ 874-5332, 888-921-3483; www.mauidreamsdiveco.com; 1993 S Kihei Rd; 1-/2-tank dives from $60/90, snorkel rental per day $5; ☼ 7am-6pm) is a first-rate, five-star PADI outfit specializing in shore dives. With this family-run operation, a dive trip is like going out with friends. And they have something geared to every level from introductory dives for the newbie to night dives and advanced open-water dives.

Maui Dive Shop (Map p378; ☎ 879-3388; www.mauidiveshop.com; 1455 S Kihei Rd; 2-tank boat dives $130, snorkel rental per day $8; ☼ 6am-9pm), the main outlet of this islandwide diving chain, is a good spot to rent or buy water-sports gear, including bodyboards, snorkels, fins and wetsuits.

Blue Water Rafting (Map p378; ☎ 879-7238; www.bluewaterrafting.com; Kihei Boat Ramp; Molokini/Kanaio trip $49/100; ☼ departure times vary) has a Molokini Express trip perfect for those who want to zip out to the crater, snorkel and be back in two hours. An adventurous half-day trip heads southward to snorkel remote coves along the Kanaio coast.

KAYAKING, CANOEING & PADDLEBOARDING

South Pacific Kayaks & Outfitters (Map p378; ☎ 875-4848, 800-776-2326; www.southpacifickayaks.com; 95 Hale Kuai St; 1-/2-person kayaks per half day $40/60, tours $65-100; ☼ 6am-9pm) is a reliable operation that leads kayak-and-snorkel tours in the Makena area. If you prefer to rent a kayak and paddle off on your own, they'll deliver it to Makena Landing (p385). They also offer paddleboard lessons (two hours for $89) and paddleboard rentals (four hours for $45).

Kihei Canoe Club (Map p376; www.kiheicanoeclub.com; Kihei Wharf; donation $25) invites visitors to share in the mana by joining members in paddling their outrigger canoes on Tuesday and Thursday mornings. No reservations are necessary; just show up at the wharf at 7:30am. The donation helps offset the cost of maintaining the canoes and entitles you to join them each Tuesday and Thursday for the rest of the month.

Maui Nui O Kama Canoe Club Cultural Tour (Map p376; ☎ 242-8536; 1191 N Kihei Rd; outing $40; ☼ 7:30am) offers memorable 90-minute narrated outrigger canoe rides led by a Native Hawaiian. Much more than just a canoe ride, the tour emphasizes cultural aspects including chant-

ing and a paddle to an ancient Hawaiian site. Reservations are required.

YOGA

Maui Yoga Path (Map p378; ☎ 874-5545; 2960 S Kihei Rd; class $20; ☼ 9-10:30am) has sessions at the Mana Kai Maui hotel that focus on the relaxing stretches and breathing exercises of Iyengar yoga.

Festivals & Events

Whale Day Celebration (www.greatmauiwhalefestival.org) This big family-oriented bash celebrates humpback whales with a parade, live music, local crafts and food booths. Kids will love the whale regatta (Maui's version of a rubber-duck race). It's held at Kalama Park, next to the big whale statue, on a Saturday in mid-February.

Sleeping

In Kihei, hotels and B&Bs can be counted on one hand while condos line up cheek to jowl. Some condominium complexes maintain a front desk or a daytime office that handles bookings, but others are booked only via rental agents. In many places along S Kihei Rd the traffic is noisy, so you may want to avoid rooms close to the road.

The following rental agents handle Kihei condos:

Bello Realty (☎ 879-3328, 800-541-3060; www.bellomaui.com)

Kihei Maui Vacations (☎ 879-7581, 800-541-6284; www.kmvmaui.com)

Resort Quest Maui (☎ 879-5445, 866-774-2924; www.resortquestmaui.com)

BUDGET & MIDRANGE

Ocean Breeze Hideaway (Map p376; ☎ 879-0657, 888-463-6687; www.hawaiibednbreakfast.com; 435 Kalalau Pl; r incl breakfast $99-115; ☒ ☎) Tucked into a residential neighborhood a short drive from the beach, this friendly B&B has two cozy rooms, one with a queen bed and ceiling fans, the other with a king bed and air-con. Each has a private entrance and refrigerator.

Two Mermaids on Maui B&B (Map p378; ☎ 874-8687, 800-598-9550; www.twomermaids.com; 2840 Umalu Pl; studio/1br incl breakfast $115/140; ☒ ☎ ☒) The two women who operate this B&B add lots of personal touches. The units have kitchenettes and cheerful tropical decor, a breakfast of organic fruit is provided and families are welcome – the backyard pool even has a shallow section just for kids. One of the 'mermaids' is a justice of the peace and can arrange wedding packages.

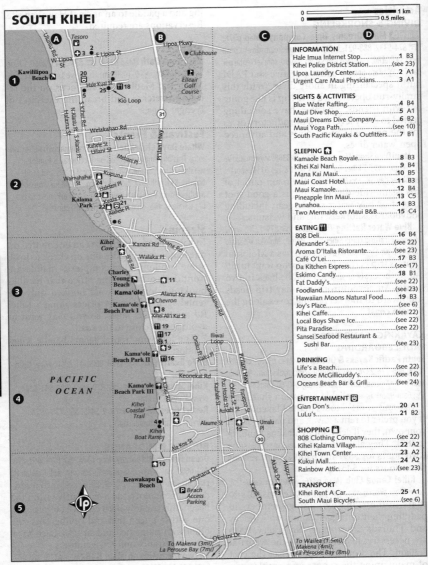

SOUTH KIHEI

INFORMATION
Hale Imua Internet Stop...................1 B3
Kihei Police District Station..........(see 23)
Lipoa Laundry Center.......................2 A1
Urgent Care Maui Physicians...........3 A1

SIGHTS & ACTIVITIES
Blue Water Rafting...........................4 B4
Maui Dive Shop................................5 A1
Maui Dreams Dive Company............6 B2
Maui Yoga Path.............................(see 10)
South Pacific Kayaks & Outfitters....7 B1

SLEEPING
Kamaole Beach Royale......................8 B3
Kihei Kai Nani..................................9 B4
Mana Kai Maui...............................10 B5
Maui Coast Hotel...........................11 B3
Maui Kamaole................................12 B4
Pineapple Inn Maui........................13 C5
Punahoa...14 B3
Two Mermaids on Maui B&B..........15 C4

EATING
808 Deli...16 B4
Alexander's...................................(see 22)
Aroma D'Italia Ristorante.............(see 23)
Café O'Lei......................................17 B3
Da Kitchen Express.......................(see 17)
Eskimo Candy................................18 B1
Fat Daddy's...................................(see 22)
Foodland.......................................(see 23)
Hawaiian Moons Natural Food......19 B3
Joy's Place....................................(see 6)
Kihei Caffe....................................(see 22)
Local Boys Shave Ice....................(see 22)
Pita Paradise.................................(see 22)
Sansei Seafood Restaurant &
   Sushi Bar...................................(see 23)

DRINKING
Life's a Beach................................(see 22)
Moose McGillicuddy's...................(see 16)
Oceans Beach Bar & Grill.............(see 24)

ENTERTAINMENT
Gian Don's.....................................20 A1
LuLu's...21 B2

SHOPPING
808 Clothing Company.................(see 22)
Kihei Kalama Village......................22 A2
Kihei Town Center.........................23 A2
Kukui Mall.....................................24 A2
Rainbow Attic...............................(see 23)

TRANSPORT
Kihei Rent A Car............................25 A1
South Maui Bicycles.....................(see 6)

Maui Sunseeker (Map p376; ☎ 879-1261, 800-532-6284; www.mauisunseeker.com; 551 S Kihei Rd; studios from $145; ☒ ☐ ☜) Catering to gay and lesbian travelers, this place consists of two adjacent properties. Opt for a 2nd floor unit in the rear one, known formerly as Wailana Inn, to snatch a fab ocean view. All units have king beds, kitchenettes and private lanai, and

there's a clothing-optional rooftop deck with a hot tub.

Kihei Kai Nani (Map p378; ☎ 879-9088, 800-473-1493; www.kiheikainani.com; 2495 S Kihei Rd; 1br $148; ☒ ☒) The staff are as friendly as they come, the units are well maintained and the pool's a whopping 60ft long. Add a low-rise appeal and convenient location opposite the beach and it adds up to one of south Maui's best bargains. Another nice touch: the free cable internet reaches all the way out to your lanai.

Nona Lani Cottages (Map p376; ☎ 879-2497, 800-733-2688; www.nonalanicottages.com; 455 S Kihei Rd; cottages from $150; ⊠) Those who prefer old-fashioned simplicity to glitzy resort amenities will feel right at home in these sweet retro cottages. They're compact but squeeze in everything you'll need: a full kitchen, a living room with daybed and a bedroom with a queen bed. Opt for one of the rear cottages and enjoy the sweet scented plumeria trees that the hosts harvest to string lei.

Punahoa (Map p378; ☎ 879-2720, 800-564-4380; www.punahoabeach.com; 2142 Ili'ili Rd; studio/1br/2br $156/239/269; 🛜) This tasteful boutique condo lies hidden on a quiet side street fronting an even quieter beach. Every unit looks down upon a sparkling slice of the ocean that's frequented by sea turtles. There's no pool, but who needs one when the beach is at your doorstep? Surfers, bring your boards – Kihei's best waves are just a few minutes' walk away.

Koa Lagoon (Map p376; ☎ 879-3002, 800-367-8030; www.koalagoon.com; 800 S Kihei Rd; 1br/2br $170/200; ⊠ 🛜) Watch the whales pass from your balcony at this seaside complex with just 42 units, every one of which shares a clear-on view of the ocean. Other perks include a pretty backyard, a relaxing beach and a pool that's not only heated but seldom crowded! Inside the comfy units are fitted with king beds and everything you'd ever need down to a washer and dryer.

Kamaole Beach Royale (Map p378; ☎ 879-3131, 800-421-3661; www.mauikbr.com; 2385 S Kihei Rd; 1br/2br/3br from $170/200/250; 🛜) Set back from the road, this complex opposite Kama'ole Beach Park I is quieter than most. Another plus: most of the condos in the rental pool are fresh off a renovation that's perked them up with pizazz. Request a unit on the top floor to score the best ocean view. Or just head up to the roof garden where there's a BBQ grill and a sweet view.

Mana Kai Maui (Map p378; ☎ 879-2778, 800-367-5242; www.crhmaui.com; 2960 S Kihei Rd; r/1br from $190/300; ⊠ 🛜 🖵) The rooms are small but the views are grand. Perched on a point overlooking Keawakapu Beach, this complex boasts the most incredible sunsets. Matter of fact, when the sun drops you'll find everyone out on their deck oohing and aahing. And you can swim and snorkel from the beach right outside the door.

Maui Kamaole (Map p378; ☎ 874-5151, 800-367-5242; www.crhmaui.com; 2777 S Kihei Rd; 1br/2br from $225/280; ⊠ 🛜 🖵) Bougainvillea draped over the balconies and birdsong in the gardens set the

MAUI

MOLOKINI CRATER

No underwater site draws more visitors than Molokini, the volcanic crater that lies midway between the islands of Maui and Kaho'olawe. Half of the crater rim has eroded away, leaving a pretty crescent moon that rises 160ft above the ocean surface, with a mere 18 acres of rocky land high and dry. But it's what's beneath the surface that draws the crowds. Snorkelers and divers will be thrilled by steep walls, ledges, white-tipped reef sharks, manta rays, turtles and abundant fish.

The legends about Molokini are myriad. One says Molokini was a beautiful woman who was turned to stone by jealous Pele, goddess of volcanoes. Another claims one of Pele's lovers angered her by secretly marrying a *mo'o* (supernatural serpent or lizard). Pele chopped the lizard in half, leaving Molokini as its tail and Pu'u Ola'i in Makena as its head. Yet another tale alleges that Molokini, which means 'many ties' in Hawaiian, is the umbilical cord left over from the birth of Kaho'olawe.

The coral reef that extends outward from Molokini is extraordinary, though it has lost some of its variety over the years. Most of the black coral that was once prolific in Molokini's deeper waters made its way into Lahaina jewelry stores before the island was declared a marine conservation district in 1977. During WWII the US Navy shelled Molokini for target practice, and live bombs are still occasionally spotted on the crater floor.

Consider the following when planning your excursion to Molokini. The water's calmest and clearest in the morning. Don't fall for discounted afternoon tours – go out early for the smoothest sailing and best conditions. For snorkelers, there's simply not much to see when the water's choppy. The main departure point for outings to Molokini is Ma'alaea (p373) but you can also get there from other ports, including Kihei (p377).

tone at this luxurious condo. Everything is low rise, the units are incredibly spacious and the quiet location off Kamaʻole Beach Park III is primo. There's so much privacy here you could sunbathe au naturel on your balcony and no one would even notice.

TOP END

Maui Coast Hotel (Map p378; ☎ 874-6284, 800-895-6284; www.mauicoasthotel.com; 2259 S Kihei Rd; r/ste from $245/275; 🅿 💻 🛜 🐾) Among the handful of hotels in condo-laden Kihei, this is the best. It's clean and comfortable with plenty of thoughtful extras from guest computers to free laundry facilities. The rooms are big, equipped with either a king or two queen beds, plus a pullout sofa. After a day of sightseeing, you can sit back with a drink and enjoy live music at the poolside bar. Ask about discounts, which can cut the standard rates in half.

Eating

If you're staying in Kihei, you probably have a condo kitchen. But, hey, take a break. You're on vacation after all and Kihei's dining scene is well worth exploring.

BUDGET

Local Boys Shave Ice (Map p378; Kihei Kalama Village, 1913 S Kihei Rd; shave ice $4; 🕙 10am-9pm) A hot day at the beach deserves a cool treat. This stall conveniently located opposite Kalama Park dishes up shave ice drenched in a rainbow of tropical flavors. Passion fruit, piña colada or perhaps the lemon-lime?

Hawaiian Moons Natural Foods (Map p378; ☎ 875-4356; Kamaʻole Beach Center, 2411 S Kihei Rd; 🕙 8am-9pm) is the perfect place to pack a healthy picnic lunch.

808 Deli (Map p378; ☎ 879-1111; 2511 S Kihei Rd; sandwiches $5-8; 🕙 7am-5pm) Kihei's latest nod to the foodie offers topnotch deli fare, and amazingly everything on the menu is priced under $8.08. A standout is the tender pesto chicken with provolone cheese and sun-dried tomatoes grilled in a panini sandwich that's so big it's cut into three slices. Lox and bagel breakfast fare, innovative salads and gelato round out the menu.

Kihei Caffe (Map p378; ☎ 879-2230; 1945 S Kihei Rd; mains $5-10; 🕙 5am-2pm) If jet lag has you up before sunrise, head to this friendly sidewalk café. After you adjust to Hawaiian time you just might find yourself coming back again to feast on the delish banana pancakes, sinful cinnamon rolls and other breakfast goodies served till closing.

Joy's Place (Map p378; ☎ 879-9258; 1993 S Kihei Rd; mains $7-12; 🕙 10am-3pm Mon-Sat) Blink and you'll miss this hole in the wall, but what a shame that'd be. Joy takes pride in her little kitchen. Operative words are organic, free range and locally harvested. The healthiest salads you'll find in south Maui, tasty sandwiches made to order and plenty of vegan options.

Da Kitchen Express (Map p378; ☎ 875-7782; Rainbow Mall, 2439 S Kihei Rd; meals $9-12; 🕙 9am-9pm) It's all about the plate lunches – tasty and huge – at this quintessentially Hawaiian diner. The justifiably famous *kalua* pork is, as they say, 'so tender it falls off da bone' and the more expensive plates are big enough to feed two.

Kihei has two 24-hour supermarkets: **Foodland** (Map p378; ☎ 879-9350; Kihei Town Center, 1881 S Kihei Rd) and **Safeway** (Map p376; ☎ 891-9120; Piʻilani Village, 277 Piʻikea Ave). **Kihei Farmers Market** (Map p376; ☎ 875-0949; 61 S Kihei Rd; 🕙 8am-4pm Mon-Fri) sells island-grown fruits and vegetables.

MIDRANGE

Vietnamese Cuisine (Map p376; ☎ 875-2088; Azeka Makai, 1280 S Kihei Rd; mains $8-14; 🕙 10am-9:30pm) It doesn't look like much from the outside but the Vietnamese chef-owner works wonders in the kitchen. The curried lemongrass dishes and the crispy egg noodles are both tasty choices. Or have some fun with your food and order *banh hoi*, a roll-your-own Vietnamese version of fajitas that come with mint leaves, assorted veggies and grilled shrimp.

Alexander's (Map p378; ☎ 874-0788; Kihei Kalama Village, 1913 S Kihei Rd; meals $8-14; 🕙 11am-9pm) If you're hanging at the beach, scoot over here for fish-and-chips, made with your choice of mahimahi, ahi or *ono* (wahoo). The fried fare's a bit greasy but the grilled fish is absolute perfection. Everything's takeout – carry it back to the beach or chow down at the picnic tables outside the eatery.

Pita Paradise (Map p378; ☎ 875-7679; Kihei Kalama Village, 1913 S Kihei Rd; mains $8-16; 🕙 11am-9:30pm) Don't be fooled by its location in the back of a mundane shopping arcade – this little patio café is pure gourmet. The owner, an ardent fisher, reels in his own fresh catch – grilled on a skewer it rivals the best of 'em. The menu is decidedly Mediterranean: falafels on pita, lamb gyros and a baklava ice-cream cake to die for.

Eskimo Candy (Map p378; ☎ 891-8898; 2665 Hale Kuai St; meals $8-17; 🕙 10:30am-7pm Mon-Fri) Off the beaten path on a side street between the beach and the highway, Eskimo Candy is a local fish market with a takeout counter and a few café tables. If you've never tried *poke* here's a great place to savor the real deal, made fresh daily. Delicious ahi wraps and fish tacos too.

Fat Daddy's (Map p378; ☎ 879-8711; Kihei Kalama Village, 1913 S Kihei Rd; mains $8-17; ⏰ 11:30am-9pm Mon-Sat, 11:30am-2pm Sun) Big plates of tangy BBQ ribs with all the fixings are the specialty at this Texas-style smokehouse. Here, the Southwest takes on a Hawaiian accent with Maui Cattle Company beef on the grill and Maui-brewed beers on tap.

Aroma D'Italia Ristorante (Map p378; ☎ 879-0133; Kihei Town Center, 1881 S Kihei Rd; mains $10-24; ⏰ 5-9pm) Just like Mama used to make…if yo mama was Italian. This place has it all – smart service, old-world decor and a chef who relies upon traditional family recipes to create delicious pastas, spicy chicken parmigiana and home-made cannoli. Mama mia!

Sansei Seafood Restaurant & Sushi Bar (Map p378; ☎ 879-0004; Kihei Town Center, 1881 S Kihei Rd; appetizers $4-15, mains $17-32; ⏰ 5:30pm-1am Tue-Sat, 5pm-1am Sun & Mon) The line runs out the door but your patience will be rewarded. The innovative appetizer menu rolls out everything from traditional sushi to blue crab ravioli. For the ultimate East-meets-West treat, order the tempura rock shrimp in garlic aioli, which lusciously fuses Japanese and French flavors. Night owls, swing by after 10pm when the sushi and appetizers are half-price.

ourpick **Café O'Lei** (Map p378; ☎ 891-1368; Rainbow Mall, 2439 S Kihei Rd; lunch $8-13, dinner $18-30; ⏰ 10:30am-9pm Tue-Sun) If you have time for only one restaurant meal in Kihei, make it here. Superb Hawaii Regional Cuisine at honest prices separates this place from other upscale Kihei dining spots. The blackened mahimahi served with fresh papaya salsa is arguably the best lunch deal ($10) on Maui. Other tasty stars include seared ahi on focaccia and the Makawao ginger steak served on a bed of Ha'iku organic greens. Good dinnertime sushi and fierce martinis too.

Drinking & Entertainment

LuLu's (Map p378; ☎ 879-9944; 945 S Kihei Rd 2nd floor) Kihei's top party venue is loud, lively and full of people having fun. Come here for a drink, shoot some pool or dance the night away. Salsa, reggae bands or DJs command the floor at night.

> **TOP PICKS – VEGETARIAN EATS**
> - **Fresh Mint** (p390) in Pa'ia
> - **Veg Out** (p408) in Ha'iku
> - **Joy's Place** (opposite) in Kihei
> - **Farmers Market Deli** (p356) in Honokowai
> - **Down to Earth Natural Foods** (p367) in Kahului

Life's a Beach (Map p378; ☎ 891-8010; Kihei Kalama Village, 1913 S Kihei Rd) Directly opposite Kalama Beach, this brightly painted, Bob Marley–lovin' shack draws a crowd, with its $1 mai tais from 3pm to 7pm along with live music or DJs.

Moose McGillicuddy's (Map p378; ☎ 891-8600; 2511 S Kihei Rd) Moose's open-air lanai is a good place to head for a sunset drink with an ocean view. Happy hour (4pm to 7pm) happily coincides with the sinking orange orb.

Oceans Beach Bar & Grill (Map p378; ☎ 891-2414; Kukui Mall; 1819 S Kihei Rd) OK, despite the name, it's not on the beach, but it is open air, with surf videos running nonstop and dancing on weekends.

Gian Don's (Map p378; ☎ 874-4041; 1445 S Kihei Rd) This glittering space with its white marble columns hosts Maui's gay community with a cabaret drag show on Friday and an 'ultra fab' DJ event on Saturday.

Shopping

Kihei Kalama Village (Map p378; 1913 S Kihei Rd) This complex opposite Kalama Park has a collection of stalls selling beach clothing and jewelry that can be fun to browse. Best of the shops in the center is **808 Clothing Company** (☎ 357-1988), which sells cool T-shirts with their own original Maui designs.

Rainbow Attic (Map p378; ☎ 874-0884; Kihei Town Center, 1881 S Kihei Rd) A secondhand shop with a bit of flair, Rainbow's the perfect place to pick up good quality aloha shirts already pre-shrunk.

Getting There & Around
BICYCLE
Bike lanes run along the Pi'ilani Hwy and S Kihei Rd, but cyclists need to watch out for inattentive drivers making sudden turns across the lanes. **South Maui Bicycles** (Map p378; ☎ 874-0068; 1993 S Kihei Rd; per day $22-60, per week $99-250;

10am-6pm Mon-Sat) rents top-of-the-line Trek road bicycles as well as basic around-town bikes. No matter what you opt for, you can count on it being well maintained.

BUS

Maui Bus (☎ 871-4838) serves Kihei with two routes. One connects Kihei with Wailea and Ma'alaea; stops include Kama'ole Beach III and the Pi'ilani Village shopping center. From Ma'alaea you can connect with buses bound for Lahaina and Kahului. The other route primarily serves the northern half of Kihei, with a half-dozen stops along S Kihei Rd. Both routes operate hourly from around 5:30am to 7:30pm and cost $1.

CAR & MOTORCYCLE

A family-owned operation, **Kihei Rent A Car** (Map p378; ☎ 879-7257, 800-251-5288; www.kiheirentacar .com; 96 Kio Loop; per day/week from $36/175) rents cars and jeeps to those aged over 21, accepts cash deposits and includes unlimited mileage.

Hula Hogs (Map p376; ☎ 875-7433, 877-464-7433; www.hulahogs.com; 1279 S Kihei Rd; per day $140) are the folks to see if you want to pack your saddle-bags and tour Maui on a Harley Road King.

WAILEA
pop 5400

Wailea breathes money. As you drive up the hill from Kihei it's like entering another world. Everything is green, manicured and precise. Don't even bother looking for a gas station or fast-food joint. Wailea is all about swank beachfront resorts, low-rise condo villas, emerald golf courses and a tennis club so chic it's dubbed 'Wimbledon West.'

One look at Wailea's beaches and it's easy to see why it's become such hot real estate. The golden-sand jewels sparkling along the Wailea coast are postcard material offering some of Maui's finest swimming, snorkeling and sunbathing.

Orientation & Information

Heading into Wailea it's best to take the Pi'ilani Hwy (Hwy 31) and not S Kihei Rd, which can be a slow drive through congested traffic. Wailea's main road is Wailea Alanui Dr, which turns into Makena Alanui Dr after Polo Beach and continues south to Makena.

If you are looking for an ATM, you'll find one at the **Shops at Wailea** (3750 Wailea Alanui Dr; 9:30am-9pm). Many hotels also have them.

Sights

Wailea's gorgeous beaches begin with the southern end of Keawakapu Beach in Kihei and continue south toward Makena. All of the beaches that are backed by resorts have public access, with free parking, showers and rest rooms.

ULUA & MOKAPU BEACHES

You'll have to get up early to secure a parking space but it's worth it. Ulua Beach offers Wailea's best easy-access snorkeling. Not only is it teeming with brilliant tropical fish but it's one of the best spots for hearing humpbacks sing as they pass offshore. Snorkelers should head straight for the coral at the rocky outcrop on the right side of Ulua Beach, which separates it from its twin to the north, Mokapu Beach. Snorkeling is best in the morning before the winds pick up and the crowds arrive. When the surf's up, forget snorkeling – go bodysurfing instead. Beach access is just north of the Wailea Marriott Resort.

WAILEA BEACH

Fronting a pair of resort hotels, this wide sparkling strand is where the lion's share of Wailea's vacationers get their tans. It offers a full menu of water activities from standup paddleboarding to windsurfing. The beach slopes gradually, making it a good swimming spot. When it's calm, there's decent snorkeling around the rocky point on the south end. Most afternoons there's a gentle shorebreak suitable for bodysurfing. Divers entering the water at Wailea Beach can follow an offshore reef that runs down to Polo Beach. The beach access road runs between the Grand Wailea and Four Seasons resorts.

POLO BEACH

At the quieter south end of Wailea, Polo Beach is seldom crowded. When there's wave action, bodyboarders and bodysurfers usually find good shorebreaks here. When calm, the rocks at the northern end of the beach provide good snorkeling. At low tide, check out the lava outcropping at the southern end for tide pools harboring spiny sea urchins and small fish. To get to Polo Beach, turn down Kaukahi St after the Fairmont Kea Lani and keep an eye out for the beach parking lot on the right.

PALAUEA BEACH

This untouristed sandy stretch just to the south of Polo Beach attracts local surfers and body-

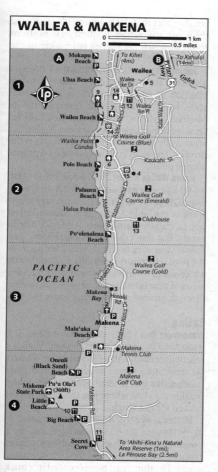

WAILEA & MAKENA

MAUI

boarders. Kiawe trees block the view of the beach from the roadside, but you can find it by looking for the line of cars along Makena Rd.

PO'OLENALENA BEACH

Beyond all the development of the Wailea resort strip lies this long crescent favored by local families on weekends. During the week it's rarely crowded. The shallow, sandy bottom and calm waters make for excellent swimming, and there's good snorkeling off both the southern and northern lava points. **Haloa Point**, a bit further north, is a popular scuba-diving spot. The beach parking lot is on Makena Alanui Rd, a half-mile south of its intersection with Makena Rd. There are no facilities except a portable toilet.

WAILEA BEACH WALK

For an unbeatable sunset stroll, take the 1.3-mile shoreline path that connects Wailea's beaches and the resort hotels that front them. The undulating path winds above jagged lava points and back down to sandy beaches.

Not only are the views superb, but in winter this is one of the best walks on Maui for spotting humpback whales – on a good day you might see more than a dozen of them frolicking in the waters offshore. Forgotten your binoculars? Just drop a coin in the telescope in front of the Wailea Marriott Resort.

Some of the luxury hotels you'll pass along the walk are worth strolling through as well – most notably the Grand Wailea Resort, which showcases $30 million worth of artwork. In front of the Wailea Point condos are the foundations of three Hawaiian house sites dating to AD 1300 and a bench perched perfectly for a sunset view.

Activities
AT SEA

Maui Ocean Activities (☎ 667-2001; Grand Wailea Resort, 3850 Wailea Alanui Dr; snorkel/kayak/paddleboard rental per hr $8/15/40; ⏰ 8am-5pm) has water-sports rentals and gives windsurfing lessons ($90).

Hawaiian Sailing Canoe Adventures (☎ 281-9301; www.mauisailingcanoe.com; departs from Polo Beach; adult/child 5-12 $100/80; ⏲ tours 8am &10am) offers two-hour sails aboard a Hawaiian-style outrigger canoe. There's a maximum of six passengers, so they're able to accommodate requests – including stopping to snorkel with turtles.

ON LAND

Wailea Golf Club (☎ 875-7450, 800-332-1614; www.waileagolf.com; 100 Golf Club Dr; green fees $135-200; ⏲ 1st tee 6:45am) consists of three championship courses. The Emerald course is a tropical garden that consistently ranks top; the rugged Gold course takes advantage of volcanic landscapes; and the Blue course is marked by an open fairway and challenging greens.

Wailea Tennis Club (☎ 879-1958; www.waileatennis.com; 131 Wailea Ike Pl; court fees from $30; ⏲ 8am-7pm Mon-Fri, 8am-5pm Sat & Sun) is an award-winning complex with 11 Plexipave courts, lessons, clinics and equipment rentals.

Festivals & Events

Hollywood celebs galore show up for the **Maui Film Festival** (www.mauifilmfestival.com), a five-day extravaganza in mid-June. Sit with the stars under the stars at various locations around Wailea, including at the open-air 'SandDance Theater' right on Wailea Beach.

Every Wednesday evening the **Shops at Wailea** (☎ 891-6770; 3750 Wailea Alanui Dr) sponsors WOW at Wailea, with live Hawaiian music and hula dancing in the ground-level concourse, and wine receptions in the art galleries.

Sleeping

our pick **Pineapple Inn Maui** (Map p378; ☎ 298-4403, 877-212-6284; www.pineappleinnmaui.com; 3170 Akala Dr; r/cottage $149/215; ❄ 🛜 ▣) This inviting boutique inn is a class act, with rooms that are as nice as those at the exclusive resorts. Flowering gardens, a saline pool, a hot tub and ocean views – there's nothing lacking here other than the high price. All the rooms have well-equipped kitchenettes and the two-bedroom cottage has a full kitchen. The beach is a five-minute drive away but with the conveniences here, you just might want to stay close to home.

Wailea Beach Marriott Resort & Spa (☎ 879-1922, 800-367-2960; www.waileamarriott.com; 3700 Wailea Alanui Dr; r from $380; ❄ 🛜 ▣) The smallest and most Hawaiian of Wailea's resorts sports an open-air lobby overlooking banyan trees and koi ponds. It's the oldest of the Wailea hotels,

but don't let that deter you, as it's fresh off a thorough renovation. Request an oceanfront room to watch sea turtles swimming in the surf below.

Fairmont Kea Lani (☎ 875-4100, 800-659-4100; www.kealani.com; 4100 Wailea Alanui Dr; ste/oceanfront villa from $500/1500; ❄ 🛜 ▣) To stargaze Hollywood-style, head to this swank resort. With its Moorish-style architecture, the Kea Lani resembles something out of *Arabian Nights*, but what really draws the rich and famous is the privacy. The villas even have their own private plunge pools.

Grand Wailea Resort Hotel & Spa (☎ 875-1234, 800-888-6100; www.grandwailea.com; 3850 Wailea Alanui Dr; r from $625; ❄ 🛜 ▣) From the extravagant artwork in the lobby to the guest rooms decked out in Italian marble, this is Maui's ode to excess. But don't think it's all highbrow. Just follow your ears to the shrieks coming from the pool. The resort boasts the most elaborate water-world wonders in Hawaii: an impressive series of nine interconnected pools with swim-through grottos and towering water slides.

Eating

Waterfront Deli (☎ 891-2039; Shops at Wailea, 3750 Wailea Alanui Dr; meals $6-10; ⏲ 7am-8pm) Wailea's sole budget option, this deli inside the Whalers General Store serves sandwiches and plate lunches. It's just takeout but there are tables outside the store where you can eat or have it packed for the beach.

Matteo's (☎ 874-1234; 100 Wailea Ike Dr; mains $10-20; ⏲ 11am-9pm Mon-Fri, 5-9pm Sat & Sun) Run by a breakaway resort chef, this authentic Italian restaurant has damn good food at reasonable prices. The thin-crust pizzas cooked in a brick oven, Maui's finest, are topped with classics like prosciutto and artichokes. Or get more serious with the likes of braised lamb and homemade rigatoni.

Mala Wailea (☎ 875-9394; Wailea Beach Marriott Resort & Spa, 3700 Wailea Alanui Dr; mains $18-35; ⏲ 5:30-9pm) Come here to enjoy a fine ocean view while dining on scrumptious fare that fuses Pacific Rim and Mediterranean flavors. Island favorites like seared sashimi in shiitake ginger sauce pair off with big Greek salads and spicy bruschetta. And the chef's 'practice aloha' commitment to support local fishers and organic farmers makes this Wailea's green standout.

SeaWatch (☎ 875-8080; 100 Wailea Golf Club Dr; breakfast & lunch $10-15; dinner mains $26-35; ⏲ 8am-10pm) One of the hottest chefs in Maui, Todd

Carlos, works magic in the kitchen of this breezy hillside restaurant. At breakfast everyone flocks here for the crabcake Benedict; at lunch the mango BBQ *kalua* pork sandwich steals the show. Dinner gets downright fancy with 'Hawaiian coastal cuisine' – think fresh seafood.

Entertainment

All of the Wailea hotels have some sort of live music in the evening.

Mulligan's on the Blue (☎ 874-1131; 100 Kauhaki St) Perched above the golf course, its nightly entertainment covers the gamut from Irish folk music to jazz. It's a good place to knock back an ale while enjoying a hilltop ocean view.

Four Seasons Resort Maui (☎ 874-8000; 3900 Wailea Alanui) The lobby lounge has Hawaiian music and hula performances from 5:30pm to 7:30pm nightly and jazz or slack key guitar later in the evening.

Wailea Beach Marriott Resort & Spa (☎ 879-1922; 3700 Wailea Alanui; adult/child 6-12 $94/49; ☑ 5-8pm Mon, Thu, Fri & Sat) Sure, it's a bit of a tourist resort–luau cliché but the Marriott's luau is the best this side of Lahaina, and it's right on the oceanfront lawn.

Shopping

Shops at Wailea (☎ 891-6770; 3750 Wailea Alanui Dr; ☑ 9:30am-9pm) This center has dozens of stores, most flashing names like Gucci and Tiffany, but you will also find some tempting locally grown shops:

Honolua Surf Co (☎ 891-8229) Hip surfer-motif T-shirts, board shorts and aloha shirts.

Lahaina Galleries (☎ 874-8583) Paintings, bronzes and wood carvings of top Maui artists.

Maui Waterwear (☎ 891-1939) A full line of tropical swimwear you'll love to flaunt.

Na Hoku (☎ 891-8040) Upscale Hawaiian jeweler specializing in island floral and marine-life designs.

Getting There & Around

Maui Bus (☎ 871-4838) operates between Wailea and Kahului hourly from 6:30am until 8:30pm. Buses leave from the Shops at Wailea and run along S Kihei Rd before heading up to the Pi'ilani Village shopping center and Ma'alaea.

A free **shuttle bus** (☎ 879-2828) runs around the Wailea resort every 30 minutes from 7am to 6pm, stopping at the Grand Wailea and Four Seasons resorts, the Shops at Wailea and the golf courses.

MAKENA
pop 500

Makena's where untamed south Maui begins. It's handsome on land and stunning in the water. Primo snorkeling, kayaking and bodysurfing, sea turtles galore and schools of dolphins too. The beaches are magnificent. The king of them all, Big Beach, is an immense sweep of glistening sand and a prime sunset-viewing locale. The secluded cove at neighboring Little Beach is Maui's most popular nude beach.

Sights & Activities
MAKENA BAY

It's a bay, it's a boat ramp and it's the gateway to a waterworld of some very pretty sights. Arrange to have your kayak – see p377 – delivered here. The outfitter will bring it right down to the water's edge at **Makena Landing** and off you go. Paddle south, past Turtle Beach and on toward Makena State Park. Gorgeous beaches on one side and, with a little luck, breaching whales on the other.

Or perhaps you'd prefer to explore Makena Bay in a wetsuit. The turtles and tropical fish alone make this a worthy shore dive but it's the cool lava caves and the friendly whitetip reef sharks that hang out in them that really perk the scenery up. To get to the caves from the landing head to the right side of the bay and continue a few yards beyond the point. Snorkelers, too, will enjoy Makena Bay's coral gardens. South of the landing is **Keawala'i Congregational Church**, one of Maui's earliest missionary churches. The current building was erected in 1855 with 3ft-thick walls made of burnt coral rock. Don't miss the adjacent graveyard, which has old tombstones adorned with cameo photographs, many of Hawaiian cowboys laid to rest a century ago. Makena Rd ends shortly after the church at a cul-de-sac on the ocean side of Maui Prince Hotel.

MALU'AKA BEACH

As you step onto this beach it's easy to see where the action's centered, and it's definitely not on the sand. So many snorkelers flock here to see the sea turtles that frequent these waters that it's been dubbed Turtle Beach. You'll find terrific coral about 50yd out. Sea turtles feed along the coral and often swim within a few feet of snorkelers. The best action is at the south end of the beach. One caveat: come on a calm day. When it's choppy, you won't see anything.

MAUI

There are beach parking lots, rest rooms and showers at both ends of the beach. At the north side, there's the lot opposite Keawala'i Congregational Church. Or, after driving south past the Maui Prince Hotel, take the first sharp right, which dead-ends at the parking lot.

MAKENA STATE PARK

If one place captures the untamed spirit of Maui, it's this coastal park. Its crowning glory, the aptly named Big Beach, is an awesome expanse of sand and surf. Neighboring Little Beach basks in the sunshine as the island's favorite nude beach. Although it's a state park, carefree Makena remains in a natural state, with no facilities except for a couple of pit toilets and picnic tables.

Oneuli (Black Sand) Beach

A potholed dirt road at the first Makena State Park access sign leads to a salt-and-pepper–sand beach. Because of a lava shelf along the shoreline, it's not good for swimming, but local families come for fishing and picnics. Kayakers take to the water here as well.

Big Beach

The ancient Hawaiians called it Oneloʻa, literally 'Long Sand.' And indeed the golden sands stretch for the better part of a mile and are as broad as they come. The waters are a beautiful turquoise. When they're calm you'll find kids bodyboarding here, but at other times the breaks belong to experienced bodysurfers, who get tossed wildly in the transparent waves.

In the late 1960s this was the site of an alternative-lifestyle encampment that took on the nickname 'Hippie Beach.' The tent city lasted until 1972, when police finally evicted everyone. More than a few of Maui's now-graying residents can trace their roots on the island to those days.

The main parking area is a mile beyond the Maui Prince Hotel. A second parking area lies 0.25 miles to the south. You can also park alongside the road and walk in; watch out for kiawe thorns in the woods behind the beach. Thefts and broken windshields are unfortunately commonplace; don't leave anything valuable in your car.

Little Beach

Also known as Pu'u Ola'i Beach, this is south Maui's au naturel beach. Mind you, nudity is officially illegal, but enforcement is at the political whim of the day. Hidden by a rocky outcrop that juts out from Pu'u Ola'i, the cinder hill that marks the north end of Big Beach, most visitors don't even know Little Beach is there. But take the short scramble up the rock that links the two beaches and bam, there it is, spread out in front of you. The crowd is mixed, about half gay and half straight. Little Beach fronts a sandy cove that usually has a gentle shorebreak ideal for bodysurfing and bodyboarding. When the surf's up, you'll find local surfers here as well. When it's calm, snorkeling is good along the rocky point to the north.

SECRET COVE

Once a secret and now a favorite for getaway weddings, it's a toss-up as to whether you'll have this little pocket cove all to yourself or it'll be packed to the brim with tuxes and tulle. But this lovely postcard-size beach of golden sand is certainly worth a peek. The cove is 0.25 miles after the southernmost Makena State Park parking lot. The entrance is through an opening in a lava-rock wall just south of house No 6900.

Festivals & Events

The **Xterra World Championship** (www.xterraplanet.com), held in late October at the Maui Prince Hotel, is a major off-road triathlon that begins with a 1-mile swim, follows with an 6.8-mile trail run and tops off with a grueling 18.6-mile bike ride up the slopes of Haleakalā.

Sleeping & Eating

Maui Prince Hotel (☎ 874-1111, 800-321-6248; www.mauiprince.com; 5400 Makena Alanui Dr; r from $400; ❄ 🛜 🏊) Largely a tour group hotel, the

Maui Prince looks like a fortress from the outside, but the interior incorporates a fine sense of Japanese aesthetics, with carp ponds and raked-rock gardens. It has a highly regarded Japanese dinner restaurant, Hakone; and an excellent Sunday brunch.

Jawz Big Beach Maui (Makena State Park; snacks $5-9; ☷ 11am-4pm) This food truck conveniently parks in the northernmost Big Beach parking lot selling shave ice and real-deal burritos to beachgoers.

Makena Grill (Makena Alanui Dr; snacks $7-10; ☷ 11am-4pm) Hours can be irregular but when this roadside smoke grill is open it serves up tasty grinds, like fish tacos and chicken kebabs. Take your goodies across the street to Secret Cove and have a picnic.

BEYOND MAKENA

Makena Rd continues as a narrow paved road for about 3 miles after Makena State Park. The road goes through the 'Ahihi-Kina'u Natural Area Reserve before deadending at La Pérouse Bay.

Sights & Activities
'AHIHI-KINA'U NATURAL AREA RESERVE

Credit this one to Maui's last lava flow, which spilled down to the sea here in 1790, shaping 'Ahihi Bay and Cape Kina'u along the way. The jagged lava coastline and the pristine waters fringing it have been designated a reserve to protect its unique marine habitat.

Thanks in part to the prohibition on fishing, snorkeling is incredible. Just about everyone heads to the little roadside cove 0.1 miles south of the first reserve sign – granted it offers good snorkeling, but there's a better, less-crowded option. Instead, drive 0.2 miles past the cove and look for a large clearing on the right. Park here and follow the coastal footpath south for five minutes to reach a black-pebble beach with fantastic coral, clear water and few visitors. Enter the water from the left side of the beach, snorkel in a northerly direction and you'll immediately be over coral gardens teeming with an amazing variety of fish. Huge rainbow parrotfish abound here and it's not unusual to see turtles and the occasional reef shark as well.

LA PÉROUSE BAY

Ocean and land merge in an eerie desolate beauty at La Pérouse Bay. The ancient Hawaiian village of Keone'o'io flourished here before

the 1790 volcanic eruption and its remains – mainly house and heiau platforms – can be seen scattered among the lava patches. From the shoreline look for pods of spinner dolphins, which commonly come into the bay in the morning. The combination of strong offshore winds and rough waters rule out swimming but it's an interesting place to explore on land. It was at this bay that the first Westerners set foot on Maui. When the French explorer Jean François de Galaup La Pérouse landed here in 1786, scores of Hawaiians from the village of Keone'o'io came out to greet him. A **monument** to La Pérouse marks the end of the road.

Makena Stables (☎ 879-0244; www.makenastables .com; 2½-3hr trail rides $145-170; ☷ 8am-6pm), just before the road ends, offers horseback rides up the slopes of 'Ulupalakua Ranch, led by a Maui-born cowpoke whose stories are as fascinating as the terrain.

From La Pérouse Bay, the **Hoapili (King's Hwy) Trail** follows an ancient footpath along the coastline across jagged lava flows. Be prepared: bring hiking boots and plenty of water. The first part of the trail is along the beach at La Pérouse Bay. Right after the trail emerges onto the lava fields, it's possible to take a spur trail 0.75 miles down to the light beacon at the tip of Cape Hanamanioa. Alternatively, walk inland to the Na Ala Hele sign and turn right onto the trail as it climbs through rough 'a'a lava inland for the next 2 miles before coming back to the coast to an older lava flow at Kanaio Beach.

NORTH SHORE & EAST MAUI

Families living off the grid, surfers challenging death-defying waves, a hiker beating a path to a secluded waterfall – this is the free-spirited side of Maui. Start up north in the windsurfing haven of Pa'ia, then follow the serpentine Hana Hwy for the jaw-droppingly dramatic drive to Hana. Maui's most Hawaiian town dishes up a taste of Hawaii the way it used to be: s-l-o-w, friendly and quintessentially local.

Beyond Hana lies Haleakalā National Park's less frequented Kipahulu section and the cool pools and forested trails of 'Ohe'o Gulch. A fitting finale to it all is the adventurous romp through the cowboy village of Kaupo and the Pi'ilani Hwy, a road so remote some maps don't even show it.

MAUI

PA'IA
pop 2500

Home to an eclectic mix of surfers and soul seekers, Pa'ia is Maui's hippest burg. Once a thriving sugar town, a century ago Pa'ia boasted 10,000 residents living in plantation camps above a now-defunct sugar mill. During the 1950s there was an exodus to Kahului, shops were shuttered and Pa'ia began to collect cobwebs. Attracted by low rent, hippies seeking paradise landed in Pa'ia in the 1970s. A decade later windsurfers discovered Ho'okipa Beach, and Pa'ia broke onto the map big time. It hasn't been the same since. Its aging wooden storefronts, now splashed in sunshine yellows and sky blues, house a wild array of shops geared to visitors. And the dining scene? Any excuse to be here at mealtime will do.

Orientation

At Pa'ia's one stoplight, the Hana Hwy (Hwy 36) intersects with Baldwin Ave (Hwy 390), which leads through the Upcountry to Makawao. Everything in Pa'ia is on these two roads, and the whole town is walkable. Traffic backs up along the Hana Hwy as commuters shuttle to and from jobs and whenever the surf is up on the North Shore. Pa'ia is the last place to gas up your car before Hana, but that's not a problem as there's a 24-hour gas station in town.

Information

Bank of Hawaii (☎ 579-9511; 35 Baldwin Ave) Has a 24-hour ATM.

Green Banana Café (☎ 579-9130; 137 Hana Hwy; per min 10¢, minimum $3; ✆ 6am-8pm) Ecofriendly place to surf the net – lots of stations, organic free-trade coffee, green munchies.

Pa'ia Laundromat (129 Baldwin Ave; ✆ 5am-8pm)

Post office (☎ 579-8866; 120 Baldwin Ave; ✆ 8:30am-4:30pm Mon-Fri, 10:30am-12:30pm Sat)

Sights

HO'OKIPA BEACH PARK

Ho'okipa is to daredevil windsurfers what Everest is to climbers. It reigns supreme as the world's premier windsurfing beach, with strong currents, dangerous shorebreaks and razor-sharp coral offering the ultimate challenge.

The beach is also one of Maui's prime surfing spots. Winter sees the biggest waves for board surfers, and summer has the most consistent winds for windsurfers. To prevent intersport beefs, surfers hit the waves in the

morning and the windsurfers take over during the afternoon.

The action in the water is suitable for pros only. But a hilltop perch overlooking the beach offers spectators a bird's-eye view of top windsurfers doing their death-defying stuff. Ho'okipa is just before the 9-mile marker; to reach the lookout above the beach take the driveway at the east side of the park.

HA BALDWIN BEACH PARK

Bodyboarders and bodysurfers take to the waves at this palm-lined county park about a mile west of Pa'ia, at the 6-mile marker. The wide sandy beach drops off quickly, and when the shorebreak is big, unsuspecting swimmers can get slammed soundly. If you see lots of bodysurfers in the water, it's probably big! Showers, rest rooms, picnic tables, and a well-used baseball and soccer field round out the facilities. The park has a reputation for drunken nastiness after the sun sets but it's fine in the daytime when there's a lifeguard on duty.

SPRECKELSVILLE BEACH

Extending west from HA Baldwin Beach, this two-mile stretch of sand punctuated by lava outcrops is a good walking beach but its nearshore lava shelf makes it less than ideal for swimming. The rocks do, however, provide protection for young kids. If you walk to the center of the beach, you'll come to a section dubbed 'baby beach,' where local families take the little ones to splash. There are no facilities. To get there, turn toward the ocean on Nonohe Pl, then turn left on Kealakai Pl just before the Maui Country Club.

TAVARES BEACH

The local favorite for a swim in the Pa'ia area, this sandy beach attracts lots of families on weekends but is seldom crowded during the week. A submerged rocky lava shelf runs parallel to the beach about 25ft from the shore and is shallow enough for swimmers to scrape on. Once you know it's there, however, the rocks are easy to avoid, so take a look before jumping in. The beach parking lot is at the first shoreline access sign on the Hana side of the 7-mile marker. There are no facilities.

Activities

At **Hana Hwy Surf** (☎ 579-8999; 149 Hana Hwy; surfboards/ boogie boards per day $20/10; ✆ 9:30am-6pm Mon-Sat, 10am-

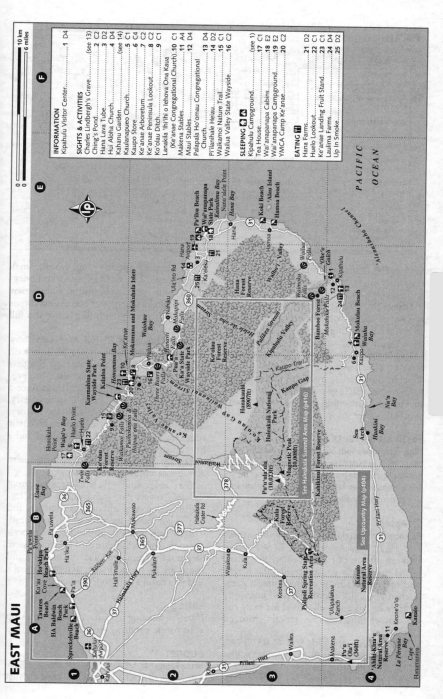

EAST MAUI

0	10 km
0	6 miles

PACIFIC

OCEAN

'Alenuihaha Channel

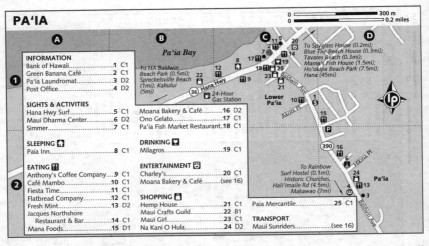

PA'IA

INFORMATION	
Bank of Hawaii	1 C1
Green Banana Café	2 C1
Pa'ia Laundromat	3 D2
Post Office	4 D2

SIGHTS & ACTIVITIES	
Hana Hwy Surf	5 C1
Maui Dharma Center	6 D2
Simmer	7 C1

SLEEPING	
Paia Inn	8 C1

EATING	
Anthony's Coffee Company	9 C1
Café Mambo	10 C1
Fiesta Time	11 C1
Flatbread Company	12 C1
Fresh Mint	13 D2
Jacques Northshore Restaurant & Bar	14 C1
Mana Foods	15 D1

Moana Bakery & Café	16 D2
Ono Gelato	17 C1
Pa'ia Fish Market Restaurant	18 C1

DRINKING	
Milagros	19 C1

ENTERTAINMENT	
Charley's	20 C1
Moana Bakery & Café	(see 16)

SHOPPING	
Hemp House	21 C1
Maui Crafts Guild	22 B1
Maui Girl	23 C1
Na Kani O Hula	24 D2

Paia Mercantile	25 C1

TRANSPORT	
Maui Sunriders	(see 16)

5pm Sun), Pa'ia's surfing headquarters, the staff keep their finger on the pulse of the surf scene and provide a daily recorded surf report.

Simmer (☎ 579-8484; www.simmerhawaii.com; 137 Hana Hwy; sailboards per day/week $50/315; ☷ 9am-7pm) is all about windsurfing and handles everything from repairs to top-of-the-line gear rentals.

Maui Dharma Center (☎ 579-8076; www.mauidharma center.org; 81 Baldwin Ave; ☷ 6:30am-6:30pm), the Tibetan Buddhist temple and stupa in the town center, shares good karma, inviting visitors to join in morning meditation, yoga sessions and other spiritual activities.

Festivals & Events
High-Tech/Lopez Split Surfbash (www.mauisurf ohana.org) Maui's largest surf contest takes place at Ho'okipa Beach on the last weekend in November or the first weekend in December, with competing short-boarders, long-boarders and bodyboarders.

Sleeping
Rainbow Surf Hostel (☎ 579-9057; www.mauigateway .com/~riki; 221 Baldwin Ave; dm/r $25/70; ☐ ☎) Within walking distance of Pa'ia center, this small hostel in a tightly packed residential neighborhood offers simple clean rooms, a guest kitchen and a TV room. It's predominantly a surfer crowd and well-suited for early risers – quiet-time rules are strictly enforced after 10pm.

Blue Tile Beach House (☎ 579-6446, 888-579-6446; www.beachvacationmaui.com; 459 Hana Hwy; r incl breakfast $90-150, ste $250) Step out the door at this exclusive oceanfront estate and you're literally on the

beach. Sleeping options range from a small straightforward room to the spacious honeymoon suite with wraparound ocean-view windows and a four-poster bed. All six rooms share a living room with fireplace and a full kitchen.

Spyglass House (☎ 579-8608, 800-475-6695; www .spyglassmaui.com; 367 Hana Hwy; r $110-180) Smack on the water at the end of a private road, Spyglass House attracts surfers and families who prefer salt spray to resort glitter. It was once a favorite haunt of LSD guru Timothy Leary, and although the psychedelics are history, this seaside retreat still maintains an eccentric edge. Stained glass, porthole windows and a hot tub are just some of the fun here.

Paia Inn (☎ 579-6000, 800-721-4000; www.paiainn .com; 93 Hana Hwy; r incl breakfast $169-239; ☐ ☒ ☎) Take a classic century-old building, soundproof the walls, spruce it up with bamboo floors, travertine bathrooms and original artwork, and you've got one classy place to lay your head. This friendly boutique inn, with seven appealing rooms, offers the ultimate Pa'ia immersion. Step out the front and Pa'ia's restaurants and shops are on the doorstep; step out the back and you're on a path to the beach.

Eating
If you're heading to Hana, be sure to pick up your picnic goodies here before moving on.

BUDGET
Mana Foods (☎ 579-8078; 49 Baldwin Ave; ☷ 8:30am-8:30pm) Dreadlocked, Birkenstocked or just

needing to stock up – everyone rubs shoulders at Mana, a health food store, bakery and deli wrapped in one. Don't miss the walnut cinnamon rolls made fresh every morning. Then look for the hot rosemary-grilled chicken and organic salad bar.

Anthony's Coffee Company (☎ 579-8340; 90 Hana Hwy; mains $4-11; 🕑 6am-2pm) The best cup of joe on this side of the island. Fresh-ground organic coffee and a delish variety of goodies from pastries to lox Benedict. Staff even pack picnics for the drive to Hana. You know everything's done right – you'll find Anthony himself on the other side of the counter grinding away.

Ono Gelato (☎ 579-9201; 115 Hana Hwy; cones $5; 🕑 11am-10pm) How cool is this? This little shop dishes up Maui-made organic gelato in island flavors like guava, mango and Kula strawberry. For the ultimate treat, order the *liliko'i* (passion fruit) quark, combining passion fruit and goat's cheese – it's awesome…really.

Fiesta Time (☎ 579-8269; 149 Hana Hwy; mains $5-13; 🕑 11am-9pm Mon-Sat, noon-8pm Sun) Surfers line up at this hole-in-the-wall for real-deal home-cooked Mexican food that's twice as good and half the price as nearby options. Quesadillas, tostadas, hot tamales – *muy delicioso!*

Café Mambo (☎ 579-8021; 30 Baldwin Ave; mains $6-18; 🕑 8am-9pm) You can't walk by this upbeat, arty café without being pulled in by the aromatic scents. Choose from fragrant Moroccan stews, mouthwatering crispy duck fajitas and creative vegetarian fare. Mambo also packs box lunches in coolers for the road to Hana (for two people $17).

Fresh Mint (☎ 579-9144; 115 Baldwin Ave; mains $8-13; 🕑 5-9pm) Spotless and tidy, this family-run restaurant serves authentic Vietnamese fare, but is totally vegetarian. Even meateaters will be amazed by the way soy takes on the flavors and texture of the foods it substitutes – just try the 'soy fish' simmered in pineapple sauce. For dessert, don't miss the mango tapioca.

MIDRANGE

Pa'ia Fish Market Restaurant (☎ 579-8030; 110 Hana Hwy; meals $9-16; 🕑 11am-9:30pm) Pick your fish from the day's catch staring at you from the refrigerated display case. The local favorite is *ono* fish and chips, but the menu includes plenty of other tempting fish preparations, from charbroiled to Cajun-blackened. Little wonder the tables here are packed like sardines.

Flatbread Company (☎ 579-8989; 89 Hana Hwy; mains $9-20; 🕑 11:30-10pm Mon-Thu, 11:30am-11pm Fri & Sat) Wood-fired pizzas made with organic sauces, nitrate-free pepperoni, Kula onions – you'll never stop at a chain pizza house again. Lots of fun combinations, from pure vegan to *kalua* pork with Surfing Goat chevre. Eat even greener on Tuesday night when a cut of the profits goes to a local environmental cause.

Jacques Northshore Restaurant & Bar (☎ 579-8844; 120 Hana Hwy; mains $10-25; 🕑 5-10pm Thu-Sun) A simple open-air restaurant for innovative seafood at honest prices. Jacques is all about fresh fish, from the top-quality sushi bar to grilled delights like the macnut-crusted mahimahi. Order the nightly special and you can't go wrong.

Moana Bakery & Café (☎ 579-9999; 71 Baldwin Ave; breakfast & lunch $10-16, dinner $15-35; 🕑 8am-3pm Sun & Mon, 8am-9pm Tue-Sat) The best place in town to linger over a relaxing lunch. Locals love that the chef is agreeable to any special requests. Not that you won't find what you're looking for on the varied menu – perhaps the fresh catch steamed in banana leaves and served with green papaya salad, or the Hana Bay crab cakes with guava puree?

TOP END

our pick Mama's Fish House (☎ 579-8488; 799 Poho Pl; mains $36-50; 🕑 11am-2:30pm & 5-9:30pm) Mama's is where you go when you want to propose or celebrate a big anniversary. Not only is the seafood as good as it gets, but when the beachside tiki torches are lit at dinnertime, the scene's achingly romantic. The island-caught fish is so fresh your server tells you who caught it, and where! Mama's is at Ku'au Cove, along the Hana Hwy, 2 miles east of Pa'ia center. Reservations are essential.

Drinking & Entertainment

Charley's (☎ 579-9453; 142 Hana Hwy) Don't be surprised to find country-singer legend Willie Nelson at the next table. A part-time Pa'ia resident, this cowboy-centric place is Willie's favorite hang. There's live music most nights.

Milagros (☎ 579-8755; 3 Baldwin Ave; 🕑 8am-10pm) *The* spot for a late-afternoon beer or the perfect margarita. The sidewalk tables are perched perfectly for watching all the action on Pa'ia's busiest corner.

Moana Bakery & Café (☎ 579-9999; 71 Baldwin Ave) If jazz is your thing, this is your place, with live music Wednesday to Saturday nights.

MAUI

Shopping

This is a fun town for browsing, with owner-run shops and boutiques selling Maui-made goodies of all sorts. It's convenient too – most shops are within a stone's throw of each other near the intersection of Baldwin Ave and the Hana Hwy.

Maui Crafts Guild (☎ 579-9697; 69 Hana Hwy) This longstanding collective of 30 Maui artists and craftspeople sells everything from pottery and jewelry to handpainted silks and natural-fiber baskets at reasonable prices.

Na Kani O Hula (☎ 573-6332; 115 Baldwin Ave) Hula *halau* (troupes) shop here for *'uli'uli* (feather-decorated gourd rattles), *'ohe halo ihu* (bamboo nose flutes) and other traditional dance and music supplies – any of which would make for a fascinating souvenir.

Hemp House (☎ 579-8880; 16 Baldwin Ave) Come here for all things hemp – well, almost all. Hemp clothing, hemp lotion and of course, hemp frisbees.

Maui Girl (☎ 579-9266; 12 Baldwin Ave) Get your itty-bitty bikinis here. These local creations really are hot – two of them even made it into the latest *Sports Illustrated* swimsuit edition.

Paia Mercantile (☎ 579-6388; 2 Baldwin Ave) All sorts of Maui-made arts and crafts are sold at this little shop next to the fish market. The sea-turtle theme plays out in everything from jewelry to photographs and paintings.

Getting There & Around

Maui Bus (☎ 871-4838) operates between Kahului and Pa'ia ($1) every 90 minutes from 5:30am to 8:30pm. You can rent Trek mountain bikes at **Maui Sunriders** (☎ 579-8970; www.mauibikeride.com; 71 Baldwin Ave; per day/week $30/100; ☻ 9am-4:30pm). The price includes a bike rack, so a travel companion could drop you off at the top of Haleakalā, or anywhere else, to cycle a one-way route.

THE ROAD TO HANA

Of all the breathtaking drives in Hawaii, this is the big kahuna.

A roller-coaster of a ride, the Hana Hwy winds down into jungly valleys and back up towering razor-edge cliffs, curling around 600 twists and turns along the way. Some 54 one-lane bridges cross nearly as many waterfalls, some eye-popping torrents and others so gentle they beg a dip. But that's just the drive. When you're ready to get out and stretch your legs the real adventure begins:

hiking trails climb into fragrant forests, short paths lead to Eden-like swimming holes, side roads wind down to sleepy seaside villages. If you've never tried smoked breadfruit, taken a dip in a spring-fed cave or gazed upon an ancient Hawaiian temple, set the alarm early – you've got a big day coming up.

Twin Falls

Just after the 2-mile marker on Hwy 360 a wide parking area with a fruit stand marks the start of the trail to Twin Falls. Local kids and tourists flock to the pool beneath the lower falls, about a 10-minute walk in. Twin Falls gets a lot of attention as being the 'first waterfall on the Road to Hana.' Truth be told, unless you're interested in taking a dip in muddy waters, this one's not worth the time. You'll find more idyllic options en route to Hana.

Huelo

Huelo Rd, a one-lane road 0.5 miles past the 3-mile marker, leads down to **Kaulanapueo Church**, which was named for the pueo (owls) that once thrived in the surrounding forest. Built of coral blocks in 1853, it's typical early Hawaiian missionary style with a tin roof and a green steeple. There are no formal opening hours, but it's usually unlocked during the day.

Huelo Rd is unmarked, so don't look for a sign. Look instead for a double row of mailboxes and a green bus shelter on the highway marking the start of the road.

SLEEPING & EATING

Tea House (☎ 572-5610, 800-215-6130; www.mauitea house.com; Hoolawa Rd; 1br cottage $135) Built with walls recycled from a Zen temple, this one-of-a-kind cottage is a real find. The place is so secluded that it's off the grid, and uses its own solar power to stoke up the lights. Yet it has everything you'll need, including a kitchen with gas burners and an open-air shower in a redwood gazebo. Meditate at a Tibetan-style stupa with a spectacular ocean view.

Huelo Lookout (☎ 573-1850; 7600 Hana Hwy; snacks $5; ☻ 7:30am-5:30pm) Drinking-coconuts, acai-berry smoothies, even real French crêpes, and it's all organic from their 12-acre farm…now that's some fruit stand. Take your goodies down the steps for a grand panorama clear out to the coast.

HITTING THE ROAD

You've probably heard how heavy traffic can be on the Hana Hwy, no parking spaces open at waterfall sights, etc. Well, that's true for many people, but it doesn't have to be for you. Most travelers take to the road between 9am and 10am. That makes for a little parade – one you don't want to be in. The trick is to set out at sunrise and you'll have the road to yourself, not to mention enough time to enjoy it. The rush-hour crowd, on the other hand, will be spending half their time looking at the clock and the rest staring nose-to-tail at the car in front of them.

Come prepared. Fill up the tank in Pa'ia; the next gas station isn't until Hana. Bring a picnic lunch; there are lots of achingly scenic places along the way to break it out. Wear a bathing suit under your clothes so you're ready for impromptu swims.

Once you're on the road, pull over to let local drivers pass – they've got places to get to and are moving at a different pace. Keep in mind that nature is alive here. Take waterfall descriptions with a few grains of salt – whether you see torrents or trickles depends on recent rainfall up in the mountains. And if it really starts to pour, watch out for rockslides and debris on the road.

Koʻolau Forest Reserve

This is where it starts to get wild! As the highway snakes along the edge of the Koʻolau Forest Reserve, the jungle takes over and one-lane bridges appear around every other bend. Koʻolau means 'windward,' and the upper slopes of these mountains squeeze passing clouds of a mighty 200in to 300in of rain annually. No surprise – that makes for awesome waterfalls as the rainwater rushes down the reserve's abundant gulches and streams.

After the 5-mile marker you'll pass through the village of **Kailua**. This little community of tin-roofed houses is the home base for the employees of the East Maui Irrigation (EMI) company. These workers maintain the extensive irrigation system that carries water from the rain forest to thirsty sugarcane fields in central Maui. Along the highway you'll see glimpses of the **Koʻolau Ditch**, the century-old system that carries up to 450 million gallons of water a day through 75 miles of ditches and tunnels to the dry central plains. For a close-up look, stop at the small pull-off just before the bridge that comes up immediately after the 8-mile marker. Just 30ft above the road you'll see water flowing through a hand-hewn stone-block section of the ditch before tunneling into the mountain.

Waikamoi Trail & Waterfalls

Put on your walking shoes for a stroll beneath majestic trees along the 30-minute **Waikamoi Nature Trail**. Look for the signposted trailhead at the wide dirt pull-off 0.5 miles past the 9-mile marker. At the start of this 0.8-mile trail you're welcomed by a sign that reads 'Quiet. Trees at Work' and a strand of reddish *Eucalyptus robusta*, one of several types of towering eucalyptus trees that grow along the path. On the ridge at the top of the loop, you'll be rewarded with fine views of the winding Hana Hwy.

Waikamoi Falls is at the bridge just before the 10-mile marker, but unless it's been raining recently don't worry about missing this one. EMI diverts water from the stream, and as a result the falls is usually just a trickle. Past Waikamoi, bamboo grows almost horizontally out from the cliffs, creating a canopy effect over the road.

Immediately following the 11-mile marker you'll pass **Puohokamoa Falls**, another zenlike waterfall. This one doesn't have any public access, but you can get a view of it right from the bridge.

If you're ready for a dip, **Haipua'ena Falls**, 0.5 miles after the 11-mile marker, has a gentle waterfall with a perfect little pool deep enough for swimming. Most people don't know this one's here, as you can't see the pool from the road. There's space for a couple of cars on the Hana side of the bridge. To reach the falls, just walk 100yd upstream.

Clean rest rooms, much appreciated right about now, and a grassy lawn with picnic tables make **Kaumahina State Wayside Park** one family-friendly stop. The park comes up 0.2 miles after the 12-mile marker. Be sure to take the short walk up the hill past the rest rooms for an eye-popping view of the coastal scenery that awaits to the south.

For the next several miles, the scenery is absolutely stunning, opening up to a new vista as you round each bend. If it's been raining recently, you can expect to see waterfalls galore crashing down the mountains.

MAUI

Honomanu Bay

You'll get your first view of this striking stream-fed bay from the roadside pull-off at the 13-mile marker.

Honomanu Bay's rocky black-sand beach is favored by surfers and fishers. The water's usually too turbulent for swimming, but on very calm days it's possible to snorkel. Keep those rips in mind before you kick out. Honomanu Stream forms a little pool just inland of the beach that's good for splashing around and on weekends local families take the young 'uns here to wade in its shallow water.

For those with a standard rental car, the best way to get to Honomanu Bay is to park at the turnoff 0.5 miles past the 13-mile marker and make a five-minute walk along the rutted access road. The road deposits you on the north side of the stream, but unless the water is high you can wade across to the rock-strewn beach.

Kalaloa Point

For a fascinating view of the coast stop at the wide pull-off on the ocean side of the highway 0.4 miles past the 14-mile marker. From here you can look clear across Honomanu Bay to watch ant-size cars descending the mountain cliffs on the other side. If there's no place to park, there's another pull-off with the same view 0.2 miles further.

Ke'anae

Congratulations, you've made it halfway to Hana. Your reward: dramatic landscapes and the friendliest seaside village on the route. Ke'anae Valley starts up at the Ko'olau Gap in the rim of Haleakalā Crater and radiates green clear down to the coast. At its foot lies Ke'anae Peninsula, created by a late eruption of Haleakalā that sent lava gushing all the way down Ke'anae Valley and into the sea. Unlike its rugged surroundings, the peninsula is perfectly flat, like a leaf floating on the water. You'll want to see Ke'anae up close. But keep an eye peeled, as sights come up in quick succession.

Ke'anae Arboretum, on the inland side of the road 0.7 miles past the 16-mile marker, follows the Pi'ina'ua Stream past an array of shady trees. Coolest of all are the painted eucalyptus trees and the golden-stemmed bamboo, whose green stripes look like the strokes of a Japanese *shodo* (calligraphy) artist. The 0.6-mile path, which takes about 30 minutes to walk, passes ginger and other fragrant plants before ending at taro patches.

Just after you pass Ke'anae Arboretum is the road leading down to **Ke'anae Peninsula**, which deposits you in the village of Ke'anae. In this slice of rural Hawaii, families who have had roots in the land for generations still tend stream-fed taro patches. Marking the heart of the village, just half a mile from the Hana Hwy, is **Lanakila 'Ihi'ihi o Iehova Ona Kaua** (Ke'anae Congregational Church), built in 1860. This is one church made of lava rocks and coral mortar whose exterior hasn't been covered over with layers of whitewash. It's a welcoming place with open doors and a guest book to sign. Pick up some homemade banana bread and head across the street, where there's a scenic coastline of jagged black rock and hypnotic white-capped waves. The rock islets visible off the coast, **Mokumana** and **Mokuhala**, are seabird sanctuaries.

Back up on the Hana Hwy, a local swimming hole known as **Ching's Pond** lies just below the bridge 0.9 miles after the 16-mile marker. You won't see anything driving by, but stop at the pull-off immediately before the bridge and behold: a deep crystal-clear pool and a little waterfall.

For a bird's-eye view of Ke'anae village and its velvety patchwork of taro fields, stop at **Ke'anae Peninsula Lookout**, an unmarked pull-off just past the 17-mile marker on the *makai* side of the road; look for the yellow tsunami speaker. If it's been raining lately, gaze to the far left to spot cascading waterfalls.

SLEEPING & EATING

YMCA Camp Ke'anae (☎ 248-8355; www.mauiymca.org; 13375 Hana Hwy; campsite/dm $17/17, cottages $125) When they're not tied up by groups, the Y's cabins, on a knoll overlooking the coast, are available to individuals as hostel-style dorms. You'll need your own sleeping bag, and cooking facilities are limited to simple outdoor grills. Another option is to pitch your tent on the grounds. The Y also has two cottages, each with full facilities, two bedrooms and a lanai with spectacular ocean views. The camp is between the 16- and 17-mile markers.

Ke'anae Landing Fruit Stand (Ke'anae Peninsula; banana bread $4.75; ☽ 8:30am-3pm) 'Da best' banana bread on Maui is baked fresh every morning, and is so good you'll find as many locals as tourists pulling up here. You can also get coconut candy, pineapple slices and drinks at this seaside stand down in the village center.

Wailua

After the Ke'anae Peninsula Lookout, you'll pass a couple of roadside fruit stands. A quarter-mile after the 18-mile marker, the unmarked Wailua Rd leads to the left into the village of Wailua. Truth be told, there's little to see other than a small church, and the village doesn't exactly welcome visitors, so you might as well stick to the highway where the real sights are.

Just before the 19-mile marker, **Wailua Valley State Wayside** lookout comes up on the right, providing a broad view into Ke'anae Valley, which appears to be a hundred shades of green. You can see a couple of waterfalls, and on a clear day you can steal a view of Ko'olau Gap, the break in the rim of Haleakalā Crater. If you climb up the steps to the right, you'll find a good view of Wailua Peninsula as well.

An even better view of Wailua Peninsula comes up at the large paved **pull-off** on the ocean side of the road 0.25 miles after the 19-mile marker. There's no sign but it's not hard to find; two concrete picnic tables mark the spot. Grab a seat, break out your snack pack and ogle the taro fields and jungle-like vistas unfolding below.

Waterfalls

The picture-perfect **Three Bears Falls**, 0.5 miles past the 19-mile marker, takes its name from the triple cascade on the inland side of the road. Catch it after a rainstorm and it roars as one mighty falls. There's a small turnout with parking for a few cars right before crossing the bridge.

Pua'a Ka'a State Wayside Park spreads along both sides of the highway 0.5 miles after the 22-mile marker. Some unlucky folks just see the rest rooms on the ocean side of the road and miss the rest. But you brought your beach towel, didn't you? Cross the highway and head inland to find a pair of delicious waterfalls cascading into pools. The best for swimming is the upper pool, visible just beyond the picnic tables. To reach it, you'll need to cross the stream, skipping across a few rocks, but it's nothing daunting.

Hanawi Falls, which is 0.1 miles after the 24-mile marker, has a split personality. Sometimes it flows gently into a quiet pool and sometimes it gushes wildly across a broad rockface. No matter the mood, it's always a beaut.

Most waterfall views look up at the cascades, but **Makapipi Falls** offers a rare chance

to experience an explosive waterfall from the top. Makapipi makes its sheer plunge right beneath your feet as you stand on the ocean side of the Makapipi Bridge. The falls is 0.1 miles after the 25-mile marker; you'll find pull-offs before and after the bridge.

Nahiku

While the village of Nahiku is down on the coast (see the boxed text, p396), its tiny 'commercial' center – such as it is – is right on the Hana Hwy, 0.8 miles past the 28-mile marker. Here you'll find a little coffee shop, fruit stand and BBQ eatery clustered together.

EATING

Up in Smoke (Hana Hwy; snacks $3-6; ☿ 10am-5pm Fri-Wed) This bustling BBQ stand is *the* place to try smoked breadfruit and *kalua* pig tacos, all cooked with kiawe wood. Hawaiian food never tasted better.

'Ula'ino Road

'Ula'ino Rd begins at the Hana Hwy just south of the 31-mile marker. Hana Lava Tube is half a mile from the highway and Kahanu Garden a mile further.

HANA LAVA TUBE

One of the odder sights on this otherwise lushly green drive are these mammoth **caves** (☎ 248-7308; www.mauicave.com; admission $12; ☿ 10:30am-4pm) formed by ancient lava flows. The caves are so formidable that they once served as a slaughterhouse – 17,000lb of cow bones had to be removed before they were opened to visitors! Winding your way through the extensive underground lava tubes, which reach heights of 40ft, you'll find a unique ecosystem of stalactites and stalagmites. The admission includes flashlights and hard hats.

KAHANU GARDEN

These extraordinary **gardens** (☎ 248-8912; www.ntbg.org; self-guided/guided tour $10/25; ☿ self-guided tour 10am-2pm Mon-Fri, guided tour 10am-noon Sat) deliver a double blast of mana. Hawaii's largest temple and Maui's most important ethnobotanical garden share this 294-acre site operated by the National Tropical Botanical Garden. The gardens preserve rare and medicinal plants from the tropical Pacific, the world's largest breadfruit tree collection, and a canoe garden containing plants brought to Hawaii by early Polynesian settlers.

MAUI

In the grounds, **Pi'ilanihale Heiau** is an immense structure with a stone platform 450ft in length. The history of this ancient temple is shrouded in mystery, but there's no doubt it was an important religious site for Hawaiians. Archaeologists believe construction began as early as AD 1200 and the heiau was built in sequences. The final grand scale was the work of Pi'ilani (the heiau's name means House of Pi'ilani), the 14th-century Maui chief who constructed many of the coastal fishponds in east Maui. The gardens and heiau, on Kalahu Point, are 1.5 miles down 'Ula'ino Rd. The road is crossed by a streambed immediately before the gardens; if it's dry you should be able to drive over it, but if it's been raining heavily don't try.

Wai'anapanapa State Park

Sun on a black-sand beach, swim in a cave, walk an ancient trail – a bounty of sights await at this fascinating park. If you're lucky, you might even spot a monk seal basking onshore.

Wai'anapanapa's centerpiece, **Pa'iloa Beach**, is a jet-black stunner. But be cautious before jumping in. It's open ocean and the bottom drops quickly, so water conditions are best suited to strong swimmers. Powerful rips are the norm, but when it's very calm the area around the sea arch offers good snorkeling.

Don't miss the lava-tube **caves** a five-minute walk from the parking lot. Their garden-like exteriors are draped with ferns, while the interiors harbor deep spring-fed pools. *Wai'anapanapa* means 'glistening waters,' and its mineral waters reputedly rejuvenate the skin. On certain nights of the year, the waters in the caves turn red. Legend says it's the blood of a princess and her lover who were killed in a fit of rage by the princess's jealous husband after he found them hiding together here. Less romantic types attribute the phenomenon to swarms of tiny bright-red shrimp called *'opaeula,* which occasionally emerge from subterranean cracks in the lava. A **coastal trail** leads south 2.5 miles from the park to Kainalimu Bay, just north of Hana Bay, offering splendid views along the way. Shortly beyond the park cabins, the trail passes blowholes and burial grounds before reaching temple ruins. As the trail fades, keep following the coast over old lava fields. Once you reach the boulder-strewn beach at Kainalimu Bay, it's about a mile further to Hana center. Honokalani Rd, which leads into Wai'anapanapa State Park, is just south of the 32-mile marker.

DETOUR: NAHIKU

Unseen by most travelers, the rural village of Nahiku was once the site of Hawaii's only rubber plantation. The plantation folded in 1916, but some of the old rubber trees can still be seen along the road, half-covered in a canopy of climbing vines. Be warned, the road is just one lane the entire way and passing traffic requires pulling over and backing up – so this isn't a detour for the faint-hearted. The turnoff onto the unmarked Nahiku Rd is just east of the 25-mile marker. After winding down 2.5 miles you'll reach the village center with its brightly painted church and smattering of old wooden houses.

SLEEPING

Fall asleep to the lullaby of the rolling surf at Wai'anapanapa State Park's **campground** on a shady lawn near the beach. One caveat: this is the rainy side of the island, so it can get wet at any time – plan accordingly. The park also has a dozen **cabins** that are extremely popular and usually book up months in advance. See p328 for details on permits and reservations.

HANA

pop 1855

Hana doesn't hit you with a bam. After the spectacular drive to get here, some visitors are surprised to find the town is a bit of a sleeper. Cows graze lazily in green pastures stretching up the hillsides. Neighbors chat over plate lunches at the beach. Even at Hana's legendary hotel, the emphasis is on relaxation.

Isolated as it is by that long and winding road, Hana stands as one of the most Hawaiian communities in the state. Folks share a strong sense of 'ohana (family), and if you listen closely you'll hear the words 'auntie' and 'uncle' a lot. There's a timeless rural character, and though 'Old Hawaii' is an oft-used cliché elsewhere, it's hard not to think of Hana in such terms. What Hana has to offer is best appreciated by those who stop and unwind. Visitors who stay awhile will experience an authentic slice of aloha.

History

It's hard to imagine little Hana as the epicenter of Maui but this village produced many of ancient Hawaii's most influential *ali'i.* Hana's great 14th-century chief Pi'ilani marched from here to conquer rivals in Wailuku and

Lahaina, and become Maui's first unified leader. The paths he took became such vital routes that even today half of Maui's highways bear his name.

The landscape changed dramatically in 1849 when ex-whaler George Wilfong bought 60 acres of land to plant sugarcane. Hana became a booming plantation town, complete with a narrow-gauge railroad connecting the fields to the Hana Mill. In the 1940s Hana could no longer compete with larger sugar operations in central Maui and the mill went bust.

Enter San Francisco businessman Paul Fagan, who purchased 14,000 acres in Hana in 1943. Starting with 300 Herefords, Fagan converted the cane fields to ranch land. A few years later he opened a six-room hotel as a getaway resort for well-to-do friends and brought his minor-league baseball team, the San Francisco Seals, to Hana for spring training. That's when visiting sports journalists gave the town its moniker, 'Heavenly Hana.' Today Hana Ranch remains the backbone of Hana's economy and its hillside pastures graze some 2000 head of cattle worked by Hawaiian *paniolo*.

Orientation & Information

Hana closes up early. If you're going to be heading back late, get gas in advance – the sole gas station, **Hana Gas** (☎ 248-7671; cnr Mill Rd & Hana Hwy; 7am-6pm), has limited opening hours.

Hana Ranch Center (Mill Rd) is the commercial center of town. It has a **post office** (☎ 248-8258); a tiny **Bank of Hawaii** (☎ 248-8015; 3-4:30pm Mon-Thu, to 6pm Fri), and the **Hana Ranch Store** (☎ 248-8261; 7am-7:30pm), which sells groceries and liquor. There's no ATM at the bank, but **Hasegawa General Store** (☎ 248-8231; 5165 Hana Hwy; 7am-7pm Mon-Sat, 8am-6pm Sun) has one. For medical needs, **Hana Health** (☎ 248-8294; 4590 Hana Hwy; 8:30am-5pm) is at the north side of town.

Sights
HANA BEACH PARK

Hana's pulse beats from this bayside park. Families come here to take the kids for a splash, to picnic on the beach and to strum their ukulele with friends. When water conditions are very calm, snorkeling and diving are good out in the direction of the light beacon. Currents can be strong, however, and snorkelers shouldn't venture beyond the beacon. Surfers head to **Waikoloa Beach**, at the northern end of the bay.

HANA CULTURAL CENTER

Soak up a little local history at this down-home **museum** (☎ 248-8622; www.hookele.com/hccm; 4974 Uakea Rd; adult/child under 12 $3/free; 10am-4pm Mon-Fri) displaying Hawaiian artifacts, wood carvings and quilts.

The museum grounds harbor still more cultural gems, including four authentically reconstructed thatched *hale*, which can be admired even outside of opening hours. Here, too, is a three-bench, c 1871 **courthouse**. Although it looks like a museum piece, you may be surprised to learn this tiny court is still used on the first Tuesday of each month when a judge shows up to hear minor cases, sparing Hana residents with traffic tickets the need to drive all the way to Wailuku.

KAIHALULU (RED SAND) BEACH

A favored haunt of nude sunbathers, this little cove on the south side of Ka'uiki Head has beautiful contrasts with rich red sand set against brilliant turquoise water. The cove is partly protected by a lava outcrop, but the currents can be powerful when the surf's up. Indeed, the name Kaihalulu means 'roaring sea.' Water drains through a break on the left side, which should be avoided. Your best chance of finding calm waters is in the morning.

The path to the beach starts across the lawn at the lower side of the Hana Community Center, where a steep 10-minute trail continues down to the cove. En route you'll pass an overgrown **Japanese cemetery**, a remnant of the sugarcane days.

HASEGAWA GENERAL STORE

For a century, this tin-roofed **store** (☎ 248-8231; 5165 Hana Hwy; 7am-7pm Mon-Sat, 8am-6pm Sun) operated by the Hasegawa family has been Hana's sole general store, its narrow aisles jam-packed with everything from fishing poles and machetes to soda pop and bags of poi. This icon of mom-and-pop shops is always crowded with locals picking up supplies, travelers stopping for snacks and sightseers buying 'I Survived the Hana Highway' T-shirts. It's a sight in itself.

WANANALUA CONGREGATIONAL CHURCH

On the National Register of Historic Places, this c 1838 **church** (cnr Hana Hwy & Hau'oli St) has such hefty walls it resembles an ancient Norman church. Take a close look and you'll notice that the rock is cut from lava. Also noteworthy is the

---

THE ULTIMATE GETAWAY

Hana may be a tight-knit Hawaiian community, but it's certainly not a closed one. Over the years celebrities have fallen in love with Hana. Aviator Charles Lindbergh found his piece of paradise in nearby Kipahulu. Beatle George Harrison retreated to his estate in Nahiku when the world started pressing in. Woody Harrelson tucks himself back in the organic-gridless-communal Kipahulu area when he's not busy acting. Singer Kris Kristofferson has long been active in the Hana community and actor Jim Nabors (aka Gomer Pyle) grows macadamia nuts nearby.

---

little cemetery at the side, where the graves are randomly laid out rather than lined up in rows. Even at rest, Hana folks like things casual.

FAGAN MEMORIAL

Rancher Paul Fagan often ended his day with a walk up Lyon's Hill to enjoy the view at sunset – and if you've got time you might want to follow in his footsteps. The big white cross topping the hill is now Hana's most dominant landmark. The 15-minute trail up Lyon's Hill starts opposite Hotel Hana-Maui.

Activities

For the ultimate bird's-eye view hop aboard a tandem ultralight aircraft with **Hang Gliding Maui** (☎ 572-6557; Hana Airport; ½/1hr flight $130/220; ☺ by appointment). Flight suits are provided; all you need is a little daring! And you actually get to fly this cool craft that looks like a motorcycle with wings – dual controls allow the passenger to take the reins once it's airborne.

If you're up for pampering, the posh **Honua Spa** (☎ 270-5290; Hotel Hana-Maui, 5031 Hana Hwy; treatments $140-250; ☺ 9am-8pm) can fill the bill with *lomilomi* (traditional Hawaiian massage) and ginger scrubs. **Luana Spa Retreat** (☎ 248-8855; 5050 Uakea Rd; treatments $40-175; ☺ by appointment) offers massages and body treatments in a Hawaiian-style open-air setting.

Hana Ranch Stables (☎ 270-5258; Mill Rd; 1hr ride $60), which books through Hotel Hana-Maui, gives horseback riders the option to trot along Hana's black-lava coastline or head for the hills into green cattle pasture.

Other activities, including **kayaking**, can be arranged through Hotel Hana-Maui. Hana Ballpark has public **tennis courts**.

Festivals & Events

East Maui Taro Festival (www.tarofestival.org) Maui's most Hawaiian town throws its most Hawaiian party. If it's native, it's here – outrigger canoe races, a taro pancake breakfast, poi making, hula dancing and a big jamfest of top ukulele and slack key guitarists. Held on a weekend in April, it's Hana at its finest; book accommodations well in advance.
Hana Relays (www.virr.com) This relay road race, held on a Saturday in early September, follows the untamed Hana Hwy for 52 breathtaking miles from Kahului to Hana Ballpark.

Sleeping

In addition to the following accommodation options, there are cabins and tent camping at Wai'anapanapa State Park (p396), just to the north of Hana, and camping at 'Ohe'o Gulch (p401), about 10 miles south.

Joe's Place (☎ 248-7033; www.joesrentals.com; 4870 Uakea Rd; r with shared/private bathroom $50/60) Hana's only road to the budget traveler offers a dozen basic rooms. The linoleum's worn but there's a fresh coat of paint on the walls and the place is kept sparkling clean. The shared facilities – a BBQ, TV den and full kitchen – provide homey opportunities to exchange tips with fellow travelers after a day of sightseeing.

Luana Spa Retreat (☎ 248-8855; www.luanaspa.com; 5050 Uakea Rd; d $150) Just you, a yurt and a view. On a secluded hill overlooking Hana Bay, this back-to-nature charmer fuses outdoor living with indoor comforts. The yurt sports a well-equipped kitchenette and a stereo with Hawaiian music. Shower outdoors in a bamboo enclosure, enjoy spectacular stargazing over the bay – this is pure romance, Hana-style.

Hana Kai-Maui (☎ 248-8426, 800-346-2772; www.hanakai.com; 1533 Uakea Rd; studios/1br from $185/210) Hana's only condo complex is just a stone's throw from Hana's hottest surfing beach. The units are nicely fitted and although the walls are thin, the sound of the surf drowns out neighboring chatter. For primo ocean views request a top-floor corner unit.

Hotel Hana-Maui (☎ 248-8211, 800-321-4262; www.hotelhanamaui.com; 5031 Hana Hwy; r from $495; ☐ ☎) This famed getaway hotel breathes tranquility. Everything's airy and open, rich with Hawaiian accents, from island art in the lobby to hand-stitched quilts on the beds. Rooms have a subdued elegance with bleached hardwood floors, ceiling fans and French doors opening to trellised patios. Delightfully absent are electronic gadgets – sans even alarm clocks! If that's not relaxing enough, there's complimentary yoga and a spa offering Hawaiian massage.

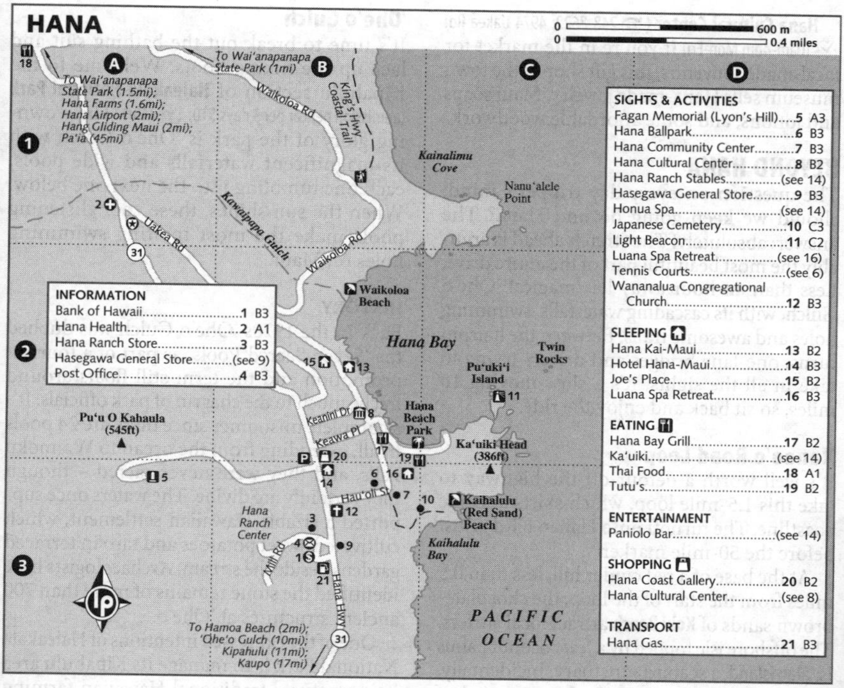
HANA
0 600 m
0 0.4 miles
A
B
C
D
1
2
3
18
To Wai'anapanapa State Park (1mi)
To Wai'anapanapa State Park (1.5mi); Hana Farms (1.6mi); Hana Airport (2mi); Hang Gliding Maui (2mi); Pa'ia (45mi)
Waikoloa Rd
King's Hwy Coastal Trail
Kainalimu Cove
Nanu'alele Point
Kawaipapa Gulch
Uakea Rd
31
Waikoloa Rd
Waikoloa Beach
Hana Bay
Twin Rocks
Pu'uki'i Island
Pu'u O Kahaula (545ft)
Keanini Dr
Keawa Pl
Hana Beach Park
Ka'uiki Head (386ft)
Hau'oli St
Kaihalulu (Red Sand) Beach
Hana Ranch Center
Kaihalulu Bay
Mill Rd
Hana Hwy
PACIFIC OCEAN
To Hamoa Beach (2mi); 'Ohe'o Gulch (10mi); Kipahulu (11mi); Kaupo (17mi)
INFORMATION
Bank of Hawaii....1 B3
Hana Health....2 A1
Hana Ranch Store....3 B3
Hasegawa General Store....(see 9)
Post Office....4 B3
SIGHTS & ACTIVITIES
Fagan Memorial (Lyon's Hill)....5 A3
Hana Ballpark....6 B3
Hana Community Center....7 B3
Hana Cultural Center....8 B2
Hana Ranch Stables....(see 14)
Hasegawa General Store....9 B3
Honua Spa....(see 14)
Japanese Cemetery....10 C3
Light Beacon....11 C2
Luana Spa Retreat....(see 16)
Tennis Courts....(see 6)
Wananalua Congregational Church....12 B3
SLEEPING
Hana Kai-Maui....13 B2
Hotel Hana-Maui....14 B3
Joe's Place....15 B2
Luana Spa Retreat....16 B3
EATING
Hana Bay Grill....17 B2
Ka'uiki....(see 14)
Thai Food....18 A1
Tutu's....19 B2
ENTERTAINMENT
Paniolo Bar....(see 14)
SHOPPING
Hana Coast Gallery....20 B2
Hana Cultural Center....(see 8)
TRANSPORT
Hana Gas....21 B3

Eating

Hana has limited grocery selections, so if you're staying awhile it's best to stock up in Kahului before heading down.

Hana Farms (☎ 248-7553; 2910 Hana Hwy; snacks $4-7; 🕑 9am-6pm) This roadside stand at the 'Welcome to Hana' sign sells Ono Farms organic coffee, delish macnut banana bread, made-to-order smoothies and fresh fruit. You'll also find a couple of covered picnic tables where you can relax and imbibe.

Tutu's (☎ 248-8224; Hana Beach Park; snacks $4-9; 🕑 8:30am-4pm) Hana Beach Park's fast-food grill serves the expected menu of shave ice, burgers and loco moco (egg, hamburger and rice) plates. Grab a table on the beach and you've got yourself a picnic.

Hana Bay Grill (Hana Beach Park; mains $7-12; 🕑 11am-5pm) This colorfully painted food truck that parks at the head of Hana Beach Park makes the perfect burger made of Maui-raised cattle. Not in a beefy mood? Order the fresh-grilled local fish plate.

Thai Food (Hana Hwy; plate lunch $9; 🕑 11am-3pm Wed-Fri) If you're lucky enough to come by on the right day, you can treat yourself to a delicious homestyle Thai lunch at this roadside stand (at the 33-mile marker) on the way into town. The menu varies, but think beef and pumpkin curry, papaya salad and pad Thai.

Ka'uiki (☎ 248-8211; Hotel Hana-Maui, 5031 Hana Hwy; dinner $50-65; 🕑 11:30am-2:30pm & 6-9pm) Don't bother with lunch – the real magic occurs here after sunset. Dinner is a locavore's treat with Hana-caught fish, Nahiku greens and other home-grown delights. Nearly everything's organic. The flavors are an innovative fusion of Hawaiian and Asian influences. Fridays are casual fun, with a Hawaiian buffet and hula show.

Drinking & Entertainment

Paniolo Bar (☎ 248-8211; Hotel Hana-Maui, 5031 Hana Hwy; 🕑 11:30am-10pm) A classy spot for a drink, this open-air bar has live Hawaiian music (6:30pm to 9pm) most evenings.

Shopping

Hana Coast Gallery (☎ 248-8636; 5031 Hana Hwy; 🕑 9am-5pm) The museum-quality collection of sculpture, paintings and woodwork makes this gallery a worthy stop, whether you're planning on top-end shopping or just browsing.

MAUI

Hana Cultural Center (☎ 248-8622; 4974 Uakea Rd; ⓨ 10am-4pm Mon-Fri) If you're in the market for local-made souvenirs, this gift shop at the town museum sells Hana-made jewelry, Maui soaps and lotions, and some affordable woodwork.

BEYOND HANA

The question on every day-tripper's mind: should we keep going beyond Hana? The answer: absolutely! The stretch ahead is arguably the most beautiful part of the entire drive. Less than an hour away lies magical 'Ohe'o Gulch, with its cascading waterfalls, swimming holes and awesome trails. Between the hairpin turns, one-lane bridges and drivers trying to take in all the sights, it's a slow-moving 10 miles, so sit back and enjoy the ride.

Haneo'o Road Loop

It's well worth a detour off the highway to take this 1.5-mile loop, which skirts a scenic coastline. The turnoff onto Haneo'o Rd is just before the 50-mile marker.

At the base of a red cinder hill, less than 0.5 miles from the start of the loop, the chocolate-brown sands of **Koki Beach** attract local surfers. The offshore isle topped by a few coconut palms is **'Alau Island**, a seabird sanctuary. Incidentally, those trees are a green refreshment stand of sorts, planted by Hana residents to provide themselves with drinking coconuts while fishing from the island.

A little further is **Hamoa Beach**, its lovely gray sands are maintained by Hotel Hana-Maui, but it's open to all. Author James Michener once called it the only beach in the North Pacific that actually looked as if it belonged in the South Pacific. When the surf's up, surfers and boogie boarders flock to the waters, though be aware of rips. When seas are calm, swimming is good in the cove. Public access is down the steps just north of the hotel's bus-stop sign. Facilities include showers and rest rooms.

Wailua Falls

As you continue south, you'll see waterfalls cascading down the cliffs, orchids growing out of the rocks, and jungles of breadfruit and coconut trees. Hands-down the most spectacular sight along the way is Wailua Falls, which plunges a mighty 100ft just beyond the road. It appears 0.3 miles after the 45-mile marker and you won't need anyone to point this one out, as folks are always lined up along the roadside snapping photos.

'Ohe'o Gulch

It's time to break out the bathing suit and lace up the hiking boots. Welcome to the Kipahulu section of **Haleakalā National Park** (admission per car per 3 days $10; ⓨ 24hr). The crowning glory of the park is 'Ohe'o Gulch with its magnificent waterfalls and wide pools, each one tumbling into the next one below. When the sun shines, these cool glistening pools make the most inviting swimming holes on Maui.

HISTORY

Back in the 1970s 'Ohe'o Gulch was dubbed the 'Seven Sacred Pools' as part of a tourism promotion and the term still floats around freely, much to the chagrin of park officials. It's a complete misnomer since there are 24 pools in all, extending from the ocean to Waimoku Falls, and they were never sacred – though they certainly are divine. The waters once supported a sizable Hawaiian settlement, which cultivated sweet potatoes and taro in terraced gardens beside the stream. Archaeologists have identified the stone remains of more than 700 ancient structures at 'Ohe'o.

One of the expressed intentions of Haleakalā National Park is to manage its Kipahulu area 'to perpetuate traditional Hawaiian farming and *ho'onanea*' – a Hawaiian word meaning to pass the time in ease, peace and pleasure. So kick back and have some fun!

INFORMATION

The national park's **Kipahulu Visitor Center** (☎ 248-7375; www.nps.gov/hale; ⓨ 8:30am-5:30pm) offers a thin menu of visitor programs, depending on the season and the staff available. The mainstay is a short cultural history talk typically presented in the early afternoon. You'll find rest rooms at the parking lot. Food and gas are not available.

Since there's no access between this section of the park and the main Haleakalā summit area (p413), your visit to the cindery summit will need to wait for another day. But hold onto your ticket, because it's good for both sections of the park.

SIGHTS & ACTIVITIES
Lower Pools

First thing on your agenda should be the **Kuloa Point Trail**, a half-mile loop that runs from the visitor center down to the lower pools and back. At the junction with Pipiwai Trail go right.

A few minutes down, you'll come to a broad grassy knoll with a gorgeous view of the Hana coast. On a clear day you can see the Big Island, 30 miles away across 'Alenuihaha Channel. This would be a fine place for a picnic lunch.

The large freshwater pools along the trail are terraced one atop the other and connected by gentle cascades. They're usually calm and great for swimming, their cool waters refreshingly brisk. The second big pool below the bridge is a favorite swimming hole.

However, be aware: conditions can change in a heartbeat. Heavy rains falling far away on the upper slopes can bring a sudden torrent through the pools at any time. If the water starts to rise, get out immediately. Several people have been swept out to sea from these pools by flash floods. Slippery rocks and unseen submerged ledges are other potential hazards, so check carefully before jumping in.

Waterfall Trails

The **Pipiwai Trail** runs up the 'Ohe'o streambed, rewarding hikers with picture-perfect views of waterfalls. The trail starts on the *mauka* side of the visitor center and leads up to Makahiku Falls (0.5 miles) and Waimoku Falls (2 miles). To see both falls, allow about two hours return. The upper section is muddy, but boardwalks cover some of the worst bits.

Along the path, you'll pass large mango trees and patches of guava before coming to an overlook after about 10 minutes. **Makahiku Falls**, a long bridal-veil waterfall that drops into a deep gorge, is just off to the right. Thick green ferns cover the sides of basalt cliffs where the fall cascades – a very rewarding scene for such a short walk.

To the left of the overlook, a worn path continues up to the top of the waterfall, where there's a remote skinny-dipping pool known to locals as 'last chance pool.' If you're considering a dip, assess the situation carefully. Rocks above the falls offer some protection from going over the edge when the water level isn't high; a cut on one side lets the water plunge over the cliff – don't go near it! Flash floods are not uncommon here – if the water starts to rise, get out immediately – a drop over this sheer 185ft waterfall could, obviously, be fatal.

Continuing along the main trail, you'll walk beneath old banyan trees, cross Palikea Stream (killer mosquitoes thrive here) and enter the wonderland of the **Bamboo Forest**, where thick

groves of trees bang together musically in the wind. Beyond them is **Waimoku Falls**, a thin, lacy 400ft waterfall dropping down a sheer rock face. When you come out of the first grove, you'll see the waterfall in the distance. Forget swimming under Waimoku Falls – its pool is shallow and there's a danger of falling rocks.

If you want to take a dip, you'll find better pools along the way. About 100yd before Waimoku Falls, you'll cross a little stream. If you go left and work your way upstream for 10 minutes, you'll come to an attractive waterfall and a little pool about neck deep. There's also an inviting pool in the stream about halfway between Makahiku and Waimoku Falls.

TOURS

For fascinating insights into the area's past, join one of the ethnobotanical tours led by **Kipahulu 'Ohana** (☎ 248-8558; www.kipahulu .org; Kipahulu Visitor Center), a collective of Native Hawaiian farmers who have restored ancient taro patches within the park. Tours include a two-hour outing ($49) that concentrates on the farm and a 3½-hour tour ($79) that adds on a hike to Waimoku Falls. The schedule varies, so call ahead.

SLEEPING

At the national park's **Kipahulu Campground**, there's so much mana you can almost hear the whispers of the ancient Hawaiians. The facilities are minimal: pit toilets, picnic tables, grills. But the setting – oceanside cliffs amid the stone ruins of an ancient village – is simply incredible. There's no water, so bring your own. Mosquito repellent and gear suitable for rainy conditions are also a must.

Permits aren't required. Camping is free but limited to three nights each month. In winter you'll probably have the place to yourself, and even in summer there's typically enough space to handle everyone who shows up.

Kipahulu

Less than a mile south of 'Ohe'o Gulch lies the little village of Kipahulu. It's hard to imagine, but this quiet community was once a bustling sugar-plantation town. After the mill shut down in 1922, most people left for jobs elsewhere. Today mixed among modest homes, organic farms and back-to-the-landers living off the grid are a scattering of exclusive estates, including the former home of famed aviator Charles Lindbergh.

MAUI

KILLER WEED

According to legend, Hana folks once killed an evil shark-man who lived on a bluff near Mu'olea, the area between mile markers 46 and 47 north of Kipahulu. After burning the shark-man's body, they dropped his ashes into a tide pool, but the shark man returned – this time in the form of *limu make o Hana*, the 'deadly seaweed of Hana.' The tide pool where the red seaweed was found was made *kapu* (taboo), though warriors learned to tip their spears with the toxin to make them more deadly.

Inspired by the legend, which was written down by a Hawaiian scholar in the 19th century, scientists from the University of Hawai'i came to the Mu'olea tide pool to look for *limu make o Hana* in the early 1960s. The legend said the seaweed resembled 'the suckers of an octopus.' What they found was not a seaweed, but a previously unknown type of soft coral, related to the sea anemone. When tested, researchers discovered the toxin it bore, which they named palytoxin, was one of the most deadly substances ever found in nature. Since palytoxin has since been found in certain toxic fish, and may be related to a symbiotic algae that grows within the coral. The active properties in *limu make o Hana* are being tested as a possible treatment for cancer.

Maui County, the Trust for Public Lands and the Office of Hawaiian Affairs have jointly purchased 70 acres at Mu'olea point, including the tide pools where the *limu* is found. The property is culturally important in other ways, too. It includes the ruins of a heiau that seems to be aligned with the Pleiades constellation, a summer residence of King David Kalakaua, and rare native plants. Hawaiian cultural organizations, including Kipahulu 'Ohana (p401), are hoping to eventually restore the heiau and establish educational programs there.

SIGHTS

Charles Lindbergh moved to remote Kipahulu in 1968. Although he relished the privacy he found here, he did occasionally emerge as a spokesperson for conservation issues. Following his death from cancer in 1974, Lindbergh was buried in the graveyard of **Palapala Ho'omau Congregational Church**. The church (c 1864) is also notable for its window painting of a Polynesian Christ draped in the red-and-yellow feather capes that were reserved for Hawaii's highest chiefs.

Lindbergh's desire to be out of the public eye may still be at play; many visitors fail to find his grave. To get there, turn left at the sign for Maui Stables, which is 0.2 miles south of the 41-mile marker and then veer left after the stables. The church is 0.2 miles further. **Charles Lindbergh's grave**, a simple granite slate laid upon lava stones, is in the yard behind the church. The inscription reads simply, '…If i take the wings of the morning, and dwell in the uttermost parts of the sea…C.A.L.'

Walk a minute or two past the graveyard to reach a hilltop vantage point with a fine view of the jagged Kipahulu coast – one look and you'll understand why Lindbergh was so taken by this area.

ACTIVITIES

Ride in the wilderness with **Maui Stables** (☎ 248-7799; www.mauistables.com; 3hr ride $150; ☺ departures 10am), on horseback trips that mix breathtaking views with Hawaiian storytelling and chanting – a real cultural immersion experience. It's between the 40- and 41-mile markers.

EATING

Laulima Farms (snacks $3-5; ☺ 10:30am-5pm) Pedal power takes on new meaning at this off-the-grid fruit stand (between the 40- and 41-mile markers), where customers take the seat on a stationary bike and rev up enough power to run the blender, juicing their own fruit smoothies. Everything sold here, from the hand-picked organic coffee to the GMO-free veggies, is homegrown. Refreshing in every way.

PI'ILANI HIGHWAY

The untamed Pi'ilani Hwy travels 25 ruggedly scenic miles between Kipahulu and 'Ulupalakua Ranch as it skirts along the southern flank of Haleakalā.

Diehards will love this road, while the more timid may wonder what they've gotten into in these lonesome boonies. Signs such as 'Motorists assume risk of damage due to presence of cattle' and 'Safe speed 10mph' give some clues that this is not your typical highway.

The road winds like a drunken cowboy but most of it is paved. The trickiest section is around Kaupo, where the road is rutted. Depending on when it was last graded, you can usually make it in a regular car, though it may rattle your bones a bit. But after hard rains, streams flow over the road, making passage difficult, if not dangerous.

Flash floods sometimes wash away portions of the road, closing down the highway until it's repaired. The **county public works department** (☎ 248-8254; ⏲ 6:30am-3pm Mon-Fri) fields calls about road conditions, or ask at the Kipahulu Visitor Center (p400) at 'Ohe'o Gulch.

The best way to approach the drive is with an early-morning start, when the road is so quiet you'll feel like the last soul on earth. Take something to munch on and plenty to drink, and check your oil and spare tire. It's a long haul to civilization if you break down – gas stations and other services are nonexistent between Hana and the Upcountry.

Kaupo

Near the 35-mile marker you'll reach Kaupo, a scattered community of *paniolo,* many of them fourth-generation ranch hands working at Kaupo Ranch. As the only lowlands on this section of coast, Kaupo was once heavily settled and is home to several ancient heiau and two 19th-century churches. However, don't expect a developed village in any sense of the word. The sole commercial venture on the entire road is **Kaupo Store** (☎ 248-8054; ⏲ 10am-5pm Mon-Sat), which sells snacks and drinks and is worth popping inside just to see the antique counter display.

Kaupo's prettiest site, the whitewashed **Hui Aloha Church** (1859), sits above the blacksand **Mokulau Beach**, an ancient surfing site. Mokulau, meaning 'Many Small Islands,' is named for the rocks just offshore.

Kaupo to 'Ulupalakua Ranch

Past Kaupo village, you'll be rewarded with striking views of **Kaupo Gap**, the southern opening in the rim of majestic Haleakalā. Near the 31-mile marker a short 4WD road runs down to **Nu'u Bay**, favored by locals for fishing and swimming; if you're tempted to hit the water, stay close to shore, as riptides inhabit the open ocean beyond.

Just east of the 30-mile marker you'll see two gateposts that mark the path to dramatic **Huakini Bay**. Park at the side of the highway and walk down the rutted dirt drive two minutes to reach this rock-strewn beach whipped by violent surf. After the 29-mile marker, keep an eye out for a natural lava **sea arch** that's visible from the road.

At the 19-mile marker the road crosses a vast **lava flow** dating from 1790, Haleakalā's last-gasp eruption. This flow, part of the Kanaio Natural Area Reserve, is the same one that covers the La Pérouse Bay area (p387). It's still black and barren all the way down to the sea.

Just offshore is Kaho'olawe and on a clear day you can even see the Big Island popping its head up above the clouds. It's such a wide-angle view that the ocean horizon is noticeably curved. As you approach 'Ulupalakua Ranch, watch out for freerange cattle grazing at the side of the road. Soon, groves of fragrant eucalyptus trees replace the drier, scrubbier terrain and you find yourself back in civilization at Tedeschi Vineyards (p412).

UPCOUNTRY

Green, fragrant and easy on the eyes, the Upcountry begs a country drive. Carpeted with rolling hills, emerald pastures and misty cloud forest, these western slopes of Haleakalā are proof positive that Maui offers much more than just a day at the beach. The possibilities for exploring it are nothing short of breathtaking. Hike up a steep mountain, zipline over deep gorges, paraglide down the hillsides, ride a horse through a lofty forest.

Upcountry is home to renegade artists and weathered cowboys, flower growers and truck farmers, all of whom can't help but feel a wee bit smug that they've scored such a golden niche of Maui for themselves. Everyone passes through a slice of the Upcountry on the way to Haleakalā National Park, but don't settle for a pass through. Look around the showy gardens, little-used trails and rambling back roads. They alone are worth the trip.

HIGHWAY 390: PA'IA TO MAKAWAO

Baldwin Ave (Hwy 390) rolls uphill for 7 winding miles between Pa'ia and Makawao, starting amid feral sugarcane fields and then cutting through pineapple fields interspersed with grassy patches where cattle graze.

Churches

Two handsome churches grace Baldwin Ave. Two miles above Pa'ia the **Holy Rosary Church** (945 Baldwin Ave), with its memorial statue of Father Damien, comes up first on the right. A mile further on the left stands the

MAUI

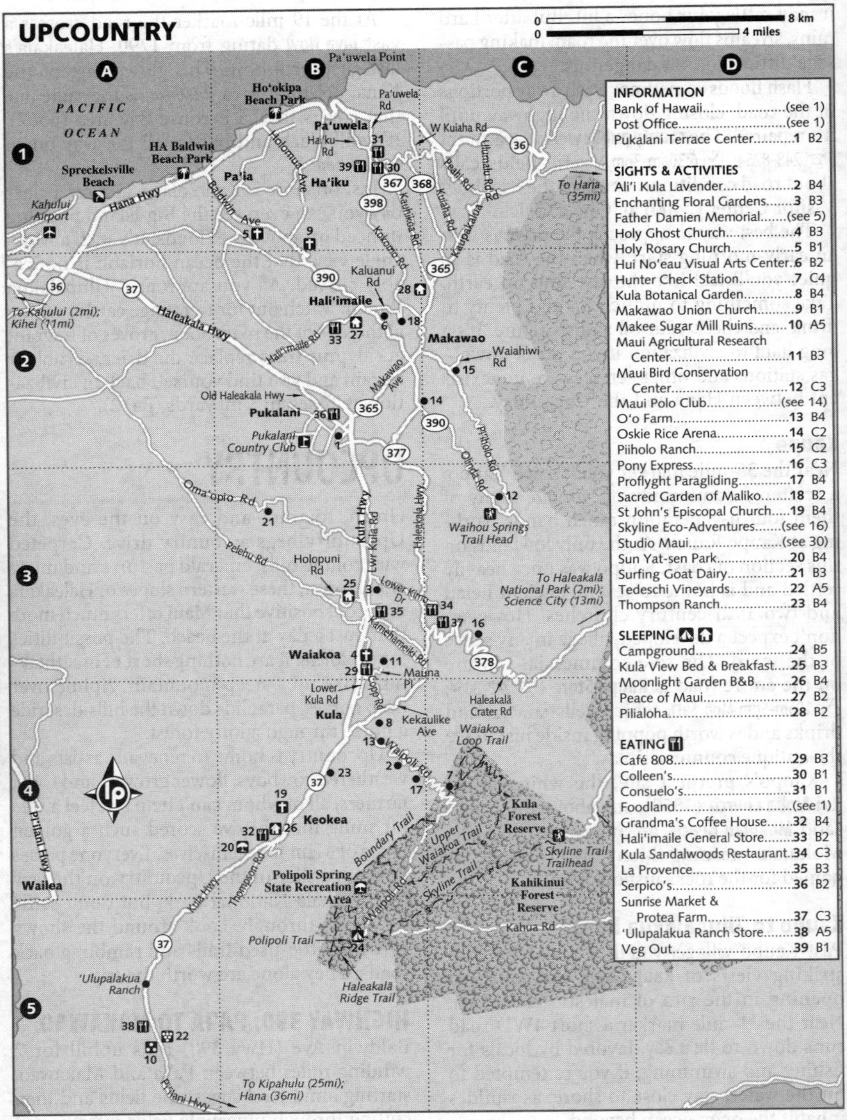

century-old **Makawao Union Church** (1445 Baldwin Ave), which was built of lava-stone blocks and is on the National Register of Historic Places.

Hui No'eau Visual Arts Center

Occupying the former estate of sugar magnates Harry and Ethel Baldwin, **Hui No'eau** (☎ 572-6560; www.huinoeau.com; 2841 Baldwin Ave; admission free; ⌚ 10am-4pm Mon-Sat) radiates artistic creativity. Famed Honolulu architect CW Dickey designed the two-story plantation home with its Spanish-style tile roof in 1917. The prestigious arts club founded here in the 1930s still offers classes in printmaking, pottery, woodcarving and other visual arts. You're welcome to visit the galleries, which exhibit the works of island artists, and walk around the grounds where you'll find stables converted into art studios. The gift shop sells quality ceramics, glassware and original prints created onsite. Pick up a walking tour map at the front desk. The center is just after the 5-mile marker.

Hali'imaile
pop 900

The little pineapple town of Hali'imaile ('fragrant twining shrub') is named for the sweet-scented maile plants used in lei-making that covered the area before pineapple took over. The heart of town is the old general store (c 1918) that's been turned into Upcountry's best restaurant. Hali'imaile Rd runs through the town, connecting Baldwin Ave (Hwy 390) with the Haleakala Hwy (Hwy 37).

SLEEPING & EATING
Peace of Maui (☎ 572-5045, 888-475-5045; www.peace ofmaui.com; 1290 Hali'imaile Rd; s/d with shared bathroom $55/65, 2br cottage $130; ☐ ☎) This aptly named place in quiet Hali'imaile is Upcountry's top budget sleep. In the middle of nowhere yet within an hour's drive of nearly everywhere, it would make a good central base for exploring the whole island. Rooms are small but comfortable, each with refrigerator, fan and TV. There's a guest kitchen, free wi-fi and a hot tub. If you need more space, the cottage is large enough to sleep a family.

ourpick Hali'imaile General Store (☎ 572-2666; 900 Hali'imaile Rd; lunch $10-25, dinner $25-42; ☎ 11am-2:30pm Mon-Fri & 5:30-9:30pm daily) Chef Bev Gannon was one of the original forces behind the Hawaii Regional Cuisine movement and a steady flow of in-the-know diners beat a track to this tiny village to feast on her inspired creations. You can tantalize the tastebuds with fusion fare, like the award-winning ginger-chili duck tostadas. The atmospheric plantation-era decor is nearly as interesting as the food and the wine list is no slacker either.

MAKAWAO
pop 6330

A ranching town since the 1800s, Makawao shows its *paniolo* roots in the Old West–style wooden buildings lining Baldwin Ave. And the cattle pastures surrounding the town remind you it's more than just history. If you want to see what a real Hawaiian rodeo is all about, swing by on the 4th of July, when

Makawao's streets fill with cowhands parading on horseback wearing festive lei.

But that's only one side of Makawao. Many of the old shops that once sold saddles and stirrups now have artsy new tenants who have turned Makawao into the most happening art center on Maui. Its galleries display the works of painters and sculptors who have escaped frenzied scenes elsewhere to set up shop in these inspirational hills. If you enjoy browsing, just about every storefront is worth poking your head into.

Orientation & Information
Most things are within a few minutes' walk of the main intersection, where Baldwin Ave (Hwy 390) meets Makawao Ave (Hwy 365), including the **post office** (☎ 572-0019; 1075 Makawao Ave; ☎ 8:30am-4:30pm Mon-Fri, 8:30-11am Sat) and **public library** (☎ 573-8785; 1159 Makawao Ave; ☎ noon-8pm Mon & Wed, 9:30am-5pm Tue, Thu & Sat). There's no bank, but there's an ATM at the **Minit Stop** (☎ 573-9295; 1100 Makawao Ave; ☎ 5am-11:30pm) gas station.

Sights & Activities
OLINDA ROAD
Pretty country roads abound in the hills around Makawao. The best of all is **Olinda Rd**, which picks up in town where Baldwin Ave leaves off, drifting up past the **Oskie Rice Arena**, where rodeos are held, and the **Maui Polo Club**, which hosts matches on Sunday afternoons in the fall. From here the winding road is little more than a path through the forest, and knotty tree roots as high as your car caresses the roadsides. The air's rich with the fragrance of eucalyptus trees and occasionally there's a clearing with an ocean vista. Four miles from town, past the 11-mile marker, the **Maui Bird Conservation Center** (closed to the public) breeds nene (the native Hawaiian goose) and other endangered birds. To make a loop, turn left onto Pi'iholo Rd near the top of Olinda Rd and wind back down into town.

WAIHOU SPRINGS TRAIL
If you're ready for a quiet walk in the woods, take this peaceful trail, which begins 4.75 miles up Olinda Rd from central Makawao. The forest is amazingly varied, having been planted by the US Forest Service in an effort to determine which trees would produce the best quality lumber in Hawaii. Thankfully these magnificent specimens never met the woodman's ax. The trail, which begins on a soft carpet of pine needles, passes Monterey cypress and eucalyptus as well as orderly

MAUI

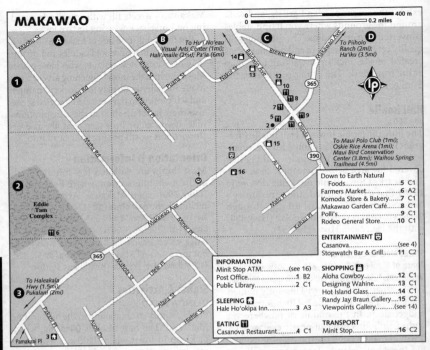

MAKAWAO

INFORMATION
Minit Stop ATM................(see 16)
Post Office.............................1 B2
Public Library.......................2 C1

SLEEPING 🏠
Hale Ho'okipa Inn................3 A3

EATING 🍴
Casanova Restaurant...........4 C1

Down to Earth Natural
  Foods..................................5 C1
Farmers Market.....................6 A2
Komoda Store & Bakery......7 C1
Makawao Garden Café.........8 C1
Polli's....................................9 C1
Rodeo General Store..........10 C1

ENTERTAINMENT 🎭
Casanova.........................(see 4)
Stopwatch Bar & Grill.........11 C2

SHOPPING 🛍
Aloha Cowboy......................12 C1
Designing Wahine................13 C1
Hot Island Glass...................14 C1
Randy Jay Braun Gallery.....15 C2
Viewpoints Gallery..........(see 14)

TRANSPORT
Minit Stop............................16 C2

rows of pine trees. After 0.7 miles, you'll be rewarded with a view clear out to the ocean, and up to this point it's easy going. It's also possible to continue steeply downhill for another 0.25 miles to reach Waihou Springs, but that part of the trail can be a muddy mess.

HORSEBACK RIDING
At **Piiholo Ranch** (☎ 357-5544; www.piiholo.com; Waiahiwi Rd; 2hr ride $120; ☼ 9am-3:30pm Mon-Sat) you can ride with real *paniolo* across the open range of this cattle ranch that's been worked by the same family for six generations. Mountain, valley and pasture views galore.

Festivals & Events
Upcountry Fair Traditional agricultural fair with a farmers market, arts and crafts, chili cookoff, *keiki* games and good ol' country music; held on the second weekend in June at the Eddie Tam Complex.
Makawao Rodeo Hundreds of *paniolo* show up at the Oskie Rice Arena on the weekend closest to Independence Day (July 4) to compete in roping and riding competitions at Hawaii's premier rodeo. Qualifying events occur all day on Thursday and Friday to determine who gets to

compete for the big prizes over the weekend. For thrills on Friday night, head up to the arena to see the daredevil bull-riding bash.
Paniolo Parade Held on the Saturday morning closest to July 4, this festive parade goes right through the heart of Makawao; park at the rodeo grounds and take the free shuttle to the town center.

Sleeping
Hale Ho'okipa Inn (☎ 572-6698; www.maui-bed-&-breakfast.com; 32 Pakani Pl; r incl breakfast $125-165; 🛜) A short walk from the town center, this historic craftsman-style house built in 1924 offers four sunny guest rooms. It's all very casual and homey with country-style furnishings in the rooms and organic fruit from the yard on the breakfast table.

Eating
our pick Komoda Store & Bakery (☎ 572-7261; 3674 Baldwin Ave; pastries $1-2; ☼ 7am-5pm Mon, Wed, Thu & Fri, to 2pm Sat) This homespun bakery, legendary for its mouth-watering cream puffs and guava-filled *malasadas* (Portuguese donut), is a must-stop. It's been a Makawao landmark since Tazeko Komoda first stoked up the oven in 1916 and

his offspring, using the same time-honored recipes, have been at it ever since. Best believe they've got it down pat! Do arrive early though – it often sells out by noon.

Rodeo General Store (☎ 572-1868; 3661 Baldwin Ave; meals $5-8; ☺ 6:30am-10pm Mon-Sat, 6:30am-8pm Sun) Stop here to grab a tasty takeout meal. The deli counter sells everything from fresh salads and Hawaiian *poke* to hot teriyaki chicken and Japanese-style *bentō* lunches ready to go. Everything is top quality and made from scratch.

Makawao Garden Café (☎ 573-9065; 3669 Baldwin Ave; mains $7-10; ☺ 11am-4pm) On a sunny day there's no better place in town for lunch than this outdoor café tucked into a courtyard at the north end of Baldwin Ave. Strictly sandwiches and salads but everything's fresh, generous and made to order by the owner herself. The mahimahi on homemade focaccia is killer.

Polli's (☎ 572-7808; 1202 Makawao Ave; mains $8-20; ☺ 11am-10pm) Locals and visitors alike flock to this old standby Tex-Mex restaurant to down a few *cervezas* while munching away on nachos, tacos and sizzling fajitas. The food's just average, but nonstop surf videos and lively chatter keep the scene high energy.

Casanova Restaurant (☎ 572-0220; 1188 Makawao Ave; lunch $8, dinner $12-30; ☺ 11:30am-2pm Mon-Sat & 5:30-10pm daily) The one Makawao restaurant that lures diners up the mountain, Casanova offers reliably good Italian fare. The crispy innovative pizzas cooked in a kiawe-fired oven are as good as they get. Juicy Maui-raised steaks and renditions of classic Italian dishes like the seafood fra diavola shore up the rest of the menu.

It says something about a town when its biggest grocer is a health food store. At **Down to Earth Natural Foods** (☎ 572-1488; 1169 Makawao Ave; ☺ 8am-8pm) you'll find all the expected staples as well as takeout fare. Locals gather to sell their homegrown produce once a week at a small **farmers market** (Eddie Tam Complex; ☺ 7-9am Sat).

Entertainment

Casanova (☎ 572-0220; 1188 Makawao Ave) This is *the* place to go after dark in the Upcountry. Casanova has a happening dance floor with live music several nights a week and DJs on others.

Stopwatch Bar & Grill (☎ 572-1380; 1127 Makawao Ave) For a fun local scene, swing by this friendly sports bar, which brings in Upcountry musicians like the Haiku Hillbillys on weekends. Any other time it's all about sports TV.

Shopping

Start your exploration by wandering down Baldwin Ave from where it intersects with Makawao Ave.

Hot Island Glass (☎ 572-4527; 3620 Baldwin Ave) Everyone comes here to watch the glassblowers (10:30am to 4pm) spin their red-hot creations. The works range from small paperweights to elaborate fine-art pieces, with an emphasis on ocean themes.

Viewpoints Gallery (☎ 572-5979; 3620 Baldwin Ave) You'll feel like you're walking into a museum at Makawao's classiest gallery, where a dozen of the island's finest artists hang their works.

Randy Jay Braun Gallery (☎ 573-1176; 1152 Makawao Ave) Braun's sepia photographs of traditional hula dancers are among the most recognized photo art in Hawaii today. Also interesting are his shots of Hawaiian cowboys.

Aloha Cowboy (☎ 573-8190; 3643 Baldwin Ave) Get your cowboy-themed retro lunch pails and rhinestone-studded leather bags here.

Designing Wahine (☎ 573-0990; 3640 Baldwin Ave) Make this your first stop if you're looking for quality classic aloha shirts and hand-dyed Ts with *paniolo* themes. Lots of island-made souvenir goodies too.

MAUI

DETOUR: LABYRINTH WALKS

Up for a meditative moment? The **Sacred Garden of Maliko** (☎ 573-7700; 460 Kaluanui Rd; admission free; ☺ 10am-5pm), a self-described healing sanctuary, has a pair of rock-garden labyrinth walks guaranteed to reset the harmony gauge. One's in an orchid greenhouse facing a contemplative Buddha statue; the other's in a *kukui* (candlenut trees) grove beside Maliko Stream. Take your time, feel each step on the pebbles underfoot, listen to the trickling stream, inhale the gentle scent of the garden. S-o-o-o soul soothing. To get there, turn east off Baldwin Ave onto Kaluanui Rd. After 0.8 miles you'll cross a one-lane bridge; 0.2 miles further look for a low stone wall – the garden is on the right just before a sharp S-curve in the road.

Getting There & Around

Maui Bus (☎ 871-4838) operates between Kahului and Makawao ($1) every 90 minutes from 6am to 9pm.

HA'IKU
pop 4500

In some ways this little town is like Pa'ia before all the tourists arrived. Like Pa'ia, Ha'iku's roots are in sugarcane. Maui's first 12 acres of the sweet stuff was planted right here in 1869, and the village once had both a sugar mill and pineapple canneries. Thanks to its affordability and proximity to Ho'okipa Beach, it's a haunt of pro surfers who have rejuvenated the town. Today the old cannery buildings are once again the heart of the community, housing a yoga studio, several surfboard shops and the kind of eateries that make a detour fun.

Activities

Studio Maui (☎ 575-9390; www.thestudiomaui.com; Ha'iku Marketplace, 810 Ha'iku Rd; classes $13-25; ☉ 7:30am-10pm) attracts a high-energy, good-karma crowd with a full schedule of yoga classes from Anusara basics to power-flow yoga, as well as ecstatic dance, New Age concerts and more.

Sleeping

Pilialoha (☎ 572-1440; mh@pilialoha.com; 2512 Kaupakalua Rd; d $135) This sunny split-level cottage blends countryside charm with all the comforts of a home away from home. The setting, nestled in a eucalyptus grove, is pretty. Everything inside is pretty too. But it's the warm hospitality and attention to detail, from the fresh-cut roses on the table to the Hawaiian music collection and cozy quilts on the beds, that shines brightest. Breakfast goodies for your first morning, and coffee for the entire stay is provided.

Eating

Veg Out (☎ 575-5320; Ha'iku Town Center, 810 Kokomo Rd; mains $5-10; ☉ 10:30am-7:30pm Mon-Fri, 11:30am-7:30pm Sat & Sun) Tucked inside a former warehouse, this rasta-casual vegetarian eatery serves up a dynamite burrito with hot tofu, beans and pineapple salsa. Also right on the mark are the taro cheeseburgers and pesto-chevre pizza.

Colleen's (☎ 575-9211; Ha'iku Marketplace; 810 Ha'iku Rd; mains $7-14; ☉ 6am-9pm) Surfers get their presunrise breakfast fix here and return in the evening to cap things off with a pint of Big Wave Golden Ale. Colleen's is pure locavore. The burgers are made with hormone-free Maui cattle, the

salads with organic Kula greens and the beer Colleen pours are Hawaiian microbrews.

Consuelo's (☎ 575-2687; 771 Ha'iku Rd; meals $9-14 ☉ 11am-4pm Mon-Fri) Consuelo whips up rea home cooking while you watch at this littl cottage opposite the post office. Dependin upon the inspiration of the moment, the chalk board menu might feature anything from Tha coconut chicken to savory fish stew – invariabl served with rice and fresh salad.

PUKALANI & AROUND
pop 7400

Aptly named, Pukalani, which translates a 'Heavenly Gate,' is the gateway to the lusl Upcountry. Most visitors just drive throug on the way to Kula and Haleakalā, and un less you need to pick up supplies you won' miss much by sticking to the bypass road. I you need to gas up, this is your last chanc before Haleakalā.

Orientation & Information

If you're coming from Kahului, take th Haleakala Hwy (Hwy 37). To reach the busines part of town, get off at the Old Haleakala Hw exit, which becomes Pukalani's main street.

Pukalani Terrace Center (cnr Old Haleakala Hwy & Pukalani St) has a coin laundry, a **post office** (☎ 572 0019) and a **Bank of Hawaii** (☎ 572-7242) with a 24 hour ATM. A couple of gas stations are on th Old Haleakala Hwy.

Sights & Activities
SURFING GOAT DAIRY

'Feta mo betta' is the motto at this 42-acre **farm** (☎ 878-2870; www.surfinggoatdairy.com; 3651 Oma'opio Rc admission free, tours $7-12; ☉ 10am-5pm Mon-Sat, 10am 2pm Sun), the source of all that luscious chevr adorning the menus of Maui's top restaurants The shop here carries an amazing variety o creamy goat cheeses; for island flavor try th mango chutney. Not everything is geared t the connoisseur – your kids will love meetin the goat kids up close in a fun 20-minute dair tour. On some of the tours they can even tr their hand at milking.

PUKALANI COUNTRY CLUB

A mile west of Pukalani Terrace Center, thi **golf course** (☎ 572-1314; www.pukalanigolf.com; 36 Pukalani St; green fees $74; ☉ 7am-dusk) has 18 hole of smooth greens with sweeping views. Here' a bargain: come after 2:30pm and golf the res of the day for just $26.

Eating

Foodland (☎ 572-0674; Pukalani Terrace Center, cnr Old Haleakala Hwy & Pukalani St; ⏰ 24hr) This supermarket is a convenient stop for those heading up the mountain for the sunrise, or coming down for supplies – there's also a Starbucks inside the store.

Serpico's (☎ 572-8498; cnr Old Haleakala Hwy & Aewa Pl; meals $7-15; ⏰ 11am-10pm) In the center of Pukalani, opposite McDonald's, this family-run eatery makes authentic New York–style pizzas and pasta dishes. If you're in a hurry, go with one of the hoagie sandwiches.

KULA

pop 9730

The navel of the Upcountry, Kula is Maui's gardenland. The very name Kula is synonymous with the fresh veggies on any Maui menu worth its salt. So bountiful is Kula's rich volcanic soil that it produces most of the onions, lettuce and strawberries grown in Hawaii. The key to these bountiful harvests is the elevation. At 3000ft, Kula's cool nights and sunny days are ideal for growing all sorts of crops.

Kula's farmers first gained fame during the California gold rush of the 1850s, when they shipped so many potatoes out to West Coast miners that Kula became known as 'Nu Kaleponi,' the Hawaiian pronunciation for New California. In the late 19th century Portuguese and Chinese immigrants who had worked off their contracts on the sugar plantations also moved up to Kula and started small farms, giving Kula the multicultural face it wears today.

Sights

Stop and smell the roses…and the lavender and all those other sweet-scented blossoms. No two gardens in Kula are alike, and each has its own special appeal.

ALI'I KULA LAVENDER

Immerse yourself in a sea of purple at **Ali'i Kula Lavender** (☎ 878-8090; www.aklmaui.com; 1100 Waipoli Rd; admission free; ⏰ 9am-4pm). Start by strolling along the garden paths where dozens of varieties of these fragrant plants blanket the hillside. Take your time, breathe deeply. Then sit for a spell on the veranda with its sweeping views and enjoy a lavender scone and perhaps a cup of lavender tea. Browse through the gift shop, sample the lavender-scented oils

and lotions, any of which would make a fine gift. If you want to really dig in, a variety of activities from garden-tea tours to wedding packages are available.

KULA BOTANICAL GARDEN

Pleasantly overgrown and shady, this mature **garden** (☎ 878-1715; 638 Kekaulike Ave; adult/child 6-12 $7.50/2; ⏰ 9am-4pm) has walking paths that wind through acres of theme plantings, including native Hawaiian specimens and a 'taboo garden' of poisonous plants. Because a stream runs through it, the garden supports water-thirsty plants you won't find in other Kula gardens. When the rain gods have been generous the whole place is an explosion of color.

ENCHANTING FLORAL GARDENS

A labor of love, **Enchanting Floral Gardens** (☎ 878-2531; 2505 Kula Hwy; adult/child 6-12 $7.50/1; ⏰ 9am-5pm) showcases the green thumb of master horticulturist Kazuo Takeda. Kula's micro-climates change with elevation and this colorful place occupies a narrow zone where tropical, temperate and desert vegetation all thrive. The sheer variety is amazing. You'll find everything from flamboyant proteas and orchids to orange trees and kava – all of it identified with both Latin and common names.

MAUI AGRICULTURAL RESEARCH CENTER

It was in this **garden** (☎ 878-1213; 424 Mauna Pl; admission free; ⏰ 7am-3:30pm Mon-Thu) at the University of Hawai'i that the state's first proteas were planted in 1965. Today you can walk through row after row of their colorful descendants. Named for the Greek god Proteus, who was noted for his ability to change form, the varieties are amazingly diverse – some look like oversized pincushions, others like spiny feathers. Nursery cuttings from the plants here are distributed to protea farms across Hawaii, which in turn supply florists as far away as Europe. To get here, follow Copp Rd (between the 12- and 13-mile markers on Hwy 37) for 0.5 miles and turn left on Mauna Pl.

HOLY GHOST CHURCH

Waiakoa's hillside landmark, the octagonal **Holy Ghost Church** (☎ 878-1261; Lower Kula Rd; ⏰ 8am-5pm) was built in 1895 by Portuguese immigrants. The church features a beautifully ornate interior that looks like it came right out of the Old World, and indeed much of it did. The gilded altar was carved by renowned

MAUI

THE MONSTER WAVE

When this monster rears its powerful head, it's big, fast, and mean enough to crunch bones. What is it? Jaws, Maui's famous big-wave surf spot. A few times a year, strong winter storms off the coast of Japan generate an abundance of energy that races unimpeded across the Pacific Ocean to Maui's north shore, translating into the planet's biggest ridable waves.

News of the mammoth swells, which reach as high as a seven-story building, attracts gutsy surfers from throughout Hawaii. With them come scores of spectators. Unfortunately, there's no legitimate public access to the cliffs that overlook Jaws, and the crowds that gather create some big headaches. Photographers, visitors and locals numbering in the thousands have been known to trample the surrounding pineapple fields and hold up harvest for a glimpse of the action, while traffic on the Hana Hwy slows to a crawl.

When Jaws (also known locally as Pe'ahi) is up, it's impossible for surfers to paddle through the break to catch a ride. But where there's a thrill, there's a way. Tow-in surfers work in pairs, using small watercraft known as WaveRunners to get people and their boards beyond the break. When even a WaveRunner is outmatched, surfers get dropped into the ocean from a helicopter.

The equation of extreme sport says that thrill doesn't come without its share of danger. There are myriad opportunities for big wave surfers to get hurt or killed. The insanely powerful waves can wash surfers into rocks, throw them into their WaveRunners, knock them against their surfboards or simply pummel them with the force of all that moving water. That said, these guys are pros and are very good at skirting the perils.

Austrian woodcarver Ferdinand Stuflesser and shipped in pieces around the Cape of Good Hope. The church is on the National Register of Historic Places.

Activities

Pony Express (☎ 667-2200; www.ponyexpresstours.com; Haleakalā Crater Rd; trail rides $95-185; ☿ 8am-5pm) offers a variety of horseback rides, beginning with easy nose-to-tail walks through pastures and eucalyptus woods. But the real prize is the trail ride in Haleakalā National Park, which starts at the summit and winds along **Sliding Sands Trail** (Map p416) clear down to the crater floor. Pony Express is on Hwy 378, 2.5 miles up from Hwy 377.

Soar above the treetops on the slopes of Haleakalā with **Skyline Eco-Adventures** (☎ 878-8400; www.skylinehawaii.com; Haleakalā Crater Rd; 1½hr outing $84; ☿ 8:30am-4:30pm). You'll glide freestyle along cables strung over five gulches for a pure adrenaline rush. A half-mile hike and a suspension bridge are tossed in for good measure. One tip: reserve early, as it often books up in advance.

If the ziplines don't get you high enough, surf the sky with **Proflyght Paragliding** (☎ 874-5433; www.paraglidehawaii.com; Waipoli Rd; paraglide $79; ☿ varies with weather). On this one you strap into a tandem paraglider with a certified instructor and take a running leap off the cliffs beneath Polipoli Spring State Recreation

Area for a 1000ft descent. The term 'bird's-eye view' will never again be the same.

Tours

You can harvest your own organic lunch on this tasty tour of **O'o Farm** (☎ 667-4341; www.oofarm .com; Waipoli Rd; lunch tour $50; ☿ 10:30am-1pm Wed & Thu), the garden of famed Lahaina restaurateur James McDonald. Then watch a top chef whip it together and feast on the bounty. Bring your own wine.

Festivals & Events

The **Holy Ghost Feast**, at the Holy Ghost Church on the last Saturday and Sunday in May, celebrates Kula's Portuguese heritage and provides a perfect opportunity for visitors to enjoy the aloha of Upcountry folk. This family event has games, craft booths, a farmers market and a free Hawaiian-Portuguese lunch on Sunday.

Sleeping

Kula View Bed & Breakfast (☎ 878-6736; 600 Holopuni Rd; studio incl breakfast $115) With her *paniolo* roots, your host knows the Upcountry like the back of her hand. She provides everything you'll need for a good stay, including warm jackets for the Haleakalā sunrise. The studio unit sits atop her country home and offers sunset ocean views. Breakfast includes fruit from the backyard and homemade muffins.

Eating

Sunrise Market & Protea Farm (☎ 878-1600; Haleakalā Crater Rd; simple eats $3-6; ⏰ 7am-3pm) Stop at this convenient shop, a quarter-mile up from the intersection of Hwys 378 and 377, to pick up post-sunrise java, breakfast burritos and hot soup. Then take a stroll behind the shop to enjoy the flowers in the protea garden.

Café 808 (☎ 878-6874; Lower Kula Rd, Waiakoa; mains $6-10; ⏰ 6am-8:30pm) Its motto, 'The Big Kahuna of Island Grinds,' says it all. This eatery, a quarter-mile south of the Holy Ghost Church, offers a wall-size chalkboard of all things local, from banana pancakes to gravy-laden plate lunches. No need to strain your brain: step up to the counter and order the roast pork and you'll see why all those cowboys are smiling.

Kula Sandalwoods Restaurant (☎ 878-3523; 15427 Haleakala Hwy; mains $8-12; ⏰ 7am-3pm) The owner-chef earned her toque from the prestigious Culinary Institute of America. At breakfast the eggs Benedict is the favorite. Lunch features garden-fresh Kula salads and heaping chicken and beefsteak sandwiches on home-made onion rolls. The restaurant is less than a mile north of Haleakalā Crater Rd.

La Provence (☎ 878-1313; 3158 Lower Kula Rd, Waiakoa; pastries $3-4, mains $8-15; ⏰ 7am-3pm Wed-Fri, 7am-2pm Sat, 8am-2pm Sun) One of Maui's top pastry chefs hangs his shingle here. Even if you are not hungry, just swing by to pick up a ham-and-cheese croissant or some flaky chocolate-filled pastries for that picnic further down the road. If you are hungry, the chevre green salads are a Kula treat to savor. This place is hard to find but worth the effort: look for the low-key sign on the Kula Hwy as you approach Waiakoa.

TOP PICKS – UPCOUNTRY-GROWN TREATS

- Maui Splash wine at **Tedeschi Vineyards** (p412)
- Chevre at **Surfing Goat Dairy** (p408)
- Maui coffee at **Grandma's** (p412)
- Lunch tour at **O'o Farm** (opposite)
- Lavender scones at **Ali'i Kula Lavender** (p409)
- Elk burgers at **'Ulupalakua Ranch Store** (p413)

POLIPOLI SPRING STATE RECREATION AREA

Crisscrossed with hiking and mountain biking trails, this misty cloud forest on the western slope of Haleakalā takes you deep off the beaten path. The shade from tall trees and the cool moist air make for a refreshing walk in the woods. Layers of clouds drift in and out; when they lift, you'll get long vistas across green rolling hills clear out to the islands of Lana'i and Kaho'olawe. Very zen-like – except for the symphony of bird calls. Everything around you is still.

It's not always possible to get all the way to the park without a 4WD, but it's worth driving part of the way for the view. Access is via Waipoli Rd, off Hwy 377, just under 0.5 miles before its southern intersection with the Kula Hwy (Hwy 37). Waipoli Rd is a narrow, switch-backing one-lane road, but the first 6 miles are paved. After the road enters the Kula Forest Reserve, it reverts to dirt. When it's muddy, the next grinding 4 miles to the campground are not even worth trying without a 4WD.

Activities

WAIAKOA LOOP TRAIL

The trailhead for the Waiakoa Loop Trail starts at the **hunter check station** 5 miles up Waipoli Rd, which is paved to this point. Walk 0.75 miles down the grassy spur road on the left to a gate marking the trail. The hike, which starts out in pine trees, makes a 3-mile loop, passing through eucalyptus stands, pine forest, and scrub land scored with feral pig trails. This is a fairly gentle easy hike. You can also connect with the Upper Waiakoa Trail at a junction about a mile up the right side of the loop.

UPPER WAIAKOA TRAIL

The Upper Waiakoa Trail is a strenuous 7-mile trail that begins off Waiakoa Loop at an elevation of 6000ft, climbs 1800ft, switchbacks and then drops back down 1400ft. It's stony terrain, but it's high and open, with good views. The trail ends on Waipoli Rd between the hunter check station and the campground. If you want to start at this end of the trail, keep an eye out for the trail marker for Waohuli Trail, as the Upper Waiakoa Trail begins across the road.

BOUNDARY TRAIL

This 4-mile trail begins about 200yd beyond the end of the paved road. Park to the right of the cattle grate that marks the boundary of the Kula Forest Reserve. It's a steep downhill walk that crosses gulches and drops deep into woods of eucalyptus, pine and cedar, as well as a bit of native forest. In the afternoon the fog generally rolls in and visibility fades.

SKYLINE TRAIL
Also partially in this park is the rugged Skyline Trail, which begins near the summit of Haleakalā National Park before descending to Polipoli Spring State Recreation Area. For details on this hike see p419.

Sleeping
Staying in Polipoli is all about roughing it. The free campground facilities are primitive, with toilets but no showers or drinking water. Tent camping requires a permit from the state and fellow campers are likely to be pig hunters. Otherwise the place can be eerily deserted, and damp. Come prepared – this is cold country, with winter temperatures frequently dropping below freezing at night.

The park also has one cabin. Unlike other state park cabins, this one has gas lanterns and a wood-burning stove but no electricity or refrigerator. See p328 for details on permits and reservations.

KEOKEA
Modest as it may be, Keokea is the last real town before Hana if you're swinging around the southern part of the island. The sum total of the town center consists of a coffee shop, an art gallery, a gas pump and two small stores, the Ching Store and the Fong Store.

Sights & Activities
Drawn by rich soil, Hakka Chinese farmers migrated to this remote corner of Kula at the turn of the 20th century. Their influence is readily visible throughout the village. Keokea's landmark **St John's Episcopal Church** (c 1907) still bears its name in Chinese characters. For a time Sun Yat-sen, father of the Chinese nationalist movement, lived on the outskirts of Keokea. A statue of Sun Yat-sen and a small **park** dedicated to him can be found along the Kula Hwy (Hwy 37), 1.7 miles beyond Grandma's Coffee House. The park has picnic tables and sweeping views of west Maui and its hillside windmills.

Thompson Ranch (☎ 878-1910; Middle Rd; 2hr ride $100; ⏲ departs at 10am) offers scenic horseback rides through the cool Upcountry bordering Polipoli Spring State Recreation Area.

Sleeping
Moonlight Garden B&B (☎ 878-6977, 866-878-6297; www .mauimoonlightgarden.com; 8980 Kula Hwy; d $135) For a relaxing taste of rural Maui, stay at Moonlight. Quiet and secluded, yet within walking distance of the village center, these two freestanding cottages sit amid fruit trees and stands of bamboo. Each is spacious with a full kitchen and cheerful Hawaiian decor, while the views from the decks sweep clear out to the sea.

Eating
Grandma's Coffee House (☎ 878-2140; 9232 Kula Hwy; pastries $3-5, deli fare $6-10; ⏲ 7am-5pm) Think Kona's the only place with primo Hawaii-grown coffee? Just check out the brew at Grandma's. This earthy café dishes up homemade pastries, hearty sandwiches and deli salads. Grandma's family has been growing coffee in Keokea for generations. If you want to see their bean-laden trees just take your goodies out to the side patio.

'ULUPALAKUA RANCH
This sprawling 20,000-acre ranch was established in the mid-19th century by James Makee, a whaling captain who jumped ship and befriended Hawaiian royalty. King David Kalakaua, the 'Merrie Monarch,' became a frequent visitor who loved to indulge in late-night rounds of poker and champagne. The ranch is still worked by *paniolo* – note the sign on the ranch store warning cowboys to wipe the shit off their boots before entering! Some 6000 head of cattle, as well as a small herd of Rocky Mountain elk, dot the hillside pastures.

The ranch is green in more ways than one. It's staged to host Upcountry's first wind energy farm and is restoring a rare native dryland forest on the upper slopes of ranch property.

Today most people come to visit Tedeschi Vineyards, Maui's sole winery, which is on 'Ulupalakua Ranch land. After the winery, it's another 25 undulating miles to Kipahulu along the remote Pi'ilani Hwy (p402).

Sights
Tedeschi Vineyards (☎ 878-6058; www.mauiwine.com; Kula Hwy; ⏲ 9am-5pm; tours 10:30am, 1:30pm & 3pm) offers free tours and tastings in the historic stone cottage where King David Kalakaua once slept. In the 1970s, while awaiting its first grape harvest, the winery decided to take advantage of Maui's prickly fruit. Today its biggest hit is the sweet

Maui Splash, a light blend of pineapple and passion fruit. Other pineapple novelties worth a taste: the dry Maui Blanc and the sparkling Hula O'Maui. This is no Napa Valley, however, and the grape wines are less of a splash.

Don't miss the fascinating little **exhibit** on ranch history and ecology at the side of the tasting room. Opposite the winery, see the stack remains of the **Makee Sugar Mill**, built in 1878.

Eating

'Ulupalakua Ranch Store (☎ 878-2561; Kula Hwy; burgers $8; ✆ grill 11am-2:30pm, store 9am-5pm) Sidle up to the life-sized wooden cowboys on the front porch and say howdy. Then pop inside and check out the cowboy hats and souvenir T-shirts. If it's lunchtime, mosey over to the grill and treat yourself to an organic ranch-raised beef or elk burger. Can't beat that for local. The store is 5.5 miles south of Keokea, shortly before the winery.

HALEAKALĀ NATIONAL PARK

With its eye-popping moonscapes, Haleakalā's like no other place in the national park system. Whether you come for sunrise, or come at the height of the day, by all means get yourself here. You simply haven't seen Maui, or at least looked into its soul, until you've made the trek up to the top of this awe-inspiring mountain. Its appeal is magnetic: ancient Hawaiians came to the summit to worship, Mark Twain praised its healing solitude, and visitors of all walks still find mystic experiences here.

Lookouts on the crater's rim provide breathtaking views of Haleakalā's volcanic surface. But there's a lot more to Haleakalā than just peering down from on high. With a pair of hiking boots you can walk down into the crater on crunchy trails that meander around cinder cones. Or saddle up and mosey down onto the crater floor on horseback. For the ultimate adventure, bring a sleeping bag and spend the night.

Haleakalā National Park stretches from the summit here all the way down to the pools of 'Ohe'o Gulch in the park's Kipahulu section south of Hana. There are separate entrances to both sections of the park, but there's no passage between them. What follows details the summit area of the park; for information on the Kipahulu section, see p400.

INFORMATION

Haleakalā National Park (www.nps.gov/hale; 3-day entry pass per car $10, per person on foot, bicycle or motorcycle $5) never closes, and the pay booth at the park entrance opens before dawn to welcome the sunrise crowd. If you plan several trips, or are going on to the Big Island, consider buying an annual pass ($25), which covers all of Hawaii's national parks.

The **Park Headquarters Visitor Center** (☎ 572-4400; ✆ 8am-4pm), less than a mile beyond the entrance, is the place to pick up brochures, buy nature books and get camping permits. You can also call ahead for recorded information on activities. There are no views at park headquarters; this is simply an information and rest-room stop. So once you've taken care of your more earthly needs, hop back into the car and continue on to reach the real wonders.

No food is sold anywhere in the park, though there are drinking fountains at the Park Headquarters Visitor Center. Be sure to bring something to eat if you're going up for the sunrise; you don't want a growling stomach to send you back down the mountain before you've had a chance to explore the sights.

It's a good idea to check **weather conditions** (☎ 866-944-5025) before driving up, as it's not uncommon for it to be cloudy at Haleakalā when it's clear on the coast. Or go straight to the crater webcam at **Haleakalā Crater Live Camera** (http://koa.ifa.hawaii.edu/crater).

Maps

National Geographic's *Haleakalā National Park Illustrated Trail Map* makes the perfect companion for hikers, showing elevations and other useful features on the routes. It's waterproof and can be purchased at Haleakalā Visitor Center (p414) for $10.

DANGERS & ANNOYANCES

The weather at Haleakalā can change suddenly from dry, hot conditions to cold, windswept rain. Although the general rule is sunny in the morning and cloudy in the afternoon, fog and clouds can blow in at any time, and the wind-chill can quickly drop below freezing. Dress in layers and bring extra clothing; don't even think of coming up without a jacket.

At 10,000ft the air is relatively thin, so expect to tire more quickly, particularly if you're hiking. The higher elevation also means that sunburn is more likely.

MAUI

SIGHTS

For info on Haleakalā Crater Rd, see p421.

Hosmer Grove

Hosmer Grove, off a side road just after the park's entrance booth, is primarily visited by campers and picnickers, but it's well worth a stop for its half-mile loop trail (p419) that begins at the edge of the campground (p420). The whole area is sweetened with the scent of eucalyptus and alive with the red flashes and calls of native birds. Drive slowly on the road in, as this is one of the top places to spot nene.

Waikamoi Preserve

This windswept native cloud forest supports one of the rarest ecosystems on earth. Managed by the Nature Conservancy, the 5230-acre Waikamoi Preserve provides the last stronghold for 76 species of native plants and forest birds. You're apt to spot the 'i'iwi (scarlet Hawaiian honeycreeper), the 'apapane (bright red Hawaiian honeycreeper) and the yellow-green 'amakihi flying among the preserve's koa and ohia trees. You might also catch a glimpse of the yellow-green 'alauahio (Maui creeper) or the 'akohekohe (Maui parrotbill), both endangered species found nowhere else on earth.

The only way to see the preserve is to join a **guided hike**. The National Park Service offers free three-hour, 3-mile guided hikes that enter the preserve from Hosmer Grove campground at 9am on Monday and Thursday. It's best to make reservations, which you can do up to one week in advance by calling ☎ 572-4459. Expect wet conditions; bring rain gear.

Leleiwi Overlook

A stop at Leleiwi Overlook (8840ft), midway between the Park Headquarters Visitor Center and the summit, offers your first look into the crater, and gives you a unique angle on the ever-changing clouds climbing up the mountain. You can literally watch the weather form at your feet. From the parking lot, it's a five-minute walk across a gravel trail to the overlook. En route you'll get a fine view of the West Maui Mountains and the isthmus connecting the two sides of Maui.

In the afternoon, if weather conditions are right, you might see the Brocken specter, an optical phenomenon that occurs at high elevations. Essentially, by standing between the sun and the clouds, your image is magnified and projected onto the clouds. The light reflects off tiny droplets of water in the clouds, creating a circular rainbow around your shadow.

Kalahaku Overlook

Whatever you do, do not miss this one. Kalahaku Overlook (9324ft), 0.8 miles above Leleiwi Overlook, offers a bird's-eye view of the crater floor and the ant-sized hikers on the trails snaking around the cinder cones below. At the observation deck, information plaques provide the skinny on each of the volcanic formations that punctuate the crater floor.

The 'ua'u (Hawaiian dark-rumped petrel) nests in burrows in the cliff face at the left side of the observation deck between May and October. Even if you don't spot the birds, you can often hear the parents and chicks making their unique clucking sounds. Of the fewer than 2000 'ua'u remaining today, most nest right here at Haleakalā, where they lay just one egg a year. These seabirds were thought to be extinct until sighted again in the crater during the 1970s.

A short trail below the parking lot leads to a field of rare native silversword ('ahinahina), ranging from seedlings to mature plants.

Haleakalā Visitor Center

Perched on the rim of the crater, the **visitor center** (🕐 6:30am-3:30pm) at a 9745ft elevation is the park's main viewing spot. And what a magical sight is awaiting you. The everchanging interplay of sun, shadow and clouds reflecting on the crater floor creates a mesmerizing dance of light and color.

The center has displays on Haleakalā's volcanic origins that explain what you're seeing on the crater floor 3000ft below. There are nature talks, books on Hawaiian culture and the environment, as well as drinking fountains and rest rooms here.

By dawn the parking lot fills up with people coming to see the sunrise show, and it pretty much stays packed all day. Leave the crowds behind by taking the 10-minute hike up **Pa Ka'oao (White Hill)**, which begins at the east side of the visitor center and provides stunning views of the crater.

Haleakalā Summit

PU'U'ULA'ULA (RED HILL) OVERLOOK

Congratulations! The 37-mile drive from sea level to the 10,023ft summit of Haleakalā you've just completed is the highest elevation gain in the shortest distance anywhere in the

---

GOING DOWNHILL

It was once one of Maui's most popular tourist activities: get a van ride to Haleakalā summit for the sunrise and then hop on a bicycle and cruise 38 miles down the 10,000ft mountain, snaking along winding roads all the way to the coast. What a rush. No pedaling involved. *Whooo-ooo.*

Except that over the years it became *too* popular. Downhill bicycle tour companies multiplied. Some mornings as many as 1000 cyclists huddled at the crater overlooks jostling for space to watch the sun rise. Then, group by group, they'd get on their bikes and take off.

Residents who needed to use the Upcountry roads for more mundane reasons, such as getting to work, were forced to slow to a crawl, waiting for a gaggle of cyclists and their support van to pull over to let them pass. The narrow roads have few shoulders, so the wait was often a long one. And, once one group of cyclists had passed, there was the next one. 'Road rage' finally made it into the vernacular in the otherwise mellow Upcountry.

Then there were the accidents. They often involved people who hadn't been on a bicycle in years, or scarcely knew how to ride. Sometimes the weather was bad, with fog cutting visibility to near zero. Whatever the reasons, ambulance calls for injured downhill cyclists became weekly occurrences. After two cyclist fatalities in 2007, Haleakalā National Park suspended all bicycle tour operations. Studies are still underway to determine if commercial cycle tours can return and operate safely. Considering the track record, and the road issues, this appears to be one park activity doomed to extinction.

---

world. You've passed through as many ecological zones as you would have on a drive from Alaska to central Mexico.

Perched atop Puʻuʻulaʻula, Maui's highest point, is the summit building providing a top-of-the-world panorama from its wraparound windows. On a clear day you can see the Big Island, Lanaʻi, Molokaʻi and even Oʻahu. When the light's right, the colors of the crater from the summit are nothing short of spectacular, with an array of grays, greens, reds and browns. A garden of silversword has been planted at the overlook, making this the best place to see these luminous silver-leafed plants in various stages of growth.

MAGNETIC PEAK

The iron-rich cinders in this flat-top hill, which lies immediately southeast of the summit in the direction of the Big Island, pack enough magnetism to play havoc with your compass. Modest looking as it is, it's also – at 10,008ft – the second-highest point on Maui.

Science City

On the Big Island's Mauna Kea, scientists study the night sky. At Haleakalā, appropriately enough, they study the sun. Off-limits to visitors, Science City, which lies just beyond the summit, is under the jurisdiction of the University of Hawaiʻi. The university owns some of the domes, and leases other land for a variety of research projects.

Department of Defense–related projects here include laser technology associated with the 'Star Wars' project, satellite tracking and identification, and a deep-space surveillance system. The Air Force's Maui Space Surveillance System, an electro-optical state-of-the-art facility used for satellite tracking, is the largest telescope anywhere in use by the Department of Defense. The system is capable of identifying a basketball-size object in space 22,000 miles away. The Faulkes Telescope, a joint University of Hawaiʻi and UK operation, is dedicated to raising interest in astronomy among students, with a fully robotic telescope that can be controlled in real time via the internet from classrooms in both Britain and Hawaii.

ACTIVITIES

Be sure to stop at the Park Headquarters Visitor Center to see what's happening during your visit. All park programs offered by the National Park Service are free. **Ranger talks** on Haleakalā's unique natural history and Hawaiian culture are given at the Haleakalā Visitor Center and the Puʻuʻulaʻula (Red Hill) Overlook; the schedule varies, but they typically take place between 7am and 1pm and there's usually half a dozen to choose from daily.

Ranger-led **walks** through Waikamoi Preserve (opposite) are held throughout the year.

Evening **stargazing programs** are offered between May and September at Hosmer Grove, typically on Friday and Saturday at 7pm. If

MAUI

MAUI

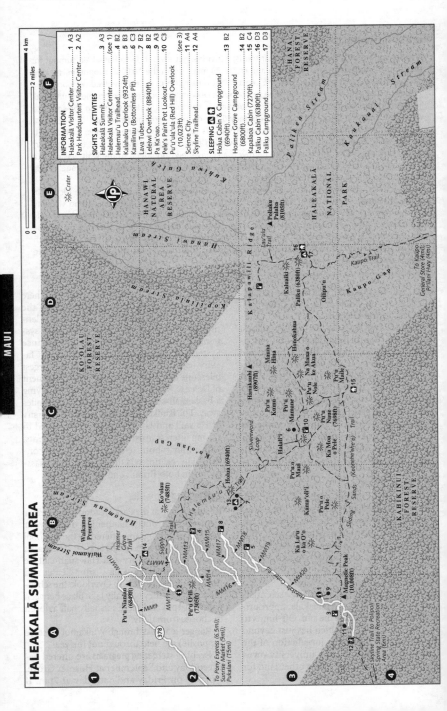

HALEAKALĀ SUMMIT AREA

INFORMATION
Haleakalā Visitor Center..............1	A3
Park Headquarters Visitor Center....2	A2

SIGHTS & ACTIVITIES
Haleakalā Summit..........................3	A3
Haleakalā Visitor Center.............(see 1)	
Halemau'u Trailhead.....................4	B2
Kalahaku Overlook (9324ft)............5	B3
Kawilinau (Bottomless Pit)............6	C3
Lava Tubes..................................7	B2
Leleiwi Overlook (8840ft)..............8	B2
Pa Ka'oao....................................9	A3
Pele's Paint Pot Lookout...............10	C3
Pu'u'ula'ula (Red Hill) Overlook...(see 3)	
(10,023ft)................................11	A4
Science City...............................11	A4
Skyline Trailhead.........................12	A4

SLEEPING
Holua Cabin & Campground	
(6940ft)..................................13	B2
Hosmer Grove Campground	
(6800ft)..................................14	B2
Kapalaoa Cabin (7270ft)...............15	C4
Paliku Cabin (6380ft)...................16	D3
Paliku Campground........................17	D3

0 — 2 miles
0 — 4 km

GINORMOUS WHATEVER YOU CALL IT

Often referred to as the world's largest dormant volcano, the floor of Haleakalā measures 7.5 miles wide, 2.5 miles long and 3000ft deep – large enough to swallow the island of Manhattan. In its prime, Haleakalā reached a height of 12,000ft before water erosion carved out two large river valleys that eventually eroded into each other to form Haleakalā Crater. Technically, as geologists like to point out, it's not a true 'crater,' but to sightseers that's all nitpicking. Valley or crater, it's one phenomenal sight.

you've got a pair of binoculars, bring them along – no telescopes are provided, but the stars themselves are phenomenal. You can see celestial objects up to the 7th magnitude, free of light interference, making Haleakalā one of the best places on the planet for a sky view. If you want to stargaze on your own, pick up a free star map at either visitor center.

For information about **horseback rides** into the crater, see p410.

Hiking

To really experience this amazing place strap on a pair of hiking boots and step into the belly of the beast. There's something for everyone, from short nature walks to hardy multiday treks. Those who hike the crater will discover a completely different angle on Haleakalā's lunar landscape. Instead of peering down from the rim, you'll be craning your neck skyward at the walls and towering cinder cones. It's a world away from anyplace else. The crater is remarkably still. Cinders crunching underfoot are the only sound, except for the occasional bark of a pueo (Hawaiian owl) or honking of a friendly nene. Whatever trail you take, give yourself extra time to absorb the wonder of it all.

To protect Haleakalā's fragile environment, keep to established trails and don't be tempted off them, even for well-beaten shortcuts through switchbacks.

Be prepared. Hikers without proper clothing risk hypothermia. The climate changes radically as you cross the crater floor – in the 4 miles between Kapalaoa and Paliku cabins, rainfall varies from an annual average of 12in to 300in! Take warm clothing in layers, sunscreen, rain gear, a first-aid kit and lots of water.

SLIDING SANDS (KEONEHE'EHE'E) TRAIL

Sliding Sands (Keonehe'ehe'e) Trail starts at the south side of the Haleakalā Visitor Center parking lot at 9740ft and descends steeply over loose cinders down to the crater floor. If you take this hike after catching the sunrise, you'll walk directly into a gentle warmish wind and the rays of the sunshine. The entire trail leads 9.2 miles to the Paliku cabins (p421) and Paliku campground (p420), passing the Kapalaoa cabin (p421) at 5.6 miles after roughly four hours.

The first 6 miles of the trail follow the south wall. There are great views on the way down, but almost no vegetation. About 2 miles down, a steep spur trail leads past silversword plants to **Ka Lu'u o ka O'o** cinder cone, about 0.5 miles north. Four miles down, after an elevation drop of 2500ft, Sliding Sands Trail intersects with a spur trail that leads north into the cinder desert; that spur connects with the Halemau'u Trail after 1.5 miles.

Continuing on Sliding Sands, as you head across the crater floor for 2 miles to Kapalaoa, verdant ridges rise on your right, giving way to ropy *pahoehoe* (smooth-flowing lava). From Kapalaoa cabin to Paliku, the descent is gentle and the vegetation gradually increases. Paliku (6380ft) is beneath a sheer cliff at the eastern end of the crater. In contrast to the crater's barren western end, this area receives heavy rainfall, with ohia forests climbing the slopes.

HALEMAU'U TRAIL

Hiking the Halemau'u Trail down to the Holua campground and back – 7.4 miles return – can make a memorable day hike. Just be sure to start early before the afternoon clouds roll in and visibility vanishes. The first mile of this trail is fairly level and offers a fine view of the crater with Ko'olau Gap to the east. It then descends 1400ft along 2 miles of switchbacks to the crater floor and on to the Holua campground (p420).

At 6940ft, **Holua** is one of the lowest areas along this trail, and you'll see impressive views of the crater walls rising a few thousand feet to the west. Large **lava tubes** here are worth exploring: one's up a short, steep cliff behind the Holua cabin, and another's a 15-minute detour further along the trail. According to legend, the latter tube was a spiritual place where mothers brought the *piko* (umbilical cords) of their newborns to gather mana for the child.

MAUI

SILVERSWORD COMEBACK

Goats ate them by the thousands. Collectors pulled them up by their roots. They were even used to decorate parade floats, for cryin' out loud. It's a miracle any of Haleakalā's famed silverswords were left at all.

It took a concerted effort to bring them back from the brink of extinction, but Haleakalā visitors can once again see this luminous relative of the sunflower in numerous places around the park.

The silversword ('ahinahina) takes its name from its elegant silver spiked leaves, which glow with dew collected from the clouds. The plant lives up to 25 years before blooming for its first and last time. In its final year it shoots up a flowering stalk that can reach as high as 9ft. During summer the stalk flowers gloriously with hundreds of maroon and yellow blossoms. When the flowers go to seed in late fall, the plant makes its last gasp and dies.

Today the silversword survives solely because its fragile environment has been protected. After years of effort, the National Park Service has finished fencing the entire park with a 32-mile fence to keep out feral goats and pigs. You can do your part by not walking on cinders close to the plant, which damages the silversword's shallow roots that radiate out several feet just inches below the surface.

If you have the energy, push on another mile to reach colorful cinder cones, being sure to make a short detour onto the **Silversword Loop**, where you'll see these unique plants in various stages of growth. In summer, you might even see silverswords in flower, their tall stalks ablaze with hundreds of maroon and yellow blossoms. But be careful – half of all silverswords today are trampled to death as seedlings, mostly by hikers who wander off trails and unknowingly step on their shallow roots. The trail continues another 6.3 miles to the Paliku cabins.

The trailhead to Halemau'u is 3.5 miles above Park Headquarters Visitor Center and about 6 miles below the Haleakalā Visitor Center. There's a fair chance you'll see nene in the parking lot. If you're camping at Hosmer Grove, you can take the little-known, unexciting **Supply Trail** instead, joining the Halemau'u Trail at the crater rim after 2.5 miles.

EXPLORING THE CINDER DESERT

A spur trail connects Sliding Sands Trail, just west of Kapalaoa cabin, with the Halemau'u Trail, about midway between the Paliku and Holua campgrounds. This spur trail takes in many of the crater's most kaleidoscopic cinder cones, and the viewing angle changes with every step. The trail ends up on the north side of the cinder desert near **Kawilinau**, also known as the Bottomless Pit. Legends say the pit leads down to the sea, though the National Park Service says it's just 65ft deep. Truth be told, there's not much to see, as you can't really get a good look down the narrow shaft.

The real prize is the nearby short loop trail, where you can sit for a while in the saddle of **Pele's Paint Pot Lookout**, the crater's most brilliant vantage point.

LAU'ULU TRAIL

Also known as the Kalapawili Ridge Trail, this trail is overgrown and barely used but if you're already deep in the crater at Paliku, then why not. The trouble is finding the trailhead, which is tucked behind the Paliku campground and cabin. From there just keep heading uphill; after an hour or two, the trail empties out onto the high-flying Kalapawili Ridge, which affords broad vistas of Hana and out to sea. Since this trail is not well maintained, allow at least five or six hours for the round-trip.

KAUPO TRAIL

The most extreme of Haleakalā's hikes is the Kaupo Trail, which starts at the Paliku campground and leads down to Kaupo on the southern coast. Be prepared for ankle-twisting conditions, blistered feet, intense tropical sun and torrential showers. Your knees will take a pounding as you descend more than 6100ft over 8.6 miles.

The first 3.7 miles of the trail drop 2500ft in elevation before reaching the park boundary. It's a steep rocky trail through rough lava and brushland, with short switchbacks alternating with level stretches. From here you'll be rewarded with spectacular ocean views.

The last 4.9 miles pass through Kaupo Ranch property on a rough jeep trail as it descends to the bottom of Kaupo Gap, exiting into a forest where feral pigs snuffle about. Here trail markings become vague, but once you reach the dirt road, it's another 1.5 miles to the end at the east side of Kaupo Store.

The 'village' of Kaupo (p403) is a long way from anywhere, with light traffic. Still, what traffic there is – sightseers braving the circle-island road and locals in pickup trucks – moves slowly enough along Kaupo's rough road to start a conversation, so you'll probably manage a lift. If you have to walk the final stretch, it's 8 miles to the 'Ohe'o Gulch (p401) campground.

Because this is such a strenuous and remote trail, it's not advisable to hike alone. No camping is allowed on Kaupo Ranch property, so most hikers spend the night at the Paliku campground and then get an early start.

HOSMER GROVE TRAIL

Those looking for a little greenery after hiking the crater will love this shaded woodland walk, and birders wing it here as well.

The half-mile loop trail starts at Hosmer Grove campground, 0.75 miles south of Park Headquarters Visitor Center, in a forest of lofty trees. The exotics in Hosmer Grove were introduced in 1910 in an effort to develop a lumber industry in Hawaii. Species include fragrant incense cedar, Norway spruce, Douglas fir, eucalyptus and various pines. Although the trees adapted well enough to grow, they didn't grow fast enough at these elevations to make tree harvesting practical. Thanks to this failure, today there's a park here instead.

After the forest, the trail moves into native shrubland, with 'akala (Hawaiian raspberry), kilau ferns and sandalwood. The 'ohelo, a berry sacred to the volcano goddess Pele, and the pukiawe, which has red and white berries and evergreen leaves, are favored by nene.

Listen for the calls of the native 'i'iwi and 'apapane, both sparrow-size birds with bright red feathers that are fairly common here. The 'i'iwi has a loud squeaking call, orange legs and a curved salmon-colored bill. The 'apapane, a fast-moving bird with a black bill, black legs and a white undertail, feeds on the nectar of ohia flowers, and its wings make a distinctive whirring sound.

SKYLINE TRAIL

This amazing otherworldly trail, which rides the crater-dotted spine of Haleakalā, begins just beyond Haleakalā's summit at a lofty elevation of 9750ft and leads down to the campground at Polipoli Spring State Recreation

MAUI

THE SUNRISE EXPERIENCE

'Haleakalā' means 'House of the Sun.' So it's no surprise that since the time of the first Hawaiians, people have been making pilgrimages up to Haleakalā to watch the sun rise. It is an experience that borders on the mystical. Mark Twain called it the 'sublimest spectacle' that he had ever seen.

Plan to arrive at the summit an hour before the actual sunrise; that will guarantee you a parking space and time to see the world awaken. Around that point the night sky begins to lighten and turn purple-blue, and the stars fade away. Ethereal silhouettes of the mountain ridges appear. The gentlest colors show up in the fragile moments just before dawn. The undersides of the clouds lighten first, accenting the night sky with pale silvery slivers and streaks of pink.

About 20 minutes before sunrise, the light intensifies on the horizon in bright oranges and reds. Turn around for a look at Science City, whose domes turn a blazing pink. For the grand finale, the moment when the disk of the sun appears, all of Haleakalā takes on a fiery glow. It feels like you're watching the earth awaken.

Come prepared – it's going to be c-o-l-d! Temperatures hovering around freezing and a biting wind are the norm at dawn and there's often a frosty ice on the top layer of cinders. If you don't have a winter jacket or sleeping bag to wrap yourself in, bring a warm blanket from your hotel. However many layers of clothes you can muster, it won't be too many.

The best photo opportunities occur before the sun rises. Every morning is different, but once the sun is up, the silvery lines and the subtleties disappear.

One caveat: a rained-out sunrise is an anticlimactic event after tearing yourself out of bed in the middle of the night to drive up a pitch-dark mountain. So check the **weather report** (☎ 866-944-5025) the night before to calculate your odds of having clear skies.

If you just can't get up that early, sunsets at Haleakalā have inspired poets as well.

TOP PICKS – HALEAKALĀ DAY HIKES

How much time do you have? Pick the ideal day hike to suit your schedule.

- **Ten hours:** If you're in good physical shape and can get an early start, the 11.2-mile hike that starts down Sliding Sands Trail and returns via Halemau'u Trail (p417) is the prize. Crossing the crater floor, it takes in a cinder desert and a cloud forest, showcasing the park's diversity.

- **Three hours:** For a half-day experience that offers a generous sampling of crater sights, follow Sliding Sands Trail (p417) down to the Ka Lu'u o ka O'o cinder cone and back. The easy bit? It takes just one hour to get down. The workout? You've got yourself a 1500ft elevation rise, making the return a strenuous two-hour climb.

- **One hour:** See Haleakalā's green side along the forested Hosmer Grove Trail (p419).

Area (p411) at 6200ft. It covers a distance of 8.5 miles and takes about four hours to walk. Get an early start to enjoy the views before clouds take over.

To get to the trailhead, go past Pu'u'ula'ula (Red Hill) Overlook and take the road to the left just before Science City. The road, which passes over a cattle grate, is signposted not for public use, but continue and you'll soon find a Na Ala Hele sign marking the trailhead.

The Skyline Trail starts in open terrain of volcanic cinder, and passes more than a dozen cinder cones and craters. The first mile is rough lava rock. After a crunchy 3 miles, it reaches the tree line (8500ft) and enters native *mamane* forest. In winter *mamane* is heavy with flowers that look like yellow sweet-pea blossoms. There's solitude on this walk. If the clouds treat you kindly, you'll have broad views all the way between the barren summit and the dense cloud forest. Eventually the trail meets the Polipoli access road, where you can either walk to the paved road in about 4 miles, or continue via the Haleakalā Ridge Trail and Polipoli Trail to the campground.

If you prefer treads to hiking boots, the Skyline Trail is an exhilarating adventure on a mountain bike.

Cycling & Mountain Biking
CYCLING
Those one-way downhill group cycle tours once wildly popular are currently banned from the park (see the boxed text, p415). Individual cyclists, however, can still pedal their way up the mountain. It's a real quad buster.

MOUNTAIN BIKING
For experienced mountain bikers the Skyline Trail (p419) is the island's ultimate wild ride,

plunging some 3000ft in the first 6 miles with a breathtaking 10% grade. The trail starts out looking like the moon and ends up in a cloud forest of redwood and cypress trees that resembles California's northern coast. The route follows a rough 4WD road that's used to maintain Polipoli Spring State Recreation Area (p411). For cripes sake, equip yourself with full pads, use a proper downhill bike and watch that you don't run any hikers down. **Crater Cycles Hawaii** (☎ 893-2020; www.cratercycles hawaii.com; 358 Papa Pl, Kahului; downhill bikes per day $75; ☼ 10am-5pm Mon-Thu & Sat, 9am-noon Fri) rents full-suspension downhill bikes, complete with a bike rack, helmet, gloves and pads.

SLEEPING
To spend the night at Haleakalā is to commune with nature. The camping options are primitive: no electricity or showers. Backcountry campgrounds have pit toilets and limited non-potable water supplies that are shared with the crater cabins. Water needs to be filtered or chemically treated before drinking; conserve it, as water tanks occasionally run dry. Fires are allowed only in grills, and in times of drought are prohibited entirely. You must pack in all your food and supplies and pack out all your trash. Keep in mind that sleeping at an elevation of 7000ft isn't like camping on the beach. You need to be well equipped – without a waterproof tent and a winter-rated sleeping bag, forget it.

Camping
The park has just one drive-up camping area: Hosmer Grove campground. Surrounded by lofty trees and adjacent to one of Maui's best birding trails, this campground at an elevation of 6800ft tends to be cloudy but

a covered picnic pavilion offers shelter if it starts to rain. Facilities include grills, toilets and running water. Camping is free on a first-come, first-served basis. No permit is required, though there's a three-day camping limit per month. It's busier in summer than in winter and is often full on holiday weekends. The campground is just after the park entrance booth.

For hikers, two backcountry campgrounds lie on the floor of Haleakalā Crater. The easiest to reach is at Holua, 3.7 miles down the Halemau'u Trail. The other is at Paliku, below a rain-forest ridge at the end of Halemau'u Trail. Weather can be unpredictable at both. Holua is typically dry with clouds rolling in during the late afternoon. Paliku is in a grassy meadow, with skies overhead alternating between stormy and sunny. Wasps are present at both campsites, so take precautions if you're allergic to stings.

Permits (free) are required for crater camping. They're issued at the Park Headquarters Visitor Center on a first-come, first-served basis between 8am and 3pm on the day of the hike. Camping is limited to three nights in the crater each month, with no more than two consecutive nights at either campground. Only 25 campers are allowed at each site, so permits can go quickly when large parties show up, a situation more likely to occur in summer.

Cabins

Three **rustic cabins** (per cabin with 1-12 people $75) dating from the 1930s lie along trails on the crater floor at Holua, Kapalaoa and Paliku. Each has a wood-burning stove, two propane burners, cooking utensils, 12 bunks with sleeping pads (but no bedding), pit toilets, and a limited supply of water and firewood.

Hiking distances to the cabins from the crater rim range from 4 to 9 miles. The driest conditions are at Kapalaoa, in the middle of the cinder desert off Sliding Sands Trail. Those craving lush rain forest will find Paliku serene. Holua has unparalleled sunrise views. There's a three-day limit per month, with no more than two consecutive nights in any cabin. Each cabin is rented to only one group at a time.

The demand is so high that the National Park Service holds a monthly lottery to award reservations! To enter, your reservation request must be received two months prior to the first day of the month of your proposed stay (eg requests for cabins on any date in July must arrive before May 1). Your chances increase if you list alternate dates within the same calendar month and choose weekdays rather than weekends. Only written (no phone) reservation requests (Haleakalā National Park, PO Box 369, Makawao, HI 96768, Attn: Cabins) are accepted for the lottery. Include your name, address, phone number, specific dates and cabins requested. Only winners are notified.

If you miss the lottery, don't write the cabins off. Cancellations often result in last-minute vacancies, and occasionally occur a few weeks in advance as well. You can check for vacancies in person at the Park Headquarters Visitor Center at any time, but calls (☎ 572-4459) regarding cancellations are accepted only between 1pm and 3pm, and you'll need to have a credit card to secure the cabin. As an added boon, if you get a vacancy within three weeks of your camping date, the cabin fee drops to $60 a day.

GETTING THERE & AROUND

Getting to Haleakalā is half the fun. Snaking up the mountain it's sometimes hard to tell if you're in an airplane or a car – all of Maui opens up below you, with sugarcane and pineapple fields creating a patchwork of green on the valley floor. The highway ribbons back and forth, and in some places as many as four or five switchbacks are in view all at once.

Haleakalā Crater Rd (Hwy 378) climbs 11 miles from Hwy 377 near Kula up to the park entrance, then another 10 miles to Haleakalā summit. It's a good paved road all the way, but it's steep and winding. You don't want to rush it, especially when it's dark or foggy. And watch out for cattle wandering across the road.

The drive to the summit takes about 1½ hours from Pa'ia or Kahului, two hours from Kihei and a bit longer from Lahaina. If you need gas, fill up the night before, as there are no services on Haleakalā Crater Rd. On your way back downhill, be sure to put your car in low gear to avoid burning out your brakes.

MAUI

KAHO'OLAWE

Seven miles southwest of Maui, the sacred but uninhabited island of Kaho'olawe (sometimes referred to as Kanaloa) has long been central to the Hawaiian-rights movement. Many consider the island a living spiritual entity, a *pu'uhonua* (refuge) and *wahi pana* (sacred place).

Yet for nearly 50 years, from WWII to 1990, the US military used Kaho'olawe as a bombing range. Beginning in the 1970s, liberating the island from the military became a rallying point for a larger resurgence of Native Hawaiian pride. Today, the bombing has stopped, the navy is gone, and healing the island is considered both a symbolic act and a concrete expression of Native Hawaiian sovereignty.

Kaho'olawe is 11 miles long and 6 miles wide, with its highest point the 1482ft Luamakika. The island and its surrounding waters are now a reserve that is off-limits to the general public because of the wealth of unexploded ordinance that remains on land and in the sea.

PATHWAY TO TAHITI

The channel between Lana'i and Kaho'olawe, as well as the westernmost point of Kaho'olawe itself, is named Kealaikahiki, meaning 'pathway to Tahiti.' When early Polynesian voyagers made the journey between Hawaii and Tahiti, they lined up their canoes at this departure point.

However, Kaho'olawe was much more than an early navigational tool. Over 540 archaeological and cultural sites have been identified. They include several heiau (an ancient stone temple) and ku'ula (fishing shrine) stones dedicated to the gods of fishers. Pu'umoiwi, a large cinder cone in the center of the island, contains one of Hawaii's largest ancient adze quarries.

A PENAL COLONY

In 1829, Ka'ahumanu, the Hawaiian prime minister, put forth her Edict of 1829, which declared that Catholics were to be banished to Kaho'olawe. Whether because of this or by coincidence, beginning in 1830, Kaulana Bay, on the island's northern side, served as a penal colony for men accused of such crimes as rebellion, theft, divorce, breaking marriage vows, murder and prostitution. History does not say if Catholics were included, and the penal colony was shut down in 1853.

INTO THE DUST BOWL

Kaho'olawe, now nearly barren, was once a lush, forested island.

Considering it good for stock raising, the territorial Hawaiian government leased the entire island to ranchers in 1858. None was successful, and sheep, goats and cattle were left to run wild. By the early 1900s, 10s of thousands of sheep and goats had denuded the better part of the island, turning it into an eroded dusty wasteland (even today, Kaho'olawe looks hazy from dust when seen from Maui).

From 1918 to 1941, Angus MacPhee, a former ranch manager on Maui, ran Kaho'olawe's most successful ranching operation. Granted a lease on the grounds to get rid of the goats, MacPhee rounded up and sold 13,000 goats, and then built a fence across the width of the entire island to keep the remaining goats at one end. He then planted grasses and ground cover and started raising cattle. It wasn't easy, but MacPhee, unlike his predecessors, was able to turn a profit.

TARGET PRACTICE

The US military had long felt that Kaho'olawe had strategic importance. In early 1941, it subleased part of the island from MacPhee for bombing practice. Following the December 7 1941 Pearl Harbor attack, martial law was declared in Hawaii and the military took control of Kaho'olawe entirely. Until the war's end, it used it to practice for invasions in the Pacific theater; in addition to ship-to-shore and aerial bombing, it tested submarine torpedoes by firing them at shoreline cliffs. It is estimated that of all the fighting that took place during WWII, Kaho'olawe was the most bombed island in the Pacific.

After the war, bombing practice continued. In 1953, President Eisenhower signed a decree giving the US navy official jurisdiction over Kaho'olawe, with the stipulation that when Kaho'olawe was no longer 'needed,' the unexploded ordinance would be removed and the island would be returned to Hawaiian control 'reasonably safe for human habitation.'

THE KAHO'OLAWE MOVEMENT

In the mid-1960s Hawaii politicians began petitioning the federal government to cease its military activities and return Kaho'olawe to the state of Hawaii. In 1976, a suit was filed against the navy, and in an attempt to attract greater attention to the bombings, nine Native Hawaiian activists sailed across and occupied the island. Despite their arrests, more occupations followed.

During one of the 1977 crossings, group members George Helm and Kimo Mitchell mysteriously disappeared in the waters off Kaho'olawe. Helm had been an inspirational Hawaiian-rights activist, and with his death the Protect Kaho'olawe 'Ohana movement arose. Helm's vision of turning Kaho'olawe into a sanctuary of Hawaiian culture became widespread among islanders.

In 1980, in a court-sanctioned decree, the navy reached an agreement with Protect Kaho'olawe 'Ohana that allowed them regular access to the island. The decree restricted the navy from bombing archaeological sites. In 1981 Kaho'olawe was added to the National Register of Historic Places as a significant archaeological area. For nearly a decade, the island had the ironic distinction of being the only such historic place being bombed by its government.

In 1982 the 'Ohana began to go to Kaho'olawe to celebrate *makahiki*, the annual observance to honor Lono, god of agriculture and peace (this celebration continues today). That same year – in what many Hawaiians felt was the ultimate insult to their heritage – the US military offered Kaho'olawe as a bombing target to foreign nations during the biennial Pacific Rim exercises.

The offer and the exercises brought what was happening to Kaho'olawe to worldwide attention. International protests over the bombings grew, and New Zealand, Australia, Japan and the UK decided to withdraw from the Kaho'olawe exercises. The plan was scrapped. In the late 1980s, Hawaii's politicians became more outspoken in their demands that Kaho'olawe be returned to Hawaii. Then in October 1990, as Hawaii's two US senators, Daniel Inouye and Daniel Akaka, were preparing a congressional bill to stop the bombing, President George Bush issued an order to immediately halt military activities.

THE NAVY SETS SAIL

In 1994, the US navy finally agreed to clean up and return Kaho'olawe to Hawaii. In a Memorandum of Understanding, the US navy promised to work until 100% of surface munitions and 30% of subsurface munitions were cleared. However, the catch was that the federally authorized cleanup would end in 10 years, regardless of the results (and regardless of Eisenhower's original promise).

Ten years later, after spending over $400 million, the navy's cleanup ended, and Kaho'olawe was transferred to the state. The government estimated that only 70% of surface ordinance and a mere 9% of subsurface ordinance had been removed.

The same year, in 2004, Hawaii established the **Kaho'olawe Island Reserve Commission** (KIRC; www.kahoolawe.hawaii.gov) to manage access and use of the island, preserve its archaeological areas and restore its habitats. KIRC's mandate is unique in state law, for it calls for the island to be 'managed in trust until such time and circumstances as a sovereign Native Hawaiian entity is recognized by the federal and state governments.' No such entity was then or is now so recognized, but KIRC works in the belief that one day a sovereign Native Hawaiian government will be, and this island will then become theirs.

HELPING THE 'OHANA

Working with KIRC as official stewards of Kaho'olawe, **Protect Kaho'olawe 'Ohana** (PKO; www.kahoolawe.org) conducts monthly visits to the island to pull weeds, plant native foliage, build infrastructure, clean up historic sights, conduct Hawaiian rituals and honor the spirits of the land. It welcomes respectful volunteers who are ready to work (not just sightsee). Visits last four to five days during or near the full moon; volunteers pay a $100 fee, which covers all food and transportation to the island. You'll need to bring your own sleeping bag, tent and personal supplies. PKO's website lists full details, schedules and contact information.

Lana'i

Among its translations, Lana'i is thought to mean 'day of conquest' and although there is debate about this, it seems appropriate. This small island (at its widest point it is only 18 miles across) has been affected more than anything by waves of conquest, whether it was the first Hawaiians (who set up fishing villages around the coast), 19th-century goats (who ate all the trees), 20th-century tycoons (who covered the place in pineapples) or modern-day visitors (looking for respite at luxury resorts).

Although in some ways the most central of the islands – on clear days you can see five islands from here – it is also the least 'Hawaiian' of the islands. The locals are a mix of people descended from immigrant pineapple workers from around the world. The relatively few buildings mostly hew to a corporate plantation style and the predictable waves of rental-car-driving tourists are missing from the miles of red-dirt roads.

Its signature Norfolk and Cook Island pines (imported) give the island an other-worldly feel that could just as well come from a remote corner of the South Pacific. And therein lies the charm of Lana'i: the entire island is the ultimate off-the-beaten-path destination. Hidden beaches, archaeological sites, oddball geology and a constant sense of isolation are perfect for those who don't want to go far to get away from it all. If you'd like to add some exotic adventure to your Hawaiian holiday, then consider adding in a few days on this unusual outpost right in the middle of the islands.

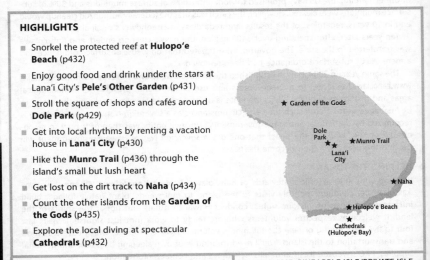

HIGHLIGHTS

- Snorkel the protected reef at **Hulopo'e Beach** (p432)
- Enjoy good food and drink under the stars at Lana'i City's **Pele's Other Garden** (p431)
- Stroll the square of shops and cafés around **Dole Park** (p429)
- Get into local rhythms by renting a vacation house in **Lana'i City** (p430)
- Hike the **Munro Trail** (p436) through the island's small but lush heart
- Get lost on the dirt track to **Naha** (p434)
- Count the other islands from the **Garden of the Gods** (p435)
- Explore the local diving at spectacular **Cathedrals** (p432)

★ Garden of the Gods

Dole Park ★★ ★Munro Trail
Lana'i City

★ Naha

★ Hulopo'e Beach

★ Cathedrals (Hulopo'e Bay)

- POPULATION: 3200   - AREA: 140.5 SQ MILES   - NICKNAME: PINEAPPLE ISLE/PRIVATE ISLE

LANA'I ITINERARIES

In Two Days
Start your first day swimming and snorkeling at **Hulopo'e Beach** (p432) or diving at nearby **Manele Bay** (p432). In the afternoon take a stroll around **Lana'i City** (p428) and watch the sun set over the majestic Norfolk Island pines at **Dole Park** (p429). On the second day rent a mountain bike or put on your hiking boots and head up the **Munro Trail** (p436) for a sweeping view of everything Lana'i has to offer.

In Four Days
Get a Jeep and do a little beachcombing along **Shipwreck Beach** (p433) and then explore the road to **Naha** (p434). That night, enjoy a superb meal at **Lana'i City Grille** (p431). On day four choose from one of the old-time **eateries** (p431) on Dole Park before a day exploring the **Garden of the Gods** (p435), the **Luahiwa Petroglyphs** (p432) and the ancient village of **Kaunolu** (p436).

For Day-Trippers
Take the early morning **ferry** (p427) from Lahaina and keep an eye out for schools of dolphins as the boat approaches **Manele Bay** (p432). Catch the shuttle into town and pour your own coffee for breakfast at **Blue Ginger Café** (p431). Stroll the shops and superb museum of **Lana'i City** (p428). In the afternoon, snorkel at **Hulopo'e Beach** (p432) before heading back to Maui on the sunset ferry.

HISTORY
Evil spirits were thought to be the only inhabitants of Lana'i prior to about 1400. Then a chief's son from Maui is credited with chasing off the evil-doers and making things safe for others from his home island. Little recorded history exists but there are traces of a thriving fishing culture along the coasts, especially to the north and east. Raiding parties from other islands were a frequent terror.

Colonialism largely bypassed Lana'i, although diseases brought by the odd missionary decimated the population from several thousand to 200 by the 1850s. Sporadic efforts were made at ranching and sugar growing by outsiders. Everything changed permanently when George Gay began buying up the place in 1902. Within a few years he owned 98% of the island (a holding that has remained almost unbroken through various owners to this day). In 1922, Lana'i passed into the hands of Jim Dole, who fatefully started a pineapple plantation that was soon the world's largest.

Under Dole (and later its corporate successor Castle & Cooke), Lana'i was not just a company town but a company island. Early managers were de facto dictators, who were known for spying on residents from their hillside mansion and ordering guards to discipline any deemed to be slackers.

In the 1980s Castle & Cooke and its hard-driving main shareholder David Murdoch made plans to shift Lana'i from pineapples to tourists. The final harvest of the former occurred in 1992, the first resorts for the latter opened in 1990.

CLIMATE
At an elevation of 1620ft Lana'i City enjoys a mild climate with average temperatures of 66°F in winter and 73°F in summer. Bring a jacket if you're coming in winter, when nighttime temperatures might dip to around 55°F. Rainfall, which is heaviest in winter, averages around 40in annually in Lana'i City and 15in along the coast. When it's overcast in Lana'i City, chances are that Hulopo'e Beach will be sunny and in the low 80s.

ACTIVITIES
Lana'i has no national, state or county parks, but its finest beach, Hulopo'e Beach, is run by the Lana'i Company as a free public park.

Almost all organized activities on the island are coordinated through the resorts. These include tennis, horseback riding, golf and scuba diving. **Adventure Lana'i Ecocentre** (☎ 565-7373; www.adventurelanai.com) offers a range of land and water activities, gear rental and will meet the Maui ferry.

LANA'I

At Sea

Snorkeling and swimming are fantastic at Hulopo'e Beach (p432), and if you manage to get there in the morning you can often watch dolphins frolicking just offshore. Shipwreck Beach (p433) is a more remote sandy idyll.

Cathedrals (p432), a dive area known for healthy reefs and clear water, is on the south coast and draws divers from as far as Maui. **Trilogy Lana'i Ocean Sports** (☎ 888-225-6284; www .visitlanai.com; beach dive $102, 2-tank boat dive $215) runs dive trips, as well as sea kayak tours (from $150) from the resorts. **Lana'i Surf Safari** (☎ 306-9837; www.lanaisurfsafari.com; surf lesson $185), run by Lana'i native Nicolas Palumbo, offers half-day surfing lessons at secluded spots.

Board rentals from $60. For more on surfing see opposite.

On Land

The ridge that cuts across Lana'i's hilly interior offers good hiking opportunities with top-notch views.

Mountain-bike rentals are available from **Adventure Lana'i Ecocentre** (☎ 565-7373; www .adventurelanai.com). The island offers plenty of dirt roads and trails, from beginner to advanced; expect challenging hills and dusty conditions.

Golf is big on Lana'i. Both of Lana'i's resorts feature world-class 18-hole designer golf courses that offer challenging locations and sweeping hill and ocean views.

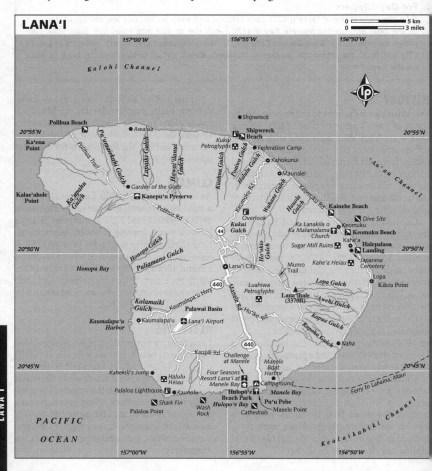

GETTING THERE & AWAY

You can get to Lana'i by air or boat.

Air

There are no direct flights to Lana'i from the mainland; see p571 for flights to Hawai'i. Lana'i airport (LNY) is about 3.5 miles southwest of Lana'i City. **Island Air** (☎ 800-323-3345; www.islandair. com) and **Mokulele Airlines** (☎ 426-7070; www.mokulele airlines.com) fly small planes between Lana'i and Honolulu half a dozen times a day. The former code shares with Hawaiian Airlines, the latter with Go! (an affiliate of Mesa Air). Because of weight limits for individual bags (40lb), take a small duffel bag in case you have to redistribute your stuff. For more on interisland flights, see p573.

Sea

Worth it just for the ride, the **Expeditions Maui-Lana'i Ferry** (☎ 661-3756, 800-695-2624; www.go-lanai.com; adult/child one-way $30/20) links Lahaina Harbor with Manele Bay Harbor on Lana'i (one hour) several times daily. In winter there's a fair chance of seeing humpback whales. Spinner dolphins are a common sight all year, especially on morning sails. Hulopo'e Beach is near the dock; Lana'i tour and activity operators will meet the ferries if you call ahead. Day trips are popular.

GETTING AROUND

Outside Lana'i City there are only three paved roads: Keomuku Rd (Hwy 44), which extends northeast to Shipwreck Beach; Kaumalapa'u Hwy (Hwy 440), which extends west past the airport to Kaumalapa'u Harbor; and Manele Rd (also Hwy 440), which flows south to Manele and Hulopo'e Bays. But to really see the island, you'll need to rent a 4WD vehicle. Lana'i's dirt roads vary from good to impassable, largely depending on the weather. Rain can turn them into scarlet-hued bogs.

Free maps from various sources are given out at the hotels and with vehicle rentals. Given the size of the (post-) Pineapple Island, you won't need much in the way of maps. Everywhere in Lana'i City is walkable.

To/From the Airport

The resorts provide a shuttle-van service (p428) that meets guests at the airport and ferry dock. Nonguests can use the shuttle for a fee, or call a taxi (p428) in advance of your arrival.

Car

The only car-rental company on the island, **Lana'i City Service** (☎ 565-7227, 800-533-7808; 1036 Lana'i Ave, Lana'i City; ⏰ 7am-7pm), is an affiliate of Dollar Rent A Car (p576). Having a monopoly on Lana'i translates into steep prices. Economy cars rent from $70 a day, 4WD Jeep Wranglers from $140. Given the paucity of paved roads, there is little reason to rent a car. Rather, you'll want a Jeep so that you can actually explore the island. Note that at least one rental house, Plantation Home (p430), includes a Jeep in the price. The resorts also arrange for cars (with City Service) and you may be able to rent from **Adventure Lana'i Ecocentre** (☎ 565-7373; www.adventurelanai.com).

Note that Lana'i City Service restricts cars to paved roads – only the 4WD Jeeps may be driven on dirt roads. Even then, the company limits which places you can drive. Check in advance, as a tow from a restricted area incurs fines, fees and possible financial ruin.

LANA'I SURF BEACHES & BREAKS *Jake Howard*

When it comes to surfing, Lana'i doesn't enjoy quite the bounty of waves as some of the other islands. Because rain clouds get trapped in the high peaks of Maui and Moloka'i there's very little rain on Lana'i, and therefore far fewer reef passes have been carved out by runoff.

Yet on the south shore the most consistent surf comes in around the Manele Point area (p432), where the main break peels off the tip of Manele and into Hulopo'e Bay. Shallow reef and submerged rocks make this a dangerous spot at low tide or in smaller surf conditions; it's probably ideal on a double overhead swell. Not too far away from here, located in front of a deserted old Hawaiian settlement, is a spot called Naha (also known as Stone Shack; p434). It offers a fun two-way peak, but does close out when it gets bigger.

Across the island, the north shore's wide-open Polihua Beach (p435) is the longest and widest sandy beach on Lana'i. Be careful of the current here, affectionately dubbed 'the Tahitian Express.' The water flowing between Moloka'i and Lana'i in the Kalohi Channel has driven many a ship into the reef, and it could easily take you on a trip to Tahiti if you're not careful.

DRIVING DISTANCES & TIMES FROM LANA'I CITY		
Destination	Miles	Time
Garden of the Gods	6	20min
Hulopo'e Beach	8	20min
Kaumalapa'u Harbor	7	20min
Keomuku	15	1hr
Lana'i Airport	3.5	10min

Also pricey is gas (sold at, you guessed it, Lana'i City Service) which can cost up to $5 per gallon, a hefty charge for the gas-guzzling Jeeps.

Shuttle
The resorts run a shuttle that links the Four Seasons Resort Lana'i at Manele Bay, Hotel Lana'i and the Lodge at Koele, as well as to the airport and ferry dock. Shuttles run about every 30 minutes throughout the day in peak season, hourly in the slower months. The first usually heads out about 7am, the last around 11pm. Fares may be included for guests and others pay $5 to $10, depending on the length of trip.

Taxi
Rabaca's Limousine Service (☎ 565-6670) charges $10 per person between the airport and Lana'i City, and $10 per person between Manele Bay and Lana'i City, the latter with a two-person minimum. Custom runs islandwide are available.

LANA'I CITY

pop 3000
Are you transported back in time or simply to another place in the Pacific or both? Pausing to get your bearings is perfectly all right in cute little Lana'i City. In fact you may need to pause to understand that it's really just a village, albeit one with irrepressible charm.

Lana'i City's main square, Dole Park, is surrounded by tin-roofed houses and shops, with not a chain in sight. It looks much the same as it did during its plantation days dating back to the 1920s. If you're not staying at one of the two resorts, you're probably staying here and that's all the better as you can wander between the surprisingly rich collection of eateries and shops, all with an authenticity not found in more touristed places. At night

stroll the quiet streets and watch the moon rise through the pine trees.

HISTORY
Lana'i is the only Hawaiian island where the largest town is in the highlands and not on the coast. Not only is Lana'i City the largest town, but for the last eight decades it has been the only town.

The village was built in the 1920s as a plantation town for the field workers and staff of Dole's Hawaiian Pineapple Company. The first planned city in Hawai'i, Lana'i City was built in the midst of the pineapple fields, with shops and a theater surrounding the central park, rows of plantation houses lined up beyond that and a pineapple-processing plant on the edge of it all. Fortunately it was done with a little pizzazz. Dole hired New Zealander George Munro, a naturalist and former ranch manager, to oversee much of the work, and he planted the tall Norfolk and Cook Island pines that give the town its green character and help suck some moisture from passing clouds.

ORIENTATION
The town is laid out in a simple grid pattern, and almost all of the shops and services border Dole Park, which marks the center of town. Most tourist activities take place about a mile north of the park at or near the Lodge at Koele. Everyone knows this hotel as the Lodge at Koele, though officially it's the 'Four Seasons Resort at Lana'i, the Lodge at Koele.'

INFORMATION
There's no local daily newspaper, but community notices, including rental-housing ads, are posted on bulletin boards outside the grocery stores.

Bank of Hawaii (☎ 565-6426; 460 8th St) Has a 24-hour ATM.

Lana'i Community Hospital (☎ 565-6411; 628 7th St) Offers 24-hour emergency medical services.

Lana'i Public Library (☎ 565-7920; 555 Fraser Ave; ⏰ 10am-5pm Mon-Fri, noon-8pm Wed) Has internet access.

Lana'i Visitors Bureau (☎ 565-7600, 800-947-4774; www.visitlanai.net; 431 7th St; ⏰ 9am-5pm Mon-Fri) The hotels can provide the same info.

Launderette Lana'i (☎ 565-7628; cnr Houston & 7th Sts; per load $4; ⏰ 6am-8pm) Self-service coin laundry.

Post office (☎ 565-6517; 620 Jacaranda St)

SIGHTS

Lana'i City is a charming place for a stroll. Although threatened by 'progress' (see the boxed text, p435), it still retains the mannered order of a planned community. There's a simple dignity to the march of shops and cafés around central **Dole Park**. The vaguely alien-looking pine trees provide plenty of shade and you can enjoy the comings and goings of the locals.

The **Lana'i Culture & Heritage Center** (☎ 565-3240; www.lanaichc.org; 111 Lana'i Ave; admission free; ☾ 8:30am-3:30pm) is a small treasure. Displays cover the island's often mysterious history; photos show its transformation into the world's pineapple supplier.

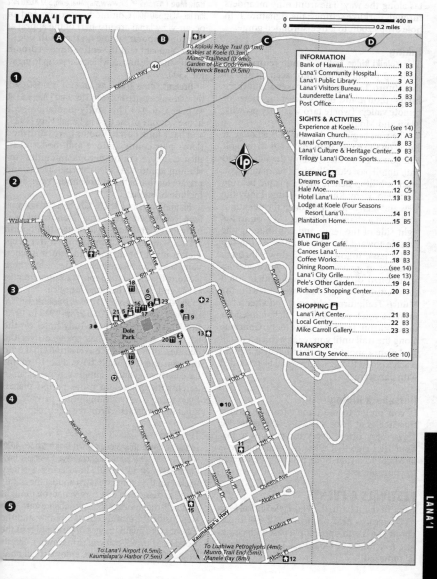

LANA'I CITY

0 —————————— 400 m
0 —————————— 0.2 miles

To Koloiki Ridge Trail (0.1mi);
Stables at Koele (0.3mi);
Munro Trailhead (0.4mi);
Garden of the Gods (6mi);
Shipwreck Beach (9.5mi)

Keomuku Hwy 44

INFORMATION
Bank of Hawaii...........................1 B3
Lana'i Community Hospital............2 B3
Lana'i Public Library.....................3 A3
Lana'i Visitors Bureau...................4 B3
Launderette Lana'i........................5 B3
Post Office...................................6 B3

SIGHTS & ACTIVITIES
Experience at Koele.................(see 14)
Hawaiian Church...........................7 A3
Lanai Company.............................8 B3
Lana'i Culture & Heritage Center...9 B3
Trilogy Lana'i Ocean Sports........10 C4

SLEEPING 🛏
Dreams Come True........................11 C4
Hale Moe....................................12 C5
Hotel Lana'i................................13 B3
Lodge at Koele (Four Seasons
    Resort Lana'i)..........................14 B1
Plantation Home..........................15 B5

EATING 🍴
Blue Ginger Café.........................16 B3
Canoes Lana'i.............................17 B3
Coffee Works..............................18 B3
Dining Room...........................(see 14)
Lana'i City Grille......................(see 13)
Pele's Other Garden....................19 B4
Richard's Shopping Center...........20 B3

SHOPPING 🛍
Lana'i Art Center.........................21 B3
Local Gentry...............................22 B3
Mike Carroll Gallery....................23 B3

TRANSPORT
Lana'i City Service..................(see 10)

3rd St

4th St

5th St

6th St

7th St

8th St

9th St

9th St

10th St

10th St

11th St

12th St

13th St

Waialua Pl

Houston St

Jacaranda St

Kiele St

Nani St

Lana'i Ave

Ilima Ave

Fraser Ave

Gay St

Pheasant Cir

Caldwell Ave

Akaki St

Akolu St

Kaumalapa'u Hwy

Awaiua Ave

Fraser Ave

Jasmine Dr

Muku Pl

Ohana Ave

Palawai Pl

Peahutu St

Queens Ave

Keoanuoa Dr

Dole Park

To Lana'i Airport (4.5mi);
Kaumalapa'u Harbor (7.5mi)

To Luahiwa Petroglyphs (4mi);
Munro Trail End (5mi);
Manele Bay (8mi)

On Sunday mornings, listen for choir music spilling out of the **Hawaiian church**.

ACTIVITIES
Golf
The **Experience at Koele** (☎ 565-4653; fees $210-225; ☼ 8am-6:30pm) curves around the resort and offers world-class golfing with knockout vistas along the way. The front nine meanders through parklike settings; the signature 17th hole drops 200ft to a tree-shrouded gorge.

Hiking
The **Koloiki Ridge Trail**, a 5-mile return hike, leads up to one of the most scenic parts of the Munro Trail (p436). It takes about three hours' return and offers sweeping views of remote valleys (where taro was once grown), Maui and Moloka'i.

The trail begins at the rear of the Lodge at Koele on the paved path that leads to the golf clubhouse. From there, follow the signposted path uphill past Norfolk Island pines until you reach a hilltop bench with a plaque bearing the poem 'If' by Rudyard Kipling. Enjoy the view and then continue through the trees until you reach a chain-link fence. Go around the right side of the fence and continue up the hillside toward the power lines. At the top of the pass, follow the trail down through a thicket of guava trees until you reach an abandoned dirt service road, which you'll turn left on. You'll soon intersect with the Munro Trail; turn right on it and after a few minutes you'll pass Kukui Gulch, named for the candlenut trees that grow there. Continue along the trail until you reach a thicket of tall sisal plants; about 50yd after that bear right to reach Koloiki Ridge, where you'll be rewarded with panoramas.

Horseback Riding
If you prefer to see Lana'i from a saddle, the **Stables at Koele** (☎ 565-7300; rides $60-300; ☼ 7am-5pm) offers everything: from a 1½-hour trail ride that takes in sweeping views of Maui, to a four-hour private ride catered to your interest.

FESTIVALS & EVENTS
Lana'i's main bash, the **Pineapple Festival** (www .visitlanai.net), is held on or near July 4 to celebrate the island's pineapple past with games and live music at Dole Park (any pineapple is imported!).

SLEEPING
Most people stay at the resorts or the hotel but there are a growing number of rental houses and B&Bs right in town and an easy walk to restaurants. There are many choices at www.vrbo.com.

Midrange
Hale Moe (☎ 565-9520; www.staylanai.com; 502 Akolu Pl; r incl breakfast $80-100) Commodious rooms and an ocean-view lanai are just part of the appeal at this contemporary home on the south side of town. You can rent the entire three-bedroom suburban-style house, which sleeps up to eight, for $300.

Dreams Come True (☎ 565-6961, 800-566-6961; www.dreamscometruelanai.com; 1168 Lana'i Ave; r $130, 4br house $520; ▯) This spiffy plantation-style house was one of the first in Lana'i City (1925) and has a long porch. Rooms have hardwood floors plus comfy antique and modern furniture. There are numerous amenities, including laundry, DVD, internet access and private marble baths. Whole house rates don't include breakfast.

Plantation Home (☎ 276-1528; craige@maui.net; cnr Gay & 13th Sts; house $225) A small, renovated two-bedroom plantation-style house, this option comes with an amazing bonus: a free Jeep. Pick it up at the airport and return it when you leave. Rooms are basic in decor but there is a long list of included sports equipment plus DVD and full kitchen and laundry.

Hotel Lana'i (☎ 565-7211; www.hotellanai.com; 828 Lana'i Ave; r $160-180, cottage $230) From 1923 to 1990, the Hotel Lana'i was the only hotel on the island. It seems little has changed over the decades, although the conversations that echo through the thin walls have. The 10 rooms have hardwood floors, antiques, pedestal sinks, patchwork quilts and more period pieces. Everything is very clean; opt for privacy and quiet in the detached cottage out back.

Top End
Lodge at Koele (Four Seasons Resort Lana'i; ☎ 565-4000, 800-321-4666; www.fourseasons.com/koele; 1 Keomuku Hwy; r from $335; ▧ ▯ ☞ ▣) Pondering a sticky wicket on the croquette lawn amidst the manicured gardens, you'd be forgiven if you thought yourself transported to an English estate. But step inside the grand central building and the touches like inlaid images of pineapples in the wood flooring tell you you're in Hawai'i. Guests in the 102 rooms and suites enjoy a small pool

a library, lawn bowls and misty mountain air. Lana'i City's heart is less than a 1-mile stroll. Activities are shared with the companion Four Seasons Resort Lana'i at Manele Bay.

EATING & DRINKING

The old-time feel of Lana'i City extends to eating hours: kitchens close by 8pm. Of the two main supermarkets, **Richard's Shopping Center** (☎ 565-6047; 434 8th St; ☻ 8am-7pm Mon-Sat) has the better wine selection, so that's good enough for us. Note: if you want vittles beyond Pop-tarts and Spam, you may want to bring them with you.

Coffee Works (☎ 565-6962; 604 'Ilima Ave; snacks $2-4; ☻ 6am-3pm Mon-Sat) Settle back on the vast deck at this long-running java-jiving caffeine house and soon most of the locals will pass by.

Canoes Lana'i (☎ 565-6537; 419 7th St; breakfast $5-9; ☻ 6:30am-1pm Thu-Tue) Breakfast is always on the menu at this old-time Hawaiian café that is little changed since pineapple pickers filled the tables. The banana pancakes are sublime, best enjoyed at the counter. The best-seller? *Loco moco* (rice, fried egg and hamburger topped with gravy).

Blue Ginger Café (☎ 565-6363; 409 7th St; breakfast & lunch $5-8, dinner $8-15; ☻ 6am-8pm) Don't worry, all the care goes into the food, not the decor at this bare-bones diner, where you can serve yourself a cup of coffee, grab a newspaper and settle back at a table outside. Muffins are some of the excellent items that arrive warm from the bakery. The long menu ranges from omelets to salads to burgers to tasty pastas and more.

our pick Pele's Other Garden (☎ 565-9628; cnr 8th & Houston Sts; lunch $5-8, dinner $10-19; ☻ 11am-2:30pm & 5-9pm Mon-Sat) More bistro than deli, this restored plantation house has tables inside and out. The talented kitchen leans Italian and serves up classic spaghetti and meatballs, crispy thin-crust pizza and a veritable minestrone of specials. Salads are made with organic local greens; the dessert star is the light but intensely flavored 'passionberry duo.' There's a fine beer list and you can probably drink until 10pm! Reserve ahead.

Lana'i City Grille (☎ 565-7211; Hotel Lana'i, 828 Lana'i Ave; mains $20-35; ☻ 5-9pm Wed-Sun) Famed Maui chef Bev Gannon is the brains behind the charming restaurant within the Hotel Lana'i. Sturdy 1930s schoolhouse furnishings give the wood-floored dining room a vintage air, the menu combines fresh seafood with various meats in ways both familiar (a perfect rib

eye) and surprising (a fan of field mushrooms, a chorizo potato puree). Specials are, well, special. The small bar pours a fine highball (often open until 11pm!) and on Friday nights there's live Hawaiian music.

Dining Room (☎ 565-7300; Lodge at Koele, 1 Keomuku Hwy; mains $45-60; ☻ 6-9:30pm) Leave your sandals in the room but bring your wallet to this very high-end restaurant with a name that will remind you where you are even after you've seen the prices. Lobster, caviar, quail and more populate a menu of expertly prepared creations presented with flawless attention to detail and service. But really, this is Lana'i and we'll take the fun and food of any of the places ringing Dole Park, first.

SHOPPING

Shops and galleries encircle Dole Park selling everything from flip-flops for locals to fine art for connoisseurs. You can spend an hour or much longer wandering.

Art lovers love **Mike Carroll Gallery** (☎ 565-7122; www.mikecarrollgallery.com; cnr 7th & Ko'ele Sts), where you can find the eponymous owner either creating a new masterpiece or busy displaying the work of another artist.

Art lovers who want to make something, wander into the **Lana'i Art Center** (☎ 565-7503; cnr 7th & Houston Sts; ☻ noon-4pm Mon-Fri), where you can enjoy a short-term class in beading or painting or peruse displays of works by local artists.

Lovers of artful clothing flock to **Local Gentry** (☎ 565-9130; 363 7th St), a clothing store with color and flair that caters to visitors and locals alike. There's no polyester schlock here.

GETTING THERE & AROUND

The resort shuttle (p428) stops at Hotel Lana'i, the Lodge at Koele and pretty much anywhere else you ask. Lana'i's only car-rental office is Lana'i City Service (p427).

HULOPO'E & MANELE BAYS

Lanai's finest beach (and one of the best in Hawai'i) is the golden crescent of sand at Hulopo'e Bay. Enjoy snorkeling in a marine preserve, walking to a fabled archaeological site or just relaxing in the shade of palms. Nearby, Manele Harbor provides a protected anchorage for sailboats and other

LANA'I

DETOUR: LUAHIWA PETROGLYPHS

Lana'i's highest concentration of petroglyphs (over 400 both ancient and modern) are carved into three dozen boulders spread over a remote slope overlooking the Palawai Basin.

To get to this seldom-visited site, head south from Lana'i City along tree-lined Manele Rd. After 2 miles, look for a cluster of six trees on the left and turn on the wide dirt road. Stay on this for 1.2 miles as you head toward the fills. When you see a house and gate, take a very sharp turn left onto a grass and dirt track for 0.3 miles. The large boulders will be on your right up the hill and there will be a turnout and small stone marker.

Many of the rock carvings are quite weathered, but you can still make out linear and triangular human figures, dogs and a canoe. Other than gusts of wind, the place is eerily quiet. You can almost feel the presence of the ancients here – honor their spirits and don't touch the fragile carvings.

---

small craft. It's just a 10-minute walk to Hulopo'e Beach.

Manele and Hulopo'e Bays are part of a marine-life conservation district that prohibits the removal of coral and restricts many fishing activities, all of which makes for great snorkeling and diving. Spinner dolphins seem to enjoy the place as much as humans. During wintertime *kona* (leeward) storms, strong currents and swells enliven the calm and imperil swimmers.

SIGHTS & ACTIVITIES
Hulopo'e Beach
One good thing about being the main beach on company-run Lana'i is that the same gardeners who manicure the Four Seasons keep things looking lovely in this free, public park. Everybody loves it – locals taking the kids for a swim, tourists on day trips from Maui and the many visitors who end up losing track of time here.

This gently curving white-sand beach is long, broad and protected by a rocky point to the south. The Four Seasons Resort Lana'i at Manele Bay sits on a low seaside terrace on the north side. Even with the hotel presence the beach is so big it never gets crowded. Generally, the most action occurs when the tour boats pull in from Maui at noon. Picnic tables shelter under palms and there are public rest rooms with solar-heated showers.

For the best **snorkeling**, head to the left side of the bay, where there's an abundance of coral and reef fish. To the left, just beyond the sandy beach, you'll find a low lava shelf with tide pools worth exploring. Often there will be somebody renting masks and fins on the beach, if not, contact **Adventure**

Lana'i Ecocentre (☎ 565-7373; www.adventurelanai .com). Look for the protected shoreline splash pool ideal for children.

Manele Harbor
During the early 20th century, cattle were herded down to Manele Bay for shipment to Honolulu. These days the herds start in Maui, traveling on day trips to Lana'i on the ferry (p427) or on one of the snorkeling cruises run by **Trilogy Lana'i Ocean Sports** (☎ 888-225-6284; www.visitlanai.com). If you want to do a little land exploration you'll find the remains of a cattle chute by walking around the point at the end of the parking lot.

But the real thrills here are beneath the surface. Coral is abundant near the cliff sides, where the bottom quickly slopes off to about 40ft. Beyond the bay's western edge, near Pu'u Pehe rock, is **Cathedrals** (Map p426), the island's most spectacular dive site, with arches and grottoes. Harbor facilities include drinking water, picnic tables, a sporadically open snack bar, rest rooms and showers.

Pu'u Pehe
From Hulopo'e Beach, a path (around 0.75 mile) leads south to the end of Manele Point, which separates Hulopo'e and Manele Bays. The point is actually a volcanic cinder cone that's sharply eroded on its seaward edge. The lava has rich rust red colors with swirls of gray and black, and its texture is bubbly and brittle – so brittle that huge chunks of the point have broken off and fallen onto the coastal shelf below.

Pu'u Pehe is the name of the cove to the left of the point, as well as the rocky islet just offshore. This islet, also called Sweetheart Rock, has a tomblike formation on top that

---

LANA'I FOR CHILDREN

The kids will love Hulopo'e Beach (opposite), where there are some cool tide pools filled with colorful little critters that will thrill the little ones; older kids will enjoy the great snorkeling. Other activities for children are centered at the resorts. The Stables at Koele (p430) has pony rides open to guests and nonguests. Both Four Seasons properties have kids' activities, including video games, sports on the property, cookies and milk and more.

---

figures into the Hawaiian legend of Pehe, a beautiful maiden who was stashed away in a cave by her lover, lest any other young men on Lana'i set eyes on her. One day when he was up in the mountains, a storm suddenly blew in and powerful waves drowned Pehe. The grief-stricken boy carried Pehe's body to the top of Pu'u Pehe, where he erected a tomb and laid her to rest. He then jumped to his death in the surging waters.

Golf

The Jack Nicklaus–branded **Challenge at Manele** (☎ 565-2222; guests/nonguests $210/225; ☼ 7am-6:30pm) offers spectacular play along seaside cliffs. The 12th hole challenges golfers to hit across a fairway that is really the ocean's surf.

SLEEPING

Camping is allowed on the grassy expanse above Hulopo'e Beach. Permits are issued by the island's owner, the **Lanai Company** (☎ 565-3273; kvelasco@castlecooke.com; 111 Lana'i Ave, Lana'i City; camping permit 3 nights $20, per person per night $6). Call or email to reserve a spot (three-night maximum stay during busy times like summer and weekends). Pick up a permit from the park attendants when you arrive.

Four Seasons Resort Lana'i at Manele Bay (Map p426; ☎ 565-3800, 800-321-4666; 1 Manele Bay Rd; www.foursea sons.com/manelebay.com; r from $445; 🅿 🖳 🛜 🖳) Of the two island resorts on offer, this one screams – well, stage-whispers – 'Hawaiian vacation!' Although the decor of the 236 rooms is just slightly overstuffed and frumpy, the views of the azure waters, the surrounds of the vast pool and the Asian-themed soaring public rooms are entrancing. Given a choice we'll take this resort first as it most says 'Hawai'i.'

EATING & DRINKING

The resort has many tables well-placed for watching the orange glint of the waters at sunset.

Harbor Café (Manele Boat Harbor; lunch $5-8; ☼ varies) Classic plate lunches, juicy teriyaki burgers and shave ice are on offer to locals and visitors looking for a deal. It's in a breezy pavilion back from the ferry dock.

Hulopo'e Court (☎ 565-7700; Four Seasons Resort Lana'i at Manele Bay; breakfast buffet $32, dinner mains $28-40; ☼ 7-11am & 6-9:30pm) The 'casual' restaurant at the resort has a long terrace overlooking the ocean and pool. The buffet breakfast is bountiful but not quite as over-the-top lavish as the prices imply. Dinner is the more interesting choice, with an emphasis on fresh seafood you can enjoy to the flicker of torches and the distant rumble of surf. The other dinner choice here is very high-end Italian.

KEOMUKU ROAD

The best drive on Lana'i, Keomuku Rd (Hwy 44), heads north from Lana'i City into cool upland hills, where fog drifts above grassy pastures. Along the way, impromptu overlooks offer straight-on views of the undeveloped southeast shore of Moloka'i and its tiny islet Mokuho'oniki, in marked contrast to Maui's sawtooth high-rises in Ka'anapali off to your right.

The surprisingly short 8-mile road gently slopes down to the coast through a mostly barren landscape punctuated by eccentrically shaped rocks. After 8 miles, the paved road ends near the coast. To the left, a dirt road leads to Shipwreck Beach, while turning right onto Keomuku Rd takes the adventurous to Keomuku Beach or all the way to Naha.

SHIPWRECK BEACH

Unlike many worldwide places named Shipwreck Beach where the name seems fanciful at best, you can't miss the namesake wreck here. A fairly large **WWII tanker** sits perched atop

---

TOP PICKS – DESERTED BEACHES

- **Shipwreck Beach** (above)
- **Halepalaoa Beach** (p434)
- **Polihua Beach** (p435)

---

rocks just offshore. Unlike a metal ship (which would have dissolved decades ago), this one was part of a series made from concrete and later dumped here by the Navy after the war.

Start by taking the dirt road that runs 1.4 miles north from the end of Hwy 44, past some beach shacks. Park in the large clearing overlooking a rocky cove which is known locally as Po'aiwa, which has good **snorkeling** amongst the rocks and reef, as well as protected **swimming** over the sandy bottom. The wreck is about 440yd to the north and you can stroll for at least 9 miles along the shore while looking for flotsam and taking in the Moloka'i and Maui views. Close to the parking area is the site of a former lighthouse on a lava-rock point, though only the cement foundation remains.

Kukui Petroglyphs

From the lighthouse foundation, trail markings lead directly inland about 100yd to the Kukui petroglyphs, a cluster of fragile carvings marked by a sign reading 'Do Not Deface'. The simple figures are etched onto large boulders on the right side of the path. Keep your eyes open here – sightings of wild mouflon sheep in the inland hills are not uncommon. Males have curled-back horns, and dominant ones travel with a harem.

Shipwreck in Awalua

The lighthouse site is the turn-around point for most people but it's possible to walk another 6 miles all the way to Awalua, where there's another shipwreck. The hike is windy, hot and dry (bring water); the further down the beach you go, the prettier it gets.

KAHOKUNUI TO NAHA

The Keomuku Rd is just the journey for those looking for real adventure on Lana'i. From the hillsides it looks barren but once you are on it, you are shaded by overhanging kiawe trees. The dirt course varies from smooth to deeply cratered (and impossibly soupy after storms). This is where your 4WD will justify its daily fee, as you explore the ruins of failed dreams and discover magical beaches. If the road is passable, driving the entire length should take about an hour. The reef-protected shore is close to the road but usually not quite visible.

Maunalei to Keomuku

Less than a mile from the end of Hwy 44 and the paving is **Maunalei**. An ancient heiau

(stone temple) sat there until 1890, when the Maunalei Sugar Company dismantled it and used the stones to build a fence and railroad. Shortly after the temple desecration, the company was beset by misfortune, as salt water filled the wells and disease decimated the workforce.

Another 6 miles further along is **Keomuku**, the center of the short-lived sugarcane plantation. There's little left to see other than the somewhat reconstructed **Ka Lanakila o Ka Malamalama Church**, which was originally built in 1903. Under the dense tropical vegetation can be found other plantation ruins, including a steam locomotive and buildings, as well as clouds of mosquitoes.

Keomuku to Naha

Just under 2 miles further along the road, you reach **Halepalaoa Landing**, which was where the sugar company planned to ship out its product. But little was accomplished during its short life (1899–1901), other than to shorten the lives of scores of Japanese workers, who are buried in a small **cemetery**. On the ocean side, you'll see the remains of Club Lana'i, a 1970s recreation spot that failed under dubious circumstances surrounding its finances. However there's a **pier** here that's maintained and which provides a good stroll out from the shore. In season you may hear whales breaching just offshore.

Running southeast from the pier is the shaded **Halepalaoa beach** that seems to have come from desert-island central casting and which runs to Lopa. There's rarely anyone here.

Another 4 miles brings you to **Naha**, which is both the end of the road and the site of ancient fishponds just offshore. With the wind whistling in your ears, it's an otherworldly place that seems utterly incongruous, given the view of developed Maui just across the waters. Look for traces of a flagstone path that ran from here right up and over the hill to the Palawai Basin.

ROAD TO GARDEN OF THE GODS

Strange rock formations, views that would overexcite a condo developer and more deserted beaches are the highlights of northwestern Lana'i.

ECHOES OF A FRUIT

Lana'i is defined by the pineapple, ironic given that the spiky fruit is now imported to the island's resorts and two markets. But evidence of its reign is everywhere. When you fly in, you pass over the ghostly outlines of vast fields that once produced one out of every three pineapples consumed worldwide. Much of the land – and island – now lies fallow.

Coming to terms with that past is an ongoing issue for the island today. Lana'i City is still very much the charming company town built by Jim Dole in the 1920s, but like the fields that were once its reason to exist, its very essence is in danger of going fallow. The stately order of vintage buildings around Dole Park is threatened by time and replacement. New buildings out of step with the old are proposed – and some are constructed (such as the current post office, which could be in Wichita). In 2006, the Historic Hawai'i Foundation, the leading advocate for cultural and historic preservation in the state, named the entire town as one of the most endangered places in Hawai'i.

Meanwhile, the two resorts opened in 1990 are successful but haven't spawned the kind of additional development envisaged by Castle & Cooke, the corporate successor to Dole which still controls much of the island. Condos on Manele Bay sell for $2.5 million, more than twice what Dole paid for all of Lana'i in 1922. Sales are slow.

What next for Lana'i is a common question. Little of the island remains in a natural state – 10,000 goats brought by missionaries denuded much of the island in the decades before Dole even planted his first pineapple. Sheep ranches took care of the rest. Perhaps the pineapple shouldn't be relegated to just a nickname. 'Let's plant some pineapples so visitors can see how this place worked,' said one longtime resident. 'It's crazy that the pineapple at the resorts is imported. Let's at least claim that part of our history.'

It's all reached via the Polihua Rd, which starts near the Lodge at Koele's stables. The stretch of road leading to Kanepu'u Preserve and the Garden of the Gods is a fairly good, albeit often dusty, route that generally takes about 20 minutes from town. To travel onward to Polihua Beach, though, is another order of magnitude in difficulty. Depending on when the road was last graded, the trip could take anywhere from 20 minutes to an hour, as you head 1800ft down to the coast in what is at times little more than a controlled skid.

KANEPU'U PRESERVE

The 590-acre Kanepu'u Preserve is the last native dryland forest of its kind across all Hawai'i. Just 5 miles northwest of Lana'i City, the forest is home to 49 species of rare native plants, including the endangered *'iliahi* (Hawaiian sandalwood) and *na'u* (fragrant Hawaiian gardenia). Look for the short, self-guided interpretive trail, which is inside the first of two fences protecting the preserve.

Dryland forests once covered 80% of Lana'i until introduced goats, deer and pigs made a feast of the foliage, leaving many native species near-extinct. Credit for saving this slice of the forest goes to ranch manager George Munro, who fenced hoofed animals out

in the 1920s. In 1991, the Lana'i Company granted the Nature Conservancy oversight of the forest.

GARDEN OF THE GODS

The only fertilizer that might work in this garden is cement. All manner of volcanic rocks are strewn about this landscape of maroon-and rust-colored earth. Many have strange shapes that stand out against the seemingly Martian landscape and you may fully expect the plucky little Mars Explorer probe to come buzzing past.

It's utterly silent up here and you can see up to four other islands across the white-capped waters. The colors change with the light – pastel in the early morning, rich hues in the late afternoon. Amidst the salmons and siennas, look for rocks oddly perched atop others.

POLIHUA BEACH

This broad, 1.5-mile-long white-sand beach at the northwestern tip of the island takes its name from the green sea turtles that nest here. Polihua means 'eggs in the bosom.' Although the beach itself is gorgeous, strong winds kicking up the sand and tiny shells often make it stingingly unpleasant; water conditions are treacherous.

LANA'I

MUNRO TRAIL

This exhilarating 12-mile adventure can be hiked, mountain biked or negotiated in a 4WD vehicle. For the best views, get an early start. Those hiking or biking should be prepared for steep grades and allow a whole day. If you're driving and the dirt road has been graded recently, give yourself two to three hours. However, be aware that rains turn the dirt into a red-colored swamp that claims many a 4WD. Watch out for sheer drop-offs.

To start, head north on Hwy 44. About a mile past the Lodge at Koele, turn right onto the paved road that ends in half a mile at the island's **cemetery**. The Munro Trail starts left of the cemetery, passing through eucalyptus groves and climbing the ridge where the path is studded with Norfolk Island pines. These trees, a species that draw moisture from the afternoon clouds and fog, were planted in the 1920s as a watershed by naturalist George Munro, after whom the trail is named.

Before the Munro Trail was upgraded to a dirt road, it was a footpath and historically was a place of taro farms, which drew on the frequent rainfall.

The trail looks down on deep ravines cutting across the east flank of the mountain, and passes **Lana'ihale** (3370ft), Lana'i's highest point. On a clear day, you can see all the inhabited Hawaiian Islands (except for distant Kaua'i and Ni'ihau) along the route. Stay on the main trail, descending 6 miles to the central plateau. Keep the hills to your left and turn right at the big fork in the road. The trail ends back on Manele Rd (Hwy 440) between Lana'i City and Manele Bay.

KAUMALAPA'U HIGHWAY

Kaumalapa'u Hwy (Hwy 440) connects Lana'i City to the airport before ending at Kaumalapa'u Harbor, the island's deepwater barge dock. The road itself is about

as exciting as a can of pineapple chunks in heavy syrup but it runs close to Lana'i's best archaeological site.

KAUNOLU

Perched on a majestic bluff at the southwestern tip of the island, the ancient fishing village of Kaunolu thrived until its abandonment in the mid-19th century after missionary transmitted disease had decimated the island. The waters of Kaunolu Bay were so prolific that royalty came here to cast their nets.

Now overgrown and visited by few, Kaunolu boasts the largest concentration of stone ruins on Lana'i. A gulch separates the two sides of the bay, with remnants of former house sites on the eastern side, obscured by thorny kiawe. The stone walls of **Halulu Heiau** at the western side of the gulch still dominate the scene. The temple once served as a pu'uhonua (place of refuge), where taboo-breakers fled to elude their death sentences. There are over 100 building sites here.

Northwest of the heiau, a natural stone wall runs along the perimeter of the sea cliff. Look for a break in the wall at the cliff's edge, where there's a sheer 80ft drop known as **Kahekili's Jump**. The ledge below makes diving into the ocean a death-defying thrill, but is recommended for professionals only. It's said that Kamehameha the Great would test the courage of upstart warriors by having them leap from this spot. More recently, it has been the site of world-class cliff-diving championships.

To get to Kaunolu, follow Kaumalapa'u Hwy (Hwy 440) 0.6 miles past the airport, turning left onto a partial gravel and dirt road that runs south through abandoned pineapple fields for 2.2 miles. A carved stone marks the turn onto a much rougher but still very 4WD-capable road down to the sea. After 2.5 miles you'll see a sign for a short **interpretive trail**, which has well-weathered signs explaining the history of Kaunolu. Another 0.3 mile brings you to a parking area amidst the ruins. One complication of a visit to this spot is that some rental firms may not allow you to drive here. Check first.

Moloka'i

The popular local T-shirt that proclaims 'Moloka'i time is when I want to show up,' sums up this idiosyncratic island perfectly: feisty and independent while not taking life too seriously.

Moloka'i is often cited as the 'most Hawaiian' of the islands and in terms of bloodlines this is true – more than 50% of the residents are at least part Native Hawaiian. But whether the island fits your idea of 'most Hawaiian' depends on your definition. If your idea of Hawaii includes great tourist facilities, forget it. There's not a single resort, not one! And definitely no restaurants ready for glossy-magazine gush. If you want a helicopter tour of the island's stunning Pali Coast, you have to go to another island to catch the helicopter.

But if your idea of 'most Hawaiian' is a place that best celebrates the appeal of the island's geography and indigenous culture, then Moloka'i is for you. It regularly ranks as one of the least spoiled islands worldwide. The attitude expressed on the T-shirt means that ancient Hawaiian sites in the island's beautiful, tropical east are jealously protected and restored; island-wide consensus favors economic hardship over development of the often sacred west.

In a cynical world, people don't realize that Moloka'i's moniker, 'the friendly isle,' is exactly right. There are the waves you get as you explore the uncrowded corners, and the advice about which fresh fish is best when you're buying food for your holiday rental. More importantly, you'll start to slow down and understand that 'Moloka'i time' simply needs to last as long as possible.

HIGHLIGHTS

- Hear echoes of Hawai'i's past while hiking in the **Halawa Valley** (p453)
- Discover underwater delights at **Twenty Mile Beach** (p451)
- Kick back at a picnic table with a superb plate lunch at **Puko'o** (p451)
- Follow in the footsteps of a saint on the **Kalaupapa Peninsula** (p458)
- Make friends bust a nut by sending a **Post-a-nut** (p457) from Ho'olehua
- Kayak past the world's tallest sea cliffs on the remote **Pali Coast** (see the boxed text, p454)
- Get your skin blasted clean on windswept and untrammeled **Papohaku Beach** (p465)
- Relive plantation Hawai'i wandering unrefined **Kaunakakai** (p444)

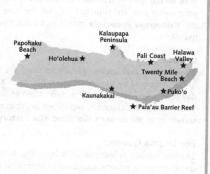

| POPULATION: 7500 | AREA: 260 SQ MILES | NICKNAME: THE FRIENDLY ISLE |

MOLOKA'I

HISTORY

Moloka'i was possibly inhabited by the 7th century. Over the following years it was a vital locale within the Hawaiian Islands and played a key role in local culture. It was known for its warriors, and its chiefs held great sway in the ever-shifting alliances between O'ahu and Maui. Much of the population lived in the east, where regular rainfalls, fertile soil and rich waters ensured abundant food.

Some of the most amazing historical sites in the islands can be found here today, including the enormous 'Ili'ili'opae Heiau (p450) and the series of fishponds just offshore (see the boxed text, p450).

At first European contact in 1786, the population was about 8000, close to today's total. Missionaries turned up in the east in the 1830s. Meanwhile the possibilities of the vast western plains drew the interest of early capitalists and colonists. By the 1900s there were large plantations of sugarcane and pineapples as well as cattle ranches. All the big pineapple players – Libby, Dole and Del Monte – had operations here but had ceased all production by 1990. Given the large local population, relatively few immigrant laborers were brought to Moloka'i, one of the reasons the island has such a high (50%) number of Native Hawaiians.

Cattle were important for all of the 20th century. The Moloka'i Ranch owns much of the western third of the island but changing investors coupled with some unsuccessful dabbles in tourism (see the boxed text, p463) caused the ranch to shut down in 2008, throwing hundreds out of work.

Tourism plays a minor role in the local economy and besides small-scale farming, the main employer now is Monsanto, which keeps a very low profile at its farms growing genetically modified (GM) seeds.

CLIMATE

At Kaunakakai, the average daily temperature is 70°F in winter and 78°F in summer. The average annual rainfall is 14in fairly consistently across the year. Still, these statistics say nothing of Moloka'i's microclimates. The east coast sees more rain and wind than Kaunakakai, with the most rain falling in the Halawa Valley. Central Moloka'i at lower elevations is pretty sheltered from wind, while upper elevations get the most rain on the island. The West End sees little rain, gets more sun and is exposed to the wind.

NATIONAL, STATE & COUNTY PARKS

The stunning Kalaupapa Peninsula, and a tour of the leprosy settlement there are reason enough to visit Moloka'i. All are within Kalaupapa National Historical Park (p458), and should not be missed. Overlooking it all,

---

MOLOKA'I ITINERARIES

In Two Days

Drive the gorgeous 27 miles east to the **Halawa Valley** (p453), including a hike to the waterfall. Follow with lunch and kicking back at **Mana'e Goods & Grindz** (p451) and a snorkel at **Twenty Mile Beach** (p451). Wander **Kaunakakai** (p446) gathering vittles for dinner under the stars at your rental pad. On your last day, let the sure-footed mules give you the ride of your life to the **Kalaupapa Peninsula** (p461) and crack open some fun at **Purdy's Macadamia Nut Farm** (p456).

In Four Days

After the two days above, spend your third day in the ancient rain forests of **Kamakou Preserve** (p455), followed by the island's best dinner at **Kualapu'u Cookhouse** (p456). In the morning of day four, enjoy some locally grown coffee at the **Moloka'i Coffee Company** (p456) then head northwest to the culturally significant beaches of Mo'omomi (p457), before finding the ultimate souvenirs at **Maunaloa's Big Wind Kite Factory** (p462).

For Drama Queens

See the world's tallest sea cliffs from the bottom up on the **Pali Coast** (see the boxed text, p454) either by private tour boat or from your own sea kayak. See the same cliffs from the top down – and marvel at the wild landscape or ancient rain forest and wild waterfalls – from the **Pelekunu Valley Overlook** (p455).

verdant Pala'au State Park (p458) has views down to Kalaupapa and woodsy hikes to erotic rock formations.

Out west, the county's Papohaku Beach Park (p465) is a good enough reason to make the trek, plus it fronts one of Hawaii's longest and best beaches.

Camping

Moloka'i's most interesting places to camp, in terms of setting and setup, is the county's Papohaku Beach Park (p465) on the untrammeled West End. The next best would be the small church-owned Waialua Pavilion & Campground (p452) in lush East Moloka'i. Camping at the county's One Ali'i Beach Park (p445) is not recommended.

County permits (adult/child Monday to Thursday $5/2, Friday to Sunday $8/5) are issued by the **Department of Parks & Recreation** (Map p444; ☎ 553-3204; www.co.maui.hi.us; Mitchell Pauole Center, Ainoa St, Kaunakakai; ☑ 8am-1pm & 2:30-4pm Mon-Fri), either online or in person. Permits are limited to three consecutive days in one park, with a yearly maximum of 15 days.

You can enjoy the views from Pala'au State Park (p458) and be ready for an early start on a visit to Kalaupapa from a peaceful camping area near the trailhead. For a true wilderness experience, consider the remote camping at Waikolu Lookout (p455). State permits ($5 per campsite per night, five-day maximum) are obtained from the **Division of State Parks** (☎ 587-0300; www.hawaiistateparks.org). Mail-in forms are available on their website. Alternatively, you can go through the district office on Maui (p328); note that permits cannot be obtained on Moloka'i.

None of these campgrounds listed are near sources of food or drink. If you forget a piece of camping equipment, Moloka'i Fish & Dive (right) stocks plenty. For full details on Moloka'i accommodations, see the boxed text, p447.

ACTIVITIES

Moloka'i has wild ocean waters, rough trails, remote rain forests and the most dramatic oceanside cliffs in Hawaii. It's a perfect destination for adventure – just don't expect to be spoon-fed.

There are two main operators and outfitters who pretty much handle every activity on the island and often work together:

Moloka'i Fish & Dive (Map p444 ☎ 553-5926, 336-1088; www.molokaifishanddive.com; Ala Malama Ave, Kaunakakai; ☑ 8am-6pm Mon-Sat, to 2pm Sun) The largest of the two operators has an intriguing shop.
Moloka'i Outdoors (Map pp440-1; ☎ 553-4477, 877-553-4477; www.molokai-outdoors.com; Hotel Moloka'i, Kamehameha V Hwy, Kaunakakai; ☑ 8:30am-4pm)

For the following activities, unless stated otherwise, either Moloka'i Fish & Dive or Moloka'i Outdoors can set you up.

At Sea

During the summer, you'll find waters are calm on the north and west shores, and made rough by the persistent trade winds on the south shore outside of the Pala'au barrier reef. Plan on getting out early, before the winds pick up. Winter storms make waters rough all around the island (outside of the reef), but, even so, the calm days between winter storms can be the best times to get out on the water.

FISHING

The sportfishing is excellent in Moloka'i waters, especially around the Penguin Banks of the southwestern tip. Bait casting is good on the southern and western shores. Boats dock and leave from the Kaunakakai Wharf; see p443 for a list of charter boats. Rates run about $25 per person per hour with various time and passenger minimums (eg six-person, four-hour minimum would be $600). Close to shore expect to find large fish including 'omilu, a type of trevally. Further out you'll find a'u (marlin) and the ever-popular various species of ahi (yellowfin tuna).

KAYAKING

The northeastern shore, sheltered by the reef, is best for kayaking. At the very tip, Halawa Beach (p453) is a good launching point when seas are calm. In the summer, expert paddlers can venture around to the northern shore to witness the grandeur of the world's tallest sea cliffs (for more information see the boxed text, p454).

Note that rental-car companies do not allow kayaks to be carried atop their vehicles. Outfitters will deliver kayaks for fees ranging from $20 to $50. Moloka'i Fish & Dive (above) runs a guided five-hour trip ($90) that paddles with the wind, finishing with a boat tow back to the dock.

MOLOKA'I

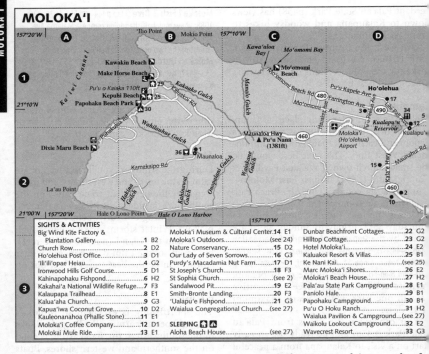

SNORKELING & SCUBA DIVING

Moloka'i's 32-mile Pala'au barrier reef – Hawaii's longest – lies along the south side of the island, promising top-notch snorkeling and excellent diving in uncrowded waters all year long, when conditions allow. To reach the good spots, you'll need a boat.

During the summer, the West End beaches are easily accessible, magical spots for snorkeling, with clear, flat waters. Here, Dixie Maru Beach (p465) and the rocks at Kawakiu Beach (p463) are both prime spots. In the east, Twenty Mile Beach (p451) is quite a good snorkeling stop.

For boat charters, see p443 or go with one of the operators ($70, three to four hours) listed earlier (see p439).

SURFING

When it's breaking, the stretch from Rock Point (p452) to Halawa Beach (p453) on the east end, and Kepuhi Beach (p464) on the West End are reliable spots. Leave Kawakiu Beach's (p463) winter waves to the experts. For secret spots, see the boxed text, p442. Moloka'i Fish & Dive and Moloka'i Outdoors

(see p439) charge around $15 per day fo surfboard rentals.

SWIMMING

Most year-round spots for a swim are on th northeastern coast, with Twenty Mile Beacl (p451), a cove just a mile past Waialua, an Puko'o (p451) being the best. At the very east ern tip, Halawa Beach (p453) is good onl when the seas are calm. On the West End sheltered Dixie Maru Beach (p465) is goo for a dip almost all year, while Kawakiu Beacl (p463) is only good in the summer.

WHALE WATCHING

Witness the sudden drama of humpbac whales breaching from December to April Both Moloka'i Fish & Dive and Moloka' Outdoors (see p439) and the boat charter op erators (p443) offer trips. Rates start at $70.

WINDSURFING & KITESURFING

Moloka'i has plenty of wind – advanced surf ers can harness it in the Pailolo and Ka'iw Channels. Most people grabbing the win come to the island with their own gear.

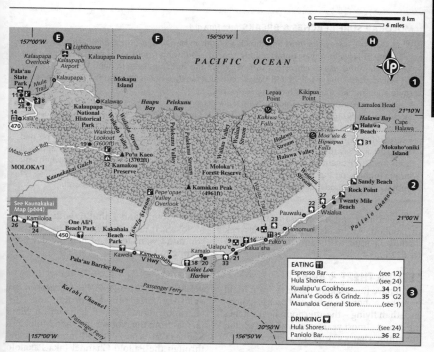

EATING 🍴
Espresso Bar....................................(see 12)
Hula Shores......................................(see 24)
Kualapu'u Cookhouse...............**34** D1
Mana'e Goods & Grindz...........**35** G2
Maunaloa General Store...........(see 1)

DRINKING 🍷
Hula Shores......................................(see 24)
Paniolo Bar.................................**36** B2

On Land

GOLF

The nine-hole Ironwood Hills Golf Club
(p458) is like something out of a Chevy Chase
movie – in a good way. The 18-hole Kaluakoi
Golf Course at the West End was closed as
part of the Moloka'i Ranch shutdown (see the
boxed text, p463).

HIKING

Much like the island itself, the hiking here
is pristine, remote and rugged, with very little traffic. Moloka'i's most-hiked trail is the
legendary descent to the Kalaupapa Peninsula
(p461).

Kamakou Preserve (p455) features unique
rain-forest hikes in the island's untamed interior
and out to scenic valley overlooks. At low tide,
it's possible to do some beach walking from
Hale O Lono Point to La'au Point. Hiring a
guide is required to hike to the falls in the lush
Halawa Valley (p453).

For trail maps and the general lowdown
on hiking, swing by Moloka'i Bicycle (p443).
Walter Naki (☎ 558-8184) is a local who leads
custom hikes across the island.

MOUNTAIN BIKING & CYCLING

There are over 40 miles of trails on Moloka'i
good for mountain biking. The roads of the
thick Moloka'i Forest Reserve (p454) are prime
for mountain biking, as are trails on the arid
West End, many with ocean views. As for cycling, pretty much all of Moloka'i's paved highways would make for a scenic ride, especially
the trip to the Halawa Valley (p453). For trail
maps and the general lowdown, visit Moloka'i
Bicycle (p443).

TENNIS

Enjoy free, public tennis courts at the Mitchell
Pauole Center (p446). Wavecrest Resort (p450)
and Paniolo Hale (p464) condo complexes also
have courts.

YOGA

Karen Noble (☎ 558-8225; www.molokai.com/yoga)
holds intimate monthly Ashtanga Vinyasa
yoga retreats on her lush property situated
in Honomuni, East Moloka'i. Weekly classes
are also offered, as are private retreats, which
feature accommodation in simple screened
huts, and vegetarian foods. Jump right into

MOLOKA'I SURF BEACHES & BREAKS *Jake Howard*

What Moloka'i, one of the most breathtaking islands in Hawaii if not the entire Pacific, possesses in beauty, it lacks in waves. Unfortunately, due to shadowing from the other islands, there just isn't much in the way of consistent surf. Yet when the surf's up, keep in mind that the Friendly Isle encompasses the ideals of 'old Hawaii' in which family remains the priority, so remember to smile a lot and let the locals have the set waves.

On the western end of Moloka'i, winter swells bring surf anywhere between 2ft and 10ft (and, very rarely, 15ft). The break known as **Hale O Lono** is one such exposed area. It comprises several fun peaks and is the starting point for the annual 32-mile Moloka'i-to-O'ahu outrigger and paddleboard races. On central Moloka'i's north shore, there are decent waves to be had at Mo'omomi Bay (p457). As the area is an archaeological site, entry is dependent on approval from the Department of Hawaiian Home Lands. For information ask at the airport when you arrive. **Tunnels**, on the southern side of Pu'u o Kaiaka (p464) to the west, is a popular break for bodysurfing and bodyboarding, and is also the only sand-bottom spot on the island.

the ocean after finishing class in the open-air pavilion. All-inclusive prices for a week (including mud baths and other delights) are $1250.

GETTING THERE & AWAY

If you have time, taking the ferry from Maui (right) is a more sociable and scenic experience than flying – the afternoon boat catches the sunset almost year-round, and in winter, breaching whales glorify the scene.

Air

Moloka'i (Ho'olehua) Airport (MKK) is small: you claim your baggage on a long bench. Single-engine planes are the norm; sit right behind the cockpit area for spectacular views forward. Because of weight limits for individual bags (40lb), pack a small duffel bag in case you have to redistribute your stuff. For more information on interisland flights, see p573.

The main airlines servicing Moloka'i have frequent service to Honolulu and one or two flights a day to Kahului on Maui. Unless you have a through ticket from the mainland, it's usually much cheaper to buy from the carriers listed here, rather than their larger airline partners.

Island Air (☎ 800-652-6541; www.islandair.com) Partner with Hawaiian Airlines; flies planes with two, yes two, engines.

Mokulele Airlines (☎ 426-7070, 866-260-7070; www .mokuleleairlines.com) Partner with go! airlines.

Pacific Wings (☎ 888-575-4546; www.pacificwings .com) Often the cheapest.

George's Aviation (☎ 834-2120, from outside Hawai'i 866-834-2120; www.georgesaviation.com) is a very small carrier that makes one round-trip daily linking Honolulu and Kahului, with a stop in Moloka'i. It arranges charters, in case, say, you don't want to spend half the day connecting to Lana'i.

Sea

Moloka'i Ferry (☎ 866-307-6524; www.molokaiferry.com; adult/4-12yr $55/28) runs a morning and late-afternoon ferry between Lahaina on Maui (across from the Pioneer Inn) and Moloka'i's Kaunakakai Wharf. The 90-minute crossing through the Pailolo Channel (aka Pakalolo Channel for all the pot smuggling) can get choppy; in fact, you can enjoy the thrill of a water park just by sitting on the top deck and getting drenched. Buy tickets online, by phone or on the *Moloka'i Princess* a half-hour before departure. Fares fluctuate with the price of gas.

GETTING AROUND

Renting a car here is essential, if you intend to fully explore the island or if you are renting a house or condo and will need to do shopping. All of Moloka'i's highways and primary routes are good, paved roads.

Exploring unmarked roads is not advisable. Folks aren't too keen on strangers cruising around on their private turf and can get churlish. On the other hand, if there's a fishpond you want to see, and someone's house is between the road and the water, it's usually easy to strike up a conversation and get permission to cross. If you're lucky they might even share some local lore and history with you, particularly the old-timers.

Good free maps of Moloka'i don't exist. *Franko's Moloka'i Guide Map* is massively detailed and highly useful. James A Bier's *Map of Moloka'i & Lana'i* has an excellent index. Both fold up small, cost under $6 and are widely available on the island.

To/From the Airport & Ferry

The various car-rental agencies will generally arrange transport for you between the airport, ferry dock and their locations as required. Note that the chains at the airport should be called directly at their Moloka'i offices to arrange ferry pick-up. See below for more details on rental cars.

A taxi (see right) from the airport costs around $20 to Kaunakakai, and $25 to the West End.

One of Moloka'i's trademarks is the sign you see leaving the airport: 'Aloha. Slow down, this is Moloka'i. Mahalo.'

Bicycle

Moloka'i Bicycle (Map p444; ☎ 553-3931, 800-709-2453; molbike@aloha.net; 80 Mohala St, Kaunakakai; ⏰ 3-6pm Wed, 9am-2pm Sat) is the place to go for all things cycling. The owner has a great depth of knowledge about biking across the breadth of the island. He'll do pick-ups and drop-offs outside of his opening hours. As well as offering repairs, parts and sales, there is a full range of rentals starting at $23/85 per day/week for mountain bikes. Glam models go for more. Prices include helmets, locks, pump, maps and much more.

Car

Keep in mind that rental cars are technically not allowed on unpaved roads, and there can also be restrictions on camping. If you intend to explore more-remote parts of the island such as Mo'omomi Bay, you'll at least need a vehicle with high clearance, and probably

a 4WD. Book well in advance, especially if planning a weekend visit. But if you're feeling lucky in low season, walk-up rates at the airport can be half that found online.

There are gas stations in Kaunakakai; one in Maunaloa is open very limited hours. Expect sticker shock at the pump.

Alamo Rental Car (www.alamo.com) took over as the sole operator at the airport in 2009. See p576 for toll-free reservation numbers and general rental information.

Island Kine Auto Rental (☎ 553-5242, 877-553-5242; www.molokai-car-rental.com), a local outfit, offers a full range of vehicles at good rates. Pick-ups can be arranged from anywhere.

Taxi

Hele Mai Taxi (☎ 336-0967) services Moloka'i.

Tours

Tours on Moloka'i come in two flavors: those you do because you want someone else to do the driving etc; and the tours that you do because they are the only way to have the experience, such as a trek up the Halawa Valley (p453), Kalaupapa (p461) or the guided tours of the Nature Conservancy's Kamakou Preserve (p455) and Mo'omomi Beach (p457).

The two main activity operators (see p439) offer various tours including custom drives to pretty much any place on the island. An excursion to a plumeria farm ($15 per person), where you can make lei, and see the fragrant flowers in all their bounteous glory, is fun.

Much of Moloka'i's coastline is only accessible by boat. The wild beauty of the impenetrable North Shore Pali, home to the world's tallest sea cliffs (see the boxed text, p454), is unforgettable. The activity operators and boat charters (below) all arrange trips that take the better part of a day, often include a stop for snorkeling, and don't run in the winter, lest storms send you to Gilligan's Island.

BOAT CHARTERS

Boat charters generally leave from Kaunakakai Wharf and, if you're traveling in a group, can be tailored to your desires. Rates start at about $100 per hour for whole boat charters, with a four-hour minimum. Try one of these personable outfits:

Alyce C Sportfishing Charters (☎ 558-8377; www.alycecsportfishing.com) Joe Reich has over 30 years of

DRIVING DISTANCES & TIMES

Average driving times and distances from Kaunakakai are listed below.

Destination	Miles	Time
Halawa Valley	27	1¼hr
Ho'olehua Airport	6.5	10min
Kalaupapa Trailhead	10	20min
Maunaloa	17	30min
Papohaku Beach	21.5	45min
Puko'o	16	20min
Twenty Mile Beach	20	40min

experience and also does whale-watching jaunts and round-island runs on his 31ft boat.

Fun Hogs Sportfishing (☎ 567-6789; www .molokaifishing.com) Fish your heart out on *The Ahi*, a 27ft sportfishing boat. Snorkeling and whale watching are also offered. Mike Holmes is a legendary local long-distance canoeist.

Hallelujah Hou Fishing (☎ 336-1870; www.hallelu jahhoufishing.com) Captain Clayton Ching runs all types of fishing trips, plus he's a real captain in the sense that he can marry you on ship *or* shore.

Ma'a Hawai'i – Moloka'i Action Adventures (☎ 558-8184) Walter Naki, of trekking fame, also offers deep-sea fishing, whale watching and North Shore tours.

KAUNAKAKAI

pop 2700

View a photo of Moloka'i's main town from 50 years ago and the main drag won't look much different than it does today. Worn wood-fronted buildings with tin roofs that roar in the rain seem like refugees from a Clint Eastwood Western. But there's no ar- tifice here – it's the real deal. Pretty much all of the island's commercial activities are here

and you'll visit often, if nothing else for its shops and services.

Walking around the town can occupy a couple of hours if you take time to get into the rhythm of things and do a little explor- ing. A popular local T-shirt reads 'Moloka'i Traffic Jam: Two Drivers Stopped in the Middle of the Road Talking Story.' And while there are stop signs, there are no stoplights.

If possible, stop by on Saturday morn- ings when the street market draws much of the island.

INFORMATION
Bookstores
Kalele Bookstore (☎ 567-9094; Ala Malama Ave) An overdue bookstore for the island that opened in 2009.

Emergency
Police, Fire & Ambulance (☎ 911)

Internet Access
The library (see opposite) has internet access.
Moloka'i Mini Mart (☎ 553-4447; Mohala St; ☯ 6am-11pm) Convenience store with internet access (per min 8¢) plus printing.

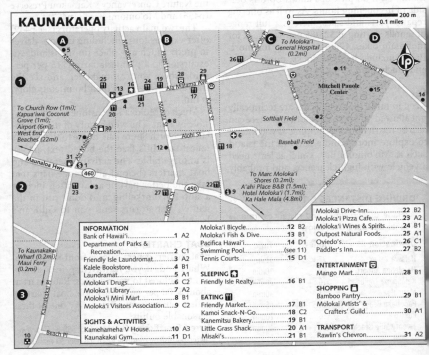

KAUNAKAKAI

0 ————— 200 m
0 ————— 0.1 miles

INFORMATION	
Bank of Hawai'i	1 A2
Department of Parks & Recreation	2 C1
Friendly Isle Laundromat	3 A2
Kalele Bookstore	4 B1
Laundramat	5 A1
Moloka'i Drugs	6 C2
Moloka'i Library	7 A2
Moloka'i Mini Mart	8 B1
Moloka'i Visitors Association	9 C2

SIGHTS & ACTIVITIES	
Kamehameha V House	10 A3
Kaunakakai Gym	11 D1
Moloka'i Bicycle	12 B2
Moloka'i Fish & Dive	13 B1
Pacifica Hawai'i	14 D1
Swimming Pool	(see 11)
Tennis Courts	15 D1

SLEEPING 🛏	
Friendly Isle Realty	16 B1

EATING 🍴	
Friendly Market	17 B1
Kamoi Snack-N-Go	18 C2
Kanemitsu Bakery	19 B1
Little Grass Shack	20 A1
Misaki's	21 B1

Molokai Drive-Inn	22 B2
Moloka'i Pizza Cafe	23 B2
Moloka'i Wines & Spirits	24 B1
Outpost Natural Foods	25 A1
Oviedo's	26 C1
Paddler's Inn	27 B2

ENTERTAINMENT 🎭	
Mango Mart	28 B1

SHOPPING 🛍	
Bamboo Pantry	29 B1
Molokai Artists' & Crafters' Guild	30 A1

TRANSPORT	
Rawlin's Chevron	31 A2

Laundry

Friendly Isle Laundromat (Kaunakakai Pl; ⏰ 7am-9pm)

Laundramat (Makaena Pl; ⏰ 7am-9pm) Bring your own soap to this place with an oddly spelt name.

Libraries

Moloka'i Library (☎ 553-1765; Ala Malama Ave; ⏰ 9:30am-5pm Mon-Fri, Wed noon-8pm) Buy a library card for 3 months ($10) or 5 years ($25) and enjoy internet use and library privileges here and at 50 other branches statewide.

Media

In lieu of a daily newspaper, bulletin boards (especially at the Friendly Market) around Kaunakakai are the prime source of news and announcements.

Molokai Dispatch (☎ 552-2781; www.themolokaidis patch.com) Free weekly with an activist slant published each Thursday; watch the events calendar for local happenings.

Medical Services

Moloka'i Drugs (☎ 553-5790; Moloka'i Professional Bldg, Kamoi St; ⏰ 9am-5:45pm Mon-Fri, to 2pm Sat) Sells local books and maps, along with drugstore fare.

Moloka'i General Hospital (☎ 553-5331; 280 Puali St; ⏰ 24hr) Emergency services.

Money

Banks with 24-hour ATMs can be found along Ala Malama Ave. **Bank of Hawai'i** (☎ 553-3273; Ala Malama Ave) is the largest.

Post

Post office (☎ 553-5845; Ala Malama Ave) The one out west is more fun (see p457).

Tourist Information

Moloka'i Visitor Center (www.visitmolokai.com) A website with excellent links.

Moloka'i Visitors Association (MVA; ☎ 553-3876, 800-800-6367; www.molokai-hawaii.com; 2 Kamoi St; ⏰ 8am-4:30pm Mon-Fri) This simple office can help with information about member businesses.

SIGHTS

Kaunakakai is its own attraction. Specifically look for gems of old buildings such as the **Moloka'i Library** (Ala Malama Ave), which dates from 1937. **Kaunakakai Wharf** is the busy commercial lifeline for Moloka'i. Okay, it's not that busy... A freight barge chugs in, skippers unload catches of mahimahi (white-fleshed fish also called 'dolphin'), and a buff gal practices for

a canoe race. A roped-off area with a floating dock provides a kiddie swim area. On the west side of the wharf, near the canoe shed, are the stone foundations of oceanfront **Kamehameha V house**, now overgrown. The house was once called 'Malama,' which today is the name of Kaunakakai's main street through town.

As Moloka'i was the favorite island playground of King Kamehameha V, he had the royal 10-acre **Kapua'iwa Coconut Grove** (Map pp440–1) planted near his sacred bathing pools in the 1860s. Standing tall, about a mile west of downtown, its name means 'mysterious taboo.' Be careful where you walk (or park) when you visit, because coconuts frequently plunge silently to the ground, landing with a deadly thump.

Across the highway is **Church Row** (Map pp440–1). Any denomination that attracts a handful of members receives its own little tract of land here. The number of churches will tell you how big that religion is here. Look for **St Sophia Church** (Map pp440–1), a little wooden gem built with the hard-won earnings of immigrant Catholic pineapple workers. It's been named one of Hawaii's most endangered historic sites as the present congregation hopes to replace it with a new building by 2012.

Three miles east of town, **One Ali'i Beach Park** (Map pp440–1) is split into two parks. Side I has a coconut palm–lined shore, a playing field, a picnic pavilion and bathrooms, and although not especially attractive it's very popular with local families for the huge weekend BBQs. Two memorials commemorate the 19th-century immigration of Japanese citizens to Hawaii. Side II is a greener and more attractive picnic area. The water is shallow and silty.

The downtown **softball and baseball fields** are often the most active spot on the island. For some local flavor, go down there and cheer on the Moloka'i Farmers as they compete against their high-school rivals, the Lana'i Pinelads.

Moloka'i has a burgeoning foodie scene. Some noteworthy sea salt is produced close to the center in the front yard of a house belonging to well-known (among salties) salt-maker Nancy Gove. Her **Pacifica Hawai'i** (☎ 553-8484; www.pacificahawaii.com; Kolapa Pl) salt comes in various flavors – ask for a sample of smoked salt. Tours ($12.50, one hour, by appointment) reveal that there are more mysteries to making salt from ocean water than you'd imagine.

MOLOKA'I

ACTIVITIES

While activities in Kaunakakai proper are limited, it is *the* place to rent gear or arrange tours.

Moloka'i Fish & Dive (☎ 553-5926, 336-1088; www .molokaifishanddive.com; Ala Malama Ave; ☽ 8am-6pm Mon-Sat, to 2pm Sun) has a shop that's worth a stop for its eclectic array of goods, even if you're not planning an activity. Its full range of rental gear is on display (mask and fins per day/ week $10/35, fishing pole $13/35, beach chair $5/20). For details on its vast range of tours and activities, see p439.

Kaunakakai Gym (☎ 553-5141; Mitchell Pauole Center; ☽ 11am-3pm Mon-Fri, 10am-3pm Sat) has an indoor swimming pool. There are also two outdoor tennis courts, free to the public. You're not likely to have to fight the crowds for a court.

FESTIVALS & EVENTS

If you're planning a visit during these culture-rich festivals, make sleeping reservations many months in advance. See www.molokaievents .com for more details.

Ka Moloka'i Makahiki (☎ 553-3673) Moloka'i is the only island still holding the ancient *makahiki* festival. It is celebrated in late January with traditional ceremony, an Olympics-esque competition of ancient Hawaiian sports, crafts and activities.

Moloka'i Ka Hula Piko (www.molokaievents.com/ka hulapiko) As Moloka'i is known as the birthplace of hula, its hula festival in May has some profound roots. It opens with a solemn ceremony at 3am at Pu'u Nana (the site of Hawaii's first hula school), followed by a day-long festival including performance, food and crafts.

Na Wahine O Ke Kai (www.nawahineokekai.com) Much the same as the Moloka'i Hoe (see below), but with all-female teams. Best time (2004): 5 hours, 22 minutes, 11 seconds. Held in late September.

Moloka'i Hoe (www.molokaihoe.org) Grueling outrigger canoe race from remote Hale O Lono Point, with six-person teams paddling furiously across the 41-mile Ka'iwi Channel to O'ahu. Best time (2008): 4 hours, 38 minutes, 35 seconds. Considered the world championship of men's long-distance outrigger canoe racing. Held in October.

SLEEPING

Few travellers actually stay in Kaunakakai. Most stay further along the coasts near the beaches and ocean. For full details on Moloka'i accommodations, see the boxed text, opposite.

A'ahi Place Bed & Breakfast (☎ 553-8033; www .molokai.com/aahi; cabins $35) This very simple, clean cedar cottage is in a small subdivision, 1 mile east of Kaunakakai. Kind of like a camp cabin

(with lots of wood paneling), this place has a full kitchen, washing machine and garden lanai (veranda). More than two people will feel crowded, whether in the barebones 'back-packers cabin' or the somewhat more swank main cabin. Breakfast is $10.

Ka Hale Mala (☎ /fax 553-9009; www.molokai-bnb .com; apt $80, incl breakfast $90) Enjoy the spacious-ness of a 900-sq-ft, one-bedroom apartment with a fully equipped kitchen and living room with an exposed-beam ceiling. The two-story house is secluded by lush plant-ings, including trees laden with low-hanging fruit. The owners add to the bounty with or-ganic vegetables and beautiful breakfasts. Rates are for two people; extra persons (up to two) are $20. It's about 5 miles east of Kaunakakai and the charming owners do airport and ferry pick-ups.

Hotel Moloka'i (Map pp440-1; ☎ 553-5347, 800-535-0085; www.hotelmolokai.com; Kamehameha V Hwy; r $120-220; ☞ ☒) It's easy to call Moloka'i's only hotel a survivor, given it outlasted interlopers in the west. But it does have a certain veteran feel about it, from the quirky rooms with a faux-native design that gives them tunnel-like qualities, to the compact grounds with a small pool and hammocks along the reef-protected limpid, silty shore. Upstairs rooms are slightly larger and brighter; some units have fridges and microwaves.

Marc Moloka'i Shores (Map pp440-1; ☎ 553-5954, res-ervations 800-535-0085; www.marcresorts.com; Kamehameha V Hwy; 1br $125-200, 2br $150-250; ☒) Managed by the same outfit as the Hotel Moloka'i, this 1970s condo development has units ranging from atrocious to charming, depending on the whims of the individual owners. If you decide to stay here, choose your unit very carefully. All have full kitchens, cable TV, lanai and ceil-ing fans. The grounds are the best feature and have a large pool, shuffleboard, BBQ areas and more. Like elsewhere on this stretch of coast, the water is shallow and muddy.

Although camping is permitted at One Ali'i Beach Park (p445), drawbacks include strong winds, no privacy from the highway and late-night high jinks, and it's not recommended. See p439 for permit details.

EATING

Foodie sensations had passed by Moloka'i until recently. But there are glimmers of change here, with a few interesting options (including a great place in Kualapu'u and a fine lunch counter on the way to the Halawa Valley). But your best bet is to cook for yourself – the markets in Kaunakakai are well stocked and Moloka'i has some unique foods (see the boxed text, p448).

Budget

The snack bar inside Outpost Natural Foods (p448) is good.

Kamoi Snack-N-Go (☎ 553-5790; Moloka'i Professional Bldg, Kamoi St; scoops $2; ☼ 10am-9pm Mon-Sun) This candy store is loaded with sweets and, more importantly, Honolulu-made Dave's Hawaiian Ice Cream. The banana fudge is truly a treat.

Kanemitsu Bakery (☎ 553-5855; Ala Malama Ave; ☼ 5:30am-6:30pm Wed-Mon) Famous throughout the islands for its Moloka'i sweetbread and lavosh crackers (the macnut ones are extraordinary). Otherwise, you'll be surprised such good stuff can come from such a drab place. Every night but Monday, slip down the alley to the bakery's back door at 10pm and buy hot loaves, sliced open with one of five spreads, from the taciturn baker. Note: the best stuff is often gone by 1pm each day.

Moloka'i Drive-Inn (☎ 553-5655; Kamehameha V Hwy; meals $3-7; ☼ 6am-10pm) Always popular, this timeless fast-food counter is best for classic plate lunches and simple local pleasures like teri-beef sandwiches, omelettes with Spam or Vienna lunch meat and fried saimin noodles. Serious talking story and gossip entertains while you wait.

ourpick Little Grass Shack (Ala Malama Ave; plate lunches $8; ☼ 11am-2pm Mon-Fri) Fish landed at the dock down the road are turned into works of simple culinary art in this unprepossessing trailer that sets up on a vacant lot weekdays at lunch. The Shack's fish tacos couldn't be fresher and its sauces pack both punch and creative flavors. For extra kick, dozens of hot sauces are arrayed near the patio tables and chairs.

Oviedo's (☎ 553-5014; Ala Malama Ave; mains $11; ☼ 10am-5:30pm Mon-Fri, to 4:30pm Sat & Sun) A local treasure, this Filipino place has seen thousands cross through its banging screen door for a selection of stews and other long-cooked tender meats like succulent roasted pork. The pork *adobo* (meat cooked in vinegar, *shōyu*, garlic and spices) packs a punch, while the pig feet, tripe stew and turkey tail are for connoisseurs. Portions are large enough to share.

Midrange

Moloka'i Pizza Cafe (☎ 553-3288; Kaunakakai Pl; meals $9-15; ☼ 10am-10pm Mon-Thu, to 11pm Fri & Sat, 11am-10pm Sun) Order at the counter or have a seat in the unadorned dining area, at this pizza joint offering everything from salad and sub sandwiches to burgers and pasta. Divert yourself with a festival of coin-operated games with dubious 'prizes.' Lazy cooks get their pizza half-baked (it's neither thick, thin, nor even just right) and finish cooking it in their rental unit.

SLEEPING ON MOLOKA'I

Moloka'i's hotel choices are limited to one, in Kaunakakai. Almost everybody stays in a B&B, cottage, condo or house. Quality ranges from rustic to swank, with the best places having private grounds located right on the ocean. Listings are found throughout this chapter, although the nicest properties are usually in the verdant and coastal east. (With the closure of Moloka'i Ranch, condos in the west can seem desolate.) For information on camping, see p439. There are no hostels.

Maui County has had a running battle with private owners who want to do vacation rentals. Primarily this is due to complaints on Maui and not on Moloka'i but county rules still rule here (and are another reason that locals feel under-represented politically). Although condos are legally in the clear, the situation is somewhat murkier for houses and B&Bs. Most owners ignore the law and at the time of research no effort had been made to enforce it on Moloka'i.

Some good sources of rental and accommodation information and reservations:

Friendly Isle Realty (☎ 553-3666, 800-600-4158; www.molokairesorts.com; 75 Ala Malama Ave) Books for more than 70 condos island-wide.

Moloka'i Vacation Properties (☎ 553-8334, 800-367-2984; www.molokai-vacation-rental.com) Well-respected local agent with houses and condos.

Vacation Rentals By Owner (www.vrbo.com) Over 100 listings island-wide, from $55 to $1200 per night (average $125).

Paddler's Inn (☎ 553-5256; 10 Mohala St, mains $8-20; ⏰ 7am-2am) This casual bar with the large concrete beer garden has a long menu that's served until about 9pm. There are few surprises, from the deep-fried pub grub to the burgers, steaks and simple pastas. Service is surprisingly crisp, a quality you may lack after a few runs at the vast cocktail menu.

Hula Shores (Map pp440-1; ☎ 553-5347; Hotel Moloka'i, Kamehameha V Hwy; breakfasts & lunches $5-9, dinners $14-20; ⏰ 7-10:30am & 11am-2pm daily, 6-9pm Sat-Thu, 4-9pm Fri) You can't beat the oceanfront location but you can beat the food at Hotel Moloka'i's restaurant. Breakfasts are best; try the banana pancakes made with fruit from just up the road. Lunch and dinner is a mixed bag of sandwiches, salads and mains like chicken with a sauce, fish with a sauce etc. The views of Lana'i, the tiki torches and the sound of the small waves divert your attention.

Markets

Friendly Market (☎ 553-5595; Ala Malama Ave; ⏰ 8:30am-8:30pm Mon-Fri, to 6:30pm Sat) The best selection of any supermarket on the island. In the afternoon fresh fish from the docks appears.

Moloka'i Wines & Spirits (☎ 553-5009; Ala Malama Ave; ⏰ 9am-8pm Sun-Thu, to 9pm Fri & Sat) Has many Hawaiian and mainland microbrews plus inexpensive wines and upscale cheeses and deli items. This is the place to get all you need for silly tropical drinks. Fire up the blender!

Misaki's (☎ 553-5505; 78 Ala Malama Ave; ⏰ 8:30am-8:30pm Mon-Sat, 9am-noon Sun) The long hours are the key to success at this living museum of grocery retailing.

Outpost Natural Foods (☎ 553-3377; 70 Makaena Pl; ⏰ 9am-6pm Mon-Thu, to 4pm Fri, 10am-5pm Sun) Organic produce, a good selection of packaged and bulk health foods and excellent local fare. Its deli (meals $4 to $6, open 10am to 3pm weekdays) makes fresh vegetarian burritos, sandwiches, salads and smoothies.

The Saturday morning market (see opposite) is a good source for local produce and prepared foods. Bamboo Pantry (opposite) has specialty foods.

DRINKING & ENTERTAINMENT

Bring board games, books and a gift for gab as nighttime fun is mostly DIY on Moloka'i.

Paddler's Inn (left) serves booze inside and out until 2am. On Friday nights there is often a live Hawaiian band; at other times satellite sports prevails.

Out at the Hotel Moloka'i, Hula Shores (left) has a simple bar and is popular for a sunset drink at least once. On many nights there is live music or, for those dreaming the impossible dream, karaoke. But the real draw are the local *kapuna* (elders) who gather at a long table to play Hawaiian music on 'Aloha Fridays' from 4pm to 6pm. It always draws a crowd and the performers range from those with some languid and traditional hula moves to jam sessions with a ukulele.

Most rentals have DVD players. Although you can rent DVDs from **Mango Mart** (☎ 553-8170; Ala Malama Ave; ⏰ 8am-8pm Mon-Sat, to 6pm Sun), you are better off bringing your own unless your tastes run towards flicks rarely mentioned on Oscar night.

TOP PICKS – LOCAL TREATS

Fruit trees grow in profusion in the east end of Moloka'i; if you're lucky you'll have plenty to pick from your rental. Organic farms are sprouting as well and you'll find their produce at the Saturday morning market (opposite) and at Outpost Natural Foods (above) in Kaunakakai. Other local foods to look for:

- **Moloka'i Coffee Company coffee** (p456), grown and roasted on the island
- **Kumu Farms Macadamia Nut Pesto** at Friendly Market (above), superb and bursting with basil goodness
- **lavosh** from Kanemitsu Bakery (p447) – the macadamia nut and taro varieties are crunchy and delicious
- **Molokai Roadside Marinade**, sold at Friendly Market (above) – turns any steak into a succulent, tangy treat
- **Pacifica Hawai'i sea salt** (p445)
- **Purdy's macadamia nuts** (p456)

SHOPPING

Saturday morning market (Ala Malama Ave; 8am-2pm) This weekly market at the west end of Ala Malama Ave is the place to browse local crafts, try new fruits, stock up on organic produce and pick up some flowers. You'll find much of Moloka'i here before noon.

Bamboo Pantry (553-3300; 107 Ala Malama Ave; 9:30am-5:30pm Mon-Fri, to 3:30pm Sat) Gourmet and fancy packaged foods share shelf space with various cookbooks, kitchen gadgets and housewares.

Moloka'i Artists' & Crafters' Guild (553-8520; 2nd fl, Moloka'i Center, 110 Ala Malama Ave; 9:30am-5pm Mon-Fri, 9am-2:30pm Sat) Run by local artists, this small shop is as packed with art as a Jackson Pollock painting is packed with brushstrokes. Works in all mediums are here and quality ranges from the earnest to the superb. The T-shirts with local sayings are the real sleepers in the souvenir department.

GETTING THERE & AROUND

Kaunakakai is a walking town. **Rawlin's Chevron** (553-3214; cnr Hwy 460 & Ala Malama Ave; 6:30am-8:30pm Mon-Sat, 7am-6pm Sun) offers credit card–operated pumps, making it the only round-the-clock gas station on the island.

EAST MOLOKA'I

The oft-quoted road sign 'Slow down, this is Moloka'i' really applies as you head east. Whether you are on the island for a day or a week, the 27-mile drive on Hwy 450 (aka Kamehameha V Hwy) from Kaunakakai to the Halawa Valley is simply a must.

Unlike the arid west, this is tropical Moloka'i, with palm trees arching over the road and banana, papaya, guava and passion fruits hanging from the lush foliage ripe for the picking. As you drive, you'll catch glimpses of ancient fishponds, the neighboring islands of Lana'i and Maui, stoic old wooden churches, modest family homes, beaches and much more. But don't take your eye off the road for long or you'll run over a dog sleeping on the yellow line.

This being Moloka'i, this intoxicating drive is rarely crowded and cars tend to mosey. Of course for the final third, when the smoothly paved road narrows down to one sinuous lane, you have little choice but to slow down, but that's just as well, as each curve yields a new

> **MOLOKA'I FOR CHILDREN**
> - Free sport kite-flying lessons at the **Big Wind Kite Factory** (p462)
> - Rent a house for running-around room, plus usually a TV, DVD and often games
> - Explore under the sea in the calm, shallow waters of **Twenty Mile Beach** (p451)

vista. The final climb up and over into the remote Halawa Valley is breathtaking.

On the practical side, bring gear so you can swim and snorkel at beaches that catch your fancy along the way. There's no gas east of Kaunakakai but there is an excellent small grocery and lunch counter about halfway, in Puko'o. Most of the choicest rentals are found along the drive; see the boxed text, p447, for a list of agents. Mile markers make it easy to find things.

KAWELA

Kakahaia Beach Park is a grassy strip wedged between the road and sea in Kawela, shortly before the 6-mile marker. It has a couple of picnic tables and is always popular for that high point in the local's weekend calendar: the family picnic. This park is the only part of the **Kakahai'a National Wildlife Refuge** (www.fws.gov/kakahaia) open to the public. Most of the 20-acre refuge is inland from the road. It includes freshwater marshland, with a dense growth of bulrushes and an inland freshwater fishpond that has been expanded to provide a home for endangered birds, including the Hawaiian stilt and coot.

KAMALO

Even if you are already married, swear you won't get married, or have no one to marry, you'll be swept away by the quaint charm of little **St Joseph's Church**, one of only two of the four island churches that missionary and prospective saint, Father Damien, built outside of the Kalaupapa Peninsula that still stand (the other, Our Lady of Seven Sorrows, is 4 miles further on; see p450). This simple, one-room wooden church, dating from 1876, has a steeple and a bell, five rows of pews and some of the original wavy glass panes. A lei-draped statue of Father Damien and a little cemetery are beside the church. It is just past the 10-mile marker, where the road – like the snakes St Patrick chased out of Scotland – becomes sinuous.

Just over three-quarters of a mile after the 11-mile marker, a small sign, on the *makai* (seaward) side of the road, notes the **Smith-Bronte Landing**, the site where pilot Ernest Smith and navigator Emory Bronte safely crash-landed their plane at the completion of the world's first civilian flight from the US mainland to Hawaii. The pair left California on July 14, 1927, destined for O'ahu and came down on Moloka'i 25 hours and two minutes later. A little memorial plaque is set among the kiawe trees and grasses.

'UALAPU'E

A half-mile beyond Wavecrest Resort condo development, at the 13-mile marker, you'll spot **'Ualapu'e Fishpond** on the *makai* side of the road. This fishpond has been restored and restocked with mullet and milkfish, two species that were raised here in ancient times. It's a good place to ponder the labor involved in moving these thousands of volcanic rocks.

With a striking view of green mountains rising up behind, and the ocean lapping gently out front, the **Wavecrest Resort** (www.wavecrest aoao.com; 1br per day/week from $100/600, 2br $150/800; 🖥) is just around the bend on a small drive in from the main road. This place is as low-key as its host island. There is no beach but the views are sweeping. Each unit is rented

FISH IN A POND

Starting just east of Kaunakakai and continuing past the 20-mile marker are dozens of *loko i'a* (fishponds), huge circular walls of rocks that are part of one of the world's most advanced forms of aquaculture. Monumental in size, backbreaking in creation, the fishponds operate on a simple principal: little fish swim in, big fish can't swim out. Some are obscured and overgrown by mangroves but others have been restored by locals anxious to preserve this link to their past. The **Kahinapohaku fishpond**, about half a mile past the 19-mile marker, is in excellent shape and is tended to by *konohiki* (caretakers) who live simply on site. Another good one is at the 13-mile marker in 'Ualapu'e.

(and decorated) by the owner. Find links on the website or go through one of the agents (see the boxed text, p447). All units have full kitchen, sofa bed, lanai or balcony, and use of the tennis court.

KALUA'AHA

The barely perceptible village of Kalua'aha is less than 2 miles past Wavecrest. The ruins of **Kalua'aha Church**, Moloka'i's first Christian church, are a bit off the road and inland but just visible, if you keep an eye peeled. It was built in 1844 by Moloka'i's first missionary, Harvey R Hitchcock. **Our Lady of Seven Sorrows** (☽ service 7:15am Sun) is a church a quarter of a mile past the Kalua'aha Church site. The present Our Lady of Sorrows is a reconstruction from 1966 of the original wood-frame building, constructed in 1874 by the missionary Father Damien.

'ILI'ILI'OPAE HEIAU

Where's Unesco when you need it? 'Ili'ili'opae is Moloka'i's biggest heiau, and is thought to be the second largest in Hawaii. It also might possibly be the oldest religious site in the state. Yet this remarkable treasure is barely known, even by many locals.

The dimensions are astonishing: over 300ft long and 100ft wide, and about 22ft high on the eastern side, and 11ft high at the other end. The main platform is strikingly level. Archaeologists believe the original heiau may have been three times its current size, reaching out beyond Mapulehu Stream. Like the fishponds, this heiau represents an extraordinary amount of labor by people with no real tools at their disposal.

Once a *luakini* (temple of human sacrifice), 'Ili'ili'opae is today silent except for the singing of birds. African tulip and mango trees line the trail to the site, a peaceful place filled with mana (spiritual essence), whose stones still seem to emanate vibrations of a mystical past. Remember: it's disrespectful to walk across the top of the heiau.

Visiting this heiau is a little tricky, since it's on private property. Park on the highway (to avoid upsetting the neighbors) and walk up the short dirt path. Pass the roundabout around a patch of trees, and continue up the rocky road. Soon after, you'll see a trail on the left-hand side, opposite a house, that will take you across a streambed. Head to the steps on the northern side of the heiau.

LIVE LIKE A LOCAL

You've probably noticed that most of what there is to do on Moloka'i happens outdoors and often involves group functions. So how do you hook up with the local folks, that is, talk some story and get a feel for local culture? Start with *Molokai Dispatch,* which lists events of all kinds, including school benefits, church events or 4-H livestock competitions. Then go buy some crafts, get a taste of some home cooking, or cheer on your favorite heifer. Other good sources in Kaunakakai are the bulletin boards outside Friendly Market (p448), Outpost Natural Foods (p448) and the library (p445). There are inevitably community groups selling goods to raise money along Ala Malama Ave; have a chat with these folk. Ball games at softball and baseball fields are also real community events.

If you're lucky you'll enjoy an experience we had a few years back when we dropped by a Democratic Party picnic at the softball field and ended up talking story for a long while with Senator Daniel Inouye, an unforgettable experience that would have been tough to replicate on other islands where the crowds would have been larger and possibly more unctuous.

The turnoff is on the *mauka* (inland) side of the highway, just over half a mile past the 15-mile marker, immediately after Mapulehu Bridge. Look for the dirt track into the trees and a fire hydrant. For more info about crossing the property, call **Pearl Hodgins** (☎ 336-0378).

PUKO'O

Puko'o was once the seat of local government (complete with a courthouse, jail, wharf and post office), but the center of island life shifted to Kaunakakai when the plantation folks built that more centrally located town. Nowadays, Puko'o is a sleepy, slow-paced gathering of a few structures just sitting on a bend on the road (near 'Ili'ili'opae Heiau), but has surprises like the cozy **beach** accessible just before the store, near the 16-mile marker. Take the short, curving path around the small bay, where fish leap out of the water, and you'll come to a stretch of sand with swimmable waters, backed by kiawe (relative of the mesquite tree) and ironwood trees.

Sleeping & Eating

Hilltop Cottage (☎ 558-8161, 336-2076; www.molokai hilltopcottage.com; Kamehameha V Hwy; cottage $140; 🖳) Instead of sleeping down near the water, put your head in the clouds here. The wraparound lanai is almost as big as the living space and you can savor the views of the neighbor islands by day or the millions of stars drowned out by light in cities and suburbs by night. There's one nicely furnished bedroom, a full kitchen, laundry facilities and a four-night minimum stay.

ourpick Mana'e Goods & Grindz (☎ 558-8498; 16-mile marker, Kamehameha V Hwy; meals $4-9; 🕑 8am-5pm). Even if it wasn't your only option, you'd still want to stop here. The plate lunches here are something of a local legend: tender yet crispy chicken katsu (deep-fried fillets), specials like pork and peas, and standards like excellent teriyaki burgers. Sauces are homemade, the potato salad superb and the mac salad is simply the island's best (it's not too gloopy). Picnic tables are shaded by trees and there's a little garden nearby. The store manages to pack an amazing amount of groceries, goods and a few DVDs in a small space. The bit of Hwy 450 between the entrance and exit to the parking area is easily the least used stretch.

WAIALUA

After a few bends along the increasingly rugged coast, Waialua is a little roadside community just past the 19-mile marker. The attractive **Waialua Congregational Church** was built of stone in 1855. Onward north from there, the road is wafer-thin, winding its way through an undulating coast that's forlorn, mysterious and fronted by white-flecked turquoise surf. The well-tended **Kahinapohaku fishpond** (see the boxed text, opposite) is a half-mile past the 19-mile marker.

There are few prizes for guessing what mile marker is found at **Twenty Mile Beach**, although its alias, Murphy's Beach, might keep you guessing. Well protected by a reef, the curve of fine sand fronts a large lagoon that is great for **snorkeling**. Near shore there are rocks and the water can be very shallow, but work your way out and you'll be rewarded with schools of fish, living sponges, octopuses and much more.

The pointy clutch of rocks sticking out, as the road swings left before the 21-mile marker, is called **Rock Point** (aka Pohakuloa Point). This popular surf spot is the site of local competitions and it's the place to go if you're looking for east-end breaks. The recent burst of creativity in place names extends to the fine little swimming cove about 500yd beyond the 21-yard marker: **Sandy Beach** (aka Kumimi Beach). Look for a taro farm back in a verdant notch in the coast near here.

Sleeping

Some of Moloka'i's more popular rental houses are here. All offer your own little stretch of reef-protected beach, lots of privacy and nighttime views of the resorts, shops and traffic jams of Ka'anapali (Maui) flickering across the Pailolo Channel.

Waialua Pavilion & Campground (☎ 558-8150; eeejsimms@aloha.net; Kamehameha V Hwy; sites per person $10) The Congregational Church maintains a small grassy, oceanfront area with BBQ grills, bathrooms and showers. It's a serene spot with views to sea and heaven, with only the occasional passing 4WD disturbing the peace.

Dunbar Beachfront Cottages (☎ 558-8153, 800-673-0520; www.molokai-beachfront-cottages.com; Kamehameha V Hwy; 2-bedroom cottages $170) The layout and furnishings are tidy and functional at these two vacation cottages near the 18-mile marker. Each cottage sleeps four people and comes with fully equipped kitchen, TV, VCR, ceiling fans, laundry, lanai and barbecue grills. The Pu'unana unit sits on stilts, while Pauwalu is more grounded. Both have good views.

Moloka'i Beach House (☎ 261-2500, 888-575-9400; www.molokaibeachhouse.com; Kamehameha V Hwy; per day/week $250/1600; 🖳) Like most of the houses in the east, this simple wooden affair holds a few surprises. Here it is rooms that follow one after another until you realize you've got three bedrooms and a huge living/family room. It's not posh but it's very relaxed. There's cable and highspeed internet, plus the usual DVD, BBQ etc. The grassy yard backs up to a narrow palm-shaded beach.

Aloha Beach House (☎ 828-1100, 888-828-1008; www.molokaivacation.com; Kamehameha V Hwy; per day/week $290/2135; 🖳) Recently built in traditional plantation style, a breezeway links the two bedrooms. The excellent kitchen flows into the living room, which flows out onto the large covered porch, which flows onto the lawn and the beach and... There's cable internet and lots of beach toys. It's just past the 19-mile marker, next to the campground and close to Moloka'i Beach House.

WAIALUA TO HALAWA

After the 22-mile marker the road starts to wind upwards. It's a good paved road, albeit very narrow. Take it slow and watch for other cars coming around the cliff-hugging corners; there's always a place to pull over so you can pass.

The terrain is rockier and less verdant here than over the preceding miles. The road levels out just before the 24-mile marker, where there's a view of the spiky islet of **Mokuho'oniki**, a seabird sanctuary and natural photo spot. If you hear a boom, it's a hapless gull setting off one of the shells left over from WWII target practice.

As you crest the hill, the fenced grassland is part of **Pu'u O Hoku Ranch** (☎ 558-8109; www.puuohoku.com; 2-bedroom cottage per day/week $140/840, 4-bedroom house $160/960; 🖳), which at 14,000 acres, is Moloka'i's second-largest ranch. Founded by Paul Fagan of Hana, the name means 'where hills and stars meet.' Guests who stay here enjoy views across the Pacific, and absolute isolation. A lodge that sleeps you and 21 of your closest friends is available for $1250 per night. There is a three-night minimum stay.

The ranch is also a certified **organic farm** growing tropical fruits and 'awa (kava, a native plant used to make an intoxicating drink). If you are staying in one of the east Moloka'i rentals, they will drop off a 10lb box of organic fruits and vegetables ($25) on their way to town on Thursdays; otherwise their goods can be found at Kaunakakai's Saturday morning market (p449). A small **store** (🕘 9am-5pm Mon-Fri) along the road has snacks, drinks and some of the ranch's fine produce.

A hidden grove of sacred *kukui* (candlenut trees) on the ranch property marks the grave of the prophet Lanikaula, a revered 16th-century kahuna (priest, healer). One of the reasons the battling armies of Maui and O'ahu steered clear of Moloka'i for centuries was the powerful reputations of kahuna like Lanikaula, who were said to have been able to pray their enemies to death. Many islanders claim to have seen the night lanterns of ghost marchers bobbing along near the grove.

Past the 25-mile marker, the jungle closes in, and the scent of eucalyptus fills the air.

About 1.25 miles further on, you round a corner and the fantastic panorama of the Halawa Valley sweeps into view. Stop and enjoy the view for a bit. Depending on recent rains, the Moa'ula and Hipuapua Falls will either be thin strands or gushing white torrents back up the valley. In winter, look across the swirl of waves and volcanic sand below for the spectacle of whales breaching.

The recently paved road descends into the valley at a steep but manageable rate. Cyclists will love the entire ride, with the exception of staying alert for errant drivers in rental cars mesmerized by the views.

HALAWA VALLEY

Halawa Valley enjoys end-of-the-road isolation, which residents guard jealously, and stunningly gorgeous scenery. It was an important settlement in pre-contact Moloka'i, with a population of over 1000 and a complex irrigation system watering over 700 taro patches. Little remains of its three heiau sites, two of which are thought to have been *luakini,* and you'll probably feel the charge down here.

As late as the mid-19th century, the fertile valley had a population of about 500 and produced most of Moloka'i's taro, as well as many of its melons, gourds and fruits. Taro production came to an abrupt end in 1946, when a massive tsunami swept up the Halawa Valley, wiping out the farms and much of the community. A second tsunami washed the valley clean in 1957. Only a few families now remain.

Sights & Activities

It's possible to swim at the base of the 250-foot, twin **Moa'ula and Hipuapua Falls**, which cascade down the back of this lush valley. They are reached via a straightforward 2-mile trail lined with historical sites. To protect these sites, and because the trail crosses private property, visiting the falls requires a **hike** with a local guide. The $80-per-person fee includes a wealth of cultural knowledge and walks can easily take five hours. Prepare for muddy conditions and wear stout shoes so you can navigate over river boulders. You may be able to organize a guide with **local residents** (☎ 553-9803), through **Kalani Pruet** (☎ 336-1149) or with the ever-present Moloka'i Fish & Dive (p439). Prepare for voracious mosquitoes.

Sunday services are still occasionally held in Hawaiian at the saintly little 1948 green-and-white **church**, where visitors are welcome anytime (the door remains open). Nearby, don't be surprised if you see a bucket filled with fabulous heliconias and other stunning tropical flowers that are yours for the taking. They are grown by **Kalani Pruet** (☎ 336-1149; kalanipruet@yahoo.com), who runs a flower farm, offers waterfall hikes and makes a mean smoothie from fruit he gathers.

Halawa Beach was a favored surfing spot for Moloka'i chiefs, and remains so today for local kids, although often you won't see a soul. The beach has double coves separated by a rocky outcrop, with the north side a bit more protected than the south. When the water is calm, there's good swimming and folks launch sea kayaks here, but both coves are subject to dangerous rip currents when the surf is heavy.

Up from the beach, Halawa Beach Park has picnic pavilions, restrooms and nondrinkable running water. Throughout the valley, there's an eerie feel that you can't quite shake, as if the generations that came before aren't sure what to make of it all. Some locals aren't entirely welcoming of visitors.

CENTRAL MOLOKA'I

Central Moloka'i is really two places. In the west there's the dry and gently rolling Ho'olehua Plains, which stretch from the remote and rare sand dunes of Mo'omomi Beach to the former plantation town and current coffee-growing center of Kualapu'u. To the east, the terrain rises sharply to the misty, ancient forests of Kamakou. Enjoy one of the island's great adventures here by going on a hike that takes you back in evolutionary time.

After the Halawa Valley drive in the east, Moloka'i's most popular drive runs from Kualapu'u (with its superb little café) up Hwy 470 to Pala'au State Park, site of the Kalaupapa Overlook, where you'll find one of the island's most captivating views.

KAMAKOU AREA

The best reason to rent a 4WD vehicle on Moloka'i is to thrill to the views from the Waikolu Lookout before venturing into the verdant mysteries of the Nature Conservancy's Kamakou Preserve, where

---

DETOUR: MOLOKA'I'S PALI COAST

The world's tallest sea *pali* (cliffs) rise from the Pacific for an awe-inspiring 14 miles from the Kalaupapa Peninsula, in central Moloka'i, east almost to Halawa Beach. The average drop of these sheer cliffs is 2000ft, with some reaching 3300ft. And these intimidating walls are not monolithic; vast valleys roaring with waterfalls cleave the dark rock faces. It's Moloka'i's most dramatic sight and also the most difficult to see.

From land, you can get an idea of the drama in the valleys from the remote **Waikolu Lookout** (opposite) and the **Pelekunu Valley Overlook** (opposite) in the Kamakou area.

But to really appreciate the cliffs, you won't want to settle for the backsides. From the Pacific you can get a full appreciation of their height. You can organize a **boat trip** (p443) or really earn your adventure cred by paddling yourself here in a **kayak** (p439). In summer when conditions allow, you can leave from Halawa Beach (p453) but this is only for expert kayakers and will require a few days plus camping on isolated stone beaches. You can get advice from Moloka'i Fish & Dive (p439).

A visit to **Kalaupapa Peninsula** (p458) also gives you an idea of the spectacle. Or you can appreciate the drama of the cliffs from the air. Many of Maui's **helicopter tours** (p366) include Moloka'i's Pali Coast.

---

you'll find the island's highest peaks. Exploring this secret side of Moloka'i is an unforgettable experience. Besides gazing down into two deep valleys on the island's stunning and impenetrable north coast, you'll explore a near-pristine rain forest that is home to more than 250 native plants (over 200 endemic) and some of Hawaii's rarest birds. Although you won't reach the island's highest point, 4961ft of Kamakou Peak, you'll still get your head in the clouds.

Orientation

The turnoff for the Kamakou Area is between the 3- and 4-mile markers on Hwy 460, immediately east of the Manawainui Bridge. The paved turnoff is marked with a sign for the Homelani Cemetery. The pavement quickly ends, and the road deteriorates into 4WD-only conditions.

About 5.5 miles from Hwy 460 and well past the cemetery, you'll cross into the Moloka'i Forest Reserve. After a further 1.5 miles, there's an old water tank and reservoir off to the left. Another 2 miles brings you to the Sandalwood Pit, and one mile past that to Waikolu Lookout and the boundary of the Kamakou Preserve.

Moloka'i Forest Reserve

As you climb and enter the Moloka'i Forest Reserve, the landscape starts off shrubby and dusty, becoming dark, fragrant woods of tall eucalyptus, with patches of cypress and

Norfolk pines. Don't bother heading down the roads branching off Maunahui Rd, as the scenery will be exactly the same. Although there's no evidence of it from the road, the Kalamaula area was once heavily settled. It was here that Kamehameha the Great (Kamehameha I) knocked out his two front teeth in grieving the death of a female high chief, whom he had come to visit. Local lore says that women once traveled up here to bury their afterbirth in order to ensure that their offspring reached great heights.

If you're up for talking story with a longtime island character, and checking out his beautiful creations, stop at Robin Baker's **woodcarving shed**. You'll see his gates on the left.

SANDALWOOD PIT

A grassy depression on the left side of the road marks the centuries-old Sandalwood Pit (Lua Na Moku 'Iliahi). In the early 19th century, shortly after the lucrative sandalwood trade began, the pit was hand-dug to the exact measurements of a 100ft-long, 40ft-wide and 7ft-deep ship's hold, and filled with fragrant sandalwood logs cleared from the nearby forest.

The *ali'i* (royalty) forced the *maka'ainana* (commoners) to abandon their crops and work the forest. When the pit was full, the wood was strapped onto the backs of the laborers, who hauled it down to the harbor for shipment to China. After all the mature trees were cut down, the *maka'ainana* pulled up every new sapling, sparing their children the misery of forced harvesting.

WAIKOLU LOOKOUT

At 3600ft, Waikolu Lookout provides a breath-taking view into the steep Waikolu Valley and out to the ocean beyond. After rains, the white strands of numerous waterfalls accent the sheer cliffs and fill the valley with a dull roar. Morning is best for clear views, but if it's foggy, have a snack at the picnic bench and see if it clears.

The wide, grassy **Waikolu Lookout campground** is directly opposite the lookout. If you can bear the mist and cold winds that sometimes blow up from the canyon, this could make a base camp for hikes into the preserve. The site has a picnic pavilion. Bring water. No open fires are allowed and state camping permits are required (see p439).

Kamakou Preserve

Since 1982, the Nature Conservancy has managed the Kamakou Preserve, which includes cloud forest, bogs, shrub land and habitat for many endangered plants and animals. Its 2774 acres of native ecosystems start immediately beyond the Waikolu Lookout.

Much of the preserve is forested with 'ohi'a lehua, a native tree with fluffy red blossoms, whose nectar is favored by native birds. It is home to the 'apapane (bright red Hawaiian honeycreeper), 'amakihi (yellow-green honey-eater) and pueo (Hawaiian owl). Other treasures include tree ferns, native orchids and silvery lilies.

Hiking back through three million years of evolution on the **Pepe'opae Trail** is Kamakou's star attraction. This undisturbed Hawaiian montane bog is a miniature primeval forest of stunted trees, dwarfed plants and lichens that feels like it's the dawn of time. This bog receives about 180in of rain each year, making it one of the wettest regions in the Hawaiian

Islands. The trail ends at the **Pelekunu Valley Overlook**, where you'll enjoy a valley view of fantastic depth, and, if it's not foggy, the ocean beyond.

Almost the entire mile-long trail is along an extremely narrow boardwalk that feels at times like tightrope walking. It is covered with a coarse metal grating to prevent hikers from slipping, but you should still wear shoes with a good grip.

There are two ways to reach the Pepe'opae Trail from Waikolu Lookout. You can walk through the forest for an hour or drive about 2.5 miles along the main jeep road to the sign-posted trailhead. When in doubt, stay to the left, ignoring side roads.

Visitors should sign in and out at the preserve's entrance. Look for entries from others on everything from car breakdowns to trail conditions and bird sightings. Posted notices announce if any part of the preserve is closed. Bring rain gear, as the trails in Kamakou can be wet and muddy.

TOURS

Excellent monthly Saturday hikes with the **Nature Conservancy** (☎ 553-5236; www.nature.org/hawaii; Moloka'i Industrial Park, 23 Pueo Pl, Kualapu'u; suggested donation $25) explore the preserve's history and ecology. Transportation is provided. Hikes have an eight-person maximum and tend to book up several months in advance.

Getting There & Away

Kamakou is protected in its wilderness state in part because the rutted dirt road leading in makes it hell to reach. A 4WD vehicle is obligatory and even then the narrow, rutted track with its sheer edges and tendency to turn into a bog after rains is a challenge. Check conditions with the **Nature Conservancy**

GETTING THE GOAT (AND SAVING THE REEF)

Hunting on Moloka'i is done mostly for good reasons. Non-native feral goats, pigs and deer have run amok in the highlands and are voraciously chewing their way through the foliage. This has led to deforestation and greatly increased the runoff from the frequent rains. These flows of mud slop down to the south coast along the east end of Moloka'i, choking the Pala'au barrier reef, which in parts is massively degraded. Some of the old fishponds have been filling with silt at the rate of a foot per year. Talk about Indonesian butterflies! A goat eats a shrub on a remote Moloka'i peak and coral dies off the coast.

Locals have been encouraged to hunt the critters, especially the feral pigs, which often star in family BBQs. Still, amateur efforts are not enough and the Nature Conservancy has ferried hunters by helicopter to remote parts of the mountains.

office (☎ 553-5236; www.nature.org/hawaii). The 10-mile drive from Hwy 460 to Waikolu Lookout takes about 45 minutes to drive.

KUALAPU'U

Kualapu'u is the name of both a 1017ft hill, and a nearby village. In a fact that only a booster could love, the world's largest rubber-lined reservoir lies at the base of the hill. Its 1.4 billion gallons of water are piped in from the rain forests of eastern Moloka'i and it is the only source of water for the Ho'olehua Plains and the dry West End. Operations were threatened when its owner, the Moloka'i Ranch, ceased operations in 2008 (see the boxed text, p463).

In the '30s Del Monte's pineapple-plantation headquarters were located here and a company town grew. Pineapples ruled for nearly 50 years, until Del Monte pulled out of Moloka'i in 1982, and the economy crumbled.

While farm equipment rusted in overgrown pineapple fields, small-scale farming developed: watermelons, dryland taro, macadamia nuts, sweet potatoes, seed corn, string beans and onions. The soil is so rich here, some feel Moloka'i has the potential to be Hawaii's 'breadbasket.' In 1991 coffee saplings were planted on formerly fallow pineapple fields, and now cover some 600 acres.

The **Moloka'i Coffee Company** (☎ 567-9490; www.coffeesofhawaii.com; cnr Hwys 470 & 490; ⏰ 7am-5pm Mon-Fri, 8am-4pm Sat, to 2pm Sun) grows and roasts its own coffee. Stop by for a tour of the plant and savor the air redolent with rich smells. Tours, like the coffee, come in several flavors. There's a morning **walking tour** (adult/child $20/10; ⏰ tours 10am Mon-Fri, 9am Sat) and a mule-drawn **wagon tour** (adult/child $35/10; ⏰ tours 8am & 1pm Mon-Fri, 8am Sat). Ask about more-strenuous guided hikes.

Next to the grande-sized gift shop, the **Espresso Bar** (snacks $2-6) serves a range of drinks made with the house brew. There's also baked goods like doughnuts and Danishes, sandwiches and soup. The cakes are tasty. Relax on the shaded, breezy deck.

our pick **Kualapu'u Cookhouse** (☎ 567-9655; Hwy 490; meals $5-20; ⏰ 7am-8pm Tue-Sat, 9am-2pm Sun, 7am-2pm Mon), which is sometimes called the Kamuela Cookhouse, serves the island's best food. Looks are definitely deceiving at this simple wood house a couple of steps above shack status. Folding chairs feature inside, worn picnic tables and insect traps are out-side. Even the menu barely suggests what lies ahead. But when your plate lunch of the best and tenderest teriyaki beef you've ever had appears, you'll be hooked. Breakfasts are huge and feature perfect omelettes. Panko-crusted Monte Cristo sandwiches join the plate lunch brigade, while at dinner inventive fare like ahi in a lime cilantro sauce or perfectly juicy prime rib star. At night locals sometimes serenade with Hawaiian music. Beer and wine can be purchased at the grocery across the street.

HO'OLEHUA

Ho'olehua is the dry plains area that separates eastern and western Moloka'i. Here, in the 1790s, Kamehameha the Great trained his warriors in a year-long preparation for the invasion of O'ahu.

Ho'olehua was settled as an agricultural community in 1924, as part of the first distribution of land under the Hawaiian Homes Commission Act, which made public lands available to Native Hawaiians. Water was scarce in this part of Moloka'i and Ho'olehua pineapple farms drew settlers as the spiky fruit required little irrigation. But the locals were soon usurped by the pineapple giants Dole, Del Monte and Libby. Most were forced to lease their lands to the plantations.

Today the plantations are gone but locals continue to plant small crops of fruits, vegetables and herbs. And Hawaiians continue to receive land deeds in Ho'olehua in accordance with the Hawaiian Homes Commission Act.

Sights & Activities

PURDY'S MACADAMIA NUT FARM

our pick **Purdy's Macadamia Nut Farm tour** (☎ 567-6601; www.molokai-aloha.com/macnuts; admission free; ⏰ 9:30am-3:30pm Mon-Fri, 10am-2pm Sat) lets you poke your pick of macadamia nuts as Tuddie Purdy takes you into his 80-year-old orchard and personally explains how the nuts grow without pesticides, herbicides or fertilizers.

Everything is done in quaint Moloka'i style: you can crack open macadamia nuts on a stone you poke with a hammer and sample macadamia blossom honey scooped up with slices of fresh coconut. Nuts (superb!) and honey are for sale. Linger and Purdy will go into full raconteur mode.

To get to the farm, turn right onto Hwy 490 from Hwy 470. After 1 mile, take a right onto Lihi Pali Ave, just before the high school. The farm is a third of a mile up, on the right.

POST-A-NUT

Why settle for a mundane postcard, or worse an emailed photo of you looking like a tan-lined git, when it comes to taunting folks in the cold climes you've left behind? Instead, send a coconut. Gary, the world-class post-master of the **Ho'olehua post office** (☎ 567-6144; Pu'u Peelua Ave) has baskets of them for free. Choose from the oodles of markers and write the address right on the husk. Add a cartoon or two. Imagine the joy when a loved one waits in a long line for a parcel and is handed a coconut! Depending on the size of your nut, postage costs $8 to $12 and takes three to six days to reach any place in the US; other countries cost more and take longer.

MO'OMOMI BEACH

When you think of Hawai'i you think of beaches so it is surprising that the islands have very few sand dunes. One of the few un-disturbed, coastal sand-dune areas left in the state is found on remote Mo'omomi Beach. Among its native grasses and shrubs are at least four endangered plant species that exist nowhere else on earth, including a relative of the sunflower. It is one of the few places in the populated islands where green sea turtles still find suitable breeding habitat.

Managed by the Nature Conservancy, Mo'omomi is not lushly beautiful, but wind-swept, lonely and wild. It's a classic Moloka'i sight: alluring and worth the effort to visit. Follow Farrington Ave west, past the inter-section with Hwy 480, until the paved road ends. If you are in a regular car and it has been raining, your journey will end here as there is often a richly red mud swamp here.

When passable, it's 2.5 miles further along a dirt road that is in some areas quite smooth and in others deeply rutted. In places, you may have to skirt the edge of the road and straddle a small gully. It's ordinarily sort of passable in a standard car, although the higher the vehicle the better. It's definitely best to have a 4WD. If you get stuck in a car, you may gift your rental company with a windfall in fees and fines.

Look for the picnic pavilion that announces you've found **Mo'omomi Bay**, with a little sandy beach used by sunbathers. The rocky east-ern point, which protects the bay, provides a fishing perch, and further along the bluffs, a sacred ceremony might be under way. There are toilets, but no drinking water.

A broad, white-sand beach (often mistak-enly called Mo'omomi) is at **Kawa'aloa Bay**, a 20-minute walk further west. The wind, which picks up steadily each afternoon, blows the dune sand into interesting ripples and waves. Like a voyeur, you're here just to look around. Swimming is dangerous.

The high hills running inland are actu-ally massive sand dunes – part of a mile-long stretch of dunes that back this part of coast. The coastal cliffs, which have been sculptured into jagged abstract designs by wind and water, are made of sand that has petrified due to Mo'omomi's dry conditions.

Because of the fragile ecology of the dunes, visitors should stay along the beach and on trails only.

Tours

The **Nature Conservancy** (☎ 553-5236; www.nature .org/hawaii; Moloka'i Industrial Park, 23 Pueo Pl, Kualapu'u; sug-gested donation $25) leads excellent monthly guided hikes of Mo'omomi. Transportation is pro-vided to and from the preserve. Reservations are required and spots fill up far in advance so get in early.

KALA'E

Rudolph Wilhelm Meyer, a German immi-grant who had plans to make it big in the California gold rush, stopped off in Hawai'i en route (he was going the long way around). He never left, and married a member of Hawaiian royalty who had huge tracts of land on Moloka'i. Meyer busied himself growing potatoes and cattle for export, serving as overseer of the Kalaupapa leprosy settle-ment and as manager of King Kamehameha V's ranch lands. In 1876, when a new treaty allowed Hawaiian sugar planters to export sugar duty-free to the US, Meyer turned his lands over to sugar, and built the mill. It op-erated for only a decade until falling prices killed its viability.

The mill has enjoyed a series of restorations over time. Features include a 100-year-old steam engine, a mule-powered cane crusher and other working artifacts. It now houses the **Moloka'i Museum & Cultural Center** (☎ 567-6436; adult/concession $2.50/1; ☯ 10am-2pm Mon-Sat), which has a small but intriguing display of Moloka'i's history with period photos, cul-tural relics and a 10-minute video. Meyer and his descendants are buried in a little family plot out back.

Ironwood Hills Golf Course

The 'pro shop' in the dilapidated trailer tells you everything you need to know about this wonderfully casual nine-hole **golf course** (☎ 567-6000; green fees 9/18 holes $18/24; ⏱ 8am-5pm) that was originally built for plantation managers in the 1920s. Electric cart rental is $8; clubs are $5.

PALA'AU STATE PARK

Thrill to views over the Kalaupapa Peninsula, listen to winds rustle through groves of ironwood and eucalyptus trees and partake of sacred rocks that represent human genitals. This misty state park is at the end of Hwy 470, near the Kalaupapa trailhead. It's good for a picnic, some photos and possibly a chance to get pregnant.

Sights & Activities

KALAUPAPA OVERLOOK

The Kalaupapa Overlook provides a scenic overview of the Kalaupapa Peninsula from the edge of a 1600ft cliff. The best light for photography is usually from late morning to mid-afternoon.

It's easy to get the lay of the land from the lookout; you'll get a good feel for just how far you travel when you descend nearly 1700ft on the trail. Interpretive plaques identify significant landmarks below and explain Kalaupapa's history. The village where all of Kalaupapa's residents live is visible, but Kalawao, the original settlement and site of Father Damien's church and grave, is not.

Kalaupapa means 'flat leaf,' an accurate description of the lava-slab peninsula that was created when a low shield volcano poked up out of the sea, long after the rest of Moloka'i had been formed. The dormant Kauhako Crater, visible from the overlook, contains a little lake that's more than 800ft deep. At 400ft, the crater is the highest point on the Kalaupapa Peninsula. A lighthouse stands erect near the northern tip of land. It once boasted the most powerful beam in the Pacific but now only holds an electric light beacon.

There's a vague **trail** of sorts that continues directly beyond the last plaque at the overlook. The path, on a carpet of soft ironwood needles, passes through diagonal rows of trees planted during a Civil Conservation Corps (CCC) reforestation project in the 1930s. Simply follow this trail for 20 minutes or so until it peters out.

KAULEONANAHOA

Kauleonanahoa (the penis of Nanahoa) is Hawaii's premier **phallic stone**, standing proud in a little clearing inside an ironwood grove, about a five-minute walk from the parking area. The legend goes that Nanahoa hit his wife Kawahuna in a jealous rage and when they were both turned to stone, he came out looking like a dick, literally.

Reputedly, women who come here with offerings of lei and dollar bills and stay overnight will soon get pregnant. There's no mention of what happens to men who might try the same thing with some nearby stones that have been carved into a female counterpart to the main rock.

Before the trees were planted, the stone, which has had some plastic surgery through the years to augment its effect, stood out like a drama queen atop the ridge.

Sleeping

Camping is allowed in a peaceful grassy field a quarter of a mile before the overlook, with a picnic pavilion and a portable toilet (although there are good bathrooms near the main parking area). It rains a lot here and outside of the summer dry season, your tent will likely be drenched by evening showers. See p439 for permit information.

KALAUPAPA NATIONAL HISTORICAL PARK

The spectacularly beautiful **Kalaupapa Peninsula** is the most remote part of Hawaii's most remote island. The only way to reach this lush green peninsula edged with long, white-sand beaches is on a twisting trail down the steep *pali*, the world's highest sea cliffs, or by plane. This remoteness is the reason it was for more than a century where leprosy patients were forced into isolation. From its inception until separation ended in 1969, 8000 patients were forced to come to Kalaupapa. It is still home to a couple of dozen patients (respectively called 'residents') who have chosen to remain in the only home they have ever known and have resisted efforts to move them away. The peninsula has been designated a national historical park and is managed by the Hawaii Department of Health and the **National Park Service** (www.nps.gov/kala).

At the bottom of the cliffs, a guided tour of the settlement and the peninsula is Moloka'i's most well-known attraction. But the tour, interesting as it is, is not the highlight: this is one case where getting there truly is half the fun. Riding a mule or hiking down the steep trail, winding through lush green tropical forest, catching glimpses of the sea far below, is unforgettable.

HISTORY

Ancient Hawaiians used Kalaupapa as a refuge when caught in storms at sea. The peninsula held a large settlement at the time of early Western contact, and the area is rich in archaeological sites, currently under investigation. A major discovery in 2004 indicated that Kalaupapa heiau had major ritual significance, with possible astronomical purposes.

In 1835 doctors in Hawai'i diagnosed the state's first case of leprosy, one of many diseases introduced by foreigners. Before modern medicine, leprosy manifested itself in dripping, foul-smelling sores. Eventually, patients experienced loss of sensation and tissue degeneration that could lead to small extremities becoming deformed or falling off altogether. Blindness was common. Alarmed by the spread of the disease, King Kamehameha V signed into law an act that banished people with leprosy to Kalaupapa Peninsula, beginning in 1865.

Hawaiians call leprosy *mai ho'oka'awale*, which means 'separating sickness,' a disease all the more dreaded because it tore families apart. Some patients arrived at the peninsula in boats, whose captains were so terrified of the disease and the rough waters they would not land, but instead dropped patients overboard. Those who could, swam to shore; those who couldn't, perished.

Once the afflicted arrived on Kalaupapa Peninsula, there was no way out, not even in a casket. The original settlement was in Kalawao, at the wetter eastern end of the peninsula. Early conditions were unspeakably horrible, with the strong stealing rations from the weak, and women forced into prostitution or worse. Life spans were invariably short, and desperate.

Father Damien (see the boxed text, p460) arrived at Kalaupapa in 1873. He wasn't the first missionary to come, but he was the first to stay. What Damien provided most of all was a sense of hope and inspiration to others.

Brother Joseph Dutton arrived in 1886 and stayed 44 years. In addition to his work with the sick, he was a prolific writer who kept the outside world informed about what was happening in Moloka'i. Mother Marianne Cope arrived a year before Damien died. She stayed 30 years, helping to establish a girls' home and encouraging patients to live life to the fullest. She is widely considered to be the mother of the hospice movement.

The same year that Father Damien arrived, a Norwegian scientist named Dr Gerhard Hansen discovered *Mycobacterium leprae*, the bacteria that causes leprosy, thus proving that the disease was not hereditary, as was previously thought. Even in Damien's day, leprosy was one of the least contagious of all communicable diseases: only 4% of human beings are even susceptible to it.

In 1909 the US Leprosy Investigation Station opened at Kalawao. However, the fancy hospital was so out of touch – requiring the patients to sign themselves in for two years, live in seclusion and give up all Hawaiian-grown food – that even in the middle of a leprosy colony, it attracted only a handful of patients. It closed a few years later.

Since the 1940s sulfa antibiotics have successfully treated and controlled leprosy, but the isolation policies in Kalaupapa weren't abandoned until 1969, when there were 300 patients here. The last arrived in 1965 and today the remaining residents are in their 60s or older.

While the state of Hawaii officially uses the term 'Hansen's disease' for leprosy, many Kalaupapa residents consider that to be a euphemism that fails to reflect the stigma they have suffered and continue to use the old term 'leprosy.' The degrading appellation 'leper,' however, is offensive to all. 'Resident' is preferred.

INFORMATION

State laws dating back to when the settlement was a quarantine zone require everyone who enters the settlement to have a 'permit' and to be accompanied at all times by a guide. The laws are no longer necessary for health reasons but they continue to be enforced in order to protect the privacy of the residents. There's no actual paper permit. Your reservation with Damien Tours or Molokai Mule Ride acts as your permit. Because the exiled patients were not allowed to keep children if they had them,

MOLOKA'I

MOLOKA'I'S SAINT

Barring unexpected divine intervention, 2009 will be the year Moloka'i gets its first saint. The story of Joseph de Veuster, the Belgian priest who sacrificed everything to care for leprosy patients, has been the subject of many books and TV movies, few of which rise above the treacly clichés inherent to such a story. And yet Father Damien's story, once learned, makes the honor of sainthood seem like the bare minimum he deserves.

In 1873, the famously strong-willed priest traveled, at age 33, to the Kalaupapa Peninsula, the leprosy settlement he'd heard called 'the living tomb.' Once on this remote place of exile he found scores of people who'd been dumped ashore by a government not quite cruel enough to simply drown them at sea. Soon he had the residents helping him construct more than 300 houses, plant trees and much more. He taught himself medicine and gave his flock the care they desperately needed. In 1888 he installed a water pipeline over to the sunny western side of the peninsula, and the settlement moved from Kalawao to where it remains today.

Father Damien contracted Hansen's disease in 1885, 12 years after he arrived, and died four years later at age 49, the only outsider ever to contract leprosy on Kalaupapa. The Vatican has recognized two miracles attributed to him. Both were people diagnosed with terminal illnesses decades after his death and who attributed their recoveries to their prayers and faith in Father Damien.

Excitement over Father Damien's sainthood is widespread on Moloka'i and fundraising efforts to pay for group travel to Rome for the ceremonies are constant. Many hope that his beatification will provide rescue from the dodgy local economy through an increase in curious visitors, although this may require a miracle that even the sainted priest can't deliver.

---

the residents made a rule that no one under the age of 16 is allowed in the settlement – this is strictly enforced, as are the permit requirements. Only guests of Kalaupapa residents are allowed to stay overnight.

SIGHTS & ACTIVITIES

At the bottom of the near-vertical *pali* is a deserted **beach** with stunning views of the steep cliffs you've just come down. The mule ride ends here and you'll board a small bus for the tour. Remember your mule's name so that the guides will put you back on the right one for the trip up! If you're hiking (see opposite), you wait for the mandatory tour here.

The settlement is very quiet, and residents tend to stay indoors while the tour is going on. With their history of being persecuted and stigmatized, you can't blame them for avoiding curious tourists, but the guide says that residents welcome visitors because it helps prevent their story from being forgotten. Restoration of village buildings is ongoing, and the homes that have been restored are small and tidy, with covered lanai, clapboard siding, and tin roofs. Other sights are mainly cemeteries, churches, and memorials. **Fuesaina's Bar**, run by Gloria Marks, the wife of the late Richard Marks, sells drinks and snacks (this was closed during our visit due to Marks' recent death). A park **visitor center** doubles as a small museum and

bookstore, with displays of items made and used by former residents ('Kalaupapa Patients Adapt & Innovate') and books and films about the settlement for sale.

On the way to the east side of the peninsula is **St Philomena Church** (better known as Father Damien's Church), in Kalawao, which was built in 1872. You can see where Damien cut open holes in the floor as a way to welcome the sick, whose disease made them need to spit frequently. The graveyard at the side contains Damien's gravestone and original burial site, although his body was exhumed in 1936 and returned to Belgium. In 1995, his right hand was reinterred here. The large black cross on the revered Father's grave is adorned with shells and leis.

The tour stops for lunch at Kalawao after a short drive through lush greenery dotted with colorful lantana vines. On the way, keep your eyes open for a heiau just past the water wells; the remains of the ancient temple are on the same side as the wells. The amazing view from Kalawao could be reason enough to visit the peninsula. It gives you a glimpse of Moloka'i's Pali Coast (see the boxed text, p454), which features the jarring spectacle of the world's highest sea cliffs. Some boast near-vertical drops of 3300ft.

This is a popular film location for producers needing an almost otherworldly landscape, including the one's scouting for 'Skull Island' in the second – and less impressive – *King Kong* from 1976. This impenetrable section of the northern shore contains two majestic valleys and **Kahiwa Falls**, the state's longest waterfall.

TOURS

Everyone who comes to the Kalaupapa Peninsula is required to visit the settlement with **Damien Tours** (☎ 567-6171; tours $40; ☽ Mon-Sat). Reservations must be made in advance (call between 4pm and 8pm). Tours last 3½ hours, are done by bus and are accompanied by lots of stories about life in years past. If you're not on the mule ride, bring your own lunch and a bottle of water. The much-loved Richard Marks, longtime resident and tour guide, died in 2008.

Mule Rides

Molokai Mule Ride (☎ 567-6088, 800-567-7550; www .muleride.com; rides $165; ☽ Mon-Sat) offers the only way down the *pali* besides hiking; but be prepared – this is not an easy ride. You'll be sore afterwards even if you're an experienced rider, and it's a safe bet that you've never experienced a ride like this one. At some points, the trail is only eight to 10 inches wide, nearly vertical in places, and it's simply amazing how the mules carefully pick their way down. The mule skinners happily announce on the second switchback that it's here that some people just get off and walk back to the barn, not willing to trust their lives to the sure-footed animals. So settle back and enjoy a natural thrill ride. You'll need to be quick with the camera if you want to get shots of the amazing views, because the mules don't stop for photo ops. (Hiking down would offer better chances for good pictures.) It takes about 45 minutes going down and one hour going up. The ride back is as challenging as the ride down, but it's definitely easier than hiking. Tours include a short riding lesson from real *paniolo* (Hawaiian cowboys), and lunch. Make reservations well in advance. Round-trip airport transfers are $18 per person (two-person minimum).

GETTING THERE & AWAY

The mule trail down the *pali* is the only land route to the peninsula, either on foot or by the mule rides. It is possible to combine hiking and flying. The island's activity/tour operators (p439) and Molokai Mule Ride (above) can organize all details of your visit.

Air

The beauty of flying in on these small prop planes is the aerial view of the *pali* and towering waterfalls. Passengers need to first book a tour with Damien Tours (left) before buying air tickets, otherwise you will be stuck at the airport. Even then you are still likely to be stuck at the airport as the flight schedules don't mesh well with tours. The morning flight down from Ho'olehua may arrive before 7:30am and you'll have to wait at the landing strip for the tour bus at 10am. If you are coming from another island, you may need to fly to Moloka'i the night before. Return trips 'up top,' as they say locally, to Ho'olehua are more convenient and allow for easy connections to Honolulu and Maui. **Pacific Wings** (☎ 888-575-4546; www.pacificwings.com) and its PW Express subsidiary have a range of fares and tour packages.

Note: charter carrier Paragon Air receives many complaints and is rated 'unsatisfactory' by the Better Business Bureau.

Foot

The trailhead is on the east side of Hwy 470, just north of the mule stables, and marked by the Pala'au park sign and parked Kalaupapa employee cars. Your car will be safest parked across from the mule stables. The 3-mile trail has 26 switchbacks, 1400 steps and drops 1664ft in elevation from start to finish. It's best to begin hiking by 8am, before the mules start to go down, to avoid walking in fresh dung, though you have no choice on the return trip. Allow an hour and a half to descend comfortably. It can be quite an adventure after a lot of rain, though the rocks keep it from getting impossibly muddy. You can also hike down and fly back up.

WEST END

Seemingly deserted and just a couple of missed rainfalls from becoming the desert, Moloka'i's West End has an outsize role in the island's past, present and future.

It has a powerful place in Hawaiian history and culture. Pu'u Nana is the site of Hawaii's first hula school, and the Maunaloa Range was also once a center of sorcery. In recent decades, much of the land has been controlled by the Moloka'i Ranch, and its fortunes for better and more recently for much worse have

MOLOKA'I

affected the entire island. Hale O Lono Harbor is the launching site for the two long-distance outrigger canoe races (p446). The island's longest beach, Papohaku Beach, dominates the west coast.

Once you pass the airport, Hwy 460 starts to climb up through dry, grassy rangeland without a building in sight. The long mountain range that begins to form on your left past the 10-mile marker is Maunaloa, which means 'long mountain.' Its highest point, at 1381ft, is Pu'u Nana.

Given the woes of Moloka'i Ranch (see the boxed text, opposite) the atmosphere out west is a bit bleak. With the exception of one superlative store, Maunaloa might as well hold tumbleweed races, while the Kaluakoi resort area is beset by financial troubles. Still, you can ignore all the earthly turmoil on one of the many fine beaches.

HISTORY

During the 1850s, Kamehameha V acquired the bulk of Moloka'i's arable land, forming Moloka'i Ranch, but overgrazing eventually led to the widespread destruction of native vegetation and fishponds. Following his death, the ranch became part of the Bishop Estate, which quickly sold it off to a group of Honolulu businesspeople.

A year later, in 1898, the American Sugar Company, a division of Moloka'i Ranch, attempted to develop a major sugar plantation in central Moloka'i. The company built a railroad system to haul the cane, developed harbor facilities, and installed a powerful pumping system to draw water. However, by 1901 the well water used to irrigate the fields had become so saline that the crops failed. The company then moved into honey production on such a large scale that at one point Moloka'i was the world's largest honey exporter. In the mid-1930s, however, an epidemic wiped out the hives and the industry. Strike two for the industrialists.

Meanwhile, the ranch continued its efforts to find *the* crop for Moloka'i. Cotton, rice and numerous grain crops all took their turn biting Moloka'i's red dust. Finally, pineapple took root as the crop most suited to the island's dry, windy conditions. Plantation-scale production began in Ho'olehua in 1920. Within 10 years, Moloka'i's population tripled, as immigrants arrived to toil in the fields.

In the 1970s, overseas competition brought an end to the pineapple's reign on Moloka'i. Dole closed its operation in 1976, and the other island giant, Del Monte, later followed suit. These closures brought hard times and the highest unemployment levels in the state. Then cattle raising, long a mainstay, suddenly collapsed as, due to a controversial state decision in 1985, every head of cattle on Moloka'i was destroyed after an incidence of bovine tuberculosis. The majority of the 240 smaller cattle owners then called it quits. The Moloka'i Ranch still owns some 64,000 acres – about 40% of the island – and more than half of the island's privately held lands. What will happen with these fallow holdings is the question of the moment; see the boxed text, opposite.

MAUNALOA
pop 200
In the 1990s, the Moloka'i Ranch bulldozed the atmospheric old plantation town of Maunaloa, leveling all but a few buildings. New buildings mimicking old, plantation-style homes were erected. This drove up rents and forced out some small businesses, again provoking the ire of island residents.

Ironically, the new development is now all but closed. Shuttered are the hotel, luxury beach campsite, cinema and even the local outlet of Kentucky Fried Chicken.

Attractions are few, unless you're an urban planner doing research. The **gas station** is open just a few sporadic hours a day while the **Maunaloa General Store** (🕑 8am-6pm Mon-Sat, to noon Sun) has a limited selection of pricey groceries and alcohol. But there is one excellent reason to visit the quiet streets, one that will literally blow you away…

our pick **Big Wind Kite Factory & Plantation Gallery** (☎ 552-2364; www.bigwindkites.com; 120 Maunaloa Hwy; 🕑 8:30am-5pm Mon-Sat, 10am-2pm Sun) custom makes kites for high fliers of all ages. It has hundreds ready to go in stock or you can choose a design and watch production begin. Lessons are available, lest you have a Charlie Brown experience with a kite-eating tree. There's a lot of other goods to browse as well, including the island's best selection of Hawaiian-themed books. Artworks, clothing and crafts have providence from just down the road to Bali.

KALUAKOI RESORT AREA
You can almost picture this place when times were good. A low-key resort fronted a perfect

TOO QUIET ON THE WESTERN FRONT

Even before Moloka'i Ranch began efforts to develop its lands on the West End in the 1970s, local people weren't so fond of the company. They resented the ranch for restricting access to land, which in turn restricted a number of traditional outdoor activities and visitation to sacred cultural and historical sites. And few were impressed by the Kaluakoi Hotel, which was built on Kepuhi Bay.

By 1975 feelings had mounted to such a degree that people took to the streets, marching from Mo'omomi Beach to Kawakiu Beach to demand access to private, and heretofore forbidden, beaches on the West End. The protest was successful and convinced Moloka'i Ranch to provide public access to Kawakiu. At the same time locals successfully scuttled plans to build, of all things, an O'ahu suburb here that would have been linked to the neighboring island by a new airport and ferry system.

In the 1990s the ranch operated a small wildlife-safari park, where tourists snapped pictures of exotic animals, and trophy hunters paid $1500 a head to shoot African eland and blackbuck antelope. Rumors abound of how local activists, long resistant to the type of tourist-oriented development that has all but consumed neighboring Maui, made life so difficult for the ranch that the safari park was shut down.

Beginning in 2001, the current owners of Moloka'i Ranch, the Singapore-based Moloka'i Properties, began a campaign to revitalize the holdings. They developed plans to reopen the Kaluakoi Hotel (and did reopen the golf course) and transfer the title to cultural sites and recreational areas amounting to 26,000 acres to a newly created Moloka'i Land Trust, essentially turning it into public land. It would also have given up the right to develop another 24,000 acres of its own lands.

But there was one small detail…what Moloka'i Properties wanted in return: the right to develop 200 one-acre lots on pristine La'au Point into a luxury subdivision marketed to multimillionaires. Most locals had an immediate and negative reaction to this. It was the 1970s all over again. Signs saying 'Save La'au Point' sprouted island-wide (and can still be seen).

Despite numerous community meetings and plans, Moloka'i Properties got nowhere as the residents of the Hawaiian island with the highest unemployment thumbed their noses at the promise of hundreds of resort and service jobs.

In 2008 Moloka'i Properties essentially took its toys and went home. It pulled the plug on all its operations, laid off dozens, closed its hotel and golf course and furthered the ghost-town feel of Maunaloa and the Kaluakoi resort area. Only a last-minute rescue by Maui County kept the water running.

With the global economy in the dumps, it's unlikely that Moloka'i Properties will be back anytime soon with new development schemes. Meanwhile, local activists have floated fanciful schemes to buy up Moloka'i Ranch without identifying where the hundreds of millions of dollars needed might be found.

crescent of sand while upscale condos lined the fairways of an emerald-green championship golf course.

Well that was then (the late 20th century) and the now is rather bleak. The resort was closed years ago and is in a state of advanced decay. The golf course died when Moloka'i Ranch pulled the plug in 2008. Those fairways are now returning to nature. Meanwhile the condo complexes do their best to put a good face on the situation as the individual owners try to play up the quiet aspects of the complex in their efforts to market their vacation rentals. Surrounding house lots have sold very slowly, although a few large mansions lurk behind walls along the beaches.

As with the rest of the west, you're best off bringing a picnic from Kaunakakai and enjoying the beautiful beaches. Everything is accessed off a good road that branches off Hwy 460 at the 15-mile marker and curves its way down to the shore.

Sights & Activities
KAWAKIU BEACH
The northernmost of Kaluakoi's beaches is also the best. Kawakiu Beach is a broad crescent beach of white sand and bright-turquoise waters. It's partially sheltered from the winds

that can bedevil the beaches to the south and when seas are calm, usually in summer, Kawakiu is generally safe for swimming. When the surf is rough, there are still areas where you can at least get wet. On the southern side of the bay, there's a small, sandy-bottomed wading pool in the rocks. The northern side has an area of flat rocks over which water slides, to fill up a shallow shoreline pool. Spindly kiawe trees provide shade. Outside of weekends, you may well have the place to yourself.

To get there, turn off Kaluakoi Rd onto the road to the Paniolo Hale condos, but instead of turning left down to the condos, continue straight toward the old golf course. Where the paved road ends, there's space to pull over and park. You'll come first to a rocky point at the southern end of the bay. Before descending to the beach, scramble around up here for a scenic view of the coast, south to Papohaku Beach and north to 'Ilio Point.

MAKE HORSE BEACH

To the south, Make Horse Beach supposedly takes its name from days past, when wild horses were run off the tall, dark cliff on its northern end; *make* (mah-*kay*) means 'dead.' This pretty, tiny white-sand cove is a local favorite, and more secluded than Kepuhi to the south. It's a sublime spot for sunbathing and sunset, but usually not for swimming as, again, the currents are fierce. On the calmest days, daredevils leap off the giant rock ledge at the beach's southern end.

To get here, turn off Kaluakoi Rd onto the road to the Paniolo Hale condos and then turn left toward the condo complex. You can park just beyond the condos and walk, or follow the dirt road heading off to the right for a quarter of a mile to a parking area. From there, cross the golf course remains to the beach. In some of the distant reaches, clothing has been deemed optional.

KEPUHI BEACH

You can see why they built the Kaluakoi Hotel here: the beach is a rocky, white-sand dream. However, swimming here can be a nightmare. Not only can there be a tough shorebreak but strong currents can be present even on calm days. During winter, the surf breaks close to shore, crashing in sand-filled waves that can be a brutal exfoliant.

A five-minute hike up to the top of **Pu'u o Kaiaka**, a 110ft-high promontory at the south-

ern end of Kepuhi Beach, rewards strollers with a nice view of Papohaku Beach. At the top, you'll find the remains of a pulley that was once used to carry cattle down to waiting barges for transport to O'ahu slaughterhouses. There was also a 40ft heiau on the hilltop that in 1967, when the US army bulldozed it (and gave the superstitious another reason to ponder the local run of bad luck). There's plenty of parking in the resort's cracked parking lots.

Sleeping

Units in the condominium complexes are rented either directly from the owners or through various agents (see the boxed text, p447). There is a small convenience store with a few basics, otherwise you'll need to shop in Kaunakakai, 20 miles distant. The closest restaurant is the splendid Kualapu'u Cookhouse (p456), 15 miles east in Kualapu'u.

Although the two condo complexes listed here are maintaining their properties well, we need to again note that much of the rest of the area has a run-down and eerie feel. We can't recommend the Kaluakoi Resort, which has rental units in one wing of the failed resort: for one, its cooking facilities are meager and there's nowhere locally to eat. And a final note: Moloka'i Ranch supplied water to the West End and at the time of research efforts were being made to secure a permanent replacement.

Paniolo Hale (www.paniolohale.org; studios from $100, 1br from $130, 2br from $180; 🖳) Separated from the environs of the failed resort by the weedy expanse of the former golf course, this is an attractive option. Large trees shade this plantation-style complex, giving it a hidden, secluded air. Each unit has a long, screened-in lanai overlooking the quiet grounds; as always with condos, shop around to get one that's been recently renovated. It is a short walk to Make Horse Beach.

Ke Nani Kai (www.knkrentals.com; Kaluakoi Rd; 1br/2br from $135/140; 🖳) This tidy operation shames the rest of the resort complex. The 100-plus units are large and well-maintained (though your interior-decor mileage may vary depending on the owner). The pool is big. Note that the ocean is not right outside, so the premium for 'ocean view' units is debatable. Kepuhi and Papohaku beaches are short walks away.

WEST END BEACHES

Windy, isolated and often untrod, the West End beaches define moody and atmospheric

Together with the beaches in the Kaluakoi Resort area, they can easily occupy a day of beachcombing and beach-hopping.

From this stretch of coast the hazy outline of O'ahu is just 26 miles away. Diamond Head is on the left, Makapu'u Point on the right. You can, reportedly, see the famous 'green flash' (the green color results from atmospheric refraction of the setting or rising sun) during sunset here. Another flash of green worth spotting are the green sea turtles that sometimes pass by.

To get to the West End beaches, take the turnoff for the Kaluakoi Resort Area at the 15-mile marker. Pass the former golf course and follow Pohakuloa Rd south.

Papohaku Beach Park

Straight as a toothpick, the light-hued sands of Papohaku Beach run for an astounding 2.5 miles. The sand is soft and you can often stroll from one end to another without seeing another soul.

But just when you think you may have found the ultimate strand, consider a few leveling details. That intoxicating surf is also a viper's nest of undertow and unpredictable currents. And there's no easy shade. You can bring an umbrella but the often strong winds may send it O'ahu-bound. Those same breezes kick up the fine sand, which can simply hurt on blustery days.

So come here for the solitude but do so with your eyes figuratively, if not literally, wide open.

There are seven turnoffs from Kaluakoi and Pohakuloa Rds that access the beach and which have parking. The first leads to **Papohaku Beach Park**, a grassy place with picnic facilities under gnarled ironwood and kiawe trees. Bathroom and shower facilities are rugged. You can **camp** here but be sure to read the signs that explain which areas are soaked by the automatic sprinklers on which days. See p439 for information on camping permits.

There are seldom any other campers here and the view of the stars at night and the sound of surf is mesmerizing. However the park can be popular with rowdy folks young and old and occasionally some try to stay the night. Guards are meant to check permits but you may be happier here if you are not alone.

Dixie Maru Beach

South of Papohaku, beach access is to small sandy coves surrounded by rocky outcrops. At the south end of the paved road there's a parking lot with access to a small, round inlet, which the ancient Hawaiians knew as Kapukahehu. It is now called Dixie Maru, after a ship that went down in the area long ago. Dixie Maru is the most protected cove on the west shore, and the most popular **swimming** and **snorkeling** area. The waters are generally calm, except when it is stormy.

If you're up for just finding your way as you go, it's possible to **hike** south 3 miles along the coast to La'au Point, and see what all the fuss was about (see the boxed text, p463). You'll pass a couple of secluded mansions, the failed luxury camping resort and several utterly untouched beaches.

NI'IHAU

Relatively small in population when Captain Cook anchored off it on January 29, 1778, Ni'ihau has fewer than 300 inhabitants today.

Part of the US, Ni'ihau, which is privately owned by the Robinson family, has long been dubbed by passing tour boats as the 'Forbidden Island.' Its 'forbidden' mystique – caused by lack of access to the public – also has a fascinating back story. Still today, only Robinson family members and Native Hawaiian residents and their guests are allowed there, plus a few government employees.

The fact that the Robinson family has been able to keep Ni'ihau relatively isolated has helped allow a culture all its own to be preserved: Hawaiian is the primary spoken language, adding to its time-capsule quality, as is a religious temperance introduced by the Robinsons that's been in place now for roughly 146 years.

HISTORY

The culture of Ni'ihau and its people are inexorably linked to the Robinsons. Since their purchase of the majority of the island from King Kamehameha V in 1863, a purchase he is said to have approved of in part because of the antidrinking practices of the Robinson family, the isolated Ni'ihau has remained the only majority Native Hawaiian–speaking island in existence.

Deciding there was too much drinking in Scotland (and haggis and bagpipes, according to Keith Robinson, great-grandson of Ni'ihau co-purchaser Eliza Sinclair), the family hauled anchor between 1830 and 1850 and headed off to New Zealand, then to Tahiti and Vancouver in search of a homeland in keeping with their moral ideals. After starting negotiations with King Kamehameha IV, they finally bought Ni'ihau in 1864 for roughly $10,000 in gold from King Kamehameha V. With the purchase marked a new era of ranching on Ni'ihau: Sinclair brought Ni'ihau's first sheep from New Zealand.

Great-great-grandsons Keith and Bruce Robinson are highly protective of Ni'ihau's isolation and its people. The family owns a significant amount of Kaua'i land and a sugar company.

Keith and Bruce Robinson are unpretentious outdoorsmen. Both are fluent in Native Hawaiian, just like any Ni'ihau resident. Bruce Robinson is married to a Ni'ihauan woman.

Thanks to its isolation since the purchase and the quarantine during the 1950s outbreak of polio, the island has been able to divert many diseases from its shores, including AIDS. To this day, residents' medical care needs are met either by the Robinsons' insurance or the Department of Social Services.

POPULATION & LIFESTYLE

Ni'ihau's population is mostly Native Hawaiian. The island's population has dropped from 600 in the 1980s to 160 in 2007 (the latest available data). Most residents live in Pu'uwai ('heart'), a settlement on the dry western coast. It's a simple life; water is collected in catchments, and the toilets are in outhouses. Residents hardly live 'without,' however. Though all residents are 'off the grid,' most have found ingenious ways to harness power, and several utilize hydro or wind sourcing, often backed-up by gasoline generators. Cell-phone signals reach some of the island, which also relies on a radio communication system.

Ni'ihau has a schoolhouse where teachers host classes from kindergarten through 12th grade. Courses are taught in Hawaiian until fourth grade. Students learn English as a second language.

Ni'ihau business and Sunday church services are conducted in Hawaiian. Throughout the islands, the Hawaiian language spoken by Ni'ihauans is known as the purest remaining form, differing at times from the evolving language that has come out of University of Hawaii-Hilo's College of Hawaiian Language, which has developed words to define modern terms. Some people have critiqued the new UH-Hilo terms as sounding too similar to Western languages. An example is the word kamepiula for computer; in an attempt to stay truer to non-Westernized Hawaiian language, critics opt for using the two older Hawaiian words lolo uila, which literally means 'electrical mind.'

GEOGRAPHY & ENVIRONMENT

A mere 17 miles from Kaua'i, Ni'ihau is the smallest of the inhabited Hawaiian Islands: 18 miles long and 6 miles at the widest point, with a total land area of almost 70 sq miles and 45 miles of coast. Ni'ihau rainfall averages a scant 12in annually because the island is in Kaua'i's rain shadow. Its highest peak, Paniau, is only 1250ft tall and cannot generate trade wind–based precipitation.

Unique to the island are its shells: warm-hued and delicate sea jewels from the island are strung into exquisite and coveted lei costing from $125 to $25,000. In late 2004, Governor Linda Lingle signed a bill mandating that only items made of 100% Ni'ihau shells and crafted entirely in Hawaii can carry the Ni'ihau label. Residents of Ni'ihau make exquisite lei for sale at the Ni'ihau Helicopters office, which they use for bartering trips to and from Kaua'i.

Almost 50 endangered monk seals live on Ni'ihau, monitored by Bruce Robinson. Unfortunately, the draw of the pristine has threatened Ni'ihau. Its waters have suffered depletion by sport and commercial fishers who sail in to fish and pick 'opihi (edible limpet) from the island's shorebreaks. The outside world also has threatened Ni'ihau fisherman and residents, who couldn't eat fish between January and March of 2009, after a dead baby humpback whale and thousands of fish were found washed up on a Ni'ihau shore. Though officials conducted necropsies, and despite speculation that the state's poisoning of neighboring Lehua island days earlier (to kill rabbits and rats who were eating endangered plants) was the reason, no cause has been determined.

ECONOMY & POLITICS

The island economy has long depended on Ni'ihau Ranch, the sheep and cattle business owned by the Robinsons. But it was always a marginal operation on windy Ni'ihau, with droughts devastating herds. In 1999 Ni'ihau Ranch closed.

The family has been able to keep the island relatively undeveloped by allowing some temporary US government projects. Keith Robinson joked of the preference in allowing military projects onto the island over development: 'The military comes and goes. After a military project is over, it usually gets rusted down to nothing.'

Allowing some tourist access is one of the prices to pay for owning a private island. Much of the tourist access the Robinsons allow is to help pay for services for Ni'ihauans, such as a recently purchased helicopter used for Medevac services.

While it's difficult to find a comparative relationship to explain the dynamic between the Robinsons and Ni'ihauans, the Robinsons view themselves as protectors. And though that's the kind of paternalism that can rub outside Native Hawaiian groups the wrong way, for the most part Ni'ihauans don't seem to mind.

In fact, the common thread between the Robinsons and Ni'ihauans seems a steadfast allegiance from both sides. That carries over even on Kaua'i, as Ni'ihauans who've emigrated seem to stay in Robinson territory, on Kaua'i's Westside. Many who move to Kaua'i work for the Robinsons and live on their property, often in the Makaweli area. Kaua'i's only church conducted in Hawaiian also is on Kaua'i's Westside in Waimea, attended mostly by Ni'ihauans.

For the Ni'ihauans who don't make it to Kaua'i, samplings of Kaua'i are brought to them via barge roughly twice a month. Soda and poi (fermented taro paste) are among items brought over.

Politically, Ni'ihau falls under the jurisdiction of Kaua'i County. In 2004, George W Bush got 39 of 40 votes cast by Ni'ihauans. In 2008, Ni'ihau's precinct was one of only three of Hawaii's 538 precincts to vote for John McCain over President Barack Obama. McCain received 35 votes and Obama received four votes, despite Hawaii being Obama's strongest state in the nation.

VISITING NI'IHAU

Although outsiders are not allowed to visit Ni'ihau on their own, the Robinsons offer **helicopter tours** (Ni'ihau Helicopters; ☎ 877-441-3500; www.niihau.us; 12550A Kaumuali'i Hwy, Makaweli; half-day per person $365; ☽ office 8am-2pm Mon-Fri), which take off from Burns Field in Port Allen. A half-day excursion includes lunch, snorkeling and swimming off the island's shores; bookings must be made well in advance. The Robinsons also offer **hunting safaris** as part of the island's conservation and wildlife management program (see the website for more information).

Kaua'i

Kaua'i people have always been staunch individualists. In ancient times, the locals defended their *'aina* (land) from King Kamehameha and spoke a distinct dialect of the Hawaiian language. Today the people continue to push back – fighting urbanization and commercialization. As they say, 'We're not Waikiki and we don't want to be!'

Born five million years ago (and five million years ahead of Hawai'i), Kaua'i boasts an epic landscape seen nowhere else: dramatic, zigzagging, hanging valleys cut by wave and wind; velvety emerald flora blanketing weathered extinct volcanoes; Mt Wai'ale'ale's inaccessible summit, the world's wettest spot (a tie with Cherrapunji, India) and Waimea Canyon's gaping chasm, displaying the island's genesis in layers of ancient lava. The least populated of the major islands, Kaua'i attracts antiurbanites, be they surfers, farmers, career-changers or nouveau hippies. Living in Honolulu guarantees access to nightlife, neurosurgeons, a university and an Apple Store. On Kaua'i, one forgoes all of that – by choice.

Traditional plantation immigrants remain (mostly in Lihu'e and other former sugar towns) but the North Shore population now looks markedly wealthy, mainland-transplanted and white. Indeed, tourism and real estate are booming, but don't come for the manmade attractions. With only one coastal highway, no town larger than 10,000 residents and no skyscrapers, your attention will target what Kauaians hold sacred: the beautiful *'aina*.

HIGHLIGHTS

- Delight your kids at **Lydgate Beach Park** (p489)
- Scope eye-popping native greenery at **Limahuli Garden** (p524)
- Take a leap of faith ziplining in **Lihu'e** (p481)
- See striking sandstone cliffs along the **Maha'ulepu Coast** (p534)
- Enter the soggy, muddy, misty otherworld of the **Alaka'i Swamp** (p556)
- Surf or swim at gorgeous **Hanalei Bay** (p516)
- Test yourself on the epic **Kalalau Trail** (p525)
- Behold colossal **Waimea Canyon** (p550)
- Check out local art and 'nightlife' in **Hanapepe** (p544)
- Cycle or walk the east coast along **Ke Ala Hele Makalae** (p502)

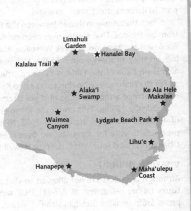

★ Limahuli Garden
★ Hanalei Bay
★ Kalalau Trail
★ Alaka'i Swamp
★ Ke Ala Hele Makalae
★ Waimea Canyon
★ Lydgate Beach Park
★ Lihu'e
★ Hanapepe
★ Maha'ulepu Coast

POPULATION 63,000	AREA: 555 SQ MILES	NICKNAME: GARDEN ISLE

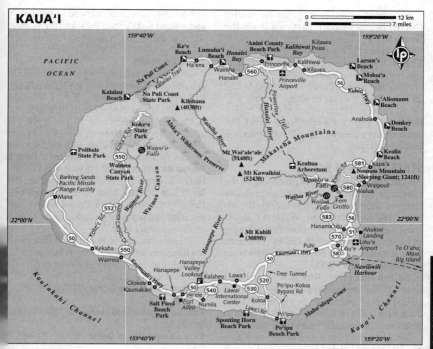

KAUA'I

0 ———— 12 km
0 ———— 7 miles

HISTORY

Like the other Hawaiian Islands, Kaua'i saw a sea change in all aspects of life with the arrival of Captain Cook, sugar plantations, statehood and tourism. While Kaua'i developed as a sugar town through the early 1900s, it became iconic as a tropical paradise after WWII, when Hollywood glamorized Lumaha'i Beach in Mitzi Gaynor's *South Pacific* (1958) and Coco Palms Resort in Elvis Presley's *Blue Hawaii* (1961).

By the 1970s, tourism began replacing sugar as the island's economic driver. Within two decades, Kaua'i's Gay & Robinson was the island's sole remaining plantation. In 2008, even this die-hard announced plans to end sugar operations after 119 years in business. While the biggest agricultural industries are coffee and seed corn, an earnest contingent of small farmers is trying to steer clear of corporate monocropping and toward locally owned, locally eaten crops (and a drop in the island's 90% dependence on imported food).

When Hurricane 'Iwa slammed the Hawaiian Islands in 1982, Kaua'i was hard hit, but that was only a prelude to Hurricane 'Iniki, which devastated the island a decade later. 'Iniki caused more than $1.8 billion (1992 USD) in damages and remains the most powerful hurricane to reach Hawaii in recorded history.

Among the largest four Hawaiian Islands, Kaua'i is the most rural and strives to keep it that way. However, in the mid-2000s, resort and luxury-end development went gangbusters, with over 5000 residential units and 6100 resort units set for development, including the massive Kukui'ula complex in Po'ipu.

CLIMATE

Mt Wai'ale'ale (5148ft), almost smack in the island's center, is considered the second-wettest place on earth, averaging 460in of rain annually. However, around the island, rainfall varies markedly by location and season. The South Shore and especially the Westside tend to be dry and sunny, while the North Shore and Eastside see regular showers. An even bigger factor is elevation, and you'll notice an increase in precipitation as you head *mauka* (inland).

KAUA'I

Seasonally, rain is a given in winter (November to March), particularly on the North Shore. The upside is that showers are usually sporadic, interspersed with sunshine. That said, winter downpours can be torrential, causing dangerous flash floods.

Since the island is only 33 miles wide and 25 miles long, it's easy to escape to your preferred climate. Temperatures drop at higher elevations (eg at Koke'e State Park) but never to any extremes. See p563 for more on Hawaii's climate.

STATE & COUNTY PARKS

About 30% of the island is protected by the state as parks, forest reserves and natural-area reserves. Must-see state parks include the adjacent Westside standouts, Waimea Canyon (p550) and Koke'e (p553) State Parks, for the awesome chasm, steep cliffs and native forests. Hiking trails abound, but some trailheads are accessible only by 4WD.

Na Pali Coast State Park is another headliner, as the steep, slippery Kalalau Trail (p525) is now practically de rigueur. Ha'ena State Park (p524) is another favorite thanks to Ke'e Beach, a fantastic snorkeling spot.

Most of Kaua'i's best and easiest-to-access beaches are designated as county parks, such as Po'ipu Beach Park (p530), on the sunny South Shore; multiple parks at knockout gorgeous Hanalei Bay (p516) and serene 'Anini Beach Park (p511), both on the North Shore; and family-friendly Lydgate Beach Park (p489), on the Eastside.

Camping
STATE PARKS
State park campsites can be found at Na Pali Coast State Park (p525), Koke'e State Park (p554) and Polihale State Park (p550).

Permits are required from the **Division of State Parks** (Map p479; ☎ 274-3444; www.hawaiistateparks.org; Department of Land & Natural Resources, State Bldg, 3060 Eiwa St, Room 306, Lihu'e, Hawaii 96766; ☽ 8am-3:30pm Mon-Fri), obtainable either in person or by mail. Fees range from $5 to $10 per night and time limits are enforced.

For remote backcountry camping around Waimea Canyon and Koke'e, there is no charge. The **Division of Forestry & Wildlife** (Map p479; ☎ 274-3433; www.hawaiitrails.org; Department of Land & Natural Resources, State Bldg, 3060 Eiwa St, Rm 306, Lihu'e, Hawaii 96766; ☽ 8am-4pm Mon-Fri) issues free, backcountry camping permits for four sites in Waimea

Canyon, two sites (Sugi Grove and Kawaikoi) in and around Koke'e State Park, and the Waialae site near the Alaka'i Wilderness Preserve.

COUNTY PARKS
Among the seven county parks with campgrounds, the most pleasant are Ha'ena Beach Park (p524), Black Pot Beach Park (Hanalei Pier) (p516) and 'Anini Beach Park (p511).

Camping permits cost $3 per night per adult camper (children under 18 free) and are issued in person or by mail (at least one month in advance) at the **Division of Parks & Recreation** (Map p479; ☎ 241-4463; www.kauai.gov; Lihu'e Civic Center, Division of Parks & Recreation, 4444 Rice St, Suite 150, Lihu'e, Hawaii 96766; ☽ 8:15am-4pm). Requirements include a signed waiver, application and payment by cash, cashier's check or money order only.

Permits can also be obtained at four satellite locations on weekdays from 8am to noon, but only cashier's checks or money orders are accepted for payment:

Hanapepe Recreation Center (☎ 335-3731; 4451 Puolo Rd)
Kalaheo Neighborhood Center (☎ 332-9770; 4480 Papalina Rd)
Kapa'a Neighborhood Center (☎ 822-1931; 4491 Kou St)
Kilauea Neighborhood Center (☎ 828-1421; 2460 Keneke St)

ACTIVITIES
No one comes to Kaua'i to admire the architecture – unless you're talking about the incomparable designs of Mother Nature. Whether you are a water baby or a landlubber, an athlete or a couch potato, you'll find fun activities for all abilities and levels of adventure.

At Sea
Note that North Shore and Westside beaches see high surf and hazardous conditions in winter (October to April), when South Shore and Eastside waters are calm. The pattern reverses in summer. For the nitty-gritty on Kaua'i's beaches and ocean safety, see www.kauaiexplorer.com.

BODYBOARDING & BODYSURFING
Bodyboarding is the best way to learn the art of catching waves. On the South Shore, find lively sets at Po'ipu Beach (p530), Brennecke Beach (p530) and, for the skilled, Shipwreck Beach (p531). On the Eastside, newbie

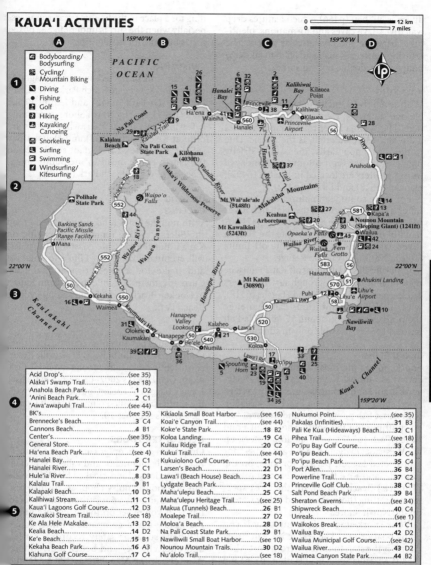

KAUA'I ACTIVITIES

0 — 12 km
0 — 7 miles

Legend:

- Bodyboarding/Bodysurfing
- Cycling/Mountain Biking
- Diving
- Fishing
- Golf
- Hiking
- Kayaking/Canoeing
- Snorkeling
- Surfing
- Swimming
- Windsurfing/Kitesurfing

...hould start at Kalapaki Beach (p479) near ...ihu'e, while experts can test themselves at ...ealia Beach (p504) and Hanalei Bay (p516), ...ear the pavilion.

...IVING

...hile Kaua'i waters cannot quite compare ... the calm, clear waters off the Big Island's Kona Coast, diving is still excellent. A top shore-diving site is Koloa Landing (p532), a great easy-entry beginner spot. Others are Po'ipu Beach Park (p530), Ke'e Beach (p524), Makua (Tunnels) Beach (p524) and Ahukini Landing (Map p478).

Most boat dives explore the waters off Po'ipu, but the the hottest site for experienced divers is Ni'ihau (p466), which features deep wall dives, lava caves and formations, plentiful marine life and crystal-clear waters. The crossing between Kaua'i and Ni'ihau takes 2½ hours and is doable only in summer.

KAYAKING

With seven rivers, including the only navigable one statewide, river kayaking is the rage here. The Wailua River tour, which includes a dip at a 130ft waterfall, is the classic. Due to the river's popularity, the county strictly regulates its use (eg no tours on Sundays). Most outfitters are located in Wailua (p492), Hanalei (p518) and Lihu'e (p482).

For more solitude in nature, visit Kaua'i's other rivers, especially the Hanalei River (p518) and Kalihiwai Stream (Map p471). A handful of tours (p482) navigate the Hule'ia River, which passes through the off-limits Hule'ia National Wildlife Refuge.

Officially all sea kayaking off Kaua'i must be done on tour because of rough surf. Beginners can learn in Po'ipu (p533) and Hanalei (p518), while the fit and ambitious can challenge themselves on the grueling 17-mile Na Pali journey (p519), possible only in summer.

SNORKELING

Snorkeling is the most unsnobby of ocean activities: almost anyone can do it. Easy-access shore snorkeling is a great way to start. Sweet spots include Po'ipu Beach Park (p530), with dense fish populations and frequent turtle spottings, on the South Shore; Salt Pond Beach Park (p542), with shallow waters, on the Westside; Lydgate Beach Park (p489), for a protected lagoon perfect for kids, on the Eastside; and Ke'e Beach (p524) and Makua (Tunnels) Beach (p524), for the most spectacular setting (both above and below water), on the North Shore.

Your snorkeling options multiply if you go by boat or raft. The scenic Na Pali Coast circuit is the star; tours leave from Port Allen (p540), Kikiaola Small Boat Harbor (p546) and Hanalei Bay (p516), which is recommended for maximum North Shore viewing.

SURFING

Kaua'i's North Shore might be less famous than O'ahu's but it's still a surfing mecca (and home turf of the Irons brothers) – the same can be said of Waikiki and Po'ipu. Actually, Kaua'i's breaks are crowded (with lots of jos-

tling for a place in the line-up) year-round, especially when the surf is under 6ft. See boxed text, opposite, for insider tips.

SWIMMING

You can find protected swimming lagoons year-round at Lydgate Beach Park (p489), Salt Pond Beach Park (p542) and 'Anini Beach Park (p511). On the North Shore, swimming is feasible only in summer, when waters are calm at Ke'e Beach (p524) and Hanalei Bay (p516). In winter, when giant swells pound the North Shore, head to the South Shore, especially Po'ipu Beach Park (p530).

On Land

CYCLING

With no bike lanes (and sometimes no road shoulders), cycling remains challenging on Kaua'i. But the Eastside coastal path (p502) will eventually run from Lihu'e to Anahola and make for a sweet recreational ride. Currently, there's a 4-mile stretch from Kapa'a to Donkey Beach, and 2.5 miles along Lydgate Beach Park.

GOLF

While Kaua'i has only nine courses, the Prince Course (p513) at the St Regis Princeville Resort consistently ranks number one statewide (as it did in Golf Digest's 2007–08 Best in State list). Kaua'i Lagoons' Kiele Course (p482) made the ninth spot, while Po'ipu Bay Golf Course (p534) was number 10.

HELICOPTER TOURS

Only from a helicopter can you see Kaua'i' inaccessible mountains and valleys, especially the mysterious, cloud-cloaked Mt Wai'ale'ale. But notoriously noisy choppers disturb residents and amplify your carbon footprint (see p483). If you're set on flying, choose one of the Lihu'e-based companies, which generally have superior safety records, cost less and offer cheaper and better tour options. Also check the **Stop Disrespectful Air Tourism** (www.stopdat.org) website for recommended helicopter companies.

HIKING

If you don't explore the island on foot, you're missing out on Kaua'i's finest (and free) terrestrial offerings. Trails range from easy walks to precarious treks, so there's something for all skill levels. For the most variety, head to

KAUA'I SURF BEACHES & BREAKS Jake Howard

The Garden Isle is one of Hawaii's most challenging islands for surfers. On the North Shore, a heavy local vibe is pervasive; though **Hanalei Bay** (p516) offers some of the best waves among the islands, it is also closely guarded local turf. With the St Regis Princeville Resort overlooking the break however, residents may be a bit more understanding of out-of-towners in the water at Hanalei than at other North Shore spots – but surfing with respect is a must. Between local resistance and the inaccessibility of the Na Pali Coast, not to mention a sizable tiger shark population, you may want to pass on surfing the North Shore.

As a general rule, surf tourism is relegated to the South Shore around Po'ipu (p533). Chances are good that you'll be staying in this popular area anyway, which is perfect, as there are some fun waves to be had here. Breaking best in the summer on south swells, spots like **BK's**, **Acid Drop's** and **Center's** (Map p471) challenge even the most experienced surfers. First-timers can get their feet wet at nearby **Brennecke's** (p530). Only bodyboarding and bodysurfing are permitted here – no stand-up surfing – and it's a great place to take the family.

On the Northeast Coast, **Unreals** breaks at Anahola Bay. It's a consistent right point that can work well on an easterly wind swell, when *kona* (leeward) winds are offshore.

Surfing lessons and board hire are available mainly in Hanalei (p518) and in Po'ipu (p533). To find the swells, call the **surf hotline** (335-3720).

Waimea Canyon State Park (p551) and Koke'e State Park (p554). Don't miss the Pihea Trail (p556), which connects to the Alaka'i Swamp Trail, for a look at pristine native forestland. Hardier trekkers can combine the Nu'alolo Trail with the Awa'awapuhi Trail (p556) for breathtaking views of the Na Pali Coast.

Along the Na Pali Coast, the once-remote Kalalau Trail (p525) now attracts anyone with two legs – but only for the doable first section to Hanakapi'ai Beach. Eastside hikes head inland and upward, such as the Nounou Mountain Trails (p494), which afford sweeping mountain-to-ocean views.

About three dozen trails are managed by **Na Ala Hele** (Map p479; 274-3442; www.hawaiitrails.org; Department of Land & Natural Resources, Division of Forestry & Wildlife, Room 306, 3060 Eiwa St, Lihu'e, Hawaii 96766).

Guided Hikes

The **Sierra Club** (651-0682; www.hi.sierraclub.org/kauai /kauai.html) leads guided hikes (suggested donation $3) ranging from beach-cleanup walks to rigorous overnighters. Koke'e Museum (p554) leads 'Wonder Walks' (by donation) in summer. For the ultimate learning experience, hike with geologist Chuck Blay's company, **Kaua'i Nature Tours** (742-8305; 888-233-8365; www.kauai naturetours.com; tours adult $100-130, child 7-12 $75-85).

ZIPLINING

For a bird's-eye view of Kaua'i's forests and lots of effortless thrills, go ziplining. Lihu'e is zip central, with three reputable outfits

(p481), including one with the island's only canopy-based ziplines (once you're in the trees, you don't touch ground till the end). On the North Shore, there's one zip park, Princeville Ranch Adventures (p514), near Princeville. Note that some tours focus on zipping while others do fewer zips but add swimming and other fun.

GETTING THERE & AWAY
Air

All commercial flights land at **Lihu'e Airport** (LIH; Map p478; 246-1448; www.hawaii.gov/dot/air ports/kauai/lih; visitor hotline 6:30am-9pm). The small airport is simple to negotiate, and the only problem you might encounter is rush-hour traffic as you exit Lihu'e. Try to avoid arriving in the late afternoon, as traffic will be crawling in either direction.

The vast majority of incoming flights from overseas and the US mainland arrive on O'ahu at Honolulu International Airport. From there, travelers must catch an interisland flight to Kaua'i.

Here are the four interisland carriers:

go! (airline code YV; 888-435-9462; www.iflygo.com) Discount carrier.

Hawaiian Airlines (airline code HA; 800-367-5320; www.hawaiianair.com) Biggest airline with the most flights and fares comparable to go!'s.

Island Air (airline code WP; US mainland 800-323-3345, Neighbor Islands 800-652-6541; www.islandair .com) Only one or two flights to/from Lihu'e per day.

SUPERFERRY NON GRATA

In August 2007, when the Hawaii Superferry sailed toward Nawiliwili Harbor for its first arrival, some 300 Kaua'i protesters blocked its entry. Three dozen people even swam into the gargantuan ferry's path, shouting, 'Go home, go home!' Ultimately, service to Maui (but not to Kaua'i) was launched in December 2007, but the whole enterprise was indefinitely terminated in March 2009, when the Hawai'i Supreme Court deemed Superferry's environmental impact statement (EIS) invalid.

Why was opposition to the ferry so furious? Many protesters were suspicious of the political process that ushered the Superferry to Hawaii – or, as they claim, Governor Linda Lingle's disregard of state environmental laws, as she gave the Superferry a green light without an EIS. When the State Supreme Court eventually mandated an EIS, Lingle got a bill passed that changed the environmental requirements, which allowed the ferry to continue operating while the statement was being prepared.

Actually, the opponents themselves were not 'antiferry' but, rather, anti-Superferry. They wanted smaller, passenger-only, publicly owned and slower-moving boats. Their main concerns were nighttime collisions with whales, worsened traffic on Neighbor Islands, spread of environmental pests and plundering of natural resources by nonresidents. Indeed, during the Superferry's brief run between O'ahu and Maui, O'ahu residents were frequently caught taking home 'opihi (a prized edible limpet), crustaceans, algae, rocks, coral and massive quantities of reef fish.

That said, not all locals were opposed. In fact, many locals (especially O'ahu residents) viewed the Superferry as a convenient way to visit friends and family on Neighbor Islands. They also cited the need for an alternate, fuel-efficient mode of transportation between the islands (though the enormous vessels are actually gas guzzlers). They also pointed to the existing Matson barges already carrying potential pests between the islands.

For a compelling, if overwhelmingly detailed, account, read *The Superferry Chronicles* (Koohan Palk and Jerry Mander), which also analyzes the ferry's ties to US military and commercial interests.

Mokulele Airlines (airline code MW; ☎ 426-7070; www.mokuleleairlines.com) Partner with Alaska Airlines.

The following airlines fly directly to Lihu'e Airport from the US mainland:

Alaska Airlines (airline code AS; ☎ 800-252-7522; www.alaskaair.com)

American Airlines (airline code AA; ☎ 800-223-5436; www.aa.com)

United Airlines (airline code UA; ☎ 800-241-6522; www.ual.com)

US Airways (airline code US; ☎ 800-428-4322; www.usairways.com)

Sea

In late 2007, the **Hawaii Superferry** (www.hawaiisuperferry.com) launched its first commuter ferry, the *Alakai*, amid controversy. While the O'ahu–Maui route was active for just over a year, all service was indefinitely terminated in March 2009 due to legal trouble (see above for more information).

The only company running interisland cruises is **Norwegian Cruise Line** (☎ 800-327-7030; www.ncl.com) and its *Pride of America* liner, distinctly painted with Old Glory. Seven-day trips (starting in Honolulu and stopping in Maui, Hawai'i Island and Kaua'i) range from about $1200 (no view) to $1650 (balcony). The ship docks at Nawiliwili Harbor on Thursdays for one night.

GETTING AROUND
To/From the Airport

For car rentals, check in at the appropriate booth outside the baggage-claim area. Vans transport you to nearby car lots. If there's a queue, go directly to the lot, where check-ins are quicker.

Bicycle

Cyclists will encounter the gamut of terrain and weather. Winter months are particularly wet, but showers are common year-round. Worse problems are the lack of bicycle lanes and the narrow, winding and busy roads.

An 18-mile coastal bicycle path is slated to run from Lihu'e all the way to Anahola by the late 2000s, and the path is partly completed. Selective bike transportation is feasible but the path currently seems geared toward recreation, rather than commuting.

Bicycle-rental shops are found in Waipouli (p498), Kapa'a (see boxed text, p502) and Hanalei (p522). In general, bicycles are required to follow the same state laws and rules of the road as cars.

Bus

The county's **Kaua'i Bus** (☎ 241-6410; www.kauai.gov; 3220 Ho'olako St; per trip adult/senior & youth 7-18 $1.50/75¢; ⏱ 5:15am-7:15pm Mon-Fri, reduced schedule Sat, no service Sun) is fine for traveling along major highway towns and stops, but its routes and runs are limited. Schedules are available online. All buses stop in Lihu'e. The number of trips per route varies; for example, for intra-Lihu'e travel, there is an average of eight departures on weekdays, but for longer routes, such as Lihu'e to Po'ipu, you are stuck with one daily departure from each end.

A few caveats: drivers accept only the exact fare; a monthly pass costs $15; you can transport a bodyboard (but not a surfboard), folding baby stroller or bicycle; stops are marked but might be hard to spot, and the schedule does not include a map.

Buses are air-conditioned and equipped with bicycle racks and wheelchair ramps.

Car & Motorcycle

Kaua'i has one belt road running three-quarters of the way around the island, from Ke'e Beach in the north to Polihale in the west. The *Ready Mapbook of Kaua'i* ($11) is an invaluable road atlas, sold online at www.hawaii mapsource.com and at island bookstores.

HIGHWAY NICKNAMES

Locals call highways by nickname rather than by number. Here's a cheat sheet:

Hwy 50 Kaumuali'i Hwy
Hwy 51 Kapule Hwy
Hwy 56 Kuhio Hwy
Hwy 58 Nawiliwili Rd
Hwy 520 Maluhia Rd (Tree Tunnel) and Po'ipu Rd
Hwy 530 Koloa Rd
Hwy 540 Halewili Rd
Hwy 550 Waimea Canyon Dr
Hwy 552 Koke'e Rd
Hwy 560 Kuhio Hwy (continuation of Hwy 56)
Hwy 570 Ahukini Rd
Hwy 580 Kuamo'o Rd
Hwy 581 Kamalu Rd and Olohena Rd
Hwy 583 Ma'alo Rd

DRIVING DISTANCES & TIMES

Average driving distances and times from Lihu'e are listed below. Allow more time during morning and afternoon rush hours and on weekends.

Destination	Miles	Time
Anahola	14	25min
Hanalei	31	1hr
Hanapepe	16	30min
Kapa'a	8	15min
Ke'e Beach	40	1¼hr
Kilauea Lighthouse	25	40min
Po'ipu	10	20min
Port Allen	15	25min
Princeville	28	45min
Waimea	23	40min
Waimea Canyon	42	1½hr

Congestion is rampant, especially between Lihu'e and Kapa'a, where rush-hour traffic is a given. To combat traffic, a 'contraflow' lane is created weekdays from 5am to 10:30am on Kuhio Hwy (Hwy 56) in the Wailua area; this turns a northbound lane into a southbound lane by reversing the flow of traffic, so that commuters to Lihu'e have an extra lane open.

Gas prices are steeper on Kaua'i than on O'ahu. Prices vary across the island, so check www.kauaiworld.com/gasprices for the current highs and lows.

Car-rental companies are located at Lihu'e Airport. The familiar major agencies are generally reliable:

Alamo (☎ 800-327-9633, Lihu'e 246-0645; www .alamo.com)

Avis (☎ 800-331-1212, Lihu'e 245-7995; www.avis.com)

Budget (☎ 800-527-0700, Lihu'e 245-9031; www .budget.com)

Dollar (☎ 800-800-4000, Lihu'e 246-0622; www.dollar .com)

Hertz (☎ 800-654-3011, Lihu'e 245-3356; www.hertz .com)

National (☎ 888-868-6207, Lihu'e 245-5636; www .nationalcar.com)

Thrifty (☎ 800-847-4389, Lihu'e 866-450-5101; www .thrifty.com)

Motorcycle and moped rentals are popular, despite frequent showers. **Kaua'i Harley-Davidson** (Map p478; ☎ 241-7020, 877-212-9253; www.kauaih-d .com; 3-1866 Kaumuali'i Hwy, Lihu'e; per day $167-188) does brisk business renting its 26-bike fleet,

KAUA'I ITINERARIES

In Two Days

Start day one immersed in glorious greenery at the **National Tropical Botanical Garden** (p531), then stop at the **Koloa Fish Market** (p529) for *poke* (cubed raw fish mixed with sesame oil, salt, chili pepper or other condiments) and plate lunches before hitting **Po'ipu Beach Park** (p530) for a lazy afternoon. Don't miss the South Shore sunset. On day two, head up to **Waimea Canyon** (p550), hike at **Koke'e State Park** (p554) and browse local art at **Hanapepe's galleries** (p544).

In Four Days

After following the two-day itinerary, rise early and take the road trip of your life along the epic North Shore. At the 'End of the Road,' test your surefootedness on the first leg of the **Kalalau Trail** (p525). In the afternoon, meet native flora at **Limahuli Garden** (p524) and then soak up that surf-town vibe in **Hanalei** (p516). On day four, splash yourself awake with a **surf lesson** (p518) at Hanalei Bay. End your trip with a bike ride along the Eastside **coastal path** (p502), followed by shopping and eating in lively **Kapa'a** (p499).

For Hikers

If hiking's your thing, Kaua'i's diverse trails and terrain can intrigue you for a lifetime. For starters, head up to the island's hiking hotbed, **Koke'e State Park** (p554), where the muddy bog of the **Alaka'i Swamp Trail** (p556) and the unnervingly steep **Nu'alolo loop hike** (p556) are utterly unique. Walk along the rugged, undeveloped **Maha'ulepu Coast** (p534) and see ancient sandstone cliffs and pristine beaches. Trek up **Nounou Mountain** (p494) for sweeping views of the Eastside, plus a butt-kicking workout. Stroll the endless carpet of sand along **Kekaha Beach Park** (p549), which you might have all to yourself. The island's signature hike navigates the sheer Na Pali cliffs along the **Kalalau Trail** (p525).

despite its going rate of almost $200 per day plus a $1000 security deposit. More affordable are mopeds, available at **Kauai Scooter Rental** (Map p478; ☎ 245-7177; www.kauaimopedrentals .com; 3371 Wilcox Rd; ☼ 8am-5pm) for $59 per day (from 8am to 5pm) and $75 for 24 hours. Staffers train new moped users until they're confident enough to hit the road – and there's no obligation if you change your mind. See the Transportation chapter for more on getting around by car (p575) or motorbikes (p577).

Taxi

Locals rarely use taxicabs so you'll find only a dozen companies. The standard flag-down fee is $3, plus 30¢ per ⅛ additional mile. Cabs line up at the airport during normal business hours, but they don't run all night or cruise for passengers; outside the airport, you'll need to call ahead.

Taxi companies include **Akiko's Taxi** (☎ 822-7588), in the Lihu'e-Kapa'a area; **North Shore Cab** (☎ 826-4118; www.northshorecab.com), based in Princeville; and **Southshore Cab** (☎ 742-1525), in Po'ipu.

LIHU'E

pop 5675

Your first impression of Lihu'e, the island capital, will likely be lukewarm. That's because this is a drive-in, drive-out town, with no distinct center. Here, the parts are greater than the sum – and you'll find gems scattered throughout. First, there's a plethora of economical eateries and shops, including longtime family-run businesses hidden in nondescript buildings. Second, the town beach is a beauty, ideal for almost all water sports. Third, there's a down-to-earth quality to this workaday town that's missing in the resort towns north and south. By necessity, you'll pass through Lihu'e – not a knockout but worth getting to know.

HISTORY

Lihu'e arose as a plantation town back when sugar was king and the massive Lihu'e Plantation sugar mill was Kaua'i's largest. The plantation relied solely on rainwater during its early years, but then William Harrison Rice, who bought the company in the early

1860s, became the first planter in Hawaii to irrigate sugarcane fields.

The plantation closed in 2001, ending more than a century of operation. But, in Lihu'e and its vicinity, the ethnic makeup still reflects the island's plantation history, with substantial numbers of Japanese and Filipino residents, as well as Caucasians and mixed-race people.

Now Lihu'e's economy relies not only on tourism but on retail, which is obvious from all the big-box stores at Kukui Grove Shopping Center. You might not think an island of 63,000 needs a Costco but, in October 2006, it got one.

ORIENTATION

Lihu'e's focal points are Nawiliwili Bay, the island's only major harbor, and Lihu'e Airport, the island's only major airport. Rice St, considered the town's main drag, runs east–west and passes the government buildings and post office, while Kuhio Hwy (Hwy 56) leads to shops and restaurants toward the north.

INFORMATION
Bookstores

Borders (Map p478; ☎ 246-0862; Kukui Grove Shopping Center, 4303 Nawiliwili Rd; ◷ 9am-10pm Mon-Thu, to 11pm Fri & Sat, to 8pm Sun) Large chain with wide range of books, CDs and DVDs; lots of local selections unavailable on the mainland. In-store Starbucks café.

Tropic Isle Music Co (Map p478; ☎ 245-8700; www.tropicislemusic.com; Anchor Cove Shopping Center, 3416 Rice St; ◷ 9am-9pm) Huge selection of Hawaii-specific books, CDs, stationery, food, toiletries, fabrics – you name it. See website for complete online store.

Emergency

Police, Fire & Ambulance (☎ 911)
Police Station (Map p479; ☎ 241-1771; 3060 Umi St) For nonemergencies, incident reporting and information.
Sexual Assault Crisis Line (☎ 245-4144)

Internet Access

Unless you have your own computer, free internet access is rare in Lihu'e. One option is **Kukui Grove Shopping Center** (Map p478; Kukui Grove Shopping Center, Kuhio Hwy; ◷ 9:30am-7pm Mon-Thu & Sat, to 9pm Fri, to 6pm Sun; ☍), where the mall's free wi-fi zone runs from Sears through the food court and central walkway. If you can't do without a table and espresso, pay for access at the mall's two Starbucks locations.

For dinosaur-age dial-up service, **Hawaii Link** (Map p478; ☎ 246-9300; www.hawaiilink.net; 2950 Kress St; ◷ 10am-6pm Mon-Fri, 9am-noon Sat) offers a $10 dail-up account deal for two weeks.

Laundry

Lihu'e Laundromat (Map p479; ☎ 332-8356; Rice Shopping Center, 4303 Rice St; ◷ 24hr)

Media
NEWSPAPERS

Garden Island (www.kauaiworld.com) Kaua'i's daily newspaper is very lean and locally focused, but it's a good source for current island events and issues.

RADIO

KITH 98.9FM Contemporary island music, including Hawaiian and reggae, plus local-favorite covers of American pop classics. Upbeat choice for island cruising.

KKCR 90.9FM (www.kkcr.org) Kaua'i Community Radio is 100% volunteer run, listener supported and noncommercial. Excellent spectrum of music programming, plus call-in talk shows, interviews and live in-studio performances. No NPR or PRI national programs. It's based in Hanalei, but you can listen islandwide at 91.9FM.

KQNG 93.5FM (www.kongradio.com) Known as KONG radio, this popular station plays mainstream US pop and contemporary island music. DJs Ron Wiley (mornings) and Marc Valentine (afternoons) are island institutions.

KQNG 570AM News, sports and talk, including syndicated shows by Rush Limbaugh, Dr Dean Edell, Mitch Albom and Al Franken.

KTOH 99.9FM Oldies, classic hits from the 1960s to 1990s.

KUAI 720AM The best station for news, every hour on the hour, plus extended coverage at 7am, noon and 5pm on weekdays.

TELEVISION

KVIC A televised loop of Kaua'i tourist information on channel 3.

Medical Services

Longs Drugs (Map p478; ☎ 245-7771; Kukui Grove Shopping Center, 3-2600 Kaumuali'i Hwy; ◷ store 7am-10pm Mon-Sat, 8am-8pm Sun, pharmacy 8am-9pm Mon-Sat, 9am-6pm Sun)

Wilcox Memorial Hospital (Map p478; ☎ 245-1010, TTY 245-1133; 3420 Kuhio Hwy) Kaua'i's only major hospital. Emergency services 24 hours.

Money

Banks with 24-hour ATMs:
American Savings Bank (Map p478; ☎ 246-8844; Kukui Grove Shopping Center, 3-2600 Kaumuali'i Hwy)
Bank of Hawaii (Map p479; ☎ 245-6761; 4455 Rice St)

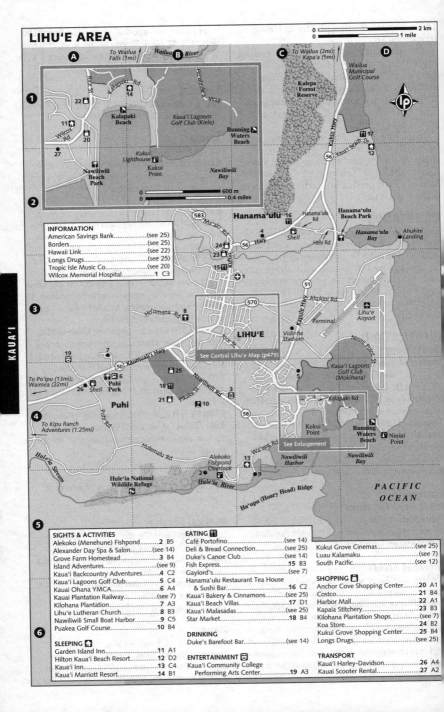

LIHU'E AREA

To Wailua Falls (1mi)

Wailua River

To Wailua (2mi); Kapa'a (5mi)

Wailua Municipal Golf Course

Kalepa Forest Reserve

Rice St

Kalapaki Rd

Ho'olaulea Way

Kuhio Hwy

Kauai Beach Dr

Kalapaki Beach

Kaua'i Lagoons Golf Club (Kiele)

Wilcox Rd

Running Waters Beach

Nawiliwili Beach Park

Kukui Lighthouse

Kukui Point

Nawiliwili Bay

Ma'alo Rd

Hanama'ulu

Hanama'ulu Rd

Hanama'ulu Beach Park

Hanama'ulu Bay

Ahukini Landing

Shell

Hehi Rd

Ho'omana Rd

Rice St

Ahukini Rd

Lihu'e Airport

LIHU'E

Kapule Hwy

Vidinha Stadium

Terminal

See Central Lihu'e Map (p479)

Kaumuali'i Hwy

Nawiliwili Rd

Pikake St

Kaua'i Lagoons Golf Club (Mokihana)

Nīnini Point St

To Po'ipu (13mi); Waimea (22mi)

Shell

Puhi Park

Puhi

Puhi Rd

To Kipu Ranch Adventures (1.25mi)

Kalapaki Rd

Kukui Point

Running Waters Beach

Nīnini Point

See Enlargement

Hule'ia Stream

Hulemalu Rd

Alekoko Fishpond Overlook

Wa'apa Rd

Nawiliwili Harbor

Nawiliwili Bay

PACIFIC OCEAN

Hule'ia National Wildlife Refuge

Hule'ia River

Ha'upu (Hoary Head) Ridge

0 — 600 m
0 — 0.4 miles

0 — 2 km
0 — 1 mile

KAUA'I

INFORMATION
American Savings Bank	(see 25)
Borders	(see 25)
Hawaii Link	(see 22)
Longs Drugs	(see 25)
Tropic Isle Music Co	(see 20)
Wilcox Memorial Hospital	1 C3

SIGHTS & ACTIVITIES
Alekoko (Menehune) Fishpond	2 B5
Alexander Day Spa & Salon	(see 14)
Grove Farm Homestead	3 B4
Island Adventures	(see 9)
Kaua'i Backcountry Adventures	4 C2
Kaua'i Lagoons Golf Club	5 C4
Kauai Ohana YMCA	6 A4
Kauai Plantation Railway	(see 7)
Kilohana Plantation	7 A3
Lihu'e Lutheran Church	8 B3
Nawiliwili Small Boat Harbor	9 C5
Puakea Golf Course	10 B4

SLEEPING
Garden Island Inn	11 A1
Hilton Kaua'i Beach Resort	12 D2
Kaua'i Inn	13 C4
Kaua'i Marriott Resort	14 B1

EATING
Café Portofino	(see 14)
Deli & Bread Connection	(see 25)
Duke's Canoe Club	(see 14)
Fish Express	15 B3
Gaylord's	(see 7)
Hanama'ulu Restaurant Tea House & Sushi Bar	16 C2
Kaua'i Bakery & Cinnamons	(see 25)
Kaua'i Beach Villas	17 D1
Kaua'i Malasadas	(see 25)
Star Market	18 B4

DRINKING
Duke's Barefoot Bar	(see 14)

ENTERTAINMENT
Kaua'i Community College Performing Arts Center	19 A3

SHOPPING
Kukui Grove Cinemas	(see 25)
Luau Kalamaku	(see 7)
South Pacific	(see 12)
Anchor Cove Shopping Center	20 A1
Costco	21 B4
Harbor Mall	22 A1
Kapaia Stitchery	23 B3
Kilohana Plantation Shops	(see 7)
Koa Store	24 B2
Kukui Grove Shopping Center	25 B4
Longs Drugs	(see 25)

TRANSPORT
Kaua'i Harley-Davidson	26 A4
Kauai Scooter Rental	27 A2

CENTRAL LIHU'E

Post
Longs Drugs (Map p478; ☎ 245-7771; Kukui Grove Shopping Center, 3-2600 Kaumuali'i Hwy; ☒ 7am-10pm Mon-Sat, 8am-8pm Sun) In-store postal center offers photocopying, FedEx and UPS, and US Postal Service (rates are slightly lower at a post office).
Post office (Map p479; ☎ 800-275-8777; 4441 Rice St; ☒ 8am-4:30pm Mon-Fri, 9am-1pm Sat) Main post office holds poste restante (general delivery) mail for a maximum of 30 days.

Tourist Information
Kaua'i Visitors Bureau (Map p479; ☎ 245-3971, 800-262-1400; www.kauaidiscovery.com; Suite 101, 4334 Rice St) offers a monthly calendar of events, bus schedules and list of county-managed Sunshine Markets (farmers markets) for the sale of Kaua'i produce. Order a free 'vacation planning kit' online.

SIGHTS
Kalapaki Beach
This well-protected sandy **beach** (Map p478) is underrated, considering its easy-access location and remarkable versatility. The calmer waters toward the east are good for

swimming, while the swells toward the west draw bodyboarders and surfers. Due to its sandy (rather than reef) bottom, waters are poor for snorkeling. Overall, it's a gem, not only for ocean sports but also for picnicking, watching the surf action, grabbing a drink at Duke's Barefoot Bar (p486) and just hanging out. It's easily overlooked because it's hidden behind a row of touristy shops and the Kaua'i Marriott Resort (p485).

Due to the proximity of Nawiliwili Harbor, the island's major port, you'll see ship traffic, barge containers and other industrial objects in the distance. Thus the beach is less exotic than those on the North and South Shores, but the forgiving wave action here is a real plus. Parking close to the water is available at the hotel's north end (signs direct you to public/beach parking). Just south, **Nawiliwili Beach Park** is not worth a stop, as its proximity to Nawiliwili Harbor and a seawall give it an industrial vibe.

Kilohana Plantation
If you're curious about how Kaua'i's powerful sugar barons lived, visit this handsome **plantation**

KAUA'I

estate (Map p478; www.kilohanakauai.com; Kaumuali'i Hwy; admission free; ☺ 9:30am-9:30pm Mon-Sat, to 5pm Sun), which today contains a variety of classy attractions, including Gaylord's restaurant (p486), a stellar luau show (p487), upscale shopping and Clydesdale-horse-drawn **carriage rides** (☎ 246-9529; 20min ride adult/child $12/6; ☺ 11am-5pm) across the 35-acre grounds. The meticulously kept property feels welcoming and guests are invited to wander around.

Plantation owner Gaylord Parke Wilcox, once the head honcho of Grove Farm Homestead, built the house in 1936. The 15,000 sq ft Tudor-style mansion has been painstakingly restored and its legacy as one of Kaua'i's distinguished historic houses is unquestioned. Antique-filled rooms and Oriental carpets on hardwood floors lead you past cases of poi (fermented taro) pounders, koa bowls and other Hawaiiana to a row of gallery shops.

Our favorite attraction is the **Kauai Planation Railway** (☎ 245-7245; www.kauaiplantationrailway.com; 40min ride adult/child 3-12 $18/14; ☺ departures on the hr, 10am-2pm), which features open-air replica cars and a restored historic train that passes fields of tropical crops and modest pastures with cattle and horses. The big thrill for city-slicker kids is stopping to feed an eager herd of pigs.

Kaua'i Museum

The island's largest **museum** (Map p479; ☎ 245-6931; www.kauaimuseum.org; 4428 Rice St; adult/child 6-12/student 13-17/senior $10/1/3/8; 1st Sat of month free; ☺ 9am-4pm Mon-Fri, 10am-4pm Sat) is no bigger than the average house, but its humbleness is

rather charming. It's worth a stop for a quick grounding in Kaua'i's history, especially if you catch a free **guided tour** (☺ 10:30am Tue-Fri); call for reservations. Free **Hawaiian quilting demonstrations** (☺ 9am-noon Wed & Thu) and **lauhala-hat weaving demonstrations** (☺ 1pm Mon & Wed) are given year-round.

Straightforward, well-written displays explain the Hawaiian Islands' volcanic genesis and the formation of the island chain from the ocean floor, as well as Kaua'i's unique ecosystems. Collections include early Hawaiian artifacts such as *kapa* (cloth made by pounding the bark of the paper mulberry tree), wooden bowls and ceremonial lei. Upstairs the collection covers the sugar and pineapple plantation era. One telling display juxtaposes replicas of a plantation worker's spartan shack and the spacious bedroom of an early missionary's house, furnished with an extravagant koa four-post bed and Hawaiian quilts.

Wailua Falls

Is it worth the winding 4-mile drive to the **falls** (off Map p478) made famous in the opening credits of *Fantasy Island*? The view is rather distant but to many, this gushing double waterfall (Wailua means 'Two Waters') misting the surrounding tropical foliage is a fantastic photo op, especially when the falls merge into one wide cascade after downpours. While officially listed as 80ft, the falls have been repeatedly measured at between 125ft and 175ft.

At the lookout spot, a sign reads: 'Slippery rocks at top of falls. People have been killed.' Heed it. Many have slipped while trying to scramble down the steep, untamed path.

To get here from Lihu'e, follow Kuhio Hwy north and turn left onto Ma'alo Rd (Hwy 583), which ends at the falls after 4 miles.

Alekoko (Menehune) Fishpond

Don't expect a splash and dip – only a distant, if gorgeous, view of this tranquil 39-acre **pond** (Map p478), an ancient *loko wai* (freshwater fishpond). According to legend, Kaua'i's *menehune* (the 'little people' who built many of Hawaii's fishponds, heiaus and other stonework, according to legend) formed the fishpond overnight when they built the 900ft stone dam across a bend in the Hule'ia River. Holes in the structure allowed young fish to enter the pond but not to escape once grown. Today you can't actually see the dam because it's covered by a thick green line of mangrove trees.

The pond was productive with mullet until 1824, when Kaua'i's leader Kaumuali'i died and *ali'i* (chiefs) from O'ahu and Maui ruled the island as absentee landlords. With no *ali'i* to feed and maintain the pond, it sorely declined. Later the surrounding area was planted with taro and rice. Today it is privately owned and not in use.

The US Fish & Wildlife Service owns the lands surrounding the fishpond (about 240 acres of river basin and steep forested slopes along the north side of Hule'ia River). In 1973 the area was designated the **Hule'ia National Wildlife Refuge** (http://pacificislands.fws.gov/wnwr/khuleianwr.html) and now provides breeding and feeding grounds for endemic water birds. The refuge is closed to the public, but kayak tours (p482) along Hule'ia River drift through it.

To get to the overlook, drive up Hulemalu Rd for 0.5 miles.

Ninini Point

If you've seen and done everything and still want to explore, here's a modest excursion to an **untouristy spot** (Map p478) where 360-degree vistas show jets swooping in the sky above and waves crashing against the rocks below. Looking east, soaring cliffs cut off rainbows and, closer in, golfers tee off near a beckoning scoop of beach. These terrific views from Ninini Point are made more so by its 100ft **lighthouse** marking the northern entrance to Nawiliwili Bay. Here, Hawaiians still fish, pick *opihi* (edible limpet) and gather *limu* (edible seaweed).

The road to the lighthouse begins off Kapule Hwy, just over 0.5 miles south of the intersection with Ahukini Rd and marked with two concrete slabs. You'll walk for just over 2 miles, past a guard gate (usually empty) and Hole 12 of the Mokihana Golf Course, most of it rutted dirt road, before you reach the short spur to the lighthouse.

Running Waters Beach (the little slice of sand visible from Ninini Point) is not swimmable but makes a nice picnic spot. To find it, return to Hole 12 and park in the lot just before it, then follow the signs for 'Shore Access.' Turn right at Whaler's Brew Pub and descend to its parking lot, where you'll see another 'Shore Access' sign to your left. It's a steep, quick walk to the beach below.

Grove Farm Homestead

History buffs might enjoy this **plantation museum** (Map p478; ☎ 245-3202; Nawiliwili Rd; 2hr tour adult/child under 12 $5/2; ☉ tours 10am & 1pm Mon, Wed & Thu), open only for prearranged tours, but kids might grow restless. Grove Farm was among the most productive sugar companies on Kaua'i and George Wilcox, the son of missionaries Abner and Lucy Wilcox, built this well-preserved farmhouse in 1864. It feels suspended in time, with rocking chairs sitting dormant on a covered porch and untouched books lining the shelves of the musty library.

Lihu'e Lutheran Church

Hawaii's oldest Lutheran **church** (Map p478; ☎ 245-2145; 4602 Ho'omana Rd; ☉ services 8am & 10:30am Sun) is a quaint clapboard house, with an incongruously slanted floor that resembles a ship's deck and a balcony akin to a captain's bridge. German immigrants built this church, styling it after their own late-19th-century boat. The building is actually a faithful 1983 reconstruction of the 1885 original, which was leveled in Hurricane 'Iwa in 1982. The church is located along a curvy country lane just off Kaumuali'i Hwy (Hwy 50).

ACTIVITIES
Ziplining & Multiactivity Tours

The 'sport' of ziplining arose in Costa Rican jungles, but it's similarly suited to Kaua'i's tree-filled rainforests. Weight and age restrictions vary widely.

our pick **Just Live** (☎ 482-1295; www.justlive.org; Kuhio Hwy; tours $79-125) Only this outfit offers canopy-based zipping, meaning you never touch ground after your first zip. The 3½-hour zip tour includes seven ziplines and five bridge crossings, 60ft to 80ft off the ground in 200ft

COURTING HOLLYWOOD

The state woos Hollywood to shoot in Hawaii, offering a 20% tax break for production work on Neighbor Islands. In 2007, Ben Stiller filmed the $100-million *Tropic Thunder* on Kaua'i, hiring 350 local crew members (in a total crew of 778), plus hundreds of local extras. The cast and crew rented houses or stayed at the two Wailua hotels for some 13 weeks. They patronized local restaurants, bars and countless businesses. They filmed across the island, from Grove Farm in Lihu'e to Hanalei. Overall, the film is estimated to have contributed a whopping $60 million to the island's economy.

However, some islanders allege that the film sets caused environmental damage, such as altered streams, flattened bamboo groves, scorched 'war zones' and toxic damage from pyrotechnics. They criticize the lack of oversight by the State Department of Land & Natural Resources (or any other authority).

We could not prove the allegations either way, but conclude that Kaua'i's movie 'industry' will always entail a fine balance. Some embrace the island's long history on the silver screen. Some value the big economic boost. Some view the 'commodification' of the *'aina* (land) as never justifiable. Opinions differed over *Tropic Thunder* and will differ again the next time Hollywood comes to town.

Norfolk Island pines. Profits from commercial tours go toward community youth programs. Minimum age is nine.

Kaua'i Backcountry Adventures (Map p478; ☎ 245-2506, 888-270-0555; www.kauaibackcountry.com; Kuhio Hwy; tour incl lunch $125) Offers a 3½-hour zipline tour with seven lines, elevated as high as 200ft above the ground and running as far as 900ft (three football fields). Afterward, refuel on a picnic lunch at a swimming pond. Groups run as large as 11. Minimum age is 12.

Outfitters Kaua'i (Map pp532-3; ☎ 742-9667, 888-742-9887; www.outfitterskauai.com; Po'ipu Plaza, 2827A Po'ipu Rd; 4hr tour adult/child 7-14 $125/99, 8hr tour incl lunch adult/child under 15 $175/135). Offers two multiactivity tours that combine zipping, hiking, waterfall swimming and the ever idealized 'rope-swinging'. Half-day tour includes four zips; full-day tour includes only one. Minimum zipping age is seven.

Kayaking & Canoeing

The only way to navigate the Hule'ia River and see the Hule'ia National Wildlife Refuge is on a commercial tour. The best are offered by **Outfitters Kaua'i** (Map pp532-3; ☎ 742-9667, 888-742-9887; www.outfitterskauai.com; Po'ipu Plaza, 2827A Po'ipu Rd, Po'ipu Beach; tours adult/child 3-14 with lunch $108/84, without lunch $104/78), which combine kayaking and hiking. It's a cinch, downwind for only 2 miles, with a return trip not by kayak but by motorized canoe.

Island Adventures (Map p478; ☎ 246-6333; www .kauaifun.com; Nawiliwili Small Boat Harbor; tour incl lunch adult/child 6-12 $89/69) offers a 4½-hour tour in the Hule'ia National Wildlife Refuge, where you'll paddle 2.5 miles into the wildlife refuge, hike to two private waterfalls, swim and picnic. If

you can't hike eight to 10 flights of uneven steps, take a pass.

Tubing

Part historical site, part lazy-man cruise, 'tubing' means floating down former sugar-plantation irrigation ditches in old-fashioned inner tubes. **Kaua'i Backcountry Adventures** (Map p478; ☎ 245-2506, 888-270-0555; www.kauaibackcountry .com; Kuhio Hwy; 3hr tour incl lunch $100; ⏱ departures 9am, 10:30am, 1pm & 2:30pm Mon-Sat, 9am & 1pm Sun) offers the island's only tubing tour, which ends with lunch at a swimming hole. Great for the whole family (including kids as young as five).

ATVs

Can driving an ATV across private, pristine ranchland really constitute an 'ecotour'? On two tours offered by **Kipu Ranch Adventures** (off Map p478; ☎ 246-9288; www.kiputours.com; tours driver/ child/senior & passenger from $125/72/100) you do see gorgeous, otherwise-inaccessible landscape, including the Ha'upu mountain range, Kipu Kai coast and Hule'ia River, plus wild pigs, pheasants, peacocks and turkeys. But gas-powered vehicles are hard to endorse. For a green alternate, try Kaua'i ATV Tours (p528).

Golf

The original two Jack Nicklaus–designed 18-hole par-72 courses at **Kaua'i Lagoons Golf Club** (Map p478; ☎ 241-6000, 800-634-6400; www.kauaila goonsgolf.com; Kaua'i Marriott, 3351 Ho'olaule'a Way; green fees morning $125-175, afternoon $105-125, club rental $55) were called Kiele and Mokihana. In 2008, both courses began undergoing a major renovation that will last through 2010. During this period, only one combined 18-hole experience is available. Guests of the Kaua'i Marriott receive discounted rates (morning/afternoon $115/95).

The lush cliffs of Mt Ha'upu serve as a backdrop to the Robin Nelson–designed **Puakea Golf Course** (Map p478; ☎ 245-8756, 866-773-5554; www .puakeagolf.com; 4315 Kalepa Rd; green fees incl cart before 11am $135, 11am-2pm $79, after 2pm $59, club rental $40), which first opened in 1997 (with an odd 10 holes) and became an 18-hole course in 2003. It's located near Kukui Grove Shopping Center.

Fishing

Most charters depart from Nawiliwili Small Boat Harbor (Map p478). The following outfits are top-notch:

OUR PICK **Lahela Ocean Adventures** (☎ 635-4020; www.sport-fishing-kauai.com; 4hr shared charter per person $219, 4hr private per 6 passengers $625) Captain Scott Akana is named by other fisherman as the island's 'best' and a real 'pro.' Spectators ride at half-price. Detailed website answers all your questions and more.

Happy Hunter Sport Fishing (☎ 639-4351, 634-2633; www.happyhuntersportfishing.com; 4hr private charter per 6 passengers $625) Captain Harry Shigekane has 30 years' experience and sails a fantastic 41ft Pacifica. Private charters only.

Helicopter Tours

The best selection and quality of chopper tours fly from Lihu'e Airport (Map p478).

The going rate for a 50- to 60-minute flight is around $200. Go online for major discounts.

A good choice for couples or threesomes is **Mauna Loa Helicopters** (☎ 245-4006; www.maunaloa helicopters.com; 1hr tour $199-239), which also runs a flight school. Highly qualified pilots don't skimp on full 60-minute private tours for up to three passengers. Small groups allow for more-personalized interaction between pilot and passengers. You can choose a doors-off tour for $10 to $20 more per person. Singles should choose another, nonprivate tour, as the cost would be prohibitive.

The following tours allow six passengers, which can seem crowded (if you get stuck in the middle), but they give hour-long (or close) rides and have well-qualified pilots:

Island Helicopters (☎ 245-8588, 800-829-8588; www.islandhelicopters.com; 50-55min tour $178) Long-time, small company.

Jack Harter Helicopters (☎ 245-3774, 888-245-2001; www.helicopters-kauai.com; 60-65min tour $229-259) You get your money's worth of air time here. Choose from standard enclosed, six-passenger AStars ($229) or doors-off, four-passenger Hughes 500s ($259). Longer 90- to 95-minute tours offered.

OUR PICK **Safari Helicopters** (☎ 246-0136, 800-326-3356; www.safarihelicopters.com; 55-/90min tours from $160/250) Besides fair prices, this outfit offers a fascinating tour that lands on a cliff overlooking Olokele Valley in Waimea. The landowner, Keith Robinson (whose family owns Ni'ihau and 2000 Kaua'i acres), chats with passengers about his conservation work with endangered species.

WHY FLY?

When did you last hear a helicopter overhead? Chances are, you can't remember. Unfortunately, island residents have a different answer: chopper noise is a daily occurrence.

Noise pollution might seem piddly next to greenhouse gases and global warming, but if your ears are constantly barraged by droning helicopters (or, worse, loud biplanes), your quality of life surely suffers. Furthermore, crashes have occurred near towns, including Ha'ena and Wainiha, causing those on the ground to worry about their safety.

The Sierra Club and other island advocacy groups have long pushed for limits on commercial aircrafts' freedom to fly over residential neighborhoods and FAA-designated noise-abatement areas. But for now it's a voluntary system. Thus the Sierra Club recommends that passengers ask pilots to avoid sensitive areas, such as the Kalalau Trail and popular beaches.

To stop 'disrespectful air tourism,' a group called **StopDAT** (www.stopdat.org) is seeking to pinpoint the best and worst tour companies. Advocates emphasize common courtesy: would you want tourists constantly flying over your hometown? They decry those who come for Kaua'i's rural serenity yet contribute to the opposite qualities by taking noisy tours.

In case you're wondering just how much carbon you'll need to offset that 60-minute tour: most helicopter companies fly Eurocopter AStars, which consume 38 to 40 gallons of fuel per hour's flight, carrying seven passengers. Smaller choppers, such as the Robinson R44s flown by Mauna Loa Helicopters, seat up to four and use less than 25 gallons for a similar tour.

Spas

The **Alexander Day Spa & Salon** (Map p478; ☎ 246-4918; www.alexanderspa.com; Kaua'i Marriottt Resort; 50min massage $115; ☺ 8am-7pm) strives to pamper guests in the most ecofriendly way, using biodegradable water cups, recycled paper products and CFL (compact fluorescent light) bulbs.

Swimming

Lap swimmers, get your fix at this open-air, Olympic-sized pool at the new **Kauai Ohana YMCA** (Map p478; ☎ 246-9090; Kaumuali'i Hwy; day pass $10; ☺ 5:30am-9am & 11am-7pm Mon-Fri, 7am-7pm Sat, 10am-6pm Sun). Teach tots to swim in a nifty learning pool with 1ft to 4ft steps. A weight room is also available. YMCA members from any state, show your card to pay only $5. It's across Kilohana Plantation.

FESTIVALS & EVENTS

E Pili Kakou I Ho'okahi Lahui (www.epilikakou-kauai .org) Annual two-day hula retreat in late February features top *kumu hula* (hula teachers) from across the islands. Current venue is the Hilton Kaua'i Beach Resort.

Spring Gourmet Gala (☎ 245-8359) Save your appetite for the island's highest-end gourmet event ($100 per person), featuring food-and-wine pairings by famous Hawaii chefs, in early April. Funds support the Kaua'i Community College's culinary arts program. The 300 tickets sell out fast.

May Day Lei Contest & Fair (☎ 245-6931; www .kauaimuseum.org) Established in the early 1980s, the annual Kaua'i Museum lei contest on May 1 spawns legendary floral art.

Kaua'i Polynesian Festival (☎ 335-6466; www .kauaipolynesianfestival.org) This four-day event in late May features rockin' competitions in expert Tahitian,

Maori, Samoan and hula dancing, plus food booths and cultural workshops, held at various locations.

Fourth of July Concert in the Sky (☎ 246-2440) Enjoy island foods, entertainment and a fireworks show set to music at Vidinha Stadium (Map p478), from 3pm to 9pm.

Kaua'i County Farm Bureau Fair (☎ 332-8189) Old-fashioned family fun at Vidinha Stadium (Map p478) in late August, with carnival rides and games, livestock show, petting zoo, hula performances and lots of local-food booths.

Aloha Festivals Ho'olaule'a & Parade (☎ 245-8508; www.alohafestivals.com) This statewide event in early September starts on Kaua'i with a parade from Vidinha Stadium (Map p478) to the county building lawn. The *ho'olaule'a* (celebration) includes an appearance by the royal court.

Kaua'i Composers Contest & Concert (☎ 822-2166; www.mokihana.kauai.net) The signature event of the Kaua'i Mokihana Festival, this contest in mid- to late September showcases homegrown musical talent.

'Kaua'i Style' Hawaiian Slack Key Guitar Festival (☎ 239-4336; www.slackkeyfestival.com) Held in mid-November, this opportunity to see master slack key guitarists for free is not to be missed.

Lights on Rice Parade (☎ 246-1004) Disney had its Main Street Electrical Parade. Kaua'i has this charming parade of illuminated floats in early December.

SLEEPING

Lihu'e's sleeping options are limited mostly to a few hotels, from the high-end Marriott to no-frills motels in the nondescript town center. Unlike on the Eastside, few B&Bs and inns operate in residential neighborhoods. For vacation-rental homes, contact **Kauai Vacation Rentals** (Map p479; ☎ 245-8841; 800-367-5025; www.kauaivacationrentals.com; 3-3311 Kuhio Hwy), where owner Lucy Kawaihalau is one of the

---

LIVE & LET LIVE

Before you get too annoyed at the thousands of wild chickens on Kaua'i, try to understand their backstory. The first chickens to populate Hawaii were jungle fowl *(moa)*, introduced by the first Polynesians. These vividly colored birds later cross-bred with domestic chickens brought by Westerners. During plantation days, Kaua'i's wild-chicken population was kept in check by field fires (a regular event before harvest, to allow more efficient reaping). However, when the sugar industry went bust in the 1980s, the chicken population boomed.

When Hurricane 'Iwa and Hurricane 'Iniki struck in 1982 and 1992 respectively, they obliterated the cages of Kaua'i's fighting cocks, adding even more chickens to the wild. With no mongoose or snake population to prey on fowl, wild chickens proliferated.

You'll see them perched in trees, running across fields, roaming parking lots and otherwise strutting their stuff across the island. Most locals have adopted an attitude of acceptance toward the chickens, but warn of their *lolo* (crazy) schedules: instead of crowing only at dawn, they cock-a-doodle-doo at random times and seem confused by a full moon or any late-night light. Before you book accommodations, ask whether there are chickens living within earshot. Or just wear earplugs.

island's most experienced and dedicated rental agents.

Kaua'i Palms Hotel (Map p479; ☎ 246-0908; www .kauaipalmshotel.com; 2931 Kalena St; r from $75-85; ⟨ ⟩ office 7am-8pm; ⟨ ⟩) The island version of Motel 6, Kaua'i Palms is Lihu'e's best budget option. The 28 rooms include fridge, cable TV and windows on opposite walls to allow cooling cross-breezes. Pay more for rooms with kitchenettes and air-con. Wi-fi available only in lobby.

ourpick Garden Island Inn (Map p478; ☎ 245-7227, 800-648-0154; www.gardenislandinn.com; 3445 Wilcox Rd; r $99-150, ste $145-180; ⟨ ⟩ ⟨ ⟩ ⟨ ⟩) You won't find the Marriott's beachfront cachet and megapool here. But this two-storey inn across the street holds its own for value and friendliness. Rooms are modest but cheerful, with tropical decor, overhead fans, quality double beds and kitchenettes. The real gems are the suites on the 2nd and 3rd floors, with large ocean-view lanais.

Kaua'i Inn (Map p478; ☎ 245-9000, 800-808-2330; www.kauai-inn.com; 2430 Hulemalu Rd; r with kitchenette incl breakfast $129-149; ⟨ ⟩ ⟨ ⟩ ⟨ ⟩ ⟨ ⟩) This large inn offers a simple home base away from traffic and crowds. While not fancy (air-con costs $10 per day), the 48 rooms include refrigerator and microwave. Ground-floor rooms have back porches, while 2nd-floor rooms are larger but sans lanai. Rooms vary in decor and bed count.

Kaua'i Beach Villas (Map p478; ☎ 800-367-5025; www.kauaivacationrentals.com; 1br $810-1250 per week, 2br $1050-1750; ⟨ ⟩ ⟨ ⟩) Just north of the Hilton, these condos are like Starbucks coffee. Not fantastic, but definitely better than average. Units include full kitchen, washer-dryer, and lots of space (the two-bedroom/two-bathroom units give two couples ample privacy). Buildings F, G, and H are closest to the ocean and afford the best views. Kauai Vacation Rentals, which manages 30 of the 60 condos, can steer you to an appropriate unit.

Hilton Kaua'i Beach Resort (Map p478; ☎ 245-1955, 888-805-3843, www.hilton.com; 4331 Kaua'i Beach Dr; r $189-229; ⟨ ⟩ ⟨ ⟩) While it doesn't quite live up to the 'resort' in its name, the 350-room Hilton is a decent business-class hotel. The location, north of Lihu'e, might strike you as 'middle of nowhere' because there's no beach akin to the Marriott's first-class Kalapaki Beach, but it does offer a quieter setting and lower rates. There are restaurants and a spa on-site.

ourpick Kaua'i Marriott Resort (Map p478; ☎ 245-5050, 800-220-2925; www.marriotthotels.com; 3610 Rice St; r $219-429; ⟨ ⟩ ⟨ ⟩) For the complete resort experience, the Marriott won't disappoint. It's got user-friendly Kalapaki Beach, two top golf courses, the island's liveliest oceanfront restaurant and a gargantuan pool that could provide all-day entertainment. With 366 hotel rooms and 464 timeshare rooms, finding your door can be a major hike. Room decor and amenities are standard and rather staid. If you can afford an oceanfront unit, go for it. The view is worth it.

EATING & DRINKING
Budget

Hamura Saimin (Map p479; ☎ 245-3271; 2956 Kress St; noodles $3.75-4.50; ⟨ ⟩ 10am-10pm Mon-Thu, to midnight Fri & Sat, to 9pm Sun) An island institution, Hamura's is a hole-in-the-wall specializing in homemade saimin (local-style noodle soup). Service can be abrupt (think Soup Nazi from *Seinfeld*) so don't hem and haw. Expect crowds at lunchtime, slurping noodles elbow-to-elbow at orange U-shaped counters. It's stifling inside with noodles boiling and no air-con, but save room for the other specialty, *liliko'i* (passion fruit) chiffon pie.

ourpick Tip Top Café & Sushi Katsu (Map p479; ☎ 245-2333; 3173 Akahi St; breakfast mains $4.50-10, lunch mains $5.50-11; ⟨ ⟩ café 6:30am-2pm, Sushi Katsu 11am-2pm & 5:30-9pm Tue-Sun) We give this retro diner a C for atmosphere and an A for good ol' fashioned eats. The main draws are its famous pancakes and oxtail soup. Meat eaters, go local with *loco moco* (two fried eggs, hamburger patty, rice and gravy), saimin and beef stew. Sushi Katsu offers value-priced sushi and Japanese dishes.

Deli & Bread Connection (Map p478; ☎ 245-7115; Kukui Grove Shopping Center; 3-2600 Kaumuali'i Hwy; sandwiches $5-7; ⟨ ⟩ 9:30am-7pm Mon-Thu & Sat, to 9pm Fri, 10am-6pm Sun) Choose from the gamut of all-American, meal-sized sandwiches, including classics like hot tuna melts and classic clubs. Vegetarians won't starve with a nonmeat burger layered with mushrooms, pesto and melted mozzarella. Fringe benefit: it's at the mall but not a chain.

Garden Island Barbecue & Chinese Restaurant (Map p479; ☎ 245-8868; 4252 Rice St; plate lunches $5-6.25, mains $7-9; ⟨ ⟩ 10am-9pm) Tasty, filling, cheap Chinese food. No surprise, it's a hit. For a true local (if lowbrow) experience, try this bustling family-style eatery. The lengthy menu includes Chinese, Japanese and Hawaiian dishes, which is a red flag on the mainland but rather common in Hawaii. Try the simpler veg dishes, eg black mushrooms with Chinese broccoli.

our pick **Fish Express** (Map p478; ☎ 245-9918; 3343 Kuhio Hwy; lunch $6-7.50; ☒ 10am-6pm Mon-Sat, to 5pm Sun, lunch served to 3pm daily) Fish lovers, this is a no-brainer. One day, order chilled deli items, from fresh ahi *poke* to green seaweed salad, by the pound. The next day, try a healthful plate lunch of blackened ahi with guava-basil sauce, plus rice and salad ($8.50) or a gourmet *bentō* (Japanese boxed meal). You might end up here every day.

Pho Kauai (Map p479; ☎ 245-9858; Rice Shopping Center, 4303 Rice St; bowls under $8; ☒ 10am-9pm Mon-Sat) Hidden in a strip mall, this no-frills eatery serves steaming bowls of well-made *pho* (Vietnamese noodle soup). Choose meat or veg toppings, such as curry chicken, grilled shrimp, snow peas or eggplant. No credit cards.

Don't miss a taste (or two, or a dozen) of fresh Portuguese *malasada* (doughnut without a hole). Sugar-coated but not too sweet, the best of these palm-sized beauties combine lightness with satisfying heft. Try the island's two best *malasada* makers:

our pick **Kaua'i Malasadas** (Map p478; Kukui Grove Shopping Center, 3-2600 Kaumuali'i Hwy; 3 pieces $1.25; ☒ from 9am Mon-Sat) This charming one-woman stand in front of Kmart is a must. She sells sugar or cinnamon-sugar varieties, kept toasty under a heat lamp and available from morning until *pau* (finished), ie sold out.

Kaua'i Bakery & Cinnamons (Map p478; 246-4765; www.kauaibakery.com; Kukui Grove Shopping Center, 3-2600 Kaumuali'i Hwy; pastries 49¢-$1.75, cakes & pies $8-16; ☒ 7am-7pm Mon-Thu & Sat, to 9pm Fri, to 6pm Sun) At this family-run, full-service bakery in the mall, savor cream- or chocolate-filled *malasadas*, plus old-fashioned cinnamon rolls, apple turnovers, bread pudding and much more.

Midrange & Top End

Hanama'ulu Restaurant Tea House & Sushi Bar (Map p478; ☎ 245-2511, 245-3225; 3-4291 Kuhio Hwy; mains $7-10, special platters $17-20; ☒ 11:30am-9:30pm Tue-Sun) This fixture on the outskirts of Lihu'e stands out mainly for its historic teahouse setting. The food is good, but not great, and the menu suspiciously includes Chinese dishes, but that's the island way. They're known for crispy fried dishes, from Chinese ginger chicken to Japanese tempura and *tonkatsu* (breaded cutlets). Avoid the dismal front dining room; request seating in the quaint tea house in back.

Duke's Canoe Club (Map p478; ☎ 246-9599; Kaua'i Marriott Resort; appetizers $8-11, mains $18-30; ☒ 5-10pm) Even in chic Princeville and Po'ipu, you won't find an evening spot more fun and lively than Duke's, its holding court on Kalapaki Beach. The steak-and-seafood menu is not very innovative, but dishes are well executed. The fresh catch baked 'Duke's style' with garlic, lemon and basil glaze is a winner. Expect a touristy crowd (matching alohawear is not uncommon).

Duke's Barefoot Bar (Map p478; ☎ 246-9599; Kaua'i Marriott Resort, Kalapaki Beach; tropical drinks $7.25, wine per glass $6-16; ☒ 11am-11pm) For either drinks or a meal, this is a convivial, Waikiki-style tropical bar, with ringside views of Kalapaki Beach. It's a thrifty substitute for Duke's Canoe Club, with similar full-fledged menu items, including fresh-fish tacos ($11), crab wontons ($8) and 'hula pie' ($6.50), a now-legendary mound of macadamia ice cream atop chocolate-cookie crust.

Café Portofino (Map p478; ☎ 245-2121; www.cafeportofino.com; Kaua'i Marriott Resort, Kalapaki Beach; appetizers $8-12, mains $16-29; ☒ 5-9:30pm) A textbook example of 'romantic,' this oceanfront restaurant appeals to particular tastes. Some appreciate the white tablecloths, low lighting and solo harpist, but others find Chef Maximillian Avocadi's food overpriced and the formal atmosphere too staid. The traditional Italian menu features fine pastas and lots of veal, such as house specialty *osso bucco* (veal shank).

Gaylord's (Map p478; ☎ 245-9593; www.kilohanakauai.com/gaylords.htm; Kilohana Plantation, Kaumuali'i Hwy; lunch $8-14, dinner $20-35; ☒ 11am-2pm & 5:30-9pm Mon-Sat, 9am-2pm & 5:30-9pm Sun) Discerning minds generally praise the Kilohana Plantation (p479) setting amid the manicured lawns, white tablecloths and formal dining room. But picky palates do differ on the quality of dishes such as filet mignon bathed in *liliko'i* sauce, and shiitake and prime rib salad with Maui onions and Kamuela tomatoes. We want to love this place, but it needs more consistency.

Kaua'i Pasta (Map p479; ☎ 245-2227; 4-939B Kuhio Hwy; mains $9-15; ☒ 11am-2pm & 5-9pm) For a happy medium between a fast-food joint and a resort splurge, this centrally located Italian bistro is your ticket. Colorful salads meld diverse flavors, such as peppery arugula, creamy goat cheese and sweet tomatoes. Hot focaccia sandwiches, classic pasta mains and luscious tiramisu would pass muster with mainland foodies.

For groceries, Lihu'e's branch of the **Big Save** (Map p479; ☎ 245-6571; 4444 Rice St; ☼ 7am-11pm) island chain is decent but lacks a deli. **Star Market** (Map p478; ☎ 245-7777; Kukui Grove Shopping Center; ☼ 6am-11pm) carries much the same stock. **Vim 'n Vigor** (☎ 245-9053; 3-3122 Kuhio Hwy; ☼ 9am-7pm Mon-Fri, to 5pm Sat) carries vitamins and supplements, health foods, organic produce and bulk staples. Finally, the food department of Costco (p488) might surprise you with fresh *poke* and gourmet cakes by Icing on the Cake (p496).

ENTERTAINMENT
Shows

Luau Kalamaku (☎ 877-622-1780; www.luau kalamaku.com; Kilohana Plantation; adult/child 3-11/teen 12-18 $95/45/65; ☼ luaus 5pm Tue & Fri) Skip the same-old commercial show for mesmerizing dinner theater with a dash of Cirque du Soleil (think lithe dancers, flashy leotards and pyrotechnics) thrown in. The thrilling stageplay about one family's epic voyage to Hawaii features hula and Tahitian dancing, and showstopping, nail-biting Samoan fire dancing. The buffet dinner is above average, despite the audience size (typically 550, maximum 1000), and there's little cringe-worthy 'embarrass the tourist' forced dancing.

South Pacific (Map p478; ☎ 246-0111; Hilton Kaua'i Beach Resort, 4331 Kaua'i Beach Dr; adult/child incl tax $71/63; ☼ shows 5:30pm Wed) If you've never seen Rodgers and Hammerstein's *South Pacific*, it's worth your while to catch this dinner-theater production directed by Brenda Turville and produced by Alain Dussaud and the Hawaii Association of Performing Arts. Line up early; seating is first-come, first-served.

Cinemas

For mainstream first-run movies, **Kukui Grove Cinemas** (Map p478; ☎ 245-5055; Kukui Grove Shopping Center, 3-2600 Kaumuali'i Hwy; adult/child $6/4, before 5pm $4) is your standard shopping-mall fourplex. It's also a venue for the **Hawaii International Film Festival** (www.hiff.org).

Concerts

The **Kaua'i Community College Performing Arts Center** is home of the **Kaua'i Concert Association** (☎ 245-7464; www.kauai-concert.org) and offers classical, jazz and dance concerts (tickets $30 to $45) at 7pm. Past performers include African singer Angélique Kidjo, the Rubberbanddance Group and Alison Brown on banjo.

SHOPPING

Koa Store (Map p478; ☎ 245-4871, 800-838-9264; www .thekoastore.com; 3-3601 Kuhio Hwy; ☼ 9am-6pm Mon-Sat, 10am-5pm Sun) Other koa galleries carry higher-end masterpieces, but here you'll find lots of affordable souvenirs, such as sleek chopsticks and desk accessories. Many items come in three grades, from the basic straight-grain koa to the rare, almost-three-dimensional, premium 'curly' koa. All woodcraft are genuine koa (not the cheap fakes sold at tourist traps).

Kapaia Stitchery (Map p478; ☎ 245-2281; 3-3551 Kuhio Hwy; ☼ 9am-5pm Mon-Sat) A quilter's heaven, this longtime shop features countless cotton fabrics, plus island-made patterns and kits. Stop here also for handmade gifts, such as children's clothing, Japanese kimonos, potholders and an assortment of bags.

Edith King Wilcox Gift Shop (Map p479; www.kauai museum.org/store; Kaua'i Museum, 4428 Rice St; ☼ 9am-4pm Mon-Fri, 10am-4pm Sat) Kaua'i Museum's gem of a gift shop features a variety of genuine Hawaiian crafts, such as Ni'ihau shell jewelry, koa woodwork and *lauhala* (a type of Hawaiian leaf weaving) hats, plus books on Hawaii and collectible ceramics. Enter the shop, free of charge, through the museum lobby.

Kilohana Plantation (Map p478; www.kilohanakauai .com/shopping.htm; Kaumuali'i Hwy; ☼ most shops 10am-9pm Mon-Sat, to 4pm Sun) Nestled in an elegant historic manor, these classy shops will please the discriminating shopper. Find high-end jewelry, original art, woodwork, raku pottery and aloha shirts. The picturesque historic setting is reason enough to stop here.

Two statewide chain stores are worth mentioning: on the positive side, **Longs Drugs** (Map p478; ☎ 245-7771; Kukui Grove Shopping Center, 3-2600 Kaumuali'i Hwy; ☼ 7am-10pm Mon-Sat, 8am-8pm Sun) is much more than drugstore. Go here for an impressive selection of locally made products, from children's books to macadamia nuts to snacks galore.

As for **Hilo Hattie** (Map p479; ☎ 245-3404; www .hilohattie.com; 3-3252 Kuhio Hwy; ☼ 8:30am-6:30pm), that tourist beacon along Kuhio Hwy, all we can say is caveat emptor. While it is a convenient one-stop shop for generic souvenirs (for example, macadamias), beware of exorbitant prices and a plethora of mediocre items made in China and the Philippines. Decades ago, Hilo Hattie hired local seamstresses to sew aloha attire, but that is not the

---

TOP PICKS – KAUA'I-MADE GIFTS

- **Nature CD recordings** (www.soundshawaiian.com) of Kaua'i birdsong and other enchanting soundscapes
- Botanical bath and body products by **Malie Organics Boutique** (p540)
- Koa handcrafts and furniture at the **Koa Store** (p487) and **Davison Arts** (p504)
- Recycled-fabric bags by **Denise Tjarks** (www.denisetjarks.com)
- Fresh homemade chips from **Taro Ko Chips Factory** (p543)
- Silver and sea-glass jewelry by **Caitlin Ross Odom** (www.caitlinrossodom.com)
- Award-winning *liliko'i*-wasabi mustard from **Aunty Lilikoi Passion Fruit Products** (p548)
- Kaua'i-themed T-shirts from **Pohaku T's** (p529) and **Puahina Moku o Kaua'i** (p544)
- Genuine **Ni'ihau shell jewelry** (www.niihau.us)
- 'Alaea salt and other seasonings from **Aloha Spice Company** (www.alohaspice.com)

---

case these days, with foreign-made clothing. Better value can be found elsewhere.

If you're seeking cheap shirts and trinkets, **Costco** (☎ 241-4000; www.costco.com; 4300 Nuhou St; ☑ 11am-8:30pm Mon-Fri, 9:30am-6pm Sat, 10am-6pm Sun) is far superior and carries some quality locally made merchandise.

Lihu'e's only major mall is **Kukui Grove Shopping Center** (Map p478; ☎ 245-7784; 3-2600 Kaumuali'i Hwy), which contains mostly chain stores such as Macy's, Sears, Longs Drugs, Borders, Kmart, Radio Shack and banks. Near Nawiliwili Harbor, **Anchor Cove Shopping Center** (Map p478; ☎ 246-0634; 3416 Rice St) and **Harbor Mall** (Map p478; ☎ 245-6255; 3501 Rice St) draw mainly tourists from cruise ships and the nearby Marriott. Take a pass.

GETTING THERE & AROUND
Bus
The Kaua'i Bus serves Lihu'e with a shuttle that runs hourly from 6am to about 7pm, with stops at all the obvious destinations, such as Kukui Grove Shopping Center, Lihu'e Airport, Vidinha Stadium, Wal-Mart, Wilcox Memorial Hospital and Big Save. In addition to this, there is a lunch shuttle that runs at 15-minute intervals within central Lihu'e.

Car & Motorcycle
Kaua'i is a driving town, so most businesses have parking lots and street parking is relatively easy to find. Metered parking in Lihu'e costs 25¢ for 30 minutes. For information about car and motorcycle rentals, see p475.

EASTSIDE

If you look past the strip malls and highway traffic, the Eastside will fascinate you on many levels. Its geography runs the gamut, from mountaintop forests and grassy pastureland to pounding surf and a majestic river. In ancient times, the Wailua River was sacred and royalty lived on its fertile banks; today, Kaua'i's population is concentrated here, creating enough critical mass for varied restaurants, shops, accommodations and people. From Wailua to Kapa'a, the 'Coconut Coast' has a busier, more workaday vibe than swankier resort strongholds in Po'ipu and Princeville – and that's no insult. On the northwest coast, a rustic world appears in Anahola, a residential and farming region where Native Hawaiians constitute 70% of all residents.

WAILUA
pop incl Wailua Homesteads 6650
Wailua makes an ideal home base, giving you a choice between oceanfront condos for a 24/7 soundtrack of waves, and upcountry B&Bs and vacation rentals surrounded by lush gardens and rolling hills. Other attractions include a whimsical kiddie playground, a gigantic Hindu monastery and the state's only navigable river.

Orientation
Don't look for a town center. Most attractions are scattered along Kuhio Hwy (Hwy 56) or along Kuamo'o Rd (Hwy 580), which leads

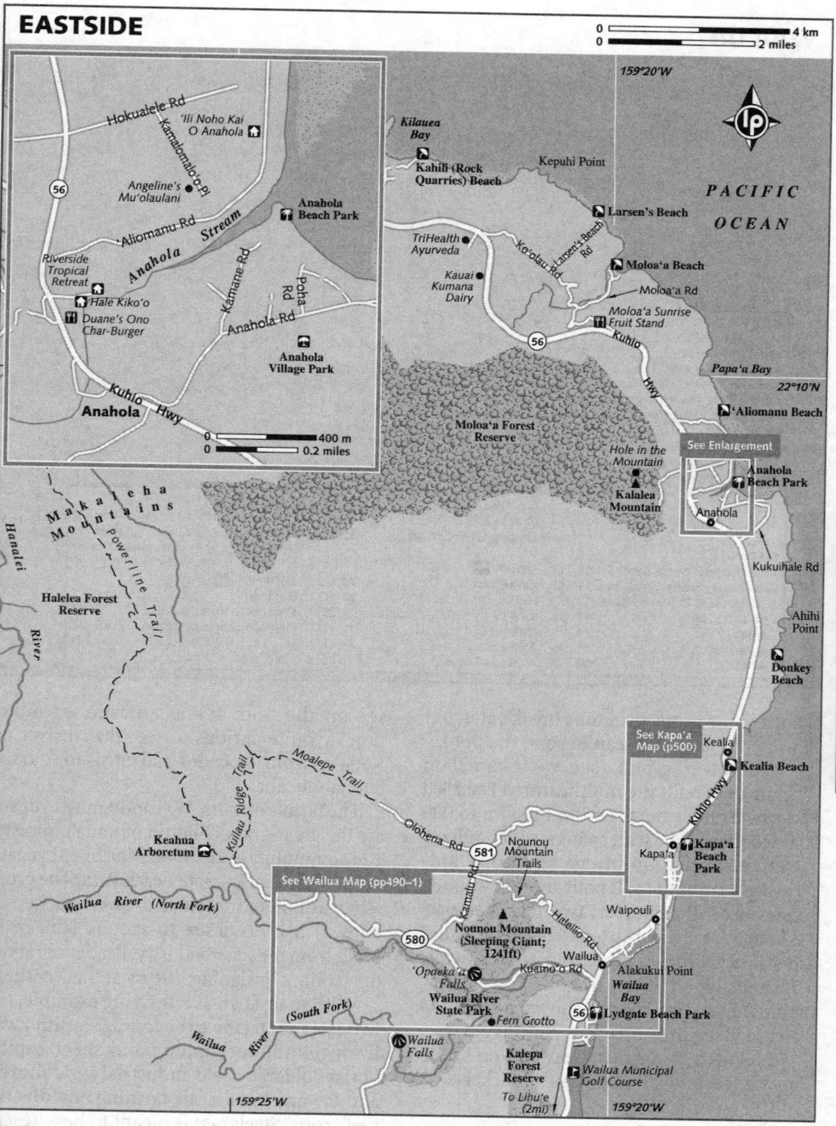

mauka (inland). To get to Kapa'a or beyond, take the Kapa'a Bypass Rd, which runs from Coconut Plantation to north Kapa'a.

Sights

See the **Kaua'i Heritage Trail** (wailuaheritagetrail.org) website and map for an overview of major sights.

LYDGATE BEACH PARK

With safe swimming, beginner snorkeling and two children's playgrounds, this popular **beach park** can entertain restless kids all afternoon. If you're seeking a secluded, pristine beach, Lydgate might seem too built-up. But most families will appreciate multiple diversions. Remember, the shallow seawater pool is calm

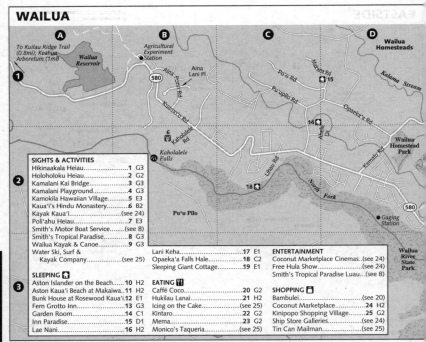

WAILUA

SIGHTS & ACTIVITIES
Hikinaakala Heiau.........................1 G3
Holoholoku Heiau..........................2 G2
Kamalani Kai Bridge.......................3 G3
Kamalani Playground.......................4 G3
Kamokila Hawaiian Village.................5 E3
Kaua'i's Hindu Monastery..................6 B2
Kayak Kaua'i..........................(see 24)
Poli'ahu Heiau............................7 E3
Smith's Motor Boat Service...........(see 8)
Smith's Tropical Paradise.................8 G3
Wailua Kayak & Canoe......................9 G3
Water Ski, Surf &
  Kayak Company.......................(see 25)

SLEEPING
Aston Islander on the Beach.............10 H2
Aston Kaua'i Beach at Makaiwa...........11 H2
Bunk House at Rosewood Kaua'i...12 E1
Fern Grotto Inn.........................13 G3
Garden Room.............................14 C1
Inn Paradise............................15 D1
Lae Nani................................16 H2

Lani Keha...............................17 E1
Opaeka'a Falls Hale.....................18 C2
Sleeping Giant Cottage..................19 E1

EATING
Caffé Coco..............................20 G2
Hukilau Lanai...........................21 H2
Icing on the Cake...................(see 25)
Kintaro.................................22 G2
Mema....................................23 G2
Monico's Taqueria...................(see 25)

ENTERTAINMENT
Coconut Marketplace Cinemas..(see 24)
Free Hula Show......................(see 24)
Smith's Tropical Paradise Luau...(see 8)

SHOPPING
Bambulei............................(see 20)
Coconut Marketplace.............24 H2
Kinipopo Shopping Village........25 G2
Ship Store Galleries................(see 24)
Tin Can Mailman...................(see 25)

thanks to the protective stone breakwater, but beware of the open ocean beyond the pool.

A volunteer group (see www.kamalani .org) in 1994 built the multifeatured **Kamalani Playground** (at the north end), a massive 16,000 sq ft wooden castle with swings, slides, mirror mazes, a suspension bridge and other kid-pleasing contraptions. It built another wooden masterpiece, the simpler, two-level **Kamalani Kai Bridge** (at the south end) in 2001. Other amenities include game-sized soccer fields, a 2.5-mile bicycle/pedestrian path, pavilions, picnic tables, rest rooms, showers, drinking water, a lifeguard and ample parking.

To get here, turn *makai* (seaward) on Kuhio Hwy between the 5- and 6-mile markers.

STEELGRASS FARM
Learn more about diversified agriculture and cacao growing at this family **farm** (☎ 821-1857; www.steelgrass.org; adult/child 12 & under $60/free; ⏱ 9am-noon Mon, Wed & Fri), which offers a unique chocolate farm tour. Steelgrass Farm's two other crops are timber bamboo and vanilla, but the 8-acre farm features literally hundreds of thriving tropical species, which you'll also

see on the tour. It's a fantastic introduction if you're curious to see what thrives on Kaua'i – from avocados and citrus to soursop and jaboticaba.

The farm's owners, Will and Emily Lydgate, are the great-grandchildren of Kaua'i minister and community leader John Mortimer Lydgate, the namesake of Lydgate Beach Park. The property was not an inheritance, as JM (as he was known) had no desire to acquire land or to profit from the sugar industry. Read more about the family's intriguing history at the website.

With their farm as a thriving example, the Lydgates are trying to encourage a shift away from the monocropping and sheer capital outlays of large-scale, industrial agriculture – and toward small-scale farming and diversified crops. Steelgrass is meant to be a 'teaching farm' to experiment with workable crops such as cacao.

Contact the family for farm location and directions.

SMITH'S TROPICAL PARADISE
Other gardens might have fancier landscaping or loftier goals, but you can't beat Smith's for

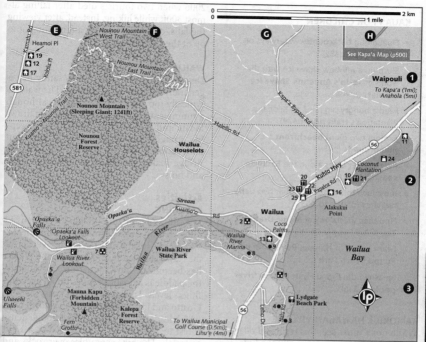

value. For $6 you can leisurely stroll a loop trail past a serene pond, grassy lawns and island-themed gardens. The setting can seem Disney-esque, with an Easter Island replica and tour trams, but it's appealingly unpretentious and large enough to accommodate all. The Smith's family-run luau (p497) is held on the garden grounds.

KAUA'I'S HINDU MONASTERY

On an island virtually devoid of Hinduism, this one-of-a-kind Hindu **monastery** (☎ 822-3012; www.himalayanacademy.com; 107 Kaholalele Rd; ☏ 9am-noon) welcomes both serious pilgrims and curious sightseers. Set on 458 acres of buoyantly thriving rainforest above the Wailua River, the astoundingly green setting (enhanced by the monks' back-breaking gardening) equals that of a commercial garden. The temples, Ganesh statues and other structures are devoted to the god Shiva. While visitors can access a limited area (self-guided tour) from 9am to noon daily, we highly recommend taking a free guided tour offered once a week; call ☎ 888-735-1619 for tour dates and parking reservations.

Currently the temple in use is **Kadavul Temple**, where guests can see the world's largest single-pointed quartz crystal, a 50-million-year-old, six-sided wonder that weighs 700lb and stands over 3ft tall. In the temple, meditating monks have been rotating in three-hour vigils round the clock since the temple was established in 1973.

Under construction is the ambitious **Iraivan Temple**, a monumental and almost incongruously imposing structure that's being entirely handcarved from white granite by a village of artisans founded in Bangalore, India.

KEAHUA ARBORETUM

Sitting pretty at the top of Kuamo'o Rd, this **arboretum** resembles storybook countryside, with grassy fields, gurgling stream and groves of teak, eucalyptus and other tall trees. Locals enjoy swimming or splashing in the freshwater stream and pools, but remember that the water can contain the leptospirosis bacterium. The road continues past the arboretum parking lot, but you must cross water – not recommended if you're driving a standard car, especially if it's rainy.

KAUA'I FOR CHILDREN

- Float along backcountry waterways on **inner tubes** (p482)
- Slurp up a rainbow shave ice with the works at **Jo-Jo's Anuenue Shave Ice & Treats** (p549)
- Feed a hungry pig herd on Kilohana Plantation's **train ride** (p479)
- Explore two **giant beachfront playgrounds** (p489)
- Ride coaster bikes along the **Eastside coastal path** (p502)
- Introduce tots to the ocean at two **baby beaches** (p501 and p531)
- Find that special toy at **Magic Dragon Toy & Art Supply Co** (p515)
- Learn to surf at **Hanalei Bay** (p518) or **Po'ipu Beach Park** (p533)
- Splash in the Grand Hyatt Kaua'i's **'river pools'** (p536)

KAUA'I

KAMOKILA HAWAIIAN VILLAGE

While not a must-see, this **replicated village** is a pleasant diversion, especially for kids. It's located along the Wailua River and includes traditional structures, from Canoe House to Chief's Assembly House, amid thriving gardens of guava, mango and banana trees. Use your imagination! You're on your own here, but the site is modest and the simple map given is sufficient.

Kamokila also offers **outrigger canoe tours** (adult/child $30/20; departures hourly 9:30am-2:30pm), which include a paddle, hike and waterfall swim. Because you start farther upriver from the mouth, the trip is shorter than going by kayak (see right) and a Hawaiian guide is guaranteed.

To get here, turn south from Kuamo'o Rd, opposite 'Opaeka'a Falls. The half-mile road leading to the village is very steep and narrow.

'OPAEKA'A FALLS

While not a showstopper, this 40ft **waterfall** makes an easy roadside stop, less than two miles up Kuamo'o Rd. For the best photographic conditions, go in the morning. Don't be tempted to try trailblazing to the base of the falls. The steep cliffs are perilous, as shown in 2006 when two tourists died after falling almost 300ft while hiking. Instead, after viewing the falls, cross the road for a fantastic photo op of the Wailua River.

WAILUA BAY

Despite its natural beauty, this sandy bay is generally a 'drive-by' attraction. The water is typically too rough for swimming, although a summer surf break toward the south draws locals and also surf students. The sweeping stretch of sand is nice for walking but its location at the heavily trafficked Wailua Bridge makes the beach annoyingly visible and noisy.

Activities

KAYAKING

Majestic and calm, the Wailua River spans 12 miles, fed by two streams originating on Mt Wai'ale'ale. It's the only navigable river across the Hawaiian Islands, and kayaking the Wailua has become a tourist must-do. Fortunately, the paddle is a doable 5 miles for all ages and fitness levels. Tours usually don't pass the Fern Grotto and instead take the river's north fork, which leads to a mile-long hike through dense forest to Uluwehi Falls (Secret Falls), a 130ft waterfall. The hike scrambles over rocks and roots, and if muddy it will probably cause some slippin' and slidin'. Tip: wear sturdy, washable, nonslip sandals such as Chacos.

Most tours last four to five hours and depart around 7am or noon (call for exact check-in times). The maximum group size is 12, with paddlers going out in double kayaks. The pricier tours include lunch, but on budget tours you can store your own food in coolers and waterproof bags. Bring a hat, sunscreen and mosquito repellent.

Experienced paddlers might want to rent individual kayaks and go out on their own. Prices wildly vary. Note that not all tour companies are also licensed to rent individual kayaks.

No kayak tours or rentals are allowed on Sundays. Of course, noncommercial kayaks are always allowed on the river.

Of the following companies, Kayak Kaua'i and Outfitters Kaua'i are big and established with many other tour offerings. But the two recommended little guys offer better value for this basic tour.

our pick **Kayak Wailua** (☎ 822-3388; www.kayakwailua.com; Kuhio Hwy, Wailua; tour per person $40) This small, family-owned outfit specializes in Wailua River tours. It keeps boats and equipment in tip-top shape and provides dry bags for your belongings and a nylon cooler for your BYO snacks. If you prefer to speed ahead of the group, it's flexible enough to accommodate different preferences.

our pick **Wailua Kayak Adventures** (☎ 822-5795, 639-6332; www.kauaiwailuakayak.com; Kuhio Hwy, Waipouli; per day single/double kayaks $25/50, tour per couple $85; ☺ check-in 7am & 1pm) Go here for the cheapest individual kayak rentals. It offers three budget-friendly Wailua River tours (which include generous snacks at the waterfall). Call for times, as they vary slightly for each tour. Located behind Lemongrass restaurant in Waipouli.

Wailua Kayak & Canoe (☎ 821-1188; Wailua River State Park; single/double kayak per 5hr $45/75, tour per person $55-90) Located at the boat ramp on the north bank, this outfit is very convenient for individual rentals (no need to transport the kayak). Tour quality is fine but the prices have skyrocketed since 2006.

Kayak Kaua'i (☎ 826-9844, 800-437-3507; www .kayakkauai.com; Coconut Marketplace, Wailua; double kayak per person per day $27, tour per adult/child under 12 $85/60; ☺ check-in 7:45am & 12:15pm) This longstand-ing and reputable outfit, with shop locations in Wailua and Hanalei, offers river and sea kayaking tours, including the Na Pali challenge. Rates run high, but lunch is included. A good choice if you need a Japanese- or Spanish-speaking guide.

Outfitters Kaua'i (Map pp532-3; ☎ 742-9667, 888-742-9887; www.outfitterskauai.com; Po'ipu Plaza, 2827A Poipu Rd, Po'ipu; kayak per person per day $40, tour adult/child 5-14 $98/78; ☺ check-in 7:45am) Known for its multiadventure tours, this established outfit is good except for its steep prices.

BOAT RIDES

If you're curious to see the legendary **Fern Grotto**, there's only one way to get up close – or least as close as you can get. **Smith's Motor Boat Service** (☎ 821-6892; www.smithskauai.com; 1½hr tour adult/child 2-12 $20/10; ☺ departures every 30min 9-11:30am, 12:30-3:30pm) since 1946 has had exclusive rights to ply the river in covered riverboats (the size of a bus) to the grotto. Bear in mind that since the heavy rains and rockslides of 2006, visitors cannot enter the grotto but must stay on the wooden platform quite a distance from the shallow cave.

THE SACRED WAILUA RIVER

To ancient Hawaiians, the Wailua River was among the most sacred places across the islands. The river basin, near its mouth, was one of the island's two royal centers (the other was Waimea) and home to the high chiefs. Here, you can find the remains of many important heiau (religious sites), including the following places.

Hikinaakala Heiau (rising of the sun) sits south of the Wailua River mouth, which is today the north end of Lydgate Beach Park (p489). In its heyday, the long, narrow temple (c AD 1200) was aligned directly north to south, but only a few remaining boulders outline its original massive shape. The neighboring **Hauola Pu'uhonua** (dew of life; place of refuge) is marked by a bronze plaque. Ancient Hawaiian kapu (taboo) breakers were assured safety from persecution if they made it inside.

Believed to be the oldest *luakini* (temple dedicated to war god Ku, often place for human sacrifice) on the island, **Holoholoku Heiau** is located a quarter-mile up Kuamo'o Rd on the left. The whole area was royal property: toward the west, against the flat-backed birthstone marked by a plaque reading 'Pohaku Ho'ohanau' (royal birthstone), queens gave birth to future kings. Only a male child born here could become king of Kaua'i. Another stone a few yards away, marked 'Pohaku Piko,' was where the *piko* (umbilical cords) of the babies were left.

Perched high on a hill overlooking the meandering Wailua River, the well-preserved **Poli'ahu Heiau**, another *luakini*, is named after the snow goddess Poli'ahu, one of the volcano goddess Pele's sisters. Poli'ahu Heiau is located immediately before the 'Opaeka'a Falls lookout, on the opposite side of the road.

Bear in mind, unmarked Hawaiian heiau might not catch your eye. Although they were originally imposing stone structures, most now lie in ruins, covered with scrub. It takes a leap of imagination for non-Hawaiians to appreciate heiau, but they are still powerful, set in places of great mana (spiritual energy).

Find an excellent brochure on the Wailua complex of heiau at www.hawaiistateparks.org/pdf /brochures/Hikinaakala.pdf. For a compelling history on the Wailua River's meaning to ancient Hawaiians, see Edward Joesting's *Kauai: The Separate Kingdom*.

The Fern Grotto, formed below an overhanging cliff at the base of **Mauna Kapu** (Forbidden Mountain), looks rather tired nowadays, having suffered from a localized drought since the 1990s, when the sugar plantations above the cliff went out of production and weren't irrigated anymore. The elongated sword ferns and delicate maidenhair seem to be struggling. If you're expecting an eye-popping emerald cascade, you might as well find old pictures.

This hokey but homespun tour attracts tour groups and the older and less adventurous set. At the grotto, guests are serenaded with 'Ke Kali Nei Au,' known as the 'Hawaiian Wedding Song' after Elvis Presley sang it in English in *Blue Hawaii*.

HIKING

Eastside hikes ascend into Kaua'i's tropical-jungle interior. Expect humid air, red dirt (or mud) and slippery patches after rains. See the Eastside Trails map (p471).

Kuilau Ridge & Moalepe Trails

The **Kuilau Ridge Trail** (Map p489; 2.1 miles; all mileage distances given are one-way) is recommended for its sheer beauty: emerald valleys, colorful birds, dewy bushes, thick ferns and glimpses of misty Mt Wai'ale'ale in the distance. After 1 mile, you'll see a grassy clearing with a picnic table; continue east in descending switchbacks until you reach the **Moalepe Trail** (Map p489; 2.25 miles). From here on, you'll see Nounou Mountain and the Makaleha Mountains.

While they are independent trails, the two are often mentioned together because they connect and can be hiked in sequence. Both are moderate hikes and among the most visually rewarding on Kaua'i. Remember, the trails don't complete a circuit so you must retrace your steps on a 9-mile out-and-back. Mountain bikers would also enjoy these forestland trails, although they're used mostly by hikers and hunters.

If you plan on doing only one trail, choose the Kuilau Ridge Trail because it takes you immediately into the forest wilderness, while the first mile of the Moalepe Trail crosses the simple, treeless pastureland of the Wailua Game Management Area. Both trails are well maintained and signposted.

The Kuilau Ridge Trail starts at a marked trailhead on the right just before Kuamo'o Rd crosses the stream at the Keahua Arboretum, 4 miles above the junction of Kuamo'o Rd and Kamalu Rd. The Moalepe Trail trailhead is at the end of Olohena Rd where it bends into Waipouli Rd.

Nounou Mountain Trails

Climbing Nounou Mountain (Sleeping Giant), you'll ascent over 1000ft, but the views of Kaua'i's Eastside panorama are a worthy reward. You can approach the mountain from the east on the **Nounou Mountain East Trail** (Map pp490–1; 1.75 miles), from the west on the **Nounou Mountain West Trail** (Map pp490–1; 1.5 miles) and from the south on the **Kuamo'o-Nounou Trail** (Map pp490–1; 2 miles). The trails meet near the center.

Visitors tend to prefer the exposed East Trail because it offers sweeping views of the ocean and distant mountains. The well-maintained trail is moderately strenuous, climbing through wild thickets of guava, *liliko'i* and ironwood. The trail is steep, with switchbacks almost to the ridge. At the three-way junction near the top, take the left fork, which will lead to the summit, marked by a picnic shelter. Now atop the giant's chest, only his head prevents you from a 360-degree view. Climbing farther is extremely risky and not recommended.

Do this hike early in the morning, when it's relatively cool and you can witness daylight spreading across the valley. The hard-packed dirt trail is exceedingly slippery when wet; look for a walking stick, which hikers sometimes leave near the trailhead.

The East Trail starts at a parking lot a mile up Haleilio Rd in the Wailua Houselots neighborhood. When the road curves left, look for telephone pole 38 with the trailhead sign.

The Nounou Mountain West Trail ascends faster but it's better if you prefer a cooler forest trail. Much of the hike is shaded by towering Norfolk Island pines and other trees. There are two ways to access the trailhead: from Kamalu Rd, near telephone pole 11, or from the end of Lokelani Rd, off Kamalu Rd. Walk through a metal gate marked as a forestry right-of-way.

The Kuamo'o-Nounou Trail runs through groves of trees planted in the 1930s by the Civilian Conservation Corps; it connects with the west trail. The trailhead is right on Kuamo'o Rd, near a grassy field between the 2- and 3-mile markers.

For guided hikes, the gold standard is geologist Chuck Blay's company, **Kaua'i Nature Tours** (☎ 742-8305; 888-233-8365; www.kauainaturetours.com; Nounou Mt tour adult/child 7-12 $115/85), which offers an all-day tour that includes lunch and transportation.

GOLF

Ranked among the finest municipal golf courses nationally, the **Wailua Municipal Golf Course** (Map p489; ☎ 241-6666; green fees weekdays/weekends & holidays $32/44, optional cart rental $18, club rental from $29) is an 18-hole, par-72 course off Kuhio Hwy north of Lihu'e. Plan ahead because morning tee times are sometimes reserved a week in advance at this popular course, designed by former head pro Toyo Shirai. After 2pm, green fees drop by half and no reservations are taken.

Just before press time, the county announced a possible major increase in fees during the next seven years. The weekday rate would jump 47% to $60 in the first year and then $5 more every other year.

WATER SKIING AND WAKEBOARDING

The only nonocean water skiing in the state is found here on the Wailua, only from the Wailua Bridge to the first big bend in the river.

Try water skiing or wakeboarding with a tow by **Water Ski, Surf & Kayak Company** (☎ 822-3574; Kinipopo Shopping Village, 4-356 Kuhio Hwy; per 30/60min $75/140; ☺ 9am-5pm Mon-Fri, to noon Sat). The company also rents water equipment, including surfboards (per day/week $10/50, $200 deposit), bodyboards ($5/20, $75 deposit) and snorkel gear ($5/15, $75 deposit).

MOUNTAIN BIKING

While the **Powerline Trail** (Map p489; which covers 13 miles, between Wailua and Princeville) is used mainly by hunters, it's a decent option for die-hard mountain bikers. Hikers might find the trek rather too long, too exposed and, especially toward the north, too monotonous. The trail (a former mainenance road for electric powerlines established in the 1930s) is never crowded and it traverses an otherwise-inaccessible north–south region. Beware of hidden, steep drop-offs hidden in the dense foliage. Expect to slog through mud and puddly ruts.

The south end of the trail begins across the stream at the Keahua Arboretum (p491), at the end of Kuamo'o Rd. Consider starting from the Princeville end, where it's less messy. Just south of Princeville, look for the Princeville Ranch Stables (p514) turnoff. This is Po'oku Rd. The trail starts about 2 miles down this road, near an obvious water tank.

Festivals & Events

Taste of Hawaii (www.tasteofhawaii.com) On the first Sunday in June, the Rotary Club of Kapa'a hosts the 'Ultimate Sunday Brunch' at Smith's Tropical Paradise. For $85 to $95 per person, indulge in gourmet samples by 50 distinguished local chefs. With additional booths offering wines, microbrews, ice cream and desserts, you're liable to stuff yourself silly here.

Aloha Festivals Royal Court Investiture (☎ 332-7888; www.alohafestivals.com) The statewide Aloha Festivals in late August is launched on each island with presentation of a royal court. Held at Kamokila Hawaiian Village, the event includes special ceremonies of traditional chanting and hula.

Sleeping

Note that many condos, B&Bs and inns require a three-night minimum and a cleaning fee. For condos, we list contact info for the agency managing the majority of units, but also check www.vrbo.com and smaller agencies. **Rosewood Kaua'i** (☎ 822-5216; www.rosewoodkauai.com), which represents not only condos but many outstanding vacation rental homes in Wailua and Kapa'a.

BUDGET

Bunk House at Rosewood Kaua'i (☎ 822-5216; www.rosewoodkauai.com; 872 Kamalu Rd; r with shared bathroom $50-60; ☎) Hostelers will be forever spoiled by these meticulously tidy bunk rooms with private entrances and kitchenettes. Expect a cleaning fee ($25). For a step up, inquire about the picturesque 'Victorian cottage' ($145), and 'thatched cottage' ($135), which are also on the storybook-pretty property, complete with white picket fence.

Lani Keha (☎ 822-1605; www.lanikeha.com; 848 Kamalu Rd; s/d from $65/75; ☎) Solo travelers and sociable types will appreciate the low-key, communal atmosphere in this longtime guesthouse. Nothing fancy, the three rooms feature lauhala-mat flooring, king beds and well-worn but clean furnishings. Gather round the kitchen and living room.

our pick Garden Room (☎ 822-5216, 822-3817; 6430 Ahele Dr; r $75; ☎) Find serenity in an immaculate studio overlooking a gorgeous pond with waterlilies and koi (Japanese carp). The aptly named room is compact (hotel-room size) but delightful, with a private entrance, kitchenette and generous welcome basket. Expect to be charmed by the host couple, longtime Kaua'i residents who make guests feel welcome.

Sleeping Giant Cottage (☎ 505-401-4403; www .wanek.com/sleepinggiant; 5979 Heamoi Pl; 1br cottage $95; 🛜) Be lord of the castle (no shared walls) at this airy plantation-style bungalow, pleasantly appointed with hardwood floor, kitchen, comfortably sized bedroom and living-dining room, plus a huge screened patio facing a backyard garden. Cleaning fee is $50; discounts for weekly or monthly stays.

MIDRANGE & TOP END

our pick Inn Paradise (☎ 822-2542; www.innparadise kauai.com; 6381 Makana Rd; studio/1br/2br incl breakfast $85/100/120; 🛜) Consistently ranked at the top on TripAdvisor, this longtime B&B sets the standard: classy units, spectacular garden view and charming innkeepers. Pick from three different-sized units, all with private entrance and kitchen or kitchenette. Reasonable rates, scrumptious breakfast fixings and shared washer-dryer clinch the deal.

our pick Opaeka'a Falls Hale (☎ 888-822-9956; www.opaekaafallskauai.ws; 120 Lihau St; 1br incl breakfast $110-130; 🖵) At a whopping 1000-plus sq ft each, these immaculate B&B units are bigger than the average city apartment. The two units overlook Wailua's emerald valleys and each includes full kitchen (stocked with breakfast fixings) and private lanai, phone and washer-dryer, plus a lovely swimming pool. DSL internet access only in the upstairs unit. Cleaning fee ($50) charged.

Fern Grotto Inn (☎ 821-9836; www.ferngrottoinn.com; 4561 Kuamo'o Rd; cottages $99-150, house $275; 🛜🖵) Charmingly retro, these remodeled, 1940s plantation-style cottages vary in size, but all feature hardwood floors, tasteful furnishings, TV/DVD, shared laundry, and kitchen or kitchenette. Rates are slightly high, but the location near the Wailua River dock reduces driving. Friendly owners go the extra mile to ensure guests' comfort.

Aston Islander on the Beach (☎ 822-7417, 877-997-6667; www.astonhawaii.com; 440 Aleka Pl; r $140-230; 🛜🖵) Among midrange hotels, you can't top the Islander. It's not a resort, so don't expect frills, but the 186 rooms seem modern and upscale, with granite countertops, flat-panel TVs and stainless-steel and teak furnishings. For internet access, room connections cost $10 per 24 hours, but there's free wi-fi in lobby. Deep discounts online.

Aston Kaua'i Beach at Makaiwa (☎ 822-3455, 800-760-8555 www.astonhawaii.com; 650 Aleka Loop; r $150-380; 🛜🖵) For a presentable business-class hotel, look no further. The 300-plus-room Kaua'i Beach has a classy, efficient feel, from the soaring lobby full of plush seating to the pleasant pool. Rooms pamper the business traveler with dark woods, black-marble counters and work desk with rolling chair. A $12 hotel fee buys you parking, local calls, internet access and daily paper. Book online.

Lae Nani (☎ 822-4938, 800-688-7444; www.outrigger.com; 410 Papaloa Rd; 1br/2br from $215/235; 🛜🖵) Conveniently located on Papaloa Rd, this five-building condo is particularly appealing, with a small but pretty stretch of beach (swimmable only during calm surf). Outrigger manages almost 60 of the 84 units and provides on-site support, but also check with other agents. Buildings 3 and 5 include the most oceanfront units; building 1 is far from the highway and parking lot.

Eating

Without a commercial center, Wailua is not a hang-out town, but it boasts a handful of notable eateries.

our pick Icing on the Cake (☎ 823-1210; www.icing onthecakekauai.com; Kinipopo Shopping Village, 4-356 Kuhio Hwy; cookies $1.25-1.75, cakes 6in/9in from $25/40) Pastry chef Andrea Quinn has a knack for elegant designs and sophisticated flavors. Nothing is too cute or too sweet. While she specializes in made-to-order cakes, walk-in customers will find gourmet treats such as cocoa-nib shortbread, pecan brownies and exquisite coconut macaroons. Check the website for retail locations islandwide.

Kintaro (☎ 822-3341; 4-370 Kuhio Hwy; appetizer $3.50-6, meals $14-20; 🕙 5:30-9:30pm Mon-Sat) Night after night, this local favorite packs 'em in. No wonder: from thick-cut slices of sashimi to a shrimp-fish-veg tempura combination, mains shine in quality and quantity. The owner is Korean, but the cuisine is authentic Japanese. A specialty is sizzling, crowd-wowing *teppanyaki*, when chefs show their stuff tableside on steel grills.

Caffé Coco (☎ 822-7990; www.restauranteur.com /caffecoco; 4-369 Kuhio Hwy; salads & sandwiches $5-14.5, meals $16-21; 🕙 11am-9pm Tue-Fri, 5-9pm Sat & Sun) At this rustic little hideaway, chefs fuse Asian

---

COCO PALMS ON HOLD

Old-timers might recall **Coco Palms Resort** (Map pp490-1, cnr of Kuhio Hwy & Kuamo'o Rd) as Hollywood's go-to wedding site during the 1950s and '60s. Built in 1953, it was Kaua'i's first resort and its lush grounds epitomized tropical paradise. The highest-profile onscreen wedding here was when Elvis Presley wed Joan Blackman in the 1961 film *Blue Hawaii*. In 1992, Hurricane 'Iniki demolished the then-396-room hotel, which then sat in benign neglect for years. In spring 2006, a new owner announced a $220 million plan to resurrect Coco Palms as a condo-hotel, but it fell through. By fall 2007, the 19-acre property was back on the market.

The site remains abandoned except for weddings performed by **Larry Rivera** (☎ 822-3868; larryrivera@hawaiian.net), a local musician and celebrity who made his career at Coco Palms. He re-creates elaborate *Blue Hawaii* fantasy weddings on the grounds. To read more about this historic resort, see www.coco-palms.com, an unofficial website created by its fans.

Middle Eastern and other flavors into healthful dishes that would delight the *Yoga Journal* crowd. Ahi is a standout, prepared with Moroccan spices and a curried veggie samosa, or seared and rolled in black sesame with wasabi cream. Luscious and yet guilt-free desserts include vegan treats. Warning: voracious mosquitoes on attack.

our pick **Monico's Taqueria** (☎ 822-4300; Kinipopo Shopping Village, 4-356 Kuhio Hwy; mains $8-14; 11am-3pm & 5-9pm) Finally, 'real' Mexican food on Kaua'i. Everything tastes fresh and rings true, from the generous plates of burritos and tacos to the freshly made chips, salsa and sauces. Thumbs up for the affordable fish mains.

Mema (☎ 823-0899; 4-369 Kuhio Hwy; mains $9-18; 11am-2pm Mon-Fri, 5-9pm daily) While not stark-raving awesome, Mema serves decent dishes that can be tailored to your meat-philic or meat-phobic preference: you choose either tofu, chicken, pork, beef, fish or shrimp. The cozy dining room is modest but a cut above the standard local-diner setting.

our pick **Hukilau Lanai** (☎ 822-0600; www.hukilaukauai.com; Kaua'i Coast Resort at the Beachboy, 520 Aleka Loop; dinner $16-27; 5-9pm Tue-Sun) To ramp it up from the typical T-shirt-casual joint, we recommend this relaxed, elegant favorite. The menu features top local ingredients, from Kilauea goat cheese to Lawa'i Valley *warabi* (fiddlehead fern). Standout selections include feta-and-sweet-potato ravioli and ahi *poke* nachos. For an affordable splurge, arrive from 5pm to 6pm for the early-bird six-course, wine-paired tasting menu ($40; food-only menu $28).

Entertainment

The best nightlife in Wailua is curling up in bed before the roosters wake you. Or, if the price isn't a deterrent, a commercial luau might be a decent diversion. **Smith's Tropical Paradise** (☎ 821-6895; www.smithskauai.com; Wailua River Marina; luau adult/child 3-6/child 7-13 $75/19/30; luaus 5pm Mon, Wed & Fri) launched their luau in 1985, and it is today a Kaua'i institution, attracting droves of tourists. It's a lively affair, run with lots of aloha spirit by four generations at the lovely 30-acre garden. The multicultural show features Hawaiian, Tahitian, Samoan, Filipino, Chinese, Japanese and New Zealand dances.

While touristy, the Coconut Marketplace's **free hula show** (☎ 822-3641; 5pm Wed) is fun and lively, featuring Leilani Rivera Bond (www.leilanirivera.com) and her *halau* (troupe). She's the daughter of famous Coco Palms entertainer Larry Rivera, who joins the show on the first Wednesday monthly.

An anytown option is a movie at a mall. **Coconut Marketplace Cinemas** (☎ 821-2324; 4-484 Kuhio Hwy; adult/child/senior $7.25/4.25/5.50, before 6pm $4.25) screens first-run flicks.

Shopping

Coconut Marketplace (www.coconutmarketplace.com; 9am-9pm Mon-Sat, 10am-6pm Sun) This touristy place feels like a throwback, a once-popular venue with too many vacant spaces. Amid midrange island attire, jewelry, T-shirts and gifts is one worthy stop: Ship Store Galleries.

Bambulei (☎ 823-8641; www.bambulei.com; 4-369D Kuhio Hwy; 10am-6pm Mon-Fri, to 5pm Sat) This irresistible women's boutique is chock-full of feminine gear made for women who've outgrown the teenage surfer-chick look. The drapey sweaters, platform sandals and kimono-fabric accessories aren't haute couture, but they're affordable and unique. Also find vintage clothing and retro home decor.

our pick **Tin Can Mailman** (☎ 822-3009; www.tincanmailman.net; Kinipopo Shopping Village, 4-356 Kuhio Hwy;

11am-7pm Mon-Fri, noon-4pm Sat) Brimming with rare books and antiques, this jam-packed shop will delight Hawaiiana collectors, with vintage LPs, aloha shirts, maps, photos, postcards, jewelry and other fascinating artifacts.

Ship Store Galleries (☎ 822-4999, 800-877-1948; www.shipstoregalleries.com; Coconut Marketplace, 4-484 Kuhio Hwy; 9am-5pm Tue-Sat) Browsers are welcome at this spacious showroom, where notables include maritime artist Raymond Massey (who's created an extensive, fascinating series on seafaring to the Hawaiian Islands), Leslie Tribolet (who does mesmerizing portraits), Dolores 'Dee' Kirby (whose unostentatious landscapes are keepers) and Marco Cannella, whose riffs on the Old Masters' still lifes have a local twist.

WAIPOULI

Sandwiched between Wailua and Kapa'a, Waipouli is less a town than a cluster of restaurants, grocers, a drugstore and other basic businesses. You're likely to stop here to stock up.

Information

There are ATMs inside Foodland supermarket in Waipouli Town Center and, just a minute north, inside Safeway in Kaua'i Village. Both are located on the *mauka* side of Kuhio Hwy.

For a pharmacy and general merchandise, **Longs Drugs** (☎ 822-4915; Kaua'i Village; store 7am-10pm Mon-Sat, 8am-8pm Sun, pharmacy 8am-9pm Mon-Sat, 9am-6pm Sun) offers reasonable prices and a wide selection of household products, beach supplies, grocery items and souvenirs.

For internet access, get wi-fi with a drink purchase at the **Coffee Bean & Tea Leaf** (☎ 822-4754; www.coffeebeanhawaii.com; Waipouli Town Center, 4-771 Kuhio Hwy; drinks from $4; 6am-9pm, to 9:30pm Fri & Sat;), a Starbucks clone.

Activities

Bear in mind that rentals are here but the actual activities are elsewhere.

SURFING

Don't miss the chance to meet surf guru Ambrose Curry of **Ambrose's Kapuna** (☎ 822-3926; www.ambrosecurry.com; 770 Kuhio Hwy; per hr $35), who offers to 'take people surfing' (not to 'give surf lessons'). If you're baffled, then you have much to learn from this longtime surfer-philosopher, once aptly dubbed a tribal elder. Originally from California, Curry has lived

on Kaua'i since 1968 and is also an artist and board shaper.

SNORKELING

The cool thing about **Snorkel Bob's** (☎ 823-9433; www.snorkelbob.com; 4-734 Kuhio Hwy; basic snorkel sets per day/week $2.50/9, better sets $8/32, bodyboards $6.50/26; 8am-5pm Mon-Sat) is that if you're island-hopping you can rent gear on Kaua'i and return it on the Big Island, O'ahu or Maui.

CYCLING

Kauai Cycle (☎ 821-2115; www.kauaicycle.com; 4-934 Kuhio Hwy, Waipouli; per day/week cruiser $20/110, mountain or road bike $30/165; 9am-6pm Mon-Fri, to 4pm Sat) sells, services and rents bikes maintained by experienced cyclists. Prices include helmet and lock.

SPAS

Enter a world of Japanese shoji screens, soft lighting, earth tones and botanical aroma-therapy at **Aveda Spa** (☎ 823-1488; www.kauaispasalon.com; Outrigger Waipouli Beach Resort & Spa, 4-820 Kuhio Hwy; 1hr massage or facial $135, haircuts $45-65; 9am-6pm Mon-Sat, 10am-6pm Sun) – and the Eastside's traffic will drift away. Treatments include relaxing extras: imagine lounging in a cushy massage chair while getting a pedicure ($70 to $115). Take advantage of numerous monthly specials.

Courses

Kaua'i Heritage Center (☎ 346-7574; www.kaieie.org) offers lectures and workshops by Kehaulani Kekua, a respected and very articulate *kumu hula* (teacher of hula). The Friday lectures are free, while the hands-on Saturday workshop cost $30. Nowhere else can you find such genuine teachings on the ancient Hawaiian lunar calendar or the significance of Kaua'i's hula heiau.

Sleeping

Waipouli is sandwiched between Wailua and Kapa'a, both with plenty of options, so also check those sections.

Outrigger Waipouli Beach Resort & Spa (☎ 822-6000, 800-688-7444; www.outriggerwaipouli.com; 4-820 Kuhio Highway; 1br/2br from $295/425;) The surrounding strip malls and traffic belie this condo's cachet as the Eastside's newest and fanciest. Units are law-firm handsome and consistently well furnished, with 37in flat-screen TVs, washer-dryer and 'extra' bathroom per unit. There's no swimmable beach but a saltwater 'river pool' and sand-bottom hot tubs somewhat compensate. Outrigger represents 100 of the 196 total units, but also check www.vrbo.com.

Eating & Drinking

our pick **Sweet Marie's Hawaii** (☎ 823-0227; www .sweetmarieskauai.com; 4-788 Kuhio Hwy; baked goods $2.25-10.00, cakes from 6in/8in $50/75; ☽ 7am-5pm Tue-Sat) Believe it or not, Chef Marie Cassel's melt-in-the-mouth white-chocolate *liliko'i* cake or gooey coconut–vanilla bean tapioca are 100% gluten-free. Whether or not you eschew wheat, you'll savor Cassel's delicious and innovative desserts and custom cakes for special diets (including gluten-, soy- and dairy-free). Located across from Foodland.

Papaya's Natural Foods (☎ 823-0190; Kaua'i Village, 4-831 Kuhio Hwy; dishes $5-8, salad per lb $7; ☽ 9am-8pm Mon-Sat, deli to 7pm Mon-Sat) At Kaua'i's biggest health-food store, you'll find the nouveau-hippie contingent, locavore-leaning mainland transplants and vegetarian-vegan types. Produce is expensive because it's either organic or local. Stock up on bulk items (including grind-your-own peanut butter), vitamins and supplements, bottled water and healthful deli fixings.

King & I (☎ 822-1642; Waipouli Plaza, 4-901 Kuhio Hwy; mains $7-11; ☽ 4:30-9:30pm) Ranked number one by locals, this friendly, family-run restaurant offers a lengthy menu featuring flavors such as curries popping with kaffir lime and lemongrass, as fiery (or not) as you like. Vegetarians will find loads of options, like flavorful eggplant and tofu in chili oil or a mound of traditional *pad thai* with tofu.

Kaua'i Pasta (☎ 822-7447; 4-939B Kuhio Hwy; mains $9-15; ☽ 5-9pm Tue-Sun) With no view to speak of, the food had better be good. And, judging from steady local clientele (the real test), it is. The chef, who cut his teeth at Roy's (p537) in Po'ipu, serves savory *panini* (hot sandwiches), classic pasta dishes and a perfectly simple (or simply perfect) Caprese salad with local basil and tomatoes and fresh mozzarella.

For groceries, chain giant **Safeway** (☎ 822-2464; Kaua'i Village, 4-831 Kuhio Hwy; ☽ 24hr) caters to mainland tourists with its familiar brands, plus American-style deli and bakery. A slightly better option is local chain **Foodland** (Waipouli Town Center; ☽ 6am-11pm), with a decent selection of gourmet and health brands such as Kashi and Scharffen Berger. Neither stocks much local produce.

Foodies will prefer Papaya's Natural Foods for local and organic produce, plus other is-

land specialties such as Kilauea honey and goat cheese. Another recommendation for local produce and national health brands is Cost U Less (p503) in nearby Kapa'a.

Shopping

Waipouli's two main shopping malls are Waipouli Town Center and Kaua'i Village. One notable boutique is the irresistible **Marta's Boat** (☎ 822-3926; 770 Kuhio Hwy; ☽ 10am-6pm Mon-Sat), which will delight 'princesses of all ages' with feminine and sexy threads from Paris, LA and New York. Distinctive lingerie and frocks shine, but locally made jewelry and excruciatingly cute little girls' outfits also enchant. Expect big-city price tags. The 'Surf for World Peace' T-shirts (handpainted by owner Marta Curry's husband, surfer and artist Ambrose Curry (opposite) make cool souvenirs.

KAPA'A
pop 9470

The only walkable town on the Eastside, Kapa'a is a charmer. The eclectic population of old-timers, new transplants, nouveau hippies and tourists coexists smoothly. Retro diners and domestic shops mingle with live jazz, Bikram yoga and your choice of espresso drinks. A new bike-foot path runs along the part-sandy, part-rocky coast, the island's best vantage point for sunrises. Kapa'a's downfall: it sits right along the highway. Try crossing the road during rush hour!

To avoid the paralyzing Kapa'a to Wailua crawl, take the Kapa'a Bypass Rd. Note that except in the heart of Kapa'a, you will definitely need a car.

Information
INTERNET ACCESS

Business Support Services (☎ 822-5504; fax 822-2148; 4-1191 Kuhio Hwy; per 15min $2.50; ☽ 8am-6pm) No atmosphere but cheap internet access, plus faxing, copies and stamps.

Java Kai (☎ 823-6887; 4-1384 Kuhio Hwy; ☽ 6am-7pm; ☞) Good coffee but the café can be stuffy as a sauna; limited patio seating.

Small Town Café (☎ 821-1604; 4-1495 Kuhio Hwy; internet per 10min $1, wi-fi free; ☽ 5:30am-1pm) Rustic, island-style coffee bar with lots of seating, indoor and outdoor.

LAUNDRY

Kapa'a Laundry Center (☎ 822-3113; Kapa'a Shopping Center, 4-1105 Kuhio Hwy; ☽ 7:30am-9:30pm, last wash 8pm)

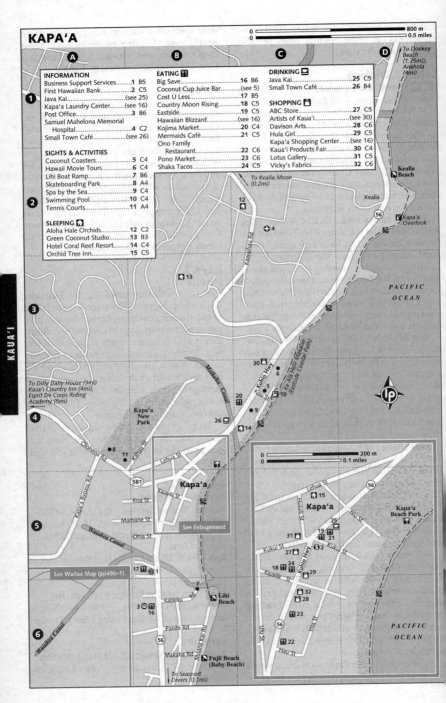

KAPA'A

INFORMATION	
Business Support Services...........1	B5
First Hawaiian Bank...................2	C5
Java Kai...............................(see 25)	
Kapa'a Laundry Center..........(see 16)	
Post Office...........................3	B6
Samuel Mahelona Memorial	
Hospital..............................4	C2
Small Town Café...................(see 26)	

SIGHTS & ACTIVITIES	
Coconut Coasters.....................5	C4
Hawaii Movie Tours..................6	C4
Lihi Boat Ramp.......................7	B6
Skateboarding Park..................8	A4
Spa by the Sea........................9	C4
Swimming Pool......................10	C4
Tennis Courts........................11	A4

SLEEPING	
Aloha Hale Orchids.................12	C2
Green Coconut Studio..............13	B3
Hotel Coral Reef Resort............14	C4
Orchid Tree Inn......................15	C5

EATING	
Big Save...............................16	B6
Coconut Cup Juice Bar.........(see 5)	
Cost U Less...........................17	B5
Country Moon Rising..............18	C5
Eastside...............................19	C5
Hawaiian Blizzard................(see 16)	
Kojima Market.......................20	C4
Mermaids Café......................21	C5
Ono Family	
Restaurant..........................22	C6
Pono Market.........................23	C6
Shaka Tacos.........................24	C5

DRINKING	
Java Kai...............................25	C5
Small Town Café...................26	B4

SHOPPING	
ABC Store............................27	C5
Artists of Kaua'i................(see 30)	
Davison Arts.........................28	C6
Hula Girl.............................29	C5
Kapa'a Shopping Center......(see 16)	
Kaua'i Products Fair...............30	C4
Lotus Gallery.........................31	C5
Vicky's Fabrics.......................32	C6

KAUA'I

MEDICAL SERVICES
Samuel Mahelona Memorial Hospital (☎ 822-4961; fax 823-4100; 4800 Kawaihau Rd) Primarily a long-term-care facility, this longstanding hospital expanded services to include basic emergency care in late 2005. Serious cases are transferred to Lihu'e's Wilcox Memorial Hospital.

MONEY
First Hawaiian Bank (☎ 822-4966; 4-1366 Kuhio Hwy) Has a 24-hour ATM.

POST
Post office (☎ 800-275-8777; Kapa'a Shopping Center, 4-1101 Kuhio Hwy; ✆ 8am-4pm Mon-Fri, 9am-2pm Sat)

Sights
KAPA'A BEACH PARK
From the highway, you'd think that Kapa'a is beachless. But along the coast is a mile-long ribbon of beach that's very low-key and local. While the whole area is officially a county park called Kapa'a Beach Park, that name is commonly used only for the northern end, where there's a grassy field, picnic tables and a public pool.

The best sandy area is at the south end, informally called **Lihi Beach**, where you'll find locals hanging out and talking story. A good starting point for the paved coastal path is the footbridge just north of the beach. To get here, turn *makai* (seaward) on Panihi Rd from the highway.

Further to the south is **Fujii Beach**, nicknamed **Baby Beach** because an offshore reef creates a shallow, placid pool of water that's perfect for toddlers. Located in a modest neighborhood that attracts few tourists, this is a real locals' beach, so don't make a loud scene.

Activities
There are free **tennis courts** and a **skateboarding park**, along with a field for baseball, football and soccer in Kapa'a New Park, and a public **swimming pool** (☎ 822-3842; admission free; ✆ 10am-5:30pm Thu-Mon) at Kapa'a Beach Park.

FISHING
Join gregarious Captain Terry of **Hawaiian Style Fishing** (☎ 635-7335; 4hr charter per person $100) on his 25ft boat. He takes four anglers at most and shares the catch. Charters depart from the small Lihi Boat Ramp at the end of Kaloloku Rd, off Kuhio Hwy.

HORSEBACK RIDING
Dale Rosenfeld qualifies as a 'horse whisperer' and the tours offered by her **Esprit De Corps Riding Academy** (☎ 822-4688; www.kauaihorses.com; Kualapa Pl; tours $130-390, lessons per hr $55) are small, personalized and varied (longer tours for more-skilled riders). Groups never exceed five people; riders must be aged 10 and above. She also offers honeymoon rides and weddings on horseback.

SPAS
For a satisfying alternative to pricey resort spas, try **Spa by the Sea** (☎ 822-2171; www.spabytheseakauai.com; 4-1558 Kuho Hwy; 50min massage or facial $110), which shares a building near the ocean with a chiropractor and physical therapist. Massage therapists are all handpicked and highly qualified. If you're torn between a massage or facial, the Menehune Meditation ($115) includes 30 minutes of each.

DIVING & SNORKELING
Eastside waters are less protected by reefs and more choppy due to easterly onshore winds. Therefore diving and snorkeling are very limited here. Still, there's a small branch of Po'ipu-based **Seasport Divers** (☎ 823-9222, 800-685-5889; www.seasportdivers.com; 4-976 Kuhio Hwy), where you can rent diving, snorkeling and other ocean gear.

Tours
In air-conditioned 'theaters on wheels,' movie buffs can cruise the island with **Hawaii Movie Tours** (☎ 822-1192, 800-628-8432; www.hawaiimovietour.com; 4-885 Kuhio Hwy; adult/child under 12 from $89/79; ✆ office 7:30am-6pm), stopping at film sites while viewing movie clips on a video monitor. The standard land tour is fine, but it's worth paying extra for the 4WD option (adult/child five to 11 $95/85), an adventurous ride that takes you off-road to the base of Mt Wai'ale'ale (*Jurassic Park* territory) and includes lunch at Lydgate Beach Park (p489).

On the **Kapa'a Town Walking Tour** (☎ 245-3373; www.kauaihistoricalsociety.org; adult/child $15/5; ✆ tours 10am & 4pm Tue, Thu & Sat), knowledgeable local guides point out landmarks, describe Kapa'a's sugar and pineapple boom days and, best of all, talk story and answer questions. Advance reservations are required.

Festivals & Events
Heiva I Kaua'i Ia Orana Tahiti (☎ 822-9447) In early August, dance troupes from as far away as Tahiti, Japan

KAUA'I

WALK THIS WAY

The Eastside's newest road is not meant for cars, but it's **Ke Ala Hele Makalae** (The Path that Goes by the Coast), a shared-use path reserved for pedestrians, bicyclists and other nonmotorized modes. At 10ft wide and paved in concrete, it has jumpstarted locals into daily fitness walking, jogging, cycling, inline skating and, perhaps, forgoing the local habit of driving everywhere.

In Kapa'a, the path currently starts at at the **Lihi Boat Ramp** at the south end of Kapa'a Beach Park (p258) and ends just past Donkey Beach (p505) at **Ahihi Point** (Map p489), a 4-mile stretch. But this constitutes only a small piece of the ambitious facility, which will run over 16 miles all the way from Lihu'e to Anahola Beach Park (p505).

While a vocal minority has complained about pouring concrete along the coast, especially near the Wailua River, which is sacred to Native Hawaiians, most appreciate the easy-access path, which is now like a town square in motion. Proponents point out that an official path is critical to preserving public shoreline access (a legal right in Hawaii). Often, such access is blocked when private landowners post no-trespassing signs or set up gates, or when trails are deemed unsafe by authorities.

Sunrise walks are brilliant but, for an added kick, rent a coaster bike! **Coconut Coasters** (☎ 822-7368; www.coconutcoasters.com; 4-1586 Kuhio Hwy; bike rentals per 1hr/4hr from $8.50/18; 7am-6pm Tue-Sat, 9am-4pm Sun) specializes in hourly rentals for the path. Classic single-speed coasters are just right for the gentle slope north, but you can upgrade to a three-speed model ($9.75 per hour) for an extravagant ride. Owners Melissa and Spark Costales meticulously maintain their fleet and exude aloha spirit. For daily or weekly rentals of coaster, mountain or road bikes, try Kauai Cycle (p498), located at the south end of the path.

A nonprofit community group called **Kaua'i Path** (www.kauaipath.org) is promoting and maintaining the path; see the website for more info. Note: the path is wheelchair accessible.

and Canada join groups from Hawaii at Kapa'a Beach Park for this Tahitian dancing and drumming competition.
Coconut Festival (☎ 651-3273; www.kbakauai.org) Celebrate all things coconut! Events during this free two-day festival in early October include coconut-pie-eating contests, coconut cook-off, cooking demonstrations, music, hula, crafts and food.

Sleeping

If you're seeking accommodations right in town, pickings are slim. Kapa'a has only one hotel and almost all B&Bs and inns are situated way beyond walking distance. In case you're wondering about the ideally located Pono Kai Resort, we're sorry to say that it's primarily a midrange timeshare, with a limited number of exorbitantly priced vacation rentals.

That said, driving *mauka* to residential neighborhoods leads through picturesque pastures, sweeping views and excellent B&Bs and inns. Remember to ask about minimum-night requirements.

BUDGET

Aloha Hale Orchids (☎ 822-4148; www.yamadanursery .com; 5087-A Kawaihau Rd; r $55, 1br cottage $85) Trust us, you won't top this value-priced pair of units at a residential orchid nursery. The studio

is ideal for singles and contains queen bed mini-refrigerator and TV, while the airy one-bedroom cottage has a full kitchen, TV windows on all walls, washer and clothesline One drawback: no wi-fi.

Orchid Tree Inn (☎ 822-5359; www.vrbo.com/118213 Lehua St; 2br s/d $85/90;) Everything's within walking distance from this rare, in-town inn Compact but tidy units include two bedrooms full kitchen, washer-dryer and a sofa sleeper Ideal for sociable types who appreciate Asian philosophies (including the careful Taoist and feng shui influences on the garden).

our pick **Green Coconut Studio** (☎ 647-0553; ww .greencoconutstudio.com; 4698 Pelehu Rd; studio $98-10) Literally lined with windows (and wraparound veranda), this fantastically air studio allows spectacular coastal views an cooling cross-breezes. The layout makes grea use of space, allowing a comfy satellite-TV setup and a kitchenette with full-sized fridg and the gamut of appliances. There's a $7 cleaning fee for brief stays.

MIDRANGE

Hotel Coral Reef Resort (☎ 822-4481, 800-843-46 www.hotelcoralreefresort.com; 4-1516 Kuhio Hwy; r $11 289;) Kapa'a's sole hotel has one majo advantage: an oceanfront location. Otherwise it's a basic hotel, with smallish room and the expected amenities such as air-con and flat-screen TV. Budget rooms ($110 to $125) face the parking lot and Kuhio Hwy. Oceanfront rates vary wildly, from $149 to $289.

Dilly Dally House (☎ 821-0192; www.dillydallyhouse.com; 6395 Waipouli Rd; r $125-155, suite $165, cottage $185; ❄ 🌐 🐾) At this fantastic B&B, units vary in size, but all feature chic furnishings, Tempurpedic mattresses on bed-frames fit for royalty, washer-dryer, private entrance and lanai. The drive to the house might seem long and confusing at first, but the reward is panoramic mountain and ocean views. The host serves scrumptious home-cooked breakfasts.

Kaua'i Country Inn (☎ 821-0207; www.kauaicountryinn.com; 6440 Olohena Rd; 1 & 2br $130-180, 3br cottage from $249; 🌐 🐾) With gleaming hardwood floors and upscale furnishings, this inn is one class act. The four spacious suites all include cable TV/DVD, Macintosh computers, wi-fi, and kitchen or kitchenette. Kids under 12 are not allowed in suites, but are welcome in the three-bedroom cottage. Beatles fans, don't miss the chance to gawk at the owner's astounding collection of memorabilia.

Kealia Moon (☎ 822-5216; www.rosewoodkauai.com; 5111 Hassard Rd; 2br cottage $135; 🐾) A great deal for two couples or a family of four, this immaculate cottage includes two bedrooms, two bathrooms, full kitchen, washer-dryer, multiple flat-screen TVs and a simple, local-style garage patio (the island version of the front stoop). The owners, who live next door, give enormous welcome baskets.

Eating & Drinking
Roadside restaurants abound, none terrible, some terribly touristy. Here are several local-favorite picks. Note that Kapa'a's famous vegan eatery, Blossoming Lotus, closed in December 2008 after a successful five-year run.

Cost U Less (☎ 823-6803; www.costuless.com; 4525 Akia Rd; ❄ 9am-8pm Mon-Fri, to 7pm Sat, to 6pm Sun) This is the best place to stock up on supplies. Find not only mainstream brands, but also local produce and meat, plus 'natural' brands, such as Kashi and Tom's of Maine. Most items are sold in large, family size. No membership is needed.

Java Kai (☎ 823-6887; www.javakai.com; 4-1384 Kuhio Hwy; coffee drinks $1.50-4.50; ❄ 6am-5pm Mon-Sat, 7am-1pm Sun) Always busy, this Kaua'i-based microroastery is best for grabbing a cup to go. The muffins, scones and cookies are baked fresh here, but it can feel like an oven inside. Sidewalk seating is limited.

Hawaiian Blizzard (www.hawaiianblizzard.com; outside Big Save, Kapa'a Shopping Center; small cup $3; ❄ noon-5pm Mon-Fri) Keep your eyes peeled for shave-ice virtuoso Aaron Furugen's plain white van. He's been perfecting the art of shave ice since the 1980s. Kids flock here after school and neighborhood regulars hang out and talk story.

Small Town Café (☎ 821-1604; 4-1495 Kuhio Hwy; coffee drinks $3-5; ❄ 5:30am-1pm daily, 6:30-9pm Tue-Thu; 🌐) The best daytime hangout in town, this indie coffeehouse offers plentiful indoor/outdoor seating for leisurely chats or websurfing. The organic, free-trade coffee suits the hippie-boho crowd. Too bad it closes just when you're getting comfy.

Country Moon Rising (☎ 822-2533; 4-1345 Kuhio Hwy; loaf $5; ❄ 7am-5pm Mon-Thu, to 3pm Fri & Sat, 9am-3pm Sun) There's nothing like freshly baked bread, made here with organic flour and sea salt. Try the sprouted wheat sourdough (barely sour but with a pleasantly chewy bite) and the tropical sweet breads featuring taro, macnuts or pineapple. Other draws include locally grown papayas, takeout sandwiches and chilled coconuts with straws. Hours are changeable and the bakery's often open into the early evening.

Coconut Cup Juice Bar (☎ 823-8630; 4-1586 Kuhio Hwy; fruit smoothies $6-7, sandwiches $8; ❄ 9am-5pm) The nonchain alternative to Jamba Juice, this roadside juice stand is a thirst-quenching oasis. Stop here for generously endowed sandwiches, from albacore tuna to avocado veggie and fresh-squeezed organic orange or carrot juice ($6 per 16oz).

Pono Market (☎ 822-4581; 4-1300 Kuhio Hwy; plate lunch $6.50; ❄ 6am-6pm Mon-Fri, to 4pm Sat) Fill up on local *grinds* (food) at this long-time hole in the wall, now with a full-fledged espresso bar. At lunch, line up for generous plate lunches, homemade sushi rolls, fresh ahi *poke* and savory delicacies such as dried *'opelu* (pan-sized mackerel scad) and smoked marlin.

Shaka Tacos (☎ 823-0012; 4-1345 Kuhio Hwy; burritos $8-10; ❄ 7:30am-9pm Mon-Sat, to 3pm Sun; 🐾) This airy taqueria might not serve virtuoso Mexican food, but the live music on Friday evenings (from 6:30pm to 9pm) showcases two awesome musicians, jazz saxophonist

Denny Morouse, a longtime pro from New York, and talented trumpeter David Braun from Chicago. A rare example of small-town 'night' life.

Ono Family Restaurant (☎ 822-1710; 4-1292 Kuhio Hwy; breakfast mains $8.50-11, lunch mains $4.50-8.25; 🕑 7am-2pm daily & 5:30-9pm Wed-Sat) Hearty breakfasts rule at this old-time diner, where you can start your day with an ahi omelet or banana pancakes, served with warmed syrup. Lunch items, from saimin to meat-and-rice plates, are tasty but not exactly calorie conscious.

Eastside (☎ 823-9500; www.theeastsidekauai.com; 4-1380 Kuhio Hwy; lunch mains $9-13, dinner mains $19-32; 🕑 11:30am-2:30pm & 5:30-9pm) The only non-diner sit-down restaurant in town, this 2008 newcomer boasts a breezy open-air dining room, gracious staff and a brief menu of fish, chicken and meat. Think dressed-up versions of down-home eats. There are no surprises on the menu, but the nimble execution of mains makes up for it.

Mermaids Café (☎ 821-2026; 4-1384 Kuhio Hwy; wraps & plates $9.50-11; 🕑 11am-8:45pm) This walk-up counter offers does brisk business with its Asian-influenced, island-fresh wraps and plates. Southeast Asian satay or coconut-curry flavors liven up tofu or chicken, while the best-selling seared ahi and *nori* (dried seaweed) wrap would be flawless with a more restrained dollop of sauce. Limited outdoor seating.

The best place for local produce is the **farmers market** (Kapa'a New Park; 🕑 3pm Wed), among the island's largest.

Local chain **Big Save** (☎ 822-4971; Kapa'a Shopping Center; 🕑 7am-11pm), has a deli, while the smaller **Kojima Market** (☎ 822-5221; 4-1543 Kuhio Hwy; 🕑 8am-7pm Mon-Fri, to 6pm Sat, to 1pm Sun) is rather limited but does carry local meat and produce.

Shopping

our pick **Davison Arts** (☎ 821-8022; www.davisonarts .com; 4-1322 Kuhio Hwy; 🕑 9am-noon Mon, to 5pm Tue-Fri, 10am-2pm Sat) For the ultimate splurge, find worthy temptation in Hayley Davison's magnificent koa furniture and John Davison's striking paintings inspired by Kaua'i's landscapes. Eyeing that lustrous classic rocking chair? It starts at $3500.

Hula Girl (☎ 822-1950; www.welovehulagirl.com; 4-1340 Kuhio Hwy; 🕑 9am-6pm Mon-Sat, 10am-5pm Sun) Aloha-shirt aficionados will find a wide selection of quality, name-brand shirts ($40 to $125). Feel the silky-soft Tori Richard line in cotton lawn ($70 to $75). This family-run shop is a standout

for quality Hawaii souvenirs (eg clothing, jewelry, island-made ceramics, art prints, books) and simply a fun place to browse.

Lotus Gallery (☎ 822-9300; www.jewelofthelotus .com; Dragon Bldg, 4504 Kukui St; 🕑 10am-6pm Tue-Sat, closed Sun & Mon) A 19th-century bronze Ganesh sculpture. Hand-carved lingam stones. Replicas of Asian dynasty gold jewelry. This fascinating gallery features authentic art and collectibles from countries such as India, Tibet and Thailand. If you're drawn to non-Western spirituality, you'll love the exotic treasures here.

Vicky's Fabrics (☎ 822-1746; www.vickysfabrics.com; 4-1326 Kuhio Hwy; 🕑 9am-5pm Mon-Sat) Established in the early 1980s, Vicky's is a gem for quilters and homemakers. Find a wide selection of Hawaiian, Japanese and batik print fabrics. Longtime owner and seamstress Vicky also offers some handmade quilts, pincushions and bags.

Artists of Kaua'i (☎ 652-7430; www.artistsofkauai .ifp3.com; Kuhio Hwy; 🕑 9am-5pm Wed-Sun) Seven Kaua'i artists share a gallery to display their outstanding works in oils, pencil, watercolor and photography. Find it within Kaua'i Products Fair grounds.

It's just a chain convenience store, but **ABC Store** (☎ 823-0081; 4-1359 Kuhio Hwy; 🕑 6am-11pm) is locally owned and carries a mesmerizing array of macadamia nuts, sundries, snacks, beer and souvenirs at competitive prices.

Kaua'i Products Fair, the outdoor market at the north end of town, has too many stall hawking cheap imitations of island arts and crafts, marked as Kaua'i made. It might no be worth the bother.

KEALIA BEACH

Visible from the highway at the 10-mil marker, this wide, long sandy beach is prim turf for local surfers and bodyboarders. Th sandy bottom slopes offshore very gradually making it possible to walk out far to catc long rides back. But the pounding barrels ar treacherous and definitely not recommende for novices. A breakwater protects the nort end, so swimming and snorkeling are occa sionally possible there.

Parking is plentiful in a paved lot, but th beach is also accessible by bike or foot alon the coastal path (p502), which runs alon the beach. There are rest rooms, picnic table and pavilions, but no trees or natural shad Sunscreen is a must.

DETOUR: DONKEY BEACH

Unofficially known as a nude site, this **beach** is secluded and scenic, although rarely swimmable. Summer swells might be manageable, but stay ashore if you're an inexperienced ocean swimmer. It's a rugged place to escape the highway and cars, with rocks scattered at the water's edge, windswept ironwood trees, and *naupaka* (a native Hawaiian shrub with a five-petaled white flower that looks as if it has been torn in half) and *'ilima* (a yellow flowering ground cover), adding dashes of color.

To get here, either take the coastal path (p502) or drive to a small lot about halfway between the 11- and 12-mile markers and then find the 'Public Shoreline Access' sign. Rest rooms are open at the parking lot.

Note: nudity is illegal in Hawaii.

ANAHOLA
pop 1930

Blink and you'll miss the predominantly Native Hawaiian village of Anahola, where there are subdivisions of Hawaiian Homestead lots at the southern and northern ends. Pineapple and sugar plantations once thrived here but today the area is mainly residential. The few who lodge here will find themselves in rural seclusion among true locals.

Grouped together at the side of Kuhio Hwy, just south of the 14-mile marker, Anahola's modest commercial center includes a **post office** (8am-4pm Mon-Fri, 9:30-11:30am Sat), burger stand and convenience store.

Sights & Activities
ANAHOLA BEACH PARK

Hidden from the highway, this locals' beach makes an easy getaway – more secluded yet still drive-up accessible. Because this county park sits on Hawaiian Home Lands, you'll probably share the beach with Hawaiian families, especially on weekends. Remember, it's their beach: respect the locals. The wide bay, fringed with a decent swath of lovely sandy beach, is a surfers' hot spot on the choppier south end. But toward the north, waters are calm enough for swimming. There are two ways to get here: for the south end, turn off Kuhio Hwy onto Kukuihale Rd at the 13-mile marker, drive a mile down and then turn onto the dirt beach road. For the north end, take Aliomanu Rd at the 14-mile marker and park in the sandy lot.

ALIOMANU BEACH

Secluded 'Aliomanu Beach is another spot frequented primarily by locals, who pole- and throw-net fish and gather *limu* (seaweed). It's a mile-long stretch of beach; you can get to the prettier north end by turning onto 'Aliomanu Rd (Second), just past the 15-mile marker on Kuhio Hwy. Don't take 'Aliomanu Rd (First), a mile south, by mistake! Then, turn left onto Kalalea View Dr, go 0.5 miles and turn right at the beach access sign.

HOLE IN THE MOUNTAIN

Ever since a landslide altered this once-obvious **landmark**, the *puka* (hole) in Pu'u Konanae has been a mere sliver. From slightly north of the 15-mile marker along Hwy 56, look back at the mountain, down to the right of the tallest pinnacle: on sunny days you'll see a smile of light shining through a slit in the rock face. Legend tells the original hole was created when a giant threw his spear through the mountain, causing the water stored within to gush forth as waterfalls.

BODYWORK

Angeline's Mu'olaulani (822-3235; www.angeline lomikauai.com; Kamalomalo'o Pl; massage treatment $150; 9am-3pm Mon-Fri by appointment only) Experience authentic *lomilomi* (traditional Hawaiian massage; literally 'loving hands') at this longstanding bodywork center run by the Native Hawaiian Locey family. With outdoor shower, open-air deck, massage tables separated by curtains, and simple sarongs to cover up, Angeline's is a rustic contrast to plush resort spas. The signature treatment comprises a steam, vigorous salt scrub and a special four-hands *lomilomi*.

TriHealth Ayurveda (828-2104, 800-455-0770; http://trihealthayurvedaspa.com; Kuhio Hwy; treatments $130-275; by appointment) In a simple bungalow just off the highway, you can sample traditional ayurvedic therapies, practiced by therapists trained both locally and in Kerala, India. Kudos if you can withstand a full-body

KAUA'I

(head and all) session in that intimidating horizontal steamer. Located between the 20- and 21-mile markers.

Eating & Sleeping

For information about camping in Anahola Beach Park, see p470.

Duane's Ono Char-Burger (☎ 822-9181; 4-4350 Kuhio Hwy; burgers $5-7; ☻ 10am-6pm Mon-Sat, 11am-6pm Sun) If you're a fan of In-N-Out and Dairy Queen, you'll go nuts over this indie drive-in. Try the 'old fashioned' (cheddar, onions and sprouts) or the 'local girl' (Swiss cheese, pineapple and teriyaki sauce). Add crispy thin fries and melt-in-your-mouth onion rings. See autographed photos of famous fans, from Chuck Norris to Steve Tyler.

our pick Hale Kiko'o (☎ 822-3922; www.halekikoo .com; 4-4382-B Kuhio Hwy; studio units s $70-80, d $75- 90; ☞) Along an unnamed, unpaved land, find two charming, modern studios, each with full kitchen. The downstairs unit is large enough for living room and features stylish slate floors, lava-rock pillars, garden patio and artsy outdoor shower. The upstairs unit is more ordinary, but brighter, with windows aplenty and a deck. Cleaning fee ($75) charged.

'Ili Noho Kai O Anahola (☎ 821-0179, 639-6317; www.kauai.net/anahola; 'Aliomanu Rd; r with shared bath- room incl breakfast $100-120) This simple guesthouse fronting Anahola Beach ain't cheap, but from here you can stroll from bed to beach in a New York minute. The four compact but tidy rooms (sharing two bathrooms) surround a central lanai, where guests talk story and fill up on home-cooked breakfasts. The hosts are Native Hawaiian activists now running a B&B on Hawaiian Home Lands for which they fought long and hard.

Riverside Tropical Retreat (☎ 823-0705; www.vrbo .com/9186; 4-4382 Kuhio Hwy; ste $125; ☞) Spiritual seekers would appreciate this rustic bungalow, surrounded by green forest, river, mountains and pasture. The one-bedroom suite is well worn rather than spanking new, but includes kitchenette and lots of louvers for ventila- tion. On-site ayurvedic treatments offered. Cleaning fee ($80) charged.

KO'OLAU ROAD

Ko'olau Rd is a peaceful, scenic loop drive through rich green pastures, dotted with soar- ing white egrets and bright wildflowers. It makes a nice diversion and is the way to reach untouristed Moloa'a Beach or Larsen's Beach (no facilities at either). Ko'olau Rd connects with Kuhio Hwy 0.5 miles north of the 16- mile marker and again 180yd south of the 20-mile marker.

For a quick bite, the **Moloa'a Sunrise Fruit Stand** (☎ 822-1441; Kuhio Hwy & Ko'olau Rd; juices & smoothies $3-6.25, sandwiches $5.50-7; ☻ 7:30am-6pm Mon-Sat, 10am-5pm Sun) offers healthful sand- wiches on multigrain bread, taro burgers and brown-rice vegetarian sushi. It's located past the 16-mile marker.

Moloa'a Beach

Off the tourist path, this classically curved bay appeared in the pilot episode of *Gilligan's Island*.

To the north, there's a shallow protected swimming area good for families; to the south, the waters are rougher but there's more sand. When the surf's up, stay dry and safe – go beach walking instead. Toward the back of the beach, which is fed by Moloa'a Stream, there's plenty of shade, making for an ideal picnic or daydreaming spot.

To get here, follow Ko'olau Rd and turn onto Moloa'a Rd, which ends 0.75 miles down at a few beach houses and a little parking area.

Larsen's Beach

This long, golden-sand **beach**, named after L David Larsen (former manager of C Brewer's Kilauea Sugar Company), is good for solitary strolls and beachcombing.

Although shallow, snorkeling can be good when the waters are very calm, usually only in the summer. Beware of a vicious current that runs westward along the beach and out through a channel in the reef.

When the tide is low, you might share Larsen's with Hawaiian families collecting an edible seaweed called *limu kohu*. The sea- weed found here is considered to be some of the finest in all of Hawaii. Otherwise, it will be you, the sand and the waves.

To get here, turn onto Ko'olau Rd from whichever end (ie where it intersects either Kuhio Hwy or Moloa'a Rd), go just over a mile then turn toward the ocean on a dirt road (easy to miss from the south: look for it just before the cemetery) and take the im- mediate left. It's 1 mile to the parking area and then a five-minute walk downhill to the beach.

NORTH SHORE

Forget Eden. Arguably the most pristine part of the island, the North Shore's quilted green slopes and valleys are effortlessly fertile. Somewhere between Hanalei Valley and the 'end of the road,' the seemingly untouched landscape makes it easy to imagine what it must have been like for the Hawaiian gods taking in from above the sand, sea and mountains below. Savour life here: swim through the turquoise sea, bite into juicy farmers-market fruits and nap away the afternoons on warm sugar-sand. To be sure, the sleepy little enclave that is the North Shore is an unassuming treasure.

KILAUEA
pop 2090

Many North Shore visitors treat Kilauea as an ephemeral stop in which to gas up, grab lunch and snap a few photographs on their way north – perhaps they're a little too hasty.

The most northern point of the island offers lush vegetation, great eateries and some of the best souvenir shopping around. It's home to wine vendors, fish markets, a scenic wildlife refuge and one of the island's best fruit stands, but perhaps the fact that it has one of the most well-known (and counterintuitively named) 'secret' beaches on the island will justify you giving it a look-see.

Sights & Activities
KAHILI (ROCK QUARRIES) BEACH & POOLS OF MOKOLEA

Best for a sunny calm day, this scenic little stretch of beach is a little hard to get to and tucked away between two cliffs where the Kilauea Stream meets the ocean. Public access is via Wailapa Rd, which begins midway between the 21- and 22-mile markers on Kuhio Hwy. Follow Wailapa Rd north for less than 0.5 miles beyond Kuhio Hwy and then turn left on the unmarked dirt road (4WD recommended) that begins at a bright-yellow water valve.

KAUAPEA (SECRET) BEACH

No, that's not Adam and Eve, it's likely a visiting couple wearing less than fig leaves, as this is a spot renowned for nude (albeit illegal) sunbathing. Kauapea remains reclusive, despite the fact that it's lost its virgin-quality mystique. To be sure, the oft-dubbed 'secret'

beach hardly lives up to its moniker these days. If you can handle nudity, this might just be the beach for you.

Accessing the beach requires a trek of about 15 minutes, which, during inclement weather, is dangerous. Turn right at Kalihiwai Rd and turn at the first dirt road. Follow the trail to the bottom. If the swells are down, you can consider strolling left instead of right where the trail meets the beach. Take caution and have respect for the ocean. Continue if water is calm to the lava rocks, about a quarter-mile down.

KILAUEA POINT NATIONAL WILDLIFE REFUGE

Home to some of Hawai'i's endangered wildlife, this **refuge** (☎ 828-1413; www.fws.gov/kilaueapoint; Lighthouse Rd; adult/child under 16 $5/free; ☯ 10am-4pm, closed federal holidays; P) also has sweeping views, as seen from the 52ft white tower of the lighthouse abutting 216ft sea cliffs. Plummeting rare birds and soaring 8ft-wingspan great frigates, along with views of breaching whales, make this historic landmark a treasure. The list of reasons to at least stop goes on and on (it houses the world's largest clamshell lens, a beacon up to 90 miles out to sea). You'll also see Moku'ae'ae Island, which is teeming with protected wildlife –often the endangered monk seal can be seen warming itself in the sun.

NA 'AINA KAI BOTANICAL GARDENS

In a somewhat over-the-top approach, this husband-and-wife **operation** (☎ 828-0525; www.naainakai.com; 4101 Wailapa Rd; tours $25-70; ☯ by reservation Tue-Fri) pays tribute to Hawaiian culture on 240 acres of botanical gardens. Also on the grounds: a beach, a bird-watching marsh and forest of 60,000 South and East Asian hardwood trees.

Turn right onto Wailapa Rd, between the 21- and 22-mile markers on Kuhio Hwy.

KAUAI KUNANA DAIRY

For a snapshot of farm bliss, this **microdairy** (☎ 651-5046; www.kauaikunanadairy.com; ☯ tours by appointment only) offers a tour harking back to a simpler time, with fruits, vegetables and, of course, goat cheese.

CHRIST MEMORIAL EPISCOPAL CHURCH

This charming **church** (☎ 826-4501; 2518 Kolo Rd) is one of two of Kilauea's lava-built churches (the

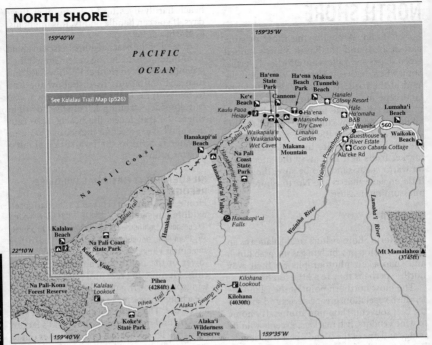

NORTH SHORE

other is St Sylvester's Catholic Church) and boasts 11 English stained-glass windows.

PINEAPPLE YOGA
Set out by Ashtanga Yoga Master Sri K Pattabhi Jois Institute in Mysore, this **yoga studio** (☎ 652-9009; www.pineappleyoga.com; drop-in classes $15; ☒ 7:30-9:30am Mon-Sat) is located in the parish house of the Christ Memorial Church, across the street from the Menehune Mart gas station.

Sleeping
Sleepy Kilauea has some unique B&Bs. What these lack in ocean views, they make up with lush, tropical farm settings.

Green Acres Cottages (Map pp508–9; ☎ 828-0478, 866-484-6347; www.greenacrescottages.com; 5-0421C Kuhio Hwy; cottages $75; P ☎) Kilauea on a budget? You got it. Each cottage has its own private entrance and kitchenette. Though somewhat small, cottages are bright and airy. On-site is a communal hot tub for use by the three cottages. The place is located on a citrus orchard, and guest can pick their own fruit.

our pick Manu Mele Cottage (Map pp508–9; ☎ 828-6797, 652-2585; www.kauaibirdsongcottage.com; cottages

$150; P) Hawaiian-inspired embellishments make this secluded little spot a find. Its name means 'bird song' in Hawaiian. There's a one-time cleaning fee of $100.

North Country Farms (Map p510; ☎ 828-1513; www.northcountryfarms.com; cottages $150; P) You've got to call for an appointment, but if it has openings this is a good deal – you can even stroll around in the morning and pick fruit from the farm. Though it claims to be minutes from the beach, keep in mind the farm is inland, and it is 'just minutes' if you're driving. The two cottages are similar to each other, but each is unique in its own charming way.

Plumeria Moon (Map pp508–9; ☎ 828-0228; www.kauaivacationhideaway.com/plumeria; 4180 N Waiakalua St; cottages $295; P ☒ ☎) One-bedroom cottages here are ideal for honeymooners. It has a private hot tub and BBQ grill. The owner boasts that vacationers can go their whole holiday without running into another soul.

Eating
Charming Kilauea town offers ample options for good eats. Whether it's a gourmet slice o' pie or high-end organic meals, you'l

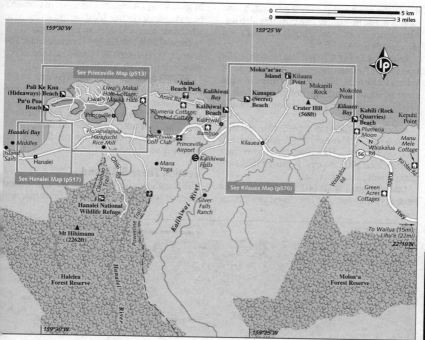

likely find *grinds* for any palate at the Kilauea Plantation or Kong Lung Centers.

our pick **Kilauea Video Ice Cream & Candy** (☎ 828-3822; Kilauea Plantation Center, 4270 Lighthouse Rd; ☺ noon-:30pm; ℗) The owner of this buzzing little hop has a lot of pride in his family, his business and his products. A perfect pick-me-up, whether it's creamy tropical ice cream or a ve-culture, low-calorie Carpigiani gelato, everything here is served up in a low-key, appy-go-lucky style.

Banana Joe's Fruitstand (☎ 828-1092; www.banana ekauai.com; 5-2719 Kuhio Hwy; smoothies $3-12; ☺ 9am-om Mon-Sat) Expect more than one variation f the fruit you're craving (there are at least ree different kinds of papaya alone). Joe kes exotic fruits to the next level – it just stes better at this little stand. Try some icy r blended fruit delicacies here, or do yourself favour and try the banana frosty du jour, the apaya bread or the coconut tapioca.

Healthy Hut (☎ 828-6626; Kilauea Plantation Center, 70 Lighthouse Rd; ☺ 8:30am-9pm) Wheat-free read, dairy-free yogurt. Got allergies? This ot can probably help keep them at bay dur-g your trip.

Kilauea Bakery & Pau Hana Pizza (☎ 828-2020; Kong Lung Center, 2484 Keneke St; pastries $4, pizza $15-33; ☺ 6:30am-9pm, pizza from 10:30am) Smoothies, cookies, fresh scones or pizza, it's all good and you'll find that whatever's baking smells wonderful.

Kilauea Fish Market (☎ 828-6244; Kilauea Plantation Center, 4270 Lighthouse Rd; plates & wraps $8-14; ☺ 11am-8pm Mon-Sat) Healthy versions of over-the-counter plate lunches are served at this island-style deli; delicious ahi burritos are a specialty.

Kilauea Town Market (☎ 828-1512; Kong Lung Center, 2484 Keneke St; ☺ 8am-8pm Sun-Thu, to 8:30pm Fri & Sat) Here, you'll find organic wines, local fruit, herbs and nitrate-free snacks galore.

Lighthouse Bistro (☎ 828-0480; Kong Lung Center, 2484 Keneke St; mains lunch $12-20, dinner $18-36; ☺ noon-2pm Mon-Sat & 5:30-9pm daily) This is a well-done town bistro with great wine, local produce and good ambience. The entertainment helps justify the pricey *pupu* and mains.

Shopping
Island Soap & Candle Works (☎ 828-1955; www.island soap.com; Kong Lung Center, 2484 Keneke St; ☺ 9am-9pm; ℗) Though there are several of these shops,

this is the most unique on the island, as the soap is made in-house. The business also donates leftovers to local schools for crafts – a plus in our book.

Kong Lung Co (☎ 828-1822; Kong Lung Center, 2484 Keneke St; ☽ 11am-6pm; ℗) This Asian-inspired art and clothing boutique features a wide array of Eastern-fusion tchotchkes as well as pricey souvenirs, reclaimed kimono quilts and children's clothes

Banana Patch Studio (☎ 828-6522; Kong Lung Center, 2484 Keneke St; ☽ 10am-6pm; ℗) A good place to pick up touristy, 'Hawaiian-style' souvenirs bearing local phraseology. Featured items are thei ceramic knickknacks.

Cake Nouveau (☎ 828-6412; Kong Lung Center, 2484 Keneke St; ☽ 11am-6pm; ℗) The closest you'll come

in town to an LA-inspired selection of women's boutique-style clothes. Ideal for those who have a hot date later and a pretty big budget.

Coconut Style (☎ 828-6899; Kong Lung Center, 2484 Keneke St; ☽ 11am-6pm; ℗) Batik, sarongs and a smattering of Bali-inspired island-wear.

our pick Oskar's K-Town Underground (☎ 828-6858; Kilauea Plantation Center, 4270 Lighthouse Rd; www.oskarskauai.com; ☽ 10am-7pm Mon-Sat, 11am-6pm Sun; ℗) A tad hodgepodge, but a great little shop if you have forgotten some necessities for baby or mom. Has a great, though small, selection of gently used and recycled baby clothes.

Getting There & Around

The Kaua'i Bus isn't yet up to par as the most efficient way to get to Kilauea. Taxis function

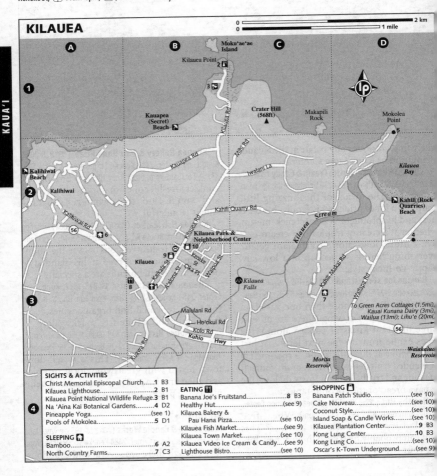

KILAUEA

SIGHTS & ACTIVITIES	
Christ Memorial Episcopal Church	1 B3
Kilauea Lighthouse	2 B1
Kilauea Point National Wildlife Refuge	3 B1
Na 'Aina Kai Botanical Gardens	4 D2
Pineapple Yoga	(see 1)
Pools of Mokolea	5 D1

SLEEPING	
Bamboo	6 A2
North Country Farms	7 C3

EATING	
Banana Joe's Fruitstand	8 B3
Healthy Hut	(see 9)
Kilauea Bakery & Pau Hana Pizza	(see 10)
Kilauea Fish Market	(see 10)
Kilauea Town Market	(see 10)
Kilauea Video Ice Cream & Candy	(see 9)
Lighthouse Bistro	(see 10)

SHOPPING	
Banana Patch Studio	(see 10)
Cake Nouveau	(see 10)
Coconut Style	(see 10)
Island Soap & Candle Works	(see 9)
Kilauea Plantation Center	9 B3
Kong Lung Center	10 B3
Kong Lung Co	(see 10)
Oskar's K-Town Underground	(see 9)

KAUA'I

BEACHSIDE SUSTAINABLE SUSTENANCE

Cooking for the allergic, the health nut or the ayurvedic devotee is all in a day's work for North Shore chef AJ Deraspe, of **Foraging Fork** (☎ 635-5865; www.foragingfork.com; dinner per couple $300). Following the mantra 'from the soil to the soul,' Deraspe is an inventive, hard-core foodie and a well-educated gourmet to boot, with a penchant for local, organic and sustainable farming. Whether it's a meal drop-off, romantic dinner or larger beach party, Deraspe can cater (pun intended) to almost every diet known to man (he got his ayurvedic training in India and Nepal). Vegan, raw, gluten-free, religious restrictions, you name it, chances are he can whip it up. He can also bring his exotic meals to you for a dinner on the beach or in a garden, should you choose.

Other private, beachside outfits:

- **Dining in Nature** (☎ 808-345-6931; www.dininginnature.com; dinner per couple $295) Here locavores can find a menu suited to their palate. Sustainable chefs Chris Hamby and Valerie Adair specialize in gluten-free gourmet for those with even the most rigid of diets. They'll bring the linen and silver and leave you with a photo memento and beach bonfire. Limousine package available.

- **Heavenly Creations** (☎ 821-9300; www.heavenlycreations.org; dinner per couple $285) Combinations can include blackened shrimp with *liliko'i* glaze, local goat cheese, olive or artichoke tapenade, fresh local fish with macadamia and grilled pineapple with coconut ice cream for dessert.

---

out of the airport mostly. Rental cars are about the only way to go. For information, see p474.

KALIHIWAI
pop 720

A wide and beautiful setting at the end of a small, picturesque valley, Kalihiwai offers great swimming (when calm), sunbathing and a great opportunity for a short kayak trek. Like all North Shore beaches, the surf can pound here, so beware, particularly as there are no lifeguards.

Remote, small and surrounded by lush grounds, **Kalihiwai Beach** is an ideal frolicking spot for sunbathing, sandcastle building and, swells permitting, swimming, bodyboarding and surfing along the cliff on the east side. To get here, take the first Kalihiwai Rd, 0.5 miles west of Kilauea.

Stay fit on vacation with **Pilates Kaua'i** (☎ 639-3074; www.pilateskauai.com; 2540 Halocline Rd; 1hr session per person in a group of 3 or more $30, per couple/single $45/75; ☑ by appointment only) and redefine the concept of bikini- or Speedo-worthy with fitness expert Laurie Antonellis.

Take in the island with a tropical jaunt on horseback at animal-friendly **Silver Falls Ranch** (Map pp508-9; ☎ 828-6718; www.silverfallsranch.com; Kamo'okoa Rd; 1½/2/3hr ride $95/115/135). Opt for the waterfall swim and picnic lunch for the best value.

our pick **Bamboo** (Map p510; ☎ 828-0811; 3281 Kalihiwai Rd; www.surfsideprop.com; 1br house per week $1100; ℗ 🛜) is pricey, perhaps, but that's to be expected. Overlooking the Kalihiwai Valley and a 10-minute walk to either 'Anini or Kalihiwai beaches, this is a charming getaway attached to a larger house inhabited by the owners. The private entrance stairs are steep to this cozy but well-appointed spot, which works well for two people.

'ANINI

A popular destination for locals spending the day or weekend camping, fishing, diving or just 'beaching' it, 'Anini is unsullied, revered and golden. To get here, cross Kalihiwai Bridge, turn onto the second Kalihiwai Rd and then bear left onto 'Anini Rd.

Sights & Activities

our pick **'Anini Beach Park** is one not to miss, as it wears many proverbial hats: it's an ideal windsurfing, snorkeling, camping, swimming and low-key just-cruisin' spot, plus it has some of the most reliable conditions, bubbling over a lagoon, and protected by one of the longest and widest fringing reefs in the Hawaiian Islands. At its widest point, the reef extends over 1600ft offshore. The park is unofficially divided into day-use, camping and windsurfing areas. While weekends might draw crowds,

KAUA'I

weekdays are low key. Facilities include rest rooms, showers, changing rooms, drinking water, picnic pavilions and BBQ grills.

You can learn what it's like to walk on water at **Windsurf Kaua'i** (☎ 828-6838; windsurfkauai@aol .com; 3hr lesson $100, board rental per hr $25; ☺ rentals 10am-4pm, lessons 9am & 1pm Mon-Fri). Teacher Celeste Harvel knows what she's doing and is enthusiastic about inspiring you. Lessons by appointment only (9am and 1pm Monday to Friday).

Sleeping

High-end vacation rentals abound in 'Anini, though they're a tad harder to find now under a new county bill which restricts vacation rentals only in specific zones on the island.

Camping at the justifiably popular 'Anini Beach Park is another option. For information on permits, see p470.

our pick **Orchid Cottage** (☎ 828-0811; www.surfside prop.com; 3585 'Anini Rd; 1br house per week $1199; P ⓡ) This private, idyllic getaway is in a small-but-lovely guesthouse a minute's walk from 'Anini Beach Park. Pick your own fruit and enjoy partial ocean views. Includes washer-dryer, TV, VCR, ministereo, kayaks, bicycles, snorkel gear and beach chairs. There's an $85 cleaning fee, a three-night minimum stay (one week during holidays), a three-person-max rule, $250 security deposit and free long-distance calling to Canada and mainland USA.

Liwai's Makai Hale Cottage (☎ 822-4500; 4343 'Anini Rd; 2½br house per week $1950; P ⓡ) Location, location, location. A good deal for four people, this secluded gem is just 120ft away from the most reclusive part of 'Anini Beach and perfect for those with children. It's ideal for a family or any group yearning for a beach vacation where leaving the property is nearly unnecessary. It comes complete with a full kitchen, TV, washer-dryer and ministereo system. The large deck overlooking the water is the cherry on top. Free long-distance calls to mainland US is available. The cost for each additional person (six-person max) is $150. The security deposit is $500 and cleaning fee $175. Between December 15 and January 5, the cost is $2800 per week with a two-week minimum stay.

Liwai's Mauka Hale (☎ 822-4500; 4343A 'Anini Rd; 2br house per week $1600; P) First, the perks: a 400 sq ft deck overlooking the ocean, a mere 160ft away. This polished home has a queen bed in its master bedroom with half bath-room, a second bedroom with two twin beds and another full bathroom with washer and dryer. For more than two people, there's a $125 fee for additional person (and a four-person max). Security deposit is $500 and between December 15 and January 5 it costs $2400 per week, with a two-week minimum stay. There's also a $150 cleaning fee.

Plumeria Cottage (☎ 828-0811; www.surfsideprop .com; 3585 'Anini Rd; 2½br house per week $1525; P ⓡ) A charming and unique spot that's both comfortable and chic, and worth the splurge for the location (it's a short walk to the beach), with sumptuous embellishments, sweeping views and amicable caretakers.

PRINCEVILLE
pop 1700

Kilauea's rich cousin, Princeville is as close as Kaua'i will get to having its own Vegas, with its penchant for resorts, large sculpture and golf courses. Lavish has found its resting place at the St Regis Princeville, formerly the Princeville Resort.

Often the most referred-to spot on the North Shore by tourists (perhaps because it doesn't carry the risk of mispronunciation) it grew in population and popularity as a result of its first flagship resort in 1985.

Though it might appear the name 'Princeville' came around the same time as the resort community, the name goes back to the young Prince Albert, son of Queen Emma and Kamehameha IV when he was given the area to manage as training to take the throne.

Orientation & Information

The North Shore's only airport is in Princeville, as is the **Chevron Gas Station** (Kuhio Hwy; ☺ 6am-10pm Mon-Sat, to 9pm Sun), the last option before the end of the road. The **post office** (☎ 800-275-8777; Princeville Center; ☺ 10:30am-3:30pm Mon-Fri, to 12:30pm Sat) is located in the shopping center.

Sights
PALI KE KUA (HIDEAWAYS) & PU'U POA BEACHES

Princeville is mostly cliffs overlooking the ocean, with rocky and dangerous coast at the base. There are, however, two worthwhile beaches, both of which, unfortunately, are difficult to access and require parking at the parking lot after the St Regis gatehouse. A

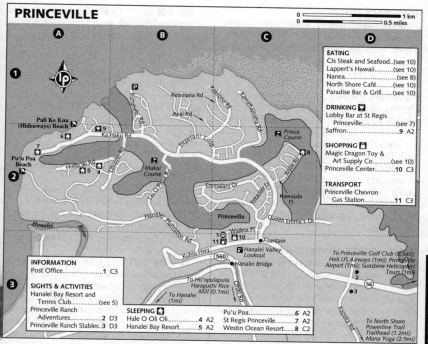

PRINCEVILLE

EATING
CJs Steak and Seafood..(see 10)
Lappert's Hawaii.........(see 10)
Nanea.......................(see 8)
North Shore Café........(see 10)
Paradise Bar & Grill.....(see 10)

DRINKING
Lobby Bar at St Regis
Princeville.................(see 7)
Saffron.......................**9** A2

SHOPPING
Magic Dragon Toy &
Art Supply Co..........(see 10)
Princeville Center..........**10** C3

TRANSPORT
Princeville Chevron
Gas Station................**11** C3

INFORMATION
Post Office......................**1** C3

SIGHTS & ACTIVITIES
Hanalei Bay Resort and
Tennis Club...............(see 5)
Princeville Ranch
Adventures................**2** D3
Princeville Ranch Stables..**3** D3

SLEEPING
Hale O Oli Oli................**4** A2
Hanalei Bay Resort.........**5** A2
Pu'u Poa.......................**6** A2
St Regis Princeville..........**7** A2
Westin Ocean Resort.....**8** C2

To Princeville Golf Club (0.5mi);
Heli US Airways (1mi); Princeville
Airport (1mi); Sunshine Helicopters
Tours (1mi)

To Hoʻopulapula
Haraguchi Rice
Mill (0.1mi);
To Hanalei
(1mi)

To North Shore
Powerline Trail
Trailhead (1.2mi);
Mana Yoga (2.5mi)

KAUA'I

path between two fences leads you to **Pali Ke Kua Beach** (also called Hideaways) and a path to the left of the gatehouse leads you to **Pu'u Poa Beach.**

QUEEN'S BATH
This beautiful but deadly spot – formed by a lava-rock shelf – has natural pools that provide a natural swimming and snorkeling hole. Often hit by powerful waves, it's notorious for pulling visitors out to sea. Though the surf at times splashes in softly, any description not stating that it's the most deadly swimming hole on the island would be amiss. If you decide to go, please be smart about it. Four tourists died there in 2008, two of whom were walking along the ledge used to access it when a large wave swept them out to sea. For tips on being water-savvy, go to www.kauaiexplorer.com.

ST REGIS PRINCEVILLE
The work that's gone into this high-end resort is reason enough to get a peek. The sunset is without a doubt among the most beautiful the island has to offer at this locale, where a deck overlooks glorious views of **Makana Mountain** and the wall of the Wainiha Valley.

HANALEI VALLEY LOOKOUT
Take in views of farmland that's been cultivated for more than 1000 years, the broad brushstroke of valley, river and taro, plus a smattering of rare wildlife. Park across from the Princeville Center (Map p513) so you don't have to cross the street, but take care to watch for other pedestrians when pulling out onto the busy highway.

Activities
GOLF
St Regis Princeville Golf Club (☎ Prince 826-5000, Makai 826-3580; www.princeville.com; 5-3900 Kuhio Hwy; green fees nonguest/guest Prince $175/150, Makai $125/110) offers some of the most scenic views imaginable, making it difficult to say anything other than the Prince Golf Course is among the most breathtaking in the world. This 18-hole par-72 course has been featured on several 'best of' lists and is set against sea cliffs. The 27-hole par-72 Makai Course (c 1971) is also beautiful and challenging for the avid golfer.

HORSEBACK RIDING

Princeville Ranch Stables (☎ 826-6777; www.princeville ranch.com; Kuhio Hwy; tours $65-170; ☼ tours Mon-Sat) is great even for those who have never seen an equestrian day. Wear jeans, sunblock and insect repellent.

MOUNTAIN BIKING

The **Powerline Trail** is a serious 11.2-mile ride that has steep climbs, deep ruts and puddles deeper than bike tires. Ample scenery makes the reward all that much sweeter along the trail, but the real reason to do this is the athletic challenge. Opt to ride in and turn-around back out, or arrange for pick-up at the **Kapa'a trailhead** or the **Opaeka'a Falls** lookout. To get there, take the road to the Princeville Ranch Stable and follow to the end to find the trailhead.

MULTIACTIVITY ADVENTURES

Princeville Ranch Adventures (☎ 826-7669, 888-955-7669; www.adventureskauai.com; tours $79-125) is a family-friendly enterprise that can bring out your adventurous side, whether it's for a hike, kayak or zipline excursion. Minimum requirements are 12 years and 80lb.

HELICOPTER RIDES

Leaving out of both Lihu'e and Princeville Airport, **Heli USA Airways** (☎ 826-6591, 866-936-1234; www.heliusahawaii.com; 55min tour $267) offers convenience if you're on the North Shore; however, it was one of two companies on-island to have a fatal crash in 2007, so its safety record is less than perfect. Also operating out of both airports is **Sunshine Helicopters** (☎ 270-3999; www.sunshinehelicopters.com/kauai/tours/princeville_adventure.html; 40-50min tours $345, online booking $285).

YOGA

Mana Yoga (☎ 826-9230, www.manayoga.com; 3812 Ahonui Pl; classes $20, private sessions per hr $80; ☼ 8:30am Mon & Wed; ℗) It's no gimmick; Michaelle Edwards created her own version of yoga that has been known to make spines sing. Her studio doubles as a yoga retreat, too. Single/double studios are $85/$95; see www.kauainorthshorevacationrentals.com for more details.

Sleeping

Princeville is high end. Whether you're renting a condo or are in a resort, expect to dole out some cash.

Hale O Oli Oli (☎ 714-803-8073; 4126 Kekuanaoa Rd; 3br per week $950) Not your typical Princeville rental, this mellow, clean home is chock-full of beach toys like surfboards and snorkel gear, as well as bikes. Reasonably priced, it's a spacious 1600 sq ft that, though not beachside, is a few blocks from the Hanalei Bay Resort. Two of the three bedrooms in the upstairs living quarters have queen beds; the third has two twins. Bonuses include that for Princeville, rife with side-by-side dwellings, this is private, freestanding and sits on a 10,000 sq ft lot with fruit trees bearing avocado, banana and tangerines. Security deposit $200, cleaning fee $150.

Hanalei Bay Resort (☎ 826-6522; www.hanaleibay resort.com; 5380 Hono'iki Rd; r $205; 1br unit from $370; ⊠ 🛜 🐾) Location is the name of the game, and though steeply priced, there's good reason: it's one of the mainstays of 'luxury' most associated with the area.

Pu'u Poa (☎ 826-9394, 800-535-0085; www.marc resorts.com; Ka Haku Rd; 2br unit $275-500; 🖥 🐾) For the price, you can do better, unless you absolutely have to stay near the St Regis Princeville. Though decor varies, most condos offer two bedrooms with a queen bed and two twins, full kitchen and sleeper sofa. Internet kiosk on-site.

ourpick Westin Ocean Resort (☎ 827-8700; www.starwoodhotels.com/wesstin/property/overview/index.html; 3838 Wyllie Rd; villas $225-780; ℗ ⊠ 🛜 🐾) Take advantage of this somewhat cheaper (though that word seems out of place) St Regis property. Condolike 'villas' boast full kitchens, flat-screen TVs and washer-dryer.

St Regis Princeville (☎ 826-9644, 800-325-3589; www.princevillehotelhawaii.com; 5520 Ka Haku Rd; r $750-6500; ℗ ⊠ 🛜 🐾) Scheduled to be open by the time you read this, the St Regis Princeville has four restaurants, including the first Jean-Georges Vongerichten restaurant in Hawaii and a locally revered lobby bar (opposite). A 5000 sq ft infinity pool overlooks Pu'u Poa (Hideaways Beach) and Hanalei Bay. You're right to expect that even the 'cheapest' rooms are opulent. Decorated with a contemporary Hawaiian design, each has custom-designed furniture, one-way viewing glass and marble bathrooms. The higher-range options include your own round-the-clock butler service, which comes with a personal unpacker. The resort also is home to the Halele'a Spa (House of Joy), an 11,000 sq ft palatial escape for massages, replete with couples and VIP treatment rooms. The spa also houses a nail and hair salon and 24-hour fitness center.

Eating
BUDGET
North Shore Café (☎ 826-1122; Princeville Center; breakfast $2.75-5; lunch & dinner $8-22; ☻ 6am-8pm Mon-Sat) For the cheapest hot breakfast in town this gas-station watering hole offers up popular breakfast sandwiches and makes a decent pizza. It's inside the North Shore General Store & Café.

Lappert's Ice Cream (☎ 826-7393; Princeville Center; ☻ 10am-9pm) The sweet smell from the waffle cones beckons, and the delectable locally inspired options are sure not to disappoint. Don't miss out. Get the Kauai Pie Kona coffee ice cream, toasted coconut, macnuts, fudge and vanilla cake.

The **Foodland Market** (☎ 826-9880; Princeville Center; ☻ 6am-11pm) has the basics: deli, bakery, produce and beer.

MIDRANGE & TOP END
Paradise Bar & Grill (☎ 826-1775; Princeville Center; mains $11-25; ☻ 11am-11pm) Pub food with a little 'tude, but if you've got the time, the burgers and fish are juicy and fresh.

CJ's Steak & Seafood (☎ 826-6211; Princeville Center; dinner mains $22-38; ☻ 6-9:30pm) CJ's is a Princeville standard, thanks to its cuisine of prime rib, shrimp, lobster and fresh fish, all done up expertly without the frills (you won't find any wasabi marinades here).

our pick **Nanea** (☎ 827-8700; Westin Princeville Ocean Resort Villas Clubhouse; dinner mains $31-38; ☻ 630-10:30am & 5:30-9:30pm; P) A new kid in town, Nanea has ironed out its kinks and is a bit of a show-off with its elegant Hawaii fusion cuisine, locally grown produce and inventive uses of island honey and Kilauea goat cheese.

Drinking & Entertainment
St Regis Princeville (☎ 826-2788; www.princeville hotelhawaii.com; 5520 Ka Haku Rd; ☻ 6pm Mon & Thu) This swanky place offers the chance to eat, drink and be merry while strolling around the oceanfront pool of its opulent digs, should you have missed the chance to stay here as a guest. For the only beach luau on-island, go to the South Shore's Sheraton.

Saffron (☎ 826-6225; 5300 Ka Haku Rd; www.saffron hawaii.com; ☻ 6-9pm Mon-Thu, to 10pm Fri & Sat) When you're ready for some Euro-style tapas and early evening cocktails, come to this place.

Sink into a couch on Wednesdays and Saturdays and sip cocktails while listening to live music ranging from contemporary Hawaiian to classical guitar.

Lobby bar at St Regis Princeville (☎ 826-9644, 800-325-3589; www.princevillehotelhawaii.com; 5520 Ka Haku Rd; ☻ 3-11pm) The much anticipated Spring 2009 reopening and 'reconcepted' cocktail-hour staple offers undeniably unforgettable views that are, dare we say, the best of Hanalei Bay, making this a the ultimate choice for sunset cocktails. It was closed for renovations when we visited, so call ahead to check that it's open.

Shopping
Magic Dragon Toy & Art Supply Co (☎ 826-9144, Princeville Center; ☻ 9am-6pm P) Kites, paints, pinwheels – this place is great for kids or the kid in you. Stuffed toys, including depictions of Frida Kahlo and Salvador Dalí, make this intriguing shop among the most original in the Princeville Center.

HANALEI VALLEY
Dense with deep *kalo loi* (taro fields), there is a mist that hovers above the gem green valley where fertile ground has been the lifeblood of taro for centuries. Here, expect sightings of native Hawaiian wildlife, gushing waterfalls, stubborn mountains and afternoon rainbows.

The 1912 landmark **Hanalei Bridge** (Map p513) is the first of seven bridges to cross the Hanalei River and lead you to the famed 'end of the road.' The bridge forces you to stop and appreciate the sleepiness of the North Shore. Thanks to this landmark, big trucks, buses or road-ragers can't ravage this serene little entrance to Hanalei.

Undulating, winding strips of road canopied by mammoth trees with glimpses here and there of ocean, valley or river – the **Hanalei Valley Scenic Drive** makes driving special when heading north on 'the road' to its end (in Ha'ena). Princeville offers some of the first famous North Shore views from its **Hanalei Valley Lookout**. To get here, turn left onto Ohiki Rd immediately after the Hanalei Bridge. You can enter the refuge on the Ho'opulapula Haraguchi Rice Mill Tour (p519).

Take in the reward of a breathless hike atop the **Okolehao Trail** (Map pp508–9), where 2.5 miles and a 1250ft climb never offered such rewards. Expect to pay with a little sweat and

DRIVING WITH ALOHA

Lauded as the most scenic and breathtaking drive on the island, the drive to the 'end of the road' is impossibly beautiful. However, though you might want to pull over for that must-have photograph, please avoid being 'that person,' as many accidents have occurred from visitors pulling over to take that photo op. (You'll likely see at least one other visitor doing this.) If you're heading to the road's end (Ke'e Beach), take it slowly and enjoy the crossing of each of the seven one-lane bridges, the first of which is in Hanalei.

When crossing these bridges, do as the locals do:

- When the bridge is empty and you reach it first, you can go.
- If there's a steady stream of cars already crossing as you approach, then simply follow them.
- When you see cars approaching from the opposite direction, yield to the entire queue of approaching cars for at least five cars, if not all.
- Give the *shaka* sign ('hang loose' hand gesture, with index, middle and ring fingers downturned) as thanks to any opposite-direction drivers who have yielded.

two hours of your day for sweeping views of Hanalei Bay. To get to the trailhead, take your first left after Hanalei's first one-way bridge heading north, along Rice Mill Rd. Go down the road about 0.5 mile to a parking lot across from the start of the trail.

HANALEI
pop 480
The surfer-chic town of Hanalei has more than its fair share of adults with Peter Pan syndrome and kids with seemingly Olympian athletic prowess. A stroll down beachfront Weke Rd and you'll see men in their 60s wax their surfboards and young 'uns carry their 'guns' (ie big-wave surfboards) to the beach. Without a doubt, beach life is *the* life here.

Orientation & Information
Hanalei has no bank, but there is an ATM in the Ching Young Village's Big Save supermarket.

Bali Hai Photo (☎ 826-9181; Ching Young Village; per hr $9; ☷ 8am-8pm Mon-Fri, 9am-5pm Sat, 10am-5pm Sun) Internet access.
Java Kai (☎ 826-6717; Hanalei Center; www.javakai .com; 2hr $12; ☷ 6:30am-6pm; ☷) Lively, open-air hangout spot for wi-fi.
Post office (☎ 800-275-8777; 5-5226 Kuhio Hwy) On the *makai* (seaward) side of the road, just west of the Big Save shopping center.

Sights
HANALEI BAY
Palisades, a crescent-shaped bay and a boatload of surfers make Hanalei Bay typify what many envision when thinking of Kaua'i.

Made up of four beaches, there's something for almost everyone here: sunbathing, bodyboarding and surfing. The winter months can make this stretch of water an experts-only spot, though in summer months the water is sometimes so calm it's hard to distinguish between sky and sea, except for the smattering of yachts bobbing on the horizon. Black Pot Beach Park (Hanalei Pier) and Wai'oli (Pine Trees) Beach Park offer rest rooms, showers, drinking water, picnic tables and grills. Family-wise, Hanalei Beach Park Pavilion is best, with facilities and lifeguards.

HANALEI BEACH PARK PAVILION
Lifeguarded and boasting sweeping views, this is a great place for a picnic, sunset or lazy day at the beach. Ideally located, its downside is parking, which can be a challenge. Park along Weke Rd if you have to, as it can get crowded.

BLACK POT BEACH PARK (HANALEI PIER)
This is one of the most crowded beaches within the already-popular Hanalei Bay. Of course its appeal is undeniable. Keep an eye out for particularly stunning views of Namolokama over the bay when Wai'oli Falls has been rejuvenated by a previous night's rain.

WAI'OLI (PINE TREES) BEACH PARK
A less popular but equally beautiful spot Pine Trees beach is dominated by locals. The shorebreak is harder here than any other spot on Hanalei Bay and swimming is dangerous except during the calmest summer surf. There are rest rooms and showers.

WAIKOKOS

Catch right and lefts at **Waikokos break** (off Map p517), protected by a reef on the western bend of Hanalei Bay. To get there, park on the side of the main highway and trek a short walk near the 4- and 5-mile markers. Winter surfing is sometimes good off Makahoa Point, the western point of the bay.

MIDDLES

The area known as Middles (Map pp508–9) is set in the middle of two breaks: between Waikokos and Pine Trees, outside (as in 'outside the reef') and to the left. An area on the inside of the reef going north is dubbed 'Grandpas' by surfers.

WAI'OLI HUI'IA CHURCH & WAI'OLI MISSION HOUSE

Built in 1912, this historic church and accompanying 1936-built house lend some context to the picturesque, verdant green grass with Mt Namolokama as a backdrop. The church's setting and artifacts give a small glimpse of the days of missionaries on the island.

Activities
DIVING

Ocean Quest Watersports (☎ 742-6991, 800-972-3078; www.fathomfive.com; ✆ dives 7am, 7:30am & 1pm Mon-Fri, North Shore dives Mar-Oct) is the satellite location of the Fathom Five outfit in Koloa, and is geared for a North Shore dive at Tunnels. It's PADI certified. Newbies can do introductory dives

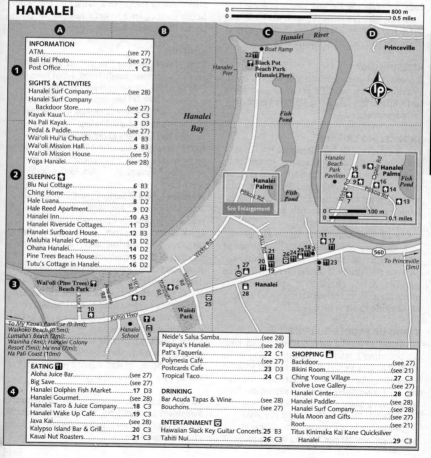

HANALEI

0   800 m
0   0.5 miles

KAUA'I

INFORMATION
ATM...(see 27)
Bali Hai Photo..................................(see 27)
Post Office...1 C3

SIGHTS & ACTIVITIES
Hanalei Surf Company.....................(see 28)
Hanalei Surf Company
  Backdoor Store.............................(see 27)
Kayak Kaua'i...2 C3
Na Pali Kayak...3 D3
Pedal & Paddle................................(see 27)
Wai'oli Hui'ia Church...........................4 B3
Wai'oli Mission Hall.............................5 B3
Wai'oli Mission House.......................(see 5)
Yoga Hanalei...................................(see 28)

SLEEPING
Blu Nui Cottage.....................................6 B3
Ching Home...7 D2
Hale Luana...8 D2
Hale Reed Apartment...........................9 D2
Hanalei Inn...10 A3
Hanalei Riverside Cottages................11 D3
Hanalei Surfboard House.....................12 B3
Maluhia Hanalei Cottage...................13 D2
Ohana Hanalei.....................................14 D2
Pine Trees Beach House.....................15 D2
Tutu's Cottage in Hanalei..................16 D2

EATING
Aloha Juice Bar................................(see 27)
Big Save...(see 27)
Hanalei Dolphin Fish Market.............17 D3
Hanalei Gourmet.............................(see 28)
Hanalei Taro & Juice Company..........18 C3
Hanalei Wake Up Café........................19 C3
Java Kai...(see 28)
Kalypso Island Bar & Grill...................20 C3
Kauai Nut Roasters.............................21 C3

Neide's Salsa Samba.........................(see 28)
Papaya's Hanalei..............................(see 28)
Pat's Taqueria..................................(see 28)
Polynesia Café..................................(see 27)
Postcards Cafe....................................22 C1
Tropical Taco.......................................24 C3

DRINKING
Bar Acuda Tapas & Wine.................(see 28)
Bouchons...(see 27)

ENTERTAINMENT
Hawaiian Slack Key Guitar Concerts.25 B3
Tahiti Nui..26 C3

SHOPPING
Backdoor...(see 27)
Bikini Room.......................................(see 21)
Ching Young Village............................27 C3
Evolve Love Gallery..........................(see 27)
Hanalei Center...................................28 C3
Hanalei Paddler................................(see 28)
Hanalei Surf Company......................(see 28)
Hula Moon and Gifts.......................(see 27)
Root..(see 21)
Titus Kinimaka Kai Kane Quicksilver
  Hanalei...29 C3

Hanalei River
Boat Ramp
22
Black Pot Beach Park (Hanalei Pier)
Hanalei Pier
Princeville
Hanalei Bay
Fish Pond
Hanalei Beach Park Pavilion
Hanalei Palms
15 8
9
7
16
14
13
0   100 m
0   0.1 miles
Pilikoa Rd
Opelu Rd
Weke Rd
Aku Rd
Hanalei Palms
Pilikoa Rd
See Enlargement
11 17
26 24 18
21
20 19
1 27
23
(560)
To Princeville (3mi)
Hanalei
28
25
Ama'ama Rd
12
6
Weke Rd
Hee Rd
Mahimahi Rd
Malolo Rd
Wai'oli (Pine Trees) Beach Park
10
Kuhio Hwy
4
Hanalei School
5
Waioli Park

*To My Kaua'i Paradise (0.3mi);
Waikoko Beach (0.5mi);
Lumaha'i Beach (2mi);
Wainiha (4mi); Hanalei Colony
Resort (5mi); Ha'ena (7mi);
Na Pali Coast (10mi)*

with a one-hour academic lesson; one-tank/two-tank dives cost around $100/140. The staff will bring the gear to you.

If you're certified, a one-tank dive costs $79 and a two-tank dive $119 per person at **North Shore Divers** (☎ 828-1223; www.northshoredivers.com; ⏰ dives 8am Mon-Fri, North Shore dives Mar-Oct; 1st-time divers 1-/2-tank dives $109/169.). For an unforgettable experience, try night diving (summer only) for $99. An open-water certification course is $450. Meet at the beach.

KAYAKING

Though not the largest or most sacred river in the state (the Wailua River holds that honour) the Hanalei River's 6 miles (roughly) are scenic, calm and safe, and ideal for novice kayakers or stand up paddlers. For kayak rentals, try **Pedal & Paddle** (☎ 826-9069; www.pedalnpaddle.com; Ching Young Village; per day/week single kayaks $15/60, double kayaks $35/140; ⏰ 9am-6pm). It offers the gamut of sports and camping equipment.

KITESURFING

It looks hard-core, fun and you want to try it. We don't blame you. To get a taste, try **Aloha Surf & Kitesurfing School** (☎ 635-9293; 3 lessons $195; ⏰ by appointment only).

SNORKELING CRUISES

For snorkeling, **Na Pali Catamaran** (☎ 826-6853, 866-255-6853; www.napalicatamaran.com; 4hr tours adult/child $135/110; ⏰ morning & afternoon May-Sep) is great: depending on the waves and the time of year, you might get to venture into some sea caves. Remember though, it pounds and there's no reprieve from the elements.

Captain Sundown (☎ 826-5585; www.captainsundown.com; 6hr tour adult/child 10-12 $162/148) is out of Lihu'e most of the year, so take advantage and use this outlet if you're here during the summer. A true character, Captain Bob has more than 38 years' experience and takes a lot of pride in what he does.

STAND UP PADDLE SURFING

For stand up paddle surfing (often called 'paddle boarding'), try the following:

our pick **Andrea Smith** (☎ 635-0269; 1½hr private lesson $80; ⏰ 8am-12pm Mon-Fri) For lessons, hitch up with surfer extraordinaire Andrea for a pleasant introduction to this core-flexing sport.

Kayak Kauai (☎ 826-9844; rental per 24hr $45; ⏰ 8am-5:30pm, to 8pm summer) Offers an array of athletic equipment and gear, including stand up paddle

surfing rentals. Find it across the street from Postcards Café.

Mitchell Alapa (☎ 482-0749; private lesson $65 ⏰ 8am-2pm) A long-time Kaua'i surfer.

OUTRIGGER CANOEING

Hawaiian Surfing Adventures (☎ 482-0749; www.hawaiiansurfingadventures.com; 2hr tours per person for 1/2/3/4 people $200/100/75/45; ⏰ 8am-2pm) A great workout and a great glimpse into this inspired Polynesian tradition, chances are you'll see marine life too.

HAWAIIAN SAILING CANOE

our pick **Island Sails** (Map pp508-9; ☎ 212-6053; http://islandsailskauai.com/home; 1½hr tours, morning snorkel trip; adult/child $85/65; ⏰ 9-10:30am, 3:30-5pm, 5:30pm-sunset) Snorkeling in the morning, cruising in the afternoon or taking in a sunset on the water, here's your chance to get a taste of the traditional Polynesian sailing canoe.

SURFING

Hanalei Surf Company (Map p517; ☎ 826-9000; www.hanaleisurf.com; Hanalei Center, 5-5161 Kuhio Hwy; 2½hr lesson $65-150, per day/week surfboards $15/65, bodyboards $5/20; ⏰ 8am-9pm) Surf instructors Russell Lewis and Ian Vernon have an excellent reputation and are especially suited for advanced surfers.

Hanalei Surf Company Backdoor Store (☎ 826-9000; www.hanaleisurf.com; Ching Young Village; 2hr lesson per person group/couple $65/75, private $150, surfboards per day $20, bodyboards $6; ⏰ 8am-9pm, lessons by appointment)

Hawaiian School of Surfing (☎ 652-1116; 1½hr lesson $65; ⏰ lessons 8am, 10am & noon) Stop by or call in advance for a lesson by legendary pro big-wave surfer Titus Kinimaka or, more likely, one of his guys, who line up the boards and red rashguards daily at the pier. No more than three students per instructor.

Hawaiian Surfing Adventures (☎ 482-0749; www.hawaiiansurfingadventures.com; 2hr lesson group/private $55/75, surfboards per day/week $30/100; ⏰ 8am-2pm) Generous lesson includes a half-hour on land, one hour in the water and another hour of solo practice. Look for the yellow rashguards on the beach.

Kayak Kaua'i (Map p517; ☎ 826-9844; www.kayakkauai.com; Kuhio Hwy; 1hr lesson $50, per day surfboards/bodyboards $20/6; ⏰ 10am & 2pm) If you rent gear for four days, you get three more days free.

Need some equipment? The **Watersports Swapmeet** (⏰ 9am-12pm, 1st Saturday of the month), at the Hanalei Center, is great for getting some cheaper, used gear.

DETOUR: THE NA PALI KAYAK TREK

The Na Pali Coast has reasonable claim to offering the most scenic scenery of all of Kaua'i. Any trip to Kaua'i without experiencing it would be incomplete; and if you're able, kayaking it arguably offers one of the most unforgettable challenges on the planet.

Kayaking the Na Pali Coast is strenuous and dangerous, and therefore not for everyone. Going with a guide helps manage the dangers, going without means you're more than just familiar with ocean (not river) kayaking. It also means you know better than to go alone. Always check several days of weather forecasting and ocean conditions before going (☎ 245-3564). Hanakapi'ai Beach is about a mile in. About six more miles and you can set up camp at Kalalau. If you started very early, you can aim for setting up camp at Miloli'i, (with a permit) which is at the 11-mile point, two miles past Nu'alolo Kai. From there you have the often surfless, hot, flat stretch of Polihale, for what feels like much longer than 3 miles.

Always start on the North Shore, end on the Westside (due to currents) and never go in winter (potentially deadly swells).

If you want to do the Na Pali Kayak Trek with a guide, try the following operators:

■ **Kayak Kaua'i** (Map p517; ☎ 826-9844, 800-437-3507; www.kayakkauai.com; Kuhio Hwy; per day/week single kayaks $28/112, double kayaks $52/208; ☯ 8am-5pm, to 8pm summer) Tours include a Na Pali Coast thriller for $185 from May to September, Blue Lagoon kayak and snorkel for $60, or an open-ocean paddle on the South Shore winter for $115.

■ **our pick Na Pali Kayak** (Map p517; ☎ 826-6900, 866-977-6900; www.napalikayak.com; Kuhio Hwy; tours $175) The Na Pali Coast trip is the only tour these folks lead and their guides have over a decade of experience paddling these waters.

■ **Outfitters Kaua'i** (Map pp532-3; ☎ 742-9667, 888-742-9887; www.outfitterskauai.com; Po'ipu Plaza, 2827A Po'ipu Rd; Na Pali Coast tour $185; ☯ reservations 8am-9pm) Located in Po'ipu, but it offers tours islandwide.

YOGA

Yoga Hanalei (☎ 826-9642; www.yogahanalei.com; Hanalei Center, 2nd fl, 5-5161E Kuhio Hwy, upstairs; per class $15) is good for Ashtanga yoga; try Bhavani Maki.

Tours

our pick Ho'opulapula Haraguchi Rice Mill Tour (Map pp508-9; ☎ 651-3399; www.haraguchiricemill.org; Kuhio Hwy; 3hr tour incl lunch per person $65; ☯ tours 10am Wed) The Haraguchi family, which also owns the Hanalei Taro & Juice Company, offers tours (by appointment only) of its historic rice mill and wetland taro farm. See the otherwise inaccessible Hanalei National Wildlife Refuge and learn about Hawaii's immigrant history. Tours are limited to 14. The family helps run the biennial (even-numbered years) **Hanalei Taro Festival**, all about growing and cooking this surprisingly tasty native staple.

Sleeping

MIDRANGE & TOP END

Ohana Hanalei (☎ 826-4116; www.hanalei-kauai .com; Pilikoa Rd; r per day/week $95/615) It's amazing how cheap this studio is given the location, a mere half-block from the beach. It has its own kitchenette, private entrance, phone, cable TV and convenient parking.

Bed, Breakfast & Beach at Hanalei (☎ 826-6111; www.bestvacationinparadise.com; 5095 Pilikoa Rd; r $105-$120) The location is ideal, but the owner can seem a bit picky (no groups of two or more; one couple per reservation). That might not matter, though, if you plan on spending much of your time across the street at Hanalei Bay. Homemade breakfast sweetens the deal.

our pick Hanalei Inn (☎ 826-9333; www.hanaleiinn .com; 5-5468 Kuhio Hwy; r $119; ☯) With four studios to choose from, each with kitchen and a killer locale, this place is a steal. Stay for a week, pay no taxes.

Maluhia Hanalei Cottage (☎ 415-382-8918, 415-310-1919; www.hanaleivacationrental.com; Pilikoa Rd; 2-/3br ste per day $150/235, week $1050/1600) This cottage has a kitchenette, posh decor and is centrally located. There's a partly refundable security deposit of $500.

Pine Trees Beach House (☎ 826-9333; www.hanalei bayinn.com; 5404 Weke Rd; r $199/$259; ☯) On the frontage road of Hanalei Bay. Four people can fit comfortably in the upstairs rental, replete with two queen beds and one futon; a

KAUA'I

HOMAGE TO KALO

According to Hawaiian cosmology, *Papa* (earth mother) and *Wakea* (sky father; who also gave birth to the Hawaiian Islands), gave birth to *Haloa*, a stillborn and brother to man. Haloa was planted in the earth, and from his body came taro, or *kalo*, a plant that has long sustained the Hawaiian people and been a staple for oceanic cultures.

Kalo is still considered a sacred food, full of tradition and spirituality for Native Hawaiians. The North Shore's Hanalei is home to the largest taro-producing farm in the state, where the purple, starchy potatolike plant is grown in pondfields known as *lo'i kalo* (Hawaiian wet taro fields). After crossing the first of several one-way bridges in Hanalei, to the left you'll notice the *kalo* growing.

Kalo regained the spotlight in the '70s thanks to the 'Hawaiian Renaissance,' a time during which some aspects of the Hawaiian culture enjoyed a modest, long-overdue resurgence and reclaimed practice. Though dismissed by some outsiders as little more than a glorified, garnet-colored potato, *kalo* is rich in nutrients. It is often boiled and pounded into poi, an earthy, starchy and somewhat sweet and sticky puddinglike food.

Families enjoy poi, defined as the 'staff of life' in the Hawaiian dictionary, a number of ways. Some prefer it fresh, while others prefer sour poi, or poi *'awa 'awa* (bitter), possibly from the method in which poi used to be served – often it sat in a bowl on the table for quite some time.

All traditional Hawaiian households show respect for taro: when the poi bowl sits on the table, one is expected to refrain from arguing or speaking in anger. That's because any bad energy is *'ino* (evil) – and can spoil the poi.

A tip: because of the spiritual relevance and cultural history of *kalo*, it's disrespectful to dismiss it as bland. If you happen upon one of many luaus on the island that include *kalo*-based poi in their smorgasbord, don't jump on the bandwagon to call it 'wallpaper paste.' It's an insult.

downstairs studio apartment can sleep two with its queen bed and a pull-out couch.

Hale Luana (☎ 826-6931; Opelu Rd; ste $150) Enjoy some budget-friendly digs, which offer a private entrance to this one-bedroom suite. There's a one-time cleaning fee of $85.

Hanalei Surfboard House (☎ 826-9825; www.hanal eisurfboardhouse.com; 5459 Weke Rd; r $175-225; ❒ 🛋) A surfer haven, this place has kitchenette, TV and unique decor, from vintage Hawaiiana to a shower floor handcrafted with Kaua'i sand. The more expensive detached unit features air-con and surround-sound stereo.

Ching Home (☎ 826-9622, 800-488-3336; 5119 Weke Rd; studio/r/ste per week $600/850/950) Clean, hip and perfect for surfers looking for an ideal and less-than-private locale, across from Hanalei Pavilion. Upstairs is the airy one-bedroom suite.

ourpick Hanalei Riverside Cottages (☎ 826-1675; www.hanaleidolphin.com/kauaivacationrental.html; 5-5016 Kuhio Hwy; 2br per week $1000; 🛋) Launch a canoe, kayak or stand up paddleboard right from your backyard on the Hanalei River. Airy, scenic and a stone's toss from the little shops of Ching Young Village. Cottage 3 has its own wi-fi, while the others poach off the signal.

Hale Reed Apartment (☎ 415-459-1858; www .hanalei-vacation.com; 4441 Pilikoa Rd; 2br apt per week from $1000-1500; 🛋) Location is key here, and you're just a short walk to the beach. This ground floor apartment boasts a full kitchen, queen bed and patio perfect for cooking, and it can sleep four people in total. There's a partly refundable $300 to $500 security deposit.

Tutu's Cottage in Hanalei (☎ 826-6111; www.best vacationinparadise.com; 5095 Pilikoa Rd.; 2br per week $1375) What this place lacks in ocean views it makes up for in location. Not necessarily a good option for those travelling with children.

Blu Nui Cottage (☎ 826-9622, 800-488-3336; 4435 Mahimahi Rd; 2br per week $1500) There's no view, but in Hanalei you're always close to the beach.

Eating & Drinking
BUDGET

ourpick Hanalei Taro & Juice Company (☎ 826-1059; 5-5070B Kuhio Hwy; smoothies $3-4.50, sandwiches $6.50; ☯ 10:30am-5pm Mon-Sat) Try anything taro-based (such as spicy taro hummus or taro smoothies) and you're all good.

Java Kai (☎ 826-6717; Hanalei Center; specialty coffee drinks $5, smoothies $6; ☯ 6:30am-6pm) Try the 'shark bite' – you'll thank us if you like creamy-sweet things. If not, the rich espresso roasts or coconut macaroons may appeal.

Pat's Taquería (☎ 346-4710; parking lot, Hanalei pier; ☺ 12-3pm) A short-but-sweet menu consists of the basics: tacos and quesadillas. But he hustles a mean Mexican meal-to-go for $4 to $7 (cash only)..

Aloha Juice Bar (☎ 826-6990; Ching Young Village; smoothies $5; ☺ 9am-4pm) Smoothies, juices and, of course, fruit.

Hanalei Wake Up Café (☎ 826-5551; cnr Kuhio Hwy & Aku Rd; breakfast $5-7; ☺ 6-11:30am) The best place for early birds to find a hot breakfast.

Kauai Nut Roasters (☎ 284-2741; 4489 Aku Rd; packages $6-7; ☺ 11am-7pm Mon-Sat, noon-5pm Sun) Some of the most delicious treats you can find are in these unassuming little packages, bursting with sweetness. Coconut, wasabi, lavender, sesame, butterscotch or praline flavors rank tops.

Papaya's Hanalei (☎ 826-0089; Hanalei Center, 5-5161 Kuhio Hwy; ☺ 9am-8pm) Fruit stands are best, but this grocer has the best selection of organic snacks. It also boasts choices with a locavore touch: Kilauea greens ($6), Anahola granola ($8) and Kauai Kunana Dairy *liliko'i* goat cheese ($8) are among favorites.

Tropical Taco (☎ 827-8226; 5-5088A Kuhio Hwy; mains $7-9; ☺ 11am-5pm Mon-Sat) Definitely not the best Mexican option, but conveniently located. Cash only.

Hanalei Gourmet (☎ 826-2524; www.hanaleigourmet.com; Hanalei Center; sandwiches $7-10, dinner mains $14-26; ☺ 8am-9:30pm, to 10:30pm summer) Chicken salad stuffed in a halved papaya or avocado and served with a frosty brew makes for a pleasant lunch.

Neide's Salsa Samba (☎ 826-1851; Hanalei Center; dishes $9-17; ☺ 11am-2:30pm & 5-9pm) The more original items on the menu include *muqueca* (fresh fish with coconut sauce), *ensopado* (baked chicken and vegetables), and *bife acebolado* (beefsteak with onions).

If you're self-catering, **Big Save** (☎ 826-5652; Ching Young Village; ☺ 7am-9pm) has an ATM and any necessary basic grocery items you might need.

MIDRANGE & TOP END
Polynesia Café (☎ 826-1999; Ching Young Village; mains 11-17; ☺ 8am-9pm) Fresh and buttery ingredients in a casual patio setting, where you can feast on seared ahi tacos or rich macnut-ncrusted *opah* (moonfish) with rice.

Breakfast is also great here, with eggs Benedict and a heavy breakfast burrito that will keep even the perpetually hungry pretty full. Also choose from a smattering of homemade desserts – perfect for picnic lunches to take to the beach.

Hanalei Dolphin Fish Market (☎ 826-6113; 5-5016 Kuhio Hwy; lunches $12-14; sushi rolls $10-14; ☺ 10am-7pm) Grab your *poke* and plate lunches here.

Kalypso Island Bar & Grill (☎ 826-9700; www.kalypsokauai.com; G4-5156 Kuhio Hwy; mains $12-30; ☺ 11am-9pm) Ambience and sincere, attentive service make the 'Hawaiian' pub fare (aloha, coconut shrimp!) easier to take.

Postcards Café (☎ 826-1191; www.postcardscafé.com; 5-5075 Kuhio Hwy; mains $18-27; ☺ 6-9pm) Postcards has a cottagelike ambience and its *pupu* platter is worth a try, with taro fritters, seafood rockets, summer rolls and seared ahi.

Bouchons (☎ 826-9701; www.sushiandblues.com; Ching Young Village; sushi rolls $8-16; ☺ 6pm-2am, sushi bar noon-9pm, happy hour 3:30-5:30pm) The service isn't all that attentive, but if you've got a hankering for sushi and sake, this is the place to get it. Take your time and go for happy hour.

Bar Acuda Tapas & Wine (☎ 826-7081; Hanalei Center; tapas, $8-15; mains $22-30; ☺ 11:30am-2:30pm & 6-9:30pm Tue-Sat) A trendy wine and tapas scene presents ornately plated food that's noteworthy, but expensive. Pluses include inventive uses of local products, like North Shore honeycomb, Kunana Farms goat cheese, plus Mizuna greens and apples.

Entertainment
Hawaiian Slack Key Guitar Concerts (☎ 826-1469; www.hawaiianslackkeyguitar.com; Hanalei Community Center; adult/child & senior $10/8; ☺ 4pm Fri & 3pm Sun) You'll find slack key guitar and ukulele concerts performed by longtime musicians Doug and Sandy McMaster year-round here, in a refreshingly informal atmosphere.

Shopping
Ching Young Village has some great spots for outfitting yourself in some Kaua'i chic, while the Hanalei Center is where many a Kaua'i surfer girl, and most of the clothing that typifies the North Shore, can be found.

our pick **Hanalei Paddler** (☎ 826-8797; Hanalei Center; ☺ 9am-8pm) Don't miss out on the surfer-chic workout threads by Andrea Smith (www.brasilbazar.com). Paddlers and surfer girls alike show up here in droves.

Hanalei Surf Company (826-9000; www.hanalei surf.com; Hanalei Center, 5-5161 Kuhio Hwy; 8am-9pm) Surf, surf, surf is its MO. Surfer-girl earrings, bikinis, rashies and guys' surf shorts, slippers and all the surf gear you might need: wax, shades and even the board itself.

Backdoor (826-1900; Ching Young Village; 5-5190 Kuhio Hwy; 9am-9pm) The same owner as Hanalei Surf Company extends the range to Los Angeles–inspired name brands and the skating lifestyle, harkening back to the days of Tony Hawk, Velcro and checker-pattern vans.

our pick Evolve Love Gallery (826-6441; Ching Young Village; 10am-6pm) Chock-full of vibrant, inspired paintings, batiks and some serious sea bling. Ni'ihau shell and pearls are among the jewels adorning the work.

Bikini Room (826-9965; www.thebikiniroom.com; 10am-5pm, to 2pm Sun) They're itsy bitsy and teeny weenie, but include cheetah and a variety of wild, vibrant prints instead of the usual polka dot. Great for those blessed with a body that just won't quit.

Root (826-2575; 4489 Aku Rd; 9:30am-7:30pm, noon-5pm Sun) This North Shore spot opted out of carrying swimwear. Instead it offers unique lingerie, sleepwear, beachwear, shoes, surfer clothes and yoga gear.

Titus Kinimaka Kai Kane Quiksilver Hanalei (826-5594; 5-5088 Kuhio Hwy; 9am-9pm Mon-Sat, 10am-5pm Sun) This surf shop has a distinct Hawaiian and Polynesian style. It carries paddling gear and surfboards, along with some of the coolest aloha shirts around.

Hula Moon & Gifts (826-9965; Ching Young Village; 10am-6pm) Woodwork, great gift ideas and jewelry make this a fun spot to peruse on a rainy day.

Getting There & Around

Parking can be a headache, and absent-minded pedestrians even more so. So do as the locals do and hop on a bike. For bicycle rentals, try **Pedal & Paddle** (826-9069; www.pedalnpaddle.com; Ching Young Village; 9am-6pm) for cruisers (per day/week $10/30) and mountain bikes ($20/80). **Kayak Kaua'i** (826-9844; www.kayakkauai.com; Kuhio Hwy; 8am-5pm) also has cruisers ($15/60).

AROUND HANALEI
Lumaha'i Beach

Movie tours may claim that Lumaha'i Beach is where Burt Lancaster and Deborah Kerr kissed in *that* scene in *From Here to Eternity*, but it's not (the scene was shot at Halona Cove on O'ahu). Lumaha'i enjoys a rather more infamous status as one of the most dangerous on-island spots, as many have drowned here.

Rather than a swim, we recommend a safe-but-still-scenic stroll (which still requires

---

TAHITI NUI'S GLORY DAYS

The **Tahiti Nui** (826-6277; Tahiti Nui Bldg, Kuhio Hwy; 2pm-2am) has changed hands and menus, and seen its fair share of dated hairdos, barflies and beer bellies. But there's a part of 'the Nui' that always seems to remain the same. It's the liveliest spot in little Hanalei, and, though certainly a dive, it remains *the* North Shore joint par excellence for regulars and visitors alike.

In 1964 a Tahitian woman named Louise Hauata and her husband Bruce Marston, founded the now iconic Tahiti Nui, a classic South Seas–style restaurant and bar. Its popularity grew and so did its draw – luring such names as Jacqueline Kennedy, who legendarily arrived unexpectedly, preceded by secret service agents. Yet despite the fact that it's seen its share of A-listers, you'd never guess it at first glance.

Bruce died in 1975, but Louise continued the spot's luau tradition, augmenting it with renditions of Tahitian songs in English, French or their original language. She was also well known for giving much aloha to her community in times of need.

Louise died in 2003, and Tahiti Nui is now run by her son, Christian Marston, her nephew, William Marston, and the president and CEO, John Austin, who is married to celebrated singer Amy Hanaiali'i Gilliom.

The Nui remains a lively, loud hangout long after its happy hours (from 4pm to 6pm Monday to Saturday and all day Sunday) and police regularly set up shop outside its doors around 2am to ensure no one's drinking and driving.

Though this crowded shacklike bar is divey, the staff are some of the most down-to-earth bartenders on the island. In a way, this gnarly, well-loved and well-worn hot spot is much like a favourite old running shoe that just keeps on going.

MANO A MANO

No doubt being attacked by a *mano* (shark) could be deadly: precautions, such as avoiding swimming in murky, post-rain waters, should be taken to avoid them. Statistically speaking, you're more likely to die from a bee sting than a shark attack, and you should be more concerned about contracting leptospirosis or staphylococcius in those infamous muddy waters than becoming a midday snack.

Rather than letting any hard-wired phobia of large predators get you down, try considering the creature from an another perspective while in Hawaii: the *mano* as sacred. For many local families, the *mano* is their *'aumakua* (guardian spirit). *'Aumakua* are family ancestors whose *'uhane,* or spirit form, lives on in the form of an animal, watching over members of their living *'ohana.* Revered for their ocean skill, *mano* were also considered the *'aumakua* of navigators. Even today, *mano 'aumakua* have been said to guide lost fishermen home, or toward areas of plentiful fish, to make for a bountiful sojourn.

---

water savvy). There are two ways onto Lumaha'i Beach. The first and more scenic is a three-minute walk that begins at the parking area 0.75 miles past the 4-mile marker on the Kuhio Hwy. The trail slopes to the left at the end of the retaining wall. On the beach, the lava-rock ledges are popular for sunbathing and photo ops, but beware: bystanders have been washed away by high surf and rogue waves.

The other way to access Lumaha'i is along the road at sea level at the western end of the beach, just before crossing the Lumaha'i River Bridge. The beach at this end is lined with ironwood trees.

Wainiha

Wainiha Valley remains as it did in the old days: a holdout for Native Hawaiians, though some vacation rentals have encroached onto the area. It is so isolated that its undeveloped areas aren't necessarily the safest of spots: the area has recently become more known for incidents of drug dealings, rather than natural beauty.

Sleeping & Eating

Coco Cabana Cottage (Map pp508-9; ☎ 826-5141; www.kauaivacation.com/coco_cabana.htm, 4766 Ananalu Rd; per night $125; 🛜) A hot tub, chirping birds, airy ambience and nearby, swimmable Wainiha River make for a lovely secluded stay. This cute little cottage is perfect for a couple wanting privacy and coziness. Has a queen-ize bed, wi-fi and phone. There's a $200 security deposit.

Hale Ho'omaha B&B (Map pp508-9; ☎ 826-7083, 00-851-0291; www.aloha.net/~hoomaha; 7083 Alamihi Rd; $150-175; 🖳) It's not so private but if you're

down with the whole sharing-space thing, then the common spaces are pretty sweet. Here plantation style meets the 1960s, including a 'great room,' with bar and above-ground deck hot tub. Bedrooms are warmly decorated and bathrooms have dual shower heads for those honeymooners out there.

Guesthouse at River Estate (Map pp508-9; ☎ 826-5118, 800-390-8444; www.riverestate.com; house per night $275; 🆒) Airy, huge and open – it's pricey, but one look and you'll see why. Featured in *National Geographic Adventure* magazine and *Los Angeles Times* travel sections, it almost feels like you're on the set of *Real World, Kaua'i* (because of the lush digs, not because there's a bunch of drunk kids). It features a master bedroom with a king bed, second room with queen bed, decked-out kitchen, wraparound lanai, washer-dryer, TV, air-con and anything else you could possibly need.

Red Hot Mama's (☎ 826-7266; 5-6607 Kuhio Hwy; meals $8.50; 🕙 11am-5pm Mon-Sat) The name means just that: red hot is what you get. Burritos, Tex-Mex and to-go sandwiches are decent.

Wainiha General Store (☎ 826-6251; 5-6600 Kuhio Hwy; 🕙 10am-dusk) The general store offers last-minute necessities or beach picnic items before the end of the road.

HA'ENA

Ha'ena is the last community on the North Shore. Remote, resplendent and idyllic, it's also the site of controversy, as many of the luxury homes on the point were built on top of ancient Hawaiian burials (*'iwi kupuna*). In 2007 this topic was brought to the attention of the media, following more mobilization of the Hawaiian community, which has continued a program of peaceful civil disobedience.

KAUA'I

Sights & Activities

LIMAHULI GARDEN

About as beautiful as it gets for living education, this **garden** (Map pp508-9; ☎ 826-1053; www.ntbg.org; self-guided/guided tour $15/20; ⏰ 9:30am-4pm Tue-Fri & Sun) offers a pleasant overview of native botany and the *ahupua'a* (land division) system of management of ancient Hawai'i. The valley was gifted to the National Tropical Botanical Garden by the Wichman family, and is run by one of its descendants, Chipper Wichman, a passionate preservationist and philanthropist. Self-guided tours allow you to take in the scenery meditatively. Occasional service projects allow a glimpse into the 985-acre preserve for native ecosystem restoration.

MANINIHOLO DRY CAVE

Directly across Ha'ena Beach Park, **Maniniholo Dry Cave** (Map pp508–9) is deep and broad and high enough to explore. A constant seep of water from the cave walls keeps the interior damp and humid. Drippy and creepy, the cave is named after the head fisherman of the *menehune* who, according to legend, built ponds and other structures overnight.

MAKUA (TUNNELS) BEACH

Another one of the North Shore's almost-too-beautiful beaches, **Tunnels** (Map pp508–9) is small, bursting with surfers and offers summer-only snorkeling in its lacelike reef, which is among the best on the island. In the winter, the season when tubes break, check with a lifeguard before going in.

HA'ENA BEACH PARK

Not necessarily for swimming, this beach (Map pp508–9) is good for taking in some sun. Ask the lifeguard about conditions before going in from October to May. To the left is **Cannons**, a particularly good wall dive.

YOGA & MASSAGE

If you're tired or need to revitalize, the **Hanalei Day Spa** (☎ 826-6621; www.hanaleidayspa.com; Hanalei Colony Resort; massage per 60/90 min $115/195; ⏰ 11am-7pm Mon-Sat) offers massage and body treatments.

Sleeping & Eating

Ha'ena Beach Park is a popular camping spot and base for exploring the North Shore, including the Na Pali Coast. To camp, permits are required. See p470 for county camping permit information.

There's an abundance of vacation rentals to be found. As of writing, the county is formally permitting vacation rental operations – always ask to make sure an operation is legal (to ensure they're still up and running for your scheduled vacation time).

Mermaid House (☎ 826-8968, 866-369-8968; 7341 Ale Lea Rd; www.kauai-beach-rental.com; 3br $225-250) A stone's toss from Makua (Tunnels) Beach, this place is perfect if you're planning on hiking Kalalau Trail, though you're a tad far from the main town strip.

A River House & Bird's Nest (☎ 826-9675; www.wainihariverhouse.com; 5121 Powerhouse Rd; house from $1610) It's got a jungle-paradise feel, is just a mile from glorious Makua (Tunnels) Beach and close to the Kalalau trailhead. Avocados, lychees, bananas, papayas and mountain apples (a delicacy even to locals) abound. Boasts a queen bed, full bath, refrigerator and hot plate. Also has a screened-in sleeping area called the Bird's Nest, with full bed and half bathroom. Weekly only.

Hanalei Colony Resort (Map pp508-9; ☎ 826-6235, 800-628-3004; www.hcr.com; Hwy 560; 2br from $210; ❌🖥🎬) The only resort west of Princeville, this is a high-end series of condominiums near Makua (Tunnels) Beach. Sure, the '70s decor in many of the units can seem a bit dated, but the location is waterfront and about as reclusive as it gets. Go to the website to have them stock your kitchenette with groceries.

Mediterranean Gourmet (☎ 826-9875; Hanalei Colony Resort; www.mediterraneangourmet.biz; dinner mains $15-25; ⏰ 11am-9pm) This is a fish out of water, but what a fish. Try roasted lamb and stuffed grape leaves, and leave room for dessert: baklava, cheesecake or a cup of muddy Turkish coffee.

HA'ENA STATE PARK

Wind beaten and lava carved, Ha'ena State Park burns with the allure, mystique and beauty usually associated with some divine tale. Pele is said to have overlooked the area as a home because of the water housed in its wet and dry caves. The 230-acre park is home to the 1280ft cliff commonly known in the tourism industry as 'Bali Hai,' its name in the film *South Pacific*. Its real name is Makana ('gift')

Sights

KE'E BEACH

Perhaps the most memorable North Shore sunsets happen at this spiritual place, where the first Hawaiians to practice hula came. It offers a refreshing dip after hiking the nearby Kalalau Trail in summer months. Beware that Ke'e Beach has appeared calm to swimmers when otherwise. Ke'e has a keyhole in its reef, where some have been sucked through. Summer brings car break-ins in the parking lot, so leave cars (especially those that are obviously rentals, such as Mustangs, Sebrings and PT Cruisers) free from valuables. There are showers and rest rooms on-site.

WET CAVES

Two wet caves are within the boundaries of Ha'ena State Park. The first, **Waikapala'e Wet Cave**, is just a short walk from the road opposite the visitor-parking overflow area. The second, **Waikanaloa Wet Cave**, is on the south side of the main road.

KAULU PAOA HEI'AU

The roaring surf worked as a teacher to those who first practised the spiritual art of hula, chanting and testing their skill against nature's decibel levels. **Ke'e beach** is home to one of the most cherished heiau, and it's also where volcanic goddess Pele fell in love with Lohiau. Leis and other offerings for Pele can be found on the ground, and should be left as is. Enter the heiau through its entryway. Do not cross over its walls, as it is disrespectful and said to bring bad luck.

NA PALI COAST STATE PARK

Kalalau, Honopu, 'Awa'awapuhi, Nu'alolo and Miloli'i (all Map p541) are the five major valleys on the Na Pali Coast, easily the most distinguishable example of beauty as nature on the island, if not within the entire archipelago. Don't miss seeing the 22-mile stretch by chopper, watercraft or old-school style – on foot.

History

Archaeologists maintain that the extreme, remote Nualolo Valley housed a civilization dating back more than a thousand years after ancient weapons and hunting tools were recovered from the area. Irrigation ditches and agricultural terraces suggest the Kalalau Valley was the most advanced within the island chain.

At the turn of the century, the majority of the inhabitants of the valley had moved to more centrally located spots on the island.

Hiking

For rewarding views of the Na Pali Coast, hiking along the 11-mile Kalalau coastal trail into Hanakapi'ai, Hanakoa and Kalalau Valleys is an adventure that's sure not to disappoint. Unfit for roads, the Na Pali Coast leads to the opposite side of the island, in Koke'e State Park. You won't want to miss hiking the west side of the island for those views. If you're one of those 'ultimate' fitness fanatics, perhaps the Na Pali Coast by sea on a 17-mile kayak adventure is up your alley (p519).

KALALAU TRAIL

How else could you brave the steep sea cliffs than by foot for 22 miles? Winding along the Na Pali (the cliffs) offers glimpses of some of the most pristine, extreme views from which to behold its deep, riveting pleats. This trail is without a doubt the best way to connect directly with the elements, though keep in mind the trek, if you opt to complete the full 22-mile round-trip into the valley, is a steep, rough hike.

There are three hike options: Ke'e Beach to Hanakapi'ai Beach, Hanakapi'ai Beach to Hanakapi'ai Falls and Hanakapi'ai Beach to Kalalau Valley. There are hunters who can do the entire trail in and out in one day, but most people will either want to opt for the Hanakapi'ai Beach or Hanakapi'ai Falls hike or bring camping gear to make it to Kalalau Beach.

The state parks office in Lihu'e can provide a Kalalau Trail brochure with a map. Another good source sponsored by the county is www .kauaiexplorer.com. Keep in mind that even if you're not planning to camp, a permit is officially required to continue on the Kalalau Trail beyond Hanakapi'ai. Free day-use hiking permits are available from the Division of State Parks, which also issues the required camping permits for the Hanakapi'ai (one night maximum) and Kalalau (five nights maximum) Valleys. For more information on permits see p470. You'll need ample time – possibly as much as six to 12 months – in advance to get permits.

Ke'e Beach to Hanakapi'ai Beach

It shouldn't take more than two hours to complete this 4-mile (round-trip) trek – the most popular and most crowded hike. The first 2 miles of the Kalalau Trail ends at Hanakapi'ai Beach (no swimming allowed).

KAUA'I

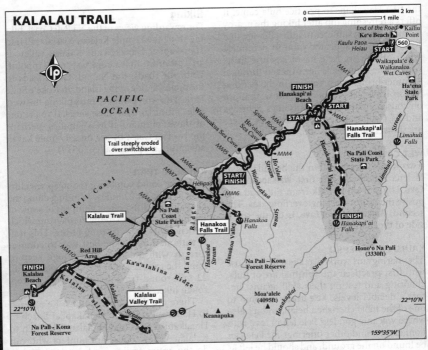

Hanakapi'ai Beach to Hanakapi'ai Falls

This trek begins after you've completed the Ke'e Beach to Hanakapia'i Beach 2-mile jaunt. Once you get to Hanakapi'ai Beach, crowds lessen, as the work-reward ratio compounds. The next 2 miles takes you deeper into the forest, with an increasingly sublime riverscape. Though you might be tempted to take a swim at Hanakapia'ai Beach, it's best to wait until the falls for such a treat as Hanakapi'ai Beach has notoriously dangerous waters (and the waters of Hanakapi'ai Falls are well worth waiting for).

Hanakapi'ai Beach to Kalalau Valley

Past Hanakapi'ai, the real challenge begins as another 9 miles ensue. At this point, there's no turning back. The trail weaves in and out of several valleys, giving alternately shaded and sunny vistas across the Pacific. Hanakoa makes a convenient rest or camping point, as it's about halfway in. Near the end, the trail takes you across the front of Kalalau Valley, where you can feel dwarfed by 1000ft lava-rock cliffs before proceeding to the campgrounds on the beach, just west of the valley. You will need a permit, see p525.

Getting There & Away

The parking lot at Ke'e Beach trailhead is quite large but fills quickly during the jammed summer months. Break-ins are rampant; some people advise leaving cars empty and unlocked to prevent damage such as window smashing. Campers, consider parking at the campground at Ha'ena Beach Park (Map pp508–9) or storing your belongings elsewhere and catching a cab to the trailhead; try **Kauai Taxi Company** (☎ 246-9554).

SOUTH SHORE

Tourists adore Po'ipu, and it's no surprise why: sun, surf and sand. The quintessential elements of a beach vacation are guaranteed here, where the weather's less rainy and the waves less changeable than on the North Shore. Since the 1970s, huge condos and hotels have mushroomed along the shore, spawning a critical mass of tourists that will either entertain or annoy you.

The South Shore also boasts two world-renowned botanical gardens, as well as the

THIS AIN'T NO DISCO

The Kalalau Trail is hella Rugged (yes, with a capital R) and therefore it's not for everyone. Being prepared is a tough call too, as you won't want to pack too much but you will need to stay hydrated, prepped for rain, and you *must* take your trash out with you. You may see hikers with machetes, walkie-talkies, climbing rope and reef shoes; but even the trekkers with the most bad-ass gear should know not to expect a rescue by emergency responders; these precipices are to be taken seriously. Anyone with a police scanner can tell you 'plenty story' about the braggart from the mainland who was warned by friends/family/an onlooker but said something along the lines of these famous last words: 'Naw, I'm from Colorado, this is nothing.' Finally, mosquitoes here are bloodthirsty and the sun can really ravage, so always wear insect repellent and sunblock.

undeveloped Maha'ulepu Coast, where lithi-fied sand-dune cliffs and pounding surf make for an unforgettable walk. What's missing is a town center – or any town at all. Thus, you're bound to stop in Koloa, a former plantation town that's now the South Shore's lively little commercial center.

KOLOA
pop 1940

On the South Shore, all roads lead to Koloa, which was a thriving plantation town until it withered after WWII, when sugar gave way to tourism. Today its quaint 'Old West' neighbor-hood contains a pleasant set of affordable shops and restaurants – a welcome complement to the budget-breaking selection in Po'ipu. The adjacent residential towns of Lawa'i (pop 1985) and Omao (pop 1220) are low-key, neighborly and blooming with foliage.

History

When William Hooper, an enterprising 24-year-old Bostonian, arrived on Kaua'i in 1835, he took advantage of two historical circumstances: the Polynesians' introduc-tion of sugarcane to the islands and Chinese immigrants' knowledge of refining sugar. With financial backing from Honolulu busi-nesspeople, he leased land in Koloa from the king and paid island *ali'i* (royalty, chiefs etc) a stipend to release commoners from their traditional work obligations. He then hired the Hawaiians as wage laborers and Koloa became Hawaii's first plantation town.

Orientation & Information

From the west, Koloa Rd (Hwy 530), which runs between Lawa'i and Koloa, is the best way in and out. From Lihu'e, take the scenic Maluhia Rd (Hwy 520) through the enchant-ing Tree Tunnel.

Services are minimal:

First Hawaiian Bank (☎ 742-1642; 3506 Waikomo Rd) At the east end of town.

Post office (☎ 800-275-8777; 5485 Koloa Rd) Serves both Koloa and Po'ipu.

Sights

LAWAI INTERNATIONAL CENTER

Magical. Enchanting. Stirring. Such words are often used to describe this quiet **spiritual site** (☎ 639-4300; www.lawaicenter.org; 3381 Wawae Rd; ☼ call for schedule) in the Lawa'i Valley, north-west of Koloa and Po'ipu. Originally the site of a Hawaiian heiau, the site's strong mana (spiritual essence) attracted future generations of worshippers, including Japanese plantation families since the late 1800s.

In 1904, these immigrants placed 88 mini-ature Shingon Buddhist shrines (about 2ft tall) along a steep hillside path to symbol-ize 88 pilgrimage shrines in Shikoku, Japan. For years, island pilgrims would journey here from as far as Hanalei and Kekaha. But the site was abandoned by the 1960s, and half of the shrines lay scattered in shards.

In the late 1980s, some volunteers formed a nonprofit group, acquired a 32-acre property and embarked on a backbreaking project to repair or rebuild the shrines. Today, all 88 are beautifully restored, and leisurely tours include a detailed history and trail walk. Despite the Buddhist shrines, the center is a nondenominational sanctuary for all cultures. Visits are allowed only during twice-monthly Sunday tours; call for details.

TREE TUNNEL

Driving from Lihu'e to Po'ipu, take Maluhia Rd (Hwy 520) not only for a shortcut but also to pass through the romantic Tree Tunnel, a mile-long canopy of towering swamp mahogany trees (a type of eucalyptus).

KAUA'I

Pineapple baron Walter McBryde planted the trees as a community project in 1911, when he had leftover trees after landscaping his estate at Kukuiolono (p538).

KOLOA HISTORIC BUILDINGS

East of town, find the **Koloa Jodo Mission** (742-6735; 2480 Waikomo Rd; services 6pm Mon-Fri, 9:30am Sun), which follows Pure Land Buddhism, a nonmeditating form, popular in Japan since the 12th century. The Buddhist temple on the left is the original, which dates back to 1910, while the larger temple on the right is currently used for services.

St Raphael's Catholic Church (742-1955; 3011 Hapa Rd), Kaua'i's oldest Catholic church, is the burial site of some of Hawaii's first Portuguese immigrants. The original church, built in 1854, was made of lava rock and coral mortar with walls 3ft thick – a type of construction visible in the ruins of the adjacent rectory. When the church was enlarged in 1936 it was plastered over, creating a more typical whitewashed appearance.

Activities

Obviously Koloa is landlocked, but it's home to two excellent ocean-sports outfits.

DIVING

our pick **Fathom Five Divers** (742-6991, 800-972-3078; www.fathomfive.com; 3450 Po'ipu Rd; shore dives $70-140, boat dives $120-330), the island's best dive outfit, is run by a husband-and-wife team, Jeannette and George Thompson. They offer the whole range, from Ni'ihau boat dives ($345) to night dives to certification courses. Newbies can expect reassuring hand holding during their introductory shore dives. Groups max out at six and they avoid mixing skill levels. Call well in advance.

SNORKELING

The king of snorkel gear is **Snorkel Bob's** (742-2206; www.snorkelbob.com; 3236 Po'ipu Rd; rental mask, snorkel & fins per week $9-35; 8am-5pm), which rents and sells enough styles and sizes to assure a good fit. If, after renting, you want to buy an item, your rental payment deflects part of the cost.

ATV

Kaua'i ATV (742-2734, 877-707-7088; www.kauaiatv.com; 5330 Koloa Rd; tours $125-175) commendably

offers two-seater and four-seater bio-diesel vehicles for a reasonable upgrade of $10 per person. Therfore, we recommend these ATV tours only if you opt for the green machines over the gas-powered ones, which constitute most of their fleet. Riding in upcountry pastureland, you're guaranteed to get dirty, whether merely dusty or soaked in mud. Use their loaner clothing.

Festivals & Events

In late July, **Koloa Plantation Days Celebration** (652-3217; www.koloaplantationdays.com), the South Shore's biggest annual celebration, spans nine days of family fun with the gamut of attractions (many free), including a parade, block party, rodeo, craft fair, canoe race, golf tournament and guided walks.

Sleeping

The following are in the Koloa, Omao and Lawa'i residential neighborhoods.

our pick **Boulay Inn** (742-1120, 635-5539; www.boulayinn.com; Omao Rd; 1br $85;) Your money goes far with this airy one-bedroom apartment in quiet residential Omao. The 500 sq ft space is comfy rather than fancy, sitting atop a garage (no shared walls with the main house). Features include wraparound lanai, full kitchen, private phone line, high ceilings and free use of washer-dryer. A cleaning fee ($50) is charged.

Cozy Kauai Cottage (742-1778, 877-742-1778; www.kauaivacationproperties.com/cottage.htm; Omao Rd; cottage s/d $75/100;) A pastoral retreat with modern amenities, this simple, compact cottage (best for a slim single or couple) is efficiently arranged to include a full kitchen, separate bedroom and comfy living area. The hardwood floor, granite counters and dimmer lights add style, while lots of windows let in cool breezes. Cleaning fee ($40) charged.

Hale Kipa O Koloa (742-1802; www.koloakauaicottage.com; 5481 Waiau Rd, Koloa; 2br cottage $125;) Great for families or groups, this plantation-style house is close to town and affords much privacy. With two bedrooms, two bathrooms, a full kitchen and washer-dryer, it's just like home. The inland location can be hot, but this cottage features high, insulated ceilings, cool tile floors and clean white walls. Additional guests cost $15 per night more.

Kaua'i Banyan Inn (888-786-3855; www.kauaibanyan.com; 3528-B Mana Hema Pl; r $130-150;) Although a tad pricey for the neighborhood, the five units are chic enough for the most discerning guests. Each impeccable unit features polished hardwood floors, kitchenette, vaulted ceilings, private lanai and furnishings you'd buy for your own home. Cleaning fee ($45) charged. No kids under 10.

Marjorie's Kaua'i Inn (☎ 332-8838, 800-717-8838; www.marjorieskauaiinn.com; Hailima St, Lawa'i; r $130-175; 🚭 🛜) The magnificent vista of Lawa'i Valley from this classy inn will change your life. Well, maybe that's a stretch, but it'll be a trip highlight, for sure. The rooms themselves show off stylish furnishings and each includes large private lanai and kitchenettes. You're nowhere near the beach, but the elegant 50ft lap pool and poolside BBQ grill compensate nicely.

Eating

Lappert's Ice Cream(☎ 742-1272; Koloa Rd; single-scoop ice cream $3.65; 🕙 6am-10pm) The late Walter Lappert's signature ice cream is tropical themed, chunky and kid-pleasingly sweet.

ourpick Koloa Fish Market (☎ 742-6199; 5482 Koloa Rd; lunch $4-7; 🕙 10am-6pm Mon-Fri, to 5pm Sat) Line up with locals at this hole-in-the-wall serving outstanding *poke*, Japanese-style *bentō*, sushi rolls and Hawaiian plate lunches. Don't miss the thick-sliced, perfectly seared ahi and rich slabs of homemade *haupia* (coconut pudding).

Pizzetta (☎ 742-8881; 5408 Koloa Rd; pizza $17-25, pasta $11-18; 🕙 11am-9pm) If this family trattoria had *any* competition, we'd be more critical, but affordable eateries are scarce around here. Choose from decent gourmet pizzas such as the El Greco (sun-dried tomatoes, artichoke hearts and feta) and filling pastas that won't ravage your wallet. Expect a mainly touristy clientele.

If your accommodations include a kitchen, you might eat best if you eat in. Local chain supermarket **Big Save** (cnr Waikomo Rd & Koloa Rd; 🕙 6am-11pm) has one of its best branches here. Don't miss the value-priced ahi *poke*. Nearby, **Sueoka Store** (☎ 742-1611; 5392 Koloa Rd; 🕙 7am-9pm) holds its own with the basics, plus packaged Japanese takeout snacks. Like all health-nut venues, **Koloa Natural Foods** (☎ 742-8910; 5356 Koloa Rd; 🕙 10am-8pm Tue-Sat, to 4pm Sun & Mon) ain't cheap, but it carries major natural brands, bulk and packaged items and supplements.

Shopping

Christian Riso Fine Arts (☎ 742-2555; www.christianrisofineart.com; 5400 Koloa Rd; 🕙 10am-9pm) Browsers are welcome at this informal gallery of paint-

TOP PICKS – BUDGET SLEEPS

- **Aloha Hale Orchids** (p502)
- **Garden Room** (p495)
- **Boulay Inn** (opposite)
- **Waimea Rock Cabin** (p547)
- **Bunk House at Rosewood Kaua'i** (p495)
- **Westside Dwelling** (p543)
- **Orchid Tree Inn** (p502)
- **Mindy's Guesthouse** (p549)
- **Cozy Kauai Cottage** (opposite)
- **Green Acres Cottages** (p508)

Note: these picks apply to single or double travelers. Groups can find a plethora of cost-cutting options if they share larger condo or residential units.

ings and drawings by island artists, fine jewelry (including Ni'ihau shell necklaces) and fun collectibles like handpainted walking sticks. The shop specializes in custom framing using Hawaiian hardwoods such as koa and kamani.

Pohaku T's (☎ 742-7500; www.pohaku.com; 3430 Po'ipu Rd; 🕙 10am-8pm Mon-Sat, to 6pm Sun) This well-stocked shop specializes in Kaua'i-made clothing, crafts and island-themed tees and tanks. Signature shirt designs feature classic island themes – petroglyphs, *honu*, navigational maps – on stonewashed or overdyed colors. Cotton aloha shirts are locally handsewn yet affordable.

Island Soap & Candle Works (☎ 742-1945, 888-528-7627; www.kauaisoap.com; 5428 Koloa Rd; 🕙 9am-10pm) For a delicious treat with zero calories, breathe deeply inside this flowery, fruity sensation of a shop. Established in 1984 to recreate the art of soap- and candle-making, the company has grown but still makes everything by hand.

Progressive Expressions (☎ 742-6041; www.progressiveexpressions.com; 5420 Koloa Rd; 🕙 9am-9pm) Established in 1972, this was the South Shore's first surf shop. Original owners Marty and Joe Kuala sold the shop to the Hanalei Surf Company in 2005 but Joe still designs and crafts boards sold here.

Getting There & Away

Almost all car, motorcycle and moped rental agencies are in Lihu'e, but **Kaua'i Scooter Rental**

(☎ 245-7177; www.kauaimopedrentals.com; 3414 Po'ipu Rd; ⊗ 8am-5pm) has a branch location in Koloa, just south of the Chevron station.

PO'IPU
pop 1075
Po'ipu (which ironically can mean 'completely overcast' in Hawaiian) is world renowned for its dependable sun and easy-access beaches. When it does rain here, you can bet it's pouring on the North Shore. Alas, no Po'ipu 'town' exists – so dining is limited and traveling by foot is challenging, except along the beaches.

The coast is already blanketed with condos, time-shares, hotels and vacation-rental homes, but a massive luxury development, **Kukui'ula** (www.kukuiula.com) will soon add a golf course, 1000 acres of custom homes, Kukui'ula Village (a 90,000 sq ft high-end shopping center) and further transform this once-lazy beach town.

Orientation & Information
There are two entry roads from Kaumuali'i Hwy. Coming from Lihu'e, take Maluhia Rd to the Ala Kino'iki bypass road, which will lead you to the eastern side of Po'ipu. Coming from the Westside, take Koloa Rd to Po'ipu Rd (Hwy 520), which leads to a roundabout. If you veer west, you'll be on Lawa'i Rd (toward National Tropical Botanical Garden); if you veer east, you will remain on Po'ipu Rd, where most beaches and accommodations are located.

For cash, **Bank of Hawaii** (☎ 742-6800; Po'ipu Shopping Village, 2360 Kiahuna Plantation Dr; ⊗ 8:30am-4pm Mon-Thu, to 6pm Fri) is available but they don't cash checks or traveler's checks at this branch.

Check the website of the **Po'ipu Beach Resort Association** (www.poipubeach.org) for general information on Po'ipu and the whole South Shore.

Sights
Note that you can't see any beaches from Po'ipu Rd (all you see are condos and parking lots). To reach the beaches, you must turn *makai* (seaward) on side streets, such as Ho'owili Rd to reach Po'ipu Beach Park and Kapili Rd for the Sheraton beach.

PO'IPU BEACH PARK
No monster waves or idyllic solitude here. But if you're seeking a safe, lively, family-friendly **beach**, this is it. Located at the end of Ho'owili Rd, it features a lifeguard station and shallow, gentle waters for swimming, snorkeling and beginner diving. The sandy beach is compact (you can see one end from the other) and is jammed on weekends, but you'll have ample elbow room on weekdays. Around the beach are grassy lawns, a children's playground, picnic pavilions and tables, rest rooms and showers. What's lacking are eating options.

Check out **Nukumoi Point**, a finger of land toward the west, where you can explore tide pools and perhaps see *honu* (green sea turtles). The best snorkeling is west of the point, where you'll find swarms of curious fish.

To get here, go to the end of Ho'owili Rd. Parking is right across the street from the beach.

BRENNECKE'S BEACH
Any time, any day, this little beach attracts a big cadre of bodyboarders, bobbing in the water, waiting for the next set. Tourists often sit on the roadside stonewall to enjoy the action. No surfboards are allowed near shore, so bodyboarders rule. If you want to join in, note that waves break dangerously close to shore. Surf is highest in summer, but the winter action is respectable, too. The beach flanks the eastern edge of Po'ipu Beach Park.

PO'IPU BEACH
Despite its nicknames of **Sheraton Beach** and **Kiahuna Beach**, this long swath of sand is not private. It merely fronts the hotel and condo, both of which scored big-time with their location along Po'ipu Beach, which lies west of Po'ipu Beach Park. The waters here are too rough for kids, although an offshore reef tames the waves enough for strong swimmers and snorkelers.

Experienced surfers and bodyboarders can attempt the breaks near the Sheraton, but the waters are famous for sneaker sets (rogue waves that appear from nowhere) and the rocky coast makes it difficult to get offshore and back. South Shore spots tend to be fickle and highly susceptible to winds, tides and swells. **Cowshead**, the rocky outcropping at the west end of the beach, is an extremely challenging break unless you know how to approach the channel. Expert surfers can attempt offshore spots such as **First Break** in front of the Sheraton, but beginners should always remain inshore. **Waiohai**, at the east end of the beach in front of the Marriott Waiohai Beach Club time-share, also sees major swells.

To get to the beach, drive to the end of Ho'onani Rd.

SHIPWRECK BEACH

Unless you're an expert surfer, body-boarder or bodysurfer, keep your feet dry at Shipwrecks. Instead, come for an invigorating walk along the half-mile crescent of light gold sand. You'll have company, as the Grand Hyatt Kaua'i Resort & Spa overlooks much of the beach along Keoneloa Bay. Row after row of waves crash close to shore, giving this beach a rugged, untamed vibe. Toward the left of the bay looms **Makawehi Point**, a gigantic lithified sand dune, which you can ascend in 10 minutes.

In the movie *Six Days Seven Nights,* stunt doubles for Harrison Ford and Anne Heche leap off Makawehi Point. In real life, a few daredevils similarly dive off the rocky cliff, as shown in thrilling YouTube clips, but no one mentions the severe casualties and deaths. In a word: don't.

To get here, head toward the Grand Hyatt, turn *makai* (seaward) on Ainako St and park in the small lot at the end.

BABY BEACH

Introduce tots to the ocean at this **baby beach** (there's another in Kapa'a; see p524), where the water is barely thigh-high. The sandy shore runs behind a row of beach homes on Ho'ona Rd (west of Koloa Landing), so access is easy but parking is tricky (don't block driveways). Look for the beach access sign that marks a path to the beach.

LAWA'I (BEACH HOUSE) BEACH

This tiny **beach** gets some major action with snorkelers and surfers. Located almost adjacent to Lawa'i Rd (beside the iconic Beach House restaurant), it's in plain view of passersby and not especially scenic or sandy. But during calm surf, the waters are rich snorkeling turf – and crowded with a contingent of tourists from nearby time-shares and condos. There are rest rooms, a shower and public parking across the street. On balance, however, choose this beach only if you're staying nearby.

NATIONAL TROPICAL BOTANICAL GARDEN

If you're interested in plants and their preservation, a visit to these **gardens** (NTBG; ☎ 742-2623; www.ntbg.org; 4425 Lawa'i Rd; admission $20-85; ☼ 8:30am-5pm) is a must. The gardens are not just stunningly beautiful, but they are also sanctuaries for native plants and living laboratories for staff scientists and international experts.

Of the two Po'ipu gardens, the 80-acre **Allerton Garden** is the showy star, but it requires a pricey **guided tour** (adult/10-12yr $45/20). Tour guides are generally knowledgeable and enthusiastic, leisurely guiding groups (up to 20) through meticulously landscaped grounds. Highlights include otherworldly Moreton Bay fig trees (seen in *Jurassic Park*), golden bamboo groves, a pristine lagoon and valley walls blanketed with purple bougainvillea during summer. The manmade statuary and water elements somehow blend into the landscape.

The adjacent **McBryde Garden** is less manicured and fancy than Allerton Garden, showcasing palms, flowering and spice trees, orchids and rare native species, plus a pretty stream and waterfall. For budget watchers, the **self-guided tour** (adult/6-12yr/under 5yr $20/10/free) allows you to the vast grounds without watching your clock.

MOIR GARDENS

If cacti are your fancy, this modest **garden** (☎ 742-6411; Kiahuna Plantation, 2253 Po'ipu Rd; admission free; ☼ sunrise-sunset) on the grounds of the Kiahuna Plantation condo is worth a look-see. It's a low-key, approachable collection of mature cacti and succulents, interspersed with winding paths, a lily pond and colorful shocks of orchids.

The gardens, established in the 1930s, were originally the estate of Hector Moir, manager of Koloa Sugar Plantation, and Alexandra 'Sandie' Knudsen Moir. The Moirs were avid gardeners who switched from flowering plants to drought-tolerant ones that could naturally thrive in dry Po'ipu.

A sideshow rather than a showstopper, it's worth a stroll if you're staying nearby or dining at the restaurant.

SPOUTING HORN BEACH PARK

It resembles a geyser, but Spouting Horn is really a hole at the top of lava cave. When ocean waves pound the shore, they flood the cave and exit through the hole, erupting skyward as a fountain. The waves are unpredictable, so you might need to wait for some action. Fountains are typically under 30ft and last only seconds, but they can reach twice that height during high surf.

To get here, turn right off Po'ipu Rd onto Lawa'i Rd and continue for 1.75 miles.

KAUA'I

PO'IPU

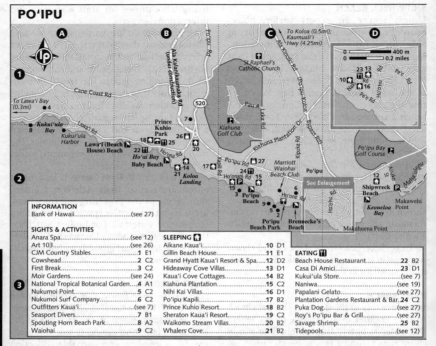

INFORMATION
Bank of Hawaii.............................(see 27)

SIGHTS & ACTIVITIES
Anara Spa....................................(see 12)
Art 103..(see 26)
CJM Country Stables.......................**1** E1
Cowshead.....................................**2** C2
First Break....................................**3** C2
Hideaway Cove Villas.....................(see 24)
Moir Gardens................................(see 24)
National Tropical Botanical Garden....**4** A1
Nukumoi Point..............................**5** C2
Nukumoi Surf Company..................**6** C2
Outfitters Kaua'i............................(see 7)
Seasport Divers.............................**7** B1
Spouting Horn Beach Park...............**8** A2
Waiohai.......................................**9** C2

SLEEPING 🏠
Aikane Kaua'i...............................**10** D1
Gillin Beach House.........................**11** E1
Grand Hyatt Kaua'i Resort & Spa.....**12** D2
Hideaway Cove Villas.....................**13** D1
Kaua'i Cove Cottages.....................**14** B2
Kiahuna Plantation.........................**15** C2
Nihi Kai Villas...............................**16** D1
Po'ipu Kapili................................**17** B2
Prince Kuhio Resort.......................**18** B2
Sheraton Kaua'i Resort...................**19** C2
Waikomo Stream Villas...................**20** B2
Whalers Cove...............................**21** B2

EATING 🍴
Beach House Restaurant..................**22** B2
Casa Di Amici...............................**23** D1
Kukui'ula Store.............................(see 7)
Naniwa.......................................(see 19)
Papalani Gelato............................(see 27)
Plantation Gardens Restaurant & Bar.**24** C2
Puka Dog.....................................(see 27)
Roy's Po'ipu Bar & Grill..................(see 27)
Savage Shrimp..............................**25** B2
Tidepools....................................(see 12)

PRINCE KUHIO PARK

The simple **green space** honoring Kaua'i's Prince Jonah Kuhio Kalaniana'ole, born around here in 1871, is looking forlorn nowadays. The lawn is often brown and dry, and visitors rarely enter the grounds, which contain the ruins of an ancient Hawaiian heiau and fishpond. That said, no local would discount the prince's considerable contributions to Hawaii and the Hawaiian people. He was the Territory of Hawaii's first delegate to the US Congress and he spearheaded the Hawaiian Homes Commission Act, which set aside 200,000 acres of land for indigenous Hawaiians, many of whom are still waiting for it.

KOLOA LANDING

Koloa Landing, at the mouth of Waikomo Stream, was once Kaua'i's largest port. In the 1850s farmers used it to ship Kaua'i-grown sugar, oranges and sweet potatoes, and it was the third-busiest whaling port among the Hawaiian Islands, surpassed only by Honolulu and Lahaina, Maui. The landing waned after the road system was built

and it was abandoned in the 1920s. Today only a small boat ramp remains.

Underwater, it's another story: Koloa Landing is popular for **snorkeling** and the best **shore-diving** spot on the South Shore. Its protected waters reach depths of about 30ft and it's generally calm all year. See underwater tunnels, a variety of coral and fish, sea turtles and monk seals. The best sights are located toward the west.

ART 103

For local art that goes beyond the no-brainer, easy-sell tropical motifs, visit this classy new **gallery** (www.art103.com; Kukui'ula Village, Ala Kalanikaumaka Rd, Suite 102/103; 🕐 noon-8pm Mon-Thu, 11am-9pm Fri & Sat, noon-6pm Sun, also by appointment). Owner and art photographer Bruna Stude (www.brunastude.com) has assembled an impressive collection by both emerging and established names. The adjoining annex, **A+**, is modeled after museum shops, and offers more affordable drawings, ceramics, fiber art and other collectibles. Everything is original – no commercial giclée (fine cut) prints.

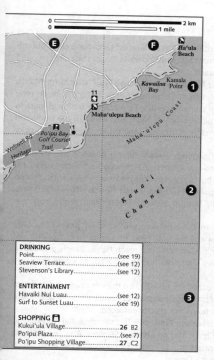

Activities

DIVING

The Po'ipu coast offers the island's best dive sites, including **Sheraton Caverns**, a series of partially collapsed lava tubes 10ft or more in height, with shafts of glowing sunlight illuminating their dim interior; **General Store**, with sharks, octopuses, eels and the remains of an 1892 shipwreck; and Nukumoi Point (p530), a shallow site and habitat for green sea turtles.

Dive boats and catamaran cruises usually depart from Kukui'ula Harbor, 0.5 miles east of Spouting Horn.

Seasport Divers (☎ 742-9303, 800-685-5889; www .seasportdivers.com; Po'ipu Plaza, 2827 Po'ipu Rd; 2-tank dive $115-145; ☼ check-in 7:30am & 12:45pm) leads a range of dives from shore or boat, including a three-tank dive to Ni'ihau ($265), offered only in summer. All dives are guided by instructor-level divemasters; any group with noncertified divers includes an additional instructor. Groups are limited to 18 but the count is typically eight to 12.

Consider nearby Fathom Five Divers (p528), our top pick for diving tours.

KAYAKING

Outfitters Kaua'i (☎ 742-9667, 888-742-9887; www.out fitterskauai.com; Po'ipu Plaza, 2827-A Po'ipu Rd; ☼ reservations taken 8am-9pm) offers a sea-kayaking tour (per adult/child 12 to 14 $135/110); the eight-hour paddle makes a good training prelude to the grueling Na Pali voyage.

SURFING

Po'ipu is a popular spot for lessons because it's got some killer breaks and year-round sun. Beware of large classes, though; four is maximum density. For lessons, we recommend the following outfits, which all meet at the beach:

Garden Island Surf School (☎ 652-4841; www .kauai-surfinglessons.com; 2hr lesson group/couple/private $75/120/150; ☼ lessons 8am, 10am, noon & 2pm) The lesson includes one hour with instructor and one hour free surfing. Four students per group; minimum age is eight for groups and five for privates.

our pick **Kaua'i Surf School** (☎ 651-6032; www .kauaisurfschool.com; 2hr lesson group/private $75/175). With 90 minutes of teaching and 30 minutes of free practice, you get your money's worth. A good outfit for kids, with a special one-hour private lesson for kids aged four to 12. Also offers multiday surf clinics and surf escort services.

Surf Lessons by Margo Oberg (☎ 332-6100, 639-0708; www.surfonkauai.com; 2hr lesson group/semiprivate/private $68/90/125) One of the longest-running surf schools on Kaua'i, this operation has a fine rep but classes can reach six.

Rentals are found at these shops:
Nukumoi Surf Company (☎ 742-8019; www .nukumoi.com; 2100 Ho'one Rd; soft-top board rental per hr/day/week $5/20/60, hard boards $7.50/30/80, body-boards per day/week $5/15; ☼ 7:45am-6:30pm Mon-Sat, 10:45am-6pm Sun) Conveniently located right across from Po'ipu Beach Park.

Progressive Expressions (☎ 742-6041; 5420 Koloa Rd, Koloa; board rental per day/week $20/100; ☼ 9am-9pm) Koloa surf shop rents all types of boards, same price.

HORSEBACK RIDING

If you want a break from hoofin' it yourself, you can hop on a horse at **CJM Country Stables** (☎ 742-6096; www.cjmstables.com; 2hr tours $98-125; ☼ tours 9:30am & 2pm Mon-Sat). The rides are the slow, nose-to-tail, follow-the-leader variety, so they're safe but would bore experienced riders, who can arrange private rides.

GOLF

The economical **Kiahuna Golf Club** (☎ 742-9595; www.kiahunagolf.com; 2545 Kiahuna Plantation Dr; green

A COAST LIKE NO OTHER

The windswept Maha'ulepu Coast resembles no other on Kaua'i: lithified sand-dune cliffs, pounding surf and three pristine beaches still free from mass tourism. Known as Kaua'i's last undeveloped accessible coast, it lies just east of Shipwreck Beach.

The best way to explore the coast is hiking the **Maha'ulepu Heritage Trail** (www.hikemahaulepu .org), a pleasant hike that runs for almost 4 miles from Shipwreck Beach to Ha'ula Beach (you can turn back at any point for a shorter, but still stunning, walk). To reach the trailhead, park in the Grand Hyatt lot at the end of Ainako St. From the beach, head east through the ironwood trees. Along the coast, you will pass spectacular cliffs of lithified sand dunes, tide pools in rocky coves and even the ruins of a heiau.

The Maha'ulepu coast comprises a string of beaches – **Maha'ulepu Beach** (Gillin's Beach), **Kawailoa Bay** and **Ha'ula Beach** – from west to east. Waters are choppy and better suited for experienced swimmers than once-a-year tourists, but hiking is enticing year-round. Near Maha'ulepu Beach you'll see the sole house on the entire coast, the **Gillin Beach House** (742-7561; www .gillinbeachhouse.com; per week from $3090), originally built in 1946 by Elbert Gillin, a civil engineer with the Koloa Sugar Plantation.

Kawailoa Bay is surrounded by sand dunes to the west and protected by jutting sea cliffs to the east. Windsurfers and kitesurfers skim across the surf here. Ironwood trees backing the beach make a pleasant spot for picnicking. Continue on until you reach Ha'ula Beach, a stunning curved bay with pounding, white-crested waves. The coastline is exposed, so come prepared for sun and wind.

If you must drive, go past the Grand Hyatt, proceed for 1.5 miles on the unpaved road and turn right where it dead-ends at a **gate** (7:30am-6pm, to 7pm summer). Continue past the gatehouse until you reach the beach parking area. Access hours are strictly enforced.

Two excellent resources are the **Maha'ulepu Heritage Trail** (www.hikemahaulepu.org) website and *Kaua'i's Geologic History: A Simplified Guide* by Chuck Blay and Robert Siemers. Also see **Malama Maha'ulepu** (www.malama-mahaulepu.org), a nonprofit group working to preserve the area, which is owned by Steve Case, the cofounder of America Online.

fees incl cart before/after 3pm $95/65, club rental $40) is a relatively forgiving 18-hole, par-70 Robert Trent Jones Jr course. Established in 1983, this compact, inland course uses smaller targets and awkward stances to pose challenges.

The South Shore's jewel is the **Po'ipu Bay Golf Course** (742-8711, 800-858-6300; www.poipu baygolf.com; 2250 Ainako St; green fees incl cart nonguest/ guest $220/150, club rental $50). This 18-hole, par-72 course adjacent to the Grand Hyatt covers 210 seaside acres. Rates drop at noon ($135) and again at 2:30pm ($80).

SPAS

When **Anara Spa** (742-1234; www.anaraspa.com; Grand Hyatt Kaua'i Resort & Spa, 1571 Po'ipu Rd; massage per hr $155-235, facials $165-225) was renovated in 2007, it was an extreme makeover, with the spa emerging as a 20,000 sq ft tropical fantasyland, with gardens and waterfalls to sooth the eyes while the face and body indulges in a splurge-worthy menu of delicious services. Access to the lap pool and fitness center is free with a 50-minute spa treatment.

Tours

Unless you're as water-phobic as a cat, we recommend a snorkeling tour (see p540 and p546) to maximize your cruise experience. But if you're seeking a sunset tour, **Cap Andy's Sailing Adventures** (335-6833, 800-535-0830; www.napali.com; Port Allen Marina Center, Waialo Rd; adult/ child 2-12 $69/50) departs from Kukui'ula Harbo between 4pm and 5pm for a scenic two-hou cruise.

Festivals & Events

Prince Kuhio Celebration of the Arts (240-6369; http://princekuhio.wetpaint.com) Day-long celebration, in late March, to honor Prince Jonah Kuhio Kalaniana'ole, who was born in 1872 on the site of Prince Kuhio Park (p532).
Garden Isle Artisan Fair (245-9021) When on Kaua'i, buy Kaua'i-made. At this triannual fair in mid-March, mid-August and mid-October, you'll find handcrafted items, Hawaiian music and local *grinds*. Usually located opposite Po'ipu Beach Park.
Kaua'i Mokihana Festival Hula Competition (822-2166; www.mokihana.kauai.net) Three days of serious hula performances at the Grand Hyatt in late

September, both *kahiko* (ancient) and *'auana* (modern). At $5 to $10, it's a must-see.

Hawaiiana Festival (☎ 240-6369; www.aloha festivals.com) Part of the Aloha Festival, this mid-October three-day event features Hawaiian crafts, demonstrations, hula and a luau.

New Year's Eve Fireworks (☎ 742-7444; www .poipubeach.org) Free fireworks on the beach at Po'ipu Beach Park on December 31.

Sleeping

The majority of accommodations in Po'ipu are condos, which are available for all budget levels. Rates can vary depending on the owner or agency renting each unit, so we list typical or average rates. Vacation-rental homes can offer more privacy and drive-up access to your door. The two major hotels are high-end Grand Hyatt and the business-class Sheraton Kaua'i. Just before press time, a new luxury hotel, **Koa Kea** (www.koakea.com; r from $445) was set to open in April 2009. With 121 rooms and a beachfront location (near Kiahuna Plantation), this boutique hotel is gorgeously appointed and strives for a personal, family-oriented atmosphere..

Check out the **Po'ipu Beach Resort Association** www.poipubeach.org) website for additional listings; note that condo links often go merely to agencies, however. If you decide on a specific condo, always check **Vacation Rentals by Owner** (www.vrbo.com) for additional rentals; owners might offer better deals than agencies.

That said, you don't incur extra fees if you book with agencies and they can steer you to appropriate properties, especially if you're seeking a vacation-rental home. We recommend the following:

Parrish Collection Kaua'i (☎ 742-2000, 800-742-412; www.parrishkauai.com; 3176 Po'ipu Rd, Ste 1, oloa, Hawaii 96756) Well established agency for condos nd vacation homes. Friendly, accommodating staff. ain, on-site agency for Waikomo Stream Villas and Nihi ai Villas.

Po'ipu Connection Realty (☎ 800-742-2260; www oipuconnection.com; PO Box 1022, Koloa, Hawaii 96756) ondo listings only; good prices and personalized service.

Po'ipu Beach Vacation Rentals (☎ 742-2850, 0-684-5133; www.pbvacationrentals.com; PO Box 58, Koloa, Hawaii 96756) Good prices; limited selection cludes condos and vacation homes.

kane Po'ipu Beach Houses (☎ 742-1778, 877-2-1778; www. kauaivacationproperties.com/poipu.htm) oose from a choice crop of dreamy beach houses near ennecke's Beach.

BUDGET

Prince Kuhio Resort (5061 Lawa'i Rd; studios $85-140, 1br $110-175; 🐾 🏊) This 90-unit condo is a budget property, so don't expect spiffy furnishings and floors. But it's a great value for the location across the road from Lawa'i (Beach House) Beach. All units have full kitchens and breezy windows, while pleasantly landscaped grounds surround a decent-size pool. Units vary markedly in quality. Find low rates at Po'ipu Connection Realty, Po'ipu Beach Vacation Rentals and www.vrbo.com.

MIDRANGE

Waikomo Stream Villas (☎ 742-2000, 800-742-1412; www.parrishkauai.com; 2721 Po'ipu Rd; 1br $105-159, 2br $149-259; 🏊) Because it's neither beachfront nor oceanfront, this condo is a real steal. The 60 units are modern, clean and huge (averaging 1100 to 1500 sq ft), with lanai, full kitchen, washer-dryer and high-speed internet access. With Waikomo Stream running through the gorgeous garden grounds, it's very pleasant – despite proximity to the Po'ipu Rd roundabout.

Kaua'i Cove Cottages (☎ 651-0279, 800-631-9313; www.kauaicove.com; 2672 Pu'uholo Rd; studios $129-165) Near Koloa Landing, this trio of 'cottages' (triplex is more apt) deftly blends modern amenities into cozy tropical bungalows. Although studio size is limited, the efficient layout allows bamboo canopy beds, vaulted ceilings, fully loaded kitchenette and lots of windows. Convenient parking is right outside your doorstep. The only drawbacks: no wi-fi and a $75 cleaning fee.

our pick **Hideaway Cove Villas** (☎ 635-8785, 866-849-2426; www.hideawaycove.com; 2307 & 2315 Nalo Rd; studios $140-205, 1br $170-220, 2br $195-310; 🐾 📶) Near Po'ipu Beach Park, these impeccable, modern and professionally managed units are a cut above their peers. All feature private lanai, fine hardwood flooring, genuine art and antiques, name-brand appliances. The Casa Di Amici restaurant is next door, but seems never to be an issue. Cleaning fees range from $90 to $130.

Nihi Kai Villas (☎ 742-2000, 800-742-1412; www .parrishkauai.com; 1870 Ho'one Rd; 2br $159-380; 🏊) For moderate spenders who want walkable beach access, here's the ticket. Po'ipu Beach Park is just down the block, although proximity depends on unit location (ie price). Of 70 units, half are well managed by the on-site Parrish agency. At 1000 to 2000 sq ft,

KAUA'I

they're comfortable, with full kitchens, two or more private lanai, washer-dryer and cable internet access.

Kiahuna Plantation (☎ 742-6411, 800-542-4862; www.outrigger.com; 2253 Po'ipu Rd; 1br $160- 360, 2br $240-460; ⬛) This aging beauty is still a hot property because it's among the rare accommodations flanking a swimmable beach. Of course, only a few units actually sit on the beach (money talks). Units are comfy, with fully equipped kitchen, living room and large lanai, but furnishings seem worn. On-site agencies include Outrigger and Castle Resorts (☎ 742-2200; www.castleresorts.com; one-bedroom units $140 to $510, two-bedroom units $390 to $560), but Kiahuna Beachside (☎ 937-6642; www.kiahuna.com; one-bedroom units $365 to $490, two-bedroom units $565) manages the best beachfront properties.

TOP END

ourpick **Po'ipu Kapili** (☎ 742-6449, 800-443-7714; www.poipukapili.com; 2221 Kapili Rd; 1br/2br from $230/345; ⬛) An all-around winner, this 60-unit condo features gorgeously landscaped ground, and spacious units (1120 to 1820 sq ft) that are consistent in quality, with lots of hardwood, big plush beds, extra bathroom, quality electronics and wired internet access. The closest sandy beach, fronting the Sheraton, is within walking distance.

ourpick **Aikane Kaua'i** (☎ 742-1778, 877-742-1778; www.kauaivacationproperties.com; 2271 Nalo Rd; 3br house $250-300; ⬛ ⬛) A stroll away from Brennecke's Beach, this beach house lets you spread out, with high ceilings, ocean-facing balcony, full kitchen and three bedrooms, each with its own bathroom. It's a 'green' house, insulated and running exclusively on solar energy. Rates vary by number of guests. The cleaning fee is $150 to $195.

Sheraton Kaua'i Resort (☎ 742-1661, 800-782-9488; www.sheraton-kauai.com; 2440 Ho'onani Rd; r garden/ocean from $240/460; ⬛ ⬛ ⬛) The business-class Sheraton has one enviable advantage: a prime stretch of sandy, swimmable, sunset-perfect beach. Rooms are decent, if unmemorable, and the low-end Garden View or Partial Ocean View wings are nowhere near the beach. Eco-efforts include recycling bins and free breakfast coupons for guests who forgo maid service that day.

Grand Hyatt Kaua'i Resort & Spa (☎ 742-1234, 800-554-9288; www.kauai.hyatt.com; 1571 Po'ipu Rd; r garden view $280-430, deluxe ocean view $470-720; ⬛ ⬛) Po'ipu's

glamour gal is 602-rooms strong and she love to show off, with a soaring lobby, tropic gardens, massive spa, world-renowned go course, oceanfront restaurants and meande ing 'river pools.' Inside, the room decor typically tropical, but obviously a class abov What's missing is a swimmable *real* beach, n just the manmade one.

Whalers Cove (☎ 742-7571, 800-225-2683; ww .whalers-cove.com; 2640 Pu'uholo Rd; 1br/2br from $349/47 ⬛ ⬛ ⬛) Po'ipu's most luxurious condo sui discriminating travelers who want luxur without a smidgen of tourist fuss. Units ar palatial (1300 sq ft on average), elegant an utterly immaculate, often with gleamin marble floors, granite counters and mansio worthy furniture. Truly gawk-worthy is th amount of prized koa wood used for doo and furnishings.

Eating
BUDGET

ourpick **Papalani Gelato** (☎ 742-2663; www.papala gelato.com; Po'ipu Shopping Village, 2360 Kiahuna Plantati Dr; single scoop $3.75; ⏱ 11:30am-9:30pm) Wit mouth-watering flavors (all homemade or site), you can't go wrong with classic vanil bean or pistachio gelato. But, for local colo try the creamy sorbetto, made with fresh island-grown starfruit, lychee, mango, guav or avocado.

Puka Dog (☎ 742-6044; www.pukadog.com; Po'i Shopping Village; hot dogs $6.50; ⏱ 11am-6pm) There only one house specialty here, and it's hot dog, for cryin' out loud. Even Anthon Bourdain couldn't resist a sample: toast bun, choice of Polish sausage or veggie do 'secret' sauce and tropical fruit relish (fro mango to pineapple). Purists might find th toppings overwhelming.

Savage Shrimp (☎ 635-0267; Lawa'i Rd near Prin Kuhio Park; meals $10; ⏱ 11am-2pm) Follow yo nose to the roadside white van for heapir plates of Brazilian-style shrimp cooked wi garlic, coconut milk, cilantro and tomatoe Be prepared for blazing sun and greasy finge (the shrimp is unpeeled).

MIDRANGE & TOP END

Plantation Gardens Restaurant & Bar (☎ 742-212 www.pgrestaurant.com; Kiahuna Plantation, 2253 Po'ipu R appetizers $9-14, mains $19-27; ⏱ 5:30-9pm) Set in historic plantation house, this restaurant lovely without trying too hard. The menu mercifully concise and features locally grow

---

EYE OF THE STORM

Almost two decades after the **Hurricane 'Iniki** blasted the island, residents can still give blow-by-blow accounts of their survival on September 11, 1992. 'Iniki blew in with sustained winds of 145mph and gusts of 165mph or more (a weather-station meter in mountainous Koke'e broke off at 227mph). It snapped trees by the thousands and totally demolished 1420 homes (and swept over 60 out to sea). Another 5000 homes were severely damaged, while thousands more sustained minor damage. Most of the island lacked electricity for over a month, and some areas lacked power for up to three months. Thirty-foot waves washed away entire wings of beachfront hotels, particularly those in Po'ipu and Princeville.

During the immediate aftermath, residents were remarkably calm and law-abiding, despite the lack of power, radio or TV. Communities held parties to share and consume perishable food. Looting was minor and when grocers allowed affected residents to take what they needed, they insisted on paying.

Miraculously, only four people died, but the total value of the damage to the island was $1.8 billion (1992 USD). The tourism industry bounced back by the late 1990s and today is thriving. While locals notice the changed landscape, newcomers would never realize the havoc wreaked 15 years ago. Unfortunately a couple of Kaua'i's native bird species have not been spotted since 'Iniki.

Because 'Iniki struck during daylight, many residents recorded the event in real time with camcorders. The best footage was compiled into an hour-long video ($24.95), which you can order at www.video-hawaii.com/iniki.html.

---

ingredients, kiawe (a relative of the mesquite tree) grilling for a rich, smoky flavor, and lots of fresh seafood. Lit by tiki torches at night, the setting is ideal for large gatherings.

our pick **Casa di Amici** (☎ 742-1555; 2301 Nalo Rd; dinner mains $23-29; ⏱ from 6pm) Often overlooked due to an obscure location, this restaurant is an unpretentious gem. The chef focuses on using the highest quality ingredients, from locally grown greens to black truffles from Italy to homemade sausage. The menu's traditional Italian pastas and meats are joined by multicultural standouts such as the grilled miso-ginger ahi and paella risotto.

Naniwa (☎ 742-1661; Sheraton Kaua'i Resort, 2440 Ho'onani Rd; dinner mains $28-33, sushi $11-16; ⏱ 5:30-9pm Tue-Sat) Despite the island's sizable Japanese population, Japanese restaurants are woefully scarce. The only major sushi bar on the South Shore, Naniwa serves flawlessly fresh, impeccably presented sushi. Your wallet will take a hit, with *nigiri* (oval-shaped sushi) going for 11 per pair.

Beach House Restaurant (☎ 742-1424; www.the-beach-house.com; 5022 Lawa'i Rd; dinner mains $26-40; ⏱ winter 5:30-9:30pm, summer 6-10pm) Overrated, perhaps, but the Beach House is the iconic spot for sunset dining and worth a splurge. Current Chef Todd Barrett's specialties include macnut crusted mahimahi and watermelon salad with gorgonzola cheese and just-picked Omao greens. Book well in advance.

Tidepools (☎ 742-6260; Grand Hyatt Kaua'i Resort & Spa, 1571 Po'ipu Rd; mains $28-40; ⏱ 5:30-10pm) Surrounded by waterfalls and lagoons filled with koi, the Grand Hyatt's signature restaurant is more romantic oasis than lively nightspot. The surprisingly brief menu presents decent but derivative examples of island fusion, from grilled peppered ahi with coconut-jasmine rice to grilled chicken breast with Okinawan sweet-potato purée. A serene 'special occasion' spot.

Roy's Po'ipu Bar & Grill (☎ 742-5000; www.roysrestaurant.com; Po'ipu Shopping Village; mains $37-47; ⏱ 5:30-9:30pm) Still iconic, still wildly popular, Roy's continues to please the foodies. Signature dishes include the melt-in-your-mouth *miso-yaki* (miso-marinated) butterfish appetizer and the pesto-steamed 'ono (white-fleshed wahoo) sizzled in cilantro-ginger-peanut oil. Expect a shopping-mall setting and notoriously high-decibel dining room.

For groceries, indie supermarket **Kukui'ula Store** (☎ 742-1601; Po'ipu Plaza, 2827 Po'ipu Rd; ⏱ 8:30am-8:30pm Mon-Fri, to 6:30pm Sat & Sun) resembles a bodega from the outside, but stocks a good selection of basics and wholesome foods. For more selection, go to Koloa's grocers and fish market.

Drinking & Entertainment
BARS
our pick **Point** (☎ 742-1661; Sheraton Kaua'i Resort; ⏱ 11am-midnight, closed lunch Mon & Tue) An informal

hangout for sunset viewing and people-watching, this bar mixes a great *mojito* ($9.50 to $11.50) or pours from the tap. For lunch and dinner, cut costs by eating from the excellent menu of appetizers and sandwiches.

Stevenson's Library (☎ 742-1234, 800-554-9288; Grand Hyatt Kaua'i Resort & Spa; 1571 Po'ipu Rd; ☽ 6pm-midnight) Resembling a too-cool-for-you gentleman's club, this handsome lounge is rather incongruous to the island scene but serves good (if pricey) sushi, desserts and drinks. Kids are permitted until 9pm, meaning that a romper-room vibe occasionally prevails till then. Highlights include the gleaming 27ft koa-wood bar and live jazz from 8pm to 10pm.

Seaview Terrace (☎ 742-1234, 800-554-9288; Grand Hyatt Kaua'i Resort & Spa; 1571 Po'ipu Rd; ☽ 4:30-8:30pm) For free resort 'entertainment,' arrive before sunset on Tuesday, Friday or Saturday for a torch-lighting ceremony and either Hawaiian music or *na keiki* (children's) hula shows. Call for start time, which varies by season.

LUAU
Between the two, the Sheraton's show gives you more for your money. Also consider driving to Lihu'e for Kilohana Plantation's new and different Luau Kalamaku (p487).

our pick Surf to Sunset Luau (☎ 742-8205; www.sheraton-kauai.com; Sheraton Kaua'i Resort, 2440 Ho'onani Rd; adult/child 6-12 $75/37.50; ☽ check-in 6pm Fri) We rate the Sheraton's 'Surf to Sunset' luau A (excellent) for oceanfront setting and B (good) for the food and show, which is the standard Polynesian revue. For a commercial luau, the audience size is small at 200 to 300. Beware: the humorous emcee expects lots of audience participation.

Havaiki Nui Luau (☎ 240-6456; www.grandhyatt kauailuau.com; Grand Hyatt Kaua'i Resort & Spa, 1571 Po'ipu Rd; adult/junior 13-20/child 5-12/under 5 $94/84/57/free; ☽ check-in 5:15pm Sun & Thu) The Havaiki Nui Luau is a well-oiled production befitting the Grand Hyatt setting, but the price is steep, especially if rain forces the show indoors.

Getting There & Around
To get here from Lihu'e, the quickest way is to exit on Maluhia Rd. Once in Po'ipu, you'll see that it's a sprawled-out town, necessitating a car to go anywhere besides the beach. Navigating is easy, with just two main roads: Po'ipu Rd along eastern Po'ipu and Lawa'i Rd along western Po'ipu. Most attrac-

tions, including Po'ipu Beach Park, have free parking lots.

The Kaua'i Bus (p475) runs through Koloa and into Po'ipu, stopping along Po'ipu Rd at Ho'owili Rd (the turnoff to Po'ipu Beach Park). It's an option to get here from other towns but a limited in-town mode.

Because Po'ipu lacks a town center, destinations are scattered. Walking is viable along the main roads and along the beaches, but the vibe is more suburbia than surf town.

KALAHEO
pop 3915
From the highway, Kalaheo is a one-stoplight cluster of eateries and little else. But along the backroads, this neighborly town offers peaceful accommodations away from the tourist crowd. If you plan to hike at Waimea Canyon and Koke'e State Parks but also want easy access to Po'ipu beaches, Kalaheo's central location is ideal.

The town's post office and handful of restaurants are clustered around the intersection of Kaumuali'i Hwy and Papalina Rd.

Sights
KUKUIOLONO PARK
Unless you stay in Kalaheo, you would miss this little **park** (☽ 6:30am-6:30pm), which offers a nine-hole golf course (opposite), modest Japanese garden, sweeping views and grassy grounds for strolling or jogging. In 1860 King Kamehameha III leased the land to Duncan McBryde, whose son, Walter, the pineapple baron, eventually purchased the 178-acre estate. He built the public golf course in 1929 and deeded the entire site for use as a public park upon his death. Walter McBryde is buried near the eighth hole of the golf course. To get here, turn left onto Papalina Rd from Kaumuali'i Hwy (heading west).

HANAPEPE VALLEY LOOKOUT
The scenic **lookout** (Map p469) that pops up shortly after the 14-mile marker offers a view deep into Hanapepe Valley. The red-clay walls of the cliffs are topped by a layer of green cane, like frosting on a cake. This sight is but a teaser of the dramatic vistas awaiting at Waimea Canyon.

While old king sugar might still dominate Hanapepe Valley, look across the highway toward the ocean to see Kaua'i's current major commercial crop, coffee.

Activities

Golf practically for free at **Kukuiolono Golf Course** (☎ 332-9151; Kukuiolono Park; green fees adult/child $9/3, pull carts $6; ⏲ 6:30am-6:30pm), an unassuming nine-hole, par-36 golf course with spectacular ocean and valley views – and zero attitude. Grab a bucket of balls for $2 and hit the driving range – first-come, first-served.

For an indoor workout, work with owner Theresa Ouano (the epitome of fitness) at **Poise Pilates** (☎ 651-5287; www.poisepilates.org; 4432 Papalina Rd; 55min private session $70, mat class $20), a cheerful, well-equipped studio. Prices drop if you buy in multiples.

Sleeping

Seaview Suite (☎ 332-9744; www.seakauai.com; 3913 Uluali'i St; studio/1br $75/95; 🖦) Choose from two comfy ground-floor units with lovely sunset and ocean views. The one-bedroom suite includes full kitchen, separate living and dining areas and bedding for four. The compact studio, with fully equipped kitchenette, is a steal. Discounted rates if you rent both.

Hale Ikena Nui (☎ 332-9005, 800-550-0778; www.kauaivacationhome.com; 3957 Uluali'i St; r incl breakfast $75, 1br $95; 🖦) Located at the end of a cul de sac, this spacious in-law apartment (1000 sq ft) includes a living area with sofabed, full kitchen and washer-dryer. Singles can rent the B&B room, which is less private but includes private bathroom and use of the main house. Bonus: an irresistible dog named Bear.

Kauai Garden Cottages (☎ 332-0877; www.kauaigardencottages.com; 5350 Pu'ulima Rd; studio $100; 🖦) Perched high in the Kalaheo upcountry, this meticulously designed pair of studio units gleams with rich Indonesian hardwood floors under soaring cathedral ceilings with cheerful stained-glass accents. The rooms adjoin a vast lanai overlooking a stunningly green valley that gives new meaning to 'valley view.' Two-for-one deal: rent both rooms for only $150 nightly.

our pick Hale O Nanakai (☎ 652-8071; www.nanakai.com; 3726 Nanakai Pl; r incl breakfast $75-150, 1br $150-175; 🖦) Guests take first priority at this lovingly designed B&B with accommodations for every budget. Traditional B&B rooms all feature plush carpeting, Sleep Number beds, flat-screen HDTV and generous continental breakfast. Guests share a huge deck and common area with awesome coastal views. For more privacy, choose the downstairs apartment.

Bamboo Jungle House (☎ 332-5515, 888-332-5115; www.kauai-bedandbreakfast.com; 3829 Waha Rd; r incl breakfast $130-170; 🖦 🖦) In a lovely plantation-style house, the classic B&B experience awaits: friendly hosts, home-cooked breakfasts and 8am gatherings 'round the morning table. The three rooms are immaculate, with snow white walls, fluffy canopy beds and sparkling French doors. Outside, enjoy a 38ft lap pool amid jungly foliage and lava-rock waterfall. It's geared towards couples, and children aren't allowed.

Eating

our pick Mark's Place (☎ 332-0050; 2-3687 Kaumuali'i Hwy; plates $6-7; ⏲ 10am-8pm Mon-Fri) If you're curious about the legendary plate lunch, skip breakfast and come here famished at noon. Classic plate lunches feature generous portions of meaty mains (from teriyaki beef to Korean chicken), plus rice and salad. Healthier gourmet options are available. Located off the highway, east of Kalaheo.

our pick Kalaheo Café & Coffee Co (☎ 332-5858; www.kalaheo.com; 2-2560 Kaumuali'i Hwy; breakfast & lunch $6-10, dinner $16-26; ⏲ 6am-2:30pm daily, 5:30-8:30pm Wed-Sat) Big thumbs up for this roadside café, which boasts a spacious dining room, easy parking and a satisfying menu of healthy California-style cooking. Breakfast favorites include a well-stuffed veggie wrap and build-your-own omelets, while the lunch hour brings fresh Kalaheo greens and Dagwood-sized sandwiches. The last temptation? Homemade fruit crisp.

Brick Oven Pizza (☎ 332-8561; Kaumuali'i Hwy; 10-/12-/15in pizzas from $11.50/16/24; ⏲ 11am-10pm Tue-Sun, 4-10pm Mon) Why did Brick Oven become Kaua'i's tourist mecca for pizza? Its pies are fine, but real pizza aficionados might be underwhelmed. That said, vegetarians will welcome the truly meatless combo piled with premium veggies and stock-free sauce. And hot pizza does hit the spot after hiking the canyon.

Pomodoro (☎ 332-5945; Rainbow Plaza, Kaumuali'i Hwy; mains $16-27; ⏲ 5:30-9:30pm Mon-Sat) Unless you know it's there, you'd never expect such a romantic restaurant in an unmemorable business mall. But locals always cite Pomodoro for traditional dishes such as veal parmigiana ($27) and linguini with white or red clam sauce ($22). With candlelit tables and white tablecloths, the setting is intimate yet neighborhood-casual.

KAUA'I

WESTSIDE

Kaua'i doesn't get more local than the Westside, where revered traditions and local-style family pride reigns supreme. Here, you're more likely to hear fluent Hawaiian, spot real-life *paniolo* (cowboys) and see old-school fisherman sewing their nets from scratch. Deep, riveting red canyons and a seemingly infinite expanse of ocean offers the widest range of atmosphere and ambience found on Kaua'i. The least touristy and the most tried and true, the Westside isn't for everyone; it's good like that.

'ELE'ELE & NUMILA

pop 2040

You might pass the small town of Numila and its bigger, albeit still small, neighbour, 'Ele'ele, without much thought. A pleasant, rural area, it offers a few convenient stops at the 'Ele'ele shopping center, including a **post office** (8am-4pm Mon-Fri, 9-11am Sat), as well as a divey (but decent) eatery, **Toi's Thai Kitchen** (☎ 335-3111; 'Ele'ele Shopping Center, 4469 Waialo Rd; mains $13-20; lunch 10:30-1:40pm, dinner 5:30-9pm Tue-Sat). The most noticeable of the bunch of small shops and restaurants is **Grinds Café** (☎ 335-6027; www.grindscafe.net; 'Ele'ele Shopping Center, 4469 Waialo Rd; breakfast $5-10, lunch $5-12; 5:30am-6pm) – it's usually busy on weekend mornings, so better to go for a dawn-patrol espresso or Sunday-afternoon latte.

Though it lacks the cachet imparted on the reputable Kona coffee, **Kaua'i Coffee Company** (☎ 335-0813, 800-545-8605; www.kauaicoffee.com; Halewili Rd; 9am-5pm) produces a sturdy cup of joe. Take the self-guided tour of the well-manicured plantation, which functions on 100% renewable energy. The drive once you're off the highway might seem long, but take in the eye candy, as it's adorned by neatly placed coffee trees and ablaze with bougainvillea.

Partnering with sustainable farmers, **Malie Organics Boutique** (☎ 866-767-5727 4353 Wai'alo Rd; www.malie.com; 9am-4pm Mon-Fri) has a claim to fame in its succulent body butters and exquisite essences. Try the Koke'e-inspired fragrance; a portion of the proceeds from that Koke'e line go specifically towards the preservation of Koke'e State Park.

PORT ALLEN

Though the area is developing to take advantage of its exquisite waterfront, Port Allen

DETOUR: PU'U ROAD SCENIC DRIVE

While the epic journeys along the North Shore and up to Waimea Canyon rank as Kaua'i's top two scenic drives, the South Shore upcountry might surprise you. **Pu'u Road** in Kalaheo makes a loop past bucolic ranches, generations-old trees and grassy pastureland – with the great Pacific as a fitting backdrop. The lush countryside is a surprise after the dry, red-dirt terrain along the highway.

Pu'u Rd intersects Papalina Dr in two places (either can be your starting point). It's a winding, one-lane country road with blind curves, so go slow and honk on the hairpins.

remains mostly an industrial area that serves as a departure point for most Na Pali tours.

Sights & Activities

GLASS BEACH

Trash as art – many a visitor has pored through the colorful well-worn remnants of glass along the shoreline of the aptly named Glass Beach, east of Port Allen. Glass 'pebbles', along with abandoned metals (some with newfound patina, some not so much), have washed up from an old dumpsite nearby, showing that decades of weather, too, can make art. To get to the little cove, take Aka'ula St, the last left before entering the Port Allen commercial harbor, go past the fuel-storage tanks and then curve to the right down a rutted dirt road that leads 100yd to the beach.

DIVING

Mana Divers (☎ 335-0881; www.manadivers.com; Bay 3, Port Allen Boat Harbour, 4310 Waialo Rd) Offers boat dives, night dives and dive charters to Ni'ihau, Lehua Rock and Mana Crack during the months of May through September. It also offers open-water certification courses.

SNORKELING & WHALE WATCHING

The majority of Na Pali tours leave from Port Allen and, depending on the season, offer a variety of ways in which to enjoy this spectacular coastline, from snorkeling in summer to whale watching in winter.

You'll either go by Zodiac (raft) or catamaran the former of which offers little res

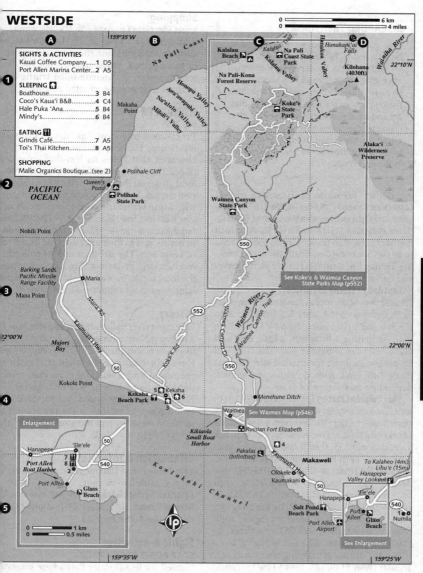

WESTSIDE

SIGHTS & ACTIVITIES
Kauai Coffee Company.....1 D5
Port Allen Marina Center..2 A5

SLEEPING 🏠
Boathouse.......................3 B4
Coco's Kaua'i B&B............4 C4
Hale Puka 'Ana.................5 B4
Mindy's............................6 B4

EATING 🍴
Grinds Café......................7 A5
Toi's Thai Kitchen............8 A5

SHOPPING
Malie Organics Boutique..(see 2)

KAUA'I

ite from the waves and sun, the latter of
hich offers shaded benches, toilet, and, of
ourse, an unending supply of drinks and
upu. Regardless of your choice, take the
information given by guides with a grain
of salt – many tell tales of cannibalism and
ush inaccuracies about the *ali'i* in order to
nsationalise the experience.

our pick **Holoholo Charters** (☎ 335-0815, 800-848-
6130; www.holoholocharters.com; Port Allen Marina Center,
Waialo Rd; adult/5 to 12yr $135/95; ⌚ 6am-8pm) is
among the best for delivering on its promises of sea-cave jaunts, *honu* sightings and
augmented cultural lore. The two-hour sunset cruise offers the best deal, at $79. Save
10% by booking online.

DISCARDED TREASURES

Blue glass fishing buoys, which used to be attached to fish nets, are prized 'finds' on Kaua'i. Used by Japanese fisherman after WWII, they occasionally wash up on Hawaiian shores. Storms and time separated the buoys from the nets. Now rare, as plastics and other materials have made the glass obsolete, the buoys that wash ashore are prized on Kaua'i and used as garden and home decor around the island, especially in fishing homes.

Another favourite is Hawaiian-owned **Catamaran Kahanu** (☎ 645-6176, 888-213-7711; www.catamarankahanu.com; Port Allen Marina Center, Waialo Rd; 5hr tour adult/child 4-11 $122/80, 3½hr tour $80/60), which includes Hawaiian trades into its tour, thanks to basket-weaving demonstrations and making 'fishing lines' from *ti* (native plant) leaves and coconut fiber.

Capt Andy's Sailing Adventures (☎ 335-6833, 800-535-0830; www.napali.com; Port Allen Marina Center, Waialo Rd; 5hr snorkeling trip adult/child 2-12 $139/99) heads to Na Pali and prices often drop by $10 online. Plan on getting a little wet, a little cold and also a little sun along the way. The crew will be on the lookout for marine life, such as flying fish, sea turtles, dolphins and whales, depending on the time of year.

Blue Dolphin Charters (☎ 335-5553, 877-511-1311; www.kauaiboats.com; Port Allen Marina Center, Waialo Rd; internet/regular booking $175/196) offers a seven-hour snorkeling tour or five-hour Na Pali trip. For an additional $35, they'll take you on a one-tank dive – even if it's your first time.

Kaua'i Sea Tours (☎ 826-7254, 800-733-7997; www.kauaiseatours.com; Aka'ula St, Port Allen) lets you opt for the summer Na Pali tour by catamaran (adult/child from $139/99) or the rougher, three-hour tour by raft (internet/regular adult from $99/109, child $69/73), or a three- to four-hour sightseeing tour of Na Pali or a five-hour dinner snorkeling tour (internet/regular from $139/148, teen $129/137, child $99/109).

If a more rugged experience is your thing, then a Zodiac raft tour might be for you; try **Captain Zodiac Raft Adventures** (☎ 335-6833, 800-535-0830; www.napali.com; Port Allen Marina Center, Waialo Rd; adult/child $129/89), Captain Andy's sister outfit, which offers a 5½-hour tour year-round.

Shopping

Kauai Chocolate Company (☎ 335-0448; www.kauachocolate.com; 4341 Waialo Rd; ☻ 11am-5pm Mon-Sa noon-5pm Sun) Save some room for at least on of these prized, exotic treats, whether it's mouth-watering ganache-filled truffle or passion-fruit sugar-encrusted pastille.

HANAPEPE
pop 2155

Proclaimed by its own as 'Kaua'i's bigges little town,' Hanapepe carries a well-brande character that belies its less-than-crowde population. Here you'll find some of the mos local *grinds* on the island, hailing from planta tion days and a homecooked tradition. Com with a thin wallet and an empty stomach an you'll do just fine. Near Salt Pond Beach Par families continue the tradition of salt pannin in basins, just as their ancestors did hundred of years ago. The spiritual task of collectin reddish, large crystals of Hawaiian salt mear the local seasoning (which cannot be bough continues to be a source of local pride.

History

Like most river valleys Hanapepe was host t a thriving Native Hawaiian community an like most places, that tradition was supplante Hanapepe was once the main port town c the island and a bustling economic cente until the new harbour was built in Lihu' Hanapepe was downsized, but survived an found renewed vitality in the restoration its old main street and transformation by th Friday Night Art Walk.

Orientation & Information

Veer *mauka* onto Hanapepe Rd at the 'Kaua'i Biggest Little Town' sign.
American Savings Bank (☎ 335-3118; 4548 Kona R
Bank of Hawaii (☎ 335-5021; 3764 Hanapepe Rd) Or the western end of Hanapepe Rd.

Sights & Activities
SALT POND BEACH PARK

Named for its saltwater flats where seawat is drained and harvested for salt, this whit sand beach is great for lounging about, wi full facilities, camping access and lifeguard Popular for local families, it also serves as th end and celebration of the Expedia Wor Challenge, which draws some of the mo skilled one-man outrigger canoers fro around the globe.

If you're toting children, a potentially quick and fun stop is **Kaua'i Cookie Company** (☎ 335-5003 1-3529 Kaumuali'I Hwy, Ste A), an island hallmark. Kona coffee and chocolate chip are the standard faves. Find it across from Omoide Bakery & Wong's Chinese Deli.

Though the timing might be tricky, if the stars align hours-wise, a fail-safe child-pleaser is **Sparky's Peace Garden, Storybook Theatre** (☎ 335-0712; 3814 Hanapepe Rd; www.storybook.org; ⊙ vary), as a quick stop at this multiuse theatre and interactive classroom offers distraction and a change of scenery. Call ahead, as hours vary.

FLYING
For a real adrenaline rush, take an ultralight lesson with **Birds in Paradise** (☎ 822-5309; www .birdsinparadise.com; Burns Field, Puolo Rd; 50min/1½hr lesson $135/335). You can also do a round-the-island lesson on one of these powered hang gliders for $300. Take the road for Salt Pond Beach Park to reach the airport.

Tours
Find a copy of Hanapepe's *Walking Tour Map* ($2), which describes the town's historic buildings. Look for the Swinging Bridge landmark, which crosses the Hanapepe River. Its funky old predecessor fell victim to 'Iniki, but thanks to a community-wide effort this new bridge was erected in 1996.

HELICOPTER RIDES
Inter-island Helicopters (☎ 335-5009, 800-656-5009; www.interislandhelicopters.com; 1-3410 Kaumuali'i Hwy; regular/waterfall flights $260/$355) offers door-free flights over the Westside, providing views that rival some of the most rugged found; its flight record is less than perfect, however.

Sleeping
Though there aren't any hotels to speak of, Salt Pond Beach Park offers convenient camping. See p470 for permit information.

Westside Dwelling (☎ 652-9900; apt $80) It's not a vacation rental by any means – it's more like borrowing a friend's apartment. Set in the Hanapepe River Valley, this place is about a 2-mile drive from Salt Pond Beach Park and it's near the river, down Awawa Rd. You'll need a car as it's not centrally located. Three-night minimum stay.

Hanapepe Riverside Inn (☎ 261-1693; 4466 Puolo d; 1br $97) Clean, simple and chock-full of the basics, this decent little upstairs unit has a full

kitchen, king-size bed, washer-dryer access and Hanapepe River views. The only problem is booking, as you have to go through a service. Maximum two people and three-night minimum stay.

Eating
Taro Ko Chips Factory (☎ 335-5586; 3940 Hanapepe Rd; small bag $2.50; ⊙ 8am-5pm) This is the place to stop if you want a unique alternative to getting your French fries fix. Thinly sliced *kalo* that's seasoned, slathered with oil and tortured in a deep wok makes for some crispy, somewhat sweet but mostly salty crunching.

Hawaiian Hut Delights (☎ 335-3781; 3805 Hanapepe Rd; ⊙ noon-5pm Mon-Fri) If you're just passing through and want some portable sustenance, try this place for an old-school local snack like *li hing mui* (salty dried plums; also a flavor of crack seed) or a quickie rainbow shave ice (from $2) on-the-go.

Lappert's Ice Cream (☎ 335-6121; www.lapperts .com; 1-3555 Kaumuali'i Hwy; ice cream $4; ⊙ 10am-6pm) There's not much that beats natural ice cream, so don't miss the Kauai pie with Kona coffee ice cream, chocolate fudge, macadamia nuts, coconut flakes and vanilla cake crunch.

Tahina's Tasty Treats (☎ 335-0260; 4505 Puolo Rd; lunches $7.75; ⊙ 11am-5pm Mon-Fri) Ahi, mahimahi or *opah* (moonfish) make for a yummy approach to the English tradition of fish and chips, while other options such as fried oysters or shrimp make for a more unusual experience. It also has *boba* (tapioca) drinks, creamy milkshakes and typical shave-ice flavours.

Da Imu Hut Café (☎ 335-0200; 1-3959 Kaumuali'i Hwy; ⊙ 10am-2pm, 5-8pm Mon-Fri & 10am-1pm Sat) Specializing in local food, this is the perfect place to pick up lunch for a drive up to the canyon or a beach picnic.

Bobbie's Island Restaurant (☎ 335-5152; 3620 Hanapepe Rd; plate lunch $5.95; ⊙ 10am-2:30pm Mon-Fri & 5-8:30pm Mon, Thu, Fri) With fish and chips, local-style plate lunches and a killer roast pork gravy, this is a predominantly locals' spot and boasts such comforting, high-calorie eats as *loco moco* (rice, fried egg and hamburger with gravy) and pork *katsu* (great for a rainy day or posthike meal).

Kaua'i Pupu Factory (☎ 335-0084; 1-3566 Kaumuali'i Hwy; plate lunch $6.25, ahi poke per lb $9; ⊙ 9am-5:30pm Mon-Fri, to 3pm Sat) A down-home-style local. If you've got a big group, get enough for everyone, pack a cooler and head to the beach.

HANAPEPE ART WALK

Any given Friday in old Hanapepe town offers a candid peek into its art-world milieu, as galleries keep later hours, offering a chance to stroll, peruse and dine. The pace picks up around 5pm – when the former main drag is transformed by its already-heady mix of musicians, art installations and visitors. Meander through the galleries on the **Friday Night Art Walk** (6-9pm Fri); the galleries house everything from the works of Sunday artists, island-inspired originals, Hawaiiana vintage and kitsch to photography, watercolours and a sampling of Asian and island art. Though art aficionados may snub some of the collections as less than cutting edge, remember: Hanapepe is small town – and proud of it. Some galleries:

Arius Hopman Gallery (☎ 335-0227; www.hopmanart.com; 3840C Hanapepe Rd; 10:30am-3:30pm Mon-Thu, to 9pm Fri) An eye for recognizing, composing and presenting nature's beauty means Hopman's photography certainly beats any postcard shot taken on the island.

Art of Marbling/Robert Bader Wood Sculpture (☎ 482-1472; 3890 Hanapepe Rd; 10am-5pm Sat-Thu, to 9pm Fri) Becky J Wold's work on silk and her husband's work in wood make for unique collecting, whether it's a small paper or Cook Island Pine work.

Banana Patch Studio (☎ 335-5944; 800-914-5944; www.bananapatchstudio.com; 3865 Hanapepe Rd; 10am-4:30pm Sat-Thu, to 9pm Fri) Koi pond watercolours, vibrant island art, souvenir ceramic tiles.

ourpick Dawn Traina Gallery (☎ 335-3993; 3840B Hanapepe Rd; 6-9 Fri or by appointment) Housed in one of the more understated galleries, her detailed research of Hawaiian culture shines through in drawings, paintings and other art.

Kauai Fine Arts (☎ 335-3778; www.brunias.com; 3751 Hanapepe Rd; 9:30am-4:30pm Mon-Thu & Sat, to 9pm Fri) If you're sending something home or want to get your hands on a unique map – including navigational charts – this is a great little spot to peruse. Also sells prints, Ni'ihau lei and other works.

Many will find that the art walk from gallery to gallery matches the gentle ambience of Old Hanapepe's modest Christmas-lit strip, which has low-key street performances, such as the Westside cult classic the **Happy Enchalata** (www.myspace.com/thehappyenchalata) or guitarist Westside Smitty, usually fronting the Talk Story Bookstore. The walk also pairs well with low-rent street vendors like Heather's Monster Tacos, a makeshift tent usually across from the Swinging Bridge. This surly, one-woman outfit (who has redeemed herself according to locals thanks to her home-made tortillas) offers an experience all her own: 'authentic' Tex-Mex that's way out of context. If you'd rather sit or have a more island-style meal, this is the only night of the week that the justifiably popular Hawaiian-American fusion **Hanapepe Café & Bakery** (☎ 335-5011, 3830 Hanapepe Rd) is open for dinner. Drop in, make reservations and then do some window-shopping or art perusing, safe in the knowledge that your name's on the list.

ourpick Omoide Bakery & Wong's Chinese Deli (☎ 335-5066, 335-5291; 1-3543 Kaumuali'i Hwy; mains $7.50-9.75; 9:30am-9pm Tue-Sat) This well-known spot also serves up fresh-baked, white-flour-based comfort eats like sesame-and-black bean *manju* (Japanese cake filled with sweet bean paste) and Portuguese sweet bread (similar to what US mainlanders think of as Hawaiian or pineapple bread).

ourpick Hanapepe Café & Bakery (☎ 335-5011; 3830 Hanapepe Rd; dinner $18-25; bakery 7am-3pm, café 11am-3pm, dinner 6-9pm Fri) With walls covered with the work of local artists and an air full of either the scent of freshly baked goods or the sound of live music, this quaint stop is a must. Seafood seekers and vegetarians will appreciate the menu here. Breakfasts such as

frittata with red potatoes ($8) pair well with spicy espresso, and build-your-own burger make a great $7 lunch.

Shopping

You'll find the artists who put the pep back in Hanapepe in many of the old main-street galleries (see boxed text, above).

ourpick Puahina Moku o Kaua'i (☎ 335-977 www.warriordesignshawaii.com; 3741 Hanapepe Rd) With an eye for recognizing the need for traditiona Hawaiian motifs fused with contemporar clothes, you'll find wearable keepsakes here

Kama'aina Cabinets Koa Wood Gallery Gifts Furniture (☎ 335-5483; 3848 Hanapepe Rd; 11am 6pm Mon-Thu & Sat, to 9pm Fri) Even if you've been lucky enough to see a koa tree on one of you

Westside hikes, it's still nice to see it in an elegant, polished form.

Amy Lauren's Gallery (☎ 634-8660; www.amylaurens gallery.com; 3890 Hanapepe Rd; ☺ 11am-5pm Mon-Fri, to 9pm Fri) Here's a chance to buy originals instead of gicleé, though the latter are usually more affordable. This boutique-style gallery is somewhat of a newbie, but still worth a perusal for its vibrant colours and on-site artists.

Jacqueline on Kaua'i (☎ 335-9911; 3837 Hanapepe Rd; ☺ 9am-9pm) Friendly and a bit eclectic, Jacqueline leaves her mark on her work in this consignment-store-cum-boutique, where she sews the nonconsignment products herself, including Japanese-inspired silk robes and custom-made aloha shirts while you wait ($45 to $52, usually about one to two hours).

JJ Ohana (☎ 335-0366; 3805B Hanapepe Rd; www .jjohana.com; ☺ 8am-6pm Mon-Thu, to 9pm Fri) Staffed by a friendly local family who sells everything from the $2 hot dog to the $7000 Ni'ihau-shell necklace, this place is worth a peek for sure.

Talk Story Bookstore (☎ 335-6469; www.talkstory bookstore.com; 3785 Hanapepe Rd; ☺ 11am-5pm Mon-Thu, to 9pm Fri) The dusty, often hot and oddball-ridden 'westernmost bookstore in the United States' carries everything from vintage erotica, pulp fiction and trashy novellas to archaic piano books and high-school-required reading.

WAIMEA
pop 1790

One of several Waimeas in Hawai'i, this is not the surfing mecca nor is it the upscale cowboy town. This is the most historic Westside town, and its history can be seen from the ground up.

'Waimea' means reddish-brown water, and it refers to the river that picks up salt from the canyon and colours the ocean red. It was here that Captain Cook landed in 1778.

As is common in Hawaii, sugar played a role in the development of Waimea and the skeleton of the old Waimea mill can still be seen across the tech centers that house defence contractors working at the Pacific Missile Range Facility. The juxtaposition of what was the old economy and what some see as the economy of the future can be seen as symbolic.

Information

Aloha-N-Paradise (☎ 338 1522; 9905 Waimea Rd; ☺ 7am-5pm Mon-Fri, 8am-noon Sat) Next to the post office; offers internet access (per half-hour $4) and all-day

---

PIE-EATING CONTEST

Liliko'i (passion fruit), is a delectable, lightly sweet and somewhat tart flavour enhancer for muffins, mousses and pies. Take a detour and compare two of the self-proclaimed best *liliko'i* pies on the island, both of which can be found on the Westside, at either Hanapepe's Omoide Bakery & Wong's Chinese Deli (opposite) or Aunty Lilikoi (p548) in Waimea.

---

wi-fi with your own laptop. In the back a barista serves up locally roasted coffee drinks and pastries, while the front room has a seating area and art gallery for perusal.

First Hawaiian Bank (☎ 338-1611; 4525 Panako Rd) On Waimea's central square.

Na Pali Explorer (☎ 338-9999, 877-335-9909; www .napali-explorer.com; Kaumuali'i Hwy; per 30min $3; ☺ 7am-5pm) One-stop shop for internet access, simple souvenirs, light snacks and snorkel-cruise and sportfishing bookings.

Sights

WEST KAUA'I TECHNOLOGY & VISITORS CENTER

A good historical orientation point to the Westside, this two-phase complex doubles as a **visitor center** (☎ 338-1332; 9565 Kaumuali'i Hwy; admission free; ☺ 9:30am-5pm Mon-Fri) and offers a free, 2½-hour walking tour at 9:30am Mondays.

LUCY WRIGHT PARK

Though this park was the **landing site** of Captain Cook, the people chose to name it in honour of Lucy Wright, a revered schoolteacher. Here you'll find access to the river and beach, as well as camping facilities, though not much in the way of scenery. See p470 for information about camping permits.

KIKI A OLA (MENEHUNE DITCH)

Not much remains to be seen of this unique and still-functional ditch or **aqueduct**, but its archaeological significance begs repeating. It is the only example of precontact cut and dressed stonework in Hawaii, said to be the work of the *menehune*, who completed it within one night for the *ali'i*.

RUSSIAN FORT ELIZABETH

Russia befriended Kaua'i's King Kaumuali'i in the early 1800s; the relationship stood to help Kaumuali'i overcome King Kamehameha, and

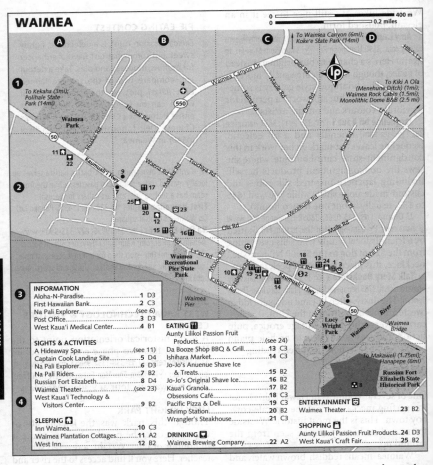

Russians to use Hawaii as an oceangoing stop during their reign as prominent fur traders. The fort was begun in September 1816, but within a year was stopped – perhaps due to King Kamehameha's orders or to general suspicion of the Russians. Hawaiian troops used the fort until 1864. Now its remains look much like a sea-battered lava-rock wall.

Activities

SNORKELING

There are three outfits offering Na Pali Coast snorkel tours from Kikiaola Small Boat Harbour.

our pick Na Pali Riders (☎ 742-6331; www.napali riders.com; 9600 Kaumuali' Hwy; morning tour adult/child $109/98, afternoon tour $87) is hosted by Captain Chris Turner, who is passionate about what he does and likes to think of his tour as being *National Geographic* style. Turner offers an intimate setting, healthy snacks and a CD of photographs and movie taken on the trip, along with the feeling that you're going out with some of your favourite ragamuffin friends.

Liko Ho'okano (☎ 338-0333, 888-732-5456; www .liko-kauai.com; 9875 Waimea Rd; 4hr cruise adult/child 4-12 $120/80) is run by a Kaua'i-born-and-raised Native Hawaiian, whose ancestors hailed from the 'forbidden island' of Ni'ihau. This outfit sails its 49ft power catamaran to the Na Pali Coast. The maxiumum group size is 34 and tours go as far as Ke'e Beach.

Na Pali Explorer (☎ 338-9999, 877-335-9909; www .napali-explorer.com; Kaumuali'i Hwy; 5hr tour adult/child 5-

12 $125/85) does snorkeling trips on rigid-hull inflatable rafts (hard bottom, inflatable sides), smoother than the all-inflatable Zodiacs. Expect between 16 and 35 passengers. The 48ft raft includes a rest room and canopy for shade.

SURFING

Between the 21- and 22-mile markers, you'll notice cars parked on the side of the highway in an area known as Makaweli. This is the access point to the fiercely defended local surf spot dubbed Pakala, or Infinities, said to offer the 'longest lefts' anywhere on-island. It's also teeming with tiger sharks. As it's one of the few locals' breaks left, we'd recommend leaving it alone. Instead, try Kekaha or Polihale beach parks.

MASSAGE & YOGA

A Hideaway Spa (☎ 338-0005; www.ahideawayspa.com; Waimea Plantation Cottages, unit 40, 9400 Kaumuali'i Hwy; massage $95-145; beachside add $20, spa & skin treatments $55-130; ☉ 9am-6pm Mon-Sat) offers traditional Hawaiian massage techniques such as *lomi-lomi* and also features ayurvedic treatments, as well as oceanfront **yoga classes** (☉ 5pm Tue, 8:30am Sat), which are ideal for newbies.

Festivals & Events

Waimea Town Celebration (☎ 338-1332; www.wk bpa.org) Free fun in mid-February includes rodeo, canoe race, food, crafts, and lei and hula competitions.

Waimea Lighted Christmas Parade (☎ 338-9957) Watch lighted floats through Waimea town. Parade starts at dusk, a week before Christmas.

Sleeping
BUDGET & MIDRANGE

Waimea Rock Cabin (☎ 822-7944, 338-9015; www.a1va cations.com/kauaiwaimearockcabin/1; Menehune Rd; cabin per day/week $50/300) If you don't plan on spending a lot of time at home base, this is a great, budget-friendly stay for those who plan to be hiking the canyon. It's about 1.5 miles northeast of town. There's a $50 cleaning fee.

ourpick Coco's Kaua'i B&B (☎ 338-0722; www.cocos kauai.com; btwn 21- & 22-mile markers; cottages $110, incl breakfast $125; P ☒ ☐ ☜) Off the grid (call in advance) and keeping it low-key at this getaway is all part of its appeal. Owned by one of the Robinson family descendants, you're basically on the quiet side of the sugar plantation. It features a king bed, private hot tub, BBQ, air conditioning, garden and kitchenette. There's a minimum two-night stay.

Inn Waimea (☎ 338-0031; www.innwaimea.com; 4469 Halepule Rd; cottages $150, r from $110; P ☜) Perfectly situated in the heart of town, this place is uniquely appointed and offers wheelchair access (it's ADA certified). Thre's a three-night minimum for the cottages and two nights for the room.

West Inn (☎ 338-1107, 866-937-8466; www .thewestinn.com; 9686 Kaumuali'i Hwy; r $139; P ☒ ☜) Likening it to a 'Best Western' is probably the best way to describe this average, clean, two-storey motel-like place, across the street from the Waimea Theater. Choose either king or double bed. Though it has wi-fi, you must have your own network card. For the price, there are better options elsewhere.

Waimea Plantation Cottages (☎ 338-1625, 800-992-7866; www.waimea-plantation.com; 9400 Kaumuali'i Hwy; 1-/2-/3br cottages from $220/275/325; ☜ ☒)These cottages are expensive, no doubt, but charming. The decor offers saliently Westside features, hailing from the tradition of plantation styles while featuring upmarket and modern Hawaiiana-inspired embellishments and several Occidental accoutrements some may not want to live without. The fact that it's a stone's toss from Waimea Brewing Company is a plus for those after a dose of nightlife.

West Kaua'i Guesthouse (☎ 346-5890; www.west kauaihouse.com; apt $135; P ☒ ☜) Fully furnished and air-conditioned, this getaway does share a wall (it's a duplex), but it also has a full kitchen and washer-dryer, as well as charcoal grill. With two bedrooms and one bathroom, it can sleep up to six people. The cleaning fee is $50.

ourpick Monolithic Dome B&B (☎ 651-7009; r $129; P ☜) Located near the Menehune Ditch, this place has got all the modern conveniences you wouldn't associate with a monolithic dome. The bathroom has frescoes on the walls, the queen bed has memory foam and high-thread count sheets, plus there's also wifi throughout. It's roughly 2 miles behind Big Save on the *mauka* side of the road, but you must call in advance. The cleaning fee is $75.

Eating

Obsessions Café (☎ 338-1110; 9875 Waimea Rd; breakfast & lunch $6-7; ☉ 8am-2pm) A much-revered local-style breakfast indulgence – the *loco moco* ($6.95) – is served up here the way it should be: smothered in gravy. Normally a hamburger patty with eggs, the 'ultimate' version here also has Portuguese sausage, cheddar cheese, onions and mushrooms. Lighter fare includes the Chinese chicken salad ($6), but sedation-inducing sandwiches such as the Reuben – with corned beef, sauerkraut and Swiss cheese ($6.75) are the specialty.

Shrimp Station (☎ 338-1242; 9652 Kaumuali'i Hwy; dishes $6-15; 🕙 11am-5pm) If you don't happen to remember that scene in *Forrest Gump* where Bubba rattles off a list of ways to fix shrimp, the menu here might jog your memory. Sautéed scampi-style, beer battered, coconut-flake grilled, in taco form or ground up into a 'shrimp burger' and coupled with papaya-ginger tartar sauce and fries – it's *the* spot for shrimp. It also stocks ice cream and desserts such as push-up rainbow pops and Neapolitan sandwiches.

Da Booze Shop BBQ & Grill (☎ 338-9953; 9883 Waimea Rd; box lunch $7.95, keiki menu $2.40; 🕙 10:30-9pm Mon-Sat, to 5pm Sun) While Da Booze Shop has plate lunches like many other local-style outlets, it's the hickory-smoked BBQ rib specials ($8.50), which combine typical, mainland US meat-eater *grinds* with Westside flair, that appeal. Try the sandwich platter with chicken and pork, rice, macnut salad (of course) and the homemade BBQ sauce, or the thriftier BBQ burger deluxe ($4.50).

Kaua'i Granola (☎ 338-0121; 9633 Kaumuali'i Hwy; www.kauaigranola.com/GranolaHome.html; granola $8; 🕙 10am-5pm) This former piecrust creator for Aunty Lilikoi has found her niche. And you can find sugarcane-sweetened 'sugar cane snax,' tropical trail mixes and dried fruits – ideal for when you're heading up to the canyon. Around Christmas time, don't miss out on her aloha-shirt-clad and hula-skirted gingerbread men and women – they make adorable, edible gifts.

our pick **Ishihara Market** (☎ 338-1751; 9894 Kaumuali'i Hwy; plate lunch $8.75; 🕙 6am-8:30pm Mon-Fri, 7am-8:30pm Sat & Sun) It's an ad hoc lesson in local cuisine perusing this market, which is easily the island's most local eatery. It also has sushi *bentō*, daily specials and marinated ready-to-go meats for those wanting to barbecue. Parking is kind of crazy, so be patient or park on the street and walk the half-block.

Pacific Pizza & Deli (☎ 338-1020; 9850 Kaumuali'i Hwy; pizza $9.35-25; 🕙 11am-9pm Mon-Sat) While the hapa-haole (half-Caucasian) pizza or calzone is a hands-down favourite, with its pesto sauce, sun-dried tomatoes, mushrooms, Canadian bacon, zucchini and pineapple, the supreme still offers some island influence (it includes

Portuguese sausage). The Mexican pizza (refried beans, sour cream, cheese) shouldn't disappoint vegetarians with a craving for abundantly topped slices.

Wrangler's Steakhouse (☎ 338-1218; 9852 Kaumuali'i Hwy; dinner mains $17-25; 🕙 11am-9pm Mon-Fri, 4-9pm Sat) Try it local style: grab a plantation lunch (which starts from $9) in a *kaukau* tin full of shrimp tempura, teriyaki, and BBQ meat, along with rice and kimchi. Included in that price is soup and salad. The restaurant also has a little gift shop where you can buy *kaukau* tins ($30), stackable food containers with three compartments for meat, veg etc – a nice souvenir for local-culture enthusiasts.

Drinking & Entertainment

our pick **Waimea Brewing Company** (☎ 338-9733; www.waimea-plantation.com/brew; Waimea Plantation Cottages, 9400 Kaumuali'i Hwy; 🕙 11am-10pm Sun-Thu, to 2am Fri & Sat) Tiki torches, live music and an inviting plantation-style architecture beckons, as does a long rotating list of tasty microbrews: Wai'ale'ale Golden Ale, *liliko'i* ale, Palaka Porter, Na Pali Pale Ale and Canefire Red. Try a 'sampler platter' for a 6oz taste of all drafts on hand.

Waimea Theater (☎ 338-0282; 9691 Kaumuali'i Hwy; 🕙 7:30pm Wed-Sun) Perfect for a rainy day or early evening reprieve from the sun and sea. Kaua'i is a little behind with the new releases, but as this is one of two functioning theaters on the island, so it's much appreciated. This is also a venue for the Hawaii International Film Festival (www.hiff.org).

Shopping

West Kaua'i Craft Fair (Kaumuali'i Hwy; 🕙 9am-4pm) Just near the entrance to the Old Sugar Mill you'll find Swarovski-crystal Limoges-inspired pillboxes, koa-wood bowls, Ni'ihau-shell leis, local honeys, *malasadas*, pineapples, longan, starfruit, banana, papaya and lychee.

Aunty Lilikoi Passion Fruit Products (☎ 866-545-4564; www.auntylilikoi.com; 9875 Waimea Rd; condiments per 10oz $5; 🕙 10am-5pm) In 2008 Aunty Lilikoi did it again, taking the gold medal in the Napa Valley International Mustard Competition for her *liliko'i*-wasabi mustard, making it clear that if it's a product with *liliko'i*, Aunty's got it down. Find something for almost any occasion: *liliko'i* syrup (great for banana pancakes), *liliko'i* massage oil (great for honeymooners) and the tasty *liliko'i* chap stick (great for après surf).

SHAVE ICE: WHAT'S IN A NAME?

Ah, the drama behind the shave-ice shops that bear the name 'Jo-Jo.' In Waimea, there are two Jo-Jo's businesses, and both claim 'original' status, but for different reasons. To complicate matters, both are across the street from Waimea High School (the one owned by Aunty Jo-Jo, which we prefer, is closer to the ocean).

As with any feud, there are differing versions of events. A 'somewhere-in'the-middle' version of the tale goes something like this: in the 1990s, Aunty Jo-Jo sold her wildly popular, seven-year-old shave ice shop (known as 'Jo-Jo's Clubhouse') to another family. The family bought the shop largely because of the success borne of the household name 'Aunty Jo Jo' had created. Over time, locals began to complain that **Jo-Jo's Original Shave Ice** (☎ 635-7615; 9740 Kaumuali'i Hwy; shave ice $2-4; ☼ 10am-6pm) just wasn't the same (probably due to the fact that the new owners hadn't been given all the old recipes – not for the delectable *haupia* topping, let alone the homemade syrups). Among locals, popularity has dwindled, although tourists still flock to this 'original' Jo-Jo's.

In 2007, Aunty Jo-Jo opened a new shop (catty-corner from her old digs), **Jo-Jo's Anuenue Shave Ice & Treats** (☎ 338-9963; 4491 Pokole Rd; shave ice $4-8; ☼ 11am-5pm), which peeved the people who bought her namesake buisness nearby, although they couldn't produce the contract that they claim includes a noncompete clause. That, coupled with the fact that patrons were becoming annoyed at the new owners' less-than-steadfast dedication toward maintaining a 'local' menu (for example, they seem to be perpetually 'out' of their *halo-halo* ingredients – a Hawaii shave ice staple) and that they're a haole-run business attempting local *grinds*, hasn't helped their odds with residents so far.

KEKAHA
pop 3175

There's no town center in Kekaha (home to many military families), but Kekaha Beach Park offers one of the most beautiful sunsets on the island. If you're looking for a town with a scenic beach near the base of Waimea Canyon, this is nice. It is, however, off the beaten track and too remote for some.

Kaumuali'i Hwy borders the coastline while Kekaha Rd (Hwy 50), the main drag, lies parallel and a few blocks inland. All you'll find in town are a post office and a couple of stores. At its eastern end, Kekaha Rd and Kaumuali'i Hwy meet near the Kikiaola Small Boat Harbor, a state harbour with a launch ramp.

In an area known for its unrelenting sun and vast beaches, the Westside's **Kekaha Beach Park** is no exception. Just west of Kekaha town, this long beach is ideal for running, walking or beachcombing. Before jumping in, find a lifeguard station and make sure it's OK, as the sea here lacks the reef protection other beaches provide. When the surf is high, currents are extremely dangerous. Under the right conditions, it can be good for surfing and bodyboarding.

Sleeping

For more lodging listings, see **Kekaha Oceanside** (www.kekahaoceansidekauai.com).

BUDGET & MIDRANGE

Mindy's Guesthouse (☎ 337-9275; 8842 Kekaha Rd; s/d $75/85; ☞) Adorable, clean and featuring its own private deck – Mindy's is a steal for the price. A 2nd-storey apartment with a full bed, wi-fi and large kitchen feels spacious and open. Though there's no air conditioning, it's got ceiling fans throughout. The price includes fruit and coffee in the morning.

Boathouse Guesthouse (☎ 332-9744; www.seakauai .com; 4518A Nene St; r $85) Within walking distance of Kekaha Beach, the Boathouse is much like staying in the guesthouse of your favourite (and clean) neighbours. Though a studio, it feels spacious and has its own covered lanai, kitchenette, king bed and TV. Ideal for one person or couple, with a washer-dryer on-site.

Hale Puka 'Ana B&B (☎ 652-6852; 8240A Elepaio Rd; www.kekahakauaisunset.com; ste $169-229; ☶ ☒ ☐ ☞) There are three choices here: the high end Ali'i Suite ($229 plus tax) has ocean views, a private lanai, cherrywood and bamboo-inspired fixtures; the Hoku Suite ($199 plus tax) also has ocean views, but is smaller; the Ku'uipo Suite ($169 plus tax) is on the ground floor. Included breakfasts range from healthy (fresh fruit) to guilty pleasure (bacon and egg on a croissant) with coffee, tea and juice.

KAUA'I

BARKING SANDS

Between Kekaha Beach Park and Polihale State Park, the beach stretches for approximately 15 miles. However, since the September 11, 2001 terrorist attacks, consistent public access has waned, as it is home to the US navy base at **Barking Sands Pacific Missile Range Facility** (PMRF; ☎ general information 335-4229, beach access 335-4111). The missile-range facility at Barking Sands provides the aboveground link to a sophisticated sonar network that tracks more than 1000 sq miles of the Pacific. Established during WWII, it's been developed into the world's largest underwater listening device.

POLIHALE BEACH PARK

A rugged access road and inconsistent weather have made this state park somewhat of a headache for the Department of Land & Natural Resources, which closed off the beach for several months in 2008 and consequently prohibited camping, after flooding created potential health risks.

There aren't any car-rental vendors who offer insurance for visitors to drive the 5-mile-long dirt road that accesses the park from Mana village off Kaumuali'i Hwy, another snag in the debate over universal access rights to this surfing haven. Locals threatened to protest when a gate was put up to keep visitors out last year, claiming they know the area better than nonresidents and should therefore be allowed access.

Whether you decide to drive for a day trip or more, it's worth remembering that camping is, at times, allowed with a permit, although the entryway, toilet and shower facilities access are inconsistent – and finding a ride back should your rental transport fail is risky.

WAIMEA CANYON STATE PARK

Of all Kaua'i's unique wonders, none can touch Waimea Canyon for utter grandeur. While one expects to find tropical beaches and gardens here, few expect a gargantuan chasm of ancient lava rock, 13 miles long and 2500ft deep to the riverbed (or 3700ft above sea level). Flowing through the canyon is the Waimea River, Kaua'i's longest, which is fed by three eastern tributaries that bring reddish-brown waters from the mountaintop bog, Alaka'i Swamp.

Waimea Canyon was formed when Kaua'i's original shield volcano, Wai'ale'ale,

slumped along an ancient fault line, creating a sharp east-facing line of cliffs. Then another shield volcano, Lihu'e, developed the island's east side, producing new lava flows that ponded against the cliffs. Thus the western canyon walls are taller, thinner and more eroded – a contrast most theatrically apparent while hiking along the canyon floor. The black and red horizontal striations along the canyon walls represent successive volcanic eruptions; the red color indicates that water seeped through the rocks, creating rust from the iron inside.

Drives on a clear day are phenomenal. But don't be disappointed by rain, as that's what makes the waterfalls gush. Sunny days following rain are ideal for prime views, though slick mud makes it a challenge.

The southern boundary of Waimea Canyon State Park is about 6 miles up the road from Waimea. You can reach the park by two roads: Waimea Canyon Dr (Hwy 550) starts in Waimea just beyond the 23-mile marker, while Koke'e Rd (Hwy 552) starts in Kekaha off Mana Rd. They merge between the 6-mile and 7-mile markers.

State officials generally prefer visitors to use Waimea Canyon Dr, which is 19 miles long and passes the canyon lookouts with terrific views into Kalalau Valley on the Na Pali Coast. Koke'e Rd is shorter by 3 miles and also offers scenic views, but not of the canyon.

Dangers & Annoyances

Rain creates hazardous conditions in the canyon. The red-dirt trails quickly become slick and river fords rise to impassable levels. Try hiking poles or a sturdy walking stick to ease the steep descent into the canyon.

Note the time of sunset and plan to return well before dark. Note that daylight will fade inside the canyon long before sunset.

While packing light is recommended, take enough water for your entire trip, especially the uphill return journey. Do not drink fresh water along the trails without treating it. Cell phones do not work here. If possible, hike with a companion or at least tell someone your expected return time.

Sights

Along Waimea Canyon Dr, you can see naturally growing examples of native trees, including koa and ohia, as well as invasive species such as kiawe. The valuable hardwood koa proliferates at the hunter's check station along the way. Look for the trees with narrow, crescent-shaped leaves.

SCENIC LOOKOUTS

At 0.3 miles north of the 10-mile marker, and an elevation of 3400ft, is the **Waimea Canyon Lookout** – the most scenic of the lookout points. Keep your eyes peeled for the canyon running in an easterly direction off Waimea, which is Koai'e Canyon. That area is accessible to backcountry hikers.

The 800ft waterscape known as **Waipo'o Falls** can be seen from a couple of small, unmarked lookouts before the 12-mile marker and then from a lookout opposite the picnic area shortly before the 13-mile marker. The picnic area includes BBQ pits, rest rooms, drinking water, a pay phone and Camp Hale Koa, a Seventh Day Adventist camp. **Pu'u Hinahina Lookout**, at 3640ft, offers two lookouts near the parking lot at a marked turnoff between the 13- and 14-mile markers, while **Pu'u o Kila Lookout**, located past Kalalau Lookout, is the start of the Pihea Trail. Sometimes the road is closed.

At mile marker 18 is the view of the Kalalau Valley from **Kalalau Lookout**, the largest of the Na Pali. Views from the lookout change minute by minute, depending on the ever-present clouds. At 4000ft elevation, the air here is much cooler than along the coast or in the valleys – so bring a sweatshirt or jacket.

Activities
HIKING

Enjoy several, rugged trails that lead deep into Waimea Canyon: keep in mind they're shared with pig and deer hunters and that it's most busy during weekends and holidays.

The Kukui and Koai'e Canyon trails, two of the steepest on Kaua'i, connect at Wiliwili Camp, 2000ft into the canyon. If the entire trek sounds too strenuous, hike just 1 mile down the Kukui Trail, as you'll reach a bench with an astounding view.

The hiking mileage given for each following trail is for one-way only.

Iliau Nature Loop

This trail was named for the *iliau*, a plant endemic to Kaua'i's Westside, which grows along the route and produces stalks up to 10ft

high. Canyon walls, waterfalls and bursting *iliau* are all reasons to give it a try.

The marked trailhead for the 10-minute Iliau Nature Loop comes up shortly before the 9-mile marker. Be sure to pass the bench to the left and walk about three minutes for a top-notch vista into Waimea Canyon.

Kukui Trail

Don't let the fact that it's 2.5 miles in (five total) fool you. The climb back out of the valley can be harrowing – it's definitely for seriously fit and agile hikers only. The narrow switchback trail covers 2000ft and doesn't offer much in the way of sweeping views, though there's a river at the canyon floor.

Keep your eyes peeled for a small sign directing hikers to turn left, and hike the steep slope down, with the hill at your back.

When you hear the sound of water, you're closing in on the picnic shelter and Wiliwili Camp area, where overnight camping is allowed, but mostly hunters stay.

To get there, find the Iliau Nature Loop trailhead just before the 9-mile marker. It officially starts just beyond it at a hunter checking station on the right.

Kalalau Lookout to Pu'u 'o Kila Lookout

This mellow, 2-mile hike offers a pleasant walk along the closed road linking two lookouts. A two-lane strip of asphalt, currently closed to traffic, connects the park's premier viewpoints of the Kalalau Valley, and in early morning and late afternoon, as the fog is wafting overhead, it is a delightful birding walk. You won't see as many species as in the forest itself, but it's worth the amble.

Koai'e Canyon Trail

Further along about 0.5 mile from the Kukui Trail is the Koai'e Canyon Trail (6 miles round-trip), a moderate trail that takes you down the south side of the canyon to some swimming holes – which are best avoided after rain, because of incredibly quickly rising waters and hazardous flash floods.

The trail offers three camps. After the first, Kaluaha'ulu Camp, stay on the eastern bank of the river – do not cross it. Later you'll come upon the overgrown Na Ala Hele trailhead for the Koai'e Canyon Trail. Watch for greenery and soil that conceals drop-offs alongside the path.

KAUA'I

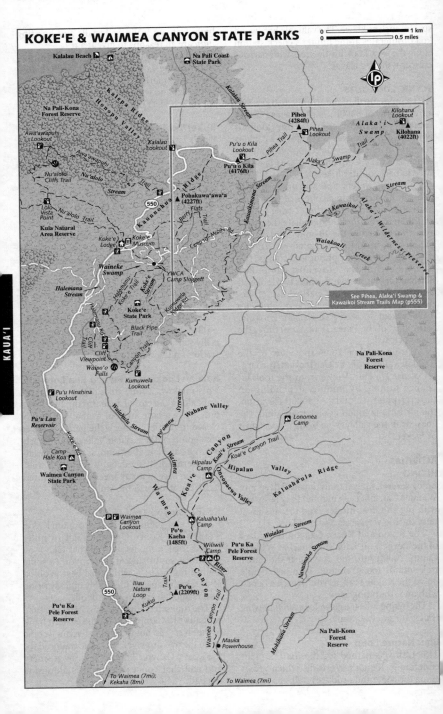

KOKE'E & WAIMEA CANYON STATE PARKS

0 ————— 1 km
0 ————— 0.5 miles

Kalalau Beach

Na Pali Coast State Park

Na Pali-Kona Forest Reserve

Honopu Valley

Kalepa Ridge

'Awa'awapuhi Lookout

Kalalau Stream

Kalalau Lookout

Nu'alolo Cliffs Trail

'Awa'awapuhi Trail

Nu'alolo Stream

Pihea (4284ft)

Pihea Lookout

Alaka'i Swamp

Kilohana Lookout

Kilohana (4022ft)

Pu'u o Kila Lookout

Pihea Trail

Alaka'i Swamp

Alaka'i Swamp

Pu'u o Kila (4176ft)

Kawaikinana Stream

Alaka'i Stream

Alaka'i Wilderness Preserve

Lolo Vista Point

Nu'alolo Trail

Kaunuohua Ridge

550

Pohakuwa'awa'a (4227ft)

Berry Flats

Kawaikoi

Waiakoali

Kawaikoi Creek

Kuia Natural Area Reserve

Koke'e Lodge

Koke'e Museum

Camp of Mokihana Rd

See Pihea, Alaka'i Swamp & Kawaikoi Stream Trails Map (p555)

Waineke Swamp

YWCA Camp Sloggett

Halemanu Stream

Halemanu-Koke'e Trail

Koke'e Stream

Koke'e State Park

Kumuwela Ridge

Na Pali-Kona Forest Reserve

Halemanu Rd

Black Pipe Trail

Cliff Trail

Cliff Viewpoint

Canyon Trail

Kumuwela Lookout

Waipo'o Falls

Pu'u Hinahina Lookout

Waialulu Stream

Po'omau Stream

Wahane Valley

Lonomea Camp

Pu'u Lua Reservoir

Koke'e Rd

Camp Hale Koa

Waimea Canyon State Park

Waimea Canyon

Koaie

Koaie Stream

Koaie Canyon Trail

Hipalau Camp

Waimea

Hipalau Valley

Kaluaha'ula Ridge

Oneapuewa Valley

Waimea Canyon Lookout

Kaluaha'ulu Camp

Po'o Kaeha (1485ft)

Wiliwili Camp

Pu'u Ka Pele Forest Reserve

Waialae Stream

Nawaimaka Stream

Waimea River

550

Iliau Nature Loop

Kukui Trail

Pu'u (2209ft)

Waimea Canyon Trail

Canyon

Mokihana Stream

Na Pali-Kona Forest Reserve

Pu'u Ka Pele Forest Reserve

Mauka Powerhouse

To Waimea (7mi); Kekaha (8mi)

To Waimea (7mi)

KAUA'I

TOP PICKS – WESTSIDE HIKES

- Iliau Nature Loop (p551)
- Pihea Trail to Alaka'i Swamp Trail p556)
- Nu'alolo Cliffs Trail (p556)
- 'Awa'awapuhi Trail (p556)
- Canyon Trail (p555)
- Okolehao Trail (p515)

Next up is Hipalau Camp. Following this the trail is hard to find. Keep heading north. Do not veer toward the river, but continue ascending at approximately the same point midway between the canyon walls and the river.

Growing steeper, the trail then enters Koai'e Canyon, recognizable by the red-rock walls rising to the left. The last camp is Lonomea. Find the best views at the emergency helipad, a grassy area perfect for picnicking. When ready, retrace your steps.

Waimea Canyon Trail

A difficult trail in this area is the 11.5-mile (one-way) Waimea Canyon Trail, which fords Waimea River. It starts at the bottom of Waimea Canyon at the end of Kukuio Trail and leads out to Waimea town. An entry permit is required at the self-service box at the Kukui Trail register.

You might see locals carrying inner tubes so they can exit via the river rather than hiking back out.

CYCLING

Coast downhill for 13 miles, from the rim of Waimea Canyon (elevation 3500ft) to sea level with **Outfitters Kaua'i** (☎ 742-9667, 888-742-9887; www.outfitterskauai.com; Po'ipu Plaza, 2827A Po'ipu Rd, Po'ipu; tour adult/child 12-14 $94/75; ☺ check-in 6am & 2:30pm), who will supply all the necessary cruisers, helmets and snacks. Remember, you'll be a target for the setting sun during the afternoon ride.

Mountain bikers can also find miles of bumpy, 4WD hunting-area roads off Waimea Canyon Dr. Even when the yellow gates are closed on nonhunting days, cyclists are still allowed to go around and use them – except for Papa'alai Rd, which is managed by the Department of Hawaiian Home Lands and open for hunting, but not recreational use.

Sleeping

All four camps on the canyon trails are part of the forest reserve system. They have open-air picnic shelters and pit toilets, but no other facilities; all freshwater must be treated before drinking. See p470 for camping permit information.

KOKE'E STATE PARK

The expansive Koke'e State Park is a playground to those who revere the environment. Home to inspirational views, it also offers an abundance of plant life and animals. You'll also enjoy some reprieve from the sun and no doubt the microclimates will leave you paying attention to the shifts in ambient air.

In ancient times, only Hawaiian bird catchers resided up in this part of the island. The trail that once ran down the cliffs from Koke'e (ko-*keh*-eh) to Kalalau Valley on the Na Pali Coast is extraordinarily steep, and has taken the life of at least one Western trekker. Though one of the park's locally revered charms is its choppy, almost impossible 4WD roads, the state has been working (despite misgivings by many Kaua'i residents) to pave much of Koke'e. Advocates against this decision have argued it would rob the area of its reclusively rugged character.

Another potential moneymaker (of equally controversial status) is the state's plan to further modernize Koke'e by adding a helicopter landing pad, which would, in turn, increase air-tourism revenues.

Orientation & Information

This park's boundary starts beyond the Pu'u Hinahina Lookout. After the 15-mile marker, you'll pass a brief stretch of park cabins, restaurant, museum and campground.

The helpful people at the Koke'e Museum sell inexpensive trail maps and provide basic information on trail conditions; you can also call them for real-time **mountain weather reports** (☎ 335-9975).

Remember, the nearest place for provisions and gas is Waimea, 15 miles away.

Dangers & Annoyances

All of the suggestions listed for Waimea Canyon State Park (p550) apply. Further, the higher elevation produces a cooler and wetter climate, so take appropriate attire.

KAUA'I

CAMPING IN KOKE'E

Even though it's Hawaii, don't be fooled into thinking you'll be warm all the time. Koke'e campgrounds are at an elevation of almost 4000ft, and nights are cold. Take a sleeping bag, waterproof jacket, change of warm clothing, extra socks and hiking shoes (instead of sneakers). See p561 for further details on the camping options.

The most accessible camping area is the **Koke'e State Park Campground**, which is north of the meadow, just a few minutes' walk from Koke'e Lodge. The campsites sit in a grassy area beside the woods, (perfect for laying out a blanket and taking a nap) along with picnic tables, drinking water, rest rooms and showers. Further off the main track, **Kawaikoi** and **Sugi Grove** campgrounds are about 4 miles east of Koke'e Lodge, off the 4WD-only Camp 10–Mohihi Rd in the forest reserve adjacent to the state park. Each campground has pit toilets, picnic shelters and fire pits. There's no water source, so you'll need to bring your own or treat the stream water. These forest-reserve campgrounds have a three-night maximum stay and require camping permits (free) in advance from the Division of Forestry & Wildlife.

The Kawaikoi campground sits on a well-maintained 3.5-acre grassy field, and it is recommended if you are camping in a large group (ie 10 or more). The Sugi Grove site is picturesque, under Sugi trees (commonly called a pine but actually a cedar), a fragrant softwood native to Japan. This site is shaded, making it ideal during hot summer months, and it is closer to Kawaikoi stream.

Sights

KOKE'E MUSEUM

At this **museum** (☎ 335-9975; www.kokee.org; entry by donation $1; ☒ 10am-4pm) you'll find detailed topographical maps, local historical photographs and a tribute to the late photographer and educator David Boynton (and contributor to Lonely Planet), who died in 2007 after he was hiking along a cliff trail to one of his most cherished spots on the Na Pali coastline.

You also can obtain a brochure for the short nature trail out back. It offers interpretive information corresponding to the trail's numbered plants and trees, including many native species. You'll probably notice in front an array of chickens who have in the past decade polluted the pristine Koke'e mornings with noise. Please don't feed them.

KALALAU LOOKOUTS

Look for the 18-mile marker, where the ethereal 4000ft **Kalalau Lookout** stands up to the ocean, sun and winds with brave, severe beauty.

Hope for a clear day for ideal views, but know that even a rainy day can make for some settling clouds that could later disappear – followed by powerful waterfalls, and, of course, rainbows.

Though it might be hard to imagine as the terrain is so extreme, as late as the 1920s Kalalau Valley was home to many residents – who farmed rice there, no less.

The only way into the valley nowadays is along the coastal Kalalau Trail (p525) from Ha'ena on the North Shore or by kayak (p519).

The paved road continues another mile to Pu'u o Kila Lookout, where it dead-ends at a parking lot. This road faces periodic closings.

Hiking

Generally speaking, Koke'e is unspoiled. Its sheer size might make it a bit challenging to nail down where you want to start. Know that if you want to avoid hunters (and their dogs), it's best to opt for trails like Alaka'i Swamp or the Cliff Trail to Waipo'o Falls; though those might have some other hikers on it, they're still relatively remote. Koke'e boasts 45 miles of trails that range from delving deep into the rain forest or merely skimming the perimeter, with views that can cause a vertiginous reaction in even the most avid mountain-sport enthusiasts.

Trekking around Koke'e offers a rare view at an abundance of endemic species of wildlife and plants, including the largest population of Kaua'i's native fern, the fragrant *laua'e*, alluded to in many of the island's chants and traditions. Also here you might see some of Kaua'i's rare and endangered native forest birds.

The starting point for several scenic hikes, Halemanu Rd is just north of the 14-mile marker on Waimea Canyon Dr. Whether or not the road is passable in a non-4WD vehicle depends on recent rainfall. Note that many rental-car agreements are null and void when off-roading.

During summer weekends, trained volunteers lead **Wonder Walks** (nominal donation; Jun-Sep), guided hikes on various trails at Waimea Canyon and Koke'e State Parks. Contact the **museum** (☎ 335-9975; www.kokee.org) for schedules and reservations.

CLIFF & CANYON TRAILS

The **Cliff Trail** (0.1 miles), is a perfect intro to the canyon's vast views. Being short, it's a relatively easy walk for the rewarding Waimea Canyon views it offers.

The **Canyon Trail** (1.8 miles) continues from there; you'll go down a semisteep forest trail, a grove, a lugelike tunnel that opens up to a vast, red-dirt promontory with cliffs to one side and charming log-steps to guide you further. Shortly thereafter it takes some steep finagling to get to **Waipo'o Falls**. If that's too much, you can always turn back around here. To get to the trailhead, walk down Halemanu Rd for just over 0.5 miles. Keeping Halemanu Stream

to your left, ignore a hunting trail-of-use on the right. Then turn right onto the footpath leading to both the Cliff and Canyon Trails. At the next junction, the Cliff Trail veers right and wanders for less than 0.25 miles uphill to the Cliff Viewpoint.

For the Canyon Trail, backtrack to the previous junction. Note to avoid holding onto any foliage for stability. Otherwise, after hopping boulders across the stream, follow the trail to **Kumuwela Ridge** at the canyon rim. The trail ends at **Kumuwela Lookout**, where you can rest at a picnic table before backtracking to Halemanu Rd.

Black Pipe Trail

To vary your return from Canyon Trail, make a right at the intersection of Black Pipe Trail and Canyon Trail at the top of the switchback where you leave the canyon rim. The trail ends at the 4WD-only Halemanu Rd, where you walk back to the Canyon trailhead.

Halemanu-Koke'e Trail

Another trail off Halemanu Rd, which starts further down the road than the Cliff and

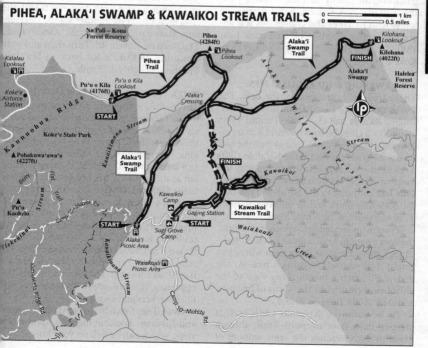

PIHEA, ALAKA'I SWAMP & KAWAIKOI STREAM TRAILS

ALAKA'I SWAMP

A sort of soggy paradise, nothing really provides that out-of-the-ordinary experience the way a hike along the Alaka'i Swamp, designated a wilderness preserve in 1964, does. Almost the entire trail is linked with wood planks, to help encourage use of the approved trail and to discourage off-trail trekking. The Department of Land & Natural Resources' Forestry & Wildlife Division started laying planks around 1989 – a time-consuming (and crazy, according to some) process that was delayed when Hurricane 'Iniki hit in 1992. Today the project continues, with a plan to cover more of the Pihea Trail.

You'll traverse truly fantastic terrain on this hike – misty bogs where plants will dwarf you. On a clear day, look for outstanding views of the Wainiha Valley and whales breaching in the ocean in the distance. If it's raining, don't fret: search for rainbows, enjoy the mist and respect the area by avoiding loud talking with your fellow hikers. This is a spiritual place: Queen Emma was said to have been so moved by tales from the Alaka'i she ventured there, only to chant in reverence during the sojourn.

The Kaua'i 'o'o, the last of four species of Hawaiian honey eaters, was thought to be extinct until a nest with two chicks was discovered in Alaka'i Swamp in 1971. Sadly, the call of the 'o'o – that of a single male – was last heard in 1987.

Canyon Trails, is Halemanu-Koke'e Trail (1.25 miles). An easy recreational nature trail, it passes through a native forest of koa and ohia trees, which provide a habitat for native birds. One of the common plants found on this trail is banana poka, a member of the passion-fruit family and an invasive pest. It has pretty pink flowers, but it drapes the forest with its vines and chokes out less aggressive native plants. The trail ends near YWCA Camp Sloggett, about 0.5 miles from Koke'e Lodge.

AWA'AWAPUHI & NU'ALOLO CLIFFS

These trails offer the best of the best. The **Awa'awapuhi Trail** (3.25 miles) and the more challenging **Nu'alolo Trail** (3.75 miles) afford views along 2000ft cliffs. Perhaps nowhere is more exhilarating (and vertigo-inducing) than the spot where the trails connect – the Nu'alolo Cliffs Trail (2 miles) has points where you may feel more of an acrobat than a hiker! The **Nu'alolo Cliffs Trail** connects to the Nu'alolo Trail near the 3.25-mile mark and to the Awa'awapuhi Trail just short of the 3-mile mark.

If you're undecided as to which trail to take, the Awa'awapuhi Trail is much less technical – though there are some steep steps where you might find yourself hugging a tree. At the end you'll reach a breathtaking view of the cliffs below (much like the 'Cliffs of Insanity' featured in *The Princess Bride*).

To be sure, the Nu'alolo Cliff Trail is steeper than Awa'awapuhi Trail, though arguably each requires the same amount of endurance. To do this 11-mile hike as a loop, begin with the Nu'alolo Trail (trailhead is just south of Koke'e Museum) and hike to the bottom of the ridge and look for a sign that says 'Nu'alolo Cliff Trail.' Follow that right, scaling rocks and cutting through tall, eye-level grass, back up through several switchbacks, up through a ridge until it intersects with the Awa'awapuhi Trail, another signed intersection. Make a right following the 'Awa'awapuhi Trailhead on Koke'e Rd. Turn right and walk alongside of Koke'e Rd back to Nu'alolo Trailhead roughly 0.75 mile.

PIHEA TRAIL TO ALAKA'I SWAMP TRAIL

This 6-mile round-trip trek begins at Pu'u o Kila Lookout. A mere 1 mile in and you'll see the **Pihea Lookout**. Past the lookout and a short scramble downhill the boardwalk begins. After another 1.5 miles you will come to a **crossing** with the Alaka'i Swamp Trail. A left at this crossing will put you on that trail to the **Kilohana Lookout**. Continuing straight on the Pihea Trail will take to you the Kawaikoi campground along the Kawaikoi stream. Most hikers start on the Pihea Trail because the trailhead is accessible by the paved road to Pu'u o Kila Lookout; however, sometimes this road is closed. For another trailhead, begin at the Alaka'i Swamp Trail starting point (see opposite). The trails are well maintained, with mile markers and signs.

Note: The stretch between Alaka'i Crossing and Kilohana Lookout includes hundreds of steps, which can be hell on your knees.

KAUA'I

ALAKA'I SWAMP TRAIL

The Alaka'i Swamp trailhead begins on a ridge above Sugi Grove on Camp 10–Mohihi Rd. While this trailhead covers less steep terrain than the beginning of the Pihea trailhead, you will need a 4WD to get there, as well as the ability to follow a map along an unmarked dirt road.

Parking at the clearing at the trailhead, the trail begins as a wide grassy path for roughly 0.5 miles where the boardwalk begins and continues through small bogs and intermittent forests until you reach the **Alaka'i Crossing**, where the Pihea and Alaka'i Swamp trails intersect. Continuing straight through the crossing, the boardwalk becomes a series of steep steps to the Kawaikoi Stream and a steep series of switchbacks up the other side. Past there the boardwalk is relatively flat, continuing through the almost otherworldly terrain of the Hawaiian Bogs of knee-high trees and tiny endemic carnivorous plants.

The boardwalk ends at Kilohana Lookout, where, with a little bit of luck, you will see views of Wainiha Valley, and beyond to Hanalei Bay.

KAWAIKOI STREAM TRAIL

Go to Sugi Grove by going down Camp 10 Rd (4WD only) and crossing **Kawaikoi Stream**. It's a nice little nature walk that follows the stream through the forest and rises up on a bluff at the end of the stream and then loops around back down to the stream at a cold dark swimming hole and then returns you back to where you started.

Festivals & Events

Hula *halau* from all over Hawaii participate in the one-day **Eo e Emalani I Alaka'i** (335-9975; www.kokee.org/details.html), an outdoor dance festival at Koke'e Museum in early October that reenacts the historic 1871 journey of Queen Emma to Alaka'i Swamp. The festival includes a royal procession, hula, music and crafts.

Sleeping & Eating

For camping options, see p554.

Koke'e State Park Cabins (335-6061; cabin $50) Minimally maintained, the 12 cabins are for folks seeking a remote, rustic and somewhat grimy experience. Chalk it up to reliving dorm life (minus the phone, TV or loud music). All cabins include a double and four twin beds, kitchen, shower, wood stove (your only heat source), linens and blankets.

YWCA Camp Sloggett (245-5959; www.camping kauai.com; campsites per person $15, dm $25, 1br cabin $85) Choose either a cabin or bunkhouse, or camp on the grass. The cabin has a king bed, full kitchen, bathroom and woodburning fireplace, while the bunker has a kitchenette, two bathrooms and a fire pit. You provide the sleeping bags and towels. To tent camp, no reservations are needed.

Koke'e Lodge (335-6061; snacks $3-7; 9am-3:30pm) This restaurant's strong point is convenience. Still, convenience goes a long way up in Koke'e, where you're a 30-minute drive away from other dining out options. Expect cereal, diner-food and a gift shop with souvenirs and a small assortment of sundries for sale if you forgot toiletries

KAUA'I

PAPAHANAUMOKUAKEA MARINE NATIONAL MONUMENT

On June 15, 2006, President Bush declared the Northwestern Hawaiian Islands (NWHI) the USA's first Marine National Monument. Encompassing around 140,000 sq miles and containing 33 islands and atolls, it is now the largest protected marine area in the world, seven times larger than all US marine sanctuaries combined.

The NWHI begin about 155 miles northwest of Kaua'i and stretch for 1200 miles. They contain the largest and healthiest coral-reef system in the US, which is home to 7000 marine species. Half of fish species and a quarter of all species are endemic to Hawaii, and new species are discovered on every scientific voyage. NWHI is also a rare 'predator-dominated ecosystem,' in which sharks, groupers and others make up over 50% of the biomass (compared to 3% in the main Hawaiian islands). The islands also support around 14 million seabirds, including 19 species of native seabirds, and they are the primary breeding ground for the endangered Hawaiian monk seal (p92) and green sea turtles.

However, the islands are not absolutely pristine. Pacific Ocean currents bring an estimated 45 to 60 tons of debris to the islands annually, and cleanups from 1998 to 2008 have removed over 560 tons of entangled fishing nets, plastic bottles and trash.

The NWHI are grouped into 10 island clusters, which contain atolls (low sandy islands formed on top of coral reefs) and some single-rock islands. From east to west, the clusters are Nihoa Island, Mokumanamana (Necker Island), French Frigate Shoals, Gardner Pinnacles, Maro Reef, Laysan Island, Lisianski Island, Pearl and Hermes Atoll, Midway Atoll and Kure Atoll. The total land area of the Northwestern Hawaiian Islands is just under 5 sq miles.

Human history on the islands extends back to the first Polynesian voyagers to arrive in Hawaii. In modern times, the most famous island has been, of course, Midway Atoll, which remains the only island open to visitors.

Today, the monument is being managed in a unique joint effort by three agencies: the National Oceanic & Atmospheric Administration, the US Fish & Wildlife Service, and the Hawaii Department of Land & Natural Resources. However, the monument's 15-year management plan, approved in December 2008, has already raised concerns among Native Hawaiian groups and the Sierra Club. The plan exempts from its regulations the US military (which conducts missile tests and Navy training within monument waters), and the plan allows for increasing visits to Midway and trips for scientific research – all of which could damage areas the monument is charged with preserving.

NIHOA & MOKUMANAMANA

Nihoa and Mokumanamana (Necker Island), the two islands closest to Kaua'i, were home to Native Hawaiians from around AD 1000 to 1700. Nearly 150 archaeological sites have been identified, including stone temple platforms, house sites, terraces, burial caves and carved stone images. Speculation is that about 175 people may have lived on Nihoa and traveled to the much smaller Mokumanamana for religious ceremonies.

That anyone could live at all on these rocks is remarkable. Nihoa is only 1 sq km in size, and Mokumanamana is one-sixth that size. Nihoa juts from the sea steeply, like a broken tooth, and is the tallest of the Northwestern Hawaiian Islands, with one peak reaching 903ft.

Two endemic land birds live on Nihoa. The Nihoa finch, which – like the Laysan finch – is a raider of other birds' eggs, has a population of a few thousand. The gray Nihoa millerbird, related to the Old World warbler family, numbers between 300 and 700.

FRENCH FRIGATE SHOALS

With 67 acres of land surrounded by 230,000 acres of coral reef, the French Frigate Shoals contains the monument's greatest variety of coral (over 41 species). It is also where most of Hawaii's green sea turtles and Hawaiian monk seals come to nest. The reef forms a classic comma-shaped atoll on top of an eroded volcano, in the center of which the 135ft-tall La Perouse Pinnacle rises like a ship; this rock was named after the French explorer who was almost wrecked here in 1786. A small sand island, Tern Island is dominated by an airfield, which was built as a refueling stop during WWII. Today, Tern Island is a US Fish & Wildlife Service field station housing two full-time refuge managers and a few volunteers.

LAYSAN ISLAND

Not quite 1.5 sq miles, Laysan is the second-biggest of the Northwestern Hawaiian Islands. The grassy island has the most bird species in the monument, and to see the huge flocks of Laysan albatross, shearwaters and curlews – plus the endemic Laysan duck chasing brine flies around the supersalty inland lake – you'd never know how close this island came to becoming a barren wasteland.

Beginning in the late 19th century, humans began frequenting Laysan to mine phosphate-rich guano – or bird droppings – to use as fertilizer; they also killed hundreds of thousands of albatross for their feathers (to adorn hats) and took eggs for albumen, a substance used in photo processing. Albatross lay just one egg a year, so an 'egging' sweep could destroy an entire year's hatch. Traders built structures and brought pack mules and, oddly enough, pet rabbits.

The rabbits ran loose and multiplied (as is their wont), and within 20 years their nibbling destroyed 21 of the island's 25 plant species. Without plants, three endemic Laysan land birds – the Laysan flightless rail, Laysan honeycreeper and Laysan millerbird – perished. About 100 Laysan finches and the last 11 Laysan ducks seemed doomed to follow. Then, in 1909, public outcry led President Theodore Roosevelt to create the Hawaiian Islands Bird Reservation, and the Northwestern Hawaiian Islands have been under some kind of protection ever since.

By 1923 every last rabbit was removed, and the rehabilitation of Laysan began. Incredibly, with weed-abatement assistance, native plantlife recovered, and so did the birds. The Laysan finch is again common, and the Laysan duck numbers about 300 (another small population has been established on Midway). About 160,000 pairs of Laysan albatross now live on the island, making it again one of the world's largest colonies. Nearly the same sequence of events unfolded on nearby Lisianski Island and, together, these islands are a success story that Fish & Wildlife officials consider one of their finest achievements.

MIDWAY ISLANDS

The Midway Islands were an important naval air station during WWII, but they are best known as the site of a pivotal battle in June 1942, when American forces surprised an attacking Japanese fleet and defeated it. This victory is credited with turning the tide in the Pacific theater. Postwar, Midway became a staging point for Cold War air patrols.

By 1996 the military no longer needed Midway, and transferred jurisdiction to the US Fish & Wildlife Service (FWS). Before leaving, it conducted an extensive cleanup program to remove debris, contaminants, rats and nonnative plants. Midway was then developed for tourism: barracks became hotel rooms, the mess hall a cafeteria. A museum and restaurant were added. A gym, theater (for movies), bowling alley and library were part of the original military facility. On Sand Island, various military structures (like gun emplacements) were designated a National Historical Landmark. Until 2002, up to 100 visitors a day were allowed, then the concessionaire pulled out (due to financial losses) and visitation ended. Today, it has resumed.

The prime highlight at Midway is the more than two million seabirds who nest here, including the world's largest colony of Laysan albatross, which are so thick between November and July that they virtually blanket the ground. Also, Midway's coral reefs are unusually rich and are frequented by dolphins, sea turtles and Hawaiian monk seals.

VISITING THE MONUMENT

The **Papahanaumokuakea Marine National Monument** (www.hawaiireef.noaa.gov) can be visited online or in Hilo, Hawai'i, at the **Mokupapapa Discovery Center** (p290). In 2008, regular visitation to Midway had resumed. Facilities are managed by the **US Fish & Wildlife Service** (www.fws.gov/midway), which issues visitation permits to organizations that comply with regulations. Current facilities and visitor impacts are being closely monitored, so expect changes. For now, the **Oceanic Society** (☎ 800-326-7491; www.oceanic-society.org) offers a dozen one-week trips a year from November through June (to coincide with albatross season). Group sizes are kept to 15 people, and trips cost around $5000 per person (you fly from Honolulu).

Good places to learn more about the monument include **Northwestern Hawaiian Islands Multi-Agency Education Project** (www.hawaiianatolls.org) and **Kahea** (www.kahea.org/nwhi).

Directory

CONTENTS

ACCOMMODATIONS

With prices to suit all budgets, Hawaii accommodations are as varied as they come – choose from campgrounds, rustic cabins, hostels, rural and upscale B&Bs, a wide range of hotels, all-inclusive resorts, condominiums and 'vacation rental' homes.

During high season – mid-December through March and June through August – lodgings are the most expensive and in demand. In low or shoulder seasons expect discounts and easier booking, though family-friendly resorts rarely lower their rates. Certain big holidays (p566) and major events (p27) command premium prices, and for these, lodgings can book up a year ahead. Reviews throughout this book note when there are large fluctuations between high- and low-season rates. Also, large hotels and resorts in tourist hot spots commonly offer year-round internet specials well below advertised 'rack rates.'

That said, jockeying for the 'best rate' in Hawaii is a popular sport that some elevate to an avocation. Be bold and inquisitive; work every angle you can think of. Also check out **Trip Advisor** (www.tripadvisor.com) for accommodations reviews and traveler advice.

For last-minute deals:
- www.expedia.com
- www.hotels.com
- www.hotwire.com
- www.orbitz.com
- www.priceline.com
- www.travelocity.com

In this guide, unless otherwise stated our reviews indicate high-season rates for single occupancy doubles or, when there's no difference in the rate for one or two people, simply the room. A double room in our budget category usually costs $100 or less; midrange doubles cost $100 to $250; and top-end rooms start at $250.

Unless noted, breakfast is *not* included, bathrooms are private and all lodging is open year-round; rates generally don't include taxes of a whopping 11.41%.

For an explanation of the icons and abbreviations used in this book see the Quick Reference on the inside front cover.

A reservation guarantees your room, but most reservations require a deposit, after which, if you change your mind, the establishment will only refund your money if it's able to rebook your room within a certain period. Note cancellation policies and other restrictions before making a deposit.

B&Bs & Vacation Rentals

In Hawaii 'B&B' is a wide-ranging category; these accommodations can run from spar

---

BOOK YOUR STAY ONLINE

For more accommodation reviews and recommendations by Lonely Planet authors, check out the online booking service at www.lonelyplanet.com/hotels. You'll find the true, insider low-down on the best places to stay. Reviews are thorough and independent. Best of all, you can book online.

bedrooms in family households to historic homes to plush, pull-out-the-stops romantic hideaways. These are mostly family-run operations; they provide much more personal, idiosyncratic experiences than hotels, but offer fewer services. Because B&Bs discourage unannounced drop-ins, they sometimes do not appear on maps in this book. Hosts are often out during the day, so same-day reservations are hard to get – try to book B&Bs in advance (they tend to fill up in advance anyway). Many B&Bs have two- and three-night minimumstay requirements, though some will waive this if you pay a slightly higher one-night rate (since it's more work to turn over rooms nightly). Simple, rural B&Bs begin around $70 per room; most B&B rates average between $100 and $200, and historic or exclusive properties typically run from $200 to $400.

True to their name, most B&Bs offer breakfast or provide some food for guests to cook their own. Ask what kind of breakfast is served; oftentimes, 'expanded continental' or 'full buffet' is coded language indicating a hot cooked meal – most B&Bs do not have stateapproved restaurant-standard kitchens, and they can be fined if caught making omelets for guests.

Sometimes, the distinction between a B&B and a 'vacation rental' is very slim. Typically, a vacation rental means renting an entire house (with no on-site manager and no breakfast provided), but many B&Bs also rent standalone cottages, and often all these kinds of properties are handled by the same rental agencies. In some communities (such as Kailua on O'ahu, p173), there is a growing tension over the proliferation of 'unlicensed' vacation rentals/B&Bs in residential neighborhoods.

This book includes B&Bs that can be booked directly, but there are others that can be booked only through B&B reservation services. Some islands have B&B associations, such as the **Hawaii Island B&B Association** (www .stayhawaii.com) on the Big Island. Some islandwide B&B agencies:

Affordable Paradise Bed & Breakfast (☎ 261-1693; www.affordable-paradise.com) Books reasonably priced B&Bs and cottages.

All Islands Bed & Breakfast (☎ 753-3445; www .all-islands.com) Books scores of host homes.

Bed & Breakfast Hawaii (☎ 822-7771, 800-733-1632; www.bandb-hawaii.com) A larger statewide service.

Vacation Rental by Owner (www.vrbo.com) Facilitates renting vacation homes directly from the owners.

Note that some B&Bs, to preserve a romantic atmosphere, have minimum ages for, or don't allow, children. Be sure to ask about any restrictions before making reservations.

Camping & Cabins

While Hawaii has, unsurprisingly, some stellar public campgrounds, the overall quality of facilities ranges from great to terrible. It has almost no full-service private campgrounds (though hostels sometimes provide camping). The best public facilities are in national parks, next best are state parks and typically the least well cared-for are county parks. Sites are less busy during the week than on weekends.

For safety reasons, a few county and state parks are expressly not recommended because they are either very isolated or they are regular late-night carousing spots. Theft and violence aimed at campers is rare, but you should still choose your campgrounds carefully. See the recommendations in this guide, and also get advice from local county and state parks departments; they are usually very upfront about campground conditions and safety.

Hawaii's two national parks – Maui's Haleakalā National Park (p413) and the Big Island's Hawai'i Volcanoes National Park (p306) – have excellent camping. Both have free drive-up campgrounds, cabins for rent and backcountry campsites; campgrounds are rarely full.

The five largest islands offer camping at state parks. These usually have picnic tables, BBQ grills, drinking water, toilets and showers. You may obtain permits ($5 per night per site) from any Division of State Parks office. The Department of Land & Natural Resources' **Division of State Parks main office** (Map pp118-19; ☎ 587-0300; www.hawaiistateparks.org; Room 131, 1151 Punchbowl St, Honolulu; ⏰ 8am-3:30pm Mon-Fri) handles reservations for all islands.

Some county parks are in fact quite wonderful, with white-sand beaches and good facilities. The key thing to keep in mind is that just because you *can* camp somewhere doesn't necessarily mean you'll *want* to. Check out the campground before committing yourself.

The state and counties also oversee some basic housekeeping cabins. For more specifics, see the O'ahu (p101), Big Island (p205), Maui (p328), Moloka'i (p439) and Kaua'i (p470) chapters.

DIRECTORY

SMOKE-FREE HAWAII

On November 16, 2006, Hawaii became the 14th state in the US to pass comprehensive antismoking legislation. It is now illegal to light up a cigarette in any public building, or within 20ft of a building's entrance. This includes restaurants, bars, offices, hotel lobbies and many other places – though you can still smoke in your car and outside in the park. Because smoking is now largely banned, this guide does not use a nonsmoking icon (⊠). Note that if you break the law, you can be fined $50, plus a $25 court fee. (For complete information on Hawaii's nonsmoking regulations, visit www.hawaii smokefree.com.)

Condominiums

More spacious than hotel rooms, condos are individually owned apartments furnished with everything a visitor needs – from a full kitchen to washer and dryer (usually) to lanai (porch, balcony or veranda). They're almost always cheaper than all but the budget hotel rooms, especially if you're traveling with a group. Most units have a three- to seven-day minimum stay. The weekly rate is often six times the daily rate and the monthly is three times the weekly.

Most condos are rented through agencies, which are listed in individual island chapters. To save money, try booking directly first, then go through the agencies. You can also do your own web searches for online classifieds. Don't forget to ask about cleaning fees, a onetime charge that varies depending on length of stay.

Hostels

Hawaii has only two hostels associated with **Hostelling International** (HI; www.hiusa.org), and both are in Honolulu (p132). All islands and most midsize towns have a small selection of private hostels. A few are appealing, friendly and well kept, but the majority are aimed at backpackers and traveling school groups, and are essentially worn-out crash pads. Most are spartan, offer a common kitchen and internet access, and have bulletin boards thick with useful postings. Dorm beds generally cost $20. Some are listed at **The Hostel Handbook** (www.hostelhandbook.com).

Hotels

It's very common for Hawaii hotels, particularly larger beach hotels, to discount their published rack rates, typically by offerin advance-purchase internet-only discount Others discount by the season, week or da depending on demand; others throw in a fre rental car. Ask about specials before bookin Within a particular hotel, the main thing tha influences room rates is the view and floor. A ocean view can cost 50% to 100% more tha a parking-lot view (euphemistically called 'garden view'). The higher the rate, usuall the quieter the room.

Resorts

Hawaii resorts do not mess around: they ar designed to be pleasure palaces that antici pate your every need and provide 'the best' c everything (to keep you on the property ever minute of the day). They provide a myria dining options, multiple swimming pool children's programs, nightly entertainmen and fitness centers. Beaches are without blem ishes, coconut trees are trimmed of droopin fronds and every single aspect of your ex perience is managed (in an oh-so-seamles way). They are intentionally contrived vision of paradise – accept that, and they're reall quite nice.

ACTIVITIES

On land and in the sea, Hawaii provides som of the top outdoor experiences you'll fin anywhere in the world, and there are very fev things you can't do at all. Rock climbing? Nc there's really no rock climbing. White-wate rafting? No, not that either. Skiing? Actually yes. It won't ever make top 10 lists, but it ca be done on Mauna Kea (p274). After that Yep, pretty much everything else. For a prope introduction, see the Outdoor Activities 8 Adventures chapter (p73).

BUSINESS HOURS

Unless there are variations of more than half-hour in either direction, the followin are the opening hours for entries listed i this book:

Banks 8:30am to 4pm Monday to Friday; some banks open to 6pm Friday and 9am to noon or 1pm Saturday

Businesses 8:30am to 4:30pm Monday to Friday; some post offices open 9am to noon Saturday

Restaurants breakfast 6am to 10am, lunch 11:30am to 2pm, dinner 5pm to 9:30pm.

Shops 9am to 5pm Monday to Saturday, some also open noon to 5pm Sunday; major shopping areas and malls kee extended hours.

CHILDREN

A parent would like to hope that Hawaii, of all places, would be enough to satisfy any child (keiki). It offers tons of beaches and outdoor activities for all ages and abilities – plus hotels have pools, malls have arcades and movies, and the trees have coconuts and ripe fruit. It's easy to meet local kids and their families at parks and beaches, and teens have many avenues – through music, arts and other programs – to encounter Hawaii's fascinating multiethnic society.

Nevertheless, don't leave home without the usual assortment of books, treats, on-the-road amusements and home comforts.

Traveling with kids in Hawaii is as easy (and hard) as anywhere in the US. Traveling families are common, most hotels and restaurants are ready to accommodate them and locals welcome and enjoy them. So long as you keep your kids covered in sunblock and don't try to do or see too much, you don't need to worry about having a successful family trip.

Some activities (like horseback riding, surf lessons and helicopter tours) require that children be of a certain age, height or weight to participate. Always ask if restrictions apply. Each island chapter includes specific advice for the best kid-friendly activities; see O'ahu (boxed text, p109), the Big Island (boxed text, p219), Maui (boxed text, p335), Lana'i (p433), Moloka'i (p449) and Kaua'i (p492).

If you forget some critical piece of equipment, **Baby's Away** (☎ on the Big Island 800-996-9030, on O'ahu 800-496-6386, on Maui 800-942-9030; www .babysaway.com) rents cribs, strollers, playpens, high chairs and more. The easiest and most reliable way to find babysitters is to ask the hotel concierge.

For general advice about traveling with children, check out **Travel With Your Kids.com** (www.travelwithyourkids.com), which also has specific advice for O'ahu and Maui. **Go City Kids** (http://gocitykids.parentsconnect.com) covers Honolulu, and Lonely Planet's *Travel with Children* has lots of valuable tips and amusing tales.

Na keiki (children) are welcome most everywhere in Hawaii (except at some B&Bs). Children under 17 or 18 often stay free when sharing a hotel room with their parents and using existing bedding. But always ask. Cots and roll-away beds are usually available (for an additional fee) at hotels and resorts.

Many restaurants have children's menus and high chairs are usually available – but if a high chair is a necessity at every meal, bring a collapsible seat.

Car-rental companies (p576) are required to provide child-safety seats, but only if you reserve in advance; bring your own and you'll avoid any mixups.

CLIMATE CHARTS

Native Hawaiians have about as many words for rain and wind as Native Alaskans have for snow. However, if each day's weather is impossible to predict, the overall climate is remarkably even tempered.

Average temperatures in Hawaii differ only about 7°F from winter to summer. Near the coast, average highs are about 83°F and lows around 68°F. Hawaii's mountains trap tradewinds blowing from the northeast, blocking clouds and bringing abundant rainfall to each island's windward side. Conversely, those same mountains block wind and rain from the

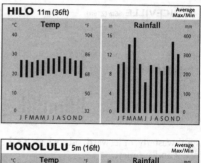

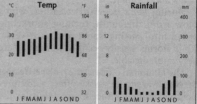

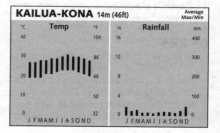

DIRECTORY

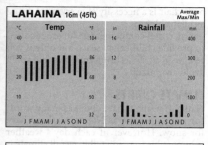

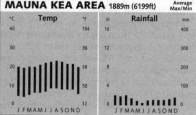

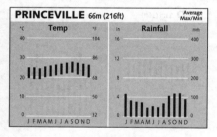

southwesterly, or leeward, side, where it's the driest and sunniest.

During *kona* (leeward) weather, winds blow from the south, turning snorkeling spots into surfing spots and vice versa. *Kona* storms usually occur in winter and are very unpredictable.

The Honolulu office of the **National Weather Service** (www.prh.noaa.gov/hnl) offers a comprehensive online weather forecast, but for the coolest infrared and satellite images, visit the **University of Hawaii Meteorology Department** (http://weathe r.hawaii.edu).

COURSES

Some resorts and shopping centers, for example Whalers Village on Maui (p353), offer free or low-cost classes and workshops in hula, traditional Hawaiian arts and the like. Since many schedules are unpredictable, keep your eyes and ears open. The hotel concierge is al-

ways a good source of information. Also check out the Big Island's East Hawai'i Cultural Center (p290) and the Volcano Art Center (p310), and Maui's Hui No'eau Visual Arts Center (p404).

For an overview of meditation, yoga and alternative healing classes and retreats on the islands, see p88.

The main venue for courses is the **University of Hawai'i** (UH; www.hawaii.edu), which has its main campus at Manoa on O'ahu and a smaller campus in Hilo on the Big Island. UH offers full-time university and summer-school courses. The summer session consists primarily of two six-week terms. For a catalog contact the **Outreach College office** (☎ 956-5666, 800-862-6628; www.outreach.hawaii.edu/summer; Room 101 Krauss Hall, 2500 Dole St, Honolulu, HI 96822).

DANGERS & ANNOYANCES

In general, Hawaii is a very safe place to visit. For travelers, the two main concerns are car break-ins (common) and natural disasters (rare but serious). Since tourism is so important to Hawaii, state officials have established the **Visitor Aloha Society of Hawaii** (VASH; ☎ 808-926-8274; www.visitoralohasocietyofhawaii.org), which provides aid to visitors who become the victims of accidents or crimes while vacationing in Hawaii.

For health concerns, see the Health chapter, p578.

Drugs

Pakalolo (marijuana) remains a billion-dollar underground industry, and the use of 'ice' (crystal methamphetamine) has been an ongoing social and law-enforcement issue since the 1990s, especially in rural communities. The 'ice epidemic' has abated recently (as a result of enforcement efforts), but ice-related crimes continue and social-service agencies still struggle to provide treatment for addicts.

Scams

The main scams directed toward visitors in Hawaii involve fake activity-operator booths and timeshare booths. Salespeople at the latter will offer you all sorts of deals, from free luaus to sunset cruises, if you'll just come to hear their 'no obligation' pitch. *Caveat emptor.*

Theft & Violence

The islands are notorious for rip-offs from parked rental cars. It can happen within seconds, whether from a secluded parking area at a trailhead or from a crowded hotel parking lot. As much as possible, do not leave anything valuable in your car, ever. If you must, pack things well out of sight *before* you arrive at your destination; thieves wait and watch to see what you put in the trunk. Locals will leave their car doors unlocked to avoid paying for broken windows.

Otherwise, the most common problem is being hassled by drunks on beaches and in campgrounds, mainly at night. Wherever you are, stay tuned to the general vibe (see also Women Travelers, p570). Don't leave valuables in your tent, and watch your belongings in hostels.

Overall, violent crime is lower in Hawaii than in most of mainland USA, but Honolulu is a major city of nearly a million people and it suffers from the gamut of typical big-city problems, including a growing homeless population. Don't forget your street smarts just because you're in Hawaii.

Natural Disasters

Hurricanes, tsunamis and earthquakes all occur in Hawaii, sometimes to devastating effect. In 2006 the Big Island was shaken by a 6.7 earthquake that caused $200 million in damage, but no deaths. In 1992 Hurricane 'Iniki wrecked large swathes of Kaua'i (p537), and in 1946 the largest tsunami in Hawaii's history killed 159 people and caused enormous damage (p285).

On average, tsunami (incorrectly called tidal waves – the Japanese term *tsunami* means 'harbor wave') have occurred once a decade over the last century and killed more people statewide than all other natural disasters combined. In 1948 Hawaii installed a tsunami warning system, aired through yellow speakers mounted on telephone poles around the islands. They're tested on the first working day of each month at 11:45am for about one minute.

Of course, it's highly unlikely that a natural disaster will occur while you're here. Usually, there is ample warning prior to hurricanes. If you hear tsunami warning sirens, head for higher ground immediately. The front sections of telephone books have maps of tsunami safety evacuation zones. Earthquakes usually provide no warning; if one occurs, get clear of buildings or brace yourself in doorways.

For more information, visit the websites of the **International Tsunami Information Centre** (http://ioc3.unesco.org/itic), the **National Hurricane Center** (www.nhc.noaa.gov), and the **Pacific Disaster Center** (www.pd c.org).

DISCOUNTS

Glossy, free tourist magazines are distributed widely; all contain discount coupons for activities and restaurants. However, for hotels and activities, usually the best deals are offered when you book in advance through their websites.

Children, students, seniors and military personnel usually receive discounts into museums and other sights. All but children need valid identification confirming their status. Since Hawaii is a popular destination for retirees, senior discounts are available more widely than others; for instance, Hawaii's biggest hotel chain, Outrigger, offers across-the-board discounts to seniors. If you have reached 'that age,' consider joining the nonprofit **American Association of Retired Persons** (AARP; ☎ 888-687-2277; www.aarp.org; 601 E St NW, Washington, DC 20049), which is a good source of travel bargains.

FOOD

Reviews in Eating sections are broken down into three price categories: 'budget' (for meals costing $12 or less), 'midrange' (where most main dishes cost $12 to $30) and 'top end' (where most dinner mains cost more than $30). These price estimates do not include taxes, tips or beverages.

For details about Hawaiian cuisine and local *grinds* (food), see the Food & Drink chapter, p61.

GAY & LESBIAN TRAVELERS

Hawaii has a heritage of Polynesian tolerance that extends to gays and lesbians – despite the sometimes homophobic statements of a few contemporary Hawaiian elders. However, locals also tend to be very private about their personal lives in general, so you will not see much public hand-holding and open displays of affection of any kind, much less between gays. Even in Waikiki (see the boxed text, p154), which is without question the home of Hawaii's main gay scene, that 'scene' is muted by mainland standards (compared with, say, San Francisco or Los Angeles). Everyday queer life is low-key – it's more about picnics and potlucks, not nightclubs.

That said, Hawaii remains a very popular destination for gay and lesbian travelers, who are served by a network of B&Bs, resorts and tours. The monthly *Odyssey* (www.odyssey hawaii.com), free at gay-friendly businesses throughout Hawaii, covers the islandwide gay scene, as does the monthly *Da Kine* (www.dakinemagazine.com).

For more information on gay Hawaii, and recommendations about places to stay, gay beaches, travel arrangements and so on, visit the following sites:

Gay Hawaii (www.gayhawaii.com)

Out in Hawaii (www.outinhawaii.com)

Pacific Ocean Holidays (☎ 545-5252, 800-735-6600; www.gayhawaiivacations.com; PO Box 88245, Honolulu, HI 96830) Arranges packages.

Rainbow Handbook Hawai'i (www.rainbowhand book.com)

HOLIDAYS

Also see the Events Calendar (p27).

New Year's Day January 1
Martin Luther King Jr Day Third Monday of January
Presidents Day Third Monday of February
Easter March or April
Memorial Day Last Monday of May
King Kamehameha Day June 11
Independence Day July 4
Admission Day Third Friday of August
Labor Day First Monday of September
Columbus Day Second Monday of October
Election Day Second Tuesday of November
Veterans Day November 11
Thanksgiving Fourth Thursday of November
Christmas Day December 25

INSURANCE

It's expensive to get sick, crash a car or have things stolen from you in the USA. For car-rental insurance, see p575, and for health insurance, see p578. Consult your home-owner's (or renter's) insurance policy before leaving home to see if and to what extent you are covered should items be stolen from your rental car. Worldwide travel insurance is available at www.lonelyplanet.com/book ings/insurance.do. You can buy, extend and claim online anytime – even if you're already on the road.

INTERNATIONAL VISITORS
Entering Hawaii

A passport is required for all foreign citizens. Unless eligible under the Visa Waiver

Program (see below), foreign travelers mu also have a tourist visa. To rent or drive a ca travelers from non-English-speaking cou tries should obtain an International Drive Permit before arriving.

Travelers entering under the Visa Waive Program must register with the US goverr ment online (https://esta.cbp.dhs.gov) a least three days before arriving; earlier is be ter, since if denied, travelers must get a vis Registration is valid for two years.

Upon arriving in the US, all foreign visitor must register in the US-Visit program, whic entails having two index fingers scanned an a digital photo taken. For information on U: Visit, see the **Department of Homeland Securit** (www.dhs.gov).

VISAS

All visitors should reconfirm entry require ments and visa guidelines before arriving The introductory portal for US visa infor mation is **Destination USA** (www.unitedstatesvis .gov). The **US State Department** (www.travel.stat .gov) maintains the most comprehensive vis information and has downloadable applica tion forms. **US Citizenship & Immigration Service** (www.uscis.gov) mainly focuses on immigrants not temporary visitors.

The Visa Waiver Program allows citizen of certain countries to enter the USA for stay of 90 days or less without first obtaining a U visa. There are 35 countries currently partici pating; they are Andorra, Australia, Austri Belgium, Brunei, Czech Republic, Denmarl Estonia, Finland, France, Germany, Hungar Iceland, Ireland, Italy, Japan, South Kore Latvia, Liechtenstein, Lithuania, Luxembourg Malta, Monaco, the Netherlands, Ne Zealand, Norway, Portugal, San Marinc Singapore, Slovakia, Slovenia, Spain, Swede Switzerland and the UK. Under this prograr you must have a return ticket (or onwar ticket to any foreign destination) that is non refundable in the USA. If your passport wa issued/renewed after October 26, 2006, yo need an 'e-passport' with digital chip; other wise, you need a machine-readable passpor

Visitors who don't qualify for the Vis Waiver Program need a visa. Basic require ments are a valid passport, recent photo, trave details and often proof of financial stability Students and adult males also must fill ou supplemental travel documents. Those plan ning to travel through other countries befor

riving in the USA are better off applying
r their US visa in their home country rather
an while on the road.

The validity period for a US visitor visa
epends on your home country. The actual
ngth of time you'll be allowed to stay in the
SA is determined by US officials at the port
f entry. If you want to stay in the USA longer
an the date stamped on your passport, go
 the Honolulu office of the **Citizenship &
nmigration Service** (☎ 800-375-5283; 595 Ala Moana
vd, Honolulu) before the stamped date to apply
r an extension.

USTOMS

ach adult visitor is allowed to bring 1L of
quor and 200 cigarettes duty-free into the
SA. In addition, each traveler is permitted
 bring up to $100 worth of gift merchandise
to the USA without incurring any duty.

Most fresh fruits and plants are restricted
om entry into Hawaii (to prevent the spread
f invasive species), and customs officials
re militant. Similarly, because Hawaii is a
bies-free state, the pet quarantine laws are
raconian. For complete details, contact the
awaiian Department of Agriculture (☎ 808-973-
60; http://hawai i.gov/hdoa).

mbassies & Consulates

he **US Department of State** (http://usembassy.state
ov) website has links for all US embassies
road.

Consulates in Honolulu (unless otherwise
ated):

ustralia (Map pp118-19; ☎ 524-5050; Penthouse,
00 Bishop St)

anada (Map pp118-19; ☎ 529-8120; Penthouse Suite,
00 Bishop St)

rance (Map pp118-19; ☎ 547-5852; Ali'i Place, Suite
00, 1099 Alakea St)

ermany (Map pp146-7; ☎ 946-3819; 252 Paoa Pl,
aikiki)

aly (Map pp118-19; ☎ 531-2277; Suite 201, 735 Bishop St)

apan (Map p114; ☎ 543-3111; 1742 Nu'uanu Ave)

orea (Map p114; ☎ 595-6109; 2756 Pali Hwy)

etherlands (Map pp118-19; ☎ 531-6897; Suite 702,
5 Fort St Mall)

ew Zealand (Map p125; ☎ 595-2200; 3929 Old Pali Rd)

hilippines (☎ 595-6316; 2433 Pali Hwy)

Money

rices quoted in this book are in US dollars
), which is the only currency used in Hawaii.
ee Quick Reference inside the front cover for

exchange rates, and Getting Started (p24) for
information on costs.

The ease and availability of ATMs have
largely negated the need for traveler's checks.
However, traveler's checks in US dollars are
accepted like cash at most midrange and top-
end businesses (but rarely at budget places).
Personal checks not drawn on a Hawaiian
bank are generally not accepted. Exchange foreign currency at the Honolulu International
Airport and larger Hawaii banks, like **Bank
of Hawaii** (www.boh.com) and **First Hawaiian Bank**
(www.fhb.com).

Major credit cards are widely accepted
(except occasionally by B&Bs), and they are
required for car rentals. Most ATM withdraw-
als using out-of-state cards incur surcharges
of $2 or so.

Post

Mail delivery to and from Hawaii usually takes
a little longer than similar services on the US
mainland via the **US postal service** (USPS; ☎ 800-
275-8777; www.usps.gov). For 1st-class mail sent
and delivered within the USA, postage rates
are 44¢ for letters up to 1oz (17¢ for each
additional ounce) and 28¢ for standard-size
postcards. International airmail rates for postcards and letters up to 1oz are 75¢ to Canada,
79¢ to Mexico and 98¢ to other countries.

You can have mail sent to you c/o General
Delivery at most big post offices in Hawaii (it's
usually held for 30 days). Most hotels will also
hold mail for incoming guests.

Practicalities

For phone, dialing and electrical advice, a
good online resource is www.kropla.com.

- Voltage is 110/120V, 60 cycles (the US
  standard).
- Hawaii's major daily newspaper is the
  Honolulu Advertiser.
- Hawaii has about 50 radio stations, and
  it receives all the major US TV networks
  and cable channels (including Japanese-
  language programs).
- Video systems use the NTSC standard
  (not compatible with the PAL system).
- As on the mainland, distances are measured in feet, yards and miles; weights in
  ounces, pounds and tons.

Telephone

Always dial '1' before toll-free (☎ 800, 888
etc) and domestic long-distance numbers.

Some toll-free numbers only work within the state or from the US mainland.

To make international calls from Hawaii, dial ☎ 011 + country code + area code + number. For international operator assistance, dial ☎ 0. To call Hawaii from abroad, the international country code for the USA is ☎ 1.

Pay phones are readily found in shopping centers and public places. Calls on a single island are considered local and cost 25¢ or 50¢. Calls from one island to another are always long distance and require dialing Hawaii's area code ☎ 808. Private prepaid phone cards are available from convenience stores, supermarkets and pharmacies.

Most of the USA's mobile-phone systems are incompatible with the GSM 900/1800 standard used throughout Europe and Asia. Check with your service provider about using your phone in Hawaii. In terms of coverage, Verizon has the most extensive network, but AT&T, Cingular and Sprint are decent. Cellular coverage is best on O'ahu, more spotty on Neighbor Islands, and nonexistent in many remote regions.

Time

Hawaii has its own time zone and does not observe daylight saving time. Noon in Hawaii equals 2pm in Los Angeles, 5pm in New York, 10pm in London, 7am the next day in Tokyo, 8am the next day in Melbourne, and 10am the next day in Auckland.

INTERNET ACCESS

Most hotels and B&Bs, and many restaurants and other businesses, now offer high-speed internet access; in this book, the 🖳 symbol indicates the availability of an internet terminal, and the 🛜 symbol indicates wi-fi. Always ask about rates; they can sometimes be exorbitant.

Most towns have cybercafés and business centers with inexpensive internet access (see Information sections). Hawaii's public libraries (www.librarieshawaii.org) provide free internet access if you have a temporary nonresident library card ($10).

For a list of wi-fi hot spots in Hawaii (plus tech and access info), visit **Wi-Fi Alliance** (www.wi-fi.org) and **Wi-Fi Free Spot** (www.wififreespot.com). If you bring a laptop from outside the USA, invest in a universal AC and plug adapter. Also confirm that your modem card will work;

for advice and technical help visit **TeleAdap** (www.telea dapt.com).

LEGAL MATTERS

You have the right to an attorney from th moment you are arrested. If you can't affor one, the state must provide one for free. Th **Hawaii State Bar Association** (☎ 537-9140, 800-808 4722; www.hawaiilawyerreferral.com) makes attorne referrals, but foreign visitors may want to ca their consulate for advice.

In Hawaii, anyone driving with a blood al cohol level of 0.08% or higher is guilty of driv ing 'under the influence,' which carries sever penalties. As with most places, the possessio of marijuana and narcotics is illegal in Hawai Public nudity (as at beaches) and hitchhikin are also illegal, but rarely enforced.

Hawaii's **Department of Commerce & Consume Affairs** (www.hawaii.gov/dcca) has a Consume Resource Center with contact numbers fo each island if you want to lodge a complain against a company or get more informatio on your rights.

MAPS

By far the most detailed street maps are th **Ready Mapbook** (www.hawaiimapsource.com) series These atlas-style books (about $11 each) cove virtually every paved and unpaved road on th main islands. Bookstores and convenienc stores in Honolulu and Waikiki also stoc street maps of the city area.

Map geeks and backcountry hikers wantin topo maps can find them at good bookstore and at national parks. Or order them from **TopoZone** (www.topozone.com) or the **US Geologica Survey** (USGS; ☎ 888-275-8747; www.usgs.gov).

Franko's Maps (www.frankosmaps.com) offers diverse range of attractive, laminated, water proof ocean sports and island sights maps including a brand-new *Obama's O'ahu* map

PHOTOGRAPHY

All camera supplies (print and slide film, dig ital memory, batteries) are readily available i Hawaii. Disposable underwater cameras (abou $15) deliver surprisingly good snaps. Long Drugs is one of the cheapest places for devel oping film and burning photo CDs and DVD (business centers burn photo CDs, too). Whil in Hawaii, develop print film as you finish eac roll, as the high temperature and humidit greatly accelerate the deterioration of expose film. One-hour print shops are everywhere.

Don't pack unprocessed film (including the roll in your camera) into checked luggage because exposure to high-powered X-ray equipment will cause it to fog. As an added precaution, 'hand check' film separately from carry-on bags at airport security checkpoints.

For a primer on taking good shots, consult Lonely Planet's *Travel Photography*.

SHOPPING

In a nation known for its kitsch, Hawaii may be the (plastic) jewel in the crown. It is also rich with high-quality handmade crafts. The question is: are you a dashboard-hula-girl-type person or a gleaming-koa-bowl-type person?

For the latter, prepare for high prices; the real stuff isn't cheap. Farmers markets are great places for well-priced crafts and local art – often sold by the artist – but it can be hard to distinguish imported from locally made articles.

The best way to ensure that what you buy is authentic Hawaiiana is to shop at well-respected art galleries and artists cooperatives. These are noted in island chapters, but a sampling of the best includes the Bishop Museum on O'ahu (p126), the Volcano Art Center on the Big Island (p310), and the Hui No'eau Visual Arts Center (p404) and Maui Crafts Guild (p392), both on Maui. On Kaua'i, the town of Hanapepe (p544) has a number of fine galleries; also visit the website www.kauaimade.org.

See p55 for more information on Hawaiian arts and crafts.

Specialty food items are a classic Hawaii gift – from chocolate-covered macadamia nuts and Kona coffee to *liliko'i* (passion fruit) preserves and crack seed (see p64), but make sure that any unsealed food item has been verified as approved for travel (or you'll be forced to surrender your pineapples and mangoes at the airport).

The same warning holds for flowers; make sure any orchids, anthuriums or proteas are inspected and approved for travel by the US Department of Agriculture; foreign visitors should check with their airline about agricultural restrictions in their home country (see p567).

SOLO TRAVELERS

Travel, including solo travel, is generally safe and easy. In general, women need to exercise more vigilance in large cities than in rural areas. Everyone, though, should avoid hiking, cycling long distances or camping alone, especially in unfamiliar places. For more safety advice, see Women Travelers (p570) and Dangers & Annoyances (p564).

TOURIST INFORMATION

In addition to the tourist bureaus listed here, you can get a good deal of useful tourist information from the two free publications **101 Things to Do** (www.101thingstodo.com) and **This Week** (www.thisweek.com).

Big Island Visitors Bureau Hilo (Map p289; ☎ 961-5797, 800-648-2441; www.bigisland.org; 250 Keawe St, Hilo 96720); Waimea (Map p264; ☎ 885-1655; 65-1158 Mamalahoa Hwy, Suite 27B, Waimea Center)

Hawaii Visitors & Convention Bureau (Map pp146-7; ☎ 800-464-2924; www.gohawaii.com; Suite 801, 2270 Kalakaua Ave, Waikiki) Will mail a free Visitor Guide.

Kauai Visitors Bureau (Map p479; ☎ 245-3971, 800-262-1400; www.kauaidiscovery.com; Suite 101, 4334 Rice St, Lihu'e)

Lana'i Visitors Bureau (Map p429; ☎ 565-7600, 800-947-4774; www.visitlanai.net; 431 7th St)

Maui Visitors Bureau (Map p369; ☎ 872-3893, 800-525-6284; www.visitmaui.com; Kahului airport) Also represents Lana'i and Moloka'i.

Moloka'i Visitors Association (Map p444; ☎ 553-3876, 800-800-6367; www.molokai-hawaii.com; Suite 200, 2 Kamoi St, Kaunakakai 96748)

O'ahu Visitors Bureau (Map pp118-19; ☎ 524-0722, 877-525-6248; www.visit-oahu.com; Suite 1520, 733 Bishop St, Honolulu)

TRAVELERS WITH DISABILITIES

Major resort hotels have elevators, TDD-capable phones and wheelchair-accessible rooms (reserve in advance). Beyond that, few generalizations can be made islandwide. For specifics, visit the **Disability & Communication Access Board** (DCAB; ☎ 586-8121; www.hawaii.gov /health/dcab; Room 101, 919 Ala Moana Blvd, Honolulu, HI 96814) website, which provides information on airlines, transportation, medical and other support services on each island.

Seeing-eye and guide dogs are not subject to the same quarantine as other pets, provided they meet the Department of Agriculture's (☎ 808-973-9560; http://hawaii.gov/hdoa) minimum requirements.

Wheelchair Getaways (☎ 800-638-1912; www.wheel chairgetaways.com) is a company that rents vans that are wheelchair-accessible on Maui, Kaua'i and the Big Island.

DIRECTORY

For a list of services available to passengers with disabilities by airline, go to the **Allgohere Airline Directory** (www.allgohere.com).

On mainland USA, the **Society for the Advancement of Travel for the Handicapped** (SATH; ☎ 212-447-7284; www.sath.org; Suite 605, 347 Fifth Ave, New York, NY 10016) publishes a quarterly magazine and has information on travel for people with disabilities.

VOLUNTEERING

Volunteer opportunities abound in Hawaii, and they provide a memorable experience of Hawaii's people and land you'll never get by just passing through. Some require time commitments, typically a week or so, but lots ask for only an afternoon or a day. Longer programs may provide meals and lodging (and charge a fee to offset costs), but none provide transportation to Hawaii.

The best central place to find out about volunteer opportunities is **Malama Hawaii** (www.malamahawaii.org), a partnership network of community and nonprofit organizations. It posts a wide-ranging calendar that also includes fundraising concerts, educational events and cultural workshops. Volunteer by pulling invasive weeds, doing trail maintenance, restoring taro patches, cleaning streams, and much more.

Hawaii State Parks (www.hawaiistateparks.org/partners) can link you with partner volunteer organizations who help preserve and maintain Hawaii's state parks.

The **National Park Service** (www.nps.gov/volunteer) coordinates volunteers at Hawai'i Volcanoes National Park (p306) on the Big Island and Haleakalā National Park (p413) on Maui.

Here is a list of more organizations gratefully accepting volunteers, some specific to one island:

Give the Reef a Break (www.iyor-hawaii.org)
Hawaii Audubon Society (www.hawaiiaudubon.com)
Hawaii Nature Center (www.hawaiinaturecenter.org) Coordinates voluntourism on O'ahu.
Hawai'i Wildlife Fund (http://wildhawaii.org)
Hawaiian Islands Humpback Whale National Marine Sanctuary (www.hawaiihumpbackwhale.noaa.gov) Holds an annual three-month Sanctuary Ocean Count.
Koke'e Resource Conservation Program (www.krcp.org) Kaua'i weed-control projects.

Protect Kaho'olawe 'Ohana (www.kahoolawe.org) Five-day trips to Kaho'olawe.
Sierra Club, Hawaii Chapter (www.hi.sierraclub.org)
Volunteer Zone (http://volunteerzone.org) Links with mainly O'ahu community groups, both volunteers and donations.
Wild Dolphin Foundation (www.wilddolphin.org)

WOMEN TRAVELERS

Hawaii presents few unique problems for women travelers and may be more relaxed and comfortable than many mainland destinations. The one place where women – especially solo travelers – might feel uneasy is in local bars, but no more or less than anywhere else in the world.

If you're camping, opt for secure, well-used camping areas over isolated locales where you might be the only camper; this advice pertains to anyone. Some county parks and their campgrounds (see p561) are notorious as latenight party spots. This can be true of beaches after dark as well, and women should be careful walking alone on beaches at night.

WORK

US citizens can pursue work in Hawaii as they would in any other state – the problem is finding a decent job. Foreign visitors in the USA on tourist visas are not legally allowed to take employment.

Finding serious 'professional' employment is difficult since Hawaii has a tight labor market. The biggest exceptions are for teachers and nurses. Joining the waitstaff of tourist-area restaurants is the most likely opportunity, but folks with language, scuba, fishing or guiding skills might investigate employment with resorts. Most housekeeping or groundskeeping jobs at megaresorts go to locals.

In addition to notice boards in hostels, cafes and natural food stores, check the classified ads in the *Honolulu Advertiser* (www.honoluluadvertiser.com). Continue surfing at **JobsHawaii.com** (www.jobshawaii.com) and at **Hire Net Hawaii** (www.hirenethawaii.com), which is run by the **State Department of Labor & Industrial Relations** (☎ 586-8700; http://hawaii.gov/labor; 830 Punchbowl St, Honolulu, HI 96813).

Transportation

CONTENTS

GETTING THERE & AWAY

Roughly 99% of visitors to Hawaii arrive by air, and the majority of flights – international and domestic – arrive at Honolulu International Airport (below), though direct flights to Neighbor Islands are increasing.

Flights, tours and rail tickets can be booked online at www.lonelyplanet.com/travelservices.

AIR

Hawaii is a very competitive market for US domestic and international airfares, which vary tremendously by season, demand, number of stopovers and ticket details. At any given time, any airline may have the cheapest fare.

Airports & Airlines

Because of the sheer distance, travelers arriving from Europe will often have to change planes on the US mainland. Major gateway airports include the following:

Atlanta International Airport (ATL; ☎ 800-897-1910; www.atlanta-airport.com)
Chicago O'Hare International Airport (ORD; ☎ 773-686-2200; www.ohare.com)
Denver International Airport (DEN; ☎ 303-342-2000; www.flydenver.com)
Los Angeles International Airport (LAX; ☎ 310-646-5252; www.los-angeles-lax.com)
New York JFK International Airport (JFK; ☎ 718-244-4444; www.panynj.gov)

San Francisco International Airport (SFO; ☎ 650-821-8211; www.flysfo.com)

The majority of incoming flights from overseas and the US mainland arrive on O'ahu at **Honolulu International Airport** (HNL; ☎ 836-6413; www.honoluluairport.com).

For more information on Neighbor Island airports, visit www.hawaii.gov/dot/airports. Following are the main ones:
Hilo International Airport (ITO; ☎ 934-5840; Hawai'i, the Big Island)
Kahului airport (OGG; ☎ 872-3893; Maui)
Kona International Airport at Keahole (KOA; ☎ 329-3423; Hawai'i)
Lana'i airport (LNY; ☎ 565-6757; Lana'i)
Lihu'e airport (LIH; ☎ 246-1448; Kaua'i)
Moloka'i airport (MKK; ☎ 567-6361; Moloka'i)

AIRLINES FLYING TO/FROM HONOLULU
Air Canada (AC; ☎ 888-247-2262; www.aircanada.com)
Air New Zealand (NZ; ☎ 800-262-1234; www.airnewzealand.com)
Air Pacific (Fj; ☎ 800-227-4446; www.airpacific.com)
Alaska Airlines (AS; ☎ 800-252-7522; www.alaskaair.com)
American Airlines (AA; ☎ 800-433-7300; www.aa.com)
China Airlines (CI; ☎ 800-227-5118; www.china-airlines.com)
Continental (CO; ☎ 800-523-3273; www.continental.com)
Delta (DL; ☎ 800-221-1212; www.delta.com)
Hawaiian Airlines (HA; ☎ 800-367-5320; www.hawaiianair.com)
Japan Airlines (JL; ☎ 800-525-3663; www.ar.jal.com)

THINGS CHANGE...
The information in this chapter is particularly vulnerable to change. Check directly with the airline or a travel agent to make sure you understand how a fare (and ticket you may buy) works and be aware of the security requirements for international travel. Shop carefully. The details given in this chapter should be regarded as pointers and are not a substitute for your own careful, up-to-date research.

TRANSPORTATION

Korean Airlines (KE; ☎ 800-438-5000; www.koreanair .com)

Northwest (NW; ☎ 800-225-2525; www.nwa.com)

Philippine Airlines (PR; ☎ 800-435-9725; www .philippineairlines.com)

Qantas Airways (QF; ☎ 800-227-4500; www.qantas .com.au)

United Airlines (UA; ☎ 800-864-8331; www.united .com)

US Airways (US; ☎ 800-428-4322; www.usairways .com/awa)

For information on most airlines, visit **Seat Guru** (www.seatguru.com). For more information on flights to individual islands, see the Getting There & Away sections near the front of each island chapter. Flights to Lana'i and Moloka'i originate only from Honolulu or Maui.

Tickets
Naturally, the internet is the first place to look for low airfares. But in Hawaii, one travel agency specializing in discount tickets and packages is **Panda Travel** (☎ 738-3898, 800-303-6702; www.pandaonline.com; 1017 Kapahulu Ave, Honolulu).

Round-the-world (RTW) tickets allow you to fly around the world using an alliance of airlines; Circle Pacific tickets are similar, but itineraries focus on the Pacific region. Only consider them if you want to visit other parts of the world in addition to Hawaii. The two main alliances are **One World** (www.oneworld.com) and the **Star Alliance** (www.staralliance.com).

For a primer in online booking agencies, see **Airinfo** (www.airinfo.aero). The big three agency websites are **Travelocity** (www.travelocity .com), **Expedia** (www.expedia.com), and **Orbitz** (www .orbitz.com). Similar and worth trying is **Cheap Tickets** (www.cheapticket.com).

Meta sites compare prices across many sources (but don't provide direct booking): try **Kayak** (www.kayak.com), **Mobissimo** (www.mobis simo.com) and **Sidestep** (www.sidestep.com). **Farecast** (http://farecast.live.com) helps predict when fares will be lowest.

Gamblers can bid for travel at **Priceline** (www .priceline.com) and **Hotwire** (www.hotwire.com), but it's worth getting advice first at **BiddingForTravel. com** (http://biddingfortravel.yuku.com).

Hook up with advance promotions and deals through **Travelzoo** (www.travelzoo.com).

US Mainland
Competition is high among airlines flying to Honolulu from major mainland cities, and the 'lowest fare' fluctuates constantly. In general, return fares from the US mainland to Hawaii cost $300 (in low season from the West Coast) to $1000-plus (in high season from the East Coast). Ongoing upheaval in the air industry makes price prediction increasingly difficult.

Most mainland flights fly to Honolulu, but there are direct flights to Maui, Kaua'i and the Big Island from San Francisco, Los Angeles, Seattle and Las Vegas. The greatest number of carriers, flights and nonstop options originate from West Coast cities. Some nonstops to Honolulu originate from the East Coast, but most often you will have to add one or even two stops (certainly if you want the cheapest fare).

For those with limited time, package tours can sometimes be the cheapest option. Basic ones cover airfare and accommodations, while deluxe packages include car rental, island hopping and activities. **Pleasant Holidays** (☎ 800-742-9244; www1.pleasantholidays.com) has departures from various US mainland points. Or, consider **Air Tech** (☎ 212-219-7000; www.airtech .com), which offers super deals between the West Coast and Hawaii (often half the usual rate). However, you must be flexible with your travel time; it offers unsold seats at the last minute and doesn't guarantee a specific flight. Currently, flights to Honolulu, Kaua'i, Maui and the Big Island depart from San Francisco and Los Angeles.

The nonstop flight time to Hawaii is about 5½ hours from the West Coast. East Coast flights range from 11 to 15 hours, depending on stops.

Australia
Hawaiian Airlines and Qantas fly nonstop between Sydney and Honolulu. Agents serving Australia include **Flight Centre** (☎ 1300-133-133; www.flightcentre.com.au) and **STA Travel** (☎ 1300-134-782; www.statravel.com.au).

Canada
Air Canada offers direct flights from Vancouver to Honolulu, Maui and the Big Island, plus flights from Edmonton and Toronto to Honolulu. Agents serving Canada include **Travel Cuts** (☎ 866-246-9762; www.travelcuts.com) and **Travelocity** (☎ 800-457-8010; www.travelocity.ca).

Japan
Japan Airlines flies direct from Tokyo to Honolulu and the Big Island; flights from Osaka

and Nagoya go to Honolulu. Northwest and Delta also fly direct to Honolulu from Tokyo and Osaka. Agents serving Japan include **STA Travel** (☎ 03-5391-2922; www.statravel.co.jp).

New Zealand, Micronesia & South Pacific Islands

Air New Zealand flies from Auckland to Honolulu. Agents serving New Zealand include both **Flight Centre** (☎ 0800-24-35-44; www .flight centre.co.nz) and **STA Travel** (☎ 0800-474-400; www.statravel.co.nz).

Air New Zealand can also connect Fiji, Tonga, the Cook Islands and Western Samoa to Honolulu through Auckland. Hawaiian Airlines flies direct from Tahiti and American Samoa to Honolulu. Air Pacific, Fiji's national airline, flies from Fiji to Honolulu, and can connect with other South Pacific islands. Finally, Continental flies nonstop from Guam to Honolulu, and it can connect other places in Micronesia through Guam.

Southeast Asia

Northwest flies to Honolulu from Bangkok, Manila, Taipei and Beijing. Korean Air, China Airlines, Philippine Airlines and others also offer numerous flights between Southeast Asian cities and Honolulu. Delta also flies direct to Honolulu from Bangkok, Taipei and Seoul.

Bucket shops in Bangkok, Singapore and Hong Kong should be able to beat standard fares, perhaps by half-price. Agents serving Southeast Asia include **STA Travel** (☎ 2148-9800; www.statravel.com.my) and **Concorde Travel** (☎ 2526-3391; www.concorde-travel.com).

UK & Continental Europe

In addition to other national carriers, American, United, Delta and Continental offer flights to Honolulu from various European cities. The most common route to Hawaii from Europe is west via New York, Chicago or Los Angeles. If you're interested in heading east with stops in Asia, consider getting a RTW ticket.

London is arguably the world's headquarters for bucket shops specializing in discount tickets. Two good, reliable agents for cheap tickets in London are **STA Travel** (☎ 0871-2300-040; www.statravel.co.uk) and **Trailfinders** (☎ 0845-058-5858; www.trailfinders.com).

SEA

A handful of cruise ships offers tours of Hawaii. Most cruises last two weeks, and airfare to and from the departure point costs extra. Longer cruises include Hawaii in wider South Pacific voyages.

Most Hawaiian cruises include stopovers in Honolulu, Maui, Kaua'i and the Big Island. Cruise lines include the following:

Holland America Cruise Line (☎ 877-932-4259; www.hollandamerica.com) The 15- to 21-day cruises depart from San Diego and Vancouver.

Princess Cruises (☎ 800-774-6237; www.princess .com) Its 10- to 14-day cruises depart from Los Angeles and Vancouver.

GETTING AROUND

Most interisland travel is by plane, but a limited number of ferries connect some islands (see p575).

AIR

The major airports handling most interisland traffic are Honolulu (on O'ahu), Kahului (on Maui), Kona and Hilo (both on the Big Island), and Lihu'e (on Kaua'i). See p571 for details.

Moloka'i and Lana'i are usually approached by ferry service from Maui.

Airlines in Hawaii

The demise of Aloha Airlines in 2008 is one indication of the upheaval that interisland air travel is currently experiencing. Expect further schedule changes and possible shake-ups. Two major interisland carriers remain – Hawaiian Airlines and newcomer go! (an affiliate of Mesa Air); both offer frequent scheduled flights in jet planes between the four main islands. Two smaller, commuter-oriented airlines – Island Air and Mokulele Airlines – provide scheduled service in both prop and jet planes to the main islands as well as to Moloka'i and Lana'i.

These commuter airlines and a few other tiny airlines – like George's Aviation and Pacific Wings – are the only ones that fly to secondary airports, such as Hana on Maui and Waimea-Kohala on Hawai'i (the Big Island). These airlines also offer charters, which can be a worthwhile way to get to places where scheduled service is infrequent and sometimes unreliable. Flights in prop planes fly so low they double as sightseeing excursions.

While it's often possible to walk up and get on a flight among the four main islands (particularly to/from Honolulu), advance reservations

---

CLIMATE CHANGE & TRAVEL

Climate change is a serious threat to the ecosystems that humans rely upon, and air travel is the fastest-growing contributor to the problem. Lonely Planet regards travel, overall, as a global benefit, but believes we all have a responsibility to limit our personal impact on global warming.

Flying & Climate Change

Pretty much every form of motor travel generates CO_2 (the main cause of human-induced climate change) but planes are far and away the worst offenders, not just because of the sheer distances they allow us to travel, but because they release greenhouse gases high into the atmosphere. The statistics are frightening: two people taking a return flight between Europe and the US will contribute as much to climate change as an average household's gas and electricity consumption over a whole year.

Carbon Offset Schemes

Climatecare.org and other websites use 'carbon calculators' that allow jetsetters to offset the greenhouse gases they are responsible for with contributions to energy-saving projects and other climate-friendly initiatives in the developing world – including projects in India, Honduras, Kazakhstan and Uganda.

Lonely Planet, together with Rough Guides and other concerned partners in the travel industry, supports the carbon offset scheme run by climatecare.org. Lonely Planet offsets all of its staff and author travel.

For more information check out our website: lonelyplanet.com.

---

are recommended, especially for peak hours (and the cheapest fares). Airline regulations concerning surfboards and oversize equipment vary and can be very restrictive; make sure to check before booking.

Interisland fare wars have been ongoing recently. To/from Honolulu, advance-purchase one-way fares to the other three main islands hover around $40. Among Neighbor Islands, fares run from $70 to $90, depending on the islands involved. Without discounts, fares range from $70 to $120. Naturally, islands with less service, or furthest from each other, cost more.

George's Aviation (☎ 834-2120, 866-834-2120; www .georgesaviation.com) Flies scheduled routes between Honolulu, Maui and Moloka'i; charters prop planes to all six islands.

go! (☎ 888-435-9462; www.iflygo.com) Flies frequently from its Honolulu hub to Kaua'i, Maui and the Big Island.

Hawaiian Airlines (☎ 800-367-5320; www.hawaiian air.com) Flies nearly 200 daily routes on 717s and 767s between Honolulu, Kaua'i, Maui and the Big Island, and they can connect to Moloka'i and Lana'i.

Island Air (☎ 800-652-6541, on O'ahu 484-2222; www .islandair.com) Flies small 37-passenger planes from hubs in Honolulu (to all islands) and Maui (to all but Lana'i).

Mokulele Airlines (☎ 426-7070, 866-260-7070; www .mokuleleairlines.com) Scheduled service to all six islands, in both prop and small jet aircraft; partners with go! airlines.

Pacific Wings (☎ 888-575-4546; www.pacificwings .com) Charter single-engine Cessnas between all the islands except for Kaua'i.

BICYCLE

Realistically, cycling as the primary mode of transportation can be challenging. All islands have narrow highways with dangerous traffic and changeable weather. Long-distance cycling is best done with the support of a tour group, but if you're adventurous and in good shape, it can be done on your own. Some islands are better for this than others, so turn to the opening Activities section of island chapters for specifics.

If you want to travel among islands, remember that interisland flights charge $35 (or more) to transport your bike.

Bringing your own bike to Hawaii costs $100 (or more) on flights from the US mainland. The bicycle can be checked at the airline counter, the same as any baggage, but you'll need to box it or prepare the bike by wrapping the handlebars and pedals in foam or by fixing the handlebars to the side and removing the pedals. For more on flying your bike, see the **International Bicycle Fund** (www.ibike.org).

In general, bicycles are required to follow the same state laws and rules of the road as cars. For more cycling information, as well as maps of current and proposed bike lanes by island, see the state **Department of Transportation** (www.state.hi.us/dot/highways/bike/bikeplan). See also the Getting Around sections of island chapters, and for a list of great rides, see p83.

BOAT

Interisland ferry service is surprisingly limited in Hawaii. Currently, only Moloka'i (p442) and Lana'i (p427) have regular, passenger-only public ferry service, and both are served only from Lahaina, Maui. In addition, **Norwegian Cruise Line** (☎ 866-234-0292; www.ncl.com) is the only company that operates a cruise between the Hawaiian Islands that starts and ends in Hawaii. Seven-day interisland cruises make round-trips from Honolulu and visit the four main islands.

From 2007 to early 2009, Hawaii Superferry (www.hawaiisuperferry.com) ran a high-speed, passenger-and-car ferry service between Honolulu and Maui (with planned service between Honolulu and the Big Island). However, it was forced to shut down in March 2009 when the State Supreme Court ruled that it had violated the state constitution by not first completing an environmental impact statement; for the complete story, see p474. Whether Superferry or a similar ferry service will ever sail again is anyone's guess, but it's unlikely in the near future.

BUS

O'ahu's excellent islandwide public system, called TheBus (p111), makes O'ahu the easiest island to navigate without a car. Schedules are frequent, service is reliable and fares are $2 per ride regardless of your destination.

Public bus systems that run on the Neighbor Islands are geared solely to resident commuters; service is infrequent and limited to main towns, sometimes bypassing tourist destinations entirely. After O'ahu's, the next best system is the Maui Bus (p335), but it doesn't stop at West Maui beaches or Haleakalā National Park.

The Big Island's Hele-On Bus (p212) is free and will get you around to most island towns (and includes Hawai'i Volcanoes National Park), but service is still too limited for sightseeing.

The limited Kaua'i Bus (p475) can take visitors between the major island towns and as far north as Hanalei, but doesn't include Waimea Canyon.

CAR

The majority of visitors to Hawaii rent their own vehicles, particularly US visitors to Neighbor Islands. So to most of you, we say: read on.

The minimum age for driving in Hawaii is 18 years, though car-rental companies usually have higher age restrictions. If you're under 25 years, you should call the car-rental agencies in advance to check their policies regarding restrictions and surcharges.

Automobile Associations

The **American Automobile Association** (AAA; Map p114; ☎ 593-2221, from Neighbor Islands 800-736-2886; www.aaa-hawaii.com; 1130 N Nimitz Hwy, Honolulu) has its only Hawaii office in Honolulu. It provides members with maps and other information. Members also get discounts on car rental, air tickets, some hotels, some sightseeing attractions, as well as emergency road service and towing (☎ 800-222-4357). AAA has reciprocal agreements with automobile associations in other countries, but be sure to bring your membership card from your country of origin.

Driver's License

An International Driving Permit, obtained before you leave home, is only necessary if you're from a non-English-speaking country.

Fuel & Towing

Fuel is readily available everywhere except along a few particular roads; these are noted in text (like Saddle Rd on the Big Island and the Road to Hana on Maui). Expect to pay at least 50¢ more per US gallon than on the mainland. Average Hawaii gas prices soared to new highs in 2008, to well over $4 a gallon, and then in early 2009 they fell to the lowest since 2005, to under $2.40 a gallon. In recent years prices have averaged between $2.70 and $3.40 a gallon.

If you get into trouble with your car, towing is mighty expensive in Hawaii; avoid it at all costs. Fees start at around $65, plus $5 to $7 for every mile you need to be towed. Don't drive your standard car on 4WD roads, which is usually prohibited by rental companies and will void damage-insurance coverage. Always ask when booking about the company's road restrictions for its vehicles.

Insurance

Liability insurance covers people and property that you might hit. For damage to the actual rental vehicle, a collision damage waiver

(CDW) is available for $15 to $20 a day. If you have collision coverage on your vehicle at home, it might cover damages to car rentals; inquire before departing. Additionally, some credit cards offer reimbursement coverage for collision damages if you rent the car with that credit card; again, check before departing. Most credit-card coverage has restrictions – whether over length of rental (some must be less than 15 days) or type (vans and 4WDs may be excluded).

Rental

Cars for rent are readily available except on Lana'i and Moloka'i, where you should reserve as early as possible. With advance reservations (highly recommended anywhere), the daily rate for a small car ranges from $20 to $40, while typical weekly rates are $130 to $170. (Rates for midsize cars or even 4WD vehicles are sometimes only a tad higher.) When getting quotes, always ask for the full rate, *including taxes*, which can add more than $5 a day and over $100 to a multiweek rental.

As with flights, getting the best deal on a car rental is all about persistence. Auto clubs and frequent-flier programs sometimes offer discounts, so ask them first. Shop around between rental companies, and check their offers against online agencies (use the same ones as for airline tickets, p572).

Rental rates usually include unlimited mileage. Sometimes, as in Honolulu, you might get a better deal if you pick up and drop off from a city (rather than an airport) location, but be careful of dropping off and picking up at different locations, which usually requires a hefty additional fee.

Having a major credit card greatly simplifies the rental process. Without one, some agents simply will not rent vehicles, while others require prepayment, a deposit of $200 per week, pay stubs, proof of return airfare and more.

Toll-free numbers for the following companies operating in Hawaii work from the US mainland:

Alamo (☎ 800-462-5266; www.alamo.com)
Avis (☎ 800-331-1212; www.avis.com)
Budget (☎ 800-527-0700; www.budget.com)
Dollar (☎ 800-800-3665; www.dollar.com)
Enterprise (☎ 800-261-7331; www.enterprise.com)
Hertz (☎ 800-654-3131; www.hertz.com)
National (☎ 800-227-7368; www.nationalcar.com)
Thrifty (☎ 800-847-4389; www.thrifty.com)

Each island has one or two local agencies (see the Getting Around sections of island chapters), and these are worth checking out – on Maui, it's the only way to rent a biofuel car (p368), and on the Big Island, it's the only way to rent a 4WD that's allowed on Mauna Kea's summit (p213).

Road Conditions & Hazards

Drunk drivers can be a hazard, and in some rural areas, so can livestock on the road. However, the main hazards are usually narrow, winding or steep roads that sometimes wash out after heavy rains. Every island has several, and they are noted in the text.

For one-lane-bridge crossings, one direction of traffic usually has the right of way while the other must obey the posted yield sign. Downhill traffic must yield to uphill traffic where there is no sign.

Street addresses on some Hawaiian highways may seem quirky, but there's a pattern. For hyphenated numbers, such as 4-734 Kuhio Hwy, the first part of the number identifies the post office district and the second part identifies the street address. Thus, it's possible for 4-736 to be followed by 5-002; you've just entered a new district, that's all.

Road Rules

As with mainland USA, driving is on the right-hand side of the road – usually. On unpaved or potholed roads, locals may hog the middle stripe until an oncoming car approaches. 'Right on red' is allowed (unless a sign prohibits it), but island drivers usually wait for the green light. Slow, courteous driving is the rule, not the exception. Locals don't honk (unless they're about to crash), they don't follow close and they let people pass. Do the same, and you may get an appreciative *shaka* (Hawaiian hand greeting sign) from other drivers.

Hawaii requires the use of seat belts (tickets are expensive), and children aged four and under must use a child-safety seat. Rental companies (left) are required to provide them on request, but only if you reserve in advance.

Speed limits are posted *and* enforced. If you're stopped for speeding, expect a ticket, as Hawaii police rarely just give warnings.

HITCHHIKING

Hitchhiking, though technically illegal statewide, is not unusual. In certain areas, it's an accepted way to get around easily (sometimes as noted in the text). However, hitchhiking anywhere is not without risks, and Lonely Planet does not recommend it. Get local advice, never hitchhike alone and size up each situation carefully before getting in a car. Travelers should understand that, by hitchhiking, they are always taking a small but serious risk.

MOPED & MOTORCYCLE

Motorcycle hire is not common in Hawaii, but mopeds are a transportation option in some resort areas. You can legally drive either vehicle in Hawaii as long as you have a valid driver's license issued by your home country. The minimum age for renting a moped is 16; for a motorcycle it's 21.

There are no helmet laws in the state of Hawaii, but rental agencies often provide free helmets, and cautious riders will use them. Also remember that the windward sides of the islands generally require foul-weather gear, since it rains often.

State law requires mopeds to be ridden by one person only and prohibits their use on sidewalks and freeways. Mopeds must always be driven in single file and may not be driven at speeds in excess of 30mph. Bizarrely, mopeds can be more expensive to rent than cars.

TAXI

All the main islands have taxis, with fares based on mileage regardless of the number of passengers. Since taxis are often station wagons or minivans, they're good value for groups (a particularly smart idea if the designated driver decides to join the party). Rates vary, as they're set by each county, but average around $3 at flag-down, then about $3 per additional mile; bags are usually 50¢ each. Outside of Honolulu and Waikiki,

and at most hotels and resorts, travelers will have to call ahead to book a taxi. Pick-ups from remote locations (such as after a long one-way hike) can sometimes be arranged in advance.

TOURS

For information on cruises to the Hawaiian Islands, see p573.

A number of companies operate half- and full-day sightseeing bus tours on each island. Specialized adventure tours, such as whale-watching cruises, snorkeling trips to Lana'i, flights over Moloka'i and boat cruises along the Kona Coast, are also available. All of these tours can be booked after arrival in Hawaii. For details, consult the Activities sections near the front of island chapters.

Helicopter tours get you to some amazing places. Prices vary depending on the destination and the length of the flight, with a 45-minute tour averaging $130 to $180 per passenger. These are mainly offered on the Big Island (see the boxed text, p214), Kaua'i (p472) and Maui (p366). For chartered sightseeing flights, see the airlines listed on p573.

If you want to visit another island while you're in Hawaii but only have a day or two to spare, consider an island-hopping tour to the Neighbor Islands. The largest company specializing in 'overnighters' is **Roberts Hawaii** (☎ on O'ahu 523-9323, from the Neighbor Islands & US mainland 800-349-3888; www.robertsovernighters.com).

Elderhostel (☎ 800-454-5768; www.elderhostel.org) offers educational programs for those aged 55 or older. Many of these focus on Hawaii's people and culture, while others explore the natural environment. Fees range from $1400 to $3500 for one- to two-week programs, including accommodations, meals and classes, but excluding airfare.

Health

CONTENTS

BEFORE YOU GO

INSURANCE

The USA offers possibly the finest health care in the world – and the most expensive. It's essential to purchase travel health insurance if your regular policy doesn't cover you overseas. For more information, check the **Lonely Planet website** (www.lonelyplanet.com/bookings/insurance.do). Find out in advance if your insurance will make payments directly to providers or reimburse you later for overseas health expenditures.

Bring any medications you may need in their original containers, clearly labeled. A signed, dated letter from your physician describing all medical conditions and medications, including generic names, is also handy.

MEDICAL CHECKLIST

- acetaminophen (eg Tylenol) or aspirin
- anti-inflammatory drugs (eg ibuprofen)
- antihistamines (for hay fever and allergic reactions)
- antibacterial ointment (eg Neosporin) for cuts and abrasions
- steroid cream or cortisone (for poison ivy and other allergic rashes)
- bandages, gauze, gauze rolls
- adhesive or paper tape
- scissors, safety pins, tweezers
- thermometer
- pocketknife
- DEET-containing insect repellent for the skin
- permethrin-containing insect spray for clothing, tents and bed nets
- sunblock

INTERNET RESOURCES

There is a wealth of travel-health advice on the internet. The World Health Organization publishes a superb book called *International Travel and Health* (www.who.int/ith/en); it's free to download. Another general-interest website, with advice for every country, is MD Travel Health (www.mdtravelhealth.com).

It's usually a good idea to consult your government's travel-health website before departure, if one is available:

Australia (www.smartraveller.gov.au)
Canada (www.phac-aspc.gc.ca)
UK (www.nathnac.org)
USA (www.cdc.gov/travel)

IN HAWAII

AVAILABILITY & COST OF HEALTH CARE

For immediate medical assistance anywhere in Hawaii, call ☎ 911. In general, if you have a medical emergency, the best bet is to go to the emergency room of the nearest hospital. If the problem isn't urgent, consider calling a nearby hospital and asking for a referral to a local physician; this is usually cheaper than an emergency-room visit. In Hawaii the nearest hospital may not be close, so the best choice may be an expensive stand-alone, for-profit, urgent-care center. See the Information sections of island chapters for local hospitals.

Pharmacies are abundantly supplied, but some medications available over the counter in your home country may require a prescription in the USA. Also, prescriptions can be shockingly expensive (so check your insurance coverage).

Covering all the islands, the **Hawaii Health Guide** (www.hawaiihealthguide.com) is the most comprehensive central resource for finding local hospitals, health services and practitioners.

INFECTIOUS DISEASES

In addition to more common ailments, several infectious diseases are present in Hawaii. Most of these diseases are acquired by mosquito or tick bites, or through environmental exposure.

RECOMMENDED VACCINATIONS

No special vaccines are required or recommended for travel to the USA. All travelers should be up-to-date on routine immunizations, listed below.

Vaccine	Recommended for	Dosage	Side effects
chicken pox	travelers who've never had chicken pox	two doses a month apart	fever; mild case of chicken pox
influenza	all travelers during flu season (Nov-Mar)	one dose	soreness at the injection site; fever
measles	travelers born after 1956 who've had only one measles vaccination	one dose	fever; rash; joint pains; allergic reactions
tetanus-diphtheria	all travelers who haven't had booster within 10 years	one dose lasts 10 years	soreness at injection site

Dengue Fever

Dengue is transmitted by aedes mosquitoes, which bite preferentially during the daytime. Since they breed primarily in artificial water containers (like barrels, plastic containers and discarded tires), dengue is especially common in densely populated, urban environments. In Hawaii the last outbreak was in 2002. For updates, consult the **Hawaii State Department of Health website** (www.state.hi.us/doh).

Dengue usually causes flulike symptoms, including fever, muscle aches, joint pains, headaches, nausea and vomiting, often followed by a rash. There is no treatment for dengue fever except to take analgesics such as acetaminophen/paracetamol (eg Tylenol) – do not take aspirin, as it increases the likelihood of hemorrhaging – and drink plenty of fluids. See a doctor to be diagnosed and monitored. Severe cases may require hospitalization for supportive care. There is no vaccine. The cornerstone of prevention is insect-protection measures.

Giardiasis

This parasitic infection of the small intestine occurs all over the world. Symptoms include nausea, bloating, cramps and diarrhea, and may last for weeks. To protect yourself, don't drink from waterfalls, ponds, streams and rivers, which may be contaminated by animal or human feces. The infection can also be transmitted from person to person if proper hand-washing is not done. Giardiasis is easily diagnosed by a stool test and readily treated with antibiotics.

Leptospirosis

Leptospirosis is acquired by exposure to water contaminated by the urine of infected animals, such as rats and feral pigs. Outbreaks often occur at times of flooding, when sudden overflow may contaminate water sources downstream from animal habitats. Even an idyllic waterfall may, in fact, be infected with leptospirosis. The initial symptoms, which resemble a mild flu, usually subside uneventfully in a few days, but a minority of cases are complicated by jaundice or meningitis. It can also cause hepatitis and renal failure, which might be fatal. Diagnosis is through blood tests and the disease is easily treated with doxycycline. There is no vaccine. You can minimize your risk by staying out of bodies of freshwater (eg pools, streams) that may be contaminated; avoid these entirely if you have open cuts or sores. Take trailhead warning signs about leptospirosis seriously. If you're camping, water purification is essential.

West Nile Virus

Hawaii has no known cases of West Nile virus in humans, but infections have occurred across the mainland US and the rising number of reported cases in California is cause for concern. The virus is transmitted by culex mosquitoes, which are active in late summer and early fall and generally bite after dusk (see also Mosquito Bites, p580). Most infections are mild or asymptomatic, but the virus may infect the central nervous system, leading to fever, headache, confusion, lethargy, coma and sometimes death. There is no treatment for West Nile virus.

For the latest update on the areas affected by West Nile, go to the **US Geological Survey website** (http://disease maps.usgs.gov).

ENVIRONMENTAL HAZARDS

Vog, a visible haze or volcanic smog from active volcanoes, is usually dispersed by trade winds. Short-term exposure is not generally hazardous, however, heavy vog can create breathing problems for some. For more, see p217.

See p79 for advice on ocean safety.

Altitude Sickness

Acute Mountain Sickness (AMS), aka altitude sickness, may develop in those who ascend rapidly to altitudes greater than 7500ft, as on Mauna Kea (see p269) and Mauna Loa (see p275) on the Big Island. Being physically fit offers no protection. Those who have experienced AMS in the past are prone to future episodes. The risk increases with faster ascents, higher altitudes and greater exertion. Symptoms may include headaches, nausea, vomiting, dizziness, malaise, insomnia and loss of appetite. Severe cases may be complicated by fluid in the lungs (high-altitude pulmonary edema) or swelling of the brain (high-altitude cerebral edema).

The best treatment for AMS is descent. If you are exhibiting symptoms, do not ascend. If symptoms are severe or persistent, descend immediately. When traveling to high altitudes, it's also important to avoid overexertion, eat light meals and abstain from alcohol. If your symptoms are more than mild or don't resolve promptly, see a doctor. Altitude sickness should be taken seriously; it can be life-threatening when severe.

Bites & Stings

Hawaii has no established wild snake population, but snakes are occasionally seen, especially in sugarcane fields.

Leeches are found in humid rainforest areas. They do not transmit any disease but their bites are often intensely itchy for weeks afterwards and can easily become infected. Apply an iodine-based antiseptic to any leech bite to help prevent infection.

Bee and wasp stings mainly cause problems for people who have allergies. Anyone with a serious bee or wasp allergy should carry an injection of adrenaline for emergency treatment. For others pain is the main problem – apply ice to the sting and take painkillers.

Fire ants and centipedes also have painful bites; the latter occasionally infiltrate buildings, so check sheets and shoes.

Commonsense behavior and dress are the most effective protections: wear long sleeves and pants, hats and shoes (not sandals).

MAMMAL BITES

Do not attempt to pet, handle or feed any animal, with the exception of domestic animals known to be free of infectious disease. Most animal injuries result when people try to touch or feed the animal.

Any mammal bite or scratch – including bats, feral pigs, goats etc – should be promptly and thoroughly cleansed with soap and water, followed by application of an antiseptic such as iodine or alcohol. You may want to start antibiotics, since animal wounds frequently become infected. Hawaii is currently rabies-free.

MARINE ANIMALS

Marine spikes, such as those found on sea urchins, scorpion fish and Hawaiian lionfish, can cause severe local pain. If this occurs, immediately immerse the affected area in hot water (as high a temperature as can be tolerated). Keep topping up with hot water until the pain subsides and medical care can be reached. The same advice applies if you are stung by a cone shell.

Marine stings from jellyfish and Portuguese man-of-war (aka 'bluebottles') also occur in Hawaii's tropical waters. Even touching a bluebottle a few hours after it's washed up onshore can result in burning stings. Jellyfish are often seen eight to 10 days after a full moon, when they float into shallow near-shore waters, such as at Waikiki. If you are stung, first aid consists of washing the skin with vinegar to prevent further discharge of remaining stinging cells, followed by rapid transfer to a hospital; antivenom are widely available.

Despite extensive media coverage, the risk of shark attack in Hawaiian waters is rare and no greater than other Pacific regions. Avoid swimming in waters with runoff after heavy rainfall (eg around river mouths) and those areas frequented by commercial fishing operators. Do not swim if you are bleeding or have open cuts, as this attracts sharks. Check with lifeguards about local risks.

MOSQUITO BITES

Where mosquito-borne illnesses have been reported, keep yourself covered and apply good insect repellent, preferably one containing DEET. In general, adults and children over 12 should use preparations containing 25 to 35% DEET, which usually lasts about hours. Children between two and 12 years of age should use preparations containing no more than 10% DEET, applied sparingly, which usually lasts about three hours. Neurologic toxicity has been reported from DEET, especially in children, but appears to be extremely uncommon and generally related to overuse. Don't use DEET-containing compounds on children under age two.

Insect repellents containing certain botanical products, including oil of eucalyptus and soybean oil, are effective but last only 1½ to two hours. Products based on citronella are not effective.

Visit the **Center for Disease Control's website** (CDC; wwww.cdc.gov/travel/contentInsectProtection.aspx) for prevention information.

SPIDER BITES

Hawaii has many spiders, but only a few non-native species cause significant human illness: particularly black widow and brown recluse spiders. The black widow is black or brown in color, measuring about 15mm in body length, with a shiny top, fat body and distinctive red or orange hourglass figure on its underside. It's found usually in woodpiles, sheds and bowls of outdoor toilets. The brown recluse spider is brown, usually 10mm in body length, with a dark violin-shaped mark on the top of the upper section of the body. It's active mostly at night, lives in dark sheltered areas such as under porches and in woodpiles, and typically bites when trapped.

If bitten by a black widow, apply ice and go immediately to the hospital. Complications of a black widow bite may include muscle spasms, breathing difficulties and high blood pressure. The bite of a brown recluse typically causes a large, inflamed wound, sometimes associated with fever and chills. If bitten, apply ice and see a physician.

Cold

To prevent hypothermia, keep all body surfaces covered, including the head and neck. Synthetic materials such as Gore-Tex and Thinsulate provide excellent insulation. Because the body loses heat faster when wet, stay dry at all times. Change inner garments promptly when they become moist. Keep active, but get enough rest. Consume plenty of food and water. Be especially sure not to have any alcohol, and avoid caffeine and tobacco.

Watch out for the 'Umbles' – stumbles, mumbles, fumbles and grumbles – which are important signs of impending hypothermia. If someone appears to be developing hypothermia, insulate them from the ground, protect them from the wind, remove wet clothing or cover with a vapor barrier such as a plastic bag, and transport immediately to a warm environment and a medical facility. Warm fluids (but not coffee or tea) may be given if the person is alert enough to swallow.

Diving & Snorkeling Hazards

Divers, snorkelers and surfers should seek specialized advice before they travel, to ensure their medical kit contains treatment for coral cuts and tropical ear infections, as well as the standard problems. Divers should check their insurance covers them for decompression illness – get specialized dive insurance through an organization such as **Divers Alert Network** (DAN; www .diversalertnetwork.org). Have a dive medical before you leave your home country – there are certain medical conditions that are incompatible with diving that your dive operator may not always ask you about.

Heat

When it's hot, drink plenty of fluids and avoid strenuous exercise.

Dehydration is the main contributor to heat exhaustion. Symptoms include feeling weak, headache, irritability, nausea or vomiting, sweaty skin, a fast, weak pulse and a normal or slightly elevated body temperature. Treatment involves getting out of the heat and/or sun, removing clothing that retains heat (cotton is okay), fanning continuously, laying the victim flat with legs raised and rehydrating with water containing one-quarter of a teaspoon of salt per liter. Recovery is usually rapid, though it's common to feel weak for days afterwards.

Heatstroke is a serious medical emergency. Symptoms come on suddenly and include weakness, nausea, a hot, dry body with a body temperature of over 106°F, dizziness, confusion, loss of coordination, fits and eventually collapse and loss of consciousness. Seek medical help and commence cooling by getting the person out of the heat, removing clothes, fanning and applying ice or cold packs to the neck, armpits and groin.

HEALTH

Language

Hawaii has two official state languages: English and Hawaiian. Although English has long replaced Hawaiian as the dominant language, many Hawaiian words and phrases are commonly used in speech and in print.

Prior to the arrival of Christian missionaries in 1820, the Hawaiians had no written language. Knowledge was passed on through complex oral genealogies, stories, chants, songs and descriptive place names. The missionaries rendered the spoken language into the Roman alphabet and established the first presses in the islands, which were used to print the Bible and other religious instructional materials in Hawaiian.

Throughout the 19th century, as more and more foreigners (particularly the Americans and the British) settled in the islands, the everyday use of Hawaiian declined. In the 1890s English was made the official language of government and education.

The push for statehood, from 1900 to 1959, added to the decline of the Hawaiian language. Speaking Hawaiian was seen as a deterrent to American assimilation, thus adult native speakers were strongly discouraged from teaching their children Hawaiian as the primary language in the home.

This attitude remained until the early 1970s when the Hawaiian community began to experience a cultural renaissance. A handful of young Hawaiians lobbied to establish Hawaiian language classes at the University of Hawai'i, and Hawaiian language immersion preschools followed in the 1980s. These preschools are modeled after Maori *kohanga reo* (language nests), where the primary method of language perpetuation is through speaking and hearing the language on a daily basis. In Hawai'i's 'Aha Punana Leo preschools, all learning and communication takes place in the mother tongue – *ka 'olelo makuahine*.

Hawaiian has now been revived from the point of extinction and is growing throughout the community. Record numbers of students enroll in Hawaiian language classes in high schools and colleges, and immersion-school graduates are raising a new generation of native speakers.

If you'd like to discover more about th[e] Hawaiian language, get a copy of Lonel[y] Planet's *South Pacific* phrasebook.

PRONUNCIATION

Written Hawaiian uses just 13 letters: fiv[e] vowels (**a, e, i, o, u**), seven consonants (**h, k, m, n, p, w**) and the glottal stop ('). The letter[s] **h, l, m** and **n** are pronounced much the sam[e] as in English. Usually every letter in Hawai[i]ian words is pronounced, and each vow[el] has a different pronunciation depending o[n] whether it is stressed or unstressed.

Consonants

p/k   similar to English, but with les[s] aspiration; **k** may be replaced with [t]

w   after **i** and **e**, usually a soft English 'v[,' thus the town of Hale'iwa is pr[o]nounced 'Hale'iva,' After **u** or **o** it[']s often like English 'w,' thus Olowalu [is] pronounced as written. After **a** or [at] the beginning of a word it can be a[n] English 'w' or 'v,' thus you'll hear bot[h] Hawai'i and Havai'i (The Big Island[)]

Unstressed vowels (without macron)

a   as in 'ago'
e   as in 'bet'
i   as the 'y' in 'city'
o   as in 'sole'
u   as in 'rude'

Glottal Stops & Macrons

Written Hawaiian uses both glottal stops (' called *'okina*, and macrons (a straight ba[r] above a vowel, eg **ā**), called *kahakō*. In mod[]ern print both the glottal stop and the ma[]cron are often omitted. In this guidebook the macrons have been omitted, but glott[al] stops have been included, as they can b[e] helpful in striving to pronounce commo[n] place names and words correctly.

The glottal stop indicates a break betwee[n] two vowels, producing an effect similar t[o] saying 'oh-oh' in English. For example, *'a'[ā]* a type of lava, is pronounced 'ah-ah,' an[d] Ho'okena, a place name, is pronounced 'H[o-]oh-kena.' A macron inidicates that the vow[el] is stressed and has a long pronunciation.

Glottal stops and macrons not only affect ronunciation, but can give a word a com-letely different meaning. For example, *ai* vith no glottal) means 'sexual intercourse,' ut *'ai* (with the glottal) means 'food.' Simi-rly, the word *ka'a* (with no macron over e second **a**) means 'to roll, turn or twist,' ut *ka'ā* (with a macron over the second **a**) a thread or line used in fishing.

ompound Words

n the written form, many Hawaiian words re compound words made up of several ifferent words. For example, the word *umuhumunukunukuapua'a* can be broken own as follows: *humuhumu-nukunuku-a-ua'a* (literally, 'trigger fish snout of pig'), neaning 'the fish with a snout like a pig.' he place name Waikiki is also a compound ord: *wai-kiki* (literally, 'freshwater sprout-g'), referring to the freshwater swamps nce found in the area. Some words are oubled to emphasize their meaning, much ke in English. For example, *wiki* means uick,' while *wikiwiki* means 'very quick.'

ommon Hawaiian Words

or more Hawaiian words, see the Glossary 584).

oha – love, hello, welcome, goodbye
ale – house
eiau – religious temple
ane – man
apu – taboo, restricted
au – traditional Hawaiian feast
ahalo – thank you
ahimahi – dolphinfish, commonly eaten
auka – a direction, toward the mountains
akai – a direction, toward the sea
no – delicious, tasty
au – finished, completed
oi – staple food made from taro
kulele – four-stringed musical instrument, used in odern Hawaiian music (literally, 'leaping flea,' because of e action of the fingers when playing)
ahine – woman

IDGIN

awaii pidgin is a distinct language, spoken y over 500,000 people. It developed on igar plantations where the *luna* (foreman) ad to communicate with laborers from any foreign countries. Early plantation idgin used a minimal and condensed form

of English as the root language, to which elements from Japanese, Hawaiian, Cantonese and Portuguese were added. It became the second language of first-generation immigrants and many Hawaiians.

As this English-based pidgin evolved, it took on its own grammatical structure and syntax. Many words were pronounced differently and combined in ways not found in English. Rather than a careless or broken form of English, it evolved into a separate language, called Hawaii Creole by linguists.

Today, there is ongoing controversy about the validity of pidgin, with opponents saying that it erodes standard English and becomes a barrier to social and educational advancement. Proponents argue that pidgin is a rich and vibrant language that should not be looked down upon or banned from schools, and that pidgin speakers are often unjustly seen as less intelligent.

In recent years numerous award-winning plays, books and poetry have been written in pidgin by local authors who are passionate in their determination to keep pidgin alive in the community.

Common Pidgin Words & Phrases

brah – shortened form of *braddah* (brother); also used as 'hey you'
broke da mout – delicious; as in 'My auntie make broke da mout kine fish!'
buggahs – guys; as in 'Da buggahs wen' go without me!'
bumbye – later on; as in 'We go movies bumbye den (then).'
bummahs – bummer; an expression of disappointment or regret
chicken skin – goose bumps from cold, fear or thrill
da kine – whatchamacallit; used whenever you can't think of the appropriate word
Fo' real? – Really? Are you kidding me?
funny kine – strange or different; as in 'He stay acking (acting) all funny kine.'
geev 'um – Go for it! Give it all you got!
Get chance? – What are my chances? As in 'She da bomb. I get chance, or what?'
How you stay? – How are you doing these days?
Howzit? – Hi, how's it going? As in 'Eh, howzit brah!'
kay den – 'OK then'; as in 'Kay den, we go beach.'
laydahs – Later on. I'll see you later; as in, 'Kay den, laydahs.'
no ack – (literally, 'no act') Stop showing off, cool it.
rubbah slippahs – (literally, 'rubber slippers') flip-flops
talk story – chitchat or any casual conversation
to da max – used to add emphasis; as in 'Da waves was big to da max!'

LANGUAGE

Glossary

For more food terms, see p70. Also see the Language chapter, p582.

'a'a – type of lava that is rough and jagged
ahi – yellowfin or bigeye tuna
'ahinahina – silversword plant with pointed silver leaves
ahu – stone cairns used to mark a trail; an altar or shrine
ahupua'a – traditional land division, usually in a wedge shape that extends from the mountains to the sea
aikane – friend
'aina – land
'akala – Hawaiian raspberry; also called a thimbleberry
akamai – clever
'akepa – endangered crested honeycreeper
aku – skipjack tuna, type of bonito
akua – god, spirit, idol
'alae kea – endangered Hawaiian coot
'alala – Hawaiian crow
ali'i – chief, royalty
aloha – the traditional greeting meaning love, welcome, good-bye
aloha 'aina – respect for the land
'ama'ama – mullet
'amakihi – small, yellow-green honeycreeper; one of the more common native birds
anchialine pool – contains a mixture of seawater and freshwater
'a'o – Newell's shearwater (a seabird)
'apapane – bright red native Hawaiian honeycreeper
'aumakua – protective deity or guardian spirit, deified ancestor or trustworthy person
awa – Hawaiian milk fish
'awa – see *kava*
'awapuhi – wild ginger
azuki bean – often served as a sweetened paste, eg as a topping for shave ice

bentō – Japanese-style boxed lunch
broke da mout – delicious; literally, 'broke the mouth'

chicken skin – goosebumps
crack seed – Chinese preserved fruit; a salty, sweet and/or sour snack

'elepaio – Hawaiian monarch flycatcher; a brownish native bird with a white rump, common to O'ahu forests

goza – rolled-up straw mats used at the beach
grinds – food; to *grind* means to eat

hala – pandanus (screwpine); the leaves *(lau)* are used in weaving mats and baskets
hale – house
hana – work; a bay, when used as a compound in place names
haole – Caucasian; literally, 'without breath'
hapa – portion or fragment; person of mixed blood
hau – indigenous lowland hibiscus tree whose wood is often used for making canoe outriggers (stabilizing arms that jut out from the hull)
Hawai'i Nei – all the Hawaiian Islands taken as a group
heiau – ancient stone temple; a place of worship in Hawaii
hele on – to get moving
Hina – Polynesian goddess (wife of Ku, one of the four main gods)
holoholo – to walk, drive or ramble around for pleasure
holua – sled or sled course
honu – green sea turtle
ho'olaule'a – celebration, party
ho'onanea – to pass the time in ease, peace and pleasure
huhu – angry
hui – group, organization
hukilau – fishing with a *seine* (a large net), involving a group of people who pull in the net
hula – Hawaiian dance form, either traditional or modern
hula 'auana – modern hula, developed after the introduction of Western music
hula halau – hula school or troupe
hula kahiko – traditional hula
humuhumunukunukuapua'a – rectangular triggerfish; Hawaii's official state fish

'i'iwi – scarlet Hawaiian honeycreeper with a curved, salmon-colored beak
'iliahi – Hawaiian sandalwood
'ili'ili – smooth, flat stones used as a hula instrument
'ilima – native plant, a ground cover with delicate yellow-orange flowers; O'ahu's official flower
'io – Hawaiian hawk
ipu – spherical, narrow-necked gourd used as a hula instrument
issei – first-generation Japanese immigrants; born in Japan

kahili – royal feathered staff
kahuna – priest, healer or sorcerer
kahuna nui – high priest
kaiseki – multicourse chef's tasting menu
kava – native plant used to make an intoxicating drink

limu – seaweed

lio – horse

loko i'a – fishpond

lolo – stupid, feeble-minded, crazy

lomi – to rub or soften

lomilomi – traditional Hawaiian massage; known as 'loving touch'

Lono – Polynesian god of harvest, agriculture, fertility and peace

loulu – native fan palms

luakini – a type of *heiau* dedicated to the war god Ku and often used for human sacrifices

luau – traditional Hawaiian feast

mahalo – thank you

mahele – to divide; usually refers to the sugar industry – initiated land divisions of 1848

mahimahi – white-fleshed dolphinfish or dorado; not related to the mammal dolphin

mai ho'oka'awale – leprosy (Hansen's disease); literally, 'the separating sickness'

mai'a – banana

maile – native plant with twining habit and fragrant leaves; often used for lei

maka'ainana – commoners; literally, 'people who tend the land'

makaha – a sluice gate, used to regulate the level of water in a fishpond

makahiki – traditional annual wet-season festival dedicated to the agricultural god Lono

makai – toward the sea; seaward

malihini – newcomer, visitor

malo – loincloth

mamane – a native tree with bright yellow flowers; used to make lei

mana – spiritual power

manini – convict tang (a reef fish); also refers to something small or insignificant

mauka – toward the mountains; inland

mele – song, chant

menehune – 'little people' who, according to legend, built many of Hawaii's fishponds, heiau and other stonework

milo – a native shade tree with beautiful hardwood

mokihana – an endemic tree or shrub, with scented green berries; used to make lei

moi – threadfish; reserved for royalty in ancient times

mo'i – king

mo'o – water spirit, lizard, reptile or dragon

mu – a 'body catcher' who secured sacrificial victims for the heiau altar

muumuu – a long, loose-fitting dress introduced by the missionaries

naupaka – native Hawaiian shrub with a five-petaled white flower

Neighbor Islands – the term used to refer to the main Hawaiian Islands outside of O'ahu

nene – a native goose; Hawaii's state bird

nisei – second-generation Japanese immigrants

niu – coconut

noni – Indian mulberry; a small tree with yellow, smelly fruit that is used medicinally

nuku pu'u – a native honeycreeper with a yellow-green underbelly

ogo – Japanese word for a crunchy, edible type of seaweed

'ohana – family, extended family; close-knit group

'ohi'a lehua – native Hawaiian tree with tufted, feathery, pom-pomlike flowers

'okole – buttocks

olo – a primitive longboard that weighed almost 100lb

ono – white-fleshed wahoo

'ono – delicious

pahoehoe – type of lava that is quick and smooth-flowing

pakalolo – marijuana; literally, 'crazy smoke'

palaka – Hawaiian-style plaid shirt made from sturdy cotton

pali – cliff

palila – endangered honeycreeper found only on Mauna Kea, Hawai'i the Big Island

paniolo – Hawaiian cowboy

pau – finished, no more

pau hana – happy hour

Pele – goddess of fire, lightning, dance, volcanoes and violence; her home is in Kilauea Caldera

pidgin – distinct local language and dialect, influenced by its multiethnic immigrants

piko – navel, umbilical cord

pili – a bunchgrass, commonly used for thatching buildings

pilo – native shrub of the coffee family

pohaku – rock

pohuehue – beach morning glory

poi – steamed, mashed taro; fermented taro

Poliahu – goddess of snow

po'ouli – endangered endemic creeper

pua aloalo – a hibiscus flower

pueo – Hawaiian owl

puhi – eel

pu'ili – bamboo sticks with long slits, used as a hula implement

puka – any kind of hole or opening; puka shells are those that are small, white and strung into necklaces

pukiawe – native plant with red and white berries and evergreen leaves

pulu – the silken clusters encasing the stems of hapu'u ferns

pupu – snack or appetizer; also a type of cowry shell

pu'u – hill, cinder cone
pu'uhonua – place of refuge
raku – a style of Japanese pottery characterized by a rough, handmade appearance
rubbah slippah – rubber flip-flops

sansei – third-generation Japanese immigrants
shaka – hand gesture used in Hawaii as a greeting or sign of local pride
stink-eye – dirty look

tabi – Japanese reef-walking shoes
taiko – Japanese drumming
talk story – to strike up a conversation, make small talk
tapa – cloth made by pounding the bark of paper mulberry, used for early Hawaiian clothing (*kapa* in Hawaiian)
ti – common native plant; its long shiny leaves are used for wrapping food and making hula skirts (*ki* in Hawaiian)

tiki – wood- or stone-carved statue, usually depicting a deity (*ki'i* in Hawaiian)
tutu – grandmother or grandfather; also term of respect for any member of that generation

'ua'u – dark-rumped petrel
ukulele – a stringed musical instrument derived from the *braguinha*, which was introduced to Hawaii in the 1800s by Portuguese immigrants
'uli'uli – gourd rattle containing seeds and decorated with feathers, used as a hula implement
'ulu maika – ancient Hawaiian bowling game
unagi – freshwater eel

wahine – woman
wikiwiki – hurry, quick
wiliwili – the lightest of the native woods

zazen – Zen meditation
zendo – communal Zen meditation hall

The Authors

JEFF CAMPBELL
Coordinating Author, History, Culture, Environment, Outdoor Activities & Adventures; Hawai'i the Big Island, Kaho'olawe, Papahanaumokuakea Marine National Monument

Jeff has been trying to reach Green Sands Beach since first hearing about it in 1990, finally digging his toes into the sparkling olive sands in 2008. In between, he fell in love on the Big Island and honeymooned on Kaua'i, camping with his ever-patient wife both times. He was the coordinating author of *Hawaii 8*. He's also been the coordinating author of Lonely Planet's *USA* three times, *Florida*, *Southwest*, *Mid-Atlantic Trips*, and more. He lives with his wife and two kids in New Jersey.

SARA BENSON
O'ahu (Honolulu, Pearl Harbor Area, Waikiki, Southwest Coast & Windward Coast)

After graduating from college in Chicago, Sara jumped on a plane to California with just one suitcase and $100 in her pocket. Then she hopped across the Pacific to Japan, eventually splitting the difference by living on Maui, the Big Island and O'ahu for a few years. She is an avid outdoor enthusiast who has worked for the National Park Service in California and as a volunteer at Hawai'i Volcanoes National Park. Already the author of over 30 travel and nonfiction books, Sara also contributed to Lonely Planet's *Honolulu, Waikiki & O'ahu* and *Hiking in Hawaii* guides.

NED FRIARY & GLENDA BENDURE
Maui

Ned and Glenda first laid eyes on Hawaii after leaving the concrete jungle of Japan, where they'd been teaching English for several years. They were so taken by Hawaii's raw natural beauty that their intended two-week stop-over turned into a four-month stay. Since then, they've returned to Hawaii more than a dozen times, exploring each island from top to bottom. Ned and Glenda wrote the first edition of Lonely Planet's *Hawaii* guide and have worked as co-authors on every edition since. They are also the authors of Lonely Planet's *Maui* guidebook.

THE AUTHORS

AMANDA C GREGG   Kaua'i (North Shore & Westside), Ni'ihau

One of Amanda Gregg's earliest memories is jumping on a Maui hotel bed with her little sister, announcing plans to someday live in Hawaii – and here she is, calling Kaua'i's Eastside home. Growing up in Massachusetts, Amanda's first love was the ocean; travel, the second. After studying in Spain, Amanda received degrees in English and fine arts and a Masters in journalism from CU-Boulder. Since then, she's worked as a beat reporter and editor on the mainland and on Kaua'i. Chasing her newest love, outrigger canoeing, she participated in the 32-mile Na Pali Challenge and 18-mile Queen Lili'uokalani Canoe Race.

SCOTT KENNEDY   O'ahu (North Shore, Central O'ahu & Wai'anae (Leeward) Coast)

Scott Kennedy grew up in the very untropical mountains of Western Canada – perhaps that's why he's always been drawn to warm places. A divemaster, amateur *mojito* connoisseur and, sometimes, surfer, he's had sand in his surf trunks on beaches from Aitutaki to Zanzibar. A decade ago, Scott first stepped foot on O'ahu and has been maintaining a long-distance relationship with Hawaii ever since. He now lives in Queenstown, New Zealand where he longs for clean waves, golden beaches and raspberry shave ice. Scott's website is www.adventureskope.com.

RYAN VER BERKMOES   Moloka'i, Lana'i

Ryan Ver Berkmoes first visited Moloka'i in 1987 and remembers being intoxicated by lush rural scenery on the drive east (or maybe it was the fumes from the heaps of mangos fermenting along the side of the road). He's been back often, usually renting a beachside house where, between novels, he looks without envy at the busy lights of Maui across the channel. For this edition of *Hawaii*, Ryan brings his journalistic skills to Lanai'i and Moloka'i, two places that had previously only tested his holiday skills.

LUCI YAMAMOTO   Food & Drink, Kaua'i (Lihu'e, Eastside & South Shore)

A fourth-generation native of Hawai'i, Luci Yamamoto grew up with hula lessons and homegrown bananas, but longed for four seasons and city sidewalks. She got as far as college in Los Angeles and law school in Berkeley, followed by a brief stint practicing law, then a career change toward writing. Over the years, especially after working on several editions of Lonely Planet's *Hawai'i the Big Island* and *Kaua'i* titles, she's come full circle from her youthful offhandedness about her extraordinary home islands. Currently living in Vancouver, she feels privileged when *kama'aina* still consider her a 'local girl.'

CONTRIBUTING AUTHORS

Dr David Goldberg wrote the material from which the Health chapter was adapted. He completed his training at Columbia-Presbyterian Medical Center in New York City and is an infectious diseases specialist and the editor-in-chief of www.mdtravelhealth.com.

Jake Howard wrote the Surfing boxed texts in the Outdoor Activities & Adventures, O'ahu, Hawai'i the Big Island, Maui, Lana'i, Moloka'i and Kaua'i chapters. Jake is a senior writer at *Surfer* magazine and lives in San Clemente, California. He has traveled and surfed extensively throughout the Hawaiian and Pacific Islands, Indonesia, and Central and South America.

Behind the Scenes

THIS BOOK

This guidebook was commissioned in Lonely Planet's Oakland office, and produced by the following:

Commissioning Editor Emily K Wolman
Coordinating Editor Maryanne Netto
Coordinating Cartographer Corey Hutchison
Coordinating Layout Designer Frank Deim
Managing Editor Geoff Howard
Managing Cartographer David Connolly, Alison Lyall
Managing Layout Designers Laura Jane, Indra Kilfoyle
Assisting Editors Jackey Coyle, Jocelyn Harewood, Victoria Harrison, Kim Hutchins, Anna Metcalfe, Sally O'Brien, Laura Stansfeld
Assisting Layout Designer Cara Smith
Cover Designer Mary Nelson Parker
Project Manager Eoin Dunlevy

Thanks to Nicholas Colicchia, Sally Darmody, Jim Hsu, Robyn Loughnane, Annelies Mertens, Wayne Murphy, Raphael Richards, Jacqui Saunders, Branislava Vladisavljevic

THANKS
JEFF CAMPBELL

Jeff owes thanks to many people, but none more so than Bobby Camara, who is a living lesson in aloha.

Mahalo nui loa! I am also extremely grateful t Lani Opunui for her wise words. Thanks for talkin story also go to Sam Rosen, Kilohana Domingo an Kenny Joyce, Ira Ono, Dr Sam Gon, Kathlyn in Ka' and Sarah and Phil in Pahoa. Park rangers wer unfailingly helpful and patient. My co-authors (an commissioning editor Emily Wolman) made m job easy, but a particular thanks to Luci (for he Big Island expertise) and to Sara (and husban Michael) for our slack key evening.

SARA BENSON

Special thanks to Ellen Gay Dela Rosa, Stephe Little, Bill Snively, Elizabeth Kumabe Maynar and the entire Keawe *'ohana*. Thanks also to Les Griffith, Lee Britos, Rebecca Pang, Bianca Mordas Lisa Mock and Seth Casey. Without supersta coordinating author Jeff Campbell, knowledgeabl co-author Luci Yamamoto, commissioning edito Emily Wolman and managing editor Sasha Baske and all of the in-house staff at LP, I never could hav finished my part of this book. The Pickett famil graciously shared their hospitality on the Windwar Coast. Finally, big thanks to Mike Connolly Jr, wh didn't mind me doing a little guidebook researc during our Hawaii honeymoon!

THE LONELY PLANET STORY

Fresh from an epic journey across Europe, Asia and Australia in 1972, Tony and Maureen Wheeler sat at their kitchen table stapling together notes. The first Lonely Planet guidebook, *Across Asia on the Cheap,* was born.

Travelers snapped up the guides. Inspired by their success, the Wheelers began publishing books to Southeast Asia, India and beyond. Demand was prodigious, and the Wheelers expanded the business rapidly to keep up. Over the years, Lonely Planet extended its coverage to every country and into the virtual world via lonelyplanet.com and the Thorn Tree message board.

As Lonely Planet became a globally loved brand, Tony and Maureen received several offers for the company. But it wasn't until 2007 that they found a partner whom they trusted to remain true to the company's principles of traveling widely, treading lightly and giving sustainably. In October of that year, BBC Worldwide acquired a 75% share in the company, pledging to uphold Lonely Planet's commitment to independent travel, trustworthy advice and editorial independence.

Today, Lonely Planet has offices in Melbourne, London and Oakland, with over 500 staff members and 300 authors. Tony and Maureen are still actively involved with Lonely Planet. They're traveling more often than ever, and they're devoting their spare time to charitable projects. And the company is still driven by the philosophy of *Across Asia on the Cheap*: 'All you've got to do is decide to go and the hardest part is over. So go!'

NED FRIARY & GLENDA BENDURE

A hearty thanks to the many fellow travelers who shared their insights along the way. A special *mahalo* goes out to Allen Tom of the Hawaiian Islands Humpback Whale National Marine Sanctuary. Thanks also to Sandi Lehua Takashiro and Keith Shibuya of Haleakalā National Park, to Glynnis Nakai of the Kealia Pond National Wildlife Refuge and to fishpond restorer Kimokeo Kapahulehua. And finally a big mai tai toast to Lonely Planet's ace commissioning editor Emily Wolman and coordinating author Jeff Campbell.

AMANDA C GREGG

Mahalo to the poetry that is Kaua'i. Thanks to Greg Benchwick, commissioning editor Emily Wolman and Luci Yamamoto for guidance and influence; to Mohala and Danita Aiu, Gil Chang and Davianna McGregor for inspiration and support; to district health officer Dileep G Bal and his wife, Muktha, for treating me like a daughter; to my family, Donald, Bettina, Kimberly and Timothy, for unconditional love and unprecedented generosity; to Imaikalani, *ku'uipo, koa haku mele*, for profound love: here's to you.

SCOTT KENNEDY

Much *mahalo* must go to all those that helped with this edition – first my wonderful commissioning editor Emily Wolman, my O'ahu co-author Sam Benson and the rest of the *Hawaii* 9 team. Cheers to the many people who helped so graciously while I was on the road: Jeff Bushman, Kyle Bernhardt, Grace Dixon, Ann Shaver, Ned Myopus, Adrian Nankivell, Toby Stanton, Chase Jarvis, Celeste Brash and Kieran O'Leary. Many thanks to Jack Johnson and Eddie Vedder for providing the soundtrack, and as always, to my wonderful wife Sophie – for everything. Aloha.

RYAN VER BERKMOES

I'd like to thank my family, and especially my mother who scrimped and saved so we could all get our first magical taste of Hawaii back in 1978 (and so I could decide which was right: the *Brady Bunch* holiday version or the tire-screeching melodrama of *Hawaii Five-0* – surprise! neither). And to Erin who helped me discover love on Molokai'i. For this book, Kepa Maly was a Hawaiian treasure and the font of Lana'i knowledge, while on Molokai'i I offer a group hug to the scores of folks who were happy to talk story for hours about the island they love.

LUCI YAMAMOTO

Mahalo nui loa: to Jon Letman of NTBG, Andrea Brower of Malama Kaua'i and Richard Sugiyama, my Kaua'i insiders; to Rosemary Smith, Chris White and Michaelle Edwards for their generosity during my research trip. Much aloha to O'ahu author Sam Benson for invaluable advice and camaraderie. To commissioning editor Emily Wolman, co-author Amanda Gregg, coordinating author Jeff Campbell and fellow island authors: you made a great team (*a hui hou!*). Special thanks, as always, to MJP and to my family.

OUR READERS

Many thanks to the travelers who used the last edition and wrote to us with helpful hints, useful advice and interesting anecdotes:

Tim Barber, Calley Beamish, Joe Bocker, Jordi Bracons, Kevin Cox, Diana Domig, Stefan Fenz, Tom Glover, H Hammer, Cathy Holt-Kentwell, Fre Hooft Van Huysduynen, Susan Hughes, Rebecca Ingham, Ulf Johnson, Erik Kawasaki, Kate Kinnear, Liz Kover, Iris Laporte, Brian Lewis, Lorna Lewis, Thomas Lippert, Thomas Lombaerts, Elizabeth Macri, Carol Morrison, Susan Pratt, Gary Russ, Michael Russell, Amy Sloma, David Tamir, Asif Tejani, Paulo Vasconcelos, Rex Watling, Linda Wise, Mario Zucca.

SEND US YOUR FEEDBACK

We love to hear from travelers – your comments keep us on our toes and help make our books better. Our well-traveled team reads every word on what you loved or loathed about this book. Although we cannot reply individually to postal submissions, we always guarantee that your feedback goes straight to the appropriate authors, in time for the next edition. Each person who sends us information is thanked in the next edition – and the most useful submissions are rewarded with a free book.

To send us your updates – and find out about Lonely Planet events, newsletters and travel news – visit our award-winning website: **lonelyplanet.com/contact**.

Note: we may edit, reproduce and incorporate your comments in Lonely Planet products such as guidebooks, websites and digital products, so let us know if you don't want your comments reproduced or your name acknowledged. For a copy of our privacy policy visit lonelyplanet.com/privacy.

ACKNOWLEDGMENTS
Many thanks to the following for the use of their content:

Globe on title page ©Mountain High Maps 1993 Digital Wisdom, Inc.

Internal photographs by Lonely Planet Images, and by Ann Cecil p8 (#1, #3), p9 (#4), p10 (#1), p13 (#2, #4), p14 (#3), p15 (#4); Linda Ching p15 (#2); Greg Elms p11 (#2), p12 (#3); Simon Foale p10 (#3); Le Foster p6, p7, p9 (#2), p16 (#1); Karl Lehmann p1 (#4), p12 (#1), p16 (#2); Merten Snijders p14 (#1)

All images are the copyright of the photographers unless otherwise indicated. Many of the images in this guide are available for licensing from Lonely Planet Images: www.lonelyplanet images.com.

OAHU

Honolulu / Waikiki
↳ Pearl Harbor / USS Arizona
↳ Hotels: Waikiki begin pg 154

- Spa / massages

North Shore

snorkeling

HAWAII BIG ISLAND

day trip
[Volcanoes Nat'l Park
Cruise / boating]

MAUI
beaches

Index

See also separate GreenDex.

000 Map pages
000 Photograph pages

INDEX

INDEX

INDEX

GreenDex

The following listings have been selected by Lonely Planet authors because they demonstrate an active sustainable-tourism policy. Some are involved in conservation or environmental education, while others are owned and operated by local operators, thereby maintaining and preserving Hawaiian identity and culture. Some of the listings are also certified by the Hawaii Ecotourism Association (www.hawaiiecotourism.org), which means they meet high standards of environmental sustainability, business ethics and cultural sensitivity. We want to keep developing our sustainable-tourism content. If you think we've omitted someone who should be listed here, or if you disagree with our choices, let us know at www.lonelyplanet.com/contact. For more information about sustainable tourism and Lonely Planet, see www.lonelyplanet.com/responsibletravel.

MAP LEGEND
ROUTES

Freeway	Mall/Steps
Primary	Tunnel
Secondary	Pedestrian Overpass
Tertiary	Walking Tour
Lane	Walking Trail
Under Construction	Walking Path
Unsealed Road	Track
One-Way Street	

TRANSPORT

Ferry	Rail

HYDROGRAPHY

River, Creek	Reef
Intermittent River	Canal
Swamp	Water

BOUNDARIES

Marine Park	Cliff

AREA FEATURES

Airport	Land
Area of Interest	Market
Beach	Park
Building	Reservation
Campus	Rocks
Cemetery, Christian	Sports
Forest	Urban

POPULATION

⊙	CAPITAL (NATIONAL)	◉	CAPITAL (STATE)
●	Large City	●	Medium City
	Small City	●	Town, Village

SYMBOLS

Sights/Activities
- Beach
- Bodysurfing
- Buddhist
- Canoeing, Kayaking
- Christian
- Diving, Snorkeling
- Golf
- Hindu
- Monument
- Museum, Gallery
- Point of Interest
- Pool
- Ruin
- Shinto
- Snorkeling
- Surfing, Surf Beach
- Taoist
- Trail Head
- Windsurfing
- Winery, Vineyard
- Zoo, Bird Sanctuary

Eating
- Eating

Drinking
- Drinking
- Café

Entertainment
- Entertainment

Shopping
- Shopping

Sleeping
- Sleeping
- Camping

Transport
- Airport, Airfield
- Bus Station
- Cycling, Bicycle Path
- General Transport
- Parking Area
- Petrol Station

Information
- Bank, ATM
- Embassy/Consulate
- Hospital, Medical
- Information
- Internet Facilities
- Police Station
- Post Office, GPO
- Toilets

Geographic
- Lighthouse
- Lookout
- Mountain, Volcano
- National Park
- Beach Park
- Pass, Canyon
- Picnic Area
- Shelter, Hut
- Trig Station
- Waterfall

LONELY PLANET OFFICES

Australia
Head Office
Locked Bag 1, Footscray, Victoria 3011
☎ 03 8379 8000, fax 03 8379 8111
talk2us@lonelyplanet.com.au

USA
150 Linden St, Oakland, CA 94607
☎ 510 250 6400, toll free 800 275 8555
fax 510 893 8572
info@lonelyplanet.com

UK
2nd fl, 186 City Rd,
London EC1V 2NT
☎ 020 7106 2100, fax 020 7106 2101
go@lonelyplanet.co.uk

Published by Lonely Planet Publications Pty Ltd
ABN 36 005 607 983

Although the authors and Lonely Planet have taken all reasonable care in preparing this book, we make no warranty about the accuracy or completeness of its content and, to the maximum extent permitted, disclaim all liability arising from its use.

MIX
Paper from responsible sources
FSC™ C021741
www.fsc.org